TheStreet.com Ratings' Guide to Life and Annuity Insurers

TheStreet.com Ratings' Guide to Life and Annuity Insurers

A Quarterly Compilation of Insurance Company Ratings and Analyses

Fall 2009

GREY HOUSE PUBLISHING

TheStreet.com Ratings, Inc.
14 Wall Street, 15th Floor
New York, NY 10005
800-289-9222

Published by Grey House Publishing, Inc. located at 4919 Route 22, Amenia, NY, 12501; telephone 518-789-8700. Grey House Publishing neither guarantees the accuracy of the data contained herein nor assumes any responsibility for errors, omissions or discrepancies. Grey House Publishing accepts no payment for listing; inclusion in the publication of any organization agency, institution, publication, service or individual does not imply endorsement of the publisher.

Edition No. 77, Fall 2009

ISBN: 978-1-59237-462-5
ISSN: 1935-5319

Contents

Introduction

Appendix

Terms and Conditions

This Document is prepared strictly for the confidential use of our customer(s). It has been provided to you at your specific request. It is not directed to, or intended for distribution to or use by, any person or entity who is a citizen or resident of or located in any locality, state, country or other jurisdiction where such distribution, publication, availability or use would be contrary to law or regulation or which would subject TheStreet.com Ratings or its affiliates to any registration or licensing requirement within such jurisdiction.

No part of the analysts' compensation was, is, or will be, directly or indirectly, related to the specific recommendations or views expressed in this research report.

This Document is not intended for the direct or indirect solicitation of business. TheStreet.com Ratings, Inc. and its affiliates disclaims any and all liability to any person or entity for any loss or damage caused, in whole or in part, by any error (negligent or otherwise) or other circumstances involved in, resulting from or relating to the procurement, compilation, analysis, interpretation, editing, transcribing, publishing and/or dissemination or transmittal of any information contained herein.

TheStreet.com Ratings has not taken any steps to ensure that the securities or investment vehicle referred to in this report are suitable for any particular investor. The investment or services contained or referred to in this report may not be suitable for you and it is recommended that you consult an independent investment advisor if you are in doubt about such investments or investment services. Nothing in this report constitutes investment, legal, accounting or tax advice or a representation that any investment or strategy is suitable or appropriate to your individual circumstances or otherwise constitutes a personal recommendation to you.

The ratings and other opinions contained in this Document must be construed solely as statements of opinion from TheStreet.com Ratings, Inc., and not statements of fact. Each rating or opinion must be weighed solely as a factor in your choice of an institution and should not be construed as a recommendation to buy, sell or otherwise act with respect to the particular product or company involved.

Past performance should not be taken as an indication or guarantee of future performance, and no representation or warranty, expressed or implied, is made regarding future performance. Information, opinions and estimates contained in this report reflect a judgment at its original date of publication and are subject to change without notice. TheStreet.com Ratings offers a notification service for rating changes on companies you specify. For more information call 1-800-289-9222 or visit www.thestreet.com/ratings. The price, value and income from any of the securities or financial instruments mentioned in this report can fall as well as rise.

This Document and the information contained herein is copyrighted by TheStreet.com Ratings, Inc. Any copying, displaying, selling, distributing or otherwise delivering of this information or any part of this Document to any other person, without the express written consent of TheStreet.com Ratings, Inc. except by a reviewer or editor who may quote brief passages in connection with a review or a news story, is prohibited.

Message To Insurers

All survey data received on or before August 21, 2009 have been considered or incorporated into this edition of the Directory. If you have not yet completed our survey form, call Sandy Fenton at TheStreet.com Ratings, Inc., (561) 354-4400. If there are particular circumstances which you believe could affect your rating, please use the survey sheets we have sent you or send a written request to bring it to our attention. If warranted, we will make every effort to incorporate the changes in our next edition.

Welcome to TheStreet.com Ratings'
Guide to Life and Annuity Insurers

Most people automatically assume their insurance company will survive, year after year. However, prudent consumers and professionals realize that in this world of shifting risks, the solvency of insurance companies can't be taken for granted.

If you are looking for accurate, unbiased ratings and data to help you choose life and annuity insurance for yourself, your family, your company or your clients, *TheStreet.com Ratings' Guide to Life and Annuity Insurers* gives you precisely what you need.

In fact, it's the only source that currently provides ratings and analyses on 1,000 life and annuity insurers.

TheStreet.com Ratings' Mission Statement

TheStreet.com Ratings' mission is to empower consumers, professionals, and institutions with high quality advisory information for selecting or monitoring a financial services company or financial investment.

In doing so, TheStreet.com Ratings will adhere to the highest ethical standards by maintaining our independent, unbiased outlook and approach to advising our customers.

Why rely on TheStreet.com Ratings?

TheStreet.com Ratings provides fair, objective ratings to help professionals and consumers alike make educated purchasing decisions.

At TheStreet.com Ratings, integrity is number one. TheStreet.com Ratings never takes a penny from insurance companies for its ratings. And, we publish TheStreet.com Financial Strength Ratings without regard for insurers' preferences. However, other rating agencies like A.M. Best, Fitch, Moody's and Standard & Poor's are paid by insurance companies for their ratings and may even suppress unfavorable ratings at an insurer's request.

Our ratings are more frequently reviewed and updated than any other ratings. You can be sure that the information you receive is accurate and current – providing you with advance warning of financial vulnerability early enough to do something about it.

Other rating agencies focus primarily on a company's current claims paying ability and consider only mild economic adversity. TheStreet.com Ratings also considers these issues, but in addition, our analysis covers a company's ability to deal with severe economic adversity and a sharp increase in claims.

Our use of more rigorous standards stems from the viewpoint that an insurance company's obligations to its policyholders should not depend on favorable business conditions. An insurer must be able to honor its policy commitments in bad times as well as good.

Our rating scale, from A to F, is easy to understand. Only a few outstanding companies receive an A (Excellent) rating, although there are many to choose from within the B (Good) category. An even larger group falls into the broad average range which receives C (Fair) ratings. Companies that demonstrate marked vulnerabilities receive either D (Weak) or E (Very Weak) ratings.

How to Use This Guide

The purpose of the *Guide to Life and Annuity Insurers* is to provide policyholders and prospective policy purchasers with a reliable source of insurance company ratings and analyses on a timely basis. We realize that the financial stength of an insurer is an important factor to consider when making the decision to purchase a policy or change companies. The ratings and analyses in this Guide can make that evaluation easier when you are considering:

- life insurance

- annuities

- health insurance

- Guaranteed Investment Contracts (GICs) and other pension products

This Guide also includes ratings for some Blue Cross Blue Shield plans.

The rating for a particular company indicates our opinion regarding that company's ability to meet its commitments to the policyholder – not only under current economic conditions, but also during a declining economy or in an environment of increased liquidity demands.

To use this Guide most effectively, we recommend you follow the steps outlined below:

Step 1 To ensure you evaluate the correct company, verify the company's exact name and state of domicile as it was given to you or appears on your policy. Many companies have similar names but are not related to one another, so you want to make sure the company you look up is really the one you are interested in evaluating.

Step 2 Turn to Section I, the Index of Companies, and locate the company you are evaluating. This section contains all companies analyzed by TheStreet.com Ratings including those that did not receive a Financial Strength Rating. It is sorted alphabetically by the name of the company and shows the state of domicile following the name for additional verification. Once you have located your specific company, the first column after the state of domicile shows its TheStreet.com Financial Strength Rating. Turn to *About TheStreet.com Financial Strength Ratings* on page 9 for information about what this rating means. If the rating has changed since the last issue of this Guide, a downgrade will be indicated with a down triangle ▼ to the left of the company name; an upgrade will be indicated with an up triangle ▲.

Step 3 Following TheStreet.com Financial Strength Rating are some of the various indexes that our analysts used in rating the company. Refer to the table on page 10 for an interpretation of which index values are considered strong, good, fair or weak. You can also turn to the Section I introduction beginning on page 21 to see what each of these factors measures. In most cases, lower rated companies will have a low index value in one or more of the factors shown. Bear in mind, however, that TheStreet.com Financial Strength Rating is the result of a complex qualitative and quantitative analysis which cannot be reproduced using only the data provided here.

Step 4 The quality of a company's investment portfolio – bonds, mortgages and other investments – is an integral part of our analysis. So, the right hand page of Section I shows you where the company has invested its premiums. Again, refer to the Section I introduction beginning on page 24 for a description of each investment category.

Step 5   Some insurers have a bullet ● preceding the company name on the right hand page of Section I. If the company you are evaluating is identified with a bullet, turn to Section II, the Analysis of Largest Companies, and locate it there (otherwise skip to step 8). Section II contains the largest insurers rated by TheStreet.com Ratings, regardless of rating. It too is sorted alphabetically by the name of the company.

Step 6   Once you have identified your company in Section II, you will find its Financial Strength Rating and a description of the rating immediately to the right of the company name. Then, below the company name is a description of the various rating factors that were considered in assigning the company's rating. These factors and the information below them are designed to give you a better feel for the company and its strengths and weaknesses. See the Section II introduction, beginning on page 71, to get a better understanding of what each of these factors means.

Step 7   To the right, you will find a five-year summary of the company's Financial Strength Rating, capitalization and income. Look for positive or negative trends in this data. Below the five-year summary, we have included a graphic illustration of the most critical factor or factors impacting the company's rating. Again, the Section II introduction provides an overview of the content of each graph or table.

Step 8   If the company you are evaluating is not highly rated and you want to find an insurer with a higher rating, turn to the page in Section IV that has your state's name at the top. This section contains those Recommended Companies (rating of A+, A, A- or B+) that are licensed to underwrite insurance in your state, sorted by rating. From here you can select a company and then refer back to Sections I and II to analyze it.

Step 9   If you decide that you would like to contact one of TheStreet.com Recommended Companies about obtaining a policy or for additional information, refer to Section III. Following each company's name is its address and phone number to assist you in making contact.

Step 10   In order to use TheStreet.com Financial Strength Ratings most effectively, we strongly recommend you consult the Important Warnings and Cautions listed on page 17. These are more than just "standard disclaimers"; they are very important factors you should be aware of before using this Guide. If you have any questions regarding the precise meaning of specific terms used in the Guide, refer to the Glossary beginning on page 334.

Step 11   Page 315 of the Appendix contains information about State Guaranty Associations and the types of coverage they provide to policyholders when an insurance company fails. Keep in mind that while guaranty funds have now been established in all states, many do not cover all types of insurance. Furthermore, all of these funds have limits on their amount of coverage. Use the table to determine whether the level of coverage is applicable to your policy and the limits are adequate for your needs. You should pay particular attention to the notes regarding whether the coverage is for residents of the state or companies domiciled in the state.

Step 12   If you want more information on your state's guaranty fund, call the State Commissioner's Office directly at the phone number listed on page 320.

Step 13   Keep in mind that good coverage from a state guaranty association is no substitute for dealing with a financially strong company. (See the discussion of problems with the guaranty fund system on page 323). For that reason, TheStreet.com Ratings only recommends those companies which we feel are most able to stand on their own, without regard to what might happen in case the company does fail.

Step 14   Make sure you stay up to date with the latest information available since the publication of this Guide. For information on how to set up a rating change notification service, acquire follow-up reports or receive a more in-depth analysis of an individual company, call 1-800-289-9222 or visit www.thestreetratings.com.

Data Sources: Annual and quarterly statutory statements filed with state insurance commissioners and data provided by the insurance companies being rated. The National Association of Insurance Commissioners has provided some of the raw data. Any analyses or conclusions are not provided or endorsed by the NAIC.

Date of data analyzed: March 31, 2009 unless otherwise noted.

About TheStreet.com Financial Strength Ratings

TheStreet.com Financial Strength Ratings represent a completely independent, unbiased opinion of an insurance company's financial strength. The ratings are derived, for the most part, from annual and quarterly financial statements obtained from state insurance commissioners. These data are supplemented by information that we request from the insurance companies themselves. Although we seek to maintain an open line of communication with the companies being rated, we do not grant them the right to influence the ratings or stop their publication.

TheStreet.com Financial Strength Ratings are assigned by our analysts based on a complex analysis of hundreds of factors that are synthesized into five indexes: capitalization, investment safety, profitability, liquidity and stability. These indexes are then used to arrive at a letter grade rating. A good rating requires consistency across all indexes. A weak score on any one index can result in a low rating, as insolvency can be caused by any one of a number of factors, such as inadequate capital, unpredictable claims experience, poor liquidity, speculative investments, or operating losses.

The primary components of TheStreet.com Financial Strength Rating are as follows:

- **Capitalization Index** gauges capital adequacy in terms of each insurer's ability to handle a variety of business and economic scenarios as they may impact investment performance, claims experience, persistency and market position.

- **Investment Safety Index** measures the exposure of the company's investment portfolio to loss of principal and/or income due to default and market risks.

- **Profitability Index** measures the soundness of the company's operations and the contribution of profits to the company's financial strength. The profitability index is a composite of five sub-factors: 1) gain or loss on operations; 2) consistency of operating results; 3) impact of operating results on surplus; 4) adequacy of investment income as compared to the needs of policy reserves; and 5) expenses in relation to industry norms for the types of policies that the company offers.

- **Liquidity Index** values a company's ability to raise the necessary cash to settle claims and honor cash withdrawal obligations. We model various cash flow scenarios, applying liquidity tests to determine how the company might fare in the event of a spike in claims or a run on policy surrenders.

- **Stability Index** integrates a number of sub-factors that affect consistency (or lack thereof) in maintaining financial strength over time. Sub-factors include 1) risk diversification in terms of company size, group size, number of policies in force, types of policies written and use of reinsurance; 2) deterioration of operations as reported in critical asset, liability, income and expense items, such as surrender rates and premium volume; 3) years in operation; 4) former problem areas where, despite recent improvement, the company has yet to establish a record of stable performance over a suitable period of time; 5) a substantial shift in the company's operations; 6) potential instabilities such as reinsurance quality, asset/liability matching, and sources of capital; and 7) relationships with holding companies and affiliates.

Each of these indexes is measured according to the following range of values.

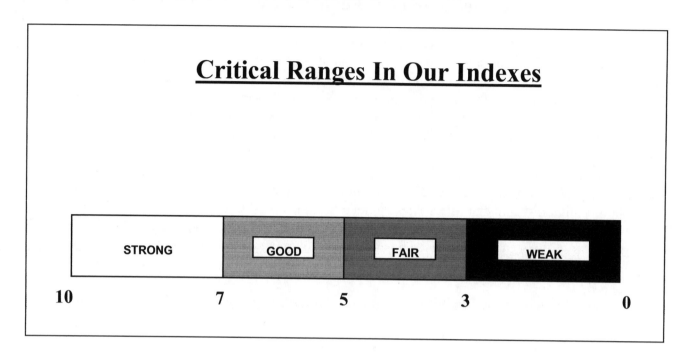

What Our Ratings Mean

A **Excellent.** The company offers excellent financial security. It has maintained a conservative stance in its investment strategies, business operations and underwriting commitments. While the financial position of any company is subject to change, we believe that this company has the resources necessary to deal with severe economic conditions.

B **Good.** The company offers good financial security and has the resources to deal with a variety of adverse economic conditions. It comfortably exceeds the minimum levels for all of our rating criteria, and is likely to remain healthy for the near future. However, in the event of a *severe* recession or major financial crisis, we feel that this assessment should be reviewed to make sure that the firm is still maintaining adequate financial strength.

C **Fair.** The company offers fair financial security and is currently stable. But during an economic downturn or other financial pressures, we feel it may encounter difficulties in maintaining its financial stability.

D **Weak.** The company currently demonstrates what we consider to be significant weaknesses which could negatively impact policyholders. In an unfavorable economic environment, these weaknesses could be magnified.

E **Very Weak.** The company currently demonstrates what we consider to be significant weaknesses and has also failed some of the basic tests that we use to identify fiscal stability. Therefore, even in a favorable economic environment, it is our opinion that policyholders could incur significant risks.

F **Failed.** The company is deemed failed if it is either 1) under supervision of an insurance regulatory authority; 2) in the process of rehabilitation; 3) in the process of liquidation; or 4) voluntarily dissolved after disciplinary or other regulatory action by an insurance regulatory authority.

+ **The plus sign** is an indication that the company is at the upper end of the letter grade rating.

- **The minus sign** is an indication that the company is at the lower end of the letter grade rating.

U **Unrated Companies.** The company is unrated for one or more of the following reasons: 1) total assets are less than $1 million; 2) premium income for the current year is less than $100,000; 3) the company functions almost exclusively as a holding company rather than as an underwriter; or 4) we do not have enough information to reliably issue a rating.

How Our Ratings Differ From Those of Other Services

TheStreet.com Financial Strength Ratings are conservative and consumer-oriented. We use tougher standards than other rating agencies because our system is specifically designed to inform risk-averse consumers about the financial strength of life and annuity insurers.

Our rating scale (A to F) is easy to understand by the general public. Users can intuitively understand that an A+ rating is at the top of the scale rather than in the middle like some of the other rating agencies.

Other rating agencies give top ratings more generously so that most companies receive excellent ratings.

More importantly, other rating agencies focus primarily on a company's *current* claims paying ability or consider only relatively mild economic adversity. We also consider these scenarios but extend our analysis to cover a company's ability to deal with severe economic adversity and potential liquidity problems. This stems from the viewpoint that an insurance company's obligations to its policyholders should not be contingent upon a healthy economy. The company must be capable of honoring its policy commitments in bad times as well.

Looking at the insurance industry as a whole, we note that several major rating firms have poor historical track records in identifying troubled companies. The 1980s saw a persistent decline in capital ratios, increased holdings of risky investments in the life and health industry as well as recurring long-term claims liabilities in the property and casualty industry. Despite these clear signs that insolvency risk was rising, other rating firms failed to downgrade at-risk insurance companies. Instead, they often rated companies by shades of excellence, understating the gravity of potential problems.

They have not issued clear warnings that the ordinary consumer can understand. Few, if any, companies receive "weak" or "poor" ratings. Surely, weak companies do exist. However, the other rating agencies apparently do not view themselves as consumer advocates with the responsibility of warning the public about the risks involved in doing business with such companies.

Additionally, these firms will at times agree *not* to issue a rating if a company denies them permission to do so. In short, too often insurance rating agencies work hand-in-glove with the companies they rate.

At TheStreet.com Ratings, although we seek to maintain good relationships with the firms, we owe our primary obligation to the consumer, not the industry. We reserve the right to rate companies based on publicly available data and make the necessary conservative assumptions when companies choose not to provide the additional data we request.

Comparison of Insurance Company Rating Agency Scales

TheStreet.com Ratings [a]	Best [a,b]	S&P [c]	Moody's	Fitch [d]
A+, A, A-	A++, A+	AAA	Aaa	AAA
B+, B, B-	A, A-	AA+, AA AA-	Aa1, Aa2, Aa3	AA+, AA, AA-
C+, C, C-	B++, B+,	A+, A, A-, BBB+, BBB, BBB-	A1, A2, A3, Baa1, Baa2, Baa3	A+, A, A-, BBB+, BBB, BBB-
D+, D, D-	B, B- C++, C+, C, C-	BB+, BB, BB-, B+, B, B-	Ba1, Ba2, Ba3, B1, B2, B3	BB+, BB, BB-, B+, B, B-
E+, E, E- F	D E, F	CCC R	Caa, Ca, C	CCC+, CCC, CCC- DD

[a] TheStreet.com Ratings and Best use additional symbols to designate that they recognize an insurer's existence but do not provide a rating. These symbols are not included in this table.

[b] Best added the A++, B++ and C++ ratings in 1992. In 1994, Best classified its ratings into "secure" and "vulnerable" categories, changed the definition of its "B" and "B-" ratings from "good" to "adequate" and assigned these ratings to the "vulnerable" category. This table contains GAO's assignment of Best's ratings to bands based on our interpretation of their rating descriptions prior to 1994.

[c] S&P discontinued CCC "+" and "-" signs, CC, C and D ratings and added the R rating in 1992.

Source: 1994 GAO *Insurance Ratings* study.

[d] Duff & Phelps Credit Rating Co. merged with Fitch IBCA in 2000, and minor changes were made to the rating scale at that time. These changes were not reflected in the GAO's 1994 study, but *are* reflected in the chart.

Rate of Insurance Company Failures

TheStreet.com Ratings provides quarterly financial strength ratings for thousands of insurance companies each year. TheStreet.com Ratings strives for fairness and objectivity in its ratings and analyses, ensuring that each company receives the rating that most accurately depicts its current financial status, and more importantly, its ability to deal with severe economic adversity and a sharp increase in claims. TheStreet.com Ratings has every confidence that its financial strength ratings provide an accurate representation of a company's stability.

In order for these ratings to be of any true value, it is important that they prove accurate over time. One way to determine the accuracy of a rating is to examine those insurance companies that have failed, and their respective TheStreet.com Financial Strength Ratings. A high percentage of failed companies with "A" ratings would indicate that TheStreet.com Ratings is not being conservative enough with its "secure" ratings, while conversely, a low percentage of failures with "vulnerable" ratings would show that TheStreet.com Ratings is overly conservative.

Over the past 20 years (1989–2008) TheStreet.com Ratings has rated 452 insurance companies, for all industries, that subsequently failed. The chart below shows the number of failed companies in each rating category, the average number of companies rated in each category per year, and the percentage of annual failures for each letter grade.

	Financial Strength Rating	Number of Failed Companies	Average Number of Companies Rated per year	Percentage of Failed Companies per year (by ratings category)*
Secure	A	1	148	0.03%
	B	2	1081	0.01%
	C	63	1642	0.19%
Vulnerable	D	208	767	1.36%
	E	178	217	4.11%

A=Excellent, B=Good, C=Fair, D=Weak, E=Very Weak

On average, only 0.08% of the companies TheStreet.com Ratings rates as "secure" fail each year. On the other hand, an average of 2.74% of the companies TheStreet.com Ratings rates as "vulnerable" fail annually. That means that a company rated by TheStreet.com Ratings as "Vulnerable" is 18 times more likely to fail than a company rated as "Secure".

When considering a TheStreet.com financial strength rating, one can be sure that they are getting the most fair, objective, and accurate financial rating available anywhere.

*Percentage of Failed Companies per year = (Number of Failed Companies) / [(Average Number of Companies Rated per year) x (years in study)]

Data as of September 2008 for Life and Annuity Insurers and Property and Casualty Insurers.
Data as of June 2008 for Health Insurers

What Does Average Mean?

At TheStreet.com Ratings, we consider the words average and fair to mean just that – average and fair. So when we assign our ratings to insurers, a large percentage of companies receive an average C rating. That way, you can be sure that a company receiving TheStreet.com B or A rating is truly above average. Likewise, you can feel confident that companies with D or E ratings are truly below average. In recent years, life and health insurers have experienced consistent, solid performance resulting in a shift in the rating distribution so that more insurers than ever are rated B or better.

Percentage for Life and Annuity Insurers in Each Rating Category

2009 TheStreet.com Ratings Distribution

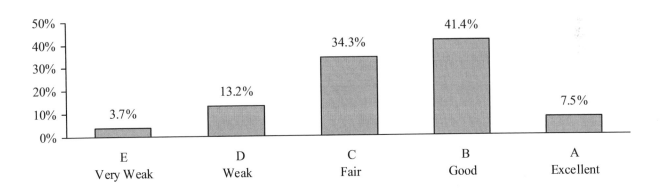

Important Warnings and Cautions

1. A rating alone cannot tell the whole story. Please read the explanatory information contained in this publication. It is provided in order to give you an understanding of our rating philosophy, as well as paint a more complete picture of how we arrive at our opinion of a company's strengths and weaknesses.

2. TheStreet.com Financial Strength Ratings represent our opinion of a company's insolvency risk. As such, a high rating means we feel that the company has less chance of running into financial difficulties. A high rating is not a guarantee of solvency nor is a low rating a prediction of insolvency. TheStreet.com Financial Strength Ratings are not deemed to be a recommendation concerning the purchase or sale of the securities of any insurance company that is publicly owned.

3. Company performance is only one factor in determining a rating. Conditions in the marketplace and overall economic conditions are additional factors that may affect the company's financial strength. Therefore, a rating upgrade or downgrade does not necessarily reflect changes in the company's profits, capital or other financial measures, but may be due to external factors. Likewise, changes in TheStreet.com indexes may reflect changes in our risk assessment of business or economic conditions as well as changes in company performance.

4. All firms that have the same Financial Strength Rating should be considered to be essentially equal in strength. This is true regardless of any differences in the underlying numbers which might appear to indicate greater strengths. TheStreet.com Financial Strength Rating already takes into account a number of lesser factors which, due to space limitations, cannot be included in this publication.

5. A good rating requires consistency. If a company is excellent on four indicators and fair on one, the company may receive a fair rating. This requirement is necessary due to the fact that fiscal problems can arise from any *one* of several causes including speculative investments, inadequate capital resources or operating losses.

6. We are an independent rating agency and do not depend on the cooperation of the companies we rate. Our data are derived, for the most part, from annual and quarterly financial statements that we obtain from federal banking regulators and state insurance commissioners. The latter may be supplemented by information insurance companies voluntarily provide upon request. Although we seek to maintain an open line of communication with the companies, we do not grant them the right to stop or influence publication of the ratings. This policy stems from the fact that this publication is designed for the protection of the consumer.

7. Affiliated companies do not automatically receive the same rating. We recognize that a troubled company may expect financial support from its parent or affiliates. TheStreet.com Financial Strength Ratings reflect our opinion of the measure of support that may become available to a subsidiary , if the subsidiary were to experience serious financial difficulties. In the case of a strong parent and a weaker subsidiary, the affiliate relationship will generally result in a higher rating for the subsidiary than it would have on a stand-alone basis. Seldom, however, would the rating be brought up to the level of the parent. This treatment is appropriate because we do not assume the parent would have either the resources or the will to "bail out" a troubled subsidiary during a severe economic crisis. Even when there is a binding legal obligation for a parent corporation to honor the policy obligations of its subsidiaries, the possibility exists that the subsidiary could be sold and lose its parental support. Therefore, it is quite common for one affiliate to have a higher rating than another. This is another reason why it is especially important that you have the precise name of the company you are evaluating.

Section I

Index of Companies

An analysis of all rated and unrated

U.S. Life and Annuity Insurers.

Companies are listed in alphabetical order.

Section I Contents

This section contains the key rating factors and investment portfolio analysis for all rated and unrated insurers analyzed by TheStreet.com Ratings. An explanation of each of the footnotes and stability factors appears at the end of this section.

Left Pages

1. Insurance Company Name

The legally registered name, which can sometimes differ from the name that the company uses for advertising. If you cannot find the company you are interested in, or if you have any doubts regarding the precise name, verify the information with the company before looking the name up in this Guide. Also, determine the domicile state for confirmation. (See column 2.)

2. Domicile State

The state which has primary regulatory responsibility for the company. It may differ from the location of the company's corporate headquarters. You do not have to be living in the domicile state to purchase insurance from this firm, provided it is licensed to do business in your state.

Also use this column to confirm that you have located the correct company. It is possible for two unrelated companies to have the same name if they are domiciled in different states.

3. Financial Strength Rating

Our rating is measured on a scale from A to F and considers a wide range of factors. Please see page 11 for specific descriptions of each letter grade. Also, refer to page 12 for information on how our ratings differ from those of other rating agencies. Most important, when using this rating, please be sure to consider the warnings beginning on page 17 regarding the ratings' limitations and the underlying assumptions. Notes in this column refer to the date of the data included in the rating evaluation and are explained on page 26.

4. Total Assets

All assets admitted by state insurance regulators in millions of dollars. This includes investments, current business assets, and separate accounts. The year-end figure is used to correspond with the figures on the right-hand pages, some of which are only available on an annual basis.

The overall size is an important factor which affects the ability of a company to manage risk. Mortality, morbidity (sickness) and investment risks can be more effectively diversified by large companies. Because the insurance business is based on probability, the number of policies must be large enough so that actuarial statistics are valid. Life insurance policies, for example, are based on mortality tables containing the expected number of deaths per thousand at various ages.

The larger the number of policyholders, the more reliable the actuarial projections will be. A large company with a correspondingly large policy base can spread its risk and minimize the effects of claims experience that exceeds actuarial expectations.

5. Capital and Surplus

The company's statutory net worth in millions of dollars. Consumers may wish to limit the size of any policy so that the policyholder's maximum benefits do not exceed approximately 1% of the company's capital and surplus. For example, when buying a policy from a company with capital and surplus of $10,000,000, the 1% limit would be $100,000. (When performing this calculation, do not forget that figures in this column are expressed in millions of dollars.)

Critical Ranges In Our Indexes and Ratios

Indicators	Strong	Good	Fair	Weak
Risk-Adjusted Capital Ratio #1	—	1.0 or more	0.75 - 0.99	0.74 or less
Risk-Adjusted Capital Ratio #2	1.0 or more	0.75 - 0.99	0.5 - 0.74	0.49 or less
Capitalization Index	7 – 10	5 - 6.9	3 - 4.9	2.9 or less
5 Year Profitability Index	7 – 10	5 - 6.9	3 - 4.9	2.9 or less
Liquidity Index	7 – 10	5 - 6.9	3 - 4.9	2.9 or less
Investment Safety Index	7 – 10	5 - 6.9	3 - 4.9	2.9 or less
Stability Index	7 – 10	5 - 6.9	3 - 4.9	2.9 or less

6. Risk-Adjusted Capital Ratio #1

This ratio examines the adequacy of the company's capital base and whether the company has sufficient capital resources to cover potential losses which might occur in an average recession or other moderate loss scenario. Specifically, the figure cited in the table answers the question: For every dollar of capital that we feel would be needed, how many dollars in capital resources does the company actually have? (See the table above for the levels which we believe are critical.) You may find that some companies have unusually high levels of capital. This often reflects special circumstances related to the small size or unusual operations of the company.

7. Risk-Adjusted Capital Ratio #2

This is similar to item 6. But in this case, the question relates to whether the company has enough capital cushion to withstand a *severe* recession or other severe loss scenario.

8. Capitalization Index

An index that measures the adequacy of the company's capital resources to deal with a variety of business and economic scenarios. It combines Risk-Adjusted Capital Ratios #1 and #2 as well as a leverage test that examines pricing risk. (See the table above for the levels which we believe are critical.)

9. **Investment Safety Index**

An index that measures the exposure of the company's investment portfolio to a loss of principal and/or income due to default and market risks. It is the composite of a series of elements, some of which are shown on the right pages. Each investment area is rated by a factor that takes into consideration both quality and liquidity. (See the table on page 22 for the levels which we believe are critical.)

10. **5-Year Profitability Index**

An index that measures the soundness of the company's operations and the contribution of profits to the company's fiscal strength. The Profitability Index is a composite of five factors: (1) gain or loss on operations; (2) consistency of operating results; (3) impact of operating results on surplus; (4) adequacy of investment income as compared to the needs of policy reserves; and (5) expenses in relation to industry averages for the types of policies that the company offers.

This factor is especially important among health insurers including Blue Cross Blue Shield companies that rely more heavily on current earnings than do life and annuity writers. After factoring out the normal cycle, companies with stable earnings and capital growth are viewed more favorably than those whose results are erratic from year to year. (See the table on page 22 for the levels which we believe are critical.)

11. **Liquidity Index**

An index which measures the company's ability to raise the necessary cash to meet policyholder obligations. This index includes a stress test which considers the consequences of a spike in claims or a run on policy surrenders. Sometimes a company may appear to have the necessary resources, but may be unable to sell its investments at the prices at which they are valued in the company's financial statements. (See the table on page 22 for the levels which we believe are critical.)

12. **Stability Index**

An index which integrates a number of factors such as: (1) risk diversification in terms of company size, number of policies in force, use of reinsurance and other items related to spread of risk; (2) deterioration of operations as reported in critical asset, liability, income or expense items such as surrender rates and premium volume; (3) former problem areas where, despite recent improvement, the company has yet to establish a record of stable performance over a suitable period of time; (4) a substantial shift in the company's operations; (5) potential instabilities such as reinsurance quality, asset/liability matching and sources of capital; plus (6) relationships to holding companies and affiliates. (See the table on page 22 for the levels which we believe are critical.)

13. **Stability Factors**

Indicates those specific areas that have negatively impacted the company's Stability Index. See page 27 for explanation of these factors.

Right Pages

1. **Net Premiums**

   The amount of insurance premiums received from policyholders less any premiums that have been transferred to other companies through reinsurance agreements. Generally speaking, companies with large net premium volume generally have more predictable claims experience.

2. **Invested Assets**

   The value of the firm's total investment portfolio, measured in millions of dollars. The year-end figure is used to correspond with the following figures, some of which are only available on an annual basis. Use the figure in this column to determine the actual dollar amounts invested in each asset category shown in columns 3 through 11 on the right-side pages. For example, if the firm has $500 million in invested assets and column 3 shows that 10% of its portfolio is in cash, the company has $50 million in cash.

   Looking at the right-side pages, columns 3 through 11 will, unless otherwise noted, add up to approximately 100%. Column 12 (investments in affiliates) is already included in other columns (usually 4, 5 or 6) depending upon the specific investment vehicle.

3. **Cash**

   Cash on hand and demand deposits. A negative cash position implies checks outstanding exceed cash balances, a situation not unusual for insurance companies.

4. **CMOs (Collateralized Mortgage Obligations) and Other Structured Securities**

   Mortgage-backed bonds that split the payments from mortgage pools into different classes, called tranches. The split may be based on maturity dates or a variety of other factors. For example, the owner of one type of CMO, called a PAC, receives principal and interest payments made by the mortgage holders between specific dates. The large majority of CMOs held by insurance companies are those issued by government agencies and carry very little risk of default. Virtually all of the CMOs included here are investment grade. However, they all carry some measure of risk based on the payment speed of the underlying mortgages.

5. **Other Investment Grade Bonds**

   All investment grade bonds other than the CMOs included in column 4. Specifically, this includes: (1) issues guaranteed by U.S. and foreign governments which are rated as "highest quality" (Class 1) by state insurance commissioners; (2) nonguaranteed obligations of governments, such as Fannie Maes, which do not carry full faith and credit guarantees; (3) obligations of governments rated as "high quality" (Class 2) by state insurance commissioners; (4) state and municipal bonds; plus (5) investment-grade corporate bonds as defined by the state insurance commissioners. The data shown in this column are based exclusively on the definition used by state insurance commissioners. However, on the companies for which a more detailed breakdown of bond ratings is available, the actual bond ratings - and not the data shown in this column - are used in our rating process to calculate the Investment Safety Index.

6. Noninvestment Grade Bonds

Low-rated issues – commonly known as "junk bonds" – which carry a high risk as defined by the state insurance commissioners. In an unfavorable economic environment, we generally assume that these will be far more subject to default than other categories of corporate bonds.

7. Common and Preferred Stock

Common and preferred equities. Although a certain amount is acceptable for the sake of diversification, excessive investment in this area is viewed as a factor that can increase the company's overall vulnerability to market declines.

8. Mortgages In Good Standing

Mortgages which are current in their payments. Mortgage-backed securities are excluded.

9. Non-performing Mortgages

Mortgages which are (a) 90 days or more past due; or (b) in process of foreclosure. If the mortgages have already been foreclosed, the asset is transferred to the next category - real estate. Clearly, a high level of nonperforming mortgages is a negative, reflecting on the quality of the entire mortgage portfolio.

10. Real Estate

Direct real estate investments including (a) property occupied by the company; and (b) properties acquired through foreclosure. A certain amount of real estate investment is considered acceptable for portfolio diversification. However, excessive amounts may subject the company to losses during a recessionary period.

11. Other Investments

Items such as premium notes, collateral loans, short-term investments, policy loans and a long list of miscellaneous items.

12. Investments in Affiliates

Bonds, preferred and common stocks, as well as other vehicles which many insurance companies use to invest in - and establish a corporate link with - affiliated companies. Since these can often be non-income-producing paper assets, they are considered less desirable than the equivalent securities of publicly traded companies. Investments in affiliates are also included in other columns (usually 4, 5 or 6). Therefore, the percentage shown here represents a duplication of some of the amounts shown in the other columns.

Footnotes:

(1) These companies have data items that are older than December 2008. They will be unrated (U) if they are not failed companies (F).

(2) Data items shown are from the company's 2007 annual statutory statement except for Risk-Adjusted Capital Indexes 1 and 2, Profitability Index, Investment Safety Index, Liquidity Index and Stability Index which have been updated using the company's September 2008 quarterly statutory statement. Other more recent data may have been factored into the rating when available.

(3) Data items shown are from the company's 2007 annual statutory statement except for Risk-Adjusted Capital Indexes 1 and 2, Profitability Index, Investment Safety Index, Liquidity Index and Stability Index which have been updated using the company's June 2008 quarterly statutory statement. Other more recent data may have been factored into the rating when available.

(4) Data items shown are from the company's 2007 annual statutory statement except for Risk-Adjusted Capital Indexes 1 and 2, Profitability Index, Investment Safety Index, Liquidity Index and Stability Index which have been updated using the company's March 2008 quarterly statutory statement. Other more recent data may have been factored into the rating when available.

(5) Data items shown are from the company's 2007 annual statutory statement. Other more recent data may have been factored into the rating when available.

(*) Breakdown of the company's investment portfolio, shown in percentages in columns 3-11 on the right hand page, does not total to 100% due to the inclusion of non–admitted assets in the bond or mortgage figures, or due to other accounting adjustments.

Stability Factors

(A) Stability Index was negatively impacted by the financial problems or weaknesses of a parent or **affiliate** company.

(C) Stability Index was negatively impacted by past results on our Risk-Adjusted **Capital** tests. In general, the Stability Index of any company can be affected by past results even if current results show improvement. While such improvement is a plus, the improved results must be maintained for a period of time to assure that the improvement is not a temporary fluctuation. During a five-year period, the impact of poor past results on the Stability Index gradually diminishes.

(D) Stability Index was negatively impacted by limited **diversification** of general business, policy, and/or investment risk. This factor especially affects smaller companies that do not issue as many policies as larger firms. It can also affect firms that specialize in only one line of business.

(E) Stability Index was negatively impacted due to a lack of operating **experience**. The company has been in operation for less than five years. Consequently, it has not been able to establish the kind of stable track record that we believe is needed to demonstrate financial permanence and strength.

(F) Stability Index was negatively impacted by negative cash **flow**. In other words, the company paid out more in claims and expenses than it received in premiums and investment income.

(G) Stability Index was negatively impacted by fast asset or premium **growth**. Fast growth can pose a serious problem for insurers. It is generally achieved by offering policies with premiums that are too low, benefits that are too costly, or agents commissions that are too high. Due to the highly competitive nature of the insurance marketplace, rapid growth has been a factor in many insurance insolvencies.

(I) Stability Index was negatively impacted by past results on our **Investment** Safety Index. This can pose a problem for insurers even after risky investments have been sold off. To illustrate, consider those companies that have sold off their junk bonds and now carry much smaller junk bond risk. For a period of time the company that had the junk bonds incorporated the expectation of higher yields into its policy design and marketing strategy. Only time will tell how the company's investment income margins and future sales will be affected by the junk bond sell off. So, while the Investment Safety Index would improve right away, the Stability Index would improve only gradually over a period of three years, if the transition to lower yielding investments is handled smoothly.

(L) Stability Index was negatively impacted by past results on our **liquidity** tests. In general, the Stability Index of any company can be affected by past results even if current results show improvement. While such improvement is a plus, the improved results must be maintained for a period of time to assure that the improvement is not a temporary fluctuation. During a five-year period, the impact of poor past results on the Stability Index gradually diminishes.

(O) Stability Index was negatively impacted by significant changes in the company's business **operations**. These changes can include shifts in the kinds of insurance offered by the company, a temporary or permanent freeze on the sale of new policies, or recent release from conservatorship. In these circumstances, past performance cannot be a reliable indicator of future financial strength.

(R) Stability Index was negatively impacted by concerns about the financial strength of its **reinsurers**.

(T) Stability Index was negatively impacted by significant **trends** in critical asset, liability, income or expense items. Examples include increasing surrender rates, increasing mortgage defaults, and shrinking premium volume.

(Z) This company is unrated due to data, as received by TheStreet.com Ratings, that are either incomplete in substantial ways or contain items that, in the opinion of TheStreet.com Ratings analysts, may not be reliable.

INSURANCE COMPANY NAME	DOM. STATE	RATING	TOTAL ASSETS ($MIL)	CAPITAL & SURPLUS ($MIL)	RISK ADJUSTED CAPITAL RATIO 1	RISK ADJUSTED CAPITAL RATIO 2	CAPITAL-IZATION INDEX (PTS)	INVEST. SAFETY INDEX (PTS)	PROFIT-ABILITY INDEX (PTS)	LIQUIDITY INDEX (PTS)	STAB. INDEX (PTS)	STABILITY FACTORS
AAA LIFE INS CO	MI	B	387.2	69.9	2.40	1.41	7.6	6.8	4.1	7.6	5.2	GT
ABILITY INS CO	NE	C-	515.6	24.6	1.94	1.15	7.2	6.1	1.7	8.7	2.7	FGT
ACACIA LIFE INS CO	DC	A-	1521.4	317.0	1.62	1.33	7.5	6.7	7.3	6.5	5.4	AFIT
ACE LIFE INS CO	CT	C	33.3	17.8	3.53	2.82	9.7	9.8	1.8	8.9	3.0	FGT
ACME LIFE INS CO	AZ	U	--	--	--	--	--	--	--	--	--	Z
ADAMS LIFE INS CO	AL	D+	2.3	1.7	1.96	1.77	8.2	6.5	2.1	10.0	2.4	DFIT
ADAMSON LIFE INS CO	AZ	U	--	--	--	--	--	--	--	--	--	Z
ADMIRAL LIFE INS CO OF AMERICA	AZ	C	14.7	9.3	4.92	4.42	10.0	8.7	5.5	7.8	4.1	AGOT
ADVANCE INS CO OF KS	KS	B	38.6	33.2	4.10	2.87	9.8	6.2	6.6	7.0	6.3	AIT
ADVANTA LIFE INS CO	AZ	D+	4.4	4.1	2.99	2.69	9.5	9.6	6.0	10.0	2.7	ADT
ADVANTAGE LIFE INS CO	TN	U	--	--	--	--	--	--	--	--	--	Z
AETNA HEALTH & LIFE INS CO	CT	B	1654.7	159.7	2.36	1.43	7.6	6.3	4.6	7.3	6.1	AI
▲ AETNA LIFE INS CO	CT	B	21125.8	3884.7	1.96	1.41	7.6	6.2	6.4	6.5	5.8	IT
AF&L INS CO	PA	E	169.8	0.2	0.05	0.04	0.0	0.0	0.2	7.6	0.0	CDIT
AGC LIFE INS CO	MO	U (1)	11339.4	5901.9	0.51	0.47	2.6	6.3	4.7	7.0	2.6	CFT
AGL LIFE ASSURANCE CO	PA	D+	4084.0	14.3	0.33	0.22	0.0	8.1	2.7	7.0	1.4	CT
AIG LIFE INS CO	DE	C+	9295.5	377.9	1.57	0.78	5.9	3.7	5.5	6.5	4.3	AFIT
AIG SUNAMERICA LIFE ASR CO	AZ	C+	22319.4	900.2	2.65	1.54	7.8	6.0	1.9	9.5	3.2	AFT
▼ ALABAMA LIFE REINS CO INC	AL	E	45.1	2.7	0.21	0.19	0.0	5.7	6.9	9.0	0.0	CDEFGIT
ALFA LIFE INS CORP	AL	B+	1087.3	150.9	3.29	1.97	8.5	7.7	5.5	7.8	6.4	A
ALL SAVERS INS CO	IN	U (1)	4.3	4.0	3.01	2.71	9.6	9.7	8.7	10.0	8.8	D
ALL SAVERS LIFE INS CO OF CA	CA	U (1)	11.6	11.4	4.40	3.96	8.0	8.9	8.5	10.0	8.0	D
ALLEGIANCE LIFE INS CO	IL	U (1)	285.4	271.3	1.19	1.06	7.1	0.9	7.9	10.0	2.9	DI
ALLIANCE HEALTH & LIFE INS CO	MI	B	37.2	16.2	0.81	0.67	4.4	8.6	1.5	2.0	4.9	CFLT
ALLIANZ LIFE & ANNUITY CO	MN	U (1)	16.3	11.4	3.85	3.47	8.0	9.8	5.4	9.5	7.0	DT
▼ ALLIANZ LIFE INS CO OF NORTH AMERICA	MN	C+	67509.3	1820.7	1.00	0.51	5.0	3.5	2.8	5.8	4.7	CI
ALLIANZ LIFE INS CO OF NY	NY	C	921.2	47.6	2.46	1.28	7.4	6.8	1.2	9.1	3.9	DGT
ALLIED FINANCIAL INS CO	TX	U (1)	0.4	0.4	2.21	1.98	8.5	9.8	3.1	10.0	3.3	DF
ALLSTATE ASR CO	IL	B	11.2	9.0	3.51	3.16	8.0	9.0	7.4	10.0	6.3	T
ALLSTATE LIFE INS CO	IL	B+	65002.0	3456.0	1.37	0.78	5.6	3.8	2.0	6.8	5.2	CIT
ALLSTATE LIFE INS CO OF NEW YORK	NY	B	7759.9	464.6	2.08	1.07	7.1	5.9	4.5	6.3	4.5	IT
ALTA HEALTH & LIFE INS CO	IN	B	31.6	21.6	9.37	8.44	4.0	9.2	6.1	6.9	4.8	AFT
AMALGAMATED LIFE & HEALTH INS CO	IL	C-	7.8	4.7	2.49	2.24	8.9	8.8	7.0	6.9	3.3	DF
AMALGAMATED LIFE INS CO	NY	A-	62.6	29.6	2.46	1.94	8.4	8.6	8.5	5.5	6.8	DL
AMBASSADOR LIFE INS CO	TX	C-	11.4	10.9	4.20	3.78	10.0	6.1	7.2	10.0	3.3	DT
AMERICAN BANKERS LIFE ASR CO OF FL	FL	B	654.2	111.8	5.22	2.97	10.0	6.7	6.2	6.8	4.7	AFT
AMERICAN CAPITOL INS CO	TX	D+	66.0	6.6	0.91	0.69	4.5	6.3	5.9	8.2	2.7	FT
AMERICAN CENTURY LIFE INS CO	OK	E	32.0	1.5	0.36	0.32	0.8	1.5	6.1	0.7	0.1	CDIL
AMERICAN CENTURY LIFE INS CO TX	TX	U (1)	0.4	0.2	1.18	1.06	7.1	8.4	7.2	6.9	6.4	DT
AMERICAN CLASSIC REINS CO	AZ	U	--	--	--	--	--	--	--	--	--	Z
AMERICAN COMMUNITY MUT INS CO	MI	B	139.7	72.8	1.50	1.14	7.2	6.9	1.8	0.8	4.9	FLT
AMERICAN CONTINENTAL INS CO	TN	C+	20.1	5.5	0.58	0.45	2.4	8.4	1.6	7.3	3.4	ACDEGT
AMERICAN CREDITORS LIFE INS CO	DE	U (1)	17.2	12.1	3.77	3.39	8.0	8.9	3.6	10.0	3.8	DT
AMERICAN EQUITY INVEST LIFE INS CO	IA	B-	13999.3	1003.6	2.41	1.23	7.3	6.1	2.8	3.7	5.0	L
AMERICAN EQUITY INVESTMENT LIFE NY	NY	B	117.8	33.6	3.68	3.32	10.0	7.2	7.2	6.6	5.2	ADFGT
AMERICAN EXCHANGE LIFE INS CO	TX	C-	438.8	425.7	1.11	0.99	6.9	1.3	9.1	10.0	3.0	DI
AMERICAN FAMILY LIFE ASR CO OF COLUM	NE	B+	67309.5	4975.9	2.34	1.38	7.6	4.9	6.7	7.3	6.4	I
AMERICAN FAMILY LIFE ASR CO OF NY	NY	B+	285.0	65.3	2.10	1.57	7.9	8.1	9.2	7.3	6.7	AD
AMERICAN FAMILY LIFE INS CO	WI	A+	3898.0	446.5	3.34	1.84	8.3	6.6	7.8	6.4	7.9	AI
AMERICAN FARM LIFE INS CO	TX	B	2.1	1.5	1.98	1.79	8.2	8.9	4.0	8.8	4.0	ADGOT
AMERICAN FARMERS & RANCHERS LIFE INS	OK	C	18.3	4.8	1.46	1.31	7.5	9.0	4.2	6.3	3.7	AD
AMERICAN FEDERATED LIFE INS CO	MS	C	17.4	5.9	1.83	1.64	8.0	8.6	6.9	9.2	4.1	AT

See Page 26 for explanation of footnotes and Page 27 for explanation of stability factors.

Arrows denote recent upgrades ▲ or downgrades ▼ (see Section VI for explanations)

30

www.thestreetratings.com

NET PREMIUM ($MIL)	IN-VESTED ASSETS ($MIL)	CASH	CMO & STRUCT. SECS.	OTH.INV. GRADE BONDS	NON-INV. GRADE BONDS	CMMON & PREF. STOCK	MORT IN GOOD STAND.	NON-PERF. MORT.	REAL ESTATE	OTHER INVEST-MENTS	INVEST. IN AFFIL	INSURANCE COMPANY NAME
						% OF INVESTED ASSETS IN:						
23.7	336.5	2.1	18.3	70.6	5.2	2.1	0.0	0.0	0.0	1.8	0.0 ●	AAA LIFE INS CO
6.1	505.8	0.2	22.1	75.1	0.1	2.5	0.0	0.0	0.0	0.0	0.0 ●	ABILITY INS CO
7.2	1,497.3	0.0	14.3	49.9	3.2	14.9	11.5	0.0	0.0	6.1	12.9 ●	ACACIA LIFE INS CO
0.2	33.9	37.4	0.0	62.6	0.0	0.0	0.0	0.0	0.0	0.1	0.0	ACE LIFE INS CO
--	--	--	--	--	--	--	--	--	--	--	--	ACME LIFE INS CO
0.0	2.5	58.5	26.9	0.0	0.0	14.6	0.0	0.0	0.0	0.0	0.0	ADAMS LIFE INS CO
--	--	--	--	--	--	--	--	--	--	--	--	ADAMSON LIFE INS CO
0.9	10.4	10.6	0.0	71.4	0.0	1.8	16.2	0.0	0.0	0.0	0.0	ADMIRAL LIFE INS CO OF AMERICA
2.7	36.8 (*)	-0.5	32.7	47.5	0.0	17.4	0.0	0.0	0.0	0.0	2.2 ●	ADVANCE INS CO OF KS
0.1	4.3	5.7	0.0	94.3	0.0	0.0	0.0	0.0	0.0	0.0	0.0	ADVANTA LIFE INS CO
--	--	--	--	--	--	--	--	--	--	--	--	ADVANTAGE LIFE INS CO
98.8	1,549.9	0.2	11.0	70.7	4.1	1.4	9.8	0.0	0.0	2.9	2.6 ●	AETNA HEALTH & LIFE INS CO
3,885.4	13,565.7	0.0	16.1	56.8	4.6	3.3	11.3	0.0	1.7	7.0	3.5 ●	AETNA LIFE INS CO
0.3	166.4	0.5	21.9	74.5	0.1	2.5	0.0	0.5	0.0	0.0	2.5	AF&L INS CO
1.5	10,133.5	0.0	0.1	3.3	0.0	96.6	0.0	0.0	0.0	0.0	99.6	AGC LIFE INS CO
32.5	69.4	5.4	1.6	9.1	0.0	0.0	0.0	0.0	0.0	83.9	0.0	AGL LIFE ASSURANCE CO
49.1	7,098.7	0.0	17.5	59.3	6.7	2.8	7.2	0.0	0.3	6.3	0.4 ●	AIG LIFE INS CO
256.6	5,061.7	-1.2	12.6	54.5	1.3	3.0	8.2	0.0	0.0	21.7	2.1 ●	AIG SUNAMERICA LIFE ASR CO
0.4	44.9	80.2	0.0	13.5	0.0	6.3	0.0	0.0	0.0	0.0	0.0	ALABAMA LIFE REINS CO INC
34.9	1,047.6	0.7	36.2	54.2	0.6	0.9	0.0	0.0	0.0	7.7	0.1 ●	ALFA LIFE INS CORP
0.0	4.2	3.2	0.0	96.8	0.0	0.0	0.0	0.0	0.0	0.0	0.0	ALL SAVERS INS CO
0.0	11.6	3.1	0.0	96.9	0.0	0.0	0.0	0.0	0.0	0.0	0.0	ALL SAVERS LIFE INS CO OF CA
1.5	284.3	0.1	0.0	1.6	3.0	95.3	0.0	0.0	0.0	0.0	95.1	ALLEGIANCE LIFE INS CO
30.7	26.7	-4.6	0.0	104.6	0.0	0.0	0.0	0.0	0.0	0.0	0.0	ALLIANCE HEALTH & LIFE INS CO
0.0	12.0	0.4	0.0	99.5	0.0	0.0	0.0	0.0	0.0	0.0	0.0	ALLIANZ LIFE & ANNUITY CO
2,643.3	53,294.0	0.0	30.7	52.6	1.4	1.4	9.2	0.0	0.7	4.1	4.8 ●	ALLIANZ LIFE INS CO OF NORTH AMERICA
77.6	420.2	0.9	32.6	66.0	0.4	0.1	0.0	0.0	0.0	0.0	0.0 ●	ALLIANZ LIFE INS CO OF NY
0.0	0.4	100.0	0.0	0.0	0.0	0.0	0.0	0.0	0.0	0.0	0.0	ALLIED FINANCIAL INS CO
0.0	9.8	0.0	0.0	97.8	0.0	2.2	0.0	0.0	0.0	0.0	0.0	ALLSTATE ASR CO
902.9	51,943.1	0.0	20.1	51.6	5.4	4.9	13.5	0.0	0.0	4.5	2.1 ●	ALLSTATE LIFE INS CO
104.2	6,869.2	-0.1	18.2	66.0	2.3	2.9	10.1	0.0	0.0	0.6	0.0 ●	ALLSTATE LIFE INS CO OF NEW YORK
7.1	16.4	-11.4	9.4	101.3	0.0	0.1	0.0	0.0	0.0	0.7	0.0	ALTA HEALTH & LIFE INS CO
1.6	6.7	5.7	30.5	54.0	0.0	0.0	0.0	0.0	0.0	9.8	0.0	AMALGAMATED LIFE & HEALTH INS CO
10.2	52.0	7.6	35.0	56.5	0.0	0.8	0.0	0.0	0.0	0.1	0.0 ●	AMALGAMATED LIFE INS CO
0.1	11.5	2.1	32.7	42.4	0.0	20.9	0.0	0.0	0.0	2.0	0.0	AMBASSADOR LIFE INS CO
20.5	597.2	2.7	3.4	65.3	4.1	9.5	9.3	0.0	3.6	2.1	0.0 ●	AMERICAN BANKERS LIFE ASR CO OF FL
0.7	65.4	11.1	23.1	50.9	0.6	9.0	0.0	0.0	0.0	5.3	3.9	AMERICAN CAPITOL INS CO
1.9	30.4 (*)	4.3	0.0	74.9	10.1	4.0	5.8	0.0	1.7	0.5	0.7	AMERICAN CENTURY LIFE INS CO
0.1	0.4	10.9	86.6	0.0	0.0	2.6	0.0	0.0	0.0	0.0	0.0	AMERICAN CENTURY LIFE INS CO TX
--	--	--	--	--	--	--	--	--	--	--	--	AMERICAN CLASSIC REINS CO
91.0	124.6 (*)	0.0	54.7	42.2	1.7	2.9	0.0	0.0	6.5	0.0	0.0 ●	AMERICAN COMMUNITY MUT INS CO
14.0	18.8 (*)	34.7	5.6	61.4	0.0	0.0	0.0	0.0	0.0	0.0	0.0	AMERICAN CONTINENTAL INS CO
0.0	17.2	9.0	0.0	13.7	0.0	1.4	0.0	0.0	0.0	76.0	0.0	AMERICAN CREDITORS LIFE INS CO
636.1	13,488.9	0.0	15.6	60.1	3.5	2.8	17.3	0.0	0.0	1.0	0.3 ●	AMERICAN EQUITY INVEST LIFE INS CO
1.8	116.0	2.9	47.8	43.7	4.7	0.0	0.0	0.0	0.0	0.9	0.0 ●	AMERICAN EQUITY INVESTMENT LIFE NY
0.3	477.0	2.1	0.0	5.1	0.0	91.4	0.0	0.0	0.0	1.5	91.4 ●	AMERICAN EXCHANGE LIFE INS CO
4,156.9	70,079.0	0.4	2.9	80.4	1.8	13.4	0.0	0.0	0.5	0.6	0.1 ●	AMERICAN FAMILY LIFE ASR CO OF COLUM
51.7	237.7	2.7	0.0	94.6	1.0	0.0	0.0	0.0	0.0	1.8	0.0 ●	AMERICAN FAMILY LIFE ASR CO OF NY
98.1	3,578.3	0.1	35.9	42.6	3.5	1.7	9.9	0.0	0.0	6.3	0.0 ●	AMERICAN FAMILY LIFE INS CO
0.1	2.1	11.3	5.6	78.1	0.0	4.8	0.0	0.0	0.0	0.2	0.0	AMERICAN FARM LIFE INS CO
0.5	17.2	1.4	27.5	70.3	0.0	0.0	0.0	0.0	0.0	0.7	0.0	AMERICAN FARMERS & RANCHERS LIFE INS
1.3	15.4	0.8	14.4	84.9	0.0	0.0	0.0	0.0	0.0	0.0	0.0	AMERICAN FEDERATED LIFE INS CO

● Bullets denote a more detailed analysis is available in Section II.

(*) Asset category percentages do not add up to 100%

INSURANCE COMPANY NAME	DOM. STATE	RATING	TOTAL ASSETS ($MIL)	CAPITAL & SURPLUS ($MIL)	RISK ADJUSTED CAPITAL RATIO 1	RISK ADJUSTED CAPITAL RATIO 2	CAPITAL-IZATION INDEX (PTS)	INVEST. SAFETY INDEX (PTS)	PROFIT-ABILITY INDEX (PTS)	LIQUIDITY INDEX (PTS)	STAB. INDEX (PTS)	STABILITY FACTORS
AMERICAN FIDELITY ASR CO	OK	A	3343.9	244.9	1.59	0.91	6.3	5.8	8.4	7.1	6.3	CI
AMERICAN FIDELITY LIFE INS CO	FL	B-	463.5	72.0	2.75	1.97	8.5	4.9	3.0	6.5	5.2	DI
AMERICAN FINANCIAL SECURITY L I C	MO	F (1)	3.1	3.0	2.98	2.68	9.5	9.7	2.0	10.0	0.0	DFGT
AMERICAN GENERAL ASSURANCE CO	IL	C	189.7	80.5	3.64	2.63	9.4	6.2	4.1	7.0	2.9	T
AMERICAN GENERAL LIFE & ACC INS CO	TN	B-	9139.2	588.9	1.87	1.00	7.0	4.9	8.1	4.8	5.0	AIL
AMERICAN GENERAL LIFE INS CO	TX	C+	38459.0	5312.5	1.42	1.09	7.1	6.3	6.8	6.8	4.6	AGT
AMERICAN HEALTH & LIFE INS CO	TX	B+	1505.6	683.7	6.08	4.25	10.0	6.6	6.5	9.2	5.2	IT
AMERICAN HERITAGE LIFE INS CO	FL	B	1317.5	200.8	1.13	0.91	6.3	6.3	6.8	6.3	5.5	CFIT
AMERICAN HOME LIFE INS CO	KS	C+	166.4	13.7	1.66	1.05	7.1	5.2	4.7	5.1	3.9	D
AMERICAN HOME LIFE INS CO	AR	E	15.0	0.8	0.29	0.26	0.1	0.0	2.0	0.1	0.1	CILT
▼ AMERICAN INCOME LIFE INS CO	IN	B+	1811.7	155.5	1.57	0.92	6.4	4.6	7.6	6.1	6.4	ACI
AMERICAN INDEPENDENT NETWORK INS CO	NY	D	22.3	8.9	2.39	2.15	8.7	8.9	8.1	8.9	1.4	AD
AMERICAN INDUSTRIES LIFE INS CO	TX	U (1)	3.2	3.0	2.99	2.56	9.3	3.0	3.6	9.1	3.0	DFIT
AMERICAN INTERNATL LIFE ASR CO OF NY	NY	C+	6514.9	335.8	1.96	0.92	6.4	3.8	2.4	7.1	4.4	AFIT
AMERICAN INVESTORS LIFE INS CO	KS	B-	15459.9	864.2	2.18	1.12	7.2	4.3	4.5	7.8	5.0	GI
AMERICAN LABOR LIFE INS CO	AZ	D	5.5	3.8	2.35	2.11	8.7	8.3	9.2	9.8	1.9	D
AMERICAN LIFE & ACC INS CO OF KY	KY	C	198.4	105.2	3.76	2.18	8.8	3.0	2.3	8.1	3.7	GIT
AMERICAN LIFE & ANNUITY CO	AR	E	37.2	1.0	0.19	0.16	0.0	1.8	3.3	2.1	0.0	CIL
AMERICAN LIFE INS CO	DE	C-	82005.8	3567.9	0.96	0.74	4.9	6.5	6.5	8.5	3.0	T
AMERICAN LIFE INS CO	IL	D+	3.2	2.0	1.97	1.77	8.2	4.9	2.0	6.9	2.4	DFT
AMERICAN MATURITY LIFE INS CO	CT	B	57.0	43.9	6.23	5.61	10.0	9.4	8.8	7.0	4.5	AT
AMERICAN MEDICAL & LIFE INS CO	NY	C	27.8	13.2	2.54	2.09	8.6	9.6	4.8	7.4	4.3	DG
AMERICAN MEDICAL SECURITY LIFE INS	WI	B	122.7	76.7	3.16	2.56	9.3	8.7	5.9	7.9	4.1	T
AMERICAN MEMORIAL LIFE INS CO	SD	B-	1968.5	85.5	1.40	0.73	5.6	3.8	5.6	6.2	4.9	ACI
AMERICAN MODERN LIFE INS CO	OH	B	62.6	17.9	1.10	1.02	7.0	7.4	2.8	8.4	5.0	A
▼ AMERICAN NATIONAL INS CO	TX	B	13984.5	1682.7	1.13	0.87	6.0	5.3	5.6	6.5	6.0	CI
AMERICAN NATIONAL LIFE INS CO OF TX	TX	B-	130.9	28.8	1.58	1.16	7.2	6.7	2.0	6.0	5.4	F
AMERICAN NETWORK INS CO	PA	F (1)	123.2	4.8	0.43	0.37	1.4	6.7	5.8	8.9	0.0	CDT
AMERICAN PHOENIX LIFE & REASSUR CO	CT	C	25.7	18.0	4.30	3.87	10.0	7.1	4.0	9.2	3.6	ADGT
AMERICAN PIONEER LIFE INS CO	FL	C-	154.7	17.2	1.19	0.83	5.6	6.6	1.8	5.9	3.3	FT
AMERICAN PROGRESSIVE L&H I C OF NY	NY	C	361.6	104.4	0.88	0.70	4.6	7.2	5.9	3.8	3.8	ACDL
AMERICAN PUBLIC LIFE INS CO	OK	B	77.0	14.1	1.26	0.93	6.4	7.7	3.8	6.4	6.3	CF
AMERICAN REPUBLIC CORP INS CO	NE	B	10.4	6.7	2.64	2.03	8.5	8.6	2.5	7.1	6.3	DGO
AMERICAN REPUBLIC INS CO	IA	A-	472.8	244.5	3.21	2.42	9.1	7.5	8.7	6.7	7.3	
AMERICAN RETIREMENT LIFE INS CO	OH	U (1)	6.4	5.5	3.13	2.82	9.7	9.6	5.1	10.0	6.1	FT
AMERICAN SAVINGS LIFE INS CO	AZ	C	23.1	11.9	1.97	1.49	7.7	3.1	7.3	7.4	3.6	DGIT
AMERICAN SERVICE LIFE INS CO	AR	U (1)	0.5	0.5	2.16	1.94	8.4	9.8	7.8	8.7	7.3	DFOT
AMERICAN UNDERWRITERS LIFE INS CO	AZ	D+	74.3	12.2	0.67	0.44	2.4	2.8	5.7	7.8	2.4	CDGIT
AMERICAN UNITED LIFE INS CO	IN	B+	12264.8	654.2	2.81	1.43	7.6	6.0	6.6	7.4	5.2	I
AMERICAN-AMICABLE LIFE INS CO OF TX	TX	B	354.6	58.1	1.22	1.05	7.1	7.9	4.7	6.2	5.5	D
AMERICO FINANCIAL LIFE & ANNUITY INS	TX	C+	3389.3	166.7	0.92	0.56	4.4	4.0	5.6	5.6	4.4	ACIT
AMERITAS LIFE INS CORP	NE	B+	4928.5	678.5	3.09	1.94	8.4	5.3	5.5	7.0	5.1	AIT
AMICA LIFE INS CO	RI	A-	950.4	154.9	3.68	2.15	8.7	7.0	6.0	6.6	6.9	A
AMIL INTERNATIONAL INS CO	TX	U (5)	--	--	--	--	--	--	--	--	--	Z
ANNUITY INVESTORS LIFE INS CO	OH	B-	1801.4	82.8	1.48	0.65	5.7	3.2	5.3	7.1	5.3	ACI
ANTHEM LIFE INS CO	IN	A-	288.0	69.4	2.04	1.48	7.7	8.1	8.3	6.9	7.1	A
ARKANSAS BANKERS LIFE INS CO	AR	D	4.8	1.6	1.09	0.98	6.8	7.7	4.8	8.8	2.3	F
ARKANSAS LIFE INS CO	AZ	C-	1.0	0.7	1.54	1.39	7.6	9.8	7.3	9.9	3.3	ADT
ASSOCIATED MUTUAL HOSP SVC OF MI	MI	C	12.9	8.3	1.91	1.58	7.9	9.5	7.1	6.9	3.9	DF
ASSUMPTION MUTUAL LIFE INS CO	MA	C	10.5	10.4	4.19	3.77	8.0	9.2	6.8	10.0	3.4	T
ASSURITY LIFE INS CO	NE	B+	2167.6	217.3	2.38	1.30	7.5	5.8	6.9	5.7	6.6	IL
ATLANTA LIFE INS CO	GA	C-	81.0	17.1	0.77	0.54	3.3	4.4	2.6	0.0	2.0	CDFILT

See Page 26 for explanation of footnotes and Page 27 for explanation of stability factors.

Arrows denote recent upgrades ▲ or downgrades ▼ (see Section VI for explanations)

32

www.thestreetratings.com

NET PREMIUM ($MIL)	IN-VESTED ASSETS ($MIL)	CASH	CMO & STRUCT. SECS.	OTH.INV. GRADE BONDS	NON-INV. GRADE BONDS	CMMON & PREF. STOCK	MORT IN GOOD STAND.	NON-PERF. MORT.	REAL ESTATE	OTHER INVEST-MENTS	INVEST. IN AFFIL	INSURANCE COMPANY NAME
172.3	2,944.9	5.2	33.5	46.6	1.5	0.9	11.1	0.0	0.1	1.1	0.0 ●	AMERICAN FIDELITY ASR CO
4.3	460.8	1.2	0.0	82.9	0.0	3.1	5.2	1.5	4.7	1.5	4.1 ●	AMERICAN FIDELITY LIFE INS CO
0.0	3.1 (*)	-0.1	0.0	95.1	0.0	0.0	0.0	0.0	0.0	0.0	0.0	AMERICAN FINANCIAL SECURITY L I C
16.4	171.3	1.0	17.6	65.8	3.6	9.5	0.0	0.0	0.0	2.5	12.5 ●	AMERICAN GENERAL ASSURANCE CO
266.5	8,746.3	0.0	14.3	56.9	6.0	3.2	13.0	0.0	0.5	6.4	1.2 ●	AMERICAN GENERAL LIFE & ACC INS CO
417.4	33,841.5	0.1	13.8	55.9	6.1	10.6	6.3	0.0	0.4	6.8	11.4 ●	AMERICAN GENERAL LIFE INS CO
31.2	1,450.7	1.3	28.4	57.5	6.6	6.2	0.0	0.0	0.0	0.1	5.2 ●	AMERICAN HEALTH & LIFE INS CO
111.0	1,205.5	-0.4	9.3	40.5	1.8	10.5	8.6	0.2	2.2	27.3	9.8 ●	AMERICAN HERITAGE LIFE INS CO
4.9	157.5	3.6	7.7	51.5	0.8	11.4	16.5	0.7	0.5	6.8	0.0	AMERICAN HOME LIFE INS CO
0.5	14.5	4.6	0.0	51.5	1.8	18.6	12.1	0.0	10.2	1.2	0.0	AMERICAN HOME LIFE INS CO
135.8	1,552.0	1.6	1.1	79.3	5.2	7.4	0.0	0.0	0.1	4.7	3.2 ●	AMERICAN INCOME LIFE INS CO
1.0	21.5	3.6	8.5	87.6	0.3	0.0	0.0	0.0	0.0	0.0	0.0	AMERICAN INDEPENDENT NETWORK INS CO
0.0	3.1	16.0	0.0	0.0	0.0	2.7	53.1	9.6	17.1	1.5	0.0	AMERICAN INDUSTRIES LIFE INS CO
32.2	6,185.1	0.0	15.9	63.8	6.3	3.7	7.5	0.0	0.4	2.4	1.1 ●	AMERICAN INTERNATL LIFE ASR CO OF NY
1,610.9	12,240.3	0.7	18.7	60.2	6.3	2.9	7.9	0.0	0.1	3.4	0.0 ●	AMERICAN INVESTORS LIFE INS CO
0.8	4.9	61.4	0.0	31.4	0.0	5.9	0.0	0.0	0.0	1.3	0.0	AMERICAN LABOR LIFE INS CO
4.0	200.7	1.2	3.4	39.6	0.0	48.1	0.0	0.0	7.6	0.1	0.0 ●	AMERICAN LIFE & ACC INS CO OF KY
1.1	36.3 (*)	1.5	34.4	45.5	1.6	12.2	0.0	0.0	0.4	0.1	0.0	AMERICAN LIFE & ANNUITY CO
-2,675.4	64,829.3	11.3	12.4	65.0	0.5	5.3	2.5	0.0	0.5	2.6	4.8 ●	AMERICAN LIFE INS CO
0.1	3.2 (*)	0.5	0.0	48.8	0.0	25.0	0.0	0.0	0.0	5.4	0.0	AMERICAN LIFE INS CO
0.0	43.8	0.0	0.0	100.0	0.0	0.0	0.0	0.0	0.0	0.0	0.0 ●	AMERICAN MATURITY LIFE INS CO
9.1	24.8	45.6	0.1	54.3	0.0	0.0	0.0	0.0	0.0	0.0	0.0	AMERICAN MEDICAL & LIFE INS CO
44.3	125.4	-1.4	3.7	97.5	0.0	0.0	0.0	0.0	0.0	0.0	0.0 ●	AMERICAN MEDICAL SECURITY LIFE INS
65.7	1,939.5	0.1	6.9	71.3	4.4	5.9	9.5	0.0	0.0	2.0	0.0 ●	AMERICAN MEMORIAL LIFE INS CO
2.5	59.2	-0.3	7.8	64.5	0.0	28.0	0.0	0.0	0.0	0.0	31.2	AMERICAN MODERN LIFE INS CO
730.3	12,662.7	-0.1	6.6	53.7	2.9	9.4	15.2	0.1	1.7	10.7	17.7 ●	AMERICAN NATIONAL INS CO
26.6	130.7	0.1	15.8	76.5	1.8	2.9	0.0	0.0	0.0	2.9	1.0 ●	AMERICAN NATIONAL LIFE INS CO OF TX
8.2	115.5 (*)	1.7	6.0	74.5	0.9	7.5	0.0	0.0	0.0	0.0	7.5	AMERICAN NETWORK INS CO
0.0	24.1	0.3	5.3	90.2	0.0	4.3	0.0	0.0	0.0	0.0	0.0	AMERICAN PHOENIX LIFE & REASSUR CO
19.8	136.7	-4.1	36.1	61.3	2.1	0.0	0.0	0.0	0.0	4.6	0.0	AMERICAN PIONEER LIFE INS CO
183.3	258.3	-5.4	39.2	60.5	4.9	0.0	0.0	0.0	0.0	0.8	0.0 ●	AMERICAN PROGRESSIVE L&H I C OF NY
10.6	69.4	3.4	44.8	45.8	0.0	2.1	1.3	0.0	1.6	1.0	0.0	AMERICAN PUBLIC LIFE INS CO
3.8	9.3	9.4	8.3	81.6	0.8	0.0	0.0	0.0	0.0	0.0	0.0	AMERICAN REPUBLIC CORP INS CO
105.5	448.6	1.7	29.5	62.0	2.5	1.6	0.0	0.0	1.4	1.4	1.6 ●	AMERICAN REPUBLIC INS CO
0.0	5.9	11.0	8.4	80.5	0.0	0.0	0.0	0.0	0.0	0.1	0.0	AMERICAN RETIREMENT LIFE INS CO
0.0	21.7	0.9	0.0	9.8	0.0	1.7	64.8	16.2	6.1	0.5	1.6	AMERICAN SAVINGS LIFE INS CO
0.2	0.5	42.1	0.0	52.5	0.0	5.4	0.0	0.0	0.0	0.2	5.4	AMERICAN SERVICE LIFE INS CO
2.0	74.9	5.9	16.3	21.8	11.8	27.1	12.5	0.0	3.5	1.1	9.7	AMERICAN UNDERWRITERS LIFE INS CO
543.8	7,067.7	-0.3	17.7	58.7	1.7	1.7	16.6	0.0	0.9	3.0	0.0 ●	AMERICAN UNITED LIFE INS CO
10.0	340.6	-0.9	59.0	24.2	0.1	11.4	0.0	0.0	0.9	4.9	11.4 ●	AMERICAN-AMICABLE LIFE INS CO OF TX
65.2	3,042.5	-0.8	27.5	49.3	1.7	9.0	10.4	0.1	0.0	2.9	3.8 ●	AMERICO FINANCIAL LIFE & ANNUITY INS
266.9	2,578.6	-0.4	13.9	47.2	3.5	9.2	15.0	0.0	2.5	9.2	3.5 ●	AMERITAS LIFE INS CORP
19.2	892.3	0.3	36.8	58.8	0.0	3.3	0.0	0.0	0.0	0.8	0.0 ●	AMICA LIFE INS CO
--	--	--	--	--	--	--	--	--	--	--	--	AMIL INTERNATIONAL INS CO
107.8	1,301.5	0.7	40.6	50.5	3.7	0.4	0.0	0.0	0.0	4.1	0.0 ●	ANNUITY INVESTORS LIFE INS CO
42.0	267.3	0.3	18.4	80.5	0.0	0.6	0.0	0.0	0.0	0.1	0.0 ●	ANTHEM LIFE INS CO
0.3	4.8 (*)	32.9	0.0	53.4	3.5	8.0	0.0	0.0	0.0	0.0	0.0	ARKANSAS BANKERS LIFE INS CO
0.1	1.0	72.5	0.0	27.6	0.0	0.0	0.0	0.0	0.0	0.0	0.0	ARKANSAS LIFE INS CO
5.5	11.7 (*)	47.6	6.2	46.7	0.0	0.8	0.0	0.0	0.0	0.0	0.7	ASSOCIATED MUTUAL HOSP SVC OF MI
0.0	10.5	29.4	0.0	68.6	0.0	0.0	0.0	0.0	0.0	2.0	0.0	ASSUMPTION MUTUAL LIFE INS CO
66.3	2,093.3	-0.3	4.9	68.4	2.8	2.8	15.8	0.0	0.6	5.0	0.1 ●	ASSURITY LIFE INS CO
16.6	22.5	1.1	14.0	59.5	0.0	9.0	0.0	0.0	16.1	0.2	0.0	ATLANTA LIFE INS CO

● Bullets denote a more detailed analysis is available in Section II.

(*) Asset category percentages do not add up to 100%

INSURANCE COMPANY NAME	DOM. STATE	RATING	TOTAL ASSETS ($MIL)	CAPITAL & SURPLUS ($MIL)	RISK ADJUSTED CAPITAL RATIO 1	RISK ADJUSTED CAPITAL RATIO 2	CAPITAL-IZATION INDEX (PTS)	INVEST. SAFETY INDEX (PTS)	PROFIT-ABILITY INDEX (PTS)	LIQUIDITY INDEX (PTS)	STAB. INDEX (PTS)	STABILITY FACTORS
ATLANTIC COAST LIFE INS CO	SC	B+	69.9	13.7	2.03	1.67	8.0	4.7	5.5	6.6	5.2	DI
ATLANTIC SOUTHERN INS CO	PR	D- (2)	18.2	8.6	2.68	1.79	8.2	7.2	7.4	7.0	1.2	AFT
AURORA NATIONAL LIFE ASR CO	CA	C+	3120.2	333.5	4.19	2.26	8.9	7.9	5.9	6.7	4.8	F
AUTO CLUB LIFE INS CO	MI	B-	429.0	47.8	1.19	0.83	5.6	6.4	4.3	5.9	5.2	I
AUTO-OWNERS LIFE INS CO	MI	A	2168.0	225.0	2.50	1.33	7.5	5.9	6.6	6.3	6.0	AIT
AUTOMOBILE CLUB OF SOUTHERN CA INS	CA	B	437.5	34.2	1.43	0.82	5.6	4.5	1.8	6.7	5.6	CGI
AVIVA LIFE & ANNUITY CO	IA	C+	25060.9	1154.6	1.25	0.67	5.4	3.5	2.8	6.2	4.5	CGIT
AVIVA LIFE & ANNUITY CO OF NY	NY	C	1432.1	95.3	1.74	0.89	6.1	4.3	2.0	5.2	4.3	IT
AXA CORPORATE SOLUTIONS LIFE REINS	DE	B	1649.4	122.2	2.65	1.40	7.6	6.8	1.0	10.0	4.7	AG
AXA EQUITABLE LIFE & ANNUITY CO	CO	B-	492.4	52.7	2.36	1.22	7.3	7.4	6.2	5.4	3.6	AFT
▼ AXA EQUITABLE LIFE INS CO	NY	C-	108227.8	2234.7	0.71	0.45	2.7	3.9	1.5	7.0	2.7	CFT
BALBOA LIFE INS CO	CA	B	44.3	31.8	1.46	1.36	7.5	7.9	6.7	7.8	6.7	A
BALBOA LIFE INS CO OF NY	NY	B	18.1	17.5	5.30	4.77	10.0	9.1	9.2	10.0	5.9	AT
BALTIMORE LIFE INS CO	MD	B	836.1	70.5	2.27	1.16	7.2	5.7	7.3	5.3	6.1	IL
BANC ONE KENTUCKY INS CO	KY	U (1)	4.0	3.8	3.02	2.72	9.6	9.2	4.5	10.0	4.2	DT
BANKERS CAPITAL LIFE INS CO	AZ	U	--	--	--	--	--	--	--	--	--	Z
BANKERS CONSECO LIFE INS CO	NY	D	261.3	26.6	2.56	1.92	8.4	5.7	1.7	7.0	1.8	D
BANKERS FIDELITY LIFE INS CO	GA	B	108.7	28.5	2.42	1.70	8.1	5.5	6.8	6.5	5.5	ADI
BANKERS LIFE & CAS CO	IL	D+	11637.0	588.2	1.07	0.59	5.1	3.0	7.7	5.4	2.7	AI
BANKERS LIFE INS CO	FL	D+	230.5	9.9	0.95	0.50	4.6	0.8	5.9	7.2	2.6	CDGIT
BANKERS LIFE INS CO OF AMERICA	TX	D-	5.3	0.7	0.49	0.44	2.3	4.8	5.8	5.8	1.3	CDFI
BANKERS LIFE OF LOUISIANA	LA	C	13.3	5.1	1.54	1.15	7.2	7.8	4.7	8.5	4.3	AG
BANNER LIFE INS CO	MD	D+	1316.3	191.5	1.21	0.91	6.3	7.0	1.4	5.3	2.5	FGT
BASNEY AUTO GROUP LIFE INS CO	AZ	U	--	--	--	--	--	--	--	--	--	Z
BCS LIFE INS CO	IL	B	178.5	80.5	3.69	2.85	9.8	8.2	8.5	6.7	5.9	ADFT
BECK LIFE INS CO	AZ	U	--	--	--	--	--	--	--	--	--	Z
BENEFICIAL LIFE INS CO	UT	C+	3445.5	438.7	2.70	1.22	7.3	4.5	8.5	5.1	4.3	IT
BENICORP INS CO	IN	F (5)	--	--	--	--	--	--	--	--	--	Z
BENTON LIFE INS CO	TN	U	--	--	--	--	--	--	--	--	--	Z
BENTON LIFE INS CO INC	LA	F (5)	--	--	--	--	--	--	--	--	--	Z
BENTON LIFE INS CO INC	LA	F (5)	--	--	--	--	--	--	--	--	--	Z
BENTON LIFE INS CO INC	LA	F (5)	--	--	--	--	--	--	--	--	--	Z
BENTON LIFE INS CO INC	LA	F (5)	--	--	--	--	--	--	--	--	--	Z
BENTON LIFE INS CO INC	LA	F (5)	--	--	--	--	--	--	--	--	--	Z
BENTON LIFE INS CO INC	LA	F (5)	--	--	--	--	--	--	--	--	--	Z
BENTON LIFE INS CO INC	LA	F (5)	--	--	--	--	--	--	--	--	--	Z
BENTON LIFE INS CO INC	LA	F (5)	--	--	--	--	--	--	--	--	--	Z
BENTON LIFE INS CO INC	LA	F (5)	--	--	--	--	--	--	--	--	--	Z
BENTON LIFE INS CO INC	LA	U	--	--	--	--	--	--	--	--	--	Z
BERKLEY LIFE & HEALTH INS CO	IA	B	27.2	25.8	6.27	5.64	8.0	8.8	8.1	10.0	4.3	AOT
BERKSHIRE HATHAWAY LIFE INS CO OF NE	NE	B-	3595.3	767.7	1.02	0.80	5.4	3.7	5.5	10.0	4.4	CFIT
BERKSHIRE LIFE INS CO OF AMERICA	MA	A	2502.2	429.3	4.95	2.92	9.9	6.5	8.8	8.1	7.8	AI
BEST LIFE & HEALTH INS CO	TX	C	15.7	9.4	1.03	0.83	5.6	7.0	5.4	3.9	3.9	DFL
BEST MERIDIAN INS CO	FL	B	168.9	30.0	2.38	1.56	7.8	7.3	7.2	6.9	5.2	DGT
BEVERLY HILLS LIFE INS CO	AZ	U	--	--	--	--	--	--	--	--	--	Z
BIG SKY LIFE INC	MT	C-	1.4	0.6	0.90	0.81	5.5	6.4	6.0	10.0	2.7	DT
BIRD INS CO	AZ	U (1)	0.5	0.5	2.15	1.93	3.0	9.6	4.1	10.0	2.9	DET
BLUE CROSS BLUE SHIELD OF KANSAS INC	KS	B	1010.3	516.8	1.58	1.24	7.4	4.9	6.2	6.1	6.3	I
BLUE SHIELD OF CALIFORNIA L&H INS CO	CA	A-	364.2	183.6	1.70	1.35	5.5	8.5	7.8	5.8	7.0	GT
BLUE SPIRIT INS CO	VT	U	--	--	--	--	--	--	--	--	--	Z
BLUEBONNET LIFE INS CO	MS	B+	39.2	34.7	6.33	5.70	10.0	8.6	9.6	9.8	6.5	AD

See Page 26 for explanation of footnotes and Page 27 for explanation of stability factors.

Arrows denote recent upgrades ▲ or downgrades ▼ (see Section VI for explanations)

34

www.thestreetratings.com

NET PREMIUM ($MIL)	IN-VESTED ASSETS ($MIL)	CASH	CMO & STRUCT. SECS.	OTH.INV. GRADE BONDS	NON-INV. GRADE BONDS	CMMON & PREF. STOCK	MORT IN GOOD STAND.	NON-PERF. MORT.	REAL ESTATE	OTHER INVEST-MENTS	INVEST. IN AFFIL	INSURANCE COMPANY NAME
3.0	65.4	1.0	32.5	42.1	0.1	4.2	11.3	0.0	6.2	2.6	0.0	ATLANTIC COAST LIFE INS CO
8.6	15.4	2.0	57.0	23.8	0.0	7.1	0.0	0.0	9.6	0.6	0.0	ATLANTIC SOUTHERN INS CO
0.4	3,104.6	0.4	15.2	74.7	0.8	1.1	0.0	0.0	0.0	7.8	0.0 •	AURORA NATIONAL LIFE ASR CO
14.7	406.0	0.4	30.7	51.4	6.9	5.0	0.0	0.0	0.0	5.6	4.7 •	AUTO CLUB LIFE INS CO
57.8	2,056.2	0.1	14.9	67.3	0.3	2.5	10.1	0.1	4.1	0.7	0.0 •	AUTO-OWNERS LIFE INS CO
41.5	387.5	0.0	24.5	68.3	5.0	0.5	0.0	0.0	0.0	1.7	0.0 •	AUTOMOBILE CLUB OF SOUTHERN CA INS
1,066.4	22,107.2	0.0	9.4	70.0	6.9	3.5	5.7	0.0	0.0	4.6	0.6 •	AVIVA LIFE & ANNUITY CO
24.9	1,345.7	-0.1	14.4	74.8	7.1	0.8	1.1	0.0	0.0	2.0	0.0 •	AVIVA LIFE & ANNUITY CO OF NY
23.3	1,380.1	31.0	9.5	58.8	0.1	0.0	0.0	0.0	0.0	0.5	0.0 •	AXA CORPORATE SOLUTIONS LIFE REINS
-2.1	482.3	-0.1	7.3	41.8	0.4	0.0	0.0	0.0	0.0	50.6	0.0 •	AXA EQUITABLE LIFE & ANNUITY CO
3,558.0	39,534.8	0.3	10.5	55.0	1.9	6.8	9.3	0.0	1.2	15.2	5.0 •	AXA EQUITABLE LIFE INS CO
3.8	40.1	2.8	30.0	22.1	0.0	43.3	0.0	0.0	0.0	1.8	43.3 •	BALBOA LIFE INS CO
0.2	16.3	-1.5	46.5	55.0	0.0	0.0	0.0	0.0	0.0	0.0	0.0	BALBOA LIFE INS CO OF NY
24.4	803.3	0.4	12.9	61.6	2.9	6.0	10.3	0.0	1.4	4.5	0.0 •	BALTIMORE LIFE INS CO
0.0	4.0	5.2	0.0	94.9	0.0	0.0	0.0	0.0	0.0	0.0	0.0	BANC ONE KENTUCKY INS CO
--	--	--	--	--	--	--	--	--	--	--	--	BANKERS CAPITAL LIFE INS CO
8.7	245.7	7.4	23.4	65.7	0.6	2.0	0.0	0.0	0.0	1.0	0.0 •	BANKERS CONSECO LIFE INS CO
14.4	103.3	6.7	0.0	78.5	4.3	7.0	0.0	0.0	0.0	3.5	0.0 •	BANKERS FIDELITY LIFE INS CO
694.5	10,999.6	4.7	21.3	55.9	7.3	2.1	8.1	0.1	0.0	0.5	0.7 •	BANKERS LIFE & CAS CO
17.8	210.9	2.5	64.3	23.0	8.5	1.4	0.0	0.0	0.4	0.3	0.0	BANKERS LIFE INS CO
0.2	4.9	2.6	0.0	68.5	0.6	0.6	0.0	0.0	20.2	7.7	0.0	BANKERS LIFE INS CO OF AMERICA
2.9	13.0	5.0	21.3	71.4	0.2	2.1	0.0	0.0	0.0	0.0	0.0	BANKERS LIFE OF LOUISIANA
27.8	1,161.0	-0.9	13.5	73.4	0.5	10.6	0.0	0.0	0.0	2.9	8.3 •	BANNER LIFE INS CO
--	--	--	--	--	--	--	--	--	--	--	--	BASNEY AUTO GROUP LIFE INS CO
47.8	150.7	2.4	47.5	49.2	0.8	0.0	0.0	0.0	0.0	0.1	3.8 •	BCS LIFE INS CO
--	--	--	--	--	--	--	--	--	--	--	--	BECK LIFE INS CO
104.6	3,302.4	0.5	48.2	37.2	7.6	0.7	0.0	0.0	0.3	4.7	0.1 •	BENEFICIAL LIFE INS CO
--	--	--	--	--	--	--	--	--	--	--	--	BENICORP INS CO
--	--	--	--	--	--	--	--	--	--	--	--	BENTON LIFE INS CO
--	--	--	--	--	--	--	--	--	--	--	--	BENTON LIFE INS CO INC
--	--	--	--	--	--	--	--	--	--	--	--	BENTON LIFE INS CO INC
--	--	--	--	--	--	--	--	--	--	--	--	BENTON LIFE INS CO INC
--	--	--	--	--	--	--	--	--	--	--	--	BENTON LIFE INS CO INC
--	--	--	--	--	--	--	--	--	--	--	--	BENTON LIFE INS CO INC
--	--	--	--	--	--	--	--	--	--	--	--	BENTON LIFE INS CO INC
--	--	--	--	--	--	--	--	--	--	--	--	BENTON LIFE INS CO INC
--	--	--	--	--	--	--	--	--	--	--	--	BENTON LIFE INS CO INC
--	--	--	--	--	--	--	--	--	--	--	--	BENTON LIFE INS CO INC
--	--	--	--	--	--	--	--	--	--	--	--	BENTON LIFE INS CO INC
--	--	--	--	--	--	--	--	--	--	--	--	BENTON LIFE INS CO INC
0.0	25.9	0.2	12.0	87.4	0.0	0.0	0.0	0.0	0.0	0.4	0.0 •	BERKLEY LIFE & HEALTH INS CO
0.0	3,492.2 (*)	0.4	47.0	10.3	22.1	23.0	0.0	0.0	0.0	0.0	24.0 •	BERKSHIRE HATHAWAY LIFE INS CO OF NE
107.9	2,338.9	0.5	1.8	81.7	1.6	0.0	14.0	0.0	0.3	0.2	0.0 •	BERKSHIRE LIFE INS CO OF AMERICA
12.4	14.3	23.7	0.0	64.5	1.7	2.3	7.9	0.0	0.0	0.0	7.9	BEST LIFE & HEALTH INS CO
12.5	151.7	4.1	47.2	41.1	1.3	0.3	0.0	0.0	1.3	4.7	0.0 •	BEST MERIDIAN INS CO
--	--	--	--	--	--	--	--	--	--	--	--	BEVERLY HILLS LIFE INS CO
0.1	1.6 (*)	2.9	0.0	119.6	0.0	24.4	0.0	0.0	0.0	0.0	0.0	BIG SKY LIFE INC
0.0	0.5	0.0	0.0	100.0	0.0	0.0	0.0	0.0	0.0	0.0	0.0	BIRD INS CO
402.2	897.3	-2.7	26.9	42.8	0.3	28.3	0.0	0.0	3.2	1.1	8.8 •	BLUE CROSS BLUE SHIELD OF KANSAS INC
257.0	309.5	0.7	35.9	63.0	0.1	0.0	0.0	0.0	0.0	0.4	0.0 •	BLUE SHIELD OF CALIFORNIA L&H INS CO
--	--	--	--	--	--	--	--	--	--	--	--	BLUE SPIRIT INS CO
1.8	37.6	0.1	42.0	38.4	0.4	0.0	0.0	0.0	0.0	19.0	0.0 •	BLUEBONNET LIFE INS CO

• **Bullets denote a more detailed analysis is available in Section II.**

(*) **Asset category percentages do not add up to 100%**

INSURANCE COMPANY NAME	DOM. STATE	RATING	TOTAL ASSETS ($MIL)	CAPITAL & SURPLUS ($MIL)	RISK ADJUSTED CAPITAL RATIO 1	RISK ADJUSTED CAPITAL RATIO 2	CAPITAL-IZATION INDEX (PTS)	INVEST. SAFETY INDEX (PTS)	PROFIT-ABILITY INDEX (PTS)	LIQUIDITY INDEX (PTS)	STAB. INDEX (PTS)	STABILITY FACTORS
BOOKER T WASHINGTON INS CO INC	AL	F (5)	--	--	--	--	--	--	--	--	--	Z
BOSTON MUTUAL LIFE INS CO	MA	B+	945.5	80.1	1.69	1.08	7.1	6.7	6.3	5.4	6.4	IL
BROKERS NATIONAL LIFE ASR CO	AR	B	27.8	17.7	2.06	1.64	8.0	8.0	8.3	7.0	5.7	D
BROOKE LIFE INS CO	MI	C	3925.2	2194.4	0.66	0.59	3.7	1.2	7.8	9.3	3.7	CGIT
BUPA INS CO	FL	D+	106.3	25.1	0.86	0.71	4.7	8.6	3.7	7.8	2.4	CD
CAMBRIDGE LIFE INS CO	MO	B-	88.7	51.6	2.45	2.03	8.5	9.4	1.9	4.2	3.9	CDFGLT
CANADA LIFE ASSURANCE CO-US BRANCH	MI	B-	4230.5	217.6	1.87	0.91	6.3	5.9	8.7	7.9	4.2	FGT
CANADA LIFE INS CO OF AMERICA	MI	B-	1826.7	184.2	3.26	1.49	7.7	5.3	6.4	9.5	4.9	FIT
CANYON STATE LIFE INS CO	AZ	U (5)	--	--	--	--	--	--	--	--	--	Z
CAPITAL RESERVE LIFE INS CO	MO	D	6.5	1.7	0.97	0.87	6.0	8.5	2.7	7.1	1.7	CGIT
CAPITAL SECURITY LIFE INS CO	OK	U	--	--	--	--	--	--	--	--	--	Z
CAPITOL LIFE & ACCIDENT INS CO	AR	U (1)	0.4	0.3	2.08	1.87	8.0	9.8	2.1	7.0	2.6	DT
CAPITOL LIFE INS CO	TX	F (1)	209.5	8.3	0.85	0.60	3.8	0.8	2.9	7.7	0.0	CDFIOT
CAPITOL SECURITY LIFE INS CO	TX	D-	4.2	0.9	0.67	0.60	3.8	9.8	7.0	9.0	1.1	ACD
CARDIF LIFE INS CO	KS	D+	60.6	14.9	2.04	1.84	8.3	8.3	1.9	8.1	2.5	FT
CAREAMERICA LIFE INS CO	CA	B	28.1	24.5	5.68	5.11	10.0	8.6	7.6	9.8	5.9	T
CARIBBEAN AMERICAN LIFE ASR CO	PR	B	63.1	21.0	3.16	2.49	9.2	8.5	6.7	8.0	4.2	AFT
CARLISLE LIFE INS CO	AZ	U	--	--	--	--	--	--	--	--	--	Z
CASS COUNTY LIFE INS CO	TX	E	3.6	0.2	0.16	0.15	0.0	0.7	4.7	7.4	0.0	CDFI
CATERPILLAR LIFE INS CO	MO	U (1)	155.6	46.9	3.51	3.02	8.0	6.1	3.9	10.0	5.2	D
CBI INS CO	AZ	U	--	--	--	--	--	--	--	--	--	Z
CELTIC INS CO	IL	B	63.8	23.3	1.36	1.10	7.2	8.6	6.1	6.6	4.9	AFT
CENSTAT LIFE ASR CO	AZ	C (5)	--	--	--	--	--	--	--	--	--	Z
CENTRAL AMERICAN LIFE INS CO	LA	C (1)	17.7	16.0	1.94	1.82	8.2	6.8	6.8	0.0	2.0	ACDFLT
CENTRAL BENEFITS NATL LIFE INS CO	OH	C-	6.8	6.8	4.27	3.85	10.0	8.9	1.8	10.0	2.5	ADFT
CENTRAL LIFE INS CO	TN	U	--	--	--	--	--	--	--	--	--	Z
CENTRAL RESERVE LIFE INS CO	OH	C	25.4	14.9	0.91	0.82	5.6	6.4	2.7	6.9	3.5	CT
CENTRAL SECURITY LIFE INS CO	TX	C	81.2	7.8	0.96	0.87	6.0	6.9	8.4	5.6	4.2	D
CENTRAL STATES H & L CO OF OMAHA	NE	B-	318.9	86.7	3.91	2.92	9.9	6.5	4.5	7.8	5.2	T
CENTRAL UNITED LIFE INS CO	AR	D+	316.3	39.3	0.68	0.57	3.6	6.8	5.9	7.1	2.8	CDF
CENTRE LIFE INS CO	MA	C+	2012.1	89.5	3.43	1.77	8.2	6.3	5.2	7.6	4.7	AFT
CENTURION LIFE INS CO	IA	B-	1699.1	1000.5	29.58	15.80	10.0	6.8	9.2	9.5	5.2	AGT
CENTURY CREDIT LIFE INS CO	MS	U (1)	32.4	31.9	6.60	5.94	4.0	9.0	8.9	10.0	6.0	D
CENTURY LIFE ASR CO	OK	D+	9.4	5.0	2.29	2.06	8.6	7.8	7.4	9.2	2.7	ADT
CHAMPIONS LIFE INS CO	TX	C-	41.3	4.9	0.32	0.27	0.2	5.6	6.8	4.7	1.9	CLT
CHARTER NATIONAL LIFE INS CO	IL	A-	133.2	10.1	3.53	3.18	8.0	9.5	8.9	7.0	5.5	AT
CHEROB LIFE INS CO	AZ	U	--	--	--	--	--	--	--	--	--	Z
CHEROKEE NATIONAL LIFE INS CO	GA	B+	30.8	11.8	2.74	2.47	9.2	7.6	8.3	8.0	5.2	AFT
CHESAPEAKE LIFE INS CO	OK	C+	78.8	43.0	2.70	2.09	8.6	8.5	2.0	6.3	4.0	FGT
CHRISTIAN FIDELITY LIFE INS CO	TX	B-	84.5	34.7	1.64	1.34	7.5	7.4	9.1	7.0	4.9	AD
CHURCH LIFE INS CORP	NY	C+	203.7	30.0	3.17	2.08	8.6	6.9	5.7	6.0	4.8	DT
CICA LIFE INS CO OF AMERICA	CO	D+ (1)	404.0	38.3	0.49	0.46	2.5	8.8	6.1	6.1	2.4	CD
CIGNA LIFE INS CO OF NEW YORK	NY	B-	398.2	104.2	3.96	2.74	9.6	7.9	8.1	7.8	5.2	AD
CIGNA WORLDWIDE INS CO	DE	C	52.6	15.7	2.32	2.09	8.6	8.7	6.5	9.2	2.6	DT
CINCINNATI EQUITABLE LIFE INS CO	OH	C-	20.3	8.5	1.38	1.27	7.4	6.5	2.0	7.4	3.1	DGT
CINCINNATI LIFE INS CO	OH	B	2476.6	253.6	2.20	1.24	7.4	5.5	2.9	6.8	4.8	IT
CITCO LIFE INS CO	AZ	U	--	--	--	--	--	--	--	--	--	Z
CITIZENS ACCIDENT & HEALTH INS CO	AZ	B-	3.0	0.9	0.87	0.78	4.0	8.8	7.6	10.0	5.1	ACT
CITIZENS FIDELITY INS CO	AR	C	51.5	6.4	0.97	0.88	6.0	4.6	6.4	7.3	3.6	DT
CITIZENS NATIONAL LIFE INS CO	TX	D+	11.7	1.9	3.04	2.73	9.6	9.6	1.8	6.4	2.6	ADT
CITIZENS SECURITY LIFE INS CO	KY	D-	126.5	6.3	0.55	0.33	1.4	0.1	1.9	5.3	1.3	CFI
CM LIFE INS CO	CT	B	7462.3	699.8	1.51	0.92	6.4	5.2	6.7	6.6	5.2	CGIT

See Page 26 for explanation of footnotes and Page 27 for explanation of stability factors.

Arrows denote recent upgrades ▲ or downgrades ▼ (see Section VI for explanations)

36

www.thestreetratings.com

NET PREMIUM ($MIL)	IN-VESTED ASSETS ($MIL)	% OF INVESTED ASSETS IN:									INVEST. IN AFFIL	INSURANCE COMPANY NAME
		CASH	CMO & STRUCT. SECS.	OTH. INV. GRADE BONDS	NON-INV. GRADE BONDS	CMMON & PREF. STOCK	MORT IN GOOD STAND.	NON-PERF. MORT.	REAL ESTATE	OTHER INVEST-MENTS		
--	--	--	--	--	--	--	--	--	--	--	--	BOOKER T WASHINGTON INS CO INC
47.6	836.2	0.3	18.9	48.5	0.1	2.4	16.8	0.0	0.6	12.4	1.4 ●	BOSTON MUTUAL LIFE INS CO
10.6	25.2	10.8	17.8	68.2	0.5	2.0	0.0	0.0	0.0	0.8	0.5	BROKERS NATIONAL LIFE ASR CO
11.9	4,123.7	0.0	2.0	6.8	0.3	90.9	0.0	0.0	0.0	0.1	90.8 ●	BROOKE LIFE INS CO
28.7	70.7	16.4	0.0	1.9	0.0	7.7	0.0	0.0	0.0	74.0	7.7	BUPA INS CO
21.4	32.6	28.4	1.7	69.9	0.0	0.0	0.0	0.0	0.0	0.0	0.0 ●	CAMBRIDGE LIFE INS CO
28.2	3,154.5	0.2	25.1	51.7	2.1	0.0	11.0	0.1	0.0	9.9	0.0 ●	CANADA LIFE ASSURANCE CO-US BRANCH
0.4	1,646.9	0.0	17.7	41.7	2.4	5.3	32.5	0.0	0.0	0.4	0.0 ●	CANADA LIFE INS CO OF AMERICA
--	--	--	--	--	--	--	--	--	--	--	--	CANYON STATE LIFE INS CO
0.1	5.9	74.7	0.0	20.2	0.0	0.0	0.0	0.0	0.0	5.1	0.0	CAPITAL RESERVE LIFE INS CO
--	--	--	--	--	--	--	--	--	--	--	--	CAPITAL SECURITY LIFE INS CO
0.0	0.3	22.9	0.0	77.1	0.0	0.0	0.0	0.0	0.0	0.0	0.0	CAPITOL LIFE & ACCIDENT INS CO
6.4	201.2	0.1	22.2	51.6	5.9	5.3	1.7	0.0	0.0	13.3	0.0	CAPITOL LIFE INS CO
0.3	3.6	11.8	0.0	88.2	0.0	0.0	0.0	0.0	0.0	0.0	0.0	CAPITOL SECURITY LIFE INS CO
1.0	54.7	1.5	57.1	39.4	0.7	0.8	0.0	0.0	0.0	0.5	0.0	CARDIF LIFE INS CO
0.7	27.1	3.3	50.2	45.9	0.0	0.0	0.0	0.0	0.0	0.5	0.0	CAREAMERICA LIFE INS CO
2.4	62.3	17.5	41.9	35.1	0.0	5.5	0.0	0.0	0.0	0.0	5.5	CARIBBEAN AMERICAN LIFE ASR CO
--	--	--	--	--	--	--	--	--	--	--	--	CARLISLE LIFE INS CO
0.0	3.5	31.7	0.0	36.0	8.7	5.7	14.3	0.0	0.0	4.3	0.0	CASS COUNTY LIFE INS CO
0.0	153.2	1.2	41.5	48.4	0.0	9.0	0.0	0.0	0.0	0.0	23.5	CATERPILLAR LIFE INS CO
--	--	--	--	--	--	--	--	--	--	--	--	CBI INS CO
20.2	62.5	-5.0	0.5	104.0	0.0	0.5	0.0	0.0	0.0	0.0	0.0	CELTIC INS CO
--	--	--	--	--	--	--	--	--	--	--	--	CENSTAT LIFE ASR CO
4.3	17.1	30.9	1.2	2.7	0.0	50.3	0.0	0.0	5.2	9.7	46.7	CENTRAL AMERICAN LIFE INS CO
0.0	6.7	15.5	0.0	84.5	0.0	0.0	0.0	0.0	0.0	0.0	0.0	CENTRAL BENEFITS NATL LIFE INS CO
--	--	--	--	--	--	--	--	--	--	--	--	CENTRAL LIFE INS CO
4.3	23.6	2.2	9.1	44.4	0.0	44.2	0.0	0.0	0.0	0.2	44.2	CENTRAL RESERVE LIFE INS CO
0.9	79.1	1.7	74.8	8.5	1.6	4.7	2.1	0.0	0.0	6.3	3.0	CENTRAL SECURITY LIFE INS CO
14.1	305.5	0.4	39.1	36.9	0.1	9.3	4.7	0.0	1.9	7.6	6.6 ●	CENTRAL STATES H & L CO OF OMAHA
22.3	264.6	-0.6	2.0	79.6	0.8	10.6	0.6	0.0	4.0	2.9	10.6 ●	CENTRAL UNITED LIFE INS CO
0.1	1,987.2	-0.3	24.8	75.3	0.1	0.0	0.0	0.0	0.0	0.1	0.0 ●	CENTRE LIFE INS CO
81.9	1,200.3 (*)	1.3	24.8	68.0	5.1	2.6	0.0	0.0	0.0	0.0	0.0 ●	CENTURION LIFE INS CO
0.0	31.8	1.7	0.0	98.3	0.0	0.0	0.0	0.0	0.0	0.0	0.0	CENTURY CREDIT LIFE INS CO
0.2	9.0	14.7	17.1	63.9	0.5	2.3	1.4	0.0	0.0	0.1	0.0	CENTURY LIFE ASR CO
0.1	40.7	1.9	61.8	5.4	0.3	20.3	1.7	0.0	5.1	3.1	19.0	CHAMPIONS LIFE INS CO
0.0	10.8	4.4	0.9	94.6	0.0	0.1	0.0	0.0	0.0	0.0	0.0	CHARTER NATIONAL LIFE INS CO
--	--	--	--	--	--	--	--	--	--	--	--	CHEROB LIFE INS CO
2.3	29.6	12.5	19.4	60.3	0.2	0.0	0.0	0.0	7.4	0.2	0.0	CHEROKEE NATIONAL LIFE INS CO
3.9	76.6	-4.0	25.7	77.9	0.4	0.0	0.0	0.0	0.0	0.6	0.0 ●	CHESAPEAKE LIFE INS CO
13.9	84.3	4.4	13.1	64.5	1.1	9.3	7.1	0.0	0.0	0.4	8.2 ●	CHRISTIAN FIDELITY LIFE INS CO
7.8	203.3 (*)	0.9	34.1	56.6	0.3	3.9	0.0	0.0	0.0	0.2	0.0 ●	CHURCH LIFE INS CORP
103.6	385.1	10.3	0.1	62.7	0.1	19.3	0.0	0.0	0.8	6.6	19.0 ●	CICA LIFE INS CO OF AMERICA
31.5	377.3	1.3	1.2	96.6	0.9	0.0	0.0	0.0	0.0	0.0	0.0 ●	CIGNA LIFE INS CO OF NEW YORK
4.6	46.1	-1.3	7.6	93.3	0.4	0.0	0.0	0.0	0.0	0.0	29.8	CIGNA WORLDWIDE INS CO
2.2	18.5	1.2	22.1	41.2	1.1	34.2	0.0	0.0	0.0	0.3	30.8	CINCINNATI EQUITABLE LIFE INS CO
48.4	1,801.2	3.4	0.8	79.1	4.0	10.2	0.0	0.0	0.0	2.5	0.0 ●	CINCINNATI LIFE INS CO
--	--	--	--	--	--	--	--	--	--	--	--	CITCO LIFE INS CO
0.0	2.7 (*)	47.2	23.3	29.7	0.0	0.0	0.0	0.0	0.0	2.5	0.0	CITIZENS ACCIDENT & HEALTH INS CO
1.2	49.7	3.7	0.6	84.0	2.4	5.6	1.3	0.0	1.8	0.6	0.0	CITIZENS FIDELITY INS CO
0.4	10.8	6.0	1.4	91.7	0.3	0.0	0.0	0.0	0.0	0.5	0.0	CITIZENS NATIONAL LIFE INS CO
6.4	96.8	14.4	1.5	56.7	6.3	8.3	0.0	0.0	8.3	5.0	5.3	CITIZENS SECURITY LIFE INS CO
287.9	5,772.9	-0.1	19.1	39.5	6.1	3.7	20.2	0.0	0.2	11.5	8.4 ●	CM LIFE INS CO

37　● Bullets denote a more detailed analysis is available in Section II.

(*) Asset category percentages do not add up to 100%

INSURANCE COMPANY NAME	DOM. STATE	RATING	TOTAL ASSETS ($MIL)	CAPITAL & SURPLUS ($MIL)	RISK ADJUSTED CAPITAL RATIO 1	RISK ADJUSTED CAPITAL RATIO 2	CAPITAL-IZATION INDEX (PTS)	INVEST. SAFETY INDEX (PTS)	PROFIT-ABILITY INDEX (PTS)	LIQUIDITY INDEX (PTS)	STAB. INDEX (PTS)	STABILITY FACTORS
COLONIAL AMERICAN LIFE INS CO	PA	B-	4.9	4.5	3.23	2.83	9.7	9.3	6.0	9.3	4.1	DFT
COLONIAL LIFE & ACCIDENT INS CO	SC	C+	2055.6	376.7	2.26	1.41	7.6	6.4	9.1	6.9	4.4	A
COLONIAL LIFE INS CO OF TX	TX	C-	16.2	13.5	4.39	3.95	10.0	7.8	7.8	7.9	2.9	ADF
COLONIAL PENN LIFE INS CO	PA	D+	692.4	40.9	0.96	0.50	4.7	1.9	1.9	0.6	2.6	ACFIL
COLONIAL SECURITY LIFE INS CO	TX	D	3.0	2.0	1.97	1.77	8.2	8.8	6.5	7.0	2.3	DT
COLORADO BANKERS LIFE INS CO	CO	B+	144.4	15.6	1.69	1.16	7.2	5.7	6.0	5.1	6.3	IL
COLUMBIA CAPITAL LIFE REINS CO	DC	C	139.3	77.2	7.28	3.68	10.0	5.4	2.6	6.8	2.9	AEFGT
COLUMBIAN LIFE INS CO	IL	C-	240.1	16.9	1.74	1.04	7.1	6.5	1.9	4.0	3.3	FLR
COLUMBIAN MUTUAL LIFE INS CO	NY	B	847.6	76.5	1.97	1.30	7.5	7.0	6.9	5.8	5.7	T
COLUMBUS LIFE INS CO	OH	B+	2512.2	208.7	2.29	1.17	7.3	5.5	6.1	5.4	6.8	AIL
COMBINED INS CO OF AMERICA	IL	B-	2421.5	626.3	2.06	1.72	8.1	7.8	6.1	6.8	4.3	AFT
COMBINED LIFE INS CO OF NEW YORK	NY	B	391.5	63.3	1.92	1.37	7.6	7.8	8.9	7.5	5.0	A
COMMENCEMENT BAY LIFE INS CO	WA	U (1)	7.1	6.0	3.13	2.82	8.0	9.8	5.8	10.0	6.0	DT
COMMERCE NATIONAL INS CO	MS	U (1)	7.4	7.3	3.74	3.36	4.0	9.8	4.9	10.0	5.1	D
COMMERCIAL TRAVELERS MUTUAL INS CO	NY	C	33.7	11.4	1.00	0.88	6.0	8.3	6.5	7.9	4.2	DF
COMMONWEALTH ANNUTIY & LIFE INS CO	MA	C-	5967.0	413.4	3.19	1.63	7.9	5.8	1.6	9.1	2.7	GT
COMMONWEALTH DEALERS LIFE INS CO	VA	C	13.0	7.5	2.65	2.38	9.1	5.3	7.7	7.9	2.6	DFT
COMMUNITY BANK LIFE & HEALTH INS CO	AR	U (1)	0.3	0.2	1.78	1.60	7.9	7.8	1.0	6.8	1.2	DFT
COMPANION LIFE INS CO	NY	B	701.5	61.1	2.37	1.24	7.4	5.4	7.0	5.4	5.8	IL
COMPANION LIFE INS CO	SC	A-	124.7	61.9	3.22	2.43	9.1	7.1	8.4	7.5	6.4	A
COMPBENEFITS INS CO	TX	B+	62.7	50.8	2.09	1.72	8.1	8.9	9.0	7.4	5.4	AD
CONCERT HEALTH PLAN INS CO	IL	D	13.2	7.8	0.94	0.78	5.2	9.6	5.4	7.0	2.2	DFT
CONGRESS LIFE INS CO	AZ	C	58.8	57.9	8.03	7.23	10.0	9.0	8.2	10.0	2.8	DT
CONNECTICUT GENERAL LIFE INS CO	CT	C+	18317.9	2093.4	2.31	1.51	7.8	5.9	6.7	6.3	4.8	AT
CONSECO HEALTH INS CO	AZ	D+	2483.9	135.2	1.53	0.79	5.8	3.3	7.4	7.7	2.7	AI
CONSECO INS CO	IL	D+	996.8	147.4	2.89	1.57	7.9	5.9	3.3	5.9	1.9	AFT
CONSECO LIFE INS CO	IN	D+	4511.5	165.6	0.82	0.43	3.6	2.1	2.0	0.6	2.4	ACIL
CONSECO LIFE INS CO OF TX	TX	D	589.8	524.7	0.55	0.51	3.1	1.6	2.4	10.0	1.8	CIT
▲ CONSTITUTION LIFE INS CO	TX	C	87.2	20.8	2.08	1.42	7.6	7.1	4.1	7.2	4.2	ADF
CONSUMERS LIFE INS CO	OH	B	33.2	15.9	1.66	1.17	7.3	9.8	1.9	7.2	5.0	FT
CONTINENTAL AMERICAN INS CO	SC	A-	105.0	33.2	2.47	1.79	8.2	7.3	8.0	8.1	6.8	D
CONTINENTAL ASSURANCE CO	IL	C	3210.9	482.5	5.37	2.76	9.6	6.2	5.6	8.4	2.6	AT
CONTINENTAL GENERAL INS CO	OH	C	222.8	38.5	2.23	1.48	7.7	7.2	6.0	6.7	3.5	T
CONTINENTAL LIFE INS CO	PA	C-	20.7	2.4	0.70	0.63	4.0	6.1	5.6	6.9	2.9	C
CONTINENTAL LIFE INS CO OF BRENTWOOD	TN	B+	149.3	56.7	1.56	1.25	7.4	6.5	9.1	6.8	5.8	ADI
CONTINENTAL LIFE INS CO OF SC	SC	E (1)	2.2	0.1	0.07	0.06	0.0	1.7	0.8	0.5	0.0	CDFLT
COOPERATIVA DE SEGUROS DE VIDA DE PR	PR	C-	358.5	15.0	0.95	0.65	4.6	6.0	1.5	3.6	3.0	L
COOPERATIVE LIFE INS CO	AR	D	6.2	1.8	1.15	1.03	7.0	5.4	7.6	6.7	2.1	T
CORNHUSKER LIFE INS CO	NE	C-	2.2	1.8	2.32	2.09	8.6	6.0	7.2	8.1	2.6	DT
COSMOPOLITAN LIFE INS CO	AR	E+ (1)	2.6	0.8	0.34	0.28	0.4	9.3	0.8	1.4	0.4	CDFLT
COTTON STATES LIFE INS CO	GA	B+	281.8	30.4	2.16	1.22	7.3	6.3	5.2	6.3	6.6	DI
COUNTRY INVESTORS LIFE ASR CO	IL	A-	192.1	153.1	16.35	8.05	8.0	8.8	4.2	10.0	5.7	
COUNTRY LIFE INS CO	IL	A+	7329.3	887.0	2.18	1.43	7.6	6.3	6.9	6.6	7.6	GI
▲ CROWN LIFE INS CO US BR	MI	C	336.3	44.3	3.37	1.77	8.2	7.3	5.8	6.0	4.0	AT
CSI LIFE INS CO	NE	B	19.8	15.3	4.34	3.91	10.0	7.6	8.4	9.5	5.8	AD
CUMBERLAND LIFE INS CO	TN	U	--	--	--	--	--	--	--	--	--	Z
CUNA MUTUAL INS SOCIETY	IA	C+	10960.4	933.4	0.93	0.72	4.8	4.8	7.1	7.1	4.5	CIT
DALLAS GENERAL LIFE INS CO	TX	C	9.8	4.3	1.42	1.11	7.2	8.5	4.0	6.4	2.9	AFT
DELAWARE AMERICAN LIFE INS CO	DE	B	88.9	28.2	3.59	2.99	10.0	7.4	6.7	7.8	5.5	ADG
DELTA LIFE INS CO	GA	D (1)	56.6	14.1	0.85	0.52	3.8	2.1	1.5	7.1	1.9	DFIT
DENNIS LIFE INS CO	AZ	U (5)	--	--	--	--	--	--	--	--	--	Z
DESERET MUTUAL INS CO	UT	C+	45.6	4.2	1.43	1.15	5.9	6.4	2.2	7.3	4.6	ADT

See Page 26 for explanation of footnotes and Page 27 for explanation of stability factors.

Arrows denote recent upgrades ▲ or downgrades ▼ (see Section VI for explanations)

38

www.thestreetratings.com

NET PREMIUM ($MIL)	IN-VESTED ASSETS ($MIL)	% OF INVESTED ASSETS IN:									INVEST. IN AFFIL	INSURANCE COMPANY NAME
		CASH	CMO & STRUCT. SECS.	OTH.INV. GRADE BONDS	NON-INV. GRADE BONDS	CMMON & PREF. STOCK	MORT IN GOOD STAND.	NON-PERF. MORT.	REAL ESTATE	OTHER INVEST-MENTS		
0.0	3.9	20.0	21.8	58.2	0.0	0.0	0.0	0.0	0.0	0.0	0.0	COLONIAL AMERICAN LIFE INS CO
266.4	1,833.0	0.0	7.3	71.0	8.3	1.8	9.0	0.0	0.9	2.5	0.0 ●	COLONIAL LIFE & ACCIDENT INS CO
0.3	15.6	3.2	46.0	41.4	3.2	3.5	0.0	0.0	0.0	2.6	0.0	COLONIAL LIFE INS CO OF TX
49.2	646.9	3.1	12.4	65.9	5.6	1.2	8.1	0.0	0.9	2.8	0.4 ●	COLONIAL PENN LIFE INS CO
0.2	2.9	1.9	14.7	79.2	0.7	0.7	0.0	0.0	0.0	2.8	0.0	COLONIAL SECURITY LIFE INS CO
14.8	131.2	1.3	28.5	67.9	1.0	0.0	0.0	0.0	0.0	1.4	0.0	COLORADO BANKERS LIFE INS CO
0.2	106.6	0.1	4.3	36.9	0.0	1.3	0.0	0.0	0.0	57.4	51.2 ●	COLUMBIA CAPITAL LIFE REINS CO
8.1	230.8	0.4	24.8	54.7	0.5	0.0	17.8	0.0	0.0	1.9	0.0	COLUMBIAN LIFE INS CO
36.2	791.2	-0.2	20.7	53.6	0.9	2.6	14.3	0.0	0.7	7.5	2.3 ●	COLUMBIAN MUTUAL LIFE INS CO
71.1	2,355.7	-0.2	24.1	59.7	2.8	4.0	3.0	0.0	0.0	6.6	2.9 ●	COLUMBUS LIFE INS CO
198.1	2,167.8	1.1	13.2	73.0	0.3	9.5	0.0	0.0	0.7	2.3	7.9 ●	COMBINED INS CO OF AMERICA
36.2	344.0	-0.2	37.7	57.9	0.5	2.0	0.0	0.0	0.0	2.2	0.0 ●	COMBINED LIFE INS CO OF NEW YORK
0.0	7.0	0.0	0.0	100.0	0.0	0.0	0.0	0.0	0.0	0.0	0.0	COMMENCEMENT BAY LIFE INS CO
0.0	7.3	24.5	0.0	75.5	0.0	0.0	0.0	0.0	0.0	0.0	0.0	COMMERCE NATIONAL INS CO
6.7	33.5	22.2	36.4	24.3	0.0	16.4	0.0	0.0	0.8	0.0	15.4	COMMERCIAL TRAVELERS MUTUAL INS CO
956.5	1,540.8	12.7	20.2	40.1	0.1	4.2	0.0	0.0	0.0	22.6	0.0 ●	COMMONWEALTH ANNUTIY & LIFE INS CO
0.0	13.8	-0.3	27.9	59.8	5.7	4.4	0.0	0.0	2.5	0.0	0.0	COMMONWEALTH DEALERS LIFE INS CO
0.0	0.2	22.1	0.0	69.6	0.0	8.3	0.0	0.0	0.0	0.0	0.0	COMMUNITY BANK LIFE & HEALTH INS CO
17.5	659.6	0.0	42.9	43.2	4.5	0.0	6.9	0.0	0.0	2.6	0.0 ●	COMPANION LIFE INS CO
36.2	122.4	33.4	27.7	30.4	0.0	8.5	0.0	0.0	0.0	0.0	0.0 ●	COMPANION LIFE INS CO
31.6	49.9	-5.0	0.0	102.3	0.0	2.7	0.0	0.0	0.0	0.0	0.0 ●	COMPBENEFITS INS CO
7.3	12.8	67.1	0.0	32.9	0.0	0.0	0.0	0.0	0.0	0.0	0.0	CONCERT HEALTH PLAN INS CO
-2.2	59.9	3.5	0.0	96.5	0.0	0.0	0.0	0.0	0.0	0.0	0.0 ●	CONGRESS LIFE INS CO
1,732.8	10,920.4	-0.9	4.0	46.7	6.6	1.6	21.8	0.0	1.2	19.0	0.9 ●	CONNECTICUT GENERAL LIFE INS CO
74.7	2,422.9	1.7	21.2	59.8	6.0	3.0	8.2	0.0	0.0	0.1	0.9 ●	CONSECO HEALTH INS CO
23.9	993.0	1.8	15.1	58.6	3.8	8.5	8.3	0.0	0.0	3.9	4.6 ●	CONSECO INS CO
82.4	4,403.8	0.0	19.7	56.6	5.8	4.6	8.6	0.0	0.0	4.9	0.8 ●	CONSECO LIFE INS CO
0.1	581.6	8.5	0.4	2.6	0.1	88.1	0.0	0.0	0.0	0.2	88.1 ●	CONSECO LIFE INS CO OF TX
7.5	83.3	-3.8	27.1	68.9	2.0	0.6	0.0	0.0	0.0	5.3	0.0	CONSTITUTION LIFE INS CO
10.3	25.7	-5.7	0.0	105.7	0.0	0.0	0.0	0.0	0.0	0.0	0.0	CONSUMERS LIFE INS CO
20.8	88.3	23.5	4.6	63.9	2.2	2.0	0.0	0.0	2.5	1.5	0.0 ●	CONTINENTAL AMERICAN INS CO
0.3	2,135.3	0.0	27.4	47.0	8.9	11.5	0.0	0.0	-0.1	5.3	0.0 ●	CONTINENTAL ASSURANCE CO
18.3	201.6	-2.4	30.8	60.0	1.3	0.7	2.3	0.0	0.4	7.1	0.0 ●	CONTINENTAL GENERAL INS CO
1.2	18.9	4.2	19.0	61.2	0.8	2.7	3.5	0.0	3.3	5.3	0.0	CONTINENTAL LIFE INS CO
40.6	144.5	1.9	26.6	62.4	2.1	6.9	0.0	0.0	0.0	0.2	6.9 ●	CONTINENTAL LIFE INS CO OF BRENTWOOD
0.1	2.1	8.7	0.0	69.3	1.2	0.0	0.0	0.0	5.4	15.4	0.0	CONTINENTAL LIFE INS CO OF SC
49.8	295.7	5.6	5.0	68.1	0.0	7.0	6.2	0.0	6.2	1.4	0.0	COOPERATIVA DE SEGUROS DE VIDA DE PR
0.1	6.2	5.4	40.8	38.3	1.8	13.2	0.0	0.0	0.3	0.1	0.0	COOPERATIVE LIFE INS CO
0.1	2.1	0.3	0.0	80.1	0.0	19.6	0.0	0.0	0.0	0.1	0.0	CORNHUSKER LIFE INS CO
4.5	1.8	97.9	0.0	0.0	0.0	0.0	0.0	0.0	0.0	2.0	0.0	COSMOPOLITAN LIFE INS CO
10.4	265.2	1.7	35.2	52.2	1.3	4.3	0.0	0.0	0.0	5.3	0.3 ●	COTTON STATES LIFE INS CO
0.0	167.7	-1.5	27.0	74.4	0.0	0.0	0.0	0.0	0.0	0.1	0.0 ●	COUNTRY INVESTORS LIFE ASR CO
257.6	6,204.8	0.0	24.4	52.8	2.9	8.1	6.0	0.0	0.7	5.2	4.4 ●	COUNTRY LIFE INS CO
2.1	316.7	2.8	22.7	73.6	0.8	0.0	0.0	0.0	0.0	0.1	0.0 ●	CROWN LIFE INS CO US BR
1.7	18.2	3.9	0.0	92.4	3.7	0.0	0.0	0.0	0.0	0.0	0.0	CSI LIFE INS CO
--	--	--	--	--	--	--	--	--	--	--	--	CUMBERLAND LIFE INS CO
727.4	7,253.4	0.6	22.9	41.0	6.5	11.6	9.5	0.0	1.5	6.4	10.7 ●	CUNA MUTUAL INS SOCIETY
3.2	9.7	13.3	18.9	66.1	0.0	1.7	0.0	0.0	0.0	0.0	0.0	DALLAS GENERAL LIFE INS CO
8.2	73.9	1.7	0.0	90.1	1.4	5.0	0.0	0.0	0.0	1.9	0.0 ●	DELAWARE AMERICAN LIFE INS CO
16.2	55.2	3.1	0.0	25.2	0.0	34.7	3.7	0.1	25.0	8.3	19.6	DELTA LIFE INS CO
--	--	--	--	--	--	--	--	--	--	--	--	DENNIS LIFE INS CO
5.1	41.9	11.8	2.3	83.0	2.8	0.1	0.0	0.0	0.0	0.0	0.1	DESERET MUTUAL INS CO

● Bullets denote a more detailed analysis is available in Section II.

(*) Asset category percentages do not add up to 100%

INSURANCE COMPANY NAME	DOM. STATE	RATING	TOTAL ASSETS ($MIL)	CAPITAL & SURPLUS ($MIL)	RISK ADJUSTED CAPITAL RATIO 1	RISK ADJUSTED CAPITAL RATIO 2	CAPITAL-IZATION INDEX (PTS)	INVEST. SAFETY INDEX (PTS)	PROFIT-ABILITY INDEX (PTS)	LIQUIDITY INDEX (PTS)	STAB. INDEX (PTS)	STABILITY FACTORS
DESTINY HEALTH INS CO	IL	E+	13.4	1.7	0.16	0.13	0.0	8.5	0.5	0.8	0.0	CDFLT
DIRECT GENERAL LIFE INS CO	SC	B-	39.2	21.1	4.07	3.67	10.0	9.4	9.3	7.6	5.1	ADG
DIRECT LIFE INS CO	GA	C	9.6	9.5	3.99	3.59	10.0	8.5	6.3	10.0	3.4	ADT
DIRECTORS LIFE ASR CO	OK	E	23.0	1.6	0.23	0.21	0.0	1.8	5.3	1.5	0.0	CDIL
DIXIE LIFE INS CO INC	LA	E-	14.4	-0.4	-0.02	-0.01	0.0	3.4	1.1	5.9	0.0	CDIT
DOCTORS LIFE INS CO	CA	U (1)	35.3	16.0	3.23	2.91	9.9	8.9	6.0	10.0	6.9	DT
DORSEY LIFE INS CO	TX	U (1)	0.5	0.1	0.67	0.60	3.8	9.8	2.2	9.6	2.4	CDF
DUO LIFE INS CO	AZ	U	--	--	--	--	--	--	--	--	--	Z
DUPAGE LIFE INS CO	AZ	U	--	--	--	--	--	--	--	--	--	Z
EAGLE AMERICAN LIFE INS CO	LA	U	--	--	--	--	--	--	--	--	--	Z
EAGLE INS CO	AZ	U	--	--	--	--	--	--	--	--	--	Z
EAGLE LIFE INS CO	IA	U (1)	6.0	6.0	3.48	3.14	3.0	9.8	3.3	10.0	4.2	DEFT
EAST ARKANSAS GEM LIFE INS CO	AZ	U	--	--	--	--	--	--	--	--	--	Z
EASTERN LIFE & HEALTH INS CO	PA	B+	44.9	24.8	3.32	2.31	9.0	6.8	5.6	7.3	5.3	AFIT
EDUCATORS HEALTH PLANS LIFE ACCIDENT	UT	C+	6.2	1.8	1.02	0.92	6.4	6.4	2.0	7.0	3.7	ADEG
EDUCATORS LIFE INS CO OF AMERICA	AZ	U (1)	0.2	0.2	2.22	2.00	8.0	9.8	2.7	10.0	2.9	DF
EDUCATORS MUTUAL INS ASN	UT	B-	64.3	32.4	2.29	1.85	8.3	7.2	6.8	6.9	5.1	D
EMC NATIONAL LIFE CO	IA	C	692.3	35.0	1.03	0.63	5.0	6.0	1.7	6.2	4.2	C
EMPHESYS INS CO	TX	C+	6.5	3.8	2.92	2.63	9.4	9.7	4.6	7.4	4.4	ADFGT
EMPIRE FIDELITY INVESTMENTS L I C	NY	A-	1138.6	52.1	2.81	2.53	9.3	9.0	2.9	7.0	5.7	T
EMPLOYEES LIFE CO MUTUAL	IL	B	297.5	17.3	1.81	1.10	7.2	4.7	5.4	5.9	4.1	DGIT
EMPLOYEES LIFE INS CO	TX	B	16.0	9.3	3.22	2.90	9.9	8.5	9.3	9.9	4.9	T
EMPLOYERS REASSURANCE CORP	KS	C-	9173.0	595.3	0.77	0.60	3.8	5.6	1.5	6.7	3.3	CT
ENTERPRISE LIFE INS CO	TX	C	20.7	7.1	1.98	1.78	8.2	8.3	2.2	9.0	3.5	GT
EPIC LIFE INSURANCE CO	WI	B+	42.6	22.1	3.87	2.68	9.5	6.8	6.3	7.4	6.6	AI
EQUITABLE LIFE & CASUALTY INS CO	UT	B-	215.2	33.4	1.71	1.21	7.3	7.5	5.5	7.1	5.0	D
▼ EQUITRUST LIFE INS CO	IA	B-	7726.0	389.2	1.43	0.69	5.6	3.5	4.3	6.2	4.7	CIT
ERIE FAMILY LIFE INS CO	PA	B	1540.7	92.6	1.41	0.75	5.6	4.1	6.6	5.2	5.6	ACGIL
▼ ESCUDE LIFE INS CO	LA	F (1)	2.2	-2.2	-1.41	-1.27	0.0	6.0	0.9	7.0	0.0	CDT
ESKAY LIFE INS CO	AZ	U	--	--	--	--	--	--	--	--	--	Z
EVANGELINE LIFE INS CO INC	LA	E+ (1)	11.9	0.5	0.24	0.13	0.0	0.0	1.5	4.6	0.0	ACFILT
FAMILY BENEFIT LIFE INS CO	MO	C+	57.8	9.2	1.32	1.19	7.3	7.2	8.1	6.1	3.0	D
FAMILY HERITAGE LIFE INS CO OF AMER	OH	B+	322.3	37.7	1.98	1.56	7.8	9.2	9.4	8.2	5.4	D
FAMILY LIBERTY LIFE INS CO	TX	C	27.1	8.2	1.92	1.73	8.1	7.6	3.0	6.8	3.1	D
▲ FAMILY LIFE INS CO	TX	C+	122.9	25.2	2.74	2.47	9.2	8.1	5.0	7.5	4.4	ADT
FAMILY SECURITY LIFE INS CO INC	MS	C-	5.8	1.3	0.77	0.70	4.6	6.5	2.7	6.9	2.9	C
FAMILY SERVICE LIFE INS CO	TX	U (1)	530.6	90.8	3.08	1.96	8.4	5.4	7.7	5.4	6.9	DFILT
FARM BUREAU LIFE INS CO	IA	B+	5605.0	371.3	1.91	0.96	6.7	4.6	7.5	4.1	6.1	ACILT
FARM BUREAU LIFE INS CO OF MICHIGAN	MI	A-	1761.1	279.1	3.16	1.69	8.0	5.9	7.8	4.9	6.9	IL
FARM BUREAU LIFE INS CO OF MISSOURI	MO	A-	374.9	44.5	3.16	1.92	8.4	7.2	5.8	5.9	6.9	G
▼ FARM FAMILY LIFE INS CO	NY	B	1020.7	85.9	1.67	0.90	6.2	4.5	6.3	5.3	6.0	CIL
FARMERS LIFE INS CO	TN	U	--	--	--	--	--	--	--	--	--	Z
FARMERS NEW WORLD LIFE INS CO	WA	B-	6446.3	546.1	1.97	1.06	7.1	5.7	5.8	5.4	4.8	A
FEDERAL LIFE INS CO (MUTUAL)	IL	C	217.5	27.5	2.51	1.41	7.6	5.9	2.2	6.0	4.1	D
FEDERATED LIFE INS CO	MN	A	978.1	219.2	3.94	2.13	8.7	6.5	8.2	7.0	7.4	AI
FIDELITY INVESTMENTS LIFE INS CO	UT	A	11382.8	650.8	5.07	3.24	10.0	7.7	8.4	7.0	6.2	T
FIDELITY LIFE ASSN A LEGAL RESERVE	IL	B+	505.8	253.5	10.32	5.60	10.0	6.7	3.8	6.9	6.2	DFGI
FIDELITY MUTUAL LIFE INS CO	PA	F (5)	--	--	--	--	--	--	--	--	--	Z
FIDELITY MUTUAL LIFE INS CO	PA	U	--	--	--	--	--	--	--	--	--	Z
▲ FIDELITY SECURITY LIFE INS CO	MO	B+	576.6	87.1	1.87	1.33	7.5	7.6	7.9	5.6	6.7	DL
FIDELITY STANDARD LIFE INS CO	AR	U (1)	0.7	0.1	0.48	0.43	2.2	7.2	3.5	8.7	2.2	CD
FINANCIAL ASSURANCE LIFE INS CO	TX	C	9.5	8.5	3.58	3.22	10.0	8.4	8.8	10.0	4.3	ADI

See Page 26 for explanation of footnotes and Page 27 for explanation of stability factors.

Arrows denote recent upgrades ▲ or downgrades ▼ (see Section VI for explanations)

40

www.thestreetratings.com

NET PREMIUM ($MIL)	IN-VESTED ASSETS ($MIL)	CASH	CMO & STRUCT. SECS.	OTH.INV. GRADE BONDS	NON-INV. GRADE BONDS	CMMON & PREF. STOCK	MORT IN GOOD STAND.	NON-PERF. MORT.	REAL ESTATE	OTHER INVEST-MENTS	INVEST. IN AFFIL	INSURANCE COMPANY NAME
1.0	8.9	28.2	0.0	71.8	0.0	0.0	0.0	0.0	0.0	0.0	0.0	DESTINY HEALTH INS CO
8.9	32.5 (*)	2.3	6.8	61.3	0.0	0.1	0.0	0.0	0.0	12.6	0.0	DIRECT GENERAL LIFE INS CO
0.0	9.2	-4.3	34.5	61.0	0.0	0.2	0.0	0.0	0.0	8.6	0.0	DIRECT LIFE INS CO
0.9	21.8	3.6	3.2	86.6	5.6	0.0	0.0	0.0	0.0	1.1	0.0	DIRECTORS LIFE ASR CO
0.3	14.3 (*)	1.3	58.0	-9.1	9.2	6.4	17.1	1.4	19.3	14.0	6.4	DIXIE LIFE INS CO INC
0.0	28.5	0.4	28.9	70.7	0.0	0.0	0.0	0.0	0.0	0.0	0.0	DOCTORS LIFE INS CO
0.0	0.4	100.0	0.0	0.0	0.0	0.0	0.0	0.0	0.0	0.0	0.0	DORSEY LIFE INS CO
--	--	--	--	--	--	--	--	--	--	--	--	DUO LIFE INS CO
--	--	--	--	--	--	--	--	--	--	--	--	DUPAGE LIFE INS CO
--	--	--	--	--	--	--	--	--	--	--	--	EAGLE AMERICAN LIFE INS CO
--	--	--	--	--	--	--	--	--	--	--	--	EAGLE INS CO
0.0	5.9	4.1	0.0	95.9	0.0	0.0	0.0	0.0	0.0	0.0	0.0	EAGLE LIFE INS CO
--	--	--	--	--	--	--	--	--	--	--	--	EAST ARKANSAS GEM LIFE INS CO
8.9	57.5	-1.5	25.2	65.1	3.8	4.2	0.0	0.0	0.0	3.3	0.0 ●	EASTERN LIFE & HEALTH INS CO
1.5	5.3 (*)	14.4	0.0	30.3	4.1	3.4	0.0	0.0	0.0	0.0	0.0	EDUCATORS HEALTH PLANS LIFE ACCIDENT
0.0	0.1	100.0	0.0	0.0	0.0	0.0	0.0	0.0	0.0	0.0	0.0	EDUCATORS LIFE INS CO OF AMERICA
12.8	60.1 (*)	6.4	0.0	56.4	2.0	13.1	0.0	0.0	2.7	0.0	8.3 ●	EDUCATORS MUTUAL INS ASN
37.9	631.7	-0.5	16.6	74.6	0.5	3.5	3.8	0.0	0.2	1.3	0.1 ●	EMC NATIONAL LIFE CO
0.6	4.7	4.2	0.0	95.8	0.0	0.0	0.0	0.0	0.0	0.0	0.0	EMPHESYS INS CO
45.1	67.4	0.2	0.0	99.8	0.0	0.0	0.0	0.0	0.0	0.0	0.0 ●	EMPIRE FIDELITY INVESTMENTS L I C
17.2	284.2	2.0	0.0	88.7	0.8	2.0	4.3	0.0	0.5	1.6	0.0	EMPLOYEES LIFE CO MUTUAL
1.9	14.8	93.9	0.0	1.4	0.2	4.5	0.0	0.0	0.0	0.0	0.0	EMPLOYEES LIFE INS CO
149.3	8,540.3	-0.1	16.6	70.0	2.8	7.4	0.0	0.0	0.0	3.4	5.6 ●	EMPLOYERS REASSURANCE CORP
0.1	18.2 (*)	0.0	62.5	40.5	1.0	0.0	0.0	0.0	0.0	0.0	0.0	ENTERPRISE LIFE INS CO
4.8	39.8	0.3	22.7	65.3	0.3	11.4	0.0	0.0	0.0	0.0	0.0	EPIC LIFE INSURANCE CO
27.6	200.2	3.1	36.8	49.8	0.6	0.0	5.3	0.0	0.2	4.4	0.0 ●	EQUITABLE LIFE & CASUALTY INS CO
320.5	7,558.3	-0.1	24.0	59.3	2.9	1.9	10.0	0.1	0.0	1.7	0.0 ●	EQUITRUST LIFE INS CO
49.8	1,477.3	-0.5	12.1	76.9	2.8	5.5	0.1	0.0	0.1	3.0	0.0 ●	ERIE FAMILY LIFE INS CO
0.6	2.2	12.9	0.0	65.4	3.3	13.5	3.3	0.0	0.0	1.7	0.0	ESCUDE LIFE INS CO
--	--	--	--	--	--	--	--	--	--	--	--	ESKAY LIFE INS CO
0.8	11.8 (*)	0.4	32.9	-3.2	3.2	0.2	28.8	1.1	35.2	15.0	0.0	EVANGELINE LIFE INS CO INC
0.4	56.8 (*)	10.6	0.0	86.4	4.1	0.3	0.6	0.0	0.9	1.9	0.0	FAMILY BENEFIT LIFE INS CO
31.7	305.3	-0.1	0.0	99.8	0.0	0.0	0.0	0.0	0.0	0.2	0.0 ●	FAMILY HERITAGE LIFE INS CO OF AMER
0.4	26.8	0.2	66.7	24.6	0.0	5.9	2.3	0.0	0.3	0.0	0.0	FAMILY LIBERTY LIFE INS CO
3.6	115.7	0.5	22.3	72.1	1.1	0.0	0.0	0.0	0.0	4.1	0.0 ●	FAMILY LIFE INS CO
0.2	5.8	1.2	50.5	32.3	4.4	4.0	0.0	0.0	7.7	0.0	0.0	FAMILY SECURITY LIFE INS CO INC
0.0	518.7	0.3	0.4	90.3	5.8	3.1	0.0	0.0	0.0	0.1	2.9	FAMILY SERVICE LIFE INS CO
164.3	4,869.3	0.1	26.2	50.8	5.3	3.7	9.2	0.1	0.0	4.7	0.0 ●	FARM BUREAU LIFE INS CO
40.7	1,666.4	-0.1	4.2	63.8	2.4	4.5	21.9	0.0	0.9	2.4	0.0 ●	FARM BUREAU LIFE INS CO OF MICHIGAN
12.7	356.8	0.0	45.1	38.9	0.6	10.5	0.0	0.0	0.0	4.9	0.6 ●	FARM BUREAU LIFE INS CO OF MISSOURI
16.5	963.9	0.2	13.0	64.3	3.7	7.3	6.4	0.0	0.5	4.5	0.0 ●	FARM FAMILY LIFE INS CO
--	--	--	--	--	--	--	--	--	--	--	--	FARMERS LIFE INS CO
147.1	5,860.6	-0.1	35.4	53.0	2.0	0.3	0.0	0.0	0.9	8.6	0.2 ●	FARMERS NEW WORLD LIFE INS CO
5.9	194.0	0.9	33.4	48.9	4.8	5.3	0.0	0.0	1.3	5.5	0.4 ●	FEDERAL LIFE INS CO (MUTUAL)
40.2	930.4	0.0	27.9	61.4	6.5	2.6	0.0	0.0	0.0	1.7	0.0 ●	FEDERATED LIFE INS CO
411.5	714.2	0.2	0.2	88.9	3.5	7.2	0.0	0.0	0.0	0.0	7.2 ●	FIDELITY INVESTMENTS LIFE INS CO
9.4	491.8	2.5	34.5	47.5	1.1	4.1	1.9	0.0	0.0	8.6	0.0 ●	FIDELITY LIFE ASSN A LEGAL RESERVE
--	--	--	--	--	--	--	--	--	--	--	--	FIDELITY MUTUAL LIFE INS CO
--	--	--	--	--	--	--	--	--	--	--	--	FIDELITY MUTUAL LIFE INS CO
88.1	512.1	1.9	50.2	42.5	0.4	1.1	1.4	0.0	0.0	2.5	0.5 ●	FIDELITY SECURITY LIFE INS CO
0.1	0.7	26.0	0.0	69.8	4.3	0.0	0.0	0.0	0.0	0.0	0.0	FIDELITY STANDARD LIFE INS CO
0.0	9.6	8.2	39.3	52.2	0.0	0.0	0.0	0.0	0.0	0.3	0.0	FINANCIAL ASSURANCE LIFE INS CO

● Bullets denote a more detailed analysis is available in Section II.

(*) Asset category percentages do not add up to 100%

INSURANCE COMPANY NAME	DOM. STATE	RATING	TOTAL ASSETS ($MIL)	CAPITAL & SURPLUS ($MIL)	RISK ADJUSTED CAPITAL RATIO 1	RISK ADJUSTED CAPITAL RATIO 2	CAPITAL-IZATION INDEX (PTS)	INVEST. SAFETY INDEX (PTS)	PROFIT-ABILITY INDEX (PTS)	LIQUIDITY INDEX (PTS)	STAB. INDEX (PTS)	STABILITY FACTORS
FINANCIAL LIFE INS CO OF GEORGIA	GA	U (1)	11.6	8.4	3.24	2.92	8.0	9.4	7.9	10.0	8.0	DF
FIRST ALLMERICA FINANCIAL LIFE INS	MA	C	1448.0	137.2	7.38	3.34	10.0	6.6	5.1	6.7	3.8	T
FIRST AMERICAN LIFE INS CO	TX	E+	9.2	0.7	0.29	0.26	0.1	4.7	7.1	1.7	0.1	CDLT
FIRST AMERITAS LIFE INS CO OF NY	NY	A-	37.7	19.6	3.68	2.81	9.7	8.5	5.6	6.8	7.2	A
FIRST AMTENN LIFE INS CO	AZ	U	--	--	--	--	--	--	--	--	--	Z
FIRST ASR LIFE OF AMERICA	LA	B	29.2	23.1	3.96	3.65	10.0	8.8	8.4	9.0	5.2	AD
FIRST BANK SYSTEM LIFE INS CO	VT	U	--	--	--	--	--	--	--	--	--	Z
FIRST BERKSHIRE HATHAWAY LIFE INS CO	NY	B	12.4	11.0	4.13	3.71	10.0	8.4	8.3	10.0	5.5	ADGT
FIRST CARTHAGE LIFE INS CO	TN	U	--	--	--	--	--	--	--	--	--	Z
FIRST CENTRAL NATL LIC OF NEW YORK	NY	B	52.9	25.5	3.76	3.39	10.0	7.1	6.0	7.0	5.7	ADFT
FIRST CITIZENS LIFE INS CO	TN	U	--	--	--	--	--	--	--	--	--	Z
▲ FIRST COMMAND LIFE INS CO	TX	B-	19.9	9.6	2.81	2.53	9.3	6.5	5.6	7.8	4.2	D
FIRST COMMUNITY LIFE INS CO	TN	U	--	--	--	--	--	--	--	--	--	Z
FIRST CONTINENTAL LIFE & ACC INS CO	TX	D-	8.8	5.1	1.49	1.38	7.6	8.9	5.9	8.3	1.2	DT
FIRST DIMENSION LIFE INS CO INC	OK	U (1)	3.8	2.0	1.66	1.49	7.7	7.7	6.4	7.6	6.6	DT
FIRST DOMINION MUTUAL LIFE INS CO	VA	U (1)	8.4	7.4	3.46	3.11	8.0	8.7	1.9	7.7	2.1	DFT
FIRST FINANCIAL ASSURANCE CO	AR	U (1)	0.1	0.1	2.07	1.86	8.0	9.8	1.9	10.0	2.1	DF
FIRST GREAT-WEST LIFE & ANNUITY INS	NY	B-	698.4	54.6	2.92	1.49	7.7	6.3	6.4	8.0	3.6	DFGT
FIRST GUARANTY INS CO	AR	C (1)	47.0	5.0	0.81	0.73	4.8	6.1	5.9	7.9	4.1	C
FIRST HEALTH LIFE & HEALTH INS CO	TX	C+	726.6	168.7	0.43	0.36	1.3	8.2	2.2	0.8	3.0	CGLT
FIRST INVESTORS LIFE INS CO	NY	A-	949.4	119.1	7.02	3.88	10.0	7.4	8.7	6.9	5.6	T
FIRST LANDMARK LIFE INS CO	NE	U (1)	2.2	2.1	2.82	2.54	8.0	9.8	7.4	10.0	7.6	DFT
FIRST LIFE AMERICA CORP	KS	D+	33.0	2.8	0.58	0.51	3.1	2.7	3.0	5.2	2.6	CI
FIRST M & F INS CO	MS	U (1)	2.3	2.3	2.86	2.57	8.0	9.8	4.6	10.0	4.8	DT
FIRST METLIFE INVESTORS INS CO	NY	C+	2056.4	161.0	4.72	2.49	9.2	6.8	1.4	10.0	4.8	
FIRST MICHIGAN LIFE INS CO	AZ	U	--	--	--	--	--	--	--	--	--	Z
FIRST MIDWEST INS CO	AZ	U	--	--	--	--	--	--	--	--	--	Z
FIRST NATIONAL INDEMNITY L I C	TX	U (1)	1.0	1.0	2.22	2.00	8.5	9.8	7.0	10.0	7.2	D
FIRST NATIONAL LIFE INS CO OF USA	NE	C-	5.3	1.1	0.75	0.67	4.4	5.0	2.1	7.5	2.9	CFIT
FIRST PENN-PACIFIC LIFE INS CO	IN	B	1877.8	197.1	2.39	1.23	7.3	5.9	7.1	5.5	5.7	AI
FIRST REHABILITATION LIFE INS AMER	NY	C	94.9	41.7	3.31	2.62	9.4	8.7	3.4	6.9	3.7	DT
FIRST RELIANCE STANDARD LIFE INS CO	NY	B	136.4	48.9	3.49	2.30	9.0	5.0	8.3	7.1	5.4	AI
FIRST SECURITY BENEFIT LIFE & ANN	NY	B	146.6	9.1	0.97	0.87	6.0	8.5	2.0	10.0	4.5	CDT
FIRST SUNAMERICA LIFE INS CO	NY	C+	7716.2	495.9	1.93	0.98	6.8	5.6	2.2	7.5	4.4	
FIRST SYMETRA NATL LIFE INS CO OF NY	NY	C+	370.1	42.9	4.00	2.10	8.7	7.0	4.1	8.0	4.8	DGT
FIRST UNITED AMERICAN LIFE INS CO	NY	A-	126.0	38.7	3.00	2.01	8.5	5.6	8.5	6.9	7.2	AI
FIRST UNUM LIFE INS CO	NY	C+	1946.2	197.0	2.16	1.31	7.5	6.2	8.2	7.1	4.8	A
FIRST VIRGINIA LIFE INS CO	VA	D	6.9	5.9	3.16	2.85	4.0	9.8	6.1	10.0	1.4	ADFT
FIRST VOLUNTEER INS CO	AZ	U	--	--	--	--	--	--	--	--	--	Z
FIVE STAR LIFE INS CO	LA	B-	172.3	45.0	1.67	1.15	7.2	6.7	5.5	6.5	5.0	T
FLEET LIFE INS CO	AZ	U (1)	25.6	24.6	5.99	5.39	8.0	9.8	7.8	10.0	8.0	D
FLORIDA COMBINED LIFE INS CO INC	FL	B+	31.8	18.3	3.87	2.74	9.6	5.5	2.1	7.8	5.0	IT
FOOTHILLS LIFE INS CO	AZ	U	--	--	--	--	--	--	--	--	--	Z
FOR LIFE INS CO	AZ	U	--	--	--	--	--	--	--	--	--	Z
FORETHOUGHT LIFE INS CO	IN	C+	3988.5	195.4	1.82	0.98	6.8	5.8	3.3	6.8	3.9	GT
FORETHOUGHT LIFE INS CO OF NY	NY	U (1)	6.2	6.2	3.54	3.18	8.0	8.6	3.3	10.0	3.5	DET
FORETHOUGHT NATIONAL LIFE INS CO	TX	U (1)	200.2	199.7	0.99	0.88	6.0	4.0	4.9	8.5	5.2	DFGIT
FORT DEARBORN LIFE INS CO	IL	A-	2870.9	288.8	1.62	1.08	7.1	6.7	3.6	7.2	7.1	GI
FORT DEARBORN LIFE INS CO OF NY	NY	B+	67.2	23.1	3.40	2.36	9.0	8.2	4.0	9.4	5.3	GT
FOUNDATION LIFE INS CO OF AR	AR	C-	6.7	1.2	0.82	0.74	4.9	1.7	5.2	9.2	2.0	DI
FRANDISCO LIFE INS CO	GA	B+	37.3	35.0	6.72	6.05	10.0	8.8	7.0	9.4	5.7	AT
FREEDOM FINANCIAL LIFE INS CO	AZ	U	--	--	--	--	--	--	--	--	--	Z

See Page 26 for explanation of footnotes and Page 27 for explanation of stability factors.

Arrows denote recent upgrades ▲ or downgrades ▼ (see Section VI for explanations)

42

www.thestreetratings.com

NET PREMIUM ($MIL)	IN-VESTED ASSETS ($MIL)	CASH	CMO & STRUCT. SECS.	OTH.INV. GRADE BONDS	NON-INV. GRADE BONDS	CMMON & PREF. STOCK	MORT IN GOOD STAND.	NON-PERF. MORT.	REAL ESTATE	OTHER INVEST-MENTS	INVEST. IN AFFIL	INSURANCE COMPANY NAME
0.0	11.3	0.0	12.4	86.7	0.0	0.0	0.0	0.0	0.9	0.0	0.9	FINANCIAL LIFE INS CO OF GEORGIA
7.8	1,336.8	0.4	24.2	56.9	0.6	1.6	0.0	0.0	0.0	16.3	0.0 ●	FIRST ALLMERICA FINANCIAL LIFE INS
0.0	8.7	4.0	92.4	0.0	0.0	3.5	0.0	0.0	0.0	0.1	0.0	FIRST AMERICAN LIFE INS CO
7.5	34.7	1.7	10.9	85.0	0.0	1.4	0.0	0.0	0.0	1.0	0.0	FIRST AMERITAS LIFE INS CO OF NY
--	--	--	--	--	--	--	--	--	--	--	--	FIRST AMTENN LIFE INS CO
1.0	28.3	14.1	0.0	69.2	0.0	16.8	0.0	0.0	0.0	0.0	16.8	FIRST ASR LIFE OF AMERICA
--	--	--	--	--	--	--	--	--	--	--	--	FIRST BANK SYSTEM LIFE INS CO
0.0	12.3	0.8	89.2	10.1	0.0	0.0	0.0	0.0	0.0	0.0	0.0	FIRST BERKSHIRE HATHAWAY LIFE INS CO
--	--	--	--	--	--	--	--	--	--	--	--	FIRST CARTHAGE LIFE INS CO
3.5	47.4	1.0	11.6	86.5	0.9	0.0	0.0	0.0	0.0	0.0	0.0 ●	FIRST CENTRAL NATL LIC OF NEW YORK
--	--	--	--	--	--	--	--	--	--	--	--	FIRST CITIZENS LIFE INS CO
0.7	18.7	0.1	0.7	83.6	3.4	11.5	0.0	0.0	0.0	0.8	0.0	FIRST COMMAND LIFE INS CO
--	--	--	--	--	--	--	--	--	--	--	--	FIRST COMMUNITY LIFE INS CO
1.8	10.7	58.8	0.0	19.1	0.0	22.1	0.0	0.0	0.0	0.0	22.1	FIRST CONTINENTAL LIFE & ACC INS CO
0.0	3.7	2.9	65.5	22.9	0.0	1.5	0.3	0.0	0.0	7.4	0.0	FIRST DIMENSION LIFE INS CO INC
0.0	8.3 (*)	-0.8	0.0	0.0	0.0	0.0	0.0	0.0	0.0	22.0	0.0	FIRST DOMINION MUTUAL LIFE INS CO
0.0	0.1 (*)	113.9	0.0	0.0	0.0	0.0	0.0	0.0	0.0	0.0	0.0	FIRST FINANCIAL ASSURANCE CO
79.2	517.0	0.3	30.2	47.1	2.8	0.0	16.3	0.0	0.0	3.1	0.0 ●	FIRST GREAT-WEST LIFE & ANNUITY INS
5.4	45.8	13.3	18.0	45.9	0.0	6.4	15.5	0.2	0.4	0.3	0.4	FIRST GUARANTY INS CO
775.2	542.8 (*)	-1.9	13.7	68.2	0.0	0.0	0.0	0.0	0.0	0.0	0.0 ●	FIRST HEALTH LIFE & HEALTH INS CO
18.6	315.9	1.3	0.0	74.0	4.0	1.1	0.0	0.0	0.0	19.7	0.2 ●	FIRST INVESTORS LIFE INS CO
0.0	2.1	0.1	0.0	99.9	0.0	0.0	0.0	0.0	0.0	0.0	0.0	FIRST LANDMARK LIFE INS CO
1.9	30.8 (*)	3.1	1.1	72.8	6.7	0.7	4.3	0.0	9.4	0.8	0.0	FIRST LIFE AMERICA CORP
0.0	2.3	76.0	0.0	24.0	0.0	0.0	0.0	0.0	0.0	0.0	0.0	FIRST M & F INS CO
189.4	442.7	-2.5	11.2	81.9	1.3	1.4	4.5	0.0	0.0	2.2	2.2 ●	FIRST METLIFE INVESTORS INS CO
--	--	--	--	--	--	--	--	--	--	--	--	FIRST MICHIGAN LIFE INS CO
--	--	--	--	--	--	--	--	--	--	--	--	FIRST MIDWEST INS CO
0.0	1.0	100.0	0.0	0.0	0.0	0.0	0.0	0.0	0.0	0.0	0.0	FIRST NATIONAL INDEMNITY L I C
0.3	5.2	9.7	10.0	59.8	0.0	20.4	0.0	0.0	0.0	0.2	0.0	FIRST NATIONAL LIFE INS CO OF USA
12.0	1,757.4	-0.2	22.6	51.0	5.9	2.3	15.3	0.0	0.0	3.1	0.0 ●	FIRST PENN-PACIFIC LIFE INS CO
22.3	78.0	-2.1	36.4	65.7	0.1	0.0	0.0	0.0	0.0	0.0	0.0 ●	FIRST REHABILITATION LIFE INS AMER
16.6	127.2	-0.9	35.6	58.1	7.1	0.0	0.0	0.0	0.0	0.0	0.0 ●	FIRST RELIANCE STANDARD LIFE INS CO
4.5	15.6	18.9	67.1	13.0	0.0	0.0	0.0	0.0	0.0	1.0	0.0	FIRST SECURITY BENEFIT LIFE & ANN
543.3	6,740.7	-0.3	34.0	53.4	2.8	1.8	7.3	0.0	0.0	1.0	0.0 ●	FIRST SUNAMERICA LIFE INS CO
67.2	301.7	1.7	39.2	57.3	1.7	0.2	0.0	0.0	0.0	0.0	0.0 ●	FIRST SYMETRA NATL LIFE INS CO OF NY
17.3	110.4	1.8	1.6	78.6	10.2	5.3	0.0	0.0	0.0	2.5	0.0 ●	FIRST UNITED AMERICAN LIFE INS CO
103.5	1,878.0	0.0	11.0	79.7	3.5	1.6	4.0	0.0	0.0	0.5	0.0 ●	FIRST UNUM LIFE INS CO
0.0	6.7	12.7	0.0	87.3	0.0	0.0	0.0	0.0	0.0	0.0	0.0	FIRST VIRGINIA LIFE INS CO
--	--	--	--	--	--	--	--	--	--	--	--	FIRST VOLUNTEER INS CO
22.8	145.2	6.9	25.6	55.2	6.4	1.2	0.0	0.0	0.0	4.7	0.1 ●	FIVE STAR LIFE INS CO
0.0	25.6	97.7	0.0	2.3	0.0	0.0	0.0	0.0	0.0	0.0	0.0	FLEET LIFE INS CO
0.0	26.0	7.8	0.0	37.5	0.0	0.0	0.0	0.0	0.0	54.7	54.7	FLORIDA COMBINED LIFE INS CO INC
--	--	--	--	--	--	--	--	--	--	--	--	FOOTHILLS LIFE INS CO
--	--	--	--	--	--	--	--	--	--	--	--	FOR LIFE INS CO
194.3	3,757.1	-0.1	34.2	58.5	2.4	1.5	2.8	0.0	0.1	0.6	0.2 ●	FORETHOUGHT LIFE INS CO
0.0	6.1	0.1	0.0	99.9	0.0	0.0	0.0	0.0	0.0	0.1	0.0	FORETHOUGHT LIFE INS CO OF NY
0.2	192.8	0.0	0.0	0.3	0.0	97.9	0.0	0.0	0.0	1.8	99.7	FORETHOUGHT NATIONAL LIFE INS CO
522.2	1,541.5	-0.5	42.1	52.0	3.8	1.8	0.0	0.0	0.0	0.9	1.8 ●	FORT DEARBORN LIFE INS CO
25.2	40.0	1.7	26.2	72.1	0.0	0.0	0.0	0.0	0.0	0.0	0.0	FORT DEARBORN LIFE INS CO OF NY
0.5	7.4	60.4	0.0	10.7	0.0	7.0	0.0	0.0	18.2	3.6	0.6	FOUNDATION LIFE INS CO OF AR
2.6	35.0	0.1	0.0	100.0	0.0	0.0	0.0	0.0	0.0	0.0	0.0 ●	FRANDISCO LIFE INS CO
--	--	--	--	--	--	--	--	--	--	--	--	FREEDOM FINANCIAL LIFE INS CO

● Bullets denote a more detailed analysis is available in Section II.

(*) Asset category percentages do not add up to 100%

INSURANCE COMPANY NAME	DOM. STATE	RATING	TOTAL ASSETS ($MIL)	CAPITAL & SURPLUS ($MIL)	RISK ADJUSTED CAPITAL RATIO 1	RISK ADJUSTED CAPITAL RATIO 2	CAPITAL-IZATION INDEX (PTS)	INVEST. SAFETY INDEX (PTS)	PROFIT-ABILITY INDEX (PTS)	LIQUIDITY INDEX (PTS)	STAB. INDEX (PTS)	STABILITY FACTORS
FREEDOM LIFE INS CO OF AMERICA	TX	C-	37.2	15.0	1.00	0.86	5.9	4.8	2.0	6.5	3.1	F
▼ FREMONT LIFE INS CO	CA	F (4)	1.8	2.0	1.42	1.28	7.4	8.4	0.4	9.1	0.8	DFT
FRINGE BENEFIT LIFE INS CO	TX	C	37.3	17.9	3.32	2.99	10.0	6.2	8.8	7.0	2.2	DT
FUNERAL DIRECTORS LIFE INS CO	TX	C+	574.9	49.8	1.50	0.83	5.8	3.5	8.1	4.9	4.5	IL
FUTURAL LIFE INS CO	AZ	D+ (1)	8.7	5.8	2.64	2.37	9.1	7.1	7.5	10.0	2.8	DT
▲ GARDEN STATE LIFE INS CO	TX	B	90.4	17.6	1.89	1.20	7.3	6.7	2.0	5.6	5.4	D
GENERAL AMERICAN LIFE INS CO	MO	C+	11331.9	1001.3	3.32	1.53	7.8	5.8	4.1	6.0	3.9	T
GENERAL FIDELITY LIFE INS CO	SC	B-	206.1	160.7	6.39	4.07	10.0	5.0	7.7	9.1	3.8	ADIT
GENERAL RE LIFE CORP	CT	B+	2682.0	465.0	2.09	1.34	7.5	6.8	4.5	8.9	6.7	AI
GENERALI USA LIFE REASSURANCE CO	MO	C	865.1	268.7	2.42	1.60	7.9	8.6	5.1	6.2	4.3	D
GENEVA LIFE INS CO	IN	U (1)	1.5	1.5	2.59	2.33	3.0	9.8	2.7	10.0	2.9	DFT
GENWORTH LIFE & ANNUITY INS CO	VA	B	24891.2	1719.3	1.37	0.87	6.0	4.8	4.6	7.7	4.0	ACFIT
GENWORTH LIFE INS CO	DE	C+	33446.7	2954.1	0.92	0.71	4.7	5.5	5.7	8.0	3.0	ACFGT
GENWORTH LIFE INS CO OF NEW YORK	NY	C	6936.4	401.9	1.75	0.87	6.1	4.2	2.0	8.0	3.9	ACIT
GEORGIA PEOPLES LIFE INS CO	AZ	U	--	--	--	--	--	--	--	--	--	Z
GERBER LIFE INS CO	NY	A-	1568.7	163.2	1.95	1.21	7.3	6.8	5.7	6.1	6.8	I
GERMANIA LIFE INS CO	TX	B-	44.1	10.7	1.79	1.61	7.9	8.1	2.7	6.7	5.2	AD
GERTRUDE GEDDES WILLIS LIFE INS CO	LA	U	--	--	--	--	--	--	--	--	--	Z
GLOBE LIFE & ACCIDENT INS CO	NE	B	2777.5	355.2	1.03	0.77	5.2	4.8	8.5	7.0	5.2	CI
GMHP HEALTH INS LMTD	GU	U (1)	1.6	1.3	2.35	2.12	8.0	3.0	1.2	9.0	1.4	DIT
GOLDEN GATE CAPTIVE INS CO	SC	U (5)	--	--	--	--	--	--	--	--	--	Z
GOLDEN RULE INS CO	IN	B	665.9	318.8	1.91	1.50	5.8	8.6	6.8	7.2	6.3	A
GOLDEN SECURITY LIFE INS CO	TN	U (1)	3.2	3.2	3.06	2.76	8.0	9.1	8.1	10.0	8.0	D
GOLDEN STATE MUTUAL LIFE INS CO	CA	D (1)	90.0	6.1	0.73	0.50	3.0	5.1	1.8	0.4	2.3	FLT
GOVERNMENT PERSONNEL MUTUAL L I C	TX	B+	783.4	81.2	2.34	1.36	7.5	5.8	6.2	5.6	6.4	DIL
GRANGE LIFE INS CO	OH	A-	258.2	34.1	2.69	1.57	7.9	7.3	5.5	5.9	6.9	AD
GREAT AMERICAN LIFE ASR CO	OH	U (1)	20.2	8.3	2.37	2.14	8.7	7.6	6.1	7.8	6.4	DFT
GREAT AMERICAN LIFE INS CO	OH	B-	9644.4	807.8	1.50	0.84	5.8	3.9	8.7	5.1	5.2	AIT
GREAT AMERICAN LIFE INS CO OF NY	NY	U (1)	46.9	7.1	1.43	1.29	7.4	6.2	6.2	6.9	6.2	DFIT
GREAT ATLANTIC LIFE INS CO	FL	U (5)	--	--	--	--	--	--	--	--	--	Z
GREAT CENTRAL LIFE INS CO	LA	C	17.5	6.5	2.05	1.39	7.6	4.3	7.8	9.1	3.6	I
GREAT FIDELITY LIFE INS CO	IN	D+	3.1	2.5	2.32	2.08	8.6	6.7	5.1	9.5	2.6	AFOT
▲ GREAT REPUBLIC LIFE INS CO	WA	D	18.4	2.9	0.91	0.82	5.6	6.8	2.9	7.7	1.7	CDFI
GREAT SOUTHEASTERN LIFE INS CO	AZ	U	--	--	--	--	--	--	--	--	--	Z
GREAT SOUTHERN LIFE INS CO	TX	C+	259.5	31.7	3.33	1.62	7.9	6.8	4.0	9.1	4.2	AGT
GREAT WEST LIFE ASR CO	MI	B	138.0	39.6	4.42	2.32	9.0	6.2	4.9	6.6	5.2	FIT
GREAT WESTERN INS CO	UT	B-	416.0	31.2	1.70	0.89	4.0	3.9	5.1	2.6	4.0	FILT
GREAT WESTERN LIFE INS CO	MT	U (1)	2.0	1.4	2.01	1.81	8.2	8.9	6.4	7.0	6.6	D
GREAT-WEST LIFE & ANNUITY INS CO	CO	B-	33902.1	918.8	1.12	0.65	5.2	5.2	5.8	7.3	3.6	CGIT
GREATER GEORGIA LIFE INS CO	GA	A-	46.3	23.2	2.10	1.56	7.8	8.4	7.3	6.8	7.1	A
GREATER MISSOURI LIFE INS CO	AZ	U	--	--	--	--	--	--	--	--	--	Z
GREGG INS CO	AR	U (5)	--	--	--	--	--	--	--	--	--	Z
GRIFFIN LEGGETT BURIAL INS CO	AR	U (1)	0.1	0.1	2.16	1.95	8.4	9.8	6.8	10.0	5.3	DFT
GUARANTEE SECURITY LIFE INS CO OF AZ	AZ	U (1)	0.8	0.7	2.08	1.87	8.3	9.8	7.6	10.0	7.8	D
▲ GUARANTEE TRUST LIFE INS CO	IL	C+	220.5	42.6	1.38	1.00	7.0	6.4	5.1	6.6	5.0	
GUARANTY INCOME LIFE INS CO	LA	B-	423.0	21.7	2.01	1.10	7.2	3.0	7.3	6.9	4.9	DGI
GUARDIAN INS & ANNUITY CO INC	DE	B	7143.6	195.7	2.53	1.27	7.4	5.2	2.5	9.2	4.7	FIT
GUARDIAN LIFE INS CO OF AMERICA	NY	A	29202.2	3550.4	2.40	1.64	8.0	6.1	7.8	6.0	7.5	I
GULF GUARANTY LIFE INS CO	MS	D	17.9	8.6	1.40	1.06	7.1	4.0	2.3	8.2	2.2	I
GULF STATES LIFE INS CO INC	LA	C-	3.0	2.4	2.39	2.15	8.7	4.4	8.8	9.1	2.9	FIT
HALLMARK LIFE INS CO	AZ	C-	1.6	0.7	0.86	0.77	5.2	8.9	1.5	0.7	1.8	ACDFGL
HANNOVER LIFE REASSUR CO OF AMERICA	FL	C+	3405.6	119.3	0.97	0.60	4.8	6.6	5.3	7.2	4.8	CGT

See Page 26 for explanation of footnotes and Page 27 for explanation of stability factors.

Arrows denote recent upgrades ▲ or downgrades ▼ (see Section VI for explanations)

44

www.thestreetratings.com

NET PREMIUM ($MIL)	IN-VESTED ASSETS ($MIL)	% OF INVESTED ASSETS IN:									INVEST. IN AFFIL	INSURANCE COMPANY NAME
		CASH	CMO & STRUCT. SECS.	OTH.INV. GRADE BONDS	NON-INV. GRADE BONDS	CMMON & PREF. STOCK	MORT IN GOOD STAND.	NON-PERF. MORT.	REAL ESTATE	OTHER INVEST-MENTS		
7.6	36.6 (*)	0.0	15.1	68.2	1.2	22.3	0.0	0.0	0.0	0.0	22.3	FREEDOM LIFE INS CO OF AMERICA
0.0	4.1	57.5	0.0	40.1	2.4	0.0	0.0	0.0	0.0	0.0	0.0	FREMONT LIFE INS CO
-0.7	37.7 (*)	1.3	1.1	61.2	0.0	9.3	20.6	0.0	0.0	11.8	0.0	FRINGE BENEFIT LIFE INS CO
32.8	542.9	0.2	6.9	73.5	2.1	7.1	2.6	0.0	5.6	2.0	1.4 ●	FUNERAL DIRECTORS LIFE INS CO
0.9	8.5	18.8	0.1	68.9	0.0	12.2	0.0	0.0	0.0	0.0	0.0	FUTURAL LIFE INS CO
8.5	72.8	-0.3	11.8	77.7	2.2	5.4	0.0	0.0	0.0	3.3	0.1	GARDEN STATE LIFE INS CO
131.4	9,767.8	0.6	23.1	42.0	2.8	3.2	2.2	0.0	0.7	25.4	5.7 ●	GENERAL AMERICAN LIFE INS CO
11.6	205.9	1.5	19.6	51.7	0.9	26.3	0.0	0.0	0.0	0.1	0.2 ●	GENERAL FIDELITY LIFE INS CO
270.4	2,392.8	0.2	1.5	89.8	5.1	3.3	0.0	0.0	0.0	0.1	3.3 ●	GENERAL RE LIFE CORP
76.5	732.9	-2.2	8.3	90.6	0.0	2.3	0.0	0.0	0.0	0.3	0.0 ●	GENERALI USA LIFE REASSURANCE CO
0.0	1.5	80.6	0.0	19.4	0.0	0.0	0.0	0.0	0.0	0.0	0.0	GENEVA LIFE INS CO
-455.0	15,778.6	0.1	18.3	42.7	5.6	7.0	16.9	0.0	0.3	9.1	5.6 ●	GENWORTH LIFE & ANNUITY INS CO
376.0	33,816.0	-0.1	17.8	47.2	3.6	9.8	13.7	0.0	0.0	8.1	10.2 ●	GENWORTH LIFE INS CO
90.1	5,595.8	-0.2	21.3	49.4	7.7	2.7	16.0	0.0	0.0	3.1	0.0 ●	GENWORTH LIFE INS CO OF NEW YORK
--	--	--	--	--	--	--	--	--	--	--	--	GEORGIA PEOPLES LIFE INS CO
107.5	1,450.7	0.2	26.6	64.7	0.9	2.1	0.0	0.0	0.0	5.4	0.0 ●	GERBER LIFE INS CO
1.4	41.0	0.3	75.4	21.2	0.7	0.7	0.0	0.0	0.0	1.6	0.0	GERMANIA LIFE INS CO
--	--	--	--	--	--	--	--	--	--	--	--	GERTRUDE GEDDES WILLIS LIFE INS CO
138.5	2,428.3	0.4	1.4	69.9	5.8	17.4	0.0	0.0	0.0	4.3	9.7 ●	GLOBE LIFE & ACCIDENT INS CO
0.0	1.6	13.9	0.0	0.0	0.0	0.0	0.0	0.0	86.1	0.0	0.0	GMHP HEALTH INS LMTD
--	--	--	--	--	--	--	--	--	--	--	--	GOLDEN GATE CAPTIVE INS CO
322.1	573.5	1.0	12.7	86.0	0.0	0.0	0.0	0.0	0.4	0.0	0.0 ●	GOLDEN RULE INS CO
0.0	3.2	0.6	0.0	99.4	0.0	0.0	0.0	0.0	0.0	0.0	0.0	GOLDEN SECURITY LIFE INS CO
28.1	74.6	2.8	0.3	46.8	1.7	6.4	32.8	0.6	2.6	5.9	0.2	GOLDEN STATE MUTUAL LIFE INS CO
12.5	757.2	0.9	4.7	62.6	3.1	1.4	15.7	0.5	1.4	9.7	0.0 ●	GOVERNMENT PERSONNEL MUTUAL L I C
11.8	224.2	2.5	40.4	50.8	2.0	0.5	0.0	0.0	0.0	3.8	0.0 ●	GRANGE LIFE INS CO
0.0	20.0	3.5	21.0	62.2	3.7	0.0	0.0	0.0	0.0	9.6	0.0	GREAT AMERICAN LIFE ASR CO
166.5	9,248.9	-0.2	32.9	53.2	6.5	2.5	1.8	0.0	0.8	2.6	2.2 ●	GREAT AMERICAN LIFE INS CO
0.0	46.3	0.0	33.3	62.9	3.8	0.0	0.0	0.0	0.0	0.0	0.0	GREAT AMERICAN LIFE INS CO OF NY
--	--	--	--	--	--	--	--	--	--	--	--	GREAT ATLANTIC LIFE INS CO
0.4	17.3	29.3	0.3	26.5	0.0	14.5	15.7	0.0	13.6	0.0	10.3	GREAT CENTRAL LIFE INS CO
0.0	3.0	9.9	11.0	45.0	3.6	7.9	22.7	0.0	0.0	0.0	0.0	GREAT FIDELITY LIFE INS CO
0.4	17.8	-0.4	0.0	94.6	1.3	4.3	0.0	0.0	0.0	0.2	0.0	GREAT REPUBLIC LIFE INS CO
--	--	--	--	--	--	--	--	--	--	--	--	GREAT SOUTHEASTERN LIFE INS CO
0.1	264.4	-1.0	29.2	60.9	2.2	5.6	0.5	0.0	0.0	2.6	0.0 ●	GREAT SOUTHERN LIFE INS CO
1.2	127.7	0.0	56.8	30.2	8.6	0.0	0.0	0.0	1.1	3.6	0.0 ●	GREAT WEST LIFE ASR CO
29.2	393.1	-0.3	3.9	77.8	5.2	6.2	2.8	0.0	0.9	3.4	0.4 ●	GREAT WESTERN INS CO
0.0	2.0	0.2	0.0	98.6	0.0	0.0	0.0	0.0	0.0	1.2	0.0	GREAT WESTERN LIFE INS CO
1,918.2	17,307.7	0.0	34.5	29.7	2.6	2.7	4.1	0.0	0.4	26.0	2.0 ●	GREAT-WEST LIFE & ANNUITY INS CO
7.5	38.5	-2.9	42.2	60.5	0.0	0.0	0.0	0.0	0.0	0.2	0.0	GREATER GEORGIA LIFE INS CO
--	--	--	--	--	--	--	--	--	--	--	--	GREATER MISSOURI LIFE INS CO
--	--	--	--	--	--	--	--	--	--	--	--	GREGG INS CO
0.0	0.1	100.0	0.0	0.0	0.0	0.0	0.0	0.0	0.0	0.0	0.0	GRIFFIN LEGGETT BURIAL INS CO
0.1	0.8	74.6	0.0	25.4	0.0	0.0	0.0	0.0	0.0	0.0	0.0	GUARANTEE SECURITY LIFE INS CO OF AZ
41.1	190.5	3.3	46.4	29.2	2.2	3.3	14.1	0.5	0.0	1.1	1.0 ●	GUARANTEE TRUST LIFE INS CO
23.6	401.9	0.3	29.6	51.5	3.2	2.3	0.9	0.0	0.8	11.5	0.8	GUARANTY INCOME LIFE INS CO
266.8	2,001.2	0.7	2.4	85.6	3.8	1.2	0.0	0.0	0.0	6.3	1.4 ●	GUARDIAN INS & ANNUITY CO INC
1,467.0	26,885.5	0.0	8.5	54.7	5.8	5.8	12.9	0.0	0.6	11.8	4.7 ●	GUARDIAN LIFE INS CO OF AMERICA
1.5	17.3	12.1	0.0	31.2	0.0	41.2	2.2	0.0	11.1	3.1	21.7	GULF GUARANTY LIFE INS CO
0.2	2.9	12.6	0.0	53.9	0.0	29.1	0.0	0.0	4.5	0.0	0.0	GULF STATES LIFE INS CO INC
0.6	1.1 (*)	9.4	0.0	79.0	0.0	0.0	0.0	0.0	0.0	0.0	0.0	HALLMARK LIFE INS CO
88.6	1,044.0	-0.2	31.2	62.8	0.4	0.9	3.8	0.0	0.0	0.9	0.0 ●	HANNOVER LIFE REASSUR CO OF AMERICA

● Bullets denote a more detailed analysis is available in Section II.

(*) Asset category percentages do not add up to 100%

INSURANCE COMPANY NAME	DOM. STATE	RATING	TOTAL ASSETS ($MIL)	CAPITAL & SURPLUS ($MIL)	RISK ADJUSTED CAPITAL RATIO 1	RISK ADJUSTED CAPITAL RATIO 2	CAPITAL-IZATION INDEX (PTS)	INVEST. SAFETY INDEX (PTS)	PROFIT-ABILITY INDEX (PTS)	LIQUIDITY INDEX (PTS)	STAB. INDEX (PTS)	STABILITY FACTORS
HARDIN COUNTY LIFE INS CO	TN	U	--	--	--	--	--	--	--	--	--	Z
HARLEYSVILLE LIFE INS CO	PA	C+	348.8	18.8	1.15	0.73	5.2	7.1	2.0	4.3	4.8	CL
HARRIS LIFE INS CO	AZ	U	--	--	--	--	--	--	--	--	--	Z
HARTFORD INTL LIFE REASR CORP	CT	B	1120.7	103.4	2.38	1.19	7.3	6.4	6.3	6.8	4.7	AFGIT
HARTFORD LIFE & ACCIDENT INS CO	CT	B-	13955.9	5601.2	1.06	1.00	7.0	4.4	7.9	7.0	5.2	AI
HARTFORD LIFE & ANNUITY INS CO	CT	B-	61552.0	2299.4	3.13	1.62	7.9	6.9	1.6	10.0	4.4	AT
HARTFORD LIFE INS CO	CT	C-	132572.4	4964.1	1.33	0.92	6.4	5.6	2.0	9.8	3.0	T
HAWKEYE LIFE INS GROUP INC	IA	C-	15.2	10.9	3.68	3.32	10.0	8.8	6.3	8.5	3.3	DT
HAWTHORN LIFE INS CO	TX	D-	9.5	1.6	0.23	0.21	0.0	5.9	2.2	3.1	0.0	ACLT
HCC LIFE INS CO	IN	B	592.2	363.2	2.96	2.51	9.3	8.6	9.4	6.9	6.0	AD
HEALTH NET LIFE INS CO	CA	B	653.2	375.9	1.98	1.62	7.9	8.4	6.4	0.3	4.2	FLT
HEALTHMARKETS INS CO	OK	U (1)	9.4	9.3	4.00	3.60	8.0	9.8	4.0	10.0	4.5	DF
▲ HEALTHPLUS INS CO	MI	C-	21.5	12.1	2.83	2.34	9.0	9.8	1.8	7.4	3.2	DEG
HEALTHSPRING LIFE & HLTH INS CO INC	TX	U (1)	7.7	7.7	3.82	3.44	8.0	9.6	6.8	7.0	6.1	DEIT
HEALTHY ALLIANCE LIFE INS CO	MO	B	666.9	303.1	1.54	1.22	5.3	8.1	9.2	5.3	6.0	L
HEARTLAND NATIONAL LIFE INS CO	IN	C	5.6	4.0	2.41	2.17	8.8	9.5	7.3	10.0	2.8	AFT
HERITAGE LIFE INS CO	AZ	U (1)	32.7	24.2	7.70	6.93	4.0	8.0	3.5	9.0	2.9	DFT
HERITAGE UNION LIFE INS CO	AZ	D	10.7	10.6	4.00	3.60	8.0	9.8	1.9	7.5	2.2	F
HIGGINBOTHAM BURIAL INS CO	AR	U (1)	1.4	0.0	0.06	0.06	0.0	0.1	0.7	8.4	0.0	CDFIT
HM LIFE INS CO	PA	B-	358.4	152.4	2.72	2.04	8.6	4.8	8.2	6.7	5.3	DI
HM LIFE INS CO OF NEW YORK	NY	B	40.4	20.2	2.03	1.62	7.9	8.9	6.6	6.3	4.9	ADFT
HOME SECURITY LIFE INS CO	MS	U	--	--	--	--	--	--	--	--	--	Z
HOMESTEADERS LIFE CO	IA	C+	1626.7	79.7	1.51	0.80	5.8	5.8	6.9	6.9	4.8	T
HORACE MANN LIFE INS CO	IL	B	4561.7	268.4	1.95	1.01	7.0	5.7	7.1	5.8	4.8	AIT
HOUSEHOLD LIFE INS CO	MI	B	813.9	317.9	4.72	3.67	10.0	8.4	6.2	7.6	4.7	AFT
HOUSEHOLD LIFE INS CO OF AZ	AZ	U (1)	843.3	47.5	1.80	0.99	6.9	6.8	1.9	10.0	3.9	F
HOUSEHOLD LIFE INS CO OF DE	DE	C	548.7	547.7	1.45	1.44	7.7	2.8	5.3	10.0	4.0	DIT
HUMANA INS CO	WI	C	4313.0	2150.9	0.92	0.77	5.1	7.9	6.8	1.0	3.0	CL
HUMANA INS CO OF KENTUCKY	KY	B-	34.2	21.1	1.33	0.93	6.4	3.4	8.8	8.4	4.6	ADGIT
HUMANA INS CO OF PUERTO RICO INC	PR	C	46.1	31.9	2.21	1.80	8.2	7.6	1.0	7.3	3.5	DT
HUMANADENTAL INS CO	WI	B-	101.4	68.3	1.73	1.38	5.9	8.2	8.0	6.5	5.2	ADT
I B A HEALTH & LIFE ASR CO	MI	C+	19.0	18.3	5.33	4.80	10.0	9.5	4.3	8.9	3.0	DFT
IA AMERICAN LIFE INS CO	GA	C	30.6	28.2	6.35	3.15	4.0	8.7	6.1	10.0	2.9	FT
IBC LIFE INS CO	TX	C-	3.3	3.0	2.84	2.55	9.3	9.8	9.6	10.0	3.3	DF
IDEALIFE INS CO	CT	B	20.5	14.4	3.96	3.56	10.0	9.1	7.4	9.6	5.0	AD
▼ ILLINOIS MUTUAL LIFE INS CO	IL	B+	1262.3	124.3	1.78	0.92	6.4	4.8	6.5	7.2	6.4	CI
INDEPENDENCE INS INC	DE	U (1)	1.7	1.7	2.68	2.41	8.0	9.2	7.6	10.0	7.8	D
INDEPENDENCE LIFE & ANNUITY CO	RI	B-	128.3	52.9	5.78	5.20	4.0	7.5	6.9	6.8	5.0	ADFT
INDEPENDENCE ONE LIFE INS CO	AZ	U	--	--	--	--	--	--	--	--	--	Z
INDIVIDUAL ASR CO LIFE HEALTH & ACC	MO	C-	45.2	11.7	1.17	0.81	5.5	6.1	3.0	6.4	3.3	
INDUSTRIAL ALLIANCE PACIFIC LIFE INS	WA	U	--	--	--	--	--	--	--	--	--	Z
ING LIFE INS & ANNUITY CO	CT	C+	54644.8	1499.7	2.07	1.00	7.0	5.1	4.7	9.2	4.6	AT
ING USA ANNUITY & LIFE INS CO	IA	C	60901.1	1340.5	1.02	0.51	5.0	3.4	1.6	9.1	3.6	CFIT
INS CO OF SCOTT AND WHITE	TX	B	3.0	2.7	2.81	2.53	9.3	9.0	6.5	10.0	4.9	DGO
INSOUTH LIFE INS CO	TN	U	--	--	--	--	--	--	--	--	--	Z
INTEGRITY CAPITAL INS CO	IN	D	7.1	2.5	1.43	1.29	7.4	9.8	3.7	9.6	2.3	ADGT
INTEGRITY LIFE INS CO	OH	C+	4942.7	363.1	1.22	0.86	5.9	5.0	5.2	8.3	4.7	T
INTERNATIONAL AMERICAN LIFE INS CO	TX	D-	1.9	0.7	0.96	0.87	6.0	9.8	4.5	9.1	1.1	AD
INTERSTATE BANKERS LIFE INS CO	IL	U (1)	0.6	0.6	2.21	1.99	8.0	9.2	1.7	8.5	1.9	DFT
INTRAMERICA LIFE INS CO	NY	B	27.2	8.8	2.03	1.82	8.2	9.6	6.3	10.0	4.9	GT
INVESTORS CONSOLIDATED INS CO INC	NH	C	15.8	6.9	2.36	2.12	8.7	9.8	5.5	10.0	3.8	A
INVESTORS GROWTH LIFE INS CO	AZ	U	--	--	--	--	--	--	--	--	--	Z

See Page 26 for explanation of footnotes and Page 27 for explanation of stability factors.

Arrows denote recent upgrades ▲ or downgrades ▼ (see Section VI for explanations)

46

www.thestreetratings.com

NET PREMIUM ($MIL)	IN-VESTED ASSETS ($MIL)	% OF INVESTED ASSETS IN:									INVEST. IN AFFIL	INSURANCE COMPANY NAME
		CASH	CMO & STRUCT. SECS.	OTH.INV. GRADE BONDS	NON-INV. GRADE BONDS	CMMON & PREF. STOCK	MORT IN GOOD STAND.	NON-PERF. MORT.	REAL ESTATE	OTHER INVEST-MENTS		
--	--	--	--	--	--	--	--	--	--	--	--	HARDIN COUNTY LIFE INS CO
14.7	321.7	0.1	18.6	79.4	0.3	0.0	0.0	0.0	0.0	1.6	0.0	HARLEYSVILLE LIFE INS CO
--	--	--	--	--	--	--	--	--	--	--	--	HARRIS LIFE INS CO
7.1	1,086.7	0.0	24.7	6.4	1.2	2.1	0.0	0.0	0.0	65.6	0.0 ●	HARTFORD INTL LIFE REASR CORP
853.0	13,636.7	0.2	11.9	35.6	1.6	40.8	5.4	0.0	0.0	4.5	35.2 ●	HARTFORD LIFE & ACCIDENT INS CO
848.0	13,987.2	1.1	19.1	55.1	1.2	1.9	4.4	0.0	0.2	17.0	0.1 ●	HARTFORD LIFE & ANNUITY INS CO
2,006.7	39,252.1	0.2	29.8	40.2	3.0	9.8	7.5	0.0	0.3	9.2	5.8 ●	HARTFORD LIFE INS CO
0.6	14.7	0.6	0.4	99.1	0.0	0.0	0.0	0.0	0.0	0.0	0.1	HAWKEYE LIFE INS GROUP INC
0.2	8.7	1.7	52.6	12.1	0.0	33.6	0.0	0.0	0.0	0.0	33.6	HAWTHORN LIFE INS CO
166.5	557.4	4.7	23.1	65.1	0.0	7.1	0.0	0.0	0.0	0.0	7.1 ●	HCC LIFE INS CO
296.9	359.0 (*)	0.0	46.8	61.0	0.0	0.9	0.0	0.0	0.0	0.0	0.0 ●	HEALTH NET LIFE INS CO
0.0	9.0	0.4	0.0	99.6	0.0	0.0	0.0	0.0	0.0	0.0	0.0	HEALTHMARKETS INS CO
9.9	16.8	16.7	0.0	83.3	0.0	0.0	0.0	0.0	0.0	0.0	0.0	HEALTHPLUS INS CO
0.0	7.7	75.2	0.0	0.0	0.0	0.0	0.0	0.0	0.0	24.8	0.0	HEALTHSPRING LIFE & HLTH INS CO INC
392.1	431.3	-3.1	35.1	64.8	1.2	0.5	0.0	0.0	0.0	1.5	0.0 ●	HEALTHY ALLIANCE LIFE INS CO
0.0	5.6	54.6	1.3	43.1	0.0	0.0	0.0	0.0	0.0	1.0	0.0	HEARTLAND NATIONAL LIFE INS CO
0.0	28.4	4.4	0.4	89.9	0.0	0.0	0.0	0.0	0.0	5.3	0.0	HERITAGE LIFE INS CO
0.0	11.9	15.4	0.0	84.6	0.0	0.0	0.0	0.0	0.0	0.0	0.0	HERITAGE UNION LIFE INS CO
0.1	1.3	60.7	0.0	19.9	9.6	7.8	0.0	0.0	0.0	2.0	0.0	HIGGINBOTHAM BURIAL INS CO
102.8	286.6	11.4	13.6	58.6	11.4	3.0	0.0	0.0	0.0	1.9	2.7 ●	HM LIFE INS CO
16.3	38.7	4.9	20.8	72.7	0.0	0.0	0.0	0.0	0.0	1.6	0.0	HM LIFE INS CO OF NEW YORK
--	--	--	--	--	--	--	--	--	--	--	--	HOME SECURITY LIFE INS CO
79.4	1,561.3	0.2	34.2	54.0	1.2	0.3	9.3	0.0	0.8	0.1	0.0 ●	HOMESTEADERS LIFE CO
91.9	3,464.9	0.1	35.6	53.8	3.2	3.5	0.5	0.0	0.0	3.5	0.4 ●	HORACE MANN LIFE INS CO
50.1	776.9	0.6	7.4	82.5	0.4	3.3	0.0	0.0	0.0	5.8	3.3 ●	HOUSEHOLD LIFE INS CO
0.0	822.9	0.0	3.5	96.2	0.3	0.0	0.0	0.0	0.0	0.0	0.0 ●	HOUSEHOLD LIFE INS CO OF AZ
0.1	571.3	0.0	1.9	31.9	0.2	66.0	0.0	0.0	0.0	0.0	66.0 ●	HOUSEHOLD LIFE INS CO OF DE
3,552.8	3,251.7	0.0	35.0	52.9	2.8	9.4	0.3	0.0	0.4	0.1	7.3 ●	HUMANA INS CO
8.0	29.4	0.9	0.0	52.9	0.0	46.2	0.0	0.0	0.0	0.0	0.0	HUMANA INS CO OF KENTUCKY
19.5	34.3	3.9	1.5	93.7	0.5	0.4	0.0	0.0	0.0	0.0	0.0 ●	HUMANA INS CO OF PUERTO RICO INC
73.2	90.0	-1.6	38.8	57.1	2.3	3.4	0.0	0.0	0.0	0.0	0.0 ●	HUMANADENTAL INS CO
0.0	18.4	0.4	0.0	99.7	0.0	0.0	0.0	0.0	0.0	0.0	0.0	I B A HEALTH & LIFE ASR CO
0.0	30.8	-2.7	0.3	17.2	0.0	0.0	0.0	0.0	0.0	85.1	0.0 ●	IA AMERICAN LIFE INS CO
0.1	3.2	59.9	0.0	40.1	0.0	0.0	0.0	0.0	0.0	0.0	0.0	IBC LIFE INS CO
0.3	19.7	0.8	0.0	78.1	0.0	0.0	0.0	0.0	0.0	21.2	0.0	IDEALIFE INS CO
50.4	1,177.2	-0.5	28.5	44.4	7.1	5.6	7.8	0.0	0.3	6.9	1.5 ●	ILLINOIS MUTUAL LIFE INS CO
0.0	1.7	0.1	0.0	0.0	0.0	0.0	0.0	0.0	0.0	99.9	0.0	INDEPENDENCE INS INC
-0.2	84.8	1.1	3.3	61.8	3.4	1.2	0.0	0.0	0.0	29.2	0.0 ●	INDEPENDENCE LIFE & ANNUITY CO
--	--	--	--	--	--	--	--	--	--	--	--	INDEPENDENCE ONE LIFE INS CO
4.9	40.2	5.0	24.8	45.1	1.2	8.3	0.0	0.0	9.1	6.5	4.7	INDIVIDUAL ASR CO LIFE HEALTH & ACC
--	--	--	--	--	--	--	--	--	--	--	--	INDUSTRIAL ALLIANCE PACIFIC LIFE INS
2,263.7	19,804.6	0.3	30.3	44.0	5.1	1.3	10.6	0.0	0.5	8.0	2.8 ●	ING LIFE INS & ANNUITY CO
1,856.3	23,457.1	0.2	37.4	35.2	6.3	1.4	13.8	0.1	0.0	4.8	1.5 ●	ING USA ANNUITY & LIFE INS CO
0.2	2.8	17.7	0.0	82.3	0.0	0.0	0.0	0.0	0.0	0.0	0.0	INS CO OF SCOTT AND WHITE
--	--	--	--	--	--	--	--	--	--	--	--	INSOUTH LIFE INS CO
0.6	6.5	100.0	0.0	0.0	0.0	0.0	0.0	0.0	0.0	0.0	0.0	INTEGRITY CAPITAL INS CO
241.8	2,443.7	-0.3	20.3	52.4	3.4	12.0	2.6	0.0	0.0	9.5	7.6 ●	INTEGRITY LIFE INS CO
0.1	1.7	8.8	0.0	91.2	0.0	0.0	0.0	0.0	0.0	0.0	0.0	INTERNATIONAL AMERICAN LIFE INS CO
0.0	0.6	21.6	78.4	0.0	0.0	0.0	0.0	0.0	0.0	0.0	0.0	INTERSTATE BANKERS LIFE INS CO
0.0	11.0	3.3	1.3	95.4	0.0	0.0	0.0	0.0	0.0	0.0	0.0	INTRAMERICA LIFE INS CO
0.4	14.8	2.8	0.0	97.2	0.0	0.0	0.0	0.0	0.0	0.0	0.0	INVESTORS CONSOLIDATED INS CO INC
--	--	--	--	--	--	--	--	--	--	--	--	INVESTORS GROWTH LIFE INS CO

● Bullets denote a more detailed analysis is available in Section II.

(*) Asset category percentages do not add up to 100%

INSURANCE COMPANY NAME	DOM. STATE	RATING	TOTAL ASSETS ($MIL)	CAPITAL & SURPLUS ($MIL)	RISK ADJUSTED CAPITAL RATIO 1	RISK ADJUSTED CAPITAL RATIO 2	CAPITAL- IZATION INDEX (PTS)	INVEST. SAFETY INDEX (PTS)	PROFIT- ABILITY INDEX (PTS)	LIQUIDITY INDEX (PTS)	STAB. INDEX (PTS)	STABILITY FACTORS
INVESTORS HERITAGE LIFE INS CO	KY	C	337.1	15.6	1.06	0.68	5.1	5.7	5.0	1.3	3.3	CLR
INVESTORS INS CORP	DE	D+	307.5	28.5	2.07	1.03	7.0	6.7	4.5	7.2	2.6	AG
INVESTORS LIFE INS CO NORTH AMERICA	TX	C-	737.8	33.5	1.69	0.89	6.1	3.6	3.5	4.9	2.7	DFLT
ISLAND INS CORP	PR	U (1)	6.1	6.0	3.52	3.16	8.0	9.8	4.1	10.0	5.1	DE
J M I C LIFE INS CO	FL	C+	90.5	49.3	5.71	5.14	4.0	8.1	6.1	9.0	3.9	DFT
JACKSON GRIFFIN INS CO	AR	D	10.0	1.2	0.52	0.47	2.6	3.7	1.0	5.3	1.6	CI
JACKSON NATIONAL LIFE INS CO	MI	B	66886.5	3510.4	2.09	1.00	7.0	3.9	6.0	6.8	5.4	IT
JACKSON NATIONAL LIFE INS CO OF NY	NY	B	2554.6	88.4	1.55	0.71	5.8	3.0	1.1	7.3	4.2	CFGIT
JAMESTOWN LIFE INS CO	VA	B-	147.6	41.7	4.43	2.81	9.7	7.1	6.0	7.8	5.3	ADT
JEFF DAVIS MORTUARY BENEFIT ASSOC	LA	C (1)	3.4	1.9	1.71	1.54	3.0	9.8	4.1	10.0	2.5	DT
JEFFERSON LIFE INS CO	TX	C-	4.8	2.8	1.79	1.43	7.6	9.6	1.4	7.9	3.2	ACDFT
JEFFERSON NATIONAL LIFE INS CO	TX	D-	1311.3	22.7	1.23	0.63	5.3	3.8	1.2	7.8	1.2	FT
JEFFERSON STANDARD LIFE INS CO	NC	U (1)	2.7	2.7	2.97	2.68	8.0	9.5	6.2	7.0	5.3	DFT
JOHN ALDEN LIFE INS CO	WI	B-	481.1	98.9	1.65	1.20	5.9	6.7	6.3	6.3	5.1	A
JOHN HANCOCK LIFE & HEALTH INS CO	MA	B	2769.4	195.1	5.34	2.69	9.5	5.5	6.7	7.5	4.0	GIT
JOHN HANCOCK LIFE INS CO	MA	B-	61635.9	2021.6	1.16	0.70	5.2	3.7	3.9	6.7	3.6	CGIT
JOHN HANCOCK LIFE INS CO (USA)	MI	B	102138.5	1779.7	1.02	0.56	5.0	3.5	1.8	9.0	4.9	CIT
JOHN HANCOCK LIFE INS CO OF NY	NY	A-	6461.4	460.7	7.21	5.98	10.0	9.1	1.7	10.0	6.0	AT
JOHN HANCOCK VARIABLE LIFE INS CO	MA	B	12033.7	552.0	1.19	0.71	5.3	4.6	5.9	5.4	4.5	CIT
JORDAN FUNERAL & INS CO INC	AL	F (5)	--	--	--	--	--	--	--	--	--	Z
KANAWHA INS CO	SC	C (1)	823.1	59.6	1.36	0.91	6.3	6.9	1.5	8.0	3.9	
KANSAS CITY LIFE INS CO	MO	B	2950.1	281.5	1.55	0.94	6.5	5.0	5.9	5.5	5.3	I
KELLEY LIFE INS CO	AZ	U	--	--	--	--	--	--	--	--	--	Z
KEMPER INVESTORS LIFE INS CO	IL	C	13503.9	163.1	1.97	1.29	4.0	7.8	1.1	7.1	3.0	T
KENTUCKY FUNERAL DIRECTORS LIFE INS	KY	C+	12.1	3.9	1.46	1.32	7.5	8.3	7.5	6.7	4.0	AD
KENTUCKY HOME LIFE INS CO	KY	B	5.1	3.9	3.41	3.07	10.0	9.8	7.9	8.2	4.7	T
KEY BANK LIFE INS LTD	AZ	U	--	--	--	--	--	--	--	--	--	Z
KILPATRICK LIFE INS CO	LA	E-	145.3	-3.6	-0.01	0.00	0.0	3.8	0.8	0.0	0.0	CDILT
LA CRUZ AZUL DE PUERTO RICO INC	PR	E-	39.9	-12.8	-0.45	-0.35	0.0	3.0	0.5	0.1	0.0	CDFLT
LAFAYETTE LIFE INS CO	IN	B-	2043.8	101.0	1.69	0.86	6.0	4.7	5.7	5.5	5.1	I
LAFOURCHE LIFE INS CO	LA	D-	22.4	2.3	0.68	0.34	2.4	0.3	4.4	6.2	1.1	ACDI
LANDCAR LIFE INS CO	UT	C+	33.3	19.5	2.30	1.58	7.9	3.4	7.3	9.5	4.2	DIT
LANDMARK LIFE INS CO	TX	E+	60.2	2.6	0.37	0.33	1.0	1.1	3.9	0.7	0.4	CDIL
LAUREL LIFE INS CO	TX	U (1)	30.2	27.5	0.76	0.68	4.4	1.0	1.3	9.3	2.1	DFIT
LEADERS LIFE INS CO	OK	B	5.4	2.9	1.83	1.65	8.0	5.0	5.2	6.5	4.1	DI
LEAFRE REINSURANCE CO	AZ	U (1)	1.4	1.4	2.49	2.24	8.0	7.0	4.7	9.3	2.8	DT
LEWER LIFE INS CO	MO	C	27.6	8.0	1.92	1.72	8.1	7.6	6.3	6.7	3.2	D
LEWIS LIFE INS CO	TX	E+	1.1	0.2	0.42	0.38	1.6	9.6	3.0	9.5	0.5	CD
LFG SOUTH CAROLINA REINSURANCE CO	SC	U (5)	--	--	--	--	--	--	--	--	--	Z
▼ LIBERTY BANKERS LIFE INS CO	OK	C-	877.2	58.6	0.69	0.47	2.6	2.1	8.5	7.7	2.6	CDGI
LIBERTY LIFE ASR CO OF BOSTON	MA	B-	11641.8	439.7	1.67	0.90	6.2	4.8	5.7	7.4	5.1	AIT
LIBERTY LIFE INS CO	SC	C	3684.7	219.4	1.48	0.82	5.7	5.6	6.3	5.0	4.1	FGT
LIBERTY NATIONAL LIFE INS CO	NE	B	5116.8	597.6	1.03	0.77	5.2	5.5	8.2	6.4	5.2	ACI
LIBERTY UNION LIFE ASR CO	MI	C-	9.9	4.2	0.90	0.72	4.8	7.9	3.7	5.5	3.2	CDFT
LIFE ASR CO OF AMERICA	IL	C-	6.1	2.5	1.28	1.15	7.2	7.5	5.2	6.9	1.6	DFGT
LIFE ASSURANCE CO INC	OK	C	7.2	2.2	1.06	0.96	6.7	9.7	8.3	9.4	3.4	T
LIFE INS CO OF AL	AL	B	84.7	16.3	1.33	0.97	6.8	7.3	8.8	7.0	5.8	T
LIFE INS CO OF BOSTON & NEW YORK	NY	B+	72.0	11.5	1.53	1.38	7.6	7.7	7.2	6.4	5.7	AD
LIFE INS CO OF LOUISIANA	LA	C+ (1)	7.0	3.5	1.93	1.74	3.0	5.0	4.6	8.0	2.2	DT
▲ LIFE INS CO OF NORTH AMERICA	PA	B-	5275.1	621.7	1.97	1.29	7.4	4.4	5.8	6.1	4.5	AI
LIFE INS CO OF THE SOUTHWEST	TX	B	6751.8	423.1	1.64	0.81	6.0	4.2	7.9	2.7	4.7	CGIL
LIFE OF AMERICA INS CO	TX	D	3.6	1.1	0.89	0.80	5.4	7.0	1.6	7.1	1.4	DGIT

See Page 26 for explanation of footnotes and Page 27 for explanation of stability factors.
Arrows denote recent upgrades ▲ or downgrades ▼ (see Section VI for explanations)

48

www.thestreetratings.com

NET PREMIUM ($MIL)	IN-VESTED ASSETS ($MIL)	CASH	CMO & STRUCT. SECS.	OTH.INV. GRADE BONDS	NON-INV. GRADE BONDS	CMMON & PREF. STOCK	MORT IN GOOD STAND.	NON-PERF. MORT.	REAL ESTATE	OTHER INVEST-MENTS	INVEST. IN AFFIL	INSURANCE COMPANY NAME
							% OF INVESTED ASSETS IN:					
8.5	319.2	0.2	24.1	64.9	0.2	1.3	7.0	0.0	0.1	2.2	1.9	INVESTORS HERITAGE LIFE INS CO
18.8	242.7	2.7	38.5	50.6	1.0	3.4	3.0	0.0	0.0	0.9	0.0 ●	INVESTORS INS CORP
-0.3	537.5	-0.5	16.2	74.8	4.6	0.3	0.0	0.0	0.0	4.8	0.1 ●	INVESTORS LIFE INS CO NORTH AMERICA
0.0	6.0	86.1	0.0	13.9	0.0	0.0	0.0	0.0	0.0	0.0	0.0	ISLAND INS CORP
-1.3	93.1	0.1	46.3	51.8	0.7	1.0	0.0	0.0	0.0	0.2	0.0 ●	J M I C LIFE INS CO
0.2	9.8	9.5	0.0	67.6	6.9	16.3	0.0	0.0	0.0	0.0	0.0	JACKSON GRIFFIN INS CO
2,507.0	47,266.7	0.0	24.4	47.4	6.5	1.7	13.5	0.0	0.2	6.4	1.9 ●	JACKSON NATIONAL LIFE INS CO
142.2	1,402.3	-0.6	30.1	65.5	4.6	0.3	0.0	0.0	0.0	0.1	0.0 ●	JACKSON NATIONAL LIFE INS CO OF NY
2.7	144.7	0.6	8.3	86.3	1.7	3.1	0.0	0.0	0.0	0.0	0.0 ●	JAMESTOWN LIFE INS CO
0.1	3.4	41.2	0.0	58.8	0.0	0.0	0.0	0.0	0.0	0.0	0.0	JEFF DAVIS MORTUARY BENEFIT ASSOC
1.2	4.6	79.7	0.0	15.5	0.0	0.0	0.0	0.0	0.0	4.8	0.0	JEFFERSON LIFE INS CO
38.8	464.5	-0.5	34.7	49.2	2.9	6.1	4.0	0.0	0.0	3.7	0.0	JEFFERSON NATIONAL LIFE INS CO
0.0	2.7	0.0	0.0	94.6	0.0	0.0	0.0	0.0	0.0	5.6	0.0	JEFFERSON STANDARD LIFE INS CO
122.0	471.0	-1.2	23.8	52.0	5.0	9.6	5.1	0.0	0.0	5.7	0.0 ●	JOHN ALDEN LIFE INS CO
2.2	801.1	0.1	6.0	65.5	3.0	0.1	12.8	0.0	1.2	11.4	0.0 ●	JOHN HANCOCK LIFE & HEALTH INS CO
1,244.6	50,354.6	0.2	14.0	48.2	5.8	4.0	17.2	0.0	2.2	8.5	3.0 ●	JOHN HANCOCK LIFE INS CO
1,749.1	29,592.2	-0.1	3.8	64.7	1.1	3.1	9.5	0.0	5.2	12.8	2.3 ●	JOHN HANCOCK LIFE INS CO (USA)
278.3	1,228.7	-0.2	0.0	96.7	0.0	0.0	0.0	0.0	0.0	3.5	0.0 ●	JOHN HANCOCK LIFE INS CO OF NY
126.6	6,472.1	0.1	12.5	49.9	4.7	4.8	15.2	0.0	4.0	8.8	3.5 ●	JOHN HANCOCK VARIABLE LIFE INS CO
--	--	--	--	--	--	--	--	--	--	--	--	JORDAN FUNERAL & INS CO INC
147.8	800.4	10.9	22.8	61.9	0.6	0.6	1.0	0.0	0.4	2.0	0.0 ●	KANAWHA INS CO
67.6	2,658.9	-0.1	25.4	46.5	4.2	3.3	14.5	0.0	1.9	4.7	2.1 ●	KANSAS CITY LIFE INS CO
--	--	--	--	--	--	--	--	--	--	--	--	KELLEY LIFE INS CO
-33.2	458.3	0.1	36.0	47.7	0.5	0.2	0.0	0.0	0.0	15.4	0.0 ●	KEMPER INVESTORS LIFE INS CO
0.3	11.9	0.9	3.9	86.1	0.6	8.4	0.0	0.0	0.0	0.0	0.0	KENTUCKY FUNERAL DIRECTORS LIFE INS
0.2	5.0	0.0	0.0	100.0	0.0	0.0	0.0	0.0	0.0	0.0	0.0	KENTUCKY HOME LIFE INS CO
--	--	--	--	--	--	--	--	--	--	--	--	KEY BANK LIFE INS LTD
4.6	136.7	2.8	0.0	50.4	14.5	6.8	16.5	0.8	3.4	5.0	4.2	KILPATRICK LIFE INS CO
17.9	11.4	29.4	0.0	3.7	66.0	0.9	0.0	0.0	0.0	0.0	0.0	LA CRUZ AZUL DE PUERTO RICO INC
88.3	1,937.4	0.4	14.3	59.7	3.8	1.1	12.0	0.0	0.1	8.7	0.0 ●	LAFAYETTE LIFE INS CO
0.5	22.3 (*)	2.1	49.4	-6.1	7.4	0.0	20.9	1.8	26.5	17.6	0.0	LAFOURCHE LIFE INS CO
0.4	33.1	1.8	0.0	8.8	1.1	35.8	41.5	5.6	0.0	5.4	0.0	LANDCAR LIFE INS CO
1.7	56.6	2.7	31.4	46.1	1.9	3.4	9.7	0.0	4.4	0.6	0.0	LANDMARK LIFE INS CO
0.0	29.9	0.0	0.0	2.5	0.0	97.5	0.0	0.0	0.0	0.0	97.5	LAUREL LIFE INS CO
0.9	3.0	20.8	51.3	14.0	11.1	2.9	0.0	0.0	0.0	0.1	0.0	LEADERS LIFE INS CO
0.0	1.4	17.0	0.0	71.2	0.0	11.8	0.0	0.0	0.0	0.0	0.0	LEAFRE REINSURANCE CO
1.5	26.6	0.2	29.0	65.3	3.2	0.0	0.0	0.0	0.0	2.3	0.0	LEWER LIFE INS CO
0.0	1.0	83.0	0.0	0.0	0.0	0.0	0.0	0.0	0.0	17.0	0.0	LEWIS LIFE INS CO
--	--	--	--	--	--	--	--	--	--	--	--	LFG SOUTH CAROLINA REINSURANCE CO
105.1	783.4	3.6	22.8	25.7	3.4	11.8	15.4	4.3	2.9	10.0	3.6 ●	LIBERTY BANKERS LIFE INS CO
261.9	8,312.7	1.0	25.3	61.7	4.4	0.5	2.3	0.0	0.0	4.8	0.0 ●	LIBERTY LIFE ASR CO OF BOSTON
187.0	3,486.9	0.9	39.9	37.4	0.1	2.1	16.1	0.0	0.0	3.4	0.0 ●	LIBERTY LIFE INS CO
114.5	4,884.2	0.0	3.1	68.3	4.4	17.1	0.3	0.0	0.1	7.1	11.2 ●	LIBERTY NATIONAL LIFE INS CO
5.5	9.3	3.7	11.2	81.7	0.3	2.7	0.3	0.0	0.0	0.1	0.0	LIBERTY UNION LIFE ASR CO
0.1	6.0	0.4	35.2	54.7	2.5	0.0	0.0	0.0	0.0	7.3	0.0	LIFE ASR CO OF AMERICA
0.5	7.4	86.4	8.5	5.1	0.0	0.0	0.0	0.0	0.0	0.0	0.0	LIFE ASSURANCE CO INC
10.3	76.3	0.0	0.0	86.7	2.4	1.7	0.0	0.0	0.7	8.6	0.0	LIFE INS CO OF AL
3.6	64.5	1.5	19.7	56.0	0.1	0.2	0.0	0.0	0.0	22.5	0.0	LIFE INS CO OF BOSTON & NEW YORK
0.2	6.2	6.8	6.5	52.0	0.7	34.0	0.0	0.0	0.0	0.1	13.0	LIFE INS CO OF LOUISIANA
591.9	4,196.4	0.4	2.4	29.5	4.8	38.2	22.5	0.0	0.0	2.3	35.7 ●	LIFE INS CO OF NORTH AMERICA
314.8	6,409.1	-0.1	27.1	49.9	4.5	0.6	13.5	0.0	0.0	4.5	0.0 ●	LIFE INS CO OF THE SOUTHWEST
0.4	4.1	28.6	6.9	44.3	4.6	0.0	15.0	0.0	0.0	0.6	0.0	LIFE OF AMERICA INS CO

● Bullets denote a more detailed analysis is available in Section II.

(*) Asset category percentages do not add up to 100%

INSURANCE COMPANY NAME	DOM. STATE	RATING		TOTAL ASSETS ($MIL)	CAPITAL & SURPLUS ($MIL)	RISK ADJUSTED CAPITAL RATIO 1	RISK ADJUSTED CAPITAL RATIO 2	CAPITAL-IZATION INDEX (PTS)	INVEST. SAFETY INDEX (PTS)	PROFIT-ABILITY INDEX (PTS)	LIQUIDITY INDEX (PTS)	STAB. INDEX (PTS)	STABILITY FACTORS
LIFE OF THE SOUTH INS CO	GA	C		63.5	17.1	0.78	0.64	4.1	7.9	6.4	8.0	3.4	CT
LIFE PROTECTION INS CO	TX	D+		13.5	11.6	4.17	3.75	10.0	5.7	6.2	10.0	2.5	AT
▲ LIFECARE ASSURANCE CO	AZ	C		846.2	62.2	1.56	0.99	6.9	6.3	9.5	9.3	3.7	D
LIFESECURE INS CO	MI	B-		57.5	19.4	1.64	1.14	7.2	8.8	1.6	9.3	4.6	DGOT
LIFESHIELD NATIONAL INS CO	OK	B-		66.3	21.2	2.86	1.90	8.4	6.7	4.3	6.8	3.5	DGT
LIFEWISE ASR CO	WA	A		70.2	40.4	2.43	1.72	8.1	7.4	8.4	7.1	6.9	A
LINCOLN BENEFIT LIFE CO	NE	B+		2007.2	295.5	3.13	1.56	7.8	8.2	2.7	10.0	5.3	T
LINCOLN HERITAGE LIFE INS CO	IL	B+		629.7	85.9	2.79	1.48	7.7	5.9	5.7	6.1	6.8	I
LINCOLN LIFE & ANNUITY CO OF NY	NY	B-		8426.1	755.2	3.34	1.67	8.0	6.3	2.0	5.9	5.2	AIT
▼ LINCOLN MEMORIAL LIFE INS CO	TX	F	(4)	124.0	-3.9	-0.18	-0.15	0.0	7.4	1.0	3.8	0.0	CDFGLT
LINCOLN MUTUAL LIFE & CAS INS CO	ND	C+		31.9	10.5	2.22	1.68	8.0	6.9	7.3	7.1	4.5	T
LINCOLN NATIONAL LIFE INS CO	IN	B-		117179.0	4566.3	1.29	0.79	5.4	4.4	7.1	6.6	4.7	CIT
▲ LOCOMOTIVE ENGRS&COND MUT PROT ASSN	MI	C-		23.0	13.5	3.69	3.32	10.0	8.0	3.3	7.5	2.5	D
LONDON LIFE INS CO	MI	B		93.3	23.0	1.54	0.68	5.8	8.0	7.7	8.0	4.4	CT
LONDON LIFE REINSURANCE CO	PA	B		737.6	68.4	2.51	1.34	7.5	7.7	6.3	9.2	5.0	AGT
LONE STAR LIFE INS CO	TX	F	(5)	--	--	--	--	--	--	--	--	--	Z
LONGEVITY INS CO	TX	D+		7.6	7.8	3.92	3.53	4.0	9.5	2.9	0.0	2.0	FLT
LOYAL AMERICAN LIFE INS CO	OH	B-		484.3	36.5	1.04	0.64	5.1	3.6	6.3	6.8	4.9	ACDGIT
M & T LIFE INS CO	AZ	U		--	--	--	--	--	--	--	--	--	Z
M LIFE INS CO	CO	B-		169.1	100.5	3.48	2.69	9.5	6.8	4.9	8.4	5.1	DT
M&I INS CO OF AZ INC	AZ	U		--	--	--	--	--	--	--	--	--	Z
MADISON NATIONAL LIFE INS CO INC	WI	C+		800.2	145.0	0.79	0.70	4.6	7.0	6.0	5.2	4.6	C
MAGNA INS CO	MS	C		42.2	12.7	2.08	1.87	8.3	8.2	3.6	6.8	3.0	DFT
MAJESTIC LIFE INS CO	LA	U		--	--	--	--	--	--	--	--	--	Z
MANHATTAN LIFE INS CO	NY	C+		350.6	33.3	1.41	1.17	7.3	8.4	4.7	6.5	4.6	ADF
▲ MANHATTAN NATIONAL LIFE INS CO	IL	C		212.9	9.2	1.05	0.94	6.5	1.9	6.0	9.2	3.6	IT
MAPFRE LIFE INS CO	PR	D+		74.8	8.9	0.26	0.21	0.0	7.4	1.3	1.1	1.2	CGL
MARQUETTE INDEMNITY & LIFE INS CO	AZ	C+		9.7	5.5	2.35	2.12	8.7	6.8	6.5	7.6	4.2	FT
▲ MARQUETTE NATIONAL LIFE INS CO	TX	D+		24.6	8.2	0.57	0.47	2.6	9.2	1.5	1.1	2.4	ACDGLT
MASSACHUSETTS MUTUAL LIFE INS CO	MA	A		112014.6	8239.8	2.65	1.45	7.7	5.7	7.7	8.2	6.1	I
MC CARTHY LIFE INS CO	AZ	U		--	--	--	--	--	--	--	--	--	Z
MCB LIFE INS CO	TN	U		--	--	--	--	--	--	--	--	--	Z
MCDONALD LIFE INS CO	TX	U	(1)	0.8	0.7	2.08	1.87	8.3	3.2	3.8	10.0	4.0	DIT
MCS LIFE INS CO	PR	D		49.0	14.2	0.40	0.35	1.2	3.7	2.8	1.1	1.8	CFLT
MEDAMERICA INS CO	PA	B-		468.2	17.6	0.89	0.57	4.1	4.5	1.3	10.0	3.5	CDGIT
MEDAMERICA INS CO OF FL	FL	C-		9.1	1.6	0.72	0.65	4.2	8.6	1.6	10.0	3.3	CDEGT
MEDAMERICA INS CO OF NEW YORK	NY	C		289.2	9.2	0.97	0.65	4.8	4.8	1.4	10.0	3.4	CT
MEDICAL BENEFITS MUTUAL LIFE INS CO	OH	B-		20.7	13.7	4.06	2.38	9.1	6.0	7.0	7.4	4.0	FG
MEDICO INS CO	NE	C		115.7	44.0	4.94	3.82	10.0	6.7	4.5	6.6	3.2	ACFT
MEGA LIFE & HEALTH INS CO	OK	B-		702.0	205.0	1.21	0.99	5.8	7.3	3.9	4.4	4.8	FLT
MELANCON LIFE INS CO	LA	D	(1)	6.6	0.8	0.53	0.48	2.8	4.0	5.6	6.4	2.3	CDT
MELLON LIFE INS CO	DE	C		26.2	24.5	5.87	5.28	10.0	9.1	7.7	10.0	3.7	DF
▲ MEMBERS LIFE INS CO	IA	C+		46.1	12.9	2.05	1.84	8.3	8.7	2.1	6.4	3.1	CDIT
MEMORIAL INS CO OF AMERICA	AR	C-		1.2	1.1	2.14	1.48	7.7	7.4	4.1	0.0	2.0	AFLT
MEMORIAL LIFE INS CO	LA	C-	(1)	2.5	1.0	1.15	1.04	7.1	5.6	7.2	9.6	3.7	C
MEMORIAL SERVICE LIFE INS CO	TX	F	(5)	--	--	--	--	--	--	--	--	--	Z
MERIT LIFE INS CO	IN	B		647.4	289.1	9.65	4.88	10.0	5.9	6.5	8.6	4.4	AIT
MERRILL LYNCH LIFE INS CO	AR	B-		9776.1	294.3	3.43	1.74	8.1	6.9	1.9	7.1	3.9	FT
METLIFE INS CO OF CT (LIFE DEPT)	CT	B		65347.5	4810.1	1.50	1.02	7.0	5.8	6.1	8.8	4.7	GIT
METLIFE INVESTORS INS CO	MO	B-		9143.0	370.4	2.59	1.25	7.4	6.1	3.7	10.0	4.6	GT
METLIFE INVESTORS USA INS CO	DE	C+		27296.1	1140.2	2.42	1.21	7.3	5.3	1.2	9.2	4.0	CIT
▼ METROPOLITAN LIFE INS CO	NY	B-		278164.2	10601.0	1.81	0.95	6.6	3.7	7.2	7.5	3.7	IT

See Page 26 for explanation of footnotes and Page 27 for explanation of stability factors.
Arrows denote recent upgrades ▲ or downgrades ▼ (see Section VI for explanations)

50

www.thestreetratings.com

NET PREMIUM ($MIL)	IN-VESTED ASSETS ($MIL)	CASH	CMO & STRUCT. SECS.	OTH.INV. GRADE BONDS	NON-INV. GRADE BONDS	CMMON & PREF. STOCK	MORT IN GOOD STAND.	NON-PERF. MORT.	REAL ESTATE	OTHER INVEST-MENTS	INVEST. IN AFFIL	INSURANCE COMPANY NAME
					% OF INVESTED ASSETS IN:							
11.0	55.6	4.8	30.9	48.9	0.0	15.3	0.0	0.0	0.0	0.8	14.1	LIFE OF THE SOUTH INS CO
0.1	13.8	5.1	7.1	63.6	0.0	23.0	0.0	0.0	0.0	1.2	0.0	LIFE PROTECTION INS CO
55.1	762.0	0.1	33.9	60.1	0.9	5.0	0.0	0.0	0.0	0.0	0.0 ●	LIFECARE ASSURANCE CO
2.5	46.6 (*)	0.1	6.4	83.9	0.0	0.0	0.0	0.0	0.0	0.0	0.0	LIFESECURE INS CO
3.2	63.0	1.9	37.6	46.7	2.2	8.7	0.0	0.0	0.0	2.9	1.4	LIFESHIELD NATIONAL INS CO
12.3	67.5	-0.8	48.8	49.6	3.2	0.0	0.0	0.0	0.0	0.0	0.0 ●	LIFEWISE ASR CO
0.0	265.2	-17.9	28.9	87.0	0.0	1.1	0.0	0.0	0.0	0.9	0.9 ●	LINCOLN BENEFIT LIFE CO
48.7	569.8	4.5	42.3	36.3	3.9	1.3	3.8	0.0	2.3	5.6	0.0 ●	LINCOLN HERITAGE LIFE INS CO
222.0	6,517.6	0.1	22.5	61.6	3.5	1.6	4.5	0.0	0.0	6.2	0.0 ●	LINCOLN LIFE & ANNUITY CO OF NY
16.4	101.5 (*)	0.7	48.9	17.7	0.6	0.8	0.5	0.0	0.0	27.1	0.0	LINCOLN MEMORIAL LIFE INS CO
1.6	31.4	-0.7	6.2	83.1	0.0	9.5	0.0	0.0	0.0	2.0	0.6	LINCOLN MUTUAL LIFE & CAS INS CO
3,060.0	61,165.6	-0.3	18.6	54.8	4.8	4.7	11.5	0.0	0.2	5.8	2.2 ●	LINCOLN NATIONAL LIFE INS CO
5.2	21.2	2.8	9.4	71.2	0.0	11.4	0.0	0.0	0.0	5.3	0.0	LOCOMOTIVE ENGRS&COND MUT PROT ASSN
1.9	53.2	1.5	0.0	98.5	0.0	0.0	0.0	0.0	0.0	0.0	0.0	LONDON LIFE INS CO
9.1	367.6	5.0	14.8	79.3	0.9	0.0	0.0	0.0	0.0	0.1	0.0 ●	LONDON LIFE REINSURANCE CO
--	--	--	--	--	--	--	--	--	--	--	--	LONE STAR LIFE INS CO
0.0	7.5 (*)	49.6	0.0	40.5	0.0	0.0	0.0	0.0	0.0	0.0	0.0	LONGEVITY INS CO
10.4	471.3	-0.3	32.8	56.6	3.2	3.1	0.0	0.0	0.0	4.5	2.9 ●	LOYAL AMERICAN LIFE INS CO
--	--	--	--	--	--	--	--	--	--	--	--	M & T LIFE INS CO
92.9	115.7	1.4	38.7	47.4	1.4	11.2	0.0	0.0	0.0	0.0	11.2 ●	M LIFE INS CO
--	--	--	--	--	--	--	--	--	--	--	--	M&I INS CO OF AZ INC
30.9	757.1 (*)	0.1	5.4	59.1	0.5	26.1	0.0	0.0	0.0	4.3	20.6 ●	MADISON NATIONAL LIFE INS CO INC
0.4	41.2	3.1	23.0	71.6	1.2	1.1	0.0	0.0	0.0	0.0	0.8	MAGNA INS CO
--	--	--	--	--	--	--	--	--	--	--	--	MAJESTIC LIFE INS CO
3.7	340.3	0.5	0.2	69.7	0.3	7.5	10.8	0.0	0.0	11.1	7.5 ●	MANHATTAN LIFE INS CO
0.1	199.1	-0.3	31.2	60.3	4.2	0.5	0.0	0.0	0.0	4.2	0.0	MANHATTAN NATIONAL LIFE INS CO
32.8	70.3	20.7	0.6	68.6	0.0	0.7	0.0	0.0	0.0	9.5	0.0	MAPFRE LIFE INS CO
0.2	9.4 (*)	0.7	38.9	45.2	0.4	14.8	0.0	0.0	0.0	1.5	0.0	MARQUETTE INDEMNITY & LIFE INS CO
2.1	21.4	23.1	8.4	68.5	0.0	0.0	0.0	0.0	0.0	0.0	0.0	MARQUETTE NATIONAL LIFE INS CO
3,019.9	81,058.8	0.3	16.3	37.9	4.5	3.2	14.7	0.0	1.3	21.9	9.6 ●	MASSACHUSETTS MUTUAL LIFE INS CO
--	--	--	--	--	--	--	--	--	--	--	--	MC CARTHY LIFE INS CO
--	--	--	--	--	--	--	--	--	--	--	--	MCB LIFE INS CO
0.0	0.8	49.5	0.0	0.0	1.3	44.0	2.4	2.9	0.0	0.0	0.0	MCDONALD LIFE INS CO
44.3	26.5	30.2	15.1	33.2	15.1	2.9	0.0	0.0	0.0	3.6	0.0	MCS LIFE INS CO
11.4	372.2	-0.2	13.1	85.3	1.3	0.5	0.0	0.0	0.0	0.0	0.5	MEDAMERICA INS CO
0.7	6.9	2.7	0.0	0.0	0.0	0.0	0.0	0.0	0.0	97.3	0.0	MEDAMERICA INS CO OF FL
9.7	269.8	-0.4	16.5	83.0	1.0	0.0	0.0	0.0	0.0	0.0	0.0	MEDAMERICA INS CO OF NEW YORK
2.5	16.4	5.0	0.0	45.9	0.0	15.6	0.0	0.0	12.5	21.1	5.5	MEDICAL BENEFITS MUTUAL LIFE INS CO
4.2	113.6	0.8	43.1	38.7	5.1	7.0	0.0	0.0	0.0	5.5	5.0 ●	MEDICO INS CO
195.4	636.3	-2.2	22.9	63.7	1.5	8.2	0.0	0.0	3.6	3.1	8.2 ●	MEGA LIFE & HEALTH INS CO
0.9	6.5	10.2	0.0	71.3	5.4	10.1	1.5	0.0	1.3	0.2	1.5	MELANCON LIFE INS CO
0.1	25.3	0.9	29.6	69.5	0.0	0.0	0.0	0.0	0.0	0.0	0.0	MELLON LIFE INS CO
1.0	40.9	0.1	24.9	68.4	0.0	0.0	0.0	0.0	0.0	6.6	0.0	MEMBERS LIFE INS CO
0.0	0.8	45.4	0.0	37.4	0.0	0.0	0.0	0.0	17.3	0.0	0.0	MEMORIAL INS CO OF AMERICA
0.4	2.4	29.5	0.0	35.7	0.0	16.0	18.7	0.0	0.0	0.0	0.0	MEMORIAL LIFE INS CO
--	--	--	--	--	--	--	--	--	--	--	--	MEMORIAL SERVICE LIFE INS CO
12.7	758.2	-0.1	11.0	59.6	7.3	2.1	19.0	0.0	0.0	1.3	0.2 ●	MERIT LIFE INS CO
69.3	2,591.5	-0.5	14.3	43.1	3.0	2.0	2.4	0.0	0.0	35.8	0.0 ●	MERRILL LYNCH LIFE INS CO
1,380.1	46,979.8	0.2	20.9	46.1	7.0	7.7	8.3	0.0	0.1	9.8	5.0 ●	METLIFE INS CO OF CT (LIFE DEPT)
563.1	2,780.2	1.4	30.6	55.7	2.8	1.9	2.7	0.0	0.0	5.0	0.1 ●	METLIFE INVESTORS INS CO
2,096.6	7,705.5	1.3	23.1	38.8	3.0	1.4	4.9	0.0	0.0	27.6	21.6 ●	METLIFE INVESTORS USA INS CO
9,196.0	213,113.3	1.6	17.9	39.1	5.5	4.2	19.0	0.0	1.7	11.2	6.0 ●	METROPOLITAN LIFE INS CO

● Bullets denote a more detailed analysis is available in Section II.

(*) Asset category percentages do not add up to 100%

INSURANCE COMPANY NAME	DOM. STATE	RATING	TOTAL ASSETS ($MIL)	CAPITAL & SURPLUS ($MIL)	RISK ADJUSTED CAPITAL RATIO 1	RISK ADJUSTED CAPITAL RATIO 2	CAPITAL-IZATION INDEX (PTS)	INVEST. SAFETY INDEX (PTS)	PROFIT-ABILITY INDEX (PTS)	LIQUIDITY INDEX (PTS)	STAB. INDEX (PTS)	STABILITY FACTORS
METROPOLITAN TOWER LIFE INS CO	DE	B	5171.2	885.3	2.52	1.12	7.2	3.0	7.4	6.6	4.3	FIT
MIAMI VALLEY INS CO	AZ	U	--	--	--	--	--	--	--	--	--	Z
MID AMERICA INS CO	AZ	U	--	--	--	--	--	--	--	--	--	Z
MID STATES LIFE INS CO	AZ	U	--	--	--	--	--	--	--	--	--	Z
MID-CONTINENT PREFERRED LIFE INS CO	OK	D+	15.9	2.1	1.94	1.74	8.1	5.2	1.9	7.1	2.5	DG
MID-WEST NATIONAL LIFE INS CO OF TN	TX	B+	228.4	101.6	2.76	2.08	8.6	6.8	6.1	6.6	5.3	ADFIT
MIDDLE TENNESSEE LIFE INS CO	TN	U	--	--	--	--	--	--	--	--	--	Z
MIDLAND NATIONAL LIFE INS CO	IA	B+	25970.2	1243.6	2.19	1.05	7.1	4.2	8.5	6.1	6.2	I
MIDWEST SECURITY LIFE INS CO	WI	B-	48.9	26.8	1.26	1.01	5.7	8.4	6.0	5.8	3.8	DFT
MIDWESTERN UNITED LIFE INS CO	IN	B	243.4	101.3	10.11	7.71	10.0	7.5	7.4	6.9	5.6	ADF
MII LIFE INC	MN	B-	148.7	9.6	1.28	1.15	7.2	5.2	0.8	9.2	3.6	FIT
MILILANI LIFE INS CO	HI	C-	2.0	1.9	2.48	2.23	8.8	9.8	8.5	10.0	2.9	D
MINNESOTA LIFE INS CO	MN	B	19313.5	1411.3	1.86	1.19	7.3	5.6	4.4	7.2	5.1	IT
MINNETONKA LIFE INS CO	AZ	U	--	--	--	--	--	--	--	--	--	Z
MISSISSIPPI VALLEY LIFE INS CO	AZ	U	--	--	--	--	--	--	--	--	--	Z
MISSOURI VALLEY LIFE AND HLTH INS CO	MO	B	11.5	11.0	4.30	3.87	10.0	9.0	9.0	10.0	4.9	DT
ML LIFE INS CO OF NEW YORK	NY	B	785.2	48.0	3.32	2.99	10.0	7.5	3.0	7.4	3.8	DT
MMA INS CO	IN	C	27.1	12.6	3.16	2.75	9.6	7.8	3.4	7.5	3.9	
MML BAY STATE LIFE INS CO	CT	A	4105.4	195.9	4.42	3.12	10.0	7.4	5.8	9.0	6.1	AT
MODERN LIFE INS CO OF ARIZONA	AZ	B	2.6	1.1	1.32	1.19	7.3	9.1	2.7	8.3	5.0	ADF
MOLINA HEALTHCARE INS CO	OH	B-	9.1	8.5	4.03	3.62	8.0	9.7	6.8	10.0	5.1	A
MONARCH LIFE INS CO	MA	F (1)	827.6	9.5	0.60	0.32	1.8	0.8	1.7	4.2	0.0	CFILT
MONITOR LIFE INS CO OF NEW YORK	NY	C-	8.7	4.9	2.24	2.02	8.5	8.9	3.5	8.7	3.2	ADF
MONUMENTAL LIFE INS CO	IA	C+	32958.8	1234.8	1.39	0.64	5.6	2.8	5.5	7.0	4.1	CFIT
▼ MONY LIFE INS CO	NY	C	9116.7	493.6	0.89	0.64	4.1	5.4	4.1	5.1	4.1	ACFT
MONY LIFE INS CO OF AMERICA	AZ	C+	3952.0	177.7	1.25	0.77	5.4	4.8	2.1	6.1	4.6	AFIT
MOTHE LIFE INS CO	LA	E-	40.8	-3.6	-0.10	-0.06	0.0	2.3	1.0	5.8	0.0	CDIT
MOTORISTS LIFE INS CO	OH	B	340.5	41.6	2.82	1.62	7.9	7.0	3.0	6.5	5.9	D
MOTORSPORT LIFE INS CO	AZ	U	--	--	--	--	--	--	--	--	--	Z
MOUNTAIN LIFE INS CO	TN	C+	8.9	3.4	1.48	1.33	7.5	8.5	6.2	9.1	4.1	FT
MTL INS CO	IL	B+	1337.3	89.1	2.41	1.23	7.3	5.6	3.2	5.4	6.2	IL
MULHEARN PROTECTIVE INS CO	LA	E (1)	9.0	0.4	0.19	0.16	0.0	1.3	2.8	7.7	0.0	CDIT
MUNICH AMERICAN REASSURANCE CO	GA	C+	5613.3	646.7	1.70	1.14	7.2	8.0	2.8	6.8	4.4	A
MUNICIPAL INS CO OF AMERICA	IL	F (5)	--	--	--	--	--	--	--	--	--	Z
MUTUAL OF AMERICA LIFE INS CO	NY	B	10756.0	779.2	3.18	1.53	7.8	6.0	4.7	7.0	5.2	I
MUTUAL OF OMAHA INS CO	NE	B+	4625.4	2061.9	0.98	0.92	6.4	5.8	8.6	7.0	6.0	ACI
MUTUAL SAVINGS LIFE INS CO	AL	C	429.8	23.6	1.30	0.83	5.6	4.8	7.6	6.0	4.2	T
NAP LIFE INS CO	TX	U (1)	2.2	2.2	2.83	2.55	8.0	9.1	7.6	10.0	6.4	D
NATIONAL ANNUITY CO	UT	F (5)	--	--	--	--	--	--	--	--	--	Z
NATIONAL BENEFIT LIFE INS CO	NY	A-	738.4	318.1	9.78	5.36	10.0	6.6	7.4	7.3	5.7	AIT
NATIONAL FAMILY CARE LIFE INS CO	TX	C	14.6	8.1	2.72	2.45	9.2	9.8	7.1	7.1	3.9	F
NATIONAL FARM LIFE INS CO	TX	B	260.4	19.9	1.81	1.04	7.1	5.4	5.7	3.2	4.7	DIL
NATIONAL FARMERS UNION LIFE INS CO	TX	B-	257.9	42.9	4.26	2.29	8.9	6.3	7.5	6.1	5.1	ADF
NATIONAL FOUNDATION LIFE INS CO	TX	C-	41.0	8.0	0.66	0.50	3.0	6.4	1.8	7.2	3.0	CFT
NATIONAL GUARDIAN LIFE INS CO	WI	B+	1663.4	155.3	1.33	0.86	5.9	5.4	7.1	6.8	5.9	CI
NATIONAL HEALTH INS CO	TX	F (1)	25.8	16.9	2.93	2.26	8.9	7.7	6.4	7.4	0.0	CT
NATIONAL HOME LIFE & ACCIDENT INS CO	IN	U (1)	0.6	0.4	0.73	0.66	4.3	9.8	5.3	10.0	4.3	CD
NATIONAL INCOME LIFE INS CO	NY	B	44.9	9.8	1.65	1.12	7.2	7.7	6.7	6.9	5.9	A
NATIONAL INTEGRITY LIFE INS CO	NY	B-	4163.6	192.0	2.98	1.34	7.5	5.5	4.0	9.0	5.1	G
NATIONAL LIFE INS CO	VT	B	7951.0	789.0	1.40	1.00	7.0	6.2	7.3	5.7	6.3	I
NATIONAL LIFE INS CO	PR	C+	145.6	24.6	0.99	0.71	4.9	6.4	5.0	6.2	4.7	C
NATIONAL MASONIC PROVIDENT ASN	OH	U (1)	1.3	0.7	1.51	1.36	7.5	8.9	1.7	7.7	1.9	DFT

See Page 26 for explanation of footnotes and Page 27 for explanation of stability factors.

Arrows denote recent upgrades ▲ or downgrades ▼ (see Section VI for explanations)

52

www.thestreetratings.com

NET PREMIUM ($MIL)	IN-VESTED ASSETS ($MIL)	% OF INVESTED ASSETS IN:									INVEST. IN AFFIL	INSURANCE COMPANY NAME
		CASH	CMO & STRUCT. SECS.	OTH.INV. GRADE BONDS	NON-INV. GRADE BONDS	CMMON & PREF. STOCK	MORT IN GOOD STAND.	NON-PERF. MORT.	REAL ESTATE	OTHER INVEST-MENTS		
13.9	5,345.6	0.4	24.0	35.8	2.3	3.6	3.7	0.0	21.0	9.3	0.6 •	METROPOLITAN TOWER LIFE INS CO
--	--	--	--	--	--	--	--	--	--	--	--	MIAMI VALLEY INS CO
--	--	--	--	--	--	--	--	--	--	--	--	MID AMERICA INS CO
--	--	--	--	--	--	--	--	--	--	--	--	MID STATES LIFE INS CO
4.2	12.2 (*)	1.0	5.7	66.2	2.6	1.7	2.9	2.5	0.0	12.2	0.0	MID-CONTINENT PREFERRED LIFE INS CO
58.5	204.3	-1.7	19.7	73.4	5.2	1.1	0.0	0.0	0.0	3.1	0.9 •	MID-WEST NATIONAL LIFE INS CO OF TN
--	--	--	--	--	--	--	--	--	--	--	--	MIDDLE TENNESSEE LIFE INS CO
716.8	23,770.1	0.1	31.3	56.3	4.7	2.1	0.9	0.0	0.1	4.5	0.0 •	MIDLAND NATIONAL LIFE INS CO
25.1	47.6	-5.1	11.2	92.7	0.0	0.0	0.0	0.0	1.2	0.0	0.0	MIDWEST SECURITY LIFE INS CO
1.2	240.4	0.2	29.0	59.5	2.0	0.5	3.2	0.0	0.0	5.5	0.6 •	MIDWESTERN UNITED LIFE INS CO
0.1	131.0	-2.8	31.1	64.3	0.7	6.7	0.0	0.0	0.0	0.1	0.0	MII LIFE INC
0.0	2.1	100.0	0.0	0.0	0.0	0.0	0.0	0.0	0.0	0.0	0.0	MILILANI LIFE INS CO
1,280.7	9,703.3	-0.2	30.2	39.7	2.3	5.1	12.9	0.0	0.2	9.9	3.7 •	MINNESOTA LIFE INS CO
--	--	--	--	--	--	--	--	--	--	--	--	MINNETONKA LIFE INS CO
--	--	--	--	--	--	--	--	--	--	--	--	MISSISSIPPI VALLEY LIFE INS CO
0.2	11.0	0.6	45.0	54.4	0.0	0.0	0.0	0.0	0.0	0.0	0.0	MISSOURI VALLEY LIFE AND HLTH INS CO
0.1	175.3	-1.6	15.4	45.7	1.0	0.9	0.0	0.0	0.0	38.5	0.0 •	ML LIFE INS CO OF NEW YORK
5.0	24.2	4.3	25.6	58.6	1.5	0.3	3.1	0.0	0.0	6.7	4.7	MMA INS CO
10.7	285.7	0.0	16.9	44.6	2.3	0.0	3.0	0.0	0.0	33.9	0.0 •	MML BAY STATE LIFE INS CO
0.2	1.1	0.4	0.0	99.6	0.0	0.0	0.0	0.0	0.0	0.0	0.0	MODERN LIFE INS CO OF ARIZONA
0.0	8.9 (*)	36.1	0.0	59.3	0.0	0.0	0.0	0.0	0.0	0.0	0.0	MOLINA HEALTHCARE INS CO
9.4	621.6	-0.1	16.5	66.5	0.8	0.0	0.0	0.0	0.0	16.2	0.0	MONARCH LIFE INS CO
0.4	8.3	4.5	41.9	53.2	0.0	0.0	0.0	0.0	0.0	0.3	0.0	MONITOR LIFE INS CO OF NEW YORK
486.5	25,695.9	-0.1	17.8	51.0	6.9	4.0	12.0	0.0	0.0	7.9	4.3 •	MONUMENTAL LIFE INS CO
104.3	8,411.5	0.0	7.3	52.6	2.6	8.7	15.7	0.0	0.0	13.1	5.4 •	MONY LIFE INS CO
53.3	2,035.9	-0.1	8.7	65.6	3.2	7.9	8.7	0.0	0.0	6.1	2.0 •	MONY LIFE INS CO OF AMERICA
0.8	40.8 (*)	3.9	37.3	-6.6	7.7	6.3	26.3	0.8	29.2	10.4	6.3	MOTHE LIFE INS CO
15.4	314.7	0.3	48.6	45.7	0.7	2.1	0.0	0.0	0.0	2.5	0.0 •	MOTORISTS LIFE INS CO
--	--	--	--	--	--	--	--	--	--	--	--	MOTORSPORT LIFE INS CO
0.4	8.0	73.0	0.0	20.9	0.0	0.0	0.0	0.0	6.1	0.0	0.0	MOUNTAIN LIFE INS CO
36.4	1,251.4	0.0	14.0	49.1	3.4	0.9	20.5	0.0	0.6	11.5	0.0 •	MTL INS CO
1.1	8.8	21.3	12.2	28.2	0.0	33.7	4.6	0.0	0.0	0.1	0.0	MULHEARN PROTECTIVE INS CO
322.7	5,054.7	0.2	20.6	77.0	0.8	0.9	0.2	0.0	0.0	0.2	0.2 •	MUNICH AMERICAN REASSURANCE CO
--	--	--	--	--	--	--	--	--	--	--	--	MUNICIPAL INS CO OF AMERICA
304.3	6,578.4	0.5	40.3	50.3	1.6	1.0	0.0	0.0	4.1	2.2	0.1 •	MUTUAL OF AMERICA LIFE INS CO
401.3	4,410.4	0.2	22.7	22.0	1.6	41.6	5.4	0.0	0.9	5.6	40.7 •	MUTUAL OF OMAHA INS CO
11.4	406.1	0.2	11.4	82.3	0.0	1.4	0.0	0.0	0.2	4.4	1.2	MUTUAL SAVINGS LIFE INS CO
0.0	2.2 (*)	7.2	19.4	64.2	0.0	0.0	0.0	0.0	0.0	0.0	0.0	NAP LIFE INS CO
--	--	--	--	--	--	--	--	--	--	--	--	NATIONAL ANNUITY CO
36.7	692.0	-0.3	33.6	57.2	6.2	0.7	0.0	0.0	0.0	2.7	0.0 •	NATIONAL BENEFIT LIFE INS CO
2.3	14.3	12.2	0.0	87.8	0.0	0.0	0.0	0.0	0.0	0.0	0.0	NATIONAL FAMILY CARE LIFE INS CO
5.1	249.4	0.8	9.6	66.5	3.3	4.1	6.8	0.0	0.2	8.8	0.6	NATIONAL FARM LIFE INS CO
1.8	239.6	-0.4	25.7	46.6	0.2	7.0	10.0	0.0	0.0	11.0	0.5 •	NATIONAL FARMERS UNION LIFE INS CO
13.4	41.3	-2.5	15.2	84.5	2.8	0.0	0.0	0.0	0.0	0.0	0.0	NATIONAL FOUNDATION LIFE INS CO
48.8	1,582.9	-0.2	14.4	61.8	5.3	8.4	6.9	0.0	0.4	3.1	3.6 •	NATIONAL GUARDIAN LIFE INS CO
32.8	23.9	21.1	0.0	32.2	0.0	25.1	0.0	0.0	3.2	18.5	0.0	NATIONAL HEALTH INS CO
0.0	0.6	100.0	0.0	0.0	0.0	0.0	0.0	0.0	0.0	0.0	0.0	NATIONAL HOME LIFE & ACCIDENT INS CO
7.4	35.9	-0.6	0.9	91.6	0.0	0.7	0.0	0.0	0.0	7.4	0.0	NATIONAL INCOME LIFE INS CO
217.7	1,525.8	0.2	27.0	59.8	6.1	2.8	0.3	0.0	0.0	4.0	0.0 •	NATIONAL INTEGRITY LIFE INS CO
125.5	6,903.4	-0.2	25.8	40.4	3.2	6.7	11.7	0.0	0.7	11.9	5.7 •	NATIONAL LIFE INS CO
24.1	129.8	3.3	25.3	51.2	2.0	6.0	0.2	0.0	9.1	2.9	5.6 •	NATIONAL LIFE INS CO
0.0	1.3	1.3	0.0	91.5	0.0	6.2	0.0	0.0	0.0	1.1	0.0	NATIONAL MASONIC PROVIDENT ASN

• Bullets denote a more detailed analysis is available in Section II.

(*) Asset category percentages do not add up to 100%

INSURANCE COMPANY NAME	DOM. STATE	RATING	TOTAL ASSETS ($MIL)	CAPITAL & SURPLUS ($MIL)	RISK ADJUSTED CAPITAL RATIO 1	RISK ADJUSTED CAPITAL RATIO 2	CAPITAL-IZATION INDEX (PTS)	INVEST. SAFETY INDEX (PTS)	PROFIT-ABILITY INDEX (PTS)	LIQUIDITY INDEX (PTS)	STAB. INDEX (PTS)	STABILITY FACTORS
NATIONAL SAFETY LIFE INS CO	PA	C+	3.1	2.2	2.03	1.83	8.2	8.8	1.8	7.1	3.5	ADFT
NATIONAL SECURITY INS CO	AL	C	41.8	8.3	1.44	1.04	7.1	5.3	3.1	6.8	3.7	
NATIONAL SECURITY LIFE & ANNUITY CO	NY	B	86.2	16.2	2.00	1.80	8.2	6.6	2.0	10.0	4.9	DGT
NATIONAL STATES INS CO	MO	D	75.3	13.1	0.60	0.43	2.2	7.9	1.7	2.1	2.1	CFLT
NATIONAL TEACHERS ASSOCIATES L I C	TX	B	240.7	29.4	1.77	1.21	7.3	7.1	9.2	9.3	5.3	D
▲ NATIONAL WESTERN LIFE INS CO	CO	B+	6175.2	715.0	3.77	2.00	8.5	6.8	7.7	6.2	5.7	
NATIONWIDE LIFE & ANNUITY CO AMERICA	DE	B	502.6	43.1	3.42	2.01	8.5	6.8	5.6	7.1	4.5	ADFT
NATIONWIDE LIFE & ANNUITY INS CO	OH	B	4342.6	120.8	1.29	0.61	5.4	3.7	1.4	5.1	4.8	ACFIT
▼ NATIONWIDE LIFE INS CO	OH	B	74462.2	1927.9	1.98	1.00	7.0	4.7	2.3	9.2	4.6	AIT
NATIONWIDE LIFE INS CO OF AMERICA	PA	B+	4826.2	501.7	2.81	1.68	8.0	5.9	6.4	6.5	5.2	AIT
NETCARE LIFE & HEALTH INS CO	GU	E	24.1	1.7	0.21	0.15	0.0	7.5	4.2	0.8	0.0	CDLT
NEW ENGLAND LIFE INS CO	MA	B	8624.0	401.5	3.04	1.73	8.1	6.6	6.2	8.2	4.8	T
NEW ERA LIFE INS CO	TX	C	300.6	44.7	0.75	0.53	3.2	4.6	5.4	5.9	3.2	CDFT
NEW ERA LIFE INS CO OF THE MIDWEST	TX	C-	42.0	8.7	0.58	0.39	1.7	4.5	7.8	5.5	1.7	CD
NEW FOUNDATION LIFE INS CO	AR	U (1)	2.1	1.6	2.16	1.94	8.4	9.8	7.2	10.0	7.4	DF
NEW SOUTH LIFE INS CO	MS	C	6.2	6.0	3.44	3.10	10.0	9.6	8.1	10.0	2.5	DT
NEW YORK LIFE AGENTS REIN CO	AZ	U (5)	--	--	--	--	--	--	--	--	--	Z
▼ NEW YORK LIFE INS & ANNUITY CORP	DE	A-	77190.7	3312.1	1.84	0.89	6.3	4.2	6.3	7.0	6.3	CGI
NEW YORK LIFE INS CO	NY	A-	114937.8	11091.8	1.42	1.04	7.1	6.0	7.1	6.6	6.1	I
▲ NIPPON LIFE INS CO OF AMERICA	IA	A-	162.8	115.3	3.78	2.95	9.9	8.0	6.6	6.5	6.9	DF
NORLEN LIFE INS CO	AZ	U	--	--	--	--	--	--	--	--	--	Z
NORTH AMERICA LIFE INS CO OF TX	TX	E	102.6	4.0	0.28	0.19	0.0	2.4	2.6	0.0	0.0	CFILT
NORTH AMERICAN CO FOR LIFE & H INS	IA	B	8961.9	516.9	2.16	1.06	7.1	4.6	7.3	6.5	5.6	GI
NORTH AMERICAN INS CO	WI	C	16.2	10.5	3.42	3.08	10.0	8.6	5.6	7.6	3.9	ADFT
NORTH AMERICAN NATIONAL RE INS CO	AZ	U	--	--	--	--	--	--	--	--	--	Z
NORTH AMERICAN NATL LIFE INS CO	AZ	U	--	--	--	--	--	--	--	--	--	Z
NORTH CAROLINA MUTUAL LIFE INS CO	NC	D	160.0	8.5	0.66	0.42	2.3	2.5	1.5	5.3	2.1	CT
NORTH COAST LIFE INS CO	WA	D	121.2	5.5	0.68	0.52	3.2	0.6	5.5	0.3	1.8	CDIL
NORTHERN NATIONAL LIFE INS CO OF RI	RI	U (1)	3.9	3.9	3.10	2.79	9.7	9.5	5.6	10.0	5.4	DT
NORTHWESTERN LONG TERM CARE INS CO	WI	B-	413.1	56.8	1.48	0.99	6.9	5.4	1.9	9.4	5.1	DGI
NORTHWESTERN MUTUAL LIFE INS CO	WI	A-	155607.2	12156.8	2.96	1.52	7.8	5.3	8.5	6.2	7.3	I
NYLIFE INS CO OF ARIZONA	AZ	B	188.0	39.5	2.83	1.88	8.3	8.2	2.3	6.5	6.0	D
OAKWOOD LIFE INS CO	AZ	U	--	--	--	--	--	--	--	--	--	Z
OBRIEN NATIONAL LIFE INS CO	AZ	U	--	--	--	--	--	--	--	--	--	Z
OCCIDENTAL LIFE INS CO OF NC	TX	B	253.9	29.7	2.90	1.87	8.3	7.5	6.3	6.0	6.2	ADF
OCOEE LIFE INS CO	TN	U	--	--	--	--	--	--	--	--	--	Z
▲ OHIO MOTORISTS LIFE INSURANCE CO	OH	B-	8.6	8.4	3.88	3.49	10.0	9.5	7.9	10.0	2.9	G
OHIO NATIONAL LIFE ASR CORP	OH	B+	2702.3	259.4	2.16	1.11	7.2	4.8	6.8	4.9	6.4	AIL
OHIO NATIONAL LIFE INS CO	OH	B	12098.1	738.3	1.46	0.97	6.8	5.7	5.2	8.1	5.8	AI
OHIO STATE LIFE INS CO	TX	C	9.9	6.8	16.07	7.98	8.0	8.1	2.9	7.0	4.3	A
OLD AMERICAN INS CO	MO	B	235.9	16.1	1.79	0.96	6.7	3.1	4.8	3.8	5.6	DIL
OLD KENT FINANCIAL LIFE INS CO	AZ	U	--	--	--	--	--	--	--	--	--	Z
OLD RELIANCE INS CO	AZ	D-	3.9	1.7	1.19	0.92	6.4	3.2	2.0	6.7	1.1	DFI
OLD REPUBLIC LIFE INS CO	IL	B	148.8	31.5	3.31	2.19	8.8	8.3	5.3	6.9	5.1	A
OLD SPARTAN LIFE INS CO INC	SC	C+	27.4	23.9	2.52	1.59	7.9	2.9	8.4	9.8	4.7	DIT
OLD STANDARD LIFE INS CO	ID	F (5)	--	--	--	--	--	--	--	--	--	Z
OLD SURETY LIFE INS CO	OK	C	19.2	7.8	1.08	0.82	5.6	7.6	9.2	6.8	3.1	D
OLD UNITED LIFE INS CO	AZ	B-	70.5	35.7	5.05	4.55	10.0	7.2	6.8	9.4	4.0	DT
OLIVIA LIFE INS CO	AZ	U	--	--	--	--	--	--	--	--	--	Z
OM FINANCIAL LIFE INS CO	MD	C	17140.4	816.5	1.39	0.71	5.6	3.3	3.6	5.9	4.2	ACIT
OM FINANCIAL LIFE INS CO OF NEW YORK	NY	B-	460.8	35.6	2.12	1.04	7.1	3.3	5.5	6.1	4.9	ADIT
OMAHA INS CO	NE	U (1)	10.4	10.4	4.20	3.78	3.0	8.9	6.8	10.0	5.0	DET

See Page 26 for explanation of footnotes and Page 27 for explanation of stability factors.

Arrows denote recent upgrades ▲ or downgrades ▼ (see Section VI for explanations)

54

www.thestreetratings.com

NET PREMIUM ($MIL)	IN-VESTED ASSETS ($MIL)	% OF INVESTED ASSETS IN:									INVEST. IN AFFIL	INSURANCE COMPANY NAME
		CASH	CMO & STRUCT. SECS.	OTH.INV. GRADE BONDS	NON-INV. GRADE BONDS	CMMON & PREF. STOCK	MORT IN GOOD STAND.	NON-PERF. MORT.	REAL ESTATE	OTHER INVEST-MENTS		
0.1	3.0	1.0	10.6	88.4	0.0	0.0	0.0	0.0	0.0	0.0	0.0	NATIONAL SAFETY LIFE INS CO
1.8	38.9	-1.5	28.0	51.8	2.9	9.4	1.3	0.0	5.1	3.1	0.0	NATIONAL SECURITY INS CO
4.3	27.6	2.2	14.8	76.1	6.8	0.0	0.0	0.0	0.0	0.2	0.0	NATIONAL SECURITY LIFE & ANNUITY CO
16.1	63.3	0.5	0.0	83.5	1.2	0.0	0.0	0.0	3.4	11.5	0.0	NATIONAL STATES INS CO
20.3	219.4	2.3	49.4	45.9	2.3	0.0	0.0	0.0	0.0	0.3	0.0 ●	NATIONAL TEACHERS ASSOCIATES L I C
188.0	6,048.8	-0.3	34.7	57.9	1.8	2.6	1.7	0.1	0.0	1.7	2.9 ●	NATIONAL WESTERN LIFE INS CO
4.3	245.6	-0.5	30.7	45.7	1.8	0.0	15.2	0.0	0.0	7.1	0.0 ●	NATIONWIDE LIFE & ANNUITY CO AMERICA
48.3	3,267.7	-0.3	28.8	36.1	8.0	0.2	22.1	0.0	0.0	5.0	0.0 ●	NATIONWIDE LIFE & ANNUITY INS CO
2,211.3	29,379.0	-0.3	24.2	30.9	6.2	1.7	21.1	0.0	0.0	16.3	0.5 ●	NATIONWIDE LIFE INS CO
52.7	3,217.7	-0.2	26.3	38.6	3.2	2.7	16.8	0.0	0.0	12.8	1.8 ●	NATIONWIDE LIFE INS CO OF AMERICA
6.9	21.9	4.0	12.6	44.6	0.0	0.1	0.0	0.0	0.0	38.5	0.0	NETCARE LIFE & HEALTH INS CO
366.2	1,639.3	0.0	14.6	39.4	2.6	4.1	3.2	0.0	0.0	36.9	12.3 ●	NEW ENGLAND LIFE INS CO
13.8	292.2	0.2	33.3	25.8	6.7	14.8	18.2	0.0	0.9	0.3	9.8 ●	NEW ERA LIFE INS CO
11.1	40.9	-0.4	36.6	44.7	7.2	7.8	3.7	0.0	0.0	0.3	0.0	NEW ERA LIFE INS CO OF THE MIDWEST
0.0	2.0	65.4	0.0	34.2	0.0	0.3	0.0	0.0	0.0	0.0	0.0	NEW FOUNDATION LIFE INS CO
0.0	6.1	11.1	0.0	88.9	0.0	0.0	0.0	0.0	0.0	0.0	0.0	NEW SOUTH LIFE INS CO
--	--	--	--	--	--	--	--	--	--	--	--	NEW YORK LIFE AGENTS REIN CO
3,772.5	53,706.6	-0.2	32.7	43.6	7.2	2.2	10.3	0.0	0.0	4.2	1.5 ●	NEW YORK LIFE INS & ANNUITY CORP
2,920.4	99,223.2	0.0	19.6	43.6	5.0	6.6	9.8	0.0	0.4	14.9	9.4 ●	NEW YORK LIFE INS CO
54.1	152.6	-3.0	22.2	76.8	0.0	1.9	2.2	0.0	0.0	0.0	0.0 ●	NIPPON LIFE INS CO OF AMERICA
--	--	--	--	--	--	--	--	--	--	--	--	NORLEN LIFE INS CO
3.1	57.6	2.0	27.7	5.7	0.2	17.8	20.4	0.2	22.6	3.3	15.8	NORTH AMERICA LIFE INS CO OF TX
505.3	8,251.4	0.1	30.9	58.7	4.8	1.3	0.0	0.0	0.0	4.2	0.0 ●	NORTH AMERICAN CO FOR LIFE & H INS
0.4	15.5	6.6	17.6	74.9	0.0	0.9	0.0	0.0	0.0	0.0	0.0	NORTH AMERICAN INS CO
--	--	--	--	--	--	--	--	--	--	--	--	NORTH AMERICAN NATIONAL RE INS CO
--	--	--	--	--	--	--	--	--	--	--	--	NORTH AMERICAN NATL LIFE INS CO
8.6	136.0	1.6	31.9	43.2	1.5	0.8	8.7	0.6	0.0	11.8	0.0	NORTH CAROLINA MUTUAL LIFE INS CO
1.5	117.4	1.7	1.2	67.4	6.1	8.5	0.2	0.0	0.0	15.0	1.8	NORTH COAST LIFE INS CO
0.0	3.9	8.0	0.0	92.0	0.0	0.0	0.0	0.0	0.0	0.0	0.0	NORTHERN NATIONAL LIFE INS CO OF RI
43.3	396.3	0.3	31.1	57.4	0.5	10.1	0.0	0.0	0.0	0.0	0.0 ●	NORTHWESTERN LONG TERM CARE INS CO
3,166.3	134,805.6	0.2	16.5	38.4	6.7	4.3	16.1	0.0	1.1	16.4	4.0 ●	NORTHWESTERN MUTUAL LIFE INS CO
9.3	146.2	-0.6	14.8	85.1	0.7	0.0	0.0	0.0	0.0	0.0	0.0 ●	NYLIFE INS CO OF ARIZONA
--	--	--	--	--	--	--	--	--	--	--	--	OAKWOOD LIFE INS CO
--	--	--	--	--	--	--	--	--	--	--	--	OBRIEN NATIONAL LIFE INS CO
7.3	250.1	0.1	69.6	24.1	0.2	0.1	0.0	0.0	0.0	5.3	0.0 ●	OCCIDENTAL LIFE INS CO OF NC
--	--	--	--	--	--	--	--	--	--	--	--	OCOEE LIFE INS CO
0.0	8.4	2.2	0.0	97.8	0.0	0.0	0.0	0.0	0.0	0.0	0.0	OHIO MOTORISTS LIFE INSURANCE CO
57.8	2,292.1	-0.1	16.1	53.4	6.8	0.8	19.8	0.1	0.0	3.1	0.0 ●	OHIO NATIONAL LIFE ASR CORP
623.0	6,434.0	0.7	15.7	54.9	6.3	5.0	14.1	0.1	0.1	3.3	4.8 ●	OHIO NATIONAL LIFE INS CO
0.0	8.2	-2.8	0.0	100.6	0.0	0.2	0.0	0.0	0.0	2.1	0.0	OHIO STATE LIFE INS CO
14.5	219.3	-0.7	24.6	54.4	3.0	1.0	12.8	0.0	0.0	4.8	0.0	OLD AMERICAN INS CO
--	--	--	--	--	--	--	--	--	--	--	--	OLD KENT FINANCIAL LIFE INS CO
0.3	3.4	3.2	0.0	51.5	5.9	9.2	4.5	0.0	21.3	4.3	5.6	OLD RELIANCE INS CO
6.2	125.7	-0.7	0.0	98.9	0.7	0.2	0.0	0.0	0.0	0.9	0.0 ●	OLD REPUBLIC LIFE INS CO
1.4	26.0	36.2	0.0	0.0	0.0	63.8	0.0	0.0	0.0	0.0	0.0	OLD SPARTAN LIFE INS CO INC
--	--	--	--	--	--	--	--	--	--	--	--	OLD STANDARD LIFE INS CO
5.6	18.6	10.0	2.2	74.1	0.5	5.3	4.8	0.0	1.3	1.8	0.0	OLD SURETY LIFE INS CO
0.4	69.4	-1.2	13.6	78.9	2.1	6.4	0.0	0.0	0.0	0.3	0.0 ●	OLD UNITED LIFE INS CO
--	--	--	--	--	--	--	--	--	--	--	--	OLIVIA LIFE INS CO
216.7	16,403.0	-0.1	22.2	65.1	3.0	8.4	0.0	0.0	0.0	1.5	0.8 ●	OM FINANCIAL LIFE INS CO
3.5	465.6	-0.5	19.6	67.2	3.9	8.0	0.0	0.0	0.0	1.9	0.0 ●	OM FINANCIAL LIFE INS CO OF NEW YORK
0.0	10.4	0.0	0.0	100.0	0.0	0.0	0.0	0.0	0.0	0.0	0.0	OMAHA INS CO

● Bullets denote a more detailed analysis is available in Section II.

(*) Asset category percentages do not add up to 100%

INSURANCE COMPANY NAME	DOM. STATE	RATING		TOTAL ASSETS ($MIL)	CAPITAL & SURPLUS ($MIL)	RISK ADJUSTED CAPITAL RATIO 1	RISK ADJUSTED CAPITAL RATIO 2	CAPITAL- IZATION INDEX (PTS)	INVEST. SAFETY INDEX (PTS)	PROFIT- ABILITY INDEX (PTS)	LIQUIDITY INDEX (PTS)	STAB. INDEX (PTS)	STABILITY FACTORS
OMAHA LIFE INS CO	NE	U	(1)	10.4	10.4	4.20	3.78	3.0	8.9	6.8	10.0	5.0	DET
OPTIMUM RE INS CO	TX	B		72.6	24.4	1.52	0.99	6.9	5.8	6.9	7.2	5.6	I
ORANGE SECURITY LIFE INS CO	AZ	U		--	--	--	--	--	--	--	--	--	Z
ORDER UNITED COMM TRAVELERS OF AMER	OH	U		--	--	--	--	--	--	--	--	--	Z
OUACHITA LIFE INS CO	AR	U	(1)	0.1	0.1	2.19	1.97	8.0	9.8	4.0	10.0	4.2	DT
OVERTON LIFE INS CO	TN	U		--	--	--	--	--	--	--	--	--	Z
OXFORD LIFE INS CO	AZ	B-		491.0	130.0	2.01	1.62	7.9	7.4	8.7	6.7	4.9	FT
OZARK NATIONAL LIFE INS CO	AR	D		19.8	1.0	0.33	0.22	0.0	0.0	5.8	0.7	0.6	CIL
OZARK NATIONAL LIFE INS CO	MO	B		626.5	99.2	4.45	2.63	9.4	8.1	5.9	7.1	5.9	D
▲ PACIFIC BEACON LIFE REASSUR INC	HI	C+		290.6	38.4	2.27	1.32	7.5	6.8	2.6	6.2	4.9	I
PACIFIC CAPTIVE INS CO	SC	U	(5)	--	--	--	--	--	--	--	--	--	Z
PACIFIC CENTURY LIFE INS CORP	AZ	C+		335.6	330.7	29.95	21.02	10.0	7.4	7.0	10.0	4.5	T
PACIFIC GUARDIAN LIFE INS CO LTD	HI	A-	(1)	426.8	83.3	3.53	2.10	8.7	6.6	6.9	6.2	6.7	I
PACIFIC LIFE & ANNUITY CO	AZ	A-		2589.4	250.5	5.25	2.56	9.3	6.7	1.9	9.7	6.2	IT
PACIFIC LIFE INS CO	NE	A-		81524.3	2869.8	2.60	1.31	7.5	5.6	2.0	8.8	5.6	IT
PACIFIC UNION ASR CO	CA	D+		28.7	22.1	4.87	4.39	10.0	7.3	4.6	10.0	2.8	DIT
PACIFICARE LIFE & HEALTH INS CO	IN	B-		775.6	669.4	11.94	8.96	10.0	8.5	9.1	8.4	3.9	T
PAN AMERICAN ASR CO	LA	B		23.2	17.1	2.17	1.32	7.5	8.7	7.8	7.1	5.7	AT
PAN AMERICAN ASR CO INTL INC	FL	U	(1)	2.6	2.6	2.95	2.66	3.0	9.0	4.0	7.0	4.2	DEFT
PAN AMERICAN LIFE INS CO OF PR	PR	B		9.2	6.0	2.90	2.37	9.1	9.2	8.0	7.2	6.0	ADEG
PAN-AMERICAN LIFE INS CO	LA	B		1519.6	264.1	1.99	1.20	7.3	5.4	5.4	6.2	6.0	I
PARK AVENUE LIFE INS CO	DE	B		418.8	146.6	1.46	1.32	7.5	6.2	6.9	6.8	5.6	DIT
PARK TWO LIFE INS CO	AZ	U		--	--	--	--	--	--	--	--	--	Z
PARKER CENTENNIAL ASR CO	WI	B		65.7	39.8	5.37	4.84	10.0	8.6	7.1	10.0	5.0	DT
PATRIOT LIFE INS CO	ME	U	(1)	7.1	6.8	3.56	3.21	10.0	9.2	7.7	10.0	5.6	DGIT
PAUL REVERE LIFE INS CO	MA	C+		4714.3	389.8	1.66	1.09	7.1	4.8	5.3	7.8	4.8	AFIT
PAUL REVERE VARIABLE ANNUITY INS CO	MA	C		113.5	97.7	11.14	8.76	8.0	5.7	2.4	9.3	3.8	AT
PEKIN FINANCIAL LIFE INS CO	AZ	U		--	--	--	--	--	--	--	--	--	Z
PEKIN LIFE INS CO	IL	B+		863.3	112.9	2.26	1.39	7.6	7.0	6.8	6.5	6.8	A
PELLERIN LIFE INS CO	LA	D	(1)	8.0	0.6	0.37	0.33	1.0	3.0	1.5	5.9	1.0	CIT
PEMCO LIFE INS CO	WA	B-		7.2	3.1	1.64	1.48	7.7	8.9	1.9	6.4	4.8	ADFT
PENN INS & ANNUITY CO	DE	B+		1038.9	104.2	3.08	1.63	7.9	7.4	5.9	6.8	5.7	AG
PENN MUTUAL LIFE INS CO	PA	B+		9647.6	1272.0	3.55	2.11	8.7	6.7	6.2	7.3	6.0	GIT
PENN OHIO LIFE INS CO	AZ	U		--	--	--	--	--	--	--	--	--	Z
PENN TREATY NETWORK AMERICA INS CO	PA	F	(1)	1001.2	-224.0	-4.77	-3.06	0.0	8.0	0.6	7.3	0.0	CT
PENNSYLVANIA LIFE INS CO	PA	D		903.0	102.9	0.29	0.23	0.0	4.7	5.1	0.1	0.2	CFGLT
PEOPLES SAVINGS LIFE INS CO	AL	U	(1)	0.4	0.3	1.91	1.72	8.1	9.3	4.6	8.5	4.8	DT
PERFORMANCE LIFE OF AMERICA	LA	B-		28.8	13.2	2.92	2.63	9.4	9.4	7.1	9.2	3.6	ADFT
PERICO LIFE INS CO	DE	B		65.5	42.5	4.10	3.27	10.0	8.9	8.9	7.5	6.0	ADG
PHARMACISTS LIFE INS CO	IA	B+		40.4	5.5	1.11	0.80	5.4	3.4	2.3	6.0	5.0	ACDGI
PHILADELPHIA AMERICAN LIFE INS CO	TX	C		173.7	20.1	1.77	0.98	6.8	4.3	7.5	6.8	3.0	AFGIT
PHILADELPHIA-UNITED LIFE INS CO	PA	C		43.9	6.5	1.32	1.18	7.3	6.7	3.9	6.3	3.4	D
PHL VARIABLE INS CO	CT	C		4150.2	214.8	1.90	0.90	6.4	3.9	1.6	8.0	3.8	FIT
PHOENIX LIFE & ANNUITY CO	CT	B-		57.5	20.6	3.03	2.72	9.6	7.3	5.0	7.0	3.7	AFT
PHOENIX LIFE & REASSURANCE CO OF NY	NY	U	(1)	13.5	13.4	4.79	4.31	10.0	7.5	6.3	10.0	7.7	DG
PHOENIX LIFE INS CO	NY	C+		14986.3	619.1	0.97	0.57	4.8	3.7	4.1	5.2	4.6	ACFIT
PHPMM INS CO	MI	B		10.0	8.4	3.45	3.10	10.0	9.8	3.6	9.1	4.8	ADEGT
PHYSICIANS BENEFITS TRUST LIFE INS	IL	C+		19.1	9.9	2.14	1.71	8.1	8.8	6.5	6.5	4.4	ADF
PHYSICIANS LIFE INS CO	NE	A-		1249.3	83.4	2.03	1.02	7.0	4.2	6.2	5.7	5.9	FIT
PHYSICIANS MUTUAL INS CO	NE	A+		1445.1	769.8	4.75	3.63	10.0	6.6	8.4	7.4	7.9	I
PINE BELT LIFE INS CO	MS	D-		2.5	0.3	0.38	0.35	1.2	9.4	2.7	9.9	1.1	CDET
PIONEER AMERICAN INS CO	TX	B-		48.5	9.6	1.48	1.33	7.5	8.3	4.9	6.3	5.1	D

See Page 26 for explanation of footnotes and Page 27 for explanation of stability factors.
Arrows denote recent upgrades ▲ or downgrades ▼ (see Section VI for explanations)

56

www.thestreetratings.com

NET PREMIUM ($MIL)	IN-VESTED ASSETS ($MIL)	CASH	CMO & STRUCT. SECS.	OTH.INV. GRADE BONDS	NON-INV. GRADE BONDS	CMMON & PREF. STOCK	MORT IN GOOD STAND.	NON-PERF. MORT.	REAL ESTATE	OTHER INVEST-MENTS	INVEST. IN AFFIL	INSURANCE COMPANY NAME
0.0	10.4	0.0	0.0	100.0	0.0	0.0	0.0	0.0	0.0	0.0	0.0	OMAHA LIFE INS CO
7.1	82.3	7.1	0.0	81.1	0.0	4.6	0.0	0.0	7.2	0.0	1.4	OPTIMUM RE INS CO
--	--	--	--	--	--	--	--	--	--	--	--	ORANGE SECURITY LIFE INS CO
--	--	--	--	--	--	--	--	--	--	--	--	ORDER UNITED COMM TRAVELERS OF AMER
0.0	0.1	100.0	0.0	0.0	0.0	0.0	0.0	0.0	0.0	0.0	0.0	OUACHITA LIFE INS CO
--	--	--	--	--	--	--	--	--	--	--	--	OVERTON LIFE INS CO
10.4	495.3	0.4	22.7	53.2	0.9	10.4	11.7	0.0	0.1	0.8	9.6 ●	OXFORD LIFE INS CO
1.3	18.8	5.3	0.0	25.6	19.8	39.1	0.2	0.0	7.9	2.2	0.0	OZARK NATIONAL LIFE INS CO
21.7	577.5	0.7	52.9	41.7	0.0	0.1	0.0	0.0	1.6	3.2	0.0 ●	OZARK NATIONAL LIFE INS CO
12.6	266.9	0.0	26.7	65.6	5.4	0.4	0.0	0.0	0.0	1.8	0.0 ●	PACIFIC BEACON LIFE REASSUR INC
--	--	--	--	--	--	--	--	--	--	--	--	PACIFIC CAPTIVE INS CO
0.2	329.7	7.9	0.0	3.7	0.0	0.3	88.0	0.1	0.0	0.0	0.0 ●	PACIFIC CENTURY LIFE INS CORP
74.7	405.4	0.5	17.7	37.0	0.0	2.8	36.1	0.0	0.0	6.0	0.0 ●	PACIFIC GUARDIAN LIFE INS CO LTD
141.2	1,430.2	-0.3	18.5	62.2	3.9	1.3	10.9	0.0	0.0	3.6	0.1 ●	PACIFIC LIFE & ANNUITY CO
2,144.6	41,758.7	1.4	19.0	38.7	3.8	2.2	13.3	0.0	0.5	20.2	1.7 ●	PACIFIC LIFE INS CO
0.1	29.1	0.0	0.0	86.9	0.0	9.7	0.0	0.0	0.0	3.5	7.3	PACIFIC UNION ASR CO
85.6	732.0	-3.2	25.1	78.1	0.0	0.0	0.0	0.0	0.0	0.0	0.0 ●	PACIFICARE LIFE & HEALTH INS CO
0.0	20.9	-14.9	24.6	77.1	0.0	13.2	0.0	0.0	0.0	0.1	13.2	PAN AMERICAN ASR CO
0.0	2.6	0.0	0.0	100.0	0.0	0.0	0.0	0.0	0.0	0.0	0.0	PAN AMERICAN ASR CO INTL INC
4.8	6.3	31.9	17.6	50.5	0.0	0.0	0.0	0.0	0.0	0.0	0.0	PAN AMERICAN LIFE INS CO OF PR
49.6	1,459.2	0.9	19.2	53.0	10.6	6.2	0.8	0.0	0.8	8.6	3.6 ●	PAN-AMERICAN LIFE INS CO
1.2	408.6	0.6	2.2	70.8	3.1	22.2	0.0	0.0	0.0	1.0	22.2 ●	PARK AVENUE LIFE INS CO
--	--	--	--	--	--	--	--	--	--	--	--	PARK TWO LIFE INS CO
0.8	63.6	0.0	0.0	99.9	0.1	0.0	0.0	0.0	0.0	0.0	0.0 ●	PARKER CENTENNIAL ASR CO
0.0	7.1	0.6	12.4	86.8	0.0	0.0	0.0	0.0	0.0	0.2	0.0	PATRIOT LIFE INS CO
26.1	4,489.6	-0.1	9.8	77.8	4.7	5.4	1.3	0.0	0.4	0.8	3.1 ●	PAUL REVERE LIFE INS CO
0.0	103.9	0.0	0.0	88.7	10.0	0.0	0.0	0.0	0.0	1.4	0.0 ●	PAUL REVERE VARIABLE ANNUITY INS CO
--	--	--	--	--	--	--	--	--	--	--	--	PEKIN FINANCIAL LIFE INS CO
57.5	827.5	0.6	34.4	60.0	2.2	0.7	0.0	0.0	0.1	2.0	0.1 ●	PEKIN LIFE INS CO
1.0	6.3	1.9	34.3	7.7	0.0	0.3	21.8	0.0	33.8	0.2	15.7	PELLERIN LIFE INS CO
0.4	5.3	11.5	0.0	85.7	0.0	2.0	0.0	0.0	0.0	0.9	0.0	PEMCO LIFE INS CO
23.0	940.1	0.1	30.2	31.0	0.7	0.1	0.0	0.0	0.0	37.9	0.0 ●	PENN INS & ANNUITY CO
330.3	6,743.2	0.4	37.4	39.5	3.0	3.5	0.0	0.0	0.2	16.2	5.6 ●	PENN MUTUAL LIFE INS CO
--	--	--	--	--	--	--	--	--	--	--	--	PENN OHIO LIFE INS CO
32.4	882.4 (*)	0.0	22.8	71.4	0.8	0.9	0.0	0.0	0.5	0.5	0.9	PENN TREATY NETWORK AMERICA INS CO
597.8	307.7	3.4	45.2	37.7	11.7	0.0	0.0	0.0	0.0	2.5	0.0 ●	PENNSYLVANIA LIFE INS CO
0.4	0.4	1.1	0.0	0.0	0.0	0.0	0.0	0.0	0.0	98.9	0.3	PEOPLES SAVINGS LIFE INS CO
1.0	29.4	14.2	0.0	85.8	0.0	0.0	0.0	0.0	0.0	0.0	0.0	PERFORMANCE LIFE OF AMERICA
18.4	59.5	9.6	13.5	76.9	0.0	0.0	0.0	0.0	0.0	0.0	0.0 ●	PERICO LIFE INS CO
1.2	35.3	1.7	21.4	58.7	10.6	5.7	0.0	0.0	0.0	2.0	0.0	PHARMACISTS LIFE INS CO
9.4	167.6	-1.3	33.1	44.8	8.0	6.1	9.1	0.0	0.2	0.1	0.0	PHILADELPHIA AMERICAN LIFE INS CO
2.0	39.9	-0.2	50.7	38.9	1.0	5.1	0.0	0.0	0.0	4.7	2.1	PHILADELPHIA-UNITED LIFE INS CO
159.8	1,828.8	0.4	31.6	48.0	9.4	2.8	0.0	0.0	0.0	7.9	0.0 ●	PHL VARIABLE INS CO
0.5	40.6	0.1	20.0	65.7	4.6	5.2	0.0	0.0	0.0	4.4	0.0	PHOENIX LIFE & ANNUITY CO
0.0	13.4	0.1	28.0	68.0	3.9	0.0	0.0	0.0	0.0	0.0	0.0	PHOENIX LIFE & REASSURANCE CO OF NY
174.5	13,555.0	0.0	24.6	38.6	6.7	6.3	0.1	0.0	0.2	23.5	2.8 ●	PHOENIX LIFE INS CO
1.6	9.8	-1.1	0.0	101.1	0.0	0.0	0.0	0.0	0.0	0.0	0.0	PHPMM INS CO
6.5	19.2	-1.1	0.0	101.1	0.0	0.0	0.0	0.0	0.0	0.0	0.0	PHYSICIANS BENEFITS TRUST LIFE INS
51.9	1,243.3	0.0	22.5	66.0	7.0	2.3	0.0	0.0	0.0	2.3	0.0 ●	PHYSICIANS LIFE INS CO
99.5	1,399.7	0.2	21.2	59.4	7.0	10.8	0.0	0.0	0.8	0.5	6.8 ●	PHYSICIANS MUTUAL INS CO
0.5	2.3 (*)	20.9	0.0	66.7	0.0	0.0	0.0	0.0	0.0	0.0	0.0	PINE BELT LIFE INS CO
1.8	46.5	0.4	61.6	29.7	0.0	0.0	0.0	0.0	0.0	7.8	0.0	PIONEER AMERICAN INS CO

● Bullets denote a more detailed analysis is available in Section II.

(*) Asset category percentages do not add up to 100%

INSURANCE COMPANY NAME	DOM. STATE	RATING	TOTAL ASSETS ($MIL)	CAPITAL & SURPLUS ($MIL)	RISK ADJUSTED CAPITAL RATIO 1	RISK ADJUSTED CAPITAL RATIO 2	CAPITAL-IZATION INDEX (PTS)	INVEST. SAFETY INDEX (PTS)	PROFIT-ABILITY INDEX (PTS)	LIQUIDITY INDEX (PTS)	STAB. INDEX (PTS)	STABILITY FACTORS
PIONEER MILITARY INS CO	NV	C-	13.2	5.7	1.90	1.71	8.1	9.8	7.5	10.0	2.6	CDEGT
PIONEER MUTUAL LIFE INS CO	ND	B	462.6	29.8	2.20	1.15	7.2	5.1	4.3	5.1	5.9	DFIL
PIONEER SECURITY LIFE INS CO	TX	B-	95.7	74.1	1.25	1.22	7.3	3.8	7.2	7.6	5.3	DI
PLATEAU INS CO	TN	B	19.0	6.9	2.09	1.88	8.3	8.9	8.0	9.1	5.5	A
POPULAR LIFE RE	PR	C	55.7	27.1	3.91	3.48	10.0	7.8	7.8	9.7	3.7	T
PORT-O-CALL LIFE INS CO	AR	C-	1.7	1.4	2.28	2.05	8.6	8.4	5.9	10.0	3.0	DT
PRAMCO LIFE INS CO	AZ	U	--	--	--	--	--	--	--	--	--	Z
PREFERRED SECURITY LIFE INS CO	TX	U (1)	4.0	0.2	0.12	0.11	0.0	9.8	1.8	8.3	0.0	CDFT
PRENEED REINS CO OF AMERICA	AZ	B	11.4	10.2	3.53	3.18	8.5	8.6	9.0	0.9	4.9	LO
PRESERVATION LIFE INS CO	MO	U (1)	9.3	2.4	1.02	0.92	6.4	6.1	5.4	8.2	4.1	DFT
PRESIDENTIAL LIFE INS CO	NY	C-	3642.5	281.4	1.90	0.95	6.6	4.8	6.8	6.3	3.2	AFGT
PRESIDENTIAL LIFE INS CO	TX	C	4.4	1.5	1.16	0.97	6.8	3.5	5.8	6.9	3.6	DGI
PRIDE OF CARROLL LIFE INS CO	LA	U	--	--	--	--	--	--	--	--	--	Z
PRIMERICA LIFE INS CO	MA	A-	5765.7	1155.4	1.81	1.38	7.6	6.1	6.6	6.9	6.3	I
PRINCIPAL LIFE INS CO	IA	A-	109923.9	4212.2	2.29	1.15	7.2	4.8	7.3	7.1	5.4	IT
PRINCIPAL LIFE INS CO IOWA	IA	U (1)	20.6	20.6	1.37	1.37	7.6	9.8	4.0	10.0	6.0	DEGT
PRINCIPAL NATIONAL LIFE INS CO	IA	U (1)	11.8	11.6	4.44	4.00	10.0	9.8	6.0	10.0	7.7	D
PRIORITY HEALTH INS CO	MI	B	25.5	7.5	0.90	0.75	5.0	9.8	1.7	2.0	4.9	CDGLO
PROFESSIONAL INS CO	TX	C	103.4	30.7	1.85	1.35	7.5	7.0	2.0	6.8	4.2	DF
PROFESSIONAL LIFE & CAS CO	IL	D	72.2	7.8	0.82	0.36	3.3	1.1	7.0	4.1	2.2	CDILT
PROTECTIVE LIFE & ANNUITY INS CO	AL	B-	790.6	55.9	2.02	0.98	6.8	3.8	6.3	7.2	5.2	ADGIT
PROTECTIVE LIFE INS CO	TN	B-	24965.9	1774.4	0.99	0.68	4.9	4.8	6.3	7.4	4.5	ACGIT
PROTECTIVE LIFE INS CO OF NY	NY	C	779.2	96.3	2.78	1.35	7.5	5.4	5.2	6.0	2.9	FGT
PROVIDENT AMER LIFE & HEALTH INS CO	OH	C-	17.0	7.6	0.60	0.51	3.1	9.3	1.7	7.0	1.9	CDFGT
PROVIDENT AMERICAN INS CO	TX	E+	22.3	3.1	0.82	0.74	4.9	9.8	1.3	0.8	0.5	CDFGILT
PROVIDENT LIFE & ACCIDENT INS CO	TN	C+	7799.2	451.3	1.90	0.98	6.8	3.8	5.0	7.2	4.8	AI
PROVIDENT LIFE & CAS INS CO	TN	B-	709.6	125.1	4.01	2.26	8.9	6.6	7.4	7.1	5.2	AD
PRUCO LIFE INS CO	AZ	C+	21663.3	495.2	1.19	0.69	5.3	5.2	1.8	8.0	4.5	ACIT
PRUCO LIFE INS CO OF NEW JERSEY	NJ	C+	3630.3	116.3	1.70	0.84	6.1	5.2	2.0	7.7	4.3	T
PRUDENTIAL ANNUITIES LIFE ASR CORP	CT	C+	34351.4	454.5	1.44	1.09	7.1	7.6	1.9	10.0	4.0	T
PRUDENTIAL INS CO OF AMERICA	NJ	C+	227934.5	6392.6	1.19	0.74	5.3	3.6	6.4	7.5	4.1	ACIT
PRUDENTIAL RETIREMENT INS & ANNUITY	CT	C+	50465.7	1196.6	2.54	1.06	7.1	3.6	4.1	8.2	4.5	AGIT
PURITAN LIFE INS CO	TX	C+	3.0	2.0	2.16	1.95	5.8	8.8	3.0	6.5	3.3	ACDGT
PYRAMID LIFE INS CO	KS	C-	445.1	167.5	0.72	0.58	3.6	7.8	6.7	5.4	3.0	CDFT
▼ RABENHORST LIFE INS CO	LA	E+	26.1	1.0	0.26	0.24	0.0	3.7	1.2	5.8	0.0	CIT
REASSURE AMERICA LIFE INS CO	IN	C+	16481.2	454.2	0.99	0.48	4.8	3.9	6.3	5.9	4.7	ACFIT
REGAL LIFE OF AMERICA INS CO	TX	D-	14.0	7.4	0.88	0.80	5.4	7.1	2.7	8.4	1.3	ACDG
REGAL REINSURANCE COMPANY	MA	U (1)	11.9	11.5	0.60	0.60	3.8	2.9	3.9	9.2	3.8	CDI
REGENCE LIFE & HEALTH INS CO	OR	B+	80.7	37.2	2.14	1.60	7.9	6.8	8.2	6.9	6.6	AFI
REGIONS LIFE INS CO	AZ	U	--	--	--	--	--	--	--	--	--	Z
REINSURANCE CO OF MO INC	MO	C+	1128.9	1061.4	1.08	0.96	6.7	1.4	4.1	7.0	4.5	I
RELIABLE LIFE INS CO	MO	B+	747.4	56.2	1.76	0.97	6.8	4.6	6.9	4.3	6.3	ACDIL
RELIABLE LIFE INS CO	LA	E+ (1)	6.2	0.7	0.41	0.29	0.5	1.1	5.1	7.4	0.5	CIT
RELIABLE SERVICE INS CO	LA	U (1)	0.1	0.1	2.22	2.00	8.0	9.8	3.9	7.0	4.1	D
RELIANCE STANDARD LIFE INS CO	IL	B-	3584.2	489.0	1.31	0.77	5.5	3.7	8.0	7.2	4.9	ACI
RELIANCE STANDARD LIFE INS CO OF TX	TX	U (1)	512.4	454.4	1.11	1.02	7.0	7.9	3.9	10.0	5.9	T
RELIASTAR LIFE INS CO	MN	B	20409.8	1995.1	2.16	1.26	7.4	5.8	6.8	5.9	4.3	AIT
RELIASTAR LIFE INS CO OF NEW YORK	NY	C+	3182.8	189.6	2.23	1.18	7.3	6.1	1.8	6.6	4.5	FT
REMINGTON LIFE INS CO	AZ	U	--	--	--	--	--	--	--	--	--	Z
RESERVE NATIONAL INS CO	OK	B	106.2	45.3	1.98	1.40	7.6	4.6	9.3	6.5	5.8	ADI
RESNICK WULBERT & RESNICK LIFE INS	AZ	U	--	--	--	--	--	--	--	--	--	Z
RESOURCE LIFE INS CO	IL	C	64.7	14.2	1.86	1.67	8.0	7.9	1.6	9.4	2.5	DFT

See Page 26 for explanation of footnotes and Page 27 for explanation of stability factors.

Arrows denote recent upgrades ▲ or downgrades ▼ (see Section VI for explanations)

58

www.thestreetratings.com

NET PREMIUM ($MIL)	IN-VESTED ASSETS ($MIL)	% OF INVESTED ASSETS IN:									INVEST. IN AFFIL	INSURANCE COMPANY NAME
		CASH	CMO & STRUCT. SECS.	OTH.INV. GRADE BONDS	NON-INV. GRADE BONDS	CMMON & PREF. STOCK	MORT IN GOOD STAND.	NON-PERF. MORT.	REAL ESTATE	OTHER INVEST-MENTS		
1.9	14.6	50.6	0.0	49.4	0.0	0.0	0.0	0.0	0.0	0.0	0.0	PIONEER MILITARY INS CO
9.5	445.8	0.2	18.0	58.2	2.2	0.8	15.9	0.0	0.0	4.8	0.0 ●	PIONEER MUTUAL LIFE INS CO
1.2	93.0	0.1	26.4	10.2	0.0	62.0	0.0	0.0	0.0	1.0	62.0 ●	PIONEER SECURITY LIFE INS CO
2.2	18.5 (*)	40.6	0.9	57.4	0.0	2.3	0.0	0.0	1.1	0.0	0.9	PLATEAU INS CO
3.1	53.4	5.7	0.0	87.1	0.0	7.2	0.0	0.0	0.0	0.0	3.8 ●	POPULAR LIFE RE
0.0	1.6	32.2	0.4	63.8	0.0	3.5	0.0	0.0	0.0	0.0	0.0	PORT-O-CALL LIFE INS CO
--	--	--	--	--	--	--	--	--	--	--	--	PRAMCO LIFE INS CO
0.0	4.0	3.4	0.0	96.6	0.0	0.0	0.0	0.0	0.0	0.0	0.0	PREFERRED SECURITY LIFE INS CO
17.1	6.8 (*)	0.1	0.0	60.8	0.0	0.0	0.0	0.0	0.0	0.0	0.0	PRENEED REINS CO OF AMERICA
0.0	9.3 (*)	0.0	56.7	28.3	4.7	0.0	0.0	0.0	0.0	8.1	0.0	PRESERVATION LIFE INS CO
58.7	3,608.1	0.0	6.3	72.2	4.8	8.3	0.0	0.0	0.0	8.6	0.0 ●	PRESIDENTIAL LIFE INS CO
1.1	3.8	53.8	0.0	7.5	14.7	17.0	4.7	0.0	0.0	2.4	0.0	PRESIDENTIAL LIFE INS CO
--	--	--	--	--	--	--	--	--	--	--	--	PRIDE OF CARROLL LIFE INS CO
306.7	5,780.5	-0.2	32.6	46.1	5.4	15.0	0.0	0.0	0.0	1.1	17.9 ●	PRIMERICA LIFE INS CO
2,041.4	61,800.7	0.1	16.8	49.0	4.7	3.2	16.5	0.0	0.6	9.2	5.6 ●	PRINCIPAL LIFE INS CO
0.0	20.3	1.0	0.0	25.0	0.0	74.0	0.0	0.0	0.0	0.0	74.0	PRINCIPAL LIFE INS CO IOWA
0.0	11.6	27.3	0.0	72.7	0.0	0.0	0.0	0.0	0.0	0.0	0.0	PRINCIPAL NATIONAL LIFE INS CO
25.7	12.5	-5.3	0.0	105.3	0.0	0.0	0.0	0.0	0.0	0.0	0.0	PRIORITY HEALTH INS CO
17.9	94.0	-1.7	14.8	72.0	3.3	4.3	0.0	0.0	0.0	7.5	0.0 ●	PROFESSIONAL INS CO
1.1	64.9	0.7	0.6	65.2	19.4	14.1	0.0	0.0	0.0	0.1	0.0	PROFESSIONAL LIFE & CAS CO
34.6	714.2	0.2	6.1	71.1	4.6	5.6	5.6	0.0	0.0	6.8	0.0 ●	PROTECTIVE LIFE & ANNUITY INS CO
594.8	19,785.7	0.5	28.6	40.7	5.8	13.0	7.6	0.0	0.1	3.8	6.0 ●	PROTECTIVE LIFE INS CO
1.0	809.4	-0.6	46.7	48.1	5.2	0.6	0.0	0.0	0.0	0.0	0.0 ●	PROTECTIVE LIFE INS CO OF NY
11.9	15.0	4.8	23.8	71.4	0.0	0.0	0.0	0.0	0.0	0.0	0.0	PROVIDENT AMER LIFE & HEALTH INS CO
7.9	6.9	79.3	0.0	17.7	0.0	0.1	0.0	0.0	0.0	2.9	0.0	PROVIDENT AMERICAN INS CO
250.6	7,289.0	-0.1	9.2	75.9	6.6	2.1	3.9	0.0	1.0	1.5	0.0 ●	PROVIDENT LIFE & ACCIDENT INS CO
25.0	684.4	0.0	17.5	75.0	6.8	0.0	0.0	0.0	0.0	0.8	0.0 ●	PROVIDENT LIFE & CAS INS CO
717.5	6,140.0	-0.6	24.9	37.3	7.4	4.1	11.9	0.0	0.0	15.2	4.1 ●	PRUCO LIFE INS CO
72.6	1,270.4	-0.4	26.2	37.9	8.8	0.3	11.7	0.0	0.0	15.5	2.0 ●	PRUCO LIFE INS CO OF NEW JERSEY
1,503.3	2,722.8 (*)	0.0	67.8	31.5	0.0	0.5	0.0	0.0	0.0	2.3	0.0 ●	PRUDENTIAL ANNUITIES LIFE ASR CORP
3,499.3	145,026.1	0.0	19.4	44.6	8.9	5.1	13.9	0.0	0.2	7.8	7.2 ●	PRUDENTIAL INS CO OF AMERICA
23.0	21,044.8	-0.5	21.1	46.0	8.8	0.8	21.8	0.0	0.0	2.1	0.1 ●	PRUDENTIAL RETIREMENT INS & ANNUITY
1.8	2.0	8.7	0.0	83.4	0.0	5.1	0.0	0.0	0.0	2.9	0.0	PURITAN LIFE INS CO
273.8	395.6	-11.0	35.1	72.5	2.8	0.0	0.0	0.0	0.0	0.7	0.0 ●	PYRAMID LIFE INS CO
0.7	21.8	0.8	37.9	37.3	0.7	11.4	11.7	0.0	0.0	0.2	11.7	RABENHORST LIFE INS CO
95.3	15,672.0	-0.2	25.4	46.3	1.7	1.6	0.7	0.0	0.0	24.5	0.0 ●	REASSURE AMERICA LIFE INS CO
2.0	12.6	20.5	0.0	34.5	0.0	42.9	0.0	0.0	0.0	2.1	42.9	REGAL LIFE OF AMERICA INS CO
0.0	11.9	0.1	1.7	18.4	0.0	79.8	0.0	0.0	0.0	0.0	79.8	REGAL REINSURANCE COMPANY
11.2	65.1	4.3	35.4	44.2	0.0	16.1	0.0	0.0	0.0	0.0	2.4	REGENCE LIFE & HEALTH INS CO
--	--	--	--	--	--	--	--	--	--	--	--	REGIONS LIFE INS CO
11.4	1,172.4	0.1	1.9	3.5	0.2	94.5	0.0	0.0	0.0	0.0	94.2 ●	REINSURANCE CO OF MO INC
28.3	699.6	0.4	19.2	59.0	2.8	6.2	0.0	0.0	1.9	10.5	0.0 ●	RELIABLE LIFE INS CO
0.9	6.1	9.3	6.7	37.2	3.9	35.2	1.4	0.0	6.3	0.0	1.0	RELIABLE LIFE INS CO
0.0	0.1	100.0	0.0	0.0	0.0	0.0	0.0	0.0	0.0	0.0	0.0	RELIABLE SERVICE INS CO
308.9	3,299.3	-0.3	45.6	33.4	11.8	3.3	2.3	1.3	0.4	2.3	2.7 ●	RELIANCE STANDARD LIFE INS CO
0.2	510.4	0.0	0.0	11.9	0.0	88.1	0.0	0.0	0.0	0.0	98.3	RELIANCE STANDARD LIFE INS CO OF TX
2.4	18,258.2	0.1	29.8	39.4	5.0	2.4	13.7	0.0	0.1	9.6	1.6 ●	RELIASTAR LIFE INS CO
91.6	2,069.3	0.3	30.6	52.1	4.4	0.2	5.9	0.0	0.0	6.7	0.1 ●	RELIASTAR LIFE INS CO OF NEW YORK
--	--	--	--	--	--	--	--	--	--	--	--	REMINGTON LIFE INS CO
32.8	97.9	1.4	12.7	59.7	0.0	11.5	0.0	0.0	10.8	3.8	0.3 ●	RESERVE NATIONAL INS CO
--	--	--	--	--	--	--	--	--	--	--	--	RESNICK WULBERT & RESNICK LIFE INS
-1.6	67.9 (*)	-0.5	40.3	60.0	0.1	0.0	0.0	0.0	0.0	8.7	0.0	RESOURCE LIFE INS CO

● Bullets denote a more detailed analysis is available in Section II.

(*) Asset category percentages do not add up to 100%

INSURANCE COMPANY NAME	DOM. STATE	RATING	TOTAL ASSETS ($MIL)	CAPITAL & SURPLUS ($MIL)	RISK ADJUSTED CAPITAL RATIO 1	RISK ADJUSTED CAPITAL RATIO 2	CAPITAL- IZATION INDEX (PTS)	INVEST. SAFETY INDEX (PTS)	PROFIT- ABILITY INDEX (PTS)	LIQUIDITY INDEX (PTS)	STAB. INDEX (PTS)	STABILITY FACTORS
REVIOS REINS CANADA LTD	CA	C- (5)	--	--	--	--	--	--	--	--	--	Z
RGA REINSURANCE CO	MO	C+	13085.6	1057.1	1.74	1.00	7.0	6.3	2.7	5.6	4.8	T
RHODES LIFE INS CO OF LA INC	LA	E (1)	3.8	0.3	0.24	0.22	0.0	1.5	2.5	8.1	0.0	CT
RIDGEWAY LIFE INS CO	TN	U	--	--	--	--	--	--	--	--	--	Z
RIGHTCHOICE INS CO	IL	U (1)	11.7	10.6	2.04	1.83	8.0	8.9	8.8	10.0	6.4	DOT
RIHT LIFE INS CO	AZ	U	--	--	--	--	--	--	--	--	--	Z
RIVERSOURCE LIFE INS CO	MN	B	67256.2	2567.3	1.83	1.08	7.1	6.0	1.8	8.1	4.6	GIT
RIVERSOURCE LIFE INS CO OF NY	NY	B-	4196.6	193.5	2.46	1.25	7.4	6.0	2.2	7.7	4.9	FGT
ROCKETT LIFE INS CO	LA	U	--	--	--	--	--	--	--	--	--	Z
ROYAL NEIGHBORS OF AMERICA	IL	U	--	--	--	--	--	--	--	--	--	Z
ROYAL STATE NATIONAL INS CO LTD	HI	B-	47.5	27.2	4.33	3.89	10.0	7.9	5.8	9.1	5.1	D
RUDANDA LIFE INS CO	AZ	U	--	--	--	--	--	--	--	--	--	Z
S USA LIFE INS CO INC	AZ	C-	14.8	10.8	3.51	3.16	10.0	9.8	1.6	7.4	2.9	DFT
SABINE LIFE INS CO	LA	D (1)	1.7	0.3	0.48	0.44	2.3	7.2	1.8	7.5	1.5	CGT
SAFEHEALTH LIFE INS CO	CA	B-	30.5	24.1	1.70	1.40	6.0	8.4	8.2	2.0	4.0	DLOT
SAGICOR LIFE INS CO	TX	C	542.6	29.4	1.53	0.77	5.8	3.8	1.7	6.2	3.3	FGIT
▼ SAVINGS BANK LIFE INS CO OF MA	MA	B+	2093.4	145.5	1.89	1.26	7.4	7.2	5.0	6.5	6.4	
SBLI USA MUT LIFE INS CO INC	NY	C+	1467.6	108.5	1.37	0.73	5.6	3.9	5.6	4.8	4.5	CILT
SCENIC CITY LIFE INS CO	TN	U	--	--	--	--	--	--	--	--	--	Z
SCOR GLOBAL LIFE RE INS CO OF TX	TX	D+	298.6	41.0	1.65	1.04	7.1	6.7	1.9	6.6	1.5	AFT
SCOR GLOBAL LIFE US RE INS CO	TX	C-	2065.1	174.6	1.13	0.76	5.2	6.4	5.4	7.3	3.1	ACGT
SCOTT LIFE INS CO	AZ	B	99.5	97.6	10.91	9.82	10.0	8.3	8.8	10.0	5.5	AD
SCOTTISH RE LIFE CORP	DE	D+(1)	521.4	66.4	1.63	1.04	7.1	6.9	2.5	6.3	2.9	ADFT
SCOTTISH RE US INC	DE	F (1)	2238.8	197.4	0.72	0.48	2.8	6.0	1.4	4.7	0.0	ACFLT
SEARS LIFE INS CO	TX	B	75.0	53.1	6.82	5.56	10.0	7.4	3.0	8.2	5.8	
SEB TRYGG LIFE USA ASR CO LTD	AZ	U (1)	0.7	0.4	1.50	1.35	7.5	9.8	2.6	10.0	2.8	DF
SECURIAN LIFE INS CO	MN	B	144.3	123.0	13.21	9.61	10.0	8.3	7.5	7.5	5.9	DT
SECURITY BENEFIT LIFE INS CO	KS	C	8734.3	241.4	0.89	0.45	4.1	3.6	2.2	7.7	3.4	CFIT
SECURITY GENERAL LIFE INS CO	OK	F (5)	--	--	--	--	--	--	--	--	--	Z
SECURITY LIFE INS CO OF AMERICA	MN	C	82.9	25.6	1.09	0.85	5.1	8.5	8.9	5.7	3.8	CDFRT
▼ SECURITY LIFE OF DENVER INS CO	CO	B-	22467.3	1319.1	1.37	0.70	5.6	3.4	7.4	7.5	3.4	ACGIT
SECURITY MUTUAL LIFE INS CO OF NY	NY	B	2229.7	108.2	1.29	0.71	5.4	5.7	5.7	4.7	5.4	CIL
SECURITY NATIONAL LIFE INS CO	UT	D	344.8	15.4	0.34	0.22	0.0	0.5	5.7	4.6	0.9	CIL
SECURITY NATIONAL LIFE INS CO OF LA	LA	D+	2.9	0.7	0.87	0.79	5.3	3.6	5.4	9.5	3.0	ADIT
▲ SECURITY PLAN LIFE INS CO	LA	C	262.9	41.5	2.76	1.77	8.2	6.6	5.8	6.6	3.5	A
SELECTED FUNERAL & LIFE INS CO	AR	C-	140.1	20.7	2.00	1.80	8.2	7.0	7.0	6.2	3.0	T
SENIOR AMERICAN LIFE INS CO	PA	E+	20.9	4.1	1.16	1.04	7.1	7.6	2.1	7.4	0.8	AD
SENIOR HEALTH INS CO OF PENNSYLVANIA	PA	D+	3288.7	176.4	1.45	0.64	5.7	2.5	1.4	5.6	2.4	FI
SENIOR LIFE INS CO	GA	B-	28.3	10.0	2.43	2.19	8.8	7.3	8.6	7.5	3.6	D
SENTINEL AMERICAN LIFE INS CO	TX	U (1)	43.5	15.2	2.92	2.62	9.4	7.2	5.4	7.4	6.9	DFT
SENTINEL SECURITY LIFE INS CO	UT	D+	49.3	19.5	2.94	2.21	8.8	4.3	6.1	6.9	2.8	DI
SENTRY LIFE INS CO	WI	A	2809.8	262.2	4.48	2.60	9.4	7.6	7.2	7.0	6.0	AT
SENTRY LIFE INS CO OF NEW YORK	NY	B	50.3	10.2	1.52	1.37	7.6	8.3	7.7	7.4	6.2	DGT
SEQUATCHIE LIFE INS CO	TN	U	--	--	--	--	--	--	--	--	--	Z
SERVCO LIFE INS CO	TX	C	29.7	7.7	1.66	1.49	7.7	8.2	5.1	10.0	2.9	RT
SERVICE LIFE & CAS INS CO	TX	C	134.7	34.6	3.07	1.60	7.9	3.3	6.6	8.9	2.9	IRT
SETTLERS LIFE INS CO	WI	B+	417.4	53.8	3.38	1.75	8.1	6.2	7.1	7.1	6.6	ADI
SHELTER LIFE INS CO	MO	A-	933.1	170.7	3.89	2.43	9.1	7.4	8.3	6.5	7.3	A
SHENANDOAH LIFE INS CO	VA	F (2)	1614.4	78.3	1.02	0.58	5.0	4.6	6.5	4.8	5.0	CIL
SHERIDAN LIFE INS CO	OK	C	1.9	1.7	2.41	2.16	8.7	9.8	8.9	10.0	3.0	ADOT
SIERRA HEALTH AND LIFE INS CO INC	CA	B	127.5	82.0	2.42	1.95	8.4	8.6	6.8	7.9	4.0	CT
SMITH BURIAL & LIFE INS CO	AR	D-	4.7	0.6	0.46	0.42	2.0	6.9	6.6	6.0	1.2	CD

See Page 26 for explanation of footnotes and Page 27 for explanation of stability factors.

Arrows denote recent upgrades ▲ or downgrades ▼ (see Section VI for explanations)

www.thestreetratings.com

NET PREMIUM ($MIL)	IN- VESTED ASSETS ($MIL)	CASH	CMO & STRUCT. SECS.	OTH.INV. GRADE BONDS	NON-INV. GRADE BONDS	CMMON & PREF. STOCK	MORT IN GOOD STAND.	NON- PERF. MORT.	REAL ESTATE	OTHER INVEST- MENTS	INVEST. IN AFFIL	INSURANCE COMPANY NAME
--	--	--	--	--	--	--	--	--	--	--	--	REVIOS REINS CANADA LTD
624.6	7,192.1	0.9	22.0	41.0	4.8	4.6	10.7	0.0	0.0	16.0	0.0 ●	RGA REINSURANCE CO
0.8	3.8	9.6	12.0	38.1	0.0	22.7	3.8	3.3	10.5	0.0	0.0	RHODES LIFE INS CO OF LA INC
--	--	--	--	--	--	--	--	--	--	--	--	RIDGEWAY LIFE INS CO
0.0	11.7	0.0	0.0	100.0	0.0	0.0	0.0	0.0	0.0	0.0	0.0	RIGHTCHOICE INS CO
--	--	--	--	--	--	--	--	--	--	--	--	RIHT LIFE INS CO
3,495.2	27,370.5	-0.2	23.6	48.8	4.5	1.8	9.3	0.0	0.0	12.2	1.7 ●	RIVERSOURCE LIFE INS CO
221.2	1,896.1	-0.2	24.2	54.9	5.3	0.0	11.2	0.0	0.0	4.7	0.0 ●	RIVERSOURCE LIFE INS CO OF NY
--	--	--	--	--	--	--	--	--	--	--	--	ROCKETT LIFE INS CO
--	--	--	--	--	--	--	--	--	--	--	--	ROYAL NEIGHBORS OF AMERICA
1.6	46.0	17.6	0.0	72.0	0.8	9.2	0.0	0.0	0.0	0.5	4.4 ●	ROYAL STATE NATIONAL INS CO LTD
--	--	--	--	--	--	--	--	--	--	--	--	RUDANDA LIFE INS CO
0.1	14.4	2.8	0.0	96.7	0.0	0.0	0.0	0.0	0.0	0.5	0.0	S USA LIFE INS CO INC
0.2	1.6 (*)	1.9	0.0	60.7	0.0	0.0	7.8	0.0	0.4	0.0	0.0	SABINE LIFE INS CO
13.0	26.3	-3.0	0.0	102.9	0.0	0.2	0.0	0.0	0.0	0.0	0.0	SAFEHEALTH LIFE INS CO
12.7	524.9	0.0	43.4	39.0	2.0	3.3	5.5	0.0	0.0	6.8	0.0 ●	SAGICOR LIFE INS CO
45.1	1,984.8	0.0	18.0	68.3	0.9	6.2	0.1	0.0	0.1	6.4	1.3 ●	SAVINGS BANK LIFE INS CO OF MA
22.5	1,457.3	0.2	43.2	37.3	3.9	4.1	0.8	0.5	0.3	9.8	0.8 ●	SBLI USA MUT LIFE INS CO INC
--	--	--	--	--	--	--	--	--	--	--	--	SCENIC CITY LIFE INS CO
8.9	225.7	0.9	30.9	39.9	0.3	0.0	0.0	0.0	0.0	28.0	0.0 ●	SCOR GLOBAL LIFE RE INS CO OF TX
51.1	1,875.0	0.4	39.1	49.5	1.2	6.8	2.2	0.0	0.0	0.8	3.5 ●	SCOR GLOBAL LIFE US RE INS CO
0.1	97.6	3.6	19.5	73.3	0.0	3.7	0.0	0.0	0.0	0.0	0.0 ●	SCOTT LIFE INS CO
123.0	378.9	12.4	30.3	38.9	1.6	13.2	0.0	0.0	0.0	3.6	0.0 ●	SCOTTISH RE LIFE CORP
-337.5	1,743.1 (*)	4.6	31.6	56.4	2.8	6.7	0.0	0.0	0.0	0.2	3.8	SCOTTISH RE US INC
6.7	57.0	3.4	30.6	62.0	3.9	0.0	0.0	0.0	0.0	0.0	0.0 ●	SEARS LIFE INS CO
0.0	0.7	100.0	0.0	0.0	0.0	0.0	0.0	0.0	0.0	0.0	0.0	SEB TRYGG LIFE USA ASR CO LTD
10.1	137.5	0.5	23.2	76.3	0.0	0.0	0.0	0.0	0.0	0.1	0.0 ●	SECURIAN LIFE INS CO
79.4	4,445.6	4.2	34.2	32.8	3.3	4.7	0.3	0.0	0.1	20.3	16.9 ●	SECURITY BENEFIT LIFE INS CO
--	--	--	--	--	--	--	--	--	--	--	--	SECURITY GENERAL LIFE INS CO
26.9	85.5	8.2	1.0	80.6	0.2	0.0	8.7	0.0	0.0	1.5	0.0 ●	SECURITY LIFE INS CO OF AMERICA
258.2	22,104.1	0.3	42.2	31.8	5.3	1.6	8.5	0.0	0.0	10.2	0.5 ●	SECURITY LIFE OF DENVER INS CO
55.3	2,104.0	0.1	19.7	59.1	0.5	0.3	9.2	0.0	0.3	10.8	0.2 ●	SECURITY MUTUAL LIFE INS CO OF NY
10.8	331.3	0.3	2.1	33.5	1.0	3.9	30.4	5.1	7.9	16.1	3.0	SECURITY NATIONAL LIFE INS CO
0.1	2.7	20.2	23.0	26.3	16.6	9.1	3.6	0.0	1.1	0.2	0.0	SECURITY NATIONAL LIFE INS CO OF LA
7.8	249.9	1.8	15.6	72.4	0.8	7.6	0.1	0.0	0.1	1.6	1.3 ●	SECURITY PLAN LIFE INS CO
3.5	137.7	4.2	55.6	35.0	1.3	2.8	0.5	0.0	0.5	0.2	0.0	SELECTED FUNERAL & LIFE INS CO
1.2	20.2	1.0	19.3	79.7	0.0	0.0	0.0	0.0	0.0	0.0	0.0	SENIOR AMERICAN LIFE INS CO
64.6	3,232.4	-0.4	21.1	63.4	9.2	1.3	5.4	0.0	0.0	0.0	0.0 ●	SENIOR HEALTH INS CO OF PENNSYLVANIA
4.7	22.4	25.5	6.2	54.9	0.0	2.6	0.0	0.0	5.4	5.4	3.4	SENIOR LIFE INS CO
0.1	42.4	20.8	5.4	72.5	1.0	0.0	0.0	0.0	0.0	0.3	0.0	SENTINEL AMERICAN LIFE INS CO
1.4	49.2	6.6	0.0	38.8	2.5	46.2	3.5	0.0	0.4	1.9	0.0	SENTINEL SECURITY LIFE INS CO
77.4	1,804.8	0.0	13.4	83.8	1.3	0.6	0.0	0.0	0.0	0.9	0.6 ●	SENTRY LIFE INS CO
2.5	32.2	0.8	10.5	84.0	0.0	0.0	0.0	0.0	0.0	4.7	0.0	SENTRY LIFE INS CO OF NEW YORK
--	--	--	--	--	--	--	--	--	--	--	--	SEQUATCHIE LIFE INS CO
0.2	27.7	44.9	0.0	53.2	0.2	1.7	0.0	0.0	0.0	0.0	0.0	SERVCO LIFE INS CO
1.7	130.0	-2.3	18.3	40.2	0.0	4.1	15.4	0.2	15.5	8.5	0.3 ●	SERVICE LIFE & CAS INS CO
10.3	401.4	0.2	11.4	75.7	5.5	4.5	0.0	0.0	1.1	1.5	0.0 ●	SETTLERS LIFE INS CO
33.7	877.8	1.5	48.7	39.5	0.7	4.9	0.7	0.0	0.0	4.1	2.7 ●	SHELTER LIFE INS CO
209.3	1,609.5	0.1	18.2	45.8	1.7	17.8	13.6	0.0	0.2	2.6	0.0	SHENANDOAH LIFE INS CO
0.0	1.9	100.0	0.0	0.0	0.0	0.0	0.0	0.0	0.0	0.0	0.0	SHERIDAN LIFE INS CO
52.2	118.8	-3.6	0.0	100.0	0.0	0.0	0.0	0.0	3.6	0.0	0.0 ●	SIERRA HEALTH AND LIFE INS CO INC
0.1	4.6	8.7	54.1	32.4	0.0	4.8	0.0	0.0	0.0	0.0	0.0	SMITH BURIAL & LIFE INS CO

● Bullets denote a more detailed analysis is available in Section II.

(*) Asset category percentages do not add up to 100%

INSURANCE COMPANY NAME	DOM. STATE	RATING	TOTAL ASSETS ($MIL)	CAPITAL & SURPLUS ($MIL)	RISK ADJUSTED CAPITAL RATIO 1	RISK ADJUSTED CAPITAL RATIO 2	CAPITAL-IZATION INDEX (PTS)	INVEST. SAFETY INDEX (PTS)	PROFIT-ABILITY INDEX (PTS)	LIQUIDITY INDEX (PTS)	STAB. INDEX (PTS)	STABILITY FACTORS
SOUTHEAST FAMILY LIFE INS CO	AZ	U	--	--	--	--	--	--	--	--	--	Z
SOUTHERN CAPITAL LIFE INS CO	MS	U (1)	6.9	6.7	5.89	5.30	8.0	9.8	8.7	8.2	8.0	DF
SOUTHERN FARM BUREAU LIFE INS CO	MS	A	10074.1	1572.6	3.87	2.11	8.7	6.3	8.4	6.2	7.4	I
SOUTHERN FIDELITY LIFE INS CO	AR	U (1)	0.1	0.1	1.94	1.75	8.1	7.8	7.0	10.0	7.2	DF
SOUTHERN FINANCIAL LIFE INS CO	KY	C	4.6	4.0	2.78	2.50	9.3	8.7	6.2	8.6	3.3	AT
SOUTHERN FINANCIAL LIFE INS CO	LA	D+	64.9	9.0	1.07	0.60	5.1	3.0	5.8	7.0	2.6	GIT
SOUTHERN LIFE & HEALTH INS CO	WI	U (1)	96.6	32.8	1.96	1.69	8.0	4.8	5.3	6.9	4.8	DFGIT
SOUTHERN NATL LIFE INS CO INC	LA	B+	16.2	12.1	2.05	1.69	8.0	6.6	5.8	7.0	5.0	I
SOUTHERN PIONEER LIFE INS CO	AR	B	25.2	13.0	3.21	2.89	9.8	9.1	8.5	9.4	5.0	AT
▲ SOUTHERN SECURITY LIFE INS CO INC	MS	D	1.8	1.6	2.57	2.30	9.0	8.5	2.4	0.0	1.7	ACFILT
SOUTHLAND NATIONAL INS CORP	AL	C	158.4	8.8	0.79	0.71	4.7	3.6	3.2	4.1	3.5	ACIL
SOUTHWEST CREDIT LIFE INC	NM	D	1.4	0.9	1.66	1.49	7.7	9.5	1.6	9.2	2.1	ADFGT
SOUTHWEST SERVICE LIFE INS CO	TX	D-	11.3	5.7	1.10	0.98	6.8	8.9	7.5	7.5	1.3	AD
SQUIRE REASSURANCE CO LLC	MI	U (1)	10.1	10.1	4.13	3.72	3.0	8.5	6.5	7.0	5.0	DET
STANDARD INS CO	OR	B+	12858.1	1126.6	2.60	1.55	7.8	6.1	8.2	7.3	6.5	AI
STANDARD LIFE & ACCIDENT INS CO	OK	A-	484.7	187.6	4.06	2.51	9.3	5.4	7.6	6.8	5.5	ADIT
STANDARD LIFE & CAS INS CO	UT	C+	22.4	5.0	1.37	1.23	7.3	7.3	8.8	6.2	4.2	G
STANDARD LIFE INS CO OF INDIANA	IN	F (1)	2088.9	44.4	0.52	0.23	1.2	0.0	4.8	5.6	0.0	CFIT
STANDARD LIFE INS CO OF NY	NY	B-	181.5	42.4	3.11	2.08	8.6	7.4	4.8	7.2	5.3	
STANDARD SECURITY LIFE INS CO OF NY	NY	B+	365.4	110.3	2.91	2.28	8.9	6.8	7.5	5.7	6.2	ADI
STARMOUNT LIFE INS CO	LA	B	35.2	14.4	1.67	1.24	7.4	7.6	8.3	7.2	5.6	G
STARVED ROCK LIFE INS CO	AZ	U	--	--	--	--	--	--	--	--	--	Z
STATE FARM ANNUITY & LIFE INS CO	IL	U (1)	8.4	8.3	3.89	3.51	8.0	9.5	7.7	10.0	8.0	D
STATE FARM LIFE & ACCIDENT ASR CO	IL	A+	1691.4	268.3	4.57	2.66	9.5	8.0	7.7	6.7	7.9	A
STATE FARM LIFE INS CO	IL	A+	44978.4	4924.9	3.50	1.98	8.5	6.7	7.9	6.4	7.9	AI
STATE LIFE INS CO	IN	B	2921.8	183.9	1.74	0.90	6.2	4.7	6.0	3.4	5.4	CIL
STATE LIFE INS FUND	WI	B (1)	87.8	6.4	0.89	0.80	5.4	6.6	7.3	1.5	4.1	CDL
STATE MUTUAL INS CO	GA	C	384.0	28.5	1.17	0.80	5.4	4.9	5.7	5.8	4.1	D
▲ STERLING INVESTORS LIFE INS CO	GA	D+	21.7	6.6	1.24	0.84	5.7	9.7	4.3	6.8	3.2	FT
STONEBRIDGE LIFE INS CO	VT	B+	2089.0	205.8	2.05	1.13	7.2	5.4	6.0	6.4	5.9	ACFI
SULLIVAN LIFE INS CO	TX	D+	6.5	3.4	1.04	1.02	7.0	7.1	6.8	6.7	2.3	AD
SUMMIT CREDIT LIFE INS CO	AZ	U	--	--	--	--	--	--	--	--	--	Z
SUN LIFE & HEALTH INS CO	CT	C+	90.5	37.3	4.58	2.32	8.0	6.8	2.2	9.1	3.2	AFT
SUN LIFE ASR CO OF CANADA	MI	C	15401.0	738.3	0.86	0.49	3.9	2.8	2.0	5.1	3.6	CIT
SUN LIFE ASR CO OF CANADA (US)	DE	C+	39760.6	1178.6	1.24	0.69	5.4	3.8	1.9	9.3	3.3	CFIT
SUN LIFE INS & ANNUITY CO OF NY	NY	C	2472.8	209.0	2.97	1.56	7.8	5.9	1.8	9.1	3.8	FT
SUNAMERICA LIFE INS CO	AZ	C	21173.1	4182.5	0.85	0.70	4.6	4.0	7.6	9.9	3.0	CGIT
SUNSET LIFE INS CO OF AMERICA	MO	B	403.4	32.9	2.21	1.08	7.1	3.7	6.8	5.3	4.9	DFIT
SUNTRUST INS CO	AZ	U (1)	16.3	15.0	4.84	4.35	4.0	9.4	7.3	10.0	6.0	DFT
SURENCY LIFE & HEALTH INS CO	KS	U (1)	2.4	2.3	2.80	2.52	3.0	9.8	1.7	9.9	1.9	DEFT
SURETY LIFE & CASUALTY INS CO	ND	C-	6.7	2.8	1.56	1.41	7.6	5.7	8.5	8.5	2.8	D
SURETY LIFE INS CO	NE	B+	13.2	12.3	3.56	1.78	8.0	9.7	8.4	10.0	6.7	AT
SWISS RE LIFE & HEALTH AMER INC	CT	B-	12589.8	1703.5	1.28	0.96	6.7	6.8	6.5	6.5	5.3	A
SYMETRA LIFE INS CO	WA	B	19398.2	1155.8	2.16	1.11	7.2	4.6	6.2	7.3	6.0	GI
▲ SYMETRA NATIONAL LIFE INS CO	WA	B	17.4	11.1	3.45	3.11	10.0	8.0	5.0	8.5	5.4	AD
T J M LIFE INS CO	TX	C	12.1	2.2	0.87	0.78	5.2	8.2	7.2	7.2	3.6	CD
TANDY LIFE INS CO	TX	D	79.6	5.6	0.69	0.62	4.0	7.5	7.8	0.0	2.0	CLT
TEACHERS INS & ANNUITY ASN OF AM	NY	A+	194588.7	16848.6	4.28	2.31	9.0	5.9	9.1	8.3	6.9	GI
TEACHERS PROTV MUTUAL LIFE INS CO	PA	C-	58.7	7.4	1.09	0.92	6.4	7.2	5.5	7.1	3.2	T
TENNESSEE FARMERS LIFE INS CO	TN	A	1318.3	201.6	2.28	1.49	7.7	6.0	6.8	6.4	7.4	AGI
TENNESSEE LIFE INS CO	AZ	U	--	--	--	--	--	--	--	--	--	Z
TEXAS DIRECTORS LIFE INS CO	TX	C+	9.5	3.7	1.60	1.44	7.7	8.0	9.3	6.7	4.0	ADO

See Page 26 for explanation of footnotes and Page 27 for explanation of stability factors.

Arrows denote recent upgrades ▲ or downgrades ▼ (see Section VI for explanations)

62

www.thestreetratings.com

NET PREMIUM ($MIL)	IN-VESTED ASSETS ($MIL)	% OF INVESTED ASSETS IN:									INVEST. IN AFFIL	INSURANCE COMPANY NAME
		CASH	CMO & STRUCT. SECS.	OTH.INV. GRADE BONDS	NON-INV. GRADE BONDS	CMMON & PREF. STOCK	MORT IN GOOD STAND.	NON-PERF. MORT.	REAL ESTATE	OTHER INVEST-MENTS		
--	--	--	--	--	--	--	--	--	--	--	--	SOUTHEAST FAMILY LIFE INS CO
0.0	6.9	0.1	0.0	99.9	0.0	0.0	0.0	0.0	0.0	0.0	0.0	SOUTHERN CAPITAL LIFE INS CO
203.6	9,607.1	0.0	15.9	54.8	0.7	4.2	14.4	0.0	0.1	9.9	0.7 ●	SOUTHERN FARM BUREAU LIFE INS CO
0.0	0.1	91.3	0.0	0.0	0.0	8.8	0.0	0.0	0.0	0.0	0.0	SOUTHERN FIDELITY LIFE INS CO
0.0	4.5	2.0	21.1	76.6	0.1	0.2	0.0	0.0	0.0	0.0	0.0	SOUTHERN FINANCIAL LIFE INS CO
2.2	59.8	0.0	0.0	52.2	11.3	29.2	0.0	0.0	0.1	7.3	0.0	SOUTHERN FINANCIAL LIFE INS CO
0.1	93.8 (*)	0.3	2.9	37.2	0.0	38.7	0.0	0.0	0.0	4.2	34.1	SOUTHERN LIFE & HEALTH INS CO
2.8	15.4 (*)	0.0	19.7	55.3	0.0	28.0	0.0	0.0	0.0	0.2	17.5	SOUTHERN NATL LIFE INS CO INC
1.1	24.3 (*)	22.2	6.3	67.8	0.0	3.7	0.0	0.0	0.0	2.8	3.7	SOUTHERN PIONEER LIFE INS CO
0.0	1.5	12.6	0.0	59.3	0.0	0.0	27.7	0.0	0.5	0.0	0.0	SOUTHERN SECURITY LIFE INS CO INC
7.2	150.6	2.6	26.3	65.8	1.7	3.4	0.2	0.0	0.0	0.1	0.1	SOUTHLAND NATIONAL INS CORP
0.1	1.4	1.1	0.0	98.9	0.0	0.0	0.0	0.0	0.0	0.0	0.0	SOUTHWEST CREDIT LIFE INC
2.1	10.7	14.5	0.0	60.1	0.0	25.4	0.0	0.0	0.0	0.0	25.4	SOUTHWEST SERVICE LIFE INS CO
0.0	10.1	0.0	0.0	100.0	0.0	0.0	0.0	0.0	0.0	0.0	0.0	SQUIRE REASSURANCE CO LLC
923.3	9,515.3 (*)	-0.3	2.1	52.9	2.8	0.0	41.9	0.0	0.4	2.1	0.0 ●	STANDARD INS CO
32.6	468.9	-0.8	12.1	65.4	3.0	9.7	8.5	0.0	0.0	2.1	0.2 ●	STANDARD LIFE & ACCIDENT INS CO
2.0	20.7	5.2	6.8	74.7	1.3	6.7	0.0	0.0	1.5	3.8	0.0	STANDARD LIFE & CAS INS CO
24.3	2,064.6	0.3	42.1	45.7	6.7	3.5	0.0	0.0	0.0	1.7	0.0	STANDARD LIFE INS CO OF INDIANA
15.1	166.4	-0.8	0.4	50.8	0.1	0.0	49.4	0.0	0.0	0.0	0.0 ●	STANDARD LIFE INS CO OF NY
47.8	300.1 (*)	0.9	2.7	65.5	1.0	19.3	0.0	0.0	0.0	2.6	13.2 ●	STANDARD SECURITY LIFE INS CO OF NY
12.5	25.7	34.4	0.0	56.1	0.4	0.3	0.0	0.0	8.6	0.2	0.0	STARMOUNT LIFE INS CO
--	--	--	--	--	--	--	--	--	--	--	--	STARVED ROCK LIFE INS CO
0.0	8.3 (*)	0.5	0.0	73.1	0.0	0.0	0.0	0.0	0.0	0.0	0.0	STATE FARM ANNUITY & LIFE INS CO
50.7	1,590.3 (*)	0.0	18.0	69.6	1.1	0.0	0.0	0.0	0.0	7.4	0.0 ●	STATE FARM LIFE & ACCIDENT ASR CO
1,190.5	42,711.4	0.0	17.9	53.8	0.9	4.3	13.3	0.0	0.0	8.9	0.8 ●	STATE FARM LIFE INS CO
82.8	2,773.8	0.3	19.1	69.5	2.5	1.0	6.5	0.0	0.0	1.2	0.1 ●	STATE LIFE INS CO
1.9	86.3 (*)	0.0	0.0	92.4	1.4	0.0	0.0	0.0	0.0	4.4	0.0	STATE LIFE INS FUND
8.1	345.0	1.6	1.0	58.1	0.3	6.1	16.1	1.4	2.3	13.1	3.3 ●	STATE MUTUAL INS CO
2.7	15.3	42.1	0.0	56.0	0.0	0.0	0.0	0.0	0.0	1.9	0.0	STERLING INVESTORS LIFE INS CO
131.1	1,919.6	0.0	16.0	59.7	5.9	3.3	10.7	0.0	1.8	2.8	2.0 ●	STONEBRIDGE LIFE INS CO
0.1	5.5	1.2	27.8	16.8	0.0	54.2	0.0	0.0	0.0	0.0	77.6	SULLIVAN LIFE INS CO
--	--	--	--	--	--	--	--	--	--	--	--	SUMMIT CREDIT LIFE INS CO
0.0	73.7	-15.0	21.7	92.8	0.0	0.0	0.0	0.0	0.0	0.5	0.0	SUN LIFE & HEALTH INS CO
635.4	13,073.6	-0.1	12.5	42.7	3.1	3.4	23.3	0.0	5.6	9.5	0.2 ●	SUN LIFE ASR CO OF CANADA
951.4	14,668.9	-0.4	33.5	40.7	4.5	2.5	9.9	0.0	1.0	8.2	2.0 ●	SUN LIFE ASR CO OF CANADA (US)
149.3	1,364.6	1.3	7.3	77.7	5.4	0.4	7.8	0.0	0.0	0.0	0.0 ●	SUN LIFE INS & ANNUITY CO OF NY
0.9	23,935.8	-0.1	23.2	23.1	4.0	18.8	10.2	0.0	0.0	20.9	20.7 ●	SUNAMERICA LIFE INS CO
3.0	397.3	-0.1	26.0	55.5	5.5	0.7	8.9	0.0	0.0	3.5	0.0 ●	SUNSET LIFE INS CO OF AMERICA
0.0	16.1	1.0	1.7	97.3	0.2	0.0	0.0	0.0	0.0	0.0	0.0	SUNTRUST INS CO
0.0	2.4	100.0	0.0	0.0	0.0	0.0	0.0	0.0	0.0	0.0	0.0	SURENCY LIFE & HEALTH INS CO
0.3	6.2	6.1	0.0	39.9	5.3	21.3	19.6	0.0	2.1	5.8	0.0	SURETY LIFE & CASUALTY INS CO
0.0	11.3	-11.6	3.1	108.5	0.0	0.0	0.0	0.0	0.0	0.0	0.0	SURETY LIFE INS CO
635.1	11,180.2	0.2	33.1	55.5	1.6	7.4	0.0	0.0	0.0	2.3	6.6 ●	SWISS RE LIFE & HEALTH AMER INC
1,041.2	14,529.1	-0.2	24.3	56.6	6.1	5.0	6.8	0.0	0.0	1.4	0.4 ●	SYMETRA LIFE INS CO
0.1	17.1	0.1	10.8	82.0	2.9	2.9	0.0	0.0	0.0	1.3	0.0	SYMETRA NATIONAL LIFE INS CO
0.3	11.8	16.5	0.0	74.9	0.0	0.0	0.0	0.0	0.0	8.7	0.0	T J M LIFE INS CO
0.0	79.2	0.2	0.0	10.4	0.0	0.0	0.0	0.0	0.0	89.4	0.0	TANDY LIFE INS CO
2,803.3	179,454.3	0.2	38.2	36.6	3.8	3.5	11.0	0.0	0.9	6.0	3.9 ●	TEACHERS INS & ANNUITY ASN OF AM
5.4	56.8	4.7	21.7	69.1	0.0	3.5	0.1	0.0	0.2	0.5	0.0	TEACHERS PROTV MUTUAL LIFE INS CO
45.5	1,244.4	0.5	0.3	69.9	1.5	23.5	0.5	0.0	0.7	3.2	20.8 ●	TENNESSEE FARMERS LIFE INS CO
--	--	--	--	--	--	--	--	--	--	--	--	TENNESSEE LIFE INS CO
0.1	9.3	0.7	3.4	85.8	1.9	8.2	0.0	0.0	0.0	0.1	0.0	TEXAS DIRECTORS LIFE INS CO

● Bullets denote a more detailed analysis is available in Section II.

(*) Asset category percentages do not add up to 100%

INSURANCE COMPANY NAME	DOM. STATE	RATING	TOTAL ASSETS ($MIL)	CAPITAL & SURPLUS ($MIL)	RISK ADJUSTED CAPITAL RATIO 1	RISK ADJUSTED CAPITAL RATIO 2	CAPITAL-IZATION INDEX (PTS)	INVEST. SAFETY INDEX (PTS)	PROFIT-ABILITY INDEX (PTS)	LIQUIDITY INDEX (PTS)	STAB. INDEX (PTS)	STABILITY FACTORS
TEXAS IMPERIAL LIFE INS CO	TX	D+	25.6	2.2	0.56	0.50	3.0	7.5	6.9	7.4	2.7	CT
TEXAS INTERNATIONAL LIFE INS CO	TX	E+	7.0	1.6	0.37	0.29	0.5	7.2	1.1	5.2	0.5	CDFT
TEXAS LIFE INS CO	TX	B	709.0	38.0	1.74	1.06	7.1	5.8	5.0	5.6	6.0	ADIT
TEXAS MEMORIAL LIFE INS CO	TX	E-	3.5	-2.6	-1.05	-0.95	0.0	9.1	0.3	0.5	0.0	CDFGLT
TEXAS SECURITY MUTUAL LIFE INS CO	TX	U (1)	1.0	0.4	0.90	0.81	5.5	7.5	1.8	6.9	2.0	DFIT
TEXAS SERVICE LIFE INS CO	TX	C-	10.8	2.2	0.96	0.86	5.9	7.2	2.7	7.5	3.1	CD
THRIVENT FINANCIAL FOR LUTHERANS	WI	U	--	--	--	--	--	--	--	--	--	Z
THRIVENT LIFE INS CO	MN	B+	2564.9	174.6	3.42	1.55	7.8	6.0	8.1	7.9	5.2	IT
TIAA-CREF LIFE INS CO	NY	B	3031.9	342.8	3.75	1.98	8.5	5.9	6.2	6.2	6.3	GI
TIME INS CO	WI	B-	658.7	207.1	1.08	0.82	5.2	5.9	6.8	5.5	4.8	AT
TIPPECANOE LIFE INS CO	AZ	U	--	--	--	--	--	--	--	--	--	Z
TOWER LIFE INS CO	TX	C	75.5	36.8	4.77	4.29	10.0	6.9	2.9	9.0	3.8	D
TOWN & COUNTRY LIFE INS CO	UT	D+	5.2	2.8	1.81	1.62	7.9	8.8	6.0	7.1	2.4	DGT
TRANS CITY LIFE INS CO	AZ	C	19.9	10.3	3.55	3.19	10.0	6.7	7.4	9.2	3.7	DT
TRANS OCEANIC LIFE INS CO	PR	C-	29.8	7.3	0.75	0.55	3.4	6.6	6.6	8.0	2.9	CDG
TRANS WORLD ASR CO	CA	B	336.0	67.9	1.73	1.48	7.7	6.1	2.9	6.4	5.4	DI
TRANS-WESTERN LIFE INS CO	TX	U (1)	0.7	0.5	1.50	1.35	7.5	9.8	9.2	8.2	6.2	CFT
TRANSAM ASR CO	AZ	U (1)	4.4	3.3	2.40	2.27	8.9	9.5	8.2	10.0	8.4	D
TRANSAMERICA FINANCIAL LIFE INS CO	NY	B-	19205.0	780.3	1.91	0.94	6.5	4.9	2.0	9.0	5.0	I
TRANSAMERICA LIFE INS CO	IA	B-	99285.7	4634.4	1.94	0.98	6.8	4.2	2.0	7.1	4.4	FGIT
TRH HEALTH INS CO	TN	U (1)	15.3	14.4	4.81	4.33	8.0	8.7	8.3	10.0	8.0	D
TRIANGLE LIFE INS CO	NC	C	6.0	4.0	2.31	2.08	8.6	8.3	5.7	8.6	4.3	AOT
TRINITY LIFE INS CO	OK	D+	3.6	2.1	1.71	1.54	7.8	9.8	2.0	9.4	1.8	DEG
TRIPLE S VIDA INC	PR	C+	340.7	47.9	1.22	0.81	5.5	6.4	2.0	4.8	4.6	CL
TRUASSURE INS CO	IL	D+	5.4	5.2	3.25	2.92	9.9	9.8	2.9	10.0	2.5	DFGT
TRUSTMARK INS CO	IL	B	1147.8	213.0	2.92	1.69	8.0	6.0	6.5	7.3	4.2	GIT
TRUSTMARK LIFE INS CO	IL	B	362.0	186.4	4.47	3.36	10.0	7.6	7.1	6.2	5.3	ADFT
TWIN LIFE INS CO	AZ	U (5)	--	--	--	--	--	--	--	--	--	Z
U S HEALTH & LIFE INS CO INC	MI	C	30.5	9.3	1.92	1.45	7.7	9.8	6.3	8.0	4.3	DF
UBS LIFE INS CO USA	CA	C+	41.9	36.2	6.21	5.59	10.0	9.6	8.0	7.0	4.4	DT
ULLICO LIFE INS CO	TX	C+	15.2	10.7	5.33	4.80	10.0	9.7	4.7	9.5	4.7	AD
UNICARE LIFE & HEALTH INS CO	IN	B	1672.9	340.3	1.04	0.79	4.7	6.5	8.9	0.6	4.5	CFL
UNIFIED LIFE INS CO	TX	B-	133.8	11.9	1.42	1.28	7.4	8.3	7.1	7.0	5.2	G
UNIMERICA INS CO	WI	B	246.9	107.4	2.16	1.67	8.0	8.6	6.7	7.1	4.1	GT
UNIMERICA LIFE INS CO OF NY	NY	B	26.2	16.9	3.52	2.68	9.5	9.2	2.0	9.6	4.2	DGT
▲ UNION BANKERS INS CO	TX	C+	107.4	19.0	2.35	1.66	8.0	7.2	5.7	7.1	4.5	ADG
UNION CENTRAL LIFE INS CO	OH	B-	6180.0	202.2	1.21	0.65	5.3	4.4	2.6	5.2	5.0	CIT
▼ UNION FIDELITY LIFE INS CO	IL	C-	18236.1	387.6	0.69	0.34	2.5	1.0	1.6	9.2	2.5	CI
UNION LABOR LIFE INS CO	MD	C+	4145.0	107.1	1.89	1.27	7.4	8.4	3.3	7.4	4.8	F
UNION LIFE INS CO	AR	U (1)	0.1	0.1	2.22	2.00	8.0	9.8	4.2	10.0	4.4	DT
UNION NATIONAL LIFE INS CO	LA	A	459.3	72.1	3.87	2.25	8.9	7.4	6.8	6.2	7.4	AD
UNION SECURITY INS CO	IA	C+	5293.4	338.7	1.35	0.83	5.6	5.4	6.1	3.4	3.3	AFLT
UNION SECURITY LIFE INS CO OF NY	NY	B	168.5	47.0	4.00	2.67	9.5	6.7	6.6	7.7	5.6	A
UNITED AMERICAN INS CO	NE	B	1504.7	130.8	0.81	0.59	3.7	5.8	8.3	6.8	4.1	CI
UNITED ASR LIFE INS CO	TX	D-	1.6	1.2	2.09	1.88	8.3	9.8	7.1	10.0	1.1	AD
UNITED BENEFIT LIFE INS CO	OH	U (1)	3.2	3.1	3.00	2.70	8.0	9.8	2.2	10.0	3.4	DF
UNITED BURIAL INS CO OF WINNSBORO	LA	U	--	--	--	--	--	--	--	--	--	Z
UNITED FARM FAMILY LIFE INS CO	IN	A	1712.9	203.5	2.83	1.61	7.9	6.5	7.0	6.5	7.4	I
UNITED FIDELITY LIFE INS CO	TX	D+	555.0	182.8	0.41	0.38	1.6	3.8	3.1	6.2	1.6	CDFIT
UNITED FUNERAL BENEFIT LIFE INS CO	OK	D	33.1	3.0	0.65	0.58	3.6	7.0	6.9	6.8	1.9	ACDT
UNITED FUNERAL DIR BENEFIT LIC	TX	D-	32.0	1.7	0.26	0.23	0.0	5.7	7.3	7.0	0.0	CI
UNITED HEALTHCARE INS CO	CT	C+	10972.7	2736.6	0.71	0.60	3.2	7.4	8.7	1.5	3.5	ACL

See Page 26 for explanation of footnotes and Page 27 for explanation of stability factors.

Arrows denote recent upgrades ▲ or downgrades ▼ (see Section VI for explanations)

64

www.thestreetratings.com

NET PREMIUM ($MIL)	IN-VESTED ASSETS ($MIL)	CASH	CMO & STRUCT. SECS.	OTH.INV. GRADE BONDS	NON-INV. GRADE BONDS	CMMON & PREF. STOCK	MORT IN GOOD STAND.	NON-PERF. MORT.	REAL ESTATE	OTHER INVEST-MENTS	INVEST. IN AFFIL	INSURANCE COMPANY NAME
0.4	25.4	22.8	29.4	47.1	0.4	0.0	0.2	0.1	0.0	0.0	0.0	TEXAS IMPERIAL LIFE INS CO
1.7	6.7	13.7	43.4	40.7	2.3	0.0	0.0	0.0	0.0	0.0	0.0	TEXAS INTERNATIONAL LIFE INS CO
29.5	640.3	0.6	25.4	55.2	3.5	2.9	6.4	0.0	0.3	5.9	0.0 ●	TEXAS LIFE INS CO
1.4	2.5	46.4	52.2	1.4	0.0	0.0	0.0	0.0	0.0	0.1	0.0	TEXAS MEMORIAL LIFE INS CO
0.0	1.0	8.6	75.9	0.0	0.0	6.9	0.0	0.0	0.0	8.6	0.0	TEXAS SECURITY MUTUAL LIFE INS CO
1.3	8.7	40.2	27.1	20.3	0.3	1.0	0.0	0.0	10.5	0.6	0.0	TEXAS SERVICE LIFE INS CO
--	--	--	--	--	--	--	--	--	--	--	--	THRIVENT FINANCIAL FOR LUTHERANS
33.9	1,202.2 (*)	1.1	31.4	50.2	8.8	0.9	0.0	0.0	0.0	2.0	4.0 ●	THRIVENT LIFE INS CO
67.7	2,362.6	0.3	23.1	69.4	1.8	1.9	3.4	0.0	0.0	0.1	0.1 ●	TIAA-CREF LIFE INS CO
328.8	604.6 (*)	0.0	7.5	56.6	9.7	10.2	15.9	0.0	2.6	3.3	0.0 ●	TIME INS CO
--	--	--	--	--	--	--	--	--	--	--	--	TIPPECANOE LIFE INS CO
0.4	73.7	0.7	13.3	61.1	0.7	0.5	2.2	0.0	12.0	9.5	0.0 ●	TOWER LIFE INS CO
0.4	5.1	26.5	0.0	59.4	0.0	2.1	11.7	0.0	0.0	0.4	0.0	TOWN & COUNTRY LIFE INS CO
0.2	19.6	3.7	0.0	68.4	0.0	23.3	0.0	0.0	4.6	0.0	23.3	TRANS CITY LIFE INS CO
6.6	24.3	28.4	29.3	27.1	0.0	9.9	0.0	0.0	4.9	0.4	0.0	TRANS OCEANIC LIFE INS CO
3.9	328.6	1.7	0.0	78.3	0.4	11.2	3.6	0.0	4.6	0.3	11.7 ●	TRANS WORLD ASR CO
0.0	0.6 (*)	57.1	0.0	0.0	0.0	0.0	0.0	0.0	0.0	0.0	0.0	TRANS-WESTERN LIFE INS CO
0.0	4.3	33.0	0.0	47.2	0.0	19.6	0.0	0.0	0.0	0.2	43.6	TRANSAM ASR CO
1,332.8	9,201.7	0.1	24.3	49.1	5.8	2.1	12.8	0.0	0.1	5.0	1.4 ●	TRANSAMERICA FINANCIAL LIFE INS CO
2,200.9	73,007.3	0.4	23.5	41.6	6.7	3.9	14.8	0.1	0.2	8.3	6.4 ●	TRANSAMERICA LIFE INS CO
0.0	14.9	5.1	0.0	94.9	0.0	0.0	0.0	0.0	0.0	0.0	0.0	TRH HEALTH INS CO
0.9	5.7	1.2	26.5	72.2	0.1	0.0	0.0	0.0	0.0	0.0	0.0	TRIANGLE LIFE INS CO
0.5	3.8	16.2	0.0	83.9	0.0	0.0	0.0	0.0	0.0	0.0	0.0	TRINITY LIFE INS CO
27.2	305.1	1.3	12.6	77.2	1.7	4.7	0.0	0.0	0.0	2.5	0.0 ●	TRIPLE S VIDA INC
0.1	5.2	9.9	0.0	79.0	0.0	0.0	0.0	0.0	0.0	11.1	0.0	TRUASSURE INS CO
66.4	1,104.8	0.0	30.9	52.2	2.5	7.3	3.2	0.0	2.4	1.6	2.0 ●	TRUSTMARK INS CO
97.4	342.2	-3.2	12.1	75.0	3.6	12.5	0.0	0.0	0.0	0.0	0.0 ●	TRUSTMARK LIFE INS CO
--	--	--	--	--	--	--	--	--	--	--	--	TWIN LIFE INS CO
7.7	27.2	3.3	0.0	96.7	0.0	0.0	0.0	0.0	0.0	0.0	0.0	U S HEALTH & LIFE INS CO INC
0.1	36.3	1.3	0.0	98.7	0.0	0.0	0.0	0.0	0.0	0.0	0.0 ●	UBS LIFE INS CO USA
0.3	14.7	1.3	20.9	77.6	0.0	0.0	0.0	0.0	0.0	0.4	0.0	ULLICO LIFE INS CO
644.2	1,347.6	-0.1	24.5	66.9	7.9	0.7	0.0	0.0	0.0	0.0	0.0 ●	UNICARE LIFE & HEALTH INS CO
5.9	88.0	1.4	34.4	56.3	0.6	0.0	0.8	0.0	0.0	6.6	0.0	UNIFIED LIFE INS CO
62.9	225.3	0.9	21.5	77.6	0.0	0.0	0.0	0.0	0.0	0.0	0.0 ●	UNIMERICA INS CO
1.8	24.2	1.3	8.3	90.4	0.0	0.0	0.0	0.0	0.0	0.0	0.0	UNIMERICA LIFE INS CO OF NY
12.5	101.1	1.7	30.9	63.0	1.0	0.0	0.0	0.0	0.0	3.5	0.0	UNION BANKERS INS CO
225.5	4,468.0	-0.2	19.8	56.9	3.0	3.8	12.3	0.0	0.3	4.0	0.5 ●	UNION CENTRAL LIFE INS CO
79.1	17,528.0	1.6	6.2	77.3	4.0	3.7	6.5	0.0	0.0	0.7	0.0 ●	UNION FIDELITY LIFE INS CO
39.3	347.2	-0.5	53.0	38.7	0.1	3.5	4.9	0.0	0.0	0.4	3.4 ●	UNION LABOR LIFE INS CO
0.0	0.1	100.0	0.0	0.0	0.0	0.0	0.0	0.0	0.0	0.0	0.0	UNION LIFE INS CO
21.9	419.8	7.0	12.8	62.0	1.1	4.5	0.0	0.0	1.0	12.0	0.0 ●	UNION NATIONAL LIFE INS CO
277.3	3,798.1	-0.8	4.3	56.2	7.0	7.9	22.2	0.0	0.0	3.3	0.0 ●	UNION SECURITY INS CO
12.1	152.1	0.7	8.9	59.2	5.4	6.9	18.7	0.0	0.0	0.2	0.0 ●	UNION SECURITY LIFE INS CO OF NY
210.8	1,272.4 (*)	0.0	0.5	80.2	2.6	10.5	0.0	0.0	0.0	7.8	4.5 ●	UNITED AMERICAN INS CO
0.1	1.4	43.9	0.0	56.1	0.0	0.0	0.0	0.0	0.0	0.0	0.0	UNITED ASR LIFE INS CO
0.0	3.2	27.0	0.0	73.0	0.0	0.0	0.0	0.0	0.0	0.0	0.0	UNITED BENEFIT LIFE INS CO
--	--	--	--	--	--	--	--	--	--	--	--	UNITED BURIAL INS CO OF WINNSBORO
33.1	1,639.1	1.4	21.2	49.1	1.4	3.8	15.1	0.0	0.4	7.6	1.2 ●	UNITED FARM FAMILY LIFE INS CO
2.9	544.9	-0.1	11.9	18.0	2.2	49.9	8.3	0.0	0.5	9.3	49.4 ●	UNITED FIDELITY LIFE INS CO
0.4	31.6	8.3	51.9	31.7	0.0	7.0	0.3	0.0	0.0	0.8	4.6	UNITED FUNERAL BENEFIT LIFE INS CO
0.5	30.6	7.2	49.6	37.5	1.0	2.1	1.9	0.0	0.0	0.7	0.0	UNITED FUNERAL DIR BENEFIT LIC
9,354.3	7,661.2	-4.0	22.7	70.1	0.3	10.5	0.0	0.0	0.0	0.4	11.6 ●	UNITED HEALTHCARE INS CO

● Bullets denote a more detailed analysis is available in Section II.

(*) Asset category percentages do not add up to 100%

INSURANCE COMPANY NAME	DOM. STATE	RATING	TOTAL ASSETS ($MIL)	CAPITAL & SURPLUS ($MIL)	RISK ADJUSTED CAPITAL RATIO 1	RISK ADJUSTED CAPITAL RATIO 2	CAPITAL-IZATION INDEX (PTS)	INVEST. SAFETY INDEX (PTS)	PROFIT-ABILITY INDEX (PTS)	LIQUIDITY INDEX (PTS)	STAB. INDEX (PTS)	STABILITY FACTORS
UNITED HEALTHCARE INS CO OF IL	IL	B	155.4	98.6	2.65	2.17	5.9	8.9	7.1	6.9	6.0	AD
UNITED HEALTHCARE INS CO OF OH	OH	B-	182.1	81.0	1.30	1.07	4.6	8.8	8.3	5.4	5.3	D
UNITED HERITAGE LIFE INS CO	ID	B	422.8	37.4	1.84	0.92	6.4	4.1	6.3	4.8	5.7	CDIL
UNITED HOME LIFE INS CO	IN	B	60.6	15.7	2.27	2.04	8.6	7.6	2.0	6.5	6.0	D
UNITED INS CO OF AMERICA	IL	B-	2036.1	206.1	1.46	0.80	5.7	3.1	6.6	5.6	5.1	ACI
UNITED INTERNATIONAL LIFE INS	OK	U (1)	2.8	0.8	0.85	0.77	5.2	9.8	2.0	5.4	2.2	DFT
UNITED INVESTORS LIFE INS CO	MO	B+	2518.4	380.2	6.15	3.29	10.0	6.2	8.9	6.4	5.7	AGIT
UNITED LIFE INS CO	IA	B	1359.1	153.3	2.90	1.45	7.7	6.1	7.9	6.9	6.5	AFGIT
UNITED NATIONAL LIFE INS CO OF AM	IL	D	7.1	2.0	1.07	0.97	6.8	8.3	1.9	7.0	1.7	FGT
UNITED OF OMAHA LIFE INS CO	NE	B+	12875.0	1155.9	1.96	1.12	7.2	5.6	4.8	6.2	6.4	I
UNITED SECURITY ASR CO OF PA	PA	B	66.8	21.6	2.38	2.01	8.5	8.7	8.9	9.2	4.8	DG
UNITED SECURITY LIFE & HEALTH INS CO	IL	D	21.6	3.5	0.44	0.34	1.1	6.4	1.2	3.0	1.1	CFLT
UNITED STATES LIFE INS CO IN NYC	NY	C	5259.4	257.9	1.80	0.98	6.8	5.2	1.8	6.1	4.1	T
UNITED TEACHER ASSOCIATES INS CO	TX	B-	512.0	58.5	1.41	0.87	6.0	5.6	6.6	6.1	5.3	A
UNITED TRUST INS CO	AL	B	5.4	4.2	2.67	2.41	9.1	9.8	4.9	9.8	4.9	DT
UNITED WORLD LIFE INS CO	NE	B+	114.6	40.3	3.33	1.40	7.6	7.4	7.8	8.2	6.7	A
UNITY FINANCIAL LIFE INS CO	PA	B-	75.4	6.8	0.91	0.82	5.6	7.3	4.7	6.9	5.0	A
UNITY MUTUAL LIFE INS CO	NY	C	263.7	23.5	2.86	1.51	7.8	6.8	3.8	4.0	4.3	DFLT
UNIVANTAGE INS CO	UT	U (1)	1.8	1.8	2.70	2.43	8.0	9.8	8.5	10.0	6.6	DT
UNIVERSAL FIDELITY LIFE INS CO	OK	D+	9.1	3.9	1.64	1.48	7.7	7.9	5.9	7.4	2.7	DGT
UNIVERSAL GUARANTY LIFE INS CO	OH	C-	255.8	26.4	1.04	0.71	5.1	4.5	5.0	6.0	3.0	DFI
UNIVERSAL LIFE INS CO	PR	C	132.4	20.4	2.24	1.65	8.0	7.1	6.0	9.1	3.1	CDT
▼ UNIVERSAL LIFE INS CO	AL	F	13.0	0.4	0.28	0.25	0.0	4.1	0.7	9.6	0.0	ACDIT
UNIVERSAL UNDERWRITERS LIFE INS CO	KS	B-	253.7	61.1	5.96	4.59	10.0	8.1	7.9	6.9	3.5	ADFT
UNUM LIFE INS CO OF AMERICA	ME	C+	16917.0	1396.9	2.44	1.34	7.5	4.5	5.7	7.3	4.8	AI
US FINANCIAL LIFE INS CO	OH	C	564.1	51.5	1.66	0.90	6.2	6.8	2.6	3.5	3.4	LT
USA INS CO	MS	C-	8.0	1.5	0.78	0.70	4.6	5.6	3.0	9.0	1.6	CDT
USA LIFE ONE INS CO OF INDIANA	IN	B-	36.2	16.6	3.14	2.83	9.7	7.4	7.1	7.0	4.0	D
USAA DIRECT LIFE INS CO	NE	U (1)	9.2	9.2	4.01	3.61	8.0	8.4	5.2	10.0	6.8	T
USAA LIFE INS CO	TX	A	13463.6	1144.8	4.04	2.20	8.8	6.1	8.4	6.2	7.4	GI
USAA LIFE INS CO OF NEW YORK	NY	B+	401.5	39.9	2.66	1.38	7.6	5.2	6.7	5.7	6.5	DGIL
USABLE LIFE	AR	A-	298.5	113.7	1.76	1.32	7.5	6.2	8.0	6.5	6.5	GI
USIC LIFE INS CO	PR	C+	3.4	3.1	2.77	2.49	9.2	3.7	4.1	7.0	3.4	EGIT
VALUE HEALTH REINS INC	AZ	U (5)	--	--	--	--	--	--	--	--	--	Z
VANTISLIFE INS CO	CT	C+	748.5	64.1	2.02	1.11	7.2	6.1	5.8	4.9	4.3	GLT
VARIABLE ANNUITY LIFE INS CO	TX	B	52157.7	3142.5	2.91	1.38	7.6	5.5	6.6	6.8	4.9	AIT
VERSANT LIFE INS CO	MS	C+	6.3	4.3	2.42	2.18	8.8	9.2	8.8	10.0	3.9	ADT
VISTA LIFE INS CO	MI	U (1)	39.6	37.8	6.74	6.06	4.0	8.7	6.7	10.0	6.0	
WACHOVIA LIFE INS CO	AZ	U	--	--	--	--	--	--	--	--	--	Z
WASHINGTON NATIONAL INS CO	IL	D+	2274.6	448.1	1.10	0.90	6.2	4.6	3.3	6.3	2.7	AFIT
WATEREE LIFE INS	SC	D+	10.4	8.6	3.51	3.16	10.0	9.0	9.1	10.0	2.5	D
WEA INS CORP	WI	B	546.2	219.9	1.85	1.43	6.7	6.4	7.5	6.2	5.7	DI
WELLMARK COMMUNITY INS INC	IA	U (1)	18.3	16.1	5.25	3.19	8.0	4.0	5.1	10.0	5.3	DIT
WEST COAST LIFE INS CO	NE	C	3389.4	320.5	1.19	0.75	5.3	5.1	1.9	5.6	4.2	A
WESTERN & SOUTHERN LIFE INS CO	OH	B	7416.9	3113.1	1.65	1.39	7.6	3.4	6.7	7.0	4.7	AIT
▲ WESTERN AMERICAN LIFE INS CO	TX	C	32.7	2.4	0.49	0.45	2.4	6.5	6.6	4.1	2.4	CDL
WESTERN MUTUAL INS CO	UT	B-	11.6	5.6	1.59	1.26	7.4	7.5	8.8	6.7	3.5	D
WESTERN NATIONAL LIFE INS CO	TX	B-	44187.0	2832.5	1.85	0.87	6.3	3.7	6.7	5.3	4.2	AFGIT
WESTERN RESERVE LIFE ASR CO OF OHIO	OH	B	7262.7	279.2	1.92	1.15	7.2	6.2	3.0	7.5	4.5	IT
WESTERN UNITED LIFE ASR CO	WA	F (1)	714.0	26.1	1.16	0.61	5.2	3.9	1.2	6.6	0.0	DFGIT
WESTERN-SOUTHERN LIFE ASR CO	OH	B-	10339.3	861.9	1.90	0.91	6.4	4.0	8.2	5.5	5.2	GI
WESTMARK LIFE INS CO	AZ	U	--	--	--	--	--	--	--	--	--	Z

See Page 26 for explanation of footnotes and Page 27 for explanation of stability factors.

66

www.thestreetratings.com

Arrows denote recent upgrades ▲ or downgrades ▼ (see Section VI for explanations)

NET PREMIUM ($MIL)	IN-VESTED ASSETS ($MIL)	CASH	CMO & STRUCT. SECS.	OTH.INV. GRADE BONDS	NON-INV. GRADE BONDS	CMMON & PREF. STOCK	MORT IN GOOD STAND.	NON-PERF. MORT.	REAL ESTATE	OTHER INVEST-MENTS	INVEST. IN AFFIL	INSURANCE COMPANY NAME
							% OF INVESTED ASSETS IN:					
79.2	118.6	0.0	6.7	93.3	0.0	0.0	0.0	0.0	0.0	0.0	0.0 ●	UNITED HEALTHCARE INS CO OF IL
117.9	149.5	0.0	12.6	87.4	0.0	0.0	0.0	0.0	0.0	0.0	0.0 ●	UNITED HEALTHCARE INS CO OF OH
14.7	403.3	1.8	28.9	46.4	5.1	4.9	9.3	0.0	1.6	2.1	0.0 ●	UNITED HERITAGE LIFE INS CO
3.2	53.2	4.3	15.5	72.0	0.9	3.3	0.1	0.2	0.0	3.7	0.0	UNITED HOME LIFE INS CO
50.5	1,880.2	-0.2	9.9	48.3	9.4	11.0	0.0	0.0	8.9	12.8	2.4 ●	UNITED INS CO OF AMERICA
0.0	2.8	2.4	0.0	97.6	0.0	0.0	0.0	0.0	0.0	0.0	0.0	UNITED INTERNATIONAL LIFE INS
94.3	1,021.1 (*)	1.2	0.3	65.8	5.6	21.3	0.0	0.0	0.0	3.1	18.4 ●	UNITED INVESTORS LIFE INS CO
72.0	1,297.3	0.6	2.6	89.2	5.6	0.9	0.6	0.0	0.0	0.6	0.0 ●	UNITED LIFE INS CO
0.8	6.7	2.8	28.5	55.8	2.3	0.0	9.3	0.0	0.0	1.4	0.0	UNITED NATIONAL LIFE INS CO OF AM
533.8	11,240.0	-0.1	39.1	35.2	5.1	1.3	14.4	0.1	0.6	4.3	3.6 ●	UNITED OF OMAHA LIFE INS CO
4.5	52.6	2.0	19.2	70.1	0.1	8.6	0.0	0.0	0.0	0.0	8.6	UNITED SECURITY ASR CO OF PA
9.3	21.4 (*)	11.9	16.1	47.7	0.0	17.0	0.0	0.0	0.0	2.9	0.0	UNITED SECURITY LIFE & HEALTH INS CO
131.9	4,784.3	0.2	22.0	57.5	5.9	2.0	7.7	0.0	0.0	4.7	2.8 ●	UNITED STATES LIFE INS CO IN NYC
49.1	479.5	-1.0	26.1	64.8	5.1	0.2	0.0	0.0	0.8	4.0	0.0 ●	UNITED TEACHER ASSOCIATES INS CO
0.1	4.8	26.6	0.0	73.5	0.0	0.0	0.0	0.0	0.0	0.0	0.0	UNITED TRUST INS CO
0.5	85.1	14.2	18.1	63.9	3.0	0.0	0.0	0.0	0.0	0.8	0.0 ●	UNITED WORLD LIFE INS CO
6.0	71.5	4.6	22.4	73.0	0.0	0.0	0.0	0.0	0.0	0.0	0.0	UNITY FINANCIAL LIFE INS CO
6.8	249.1	7.0	23.9	59.6	2.0	2.0	0.0	0.0	0.1	5.6	0.0	UNITY MUTUAL LIFE INS CO
0.0	1.8	60.8	0.0	39.2	0.0	0.0	0.0	0.0	0.0	0.0	0.0	UNIVANTAGE INS CO
0.3	6.2	-1.4	5.9	76.7	0.0	9.6	0.0	0.0	7.3	1.9	5.7	UNIVERSAL FIDELITY LIFE INS CO
2.6	253.5	6.0	28.2	15.3	1.8	18.1	16.5	0.2	2.9	10.9	13.0 ●	UNIVERSAL GUARANTY LIFE INS CO
8.9	65.4	5.6	20.2	63.3	4.3	6.8	0.0	0.0	0.0	0.0	0.0	UNIVERSAL LIFE INS CO
0.0	13.1	8.5	21.7	47.0	0.3	12.1	7.3	0.1	0.9	2.0	0.0	UNIVERSAL LIFE INS CO
2.7	240.9	1.7	43.2	52.6	0.0	0.2	0.0	0.0	0.0	2.3	0.0 ●	UNIVERSAL UNDERWRITERS LIFE INS CO
660.2	16,158.4	0.0	10.4	75.1	7.6	1.5	4.3	0.0	0.6	0.9	0.1 ●	UNUM LIFE INS CO OF AMERICA
16.3	489.9	1.3	1.0	91.4	2.2	1.2	0.0	0.0	0.0	3.0	0.0 ●	US FINANCIAL LIFE INS CO
0.2	7.8 (*)	57.5	0.0	0.0	3.6	0.0	28.0	0.0	14.4	0.2	5.4	USA INS CO
0.3	36.1	3.0	12.2	77.0	4.1	0.7	0.1	0.0	0.4	2.6	0.1	USA LIFE ONE INS CO OF INDIANA
0.0	9.1	32.9	0.0	45.2	0.0	0.0	0.0	0.0	0.0	21.9	0.0	USAA DIRECT LIFE INS CO
860.7	12,313.0	1.1	36.7	46.2	1.2	12.4	0.0	0.0	0.0	2.3	1.5 ●	USAA LIFE INS CO
23.3	368.9	2.8	30.1	56.1	1.3	8.7	0.0	0.0	0.0	1.2	0.0 ●	USAA LIFE INS CO OF NEW YORK
97.8	226.6	-0.3	0.0	83.7	1.0	14.3	0.0	0.0	0.0	1.4	0.1 ●	USABLE LIFE
0.1	3.3	3.7	0.0	71.6	24.8	0.0	0.0	0.0	0.0	0.0	0.0	USIC LIFE INS CO
--	--	--	--	--	--	--	--	--	--	--	--	VALUE HEALTH REINS INC
92.0	648.9	0.2	23.4	70.5	2.4	1.1	0.3	0.0	0.9	1.0	1.0 ●	VANTISLIFE INS CO
1,415.5	33,418.1	-0.3	29.7	38.4	6.8	2.2	13.0	0.0	0.1	10.4	1.7 ●	VARIABLE ANNUITY LIFE INS CO
0.0	6.4	29.7	0.0	70.4	0.0	0.0	0.0	0.0	0.0	0.0	0.0	VERSANT LIFE INS CO
0.0	39.2	0.0	54.6	45.4	0.0	0.0	0.0	0.0	0.0	0.0	0.0	VISTA LIFE INS CO
--	--	--	--	--	--	--	--	--	--	--	--	WACHOVIA LIFE INS CO
51.9	2,241.6	0.7	15.2	46.9	7.1	18.1	6.6	0.0	2.6	3.0	14.7 ●	WASHINGTON NATIONAL INS CO
0.2	10.1	7.8	0.0	92.2	0.0	0.0	0.0	0.0	0.0	0.0	0.0	WATEREE LIFE INS
214.8	510.0	0.4	17.8	68.8	0.0	12.6	0.0	0.0	0.0	0.0	0.0 ●	WEA INS CORP
0.0	18.1	0.6	19.9	41.6	0.0	38.0	0.0	0.0	0.0	0.0	0.0	WELLMARK COMMUNITY INS INC
52.5	3,313.6	0.0	14.5	49.1	5.0	8.6	21.7	0.0	0.0	1.1	4.1 ●	WEST COAST LIFE INS CO
65.2	6,883.3	-0.1	10.3	35.6	1.5	40.0	0.7	0.0	1.0	11.7	30.9 ●	WESTERN & SOUTHERN LIFE INS CO
0.8	31.7	2.3	84.2	10.8	0.3	1.9	0.0	0.0	0.0	0.1	0.0	WESTERN AMERICAN LIFE INS CO
4.5	10.6	6.8	0.0	79.0	0.0	12.6	0.0	0.0	0.0	1.7	2.7	WESTERN MUTUAL INS CO
933.4	44,639.7	-0.7	25.5	52.4	7.4	1.7	5.7	0.0	0.0	8.0	1.5 ●	WESTERN NATIONAL LIFE INS CO
218.4	1,425.2	0.5	21.3	38.1	3.2	2.1	0.9	0.0	2.7	31.2	1.8 ●	WESTERN RESERVE LIFE ASR CO OF OHIO
103.7	683.9	0.4	27.5	63.3	1.1	2.5	0.0	1.7	2.5	1.0	0.0	WESTERN UNITED LIFE ASR CO
406.5	9,711.4	0.0	31.9	47.5	8.4	4.9	6.1	0.0	0.0	1.4	1.1 ●	WESTERN-SOUTHERN LIFE ASR CO
--	--	--	--	--	--	--	--	--	--	--	--	WESTMARK LIFE INS CO

● Bullets denote a more detailed analysis is available in Section II.

(*) Asset category percentages do not add up to 100%

INSURANCE COMPANY NAME	DOM. STATE	RATING	TOTAL ASSETS ($MIL)	CAPITAL & SURPLUS ($MIL)	RISK ADJUSTED CAPITAL RATIO 1	RISK ADJUSTED CAPITAL RATIO 2	CAPITAL- IZATION INDEX (PTS)	INVEST. SAFETY INDEX (PTS)	PROFIT- ABILITY INDEX (PTS)	LIQUIDITY INDEX (PTS)	STAB. INDEX (PTS)	STABILITY FACTORS
WESTPORT LIFE INS CO	AZ	C	14.5	8.2	2.81	2.53	9.3	8.8	6.7	8.0	3.4	AT
WESTWARD LIFE INS CO	AZ	C-	13.3	11.1	2.99	2.69	9.5	9.6	4.6	10.0	2.6	DT
WICHITA NATIONAL LIFE INS CO	OK	C	18.8	7.1	2.11	1.90	8.4	8.9	7.3	9.3	4.3	T
WILBERT LIFE INS CO	LA	U	--	--	--	--	--	--	--	--	--	Z
WILLIAM PENN LIFE INS CO OF NEW YORK	NY	C-	964.4	97.9	2.44	1.36	7.5	7.3	2.3	5.0	3.1	AGT
WILLIAMS PROGRESSIVE LIFE & ACC I C	LA	D+	10.6	1.7	0.70	0.63	4.0	4.1	2.9	6.6	2.5	CI
WILTON REASSURANCE CO	MN	D	670.9	146.1	1.13	0.97	6.8	6.3	1.5	8.6	2.0	AGT
WILTON REASSURANCE LIFE CO OF NY	NY	D-	1173.2	66.9	1.35	0.72	5.5	3.9	2.8	2.5	1.4	FL
WINDSOR LIFE INS CO	TX	B-	2.8	2.7	2.93	2.64	9.5	9.6	4.1	10.0	4.0	DFOT
WINNFIELD LIFE INS CO	LA	D+	37.9	6.8	1.29	0.98	6.8	3.1	6.6	6.3	2.5	IO
WONDER STATE LIFE INS CO	AR	U (5)	--	--	--	--	--	--	--	--	--	Z
WOODMEN OF THE WORLD/ASSURED LIFE	CO	U	--	--	--	--	--	--	--	--	--	Z
WORKMENS LIFE INS CO	AZ	U (1)	0.5	0.5	2.17	1.95	8.0	9.7	2.0	7.0	2.2	DF
WORLD CORP INS CO	NE	B+	23.2	22.3	5.80	5.22	10.0	8.2	6.7	9.0	6.1	DT
WORLD INS CO	NE	A-	242.3	104.0	2.00	1.64	8.0	6.0	7.7	6.6	6.2	FGIT
WORLD SERVICE LIFE INS CO	CO	U (1)	8.9	2.3	0.96	0.86	5.9	7.9	7.0	7.6	4.4	DFT
XL LIFE INS & ANNUITY CO	IL	U (1)	82.5	16.0	3.38	1.70	8.0	7.1	2.1	6.9	4.1	ADT
XL RE LIFE AMERICA INC	DE	D+	55.9	32.4	4.33	2.77	9.7	8.6	1.8	7.0	2.4	GT
YADKIN VALLEY LIFE INS CO	AZ	U	--	--	--	--	--	--	--	--	--	Z
ZACHARY TAYLOR LIFE INS CO	LA	U	--	--	--	--	--	--	--	--	--	Z
ZALE LIFE INS CO	AZ	B-	10.7	8.2	3.11	2.80	9.7	7.3	7.9	9.0	5.1	A

See Page 26 for explanation of footnotes and Page 27 for explanation of stability factors.
Arrows denote recent upgrades ▲ or downgrades ▼ (see Section VI for explanations)

68

www.thestreetratings.com

NET PREMIUM ($MIL)	IN-VESTED ASSETS ($MIL)	% OF INVESTED ASSETS IN:										INSURANCE COMPANY NAME
		CASH	CMO & STRUCT. SECS.	OTH.INV. GRADE BONDS	NON-INV. GRADE BONDS	CMMON & PREF. STOCK	MORT IN GOOD STAND.	NON-PERF. MORT.	REAL ESTATE	OTHER INVEST-MENTS	INVEST. IN AFFIL	
0.5	14.1	6.0	37.7	56.3	0.0	0.0	0.0	0.0	0.0	0.0	0.0	WESTPORT LIFE INS CO
0.0	23.4	4.4	14.7	80.9	0.0	0.0	0.0	0.0	0.0	0.0	0.9	WESTWARD LIFE INS CO
0.9	18.5	78.3	5.0	0.0	0.0	9.1	1.6	0.0	1.5	4.5	9.1	WICHITA NATIONAL LIFE INS CO
--	--	--	--	--	--	--	--	--	--	--	--	WILBERT LIFE INS CO
14.1	926.6	-0.6	15.8	78.7	0.6	0.8	0.0	0.0	0.0	4.7	0.0 ●	WILLIAM PENN LIFE INS CO OF NEW YORK
0.4	10.4	4.6	11.6	32.3	2.1	20.0	26.4	0.0	2.6	0.4	4.1	WILLIAMS PROGRESSIVE LIFE & ACC I C
22.6	612.1	5.6	15.4	64.3	0.3	13.2	0.0	0.0	0.0	0.5	15.8 ●	WILTON REASSURANCE CO
13.8	1,157.4	0.5	40.4	46.2	2.2	7.7	0.0	0.0	0.0	3.0	0.0 ●	WILTON REASSURANCE LIFE CO OF NY
0.0	2.8	3.1	0.0	97.0	0.0	0.0	0.0	0.0	0.0	0.0	0.0	WINDSOR LIFE INS CO
0.5	37.1 (*)	1.1	33.9	34.0	4.4	6.0	9.8	8.9	0.2	0.0	--	WINNFIELD LIFE INS CO
--	--	--	--	--	--	--	--	--	--	--	--	WONDER STATE LIFE INS CO
--	--	--	--	--	--	--	--	--	--	--	--	WOODMEN OF THE WORLD/ASSURED LIFE
0.0	0.5	2.7	0.0	96.6	0.0	0.8	0.0	0.0	0.0	0.0	0.0	WORKMENS LIFE INS CO
0.4	23.0	2.4	25.4	70.2	2.0	0.0	0.0	0.0	0.0	0.0	0.0	WORLD CORP INS CO
54.9	193.7	-0.3	29.2	51.3	1.6	15.5	0.0	0.0	0.0	2.7	11.4 ●	WORLD INS CO
0.0	8.9	0.3	0.0	92.0	0.0	4.2	0.0	0.0	0.0	3.6	0.0	WORLD SERVICE LIFE INS CO
0.0	70.1	0.0	46.7	50.1	3.3	0.0	0.0	0.0	0.0	0.0	0.0	XL LIFE INS & ANNUITY CO
2.1	56.3	4.9	40.7	53.9	0.6	0.0	0.0	0.0	0.0	0.0	0.0 ●	XL RE LIFE AMERICA INC
--	--	--	--	--	--	--	--	--	--	--	--	YADKIN VALLEY LIFE INS CO
--	--	--	--	--	--	--	--	--	--	--	--	ZACHARY TAYLOR LIFE INS CO
0.5	11.5	6.8	7.8	76.1	0.0	7.7	0.0	0.0	0.0	1.7	0.0	ZALE LIFE INS CO

● **Bullets denote a more detailed analysis is available in Section II.**

(*) Asset category percentages do not add up to 100%

Section II

Analysis of Largest Companies

A summary analysis of those

U.S. Life and Annuity Insurers

with capital in excess of $25 million.

Companies are listed in alphabetical order.

Section II Contents

This section contains rating factors, historical data and general information on each of the largest life and health insurers. Companies with capital and surplus of less than $25 million, Blue Cross Blue Shield plans and companies lacking year-end data do not appear in this section. You can find information on these firms in Section I.

1. **Financial Strength Rating**

   The current rating appears to the right of the company name. Our ratings are designed to distinguish levels of insolvency risk and are measured on a scale from A (Excellent) to F (Failed). Highly rated companies are, in our opinion, less likely to experience financial difficulties than lower rated firms. See *About TheStreet.com Financial Strength Ratings* on page 9 for more information.

2. **Major Rating Factors**

   A synopsis of the key indexes and sub-factors that have most influenced the rating of a particular insurer. Items are presented in the approximate order of their importance to the rating. There may be additional factors which have influenced the rating but do not appear due to space limitations or confidentiality agreements with insurers.

3. **Other Rating Factors**

   A summary of those TheStreet.com Ratings indexes that were not included as Major Rating Factors, but nevertheless, may have had some impact on the final grade.

4. **Principal Business**

   The major types of policies written by an insurer along with the percentages for each line in relation to the entire book of business, including direct premium and deposit funds (from Exhibit 1 Part 1 of the annual statutory statement). Lines of business written by life, health and annuity insurers are individual life, individual health, individual annuities, group life, group health, group retirement contracts, credit life, credit health and reinsurance. The data used to calculate these amounts are the latest available from the National Association of Insurance Commissioners.

   Note: Percentages contained in this column may not agree with similar figures displayed in Section III which are based on net premium after reinsurance.

5. **Principal Investments**

   The major investments in an insurer's portfolio. These include nonCMO Bonds (debt obligations which are rated Class 1 through Class 6 based on risk of default), CMOs and other structured securities, which consist primarily of mortgage-backed bonds, real estate, mortgages in good standing, nonperforming mortgages, common and preferred stocks, policy loans (which are loans given to policyholders), miscellaneous investments and cash.

6. Investments in Affiliates

The percentage of bonds, common and preferred stocks and other financial instruments an insurer has invested with affiliated companies. This is not a subcategory of "Principal Investments."

7. Group Affiliation

The name of the group of companies to which a particular insurer belongs.

8. Licensed in

List of the states in which an insurer is licensed to conduct business.

9. Commenced Business

The date when the company first opened for business.

10. Address

The address of an insurer's corporate headquarters. This location may differ from the company's state of domicile.

11. Phone

The telephone number of an insurer's corporate headquarters.

12. Domicile State

The state that has primary regulatory responsibility for this company. You do not have to live in the domicile state to do business with this firm, provided it is registered to do business in your state.

13. NAIC Code

The identification number assigned to an insurer by the National Association of Insurance Commissioners (NAIC).

14. Historical Data

Five years of background data for TheStreet.com Financial Strength Rating, risk-adjusted capital ratios (moderate and severe loss scenarios), total assets, capital (including capital stock and retained earnings), net premium and net income. See the following page for more details on how to read the historical data table.

15. Customized Graph (or Table)

A graph or table depicting one of the company's major strengths or weaknesses. See the following page for more details.

How to Read the Historical Data Table

Data Date:
The quarterly or annual date of the financial statements that provide the source of the data.

RACR#1:
Ratio of the capital resources an insurer currently has to the resources that would be needed to deal with a modest loss scenario.

Total Assets:
Total admitted assets in millions of dollars, including investments and other business assets.

Net Premiums:
The total volume of premium dollars, in millions, retained by an insurer. This figure is equal to direct premiums written plus deposit funds, and reinsurance assumed, less reinsurance ceded.

Data Date	Financial Strength Rating	RACR #1	RACR #2	Total Assets ($mil)	Capital ($mil)	Net Premium ($mil)	Net Income ($mil)
3-09	B	2.40	1.41	387.2	69.9	23.7	-0.6
3-08	B	2.62	1.55	299.0	67.3	18.3	0.3
2008	B	2.30	1.35	291.0	56.9	16.0	1.2
2007	B	2.71	1.61	296.3	68.7	75.3	6.6
2006	B	2.26	1.32	284.7	55.8	67.9	-2.6
2005	B-	2.09	1.23	265.5	49.2	62.5	-0.7
2004	B-	1.64	0.97	246.2	34.5	76.3	-0.7

Financial Strength Rating:
Our opinion of the financial risk of an insurer based on data from that time period.

RACR #2:
Ratio of the capital resources an insurer currently has to the resources that would be needed to deal with a severe loss scenario.

Capital:
The equity or net worth of an insurer in millions of dollars.

Net Income:
Profit gained on operations and investments, after expenses and taxes.

Row Descriptions:

Row 1 contains the most recent quarterly data as filed with state regulators and is presented on a year-to-date basis. For example, the figure for third quarter premiums includes premiums received through the third quarter. **Row 2** consists of data from the same quarter of the prior year. Compare current quarterly results to those of a year ago.

Row 3 contains data from the most recent annual statutory filing. **Rows 4-7** include data from year-end statements going back four years from the most recent annual filing. Compare current year-end results to those of the previous four years. With the exception of Total Assets and Capital, quarterly data are not comparable with annual data.

Customized Graphs

In the lower right-hand corner of each company section, a customized graph or text block highlights a key factor affecting that company's financial strength. One of fifteen types of information is found, identified by one of the following headings:

Adverse Trends in Operations lists changes in key balance sheet and income statement items which may be leading indicators of deteriorating business performance.

Exposure to Withdrawals Without Penalty answers the question: For each dollar of capital and surplus, how much does the company have in annuity and deposit funds that can be withdrawn by policyholders with minimal or no penalty? The figures do not include the effects of reinsurance or funds subject to withdrawals from cash value life insurance policies.

Group Ratings shows the group name, a composite TheStreet.com Financial Strength Rating for the group, and a list of the largest members with their ratings. The composite Financial Strength Rating is made up of the weighted average, by assets, of the individual ratings of each company in the group (including life/health companies, property/casualty companies or HMOs) plus a factor for the financial strength of the holding company, where applicable.

High Risk Assets as a % of Capital answers the question: For each dollar of capital and surplus, how much does the company have in junk bonds, nonperforming mortgages and repossessed real estate? Accumulations in the Asset Valuation Reserve or AVR, which provide some protection against investment losses, have not been included in the figure for capital. These figures are based on year-end data.

Investment Income Compared to Needs of Reserves answers the question: Is the company earning enough investment income to meet the expectations of actuaries when they priced their policies and set reserve levels? According to state insurance regulators, it would be "unusual" if an insurer were to have less than $1.25 in actual investment income for each dollar of investment income that it projected in its actuarial forecasts. This provides an excess margin of at least 25 cents on the dollar to cover any unexpected decline in income or increase in claims. This graph shows whether or not the company is maintaining the appropriate 25% margin and is based on year-end data.

Junk Bonds as a % of Capital answers the question: For each dollar of capital and surplus, how much does the company have in junk bonds? In addition, it shows a breakdown of the junk bond portfolio by bond rating – BB, B, CCC or in default. Accumulations in the Asset Valuation Reserve or AVR, which provide some protection against investment losses, have not been included in the figure for capital. These figures are based on year-end data.

Net Income History plots operating gains and losses over the most recent five-year period.

Policy Leverage answers the question: To what degree is this insurer capable of handling an unexpected spike in claims? Low leverage indicates low exposure; high leverage is high exposure.

Premium Growth History depicts the change in the insurer's net premiums written. Such changes may be the result of issuing more policies or changes in reinsurance arrangements. In either case, growth rates above 20% per year are considered excessive. "Standard" growth is under 20%; "shrinkage" refers to net declines.

Rating Indexes illustrate the score and range – strong, good, fair or weak – on each of the five TheStreet.com indexes. The indexes are **capitalization**, **stability**, **investment safety**, **profitability** and **liquidity**.

Risk-Adjusted Capital Ratio #1 answers the question: In each of the past five years, does the insurer have sufficient capital to cover potential losses in its investments and business operations in a *moderate* loss scenario?

Risk-Adjusted Capital Ratio #2 answers the question: In each of the past five years, does the insurer have sufficient capital to cover potential losses in its investments and business operations in a *severe* loss scenario?

Risk-Adjusted Capital Ratios answers these questions for both a moderate loss scenario (RACR #1 shown by the dark bar) and a severe loss scenario (RACR #2, light bar).

AAA LIFE INSURANCE COMPANY   B   Good

Major Rating Factors: Good quality investment portfolio (6.8 on a scale of 0 to 10) despite mixed results such as: no exposure to mortgages and substantial holdings of BBB bonds but small junk bond holdings. Good overall results on stability tests (5.2). Strengths include good financial support from affiliation with California State Auto Group, good operational trends, good risk adjusted capital for prior years and excellent risk diversification. Fair profitability (4.1) with operating losses during the first three months of 2009.

Other Rating Factors: Strong capitalization (7.6) based on excellent risk adjusted capital (severe loss scenario). Excellent liquidity (7.6).

Principal Business: Individual life insurance (40%), individual annuities (30%), group life insurance (17%), group health insurance (11%), and individual health insurance (2%).

Principal Investments: NonCMO investment grade bonds (71%), CMOs and structured securities (18%), noninv. grade bonds (5%), common & preferred stock (2%), and misc. investments (4%).

Investments in Affiliates: None

Group Affiliation: California State Auto Group

Licensed in: All states except AL, NC

Commenced Business: July 1969

Address: 1440 NY Ave NW Ste 200, Washington, DC 20005

Phone: (734) 779-2085 **Domicile State:** MI **NAIC Code:** 71854

Data Date	Rating	RACR #1	RACR #2	Total Assets ($mil)	Capital ($mil)	Net Premium ($mil)	Net Income ($mil)
3-09	B	2.40	1.41	387.2	69.9	23.7	-0.6
3-08	B	2.62	1.55	299.0	67.3	18.3	0.3
2008	B	2.50	1.48	369.4	71.9	146.3	-6.2
2007	B	2.71	1.61	296.3	68.7	75.3	6.6
2006	B	2.26	1.32	284.7	55.8	67.9	-2.6
2005	B-	2.09	1.23	265.5	49.2	62.5	-0.7
2004	B-	1.64	0.97	246.2	34.5	76.3	-0.7

California State Auto Group Composite Group Rating: B+ Largest Group Members	Assets ($mil)	Rating
CALIFORNIA STATE AUTO ASN INTER-INS	5100	A-
AAA LIFE INS CO	369	B
PACIFIC BEACON LIFE REASSUR INC	285	C
WESTERN UNITED INS CO	135	C+
ACA INS CO	47	C+

ACACIA LIFE INSURANCE COMPANY *   A-   Excellent

Major Rating Factors: Good overall results on stability tests (5.4 on a scale of 0 to 10) despite negative cash flow from operations for 2008. Strengths that enhance stability include good operational trends and excellent risk diversification. Good quality investment portfolio (6.7) despite significant exposure to mortgages . Mortgage default rate has been low. substantial holdings of BBB bonds in addition to small junk bond holdings. Good liquidity (6.5).

Other Rating Factors: Strong capitalization (7.5) based on excellent risk adjusted capital (severe loss scenario). Excellent profitability (7.3) with operating gains in each of the last five years.

Principal Business: Individual life insurance (86%), reinsurance (8%), and individual annuities (7%).

Principal Investments: NonCMO investment grade bonds (50%), common & preferred stock (15%), CMOs and structured securities (14%), mortgages in good standing (12%), and misc. investments (10%).

Investments in Affiliates: 13%

Group Affiliation: UNIFI Mutual Holding Co

Licensed in: All states except AL, AZ, MD, NC

Commenced Business: March 1869

Address: 7315 Wisconsin Ave, Bethesda, MD 20814

Phone: (301) 280-1000 **Domicile State:** DC **NAIC Code:** 60038

Data Date	Rating	RACR #1	RACR #2	Total Assets ($mil)	Capital ($mil)	Net Premium ($mil)	Net Income ($mil)
3-09	A-	1.62	1.33	1,521.4	317.0	7.2	-2.4
3-08	A-	2.04	1.53	1,632.3	345.4	8.5	3.0
2008	A-	2.04	1.51	1,547.4	323.2	33.3	0.0
2007	A-	2.75	1.90	1,647.3	341.4	29.8	21.4
2006	A-	3.86	2.28	1,651.4	298.1	37.6	19.3
2005	B+	3.52	2.07	1,652.6	258.8	45.4	7.7
2004	B+	3.44	1.95	1,647.3	237.3	49.4	51.0

Adverse Trends in Operations
Decrease in capital during 2008 (5%)
Decrease in asset base during 2008 (6%)
Decrease in premium volume from 2006 to 2007 (21%)
Decrease in premium volume from 2005 to 2006 (17%)
Decrease in premium volume from 2004 to 2005 (8%)

ADVANCE INS CO OF KS   B   Good

Major Rating Factors: Good overall results on stability tests (6.3 on a scale of 0 to 10). Stability strengths include good operational trends and excellent risk diversification. Good quality investment portfolio (6.2) with no exposure to mortgages and minimal holdings in junk bonds. Good overall profitability (6.6). Return on equity has been fair, averaging 5.3%.

Other Rating Factors: Strong capitalization (9.8) based on excellent risk adjusted capital (severe loss scenario). Excellent liquidity (7.0).

Principal Business: Group life insurance (54%), group health insurance (35%), and individual life insurance (11%).

Principal Investments: NonCMO investment grade bonds (47%), CMOs and structured securities (33%), and common & preferred stock (17%).

Investments in Affiliates: 2%

Group Affiliation: Blue Cross Blue Shield Kansas

Licensed in: KY

Commenced Business: July 2004

Address: 1133 SW Topeka Blvd, Topeka, KS 66629-0001

Phone: (785) 291-7052 **Domicile State:** KS **NAIC Code:** 12143

Data Date	Rating	RACR #1	RACR #2	Total Assets ($mil)	Capital ($mil)	Net Premium ($mil)	Net Income ($mil)
3-09	B	4.10	2.87	38.6	33.2	2.7	0.0
3-08	B	3.70	2.57	39.9	32.9	2.8	0.6
2008	B	4.13	2.90	38.1	33.3	11.1	0.4
2007	B	3.72	2.58	39.0	32.4	11.2	2.7
2006	B	4.01	2.76	49.5	42.3	10.6	3.9
2005	B	2.87	2.34	44.8	38.8	9.5	2.8
2004	C+	2.90	2.38	41.8	37.0	2.2	0.7

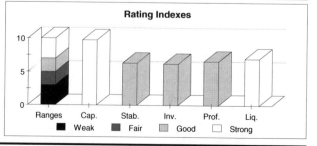

Rating Indexes

Ranges Cap. Stab. Inv. Prof. Liq.

■ Weak ▩ Fair ▨ Good □ Strong

AETNA HEALTH & LIFE INS CO   B   Good

Major Rating Factors: Good overall results on stability tests (6.1 on a scale of 0 to 10). Stability strengths include excellent operational trends and excellent risk diversification. Good quality investment portfolio (6.3) despite mixed results such as: substantial holdings of BBB bonds but moderate junk bond exposure. Fair profitability (4.6) with operating losses during the first three months of 2009.

Other Rating Factors: Strong capitalization (7.6) based on excellent risk adjusted capital (severe loss scenario). Excellent liquidity (7.3).

Principal Business: Reinsurance (100%).

Principal Investments: NonCMO investment grade bonds (71%), CMOs and structured securities (11%), mortgages in good standing (10%), noninv. grade bonds (4%), and common & preferred stock (1%).

Investments in Affiliates: 3%

Group Affiliation: Aetna Inc

Licensed in: All states except AL, GA, MT, NJ, NC

Commenced Business: October 1971

Address: 151 Farmington Avenue, Hartford, IL 06156-0417

Phone: (708) 245-4001   **Domicile State:** CT   **NAIC Code:** 78700

Data Date	Rating	RACR #1	RACR #2	Total Assets ($mil)	Capital ($mil)	Net Premium ($mil)	Net Income ($mil)
3-09	B	2.36	1.43	1,654.7	159.7	98.8	-1.0
3-08	B	3.65	2.19	1,627.7	210.0	87.6	4.3
2008	B	2.51	1.54	1,604.3	161.3	359.0	-6.7
2007	B	3.77	2.26	1,581.6	208.5	304.4	16.9
2006	B-	3.47	2.00	1,533.8	180.9	259.2	19.0
2005	C+	3.31	1.91	1,394.2	167.7	254.1	-7.0
2004	C	3.07	1.73	1,261.2	124.0	189.2	-4.3

Adverse Trends in Operations

Decrease in capital during 2008 (23%)

AETNA LIFE INSURANCE COMPANY   B   Good

Major Rating Factors: Good quality investment portfolio (6.2 on a scale of 0 to 10) despite significant exposure to mortgages . Mortgage default rate has been low. large holdings of BBB rated bonds in addition to small junk bond holdings. Good overall profitability (6.4) although investment income, in comparison to reserve requirements, is below regulatory standards. Good liquidity (6.5).

Other Rating Factors: Good overall results on stability tests (5.8) good operational trends and excellent risk diversification. Strong capitalization (7.6) based on excellent risk adjusted capital (severe loss scenario).

Principal Business: Group health insurance (65%), individual health insurance (26%), group life insurance (7%), and group retirement contracts (1%).

Principal Investments: NonCMO investment grade bonds (57%), CMOs and structured securities (16%), mortgages in good standing (11%), noninv. grade bonds (5%), and misc. investments (12%).

Investments in Affiliates: 4%

Group Affiliation: Aetna Inc

Licensed in: All states except AL

Commenced Business: December 1850

Address: 151 Farmington Ave, Hartford, CT 06156

Phone: (860) 273-0123   **Domicile State:** CT   **NAIC Code:** 60054

Data Date	Rating	RACR #1	RACR #2	Total Assets ($mil)	Capital ($mil)	Net Premium ($mil)	Net Income ($mil)
3-09	B	1.96	1.41	21,125.8	3,884.7	3,885.4	352.9
3-08	B-	2.06	1.45	21,907.8	3,366.0	3,447.9	316.8
2008	B-	1.96	1.40	20,880.6	3,743.5	13,647.5	951.2
2007	B-	2.02	1.40	33,471.0	3,239.2	10,716.9	1,163.2
2006	B-	2.22	1.50	32,339.2	3,037.2	8,667.7	981.0
2005	C+	2.43	1.61	29,120.8	2,915.2	6,744.5	825.1
2004	C+	2.35	1.51	27,017.7	2,448.2	5,256.3	566.4

Rating Indexes

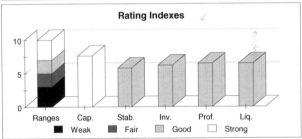

AIG LIFE INSURANCE COMPANY   C+   Fair

Major Rating Factors: Fair overall results on stability tests (4.3 on a scale of 0 to 10) including fair financial strength of affiliated American International Group and negative cash flow from operations for 2008. Fair quality investment portfolio (3.7) with large holdings of BBB rated bonds in addition to significant exposure to junk bonds. Good capitalization (5.9) based on good risk adjusted capital (moderate loss scenario).

Other Rating Factors: Good overall profitability (5.5) despite operating losses during the first three months of 2009. Good liquidity (6.5).

Principal Business: Group health insurance (40%), group retirement contracts (19%), individual life insurance (16%), individual annuities (11%), and other lines (13%).

Principal Investments: NonCMO investment grade bonds (60%), CMOs and structured securities (17%), noninv. grade bonds (7%), mortgages in good standing (7%), and misc. investments (9%).

Investments in Affiliates: None

Group Affiliation: American International Group

Licensed in: All states except AL, NC

Commenced Business: September 1962

Address: One ALICO Plaza, Wilmington, DE 19801

Phone: (302) 594-2000   **Domicile State:** DE   **NAIC Code:** 66842

Data Date	Rating	RACR #1	RACR #2	Total Assets ($mil)	Capital ($mil)	Net Premium ($mil)	Net Income ($mil)
3-09	C+	1.57	0.78	9,295.5	377.9	49.1	-14.2
3-08	B-	1.38	0.68	10,515.9	343.2	91.6	-128.9
2008	C+	1.57	0.77	9,429.4	364.4	351.3	-875.6
2007	B-	1.80	0.89	10,790.2	444.8	440.4	48.7
2006	C+	2.33	1.17	11,146.8	570.0	310.9	108.7
2005	C+	2.18	1.06	12,583.0	636.0	244.8	151.2
2004	C+	2.21	1.11	13,585.0	740.0	301.4	131.6

American International Group Composite Group Rating: C+ Largest Group Members	Assets ($mil)	Rating
AMERICAN LIFE INS CO	86338	C-
VARIABLE ANNUITY LIFE INS CO	53699	B
WESTERN NATIONAL LIFE INS CO	45803	B-
AMERICAN GENERAL LIFE INS CO	38638	C+
NATIONAL UNION FIRE INS CO OF PITTSB	33707	B

AIG SUNAMERICA LIFE ASSURANCE COMPANY

C+   **Fair**

Major Rating Factors: Fair overall results on stability tests (3.2 on a scale of 0 to 10) including fair financial strength of affiliated American International Group, weak results on operational trends and negative cash flow from operations for 2008. Good quality investment portfolio (6.0) despite mixed results such as: minimal exposure to mortgages and substantial holdings of BBB bonds but minimal holdings in junk bonds. Weak profitability (1.9) with investment income below regulatory standards in relation to interest assumptions of reserves.

Other Rating Factors: Strong capitalization (7.8) based on excellent risk adjusted capital (severe loss scenario). Excellent liquidity (9.5).

Principal Business: Group retirement contracts (54%), individual annuities (45%), and individual life insurance (1%).

Principal Investments: NonCMO investment grade bonds (54%), CMOs and structured securities (13%), mortgages in good standing (8%), policy loans (3%), and common & preferred stock (3%).

Investments in Affiliates: 2%

Group Affiliation: American International Group

Licensed in: All states except AL, NC

Commenced Business: August 1965

Address: 1 SunAmerica Center, Los Angeles, CA 90067-6022

Phone: (310) 772-6000   **Domicile State:** AZ   **NAIC Code:** 60941

Data Date	Rating	RACR #1	RACR #2	Total Assets ($mil)	Capital ($mil)	Net Premium ($mil)	Net Income ($mil)
3-09	C+	2.65	1.54	22,319.4	900.2	256.6	29.3
3-08	B	2.95	1.73	32,574.9	1,104.2	977.8	-114.4
2008	C+	3.73	2.17	24,396.3	1,274.7	3,300.0	-782.3
2007	B	3.00	1.75	35,072.4	1,154.7	4,325.5	175.4
2006	B-	2.26	1.32	32,726.5	788.9	4,146.4	147.4
2005	B-	1.81	1.04	31,514.7	950.6	3,220.5	171.5
2004	C+	1.47	0.86	29,749.4	840.0	4,017.6	99.3

American International Group
Composite Group Rating: C+
Largest Group Members

	Assets ($mil)	Rating
AMERICAN LIFE INS CO	86338	C-
VARIABLE ANNUITY LIFE INS CO	53699	B
WESTERN NATIONAL LIFE INS CO	45803	B-
AMERICAN GENERAL LIFE INS CO	38638	C+
NATIONAL UNION FIRE INS CO OF PITTSB	33707	B

ALFA LIFE INSURANCE CORPORATION *

B+   **Good**

Major Rating Factors: Good overall results on stability tests (6.4 on a scale of 0 to 10). Stability strengths include good operational trends and excellent risk diversification. Good overall profitability (5.5). Return on equity has been fair, averaging 7.0%. Strong capitalization (8.5) based on excellent risk adjusted capital (severe loss scenario).

Other Rating Factors: High quality investment portfolio (7.7). Excellent liquidity (7.8).

Principal Business: Individual life insurance (97%), individual annuities (1%), and individual health insurance (1%).

Principal Investments: NonCMO investment grade bonds (54%), CMOs and structured securities (36%), policy loans (7%), common & preferred stock (1%), and misc. investments (3%).

Investments in Affiliates: None

Group Affiliation: Alfa Ins Group

Licensed in: AK, CA, GA, HI, ME, MO, MT, ND, SD, TX, WA

Commenced Business: March 1955

Address: 2108 East South Blvd, Montgomery, AL 36116-2015

Phone: (334) 288-3900   **Domicile State:** AL   **NAIC Code:** 79049

Data Date	Rating	RACR #1	RACR #2	Total Assets ($mil)	Capital ($mil)	Net Premium ($mil)	Net Income ($mil)
3-09	B+	3.29	1.97	1,087.3	150.9	34.9	2.7
3-08	A	2.37	1.41	1,122.9	148.1	46.3	-1.2
2008	B+	3.28	1.97	1,073.4	148.1	128.9	-53.2
2007	A	3.39	2.03	1,100.2	210.8	123.4	10.3
2006	A	3.47	2.06	1,050.8	202.2	119.9	27.6
2005	A	3.20	1.88	975.4	177.2	113.2	22.7
2004	A	3.18	1.90	904.6	162.0	107.6	24.6

Adverse Trends in Operations

Decrease in asset base during 2008 (2%)
Decrease in capital during 2008 (31%)

ALLIANZ LIFE INSURANCE COMPANY OF NEW YORK

C   **Fair**

Major Rating Factors: Fair overall results on stability tests (3.9 on a scale of 0 to 10). Good quality investment portfolio (6.8) despite mixed results such as: no exposure to mortgages and large holdings of BBB rated bonds but minimal holdings in junk bonds. Weak profitability (1.2) with operating losses during the first three months of 2009.

Other Rating Factors: Strong capitalization (7.4) based on excellent risk adjusted capital (severe loss scenario). Excellent liquidity (9.1).

Principal Business: Individual annuities (98%), individual health insurance (1%), and group life insurance (1%).

Principal Investments: NonCMO investment grade bonds (66%), CMOs and structured securities (33%), and cash (1%).

Investments in Affiliates: None

Group Affiliation: Allianz Ins Group

Licensed in: DC, DE, IN, MS, MT, NC, OH

Commenced Business: April 1984

Address: One Chase Manhattan Plz 28 Fl, New York, NY 10005-1423

Phone: (212) 586-7733   **Domicile State:** NY   **NAIC Code:** 64190

Data Date	Rating	RACR #1	RACR #2	Total Assets ($mil)	Capital ($mil)	Net Premium ($mil)	Net Income ($mil)
3-09	C	2.46	1.28	921.2	47.6	77.6	-1.3
3-08	B	3.45	2.21	869.6	51.9	42.9	-7.1
2008	C	1.60	0.83	881.5	29.2	235.8	-47.5
2007	B	3.36	2.18	874.4	50.3	159.6	2.2
2006	B	4.19	2.88	849.1	62.5	154.6	3.2
2005	B	3.92	2.94	703.0	53.3	191.5	3.0
2004	B	4.33	3.90	554.2	53.9	100.4	4.4

Rating Indexes

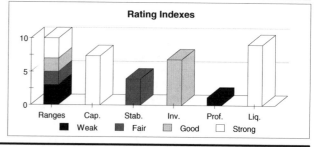

ALLIANZ LIFE INSURANCE COMPANY OF NORTH AMERICA   C+   Fair

Major Rating Factors: Fair quality investment portfolio (3.5 on a scale of 0 to 10) with substantial holdings of BBB bonds in addition to moderate junk bond exposure. Fair overall results on stability tests (4.7) including fair risk adjusted capital in prior years. Good capitalization (5.0) based on good risk adjusted capital (moderate loss scenario).

Other Rating Factors: Good liquidity (5.8). Weak profitability (2.8) with operating losses during the first three months of 2009.

Principal Business: Individual annuities (94%), individual life insurance (3%), and individual health insurance (3%).

Principal Investments: NonCMO investment grade bonds (52%), CMOs and structured securities (31%), mortgages in good standing (9%), noninv. grade bonds (1%), and misc. investments (6%).

Investments in Affiliates: 5%
Group Affiliation: Allianz Ins Group
Licensed in: All states except AL, NC
Commenced Business: December 1979
Address: 5701 Golden Hills Dr, Minneapolis, MN 55416-1297
Phone: (800) 328-5601 **Domicile State:** MN **NAIC Code:** 90611

Data Date	Rating	RACR #1	RACR #2	Total Assets ($mil)	Capital ($mil)	Net Premium ($mil)	Net Income ($mil)
3-09	C+	1.00	0.51	67,509.3	1,820.7	2,643.3	-163.1
3-08	B-	N/A	N/A	70,508.3	2,398.1	1,913.2	-65.8
2008	B-	1.12	0.58	66,374.8	2,009.3	8,351.0	-895.8
2007	B-	1.60	0.86	68,688.5	2,441.3	9,030.8	78.1
2006	B-	1.51	0.83	62,861.0	2,447.9	10,472.8	318.5
2005	B-	1.94	1.06	53,095.7	2,164.1	13,226.8	480.4
2004	B-	1.94	1.04	41,676.3	2,234.0	12,825.8	502.0

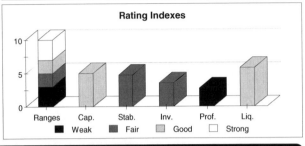

Rating Indexes

ALLSTATE LIFE INSURANCE COMPANY *   B+   Good

Major Rating Factors: Good capitalization (5.6 on a scale of 0 to 10) based on good risk adjusted capital (moderate loss scenario). Good liquidity (6.8) with sufficient resources to cover a large increase in policy surrenders. Good overall results on stability tests (5.2). Stability strengths include excellent risk diversification.

Other Rating Factors: Fair quality investment portfolio (3.8). Weak profitability (2.0) with operating losses during the first three months of 2009.

Principal Business: Reinsurance (49%), individual annuities (24%), group retirement contracts (13%), individual life insurance (12%), and group life insurance (1%).

Principal Investments: NonCMO investment grade bonds (52%), CMOs and structured securities (20%), mortgages in good standing (14%), noninv. grade bonds (5%), and misc. investments (9%).

Investments in Affiliates: 2%
Group Affiliation: Allstate Group
Licensed in: All states except AL, NC
Commenced Business: September 1957
Address: 3100 Sanders Rd, Northbrook, IL 60062-7127
Phone: (847) 402-5000 **Domicile State:** IL **NAIC Code:** 60186

Data Date	Rating	RACR #1	RACR #2	Total Assets ($mil)	Capital ($mil)	Net Premium ($mil)	Net Income ($mil)
3-09	B+	1.37	0.78	65,002.0	3,456.0	902.9	-277.3
3-08	A-	1.14	0.66	75,704.8	2,399.4	984.3	-345.7
2008	B+	1.36	0.79	67,552.1	3,248.9	4,768.2	-1,947.2
2007	A-	1.28	0.75	77,027.9	2,622.5	4,543.1	141.7
2006	A-	1.60	0.94	79,028.2	3,361.0	6,473.6	237.0
2005	A-	1.75	1.02	76,596.5	3,664.7	7,855.8	247.0
2004	A-	1.70	1.00	72,004.9	3,655.9	9,362.7	261.9

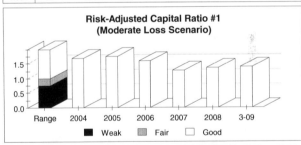

Risk-Adjusted Capital Ratio #1
(Moderate Loss Scenario)

ALLSTATE LIFE INSURANCE COMPANY OF NEW YORK   B   Good

Major Rating Factors: Good quality investment portfolio (5.9 on a scale of 0 to 10) despite large holdings of BBB rated bonds in addition to moderate junk bond exposure. Exposure to mortgages is significant, but the mortgage default rate has been low. Good liquidity (6.3) with sufficient resources to cover a large increase in policy surrenders. Fair profitability (4.5) with operating losses during the first three months of 2009.

Other Rating Factors: Fair overall results on stability tests (4.5). Strong capitalization (7.1) based on excellent risk adjusted capital (severe loss scenario).

Principal Business: Individual annuities (76%), individual life insurance (22%), and individual health insurance (2%).

Principal Investments: NonCMO investment grade bonds (66%), CMOs and structured securities (18%), mortgages in good standing (10%), common & preferred stock (3%), and misc. investments (3%).

Investments in Affiliates: None
Group Affiliation: Allstate Group
Licensed in: CO, DE, FL, IN, MT, NV, NM, NC, ND, RI, UT
Commenced Business: December 1967
Address: One Allstate Dr, Farmingville, NY 11738
Phone: (516) 451-5300 **Domicile State:** NY **NAIC Code:** 70874

Data Date	Rating	RACR #1	RACR #2	Total Assets ($mil)	Capital ($mil)	Net Premium ($mil)	Net Income ($mil)
3-09	B	2.08	1.07	7,759.9	464.6	104.2	-4.8
3-08	B	2.11	1.09	7,939.1	472.4	122.6	4.7
2008	B	1.86	0.97	7,627.5	410.5	642.3	-18.9
2007	B	2.13	1.10	7,785.8	462.4	569.6	38.2
2006	B	2.15	1.11	7,547.2	444.6	466.1	33.4
2005	B	2.04	1.04	7,301.6	410.3	1,010.4	35.9
2004	B	1.95	0.99	6,529.3	356.8	1,452.7	13.6

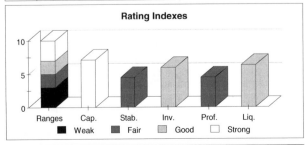

Rating Indexes

AMALGAMATED LIFE INSURANCE COMPANY *

A-   **Excellent**

Major Rating Factors: Good liquidity (5.5 on a scale of 0 to 10) with sufficient resources to handle a spike in claims. Good overall results on stability tests (6.8). Strengths that enhance stability include excellent operational trends and good risk diversification. Strong capitalization (8.4) based on excellent risk adjusted capital (severe loss scenario). Capital levels have been relatively consistent over the last five years.

Other Rating Factors: High quality investment portfolio (8.6). Excellent profitability (8.5) with operating gains in each of the last five years.

Principal Business: Group life insurance (57%), reinsurance (32%), group health insurance (10%), and individual life insurance (1%).

Principal Investments: NonCMO investment grade bonds (56%), CMOs and structured securities (35%), cash (8%), and common & preferred stock (1%).

Investments in Affiliates: None

Group Affiliation: ALICO Services Corp

Licensed in: CO, DC, DE, IN, IA, MD, MA, MI, MT, NH, NJ, NM, NC, OK, RI, SC, TN, UT, VA, WY

Commenced Business: February 1944

Address: 333 Westchester Ave, White Plains, NY 10604

Phone: (914) 367-5000 **Domicile State:** NY **NAIC Code:** 60216

Data Date	Rating	RACR #1	RACR #2	Total Assets ($mil)	Capital ($mil)	Net Premium ($mil)	Net Income ($mil)
3-09	A-	2.46	1.94	62.6	29.6	10.2	0.5
3-08	A-	2.68	2.11	60.2	30.5	9.9	0.7
2008	A-	2.54	2.02	62.4	30.9	38.1	2.1
2007	A-	2.62	2.07	57.4	30.0	36.7	4.1
2006	A-	2.49	2.01	51.8	25.7	33.2	3.0
2005	A-	2.52	2.03	51.8	22.9	33.2	2.6
2004	A-	2.41	1.92	50.8	20.3	30.8	2.0

Adverse Trends in Operations

Increase in policy surrenders from 2004 to 2005 (50%)

AMERICAN BANKERS LIFE ASSURANCE COMPANY OF FL

B   **Good**

Major Rating Factors: Good quality investment portfolio (6.7 on a scale of 0 to 10) despite mixed results such as: minimal exposure to mortgages and substantial holdings of BBB bonds but small junk bond holdings. Good overall profitability (6.2). Return on equity has been excellent over the last five years averaging 20.9%. Good liquidity (6.8).

Other Rating Factors: Fair overall results on stability tests (4.7) including fair financial strength of affiliated Assurant Inc and negative cash flow from operations for 2008. Strong capitalization (10.0) based on excellent risk adjusted capital (severe loss scenario).

Principal Business: Credit life insurance (43%), credit health insurance (34%), reinsurance (14%), individual life insurance (4%), and other lines (5%).

Principal Investments: NonCMO investment grade bonds (66%), common & preferred stock (10%), mortgages in good standing (9%), noninv. grade bonds (4%), and misc. investments (12%).

Investments in Affiliates: None

Group Affiliation: Assurant Inc

Licensed in: All states except AL, NC

Commenced Business: April 1952

Address: 11222 Quail Roost Dr, Miami, FL 33157

Phone: (305) 253-2244 **Domicile State:** FL **NAIC Code:** 60275

Data Date	Rating	RACR #1	RACR #2	Total Assets ($mil)	Capital ($mil)	Net Premium ($mil)	Net Income ($mil)
3-09	B	5.22	2.97	654.2	111.8	20.5	9.5
3-08	B	4.72	2.76	762.7	126.9	31.9	5.0
2008	B	4.99	2.86	653.1	106.7	129.9	1.7
2007	B	4.74	2.79	789.7	127.4	163.0	14.5
2006	B	3.59	2.16	776.6	105.7	171.5	28.4
2005	B	5.82	3.36	834.3	186.8	148.0	45.5
2004	B-	3.27	2.02	895.4	131.1	248.0	13.2

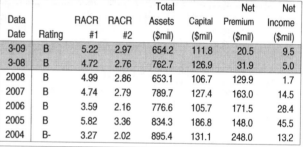

Rating Indexes

AMERICAN COMMUNITY MUTUAL INSURANCE COMPANY

B   **Good**

Major Rating Factors: Good quality investment portfolio (6.9 on a scale of 0 to 10) despite mixed results such as: no exposure to mortgages and substantial holdings of BBB bonds but minimal holdings in junk bonds. Fair overall results on stability tests (4.9) including negative cash flow from operations for 2008. Weak profitability (1.8). Excellent expense controls.

Other Rating Factors: Weak liquidity (0.8). Strong capitalization (7.2) based on excellent risk adjusted capital (severe loss scenario).

Principal Business: Group health insurance (63%), individual health insurance (35%), group life insurance (1%), and individual life insurance (1%).

Principal Investments: CMOs and structured securities (55%), nonCMO investment grade bonds (42%), real estate (7%), common & preferred stock (3%), and noninv. grade bonds (2%).

Investments in Affiliates: None

Group Affiliation: None

Licensed in: AR, CA, CT, DE, HI, IN, IA, KS, KY, LA, ME, MN, MT, NV, ND, OK, OR, RI, SD, TN, TX, VT, WY, PR

Commenced Business: December 1947

Address: 39201 W Seven Mile Rd, Livonia, MI 48152-1094

Phone: (734) 591-9000 **Domicile State:** MI **NAIC Code:** 60305

Data Date	Rating	RACR #1	RACR #2	Total Assets ($mil)	Capital ($mil)	Net Premium ($mil)	Net Income ($mil)
3-09	B	1.50	1.14	139.7	72.8	91.0	1.3
3-08	B+	2.20	1.70	152.2	96.1	86.5	-4.1
2008	B	1.56	1.20	141.9	74.5	355.8	-25.3
2007	B+	2.38	1.84	161.6	102.4	340.8	-5.9
2006	B+	2.36	1.83	178.5	106.9	338.6	-16.4
2005	B+	2.89	2.21	183.0	121.4	321.5	5.4
2004	B+	2.25	1.75	158.9	87.9	370.1	5.8

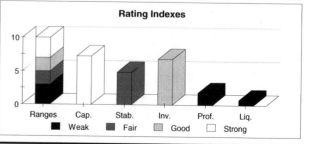

Rating Indexes

AMERICAN EQUITY INVEST LIFE INSURANCE COMPANY   B-   Good

Major Rating Factors: Good quality investment portfolio (6.1 on a scale of 0 to 10) despite substantial holdings of BBB bonds in addition to moderate junk bond exposure. Exposure to mortgages is significant, but the mortgage default rate has been low. Good overall results on stability tests (5.0). Stability strengths include excellent operational trends and excellent risk diversification. Fair liquidity (3.7).

Other Rating Factors: Weak profitability (2.8) with investment income below regulatory standards in relation to interest assumptions of reserves. Strong capitalization (7.3) based on excellent risk adjusted capital (severe loss scenario).

Principal Business: Individual annuities (99%).

Principal Investments: NonCMO investment grade bonds (60%), mortgages in good standing (17%), CMOs and structured securities (16%), noninv. grade bonds (3%), and common & preferred stock (3%).

Investments in Affiliates: None

Group Affiliation: American Equity Investment Group

Licensed in: All states except AL, DC, NC

Commenced Business: December 1981

Address: 5000 Westown Parkway, West Des Moines, IA 50266

Phone: (888) 222-1234 **Domicile State:** IA **NAIC Code:** 92738

Data Date	Rating	RACR #1	RACR #2	Total Assets ($mil)	Capital ($mil)	Net Premium ($mil)	Net Income ($mil)
3-09	B-	2.41	1.23	13,999.3	1,003.6	636.1	9.1
3-08	B	3.13	1.78	13,018.8	958.2	505.6	-24.3
2008	B-	2.59	1.39	13,593.9	983.3	2,252.6	-6.8
2007	B	3.23	1.84	12,697.2	990.8	2,060.4	15.9
2006	C+	4.18	2.38	11,471.4	992.5	1,771.0	88.5
2005	C	2.63	1.50	10,415.5	686.8	2,779.3	40.1
2004	C	2.53	1.45	7,960.8	608.9	1,665.9	47.0

Adverse Trends in Operations

Increase in policy surrenders from 2005 to 2006 (92%)
Decrease in premium volume from 2005 to 2006 (36%)

AMERICAN EQUITY INVESTMENT LIFE NY   B   Good

Major Rating Factors: Good overall results on stability tests (5.2 on a scale of 0 to 10) despite negative cash flow from operations for 2008. Other stability subfactors include good operational trends and excellent risk diversification. Good liquidity (6.6) with sufficient resources to handle a spike in claims as well as a significant increase in policy surrenders. Strong capitalization (10.0) based on excellent risk adjusted capital (severe loss scenario).

Other Rating Factors: High quality investment portfolio (7.2). Excellent profitability (7.2).

Principal Business: Individual annuities (100%).

Principal Investments: CMOs and structured securities (48%), nonCMO investment grade bonds (43%), noninv. grade bonds (5%), and cash (3%).

Investments in Affiliates: None

Group Affiliation: American Equity Investment Group

Licensed in: NC

Commenced Business: July 2001

Address: 1979 Marcus Ave Suite 210, Lake Success, NY 11042

Phone: (866) 233-6660 **Domicile State:** NY **NAIC Code:** 11135

Data Date	Rating	RACR #1	RACR #2	Total Assets ($mil)	Capital ($mil)	Net Premium ($mil)	Net Income ($mil)
3-09	B	3.68	3.32	117.8	33.6	1.8	0.3
3-08	B	3.73	3.35	118.6	33.9	0.3	0.5
2008	B	3.65	3.29	117.1	33.4	3.4	-0.3
2007	B	3.67	3.31	119.2	33.5	12.6	1.2
2006	B-	3.58	3.22	108.6	32.3	15.3	1.4
2005	C+	3.52	3.17	96.7	31.1	35.7	0.4
2004	C	4.21	3.79	64.0	31.0	26.1	0.7

Rating Indexes

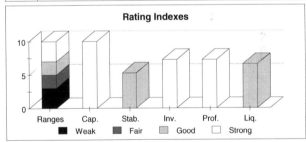

Ranges | Cap. | Stab. | Inv. | Prof. | Liq.
■ Weak   ▨ Fair   ▨ Good   □ Strong

AMERICAN EXCHANGE LIFE INSURANCE COMPANY   C-   Fair

Major Rating Factors: Fair overall results on stability tests (3.0 on a scale of 0 to 10). Low quality investment portfolio (1.3). Good current capitalization (6.9) based on good risk adjusted capital (severe loss scenario), although results have slipped from the excellent range during the last year.

Other Rating Factors: Excellent profitability (9.1) with operating gains in each of the last five years. Excellent liquidity (10.0).

Principal Business: Individual health insurance (95%) and individual life insurance (5%).

Principal Investments: Common & preferred stock (91%), nonCMO investment grade bonds (5%), and cash (2%).

Investments in Affiliates: 91%

Group Affiliation: Universal American Corp

Licensed in: ME, UT

Commenced Business: September 1965

Address: 80 E Campbell Rd Ste 345, Richardson, TX 75081-1889

Phone: (214) 520-1450 **Domicile State:** TX **NAIC Code:** 60372

Data Date	Rating	RACR #1	RACR #2	Total Assets ($mil)	Capital ($mil)	Net Premium ($mil)	Net Income ($mil)
3-09	C-	1.11	0.99	438.8	425.7	0.3	5.8
3-08	U	N/A	N/A	401.9	382.1	0.3	6.3
2008	C-	1.21	1.08	477.7	464.9	1.3	42.9
2007	U	1.19	1.05	436.5	420.9	1.4	61.5
2006	U	1.05	0.93	268.2	238.4	1.0	28.5
2005	U	1.08	0.96	157.7	155.2	0.9	4.3
2004	U	0.99	0.88	130.4	125.5	1.1	21.5

Rating Indexes

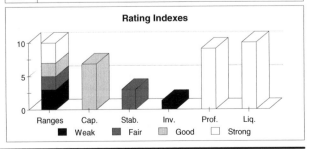

Ranges | Cap. | Stab. | Inv. | Prof. | Liq.
■ Weak   ▨ Fair   ▨ Good   □ Strong

AMERICAN FAMILY LIFE ASSUR COMPANY OF NEW YORK *   B+   Good

Major Rating Factors: Good overall results on stability tests (6.7 on a scale of 0 to 10). Stability strengths include excellent operational trends, good risk adjusted capital for prior years and excellent risk diversification. Strong current capitalization (7.9) based on excellent risk adjusted capital (severe loss scenario) reflecting improvement over results in 2005. High quality investment portfolio (8.1).

Other Rating Factors: Excellent profitability (9.2) with operating gains in each of the last five years. Excellent liquidity (7.3).

Principal Business: Individual health insurance (94%), group health insurance (5%), and individual life insurance (1%).

Principal Investments: NonCMO investment grade bonds (95%), cash (3%), and noninv. grade bonds (1%).

Investments in Affiliates: None

Group Affiliation: American Family Corp

Licensed in: DC, MI, NM, NC, OH, VA

Commenced Business: December 1964

Address: 22 Corporate Woods Blvd #2, Albany, NY 12211

Phone: (706) 660-7208 **Domicile State:** NY **NAIC Code:** 60526

Data Date	Rating	RACR #1	RACR #2	Total Assets ($mil)	Capital ($mil)	Net Premium ($mil)	Net Income ($mil)
3-09	B+	2.10	1.57	285.0	65.3	51.7	0.4
3-08	B+	1.96	1.50	240.8	54.2	47.6	3.4
2008	B+	1.94	1.45	266.5	59.3	194.1	11.6
2007	B	1.89	1.42	227.9	51.5	174.7	11.9
2006	B-	1.54	1.19	190.4	37.5	156.2	8.4
2005	B-	1.24	0.95	154.4	26.8	135.3	2.7
2004	B-	1.24	0.96	125.7	24.1	119.1	4.1

Adverse Trends in Operations

Increase in policy surrenders from 2005 to 2006 (51%)

AMERICAN FAMILY LIFE ASSURANCE CO OF COLUMBUS *   B+   Good

Major Rating Factors: Good overall profitability (6.7 on a scale of 0 to 10). Excellent expense controls. Return on equity has been excellent over the last five years averaging 38.8%. Good overall results on stability tests (6.4). Stability strengths include good operational trends and excellent risk diversification. Fair quality investment portfolio (4.9).

Other Rating Factors: Strong capitalization (7.6) based on excellent risk adjusted capital (severe loss scenario). Excellent liquidity (7.3).

Principal Business: Individual health insurance (87%), individual life insurance (11%), and individual annuities (2%).

Principal Investments: NonCMO investment grade bonds (80%), common & preferred stock (13%), CMOs and structured securities (3%), and noninv. grade bonds (2%).

Investments in Affiliates: None

Group Affiliation: American Family Corp

Licensed in: All states except AL, NC

Commenced Business: April 1956

Address: 1932 Wynnton Rd, Columbus, GA 31999

Phone: (706) 323-3431 **Domicile State:** NE **NAIC Code:** 60380

Data Date	Rating	RACR #1	RACR #2	Total Assets ($mil)	Capital ($mil)	Net Premium ($mil)	Net Income ($mil)
3-09	B+	2.34	1.38	67,309.5	4,975.9	4,156.9	472.1
3-08	B+	2.36	1.48	63,026.8	4,464.2	3,679.5	417.6
2008	B+	2.09	1.28	71,783.0	4,601.3	15,136.6	1,208.6
2007	B+	2.37	1.51	55,667.9	4,208.3	13,120.2	1,790.2
2006	B+	2.46	1.57	50,298.8	4,186.3	12,486.9	1,715.0
2005	B	2.32	1.50	46,859.4	3,705.5	12,157.3	1,248.0
2004	B	1.72	1.10	49,277.8	2,795.4	11,442.4	1,175.0

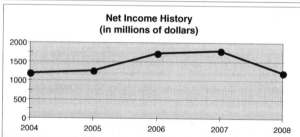

Net Income History
(in millions of dollars)

AMERICAN FAMILY LIFE INSURANCE COMPANY *   A+   Excellent

Major Rating Factors: Good quality investment portfolio (6.6 on a scale of 0 to 10) despite mixed results such as: substantial holdings of BBB bonds but moderate junk bond exposure. Good liquidity (6.4) with sufficient resources to handle a spike in claims as well as a significant increase in policy surrenders. Excellent overall results on stability tests (7.9) excellent operational trends and excellent risk diversification.

Other Rating Factors: Strong capitalization (8.3) based on excellent risk adjusted capital (severe loss scenario). Excellent profitability (7.8).

Principal Business: Individual life insurance (90%), individual annuities (9%), and group life insurance (1%).

Principal Investments: NonCMO investment grade bonds (43%), CMOs and structured securities (36%), mortgages in good standing (10%), policy loans (6%), and misc. investments (5%).

Investments in Affiliates: None

Group Affiliation: American Family Ins Group

Licensed in: AR, CO, CT, IL, IN, IA, KS, KY, MN, MS, MT, NE, NV, NH, NY, ND, OH, OK, PA, SD, TN, UT, VT, WV, WY, PR

Commenced Business: December 1957

Address: 6000 American Parkway, Madison, WI 53783-0001

Phone: (608) 242-4100 **Domicile State:** WI **NAIC Code:** 60399

Data Date	Rating	RACR #1	RACR #2	Total Assets ($mil)	Capital ($mil)	Net Premium ($mil)	Net Income ($mil)
3-09	A+	3.34	1.84	3,898.0	446.5	98.1	9.9
3-08	A+	3.72	2.05	3,922.7	509.5	101.9	10.2
2008	A+	3.33	1.81	3,860.8	446.8	392.1	-81.8
2007	A+	3.78	2.09	3,893.9	501.5	403.9	65.4
2006	A+	3.43	1.91	3,685.1	432.2	399.0	61.1
2005	A+	2.99	1.66	3,454.1	364.4	379.7	57.9
2004	A+	2.80	1.56	3,228.2	314.7	377.9	51.7

Adverse Trends in Operations

Decrease in capital during 2008 (11%)
Decrease in premium volume from 2007 to 2008 (3%)
Increase in policy surrenders from 2004 to 2005 (28%)

AMERICAN FIDELITY ASSURANCE COMPANY *   A   Excellent

Major Rating Factors: Good capitalization (6.3 on a scale of 0 to 10) based on good risk adjusted capital (severe loss scenario). Furthermore, this high level of risk adjusted capital has been consistently maintained over the last five years. Good quality investment portfolio (5.8) despite significant exposure to mortgages . Mortgage default rate has been low. substantial holdings of BBB bonds in addition to small junk bond holdings. Good overall results on stability tests (6.3) excellent operational trends, excellent risk adjusted capital for prior years and excellent risk diversification.

Other Rating Factors: Excellent profitability (8.4) with operating gains in each of the last five years. Excellent liquidity (7.1).

Principal Business: Group health insurance (46%), individual health insurance (18%), individual life insurance (14%), individual annuities (11%), and reinsurance (10%).

Principal Investments: NonCMO investment grade bonds (46%), CMOs and structured securities (34%), mortgages in good standing (11%), cash (5%), and misc. investments (4%).

Investments in Affiliates: None
Group Affiliation: American Fidelity Group
Licensed in: All states except AL, NC
Commenced Business: December 1960
Address: 2000 N Classen Blvd, Oklahoma City, OK 73106
Phone: (405) 523-2000 **Domicile State:** OK **NAIC Code:** 60410

Data Date	Rating	RACR #1	RACR #2	Total Assets ($mil)	Capital ($mil)	Net Premium ($mil)	Net Income ($mil)
3-09	A	1.59	0.91	3,343.9	244.9	172.3	14.0
3-08	A+	1.78	1.10	3,282.6	221.3	164.2	12.4
2008	A	1.67	1.01	3,311.8	239.1	652.2	38.1
2007	A+	1.77	1.09	3,211.7	213.6	577.9	23.0
2006	A+	1.90	1.16	2,959.8	200.4	493.1	25.5
2005	A+	1.75	1.05	2,932.9	184.6	457.2	19.5
2004	A+	1.76	1.07	2,736.8	176.5	442.7	25.6

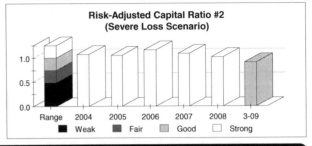

Risk-Adjusted Capital Ratio #2
(Severe Loss Scenario)

■ Weak   ▨ Fair   ▨ Good   □ Strong

AMERICAN FIDELITY LIFE INSURANCE COMPANY   B-   Good

Major Rating Factors: Good liquidity (6.5 on a scale of 0 to 10) with sufficient resources to handle a spike in claims. Good overall results on stability tests (5.2). Stability strengths include good operational trends and good risk diversification. Fair quality investment portfolio (4.9).

Other Rating Factors: Fair profitability (3.0) with investment income below regulatory standards in relation to interest assumptions of reserves. Strong capitalization (8.5) based on excellent risk adjusted capital (severe loss scenario).

Principal Business: Individual life insurance (86%), reinsurance (9%), and individual annuities (6%).

Principal Investments: NonCMO investment grade bonds (83%), mortgages in good standing (6%), real estate (5%), common & preferred stock (3%), and misc. investments (3%).

Investments in Affiliates: 4%
Group Affiliation: AMFI Corp
Licensed in: All states except AL, NM, NC, VA
Commenced Business: September 1956
Address: 4060 Barrancas Ave, Pensacola, FL 32507
Phone: (850) 456-7401 **Domicile State:** FL **NAIC Code:** 60429

Data Date	Rating	RACR #1	RACR #2	Total Assets ($mil)	Capital ($mil)	Net Premium ($mil)	Net Income ($mil)
3-09	B-	2.75	1.97	463.5	72.0	4.3	0.1
3-08	B-	2.83	2.15	474.9	77.0	4.7	0.8
2008	B-	2.87	2.04	469.8	73.2	14.6	1.2
2007	B-	2.91	2.22	477.2	77.1	15.9	1.9
2006	B-	3.84	2.94	475.0	77.5	16.4	2.6
2005	B-	4.24	3.33	464.8	76.3	16.5	2.5
2004	B-	4.50	3.51	452.9	74.0	17.2	3.0

Adverse Trends in Operations

Decrease in asset base during 2008 (2%)
Decrease in capital during 2008 (5%)
Decrease in premium volume from 2007 to 2008 (8%)
Decrease in premium volume from 2006 to 2007 (3%)
Decrease in premium volume from 2004 to 2005 (4%)

AMERICAN GENERAL ASSURANCE COMPANY   C   Fair

Major Rating Factors: Fair profitability (4.1 on a scale of 0 to 10). Return on equity has been fair, averaging 8.5%. Good quality investment portfolio (6.2) despite mixed results such as: no exposure to mortgages and large holdings of BBB rated bonds but minimal holdings in junk bonds. Weak overall results on stability tests (2.9) including weak results on operational trends.

Other Rating Factors: Strong capitalization (9.4) based on excellent risk adjusted capital (severe loss scenario). Excellent liquidity (7.0).

Principal Business: Group health insurance (53%), group life insurance (20%), credit life insurance (18%), credit health insurance (7%), and individual life insurance (1%).

Principal Investments: NonCMO investment grade bonds (65%), CMOs and structured securities (18%), common & preferred stock (10%), noninv. grade bonds (4%), and cash (1%).

Investments in Affiliates: 12%
Group Affiliation: American International Group
Licensed in: All states except AL, NC
Commenced Business: February 1930
Address: 1000 Woodfield Lake, Schaumburg, IL 60173-4793
Phone: (847) 517-6000 **Domicile State:** IL **NAIC Code:** 68373

Data Date	Rating	RACR #1	RACR #2	Total Assets ($mil)	Capital ($mil)	Net Premium ($mil)	Net Income ($mil)
3-09	C	3.64	2.63	189.7	80.5	16.4	4.5
3-08	B	3.06	2.59	280.7	146.2	14.8	1.7
2008	C	3.35	2.44	193.9	74.9	79.4	-6.5
2007	B	2.97	2.51	287.7	144.7	-104.4	28.5
2006	B	2.73	1.76	1,510.7	280.5	491.9	-6.1
2005	B	1.20	0.89	1,507.5	177.2	717.9	21.9
2004	B-	1.03	0.76	1,377.2	155.0	675.5	1.6

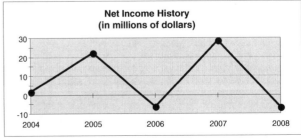

Net Income History
(in millions of dollars)

AMERICAN GENERAL LIFE & ACCIDENT INS COMPANY — B- — Good

Major Rating Factors: Good overall results on stability tests (5.0 on a scale of 0 to 10) despite fair financial strength of affiliated American International Group. Other stability subfactors include good operational trends, good risk adjusted capital for prior years and excellent risk diversification. Fair quality investment portfolio (4.9) with large holdings of BBB rated bonds in addition to junk bond exposure equal to 88% of capital. Exposure to mortgages is significant, but the mortgage default rate has been low. Fair liquidity (4.8).

Other Rating Factors: Strong capitalization (7.0) based on excellent risk adjusted capital (severe loss scenario). Excellent profitability (8.1).

Principal Business: Individual life insurance (72%), individual annuities (19%), and individual health insurance (9%).

Principal Investments: NonCMO investment grade bonds (57%), CMOs and structured securities (14%), mortgages in good standing (13%), noninv. grade bonds (6%), and misc. investments (9%).

Investments in Affiliates: 1%

Group Affiliation: American International Group

Licensed in: All states except AL, AZ, ID, MI, NJ, NC, PR

Commenced Business: December 1900

Address: MC 2450 American General Ctr, Nashville, TN 37250

Phone: (615) 749-1000 **Domicile State:** TN **NAIC Code:** 66672

Data Date	Rating	RACR #1	RACR #2	Total Assets ($mil)	Capital ($mil)	Net Premium ($mil)	Net Income ($mil)
3-09	B-	1.87	1.00	9,139.2	588.9	266.5	43.7
3-08	B	1.68	0.88	9,222.3	447.5	221.6	-84.5
2008	B-	1.81	0.96	9,134.5	563.5	955.0	-816.9
2007	B	1.93	1.01	9,134.2	546.9	883.4	203.8
2006	B	1.83	0.98	8,936.9	500.5	885.6	279.3
2005	B	2.09	1.09	8,929.0	582.9	890.2	316.6
2004	B-	2.07	1.09	8,803.4	570.7	929.1	309.3

American International Group
Composite Group Rating: C+

Largest Group Members	Assets ($mil)	Rating
AMERICAN LIFE INS CO	86338	C-
VARIABLE ANNUITY LIFE INS CO	53699	B
WESTERN NATIONAL LIFE INS CO	45803	B-
AMERICAN GENERAL LIFE INS CO	38638	C+
NATIONAL UNION FIRE INS CO OF PITTSB	33707	B

AMERICAN GENERAL LIFE INSURANCE COMPANY — C+ — Fair

Major Rating Factors: Fair overall results on stability tests (4.6 on a scale of 0 to 10) including fair financial strength of affiliated American International Group. Good quality investment portfolio (6.3) despite mixed results such as: large holdings of BBB rated bonds but moderate junk bond exposure. Good overall profitability (6.8) despite operating losses during the first three months of 2009.

Other Rating Factors: Good liquidity (6.8). Strong capitalization (7.1) based on excellent risk adjusted capital (severe loss scenario).

Principal Business: Individual life insurance (49%), individual annuities (35%), reinsurance (14%), group life insurance (1%), and individual health insurance (1%).

Principal Investments: NonCMO investment grade bonds (56%), CMOs and structured securities (14%), common & preferred stock (11%), noninv. grade bonds (6%), and misc. investments (13%).

Investments in Affiliates: 11%

Group Affiliation: American International Group

Licensed in: All states except AL, NC

Commenced Business: August 1960

Address: 2727-A Allen Parkway, Houston, TX 77019

Phone: (713) 522-1111 **Domicile State:** TX **NAIC Code:** 60488

Data Date	Rating	RACR #1	RACR #2	Total Assets ($mil)	Capital ($mil)	Net Premium ($mil)	Net Income ($mil)
3-09	C+	1.42	1.09	38,459.0	5,312.5	417.4	-1.8
3-08	B	1.33	1.03	36,618.7	4,754.7	610.1	-519.7
2008	C+	1.41	1.08	38,638.4	5,192.3	3,531.9	-4,103.6
2007	B+	1.53	1.18	36,523.2	5,694.8	2,273.1	862.3
2006	B+	1.39	1.12	34,024.8	5,447.5	2,623.5	507.0
2005	B+	1.39	1.13	30,967.9	5,010.2	2,658.6	638.0
2004	B+	1.39	1.14	28,386.4	4,705.5	2,530.9	567.3

American International Group
Composite Group Rating: C+

Largest Group Members	Assets ($mil)	Rating
AMERICAN LIFE INS CO	86338	C-
VARIABLE ANNUITY LIFE INS CO	53699	B
WESTERN NATIONAL LIFE INS CO	45803	B-
AMERICAN GENERAL LIFE INS CO	38638	C+
NATIONAL UNION FIRE INS CO OF PITTSB	33707	B

AMERICAN HEALTH & LIFE INSURANCE COMPANY * — B+ — Good

Major Rating Factors: Good quality investment portfolio (6.6 on a scale of 0 to 10) despite mixed results such as: no exposure to mortgages and large holdings of BBB rated bonds but small junk bond holdings. Good overall profitability (6.5). Excellent expense controls. Return on equity has been excellent over the last five years averaging 17.1%. Good overall results on stability tests (5.2) excellent risk diversification.

Other Rating Factors: Strong capitalization (10.0) based on excellent risk adjusted capital (severe loss scenario). Excellent liquidity (9.2).

Principal Business: Credit life insurance (41%), credit health insurance (36%), reinsurance (17%), group life insurance (4%), and group health insurance (2%).

Principal Investments: NonCMO investment grade bonds (58%), CMOs and structured securities (28%), noninv. grade bonds (7%), common & preferred stock (6%), and cash (1%).

Investments in Affiliates: 5%

Group Affiliation: Citigroup Inc

Licensed in: All states except AL, NC

Commenced Business: June 1954

Address: 307 West 7th Street, Ste 400, Fort Worth, TX 76102

Phone: (817) 348-7500 **Domicile State:** TX **NAIC Code:** 60518

Data Date	Rating	RACR #1	RACR #2	Total Assets ($mil)	Capital ($mil)	Net Premium ($mil)	Net Income ($mil)
3-09	B+	6.08	4.25	1,505.6	683.7	31.2	27.6
3-08	B+	7.69	5.38	1,711.5	915.1	63.0	32.9
2008	B+	5.78	4.09	1,519.6	656.8	282.0	96.3
2007	B+	7.53	5.33	1,676.2	886.2	292.3	101.0
2006	B	7.74	5.55	1,609.8	880.1	214.3	139.0
2005	B	7.26	5.15	1,723.0	913.6	220.0	180.2
2004	B	4.62	3.72	1,859.7	933.7	302.7	173.0

Rating Indexes

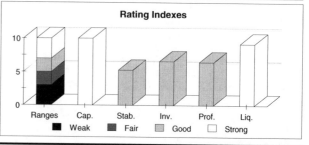

AMERICAN HERITAGE LIFE INSURANCE COMPANY   B   Good

Major Rating Factors: Good overall capitalization (6.3 on a scale of 0 to 10) based on good risk adjusted capital (severe loss scenario). However, capital levels have fluctuated somewhat during past years. Good quality investment portfolio (6.3) despite mixed results such as: minimal exposure to mortgages and substantial holdings of BBB bonds but small junk bond holdings. Good overall profitability (6.8).

Other Rating Factors: Good liquidity (6.3). Good overall results on stability tests (5.5) despite negative cash flow from operations for 2008 good operational trends and excellent risk diversification.

Principal Business: Individual health insurance (51%), individual life insurance (18%), group health insurance (18%), reinsurance (7%), and other lines (6%).

Principal Investments: NonCMO investment grade bonds (41%), policy loans (27%), common & preferred stock (11%), mortgages in good standing (9%), and misc. investments (13%).

Investments in Affiliates: 10%
Group Affiliation: Allstate Group
Licensed in: All states except AL, NC
Commenced Business: December 1956
Address: 1776 American Heritage Life Dr, Jacksonville, FL 32224-6688
Phone: (904) 992-1776 **Domicile State:** FL **NAIC Code:** 60534

Data Date	Rating	RACR #1	RACR #2	Total Assets ($mil)	Capital ($mil)	Net Premium ($mil)	Net Income ($mil)
3-09	B	1.13	0.91	1,317.5	200.8	111.0	1.8
3-08	B	1.09	0.89	1,356.7	206.0	95.0	0.7
2008	B	1.10	0.90	1,326.5	192.1	414.6	0.3
2007	B	1.08	0.88	1,376.6	204.0	460.7	12.5
2006	B	1.11	0.91	1,326.7	211.1	414.6	23.1
2005	B	1.29	1.00	1,549.9	223.8	414.4	31.1
2004	B	1.09	0.76	1,843.4	127.6	24.3	-34.5

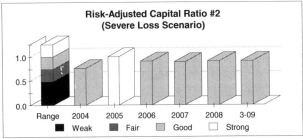

Risk-Adjusted Capital Ratio #2
(Severe Loss Scenario)

Range 2004 2005 2006 2007 2008 3-09
■ Weak ■ Fair ▨ Good □ Strong

AMERICAN INCOME LIFE INSURANCE COMPANY *   B+   Good

Major Rating Factors: Good overall results on stability tests (6.4 on a scale of 0 to 10). Stability strengths include excellent operational trends, excellent risk adjusted capital for prior years and excellent risk diversification. Good current capitalization (6.4) based on good risk adjusted capital (severe loss scenario), although results have slipped from the excellent range during the last year. Good liquidity (6.1).

Other Rating Factors: Fair quality investment portfolio (4.6). Excellent profitability (7.6) with operating gains in each of the last five years.

Principal Business: Individual life insurance (87%), individual health insurance (12%), and group health insurance (1%).

Principal Investments: NonCMO investment grade bonds (79%), common & preferred stock (7%), noninv. grade bonds (5%), policy loans (4%), and misc. investments (4%).

Investments in Affiliates: 3%
Group Affiliation: Torchmark Corp
Licensed in: All states except AL, NC
Commenced Business: August 1954
Address: 8604 Allisonville Rd Suite 151, Indianapolis, IN 46250
Phone: (254) 761-6400 **Domicile State:** IN **NAIC Code:** 60577

Data Date	Rating	RACR #1	RACR #2	Total Assets ($mil)	Capital ($mil)	Net Premium ($mil)	Net Income ($mil)
3-09	B+	1.57	0.92	1,811.7	155.5	135.8	18.0
3-08	A-	2.21	1.34	1,730.5	196.7	129.7	21.6
2008	A-	2.37	1.43	1,828.1	228.1	531.9	98.8
2007	A-	2.54	1.53	1,705.9	221.2	507.1	96.3
2006	A-	2.38	1.46	1,542.4	193.3	468.7	75.8
2005	A-	2.75	1.69	1,439.3	208.2	438.0	93.9
2004	A-	2.43	1.54	1,295.3	182.0	407.0	75.2

Adverse Trends in Operations

Decrease in capital during 2006 (7%)

AMERICAN INTERNATIONAL LIFE ASSURANCE CO OF NY   C+   Fair

Major Rating Factors: Fair overall results on stability tests (4.4 on a scale of 0 to 10) including fair financial strength of affiliated American International Group and negative cash flow from operations for 2008. Fair quality investment portfolio (3.8) with large holdings of BBB rated bonds in addition to significant exposure to junk bonds. Good capitalization (6.4) based on good risk adjusted capital (severe loss scenario).

Other Rating Factors: Weak profitability (2.4) with operating losses during the first three months of 2009. Excellent liquidity (7.1).

Principal Business: Group retirement contracts (40%), individual annuities (39%), group health insurance (9%), group life insurance (9%), and individual life insurance (3%).

Principal Investments: NonCMO investment grade bonds (64%), CMOs and structured securities (16%), mortgages in good standing (7%), noninv. grade bonds (6%), and common & preferred stock (4%).

Investments in Affiliates: 1%
Group Affiliation: American International Group
Licensed in: All states except AL, AR, DC, MA
Commenced Business: November 1962
Address: 70 Pine St, New York, NY 10270
Phone: (212) 770-7000 **Domicile State:** NY **NAIC Code:** 60607

Data Date	Rating	RACR #1	RACR #2	Total Assets ($mil)	Capital ($mil)	Net Premium ($mil)	Net Income ($mil)
3-09	C+	1.96	0.92	6,514.9	335.8	32.2	-1.7
3-08	B	2.14	1.03	6,907.1	396.7	48.0	-109.9
2008	C+	2.06	0.97	6,660.7	370.5	369.0	-1,028.9
2007	B	2.82	1.35	7,092.8	552.6	383.3	78.3
2006	B	2.81	1.35	7,820.8	606.1	312.0	62.1
2005	B	2.78	1.34	8,269.8	625.8	270.3	155.2
2004	B	2.11	1.06	8,344.2	565.9	451.1	94.7

American International Group Composite Group Rating: C+ Largest Group Members	Assets ($mil)	Rating
AMERICAN LIFE INS CO	86338	C-
VARIABLE ANNUITY LIFE INS CO	53699	B
WESTERN NATIONAL LIFE INS CO	45803	B-
AMERICAN GENERAL LIFE INS CO	38638	C+
NATIONAL UNION FIRE INS CO OF PITTSB	33707	B

AMERICAN INVESTORS LIFE INSURANCE COMPANY   B-   Good

Major Rating Factors: Good overall results on stability tests (5.0 on a scale of 0 to 10) despite fair risk adjusted capital in prior years. Other stability subfactors include good operational trends and excellent risk diversification. Fair quality investment portfolio (4.3) with large holdings of BBB rated bonds in addition to junk bond exposure equal to 88% of capital. Fair profitability (4.5) with operating losses during the first three months of 2009.

Other Rating Factors: Strong capitalization (7.2) based on excellent risk adjusted capital (severe loss scenario). Excellent liquidity (7.8).

Principal Business: Individual annuities (100%).

Principal Investments: NonCMO investment grade bonds (60%), CMOs and structured securities (19%), mortgages in good standing (8%), noninv. grade bonds (6%), and misc. investments (7%).

Investments in Affiliates: None

Group Affiliation: Aviva plc

Licensed in: All states except AL, NC

Commenced Business: May 1965

Address: 555 S Kansas Ave, Topeka, KS 66603-3404

Phone: (785) 232-6945 **Domicile State:** KS **NAIC Code:** 60631

Data Date	Rating	RACR #1	RACR #2	Total Assets ($mil)	Capital ($mil)	Net Premium ($mil)	Net Income ($mil)
3-09	B-	2.18	1.12	15,459.9	864.2	1,610.9	-36.2
3-08	B-	2.35	1.09	11,127.4	612.1	722.6	39.0
2008	B-	2.52	1.29	14,336.7	930.1	4,338.8	-223.7
2007	B-	2.61	1.21	10,586.3	641.7	2,429.1	100.9
2006	B-	1.72	0.84	8,829.2	422.9	1,008.2	-29.0
2005	B-	1.75	0.84	8,586.8	425.2	912.5	45.0
2004	C+	1.50	0.74	8,415.2	393.3	854.3	53.9

Adverse Trends in Operations

Increase in policy surrenders from 2005 to 2006 (60%)
Increase in policy surrenders from 2004 to 2005 (27%)

AMERICAN LIFE & ACCIDENT INSURANCE COMPANY OF KY   C   Fair

Major Rating Factors: Fair quality investment portfolio (3.0 on a scale of 0 to 10). Fair overall results on stability tests (3.7). Weak profitability (2.3). Excellent expense controls. Return on equity has been low, averaging -1.9%.

Other Rating Factors: Strong capitalization (8.8) based on excellent risk adjusted capital (severe loss scenario). Excellent liquidity (8.1).

Principal Business: Reinsurance (99%) and individual life insurance (1%).

Principal Investments: Common & preferred stock (48%), nonCMO investment grade bonds (40%), real estate (8%), CMOs and structured securities (3%), and cash (1%).

Investments in Affiliates: None

Group Affiliation: None

Licensed in: CA, GA, HI, IA, LA, MA, OK, RI, TX

Commenced Business: July 1906

Address: 3 Riverfront Plaza, Louisville, KY 40202-2975

Phone: (502) 585-5347 **Domicile State:** KY **NAIC Code:** 60666

Data Date	Rating	RACR #1	RACR #2	Total Assets ($mil)	Capital ($mil)	Net Premium ($mil)	Net Income ($mil)
3-09	C	3.76	2.18	198.4	105.2	4.0	3.8
3-08	C	3.23	1.89	246.9	129.9	6.6	2.5
2008	C	4.04	2.34	216.6	110.4	28.5	-9.0
2007	C	3.40	1.99	261.3	135.1	13.6	-19.2
2006	C	3.65	2.14	294.1	172.9	0.3	5.6
2005	C	3.80	2.23	268.6	159.3	0.3	4.6
2004	C	3.70	2.18	269.9	157.1	0.3	8.3

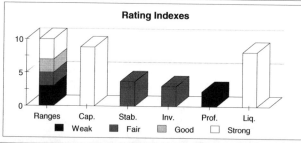

Rating Indexes

Ranges   Cap.   Stab.   Inv.   Prof.   Liq.
■ Weak   ■ Fair   ▨ Good   □ Strong

AMERICAN LIFE INSURANCE COMPANY   C-   Fair

Major Rating Factors: Fair current capitalization (4.9 on a scale of 0 to 10) based on fair risk adjusted capital (severe loss scenario), although results have slipped from the good range during the last year. Fair overall results on stability tests (3.0) including fair risk adjusted capital in prior years. Good quality investment portfolio (6.5).

Other Rating Factors: Good overall profitability (6.5). Excellent liquidity (8.5).

Principal Business: Individual life insurance (68%), individual annuities (16%), individual health insurance (12%), group retirement contracts (1%), and other lines (3%).

Principal Investments: NonCMO investment grade bonds (65%), CMOs and structured securities (12%), cash (11%), common & preferred stock (5%), and misc. investments (7%).

Investments in Affiliates: 5%

Group Affiliation: American International Group

Licensed in: FL

Commenced Business: August 1921

Address: One ALICO Plaza, Wilmington, DE 19801

Phone: (302) 594-2000 **Domicile State:** DE **NAIC Code:** 60690

Data Date	Rating	RACR #1	RACR #2	Total Assets ($mil)	Capital ($mil)	Net Premium ($mil)	Net Income ($mil)
3-09	C-	0.96	0.74	82,005.8	3,567.9	-2,675.4	94.4
3-08	B	0.92	0.78	102,254	6,588.0	9,179.5	145.6
2008	C-	1.03	0.79	86,338.1	3,902.9	29,905.9	176.9
2007	B	1.00	0.85	101,632	6,721.0	33,490.4	736.9
2006	B	0.93	0.80	84,977.1	5,734.0	25,179.1	579.1
2005	B	0.94	0.81	66,178.9	5,334.3	20,081.4	549.9
2004	B	0.82	0.72	56,392.9	4,232.6	20,123.2	268.6

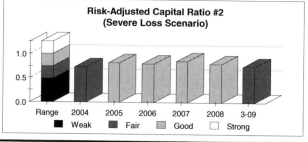

Risk-Adjusted Capital Ratio #2
(Severe Loss Scenario)

Range   2004   2005   2006   2007   2008   3-09
■ Weak   ■ Fair   ▨ Good   □ Strong

AMERICAN MATURITY LIFE INSURANCE COMPANY   B   Good

Major Rating Factors: Fair overall results on stability tests (4.5 on a scale of 0 to 10) including fair financial strength of affiliated Hartford Financial Services Inc. Strong capitalization (10.0) based on excellent risk adjusted capital (severe loss scenario). Capital levels have been relatively consistent over the last five years. High quality investment portfolio (9.4).

Other Rating Factors: Excellent profitability (8.8) with operating gains in each of the last five years. Excellent liquidity (7.0).

Principal Business: Group retirement contracts (96%) and individual annuities (4%).

Principal Investments: NonCMO investment grade bonds (100%).

Investments in Affiliates: None

Group Affiliation: Hartford Financial Services Inc

Licensed in: All states except AL

Commenced Business: March 1973

Address: 200 Hopmeadow St, Simsbury, CT 06070

Phone: (860) 843-5867 **Domicile State:** CT **NAIC Code:** 81213

Data Date	Rating	RACR #1	RACR #2	Total Assets ($mil)	Capital ($mil)	Net Premium ($mil)	Net Income ($mil)
3-09	B	6.23	5.61	57.0	43.9	0.0	0.9
3-08	B	5.64	5.08	63.1	41.6	0.0	0.3
2008	B	6.02	5.41	57.7	42.4	0.0	1.1
2007	B	5.59	5.03	65.2	41.3	0.1	1.5
2006	B	5.33	4.79	67.1	39.8	0.0	1.4
2005	B	5.07	4.57	69.5	38.4	0.0	1.0
2004	B	4.80	4.32	74.2	37.3	0.1	0.9

Hartford Financial Services Inc Composite Group Rating: C Largest Group Members	Assets ($mil)	Rating
HARTFORD LIFE INS CO	133562	C-
HARTFORD LIFE ANNUITY INS CO	65461	B-
HARTFORD FIRE INS CO	24454	B+
HARTFORD LIFE ACCIDENT INS CO	14414	B-
HARTFORD ACCIDENT INDEMNITY CO	10935	C+

AMERICAN MEDICAL SECURITY LIFE INSURANCE COMPANY   B   Good

Major Rating Factors: Good overall profitability (5.9 on a scale of 0 to 10). Excellent expense controls. Despite its volitility, return on equity has been excellent over the last five years averaging 24.7%. Fair overall results on stability tests (4.1) including weak results on operational trends. Strong capitalization (9.3) based on excellent risk adjusted capital (severe loss scenario).

Other Rating Factors: High quality investment portfolio (8.7). Excellent liquidity (7.9).

Principal Business: Group health insurance (87%), individual health insurance (12%), and group life insurance (1%).

Principal Investments: NonCMO investment grade bonds (97%) and CMOs and structured securities (4%).

Investments in Affiliates: None

Group Affiliation: UnitedHealth Group Inc

Licensed in: All states except AL, AZ, DC, ID, MD, MI, NJ, NM, NC, SC, VA

Commenced Business: March 1966

Address: 3100 AMS Blvd, Green Bay, WI 54313

Phone: (800) 232-5432 **Domicile State:** WI **NAIC Code:** 97179

Data Date	Rating	RACR #1	RACR #2	Total Assets ($mil)	Capital ($mil)	Net Premium ($mil)	Net Income ($mil)
3-09	B	3.16	2.56	122.7	76.7	44.3	5.8
3-08	B	4.75	3.52	233.9	164.3	53.2	10.3
2008	B	2.93	2.38	129.8	70.5	198.5	56.3
2007	B	4.26	3.17	237.9	153.4	282.5	57.7
2006	B	3.44	2.69	406.9	258.8	631.3	81.4
2005	B	1.69	1.33	382.6	179.4	871.2	-2.0
2004	B	2.27	1.75	373.3	200.4	707.7	15.4

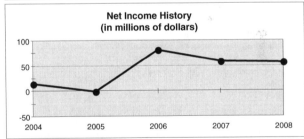

Net Income History
(in millions of dollars)

AMERICAN MEMORIAL LIFE INS CO   B-   Good

Major Rating Factors: Good overall capitalization (5.6 on a scale of 0 to 10) based on good risk adjusted capital (moderate loss scenario). Nevertheless, capital levels have fluctuated during prior years. Good overall profitability (5.6) despite operating losses during the first three months of 2009. Return on equity has been excellent over the last five years averaging 27.5%. Good liquidity (6.2).

Other Rating Factors: Fair overall results on stability tests (4.9) including fair financial strength of affiliated Assurant Inc. Fair quality investment portfolio (3.8).

Principal Business: Group life insurance (72%), individual life insurance (26%), individual annuities (1%), and group retirement contracts (1%).

Principal Investments: NonCMO investment grade bonds (71%), mortgages in good standing (9%), CMOs and structured securities (7%), common & preferred stock (6%), and misc. investments (6%).

Investments in Affiliates: None

Group Affiliation: Assurant Inc

Licensed in: All states except AL, NC

Commenced Business: October 1959

Address: 440 Mount Rushmore Rd, Rapid City, SD 57701

Phone: (605) 348-1262 **Domicile State:** SD **NAIC Code:** 67989

Data Date	Rating	RACR #1	RACR #2	Total Assets ($mil)	Capital ($mil)	Net Premium ($mil)	Net Income ($mil)
3-09	B-	1.40	0.73	1,968.5	85.5	65.7	-0.8
3-08	B-	1.51	0.80	1,963.9	89.5	69.4	1.0
2008	B-	1.42	0.75	1,996.1	86.1	281.4	-23.0
2007	B-	1.52	0.80	1,935.5	86.4	290.9	28.3
2006	B-	1.80	0.94	1,549.9	82.1	229.7	36.7
2005	C+	2.28	1.17	1,534.7	115.3	248.0	32.1
2004	C+	2.70	1.40	1,344.9	113.7	270.3	37.6

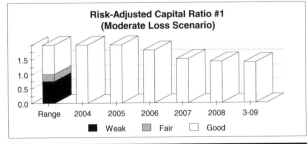

Risk-Adjusted Capital Ratio #1
(Moderate Loss Scenario)

Range 2004 2005 2006 2007 2008 3-09
■ Weak   ▨ Fair   □ Good

AMERICAN NATIONAL INSURANCE COMPANY | B | Good

Major Rating Factors: Good current capitalization (6.0 on a scale of 0 to 10) based on good risk adjusted capital (severe loss scenario), although results have slipped from the excellent range over the last two years. Good quality investment portfolio (5.3) despite significant exposure to mortgages . Mortgage default rate has been low. large holdings of BBB rated bonds in addition to small junk bond holdings. Good overall profitability (5.6) despite operating losses during the first three months of 2009.

Other Rating Factors: Good liquidity (6.5). Good overall results on stability tests (6.0) excellent operational trends and excellent risk diversification.

Principal Business: Group retirement contracts (36%), individual annuities (36%), individual life insurance (17%), reinsurance (5%), and other lines (6%).

Principal Investments: NonCMO investment grade bonds (53%), mortgages in good standing (15%), common & preferred stock (9%), CMOs and structured securities (7%), and misc. investments (15%).

Investments in Affiliates: 18%

Group Affiliation: American National Group Inc

Licensed in: All states except AL, NC

Commenced Business: March 1905

Address: One Moody Plaza, Galveston, TX 77550-7999

Phone: (409) 763-4661 **Domicile State:** TX **NAIC Code:** 60739

Data Date	Rating	RACR #1	RACR #2	Total Assets ($mil)	Capital ($mil)	Net Premium ($mil)	Net Income ($mil)
3-09	B	1.13	0.87	13,984.5	1,682.7	730.3	-9.6
3-08	B+	1.27	1.04	14,228.2	2,132.3	739.0	-13.5
2008	B+	1.21	0.95	13,586.0	1,805.7	2,243.1	-123.1
2007	B+	1.32	1.08	13,839.9	2,164.8	1,621.0	59.1
2006	B	1.37	1.12	13,239.6	2,108.1	1,389.2	92.2
2005	B	1.38	1.11	12,917.1	2,037.6	1,398.6	128.8
2004	B	1.41	1.13	12,102.8	1,867.7	1,726.2	142.0

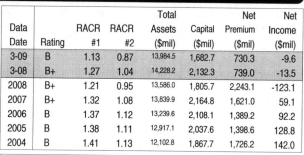

Risk-Adjusted Capital Ratio #2
(Severe Loss Scenario)

Range 2004 2005 2006 2007 2008 3-09
■ Weak ▨ Fair ▨ Good □ Strong

AMERICAN NATIONAL LIFE INSURANCE COMPANY OF TEXAS | B- | Good

Major Rating Factors: Good quality investment portfolio (6.7 on a scale of 0 to 10) despite mixed results such as: no exposure to mortgages and substantial holdings of BBB bonds but minimal holdings in junk bonds. Good liquidity (6.0) with sufficient resources to handle a spike in claims. Good overall results on stability tests (5.4) despite negative cash flow from operations for 2008 good operational trends and excellent risk diversification.

Other Rating Factors: Weak profitability (2.0) with operating losses during the first three months of 2009. Strong capitalization (7.2) based on excellent risk adjusted capital (severe loss scenario).

Principal Business: Group health insurance (66%), reinsurance (21%), individual health insurance (11%), and individual life insurance (3%).

Principal Investments: NonCMO investment grade bonds (76%), CMOs and structured securities (16%), policy loans (3%), common & preferred stock (3%), and noninv. grade bonds (2%).

Investments in Affiliates: 1%

Group Affiliation: American National Group Inc

Licensed in: All states except AL, MD, NM, NC, VA

Commenced Business: December 1954

Address: One Moody Plaza, Galveston, TX 77550

Phone: (409) 763-4661 **Domicile State:** TX **NAIC Code:** 71773

Data Date	Rating	RACR #1	RACR #2	Total Assets ($mil)	Capital ($mil)	Net Premium ($mil)	Net Income ($mil)
3-09	B-	1.58	1.16	130.9	28.8	26.6	-4.8
3-08	B-	1.97	1.58	139.8	42.0	22.0	-1.3
2008	B-	2.19	1.64	137.7	36.1	93.9	-8.4
2007	B-	2.13	1.72	140.3	44.2	75.6	-1.4
2006	B-	2.41	1.89	145.6	43.0	74.4	3.1
2005	B-	2.54	1.89	141.8	43.1	80.0	-0.2
2004	B-	2.82	2.17	142.9	48.0	83.0	-1.6

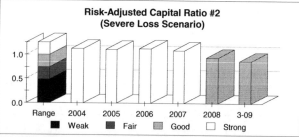

Adverse Trends in Operations

Decrease in asset base during 2008 (2%)
Decrease in capital during 2008 (18%)
Increase in policy surrenders from 2006 to 2007 (79%)
Decrease in capital during 2005 (10%)
Decrease in premium volume from 2004 to 2005 (4%)

AMERICAN PROGRESSIVE L&H INSURANCE COMPANY OF NEW | C | Fair

Major Rating Factors: Fair overall results on stability tests (3.8 on a scale of 0 to 10) including fair financial strength of affiliated Universal American Corp and fair risk adjusted capital in prior years. Fair current capitalization (4.6) based on mixed results -- excessive policy leverage mitigated by fair risk adjusted capital (moderate loss scenario), although results have slipped from the good range over the last two years. Fair liquidity (3.8).

Other Rating Factors: Good overall profitability (5.9). High quality investment portfolio (7.2).

Principal Business: Individual health insurance (97%) and individual life insurance (2%).

Principal Investments: NonCMO investment grade bonds (61%), CMOs and structured securities (39%), noninv. grade bonds (5%), and policy loans (1%).

Investments in Affiliates: None

Group Affiliation: Universal American Corp

Licensed in: AK, CT, DC, DE, FL, GA, ID, IN, IA, ME, MD, MA, MI, MS, MT, NJ, NM, NC, OK, PA, RI, SC, VA, WA

Commenced Business: March 1946

Address: 6 International Dr Suite 190, Rye Brook, NY 10573

Phone: (914) 934-8300 **Domicile State:** NY **NAIC Code:** 80624

Data Date	Rating	RACR #1	RACR #2	Total Assets ($mil)	Capital ($mil)	Net Premium ($mil)	Net Income ($mil)
3-09	C	0.88	0.70	361.6	104.4	183.3	6.2
3-08	C-	0.97	0.76	422.4	90.1	153.1	-5.0
2008	C	0.91	0.72	368.6	105.5	606.8	11.2
2007	C-	1.08	0.85	419.9	93.1	451.4	14.4
2006	D+	0.91	0.67	259.1	34.5	191.0	-1.0
2005	D+	1.00	0.67	198.6	19.4	96.3	-3.1
2004	D+	0.91	0.62	185.3	15.0	83.8	-2.3

Universal American Corp Composite Group Rating: C Largest Group Members	Assets ($mil)	Rating
PENNSYLVANIA LIFE INS CO	1103	D
AMERICAN EXCHANGE LIFE INS CO	478	C-
PYRAMID LIFE INS CO	461	C-
AMERICAN PROGRESSIVE LH I C OF NY	369	C
AMERICAN PIONEER LIFE INS CO	162	C-

AMERICAN REPUBLIC INSURANCE COMPANY *   A-   Excellent

Major Rating Factors: Good liquidity (6.7 on a scale of 0 to 10) with sufficient resources to handle a spike in claims. Strong capitalization (9.1) based on excellent risk adjusted capital (severe loss scenario). Furthermore, this high level of risk adjusted capital has been consistently maintained over the last five years. High quality investment portfolio (7.5).

Other Rating Factors: Excellent profitability (8.7) with operating gains in each of the last five years. Excellent overall results on stability tests (7.3) excellent operational trends and excellent risk diversification.

Principal Business: Group health insurance (36%), individual health insurance (34%), reinsurance (24%), individual life insurance (3%), and credit life insurance (2%).

Principal Investments: NonCMO investment grade bonds (63%), CMOs and structured securities (29%), noninv. grade bonds (2%), common & preferred stock (2%), and misc. investments (4%).

Investments in Affiliates: 2%
Group Affiliation: American Enterprise Mutual Holding
Licensed in: All states except AL, NC
Commenced Business: May 1929
Address: 601 Sixth Ave, Des Moines, IA 50309
Phone: (515) 245-2000 **Domicile State:** IA **NAIC Code:** 60836

Data Date	Rating	RACR #1	RACR #2	Total Assets ($mil)	Capital ($mil)	Net Premium ($mil)	Net Income ($mil)
3-09	A-	3.21	2.42	472.8	244.5	105.5	9.7
3-08	A-	2.86	2.16	476.2	230.6	121.6	9.1
2008	A-	3.07	2.34	475.5	235.9	459.5	17.8
2007	A-	2.71	2.07	475.3	215.8	533.9	29.7
2006	A-	2.69	2.03	495.5	203.7	483.1	0.2
2005	A-	3.50	2.60	469.7	221.2	399.1	10.1
2004	B	3.39	2.50	457.7	210.6	380.2	19.2

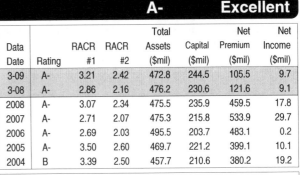

Rating Indexes

AMERICAN UNITED LIFE INSURANCE COMPANY *   B+   Good

Major Rating Factors: Good quality investment portfolio (6.0 on a scale of 0 to 10) despite significant exposure to mortgages . Mortgage default rate has been low. large holdings of BBB rated bonds in addition to small junk bond holdings. Good overall profitability (6.6). Return on equity has been fair, averaging 6.4%. Good overall results on stability tests (5.2) good operational trends and excellent risk diversification.

Other Rating Factors: Strong capitalization (7.6) based on excellent risk adjusted capital (severe loss scenario). Excellent liquidity (7.4).

Principal Business: Group retirement contracts (63%), reinsurance (14%), individual annuities (8%), group health insurance (6%), and other lines (9%).

Principal Investments: NonCMO investment grade bonds (58%), CMOs and structured securities (18%), mortgages in good standing (17%), policy loans (3%), and misc. investments (5%).

Investments in Affiliates: None
Group Affiliation: American United Life Group
Licensed in: All states except AL
Commenced Business: November 1877
Address: One American Square, Indianapolis, IN 46204
Phone: (317) 285-1877 **Domicile State:** IN **NAIC Code:** 60895

Data Date	Rating	RACR #1	RACR #2	Total Assets ($mil)	Capital ($mil)	Net Premium ($mil)	Net Income ($mil)
3-09	B+	2.81	1.43	12,264.8	654.2	543.8	0.3
3-08	A-	3.15	1.64	13,653.7	684.9	548.7	13.9
2008	B+	2.85	1.47	12,526.2	656.2	2,353.5	9.4
2007	A-	3.20	1.67	14,032.8	677.9	2,031.4	57.1
2006	B+	3.20	1.67	12,879.1	660.5	1,951.8	64.0
2005	B+	2.77	1.51	12,122.6	633.5	1,889.2	42.1
2004	B	2.87	1.57	11,548.9	644.0	1,791.4	26.3

Adverse Trends in Operations

Decrease in capital during 2008 (3%)
Decrease in asset base during 2008 (11%)
Decrease in capital during 2005 (2%)
Increase in policy surrenders from 2004 to 2005 (25%)

AMERICAN-AMICABLE LIFE INSURANCE COMPANY OF TEXAS   B   Good

Major Rating Factors: Good liquidity (6.2 on a scale of 0 to 10) with sufficient resources to cover a large increase in policy surrenders. Good overall results on stability tests (5.5). Stability strengths include excellent operational trends, good risk adjusted capital for prior years and good risk diversification. Fair profitability (4.7) with investment income below regulatory standards in relation to interest assumptions of reserves.

Other Rating Factors: Strong capitalization (7.1) based on excellent risk adjusted capital (severe loss scenario). High quality investment portfolio (7.9).

Principal Business: Individual life insurance (83%), group life insurance (10%), individual annuities (4%), and reinsurance (2%).

Principal Investments: CMOs and structured securities (59%), nonCMO investment grade bonds (24%), common & preferred stock (11%), policy loans (5%), and real estate (1%).

Investments in Affiliates: 11%
Group Affiliation: American Amicable Group
Licensed in: All states except AL, KS, MI, MN, NJ, NM, NC, SC, VA
Commenced Business: December 1981
Address: 425 Austin Ave, Waco, TX 76701
Phone: (254) 297-2777 **Domicile State:** TX **NAIC Code:** 68594

Data Date	Rating	RACR #1	RACR #2	Total Assets ($mil)	Capital ($mil)	Net Premium ($mil)	Net Income ($mil)
3-09	B	1.22	1.05	354.6	58.1	10.0	0.7
3-08	B	1.23	1.09	340.2	56.2	9.6	1.3
2008	B	1.21	1.04	353.4	57.7	40.1	4.8
2007	B	1.25	1.11	335.7	57.5	41.9	5.4
2006	B-	1.95	1.32	307.8	47.1	43.9	7.9
2005	C+	1.17	1.04	300.1	52.6	45.8	7.8
2004	C+	0.98	0.83	269.6	40.3	50.7	10.6

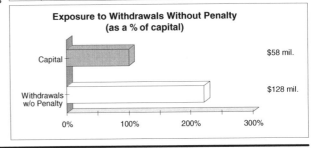

Exposure to Withdrawals Without Penalty (as a % of capital)

AMERICO FINANCIAL LIFE & ANNUITY INSURANCE   C+   Fair

Major Rating Factors: Fair current capitalization (4.4 on a scale of 0 to 10) based on fair risk adjusted capital (moderate loss scenario), although results have slipped from the good range over the last two years. Fair quality investment portfolio (4.0) with large holdings of BBB rated bonds in addition to moderate junk bond exposure. Exposure to mortgages is significant, but the mortgage default rate has been low. Fair overall results on stability tests (4.4) including fair risk adjusted capital in prior years.

Other Rating Factors: Good overall profitability (5.6). Good liquidity (5.6).

Principal Business: Individual life insurance (32%), individual annuities (32%), reinsurance (25%), group life insurance (8%), and group retirement contracts (2%).

Principal Investments: NonCMO investment grade bonds (50%), CMOs and structured securities (27%), mortgages in good standing (10%), common & preferred stock (9%), and noninv. grade bonds (2%).

Investments in Affiliates: 4%

Group Affiliation: Americo Life Inc

Licensed in: All states except AL, AZ, NM, NC

Commenced Business: July 1946

Address: 500 North Akard, Dallas, TX 75201

Phone: (816) 391-2000 **Domicile State:** TX **NAIC Code:** 61999

Data Date	Rating	RACR #1	RACR #2	Total Assets ($mil)	Capital ($mil)	Net Premium ($mil)	Net Income ($mil)
3-09	C+	0.92	0.56	3,389.3	166.7	65.2	8.7
3-08	C+	1.55	0.85	3,753.4	212.0	81.0	6.4
2008	C+	0.95	0.60	3,439.0	171.0	288.3	-20.8
2007	C+	1.74	0.95	3,735.6	225.4	339.0	8.6
2006	C+	1.75	0.93	3,575.2	216.6	300.4	18.7
2005	C+	1.57	0.83	3,519.8	190.6	338.8	40.2
2004	C	1.75	0.92	2,771.0	174.7	285.4	26.9

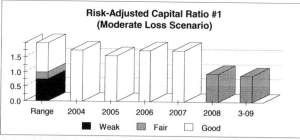

Risk-Adjusted Capital Ratio #1
(Moderate Loss Scenario)

■ Weak ▨ Fair □ Good

AMERITAS LIFE INSURANCE CORPORATION *   B+   Good

Major Rating Factors: Good overall results on stability tests (5.1 on a scale of 0 to 10). Stability strengths include excellent risk diversification. Good quality investment portfolio (5.3) despite significant exposure to mortgages . Mortgage default rate has been low. substantial holdings of BBB bonds in addition to small junk bond holdings. Good overall profitability (5.5) despite operating losses during the first three months of 2009.

Other Rating Factors: Strong capitalization (8.4) based on excellent risk adjusted capital (severe loss scenario). Excellent liquidity (7.0).

Principal Business: Group health insurance (37%), group retirement contracts (31%), individual annuities (19%), individual life insurance (10%), and reinsurance (4%).

Principal Investments: NonCMO investment grade bonds (47%), mortgages in good standing (15%), CMOs and structured securities (14%), common & preferred stock (9%), and misc. investments (14%).

Investments in Affiliates: 3%

Group Affiliation: UNIFI Mutual Holding Co

Licensed in: All states except AL, NC

Commenced Business: May 1887

Address: 5900 O Street, Lincoln, NE 68510

Phone: (402) 467-1122 **Domicile State:** NE **NAIC Code:** 61301

Data Date	Rating	RACR #1	RACR #2	Total Assets ($mil)	Capital ($mil)	Net Premium ($mil)	Net Income ($mil)
3-09	B+	3.09	1.94	4,928.5	678.5	266.9	-10.8
3-08	A-	3.37	2.22	6,200.3	878.7	405.8	9.2
2008	B+	3.19	2.02	5,142.4	710.6	1,299.0	-72.0
2007	A-	3.44	2.25	6,392.3	878.1	1,055.5	77.7
2006	A-	3.37	2.28	3,566.7	814.2	732.1	54.2
2005	A-	3.94	2.53	3,076.2	757.6	520.6	52.7
2004	A-	4.51	2.79	2,838.7	703.8	496.4	56.6

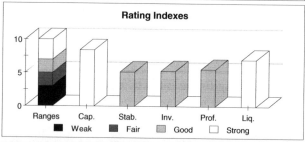

Rating Indexes

Ranges Cap. Stab. Inv. Prof. Liq.

■ Weak ▨ Fair □ Good □ Strong

AMICA LIFE INSURANCE COMPANY *   A-   Excellent

Major Rating Factors: Good overall results on stability tests (6.9 on a scale of 0 to 10). Strengths that enhance stability include excellent operational trends and excellent risk diversification. Good overall profitability (6.0) although investment income, in comparison to reserve requirements, is below regulatory standards. Good liquidity (6.6).

Other Rating Factors: Strong capitalization (8.7) based on excellent risk adjusted capital (severe loss scenario). High quality investment portfolio (7.0).

Principal Business: Individual life insurance (76%), individual annuities (21%), and group life insurance (3%).

Principal Investments: NonCMO investment grade bonds (59%), CMOs and structured securities (37%), common & preferred stock (3%), and policy loans (1%).

Investments in Affiliates: None

Group Affiliation: Amica Mutual Group

Licensed in: All states except AL, ID

Commenced Business: May 1970

Address: One Hundred Amica Way, Lincoln, RI 02867

Phone: (401) 334-6000 **Domicile State:** RI **NAIC Code:** 72222

Data Date	Rating	RACR #1	RACR #2	Total Assets ($mil)	Capital ($mil)	Net Premium ($mil)	Net Income ($mil)
3-09	A-	3.68	2.15	950.4	154.9	19.2	2.7
3-08	A-	3.74	2.18	928.2	159.9	14.2	3.2
2008	A-	3.76	2.20	940.1	156.4	61.8	8.7
2007	A-	3.77	2.21	923.1	158.6	54.9	10.1
2006	A-	3.62	2.12	891.4	147.5	57.9	11.4
2005	A-	3.65	2.12	847.5	143.3	60.3	13.5
2004	A-	3.45	2.02	800.9	128.5	67.0	10.3

Adverse Trends in Operations

Decrease in capital during 2008 (1%)
Decrease in premium volume from 2006 to 2007 (5%)
Increase in policy surrenders from 2005 to 2006 (48%)
Decrease in premium volume from 2005 to 2006 (4%)
Decrease in premium volume from 2004 to 2005 (10%)

ANNUITY INVESTORS LIFE INSURANCE COMPANY   **B-**   **Good**

Major Rating Factors: Good overall results on stability tests (5.3 on a scale of 0 to 10) despite fair financial strength of affiliated American Financial Corp. Other stability subfactors include excellent operational trends and excellent risk diversification. Good capitalization (5.7) based on good risk adjusted capital (moderate loss scenario). Capital levels have been relatively consistent over the last five years. Good overall profitability (5.3) despite operating losses during the first three months of 2009.

Other Rating Factors: Fair quality investment portfolio (3.2). Excellent liquidity (7.1).

Principal Business: Individual annuities (89%) and group retirement contracts (11%).

Principal Investments: NonCMO investment grade bonds (50%), CMOs and structured securities (41%), policy loans (4%), noninv. grade bonds (4%), and cash (1%).

Investments in Affiliates: None

Group Affiliation: American Financial Corp

Licensed in: All states except AL, NC, VA

Commenced Business: December 1981

Address: 250 E Fifth St, Cincinnati, OH 45202

Phone: (513) 357-3300 **Domicile State:** OH **NAIC Code:** 93661

Data Date	Rating	RACR #1	RACR #2	Total Assets ($mil)	Capital ($mil)	Net Premium ($mil)	Net Income ($mil)
3-09	B-	1.48	0.65	1,801.4	82.8	107.8	-1.4
3-08	B-	1.56	0.77	1,705.4	61.1	85.8	-2.4
2008	B-	1.72	0.82	1,742.2	78.6	417.4	-25.9
2007	B-	1.70	0.84	1,739.5	65.9	318.9	-1.2
2006	C+	2.02	0.98	1,601.8	65.4	276.5	25.2
2005	C	1.79	0.89	1,383.7	43.1	206.6	-3.4
2004	C	2.21	1.10	1,288.2	48.2	212.0	-0.2

American Financial Corp
Composite Group Rating: C+

Largest Group Members	Assets ($mil)	Rating
GREAT AMERICAN LIFE INS CO	9628	B-
GREAT AMERICAN INS CO	5642	C
ANNUITY INVESTORS LIFE INS CO	1742	B-
REPUBLIC INDEMNITY CO OF AMERICA	858	B-
NATIONAL INTERSTATE INS CO	730	C+

ANTHEM LIFE INSURANCE COMPANY *   **A-**   **Excellent**

Major Rating Factors: Good liquidity (6.9 on a scale of 0 to 10) with sufficient resources to handle a spike in claims. Excellent overall results on stability tests (7.1). Strengths that enhance stability include excellent operational trends and excellent risk diversification. Strong capitalization (7.7) based on excellent risk adjusted capital (severe loss scenario). Furthermore, this high level of risk adjusted capital has been consistently maintained over the last five years.

Other Rating Factors: High quality investment portfolio (8.1). Excellent profitability (8.3) with operating gains in each of the last five years.

Principal Business: Group life insurance (63%), group health insurance (35%), and individual life insurance (2%).

Principal Investments: NonCMO investment grade bonds (81%), CMOs and structured securities (18%), and common & preferred stock (1%).

Investments in Affiliates: None

Group Affiliation: WellPoint Inc

Licensed in: All states except AL, NC, SC, VA

Commenced Business: September 1953

Address: 6740 N High St Suite 200, Worthington, OH 43085

Phone: (614) 438-3959 **Domicile State:** IN **NAIC Code:** 61069

Data Date	Rating	RACR #1	RACR #2	Total Assets ($mil)	Capital ($mil)	Net Premium ($mil)	Net Income ($mil)
3-09	A-	2.04	1.48	288.0	69.4	42.0	4.3
3-08	A-	2.05	1.49	293.9	69.6	43.6	5.7
2008	A-	1.82	1.33	288.3	65.4	173.3	23.8
2007	A-	1.81	1.32	276.4	64.1	160.5	20.4
2006	A-	2.03	1.47	258.1	57.8	135.6	15.6
2005	B+	2.53	1.81	263.5	66.4	120.1	2.6
2004	B-	2.46	1.77	252.5	63.7	120.5	5.0

Adverse Trends in Operations

Decrease in asset base during 2006 (2%)
Decrease in capital during 2006 (13%)

ASSURITY LIFE INSURANCE COMPANY *   **B+**   **Good**

Major Rating Factors: Good quality investment portfolio (5.8 on a scale of 0 to 10) despite large holdings of BBB rated bonds in addition to moderate junk bond exposure. Exposure to mortgages is significant, but the mortgage default rate has been low. Good overall profitability (6.9). Return on equity has been low, averaging 4.9%. Good liquidity (5.7).

Other Rating Factors: Good overall results on stability tests (6.6) excellent operational trends and excellent risk diversification. Strong capitalization (7.5) based on excellent risk adjusted capital (severe loss scenario).

Principal Business: Individual life insurance (45%), individual health insurance (24%), group health insurance (17%), individual annuities (7%), and other lines (7%).

Principal Investments: NonCMO investment grade bonds (68%), mortgages in good standing (16%), policy loans (5%), CMOs and structured securities (5%), and misc. investments (7%).

Investments in Affiliates: None

Group Affiliation: Assurity Security Group Inc

Licensed in: All states except AL, NC

Commenced Business: March 1964

Address: 1526 K Street, Lincoln, NE 68508

Phone: (402) 476-6500 **Domicile State:** NE **NAIC Code:** 71439

Data Date	Rating	RACR #1	RACR #2	Total Assets ($mil)	Capital ($mil)	Net Premium ($mil)	Net Income ($mil)
3-09	B+	2.38	1.30	2,167.6	217.3	66.3	1.1
3-08	B+	2.50	1.45	2,182.1	246.3	57.4	3.5
2008	B+	2.44	1.35	2,161.1	223.2	236.6	1.9
2007	B+	2.66	1.54	2,189.2	245.5	236.0	14.6
2006	B	2.47	1.40	1,327.6	136.2	155.9	5.7
2005	B-	2.62	1.47	1,313.2	132.3	171.2	5.6
2004	C+	2.50	1.40	1,103.2	107.3	136.7	10.4

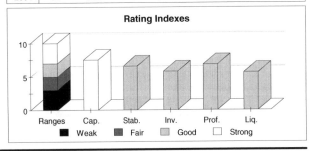

Rating Indexes

(Chart legend: Ranges, Cap., Stab., Inv., Prof., Liq. — Weak, Fair, Good, Strong)

AURORA NATIONAL LIFE ASSURANCE COMPANY · C+ · Fair

Major Rating Factors: Fair overall results on stability tests (4.8 on a scale of 0 to 10) including negative cash flow from operations for 2008. Good overall profitability (5.9) despite operating losses during the first three months of 2009. Return on equity has been low, averaging 4.2%. Good liquidity (6.7) with sufficient resources to handle a spike in claims as well as a significant increase in policy surrenders.

Other Rating Factors: Strong capitalization (8.9) based on excellent risk adjusted capital (severe loss scenario). High quality investment portfolio (7.9).

Principal Business: Individual life insurance (96%) and group life insurance (4%).

Principal Investments: NonCMO investment grade bonds (75%), CMOs and structured securities (15%), policy loans (8%), common & preferred stock (1%), and noninv. grade bonds (1%).

Investments in Affiliates: None

Group Affiliation: New California Life Holdings Inc

Licensed in: All states except AL, DC, MD, NJ, NC

Commenced Business: December 1961

Address: 2525 Colorado Ave, Bl C, Santa Monica, CA 90404-3540

Phone: (310) 264-3200 **Domicile State:** CA **NAIC Code:** 61182

Data Date	Rating	RACR #1	RACR #2	Total Assets ($mil)	Capital ($mil)	Net Premium ($mil)	Net Income ($mil)
3-09	C+	4.19	2.26	3,120.2	333.5	0.4	-1.6
3-08	C	3.28	1.71	3,240.5	306.5	0.4	4.2
2008	C+	4.12	2.21	3,125.4	327.6	1.3	14.2
2007	C	3.35	1.74	3,246.6	300.9	1.3	22.0
2006	C-	3.06	1.58	3,292.1	285.5	1.6	18.8
2005	C-	2.77	1.41	3,354.3	271.4	1.8	48.6
2004	D	2.51	1.27	3,524.2	263.6	2.3	-70.3

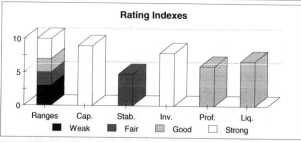

Rating Indexes

Ranges · Cap. · Stab. · Inv. · Prof. · Liq.
■ Weak ■ Fair ▨ Good □ Strong

AUTO CLUB LIFE INSURANCE COMPANY · B- · Good

Major Rating Factors: Good current capitalization (5.6 on a scale of 0 to 10) based on good risk adjusted capital (severe loss scenario), although results have slipped from the excellent range over the last two years. Good quality investment portfolio (6.4) despite mixed results such as: substantial holdings of BBB bonds but junk bond exposure equal to 58% of capital. Good liquidity (5.9).

Other Rating Factors: Good overall results on stability tests (5.2) despite fair risk adjusted capital in prior years excellent operational trends and excellent risk diversification. Fair profitability (4.3) with operating losses during the first three months of 2009.

Principal Business: Reinsurance (75%), individual life insurance (20%), individual annuities (3%), group health insurance (2%), and individual health insurance (1%).

Principal Investments: NonCMO investment grade bonds (51%), CMOs and structured securities (31%), noninv. grade bonds (7%), common & preferred stock (5%), and policy loans (2%).

Investments in Affiliates: 5%

Group Affiliation: Automobile Club of Michigan Group

Licensed in: AR, CA, CO, CT, IN, IA, KS, KY, LA, MA, MN, MS, MT, NV, NY, ND, OH, OK, OR, RI, SD, TN, UT, WA, WV, WY

Commenced Business: August 1974

Address: 17250 Newburgh Road, Livonia, MI 48152

Phone: (734) 591-9442 **Domicile State:** MI **NAIC Code:** 84522

Data Date	Rating	RACR #1	RACR #2	Total Assets ($mil)	Capital ($mil)	Net Premium ($mil)	Net Income ($mil)
3-09	B-	1.19	0.83	429.0	47.8	14.7	-0.4
3-08	B-	1.46	1.01	432.6	55.7	10.6	-0.6
2008	B-	1.18	0.82	423.3	48.8	54.3	-3.5
2007	B-	1.51	1.04	430.0	58.0	45.8	4.3
2006	C+	1.82	0.93	423.3	33.7	51.3	0.9
2005	C+	1.24	0.73	423.5	23.2	51.0	-1.8
2004	C+	1.48	0.86	417.8	26.5	56.9	1.2

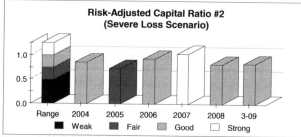

Risk-Adjusted Capital Ratio #2
(Severe Loss Scenario)

Range · 2004 · 2005 · 2006 · 2007 · 2008 · 3-09
■ Weak ■ Fair ▨ Good □ Strong

AUTO-OWNERS LIFE INSURANCE COMPANY * · A · Excellent

Major Rating Factors: Good overall results on stability tests (6.0 on a scale of 0 to 10). Strengths that enhance stability include excellent risk diversification. Good quality investment portfolio (5.9) despite significant exposure to mortgages . Mortgage default rate has been low. substantial holdings of BBB bonds in addition to minimal holdings in junk bonds. Good overall profitability (6.6). Excellent expense controls.

Other Rating Factors: Good liquidity (6.3). Strong capitalization (7.5) based on excellent risk adjusted capital (severe loss scenario).

Principal Business: Individual annuities (42%), individual life insurance (42%), group retirement contracts (7%), individual health insurance (7%), and group health insurance (1%).

Principal Investments: NonCMO investment grade bonds (67%), CMOs and structured securities (15%), mortgages in good standing (10%), real estate (4%), and common & preferred stock (2%).

Investments in Affiliates: None

Group Affiliation: Auto-Owners Group

Licensed in: AK, AR, CA, CT, GA, HI, IL, IN, IA, KS, KY, LA, MN, MS, MO, MT, NV, NH, NY, ND, OH, OK, PA, RI, SD, TN, TX, UT, VT, WA, WV, WY

Commenced Business: January 1966

Address: 6101 Anacapri Blvd, Lansing, MI 48917

Phone: (517) 323-1200 **Domicile State:** MI **NAIC Code:** 61190

Data Date	Rating	RACR #1	RACR #2	Total Assets ($mil)	Capital ($mil)	Net Premium ($mil)	Net Income ($mil)
3-09	A	2.50	1.33	2,168.0	225.0	57.8	0.1
3-08	A	2.81	1.53	2,073.9	225.9	72.6	3.1
2008	A	2.59	1.39	2,110.9	229.6	181.6	13.4
2007	A	2.89	1.59	2,009.9	224.7	205.5	20.2
2006	A	2.85	1.56	1,840.8	203.0	208.8	16.9
2005	A	2.86	1.55	1,686.4	183.8	224.4	12.4
2004	A	2.85	1.56	1,508.3	173.0	205.1	9.8

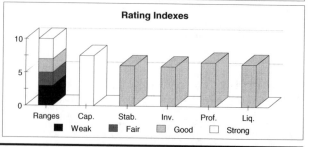

Rating Indexes

Ranges · Cap. · Stab. · Inv. · Prof. · Liq.
■ Weak ■ Fair ▨ Good □ Strong

AUTOMOBILE CLUB OF SOUTHERN CA INS   B   Good

Major Rating Factors: Good capitalization (5.6 on a scale of 0 to 10) based on good risk adjusted capital (severe loss scenario). Capital levels have been relatively consistent over the last five years. Good liquidity (6.7) with sufficient resources to cover a large increase in policy surrenders. Good overall results on stability tests (5.6) excellent operational trends and excellent risk diversification.

Other Rating Factors: Fair quality investment portfolio (4.5). Weak profitability (1.8) with operating losses during the first three months of 2009.

Principal Business: Reinsurance (100%).

Principal Investments: NonCMO investment grade bonds (68%), CMOs and structured securities (25%), and noninv. grade bonds (5%).

Investments in Affiliates: None

Group Affiliation: Interins Exch Automobile Club

Licensed in: CO

Commenced Business: December 1999

Address: 3333 Fairview Road, Costa Mesa, CA 92625

Phone: (714) 850-5111 **Domicile State:** CA **NAIC Code:** 60256

Data Date	Rating	RACR #1	RACR #2	Total Assets ($mil)	Capital ($mil)	Net Premium ($mil)	Net Income ($mil)
3-09	B	1.43	0.82	437.5	34.2	41.5	-1.7
3-08	B	1.43	0.83	363.6	28.1	18.3	-3.6
2008	B	1.53	0.89	410.7	37.6	115.0	-13.5
2007	B	1.62	0.94	349.4	32.2	69.9	-4.8
2006	C+	1.53	0.87	317.2	26.0	61.1	-12.5
2005	C+	1.32	0.77	273.0	17.9	51.4	-5.2
2004	C+	1.52	0.89	245.7	18.2	52.4	1.0

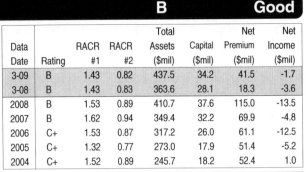

Risk-Adjusted Capital Ratio #2
(Severe Loss Scenario)

Range 2004 2005 2006 2007 2008 3-09
■ Weak ▦ Fair ▨ Good ☐ Strong

AVIVA LIFE & ANNUITY COMPANY   C+   Fair

Major Rating Factors: Fair quality investment portfolio (3.5 on a scale of 0 to 10) with large holdings of BBB rated bonds in addition to significant exposure to junk bonds. Fair overall results on stability tests (4.5). Good capitalization (5.4) based on good risk adjusted capital (moderate loss scenario). Capital levels have been relatively consistent over the last five years.

Other Rating Factors: Good liquidity (6.2). Weak profitability (2.8) with operating losses during the first three months of 2009.

Principal Business: Individual annuities (73%), individual life insurance (23%), group retirement contracts (3%), and reinsurance (1%).

Principal Investments: NonCMO investment grade bonds (70%), CMOs and structured securities (9%), noninv. grade bonds (7%), mortgages in good standing (6%), and misc. investments (8%).

Investments in Affiliates: 1%

Group Affiliation: Aviva plc

Licensed in: All states except AL, NC

Commenced Business: February 1896

Address: 611 Fifth Ave, Des Moines, IA 50309

Phone: (515) 283-2371 **Domicile State:** IA **NAIC Code:** 61689

Data Date	Rating	RACR #1	RACR #2	Total Assets ($mil)	Capital ($mil)	Net Premium ($mil)	Net Income ($mil)
3-09	C+	1.25	0.67	25,060.9	1,154.6	1,066.4	-162.5
3-08	B-	1.57	0.79	12,044.2	508.8	560.7	-32.2
2008	C+	1.43	0.77	24,683.2	1,266.5	3,752.0	-287.4
2007	B-	1.70	0.85	11,603.1	549.0	1,953.7	-3.4
2006	B-	2.04	1.02	9,669.9	508.1	1,677.8	80.6
2005	B-	2.06	1.05	8,073.1	469.7	1,834.6	95.6
2004	C+	1.60	0.89	6,785.0	351.5	1,157.7	79.4

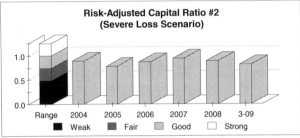

Junk Bonds as a % of Capital

Capital $1 bil.
Junk Bonds $2 bil.

0% 20% 40% 60% 80% 100% 120%
■ BB ▦ B ▨ CCC ☐ In default

AVIVA LIFE & ANNUITY COMPANY OF NEW YORK   C   Fair

Major Rating Factors: Fair quality investment portfolio (4.3 on a scale of 0 to 10) with large holdings of BBB rated bonds in addition to significant exposure to junk bonds. Fair overall results on stability tests (4.3) including fair risk adjusted capital in prior years. Good capitalization (6.1) based on good risk adjusted capital (severe loss scenario).

Other Rating Factors: Good liquidity (5.2). Weak profitability (2.0) with operating losses during the first three months of 2009.

Principal Business: Individual life insurance (67%), individual annuities (27%), group life insurance (4%), reinsurance (2%), and individual health insurance (1%).

Principal Investments: NonCMO investment grade bonds (75%), CMOs and structured securities (14%), noninv. grade bonds (7%), policy loans (2%), and misc. investments (2%).

Investments in Affiliates: None

Group Affiliation: Aviva plc

Licensed in: DC, GA, IN, IA, KS, KY, LA, MI, MN, MO, NH, NM, NC, ND, RI, SC, VA

Commenced Business: November 1958

Address: 65 Froehlich Farm Blvd, Woodbury, NY 11797-9847

Phone: (516) 364-5900 **Domicile State:** NY **NAIC Code:** 63932

Data Date	Rating	RACR #1	RACR #2	Total Assets ($mil)	Capital ($mil)	Net Premium ($mil)	Net Income ($mil)
3-09	C	1.74	0.89	1,432.1	95.3	24.9	-7.9
3-08	C	1.91	0.99	1,357.7	86.7	34.2	-2.7
2008	C	1.46	0.73	1,394.3	80.4	126.3	-22.9
2007	C	1.96	1.01	1,336.0	90.4	126.9	-18.4
2006	C	2.20	1.16	566.9	50.2	77.6	-1.3
2005	C	2.27	1.20	549.8	50.4	75.6	-0.7
2004	C+	2.05	1.09	525.5	44.0	80.2	8.0

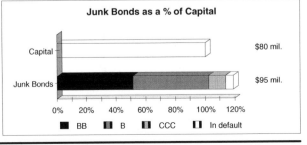

Junk Bonds as a % of Capital

Capital $80 mil.
Junk Bonds $95 mil.

0% 20% 40% 60% 80% 100% 120%
■ BB ▦ B ▨ CCC ☐ In default

AXA CORPORATE SOLUTIONS LIFE REINSURANCE COMPANY | B | Good

Major Rating Factors: Good quality investment portfolio (6.8 on a scale of 0 to 10) with no exposure to mortgages and minimal holdings in junk bonds. Fair overall results on stability tests (4.7) including fair financial strength of affiliated AXA Financial Inc. Weak profitability (1.0) with operating losses during the first three months of 2009. Return on equity has been low, averaging -79.5%.

Other Rating Factors: Strong capitalization (7.6) based on excellent risk adjusted capital (severe loss scenario). Excellent liquidity (10.0).

Principal Business: Reinsurance (100%).

Principal Investments: NonCMO investment grade bonds (58%), cash (31%), and CMOs and structured securities (10%).

Investments in Affiliates: None

Group Affiliation: AXA Financial Inc

Licensed in: All states except AL, GA, MD, ND, WA, PR

Commenced Business: January 1959

Address: 17 State St, New York, NY 10004

Phone: (212) 493-9364 **Domicile State:** DE **NAIC Code:** 68365

Data Date	Rating	RACR #1	RACR #2	Total Assets ($mil)	Capital ($mil)	Net Premium ($mil)	Net Income ($mil)
3-09	B	2.65	1.40	1,649.4	122.2	23.3	-91.8
3-08	A-	29.72	17.24	896.7	492.4	23.8	29.4
2008	B	5.92	3.41	1,540.9	254.5	98.7	-518.6
2007	A-	29.42	18.06	817.1	487.9	101.9	19.8
2006	B+	29.42	17.57	770.3	475.5	112.3	62.8
2005	C	24.11	12.89	666.3	350.0	127.2	24.5
2004	C	21.55	11.45	640.5	329.8	138.4	46.7

AXA Financial Inc
Composite Group Rating: C

Largest Group Members	Assets ($mil)	Rating
AXA EQUITABLE LIFE INS CO	111796	C
MONY LIFE INS CO	9162	C+
MONY LIFE INS CO OF AMERICA	4199	C+
AXA CORPORATE SOLUTIONS LIFE REINS	1541	B
COLISEUM REINS CO	619	C

AXA EQUITABLE LIFE & ANNUITY COMPANY | B- | Good

Major Rating Factors: Good overall profitability (6.2 on a scale of 0 to 10). Return on equity has been good over the last five years, averaging 10.5%. Good liquidity (5.4) with sufficient resources to handle a spike in claims as well as a significant increase in policy surrenders. Fair overall results on stability tests (3.6) including fair financial strength of affiliated AXA Financial Inc and negative cash flow from operations for 2008.

Other Rating Factors: Strong capitalization (7.3) based on excellent risk adjusted capital (severe loss scenario). High quality investment portfolio (7.4).

Principal Business: Individual life insurance (100%).

Principal Investments: Policy loans (51%), nonCMO investment grade bonds (42%), and CMOs and structured securities (7%).

Investments in Affiliates: None

Group Affiliation: AXA Financial Inc

Licensed in: All states except AL, NC

Commenced Business: June 1984

Address: 135 W 50th St Location 6F, New York, NY 10020

Phone: (212) 641-8231 **Domicile State:** CO **NAIC Code:** 62880

Data Date	Rating	RACR #1	RACR #2	Total Assets ($mil)	Capital ($mil)	Net Premium ($mil)	Net Income ($mil)
3-09	B-	2.36	1.22	492.4	52.7	-2.1	4.0
3-08	B+	4.83	2.49	550.4	110.5	-2.5	5.2
2008	B-	2.19	1.14	512.8	48.8	7.8	8.6
2007	B+	4.70	2.43	554.7	105.2	10.5	7.2
2006	B	4.30	2.20	541.7	97.6	7.7	6.1
2005	B	3.28	1.65	533.7	91.9	10.3	6.1
2004	B-	2.99	1.52	525.7	85.7	14.4	7.3

AXA Financial Inc
Composite Group Rating: C

Largest Group Members	Assets ($mil)	Rating
AXA EQUITABLE LIFE INS CO	111796	C
MONY LIFE INS CO	9162	C+
MONY LIFE INS CO OF AMERICA	4199	C+
AXA CORPORATE SOLUTIONS LIFE REINS	1541	B
COLISEUM REINS CO	619	C

AXA EQUITABLE LIFE INSURANCE COMPANY | C- | Fair

Major Rating Factors: Poor current capitalization (2.7 on a scale of 0 to 10) based on weak risk adjusted capital (moderate loss scenario), although results have slipped from the good range during the last year. Weak profitability (1.5). Return on equity has been low, averaging -9.2%. Weak overall results on stability tests (2.7) including negative cash flow from operations for 2008.

Other Rating Factors: Fair quality investment portfolio (3.9). Excellent liquidity (7.0).

Principal Business: Group retirement contracts (61%), individual annuities (23%), individual life insurance (14%), reinsurance (1%), and individual health insurance (1%).

Principal Investments: NonCMO investment grade bonds (54%), CMOs and structured securities (11%), policy loans (9%), mortgages in good standing (9%), and misc. investments (16%).

Investments in Affiliates: 5%

Group Affiliation: AXA Financial Inc

Licensed in: All states except AL

Commenced Business: July 1859

Address: 787 Seventh Ave, New York, NY 10019

Phone: (212) 641-8231 **Domicile State:** NY **NAIC Code:** 62944

Data Date	Rating	RACR #1	RACR #2	Total Assets ($mil)	Capital ($mil)	Net Premium ($mil)	Net Income ($mil)
3-09	C-	0.71	0.45	108,228	2,234.7	3,558.0	255.4
3-08	B	1.33	1.02	135,389	6,562.3	4,456.1	97.2
2008	C	1.03	0.65	111,796	3,155.0	14,590.2	-1,074.8
2007	B	1.41	1.08	142,433	6,569.3	19,338.3	598.6
2006	B	1.33	1.04	131,780	6,497.6	16,603.7	526.2
2005	B	1.43	1.05	115,386	5,111.1	14,427.8	774.3
2004	B	1.48	1.03	105,308	4,331.5	13,958.8	564.1

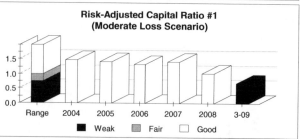

Risk-Adjusted Capital Ratio #1
(Moderate Loss Scenario)

■ Weak ▨ Fair □ Good

BALBOA LIFE INSURANCE COMPANY   B   Good

Major Rating Factors: Good overall results on stability tests (6.7 on a scale of 0 to 10). Stability strengths include excellent operational trends and excellent risk diversification. Good overall profitability (6.7). Return on equity has been excellent over the last five years averaging 15.6%. Strong capitalization (7.5) based on excellent risk adjusted capital (severe loss scenario).

Other Rating Factors: High quality investment portfolio (7.9). Excellent liquidity (7.8).

Principal Business: Group health insurance (47%), credit health insurance (27%), individual life insurance (13%), credit life insurance (12%), and group life insurance (1%).

Principal Investments: Common & preferred stock (43%), CMOs and structured securities (30%), nonCMO investment grade bonds (22%), and cash (3%).

Investments in Affiliates: 43%

Group Affiliation: Bank of America Corp

Licensed in: All states except AL, NC

Commenced Business: January 1969

Address: 18581 Teller Avenue, Irvine, CA 92612-1627

Phone: (949) 553-0700 **Domicile State:** CA **NAIC Code:** 68160

Data Date	Rating	RACR #1	RACR #2	Total Assets ($mil)	Capital ($mil)	Net Premium ($mil)	Net Income ($mil)
3-09	B	1.46	1.36	44.3	31.8	3.8	1.2
3-08	B	1.32	1.23	40.9	27.3	4.0	1.4
2008	B	1.41	1.32	43.3	30.7	16.2	4.0
2007	B	1.35	1.26	41.3	27.9	15.5	5.4
2006	B	2.63	2.25	38.9	22.4	17.6	4.4
2005	B+	2.33	2.10	71.9	47.2	19.0	7.5
2004	B+	4.74	4.25	114.2	84.5	16.2	7.7

Adverse Trends in Operations

Decrease in premium volume from 2006 to 2007 (12%)
Decrease in asset base during 2006 (46%)
Decrease in capital during 2006 (53%)
Decrease in asset base during 2005 (37%)
Decrease in capital during 2005 (44%)

BALTIMORE LIFE INSURANCE COMPANY   B   Good

Major Rating Factors: Good quality investment portfolio (5.7 on a scale of 0 to 10) despite large holdings of BBB rated bonds in addition to moderate junk bond exposure. Exposure to mortgages is significant, but the mortgage default rate has been low. Good liquidity (5.3) with sufficient resources to cover a large increase in policy surrenders. Good overall results on stability tests (6.1) excellent operational trends, good risk adjusted capital for prior years and good risk diversification.

Other Rating Factors: Strong capitalization (7.2) based on excellent risk adjusted capital (severe loss scenario). Excellent profitability (7.3) with operating gains in each of the last five years.

Principal Business: Individual life insurance (69%), individual annuities (13%), reinsurance (8%), group life insurance (6%), and group health insurance (4%).

Principal Investments: NonCMO investment grade bonds (61%), CMOs and structured securities (13%), mortgages in good standing (10%), common & preferred stock (6%), and misc. investments (9%).

Investments in Affiliates: None

Group Affiliation: Baltimore Life Holdings Inc

Licensed in: All states except AL, NC

Commenced Business: March 1882

Address: 10075 Red Run Blvd, Owings Mills, MD 21117-6050

Phone: (410) 581-6600 **Domicile State:** MD **NAIC Code:** 61212

Data Date	Rating	RACR #1	RACR #2	Total Assets ($mil)	Capital ($mil)	Net Premium ($mil)	Net Income ($mil)
3-09	B	2.27	1.16	836.1	70.5	24.4	0.9
3-08	B	2.48	1.32	808.6	72.4	20.1	0.7
2008	B	2.30	1.22	834.8	71.5	100.3	1.1
2007	B	2.51	1.34	810.3	72.4	80.7	8.5
2006	C+	2.24	1.20	801.5	64.1	71.1	5.6
2005	C	2.05	1.08	805.5	55.3	69.1	7.6
2004	C	1.66	0.88	795.2	46.1	75.1	8.6

Adverse Trends in Operations

Decrease in capital during 2008 (1%)
Decrease in premium volume from 2004 to 2005 (8%)

BANKERS CONSECO LIFE INSURANCE COMPANY   D   Weak

Major Rating Factors: Weak profitability (1.7 on a scale of 0 to 10) with operating losses during the first three months of 2009. Return on equity has been low, averaging -46.2%. Weak overall results on stability tests (1.8). Good quality investment portfolio (5.7) despite mixed results such as: no exposure to mortgages and large holdings of BBB rated bonds but minimal holdings in junk bonds.

Other Rating Factors: Strong capitalization (8.4) based on excellent risk adjusted capital (severe loss scenario). Excellent liquidity (7.0).

Principal Business: Individual life insurance (51%), individual health insurance (35%), individual annuities (12%), and reinsurance (3%).

Principal Investments: NonCMO investment grade bonds (66%), CMOs and structured securities (23%), cash (7%), common & preferred stock (2%), and misc. investments (2%).

Investments in Affiliates: None

Group Affiliation: Conseco Group

Licensed in: NC

Commenced Business: July 1987

Address: 11815 N Pennsylvania St, Carmel, IN 46032

Phone: (215) 244-1600 **Domicile State:** NY **NAIC Code:** 68560

Data Date	Rating	RACR #1	RACR #2	Total Assets ($mil)	Capital ($mil)	Net Premium ($mil)	Net Income ($mil)
3-09	D	2.56	1.92	261.3	26.6	8.7	-1.2
3-08	D	1.98	1.74	247.9	20.2	7.0	-1.0
2008	D	2.68	2.25	254.3	27.8	29.2	5.6
2007	D	2.10	1.89	241.2	21.4	25.9	-17.3
2006	D	1.48	1.34	237.1	14.6	24.8	-16.3
2005	D	1.48	1.34	181.6	14.0	25.1	-2.4
2004	D	0.99	0.89	168.0	9.1	25.7	-6.5

Net Income History
(in millions of dollars)

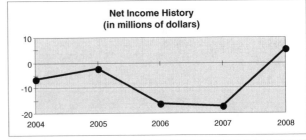

BANKERS FIDELITY LIFE INSURANCE COMPANY | B | Good

Major Rating Factors: Good overall results on stability tests (5.5 on a scale of 0 to 10) despite fair financial strength of affiliated Atlantic American Corp. Other stability subfactors include good operational trends and good risk diversification. Good quality investment portfolio (5.5) with no exposure to mortgages and small junk bond holdings. Good overall profitability (6.8).

Other Rating Factors: Good liquidity (6.5). Strong capitalization (8.1) based on excellent risk adjusted capital (severe loss scenario).

Principal Business: Individual health insurance (80%) and individual life insurance (18%).

Principal Investments: NonCMO investment grade bonds (78%), common & preferred stock (7%), cash (7%), noninv. grade bonds (4%), and policy loans (2%).

Investments in Affiliates: None

Group Affiliation: Atlantic American Corp

Licensed in: All states except AL, CO, DC, NC, VA

Commenced Business: November 1955

Address: 4370 Peachtree Rd NE, Atlanta, GA 30319

Phone: (404) 266-5500 **Domicile State:** GA **NAIC Code:** 61239

Data Date	Rating	RACR #1	RACR #2	Total Assets ($mil)	Capital ($mil)	Net Premium ($mil)	Net Income ($mil)
3-09	B	2.42	1.70	108.7	28.5	14.4	0.6
3-08	B-	2.82	2.04	115.8	33.7	14.2	1.0
2008	B	2.58	1.82	110.7	29.9	55.2	1.3
2007	B-	2.86	2.07	119.8	33.8	55.9	12.0
2006	C+	2.04	1.40	115.2	34.5	58.3	3.2
2005	C+	1.87	1.25	118.1	33.9	65.5	5.1
2004	C+	1.96	1.36	116.2	35.5	66.8	4.6

Atlantic American Corp Composite Group Rating: C+ Largest Group Members	Assets ($mil)	Rating
BANKERS FIDELITY LIFE INS CO	111	B
AMERICAN SOUTHERN INS CO	96	C+
AMERICAN SAFETY INS CO	19	C

BANKERS LIFE & CASUALTY COMPANY | D+ | Weak

Major Rating Factors: Weak overall results on stability tests (2.7 on a scale of 0 to 10) including potential financial drain due to affiliation with Conseco Group. Fair quality investment portfolio (3.0) with large holdings of BBB rated bonds in addition to significant exposure to junk bonds. Good capitalization (5.1) based on good risk adjusted capital (moderate loss scenario).

Other Rating Factors: Good liquidity (5.4). Excellent profitability (7.7) despite operating losses during the first three months of 2009.

Principal Business: Individual annuities (36%), individual health insurance (36%), reinsurance (18%), individual life insurance (8%), and group health insurance (2%).

Principal Investments: NonCMO investment grade bonds (56%), CMOs and structured securities (21%), mortgages in good standing (8%), noninv. grade bonds (7%), and misc. investments (7%).

Investments in Affiliates: 1%

Group Affiliation: Conseco Group

Licensed in: All states except AL, NC

Commenced Business: January 1879

Address: 222 Merchandise Mart Plaza, Chicago, IL 60654

Phone: (312) 396-6000 **Domicile State:** IL **NAIC Code:** 61263

Data Date	Rating	RACR #1	RACR #2	Total Assets ($mil)	Capital ($mil)	Net Premium ($mil)	Net Income ($mil)
3-09	D+	1.07	0.59	11,637.0	588.2	694.5	-7.0
3-08	D+	1.36	0.77	10,770.4	617.6	719.0	12.4
2008	D+	1.18	0.66	11,442.4	607.1	2,911.1	-27.3
2007	D+	1.56	0.88	10,612.8	685.9	2,631.6	113.7
2006	D+	1.65	0.93	9,887.3	630.2	2,493.7	53.8
2005	D+	1.64	0.94	8,907.7	579.8	2,323.5	26.6
2004	D	1.34	0.76	7,864.4	418.7	2,235.4	27.8

Conseco Group Composite Group Rating: D+ Largest Group Members	Assets ($mil)	Rating
BANKERS LIFE CAS CO	11442	D+
CONSECO LIFE INS CO	4529	D+
CONSECO HEALTH INS CO	2472	D+
WASHINGTON NATIONAL INS CO	2348	D+
CONSECO INS CO	1044	D+

BANNER LIFE INSURANCE COMPANY | D+ | Weak

Major Rating Factors: Weak profitability (1.4 on a scale of 0 to 10) with investment income below regulatory standards in relation to interest assumptions of reserves. Weak overall results on stability tests (2.5) including negative cash flow from operations for 2008. Good capitalization (6.3) based on good risk adjusted capital (severe loss scenario).

Other Rating Factors: Good liquidity (5.3). High quality investment portfolio (7.0).

Principal Business: Individual life insurance (100%).

Principal Investments: NonCMO investment grade bonds (73%), CMOs and structured securities (14%), common & preferred stock (11%), policy loans (3%), and noninv. grade bonds (1%).

Investments in Affiliates: 8%

Group Affiliation: Legal & General America Inc

Licensed in: All states except AL, NC

Commenced Business: October 1981

Address: 1701 Research Blvd, Rockville, MD 20850

Phone: (301) 279-4800 **Domicile State:** MD **NAIC Code:** 94250

Data Date	Rating	RACR #1	RACR #2	Total Assets ($mil)	Capital ($mil)	Net Premium ($mil)	Net Income ($mil)
3-09	D+	1.21	0.91	1,316.3	191.5	27.8	11.7
3-08	C-	1.18	0.91	1,277.5	196.8	46.1	-1.1
2008	D+	1.32	1.00	1,335.2	211.3	194.6	-16.1
2007	C-	1.33	1.03	1,293.4	225.4	106.5	-476.6
2006	C	1.08	0.87	1,226.4	183.2	245.2	-43.9
2005	C-	1.27	1.02	1,201.0	232.3	229.5	-62.7
2004	C+	1.96	1.57	1,172.5	321.4	228.2	-8.6

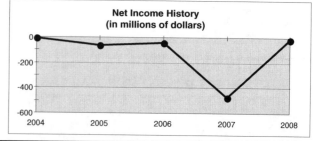

Net Income History (in millions of dollars)

BCS LIFE INSURANCE COMPANY

B **Good**

Major Rating Factors: Good overall results on stability tests (5.9 on a scale of 0 to 10) despite negative cash flow from operations for 2008. Other stability subfactors include good operational trends and excellent risk diversification. Good liquidity (6.7) with sufficient resources to handle a spike in claims. Strong capitalization (9.8) based on excellent risk adjusted capital (severe loss scenario).

Other Rating Factors: High quality investment portfolio (8.2). Excellent profitability (8.5) with operating gains in each of the last five years.

Principal Business: Group health insurance (79%), reinsurance (13%), and group life insurance (8%).

Principal Investments: NonCMO investment grade bonds (50%), CMOs and structured securities (47%), cash (2%), and noninv. grade bonds (1%).

Investments in Affiliates: 4%

Group Affiliation: BCS Financial Corp

Licensed in: All states except AL

Commenced Business: November 1949

Address: 676 North St Clair St, Chicago, IL 60611-2997

Phone: (312) 951-7700 **Domicile State:** IL **NAIC Code:** 80985

Data Date	Rating	RACR #1	RACR #2	Total Assets ($mil)	Capital ($mil)	Net Premium ($mil)	Net Income ($mil)
3-09	B	3.69	2.85	178.5	80.5	47.8	0.3
3-08	B-	3.68	2.88	187.6	82.1	51.0	1.9
2008	B	3.07	2.40	180.6	79.7	200.9	1.1
2007	B-	3.06	2.40	196.9	80.5	207.6	7.3
2006	C+	2.92	2.30	170.4	76.4	209.4	5.5
2005	C	2.91	2.28	166.7	72.8	196.4	5.2
2004	C	3.04	2.37	155.0	69.9	176.8	5.3

Adverse Trends in Operations

Decrease in capital during 2008 (1%)
Decrease in premium volume from 2007 to 2008 (3%)
Decrease in asset base during 2008 (8%)
Increase in policy surrenders from 2006 to 2007 (31%)
Increase in policy surrenders from 2004 to 2005 (39%)

BENEFICIAL LIFE INSURANCE COMPANY

C+ **Fair**

Major Rating Factors: Fair quality investment portfolio (4.5 on a scale of 0 to 10) with large holdings of BBB rated bonds in addition to junk bond exposure equal to 58% of capital. Fair overall results on stability tests (4.3). Good liquidity (5.1) with sufficient resources to handle a spike in claims as well as a significant increase in policy surrenders.

Other Rating Factors: Strong capitalization (7.3) based on excellent risk adjusted capital (severe loss scenario). Excellent profitability (8.5).

Principal Business: Individual annuities (67%), individual life insurance (31%), and reinsurance (1%).

Principal Investments: CMOs and structured securities (48%), nonCMO investment grade bonds (37%), noninv. grade bonds (8%), policy loans (4%), and common & preferred stock (1%).

Investments in Affiliates: None

Group Affiliation: Beneficial Life Group

Licensed in: All states except AL, NC

Commenced Business: June 1905

Address: 36 South State St, Salt Lake City, UT 84136

Phone: (801) 933-1100 **Domicile State:** UT **NAIC Code:** 61395

Data Date	Rating	RACR #1	RACR #2	Total Assets ($mil)	Capital ($mil)	Net Premium ($mil)	Net Income ($mil)
3-09	C+	2.70	1.22	3,445.5	438.7	104.6	14.4
3-08	C+	2.09	1.06	3,548.9	342.5	72.2	10.9
2008	C+	3.16	1.52	3,437.2	451.3	366.6	-239.7
2007	C+	2.14	1.10	3,559.6	341.1	329.3	-174.5
2006	B+	1.85	0.97	3,678.7	279.1	497.5	29.1
2005	B+	1.91	0.99	3,093.1	254.8	404.1	25.4
2004	B+	1.94	0.98	2,856.7	233.2	389.6	26.3

Rating Indexes

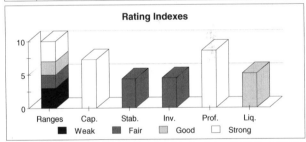

BERKLEY LIFE & HEALTH INSURANCE COMPANY

B **Good**

Major Rating Factors: Fair overall results on stability tests (4.3 on a scale of 0 to 10) including fair financial strength of affiliated W R Berkley Corp and significant changes in business operations. Strong capitalization (8.0) based on excellent risk adjusted capital (severe loss scenario). Moreover, capital levels have been consistently high over the last five years. High quality investment portfolio (8.8).

Other Rating Factors: Excellent profitability (8.1) with operating gains in each of the last five years. Excellent liquidity (10.0).

Principal Business: Individual life insurance (94%) and individual annuities (6%).

Principal Investments: NonCMO investment grade bonds (87%) and CMOs and structured securities (12%).

Investments in Affiliates: None

Group Affiliation: W R Berkley Corp

Licensed in: All states except AL, DC, NC, VA

Commenced Business: July 1963

Address: 200 Clarendon St, Boston, MA 02117

Phone: (203) 851-1755 **Domicile State:** IA **NAIC Code:** 64890

Data Date	Rating	RACR #1	RACR #2	Total Assets ($mil)	Capital ($mil)	Net Premium ($mil)	Net Income ($mil)
3-09	B	6.27	5.64	27.2	25.8	0.0	0.1
3-08	B	6.26	5.63	25.6	25.3	0.0	0.1
2008	B	6.25	5.62	26.1	25.7	0.0	0.6
2007	B	6.23	5.60	25.4	25.2	0.0	0.1
2006	B	3.90	3.51	7.8	7.6	0.2	0.1
2005	B-	3.86	3.48	7.7	7.4	0.2	0.1
2004	B-	3.84	3.45	7.6	7.4	0.1	0.1

W R Berkley Corp
Composite Group Rating: C+
Largest Group Members

	Assets ($mil)	Rating
BERKLEY INS CO	6846	C
BERKLEY REGIONAL INS CO	2665	B-
ADMIRAL INS CO	2514	C
NAUTILUS INS CO	1395	C+
CAROLINA CASUALTY INS CO	797	C

BERKSHIRE HATHAWAY LIFE INSURANCE COMPANY OF NE   B-   Good

Major Rating Factors: Good current capitalization (5.4 on a scale of 0 to 10) based on good risk adjusted capital (severe loss scenario), although results have slipped from the excellent range over the last two years. Good overall profitability (5.5) although investment income, in comparison to reserve requirements, is below regulatory standards. Fair quality investment portfolio (3.7).

Other Rating Factors: Fair overall results on stability tests (4.4) including negative cash flow from operations for 2008 and fair risk adjusted capital in prior years. Excellent liquidity (10.0).

Principal Business: Reinsurance (99%) and individual annuities (1%).

Principal Investments: CMOs and structured securities (47%), common & preferred stock (23%), noninv. grade bonds (22%), and nonCMO investment grade bonds (10%).

Investments in Affiliates: 24%

Group Affiliation: Berkshire-Hathaway

Licensed in: All states except AL, CT, MD, MS, NC, ND, VA

Commenced Business: June 1993

Address: 3024 Harney St, Omaha, NE 68131

Phone: (402) 536-3000 **Domicile State:** NE **NAIC Code:** 62345

Data Date	Rating	RACR #1	RACR #2	Total Assets ($mil)	Capital ($mil)	Net Premium ($mil)	Net Income ($mil)
3-09	B-	1.02	0.80	3,595.3	767.7	0.0	22.1
3-08	B-	1.15	1.04	3,647.8	857.5	16.2	-0.1
2008	B-	1.07	0.88	3,528.0	810.4	57.9	70.1
2007	B-	1.15	1.03	3,658.6	858.1	98.5	56.7
2006	B	1.13	1.02	3,757.5	862.0	139.9	353.1
2005	B	0.64	0.58	3,345.7	479.1	184.7	57.0
2004	B	0.71	0.63	3,495.5	566.9	201.7	-93.7

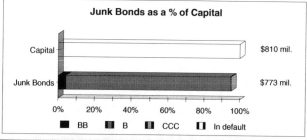

Junk Bonds as a % of Capital

Capital — $810 mil.
Junk Bonds — $773 mil.

■ BB   ▨ B   ▥ CCC   ▯ In default

BERKSHIRE LIFE INSURANCE COMPANY OF AMERICA *   A   Excellent

Major Rating Factors: Good quality investment portfolio (6.5 on a scale of 0 to 10) despite significant exposure to mortgages . Mortgage default rate has been low. large holdings of BBB rated bonds in addition to minimal holdings in junk bonds. Excellent overall results on stability tests (7.8). Strengths that enhance stability include excellent operational trends and excellent risk diversification. Strong capitalization (9.9) based on excellent risk adjusted capital (severe loss scenario).

Other Rating Factors: Excellent profitability (8.8). Excellent liquidity (8.1).

Principal Business: Reinsurance (49%), individual health insurance (48%), and individual life insurance (3%).

Principal Investments: NonCMO investment grade bonds (81%), mortgages in good standing (14%), noninv. grade bonds (2%), and CMOs and structured securities (2%).

Investments in Affiliates: None

Group Affiliation: Guardian Group

Licensed in: All states except AL

Commenced Business: May 1968

Address: 700 South St, Pittsfield, MA 01201

Phone: (413) 499-4321 **Domicile State:** MA **NAIC Code:** 71714

Data Date	Rating	RACR #1	RACR #2	Total Assets ($mil)	Capital ($mil)	Net Premium ($mil)	Net Income ($mil)
3-09	A	4.95	2.92	2,502.2	429.3	107.9	5.7
3-08	A	4.98	2.98	2,360.2	399.7	96.2	14.1
2008	A	5.21	3.11	2,455.5	423.9	419.3	28.7
2007	A	4.83	2.92	2,292.7	386.6	402.4	62.0
2006	A	4.65	2.82	2,139.1	345.4	379.5	59.2
2005	A-	4.08	2.40	1,972.0	296.1	357.9	41.2
2004	B	3.67	2.11	1,772.4	259.7	340.9	-0.2

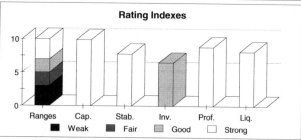

Rating Indexes

Ranges   Cap.   Stab.   Inv.   Prof.   Liq.

■ Weak   ▨ Fair   ▥ Good   ▯ Strong

BEST MERIDIAN INSURANCE COMPANY   B   Good

Major Rating Factors: Good liquidity (6.9 on a scale of 0 to 10) with sufficient resources to handle a spike in claims. Good overall results on stability tests (5.2). Stability strengths include excellent operational trends and good risk diversification. Strong capitalization (7.8) based on excellent risk adjusted capital (severe loss scenario). Capital levels have been relatively consistent over the last five years.

Other Rating Factors: High quality investment portfolio (7.3). Excellent profitability (7.2) with operating gains in each of the last five years.

Principal Business: Individual health insurance (51%), individual life insurance (43%), reinsurance (3%), group health insurance (3%), and group life insurance (1%).

Principal Investments: CMOs and structured securities (47%), nonCMO investment grade bonds (41%), policy loans (4%), cash (4%), and misc. investments (2%).

Investments in Affiliates: None

Group Affiliation: BMI Financial Group

Licensed in: GA

Commenced Business: August 1987

Address: 1320 S.Dixie Hwy, 6th Floor, Coral Gables, FL 33146

Phone: (305) 443-2898 **Domicile State:** FL **NAIC Code:** 63886

Data Date	Rating	RACR #1	RACR #2	Total Assets ($mil)	Capital ($mil)	Net Premium ($mil)	Net Income ($mil)
3-09	B	2.38	1.56	168.9	30.0	12.5	0.6
3-08	C+	1.90	1.33	156.3	25.3	30.2	1.3
2008	B	2.32	1.56	167.6	30.2	73.5	6.5
2007	C+	2.07	1.41	153.2	23.0	46.9	3.5
2006	C	2.04	1.40	139.6	20.1	41.6	4.2
2005	D+	1.62	1.14	125.6	15.5	42.2	0.1
2004	D	1.86	1.68	112.3	16.8	24.4	3.2

Adverse Trends in Operations

Increase in policy surrenders from 2007 to 2008 (53%)
Change in premium mix from 2007 to 2008 (4.4%)
Decrease in premium volume from 2005 to 2006 (2%)
Decrease in capital during 2005 (7%)

BLUE CROSS BLUE SHIELD OF KANSAS INCORPORATED — B — Good

Major Rating Factors: Good overall profitability (6.2 on a scale of 0 to 10) despite operating losses during the first three months of 2009. Good liquidity (6.1) with sufficient resources to handle a spike in claims. Good overall results on stability tests (6.3). Stability strengths include excellent operational trends and excellent risk diversification.

Other Rating Factors: Fair quality investment portfolio (4.9). Strong capitalization (7.4) based on excellent risk adjusted capital (severe loss scenario).

Principal Business: Group health insurance (75%) and individual health insurance (25%).

Principal Investments: NonCMO investment grade bonds (43%), common & preferred stock (28%), CMOs and structured securities (27%), and real estate (3%).

Investments in Affiliates: 9%

Group Affiliation: Blue Cross Blue Shield Kansas

Licensed in: KY

Commenced Business: July 1942

Address: 1133 SW Topeka Blvd, Topeka, KS 66629-0001

Phone: (785) 291-7000 **Domicile State:** KS **NAIC Code:** 70729

Data Date	Rating	RACR #1	RACR #2	Total Assets ($mil)	Capital ($mil)	Net Premium ($mil)	Net Income ($mil)
3-09	B	1.58	1.24	1,010.3	516.8	402.2	-14.6
3-08	B	1.62	1.26	1,027.4	474.7	369.9	-3.0
2008	B	1.61	1.27	1,001.8	519.0	1,514.0	24.7
2007	B	1.60	1.24	1,053.1	498.0	1,396.0	13.2
2006	B	1.55	1.21	968.3	455.5	1,289.5	-27.1
2005	B	1.89	1.46	890.7	458.8	1,166.5	61.4
2004	C+	1.79	1.38	846.3	393.6	1,135.3	66.3

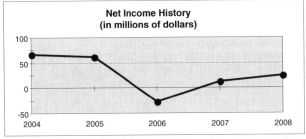

Net Income History
(in millions of dollars)

BLUE SHIELD OF CALIFORNIA LIFE & HEALTH INS CO * — A- — Excellent

Major Rating Factors: Strong capitalization (5.5 on a scale of 0 to 10) based on excellent risk adjusted capital (severe loss scenario). Furthermore, this high level of risk adjusted capital has been consistently maintained over the last five years. Good liquidity (5.8) with sufficient resources to handle a spike in claims. High quality investment portfolio (8.5).

Other Rating Factors: Excellent profitability (7.8) with operating gains in each of the last five years. Excellent overall results on stability tests (7.0) excellent operational trends, excellent risk adjusted capital for prior years and excellent risk diversification.

Principal Business: Group health insurance (58%), individual health insurance (40%), and group life insurance (1%).

Principal Investments: NonCMO investment grade bonds (63%), CMOs and structured securities (36%), and cash (1%).

Investments in Affiliates: None

Group Affiliation: Blue Shield of California

Licensed in: CO

Commenced Business: July 1954

Address: 50 Beale St, San Francisco, CA 94105

Phone: (800) 642-5599 **Domicile State:** CA **NAIC Code:** 61557

Data Date	Rating	RACR #1	RACR #2	Total Assets ($mil)	Capital ($mil)	Net Premium ($mil)	Net Income ($mil)
3-09	A-	1.70	1.35	364.2	183.6	257.0	15.2
3-08	A-	1.62	1.28	243.8	110.4	145.2	4.9
2008	A-	1.40	1.12	324.3	138.5	750.5	3.0
2007	A-	1.64	1.29	218.8	105.4	470.9	22.6
2006	A	4.30	3.32	235.7	82.6	302.6	23.9
2005	A-	4.36	3.36	197.9	141.3	198.7	21.8
2004	B+	6.38	4.81	166.1	119.6	106.8	5.7

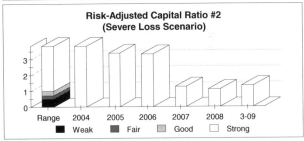

Risk-Adjusted Capital Ratio #2
(Severe Loss Scenario)

Range / 2004 / 2005 / 2006 / 2007 / 2008 / 3-09

■ Weak ■ Fair ▨ Good ☐ Strong

BLUEBONNET LIFE INSURANCE COMPANY * — B+ — Good

Major Rating Factors: Good overall results on stability tests (6.5 on a scale of 0 to 10). Stability strengths include excellent operational trends and good risk diversification. Strong capitalization (10.0) based on excellent risk adjusted capital (severe loss scenario). Moreover, capital levels have been consistently high over the last five years. High quality investment portfolio (8.6).

Other Rating Factors: Excellent profitability (9.6) with operating gains in each of the last five years. Excellent liquidity (9.8).

Principal Business: Group life insurance (97%) and group health insurance (2%).

Principal Investments: CMOs and structured securities (42%) and nonCMO investment grade bonds (38%).

Investments in Affiliates: None

Group Affiliation: Bl Cross & Bl Shield of Mississippi

Licensed in: AK, CA, ME, MO, TX

Commenced Business: June 1984

Address: 3475 Lakeland Drive, Jackson, MS 39208

Phone: (601) 932-8269 **Domicile State:** MS **NAIC Code:** 68535

Data Date	Rating	RACR #1	RACR #2	Total Assets ($mil)	Capital ($mil)	Net Premium ($mil)	Net Income ($mil)
3-09	B+	6.33	5.70	39.2	34.7	1.8	0.9
3-08	B+	6.12	5.51	35.9	31.1	1.9	0.8
2008	B+	6.15	5.53	38.4	33.7	7.4	3.7
2007	B+	5.96	5.37	34.6	30.3	7.7	3.4
2006	B+	5.70	5.13	31.2	26.9	7.8	3.1
2005	B	5.40	4.86	28.2	23.7	7.6	3.0
2004	C+	5.12	4.61	25.5	21.0	7.8	2.3

Adverse Trends in Operations

Decrease in premium volume from 2007 to 2008 (4%)
Decrease in premium volume from 2004 to 2005 (3%)

BOSTON MUTUAL LIFE INSURANCE COMPANY *

B+   **Good**

Major Rating Factors: Good quality investment portfolio (6.7 on a scale of 0 to 10) despite significant exposure to mortgages . Mortgage default rate has been low. substantial holdings of BBB bonds in addition to minimal holdings in junk bonds. Good overall profitability (6.3). Good liquidity (5.4).

Other Rating Factors: Good overall results on stability tests (6.4) excellent operational trends, good risk adjusted capital for prior years and excellent risk diversification. Strong capitalization (7.1) based on excellent risk adjusted capital (severe loss scenario).

Principal Business: Individual life insurance (59%), group health insurance (22%), group life insurance (17%), and individual health insurance (2%).

Principal Investments: NonCMO investment grade bonds (48%), CMOs and structured securities (19%), mortgages in good standing (17%), policy loans (11%), and misc. investments (4%).

Investments in Affiliates: 1%
Group Affiliation: Boston Mutual Group
Licensed in: All states except AL, NC
Commenced Business: February 1892
Address: 120 Royall St, Canton, MA 02021-1098
Phone: (781) 828-7000 **Domicile State:** MA **NAIC Code:** 61476

Data Date	Rating	RACR #1	RACR #2	Total Assets ($mil)	Capital ($mil)	Net Premium ($mil)	Net Income ($mil)
3-09	B+	1.69	1.08	945.5	80.1	47.6	2.2
3-08	B+	1.98	1.26	897.3	93.6	46.4	2.0
2008	B+	1.66	1.07	929.1	77.7	170.7	9.6
2007	B+	2.06	1.31	893.5	102.1	169.5	10.3
2006	B+	1.89	1.20	841.5	89.4	184.7	7.2
2005	B+	1.73	1.11	788.2	79.4	188.9	8.0
2004	B+	1.53	0.97	747.1	67.2	188.9	4.2

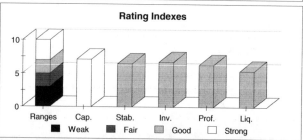

Rating Indexes

BROOKE LIFE INSURANCE COMPANY

C   **Fair**

Major Rating Factors: Fair capitalization (3.7 on a scale of 0 to 10) based on fair risk adjusted capital (severe loss scenario). Fair overall results on stability tests (3.7) including fair risk adjusted capital in prior years. Low quality investment portfolio (1.2).

Other Rating Factors: Excellent profitability (7.8) despite operating losses during the first three months of 2009. Excellent liquidity (9.3).

Principal Business: Individual annuities (99%) and reinsurance (1%).

Principal Investments: Common & preferred stock (91%), nonCMO investment grade bonds (7%), and CMOs and structured securities (2%).

Investments in Affiliates: 91%
Group Affiliation: Prudential plc
Licensed in: MN
Commenced Business: August 1987
Address: 5901 Executive Dr, Lansing, MI 48911
Phone: (517) 394-3400 **Domicile State:** MI **NAIC Code:** 78620

Data Date	Rating	RACR #1	RACR #2	Total Assets ($mil)	Capital ($mil)	Net Premium ($mil)	Net Income ($mil)
3-09	C	0.66	0.59	3,925.2	2,194.4	11.9	-20.0
3-08	U	N/A	N/A	4,187.5	2,411.9	45.0	-23.8
2008	C	0.68	0.60	4,128.9	2,244.9	218.6	216.0
2007	U	0.75	0.66	4,210.9	2,508.3	20.9	160.2
2006	U	0.71	0.63	3,864.2	2,202.6	3.1	122.1
2005	D+	0.76	0.67	3,639.7	2,208.0	7.2	330.7
2004	D+	0.71	0.63	3,346.0	1,910.6	37.7	37.6

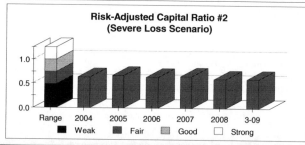

Risk-Adjusted Capital Ratio #2
(Severe Loss Scenario)

BUPA INSURANCE COMPANY

D+   **Weak**

Major Rating Factors: Weak overall results on stability tests (2.4 on a scale of 0 to 10). Fair overall capitalization (4.7) based on mixed results -- excessive policy leverage mitigated by fair risk adjusted capital (moderate loss scenario). Fair profitability (3.7). Excellent expense controls. Return on equity has been low, averaging -1.8%.

Other Rating Factors: High quality investment portfolio (8.6). Excellent liquidity (7.8).

Principal Business: Individual health insurance (73%), reinsurance (24%), and group health insurance (3%).

Principal Investments: Cash (16%), common & preferred stock (8%), nonCMO investment grade bonds (2%), and policy loans (1%).

Investments in Affiliates: 8%
Group Affiliation: British United Provident Assoc Ltd
Licensed in: GA
Commenced Business: July 1973
Address: 7001 S.W.97th Avenue, Miami, FL 33173
Phone: (305) 275-1400 **Domicile State:** FL **NAIC Code:** 81647

Data Date	Rating	RACR #1	RACR #2	Total Assets ($mil)	Capital ($mil)	Net Premium ($mil)	Net Income ($mil)
3-09	D+	0.86	0.71	106.3	25.1	28.7	1.8
3-08	D+	0.73	0.59	90.7	17.8	24.5	-1.4
2008	D+	0.80	0.66	101.5	23.1	112.0	1.6
2007	D+	0.76	0.62	91.3	19.1	104.6	-2.0
2006	C-	1.00	0.81	82.0	21.2	94.4	-6.3
2005	B	1.45	1.16	77.4	31.6	80.2	1.4
2004	B	1.49	1.18	69.1	29.4	70.3	2.3

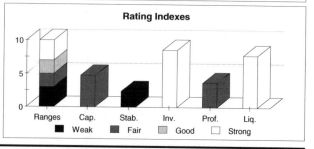

Rating Indexes

CAMBRIDGE LIFE INSURANCE COMPANY   B-   Good

Major Rating Factors: Fair liquidity (4.2 on a scale of 0 to 10) as cash from operations and sale of marketable assets may not be adequate to cover a spike in claims. Fair overall results on stability tests (3.9) including weak risk adjusted capital in prior years and negative cash flow from operations for 2008. Weak profitability (1.9). Excellent expense controls.

Other Rating Factors: Strong capitalization (8.5) based on excellent risk adjusted capital (severe loss scenario). High quality investment portfolio (9.4).

Principal Business: Individual health insurance (98%), group health insurance (2%), and reinsurance (1%).

Principal Investments: NonCMO investment grade bonds (70%), cash (28%), and CMOs and structured securities (2%).

Investments in Affiliates: None

Group Affiliation: Coventry Health Care Inc

Licensed in: AR, CA, CT, GA, IA, KY, LA, ME, MA, MO, MT, NE, NV, NH, NY, NC, ND, OR, SD, TN, TX, UT, VT, WI

Commenced Business: December 1974

Address: 237 E High St, Jefferson City, MO 65102

Phone: (714) 380-0233 **Domicile State:** MO **NAIC Code:** 81000

Data Date	Rating	RACR #1	RACR #2	Total Assets ($mil)	Capital ($mil)	Net Premium ($mil)	Net Income ($mil)
3-09	B-	2.45	2.03	88.7	51.6	21.4	3.0
3-08	B-	1.34	1.11	55.4	22.7	21.7	-3.4
2008	B-	2.13	1.76	80.4	42.0	56.7	-12.8
2007	B-	1.75	1.45	45.7	26.2	55.6	-6.1
2006	B-	0.46	0.38	25.3	7.5	61.6	-0.9
2005	B-	3.35	3.02	10.2	8.4	1.5	0.5
2004	C-	3.41	3.07	9.1	7.7	2.2	0.9

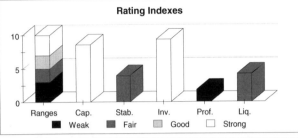
Rating Indexes

CANADA LIFE ASSURANCE CO-US BRANCH   B-   Good

Major Rating Factors: Good current capitalization (6.3 on a scale of 0 to 10) based on good risk adjusted capital (moderate loss scenario) reflecting some improvement over results in 2004. Good quality investment portfolio (5.9) despite large holdings of BBB rated bonds in addition to moderate junk bond exposure. Exposure to mortgages is significant, but the mortgage default rate has been low. Fair overall results on stability tests (4.2) including negative cash flow from operations for 2008 and fair risk adjusted capital in prior years.

Other Rating Factors: Excellent profitability (8.7) despite modest operating losses during 2005 and 2007. Excellent liquidity (7.9).

Principal Business: Reinsurance (95%), individual life insurance (3%), and group health insurance (2%).

Principal Investments: NonCMO investment grade bonds (52%), CMOs and structured securities (25%), mortgages in good standing (11%), policy loans (9%), and noninv. grade bonds (2%).

Investments in Affiliates: None

Group Affiliation: Great West Life Asr

Licensed in: All states except AL, NC

Commenced Business: August 1847

Address: 330 University Ave, Toronto Ontario, CN M5G 1R8

Phone: (770) 953-1959 **Domicile State:** MI **NAIC Code:** 80659

Data Date	Rating	RACR #1	RACR #2	Total Assets ($mil)	Capital ($mil)	Net Premium ($mil)	Net Income ($mil)
3-09	B-	1.87	0.91	4,230.5	217.6	28.2	11.0
3-08	B-	N/A	N/A	3,566.5	196.8	24.4	24.9
2008	B-	1.85	0.91	4,193.7	217.0	65.1	35.9
2007	B-	1.58	0.83	3,357.5	184.7	-20.8	-1.9
2006	B-	1.86	1.02	1,672.5	139.8	90.8	10.4
2005	C	1.61	0.82	1,867.7	113.8	8.3	-5.3
2004	D+	1.19	0.62	2,345.1	98.4	100.8	1.7

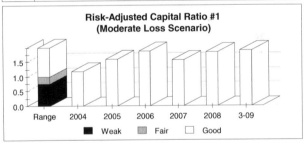
Risk-Adjusted Capital Ratio #1 (Moderate Loss Scenario)

CANADA LIFE INSURANCE COMPANY OF AMERICA   B-   Good

Major Rating Factors: Good quality investment portfolio (5.3 on a scale of 0 to 10) despite large exposure to mortgages . Mortgage default rate has been low. large holdings of BBB rated bonds in addition to small junk bond holdings. Good overall profitability (6.4). Excellent expense controls. Return on equity has been good over the last five years, averaging 12.9%. Fair overall results on stability tests (4.9) including negative cash flow from operations for 2008.

Other Rating Factors: Strong capitalization (7.7) based on excellent risk adjusted capital (severe loss scenario). Excellent liquidity (9.5).

Principal Business: Individual annuities (49%), reinsurance (34%), and individual life insurance (17%).

Principal Investments: NonCMO investment grade bonds (41%), mortgages in good standing (33%), CMOs and structured securities (18%), common & preferred stock (5%), and noninv. grade bonds (2%).

Investments in Affiliates: None

Group Affiliation: Great West Life Asr

Licensed in: All states except AL, NC, VA

Commenced Business: July 1988

Address: 201 Townsend St Suite 900, Lansing, MI 46933

Phone: (303) 737-3000 **Domicile State:** MI **NAIC Code:** 81060

Data Date	Rating	RACR #1	RACR #2	Total Assets ($mil)	Capital ($mil)	Net Premium ($mil)	Net Income ($mil)
3-09	B-	3.26	1.49	1,826.7	184.2	0.4	3.8
3-08	B-	3.17	1.55	1,987.1	169.5	1.0	6.0
2008	B-	2.36	1.18	1,801.0	124.6	4.4	11.4
2007	B-	2.98	1.47	2,049.4	170.5	5.0	21.7
2006	B-	2.97	1.47	2,183.2	180.8	4.2	35.4
2005	B-	2.43	1.16	2,402.2	145.7	6.1	26.9
2004	B-	3.21	1.46	2,635.4	169.9	12.1	-1.7

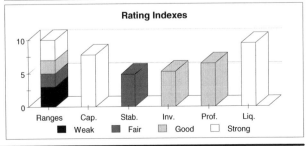
Rating Indexes

CENTRAL STATES HEALTH & LIFE COMPANY OF OMAHA   B-   Good

Major Rating Factors: Good quality investment portfolio (6.5 on a scale of 0 to 10) despite mixed results such as: minimal exposure to mortgages and substantial holdings of BBB bonds but minimal holdings in junk bonds. Good overall results on stability tests (5.2). Stability strengths include good operational trends and excellent risk diversification. Fair profitability (4.5).

Other Rating Factors: Strong capitalization (9.9) based on excellent risk adjusted capital (severe loss scenario). Excellent liquidity (7.8).

Principal Business: Credit life insurance (41%), credit health insurance (35%), individual health insurance (18%), group health insurance (3%), and individual life insurance (2%).

Principal Investments: CMOs and structured securities (39%), nonCMO investment grade bonds (37%), common & preferred stock (9%), mortgages in good standing (5%), and misc. investments (10%).

Investments in Affiliates: 7%

Group Affiliation: Central States Group

Licensed in: All states except AL, NC

Commenced Business: June 1932

Address: 1212 N 96th St, Omaha, NE 68114

Phone: (402) 397-1111 **Domicile State:** NE **NAIC Code:** 61751

Data Date	Rating	RACR #1	RACR #2	Total Assets ($mil)	Capital ($mil)	Net Premium ($mil)	Net Income ($mil)
3-09	B-	3.91	2.92	318.9	86.7	14.1	1.7
3-08	B-	4.91	3.53	307.3	98.4	17.7	4.5
2008	B-	3.86	2.92	320.0	85.1	85.5	-0.8
2007	C+	5.24	3.79	290.8	99.1	80.7	5.6
2006	C	6.71	4.59	278.1	94.2	44.3	10.0
2005	C	14.19	8.40	310.7	94.2	-20.3	7.7
2004	C	3.65	2.63	338.3	65.8	119.8	-15.4

Adverse Trends in Operations

Decrease in capital during 2008 (14%)
Decrease in asset base during 2006 (10%)
Change in premium mix from 2005 to 2006 (66.7%)
Decrease in asset base during 2005 (8%)
Decrease in premium volume from 2004 to 2005 (117%)

CENTRAL UNITED LIFE INSURANCE COMPANY   D+   Weak

Major Rating Factors: Weak overall results on stability tests (2.8 on a scale of 0 to 10) including weak risk adjusted capital in prior years and negative cash flow from operations for 2008. Fair capitalization for the current period (3.6) based on fair risk adjusted capital (severe loss scenario) reflecting some improvement over results in 2006. Good quality investment portfolio (6.8).

Other Rating Factors: Good overall profitability (5.9). Excellent liquidity (7.1).

Principal Business: Individual health insurance (60%), reinsurance (31%), individual life insurance (5%), and group health insurance (3%).

Principal Investments: NonCMO investment grade bonds (80%), common & preferred stock (11%), real estate (4%), policy loans (3%), and misc. investments (3%).

Investments in Affiliates: 11%

Group Affiliation: Central United Life Group

Licensed in: All states except AL, AZ, DC, DE, FL, ID, MN, NM, NC, SC, VA

Commenced Business: September 1963

Address: 2727 Allen Parkway,6th Floor, Houston, TX 77019-2115

Phone: (713) 529-0045 **Domicile State:** AR **NAIC Code:** 61883

Data Date	Rating	RACR #1	RACR #2	Total Assets ($mil)	Capital ($mil)	Net Premium ($mil)	Net Income ($mil)
3-09	D+	0.68	0.57	316.3	39.3	22.3	0.3
3-08	D+	0.61	0.51	328.2	37.3	24.0	0.2
2008	D+	0.67	0.56	321.4	38.1	92.6	2.3
2007	D+	0.61	0.51	332.5	37.0	100.9	5.2
2006	D+	0.52	0.44	350.2	32.3	106.7	1.7
2005	C-	0.56	0.48	371.4	36.6	111.8	5.3
2004	C-	0.58	0.49	380.5	35.4	92.1	-7.7

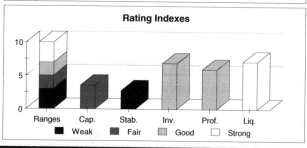

Rating Indexes

Ranges | Cap. | Stab. | Inv. | Prof. | Liq.
■ Weak ■ Fair ▨ Good □ Strong

CENTRE LIFE INSURANCE COMPANY   C+   Fair

Major Rating Factors: Fair overall results on stability tests (4.7 on a scale of 0 to 10) including fair financial strength of affiliated Zurich Financial Services Group and negative cash flow from operations for 2008. Good quality investment portfolio (6.3) with no exposure to mortgages and minimal holdings in junk bonds. Good overall profitability (5.2) despite operating losses during the first three months of 2009.

Other Rating Factors: Strong capitalization (8.2) based on excellent risk adjusted capital (severe loss scenario). Excellent liquidity (7.6).

Principal Business: Reinsurance (69%) and individual health insurance (31%).

Principal Investments: NonCMO investment grade bonds (75%) and CMOs and structured securities (25%).

Investments in Affiliates: None

Group Affiliation: Zurich Financial Services Group

Licensed in: All states except AL

Commenced Business: October 1927

Address: 1600 McConnor Parkway, Schaumburg, IL 60196-6801

Phone: (847) 874-7400 **Domicile State:** MA **NAIC Code:** 80896

Data Date	Rating	RACR #1	RACR #2	Total Assets ($mil)	Capital ($mil)	Net Premium ($mil)	Net Income ($mil)
3-09	C+	3.43	1.77	2,012.1	89.5	0.1	-0.9
3-08	C	4.01	2.20	1,861.1	88.3	1.0	4.7
2008	C+	3.45	1.95	2,021.7	90.8	1.2	3.4
2007	C-	4.22	2.68	1,658.2	93.2	3.4	9.0
2006	C-	3.39	2.18	1,672.6	75.1	4.5	6.4
2005	C-	1.96	1.20	1,687.9	66.9	5.2	-0.4
2004	C-	2.06	1.07	1,696.1	70.1	5.4	-2.7

Zurich Financial Services Group Composite Group Rating: C Largest Group Members	Assets ($mil)	Rating
ZURICH AMERICAN INS CO	29634	C-
KEMPER INVESTORS LIFE INS CO	13886	C
FARMERS INS EXCHANGE	13368	C
FARMERS NEW WORLD LIFE INS CO	6444	B-
MID-CENTURY INS CO	3273	C-

CENTURION LIFE INSURANCE COMPANY   B-   Good

Major Rating Factors: Good overall results on stability tests (5.2 on a scale of 0 to 10) despite fair financial strength of affiliated Wells Fargo Group. Other stability subfactors include good operational trends and excellent risk diversification. Good quality investment portfolio (6.8) despite mixed results such as: no exposure to mortgages and substantial holdings of BBB bonds but minimal holdings in junk bonds. Strong capitalization (10.0) based on excellent risk adjusted capital (severe loss scenario).

Other Rating Factors: Excellent profitability (9.2) with operating gains in each of the last five years. Excellent liquidity (9.5).

Principal Business: Individual annuities (60%), reinsurance (31%), credit life insurance (7%), and credit health insurance (2%).

Principal Investments: NonCMO investment grade bonds (68%), CMOs and structured securities (25%), noninv. grade bonds (5%), common & preferred stock (3%), and cash (1%).

Investments in Affiliates: None

Group Affiliation: Wells Fargo Group

Licensed in: All states except AL, MD, NC, VA

Commenced Business: July 1956

Address: 206 Eighth Street, Des Moines, IA 50309

Phone: (515) 243-2131 **Domicile State:** IA **NAIC Code:** 62383

Data Date	Rating	RACR #1	RACR #2	Total Assets ($mil)	Capital ($mil)	Net Premium ($mil)	Net Income ($mil)
3-09	B-	29.58	15.80	1,699.1	1,000.5	81.9	11.1
3-08	C+	26.32	14.33	1,548.1	966.4	22.0	12.0
2008	B-	33.08	17.65	1,621.0	993.3	135.2	47.8
2007	C+	25.94	14.03	1,521.6	949.9	94.1	45.0
2006	B-	29.86	15.87	1,045.3	915.7	49.3	57.4
2005	A-	24.47	14.18	1,082.6	870.9	137.0	37.6
2004	A	27.80	15.97	1,051.4	854.2	43.1	43.9

Wells Fargo Group
Composite Group Rating: C+

Largest Group Members	Assets ($mil)	Rating
RURAL COMMUNITY INS CO	4387	B-
CENTURION LIFE INS CO	1621	B-
CENTURION CASUALTY CO	383	B
HERITAGE INDEMNITY CO	191	C+
SCOTT LIFE INS CO	99	B

CHESAPEAKE LIFE INSURANCE COMPANY   C+   Fair

Major Rating Factors: Fair overall results on stability tests (4.0 on a scale of 0 to 10) including negative cash flow from operations for 2008. Good liquidity (6.3) with sufficient resources to handle a spike in claims. Weak profitability (2.0) with operating losses during the first three months of 2009. Return on equity has been low, averaging -10.2%.

Other Rating Factors: Strong capitalization (8.6) based on excellent risk adjusted capital (severe loss scenario). High quality investment portfolio (8.5).

Principal Business: Group health insurance (57%), individual life insurance (35%), and individual health insurance (7%).

Principal Investments: NonCMO investment grade bonds (78%) and CMOs and structured securities (26%).

Investments in Affiliates: None

Group Affiliation: HealthMarkets

Licensed in: All states except AL, NM, NC, VA

Commenced Business: October 1956

Address: 9151 Grapevine Highway, North Richland Hills, TX 76180

Phone: (817) 255-3100 **Domicile State:** OK **NAIC Code:** 61832

Data Date	Rating	RACR #1	RACR #2	Total Assets ($mil)	Capital ($mil)	Net Premium ($mil)	Net Income ($mil)
3-09	C+	2.70	2.09	78.8	43.0	3.9	-1.8
3-08	C+	4.59	3.22	97.2	40.3	21.7	-4.0
2008	C+	2.24	1.75	86.2	44.9	117.5	-8.8
2007	C+	5.48	4.93	96.0	48.3	27.3	-1.3
2006	C	4.48	3.31	99.5	44.8	61.0	2.3
2005	C	2.84	2.19	105.5	42.2	102.2	-10.2
2004	C+	2.75	2.09	90.2	25.9	50.1	-2.7

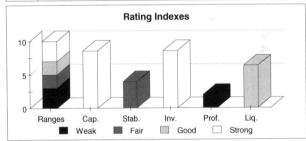

Rating Indexes

(Bar chart categories: Ranges, Cap., Stab., Inv., Prof., Liq. Legend: ■ Weak, ▨ Fair, ▨ Good, ☐ Strong)

CHRISTIAN FIDELITY LIFE INSURANCE COMPANY   B-   Good

Major Rating Factors: Fair overall results on stability tests (4.9 on a scale of 0 to 10) including fair financial strength of affiliated Amerco Corp. Strong current capitalization (7.5) based on excellent risk adjusted capital (severe loss scenario) reflecting improvement over results in 2006. High quality investment portfolio (7.4).

Other Rating Factors: Excellent profitability (9.1) with operating gains in each of the last five years. Excellent liquidity (7.0).

Principal Business: Individual health insurance (99%) and individual life insurance (1%).

Principal Investments: NonCMO investment grade bonds (65%), CMOs and structured securities (13%), common & preferred stock (9%), mortgages in good standing (7%), and misc. investments (5%).

Investments in Affiliates: 8%

Group Affiliation: Amerco Corp

Licensed in: AK, AR, CA, CT, GA, HI, IL, IN, IA, KY, LA, ME, MO, MT, NE, NV, NH, NY, OH, OK, OR, PA, SD, TN, TX, UT, VT, WA, WV, WI, PR

Commenced Business: June 1954

Address: 2721 N Central Ave, Phoenix, AZ 85004-1172

Phone: (972) 937-4420 **Domicile State:** TX **NAIC Code:** 61859

Data Date	Rating	RACR #1	RACR #2	Total Assets ($mil)	Capital ($mil)	Net Premium ($mil)	Net Income ($mil)
3-09	B-	1.64	1.34	84.5	34.7	13.9	0.7
3-08	C+	1.18	0.96	79.2	27.0	14.5	1.2
2008	B-	1.63	1.33	86.9	34.4	56.1	4.3
2007	C	1.09	0.90	79.1	25.4	58.4	4.2
2006	C-	0.94	0.78	77.5	21.0	60.3	2.7
2005	C-	1.45	1.09	78.0	22.5	60.8	1.5
2004	C-	1.32	0.97	79.6	21.0	60.5	2.4

Amerco Corp
Composite Group Rating: C

Largest Group Members	Assets ($mil)	Rating
OXFORD LIFE INS CO	503	B-
REPUBLIC WESTERN INS CO	238	C-
CHRISTIAN FIDELITY LIFE INS CO	87	B-
NORTH AMERICAN INS CO	16	C
DALLAS GENERAL LIFE INS CO	10	C

CHURCH LIFE INSURANCE CORPORATION

C+   **Fair**

Major Rating Factors: Fair overall results on stability tests (4.8 on a scale of 0 to 10). Good quality investment portfolio (6.9) despite mixed results such as: no exposure to mortgages and substantial holdings of BBB bonds but minimal holdings in junk bonds. Good overall profitability (5.7) despite operating losses during the first three months of 2009. Return on equity has been fair, averaging 5.3%.

Other Rating Factors: Good liquidity (6.0). Strong capitalization (8.6) based on excellent risk adjusted capital (severe loss scenario).

Principal Business: Group life insurance (46%), individual annuities (33%), group retirement contracts (17%), and individual life insurance (4%).

Principal Investments: NonCMO investment grade bonds (57%), CMOs and structured securities (34%), common & preferred stock (4%), and cash (1%).

Investments in Affiliates: None

Group Affiliation: Church Pension Fund

Licensed in: All states except AL, AK, KS, MS, NH, ND, PR

Commenced Business: July 1922

Address: 445 Fifth Ave, New York, NY 10016

Phone: (212) 592-9473 **Domicile State:** NY **NAIC Code:** 61875

Data Date	Rating	RACR #1	RACR #2	Total Assets ($mil)	Capital ($mil)	Net Premium ($mil)	Net Income ($mil)
3-09	C+	3.17	2.08	203.7	30.0	7.8	-0.6
3-08	C+	3.88	2.31	209.2	36.7	5.5	0.2
2008	C+	3.35	2.28	205.9	31.5	25.4	-3.1
2007	C+	4.00	2.44	201.3	37.5	27.1	2.4
2006	C+	3.75	2.37	199.4	35.0	40.4	4.2
2005	C+	3.18	2.01	201.7	29.6	40.9	0.0
2004	B-	3.15	2.01	200.6	29.3	22.5	0.7

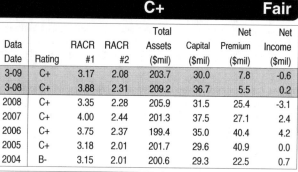

Rating Indexes

CICA LIFE INSURANCE COMPANY OF AMERICA

D+   **Weak**

Major Rating Factors: Poor capitalization (2.5 on a scale of 0 to 10) based on weak risk adjusted capital (moderate loss scenario). Weak overall results on stability tests (2.4) including weak risk adjusted capital in prior years. Good overall profitability (6.1) despite operating losses during 2008. Return on equity has been good over the last five years, averaging 11.2%.

Other Rating Factors: Good liquidity (6.1). High quality investment portfolio (8.8).

Principal Business: Individual life insurance (93%), individual health insurance (2%), individual annuities (2%), reinsurance (1%), and credit health insurance (1%).

Principal Investments: NonCMO investment grade bonds (63%), common & preferred stock (19%), cash (10%), policy loans (7%), and real estate (1%).

Investments in Affiliates: 19%

Group Affiliation: Citizens Inc

Licensed in: AR, CA, CT, DE, ID, IL, IA, KY, LA, ME, MO, MT, NE, NH, NY, OH, OR, PA, RI, SD, TN, TX, UT, VT, WV, PR

Commenced Business: June 1968

Address: 1675 Broadway, Denver, CO 80202

Phone: (512) 837-7100 **Domicile State:** CO **NAIC Code:** 71463

Data Date	Rating	RACR #1	RACR #2	Total Assets ($mil)	Capital ($mil)	Net Premium ($mil)	Net Income ($mil)
2008	D+	0.49	0.46	404.0	38.3	103.6	-3.3
2007	C-	0.49	0.48	387.5	51.6	102.6	7.4
2006	C-	0.63	0.58	341.9	42.8	95.0	4.8
2005	C-	0.52	0.49	301.2	38.4	80.4	-0.4
2004	C-	0.74	0.70	288.8	74.7	65.0	3.3

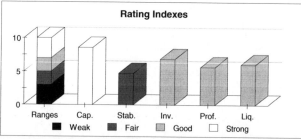

Risk-Adjusted Capital Ratio #1
(Moderate Loss Scenario)

CIGNA LIFE INSURANCE COMPANY OF NEW YORK

B-   **Good**

Major Rating Factors: Good overall results on stability tests (5.2 on a scale of 0 to 10) despite fair financial strength of affiliated CIGNA Group. Other stability subfactors include excellent operational trends and excellent risk diversification. Strong capitalization (9.6) based on excellent risk adjusted capital (severe loss scenario). Capital levels have been relatively consistent over the last five years. High quality investment portfolio (7.9).

Other Rating Factors: Excellent profitability (8.1) with operating gains in each of the last five years. Excellent liquidity (7.8).

Principal Business: Group health insurance (73%) and group life insurance (27%).

Principal Investments: NonCMO investment grade bonds (97%), CMOs and structured securities (1%), noninv. grade bonds (1%), and cash (1%).

Investments in Affiliates: None

Group Affiliation: CIGNA Group

Licensed in: AK, DE, MT, NC, RI, TX

Commenced Business: December 1965

Address: 499 Washington Blvd, Jersey City, NJ 07310-1995

Phone: (212) 618-5757 **Domicile State:** NY **NAIC Code:** 64548

Data Date	Rating	RACR #1	RACR #2	Total Assets ($mil)	Capital ($mil)	Net Premium ($mil)	Net Income ($mil)
3-09	B-	3.96	2.74	398.2	104.2	31.5	3.4
3-08	C+	4.02	2.81	390.8	94.8	29.1	9.5
2008	B-	3.83	2.68	401.2	100.0	123.0	25.8
2007	C+	3.57	2.48	381.7	85.4	115.7	16.3
2006	C	4.12	2.77	373.5	78.7	100.8	13.3
2005	C	4.62	3.08	362.7	83.1	91.9	17.5
2004	C	3.93	2.53	353.1	73.7	100.7	19.0

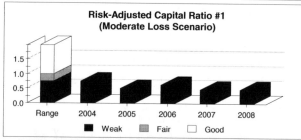

CIGNA Group Composite Group Rating: C+ Largest Group Members	Assets ($mil)	Rating
CONNECTICUT GENERAL LIFE INS CO	17733	C+
LIFE INS CO OF NORTH AMERICA	5464	C+
CIGNA LIFE INS CO OF NEW YORK	401	B-
CIGNA HEALTHCARE OF CALIFORNIA INC	156	C
CIGNA HEALTHCARE OF ARIZONA INC	126	B

CINCINNATI LIFE INSURANCE COMPANY   B   Good

Major Rating Factors: Good quality investment portfolio (5.5 on a scale of 0 to 10) despite mixed results such as: large holdings of BBB rated bonds but moderate junk bond exposure. Good liquidity (6.8) with sufficient resources to cover a large increase in policy surrenders. Fair overall results on stability tests (4.8).

Other Rating Factors: Weak profitability (2.9) with operating losses during the first three months of 2009. Strong capitalization (7.4) based on excellent risk adjusted capital (severe loss scenario).

Principal Business: Individual life insurance (81%), individual annuities (15%), individual health insurance (3%), and group life insurance (1%).

Principal Investments: NonCMO investment grade bonds (79%), common & preferred stock (10%), noninv. grade bonds (4%), cash (3%), and misc. investments (4%).

Investments in Affiliates: None

Group Affiliation: Cincinnati Financial Corp

Licensed in: All states except AL, NC

Commenced Business: February 1988

Address: 6200 S Gilmore Rd, Fairfield, OH 45014-5141

Phone: (513) 870-2000 **Domicile State:** OH **NAIC Code:** 76236

Data Date	Rating	RACR #1	RACR #2	Total Assets ($mil)	Capital ($mil)	Net Premium ($mil)	Net Income ($mil)
3-09	B	2.20	1.24	2,476.6	253.6	48.4	-1.8
3-08	B	2.65	1.51	2,815.8	453.0	42.0	-8.0
2008	B	2.54	1.44	2,477.6	290.1	176.9	-70.1
2007	B	2.88	1.65	2,550.0	476.9	157.6	39.3
2006	B	2.69	1.56	2,521.4	478.8	153.2	28.5
2005	B	2.84	1.64	2,351.7	450.8	193.8	21.0
2004	B	2.77	1.60	2,155.6	438.7	175.6	28.3

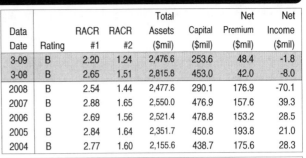

Rating Indexes

CM LIFE INSURANCE COMPANY   B   Good

Major Rating Factors: Good current capitalization (6.4 on a scale of 0 to 10) based on good risk adjusted capital (severe loss scenario), although results have slipped from the excellent range during the last year. Good quality investment portfolio (5.2) despite large holdings of BBB rated bonds in addition to moderate junk bond exposure. Exposure to mortgages is significant, but the mortgage default rate has been low. Good overall profitability (6.7) despite operating losses during the first three months of 2009.

Other Rating Factors: Good liquidity (6.6). Good overall results on stability tests (5.2) despite fair risk adjusted capital in prior years good operational trends and excellent risk diversification.

Principal Business: Individual annuities (65%) and individual life insurance (35%).

Principal Investments: NonCMO investment grade bonds (40%), mortgages in good standing (20%), CMOs and structured securities (19%), noninv. grade bonds (6%), and misc. investments (15%).

Investments in Affiliates: 8%

Group Affiliation: Massachusetts Mutual Group

Licensed in: All states except AL, NC

Commenced Business: May 1981

Address: 100 Bright Meadow Blvd, Enfield, CT 06082

Phone: (413) 788-8411 **Domicile State:** CT **NAIC Code:** 93432

Data Date	Rating	RACR #1	RACR #2	Total Assets ($mil)	Capital ($mil)	Net Premium ($mil)	Net Income ($mil)
3-09	B	1.51	0.92	7,462.3	699.8	287.9	-9.2
3-08	B	1.66	1.04	8,380.7	665.2	151.7	5.1
2008	B	1.61	1.00	7,539.9	707.8	779.1	-76.6
2007	B	1.58	0.99	8,625.4	607.8	538.3	85.7
2006	B	1.27	0.81	9,123.6	503.0	651.2	118.4
2005	B	1.04	0.67	9,167.0	434.2	782.0	93.0
2004	B	0.99	0.65	8,992.2	396.8	1,706.1	24.7

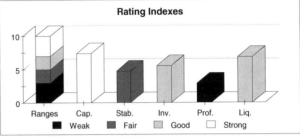

Risk-Adjusted Capital Ratio #2
(Severe Loss Scenario)

COLONIAL LIFE & ACCIDENT INSURANCE COMPANY   C+   Fair

Major Rating Factors: Fair overall results on stability tests (4.4 on a scale of 0 to 10). Good quality investment portfolio (6.4) despite mixed results such as: large holdings of BBB rated bonds but moderate junk bond exposure. Good liquidity (6.9) with sufficient resources to handle a spike in claims as well as a significant increase in policy surrenders.

Other Rating Factors: Strong capitalization (7.6) based on excellent risk adjusted capital (severe loss scenario). Excellent profitability (9.1) with operating gains in each of the last five years.

Principal Business: Individual health insurance (76%), individual life insurance (20%), group health insurance (3%), group life insurance (1%), and reinsurance (1%).

Principal Investments: NonCMO investment grade bonds (71%), mortgages in good standing (9%), noninv. grade bonds (8%), CMOs and structured securities (7%), and misc. investments (5%).

Investments in Affiliates: None

Group Affiliation: Unum Group

Licensed in: All states except AL, NC

Commenced Business: September 1939

Address: 6335 S. East Street, Suite A, Indianapolis, IN 46227

Phone: (803) 798-7000 **Domicile State:** SC **NAIC Code:** 62049

Data Date	Rating	RACR #1	RACR #2	Total Assets ($mil)	Capital ($mil)	Net Premium ($mil)	Net Income ($mil)
3-09	C+	2.26	1.41	2,055.6	376.7	266.4	25.0
3-08	C	2.44	1.55	1,948.7	367.2	254.8	21.7
2008	C+	2.34	1.47	1,988.8	379.6	1,011.7	109.3
2007	C	2.49	1.58	1,902.1	369.3	945.5	116.4
2006	C	2.62	1.66	1,773.9	370.5	879.0	110.6
2005	C-	2.59	1.67	1,668.8	351.2	822.1	99.4
2004	C-	2.40	1.58	1,504.9	294.9	773.3	104.5

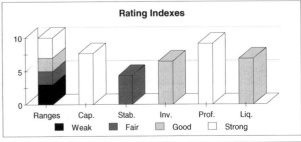

Rating Indexes

COLONIAL PENN LIFE INSURANCE COMPANY

D+   **Weak**

Major Rating Factors: Weak overall results on stability tests (2.6 on a scale of 0 to 10) including weak financial strength of affiliated Conseco Group and negative cash flow from operations for 2008. Low quality investment portfolio (1.9) containing large holdings of BBB rated bonds in addition to junk bond exposure equal to 89% of capital. Weak profitability (1.9) with operating losses during the first three months of 2009.

Other Rating Factors: Weak liquidity (0.6). Fair capitalization (4.7) based on fair risk adjusted capital (moderate loss scenario).

Principal Business: Individual life insurance (49%), group life insurance (42%), individual health insurance (4%), and reinsurance (4%).

Principal Investments: NonCMO investment grade bonds (66%), CMOs and structured securities (12%), mortgages in good standing (8%), noninv. grade bonds (6%), and misc. investments (8%).

Investments in Affiliates: None

Group Affiliation: Conseco Group

Licensed in: All states except AL, NC

Commenced Business: September 1959

Address: 399 Market St, Philadelphia, PA 19181

Phone: (215) 928-8000 **Domicile State:** PA **NAIC Code:** 62065

Data Date	Rating	RACR #1	RACR #2	Total Assets ($mil)	Capital ($mil)	Net Premium ($mil)	Net Income ($mil)
3-09	D+	0.96	0.50	692.4	40.9	49.2	-1.5
3-08	D+	1.13	0.60	709.5	45.6	48.5	-5.4
2008	D+	1.00	0.52	692.2	37.6	174.5	-0.4
2007	D+	1.17	0.62	710.9	47.2	124.8	-55.4
2006	D+	1.15	0.61	716.7	44.5	99.8	9.0
2005	D+	1.60	0.87	725.6	35.3	90.1	9.5
2004	D	1.61	0.86	774.7	36.5	81.8	13.2

Conseco Group Composite Group Rating: D+ Largest Group Members	Assets ($mil)	Rating
BANKERS LIFE CAS CO	11442	D+
CONSECO LIFE INS CO	4529	D+
CONSECO HEALTH INS CO	2472	D+
WASHINGTON NATIONAL INS CO	2348	D+
CONSECO INS CO	1044	D+

COLUMBIA CAPITAL LIFE REINS CO

C   **Fair**

Major Rating Factors: Good quality investment portfolio (5.4 on a scale of 0 to 10) with no exposure to mortgages and no exposure to junk bonds. Good liquidity (6.8) with sufficient resources to cover a large increase in policy surrenders. Weak overall results on stability tests (2.9) including fair financial strength of affiliated Goldman Sachs Group, negative cash flow from operations for 2008, weak results on operational trends and lack of operational experience.

Other Rating Factors: Weak profitability (2.6). Strong capitalization (10.0) based on excellent risk adjusted capital (severe loss scenario).

Principal Business: Reinsurance (100%).

Principal Investments: NonCMO investment grade bonds (37%), policy loans (6%), CMOs and structured securities (4%), and common & preferred stock (1%).

Investments in Affiliates: 51%

Group Affiliation: Goldman Sachs Group

Licensed in: SD

Commenced Business: February 2005

Address: 151 Meeting St Suite 301, Charleston, SC 29401-2238

Phone: (843) 577-1035 **Domicile State:** DC **NAIC Code:** 12276

Data Date	Rating	RACR #1	RACR #2	Total Assets ($mil)	Capital ($mil)	Net Premium ($mil)	Net Income ($mil)
3-09	C	7.28	3.68	139.3	77.2	0.2	0.4
3-08	C	9.03	4.62	115.1	47.7	0.2	0.0
2008	C	7.23	3.67	138.1	69.6	1.0	-6.1
2007	C-	5.90	5.31	36.4	31.2	0.1	0.6
2006	U	3.63	3.27	84.5	30.1	0.1	-0.8
2005	U	5.85	5.27	21.6	21.6	0.0	0.1
2004	N/A	N/A	N/A	0.0	0.0	0.0	0.0

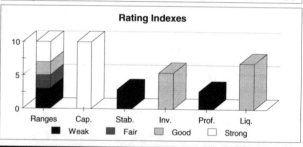

Rating Indexes

COLUMBIAN MUTUAL LIFE INSURANCE COMPANY

B   **Good**

Major Rating Factors: Good overall profitability (6.9 on a scale of 0 to 10). Good liquidity (5.8) with sufficient resources to handle a spike in claims as well as a significant increase in policy surrenders. Good overall results on stability tests (5.7). Stability strengths include excellent operational trends, good risk adjusted capital for prior years and good risk diversification.

Other Rating Factors: Strong capitalization (7.5) based on excellent risk adjusted capital (severe loss scenario). High quality investment portfolio (7.0).

Principal Business: Individual life insurance (50%), reinsurance (44%), individual annuities (2%), group health insurance (2%), and group retirement contracts (1%).

Principal Investments: NonCMO investment grade bonds (53%), CMOs and structured securities (21%), mortgages in good standing (14%), policy loans (7%), and misc. investments (5%).

Investments in Affiliates: 2%

Group Affiliation: Columbian Life Group

Licensed in: All states except AL

Commenced Business: February 1883

Address: Vestal Parkway East, Binghamton, NY 13902

Phone: (607) 724-2472 **Domicile State:** NY **NAIC Code:** 62103

Data Date	Rating	RACR #1	RACR #2	Total Assets ($mil)	Capital ($mil)	Net Premium ($mil)	Net Income ($mil)
3-09	B	1.97	1.30	847.6	76.5	36.2	1.3
3-08	B-	1.71	1.16	899.6	74.5	34.6	1.2
2008	B	2.03	1.35	846.3	79.4	143.2	6.1
2007	B-	1.72	1.18	892.8	74.2	131.7	1.7
2006	B-	3.29	1.82	385.2	43.2	76.5	0.8
2005	B-	1.96	1.39	318.6	37.2	29.6	6.2
2004	C+	1.22	0.98	318.3	39.3	31.0	0.5

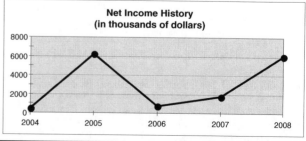

Net Income History
(in thousands of dollars)

COLUMBUS LIFE INSURANCE COMPANY *   B+   Good

Major Rating Factors: Good overall results on stability tests (6.8 on a scale of 0 to 10). Stability strengths include excellent operational trends and excellent risk diversification. Good quality investment portfolio (5.5) despite mixed results such as: large holdings of BBB rated bonds but moderate junk bond exposure. Good overall profitability (6.1).

Other Rating Factors: Good liquidity (5.4). Strong capitalization (7.3) based on excellent risk adjusted capital (severe loss scenario).

Principal Business: Individual life insurance (68%) and individual annuities (32%).

Principal Investments: NonCMO investment grade bonds (60%), CMOs and structured securities (24%), common & preferred stock (4%), policy loans (3%), and misc. investments (9%).

Investments in Affiliates: 3%
Group Affiliation: Western & Southern Group
Licensed in: All states except AL, AZ, NC, OH
Commenced Business: December 1986
Address: 400 E 4th St, Cincinnati, OH 45202
Phone: (513) 357-4000 **Domicile State:** OH **NAIC Code:** 99937

Data Date	Rating	RACR #1	RACR #2	Total Assets ($mil)	Capital ($mil)	Net Premium ($mil)	Net Income ($mil)
3-09	B+	2.29	1.17	2,512.2	208.7	71.1	7.6
3-08	B+	2.80	1.53	2,521.5	234.6	47.3	11.0
2008	B+	2.41	1.30	2,500.6	209.0	204.6	17.0
2007	B+	2.79	1.53	2,507.4	229.1	165.7	15.9
2006	B+	3.03	1.64	2,550.3	253.2	194.7	23.9
2005	B+	2.75	1.51	2,538.8	229.8	207.9	2.6
2004	B+	3.22	1.71	2,326.8	261.7	216.8	6.5

Adverse Trends in Operations

Change in premium mix from 2007 to 2008 (4.3%)
Decrease in premium volume from 2006 to 2007 (15%)
Decrease in capital during 2007 (10%)
Decrease in capital during 2005 (12%)
Decrease in premium volume from 2004 to 2005 (4%)

COMBINED INSURANCE COMPANY OF AMERICA   B-   Good

Major Rating Factors: Good overall profitability (6.1 on a scale of 0 to 10). Return on equity has been excellent over the last five years averaging 19.0%. Good liquidity (6.8) with sufficient resources to handle a spike in claims as well as a significant increase in policy surrenders. Fair overall results on stability tests (4.3) including fair financial strength of affiliated ACE Ltd and negative cash flow from operations for 2008.

Other Rating Factors: Strong capitalization (8.1) based on excellent risk adjusted capital (severe loss scenario). High quality investment portfolio (7.8).

Principal Business: Individual health insurance (78%), group health insurance (13%), individual life insurance (6%), reinsurance (3%), and group life insurance (1%).

Principal Investments: NonCMO investment grade bonds (73%), CMOs and structured securities (13%), common & preferred stock (9%), policy loans (2%), and misc. investments (2%).

Investments in Affiliates: 8%
Group Affiliation: ACE Ltd
Licensed in: All states except AL, NC
Commenced Business: December 1922
Address: 1000 North Milwakee Ave, Glenview, IL 60025
Phone: (312) 701-3000 **Domicile State:** IL **NAIC Code:** 62146

Data Date	Rating	RACR #1	RACR #2	Total Assets ($mil)	Capital ($mil)	Net Premium ($mil)	Net Income ($mil)
3-09	B-	2.06	1.72	2,421.5	626.3	198.1	38.9
3-08	B-	1.96	1.69	3,254.4	975.9	310.5	38.0
2008	B-	2.04	1.70	2,382.5	593.5	693.9	383.5
2007	C+	1.88	1.62	3,215.0	933.7	1,243.8	233.0
2006	C+	1.97	1.64	2,878.4	809.3	1,234.3	176.9
2005	C	2.13	1.73	2,786.3	868.3	1,211.3	100.9
2004	C	2.28	1.84	2,667.8	839.4	1,222.1	166.8

ACE Ltd
Composite Group Rating: C
Largest Group Members

	Assets ($mil)	Rating
ACE AMERICAN INS CO	8051	C+
ACE PROPERTY CASUALTY INS CO	5785	C
WESTCHESTER FIRE INS CO	2561	C-
PACIFIC EMPLOYERS INS CO	2446	C+
COMBINED INS CO OF AMERICA	2382	B-

COMBINED LIFE INSURANCE COMPANY OF NEW YORK   B   Good

Major Rating Factors: Good overall results on stability tests (5.0 on a scale of 0 to 10) despite fair financial strength of affiliated ACE Ltd. Other stability subfactors include excellent operational trends and excellent risk diversification. Strong capitalization (7.6) based on excellent risk adjusted capital (severe loss scenario). Capital levels have been relatively consistent over the last five years. High quality investment portfolio (7.8).

Other Rating Factors: Excellent profitability (8.9) with operating gains in each of the last five years. Excellent liquidity (7.5).

Principal Business: Individual health insurance (73%), group health insurance (14%), and individual life insurance (12%).

Principal Investments: NonCMO investment grade bonds (58%), CMOs and structured securities (38%), policy loans (2%), and common & preferred stock (2%).

Investments in Affiliates: None
Group Affiliation: ACE Ltd
Licensed in: GA, IN, NC
Commenced Business: June 1971
Address: 11 British Anerican Blvd, Latham, NY 12110
Phone: (518) 220-9333 **Domicile State:** NY **NAIC Code:** 78697

Data Date	Rating	RACR #1	RACR #2	Total Assets ($mil)	Capital ($mil)	Net Premium ($mil)	Net Income ($mil)
3-09	B	1.92	1.37	391.5	63.3	36.2	5.1
3-08	B	2.13	1.55	368.1	68.9	37.0	8.4
2008	B	1.82	1.31	376.0	59.1	145.4	26.4
2007	B-	1.87	1.36	359.9	60.1	145.0	16.9
2006	C+	1.66	1.21	337.7	51.0	138.7	14.8
2005	C+	1.76	1.29	326.1	52.1	132.9	8.1
2004	C	1.43	1.07	299.8	42.5	138.2	10.8

ACE Ltd
Composite Group Rating: C
Largest Group Members

	Assets ($mil)	Rating
ACE AMERICAN INS CO	8051	C+
ACE PROPERTY CASUALTY INS CO	5785	C
WESTCHESTER FIRE INS CO	2561	C-
PACIFIC EMPLOYERS INS CO	2446	C+
COMBINED INS CO OF AMERICA	2382	B-

COMMONWEALTH ANNUTIY & LIFE INSURANCE COMPANY   C-   Fair

Major Rating Factors: Weak profitability (1.6 on a scale of 0 to 10) with operating losses during the first three months of 2009. Return on equity has been low, averaging -19.2%. Weak overall results on stability tests (2.7) including weak results on operational trends. Good quality investment portfolio (5.8).

Other Rating Factors: Strong capitalization (7.9) based on excellent risk adjusted capital (severe loss scenario). Excellent liquidity (9.1).

Principal Business: Reinsurance (40%), individual life insurance (38%), individual annuities (16%), and individual health insurance (6%).

Principal Investments: NonCMO investment grade bonds (40%), CMOs and structured securities (20%), cash (13%), policy loans (6%), and common & preferred stock (4%).

Investments in Affiliates: None

Group Affiliation: Goldman Sachs Group

Licensed in: All states except AL, NC

Commenced Business: January 1967

Address: 440 Lincoln St, Worcester, MA 01653

Phone: (508) 855-1000 **Domicile State:** MA **NAIC Code:** 84824

Data Date	Rating	RACR #1	RACR #2	Total Assets ($mil)	Capital ($mil)	Net Premium ($mil)	Net Income ($mil)
3-09	C-	3.19	1.63	5,967.0	413.4	956.5	-246.8
3-08	C-	5.59	3.27	8,644.1	499.3	25.1	-7.1
2008	C-	5.17	2.73	5,334.8	390.6	108.9	-247.1
2007	C-	5.19	2.90	9,653.7	461.4	529.9	58.2
2006	C-	3.85	2.43	10,556.9	368.9	100.4	-35.5
2005	D+	4.05	2.15	10,084.4	374.1	33.7	-2.3
2004	D	1.95	1.45	11,534.0	555.6	80.2	79.8

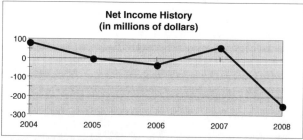

Net Income History (in millions of dollars)

COMPANION LIFE INSURANCE COMPANY   B   Good

Major Rating Factors: Good quality investment portfolio (5.4 on a scale of 0 to 10) despite mixed results such as: large holdings of BBB rated bonds but moderate junk bond exposure. Good liquidity (5.4) with sufficient resources to cover a large increase in policy surrenders. Good overall results on stability tests (5.8) excellent operational trends and excellent risk diversification.

Other Rating Factors: Strong capitalization (7.4) based on excellent risk adjusted capital (severe loss scenario). Excellent profitability (7.0) despite modest operating losses during 2004 and 2005.

Principal Business: Individual life insurance (85%), individual annuities (8%), and group life insurance (7%).

Principal Investments: CMOs and structured securities (43%), nonCMO investment grade bonds (43%), mortgages in good standing (7%), noninv. grade bonds (4%), and policy loans (3%).

Investments in Affiliates: None

Group Affiliation: Mutual Of Omaha Group

Licensed in: DC, NM, NC

Commenced Business: July 1949

Address: 303 Merrick Rd Ste 503, Lynbrook, NY 11563-2515

Phone: (800) 877-5399 **Domicile State:** NY **NAIC Code:** 62243

Data Date	Rating	RACR #1	RACR #2	Total Assets ($mil)	Capital ($mil)	Net Premium ($mil)	Net Income ($mil)
3-09	B	2.37	1.24	701.5	61.1	17.5	-1.5
3-08	B	2.39	1.27	676.3	57.6	16.5	-0.7
2008	B	2.40	1.25	699.4	61.5	70.4	2.9
2007	B	2.16	1.19	672.9	58.0	71.3	3.9
2006	B	2.46	1.27	673.8	58.0	76.7	4.1
2005	B	2.28	1.15	663.8	54.4	73.7	-0.7
2004	B	2.33	1.13	653.4	58.3	63.7	-4.4

Adverse Trends in Operations

Decrease in premium volume from 2007 to 2008 (1%)
Decrease in premium volume from 2006 to 2007 (7%)
Increase in policy surrenders from 2005 to 2006 (43%)
Decrease in capital during 2005 (7%)
Increase in policy surrenders from 2004 to 2005 (25%)

COMPANION LIFE INSURANCE COMPANY *   A-   Excellent

Major Rating Factors: Good overall results on stability tests (6.4 on a scale of 0 to 10). Strengths that enhance stability include good operational trends and excellent risk diversification. Strong capitalization (9.1) based on excellent risk adjusted capital (severe loss scenario). Furthermore, this high level of risk adjusted capital has been consistently maintained over the last five years. High quality investment portfolio (7.1).

Other Rating Factors: Excellent profitability (8.4) with operating gains in each of the last five years. Excellent liquidity (7.5).

Principal Business: Group health insurance (90%) and group life insurance (9%).

Principal Investments: Cash (33%), nonCMO investment grade bonds (30%), CMOs and structured securities (28%), and common & preferred stock (9%).

Investments in Affiliates: None

Group Affiliation: Blue Cross Blue Shield of SC Group

Licensed in: All states except AL, CO, DC, ID, NM, NC

Commenced Business: July 1970

Address: 2501 Faraway Dr, Columbia, SC 29219

Phone: (800) 753-0404 **Domicile State:** SC **NAIC Code:** 77828

Data Date	Rating	RACR #1	RACR #2	Total Assets ($mil)	Capital ($mil)	Net Premium ($mil)	Net Income ($mil)
3-09	A-	3.22	2.43	124.7	61.9	36.2	1.5
3-08	A-	3.06	2.25	125.0	64.4	34.4	1.6
2008	A-	3.52	2.68	130.4	67.5	137.8	6.7
2007	A-	3.03	2.25	122.0	63.0	135.5	9.5
2006	A-	2.52	1.88	95.9	54.4	123.9	7.4
2005	A-	2.21	1.64	87.6	47.4	113.1	6.6
2004	A-	2.48	1.83	88.4	51.0	100.9	6.1

Adverse Trends in Operations

Decrease in capital during 2005 (7%)

COMPBENEFITS INSURANCE COMPANY *   B+   Good

Major Rating Factors: Good overall results on stability tests (5.4 on a scale of 0 to 10) despite fair financial strength of affiliated Humana Inc. Other stability subfactors include excellent operational trends and excellent risk diversification. Strong capitalization (8.1) based on excellent risk adjusted capital (severe loss scenario). Moreover, capital has steadily grown over the last five years. High quality investment portfolio (8.9).

Other Rating Factors: Excellent profitability (9.0) with operating gains in each of the last five years. Excellent liquidity (7.4).

Principal Business: Group health insurance (99%) and reinsurance (1%).

Principal Investments: NonCMO investment grade bonds (102%) and common & preferred stock (3%).

Investments in Affiliates: None

Group Affiliation: Humana Inc

Licensed in: AK, AR, CA, CT, DE, GA, HI, IL, IN, IA, KS, KY, LA, ME, MA, MO, MT, NV, NH, NY, ND, OH, OK, OR, PA, SD, TX, UT, VT, WA, WV, WI

Commenced Business: November 1959

Address: 2929 Briar Park Suite 314, Houston, TX 77042

Phone: (770) 998-8936 **Domicile State:** TX **NAIC Code:** 60984

Data Date	Rating	RACR #1	RACR #2	Total Assets ($mil)	Capital ($mil)	Net Premium ($mil)	Net Income ($mil)
3-09	B+	2.09	1.72	62.7	50.8	31.6	2.5
3-08	B+	1.60	1.33	52.0	38.2	34.4	2.9
2008	B+	1.95	1.60	59.9	48.1	133.4	10.5
2007	B+	1.48	1.23	63.6	35.0	135.1	16.7
2006	B+	1.24	1.03	43.1	28.8	128.1	9.7
2005	B+	1.23	1.02	37.6	24.3	108.1	9.7
2004	B+	1.31	1.09	31.1	20.6	86.9	7.4

Humana Inc Composite Group Rating: C+ Largest Group Members	Assets ($mil)	Rating
HUMANA INS CO	4063	C
HUMANA MEDICAL PLAN INC	1085	B
KANAWHA INS CO	823	C
HUMANA HEALTH PLAN INC	402	B-
HUMANA HEALTH BENEFIT PLAN LA	254	C+

CONGRESS LIFE INSURANCE COMPANY   C   Fair

Major Rating Factors: Weak overall results on stability tests (2.8 on a scale of 0 to 10) including weak results on operational trends. Strong capitalization (10.0) based on excellent risk adjusted capital (severe loss scenario). Moreover, capital levels have been consistently high over the last five years. High quality investment portfolio (9.0).

Other Rating Factors: Excellent profitability (8.2) with operating gains in each of the last five years. Excellent liquidity (10.0).

Principal Business: Reinsurance (100%).

Principal Investments: NonCMO investment grade bonds (97%) and cash (3%).

Investments in Affiliates: None

Group Affiliation: Lehman Brothers Holdings Inc

Licensed in: All states except AL, DC, HI, MD, MI, NJ, NM, NC, ND

Commenced Business: February 1966

Address: 6681 Country Club Dr, Minneapolis, MN 55427-4698

Phone: (612) 544-2121 **Domicile State:** AZ **NAIC Code:** 73504

Data Date	Rating	RACR #1	RACR #2	Total Assets ($mil)	Capital ($mil)	Net Premium ($mil)	Net Income ($mil)
3-09	C	8.03	7.23	58.8	57.9	-2.2	0.8
3-08	C	7.94	7.14	59.5	56.8	0.3	0.3
2008	C	7.93	7.14	60.2	57.1	1.1	0.6
2007	C	7.90	7.11	59.0	56.5	1.9	0.1
2006	U	3.57	3.22	6.3	6.3	0.1	0.1
2005	C+	3.54	3.19	6.2	6.2	0.1	0.2
2004	C+	3.49	3.14	6.2	6.1	0.2	0.1

Adverse Trends in Operations

Decrease in premium volume from 2007 to 2008 (42%)
Change in asset mix during 2007 (16%)
Change in premium mix from 2006 to 2007 (22%)
Decrease in premium volume from 2005 to 2006 (38%)
Decrease in premium volume from 2004 to 2005 (26%)

CONNECTICUT GENERAL LIFE INSURANCE COMPANY   C+   Fair

Major Rating Factors: Fair overall results on stability tests (4.8 on a scale of 0 to 10). Good quality investment portfolio (5.9) despite large holdings of BBB rated bonds in addition to moderate junk bond exposure. Exposure to mortgages is significant, but the mortgage default rate has been low. Good overall profitability (6.7). Excellent expense controls. Return on equity has been excellent over the last five years averaging 23.2%.

Other Rating Factors: Good liquidity (6.3). Strong capitalization (7.8) based on excellent risk adjusted capital (severe loss scenario).

Principal Business: Group health insurance (76%), reinsurance (11%), individual life insurance (6%), individual health insurance (4%), and group life insurance (3%).

Principal Investments: NonCMO investment grade bonds (47%), mortgages in good standing (22%), policy loans (14%), noninv. grade bonds (7%), and misc. investments (11%).

Investments in Affiliates: 1%

Group Affiliation: CIGNA Group

Licensed in: All states except AL

Commenced Business: October 1865

Address: 900 Cottage Grove Rd,S-330, Bloomfield, CT 06002

Phone: (860) 726-7234 **Domicile State:** CT **NAIC Code:** 62308

Data Date	Rating	RACR #1	RACR #2	Total Assets ($mil)	Capital ($mil)	Net Premium ($mil)	Net Income ($mil)
3-09	C+	2.31	1.51	18,317.9	2,093.4	1,732.8	14.0
3-08	C+	2.82	1.80	16,533.8	1,857.1	1,608.5	20.3
2008	C+	2.39	1.58	17,733.1	2,030.2	6,979.3	1.0
2007	C	2.87	1.84	16,582.3	1,897.1	5,903.2	668.2
2006	C	3.28	2.02	17,765.4	1,990.2	4,755.8	1,032.8
2005	C	3.20	1.93	20,748.7	2,309.1	5,065.9	718.6
2004	C-	2.66	1.58	50,665.3	2,430.7	5,481.6	815.7

Rating Indexes

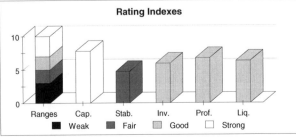

CONSECO HEALTH INSURANCE COMPANY

D+ **Weak**

Major Rating Factors: Weak overall results on stability tests (2.7 on a scale of 0 to 10) including potential financial drain due to affiliation with Conseco Group. Fair quality investment portfolio (3.3) with large holdings of BBB rated bonds in addition to significant exposure to junk bonds. Good capitalization (5.8) based on good risk adjusted capital (moderate loss scenario).

Other Rating Factors: Excellent profitability (7.4) with operating gains in each of the last five years. Excellent liquidity (7.7).

Principal Business: Individual health insurance (74%) and group health insurance (25%).

Principal Investments: NonCMO investment grade bonds (60%), CMOs and structured securities (21%), mortgages in good standing (8%), noninv. grade bonds (6%), and misc. investments (5%).

Investments in Affiliates: 1%

Group Affiliation: Conseco Group

Licensed in: All states except AL, DC, MI, NC

Commenced Business: December 1970

Address: 11815 N Pennsylvania St, Carmel, IN 46032

Phone: (317) 817-3700 **Domicile State:** AZ **NAIC Code:** 78174

Data Date	Rating	RACR #1	RACR #2	Total Assets ($mil)	Capital ($mil)	Net Premium ($mil)	Net Income ($mil)
3-09	D+	1.53	0.79	2,483.9	135.2	74.7	-2.3
3-08	D+	1.53	0.83	2,392.4	112.6	73.8	2.0
2008	D+	1.60	0.84	2,472.3	128.6	293.1	1.4
2007	D+	1.53	0.83	2,361.3	108.5	293.9	9.9
2006	D+	1.51	0.85	2,187.9	105.2	304.1	17.4
2005	D+	1.40	0.81	2,077.7	102.9	337.1	17.4
2004	D	1.42	0.82	1,980.5	110.9	364.8	3.3

Conseco Group
Composite Group Rating: D+
Largest Group Members

	Assets ($mil)	Rating
BANKERS LIFE CAS CO	11442	D+
CONSECO LIFE INS CO	4529	D+
CONSECO HEALTH INS CO	2472	D+
WASHINGTON NATIONAL INS CO	2348	D+
CONSECO INS CO	1044	D+

CONSECO INSURANCE COMPANY

D+ **Weak**

Major Rating Factors: Weak overall results on stability tests (1.9 on a scale of 0 to 10) including potential financial drain due to affiliation with Conseco Group, weak results on operational trends and negative cash flow from operations for 2008. Fair profitability (3.3) with operating losses during the first three months of 2009. Return on equity has been low, averaging 4.3%. Good quality investment portfolio (5.9).

Other Rating Factors: Good liquidity (5.9). Strong capitalization (7.9) based on excellent risk adjusted capital (severe loss scenario).

Principal Business: Individual health insurance (53%), individual annuities (25%), individual life insurance (14%), group retirement contracts (6%), and group life insurance (1%).

Principal Investments: NonCMO investment grade bonds (59%), CMOs and structured securities (15%), common & preferred stock (9%), mortgages in good standing (8%), and misc. investments (10%).

Investments in Affiliates: 5%

Group Affiliation: Conseco Group

Licensed in: All states except AL, NC

Commenced Business: December 1951

Address: 11815 N Pennsylvania St, Carmel, IN 46032

Phone: (317) 817-4000 **Domicile State:** IL **NAIC Code:** 60682

Data Date	Rating	RACR #1	RACR #2	Total Assets ($mil)	Capital ($mil)	Net Premium ($mil)	Net Income ($mil)
3-09	D+	2.89	1.57	996.8	147.4	23.9	-5.5
3-08	D+	2.90	1.58	1,133.9	149.2	28.3	3.7
2008	D+	3.09	1.69	1,044.5	159.1	108.2	18.7
2007	D+	4.01	2.25	1,242.3	233.0	167.5	-10.8
2006	D+	2.35	1.23	4,011.7	314.1	249.8	8.6
2005	D+	2.42	1.26	4,326.7	346.1	179.6	34.8
2004	D	2.18	1.11	4,899.7	352.0	67.1	18.9

Conseco Group
Composite Group Rating: D+
Largest Group Members

	Assets ($mil)	Rating
BANKERS LIFE CAS CO	11442	D+
CONSECO LIFE INS CO	4529	D+
CONSECO HEALTH INS CO	2472	D+
WASHINGTON NATIONAL INS CO	2348	D+
CONSECO INS CO	1044	D+

CONSECO LIFE INS CO OF TX

D **Weak**

Major Rating Factors: Low quality investment portfolio (1.6 on a scale of 0 to 10). Weak profitability (2.4) with operating losses during the first three months of 2009. Return on equity has been low, averaging 0.5%. Weak overall results on stability tests (1.8) including weak results on operational trends.

Other Rating Factors: Fair capitalization (3.1) based on fair risk adjusted capital (severe loss scenario). Excellent liquidity (10.0).

Principal Business: Individual life insurance (86%), individual annuities (10%), and reinsurance (3%).

Principal Investments: Common & preferred stock (88%), cash (9%), and nonCMO investment grade bonds (3%).

Investments in Affiliates: 88%

Group Affiliation: Conseco Group

Licensed in: UT

Commenced Business: September 2003

Address: (No address available)

Phone: (317) 817-3700 **Domicile State:** TX **NAIC Code:** 11804

Data Date	Rating	RACR #1	RACR #2	Total Assets ($mil)	Capital ($mil)	Net Premium ($mil)	Net Income ($mil)
3-09	D	0.55	0.51	589.8	524.7	0.1	-6.8
3-08	U	N/A	N/A	1,192.0	1,164.4	0.1	56.4
2008	D	0.60	0.56	601.0	573.2	0.3	-1,483.1
2007	U	0.77	0.69	1,291.2	1,174.4	0.4	2.9
2006	D+	0.83	0.76	1,525.0	1,392.8	0.4	-32.0
2005	U	0.92	0.82	1,669.1	1,602.1	0.4	-43.1
2004	U	0.91	0.81	1,560.8	1,508.4	0.5	-108.6

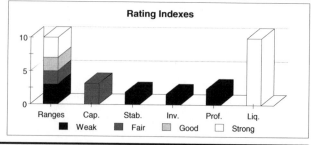

Rating Indexes

Ranges, Cap., Stab., Inv., Prof., Liq.

■ Weak ■ Fair ▨ Good ☐ Strong

CONSECO LIFE INSURANCE COMPANY

D+   **Weak**

Major Rating Factors: Low quality investment portfolio (2.1 on a scale of 0 to 10) containing large holdings of BBB rated bonds in addition to significant exposure to junk bonds. Weak profitability (2.0). Excellent expense controls. Return on equity has been low, averaging -15.7%. Weak liquidity (0.6) as a spike in claims or a run on policy withdrawals may stretch capacity.

Other Rating Factors: Weak overall results on stability tests (2.4) including weak risk adjusted capital in prior years. Fair capitalization (3.6) based on fair risk adjusted capital (moderate loss scenario).

Principal Business: Individual life insurance (71%), reinsurance (25%), and individual health insurance (3%).

Principal Investments: NonCMO investment grade bonds (56%), CMOs and structured securities (20%), mortgages in good standing (9%), noninv. grade bonds (6%), and misc. investments (10%).

Investments in Affiliates: 1%

Group Affiliation: Conseco Group

Licensed in: All states except AL, NC

Commenced Business: May 1962

Address: 11815 N Pennsylvania St, Carmel, IN 46032

Phone: (317) 817-6400   **Domicile State:** IN   **NAIC Code:** 65900

Data Date	Rating	RACR #1	RACR #2	Total Assets ($mil)	Capital ($mil)	Net Premium ($mil)	Net Income ($mil)
3-09	D+	0.82	0.43	4,511.5	165.6	82.4	5.8
3-08	D+	0.94	0.51	4,266.8	149.4	79.4	0.0
2008	D+	0.83	0.44	4,529.5	162.4	312.3	-68.2
2007	D+	0.95	0.52	4,256.1	148.2	318.8	-54.3
2006	D+	1.10	0.62	3,983.2	160.9	350.3	-157.1
2005	D+	1.69	0.95	3,935.6	263.2	375.5	46.8
2004	D	1.37	0.76	3,951.3	219.0	413.2	20.6

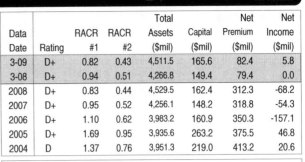

Junk Bonds as a % of Capital

Capital — $162 mil.
Junk Bonds — $251 mil.

0% 20% 40% 60% 80% 100% 120% 140% 160%

■ BB   ▨ B   ⬚ CCC   □ In default

CONTINENTAL AMEICAN INSURANCE COMPANY *

A-   **Excellent**

Major Rating Factors: Good overall results on stability tests (6.8 on a scale of 0 to 10). Strengths that enhance stability include excellent operational trends and good risk diversification. Strong capitalization (8.2) based on excellent risk adjusted capital (severe loss scenario). Moreover, capital levels have been consistently high over the last five years. High quality investment portfolio (7.3).

Other Rating Factors: Excellent profitability (8.0) with operating gains in each of the last five years. Excellent liquidity (8.1).

Principal Business: Group health insurance (56%), reinsurance (33%), group life insurance (9%), individual health insurance (1%), and individual life insurance (1%).

Principal Investments: NonCMO investment grade bonds (64%), cash (23%), CMOs and structured securities (5%), common & preferred stock (2%), and misc. investments (5%).

Investments in Affiliates: None

Group Affiliation: Continental American Ins Group

Licensed in: All states except AL, DC, KS, MI, MN, NJ, NM, NC, SC

Commenced Business: January 1969

Address: 2801 Devine St, Columbia, SC 29205

Phone: (803) 256-6265   **Domicile State:** SC   **NAIC Code:** 71730

Data Date	Rating	RACR #1	RACR #2	Total Assets ($mil)	Capital ($mil)	Net Premium ($mil)	Net Income ($mil)
3-09	A-	2.47	1.79	105.0	33.2	20.8	1.8
3-08	B	2.51	1.85	98.9	28.1	17.6	1.4
2008	A-	2.61	1.89	104.0	32.6	69.1	6.9
2007	B	2.45	1.80	102.8	27.0	64.9	5.1
2006	B-	1.94	1.44	86.2	22.7	61.7	4.8
2005	C+	1.77	1.32	72.7	18.9	53.5	3.4
2004	C+	1.63	1.21	62.5	15.9	42.4	2.7

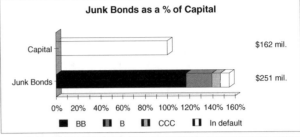

Adverse Trends in Operations

Increase in policy surrenders from 2006 to 2007 (40%)
Increase in policy surrenders from 2005 to 2006 (131%)
Increase in policy surrenders from 2004 to 2005 (47%)

CONTINENTAL ASSURANCE COMPANY

C   **Fair**

Major Rating Factors: Good quality investment portfolio (6.2 on a scale of 0 to 10) despite mixed results such as: large holdings of BBB rated bonds but moderate junk bond exposure. Good overall profitability (5.6) despite operating losses during the first three months of 2009. Return on equity has been good over the last five years, averaging 12.4%. Weak overall results on stability tests (2.6) including fair financial strength of affiliated CNA Financial Corp and weak results on operational trends.

Other Rating Factors: Strong capitalization (9.6) based on excellent risk adjusted capital (severe loss scenario). Excellent liquidity (8.4).

Principal Business: Individual life insurance (54%), group life insurance (42%), group health insurance (1%), individual annuities (1%), and individual health insurance (1%).

Principal Investments: NonCMO investment grade bonds (47%), CMOs and structured securities (27%), common & preferred stock (12%), and noninv. grade bonds (9%).

Investments in Affiliates: None

Group Affiliation: CNA Financial Corp

Licensed in: All states except AL

Commenced Business: August 1911

Address: 333 S Wabash Ave, Chicago, IL 60604

Phone: (312) 822-5000   **Domicile State:** IL   **NAIC Code:** 62413

Data Date	Rating	RACR #1	RACR #2	Total Assets ($mil)	Capital ($mil)	Net Premium ($mil)	Net Income ($mil)
3-09	C	5.37	2.76	3,210.9	482.5	0.3	-6.7
3-08	C	5.18	2.93	4,015.7	523.0	0.5	21.0
2008	C	4.60	2.53	3,333.6	487.3	1.5	-50.7
2007	C	5.17	2.91	4,120.1	471.2	2.8	27.3
2006	C	5.91	3.16	4,481.6	686.6	8.5	67.4
2005	C	5.70	2.93	5,092.0	627.0	10.9	64.7
2004	C	8.21	4.25	6,037.7	1,176.7	176.2	629.1

CNA Financial Corp
Composite Group Rating: C

Largest Group Members	Assets ($mil)	Rating
CONTINENTAL CASUALTY CO	38650	C
CONTINENTAL INS CO	3748	C+
CONTINENTAL ASSURANCE CO	3334	C
WESTERN SURETY CO	1210	C
FIRST INS CO OF HI LTD	593	C+

CONTINENTAL GENERAL INSURANCE COMPANY   C   Fair

Major Rating Factors: Fair overall results on stability tests (3.5 on a scale of 0 to 10). Good overall profitability (6.0). Excellent expense controls. Return on equity has been excellent over the last five years averaging 16.6%. Good liquidity (6.7) with sufficient resources to cover a large increase in policy surrenders.

Other Rating Factors: Strong capitalization (7.7) based on excellent risk adjusted capital (severe loss scenario). High quality investment portfolio (7.2).

Principal Business: Individual health insurance (72%), group health insurance (19%), individual life insurance (7%), individual annuities (1%), and reinsurance (1%).

Principal Investments: NonCMO investment grade bonds (60%), CMOs and structured securities (31%), policy loans (2%), mortgages in good standing (2%), and misc. investments (6%).

Investments in Affiliates: None

Group Affiliation: American Financial Corp

Licensed in: All states except AL, NC

Commenced Business: July 1961

Address: 8901 Indian Hills Dr, Omaha, NE 68114

Phone: (402) 397-3200 **Domicile State:** OH **NAIC Code:** 71404

Data Date	Rating	RACR #1	RACR #2	Total Assets ($mil)	Capital ($mil)	Net Premium ($mil)	Net Income ($mil)
3-09	C	2.23	1.48	222.8	38.5	18.3	2.2
3-08	C	2.71	1.81	238.2	50.4	21.1	1.1
2008	C	2.53	1.69	227.2	44.6	78.8	3.9
2007	C	2.74	1.84	262.0	51.3	89.8	11.8
2006	C	2.65	1.88	308.4	63.6	36.8	19.4
2005	C-	1.14	0.79	467.2	65.9	313.5	5.4
2004	D	1.29	0.92	444.7	69.0	318.1	10.3

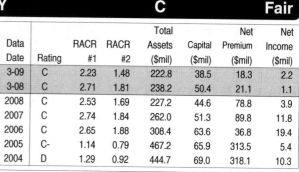

Rating Indexes

CONTINENTAL LIFE INSURANCE COMPANY OF BRENTWOOD *   B+   Good

Major Rating Factors: Good overall results on stability tests (5.8 on a scale of 0 to 10) despite fair financial strength of affiliated Genworth Financial. Other stability subfactors include good operational trends and excellent risk diversification. Good quality investment portfolio (6.5) with no exposure to mortgages and minimal holdings in junk bonds. Good liquidity (6.8).

Other Rating Factors: Strong capitalization (7.4) based on excellent risk adjusted capital (severe loss scenario). Excellent profitability (9.1) with operating gains in each of the last five years.

Principal Business: Individual health insurance (90%), group health insurance (6%), and individual life insurance (4%).

Principal Investments: NonCMO investment grade bonds (62%), CMOs and structured securities (27%), common & preferred stock (7%), noninv. grade bonds (2%), and cash (2%).

Investments in Affiliates: 7%

Group Affiliation: Genworth Financial

Licensed in: AK, AR, CA, CT, GA, HI, IL, IN, IA, KS, KY, LA, ME, MN, MS, MO, MT, NE, NV, NH, NY, ND, OH, OK, OR, RI, SD, TN, TX, UT, VT, WA, WI, WY, PR

Commenced Business: December 1983

Address: 101 Continental Plaza, Brentwood, TN 37027

Phone: (615) 377-1300 **Domicile State:** TN **NAIC Code:** 68500

Data Date	Rating	RACR #1	RACR #2	Total Assets ($mil)	Capital ($mil)	Net Premium ($mil)	Net Income ($mil)
3-09	B+	1.56	1.25	149.3	56.7	40.6	1.6
3-08	B+	1.72	1.38	169.7	60.2	45.2	1.8
2008	B+	1.65	1.32	153.0	60.0	171.1	11.9
2007	B+	1.75	1.42	155.9	60.1	175.6	7.1
2006	B+	1.97	1.54	147.7	54.2	170.9	10.3
2005	B	1.62	1.30	129.3	44.5	167.0	7.2
2004	B-	1.62	1.27	113.2	36.6	152.6	5.2

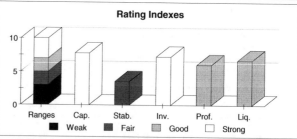

Genworth Financial Composite Group Rating: C+ Largest Group Members	Assets ($mil)	Rating
GENWORTH LIFE INS CO	34734	C+
GENWORTH LIFE ANNUITY INS CO	25964	B
GENWORTH LIFE INS CO OF NEW YORK	6999	C
GENWORTH MORTGAGE INS CORP	3023	C
GENWORTH MTG INS CORP OF NC	490	C+

COTTON STATES LIFE INSURANCE COMPANY *   B+   Good

Major Rating Factors: Good quality investment portfolio (6.3 on a scale of 0 to 10) despite mixed results such as: minimal exposure to mortgages and substantial holdings of BBB bonds but small junk bond holdings. Good overall profitability (5.2) despite operating losses during the first three months of 2009. Return on equity has been low, averaging -0.7%. Good liquidity (6.3).

Other Rating Factors: Good overall results on stability tests (6.6) excellent operational trends and excellent risk diversification. Strong capitalization (7.3) based on excellent risk adjusted capital (severe loss scenario).

Principal Business: Individual life insurance (99%) and reinsurance (1%).

Principal Investments: NonCMO investment grade bonds (52%), CMOs and structured securities (35%), policy loans (5%), common & preferred stock (4%), and misc. investments (3%).

Investments in Affiliates: None

Group Affiliation: COUNTRY Financial

Licensed in: AK, GA, HI, LA, ME, MO, ND, SD, TX, WA

Commenced Business: December 1955

Address: 244 Perimeter Ctr Pkwy NE, Atlanta, GA 30346

Phone: (770) 391-8600 **Domicile State:** GA **NAIC Code:** 62537

Data Date	Rating	RACR #1	RACR #2	Total Assets ($mil)	Capital ($mil)	Net Premium ($mil)	Net Income ($mil)
3-09	B+	2.16	1.22	281.8	30.4	10.4	-0.4
3-08	B	2.17	1.31	275.5	30.6	11.5	-0.2
2008	B+	2.31	1.36	281.2	31.7	45.5	1.4
2007	B	2.23	1.35	273.7	31.1	48.1	2.4
2006	B	2.19	1.34	261.1	28.1	50.4	0.9
2005	B	2.00	1.28	246.2	27.6	49.3	0.4
2004	C	2.08	1.33	226.7	25.2	46.8	-6.4

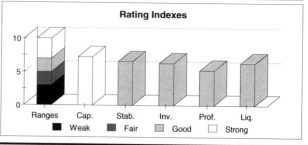

Rating Indexes

COUNTRY INVESTORS LIFE ASSURANCE COMPANY *   A-   Excellent

Major Rating Factors: Good overall results on stability tests (5.7 on a scale of 0 to 10). Strengths include potential support from affiliation with COUNTRY Financial, good operational trends and excellent risk diversification. Fair profitability (4.2). Return on equity has been low, averaging 0.8%. Strong capitalization (8.0) based on excellent risk adjusted capital (severe loss scenario).

Other Rating Factors: High quality investment portfolio (8.8). Excellent liquidity (10.0).

Principal Business: Individual annuities (79%) and individual life insurance (21%).

Principal Investments: NonCMO investment grade bonds (74%) and CMOs and structured securities (27%).

Investments in Affiliates: None

Group Affiliation: COUNTRY Financial

Licensed in: AK, AZ, AR, CA, CT, DC, FL, GA, IL, IN, IA, KS, KY, LA, MD, MA, MI, MN, MS, MT, NE, NV, NH, NY, OH, OK, OR, PA, RI, SC, TN, TX, UT, WV, WI, WY, PR

Commenced Business: November 1981

Address: 1701 N Towanda Ave, Bloomington, IL 61701

Phone: (309) 821-3000 **Domicile State:** IL **NAIC Code:** 94218

Data Date	Rating	RACR #1	RACR #2	Total Assets ($mil)	Capital ($mil)	Net Premium ($mil)	Net Income ($mil)
3-09	A-	16.35	8.05	192.1	153.1	0.0	1.0
3-08	B+	16.42	9.49	192.7	149.3	0.0	0.9
2008	A-	16.25	9.75	199.2	152.2	0.0	4.1
2007	B+	14.66	9.33	167.6	132.4	0.0	-1.4
2006	B+	14.93	9.52	158.0	133.8	0.0	-0.1
2005	B+	15.01	9.91	152.5	133.9	0.0	0.3
2004	B+	15.05	10.08	146.4	133.5	0.0	2.9

COUNTRY Financial Composite Group Rating: A Largest Group Members	Assets ($mil)	Rating
COUNTRY LIFE INS CO	7271	A+
COUNTRY MUTUAL INS CO	3378	A
COTTON STATES LIFE INS CO	281	B+
MIDDLESEX MUTUAL ASR CO	252	B-
COTTON STATES MUTUAL INS CO	245	C

COUNTRY LIFE INSURANCE COMPANY *   A+   Excellent

Major Rating Factors: Good quality investment portfolio (6.3 on a scale of 0 to 10) despite mixed results such as: minimal exposure to mortgages and large holdings of BBB rated bonds but small junk bond holdings. Good overall profitability (6.9) despite operating losses during the first three months of 2009. Return on equity has been low, averaging 3.4%. Good liquidity (6.6).

Other Rating Factors: Strong capitalization (7.6) based on excellent risk adjusted capital (severe loss scenario). Excellent overall results on stability tests (7.6) excellent operational trends and excellent risk diversification.

Principal Business: Individual life insurance (55%), reinsurance (27%), individual health insurance (15%), group retirement contracts (1%), and group life insurance (1%).

Principal Investments: NonCMO investment grade bonds (53%), CMOs and structured securities (24%), common & preferred stock (8%), mortgages in good standing (6%), and misc. investments (9%).

Investments in Affiliates: 4%

Group Affiliation: COUNTRY Financial

Licensed in: All states except AL, CO, DE, ID, NJ, NM, NC, VA

Commenced Business: December 1928

Address: 1701 N Towanda Ave, Bloomington, IL 61701-2090

Phone: (309) 821-3000 **Domicile State:** IL **NAIC Code:** 62553

Data Date	Rating	RACR #1	RACR #2	Total Assets ($mil)	Capital ($mil)	Net Premium ($mil)	Net Income ($mil)
3-09	A+	2.18	1.43	7,329.3	887.0	257.6	-20.8
3-08	A+	2.62	1.74	7,371.9	977.5	142.0	2.7
2008	A+	2.36	1.57	7,270.7	944.9	568.2	-9.7
2007	A+	2.71	1.78	7,356.2	981.0	502.3	36.0
2006	A+	2.45	1.69	6,771.1	946.7	469.4	53.6
2005	A+	2.42	1.68	6,407.4	909.2	489.6	47.3
2004	A+	2.26	1.58	6,181.1	934.4	523.8	25.5

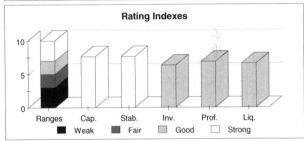

Rating Indexes
Ranges | Cap. | Stab. | Inv. | Prof. | Liq.
■ Weak   ■ Fair   ▨ Good   □ Strong

CROWN LIFE INSURANCE COMPANY US BRANCH   C   Fair

Major Rating Factors: Fair overall results on stability tests (4.0 on a scale of 0 to 10). Good overall profitability (5.8). Excellent expense controls. Good liquidity (6.0) with sufficient resources to handle a spike in claims as well as a significant increase in policy surrenders.

Other Rating Factors: Strong capitalization (8.2) based on excellent risk adjusted capital (severe loss scenario). High quality investment portfolio (7.3).

Principal Business: Individual life insurance (89%), individual health insurance (8%), group life insurance (2%), and reinsurance (1%).

Principal Investments: NonCMO investment grade bonds (73%), CMOs and structured securities (23%), cash (3%), and noninv. grade bonds (1%).

Investments in Affiliates: None

Group Affiliation: Great West Life Asr

Licensed in: All states except AL, NC

Commenced Business: October 1901

Address: 1901 Scarth St Suite 1900, Regina Saskatchwan, CN S4P4L4

Phone: (306) 751-6000 **Domicile State:** MI **NAIC Code:** 80675

Data Date	Rating	RACR #1	RACR #2	Total Assets ($mil)	Capital ($mil)	Net Premium ($mil)	Net Income ($mil)
3-09	C	3.37	1.77	336.3	44.3	2.1	0.6
3-08	U	N/A	N/A	408.5	112.3	2.3	1.2
2008	C-	3.35	1.77	342.5	43.9	8.6	7.2
2007	U	N/A	N/A	414.5	105.9	9.9	11.2
2006	U	N/A	N/A	375.0	49.9	11.1	5.8
2005	U	N/A	N/A	376.7	41.8	12.1	2.9
2004	N/A	N/A	N/A	385.2	45.9	13.1	11.6

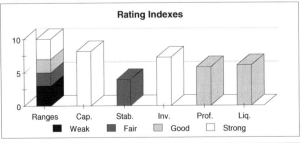

Rating Indexes
Ranges | Cap. | Stab. | Inv. | Prof. | Liq.
■ Weak   ■ Fair   ▨ Good   □ Strong

CUNA MUTUAL INSURANCE SOCIETY   C+   Fair

Major Rating Factors: Fair current capitalization (4.8 on a scale of 0 to 10) based on fair risk adjusted capital (severe loss scenario), although results have slipped from the good range during the last year. Fair quality investment portfolio (4.8) with substantial holdings of BBB bonds in addition to junk bond exposure equal to 50% of capital. Fair overall results on stability tests (4.5).

Other Rating Factors: Excellent profitability (7.1) despite operating losses during the first three months of 2009. Excellent liquidity (7.1).

Principal Business: Group retirement contracts (31%), individual annuities (22%), credit health insurance (14%), group life insurance (10%), and other lines (23%).

Principal Investments: NonCMO investment grade bonds (41%), CMOs and structured securities (23%), common & preferred stock (12%), mortgages in good standing (10%), and misc. investments (15%).

Investments in Affiliates: 11%

Group Affiliation: CUNA Mutual Ins Group

Licensed in: All states except AL

Commenced Business: August 1935

Address: 5910 Mineral Point Rd, Madison, WI 53705

Phone: (608) 238-5851 **Domicile State:** IA **NAIC Code:** 62626

Data Date	Rating	RACR #1	RACR #2	Total Assets ($mil)	Capital ($mil)	Net Premium ($mil)	Net Income ($mil)
3-09	C+	0.93	0.72	10,960.4	933.4	727.4	-21.2
3-08	B-	0.92	0.72	11,716.7	997.1	575.6	-7.0
2008	C+	1.00	0.79	11,002.5	985.2	2,433.3	-37.8
2007	B-	0.95	0.75	12,215.1	1,035.4	2,830.3	10.6
2006	B	1.01	0.87	3,393.4	790.1	1,557.5	67.5
2005	B-	0.98	0.86	3,226.1	746.9	1,407.8	118.7
2004	C+	0.90	0.81	3,124.0	724.7	1,448.0	37.6

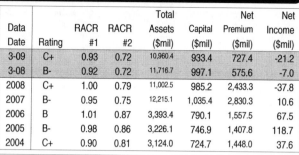

Risk-Adjusted Capital Ratio #2
(Severe Loss Scenario)

■ Weak ■ Fair ▨ Good □ Strong

DELAWARE AMERICAN LIFE INSURANCE COMPANY   B   Good

Major Rating Factors: Good overall results on stability tests (5.5 on a scale of 0 to 10) despite fair financial strength of affiliated American International Group. Other stability subfactors include excellent operational trends and excellent risk diversification. Good overall profitability (6.7). Return on equity has been good over the last five years, averaging 10.2%. Strong capitalization (10.0) based on excellent risk adjusted capital (severe loss scenario).

Other Rating Factors: High quality investment portfolio (7.4). Excellent liquidity (7.8).

Principal Business: Group health insurance (70%), group life insurance (21%), individual life insurance (7%), and reinsurance (2%).

Principal Investments: NonCMO investment grade bonds (90%), common & preferred stock (5%), policy loans (2%), cash (2%), and noninv. grade bonds (1%).

Investments in Affiliates: None

Group Affiliation: American International Group

Licensed in: All states except AL, MS, MT, NJ, NC, ND

Commenced Business: August 1966

Address: One ALICO Plaza, Wilmington, DE 19801

Phone: (302) 594-2000 **Domicile State:** DE **NAIC Code:** 62634

Data Date	Rating	RACR #1	RACR #2	Total Assets ($mil)	Capital ($mil)	Net Premium ($mil)	Net Income ($mil)
3-09	B	3.59	2.99	88.9	28.2	8.2	1.0
3-08	B+	3.21	2.75	80.9	24.3	6.1	-1.8
2008	B	3.63	3.17	83.9	27.3	26.6	2.3
2007	B+	3.64	3.23	76.4	26.3	17.0	0.9
2006	B	3.52	3.01	80.5	25.8	19.6	2.8
2005	B	3.27	2.65	78.0	23.4	20.2	3.3
2004	B+	4.77	4.03	97.0	39.2	15.3	3.7

American International Group Composite Group Rating: C+ Largest Group Members	Assets ($mil)	Rating
AMERICAN LIFE INS CO	86338	C-
VARIABLE ANNUITY LIFE INS CO	53699	B
WESTERN NATIONAL LIFE INS CO	45803	B-
AMERICAN GENERAL LIFE INS CO	38638	C+
NATIONAL UNION FIRE INS CO OF PITTSB	33707	B

EDUCATORS MUTUAL INSURANCE ASSOCIATION   B-   Good

Major Rating Factors: Good overall profitability (6.8 on a scale of 0 to 10) despite operating losses during the first three months of 2009. Good liquidity (6.9) with sufficient resources to handle a spike in claims. Good overall results on stability tests (5.1). Stability strengths include good operational trends and good risk diversification.

Other Rating Factors: Strong capitalization (8.3) based on excellent risk adjusted capital (severe loss scenario). High quality investment portfolio (7.2).

Principal Business: Group health insurance (75%), reinsurance (25%), and individual life insurance (1%).

Principal Investments: NonCMO investment grade bonds (56%), common & preferred stock (13%), cash (6%), real estate (3%), and noninv. grade bonds (2%).

Investments in Affiliates: 8%

Group Affiliation: Educators Mutual Group

Licensed in: VT

Commenced Business: June 1935

Address: 852 E Arrowhead Ln, Murray, UT 84107

Phone: (801) 262-7476 **Domicile State:** UT **NAIC Code:** 81701

Data Date	Rating	RACR #1	RACR #2	Total Assets ($mil)	Capital ($mil)	Net Premium ($mil)	Net Income ($mil)
3-09	B-	2.29	1.85	64.3	32.4	12.8	-0.7
3-08	C+	2.58	2.05	61.1	33.1	11.7	0.5
2008	B-	2.58	2.08	65.2	35.7	47.8	5.1
2007	C+	2.82	2.28	61.8	33.4	39.6	4.7
2006	C	3.25	2.46	54.0	28.5	40.4	4.9
2005	C-	1.95	1.62	50.5	24.0	43.0	4.8
2004	D	1.75	1.46	52.8	18.8	37.6	-2.7

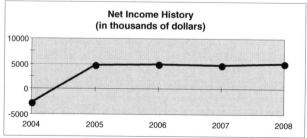

Net Income History
(in thousands of dollars)

EMC NATIONAL LIFE COMPANY   C   Fair

Major Rating Factors: Fair overall results on stability tests (4.2 on a scale of 0 to 10). Good overall capitalization (5.0) based on good risk adjusted capital (moderate loss scenario). Nevertheless, capital levels have fluctuated during prior years. Good quality investment portfolio (6.0) with minimal exposure to mortgages and minimal holdings in junk bonds.

Other Rating Factors: Good liquidity (6.2). Weak profitability (1.7) with operating losses during the first three months of 2009.

Principal Business: Individual annuities (40%), individual life insurance (30%), individual health insurance (24%), group life insurance (4%), and reinsurance (2%).

Principal Investments: NonCMO investment grade bonds (74%), CMOs and structured securities (17%), mortgages in good standing (4%), common & preferred stock (3%), and policy loans (1%).

Investments in Affiliates: None

Group Affiliation: Employers Mutual Group

Licensed in: All states except AL, NM, NC

Commenced Business: April 1963

Address: 4095 NW Urbandale Dr, Urbandale, IA 50322

Phone: (515) 280-2511 **Domicile State:** IA **NAIC Code:** 62928

Data Date	Rating	RACR #1	RACR #2	Total Assets ($mil)	Capital ($mil)	Net Premium ($mil)	Net Income ($mil)
3-09	C	1.03	0.63	692.3	35.0	37.9	-4.8
3-08	C+	1.73	1.09	691.2	51.7	32.1	-0.9
2008	C	1.27	0.78	682.7	41.3	119.3	-22.0
2007	C+	1.79	1.12	663.4	53.0	122.4	-1.2
2006	B-	1.74	1.09	679.9	52.0	143.4	-4.5
2005	B	2.31	1.40	684.3	71.7	97.7	3.3
2004	B	2.60	1.56	652.2	73.4	153.1	9.2

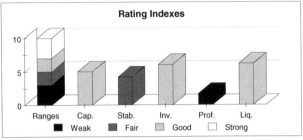

Rating Indexes

Ranges   Cap.   Stab.   Inv.   Prof.   Liq.

■ Weak   ■ Fair   ▨ Good   □ Strong

EMPIRE FIDELITY INVESTMENTS LIFE INSURANCE COMPANY *   A-   Excellent

Major Rating Factors: Good overall results on stability tests (5.7 on a scale of 0 to 10) despite weak results on operational trends. Strengths include potential support from affiliation with FMR Corp and excellent risk diversification. Weak profitability (2.9) with investment income below regulatory standards in relation to interest assumptions of reserves. Strong capitalization (9.3) based on excellent risk adjusted capital (severe loss scenario).

Other Rating Factors: High quality investment portfolio (9.0). Excellent liquidity (7.0).

Principal Business: Individual annuities (99%) and individual life insurance (1%).

Principal Investments: NonCMO investment grade bonds (100%).

Investments in Affiliates: None

Group Affiliation: FMR Corp

Licensed in: NC

Commenced Business: June 1992

Address: 200 Liberty St 1 World Financl, New York, NY 10281

Phone: (212) 335-5706 **Domicile State:** NY **NAIC Code:** 71228

Data Date	Rating	RACR #1	RACR #2	Total Assets ($mil)	Capital ($mil)	Net Premium ($mil)	Net Income ($mil)
3-09	A-	2.81	2.53	1,138.6	52.1	45.1	0.4
3-08	A-	2.32	1.90	1,542.8	51.4	72.6	0.2
2008	A-	2.78	2.50	1,197.3	51.7	204.1	-0.1
2007	A-	2.31	1.80	1,613.2	51.2	241.7	2.8
2006	A-	2.49	2.17	1,353.1	49.3	144.6	4.2
2005	A-	2.53	2.25	1,178.5	46.1	43.6	5.5
2004	B	2.27	2.04	1,137.6	40.5	39.6	5.7

FMR Corp Composite Group Rating: A Largest Group Members	Assets ($mil)	Rating
FIDELITY INVESTMENTS LIFE INS CO	11894	A
EMPIRE FIDELITY INVESTMENTS L I C	1197	A-

EMPLOYERS REASSURANCE CORPORATION   C-   Fair

Major Rating Factors: Fair current capitalization (3.8 on a scale of 0 to 10) based on fair risk adjusted capital (moderate loss scenario), although results have slipped from the good range over the last two years. Fair overall results on stability tests (3.3) including weak risk adjusted capital in prior years. Weak profitability (1.5). Excellent expense controls.

Other Rating Factors: Good quality investment portfolio (5.6). Good liquidity (6.7).

Principal Business: Reinsurance (100%).

Principal Investments: NonCMO investment grade bonds (70%), CMOs and structured securities (17%), common & preferred stock (7%), and noninv. grade bonds (3%).

Investments in Affiliates: 6%

Group Affiliation: GE Insurance Solutions

Licensed in: All states except AL, NC

Commenced Business: November 1907

Address: 5200 Metcalf Ave, Overland Park, KS 66201

Phone: (913) 676-5724 **Domicile State:** KS **NAIC Code:** 68276

Data Date	Rating	RACR #1	RACR #2	Total Assets ($mil)	Capital ($mil)	Net Premium ($mil)	Net Income ($mil)
3-09	C-	0.77	0.60	9,173.0	595.3	149.3	17.2
3-08	C-	1.16	0.90	8,784.8	805.1	250.8	13.6
2008	C-	0.90	0.70	9,697.7	681.2	686.9	-619.1
2007	C-	1.13	0.88	8,666.4	780.3	1,054.1	-331.5
2006	C-	1.26	0.80	7,644.2	421.1	1,154.6	-258.8
2005	C-	0.81	0.51	5,341.8	252.9	-148.9	-107.6
2004	C	0.76	0.48	6,043.3	259.9	1,030.2	-144.1

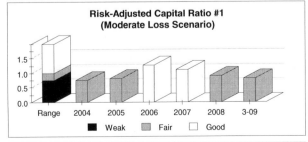

Risk-Adjusted Capital Ratio #1 (Moderate Loss Scenario)

Range   2004   2005   2006   2007   2008   3-09

■ Weak   ▨ Fair   □ Good

EQUITABLE LIFE & CASUALTY INSURANCE COMPANY | B- | Good

Major Rating Factors: Good overall profitability (5.5 on a scale of 0 to 10) despite operating losses during the first three months of 2009. Return on equity has been fair, averaging 6.6%. Good overall results on stability tests (5.0). Stability strengths include excellent operational trends and good risk diversification. Strong capitalization (7.3) based on excellent risk adjusted capital (severe loss scenario).

Other Rating Factors: High quality investment portfolio (7.5). Excellent liquidity (7.1).

Principal Business: Individual health insurance (92%) and individual life insurance (8%).

Principal Investments: NonCMO investment grade bonds (50%), CMOs and structured securities (37%), mortgages in good standing (5%), cash (3%), and misc. investments (2%).

Investments in Affiliates: None

Group Affiliation: Insurance Investment Co

Licensed in: All states except AL, CO, GA, HI, MI, MS, NM, NC, WY

Commenced Business: June 1935

Address: 3 Triad Center Suite 200, Salt Lake City, UT 84180

Phone: (801) 579-3400 **Domicile State:** UT **NAIC Code:** 62952

Data Date	Rating	RACR #1	RACR #2	Total Assets ($mil)	Capital ($mil)	Net Premium ($mil)	Net Income ($mil)
3-09	B-	1.71	1.21	215.2	33.4	27.6	-2.5
3-08	C+	2.18	1.60	209.1	40.3	26.7	0.2
2008	B-	2.00	1.43	215.3	38.8	104.2	-0.4
2007	C+	2.18	1.60	207.2	40.2	107.9	3.2
2006	C+	2.02	1.49	190.6	37.2	109.3	3.7
2005	C+	1.80	1.33	173.7	34.8	116.2	4.1
2004	C+	1.63	1.20	156.3	32.9	114.0	3.9

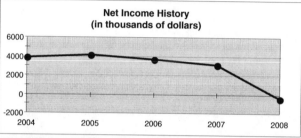

Net Income History
(in thousands of dollars)

EQUITRUST LIFE INSURANCE COMPANY | B- | Good

Major Rating Factors: Good capitalization (5.6 on a scale of 0 to 10) based on good risk adjusted capital (moderate loss scenario). Capital levels have been relatively consistent over the last five years. Good liquidity (6.2) with sufficient resources to handle a spike in claims as well as a significant increase in policy surrenders. Fair quality investment portfolio (3.5).

Other Rating Factors: Fair profitability (4.3) with operating losses during the first three months of 2009. Fair overall results on stability tests (4.7).

Principal Business: Individual annuities (98%) and reinsurance (2%).

Principal Investments: NonCMO investment grade bonds (59%), CMOs and structured securities (24%), mortgages in good standing (10%), noninv. grade bonds (3%), and common & preferred stock (2%).

Investments in Affiliates: None

Group Affiliation: Iowa Farm Bureau

Licensed in: All states except AL, NC

Commenced Business: July 1967

Address: 5400 University Ave, West Des Moines, IA 50266-5997

Phone: (515) 225-5400 **Domicile State:** IA **NAIC Code:** 62510

Data Date	Rating	RACR #1	RACR #2	Total Assets ($mil)	Capital ($mil)	Net Premium ($mil)	Net Income ($mil)
3-09	B-	1.43	0.69	7,726.0	389.2	320.5	-21.2
3-08	B	1.59	0.79	6,945.9	358.9	315.0	-40.9
2008	B	1.60	0.78	7,779.9	417.0	1,504.7	-116.9
2007	B	1.77	0.88	6,841.5	391.6	1,562.8	22.3
2006	B	2.37	1.15	5,477.3	328.0	1,855.5	24.5
2005	B	2.01	1.01	3,657.8	215.6	959.3	20.2
2004	B	1.72	0.90	2,849.3	165.8	723.4	22.9

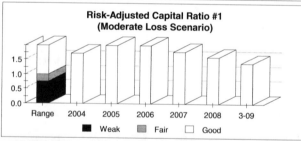

Risk-Adjusted Capital Ratio #1
(Moderate Loss Scenario)

■ Weak   ■ Fair   □ Good

ERIE FAMILY LIFE INSURANCE COMPANY | B | Good

Major Rating Factors: Good overall results on stability tests (5.6 on a scale of 0 to 10). Stability strengths include good operational trends and excellent risk diversification. Good overall capitalization (5.6) based on good risk adjusted capital (moderate loss scenario). Nevertheless, capital levels have fluctuated during prior years. Good overall profitability (6.6) despite operating losses during the first three months of 2009.

Other Rating Factors: Good liquidity (5.2). Fair quality investment portfolio (4.1).

Principal Business: Individual annuities (53%), individual life insurance (44%), group retirement contracts (2%), and group life insurance (1%).

Principal Investments: NonCMO investment grade bonds (77%), CMOs and structured securities (12%), common & preferred stock (5%), noninv. grade bonds (3%), and misc. investments (2%).

Investments in Affiliates: None

Group Affiliation: Erie Ins Group

Licensed in: DE, GA, IN, IA, LA, MA, MS, ND, OK, RI, TX, WA, WI, WY

Commenced Business: September 1967

Address: 100 Erie Insurance Pl, Erie, PA 16530

Phone: (800) 458-0811 **Domicile State:** PA **NAIC Code:** 70769

Data Date	Rating	RACR #1	RACR #2	Total Assets ($mil)	Capital ($mil)	Net Premium ($mil)	Net Income ($mil)
3-09	B	1.41	0.75	1,540.7	92.6	49.8	-8.5
3-08	B+	2.44	1.31	1,560.1	170.8	48.8	-10.5
2008	B	1.62	0.87	1,533.7	105.8	216.4	-66.4
2007	B+	2.62	1.41	1,563.9	183.5	129.8	12.5
2006	B	2.47	1.35	1,558.3	168.1	150.5	23.5
2005	B	2.20	1.21	1,592.1	147.5	144.5	15.7
2004	B	2.16	1.20	1,459.7	136.0	128.9	20.5

Adverse Trends in Operations

Change in premium mix from 2007 to 2008 (4.2%)
Decrease in asset base during 2008 (2%)
Decrease in capital during 2008 (42%)
Decrease in premium volume from 2006 to 2007 (14%)
Increase in policy surrenders from 2005 to 2006 (82%)

FAMILY HERITAGE LIFE INSURANCE COMPANY OF AMERICA * B+ Good

Major Rating Factors: Good overall results on stability tests (5.4 on a scale of 0 to 10). Stability strengths include excellent operational trends and good risk diversification. Strong capitalization (7.8) based on excellent risk adjusted capital (severe loss scenario). Moreover, capital has steadily grown over the last five years. High quality investment portfolio (9.2).

Other Rating Factors: Excellent profitability (9.4) with operating gains in each of the last five years. Excellent liquidity (8.2).

Principal Business: Individual health insurance (100%).

Principal Investments: NonCMO investment grade bonds (100%).

Investments in Affiliates: None

Group Affiliation: Southwestern/Great American Inc

Licensed in: All states except AL, MI, NJ, NM, NC, VA

Commenced Business: November 1989

Address: 6001 E Royalton Rd Suite 200, Cleveland, OH 44147-3529

Phone: (440) 922-5222 **Domicile State:** OH **NAIC Code:** 77968

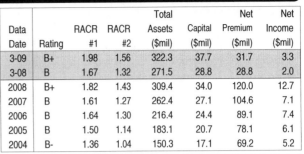

Data Date	Rating	RACR #1	RACR #2	Total Assets ($mil)	Capital ($mil)	Net Premium ($mil)	Net Income ($mil)
3-09	B+	1.98	1.56	322.3	37.7	31.7	3.3
3-08	B	1.67	1.32	271.5	28.8	28.8	2.0
2008	B+	1.82	1.43	309.4	34.0	120.0	12.7
2007	B	1.61	1.27	262.4	27.1	104.6	7.1
2006	B	1.64	1.30	216.4	24.4	89.1	7.4
2005	B	1.50	1.14	183.1	20.7	78.1	6.1
2004	B-	1.36	1.04	150.3	17.1	69.2	5.2

Rating Indexes

(Bar chart: Ranges, Cap., Stab., Inv., Prof., Liq.)
Weak ■ Fair ▨ Good ▥ Strong ☐

FAMILY LIFE INSURANCE COMPANY C+ Fair

Major Rating Factors: Fair overall results on stability tests (4.4 on a scale of 0 to 10) including fair financial strength of affiliated Central United Life Group. Good profitability (5.0) although investment income, in comparison to reserve requirements, is below regulatory standards. Strong capitalization (9.2) based on excellent risk adjusted capital (severe loss scenario).

Other Rating Factors: High quality investment portfolio (8.1). Excellent liquidity (7.5).

Principal Business: Individual life insurance (99%), reinsurance (1%), and individual annuities (1%).

Principal Investments: NonCMO investment grade bonds (72%), CMOs and structured securities (22%), policy loans (4%), noninv. grade bonds (1%), and cash (1%).

Investments in Affiliates: None

Group Affiliation: Central United Life Group

Licensed in: All states except AL, NC

Commenced Business: June 1949

Address: 1200 6th Ave Park Place Bldg, Seattle, WA 98101

Phone: (512) 404-5284 **Domicile State:** TX **NAIC Code:** 63053

Data Date	Rating	RACR #1	RACR #2	Total Assets ($mil)	Capital ($mil)	Net Premium ($mil)	Net Income ($mil)
3-09	C+	2.74	2.47	122.9	25.2	3.6	1.0
3-08	C-	2.58	2.17	126.6	23.5	4.1	1.2
2008	C	2.75	2.47	126.2	25.4	15.9	4.9
2007	D+	2.47	2.11	127.8	22.5	20.1	6.5
2006	D+	1.99	1.40	119.1	17.9	40.4	-4.9
2005	D+	1.40	1.00	104.4	17.2	21.5	-4.0
2004	C-	1.92	1.40	111.6	21.9	20.9	-1.6

Central United Life Group
Composite Group Rating: C

Largest Group Members	Assets ($mil)	Rating
MANHATTAN LIFE INS CO	354	C+
CENTRAL UNITED LIFE INS CO	321	D+
FAMILY LIFE INS CO	126	C
INVESTORS CONSOLIDATED INS CO INC	16	C

FARM BUREAU LIFE INSURANCE COMPANY * B+ Good

Major Rating Factors: Good overall results on stability tests (6.1 on a scale of 0 to 10). Stability strengths include excellent operational trends, excellent risk adjusted capital for prior years and excellent risk diversification. Good current capitalization (6.7) based on good risk adjusted capital (severe loss scenario), although results have slipped from the excellent range during the last year. Fair quality investment portfolio (4.6).

Other Rating Factors: Fair liquidity (4.1). Excellent profitability (7.5) despite operating losses during the first three months of 2009.

Principal Business: Individual annuities (51%), individual life insurance (45%), individual health insurance (2%), and group retirement contracts (2%).

Principal Investments: NonCMO investment grade bonds (51%), CMOs and structured securities (26%), mortgages in good standing (9%), noninv. grade bonds (5%), and misc. investments (8%).

Investments in Affiliates: None

Group Affiliation: Iowa Farm Bureau

Licensed in: AR, CT, IL, KS, KY, MS, NE, NV, NH, NY, OH, OR, PA, TN, VT, WV, WY, PR

Commenced Business: January 1945

Address: 5400 University Ave, West Des Moines, IA 50266-5997

Phone: (515) 225-5400 **Domicile State:** IA **NAIC Code:** 63088

Data Date	Rating	RACR #1	RACR #2	Total Assets ($mil)	Capital ($mil)	Net Premium ($mil)	Net Income ($mil)
3-09	B+	1.91	0.96	5,605.0	371.3	164.3	-9.0
3-08	B+	2.23	1.15	5,623.3	368.8	123.2	-7.8
2008	B+	2.03	1.04	5,591.9	385.4	555.3	-28.7
2007	B+	2.25	1.16	5,633.1	364.9	455.0	55.2
2006	B+	2.08	1.08	5,477.7	335.3	440.6	49.3
2005	A-	2.36	1.24	5,370.7	395.9	494.6	46.0
2004	A-	2.41	1.27	5,152.8	376.3	521.3	38.1

Adverse Trends in Operations

Increase in policy surrenders from 2006 to 2007 (318%)
Decrease in capital during 2006 (15%)
Decrease in premium volume from 2005 to 2006 (11%)
Decrease in premium volume from 2004 to 2005 (5%)

FARM BUREAU LIFE INSURANCE COMPANY OF MICHIGAN *   A-   Excellent

Major Rating Factors: Good quality investment portfolio (5.9 on a scale of 0 to 10) despite significant exposure to mortgages . Mortgage default rate has been low. large holdings of BBB rated bonds in addition to small junk bond holdings. Good overall results on stability tests (6.9). Strengths that enhance stability include excellent operational trends and excellent risk diversification. Fair liquidity (4.9).

Other Rating Factors: Strong capitalization (8.0) based on excellent risk adjusted capital (severe loss scenario). Excellent profitability (7.8).

Principal Business: Individual annuities (54%), individual life insurance (44%), group retirement contracts (1%), and group life insurance (1%).

Principal Investments: NonCMO investment grade bonds (64%), mortgages in good standing (22%), common & preferred stock (5%), CMOs and structured securities (4%), and misc. investments (5%).

Investments in Affiliates: None

Group Affiliation: Michigan Farm Bureau

Licensed in: MN

Commenced Business: September 1951

Address: 7373 West Saginaw Hwy, Lansing, MI 48909

Phone: (517) 323-7000 **Domicile State:** MI **NAIC Code:** 63096

Data Date	Rating	RACR #1	RACR #2	Total Assets ($mil)	Capital ($mil)	Net Premium ($mil)	Net Income ($mil)
3-09	A-	3.16	1.69	1,761.1	279.1	40.7	1.3
3-08	A-	3.57	1.90	1,706.0	302.9	30.2	4.7
2008	A-	3.23	1.71	1,740.9	283.7	135.5	-6.5
2007	A-	3.62	1.93	1,695.4	299.0	101.1	21.0
2006	A-	3.51	1.88	1,655.9	278.1	110.5	22.1
2005	A-	3.35	1.77	1,609.3	251.0	129.5	20.8
2004	A-	3.24	1.70	1,512.5	233.9	148.9	22.7

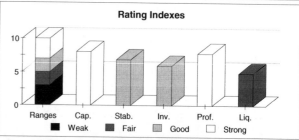

Rating Indexes

FARM BUREAU LIFE INSURANCE COMPANY OF MISSOURI *   A-   Excellent

Major Rating Factors: Good overall profitability (5.8 on a scale of 0 to 10) despite operating losses during the first three months of 2009. Return on equity has been low, averaging 3.2%. Good liquidity (5.9) with sufficient resources to cover a large increase in policy surrenders. Good overall results on stability tests (6.9) excellent operational trends and excellent risk diversification.

Other Rating Factors: Strong capitalization (8.4) based on excellent risk adjusted capital (severe loss scenario). High quality investment portfolio (7.2).

Principal Business: Individual life insurance (78%), individual annuities (21%), and group health insurance (1%).

Principal Investments: CMOs and structured securities (45%), nonCMO investment grade bonds (39%), common & preferred stock (10%), policy loans (5%), and noninv. grade bonds (1%).

Investments in Affiliates: 1%

Group Affiliation: Missouri Farm Bureau

Licensed in: MT

Commenced Business: July 1950

Address: 701 S Country Club Dr, Jefferson City, MO 65109

Phone: (573) 893-1400 **Domicile State:** MO **NAIC Code:** 63118

Data Date	Rating	RACR #1	RACR #2	Total Assets ($mil)	Capital ($mil)	Net Premium ($mil)	Net Income ($mil)
3-09	A-	3.16	1.92	374.9	44.5	12.7	0.0
3-08	A-	3.79	2.37	368.5	52.0	11.8	-0.1
2008	A-	3.25	1.98	367.9	45.3	32.8	-0.2
2007	A-	3.80	2.38	363.5	52.5	29.5	1.4
2006	A-	3.83	2.38	353.3	51.6	28.0	1.3
2005	A-	3.93	2.45	337.9	50.2	31.1	1.6
2004	A-	4.66	2.72	318.9	49.1	30.8	1.3

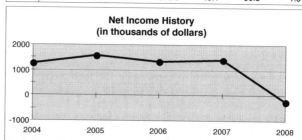

Net Income History
(in thousands of dollars)

FARM FAMILY LIFE INSURANCE COMPANY   B   Good

Major Rating Factors: Good current capitalization (6.2 on a scale of 0 to 10) based on good risk adjusted capital (severe loss scenario), although results have slipped from the excellent range over the last two years. Good overall profitability (6.3) despite operating losses during the first three months of 2009. Return on equity has been fair, averaging 8.1%. Good liquidity (5.3).

Other Rating Factors: Good overall results on stability tests (6.0) excellent operational trends and excellent risk diversification. Fair quality investment portfolio (4.5).

Principal Business: Individual life insurance (66%), individual annuities (26%), individual health insurance (7%), and group life insurance (1%).

Principal Investments: NonCMO investment grade bonds (64%), CMOs and structured securities (13%), common & preferred stock (7%), mortgages in good standing (6%), and misc. investments (9%).

Investments in Affiliates: None

Group Affiliation: American National Group Inc

Licensed in: DC, FL, MD, MA, MI, NJ, NM, NC, RI, SC, VA, WI

Commenced Business: January 1954

Address: 344 Route 9W, Glenmont, NY 12077

Phone: (518) 431-5000 **Domicile State:** NY **NAIC Code:** 63126

Data Date	Rating	RACR #1	RACR #2	Total Assets ($mil)	Capital ($mil)	Net Premium ($mil)	Net Income ($mil)
3-09	B	1.67	0.90	1,020.7	85.9	16.5	-5.1
3-08	B+	2.38	1.30	1,012.6	123.1	15.8	1.0
2008	B+	1.81	0.99	991.0	91.3	68.9	-12.5
2007	B+	2.53	1.39	1,015.0	125.1	61.3	11.5
2006	B+	2.68	1.47	1,016.4	125.7	58.4	13.4
2005	B+	2.66	1.46	981.0	120.9	63.7	15.4
2004	B+	2.73	1.48	943.3	120.5	60.0	1.6

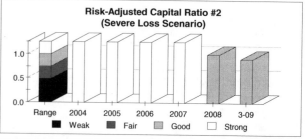

Risk-Adjusted Capital Ratio #2
(Severe Loss Scenario)

FARMERS NEW WORLD LIFE INSURANCE COMPANY   B-   Good

Major Rating Factors: Good quality investment portfolio (5.7 on a scale of 0 to 10) despite mixed results such as: no exposure to mortgages and substantial holdings of BBB bonds but small junk bond holdings. Good overall profitability (5.8) despite operating losses during the first three months of 2009. Good liquidity (5.4).

Other Rating Factors: Fair overall results on stability tests (4.8) including fair financial strength of affiliated Zurich Financial Services Group. Strong capitalization (7.1) based on excellent risk adjusted capital (severe loss scenario).

Principal Business: Individual life insurance (83%), individual annuities (13%), reinsurance (2%), and individual health insurance (1%).

Principal Investments: NonCMO investment grade bonds (53%), CMOs and structured securities (35%), policy loans (5%), noninv. grade bonds (2%), and real estate (1%).

Investments in Affiliates: None
Group Affiliation: Zurich Financial Services Group
Licensed in: All states except AL, NC
Commenced Business: May 1911
Address: 3003 77th Ave SE, Mercer Island, WA 98040-2890
Phone: (206) 232-8400 **Domicile State:** WA **NAIC Code:** 63177

Data Date	Rating	RACR #1	RACR #2	Total Assets ($mil)	Capital ($mil)	Net Premium ($mil)	Net Income ($mil)
3-09	B-	1.97	1.06	6,446.3	546.1	147.1	-20.5
3-08	B-	2.27	1.29	7,054.2	651.1	151.8	22.8
2008	B-	2.02	1.10	6,443.9	551.5	623.8	19.2
2007	B-	2.28	1.31	6,987.5	641.3	647.3	97.9
2006	B-	2.82	1.60	6,966.4	668.6	659.5	142.2
2005	B-	2.65	1.51	6,744.4	634.6	653.5	175.3
2004	B	3.75	2.07	6,828.3	1,094.6	653.2	164.2

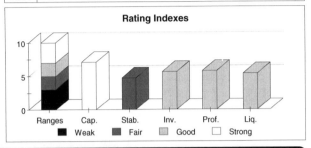

FEDERAL LIFE INSURANCE COMPANY (MUTUAL)   C   Fair

Major Rating Factors: Fair overall results on stability tests (4.1 on a scale of 0 to 10). Good quality investment portfolio (5.9) despite mixed results such as: substantial holdings of BBB bonds but moderate junk bond exposure. Good liquidity (6.0) with sufficient resources to cover a large increase in policy surrenders.

Other Rating Factors: Weak profitability (2.2) with operating losses during the first three months of 2009. Strong capitalization (7.6) based on excellent risk adjusted capital (severe loss scenario).

Principal Business: Individual life insurance (56%), reinsurance (21%), group retirement contracts (13%), group life insurance (6%), and other lines (4%).

Principal Investments: NonCMO investment grade bonds (49%), CMOs and structured securities (33%), policy loans (5%), common & preferred stock (5%), and misc. investments (7%).

Investments in Affiliates: None
Group Affiliation: None
Licensed in: All states except AL, MD, MI, NC, VA
Commenced Business: May 1900
Address: 3750 W Deerfield Rd, Riverwoods, IL 60015
Phone: (847) 520-1900 **Domicile State:** IL **NAIC Code:** 63223

Data Date	Rating	RACR #1	RACR #2	Total Assets ($mil)	Capital ($mil)	Net Premium ($mil)	Net Income ($mil)
3-09	C	2.51	1.41	217.5	27.5	5.9	-1.1
3-08	C	2.88	1.64	231.0	31.9	4.6	-0.8
2008	C	2.65	1.51	219.1	29.8	20.4	-2.6
2007	C	3.02	1.74	235.6	33.0	24.9	-0.7
2006	C+	3.44	2.01	238.5	35.2	23.5	-0.6
2005	C+	3.80	2.19	233.0	35.9	20.0	-3.1
2004	B	4.33	2.50	233.6	39.1	22.0	-1.8

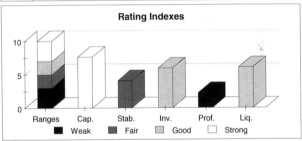

FEDERATED LIFE INSURANCE COMPANY *   A   Excellent

Major Rating Factors: Good quality investment portfolio (6.5 on a scale of 0 to 10) despite mixed results such as: large holdings of BBB rated bonds but moderate junk bond exposure. Excellent overall results on stability tests (7.4). Strengths that enhance stability include excellent operational trends and excellent risk diversification. Strong capitalization (8.7) based on excellent risk adjusted capital (severe loss scenario).

Other Rating Factors: Excellent profitability (8.2) with operating gains in each of the last five years. Excellent liquidity (7.0).

Principal Business: Individual life insurance (71%), individual health insurance (18%), individual annuities (6%), and group life insurance (5%).

Principal Investments: NonCMO investment grade bonds (61%), CMOs and structured securities (28%), noninv. grade bonds (6%), common & preferred stock (3%), and policy loans (2%).

Investments in Affiliates: None
Group Affiliation: Federated Mutual Ins Group
Licensed in: All states except AL, AZ, DE, ID
Commenced Business: January 1959
Address: 121 E Park Square, Owatonna, MN 55060
Phone: (800) 533-0472 **Domicile State:** MN **NAIC Code:** 63258

Data Date	Rating	RACR #1	RACR #2	Total Assets ($mil)	Capital ($mil)	Net Premium ($mil)	Net Income ($mil)
3-09	A	3.94	2.13	978.1	219.2	40.2	6.3
3-08	A	4.39	2.53	944.6	222.0	36.9	6.8
2008	A	4.08	2.26	954.9	218.0	123.0	12.2
2007	A	4.33	2.50	919.1	217.0	117.3	21.1
2006	A	4.37	2.59	868.7	205.2	114.0	17.1
2005	A	4.44	2.60	815.4	197.2	108.4	18.2
2004	A	4.53	2.67	762.9	190.0	102.0	22.6

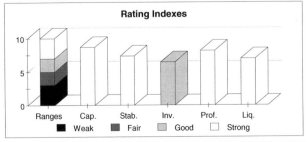

FIDELITY INVESTMENTS LIFE INSURANCE COMPANY *   A   Excellent

Major Rating Factors: Good overall results on stability tests (6.2 on a scale of 0 to 10). Strengths that enhance stability include excellent risk diversification. Strong capitalization (10.0) based on excellent risk adjusted capital (severe loss scenario). Furthermore, this high level of risk adjusted capital has been consistently maintained over the last five years. High quality investment portfolio (7.7).

Other Rating Factors: Excellent profitability (8.4). Excellent liquidity (7.0).

Principal Business: Individual annuities (99%) and individual life insurance (1%).

Principal Investments: NonCMO investment grade bonds (89%), common & preferred stock (7%), and noninv. grade bonds (3%).

Investments in Affiliates: 7%

Group Affiliation: FMR Corp

Licensed in: All states except AL, NC

Commenced Business: December 1981

Address: 175 E 400 S 8th Floor, Salt Lake City, UT 84111

Phone: (617) 563-9106 **Domicile State:** UT **NAIC Code:** 93696

Data Date	Rating	RACR #1	RACR #2	Total Assets ($mil)	Capital ($mil)	Net Premium ($mil)	Net Income ($mil)
3-09	A	5.07	3.24	11,382.8	650.8	411.5	2.2
3-08	A	4.20	2.56	15,309.5	651.0	757.1	5.5
2008	A	4.92	3.13	11,893.8	649.0	2,163.1	-7.1
2007	A	4.02	2.43	16,034.0	645.2	2,033.9	47.4
2006	A-	4.20	2.58	13,590.0	604.5	1,215.1	43.3
2005	A-	4.12	2.51	12,280.3	566.3	533.5	48.3
2004	B	4.09	2.48	11,548.9	512.9	383.0	56.4

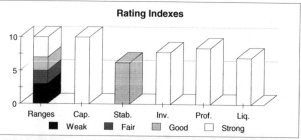

Rating Indexes

Ranges   Cap.   Stab.   Inv.   Prof.   Liq.
Weak   Fair   Good   Strong

FIDELITY LIFE ASSOCIATION A LEGAL RESERVE LIFE INSURAN   B+   Good

Major Rating Factors: Good quality investment portfolio (6.7 on a scale of 0 to 10) despite mixed results such as: minimal exposure to mortgages and substantial holdings of BBB bonds but minimal holdings in junk bonds. Good liquidity (6.9) with sufficient resources to handle a spike in claims. Good overall results on stability tests (6.2) despite negative cash flow from operations for 2008 good operational trends and excellent risk diversification.

Other Rating Factors: Fair profitability (3.8) with operating losses during the first three months of 2009. Strong capitalization (10.0) based on excellent risk adjusted capital (severe loss scenario).

Principal Business: Individual life insurance (81%), reinsurance (15%), and group life insurance (3%).

Principal Investments: NonCMO investment grade bonds (48%), CMOs and structured securities (34%), common & preferred stock (4%), policy loans (3%), and misc. investments (11%).

Investments in Affiliates: None

Group Affiliation: Fidelity Lifecorp Inc

Licensed in: All states except AL, NC, PR

Commenced Business: February 1896

Address: 1211 W. 22nd St., Ste 209, Oak Brook, IL 60523

Phone: (630) 522-0392 **Domicile State:** IL **NAIC Code:** 63290

Data Date	Rating	RACR #1	RACR #2	Total Assets ($mil)	Capital ($mil)	Net Premium ($mil)	Net Income ($mil)
3-09	B+	10.32	5.60	505.8	253.5	9.4	-0.8
3-08	B+	9.93	5.38	528.5	269.0	5.0	-1.7
2008	B+	10.55	5.75	514.7	256.8	34.3	-14.1
2007	B+	10.19	5.52	538.3	275.2	20.8	-0.1
2006	B	13.91	7.75	553.2	279.1	15.4	13.0
2005	B	7.07	4.07	579.5	267.8	15.3	9.7
2004	B	6.94	3.93	586.6	263.9	14.7	16.4

Adverse Trends in Operations

Decrease in asset base during 2008 (4%)
Decrease in asset base during 2007 (3%)
Decrease in capital during 2007 (1%)
Decrease in asset base during 2006 (5%)
Decrease in asset base during 2005 (1%)

FIDELITY SECURITY LIFE INSURANCE COMPANY *   B+   Good

Major Rating Factors: Good liquidity (5.6 on a scale of 0 to 10) with sufficient resources to cover a large increase in policy surrenders. Good overall results on stability tests (6.7). Stability strengths include excellent operational trends and excellent risk diversification. Strong capitalization (7.5) based on excellent risk adjusted capital (severe loss scenario).

Other Rating Factors: High quality investment portfolio (7.6). Excellent profitability (7.9) with operating gains in each of the last five years.

Principal Business: Group health insurance (85%), reinsurance (5%), group life insurance (3%), group retirement contracts (3%), and other lines (3%).

Principal Investments: CMOs and structured securities (50%), nonCMO investment grade bonds (43%), cash (2%), common & preferred stock (1%), and misc. investments (3%).

Investments in Affiliates: 1%

Group Affiliation: Fidelity Security Group

Licensed in: All states except AL, NC

Commenced Business: July 1969

Address: 3130 Broadway, Kansas City, MO 64111

Phone: (816) 750-1060 **Domicile State:** MO **NAIC Code:** 71870

Data Date	Rating	RACR #1	RACR #2	Total Assets ($mil)	Capital ($mil)	Net Premium ($mil)	Net Income ($mil)
3-09	B+	1.87	1.33	576.6	87.1	88.1	2.7
3-08	B	1.75	1.29	495.1	79.7	72.3	2.9
2008	B	1.88	1.35	538.4	84.6	298.0	8.3
2007	B	1.64	1.18	488.1	77.3	312.0	9.6
2006	B	2.46	1.72	480.2	68.8	164.1	9.9
2005	B	2.28	1.57	469.1	59.0	154.4	6.9
2004	B-	2.35	1.60	454.6	54.5	153.5	5.0

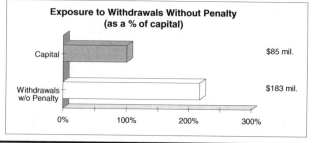

Exposure to Withdrawals Without Penalty (as a % of capital)

Capital $85 mil.

Withdrawals w/o Penalty $183 mil.

0%   100%   200%   300%

FIRST ALLMERICA FINANCIAL LIFE INSURANCE | C | Fair

Major Rating Factors: Fair overall results on stability tests (3.8 on a scale of 0 to 10). Good quality investment portfolio (6.6) despite mixed results such as: no exposure to mortgages and large holdings of BBB rated bonds but minimal holdings in junk bonds. Good overall profitability (5.1). Return on equity has been excellent over the last five years averaging 27.8%.

Other Rating Factors: Good liquidity (6.7). Strong capitalization (10.0) based on excellent risk adjusted capital (severe loss scenario).

Principal Business: Individual life insurance (71%), group retirement contracts (12%), reinsurance (10%), individual annuities (3%), and other lines (4%).

Principal Investments: NonCMO investment grade bonds (57%), CMOs and structured securities (24%), policy loans (8%), common & preferred stock (2%), and noninv. grade bonds (1%).

Investments in Affiliates: None
Group Affiliation: Goldman Sachs Group
Licensed in: All states except AL
Commenced Business: June 1845
Address: 440 Lincoln St, Worcester, MA 01653
Phone: (508) 855-1000 **Domicile State:** MA **NAIC Code:** 69140

Data Date	Rating	RACR #1	RACR #2	Total Assets ($mil)	Capital ($mil)	Net Premium ($mil)	Net Income ($mil)
3-09	C	7.38	3.34	1,448.0	137.2	7.8	5.1
3-08	C	6.41	2.87	1,881.2	155.5	11.5	6.4
2008	C	6.18	3.04	1,714.1	113.7	30.7	33.1
2007	C	6.20	2.76	2,155.8	163.7	32.4	17.0
2006	D+	5.35	2.38	2,375.9	151.8	34.8	13.0
2005	D	4.35	1.96	2,845.4	158.3	50.7	34.5
2004	D-	2.68	1.33	3,851.1	183.6	60.8	124.8

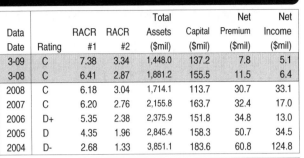

Rating Indexes

Ranges | Cap. | Stab. | Inv. | Prof. | Liq.
■ Weak ▨ Fair ▤ Good □ Strong

FIRST CENTRAL NATIONAL LIFE INSURANCE CO OF NY | B | Good

Major Rating Factors: Good overall results on stability tests (5.7 on a scale of 0 to 10) despite fair financial strength of affiliated HSBC Holdings and negative cash flow from operations for 2008. Other stability subfactors include good operational trends and excellent risk diversification. Good overall profitability (6.0). Excellent expense controls. Return on equity has been fair, averaging 8.2%. Strong capitalization (10.0) based on excellent risk adjusted capital (severe loss scenario).

Other Rating Factors: High quality investment portfolio (7.1). Excellent liquidity (7.0).

Principal Business: Credit life insurance (49%), individual life insurance (28%), credit health insurance (18%), and reinsurance (5%).

Principal Investments: NonCMO investment grade bonds (86%), CMOs and structured securities (12%), noninv. grade bonds (1%), and cash (1%).

Investments in Affiliates: None
Group Affiliation: HSBC Holdings
Licensed in: FL, NC
Commenced Business: November 1971
Address: 452 Fifth Avenue, New York, NY 10018
Phone: (908) 781-4090 **Domicile State:** NY **NAIC Code:** 79340

Data Date	Rating	RACR #1	RACR #2	Total Assets ($mil)	Capital ($mil)	Net Premium ($mil)	Net Income ($mil)
3-09	B	3.76	3.39	52.9	25.5	3.5	0.4
3-08	B	5.13	4.62	56.8	35.5	4.0	1.7
2008	B	3.71	3.34	52.5	25.3	15.0	-4.3
2007	B	4.89	4.40	55.1	33.8	13.1	5.1
2006	B	5.40	4.86	60.9	38.7	13.2	4.5
2005	B	4.94	4.45	54.6	34.1	12.7	2.8
2004	B	4.87	4.38	47.2	31.1	8.3	2.4

HSBC Holdings Composite Group Rating: C+ Largest Group Members	Assets ($mil)	Rating
HOUSEHOLD LIFE INS CO	829	B
HOUSEHOLD LIFE INS CO OF DE	575	C
HSBC INS CO OF DELAWARE	385	C
FIRST CENTRAL NATL LIC OF NEW YORK	53	B

FIRST GREAT-WEST LIFE & ANNUITY INSURANCE COMPANY | B- | Good

Major Rating Factors: Good quality investment portfolio (6.3 on a scale of 0 to 10) despite large holdings of BBB rated bonds in addition to moderate junk bond exposure. Exposure to mortgages is significant, but the mortgage default rate has been low. Good overall profitability (6.4). Return on equity has been good over the last five years, averaging 12.1%. Fair overall results on stability tests (3.6) including negative cash flow from operations for 2008.

Other Rating Factors: Strong capitalization (7.7) based on excellent risk adjusted capital (severe loss scenario). Excellent liquidity (8.0).

Principal Business: Group retirement contracts (79%), individual life insurance (13%), group health insurance (4%), and individual annuities (4%).

Principal Investments: NonCMO investment grade bonds (47%), CMOs and structured securities (30%), mortgages in good standing (16%), noninv. grade bonds (3%), and policy loans (2%).

Investments in Affiliates: None
Group Affiliation: Great West Life Asr
Licensed in: NC
Commenced Business: January 1972
Address: 50 Main St 9th Floor, White Plains, NY 10606
Phone: (914) 682-3611 **Domicile State:** NY **NAIC Code:** 79359

Data Date	Rating	RACR #1	RACR #2	Total Assets ($mil)	Capital ($mil)	Net Premium ($mil)	Net Income ($mil)
3-09	B-	2.92	1.49	698.4	54.6	79.2	0.7
3-08	B-	2.56	1.38	676.0	48.8	55.9	2.0
2008	B-	2.93	1.55	656.6	53.9	184.6	3.6
2007	B-	2.53	1.36	650.4	47.8	93.1	5.2
2006	B-	2.50	1.34	605.7	45.6	49.6	8.3
2005	B-	2.36	1.28	583.0	37.5	46.1	8.7
2004	C+	2.03	1.17	283.5	19.2	13.7	1.9

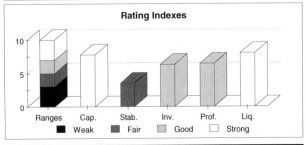

Rating Indexes

Ranges | Cap. | Stab. | Inv. | Prof. | Liq.
■ Weak ▨ Fair ▤ Good □ Strong

FIRST HEALTH LIFE & HEALTH INSURANCE COMPANY

C+ **Fair**

Major Rating Factors: Fair overall results on stability tests (3.0 on a scale of 0 to 10) including weak risk adjusted capital in prior years. Poor overall capitalization (1.3) based on excessive policy leverage and weak risk adjusted capital (moderate loss scenario). Weak profitability (2.2) with operating losses during the first three months of 2009. Return on equity has been fair, averaging 7.4%.

Other Rating Factors: Weak liquidity (0.8). High quality investment portfolio (8.2).

Principal Business: Individual health insurance (77%) and group health insurance (23%).

Principal Investments: NonCMO investment grade bonds (68%) and CMOs and structured securities (14%).

Investments in Affiliates: None

Group Affiliation: Coventry Health Care Inc

Licensed in: All states except AL, NC

Commenced Business: June 1979

Address: 300 W 11th St, Kansas City, MO 64199-3487

Phone: (816) 391-2231 **Domicile State:** TX **NAIC Code:** 90328

Data Date	Rating	RACR #1	RACR #2	Total Assets ($mil)	Capital ($mil)	Net Premium ($mil)	Net Income ($mil)
3-09	C+	0.43	0.36	726.6	168.7	775.2	-49.6
3-08	B-	0.44	0.36	527.4	121.3	500.0	-6.5
2008	C+	0.62	0.51	682.1	214.7	2,034.1	-76.8
2007	B-	0.52	0.43	481.8	131.7	1,453.5	47.4
2006	B-	0.53	0.44	350.1	43.1	470.7	7.3
2005	B	3.56	3.20	109.8	32.3	43.8	8.1
2004	C	2.82	2.54	88.2	23.8	35.9	5.9

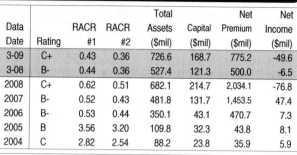

Rating Indexes

FIRST INVESTORS LIFE INSURANCE COMPANY *

A- **Excellent**

Major Rating Factors: Good liquidity (6.9 on a scale of 0 to 10) with sufficient resources to handle a spike in claims as well as a significant increase in policy surrenders. Good overall results on stability tests (5.6). Strengths that enhance stability include excellent risk diversification. Strong capitalization (10.0) based on excellent risk adjusted capital (severe loss scenario).

Other Rating Factors: High quality investment portfolio (7.4). Excellent profitability (8.7) with operating gains in each of the last five years.

Principal Business: Individual life insurance (80%), individual annuities (18%), and reinsurance (2%).

Principal Investments: NonCMO investment grade bonds (74%), policy loans (20%), noninv. grade bonds (4%), common & preferred stock (1%), and cash (1%).

Investments in Affiliates: None

Group Affiliation: First Investors Consolidated Corp

Licensed in: All states except AL, TN

Commenced Business: December 1962

Address: 110 Wall Street, New York, NY 10005

Phone: (800) 832-7783 **Domicile State:** NY **NAIC Code:** 63495

Data Date	Rating	RACR #1	RACR #2	Total Assets ($mil)	Capital ($mil)	Net Premium ($mil)	Net Income ($mil)
3-09	A-	7.02	3.88	949.4	119.1	18.6	1.7
3-08	A-	5.94	3.46	1,275.7	116.0	22.1	3.0
2008	A-	6.89	3.82	1,011.1	119.7	80.3	8.8
2007	A-	5.79	3.31	1,370.1	113.0	88.4	12.2
2006	A-	5.35	3.23	1,339.0	102.8	90.2	12.0
2005	A-	5.06	3.08	1,241.2	92.6	101.8	9.1
2004	C+	4.61	2.91	1,208.9	83.0	103.4	7.5

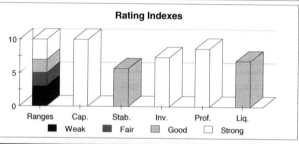

Rating Indexes

FIRST METLIFE INVESTORS INSURANCE COMPANY

C+ **Fair**

Major Rating Factors: Fair overall results on stability tests (4.8 on a scale of 0 to 10). Good quality investment portfolio (6.8) with minimal exposure to mortgages and minimal holdings in junk bonds. Weak profitability (1.4) with operating losses during the first three months of 2009.

Other Rating Factors: Strong capitalization (9.2) based on excellent risk adjusted capital (severe loss scenario). Excellent liquidity (10.0).

Principal Business: Individual annuities (96%) and individual life insurance (4%).

Principal Investments: NonCMO investment grade bonds (82%), CMOs and structured securities (11%), mortgages in good standing (4%), noninv. grade bonds (1%), and common & preferred stock (1%).

Investments in Affiliates: 2%

Group Affiliation: MetLife Inc

Licensed in: NC

Commenced Business: March 1993

Address: 200 Park Avenue, New York, NY 10166-0188

Phone: (212) 766-4923 **Domicile State:** NY **NAIC Code:** 60992

Data Date	Rating	RACR #1	RACR #2	Total Assets ($mil)	Capital ($mil)	Net Premium ($mil)	Net Income ($mil)
3-09	C+	4.72	2.49	2,056.4	161.0	189.4	-18.7
3-08	B-	1.99	1.38	1,975.5	51.5	105.5	-10.6
2008	C+	2.43	1.31	2,067.2	74.0	546.5	-56.9
2007	B-	2.27	1.56	2,025.5	58.9	598.4	-42.3
2006	B-	2.37	1.55	1,474.9	49.4	552.2	-25.1
2005	B-	2.79	1.56	877.0	43.1	293.3	-15.9
2004	B	2.34	1.24	587.5	30.0	68.7	-15.4

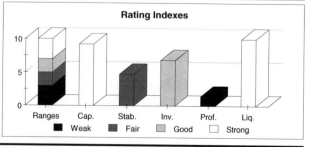

Rating Indexes

FIRST PENN-PACIFIC LIFE INSURANCE COMPANY

B **Good**

Major Rating Factors: Good overall results on stability tests (5.7 on a scale of 0 to 10). Stability strengths include good operational trends and excellent risk diversification. Good quality investment portfolio (5.9) despite large holdings of BBB rated bonds in addition to junk bond exposure equal to 52% of capital. Exposure to mortgages is significant, but the mortgage default rate has been low. Good liquidity (5.5).

Other Rating Factors: Strong capitalization (7.3) based on excellent risk adjusted capital (severe loss scenario). Excellent profitability (7.1) with operating gains in each of the last five years.

Principal Business: Individual life insurance (99%) and individual annuities (1%).

Principal Investments: NonCMO investment grade bonds (51%), CMOs and structured securities (23%), mortgages in good standing (15%), noninv. grade bonds (6%), and misc. investments (5%).

Investments in Affiliates: None

Group Affiliation: Lincoln National Corp

Licensed in: All states except AL, NC

Commenced Business: June 1964

Address: 1300 S Clinton St, Fort Wayne, IN 46802-3518

Phone: (260) 455-2000 **Domicile State:** IN **NAIC Code:** 67652

Data Date	Rating	RACR #1	RACR #2	Total Assets ($mil)	Capital ($mil)	Net Premium ($mil)	Net Income ($mil)
3-09	B	2.39	1.23	1,877.8	197.1	12.0	4.4
3-08	B	2.68	1.42	1,930.5	197.2	12.8	10.8
2008	B	2.42	1.27	1,890.9	192.5	56.9	27.3
2007	B	2.57	1.37	1,921.6	186.7	61.1	58.6
2006	B	3.88	2.06	1,898.2	275.2	68.5	62.9
2005	B	2.90	1.53	1,856.3	217.7	95.8	61.6
2004	B	2.17	1.15	1,797.0	161.8	101.1	46.8

Adverse Trends in Operations

Decrease in asset base during 2008 (2%)
Decrease in capital during 2007 (32%)
Decrease in premium volume from 2006 to 2007 (11%)
Decrease in premium volume from 2005 to 2006 (29%)
Decrease in premium volume from 2004 to 2005 (5%)

FIRST REHABILITATION LIFE INSURANCE CO OF AMERICA

C **Fair**

Major Rating Factors: Fair profitability (3.4 on a scale of 0 to 10). Return on equity has been low, averaging -0.8%. Fair overall results on stability tests (3.7). Good liquidity (6.9) with sufficient resources to handle a spike in claims.

Other Rating Factors: Strong capitalization (9.4) based on excellent risk adjusted capital (severe loss scenario). High quality investment portfolio (8.7).

Principal Business: Group health insurance (100%).

Principal Investments: NonCMO investment grade bonds (66%) and CMOs and structured securities (36%).

Investments in Affiliates: None

Group Affiliation: Rehab Services Corp

Licensed in: CT, DC, DE, FL, IN, MA, MI, MN, MS, NM, NC, ND, RI, SC, SD, TX

Commenced Business: November 1972

Address: 600 Northern Blvd, Great Neck, NY 11021-5202

Phone: (516) 829-8100 **Domicile State:** NY **NAIC Code:** 81434

Data Date	Rating	RACR #1	RACR #2	Total Assets ($mil)	Capital ($mil)	Net Premium ($mil)	Net Income ($mil)
3-09	C	3.31	2.62	94.9	41.7	22.3	0.6
3-08	C-	3.72	2.98	99.8	43.2	17.8	0.4
2008	C	3.31	2.63	90.7	42.9	83.7	7.7
2007	C-	3.46	2.77	95.2	35.5	79.5	4.9
2006	C-	3.75	3.37	94.0	32.5	46.0	-19.0
2005	B-	4.38	3.53	83.3	50.0	77.2	6.1
2004	C+	4.74	3.52	76.7	44.1	70.0	3.6

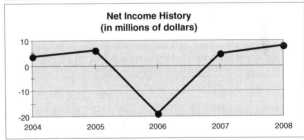

Net Income History
(in millions of dollars)

FIRST RELIANCE STANDARD LIFE INSURANCE COMPANY

B **Good**

Major Rating Factors: Good overall results on stability tests (5.4 on a scale of 0 to 10) despite fair financial strength of affiliated Delphi Financial Group Inc. Other stability subfactors include excellent operational trends and excellent risk diversification. Good quality investment portfolio (5.0) with no exposure to mortgages and small junk bond holdings. Strong capitalization (9.0) based on excellent risk adjusted capital (severe loss scenario).

Other Rating Factors: Excellent profitability (8.3) with operating gains in each of the last five years. Excellent liquidity (7.1).

Principal Business: Group health insurance (62%) and group life insurance (38%).

Principal Investments: NonCMO investment grade bonds (58%), CMOs and structured securities (36%), and noninv. grade bonds (7%).

Investments in Affiliates: None

Group Affiliation: Delphi Financial Group Inc

Licensed in: DE, NC

Commenced Business: October 1984

Address: 590 Madison Ave 29th Floor, New York, NY 10022

Phone: (215) 787-4000 **Domicile State:** NY **NAIC Code:** 71005

Data Date	Rating	RACR #1	RACR #2	Total Assets ($mil)	Capital ($mil)	Net Premium ($mil)	Net Income ($mil)
3-09	B	3.49	2.30	136.4	48.9	16.6	0.7
3-08	B	3.42	2.39	133.5	44.8	15.9	0.4
2008	B	3.54	2.36	133.4	48.5	61.5	9.3
2007	B	3.53	2.57	128.1	44.4	61.5	9.6
2006	B-	3.32	2.38	120.0	37.3	55.1	6.9
2005	C+	2.96	2.12	111.1	32.3	52.5	5.1
2004	C	3.22	2.35	101.2	29.9	42.4	3.2

Delphi Financial Group Inc
Composite Group Rating: C+

Largest Group Members	Assets ($mil)	Rating
RELIANCE STANDARD LIFE INS CO	3509	B-
SAFETY NATIONAL CASUALTY CORP	1904	C
FIRST RELIANCE STANDARD LIFE INS CO	133	B
SAFETY FIRST INS CO	15	C

FIRST SUNAMERICA LIFE INSURANCE COMPANY

C+   **Fair**

Major Rating Factors: Fair overall results on stability tests (4.4 on a scale of 0 to 10). Good current capitalization (6.8) based on good risk adjusted capital (severe loss scenario), although results have slipped from the excellent range during the last year. Good quality investment portfolio (5.6) despite mixed results such as: substantial holdings of BBB bonds but moderate junk bond exposure.

Other Rating Factors: Weak profitability (2.2) with operating losses during the first three months of 2009. Excellent liquidity (7.5).

Principal Business: Individual annuities (99%) and individual life insurance (1%).

Principal Investments: NonCMO investment grade bonds (53%), CMOs and structured securities (34%), mortgages in good standing (7%), noninv. grade bonds (3%), and common & preferred stock (2%).

Investments in Affiliates: None

Group Affiliation: American International Group

Licensed in: NV, NY, NC

Commenced Business: September 1980

Address: 733 Third Avenue, New York, NY 10017

Phone: (310) 772-6000 **Domicile State:** NY **NAIC Code:** 92495

Data Date	Rating	RACR #1	RACR #2	Total Assets ($mil)	Capital ($mil)	Net Premium ($mil)	Net Income ($mil)
3-09	C+	1.93	0.98	7,716.2	495.9	543.3	-19.1
3-08	B	1.71	0.88	6,737.4	379.0	414.7	-124.3
2008	C+	2.17	1.11	7,445.7	547.2	1,590.2	-1,132.8
2007	B	2.47	1.28	6,479.3	503.9	1,152.9	-7.1
2006	B-	2.29	1.20	5,617.3	397.0	1,224.9	18.5
2005	B-	1.70	0.91	4,658.4	268.6	1,100.5	11.0
2004	B-	2.25	1.15	3,780.6	261.7	540.0	41.5

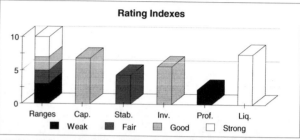

Rating Indexes

Ranges | Cap. | Stab. | Inv. | Prof. | Liq.

■ Weak   ■ Fair   ▨ Good   □ Strong

FIRST SYMETRA NATIONAL LIFE INSURANCE COMPANY OF NE

C+   **Fair**

Major Rating Factors: Fair profitability (4.1 on a scale of 0 to 10). Excellent expense controls. Return on equity has been low, averaging -0.2%. Fair overall results on stability tests (4.8). Strong capitalization (8.7) based on excellent risk adjusted capital (severe loss scenario). Moreover, capital levels have been consistently high over the last five years.

Other Rating Factors: High quality investment portfolio (7.0). Excellent liquidity (8.0).

Principal Business: Individual annuities (95%) and group health insurance (4%).

Principal Investments: NonCMO investment grade bonds (57%), CMOs and structured securities (39%), noninv. grade bonds (2%), and cash (2%).

Investments in Affiliates: None

Group Affiliation: White Mountains Group

Licensed in: NC

Commenced Business: January 1990

Address: 375 Woodcliff Dr 2nd Floor, Fairport, NY 14450

Phone: (425) 376-8000 **Domicile State:** NY **NAIC Code:** 78417

Data Date	Rating	RACR #1	RACR #2	Total Assets ($mil)	Capital ($mil)	Net Premium ($mil)	Net Income ($mil)
3-09	C+	4.00	2.10	370.1	42.9	67.2	0.5
3-08	C+	2.73	2.46	126.6	24.4	10.2	-0.7
2008	C+	4.03	2.40	306.7	42.7	181.5	-2.2
2007	C+	2.80	2.52	123.4	25.1	16.4	2.4
2006	C+	2.49	2.24	154.6	23.0	11.5	0.0
2005	C+	2.39	1.96	170.6	22.2	4.7	-3.0
2004	C+	2.10	1.69	174.1	19.5	11.1	0.9

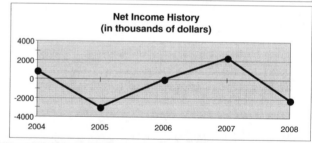

Net Income History
(in thousands of dollars)

2004 | 2005 | 2006 | 2007 | 2008

FIRST UNITED AMERICAN LIFE INSURANCE COMPANY *

A-   **Excellent**

Major Rating Factors: Good quality investment portfolio (5.6 on a scale of 0 to 10) despite mixed results such as: large holdings of BBB rated bonds but moderate junk bond exposure. Good liquidity (6.9) with sufficient resources to handle a spike in claims. Excellent overall results on stability tests (7.2) excellent operational trends and excellent risk diversification.

Other Rating Factors: Strong capitalization (8.5) based on excellent risk adjusted capital (severe loss scenario). Excellent profitability (8.5) with operating gains in each of the last five years.

Principal Business: Individual health insurance (65%), individual life insurance (32%), group health insurance (2%), and individual annuities (1%).

Principal Investments: NonCMO investment grade bonds (78%), noninv. grade bonds (10%), common & preferred stock (5%), policy loans (3%), and misc. investments (4%).

Investments in Affiliates: None

Group Affiliation: Torchmark Corp

Licensed in: NC

Commenced Business: December 1984

Address: 1020 7th North St, Liverpool, NY 13088

Phone: (315) 451-2544 **Domicile State:** NY **NAIC Code:** 74101

Data Date	Rating	RACR #1	RACR #2	Total Assets ($mil)	Capital ($mil)	Net Premium ($mil)	Net Income ($mil)
3-09	A-	3.00	2.01	126.0	38.7	17.3	1.7
3-08	A-	2.89	1.96	122.5	40.0	18.0	2.0
2008	A-	2.87	1.89	125.4	37.8	65.1	6.5
2007	A-	3.09	2.10	121.0	42.5	69.3	8.6
2006	A-	2.79	1.95	112.3	37.4	68.1	8.5
2005	B+	2.41	1.69	101.9	31.6	59.3	4.7
2004	B+	2.30	1.63	95.7	30.7	59.1	4.1

Adverse Trends in Operations

Decrease in capital during 2008 (11%)
Decrease in premium volume from 2007 to 2008 (6%)
Increase in policy surrenders from 2004 to 2005 (39%)

FIRST UNUM LIFE INSURANCE COMPANY   C+   Fair

Major Rating Factors: Fair overall results on stability tests (4.8 on a scale of 0 to 10) including fair financial strength of affiliated Unum Group. Good quality investment portfolio (6.2) despite mixed results such as: large holdings of BBB rated bonds but moderate junk bond exposure. Strong capitalization (7.5) based on excellent risk adjusted capital (severe loss scenario).

Other Rating Factors: Excellent profitability (8.2) with operating gains in each of the last five years. Excellent liquidity (7.1).

Principal Business: Group health insurance (56%), individual health insurance (26%), group life insurance (18%), and reinsurance (1%).

Principal Investments: NonCMO investment grade bonds (80%), CMOs and structured securities (11%), mortgages in good standing (4%), noninv. grade bonds (3%), and misc. investments (3%).

Investments in Affiliates: None

Group Affiliation: Unum Group

Licensed in: NC

Commenced Business: January 1960

Address: Christiana Bldg Suite 100, Tarrytown, NY 10591

Phone: (914) 524-4056 **Domicile State:** NY **NAIC Code:** 64297

Data Date	Rating	RACR #1	RACR #2	Total Assets ($mil)	Capital ($mil)	Net Premium ($mil)	Net Income ($mil)
3-09	C+	2.16	1.31	1,946.2	197.0	103.5	-6.1
3-08	C+	2.26	1.44	1,813.5	187.2	102.8	2.5
2008	C+	2.18	1.33	1,933.2	193.8	413.3	19.5
2007	C+	2.24	1.43	1,779.8	184.0	408.5	20.7
2006	C+	2.21	1.42	1,653.8	182.8	413.7	26.2
2005	C	1.97	1.25	1,497.3	160.1	390.5	18.7
2004	C-	2.02	1.29	1,377.5	166.2	407.1	13.5

Unum Group Composite Group Rating: C+ Largest Group Members	Assets ($mil)	Rating
UNUM LIFE INS CO OF AMERICA	16890	C+
PROVIDENT LIFE ACCIDENT INS CO	7741	C+
PAUL REVERE LIFE INS CO	4710	C+
COLONIAL LIFE ACCIDENT INS CO	1989	C+
FIRST UNUM LIFE INS CO	1933	C+

FIVE STAR LIFE INSURANCE COMPANY   B-   Good

Major Rating Factors: Good quality investment portfolio (6.7 on a scale of 0 to 10) despite mixed results such as: no exposure to mortgages and substantial holdings of BBB bonds but small junk bond holdings. Good overall profitability (5.5) despite operating losses during the first three months of 2009. Return on equity has been low, averaging 1.5%. Good liquidity (6.5).

Other Rating Factors: Good overall results on stability tests (5.0) excellent operational trends and good risk diversification. Strong capitalization (7.2) based on excellent risk adjusted capital (severe loss scenario).

Principal Business: Group life insurance (88%) and individual life insurance (12%).

Principal Investments: NonCMO investment grade bonds (55%), CMOs and structured securities (26%), cash (7%), noninv. grade bonds (6%), and misc. investments (6%).

Investments in Affiliates: None

Group Affiliation: 5 Star Financial LLC

Licensed in: All states except AL, NC

Commenced Business: May 1943

Address: 8440 Jefferson Hwy Ste 301, Baton Rouge, LA 70809-7652

Phone: (800) 776-2322 **Domicile State:** LA **NAIC Code:** 77879

Data Date	Rating	RACR #1	RACR #2	Total Assets ($mil)	Capital ($mil)	Net Premium ($mil)	Net Income ($mil)
3-09	B-	1.67	1.15	172.3	45.0	22.8	-3.4
3-08	C+	2.00	1.40	167.3	51.1	22.0	-1.5
2008	B-	1.81	1.26	174.8	48.4	94.5	-5.1
2007	C+	2.07	1.46	166.0	52.3	91.8	1.1
2006	C+	2.06	1.46	154.8	50.8	83.7	0.7
2005	C+	2.01	1.44	149.7	50.1	89.9	1.1
2004	C+	2.06	1.47	138.4	49.3	83.0	1.1

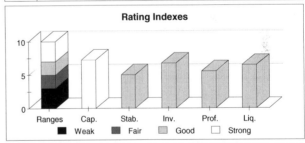

Rating Indexes

Ranges | Cap. | Stab. | Inv. | Prof. | Liq.

■ Weak ■ Fair ▨ Good ☐ Strong

FORETHOUGHT LIFE INSURANCE COMPANY   C+   Fair

Major Rating Factors: Fair profitability (3.3 on a scale of 0 to 10) with investment income below regulatory standards in relation to interest assumptions of reserves. Fair overall results on stability tests (3.9). Good current capitalization (6.8) based on good risk adjusted capital (severe loss scenario), although results have slipped from the excellent range over the last two years.

Other Rating Factors: Good quality investment portfolio (5.8). Good liquidity (6.8).

Principal Business: Individual annuities (46%), group life insurance (45%), individual life insurance (6%), and group retirement contracts (3%).

Principal Investments: NonCMO investment grade bonds (59%), CMOs and structured securities (34%), noninv. grade bonds (3%), mortgages in good standing (3%), and common & preferred stock (1%).

Investments in Affiliates: None

Group Affiliation: Forethought Financial Group Inc

Licensed in: All states except AL, NC

Commenced Business: September 1980

Address: Forethought Center, Batesville, IN 47006

Phone: (812) 933-6600 **Domicile State:** IN **NAIC Code:** 91642

Data Date	Rating	RACR #1	RACR #2	Total Assets ($mil)	Capital ($mil)	Net Premium ($mil)	Net Income ($mil)
3-09	C+	1.82	0.98	3,988.5	195.4	194.3	9.6
3-08	C+	4.57	2.53	913.9	161.3	168.5	-9.6
2008	C+	1.82	0.99	3,870.2	189.7	776.4	-71.6
2007	C+	3.59	2.00	777.4	116.4	438.9	-0.2
2006	C+	3.34	2.11	462.3	109.7	356.0	7.6
2005	C+	2.85	1.78	488.1	91.6	328.1	6.1
2004	C+	2.76	1.87	310.5	102.0	210.8	6.5

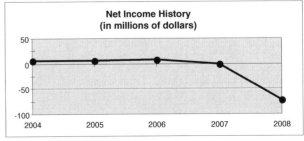

Net Income History
(in millions of dollars)

FORT DEARBORN LIFE INSURANCE COMPANY *

A-   **Excellent**

Major Rating Factors: Good quality investment portfolio (6.7 on a scale of 0 to 10) despite mixed results such as: no exposure to mortgages and large holdings of BBB rated bonds but small junk bond holdings. Fair profitability (3.6) with operating losses during the first three months of 2009. Return on equity has been low, averaging 4.1%. Strong capitalization (7.1) based on excellent risk adjusted capital (severe loss scenario).

Other Rating Factors: Excellent liquidity (7.2). Excellent overall results on stability tests (7.1) excellent operational trends and excellent risk diversification.

Principal Business: Individual annuities (46%), group life insurance (31%), group health insurance (13%), reinsurance (9%), and individual life insurance (1%).

Principal Investments: NonCMO investment grade bonds (52%), CMOs and structured securities (42%), noninv. grade bonds (4%), and common & preferred stock (2%).

Investments in Affiliates: 2%

Group Affiliation: HCSC Group

Licensed in: All states except AL, NC

Commenced Business: April 1969

Address: 300 East Randolph Street, Chicago, IL 60601-5099

Phone: (800) 633-3696   **Domicile State:** IL   **NAIC Code:** 71129

Data Date	Rating	RACR #1	RACR #2	Total Assets ($mil)	Capital ($mil)	Net Premium ($mil)	Net Income ($mil)
3-09	A-	1.62	1.08	2,870.9	288.8	522.2	-0.9
3-08	A	2.76	1.89	2,264.4	431.8	265.1	-8.3
2008	A-	1.73	1.16	2,616.4	290.3	1,253.0	-38.5
2007	A	2.88	1.98	2,238.6	468.5	963.1	42.8
2006	A-	3.01	2.04	2,105.5	443.4	1,020.4	17.7
2005	B+	3.01	2.04	1,681.4	347.1	738.8	33.3
2004	B	2.76	1.88	1,595.3	331.7	727.3	24.6

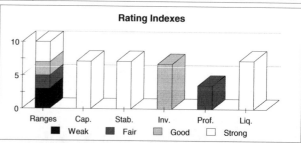

Rating Indexes

FRANDISCO LIFE INSURANCE COMPANY *

B+   **Good**

Major Rating Factors: Good overall results on stability tests (5.7 on a scale of 0 to 10). Stability strengths include good operational trends and good risk diversification. Strong overall capitalization (10.0) based on excellent risk adjusted capital (severe loss scenario). Nevertheless, capital levels have fluctuated during prior years. High quality investment portfolio (8.8).

Other Rating Factors: Excellent profitability (7.0) with operating gains in each of the last five years. Excellent liquidity (9.4).

Principal Business: Reinsurance (100%).

Principal Investments: NonCMO investment grade bonds (100%).

Investments in Affiliates: None

Group Affiliation: Franklin Financial Corp

Licensed in: HI

Commenced Business: November 1977

Address: 213 E Tugalo St, Toccoa, GA 30577

Phone: (706) 886-7571   **Domicile State:** GA   **NAIC Code:** 89079

Data Date	Rating	RACR #1	RACR #2	Total Assets ($mil)	Capital ($mil)	Net Premium ($mil)	Net Income ($mil)
3-09	B+	6.72	6.05	37.3	35.0	2.6	1.3
3-08	B+	7.18	6.46	47.1	45.0	2.6	1.4
2008	B+	6.47	5.82	35.9	33.7	11.0	4.8
2007	B+	6.96	6.26	45.6	43.6	10.5	4.6
2006	B+	6.80	6.12	40.7	39.0	9.4	4.2
2005	B+	6.61	5.95	36.2	34.7	8.4	3.7
2004	B+	6.40	5.76	32.5	31.1	8.3	3.6

Adverse Trends in Operations

Decrease in asset base during 2008 (21%)
Decrease in capital during 2008 (23%)

FUNERAL DIRECTORS LIFE INSURANCE COMPANY

C+   **Fair**

Major Rating Factors: Fair quality investment portfolio (3.5 on a scale of 0 to 10). Fair liquidity (4.9) due, in part, to cash value policies that are subject to withdrawals with minimal or no penalty. Fair overall results on stability tests (4.5).

Other Rating Factors: Good capitalization (5.8) based on good risk adjusted capital (moderate loss scenario). Excellent profitability (8.1) with operating gains in each of the last five years.

Principal Business: Individual annuities (63%), individual life insurance (19%), and group life insurance (18%).

Principal Investments: NonCMO investment grade bonds (73%), common & preferred stock (7%), CMOs and structured securities (7%), real estate (6%), and misc. investments (7%).

Investments in Affiliates: 1%

Group Affiliation: Directors Investment Group

Licensed in: All states except AL, AZ, CO, DE, MD, MI, NJ, NC, PR

Commenced Business: April 1981

Address: 6550 Directors Pkwy, Abilene, TX 79606

Phone: (915) 695-3412   **Domicile State:** TX   **NAIC Code:** 99775

Data Date	Rating	RACR #1	RACR #2	Total Assets ($mil)	Capital ($mil)	Net Premium ($mil)	Net Income ($mil)
3-09	C+	1.50	0.83	574.9	49.8	32.8	1.8
3-08	C+	1.63	0.95	508.1	48.6	26.3	0.8
2008	C+	1.51	0.85	556.6	48.6	124.1	1.0
2007	C+	1.64	0.96	500.4	48.5	99.4	3.8
2006	C+	2.24	1.43	453.4	45.4	84.7	3.3
2005	C+	2.11	1.34	416.3	41.5	83.6	3.7
2004	C	2.02	1.27	378.4	37.1	75.8	3.4

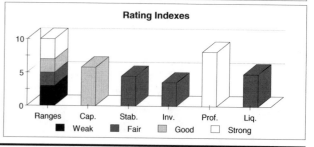

Rating Indexes

GENERAL AMERICAN LIFE INSURANCE COMPANY

C+   **Fair**

Major Rating Factors: Fair profitability (4.1 on a scale of 0 to 10). Return on equity has been low, averaging 3.5%. Fair overall results on stability tests (3.9) including fair risk adjusted capital in prior years. Good quality investment portfolio (5.8) despite mixed results such as: substantial holdings of BBB bonds but moderate junk bond exposure.

Other Rating Factors: Good liquidity (6.0). Strong capitalization (7.8) based on excellent risk adjusted capital (severe loss scenario).

Principal Business: Individual life insurance (76%), reinsurance (20%), individual annuities (2%), and individual health insurance (2%).

Principal Investments: NonCMO investment grade bonds (42%), CMOs and structured securities (23%), policy loans (17%), common & preferred stock (3%), and misc. investments (15%).

Investments in Affiliates: 6%
Group Affiliation: MetLife Inc
Licensed in: All states except AL, NC
Commenced Business: September 1933
Address: 700 Market St, St Louis, MO 63101
Phone: (314) 843-8700 **Domicile State:** MO **NAIC Code:** 63665

Data Date	Rating	RACR #1	RACR #2	Total Assets ($mil)	Capital ($mil)	Net Premium ($mil)	Net Income ($mil)
3-09	C+	3.32	1.53	11,331.9	1,001.3	131.4	46.9
3-08	B-	1.48	1.22	13,962.5	2,330.3	136.6	64.0
2008	C+	3.39	1.61	11,734.9	1,079.5	447.9	1,177.1
2007	B-	1.46	1.21	14,122.9	2,279.7	476.9	106.0
2006	B-	1.32	1.10	14,483.0	2,141.7	502.6	316.5
2005	B-	1.17	0.96	14,094.4	1,677.3	94.3	-33.6
2004	B-	0.87	0.72	14,452.9	1,297.3	689.8	-80.3

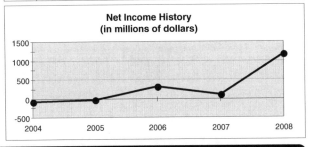

Net Income History
(in millions of dollars)

GENERAL FIDELITY LIFE INSURANCE COMPANY

B-   **Good**

Major Rating Factors: Good quality investment portfolio (5.0 on a scale of 0 to 10) with no exposure to mortgages and minimal holdings in junk bonds. Fair overall results on stability tests (3.8). Strong capitalization (10.0) based on excellent risk adjusted capital (severe loss scenario).

Other Rating Factors: Excellent profitability (7.7) with operating gains in each of the last five years. Excellent liquidity (9.1).

Principal Business: Reinsurance (96%), credit life insurance (4%), group life insurance (1%), and credit health insurance (1%).

Principal Investments: NonCMO investment grade bonds (51%), common & preferred stock (26%), CMOs and structured securities (20%), noninv. grade bonds (1%), and cash (1%).

Investments in Affiliates: None
Group Affiliation: Bank of America Corp
Licensed in: All states except AL, MD, NC
Commenced Business: July 1980
Address: 1901 Main St, Columbia, SC 29201
Phone: (800) 456-2133 **Domicile State:** SC **NAIC Code:** 93521

Data Date	Rating	RACR #1	RACR #2	Total Assets ($mil)	Capital ($mil)	Net Premium ($mil)	Net Income ($mil)
3-09	B-	6.39	4.07	206.1	160.7	11.6	2.5
3-08	B-	5.06	3.17	236.6	152.6	11.8	2.3
2008	B-	6.46	4.11	210.2	164.1	48.7	7.1
2007	B-	5.37	3.36	250.1	162.0	40.6	13.6
2006	B-	5.74	3.50	252.0	145.7	2.1	22.9
2005	C+	17.25	10.24	304.1	251.8	-1.9	14.2
2004	U	16.94	10.03	307.5	241.9	-5.0	15.3

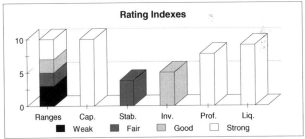

Rating Indexes

Ranges | Cap. | Stab. | Inv. | Prof. | Liq.
■ Weak ■ Fair ▨ Good □ Strong

GENERAL RE LIFE CORPORATION *

B+   **Good**

Major Rating Factors: Good overall results on stability tests (6.7 on a scale of 0 to 10). Stability strengths include excellent operational trends and excellent risk diversification. Good quality investment portfolio (6.8) with no exposure to mortgages and moderate junk bond exposure. Fair profitability (4.5) with operating losses during the first three months of 2009.

Other Rating Factors: Strong capitalization (7.5) based on excellent risk adjusted capital (severe loss scenario). Excellent liquidity (8.9).

Principal Business: Reinsurance (100%).

Principal Investments: NonCMO investment grade bonds (89%), noninv. grade bonds (5%), common & preferred stock (3%), and CMOs and structured securities (2%).

Investments in Affiliates: 3%
Group Affiliation: Berkshire-Hathaway
Licensed in: All states except AL, GA, ID, MD, MT, NJ, NC, VA
Commenced Business: August 1967
Address: 30 Oak Street, Stamford, CT 06905-5339
Phone: (203) 352-3000 **Domicile State:** CT **NAIC Code:** 86258

Data Date	Rating	RACR #1	RACR #2	Total Assets ($mil)	Capital ($mil)	Net Premium ($mil)	Net Income ($mil)
3-09	B+	2.09	1.34	2,682.0	465.0	270.4	-0.1
3-08	B+	2.30	1.73	2,646.0	438.6	275.1	-2.2
2008	B+	2.24	1.54	2,615.1	466.6	1,086.1	31.9
2007	B+	2.32	1.75	2,637.6	440.2	1,055.8	-15.5
2006	B+	1.89	1.37	2,382.8	392.4	1,039.9	28.6
2005	B+	1.83	1.32	2,219.3	368.4	1,010.7	18.8
2004	B+	1.85	1.33	2,042.5	355.9	860.0	39.7

Adverse Trends in Operations

Increase in policy surrenders from 2006 to 2007 (54%)

GENERALI USA LIFE REASSURANCE COMPANY | C | Fair

Major Rating Factors: Fair overall results on stability tests (4.3 on a scale of 0 to 10). Good overall profitability (5.1). Excellent expense controls. Return on equity has been low, averaging -0.7%. Good liquidity (6.2) with sufficient resources to handle a spike in claims.

Other Rating Factors: Strong capitalization (7.9) based on excellent risk adjusted capital (severe loss scenario). High quality investment portfolio (8.6).

Principal Business: Reinsurance (100%).

Principal Investments: NonCMO investment grade bonds (91%), CMOs and structured securities (8%), and common & preferred stock (2%).

Investments in Affiliates: None

Group Affiliation: Generali Group

Licensed in: CA, CO, FL, GA, HI, ID, IL, IN, IA, KS, KY, ME, MI, MN, MO, MT, NH, NM, OK, OR, PA, TX, UT, VT, WV, WY

Commenced Business: October 1982

Address: 150 King St W 11th Fl, Toronto Ontario, CN M5H 1J9

Phone: (416) 979-6266 **Domicile State:** MO **NAIC Code:** 97071

Data Date	Rating	RACR #1	RACR #2	Total Assets ($mil)	Capital ($mil)	Net Premium ($mil)	Net Income ($mil)
3-09	C	2.42	1.60	865.1	268.7	76.5	0.1
3-08	C	2.54	1.70	836.8	270.0	71.9	12.6
2008	C	2.35	1.56	831.1	259.5	278.1	0.7
2007	C	2.45	1.64	801.3	256.2	245.3	3.5
2006	C-	2.65	1.81	731.9	240.2	235.4	-9.2
2005	C-	2.88	1.96	671.3	244.9	196.0	-12.0
2004	C-	3.05	2.09	635.2	239.8	233.3	-1.1

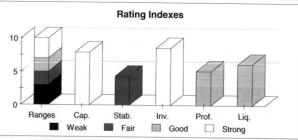

Rating Indexes

GENWORTH LIFE & ANNUITY INSURANCE COMPANY | B | Good

Major Rating Factors: Good current capitalization (6.0 on a scale of 0 to 10) based on good risk adjusted capital (severe loss scenario), although results have slipped from the excellent range during the last year. Fair overall results on stability tests (4.0) including fair financial strength of affiliated Genworth Financial and negative cash flow from operations for 2008. Fair quality investment portfolio (4.8).

Other Rating Factors: Fair profitability (4.6) with investment income below regulatory standards in relation to interest assumptions of reserves. Excellent liquidity (7.7).

Principal Business: Individual annuities (54%), individual life insurance (37%), reinsurance (6%), and individual health insurance (2%).

Principal Investments: NonCMO investment grade bonds (43%), CMOs and structured securities (18%), mortgages in good standing (17%), common & preferred stock (7%), and misc. investments (15%).

Investments in Affiliates: 6%

Group Affiliation: Genworth Financial

Licensed in: All states except AL, NC

Commenced Business: April 1871

Address: 6610 W Broad St, Richmond, VA 23230

Phone: (804) 662-2400 **Domicile State:** VA **NAIC Code:** 65536

Data Date	Rating	RACR #1	RACR #2	Total Assets ($mil)	Capital ($mil)	Net Premium ($mil)	Net Income ($mil)
3-09	B	1.37	0.87	24,891.2	1,719.3	-455.0	9.0
3-08	B	1.84	1.05	28,514.5	1,520.6	911.0	-41.4
2008	B	1.63	1.05	25,963.9	1,930.9	2,192.9	-242.0
2007	B	1.86	1.07	29,146.5	1,414.2	2,909.6	420.7
2006	B	2.13	1.03	18,729.3	587.8	2,087.9	169.6
2005	B	1.80	0.90	15,893.6	476.0	1,301.7	144.4
2004	B	2.91	1.41	17,256.6	817.2	1,478.2	105.8

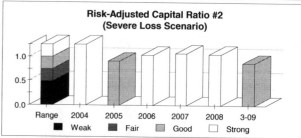

Risk-Adjusted Capital Ratio #2 (Severe Loss Scenario)

GENWORTH LIFE INSURANCE COMPANY | C+ | Fair

Major Rating Factors: Fair current capitalization (4.7 on a scale of 0 to 10) based on fair risk adjusted capital (moderate loss scenario), although results have slipped from the good range during the last year. Fair overall results on stability tests (3.0) including weak results on operational trends and negative cash flow from operations for 2008. Good quality investment portfolio (5.5).

Other Rating Factors: Good overall profitability (5.7) despite operating losses during the first three months of 2009. Excellent liquidity (8.0).

Principal Business: Individual health insurance (38%), individual annuities (30%), group retirement contracts (12%), reinsurance (11%), and other lines (9%).

Principal Investments: NonCMO investment grade bonds (47%), CMOs and structured securities (18%), mortgages in good standing (14%), common & preferred stock (10%), and misc. investments (12%).

Investments in Affiliates: 10%

Group Affiliation: Genworth Financial

Licensed in: All states except AL, NC

Commenced Business: October 1956

Address: 6604 West Broad St, Richmond, VA 23230

Phone: (800) 255-7836 **Domicile State:** DE **NAIC Code:** 70025

Data Date	Rating	RACR #1	RACR #2	Total Assets ($mil)	Capital ($mil)	Net Premium ($mil)	Net Income ($mil)
3-09	C+	0.92	0.71	33,446.7	2,954.1	376.0	-165.9
3-08	C+	1.07	0.79	34,672.8	3,102.3	612.4	-63.4
2008	C+	1.08	0.82	34,733.5	3,326.8	1,343.0	-349.2
2007	C+	1.12	0.83	34,571.6	3,142.8	768.6	182.2
2006	C+	1.26	0.91	34,770.6	2,996.9	3,190.1	634.0
2005	C+	1.15	0.84	34,936.1	3,098.4	5,634.7	636.7
2004	C+	1.08	0.83	31,489.9	3,183.9	4,834.4	1,052.8

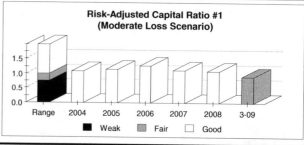

Risk-Adjusted Capital Ratio #1 (Moderate Loss Scenario)

GENWORTH LIFE INSURANCE COMPANY OF NEW YORK   C   Fair

Major Rating Factors: Fair quality investment portfolio (4.2 on a scale of 0 to 10) with large holdings of BBB rated bonds in addition to significant exposure to junk bonds. Exposure to mortgages is significant, but the mortgage default rate has been low. Fair overall results on stability tests (3.9) including fair risk adjusted capital in prior years. Good capitalization (6.1) based on good risk adjusted capital (moderate loss scenario).

Other Rating Factors: Weak profitability (2.0) with operating losses during the first three months of 2009. Excellent liquidity (8.0).

Principal Business: Individual annuities (76%), individual health insurance (12%), individual life insurance (6%), and reinsurance (6%).

Principal Investments: NonCMO investment grade bonds (50%), CMOs and structured securities (21%), mortgages in good standing (16%), noninv. grade bonds (8%), and misc. investments (6%).

Investments in Affiliates: None

Group Affiliation: Genworth Financial

Licensed in: FL, IN, NC

Commenced Business: October 1988

Address: 125 Park Ave 6th Floor, New York, NY 10017-5529

Phone: (800) 357-1066 **Domicile State:** NY **NAIC Code:** 72990

Data Date	Rating	RACR #1	RACR #2	Total Assets ($mil)	Capital ($mil)	Net Premium ($mil)	Net Income ($mil)
3-09	C	1.75	0.87	6,936.4	401.9	90.1	-33.5
3-08	C+	2.03	1.01	6,656.1	406.0	336.1	-9.3
2008	C	1.88	0.96	6,999.4	434.4	1,176.8	-258.8
2007	C+	2.16	1.09	6,465.1	408.8	844.3	110.7
2006	C+	1.39	0.71	4,905.7	210.2	579.9	-126.1
2005	B-	2.00	1.01	4,832.4	347.0	539.9	88.2
2004	B-	1.67	0.85	4,558.9	268.1	805.0	-19.8

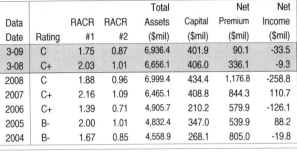

Junk Bonds as a % of Capital

Capital — $434 mil.

Junk Bonds — $430 mil.

■ BB ▨ B ▥ CCC □ In default

GERBER LIFE INSURANCE COMPANY *   A-   Excellent

Major Rating Factors: Good quality investment portfolio (6.8 on a scale of 0 to 10) despite mixed results such as: no exposure to mortgages and large holdings of BBB rated bonds but minimal holdings in junk bonds. Good overall profitability (5.7) despite operating losses during the first three months of 2009. Return on equity has been fair, averaging 9.4%. Good liquidity (6.1).

Other Rating Factors: Good overall results on stability tests (6.8) excellent operational trends and excellent risk diversification. Strong capitalization (7.3) based on excellent risk adjusted capital (severe loss scenario).

Principal Business: Individual life insurance (51%), group health insurance (37%), reinsurance (9%), individual health insurance (2%), and group life insurance (1%).

Principal Investments: NonCMO investment grade bonds (64%), CMOs and structured securities (27%), policy loans (3%), common & preferred stock (2%), and noninv. grade bonds (1%).

Investments in Affiliates: None

Group Affiliation: Nestle SA

Licensed in: All states except AL

Commenced Business: September 1968

Address: 66 Church St, White Plains, NY 10601

Phone: (914) 761-4404 **Domicile State:** NY **NAIC Code:** 70939

Data Date	Rating	RACR #1	RACR #2	Total Assets ($mil)	Capital ($mil)	Net Premium ($mil)	Net Income ($mil)
3-09	A-	1.95	1.21	1,568.7	163.2	107.5	-1.9
3-08	A-	2.45	1.54	1,466.3	199.5	104.5	-2.7
2008	A-	1.92	1.20	1,567.9	160.4	368.1	-42.1
2007	A-	2.53	1.59	1,422.1	201.2	346.3	14.1
2006	A-	2.75	1.72	1,242.8	190.8	310.6	22.6
2005	A-	2.79	1.74	1,101.0	172.8	278.8	26.0
2004	B+	2.79	1.74	937.8	148.6	252.0	25.3

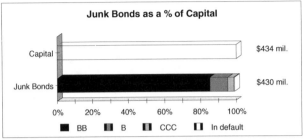

Rating Indexes

Ranges Cap. Stab. Inv. Prof. Liq.

■ Weak ▨ Fair ▥ Good □ Strong

GLOBE LIFE & ACCIDENT INSURANCE COMPANY   B   Good

Major Rating Factors: Good overall capitalization (5.2 on a scale of 0 to 10) based on good risk adjusted capital (severe loss scenario). However, capital levels have fluctuated somewhat during past years. Good overall results on stability tests (5.2). Strengths include good financial support from affiliation with Torchmark Corp, excellent operational trends and excellent risk diversification. Fair quality investment portfolio (4.8).

Other Rating Factors: Excellent profitability (8.5) with operating gains in each of the last five years. Excellent liquidity (7.0).

Principal Business: Individual life insurance (45%), group life insurance (42%), reinsurance (7%), and individual health insurance (5%).

Principal Investments: NonCMO investment grade bonds (70%), common & preferred stock (17%), noninv. grade bonds (6%), policy loans (2%), and CMOs and structured securities (1%).

Investments in Affiliates: 10%

Group Affiliation: Torchmark Corp

Licensed in: All states except AL, NC

Commenced Business: September 1980

Address: 10306 Regency Parkway Bldg, Omaha, NE 68114-3743

Phone: (405) 270-1400 **Domicile State:** NE **NAIC Code:** 91472

Data Date	Rating	RACR #1	RACR #2	Total Assets ($mil)	Capital ($mil)	Net Premium ($mil)	Net Income ($mil)
3-09	B	1.03	0.77	2,777.5	355.2	138.5	108.6
3-08	B-	0.92	0.71	2,644.1	296.0	140.2	64.1
2008	B	1.13	0.88	2,736.8	392.7	511.6	133.7
2007	B-	0.99	0.77	2,554.7	324.5	524.7	130.1
2006	B	1.11	0.87	2,403.8	338.1	484.1	123.5
2005	B+	1.17	0.94	2,274.7	363.4	456.9	144.4
2004	A-	1.16	0.93	2,103.4	326.5	448.5	131.1

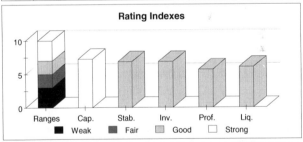

Risk-Adjusted Capital Ratio #2
(Severe Loss Scenario)

Range 2004 2005 2006 2007 2008 3-09

■ Weak ▨ Fair ▥ Good □ Strong

GOLDEN RULE INSURANCE COMPANY   B   Good

Major Rating Factors: Good overall results on stability tests (6.3 on a scale of 0 to 10). Stability strengths include good operational trends and excellent risk diversification. Good current capitalization (5.8) based on mixed results -- excessive policy leverage mitigated by excellent risk adjusted capital (severe loss scenario) reflecting improvement over results in 2004. Good overall profitability (6.8).

Other Rating Factors: High quality investment portfolio (8.6). Excellent liquidity (7.2).

Principal Business: Group health insurance (78%), individual health insurance (13%), individual life insurance (6%), and individual annuities (3%).

Principal Investments: NonCMO investment grade bonds (86%), CMOs and structured securities (13%), and cash (1%).

Investments in Affiliates: None

Group Affiliation: UnitedHealth Group Inc

Licensed in: All states except AL, NC

Commenced Business: January 1941

Address: 712 Eleventh St, Lawrenceville, IL 62439-2395

Phone: (317) 290-8100 **Domicile State:** IN **NAIC Code:** 62286

Data Date	Rating	RACR #1	RACR #2	Total Assets ($mil)	Capital ($mil)	Net Premium ($mil)	Net Income ($mil)
3-09	B	1.91	1.50	665.9	318.8	322.1	56.2
3-08	B	2.07	1.59	648.8	317.5	301.0	57.6
2008	B	1.61	1.26	613.7	267.8	1,260.6	144.7
2007	B	1.76	1.35	590.1	263.9	1,128.1	162.6
2006	B	2.10	1.59	596.6	291.7	996.6	191.5
2005	B	2.53	1.89	826.0	375.8	1,039.4	194.5
2004	B+	1.49	0.96	2,369.0	274.6	1,014.4	106.1

Adverse Trends in Operations

Change in asset mix during 2006 (4.6%)
Decrease in asset base during 2006 (28%)
Decrease in capital during 2006 (22%)
Change in asset mix during 2005 (9.0%)
Decrease in asset base during 2005 (65%)

GOVERNMENT PERSONNEL MUTUAL LIFE INSURANCE CO *   B+   Good

Major Rating Factors: Good quality investment portfolio (5.8 on a scale of 0 to 10) despite substantial holdings of BBB bonds in addition to moderate junk bond exposure. Exposure to mortgages is significant, but the mortgage default rate has been low. Good overall profitability (6.2). Good liquidity (5.6).

Other Rating Factors: Good overall results on stability tests (6.4) excellent operational trends and good risk diversification. Strong capitalization (7.5) based on excellent risk adjusted capital (severe loss scenario).

Principal Business: Individual life insurance (66%), group life insurance (28%), reinsurance (3%), individual annuities (2%), and group health insurance (2%).

Principal Investments: NonCMO investment grade bonds (62%), mortgages in good standing (15%), policy loans (10%), CMOs and structured securities (5%), and misc. investments (7%).

Investments in Affiliates: None

Group Affiliation: None

Licensed in: All states except AL, NM, NC

Commenced Business: October 1934

Address: 2211 NW Loop 410, San Antonio, TX 78217

Phone: (800) 938-9765 **Domicile State:** TX **NAIC Code:** 63967

Data Date	Rating	RACR #1	RACR #2	Total Assets ($mil)	Capital ($mil)	Net Premium ($mil)	Net Income ($mil)
3-09	B+	2.34	1.36	783.4	81.2	12.5	1.0
3-08	B+	2.99	1.76	789.0	87.9	12.9	0.1
2008	B+	2.47	1.41	787.2	83.6	52.7	-3.1
2007	B+	3.06	1.79	786.6	88.0	54.1	5.1
2006	B	3.57	2.00	775.4	84.5	55.7	5.8
2005	B	3.35	1.87	764.0	79.3	98.8	1.7
2004	B	3.53	2.03	711.5	78.3	54.3	8.4

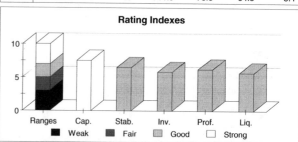

Rating Indexes

Ranges / Cap. / Stab. / Inv. / Prof. / Liq.
■ Weak ■ Fair ▨ Good ☐ Strong

GRANGE LIFE INSURANCE COMPANY *   A-   Excellent

Major Rating Factors: Good overall results on stability tests (6.9 on a scale of 0 to 10). Strengths that enhance stability include excellent operational trends and excellent risk diversification. Good overall profitability (5.5) although investment income, in comparison to reserve requirements, is below regulatory standards. Good liquidity (5.9).

Other Rating Factors: Strong capitalization (7.9) based on excellent risk adjusted capital (severe loss scenario). High quality investment portfolio (7.3).

Principal Business: Individual life insurance (86%), individual annuities (5%), reinsurance (5%), group life insurance (3%), and individual health insurance (1%).

Principal Investments: NonCMO investment grade bonds (51%), CMOs and structured securities (40%), policy loans (4%), cash (3%), and noninv. grade bonds (2%).

Investments in Affiliates: None

Group Affiliation: Grange Mutual Casualty Group

Licensed in: HI, IN, IA, KS, KY, LA, MN, MS, MT, OK, RI, SD, TX, WA, WY

Commenced Business: July 1968

Address: 650 S Front St, Columbus, OH 43216

Phone: (614) 445-2820 **Domicile State:** OH **NAIC Code:** 71218

Data Date	Rating	RACR #1	RACR #2	Total Assets ($mil)	Capital ($mil)	Net Premium ($mil)	Net Income ($mil)
3-09	A-	2.69	1.57	258.2	34.1	11.8	0.7
3-08	A-	2.63	1.62	248.0	34.3	11.1	0.1
2008	A-	2.75	1.64	254.9	33.6	41.7	-1.2
2007	A-	2.63	1.63	245.5	34.2	40.1	3.3
2006	A-	2.60	1.63	227.6	31.1	39.6	3.0
2005	A-	2.41	1.52	214.7	28.2	37.4	1.4
2004	A-	1.91	1.21	190.3	20.0	37.4	0.5

Adverse Trends in Operations

Decrease in capital during 2008 (2%)

GREAT AMERICAN LIFE INSURANCE COMPANY   B-   Good

Major Rating Factors: Good overall results on stability tests (5.2 on a scale of 0 to 10) despite fair financial strength of affiliated American Financial Corp. Other stability subfactors include excellent operational trends and excellent risk diversification. Good capitalization (5.8) based on good risk adjusted capital (moderate loss scenario). Moreover, capital levels have been consistent over the last five years. Good liquidity (5.1).

Other Rating Factors: Fair quality investment portfolio (3.9). Excellent profitability (8.7) despite operating losses during the first three months of 2009.

Principal Business: Individual annuities (87%), individual life insurance (6%), group retirement contracts (3%), individual health insurance (3%), and reinsurance (1%).

Principal Investments: NonCMO investment grade bonds (53%), CMOs and structured securities (33%), noninv. grade bonds (6%), common & preferred stock (2%), and misc. investments (6%).

Investments in Affiliates: 2%

Group Affiliation: American Financial Corp

Licensed in: All states except AL, NC

Commenced Business: December 1959

Address: 250 E Fifth St, Cincinnati, OH 45202

Phone: (800) 854-3649 **Domicile State:** OH **NAIC Code:** 63312

Data Date	Rating	RACR #1	RACR #2	Total Assets ($mil)	Capital ($mil)	Net Premium ($mil)	Net Income ($mil)
3-09	B-	1.50	0.84	9,644.4	807.8	166.5	-15.5
3-08	B-	1.30	0.81	9,254.3	681.8	203.9	-18.0
2008	B-	1.55	0.91	9,627.9	781.0	1,187.4	-30.0
2007	B-	1.40	0.88	9,295.6	732.3	1,230.3	44.0
2006	B-	1.32	0.86	8,703.7	643.8	1,087.6	120.9
2005	B-	1.47	0.92	8,074.3	638.1	644.4	147.8
2004	C	1.14	0.75	7,788.7	577.9	559.4	81.0

American Financial Corp
Composite Group Rating: C+

Largest Group Members	Assets ($mil)	Rating
GREAT AMERICAN LIFE INS CO	9628	B-
GREAT AMERICAN INS CO	5642	C
ANNUITY INVESTORS LIFE INS CO	1742	B-
REPUBLIC INDEMNITY CO OF AMERICA	858	B-
NATIONAL INTERSTATE INS CO	730	C+

GREAT SOUTHERN LIFE INSURANCE COMPANY   C+   Fair

Major Rating Factors: Fair overall results on stability tests (4.2 on a scale of 0 to 10) including fair financial strength of affiliated Americo Life Inc. Fair profitability (4.0). Excellent expense controls. Return on equity has been low, averaging -1.5%. Good quality investment portfolio (6.8) despite mixed results such as: minimal exposure to mortgages and large holdings of BBB rated bonds but small junk bond holdings.

Other Rating Factors: Strong capitalization (7.9) based on excellent risk adjusted capital (severe loss scenario). Excellent liquidity (9.1).

Principal Business: Individual life insurance (83%), group life insurance (9%), individual annuities (3%), group health insurance (3%), and group retirement contracts (1%).

Principal Investments: NonCMO investment grade bonds (61%), CMOs and structured securities (29%), common & preferred stock (6%), noninv. grade bonds (2%), and misc. investments (2%).

Investments in Affiliates: None

Group Affiliation: Americo Life Inc

Licensed in: All states except AL, NJ, NC, SC, VA

Commenced Business: September 1909

Address: 500 N Akard, Dallas, TX 75201

Phone: (214) 954-8100 **Domicile State:** TX **NAIC Code:** 90212

Data Date	Rating	RACR #1	RACR #2	Total Assets ($mil)	Capital ($mil)	Net Premium ($mil)	Net Income ($mil)
3-09	C+	3.33	1.62	259.5	31.7	0.1	0.0
3-08	C+	3.23	1.54	282.5	31.2	0.1	-0.5
2008	C+	3.20	1.51	274.1	34.2	0.2	-1.1
2007	C+	3.00	1.46	289.2	31.1	0.8	-0.3
2006	C	2.83	1.31	303.6	30.0	0.7	-1.2
2005	C-	2.56	1.18	331.8	29.1	0.9	-0.6
2004	D	1.93	0.97	75.5	26.9	0.9	-0.8

Americo Life Inc
Composite Group Rating: C

Largest Group Members	Assets ($mil)	Rating
AMERICO FINANCIAL LIFE ANNUITY INS	3439	C+
INVESTORS LIFE INS CO NORTH AMERICA	755	C-
UNITED FIDELITY LIFE INS CO	572	D+
GREAT SOUTHERN LIFE INS CO	274	C+
NATIONAL FARMERS UNION LIFE INS CO	263	B-

GREAT WEST LIFE ASR CO   B   Good

Major Rating Factors: Good quality investment portfolio (6.2 on a scale of 0 to 10) with no exposure to mortgages and moderate junk bond exposure. Good liquidity (6.6) with sufficient resources to handle a spike in claims. Good overall results on stability tests (5.2) despite negative cash flow from operations for 2008 good operational trends and excellent risk diversification.

Other Rating Factors: Fair profitability (4.9). Strong capitalization (9.0) based on excellent risk adjusted capital (severe loss scenario).

Principal Business: Individual life insurance (76%), individual health insurance (17%), reinsurance (6%), group life insurance (2%), and group health insurance (2%).

Principal Investments: CMOs and structured securities (57%), nonCMO investment grade bonds (30%), noninv. grade bonds (9%), policy loans (3%), and real estate (1%).

Investments in Affiliates: None

Group Affiliation: Great West Life Asr

Licensed in: All states except AL, NC

Commenced Business: August 1892

Address: 60 Osborne St N, Winnepeg, MB R3C 1V3

Phone: (303) 737-3000 **Domicile State:** MI **NAIC Code:** 80705

Data Date	Rating	RACR #1	RACR #2	Total Assets ($mil)	Capital ($mil)	Net Premium ($mil)	Net Income ($mil)
3-09	B	4.42	2.32	138.0	39.6	1.2	1.4
3-08	B	4.17	3.15	141.8	38.2	1.8	1.0
2008	B	4.13	2.23	135.0	37.7	5.0	-0.4
2007	B	3.99	2.98	145.6	36.8	5.5	2.8
2006	B	3.78	2.73	145.9	35.0	6.0	4.4
2005	B+	4.45	3.07	201.1	43.5	8.6	-1.2
2004	B+	5.33	3.49	188.9	40.8	8.3	2.3

Adverse Trends in Operations

Change in premium mix from 2005 to 2006 (4.9%)
Decrease in premium volume from 2005 to 2006 (31%)
Decrease in capital during 2006 (20%)
Decrease in asset base during 2006 (27%)
Decrease in capital during 2005 (15%)

GREAT WESTERN INSURANCE COMPANY

B-   **Good**

Major Rating Factors: Fair current capitalization (4.0 on a scale of 0 to 10) based on mixed results -- excessive policy leverage mitigated by good risk adjusted capital (severe loss scenario), although results have slipped from the excellent range over the last two years. Fair quality investment portfolio (3.9) with large holdings of BBB rated bonds in addition to junk bond exposure equal to 65% of capital. Fair overall results on stability tests (4.0) including negative cash flow from operations for 2008.

Other Rating Factors: Good overall profitability (5.1) despite operating losses during the first three months of 2009. Weak liquidity (2.6).

Principal Business: Group life insurance (73%), individual life insurance (24%), reinsurance (2%), and individual annuities (1%).

Principal Investments: NonCMO investment grade bonds (78%), common & preferred stock (6%), noninv. grade bonds (5%), CMOs and structured securities (4%), and misc. investments (4%).

Investments in Affiliates: None

Group Affiliation: Great Western Co

Licensed in: All states except AL, AZ, DC, DE, ID, MI, NJ, NM, NC

Commenced Business: May 1983

Address: 3434 Washington Blvd, Ogden, UT 84401

Phone: (801) 621-5688 **Domicile State:** UT **NAIC Code:** 71480

Data Date	Rating	RACR #1	RACR #2	Total Assets ($mil)	Capital ($mil)	Net Premium ($mil)	Net Income ($mil)
3-09	B-	1.70	0.89	416.0	31.2	29.2	-4.6
3-08	B	1.88	1.06	511.5	32.5	35.2	0.9
2008	B-	1.70	0.87	403.0	32.4	-14.0	6.4
2007	B	2.01	1.14	499.8	33.8	148.3	-3.4
2006	B-	2.67	1.54	433.8	37.9	130.7	6.6
2005	C+	2.46	1.40	386.6	30.8	116.9	5.6
2004	C+	2.28	1.31	337.1	24.0	103.1	5.2

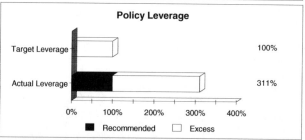

Policy Leverage

Target Leverage — 100%

Actual Leverage — 311%

0% 100% 200% 300% 400%

■ Recommended   □ Excess

GREAT-WEST LIFE & ANNUITY INSURANCE COMPANY

B-   **Good**

Major Rating Factors: Good capitalization (5.2 on a scale of 0 to 10) based on good risk adjusted capital (moderate loss scenario). Good quality investment portfolio (5.2) despite mixed results such as: substantial holdings of BBB bonds but moderate junk bond exposure. Good overall profitability (5.8). Return on equity has been excellent over the last five years averaging 23.0%.

Other Rating Factors: Fair overall results on stability tests (3.6) including weak results on operational trends and fair risk adjusted capital in prior years. Excellent liquidity (7.3).

Principal Business: Group retirement contracts (57%), individual life insurance (21%), group health insurance (14%), reinsurance (4%), and other lines (4%).

Principal Investments: CMOs and structured securities (34%), nonCMO investment grade bonds (30%), policy loans (23%), mortgages in good standing (4%), and misc. investments (8%).

Investments in Affiliates: 2%

Group Affiliation: Great West Life Asr

Licensed in: All states except AL, NC

Commenced Business: April 1907

Address: 8515 E Orchard Rd, Englewood, CO 80111

Phone: (800) 537-2033 **Domicile State:** CO **NAIC Code:** 68322

Data Date	Rating	RACR #1	RACR #2	Total Assets ($mil)	Capital ($mil)	Net Premium ($mil)	Net Income ($mil)
3-09	B-	1.12	0.65	33,902.1	918.8	1,918.2	69.1
3-08	B+	1.48	1.00	36,344.0	1,625.3	1,378.7	85.7
2008	B-	1.15	0.69	33,279.5	904.4	4,405.1	271.4
2007	B+	1.67	1.13	36,530.3	1,846.2	2,952.8	562.3
2006	B+	1.63	1.10	37,320.2	1,862.3	6,718.3	280.9
2005	B+	1.71	1.11	33,645.9	1,529.1	4,244.2	391.6
2004	B+	1.58	1.04	32,157.7	1,477.4	3,555.8	402.3

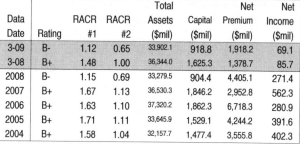

Risk-Adjusted Capital Ratio #1
(Moderate Loss Scenario)

Range 2004 2005 2006 2007 2008 3-09

■ Weak   ▨ Fair   □ Good

GUARANTEE TRUST LIFE INSURANCE COMPANY

C+   **Fair**

Major Rating Factors: Good quality investment portfolio (6.4 on a scale of 0 to 10) despite significant exposure to mortgages . Mortgage default rate has been low. substantial holdings of BBB bonds in addition to minimal holdings in junk bonds. Good overall profitability (5.1). Good liquidity (6.6).

Other Rating Factors: Good overall results on stability tests (5.0) despite fair risk adjusted capital in prior years excellent operational trends and excellent risk diversification. Strong capitalization (7.0) based on excellent risk adjusted capital (severe loss scenario).

Principal Business: Group health insurance (45%), individual health insurance (33%), individual life insurance (12%), credit health insurance (4%), and other lines (7%).

Principal Investments: CMOs and structured securities (46%), nonCMO investment grade bonds (30%), mortgages in good standing (15%), cash (3%), and misc. investments (6%).

Investments in Affiliates: 1%

Group Affiliation: Guarantee Trust

Licensed in: All states except AL, NC

Commenced Business: June 1936

Address: 1275 Milwaukee Ave, Glenview, IL 60025

Phone: (847) 699-0600 **Domicile State:** IL **NAIC Code:** 64211

Data Date	Rating	RACR #1	RACR #2	Total Assets ($mil)	Capital ($mil)	Net Premium ($mil)	Net Income ($mil)
3-09	C+	1.38	1.00	220.5	42.6	41.1	0.3
3-08	C	1.51	1.09	205.4	41.7	34.4	-0.6
2008	C	1.35	0.99	218.7	42.0	160.4	-1.3
2007	C	1.58	1.14	207.7	43.5	130.7	1.0
2006	C	1.22	0.90	193.6	35.5	152.6	2.2
2005	C	1.04	0.77	199.2	34.0	170.8	4.0
2004	C	0.82	0.62	211.2	31.5	206.8	-1.8

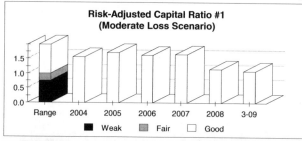

Rating Indexes

Ranges Cap. Stab. Inv. Prof. Liq.

■ Weak   ▨ Fair   ▨ Good   □ Strong

GUARDIAN INSURANCE & ANNUITY COMPANY INC   **B**   **Good**

Major Rating Factors: Good quality investment portfolio (5.2 on a scale of 0 to 10) despite mixed results such as: large holdings of BBB rated bonds but moderate junk bond exposure. Fair overall results on stability tests (4.7) including negative cash flow from operations for 2008. Weak profitability (2.5) with operating losses during the first three months of 2009.

Other Rating Factors: Strong capitalization (7.4) based on excellent risk adjusted capital (severe loss scenario). Excellent liquidity (9.2).

Principal Business: Individual annuities (50%), group retirement contracts (43%), and individual life insurance (6%).

Principal Investments: NonCMO investment grade bonds (86%), policy loans (5%), noninv. grade bonds (4%), CMOs and structured securities (2%), and misc. investments (3%).

Investments in Affiliates: 1%
Group Affiliation: Guardian Group
Licensed in: All states except AL
Commenced Business: December 1971
Address: 1209 Orange St, Wilmington, DE 19801
Phone: (212) 598-8000 **Domicile State:** DE **NAIC Code:** 78778

Data Date	Rating	RACR #1	RACR #2	Total Assets ($mil)	Capital ($mil)	Net Premium ($mil)	Net Income ($mil)
3-09	B	2.53	1.27	7,143.6	195.7	266.8	-16.6
3-08	B	2.70	1.35	9,705.3	246.3	272.0	3.3
2008	B	2.69	1.35	7,502.7	212.6	941.1	-35.1
2007	B	2.62	1.31	10,402.9	244.7	1,190.1	20.0
2006	B	2.24	1.17	10,291.2	228.6	1,214.0	20.5
2005	B	1.73	0.97	9,855.1	244.4	1,091.4	21.6
2004	B-	1.70	0.96	9,904.8	230.8	1,132.3	13.8

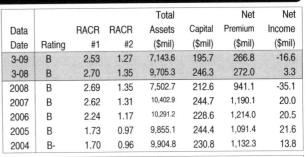

Rating Indexes

GUARDIAN LIFE INSURANCE COMPANY OF AMERICA *   **A**   **Excellent**

Major Rating Factors: Good quality investment portfolio (6.1 on a scale of 0 to 10) despite large holdings of BBB rated bonds in addition to moderate junk bond exposure. Exposure to mortgages is significant, but the mortgage default rate has been low. Good liquidity (6.0) with sufficient resources to handle a spike in claims as well as a significant increase in policy surrenders. Strong capitalization (8.0) based on excellent risk adjusted capital (severe loss scenario).

Other Rating Factors: Excellent profitability (7.8) with operating gains in each of the last five years. Excellent overall results on stability tests (7.5) excellent operational trends and excellent risk diversification.

Principal Business: Group health insurance (45%), individual life insurance (44%), group life insurance (5%), individual health insurance (4%), and reinsurance (1%).

Principal Investments: NonCMO investment grade bonds (55%), mortgages in good standing (13%), policy loans (9%), CMOs and structured securities (8%), and misc. investments (16%).

Investments in Affiliates: 5%
Group Affiliation: Guardian Group
Licensed in: All states except AL
Commenced Business: July 1860
Address: 7 Hanover Square, New York, NY 10004-4025
Phone: (212) 598-8000 **Domicile State:** NY **NAIC Code:** 64246

Data Date	Rating	RACR #1	RACR #2	Total Assets ($mil)	Capital ($mil)	Net Premium ($mil)	Net Income ($mil)
3-09	A	2.40	1.64	29,202.2	3,550.4	1,467.0	60.4
3-08	A	2.36	1.59	28,965.6	3,706.6	1,481.1	91.7
2008	A	2.46	1.69	28,973.5	3,658.9	5,926.4	437.3
2007	A	2.42	1.64	28,328.3	3,750.5	5,929.1	292.0
2006	A	2.08	1.48	26,707.0	3,490.2	6,004.5	375.8
2005	A	2.31	1.59	24,806.5	3,158.6	5,885.7	375.2
2004	A	2.29	1.56	23,336.3	2,905.3	5,607.1	285.5

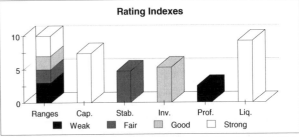

Rating Indexes

HANNOVER LIFE REASSURANCE COMPANY OF AMERICA   **C+**   **Fair**

Major Rating Factors: Fair current capitalization (4.8 on a scale of 0 to 10) based on fair risk adjusted capital (moderate loss scenario), although results have slipped from the good range during the last year. Fair overall results on stability tests (4.8) including fair risk adjusted capital in prior years. Good quality investment portfolio (6.6).

Other Rating Factors: Good overall profitability (5.3). Excellent liquidity (7.2).
Principal Business: Reinsurance (100%).
Principal Investments: NonCMO investment grade bonds (63%), CMOs and structured securities (31%), mortgages in good standing (4%), and common & preferred stock (1%).

Investments in Affiliates: None
Group Affiliation: Hannover Group
Licensed in: AZ, CO, GA, IA, KY, MI, MN, NV, OK, VT, WV
Commenced Business: October 1988
Address: 800 N Magnolia Ave, Ste 1000, Orlando, FL 32803-3251
Phone: (407) 649-8411 **Domicile State:** FL **NAIC Code:** 88340

Data Date	Rating	RACR #1	RACR #2	Total Assets ($mil)	Capital ($mil)	Net Premium ($mil)	Net Income ($mil)
3-09	C+	0.97	0.60	3,405.6	119.3	88.6	6.9
3-08	C+	1.20	0.81	2,099.3	138.4	506.8	2.0
2008	C+	1.11	0.72	3,572.6	128.1	788.3	-11.4
2007	C+	1.67	1.06	1,710.6	136.6	295.5	30.3
2006	C+	1.36	0.86	1,542.0	111.4	279.3	2.4
2005	C	1.57	0.99	1,305.9	113.1	283.8	3.4
2004	D+	1.05	0.66	1,225.1	85.9	299.9	-5.2

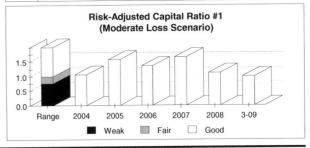

Risk-Adjusted Capital Ratio #1
(Moderate Loss Scenario)

HARTFORD INTERNATIONAL LIFE REASSURANCE CORP   B   Good

Major Rating Factors: Good quality investment portfolio (6.4 on a scale of 0 to 10) with no exposure to mortgages and small junk bond holdings. Good overall profitability (6.3). Excellent expense controls. Return on equity has been good over the last five years, averaging 14.0%. Good liquidity (6.8) with sufficient resources to handle a spike in claims as well as a significant increase in policy surrenders.

Other Rating Factors: Fair overall results on stability tests (4.7) including fair financial strength of affiliated Hartford Financial Services Inc, negative cash flow from operations for 2008 and fair risk adjusted capital in prior years. Strong capitalization (7.3) based on excellent risk adjusted capital (severe loss scenario).

Principal Business: Reinsurance (100%).

Principal Investments: Policy loans (65%), CMOs and structured securities (25%), nonCMO investment grade bonds (6%), common & preferred stock (2%), and noninv. grade bonds (1%).

Investments in Affiliates: None

Group Affiliation: Hartford Financial Services Inc

Licensed in: AZ, CA, CO, DC, DE, FL, IL, IN, IA, KS, KY, LA, MA, MI, MN, MO, NE, NH, NJ, NM, NC, ND, OH, OK, RI, SD, TN, UT, VT, WV, WI

Commenced Business: July 1981

Address: 200 Hopmeadow St, Simsbury, CT 06070

Phone: (860) 547-5000   **Domicile State:** CT   **NAIC Code:** 93505

Data Date	Rating	RACR #1	RACR #2	Total Assets ($mil)	Capital ($mil)	Net Premium ($mil)	Net Income ($mil)
3-09	B	2.38	1.19	1,120.7	103.4	7.1	0.7
3-08	B	2.44	1.25	1,161.6	108.5	3.0	1.8
2008	B	2.32	1.19	1,115.8	102.4	9.8	4.4
2007	B	2.38	1.23	1,135.9	106.4	12.6	3.7
2006	B	1.93	1.01	1,144.1	83.3	18.4	19.1
2005	B	1.97	1.04	1,197.8	82.3	20.3	20.2
2004	B	1.25	0.65	1,785.1	79.8	21.5	20.8

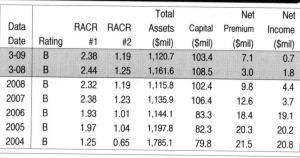

Rating Indexes

(Ranges, Cap., Stab., Inv., Prof., Liq. — Weak, Fair, Good, Strong)

HARTFORD LIFE & ACCIDENT INSURANCE COMPANY   B-   Good

Major Rating Factors: Good overall results on stability tests (5.2 on a scale of 0 to 10) despite fair financial strength of affiliated Hartford Financial Services Inc. Other stability subfactors include good operational trends, good risk adjusted capital for prior years and excellent risk diversification. Fair quality investment portfolio (4.4). Strong capitalization (7.0) based on excellent risk adjusted capital (severe loss scenario).

Other Rating Factors: Excellent profitability (7.9) with operating gains in each of the last five years. Excellent liquidity (7.0).

Principal Business: Group health insurance (56%), group life insurance (29%), reinsurance (14%), and individual life insurance (1%).

Principal Investments: Common & preferred stock (41%), nonCMO investment grade bonds (35%), CMOs and structured securities (12%), mortgages in good standing (5%), and noninv. grade bonds (2%).

Investments in Affiliates: 35%

Group Affiliation: Hartford Financial Services Inc

Licensed in: All states except AL, NC

Commenced Business: February 1967

Address: 200 Hopmeadow St, Simsbury, CT 06070

Phone: (860) 547-5000   **Domicile State:** CT   **NAIC Code:** 70815

Data Date	Rating	RACR #1	RACR #2	Total Assets ($mil)	Capital ($mil)	Net Premium ($mil)	Net Income ($mil)
3-09	B-	1.06	1.00	13,955.9	5,601.2	853.0	49.2
3-08	B	1.05	0.98	14,303.9	5,655.5	1,010.9	173.4
2008	B-	1.14	1.08	14,414.0	6,045.7	4,035.6	263.4
2007	B	1.06	1.00	14,187.5	5,786.1	4,047.8	776.8
2006	B	1.11	1.03	12,966.2	4,733.0	3,980.4	644.5
2005	B	0.94	0.90	10,134.0	4,347.5	2,726.3	788.9
2004	B+	1.00	0.96	10,838.2	5,117.9	2,474.1	771.9

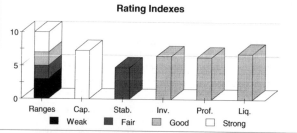

Hartford Financial Services Inc
Composite Group Rating: C
Largest Group Members

	Assets ($mil)	Rating
HARTFORD LIFE INS CO	133562	C-
HARTFORD LIFE ANNUITY INS CO	65461	B-
HARTFORD FIRE INS CO	24454	B+
HARTFORD LIFE ACCIDENT INS CO	14414	B-
HARTFORD ACCIDENT INDEMNITY CO	10935	C+

HARTFORD LIFE & ANNUITY INSURANCE COMPANY   B-   Good

Major Rating Factors: Good quality investment portfolio (6.9 on a scale of 0 to 10) despite mixed results such as: minimal exposure to mortgages and substantial holdings of BBB bonds but minimal holdings in junk bonds. Fair overall results on stability tests (4.4) including fair financial strength of affiliated Hartford Financial Services Inc. Weak profitability (1.6) with operating losses during the first three months of 2009.

Other Rating Factors: Strong capitalization (7.9) based on excellent risk adjusted capital (severe loss scenario). Excellent liquidity (10.0).

Principal Business: Individual annuities (62%), reinsurance (23%), and individual life insurance (15%).

Principal Investments: NonCMO investment grade bonds (55%), CMOs and structured securities (19%), mortgages in good standing (4%), policy loans (3%), and misc. investments (19%).

Investments in Affiliates: None

Group Affiliation: Hartford Financial Services Inc

Licensed in: All states except AL, NC

Commenced Business: July 1965

Address: 200 Hopmeadow St, Simsbury, CT 06070

Phone: (860) 547-5000   **Domicile State:** CT   **NAIC Code:** 71153

Data Date	Rating	RACR #1	RACR #2	Total Assets ($mil)	Capital ($mil)	Net Premium ($mil)	Net Income ($mil)
3-09	B-	3.13	1.62	61,552.0	2,299.4	848.0	-54.5
3-08	B+	3.54	2.08	82,527.2	2,776.9	2,156.9	-19.3
2008	B-	2.93	1.53	65,460.5	2,177.9	9,352.5	-1,983.1
2007	B+	3.26	1.90	89,347.8	2,556.6	10,313.5	284.5
2006	B+	2.32	1.49	83,086.1	1,667.7	9,842.3	338.7
2005	B+	2.30	1.43	75,100.5	1,490.3	9,152.3	219.1
2004	B+	2.18	1.32	69,726.5	1,308.0	11,619.8	256.7

Hartford Financial Services Inc
Composite Group Rating: C
Largest Group Members

	Assets ($mil)	Rating
HARTFORD LIFE INS CO	133562	C-
HARTFORD LIFE ANNUITY INS CO	65461	B-
HARTFORD FIRE INS CO	24454	B+
HARTFORD LIFE ACCIDENT INS CO	14414	B-
HARTFORD ACCIDENT INDEMNITY CO	10935	C+

HARTFORD LIFE INSURANCE COMPANY   C-   Fair

Major Rating Factors: Fair overall results on stability tests (3.0 on a scale of 0 to 10). Weak profitability (2.0) with investment income below regulatory standards in relation to interest assumptions of reserves. Good overall capitalization (6.4) based on good risk adjusted capital (severe loss scenario). However, capital levels have fluctuated somewhat during past years.

Other Rating Factors: Good quality investment portfolio (5.6). Excellent liquidity (9.8).

Principal Business: Group retirement contracts (49%), individual annuities (36%), reinsurance (6%), group health insurance (4%), and other lines (6%).

Principal Investments: NonCMO investment grade bonds (40%), CMOs and structured securities (30%), common & preferred stock (10%), mortgages in good standing (7%), and misc. investments (13%).

Investments in Affiliates: 6%

Group Affiliation: Hartford Financial Services Inc

Licensed in: All states except AL

Commenced Business: January 1979

Address: 200 Hopmeadow St, Simsbury, CT 06070

Phone: (860) 547-5000 **Domicile State:** CT **NAIC Code:** 88072

Data Date	Rating	RACR #1	RACR #2	Total Assets ($mil)	Capital ($mil)	Net Premium ($mil)	Net Income ($mil)
3-09	C-	1.33	0.92	132,572	4,964.1	2,006.7	195.2
3-08	B	1.15	0.82	156,649	4,334.6	2,432.1	-545.0
2008	C-	1.13	0.79	133,562	4,071.4	9,334.0	-2,533.3
2007	B	1.18	0.84	165,998	4,448.5	16,284.4	191.5
2006	B	1.19	0.81	146,278	3,275.6	11,541.2	553.0
2005	B+	1.32	0.92	120,590	3,021.7	10,428.3	171.5
2004	B+	1.51	1.05	112,861	3,191.9	11,507.8	535.6

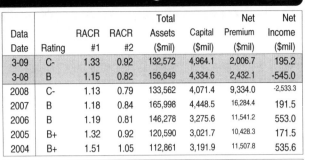

Rating Indexes

Ranges Cap. Stab. Inv. Prof. Liq.
■ Weak ■ Fair ▨ Good ☐ Strong

HCC LIFE INSURANCE COMPANY   B   Good

Major Rating Factors: Good overall results on stability tests (6.0 on a scale of 0 to 10). Stability strengths include excellent operational trends and excellent risk diversification. Good liquidity (6.9) with sufficient resources to handle a spike in claims. Strong capitalization (9.3) based on excellent risk adjusted capital (severe loss scenario).

Other Rating Factors: High quality investment portfolio (8.6). Excellent profitability (9.4) with operating gains in each of the last five years.

Principal Business: Group health insurance (85%), reinsurance (12%), individual health insurance (2%), and group life insurance (1%).

Principal Investments: NonCMO investment grade bonds (65%), CMOs and structured securities (23%), common & preferred stock (7%), and cash (5%).

Investments in Affiliates: 7%

Group Affiliation: HCC Ins Holdings Inc

Licensed in: All states except AL, ID, MD, MI, NJ, NC

Commenced Business: March 1981

Address: 300 N Meridian St Ste 2700, Indianapolis, IN 46204

Phone: (713) 996-1200 **Domicile State:** IN **NAIC Code:** 92711

Data Date	Rating	RACR #1	RACR #2	Total Assets ($mil)	Capital ($mil)	Net Premium ($mil)	Net Income ($mil)
3-09	B	2.96	2.51	592.2	363.2	166.5	15.0
3-08	B	3.12	2.62	613.0	353.8	166.0	16.7
2008	B	2.83	2.42	584.8	345.4	663.4	60.3
2007	B	2.95	2.48	623.2	336.2	649.5	64.2
2006	B	2.96	2.49	549.1	268.8	494.2	48.0
2005	B	3.55	2.84	325.3	190.6	421.1	30.4
2004	B	4.25	3.35	240.9	130.0	230.3	27.2

Adverse Trends in Operations

Decrease in asset base during 2008 (6%)

HEALTH NET LIFE INSURANCE COMPANY   B   Good

Major Rating Factors: Good overall profitability (6.4 on a scale of 0 to 10). Excellent expense controls. Return on equity has been good over the last five years, averaging 11.5%. Fair overall results on stability tests (4.2) including negative cash flow from operations for 2008. Weak liquidity (0.3) as a spike in claims may stretch capacity.

Other Rating Factors: Strong capitalization (7.9) based on excellent risk adjusted capital (severe loss scenario). High quality investment portfolio (8.4).

Principal Business: Individual health insurance (57%), group health insurance (42%), and reinsurance (1%).

Principal Investments: NonCMO investment grade bonds (61%), CMOs and structured securities (47%), and common & preferred stock (1%).

Investments in Affiliates: None

Group Affiliation: Health Net Inc

Licensed in: All states except AL, AZ, ID, MS, NJ, NC

Commenced Business: January 1987

Address: 225 N Main St, Pueblo, CO 81003

Phone: (719) 585-8017 **Domicile State:** CA **NAIC Code:** 66141

Data Date	Rating	RACR #1	RACR #2	Total Assets ($mil)	Capital ($mil)	Net Premium ($mil)	Net Income ($mil)
3-09	B	1.98	1.62	653.2	375.9	296.9	8.6
3-08	B+	2.05	1.68	798.8	345.3	325.6	-11.1
2008	B	1.92	1.57	650.1	368.8	1,241.2	14.1
2007	B+	1.67	1.37	656.0	233.6	1,065.0	-20.0
2006	B+	1.74	1.42	400.4	203.5	816.5	61.7
2005	B	2.07	1.69	359.8	191.6	640.7	42.5
2004	B-	1.89	1.56	344.1	168.6	643.1	16.6

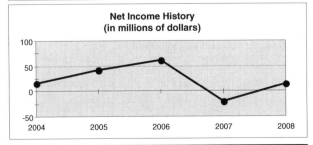

Net Income History
(in millions of dollars)

2004 2005 2006 2007 2008

HEALTHY ALLIANCE LIFE INSURANCE COMPANY | B | Good

Major Rating Factors: Good current capitalization (5.3 on a scale of 0 to 10) based on mixed results -- excessive policy leverage mitigated by excellent risk adjusted capital (severe loss scenario) reflecting improvement over results in 2007. Good liquidity (5.3) with sufficient resources to handle a spike in claims. Good overall results on stability tests (6.0) excellent operational trends and excellent risk diversification.

Other Rating Factors: High quality investment portfolio (8.1). Excellent profitability (9.2) with operating gains in each of the last five years.

Principal Business: Group health insurance (79%) and individual health insurance (21%).

Principal Investments: NonCMO investment grade bonds (65%), CMOs and structured securities (35%), and noninv. grade bonds (1%).

Investments in Affiliates: None

Group Affiliation: WellPoint Inc

Licensed in: AK, AR, CA, CO, CT, DE, FL, ID, IL, IN, IA, KS, KY, ME, MA, MO, MT, NE, NV, NH, NY, ND, OH, OK, OR, PA, RI, SD, TN, TX, UT, VT, WA, WV, WI, WY

Commenced Business: June 1971

Address: 1831 Chestnut St, St Louis, MO 63103-2275

Phone: (877) 864-2273 **Domicile State:** MO **NAIC Code:** 78972

Data Date	Rating	RACR #1	RACR #2	Total Assets ($mil)	Capital ($mil)	Net Premium ($mil)	Net Income ($mil)
3-09	B	1.54	1.22	666.9	303.1	392.1	34.8
3-08	B	1.33	1.06	624.6	248.0	388.0	19.2
2008	B	1.40	1.13	598.3	268.9	1,553.4	107.5
2007	B	1.18	0.94	541.5	214.0	1,479.1	83.0
2006	B	1.23	0.99	529.9	222.8	1,496.6	67.2
2005	B	1.16	0.94	456.5	199.5	1,407.1	63.2
2004	B	1.30	1.05	444.5	198.8	1,251.3	88.3

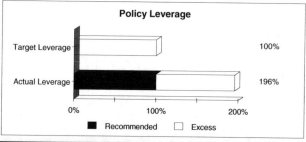

Policy Leverage

Target Leverage — 100%

Actual Leverage — 196%

0%   100%   200%

■ Recommended   □ Excess

HM LIFE INSURANCE COMPANY | B- | Good

Major Rating Factors: Good liquidity (6.7 on a scale of 0 to 10) with sufficient resources to handle a spike in claims. Good overall results on stability tests (5.3). Stability strengths include excellent operational trends and excellent risk diversification. Fair quality investment portfolio (4.8).

Other Rating Factors: Strong capitalization (8.6) based on excellent risk adjusted capital (severe loss scenario). Excellent profitability (8.2).

Principal Business: Group health insurance (82%) and reinsurance (18%).

Principal Investments: NonCMO investment grade bonds (58%), CMOs and structured securities (14%), noninv. grade bonds (11%), cash (11%), and common & preferred stock (3%).

Investments in Affiliates: 3%

Group Affiliation: Highmark Inc

Licensed in: All states except AL, NC

Commenced Business: May 1981

Address: 120 Fifth Avenue, Pittsburgh, PA 15222

Phone: (800) 328-5433 **Domicile State:** PA **NAIC Code:** 93440

Data Date	Rating	RACR #1	RACR #2	Total Assets ($mil)	Capital ($mil)	Net Premium ($mil)	Net Income ($mil)
3-09	B-	2.72	2.04	358.4	152.4	102.8	4.1
3-08	B-	2.90	2.15	329.4	141.0	95.2	0.3
2008	B-	2.70	2.03	350.1	148.5	383.9	0.0
2007	B-	3.04	2.23	318.0	141.8	315.9	4.4
2006	B-	3.37	2.48	284.8	138.7	284.9	10.5
2005	B-	2.50	1.81	400.0	125.0	286.9	8.7
2004	B-	2.58	1.86	366.0	116.8	252.0	11.5

Adverse Trends in Operations

Decrease in asset base during 2006 (29%)

HOMESTEADERS LIFE COMPANY | C+ | Fair

Major Rating Factors: Fair overall results on stability tests (4.8 on a scale of 0 to 10). Good capitalization (5.8) based on good risk adjusted capital (moderate loss scenario). Moreover, capital levels have been consistent over the last five years. Good quality investment portfolio (5.8) with minimal exposure to mortgages and small junk bond holdings.

Other Rating Factors: Good overall profitability (6.9). Good liquidity (6.9).

Principal Business: Group life insurance (95%), individual life insurance (4%), and individual annuities (1%).

Principal Investments: NonCMO investment grade bonds (54%), CMOs and structured securities (34%), mortgages in good standing (9%), noninv. grade bonds (1%), and real estate (1%).

Investments in Affiliates: None

Group Affiliation: None

Licensed in: All states except AL, NC

Commenced Business: February 1906

Address: 2141 Grand Ave, Des Moines, IA 50312

Phone: (515) 288-7481 **Domicile State:** IA **NAIC Code:** 64505

Data Date	Rating	RACR #1	RACR #2	Total Assets ($mil)	Capital ($mil)	Net Premium ($mil)	Net Income ($mil)
3-09	C+	1.51	0.80	1,626.7	79.7	79.4	1.4
3-08	C+	1.65	0.87	1,494.4	75.0	77.7	0.4
2008	C+	1.53	0.82	1,602.4	79.2	339.9	0.2
2007	C+	1.63	0.86	1,473.8	74.7	328.8	7.8
2006	C	1.60	0.84	1,337.9	67.8	329.3	4.2
2005	C	1.60	0.83	1,197.7	63.2	301.4	3.4
2004	C	1.70	0.87	1,070.2	60.5	274.6	5.9

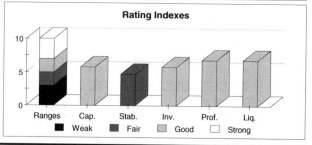

Rating Indexes

10

5

0

Ranges   Cap.   Stab.   Inv.   Prof.   Liq.

■ Weak   ■ Fair   ■ Good   □ Strong

HORACE MANN LIFE INSURANCE COMPANY | B | Good

Major Rating Factors: Good quality investment portfolio (5.7 on a scale of 0 to 10) despite mixed results such as: large holdings of BBB rated bonds but moderate junk bond exposure. Good liquidity (5.8) with sufficient resources to cover a large increase in policy surrenders. Fair overall results on stability tests (4.8).

Other Rating Factors: Strong capitalization (7.0) based on excellent risk adjusted capital (severe loss scenario). Excellent profitability (7.1) despite operating losses during the first three months of 2009.

Principal Business: Individual annuities (64%), individual life insurance (23%), group retirement contracts (10%), group life insurance (1%), and group health insurance (1%).

Principal Investments: NonCMO investment grade bonds (53%), CMOs and structured securities (36%), policy loans (3%), common & preferred stock (3%), and noninv. grade bonds (3%).

Investments in Affiliates: None
Group Affiliation: Horace Mann Educators Corp
Licensed in: All states except AL, NM, NC
Commenced Business: September 1949
Address: 1 Horace Mann Plaza, Springfield, IL 62715
Phone: (800) 999-1030 **Domicile State:** IL **NAIC Code:** 64513

Data Date	Rating	RACR #1	RACR #2	Total Assets ($mil)	Capital ($mil)	Net Premium ($mil)	Net Income ($mil)
3-09	B	1.95	1.01	4,561.7	268.4	91.9	-1.9
3-08	B	2.44	1.25	4,948.3	263.6	97.4	1.5
2008	B	2.09	1.10	4,540.8	270.4	412.7	-10.7
2007	B	2.55	1.31	5,069.9	276.6	438.0	26.1
2006	B	2.25	1.16	5,102.5	251.2	428.1	28.4
2005	B	2.30	1.18	4,649.0	230.7	887.4	24.5
2004	B	2.46	1.25	4,163.2	230.1	385.0	19.7

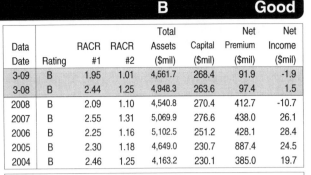

Rating Indexes

HOUSEHOLD LIFE INS CO OF DE | C | Fair

Major Rating Factors: Fair overall results on stability tests (4.0 on a scale of 0 to 10). Good overall profitability (5.3). Return on equity has been good over the last five years, averaging 12.8%. Low quality investment portfolio (2.8).

Other Rating Factors: Strong capitalization (7.7) based on excellent risk adjusted capital (severe loss scenario). Excellent liquidity (10.0).

Principal Business: Group life insurance (91%) and credit life insurance (9%).

Principal Investments: Common & preferred stock (66%), nonCMO investment grade bonds (32%), and CMOs and structured securities (2%).

Investments in Affiliates: 66%
Group Affiliation: HSBC Holdings
Licensed in: FL
Commenced Business: November 2000
Address: 200 Somerset Corporate Blvd, Bridgewater, NJ 08807
Phone: (908) 203-2127 **Domicile State:** DE **NAIC Code:** 89007

Data Date	Rating	RACR #1	RACR #2	Total Assets ($mil)	Capital ($mil)	Net Premium ($mil)	Net Income ($mil)
3-09	C	1.45	1.44	548.7	547.7	0.1	1.1
3-08	C	1.48	1.46	723.1	721.5	0.1	1.4
2008	C	1.52	1.51	574.6	573.8	0.5	120.1
2007	C	1.44	1.43	683.6	682.2	0.6	115.0
2006	C	1.39	1.38	777.4	775.9	0.5	52.1
2005	C	1.56	1.56	812.7	808.8	0.5	85.7
2004	C	1.32	1.31	697.9	678.5	0.3	80.2

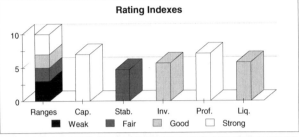

Rating Indexes

HOUSEHOLD LIFE INSURANCE COMPANY | B | Good

Major Rating Factors: Good overall profitability (6.2 on a scale of 0 to 10). Excellent expense controls. Return on equity has been excellent over the last five years averaging 15.1%. Fair overall results on stability tests (4.7) including fair financial strength of affiliated HSBC Holdings and negative cash flow from operations for 2008. Strong capitalization (10.0) based on excellent risk adjusted capital (severe loss scenario).

Other Rating Factors: High quality investment portfolio (8.4). Excellent liquidity (7.6).

Principal Business: Credit life insurance (28%), credit health insurance (26%), reinsurance (22%), group life insurance (11%), and other lines (13%).

Principal Investments: NonCMO investment grade bonds (83%), CMOs and structured securities (7%), policy loans (6%), common & preferred stock (3%), and cash (1%).

Investments in Affiliates: 3%
Group Affiliation: HSBC Holdings
Licensed in: All states except AL, NC
Commenced Business: January 1981
Address: 500 Woodward Ave., Ste 4000, Detroit, MI 48226
Phone: (810) 848-7811 **Domicile State:** MI **NAIC Code:** 93777

Data Date	Rating	RACR #1	RACR #2	Total Assets ($mil)	Capital ($mil)	Net Premium ($mil)	Net Income ($mil)
3-09	B	4.72	3.67	813.9	317.9	50.1	4.3
3-08	B	5.64	4.45	960.1	454.3	61.3	9.5
2008	B	4.81	3.73	829.1	329.5	247.0	12.7
2007	B	5.30	4.20	943.4	424.0	265.6	59.6
2006	B-	5.84	4.64	1,043.8	509.1	265.1	58.5
2005	B-	6.12	4.77	1,050.4	490.9	223.9	103.4
2004	C	5.88	4.55	1,064.1	452.8	195.1	103.2

HSBC Holdings
Composite Group Rating: C+

Largest Group Members	Assets ($mil)	Rating
HOUSEHOLD LIFE INS CO	829	B
HOUSEHOLD LIFE INS CO OF DE	575	C
HSBC INS CO OF DELAWARE	385	C
FIRST CENTRAL NATL LIC OF NEW YORK	53	B

HUMANA INS CO
C   **Fair**

Major Rating Factors: Fair overall results on stability tests (3.0 on a scale of 0 to 10) including fair risk adjusted capital in prior years. Good current capitalization (5.1) based on mixed results -- excessive policy leverage mitigated by good risk adjusted capital (severe loss scenario) reflecting some improvement over results in 2006. Good overall profitability (6.8) despite operating losses during the first three months of 2009.

Other Rating Factors: Weak liquidity (1.0). High quality investment portfolio (7.9).

Principal Business: Individual health insurance (74%), group health insurance (21%), and reinsurance (5%).

Principal Investments: NonCMO investment grade bonds (53%), CMOs and structured securities (35%), common & preferred stock (9%), and noninv. grade bonds (3%).

Investments in Affiliates: 7%

Group Affiliation: Humana Inc

Licensed in: All states except AL, NJ, NC, VA

Commenced Business: December 1968

Address: 1100 Employers Blvd, De Pere, WI 54115

Phone: (920) 336-1100 **Domicile State:** WI **NAIC Code:** 73288

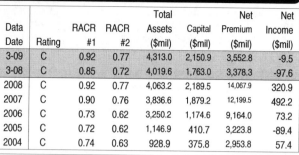

Data Date	Rating	RACR #1	RACR #2	Total Assets ($mil)	Capital ($mil)	Net Premium ($mil)	Net Income ($mil)
3-09	C	0.92	0.77	4,313.0	2,150.9	3,552.8	-9.5
3-08	C	0.85	0.72	4,019.6	1,763.0	3,378.3	-97.6
2008	C	0.92	0.77	4,063.2	2,189.5	14,067.9	320.9
2007	C	0.90	0.76	3,836.6	1,879.2	12,199.5	492.2
2006	C	0.73	0.62	3,250.2	1,174.6	9,164.0	73.2
2005	C	0.72	0.62	1,146.9	410.7	3,223.8	-89.4
2004	C	0.74	0.63	928.9	375.8	2,953.8	57.4

Rating Indexes

Ranges | Cap. | Stab. | Inv. | Prof. | Liq.
■ Weak ■ Fair ▨ Good □ Strong

HUMANA INSURANCE COMPANY OF PUERTO RICO INCORPOR/
C   **Fair**

Major Rating Factors: Fair overall results on stability tests (3.5 on a scale of 0 to 10) including weak risk adjusted capital in prior years. Weak profitability (1.0). Excellent expense controls. Strong current capitalization (8.2) based on excellent risk adjusted capital (severe loss scenario) reflecting significant improvement over results in 2004.

Other Rating Factors: High quality investment portfolio (7.6). Excellent liquidity (7.3).

Principal Business: Group health insurance (99%) and group life insurance (1%).

Principal Investments: NonCMO investment grade bonds (94%), cash (4%), CMOs and structured securities (1%), and noninv. grade bonds (1%).

Investments in Affiliates: None

Group Affiliation: Humana Inc

Licensed in: (No states)

Commenced Business: September 1970

Address: 383 F D Roosevelt Ave, San Juan, PR 00918-2131

Phone: (787) 282-7900 **Domicile State:** PR **NAIC Code:** 84603

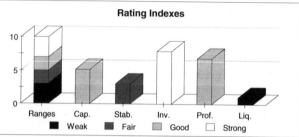

Data Date	Rating	RACR #1	RACR #2	Total Assets ($mil)	Capital ($mil)	Net Premium ($mil)	Net Income ($mil)
3-09	C	2.21	1.80	46.1	31.9	19.5	0.6
3-08	C	2.08	1.72	39.2	25.8	18.6	1.7
2008	C	2.18	1.79	44.1	31.1	77.2	7.2
2007	C	1.96	1.62	36.2	23.6	65.6	6.0
2006	E-	N/A	N/A	30.6	17.4	90.7	3.1
2005	E-	N/A	N/A	18.3	-7.2	106.3	-15.4
2004	C-	0.43	0.35	27.0	8.2	104.8	0.0

Rating Indexes

Ranges | Cap. | Stab. | Inv. | Prof. | Liq.
■ Weak ■ Fair ▨ Good □ Strong

HUMANADENTAL INSURANCE COMPANY
B-   **Good**

Major Rating Factors: Good overall results on stability tests (5.2 on a scale of 0 to 10) despite fair financial strength of affiliated Humana Inc. Other stability subfactors include good operational trends and excellent risk diversification. Good current capitalization (5.9) based on mixed results -- excessive policy leverage mitigated by excellent risk adjusted capital (severe loss scenario) reflecting improvement over results in 2006. Good liquidity (6.5).

Other Rating Factors: High quality investment portfolio (8.2). Excellent profitability (8.0) with operating gains in each of the last five years.

Principal Business: Group health insurance (92%), individual health insurance (5%), individual life insurance (2%), and individual annuities (1%).

Principal Investments: NonCMO investment grade bonds (57%), CMOs and structured securities (39%), common & preferred stock (3%), and noninv. grade bonds (2%).

Investments in Affiliates: None

Group Affiliation: Humana Inc

Licensed in: All states except AL, MD, NC

Commenced Business: October 1908

Address: 1100 Employers Blvd, De Pere, WI 54115

Phone: (920) 336-1100 **Domicile State:** WI **NAIC Code:** 70580

Data Date	Rating	RACR #1	RACR #2	Total Assets ($mil)	Capital ($mil)	Net Premium ($mil)	Net Income ($mil)
3-09	B-	1.73	1.38	101.4	68.3	73.2	4.5
3-08	B-	1.88	1.51	101.1	71.2	74.6	6.3
2008	B-	1.62	1.29	93.9	63.8	296.4	22.7
2007	B-	1.74	1.40	96.6	65.6	301.7	22.5
2006	B	1.17	0.95	90.4	63.9	277.2	21.3
2005	B-	1.31	1.05	92.2	62.4	249.7	20.3
2004	C+	1.28	1.02	77.1	57.4	205.0	17.7

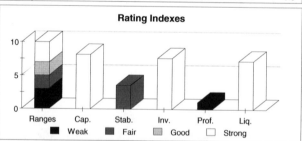

Humana Inc Composite Group Rating: C+ Largest Group Members	Assets ($mil)	Rating
HUMANA INS CO	4063	C
HUMANA MEDICAL PLAN INC	1085	B
KANAWHA INS CO	823	C
HUMANA HEALTH PLAN INC	402	B-
HUMANA HEALTH BENEFIT PLAN LA	254	C+

ILLINOIS MUTUAL LIFE INSURANCE COMPANY *   B+   Good

Major Rating Factors: Good current capitalization (6.4 on a scale of 0 to 10) based on good risk adjusted capital (severe loss scenario), although results have slipped from the excellent range during the last year. Good overall profitability (6.5) despite operating losses during the first three months of 2009. Good overall results on stability tests (6.4) good operational trends, excellent risk adjusted capital for prior years and excellent risk diversification.

Other Rating Factors: Fair quality investment portfolio (4.8). Excellent liquidity (7.2).

Principal Business: Individual health insurance (42%), individual life insurance (29%), individual annuities (28%), and group health insurance (1%).

Principal Investments: NonCMO investment grade bonds (44%), CMOs and structured securities (29%), mortgages in good standing (8%), noninv. grade bonds (7%), and misc. investments (13%).

Investments in Affiliates: 1%

Group Affiliation: None

Licensed in: All states except AL, AZ, DE, ID, NC

Commenced Business: July 1912

Address: 300 SW Adams, Peoria, IL 61634

Phone: (309) 674-8255 **Domicile State:** IL **NAIC Code:** 64580

Data Date	Rating	RACR #1	RACR #2	Total Assets ($mil)	Capital ($mil)	Net Premium ($mil)	Net Income ($mil)
3-09	B+	1.78	0.92	1,262.3	124.3	50.4	-1.0
3-08	A-	2.53	1.43	1,273.1	144.2	36.8	0.6
2008	A-	1.97	1.02	1,268.2	132.4	144.9	-9.1
2007	A-	2.59	1.48	1,253.6	145.6	151.3	17.3
2006	B+	2.52	1.42	1,235.0	147.2	153.7	25.2
2005	B+	2.28	1.30	1,158.4	130.7	126.2	0.3
2004	B+	2.22	1.26	1,116.2	122.5	106.3	6.5

Risk-Adjusted Capital Ratio #2 (Severe Loss Scenario)

Legend: ■ Weak ■ Fair ■ Good □ Strong

INDEPENDENCE LIFE & ANNUITY COMPANY   B-   Good

Major Rating Factors: Fair overall capitalization (4.0 on a scale of 0 to 10) based on mixed results -- excessive policy leverage mitigated by excellent risk adjusted capital (severe loss scenario). However, capital levels have fluctuated somewhat during past years. Good overall results on stability tests (5.0) despite fair financial strength of affiliated Sun Life Assurance Group and negative cash flow from operations for 2008 good operational trends, excellent risk adjusted capital for prior years and excellent risk diversification. Good overall profitability (6.9).

Other Rating Factors: Good liquidity (6.8). High quality investment portfolio (7.5).

Principal Business: N/A.

Principal Investments: NonCMO investment grade bonds (62%), policy loans (29%), CMOs and structured securities (3%), noninv. grade bonds (3%), and misc. investments (2%).

Investments in Affiliates: None

Group Affiliation: Sun Life Assurance Group

Licensed in: All states except AL, NC

Commenced Business: November 1945

Address: 125 High St, Boston, MA 02110-2712

Phone: (800) 633-4500 **Domicile State:** RI **NAIC Code:** 64602

Data Date	Rating	RACR #1	RACR #2	Total Assets ($mil)	Capital ($mil)	Net Premium ($mil)	Net Income ($mil)
3-09	B-	5.78	5.20	128.3	52.9	-0.2	0.3
3-08	B-	5.73	5.16	153.9	54.0	-0.2	0.8
2008	B-	5.75	5.18	131.6	52.7	-0.8	-0.6
2007	B-	5.65	5.09	162.4	53.3	-0.8	1.8
2006	C+	5.42	4.88	171.9	51.3	-0.9	2.6
2005	C	5.15	4.63	171.9	48.7	-0.9	2.9
2004	U	4.83	4.35	172.0	45.8	-0.9	3.3

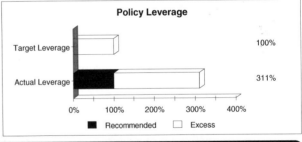

Policy Leverage

Target Leverage — 100%
Actual Leverage — 311%

Legend: ■ Recommended □ Excess

ING LIFE INSURANCE & ANNUITY COMPANY   C+   Fair

Major Rating Factors: Fair overall results on stability tests (4.6 on a scale of 0 to 10) including fair financial strength of affiliated ING America Ins Holdings Inc. Fair profitability (4.7). Return on equity has been fair, averaging 8.0%. Good quality investment portfolio (5.1) despite large holdings of BBB rated bonds in addition to junk bond exposure equal to 66% of capital. Exposure to mortgages is significant, but the mortgage default rate has been low.

Other Rating Factors: Strong capitalization (7.0) based on excellent risk adjusted capital (severe loss scenario). Excellent liquidity (9.2).

Principal Business: Group retirement contracts (90%), individual annuities (8%), and individual life insurance (1%).

Principal Investments: NonCMO investment grade bonds (44%), CMOs and structured securities (30%), mortgages in good standing (11%), noninv. grade bonds (5%), and misc. investments (9%).

Investments in Affiliates: 3%

Group Affiliation: ING America Ins Holdings Inc

Licensed in: All states except AL

Commenced Business: April 1954

Address: 151 Farmington Ave, Hartford, CT 06156

Phone: (866) 723-4646 **Domicile State:** CT **NAIC Code:** 86509

Data Date	Rating	RACR #1	RACR #2	Total Assets ($mil)	Capital ($mil)	Net Premium ($mil)	Net Income ($mil)
3-09	C+	2.07	1.00	54,644.8	1,499.7	2,263.7	6.8
3-08	B	1.92	0.95	64,652.9	1,284.0	2,877.3	-103.9
2008	C+	2.15	1.04	57,306.2	1,524.6	10,499.5	-428.4
2007	B	2.02	0.99	67,000.4	1,388.0	10,171.6	245.5
2006	B	1.90	1.00	63,590.6	1,434.9	10,250.8	125.7
2005	B	2.46	1.22	56,859.4	1,539.1	7,359.9	228.5
2004	B-	1.93	1.01	53,115.0	1,347.0	6,953.2	217.2

ING America Ins Holdings Inc
Composite Group Rating: C+

Largest Group Members	Assets ($mil)	Rating
ING USA ANNUITY LIFE INS CO	64090	C
ING LIFE INS ANNUITY CO	57306	C+
SECURITY LIFE OF DENVER INS CO	24265	B
RELIASTAR LIFE INS CO	20474	B
RELIASTAR LIFE INS CO OF NEW YORK	3207	C+

ING USA ANNUITY & LIFE INSURANCE COMPANY — C — Fair

Major Rating Factors: Fair quality investment portfolio (3.4 on a scale of 0 to 10) with substantial holdings of BBB bonds in addition to significant exposure to junk bonds. Exposure to mortgages is significant, but the mortgage default rate has been low. Fair overall results on stability tests (3.6) including negative cash flow from operations for 2008. Good capitalization (5.0) based on good risk adjusted capital (moderate loss scenario).

Other Rating Factors: Weak profitability (1.6) with operating losses during the first three months of 2009. Excellent liquidity (9.1).

Principal Business: Group retirement contracts (50%), individual annuities (47%), and reinsurance (2%).

Principal Investments: CMOs and structured securities (37%), nonCMO investment grade bonds (36%), mortgages in good standing (14%), noninv. grade bonds (6%), and misc. investments (6%).

Investments in Affiliates: 1%

Group Affiliation: ING America Ins Holdings Inc

Licensed in: All states except AL, NC

Commenced Business: October 1973

Address: 1209 Orange St, Wilmington, DE 19801

Phone: (770) 980-5100 **Domicile State:** IA **NAIC Code:** 80942

Data Date	Rating	RACR #1	RACR #2	Total Assets ($mil)	Capital ($mil)	Net Premium ($mil)	Net Income ($mil)
3-09	C	1.02	0.51	60,901.1	1,340.5	1,856.3	-401.6
3-08	B-	1.88	0.94	72,834.3	2,074.0	3,277.6	-293.3
2008	C	1.53	0.77	64,090.0	1,872.7	11,965.1	-831.4
2007	B-	2.34	1.16	74,257.1	2,552.6	11,515.7	-40.1
2006	B-	1.92	0.96	61,524.3	1,660.7	9,704.1	-1.6
2005	B-	3.00	1.45	52,423.1	1,846.6	6,502.3	6.9
2004	B-	2.54	1.22	48,007.1	1,668.3	8,907.9	96.1

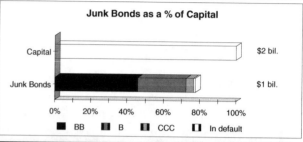

Junk Bonds as a % of Capital

INTEGRITY LIFE INS CO — C+ — Fair

Major Rating Factors: Fair overall results on stability tests (4.7 on a scale of 0 to 10). Good current capitalization (5.9) based on good risk adjusted capital (severe loss scenario), although results have slipped from the excellent range over the last two years. Good quality investment portfolio (5.0) despite mixed results such as: minimal exposure to mortgages and large holdings of BBB rated bonds but small junk bond holdings.

Other Rating Factors: Good overall profitability (5.2) although investment income, in comparison to reserve requirements, is below regulatory standards. Excellent liquidity (8.3).

Principal Business: Individual annuities (100%).

Principal Investments: NonCMO investment grade bonds (53%), CMOs and structured securities (20%), common & preferred stock (12%), policy loans (5%), and misc. investments (11%).

Investments in Affiliates: 8%

Group Affiliation: Western & Southern Group

Licensed in: All states except AL, MD, NJ, NC, VA

Commenced Business: May 1966

Address: 515 W Market St, Louisville, KY 40202

Phone: (502) 582-7900 **Domicile State:** OH **NAIC Code:** 74780

Data Date	Rating	RACR #1	RACR #2	Total Assets ($mil)	Capital ($mil)	Net Premium ($mil)	Net Income ($mil)
3-09	C+	1.22	0.86	4,942.7	363.1	241.8	0.2
3-08	B	1.27	0.89	4,773.7	285.0	265.1	10.9
2008	C+	1.30	0.95	4,850.8	375.4	749.8	-27.4
2007	B	1.59	1.14	4,692.4	355.3	550.7	30.5
2006	B	1.57	1.11	4,649.0	338.4	554.8	75.7
2005	C+	1.35	0.93	4,228.6	236.6	366.7	10.6
2004	C	1.34	0.91	4,020.8	245.0	323.9	29.3

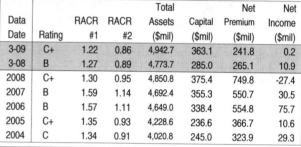

Rating Indexes

Ranges — Cap. — Stab. — Inv. — Prof. — Liq.
■ Weak ■ Fair ■ Good □ Strong

INVESTORS INSURANCE CORPORATION — D+ — Weak

Major Rating Factors: Weak overall results on stability tests (2.6 on a scale of 0 to 10) including potential financial drain due to affiliation with Scor Reinsurance Group. Fair profitability (4.5) with operating losses during the first three months of 2009. Return on equity has been low, averaging 1.5%. Good quality investment portfolio (6.7).

Other Rating Factors: Strong capitalization (7.0) based on excellent risk adjusted capital (severe loss scenario). Excellent liquidity (7.2).

Principal Business: Individual annuities (100%).

Principal Investments: NonCMO investment grade bonds (50%), CMOs and structured securities (39%), cash (3%), common & preferred stock (3%), and misc. investments (5%).

Investments in Affiliates: None

Group Affiliation: Scor Reinsurance Group

Licensed in: AZ, AR, CA, CO, CT, DC, DE, FL, GA, HI, ID, IL, IN, IA, KS, ME, MA, MI, MN, MO, MT, NE, NV, NH, NY, ND, OH, OK, OR, PA, RI, SD, TN, TX, UT, VT, WV, WI, PR

Commenced Business: July 1987

Address: Rodney Sq N, 11th & Market St, Wilmington, DE 19801

Phone: (904) 260-6990 **Domicile State:** DE **NAIC Code:** 64939

Data Date	Rating	RACR #1	RACR #2	Total Assets ($mil)	Capital ($mil)	Net Premium ($mil)	Net Income ($mil)
3-09	D+	2.07	1.03	307.5	28.5	18.8	-0.1
3-08	D+	N/A	N/A	N/A	N/A	N/A	N/A
2008	D+	2.34	1.20	246.9	28.4	30.5	0.6
2007	D+	2.76	1.41	245.2	31.7	6.3	3.8
2006	D	1.88	0.96	248.0	22.3	112.3	-2.4
2005	D	2.02	1.01	255.6	24.7	18.8	-0.6
2004	D	2.43	1.22	230.5	24.6	37.3	-1.1

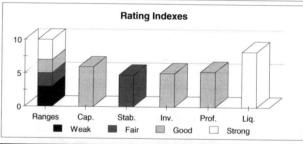

Scor Reinsurance Group Composite Group Rating: D Largest Group Members	Assets ($mil)	Rating
SCOR GLOBAL LIFE US RE INS CO	2011	C-
SCOR REINSURANCE CO	1452	D
GENERAL SECURITY NATIONAL INS CO	317	D
SCOR GLOBAL LIFE RE INS CO OF TX	315	D+
INVESTORS INS CORP	247	D+

INVESTORS LIFE INSURANCE COMPANY NORTH AMERICA   C-   Fair

Major Rating Factors: Fair quality investment portfolio (3.6 on a scale of 0 to 10) with large holdings of BBB rated bonds in addition to junk bond exposure equal to 73% of capital. Fair profitability (3.5) with operating losses during the first three months of 2009. Fair liquidity (4.9) as cash from operations and sale of marketable assets may not be adequate to cover a spike in claims.

Other Rating Factors: Weak overall results on stability tests (2.7) including weak risk adjusted capital in prior years, weak results on operational trends and negative cash flow from operations for 2008. Good capitalization (6.1) based on good risk adjusted capital (severe loss scenario).

Principal Business: N/A

Principal Investments: NonCMO investment grade bonds (75%), CMOs and structured securities (16%), policy loans (5%), and noninv. grade bonds (5%).

Investments in Affiliates: None

Group Affiliation: Americo Life Inc

Licensed in: All states except AL, NC

Commenced Business: December 1963

Address: 6500 River Place Blvd Bldg One, Austin, TX 78730

Phone: (512) 404-5000 **Domicile State:** TX **NAIC Code:** 63487

Data Date	Rating	RACR #1	RACR #2	Total Assets ($mil)	Capital ($mil)	Net Premium ($mil)	Net Income ($mil)
3-09	C-	1.69	0.89	737.8	33.5	-0.3	-0.3
3-08	C-	1.92	1.07	903.4	45.9	7.6	-0.5
2008	C-	1.79	0.95	754.8	34.2	21.8	-0.5
2007	C-	1.94	1.08	936.4	47.8	31.6	3.9
2006	C-	1.74	0.99	988.9	43.4	13.5	6.0
2005	C-	1.31	0.83	1,016.4	39.7	35.2	10.0
2004	C-	0.80	0.42	1,060.1	34.1	43.3	-1.6

Rating Indexes

IOWA AMERICAN LIFE INSURANCE COMPANY   C   Fair

Major Rating Factors: Fair overall capitalization (4.0 on a scale of 0 to 10) based on mixed results -- excessive policy leverage mitigated by excellent risk adjusted capital (severe loss scenario). Nevertheless, capital levels have fluctuated during prior years. Good overall profitability (6.1). Excellent expense controls. Return on equity has been good over the last five years, averaging 13.2%. Weak overall results on stability tests (2.9) including weak results on operational trends and negative cash flow from operations for 2008.

Other Rating Factors: High quality investment portfolio (8.7). Excellent liquidity (10.0).

Principal Business: Individual life insurance (77%), group life insurance (17%), and individual health insurance (6%).

Principal Investments: NonCMO investment grade bonds (18%).

Investments in Affiliates: None

Group Affiliation: Industrial Alliance Life Group

Licensed in: All states except AL, NC

Commenced Business: May 1980

Address: 230 John Wesley Dobbs Ave NE, Atlanta, GA 30303

Phone: (404) 588-9400 **Domicile State:** GA **NAIC Code:** 91693

Data Date	Rating	RACR #1	RACR #2	Total Assets ($mil)	Capital ($mil)	Net Premium ($mil)	Net Income ($mil)
3-09	C	6.35	3.15	30.6	28.2	0.0	0.0
3-08	C	3.16	2.35	69.5	18.4	0.6	0.5
2008	C	5.32	2.66	31.1	28.5	-39.1	4.3
2007	C	3.07	2.23	80.3	17.6	2.5	2.9
2006	C	3.97	2.92	84.4	25.5	3.1	4.9
2005	C+	1.18	1.05	1,026.0	884.6	4.1	77.7
2004	C+	1.17	1.07	944.3	808.4	4.3	167.8

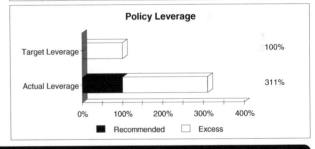

Policy Leverage

Target Leverage — 100%

Actual Leverage — 311%

0%   100%   200%   300%   400%

■ Recommended   □ Excess

J M I C LIFE INSURANCE COMPANY   C+   Fair

Major Rating Factors: Fair overall capitalization (4.0 on a scale of 0 to 10) based on mixed results -- excessive policy leverage mitigated by excellent risk adjusted capital (severe loss scenario). Nevertheless, capital levels have fluctuated during prior years. Fair overall results on stability tests (3.9) including negative cash flow from operations for 2008. Good overall profitability (6.1).

Other Rating Factors: High quality investment portfolio (8.1). Excellent liquidity (9.0).

Principal Business: N/A

Principal Investments: NonCMO investment grade bonds (52%), CMOs and structured securities (46%), noninv. grade bonds (1%), and common & preferred stock (1%).

Investments in Affiliates: None

Group Affiliation: J M Family Enterprise Group

Licensed in: All states except AL, CO, MN, NC

Commenced Business: June 1979

Address: 100 NW 12th Ave, Deerfield Beach, FL 33442

Phone: (954) 429-2007 **Domicile State:** FL **NAIC Code:** 89958

Data Date	Rating	RACR #1	RACR #2	Total Assets ($mil)	Capital ($mil)	Net Premium ($mil)	Net Income ($mil)
3-09	C+	5.71	5.14	90.5	49.3	-1.3	2.1
3-08	C+	9.64	8.67	187.4	92.3	-2.2	4.6
2008	C+	5.47	4.92	95.9	47.2	-6.6	13.9
2007	C	8.83	7.94	183.8	87.2	-9.0	5.6
2006	C	5.35	3.35	239.0	80.5	34.4	1.3
2005	C	3.58	2.58	245.8	79.1	38.1	1.2
2004	C	3.73	2.69	235.9	76.1	37.8	7.2

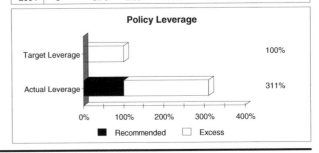

Policy Leverage

Target Leverage — 100%

Actual Leverage — 311%

0%   100%   200%   300%   400%

■ Recommended   □ Excess

JACKSON NATIONAL LIFE INSURANCE CO OF NEW YORK   B   Good

Major Rating Factors: Good overall capitalization (5.8 on a scale of 0 to 10) based on good risk adjusted capital (moderate loss scenario). Nevertheless, capital levels have fluctuated during prior years. Fair quality investment portfolio (3.0) with large holdings of BBB rated bonds in addition to junk bond exposure equal to 73% of capital. Fair overall results on stability tests (4.2) including negative cash flow from operations for 2008.

Other Rating Factors: Weak profitability (1.1) with operating losses during the first three months of 2009. Excellent liquidity (7.3).

Principal Business: Individual annuities (98%) and group retirement contracts (1%).

Principal Investments: NonCMO investment grade bonds (66%), CMOs and structured securities (30%), and noninv. grade bonds (5%).

Investments in Affiliates: None

Group Affiliation: Prudential plc

Licensed in: FL, MN, NC

Commenced Business: August 1996

Address: 5901 Executive Dr, Lansing, MI 48911

Phone: (517) 394-3400 **Domicile State:** NY **NAIC Code:** 60140

Data Date	Rating	RACR #1	RACR #2	Total Assets ($mil)	Capital ($mil)	Net Premium ($mil)	Net Income ($mil)
3-09	B	1.55	0.71	2,554.6	88.4	142.2	-7.1
3-08	B	3.24	1.52	2,976.6	149.9	122.3	17.1
2008	B	1.84	0.87	2,681.8	94.7	215.3	-309.4
2007	B	2.93	1.38	3,039.7	132.1	555.9	-4.1
2006	B-	2.96	1.37	2,680.9	134.6	449.9	3.4
2005	B-	2.94	1.34	2,281.7	132.4	344.0	11.9
2004	C	2.73	1.24	1,992.2	123.1	324.7	14.8

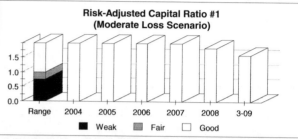

Risk-Adjusted Capital Ratio #1 (Moderate Loss Scenario)

Weak   Fair   Good

JACKSON NATIONAL LIFE INSURANCE COMPANY   B   Good

Major Rating Factors: Good overall profitability (6.0 on a scale of 0 to 10) despite operating losses during the first three months of 2009. Return on equity has been fair, averaging 8.7%. Good liquidity (6.8) with sufficient resources to cover a large increase in policy surrenders. Good overall results on stability tests (5.4) good operational trends and excellent risk diversification.

Other Rating Factors: Fair quality investment portfolio (3.9). Strong capitalization (7.0) based on excellent risk adjusted capital (severe loss scenario).

Principal Business: Individual annuities (82%), group retirement contracts (10%), individual life insurance (5%), and reinsurance (2%).

Principal Investments: NonCMO investment grade bonds (48%), CMOs and structured securities (24%), mortgages in good standing (14%), noninv. grade bonds (6%), and misc. investments (9%).

Investments in Affiliates: 2%

Group Affiliation: Prudential plc

Licensed in: All states except AL, NC

Commenced Business: August 1961

Address: 5901 Executive Dr, Lansing, MI 48911

Phone: (517) 394-3400 **Domicile State:** MI **NAIC Code:** 65056

Data Date	Rating	RACR #1	RACR #2	Total Assets ($mil)	Capital ($mil)	Net Premium ($mil)	Net Income ($mil)
3-09	B	2.09	1.00	66,886.5	3,510.4	2,507.0	-248.1
3-08	B+	2.72	1.37	73,607.1	3,951.4	2,306.2	85.1
2008	B	2.38	1.16	68,327.3	3,745.7	10,596.1	-623.4
2007	B+	2.81	1.42	73,963.9	4,024.1	11,014.6	490.0
2006	B	2.63	1.32	66,835.7	3,676.9	9,332.9	412.3
2005	B-	2.43	1.22	60,742.6	3,434.0	7,432.6	565.1
2004	C+	2.20	1.11	53,721.7	3,140.7	6,534.2	616.3

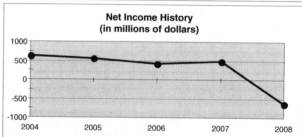

Net Income History (in millions of dollars)

JAMESTOWN LIFE INSURANCE COMPANY   B-   Good

Major Rating Factors: Good overall results on stability tests (5.3 on a scale of 0 to 10) despite fair financial strength of affiliated Genworth Financial. Other stability subfactors include good operational trends and excellent risk diversification. Good overall profitability (6.0). Excellent expense controls. Return on equity has been excellent over the last five years averaging 55.7%. Strong capitalization (9.7) based on excellent risk adjusted capital (severe loss scenario).

Other Rating Factors: High quality investment portfolio (7.1). Excellent liquidity (7.8).

Principal Business: Reinsurance (100%).

Principal Investments: NonCMO investment grade bonds (87%), CMOs and structured securities (8%), common & preferred stock (3%), noninv. grade bonds (2%), and cash (1%).

Investments in Affiliates: None

Group Affiliation: Genworth Financial

Licensed in: WA

Commenced Business: December 1982

Address: 700 Main St, Lynchburg, VA 24504

Phone: (804) 845-0911 **Domicile State:** VA **NAIC Code:** 97144

Data Date	Rating	RACR #1	RACR #2	Total Assets ($mil)	Capital ($mil)	Net Premium ($mil)	Net Income ($mil)
3-09	B-	4.43	2.81	147.6	41.7	2.7	2.3
3-08	C+	5.16	3.54	153.5	47.9	2.5	0.9
2008	B-	4.25	2.83	148.1	40.1	7.8	-3.6
2007	C+	5.06	3.52	150.0	47.0	8.1	4.4
2006	C+	13.93	7.62	244.5	141.9	-33.2	33.3
2005	C+	8.92	4.97	268.4	108.4	16.4	4.9
2004	C+	8.90	4.80	343.7	113.6	17.1	279.1

Genworth Financial Composite Group Rating: C+ Largest Group Members	Assets ($mil)	Rating
GENWORTH LIFE INS CO	34734	C+
GENWORTH LIFE ANNUITY INS CO	25964	B
GENWORTH LIFE INS CO OF NEW YORK	6999	C
GENWORTH MORTGAGE INS CORP	3023	C
GENWORTH MTG INS CORP OF NC	490	C+

JOHN ALDEN LIFE INSURANCE COMPANY   B-   Good

Major Rating Factors: Good overall results on stability tests (5.1 on a scale of 0 to 10) despite fair financial strength of affiliated Assurant Inc. Other stability subfactors include good operational trends, excellent risk adjusted capital for prior years and excellent risk diversification. Good overall capitalization (5.9) based on mixed results -- excessive policy leverage mitigated by excellent risk adjusted capital (severe loss scenario). Nevertheless, capital levels have fluctuated during prior years. Good quality investment portfolio (6.7).
Other Rating Factors: Good overall profitability (6.3). Good liquidity (6.3).
Principal Business: Group health insurance (85%), individual health insurance (12%), individual life insurance (2%), and group life insurance (1%).
Principal Investments: NonCMO investment grade bonds (52%), CMOs and structured securities (24%), common & preferred stock (10%), policy loans (5%), and misc. investments (10%).
Investments in Affiliates: None
Group Affiliation: Assurant Inc
Licensed in: All states except AL, NC
Commenced Business: January 1974
Address: 7300 Corporate Center Dr, Miami, FL 33102-0270
Phone: (305) 715-3772 **Domicile State:** WI **NAIC Code:** 65080

Data Date	Rating	RACR #1	RACR #2	Total Assets ($mil)	Capital ($mil)	Net Premium ($mil)	Net Income ($mil)
3-09	B-	1.65	1.20	481.1	98.9	122.0	3.8
3-08	B-	1.59	1.17	528.1	101.3	131.1	8.6
2008	B-	1.55	1.14	490.6	94.3	510.7	28.0
2007	B-	1.48	1.09	526.0	93.1	543.9	37.6
2006	B-	1.55	1.13	540.6	102.6	564.7	61.7
2005	C+	1.48	1.08	587.4	106.8	616.7	49.0
2004	C	1.69	1.25	667.4	150.0	737.2	47.5

Assurant Inc
Composite Group Rating: C+
Largest Group Members

Largest Group Members	Assets ($mil)	Rating
UNION SECURITY INS CO	5524	C+
AMERICAN MEMORIAL LIFE INS CO	1996	B-
AMERICAN SECURITY INS CO	1881	B
AMERICAN BANKERS INS CO OF FL	1270	B-
TIME INS CO	678	B-

JOHN HANCOCK LIFE & HEALTH INSURANCE COMPANY   B   Good

Major Rating Factors: Good quality investment portfolio (5.5 on a scale of 0 to 10) despite significant exposure to mortgages . Mortgage default rate has been low. large holdings of BBB rated bonds in addition to small junk bond holdings. Good overall profitability (6.7). Return on equity has been fair, averaging 5.1%. Fair overall results on stability tests (4.0) including weak results on operational trends.
Other Rating Factors: Strong capitalization (9.5) based on excellent risk adjusted capital (severe loss scenario). Excellent liquidity (7.5).
Principal Business: Individual life insurance (72%) and reinsurance (28%).
Principal Investments: NonCMO investment grade bonds (66%), mortgages in good standing (13%), policy loans (11%), CMOs and structured securities (6%), and misc. investments (4%).
Investments in Affiliates: None
Group Affiliation: Manulife Financial Group
Licensed in: All states except AL, ME, MD, NC
Commenced Business: October 1981
Address: 2711 Centerville Rd Ste 400, Wilmington, DE 19808
Phone: (617) 572-6000 **Domicile State:** MA **NAIC Code:** 93610

Data Date	Rating	RACR #1	RACR #2	Total Assets ($mil)	Capital ($mil)	Net Premium ($mil)	Net Income ($mil)
3-09	B	5.34	2.69	2,769.4	195.1	2.2	2.7
3-08	B	7.33	3.61	538.6	127.7	-0.7	2.7
2008	B	5.59	2.79	2,573.7	193.2	0.2	6.4
2007	B	7.19	3.55	538.9	126.3	1.2	13.2
2006	B	6.39	3.11	545.7	118.6	1.1	5.3
2005	B	3.34	1.99	546.4	115.4	0.5	-2.4
2004	B	5.98	2.82	561.6	116.0	0.2	10.6

Adverse Trends in Operations

Decrease in premium volume from 2007 to 2008 (84%)
Change in premium mix from 2006 to 2007 (12%)
Change in premium mix from 2005 to 2006 (9.9%)
Change in premium mix from 2004 to 2005 (13.1%)
Decrease in asset base during 2005 (3%)

JOHN HANCOCK LIFE INSURANCE COMPANY   B-   Good

Major Rating Factors: Good overall capitalization (5.2 on a scale of 0 to 10) based on good risk adjusted capital (moderate loss scenario). Nevertheless, capital levels have fluctuated during prior years. Good liquidity (6.7) with sufficient resources to cover a large increase in policy surrenders. Fair quality investment portfolio (3.7).
Other Rating Factors: Fair profitability (3.9) with operating losses during the first three months of 2009. Fair overall results on stability tests (3.6) including weak results on operational trends.
Principal Business: Individual annuities (26%), group retirement contracts (25%), individual health insurance (16%), individual life insurance (14%), and other lines (19%).
Principal Investments: NonCMO investment grade bonds (48%), mortgages in good standing (17%), CMOs and structured securities (14%), noninv. grade bonds (6%), and misc. investments (14%).
Investments in Affiliates: 3%
Group Affiliation: Manulife Financial Group
Licensed in: All states except AL
Commenced Business: December 1862
Address: John Hancock Place, Boston, MA 02117
Phone: (617) 572-6000 **Domicile State:** MA **NAIC Code:** 65099

Data Date	Rating	RACR #1	RACR #2	Total Assets ($mil)	Capital ($mil)	Net Premium ($mil)	Net Income ($mil)
3-09	B-	1.16	0.70	61,635.9	2,021.6	1,244.6	-260.4
3-08	A-	2.13	1.33	68,798.4	4,490.4	1,018.7	128.4
2008	B-	1.45	0.87	62,943.5	2,583.6	1,093.6	-438.2
2007	A-	2.11	1.32	69,812.5	4,407.5	4,426.1	1,123.5
2006	A-	1.83	1.16	71,776.2	3,592.3	3,357.0	523.5
2005	A-	1.71	1.12	72,433.1	3,966.3	4,072.5	654.0
2004	A-	1.85	1.12	73,282.7	4,084.5	3,999.6	481.9

Junk Bonds as a % of Capital

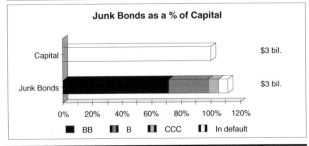

JOHN HANCOCK LIFE INSURANCE COMPANY (USA)   B   Good

Major Rating Factors: Good capitalization (5.0 on a scale of 0 to 10) based on good risk adjusted capital (moderate loss scenario). Fair quality investment portfolio (3.5). Fair overall results on stability tests (4.9) including fair risk adjusted capital in prior years.

Other Rating Factors: Weak profitability (1.8). Excellent liquidity (9.0).

Principal Business: Group retirement contracts (48%), individual annuities (36%), individual life insurance (14%), and reinsurance (2%).

Principal Investments: NonCMO investment grade bonds (65%), mortgages in good standing (10%), policy loans (9%), real estate (5%), and misc. investments (11%).

Investments in Affiliates: 2%

Group Affiliation: Manulife Financial Group

Licensed in: All states except AL, NC

Commenced Business: January 1956

Address: 38500 Woodward Ave, Bloomfield Hills, MI 48304

Phone: (416) 926-0100 **Domicile State:** MI **NAIC Code:** 65838

Data Date	Rating	RACR #1	RACR #2	Total Assets ($mil)	Capital ($mil)	Net Premium ($mil)	Net Income ($mil)
3-09	B	1.02	0.56	102,138	1,779.7	1,749.1	8.2
3-08	B+	1.02	0.57	121,385	1,477.4	3,999.4	-60.2
2008	B	1.18	0.65	103,891	1,980.6	10,536.4	-2,019.3
2007	B+	1.08	0.60	126,027	1,523.3	14,022.0	-9.8
2006	B+	1.38	0.72	108,335	1,426.5	13,031.9	161.2
2005	B+	1.11	0.57	88,364.0	945.0	10,204.0	10.8
2004	B+	1.23	0.65	73,775.9	1,164.9	9,211.6	304.1

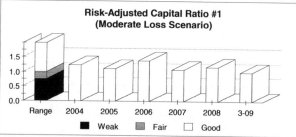

Risk-Adjusted Capital Ratio #1 (Moderate Loss Scenario)

Range 2004 2005 2006 2007 2008 3-09 — ■ Weak ▨ Fair □ Good

JOHN HANCOCK LIFE INSURANCE COMPANY OF NEW YORK *   A-   Excellent

Major Rating Factors: Good overall results on stability tests (6.0 on a scale of 0 to 10). Strengths that enhance stability include good operational trends and excellent risk diversification. Weak profitability (1.7) with operating losses during the first three months of 2009. Return on equity has been low, averaging -8.6%. Strong capitalization (10.0) based on excellent risk adjusted capital (severe loss scenario).

Other Rating Factors: High quality investment portfolio (9.1). Excellent liquidity (10.0).

Principal Business: Individual annuities (46%), group retirement contracts (37%), and individual life insurance (17%).

Principal Investments: NonCMO investment grade bonds (97%) and policy loans (4%).

Investments in Affiliates: None

Group Affiliation: Manulife Financial Group

Licensed in: NC

Commenced Business: July 1992

Address: 100 Summit Lake Dr 2nd Floor, Valhalla, NY 10595

Phone: (800) 344-1029 **Domicile State:** NY **NAIC Code:** 86375

Data Date	Rating	RACR #1	RACR #2	Total Assets ($mil)	Capital ($mil)	Net Premium ($mil)	Net Income ($mil)
3-09	A-	7.21	5.98	6,461.4	460.7	278.3	-62.0
3-08	A	3.13	2.76	7,064.6	230.0	355.3	5.2
2008	A-	3.43	2.80	6,221.3	218.3	1,397.2	-328.1
2007	A	3.03	2.62	7,320.5	223.0	1,499.7	66.4
2006	A-	2.69	2.13	6,042.2	166.3	1,294.6	63.1
2005	B+	2.07	1.61	4,594.9	100.9	1,186.6	13.2
2004	B+	1.33	1.16	3,516.8	51.0	967.5	20.6

Adverse Trends in Operations

Decrease in premium volume from 2007 to 2008 (7%)
Decrease in asset base during 2008 (15%)
Decrease in capital during 2008 (2%)
Increase in policy surrenders from 2006 to 2007 (39%)
Increase in policy surrenders from 2004 to 2005 (39%)

JOHN HANCOCK VARIABLE LIFE INSURANCE COMPANY   B   Good

Major Rating Factors: Good capitalization (5.3 on a scale of 0 to 10) based on good risk adjusted capital (moderate loss scenario). Good overall profitability (5.9). Excellent expense controls. Return on equity has been excellent over the last five years averaging 19.2%. Good liquidity (5.4) with sufficient resources to handle a spike in claims as well as a significant increase in policy surrenders.

Other Rating Factors: Fair quality investment portfolio (4.6). Fair overall results on stability tests (4.5) including fair risk adjusted capital in prior years.

Principal Business: Individual life insurance (100%).

Principal Investments: NonCMO investment grade bonds (50%), mortgages in good standing (15%), CMOs and structured securities (12%), policy loans (7%), and misc. investments (16%).

Investments in Affiliates: 3%

Group Affiliation: Manulife Financial Group

Licensed in: All states except AL, NC

Commenced Business: February 1980

Address: 197 Clarendon St, Boston, MA 02117-0717

Phone: (617) 572-6000 **Domicile State:** MA **NAIC Code:** 90204

Data Date	Rating	RACR #1	RACR #2	Total Assets ($mil)	Capital ($mil)	Net Premium ($mil)	Net Income ($mil)
3-09	B	1.19	0.71	12,033.7	552.0	126.6	17.6
3-08	B+	1.66	0.95	14,560.3	640.4	148.0	41.1
2008	B	1.18	0.71	12,432.5	544.8	581.4	43.0
2007	B+	1.60	0.92	15,151.7	609.4	663.6	168.0
2006	B+	1.67	0.96	15,051.0	676.5	852.0	117.5
2005	B+	1.43	0.93	14,100.4	752.7	894.1	165.8
2004	B+	2.17	1.28	13,399.9	810.8	1,065.2	162.2

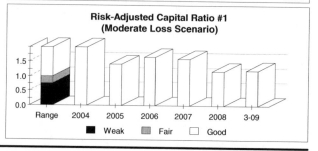

Risk-Adjusted Capital Ratio #1 (Moderate Loss Scenario)

Range 2004 2005 2006 2007 2008 3-09 — ■ Weak ▨ Fair □ Good

KANAWHA INSURANCE COMPANY   C   Fair

Major Rating Factors: Fair overall results on stability tests (3.9 on a scale of 0 to 10). Good overall capitalization (6.3) based on good risk adjusted capital (severe loss scenario). Nevertheless, capital levels have fluctuated during prior years. Good quality investment portfolio (6.9) despite mixed results such as: minimal exposure to mortgages and substantial holdings of BBB bonds but small junk bond holdings.

Other Rating Factors: Weak profitability (1.5) with operating losses during 2008. Excellent liquidity (8.0).

Principal Business: Individual health insurance (52%), group health insurance (31%), individual life insurance (10%), group life insurance (5%), and reinsurance (2%).

Principal Investments: NonCMO investment grade bonds (62%), CMOs and structured securities (23%), cash (11%), policy loans (2%), and misc. investments (3%).

Investments in Affiliates: None

Group Affiliation: Humana Inc

Licensed in: All states except AL, AZ, DE, MD, NJ, NC, VA

Commenced Business: December 1958

Address: 210 S White St, Lancaster, SC 29721

Phone: (803) 283-5300 **Domicile State:** SC **NAIC Code:** 65110

Data Date	Rating	RACR #1	RACR #2	Total Assets ($mil)	Capital ($mil)	Net Premium ($mil)	Net Income ($mil)
2008	C	1.36	0.91	823.1	59.6	147.8	-73.7
2007	C+	1.34	0.92	664.7	65.9	162.2	-30.1
2006	C+	1.82	1.23	608.8	72.3	129.4	-14.7
2005	C+	2.22	1.52	575.2	85.1	107.9	-8.9
2004	B-	2.48	1.69	539.0	83.7	102.9	-1.7

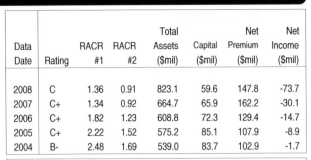

Rating Indexes

KANSAS CITY LIFE INSURANCE COMPANY   B   Good

Major Rating Factors: Good current capitalization (6.5 on a scale of 0 to 10) based on good risk adjusted capital (severe loss scenario), although results have slipped from the excellent range during the last year. Good quality investment portfolio (5.0) despite large holdings of BBB rated bonds in addition to moderate junk bond exposure. Exposure to mortgages is significant, but the mortgage default rate has been low. Good overall profitability (5.9) despite operating losses during the first three months of 2009.

Other Rating Factors: Good liquidity (5.5). Good overall results on stability tests (5.3) good operational trends, excellent risk adjusted capital for prior years and excellent risk diversification.

Principal Business: Individual life insurance (43%), individual annuities (32%), group health insurance (15%), reinsurance (5%), and group life insurance (4%).

Principal Investments: NonCMO investment grade bonds (47%), CMOs and structured securities (25%), mortgages in good standing (14%), noninv. grade bonds (4%), and misc. investments (10%).

Investments in Affiliates: 2%

Group Affiliation: Kansas City Life Group

Licensed in: All states except AL, NC, VA

Commenced Business: May 1895

Address: 3520 Broadway, Kansas City, MO 64111-2565

Phone: (816) 753-7000 **Domicile State:** MO **NAIC Code:** 65129

Data Date	Rating	RACR #1	RACR #2	Total Assets ($mil)	Capital ($mil)	Net Premium ($mil)	Net Income ($mil)
3-09	B	1.55	0.94	2,950.1	281.5	67.6	-17.7
3-08	B	2.16	1.30	3,221.1	350.4	61.9	3.1
2008	B	1.73	1.06	2,998.1	306.2	253.2	-20.1
2007	B	2.26	1.36	3,258.3	357.3	245.7	47.7
2006	B	2.13	1.31	3,314.1	371.8	238.9	49.4
2005	B	2.09	1.30	3,333.6	340.0	263.9	48.7
2004	B	1.84	1.14	3,311.0	290.3	187.2	79.4

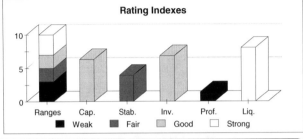

Risk-Adjusted Capital Ratio #2 (Severe Loss Scenario)

KEMPER INVESTORS LIFE INSURANCE COMPANY   C   Fair

Major Rating Factors: Fair overall capitalization (4.0 on a scale of 0 to 10) based on mixed results -- excessive policy leverage mitigated by excellent risk adjusted capital (severe loss scenario). Nevertheless, capital levels have fluctuated during prior years. Fair overall results on stability tests (3.0). Weak profitability (1.1) with operating losses during the first three months of 2009.

Other Rating Factors: High quality investment portfolio (7.8). Excellent liquidity (7.1).

Principal Business: Individual annuities (64%), reinsurance (15%), group retirement contracts (11%), individual life insurance (5%), and group life insurance (5%).

Principal Investments: NonCMO investment grade bonds (48%), CMOs and structured securities (36%), and policy loans (15%).

Investments in Affiliates: None

Group Affiliation: Zurich Financial Services Group

Licensed in: All states except AL, NC

Commenced Business: September 1947

Address: 1600 McConnor Parkway, Schaumburg, IL 60196-6801

Phone: (847) 874-7400 **Domicile State:** IL **NAIC Code:** 90557

Data Date	Rating	RACR #1	RACR #2	Total Assets ($mil)	Capital ($mil)	Net Premium ($mil)	Net Income ($mil)
3-09	C	1.97	1.29	13,503.9	163.1	-33.2	-3.6
3-08	C	1.78	1.31	16,054.7	183.0	-15.0	-4.0
2008	C	2.00	1.30	13,886.2	166.9	-108.6	-15.7
2007	C	1.81	1.30	16,700.2	186.9	3.7	-19.9
2006	C	2.04	1.48	16,589.8	222.5	-928.3	-423.0
2005	C+	3.11	1.91	17,324.2	410.8	198.4	39.9
2004	C+	3.05	1.75	16,759.0	384.5	263.8	34.1

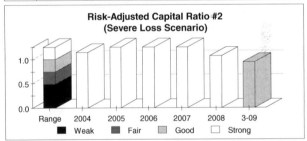

Policy Leverage

Target Leverage — 100%
Actual Leverage — 311%

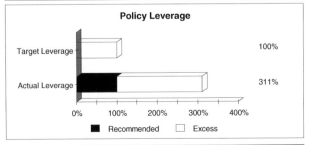

LAFAYETTE LIFE INSURANCE COMPANY — B- — Good

Major Rating Factors: Good overall capitalization (6.0 on a scale of 0 to 10) based on good risk adjusted capital (moderate loss scenario). Nevertheless, capital levels have fluctuated during prior years. Good overall profitability (5.7) despite operating losses during the first three months of 2009. Return on equity has been low, averaging 2.9%. Good liquidity (5.5).

Other Rating Factors: Good overall results on stability tests (5.1) excellent operational trends and excellent risk diversification. Fair quality investment portfolio (4.7).

Principal Business: Individual life insurance (59%), individual annuities (26%), group life insurance (8%), group health insurance (5%), and group retirement contracts (3%).

Principal Investments: NonCMO investment grade bonds (60%), CMOs and structured securities (14%), mortgages in good standing (12%), policy loans (8%), and misc. investments (6%).

Investments in Affiliates: None

Group Affiliation: Western & Southern Group

Licensed in: All states except AL, AZ, NC

Commenced Business: December 1905

Address: 1905 Teal Rd, Lafayette, IN 47905

Phone: (765) 477-7411 **Domicile State:** IN **NAIC Code:** 65242

Data Date	Rating	RACR #1	RACR #2	Total Assets ($mil)	Capital ($mil)	Net Premium ($mil)	Net Income ($mil)
3-09	B-	1.69	0.86	2,043.8	101.0	88.3	-0.1
3-08	B	1.92	1.01	1,983.1	121.1	86.9	1.5
2008	B-	1.73	0.89	2,017.2	102.9	353.5	-9.6
2007	B	1.91	1.01	1,937.3	118.2	311.9	-0.6
2006	B	2.09	1.10	1,807.0	117.4	268.7	4.7
2005	B	2.06	1.09	1,762.6	114.4	299.4	3.4
2004	B	2.02	1.07	1,672.7	110.2	272.1	1.3

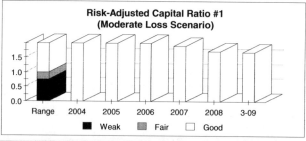

Risk-Adjusted Capital Ratio #1 (Moderate Loss Scenario)

LIBERTY BANKERS LIFE INSURANCE COMPANY — C- — Fair

Major Rating Factors: Poor current capitalization (2.6 on a scale of 0 to 10) based on weak risk adjusted capital (moderate loss scenario), although results have slipped from the fair range during the last year. Low quality investment portfolio (2.1) containing substantial holdings of BBB bonds in addition to moderate junk bond exposure. Exposure to mortgages is significant, but the mortgage default rate has been low. Weak overall results on stability tests (2.6).

Other Rating Factors: Excellent profitability (8.5) with operating gains in each of the last five years. Excellent liquidity (7.7).

Principal Business: Individual annuities (96%) and individual life insurance (4%).

Principal Investments: NonCMO investment grade bonds (26%), CMOs and structured securities (23%), mortgages in good standing (16%), common & preferred stock (12%), and misc. investments (19%).

Investments in Affiliates: 4%

Group Affiliation: Heritage Guaranty Group

Licensed in: AR, CA, CO, CT, FL, GA, HI, IL, IN, IA, KS, KY, LA, ME, MA, MN, MO, MT, NE, NV, NH, NY, ND, OH, OK, OR, PA, RI, SD, TN, TX, UT, VT, WA, WV, WI, WY

Commenced Business: February 1958

Address: 1800 Valley View Lane Ste 300, Dallas, TX 75234

Phone: (800) 745-4927 **Domicile State:** OK **NAIC Code:** 68543

Data Date	Rating	RACR #1	RACR #2	Total Assets ($mil)	Capital ($mil)	Net Premium ($mil)	Net Income ($mil)
3-09	C-	0.69	0.47	877.2	58.6	105.1	0.8
3-08	C	1.25	0.77	672.9	49.1	50.8	0.3
2008	C	0.78	0.53	807.1	63.2	185.7	2.0
2007	C	1.35	0.84	620.2	53.1	167.9	8.7
2006	D+	1.08	0.60	419.5	31.5	135.2	6.8
2005	D	0.99	0.62	308.6	26.6	72.0	0.6
2004	D	0.83	0.56	239.7	14.8	-16.3	6.4

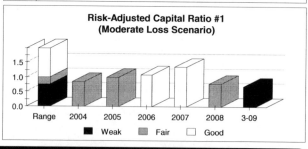

Risk-Adjusted Capital Ratio #1 (Moderate Loss Scenario)

LIBERTY LIFE ASSURANCE COMPANY OF BOSTON — B- — Good

Major Rating Factors: Good overall results on stability tests (5.1 on a scale of 0 to 10) despite fair financial strength of affiliated Liberty Mutual Group. Other stability subfactors include good operational trends and excellent risk diversification. Good current capitalization (6.2) based on good risk adjusted capital (severe loss scenario), although results have slipped from the excellent range over the last two years. Good overall profitability (5.7) despite operating losses during the first three months of 2009.

Other Rating Factors: Fair quality investment portfolio (4.8). Excellent liquidity (7.4).

Principal Business: Group health insurance (36%), individual life insurance (25%), individual annuities (23%), and group life insurance (16%).

Principal Investments: NonCMO investment grade bonds (62%), CMOs and structured securities (25%), noninv. grade bonds (4%), mortgages in good standing (2%), and misc. investments (6%).

Investments in Affiliates: None

Group Affiliation: Liberty Mutual Group

Licensed in: All states except AL

Commenced Business: January 1964

Address: 175 Berkeley St, Boston, MA 02117

Phone: (617) 357-9500 **Domicile State:** MA **NAIC Code:** 65315

Data Date	Rating	RACR #1	RACR #2	Total Assets ($mil)	Capital ($mil)	Net Premium ($mil)	Net Income ($mil)
3-09	B-	1.67	0.90	11,641.8	439.7	261.9	-15.9
3-08	B-	2.10	1.13	11,444.9	490.0	240.7	8.3
2008	B-	1.80	0.98	11,605.1	460.4	1,104.0	-27.6
2007	B-	2.08	1.12	11,185.4	482.7	941.3	35.5
2006	B-	2.10	1.14	10,457.2	449.3	1,235.6	12.9
2005	C+	2.02	1.08	9,026.1	431.7	805.4	38.5
2004	C+	1.72	0.87	8,228.4	302.6	439.9	-20.3

Liberty Mutual Group
Composite Group Rating: C+

Largest Group Members	Assets ($mil)	Rating
LIBERTY MUTUAL INS CO	32550	B-
LIBERTY LIFE ASR CO OF BOSTON	11605	B-
PEERLESS INS CO	7069	C+
OHIO CASUALTY INS CO	4869	C+
SAFECO INS CO OF AMERICA	3952	B-

LIBERTY LIFE INSURANCE COMPANY   C   Fair

Major Rating Factors: Fair overall results on stability tests (4.1 on a scale of 0 to 10) including negative cash flow from operations for 2008. Good overall capitalization (5.7) based on good risk adjusted capital (moderate loss scenario). However, capital levels have fluctuated somewhat during past years. Good quality investment portfolio (5.6).

Other Rating Factors: Good overall profitability (6.3) despite operating losses during the first three months of 2009. Good liquidity (5.0).

Principal Business: Individual life insurance (47%), individual annuities (33%), group health insurance (9%), individual health insurance (5%), and other lines (6%).

Principal Investments: CMOs and structured securities (40%), nonCMO investment grade bonds (37%), mortgages in good standing (16%), policy loans (3%), and misc. investments (3%).

Investments in Affiliates: None
Group Affiliation: RBC Holdings (USA) Group
Licensed in: All states except AL, NC
Commenced Business: July 1909
Address: BMA Tower Penn Valley Park, Kansas City, MO 64108
Phone: (816) 753-8000 **Domicile State:** SC **NAIC Code:** 61492

Data Date	Rating	RACR #1	RACR #2	Total Assets ($mil)	Capital ($mil)	Net Premium ($mil)	Net Income ($mil)
3-09	C	1.48	0.82	3,684.7	219.4	187.0	-6.5
3-08	C	1.71	0.96	3,702.3	257.4	73.9	0.2
2008	C	1.61	0.90	3,597.2	234.3	294.9	-19.1
2007	C	1.79	1.01	3,722.4	261.5	318.9	39.3
2006	C	1.78	1.01	3,770.9	268.5	461.7	20.0
2005	C	2.12	1.14	2,331.9	153.1	386.7	15.3
2004	C-	2.25	1.22	2,152.2	146.4	367.8	14.3

Rating Indexes

LIBERTY NATIONAL LIFE INSURANCE COMPANY   B   Good

Major Rating Factors: Good overall capitalization (5.2 on a scale of 0 to 10) based on good risk adjusted capital (severe loss scenario). However, capital levels have fluctuated somewhat during past years. Good quality investment portfolio (5.5) despite mixed results such as: large holdings of BBB rated bonds but moderate junk bond exposure. Good liquidity (6.4).

Other Rating Factors: Good overall results on stability tests (5.2) excellent operational trends and excellent risk diversification. Excellent profitability (8.2) with operating gains in each of the last five years.

Principal Business: Individual life insurance (71%), individual health insurance (22%), group life insurance (3%), reinsurance (3%), and individual annuities (1%).

Principal Investments: NonCMO investment grade bonds (68%), common & preferred stock (17%), policy loans (4%), noninv. grade bonds (4%), and CMOs and structured securities (3%).

Investments in Affiliates: 11%
Group Affiliation: Torchmark Corp
Licensed in: All states except AL, NC
Commenced Business: July 1929
Address: 2001 Third Ave S, Birmingham, AL 35233
Phone: (205) 325-4918 **Domicile State:** NE **NAIC Code:** 65331

Data Date	Rating	RACR #1	RACR #2	Total Assets ($mil)	Capital ($mil)	Net Premium ($mil)	Net Income ($mil)
3-09	B	1.03	0.77	5,116.8	597.6	114.5	19.2
3-08	B	1.09	0.84	5,116.7	571.0	133.3	66.0
2008	B	1.18	0.92	5,149.1	674.1	476.5	155.3
2007	B+	1.17	0.90	4,981.0	607.0	538.9	217.4
2006	B+	1.31	1.02	4,926.7	677.8	540.0	225.0
2005	B+	1.34	0.98	4,565.7	516.1	538.3	183.6
2004	B+	1.48	1.03	4,340.4	443.4	539.4	148.5

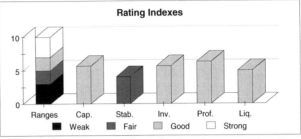

Risk-Adjusted Capital Ratio #2
(Severe Loss Scenario)

LIFE INSURANCE COMPANY OF NORTH AMERICA   B-   Good

Major Rating Factors: Good overall profitability (5.8 on a scale of 0 to 10). Return on equity has been excellent over the last five years averaging 18.0%. Good liquidity (6.1) with sufficient resources to handle a spike in claims. Fair overall results on stability tests (4.5) including fair financial strength of affiliated CIGNA Group.

Other Rating Factors: Fair quality investment portfolio (4.4). Strong capitalization (7.4) based on excellent risk adjusted capital (severe loss scenario).

Principal Business: Group health insurance (51%), group life insurance (38%), and reinsurance (10%).

Principal Investments: Common & preferred stock (38%), nonCMO investment grade bonds (30%), mortgages in good standing (22%), noninv. grade bonds (5%), and CMOs and structured securities (2%).

Investments in Affiliates: 36%
Group Affiliation: CIGNA Group
Licensed in: All states except AL, NC
Commenced Business: September 1957
Address: 1601 Chestnut ST,2 Liberty Pl, Philadelphia, PA 19192-2235
Phone: (860) 726-7234 **Domicile State:** PA **NAIC Code:** 65498

Data Date	Rating	RACR #1	RACR #2	Total Assets ($mil)	Capital ($mil)	Net Premium ($mil)	Net Income ($mil)
3-09	B-	1.97	1.29	5,275.1	621.7	591.9	7.4
3-08	C-	2.21	1.45	5,711.5	621.5	543.4	25.5
2008	C+	1.98	1.30	5,464.3	628.6	2,255.5	125.0
2007	C-	2.18	1.43	5,880.6	641.3	2,051.4	173.0
2006	D+	2.29	1.48	5,776.6	615.5	1,794.9	94.9
2005	D	2.62	1.70	5,537.9	682.4	1,750.8	123.4
2004	D	2.71	1.75	5,321.9	660.3	1,682.0	96.3

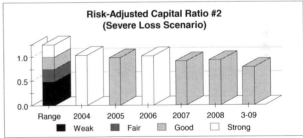

CIGNA Group Composite Group Rating: C+ Largest Group Members	Assets ($mil)	Rating
CONNECTICUT GENERAL LIFE INS CO	17733	C+
LIFE INS CO OF NORTH AMERICA	5464	C+
CIGNA LIFE INS CO OF NEW YORK	401	B-
CIGNA HEALTHCARE OF CALIFORNIA INC	156	C
CIGNA HEALTHCARE OF ARIZONA INC	126	B

LIFE INSURANCE COMPANY OF THE SOUTHWEST   B   Good

Major Rating Factors: Good capitalization (6.0 on a scale of 0 to 10) based on good risk adjusted capital (moderate loss scenario). Moreover, capital levels have been consistent over the last five years. Fair quality investment portfolio (4.2) with large holdings of BBB rated bonds in addition to junk bond exposure equal to 68% of capital. Exposure to mortgages is significant, but the mortgage default rate has been low. Fair overall results on stability tests (4.7).

Other Rating Factors: Weak liquidity (2.7). Excellent profitability (7.9).

Principal Business: Individual annuities (77%), individual life insurance (14%), and group retirement contracts (8%).

Principal Investments: NonCMO investment grade bonds (50%), CMOs and structured securities (27%), mortgages in good standing (14%), noninv. grade bonds (5%), and misc. investments (5%).

Investments in Affiliates: None

Group Affiliation: National Life Group

Licensed in: All states except AL, NC

Commenced Business: January 1956

Address: 1300 W Mockingbird Lane, Dallas, TX 75247

Phone: (800) 579-2878 **Domicile State:** TX **NAIC Code:** 65528

Data Date	Rating	RACR #1	RACR #2	Total Assets ($mil)	Capital ($mil)	Net Premium ($mil)	Net Income ($mil)
3-09	B	1.64	0.81	6,751.8	423.1	314.8	7.2
3-08	B	1.71	0.86	5,907.1	354.0	237.8	-0.5
2008	B	1.69	0.85	6,525.4	420.1	1,229.8	-37.0
2007	B	1.72	0.87	5,849.9	364.6	871.6	43.5
2006	B-	1.54	0.79	5,352.8	292.9	823.6	46.2
2005	B-	1.54	0.79	4,658.1	240.6	800.7	35.1
2004	B-	1.45	0.77	4,043.2	219.3	684.2	35.5

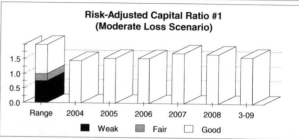

Risk-Adjusted Capital Ratio #1 (Moderate Loss Scenario)

■ Weak   ▨ Fair   □ Good

LIFECARE ASSURANCE COMPANY   C   Fair

Major Rating Factors: Fair overall results on stability tests (3.7 on a scale of 0 to 10). Good current capitalization (6.9) based on good risk adjusted capital (severe loss scenario), although results have slipped from the excellent range over the last two years. Good quality investment portfolio (6.3) despite mixed results such as: no exposure to mortgages and substantial holdings of BBB bonds but small junk bond holdings.

Other Rating Factors: Excellent profitability (9.5) with operating gains in each of the last five years. Excellent liquidity (9.3).

Principal Business: Reinsurance (100%).

Principal Investments: NonCMO investment grade bonds (60%), CMOs and structured securities (34%), common & preferred stock (5%), and noninv. grade bonds (1%).

Investments in Affiliates: None

Group Affiliation: 21st Century Life & Health Co Inc

Licensed in: AR, IA, MO, ND

Commenced Business: July 1980

Address: 2929 N 44th St Suite 1500, Phoenix, AZ 91367

Phone: (818) 887-4436 **Domicile State:** AZ **NAIC Code:** 91898

Data Date	Rating	RACR #1	RACR #2	Total Assets ($mil)	Capital ($mil)	Net Premium ($mil)	Net Income ($mil)
3-09	C	1.56	0.99	846.2	62.2	55.1	6.0
3-08	C-	1.53	1.06	682.8	52.2	51.2	4.1
2008	C-	1.46	0.97	800.0	58.0	209.3	8.7
2007	D+	1.46	1.02	637.0	48.2	189.9	10.9
2006	D+	1.48	1.06	484.6	42.8	173.0	8.5
2005	D+	1.46	1.05	352.1	36.0	146.8	5.8
2004	D+	1.48	1.12	239.1	30.1	122.7	8.6

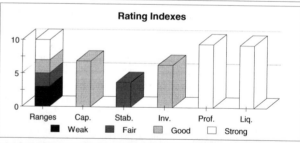

Rating Indexes

■ Weak   ▨ Fair   ▤ Good   □ Strong

LIFEWISE ASSURANCE COMPANY *   A   Excellent

Major Rating Factors: Good overall results on stability tests (6.9 on a scale of 0 to 10). Strengths that enhance stability include excellent operational trends and good risk diversification. Strong capitalization (8.1) based on excellent risk adjusted capital (severe loss scenario). Furthermore, this high level of risk adjusted capital has been consistently maintained over the last five years. High quality investment portfolio (7.4).

Other Rating Factors: Excellent profitability (8.4) with operating gains in each of the last five years. Excellent liquidity (7.1).

Principal Business: Group health insurance (61%) and group life insurance (39%).

Principal Investments: CMOs and structured securities (49%), nonCMO investment grade bonds (49%), and noninv. grade bonds (3%).

Investments in Affiliates: None

Group Affiliation: PREMERA

Licensed in: AZ, AR, CO, IL, NE, NY, OH, PA, VT, WV, PR

Commenced Business: November 1981

Address: 7007 220th SW, Mountlake Terrace, WA 98043

Phone: (206) 670-4584 **Domicile State:** WA **NAIC Code:** 94188

Data Date	Rating	RACR #1	RACR #2	Total Assets ($mil)	Capital ($mil)	Net Premium ($mil)	Net Income ($mil)
3-09	A	2.43	1.72	70.2	40.4	12.3	-0.2
3-08	A	3.70	2.72	65.8	40.3	11.2	0.7
2008	A	2.51	1.84	70.4	41.2	47.1	1.5
2007	A	3.63	2.67	67.1	39.4	39.2	5.6
2006	B+	3.52	2.58	62.8	34.4	34.4	3.6
2005	B	2.94	2.17	57.2	30.6	31.8	2.5
2004	B	2.98	2.21	62.5	31.0	32.0	2.7

Adverse Trends in Operations

Decrease in capital during 2005 (2%)
Decrease in asset base during 2005 (8%)

LINCOLN BENEFIT LIFE COMPANY *   **B+**   **Good**

Major Rating Factors: Good overall results on stability tests (5.3 on a scale of 0 to 10). Strengths include good financial support from affiliation with Allstate Group and excellent risk diversification. Weak profitability (2.7) with investment income below regulatory standards in relation to interest assumptions of reserves. Strong capitalization (7.8) based on excellent risk adjusted capital (severe loss scenario).

Other Rating Factors: High quality investment portfolio (8.2). Excellent liquidity (10.0).

Principal Business: Individual annuities (46%), individual life insurance (45%), individual health insurance (4%), group retirement contracts (3%), and group life insurance (2%).

Principal Investments: NonCMO investment grade bonds (87%), CMOs and structured securities (29%), and common & preferred stock (1%).

Investments in Affiliates: 1%

Group Affiliation: Allstate Group

Licensed in: All states except AL, NC

Commenced Business: October 1938

Address: 206 S 13th St, Suite 200, Lincoln, NE 68508

Phone: (800) 525-9287 **Domicile State:** NE **NAIC Code:** 65595

Data Date	Rating	RACR #1	RACR #2	Total Assets ($mil)	Capital ($mil)	Net Premium ($mil)	Net Income ($mil)
3-09	B+	3.13	1.56	2,007.2	295.5	0.0	1.9
3-08	B+	2.91	1.46	3,120.9	284.2	0.0	2.2
2008	B+	3.06	1.52	2,184.8	278.8	0.0	7.8
2007	B+	3.02	1.51	3,442.5	282.9	0.0	9.1
2006	B+	3.12	1.56	3,448.6	274.4	0.0	9.1
2005	B+	3.35	1.66	3,075.2	267.5	0.0	8.8
2004	B+	3.65	1.81	2,683.3	255.5	0.0	7.4

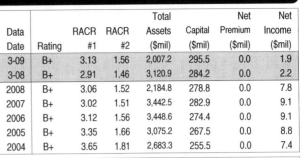

Rating Indexes

LINCOLN HERITAGE LIFE INSURANCE COMPANY *   **B+**   **Good**

Major Rating Factors: Good quality investment portfolio (5.9 on a scale of 0 to 10) despite mixed results such as: substantial holdings of BBB bonds but moderate junk bond exposure. Good overall profitability (5.7). Return on equity has been fair, averaging 7.8%. Good liquidity (6.1) with sufficient resources to handle a spike in claims as well as a significant increase in policy surrenders.

Other Rating Factors: Good overall results on stability tests (6.8) excellent operational trends and good risk diversification. Strong capitalization (7.7) based on excellent risk adjusted capital (severe loss scenario).

Principal Business: Individual life insurance (67%), individual health insurance (21%), group life insurance (8%), reinsurance (3%), and group retirement contracts (1%).

Principal Investments: CMOs and structured securities (42%), nonCMO investment grade bonds (37%), policy loans (5%), noninv. grade bonds (4%), and misc. investments (12%).

Investments in Affiliates: None

Group Affiliation: Londen Ins Group

Licensed in: All states except AL, NC

Commenced Business: October 1963

Address: Government Ctr 200 Pleasant St, Malden, MA 02148

Phone: (602) 957-1650 **Domicile State:** IL **NAIC Code:** 65927

Data Date	Rating	RACR #1	RACR #2	Total Assets ($mil)	Capital ($mil)	Net Premium ($mil)	Net Income ($mil)
3-09	B+	2.79	1.48	629.7	85.9	48.7	1.6
3-08	B+	3.54	1.94	594.1	89.6	46.8	0.9
2008	B+	2.98	1.65	621.7	86.1	200.3	2.3
2007	B+	3.60	1.99	587.1	88.9	181.3	4.2
2006	B	3.98	2.18	549.3	89.3	155.4	10.4
2005	B-	3.85	2.11	514.3	79.4	141.8	9.7
2004	C+	3.63	1.88	485.8	72.6	112.0	6.4

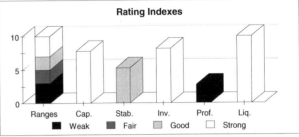

Rating Indexes

LINCOLN LIFE & ANNUITY COMPANY OF NEW YORK   **B-**   **Good**

Major Rating Factors: Good overall results on stability tests (5.2 on a scale of 0 to 10). Stability strengths include good operational trends, good risk adjusted capital for prior years and excellent risk diversification. Good quality investment portfolio (6.3) despite mixed results such as: large holdings of BBB rated bonds but moderate junk bond exposure. Good liquidity (5.9).

Other Rating Factors: Weak profitability (2.0) with operating losses during the first three months of 2009. Strong capitalization (8.0) based on excellent risk adjusted capital (severe loss scenario).

Principal Business: Individual annuities (43%), individual life insurance (23%), reinsurance (22%), group retirement contracts (9%), and other lines (4%).

Principal Investments: NonCMO investment grade bonds (61%), CMOs and structured securities (23%), policy loans (6%), mortgages in good standing (5%), and misc. investments (5%).

Investments in Affiliates: None

Group Affiliation: Lincoln National Corp

Licensed in: All states except AL

Commenced Business: December 1897

Address: 100 Madison St Suite 1860, Syracuse, NY 13202-2802

Phone: (336) 691-3000 **Domicile State:** NY **NAIC Code:** 62057

Data Date	Rating	RACR #1	RACR #2	Total Assets ($mil)	Capital ($mil)	Net Premium ($mil)	Net Income ($mil)
3-09	B-	3.34	1.67	8,426.1	755.2	222.0	-6.7
3-08	B-	3.95	2.02	8,946.6	839.6	256.3	10.1
2008	B-	3.62	1.86	8,440.9	795.2	928.6	-95.0
2007	B-	3.93	2.02	9,000.6	832.8	1,003.4	-187.8
2006	B+	1.56	0.84	1,416.1	68.8	211.8	-26.4
2005	B+	2.21	1.16	1,389.1	100.6	128.4	-1.3
2004	B+	2.30	1.20	1,431.7	107.8	150.6	-4.7

Adverse Trends in Operations

Decrease in asset base during 2008 (6%)
Increase in policy surrenders from 2006 to 2007 (178%)
Decrease in capital during 2006 (32%)
Increase in policy surrenders from 2004 to 2005 (141%)
Decrease in premium volume from 2004 to 2005 (15%)

LINCOLN NATIONAL LIFE INSURANCE COMPANY

B-   Good

Major Rating Factors: Good overall capitalization (5.4 on a scale of 0 to 10) based on good risk adjusted capital (moderate loss scenario). However, capital levels have fluctuated somewhat during past years. Good liquidity (6.6) with sufficient resources to cover a large increase in policy surrenders. Fair quality investment portfolio (4.4).

Other Rating Factors: Fair overall results on stability tests (4.7). Excellent profitability (7.1) despite operating losses during the first three months of 2009.

Principal Business: Individual annuities (55%), individual life insurance (19%), group retirement contracts (12%), reinsurance (7%), and other lines (7%).

Principal Investments: NonCMO investment grade bonds (54%), CMOs and structured securities (19%), mortgages in good standing (11%), noninv. grade bonds (5%), and misc. investments (11%).

Investments in Affiliates: 2%

Group Affiliation: Lincoln National Corp

Licensed in: All states except AL, NC

Commenced Business: September 1905

Address: 1300 S Clinton St, Fort Wayne, IN 46802

Phone: (260) 455-2000 **Domicile State:** IN **NAIC Code:** 65676

Data Date	Rating	RACR #1	RACR #2	Total Assets ($mil)	Capital ($mil)	Net Premium ($mil)	Net Income ($mil)
3-09	B-	1.29	0.79	117,179	4,566.3	3,060.0	-41.8
3-08	B-	1.45	0.93	139,496	4,749.3	5,101.8	107.1
2008	B-	1.31	0.82	119,850	4,585.4	18,432.1	-144.8
2007	B-	1.50	0.96	144,610	4,957.9	20,339.4	1,204.8
2006	B-	1.32	0.81	106,799	3,035.3	13,867.9	224.1
2005	B-	1.42	0.86	95,380.5	3,214.7	11,708.8	494.3
2004	B-	1.32	0.81	87,081.1	2,961.2	11,328.9	242.1

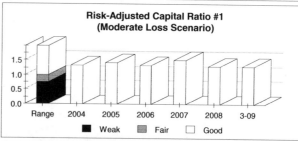

Risk-Adjusted Capital Ratio #1
(Moderate Loss Scenario)

LONDON LIFE REINSURANCE COMPANY

B   Good

Major Rating Factors: Good overall results on stability tests (5.0 on a scale of 0 to 10). Stability strengths include good operational trends and excellent risk diversification. Good overall profitability (6.3) despite operating losses during the first three months of 2009. Return on equity has been low, averaging 3.8%. Strong capitalization (7.5) based on excellent risk adjusted capital (severe loss scenario).

Other Rating Factors: High quality investment portfolio (7.7). Excellent liquidity (9.2).

Principal Business: Reinsurance (97%) and group health insurance (3%).

Principal Investments: NonCMO investment grade bonds (79%), CMOs and structured securities (15%), cash (5%), and noninv. grade bonds (1%).

Investments in Affiliates: None

Group Affiliation: Great West Life Asr

Licensed in: All states except AL, MD, NC, VA, WA

Commenced Business: December 1969

Address: 1787 Sentry Parkway, Ste 420, Blue Bell, PA 1942-22

Phone: (215) 542-7200 **Domicile State:** PA **NAIC Code:** 76694

Data Date	Rating	RACR #1	RACR #2	Total Assets ($mil)	Capital ($mil)	Net Premium ($mil)	Net Income ($mil)
3-09	B	2.51	1.34	737.6	68.4	9.1	-1.0
3-08	B+	2.61	1.39	1,245.9	70.5	12.3	0.8
2008	B	2.54	1.37	713.2	70.4	37.8	3.4
2007	B+	2.87	1.52	1,502.5	75.0	20.2	3.5
2006	B+	2.43	1.32	1,558.7	71.4	30.9	1.7
2005	B+	2.75	1.52	1,496.1	69.6	42.3	2.9
2004	B+	2.73	1.55	849.8	68.0	55.2	4.0

Adverse Trends in Operations

Decrease in asset base during 2008 (53%)
Decrease in asset base during 2007 (4%)
Decrease in premium volume from 2006 to 2007 (35%)
Decrease in premium volume from 2005 to 2006 (27%)
Decrease in premium volume from 2004 to 2005 (23%)

LOYAL AMERICAN LIFE INSURANCE COMPANY

B-   Good

Major Rating Factors: Good capitalization (5.1 on a scale of 0 to 10) based on good risk adjusted capital (moderate loss scenario). Good overall profitability (6.3) despite operating losses during the first three months of 2009. Return on equity has been good over the last five years, averaging 10.1%. Good liquidity (6.8) with sufficient resources to handle a spike in claims as well as a significant increase in policy surrenders.

Other Rating Factors: Fair overall results on stability tests (4.9) including fair financial strength of affiliated American Financial Corp and fair risk adjusted capital in prior years. Fair quality investment portfolio (3.6).

Principal Business: Individual annuities (70%), individual health insurance (22%), individual life insurance (7%), and group health insurance (1%).

Principal Investments: NonCMO investment grade bonds (56%), CMOs and structured securities (33%), policy loans (4%), common & preferred stock (3%), and noninv. grade bonds (3%).

Investments in Affiliates: 3%

Group Affiliation: American Financial Corp

Licensed in: All states except AL, NC

Commenced Business: July 1955

Address: 525 Vine Street,20th Floor, Cincinnati, OH 45202

Phone: (800) 633-6752 **Domicile State:** OH **NAIC Code:** 65722

Data Date	Rating	RACR #1	RACR #2	Total Assets ($mil)	Capital ($mil)	Net Premium ($mil)	Net Income ($mil)
3-09	B-	1.04	0.64	484.3	36.5	10.4	-0.2
3-08	B-	1.22	0.82	436.2	38.7	11.0	-1.8
2008	B-	1.13	0.73	483.9	37.7	107.2	-4.7
2007	B-	1.29	0.85	439.0	41.8	59.3	4.9
2006	C+	1.56	1.04	434.9	45.4	32.6	4.9
2005	C	1.49	0.98	447.8	43.4	38.3	4.3
2004	C	5.75	3.09	501.8	94.1	48.1	14.3

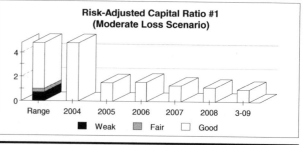

Risk-Adjusted Capital Ratio #1
(Moderate Loss Scenario)

M LIFE INSURANCE COMPANY

B- **Good**

Major Rating Factors: Good quality investment portfolio (6.8 on a scale of 0 to 10) with no exposure to mortgages and minimal holdings in junk bonds. Good overall results on stability tests (5.1). Stability strengths include good operational trends and excellent risk diversification. Fair profitability (4.9).

Other Rating Factors: Strong capitalization (9.5) based on excellent risk adjusted capital (severe loss scenario). Excellent liquidity (8.4).

Principal Business: Reinsurance (100%).

Principal Investments: NonCMO investment grade bonds (47%), CMOs and structured securities (39%), common & preferred stock (11%), noninv. grade bonds (1%), and cash (1%).

Investments in Affiliates: 11%

Group Affiliation: M Financial Holdings Inc

Licensed in: CT

Commenced Business: December 1981

Address: 1290 Broaday, Denver, CO 80203-5699

Phone: (503) 232-6960 **Domicile State:** CO **NAIC Code:** 93580

Data Date	Rating	RACR #1	RACR #2	Total Assets ($mil)	Capital ($mil)	Net Premium ($mil)	Net Income ($mil)
3-09	B-	3.48	2.69	169.1	100.5	92.9	9.6
3-08	B-	6.68	5.47	373.5	295.4	69.0	135.0
2008	B-	3.09	2.49	229.0	87.2	387.8	122.7
2007	B-	2.27	1.86	222.5	98.1	426.8	11.3
2006	B-	3.37	2.68	196.8	115.9	348.3	29.3
2005	C	2.92	2.21	193.2	98.3	369.5	-21.8
2004	C-	2.38	1.75	185.3	83.5	382.3	8.5

Adverse Trends in Operations

Decrease in capital during 2008 (11%)
Decrease in capital during 2007 (15%)
Increase in policy surrenders from 2006 to 2007 (61%)
Decrease in premium volume from 2004 to 2005 (3%)
Increase in policy surrenders from 2004 to 2005 (63%)

MADISON NATIONAL LIFE INSURANCE COMPANY INC

C+ **Fair**

Major Rating Factors: Fair capitalization (4.6 on a scale of 0 to 10) based on fair risk adjusted capital (moderate loss scenario). Fair overall results on stability tests (4.6) including fair risk adjusted capital in prior years. Good overall profitability (6.0). Return on equity has been low, averaging 4.9%.

Other Rating Factors: Good liquidity (5.2). High quality investment portfolio (7.0).

Principal Business: Group health insurance (65%), reinsurance (11%), group life insurance (7%), individual life insurance (6%), and other lines (11%).

Principal Investments: NonCMO investment grade bonds (60%), common & preferred stock (26%), CMOs and structured securities (5%), policy loans (3%), and noninv. grade bonds (1%).

Investments in Affiliates: 21%

Group Affiliation: Geneve Holdings Inc

Licensed in: All states except AL, NC

Commenced Business: March 1962

Address: 6120 University Ave, Middleton, WI 53562

Phone: (608) 238-2691 **Domicile State:** WI **NAIC Code:** 65781

Data Date	Rating	RACR #1	RACR #2	Total Assets ($mil)	Capital ($mil)	Net Premium ($mil)	Net Income ($mil)
3-09	C+	0.79	0.70	800.2	145.0	30.9	7.7
3-08	C+	0.80	0.73	746.2	142.2	31.7	4.9
2008	C+	0.76	0.69	799.1	138.2	126.9	-4.8
2007	C+	0.77	0.69	757.9	136.6	134.8	7.4
2006	B	1.97	1.53	755.1	126.4	115.0	7.8
2005	B-	0.88	0.77	759.4	129.3	97.7	-4.2
2004	B-	1.01	0.91	601.4	135.7	77.1	4.9

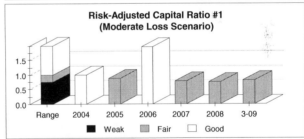

Risk-Adjusted Capital Ratio #1
(Moderate Loss Scenario)

■ Weak ▨ Fair ☐ Good

MANHATTAN LIFE INSURANCE COMPANY

C+ **Fair**

Major Rating Factors: Fair overall results on stability tests (4.6 on a scale of 0 to 10) including fair financial strength of affiliated Central United Life Group and negative cash flow from operations for 2008. Fair profitability (4.7). Return on equity has been low, averaging 4.9%. Good liquidity (6.5).

Other Rating Factors: Strong capitalization (7.3) based on excellent risk adjusted capital (severe loss scenario). High quality investment portfolio (8.4).

Principal Business: Individual life insurance (91%), reinsurance (8%), and individual annuities (1%).

Principal Investments: NonCMO investment grade bonds (70%), mortgages in good standing (11%), policy loans (11%), common & preferred stock (7%), and cash (1%).

Investments in Affiliates: 7%

Group Affiliation: Central United Life Group

Licensed in: All states except AL

Commenced Business: August 1850

Address: 111 W 57th St, New York, NY 10019

Phone: (212) 484-9300 **Domicile State:** NY **NAIC Code:** 65870

Data Date	Rating	RACR #1	RACR #2	Total Assets ($mil)	Capital ($mil)	Net Premium ($mil)	Net Income ($mil)
3-09	C+	1.41	1.17	350.6	33.3	3.7	1.4
3-08	C+	1.65	1.35	363.2	36.8	3.8	1.2
2008	C+	1.40	1.17	354.2	32.0	15.0	-1.0
2007	C+	1.64	1.35	363.1	35.7	16.8	0.5
2006	C+	1.91	1.52	362.5	34.8	16.3	0.0
2005	C+	5.18	3.31	400.5	43.6	17.7	5.5
2004	C	4.72	2.75	350.4	40.0	20.1	4.7

Central United Life Group Composite Group Rating: C Largest Group Members	Assets ($mil)	Rating
MANHATTAN LIFE INS CO	354	C+
CENTRAL UNITED LIFE INS CO	321	D+
FAMILY LIFE INS CO	126	C
INVESTORS CONSOLIDATED INS CO INC	16	C

MASSACHUSETTS MUTUAL LIFE INSURANCE COMPANY *   A   Excellent

Major Rating Factors: Good quality investment portfolio (5.7 on a scale of 0 to 10) despite substantial holdings of BBB bonds in addition to moderate junk bond exposure. Exposure to mortgages is significant, but the mortgage default rate has been low. Good overall results on stability tests (6.1). Strengths that enhance stability include good operational trends and excellent risk diversification. Strong capitalization (7.7) based on excellent risk adjusted capital (severe loss scenario).

Other Rating Factors: Excellent profitability (7.7) despite operating losses during the first three months of 2009. Excellent liquidity (8.2).

Principal Business: Group retirement contracts (44%), individual life insurance (29%), individual annuities (19%), individual health insurance (4%), and other lines (3%).

Principal Investments: NonCMO investment grade bonds (38%), CMOs and structured securities (16%), mortgages in good standing (15%), policy loans (11%), and misc. investments (20%).

Investments in Affiliates: 10%

Group Affiliation: Massachusetts Mutual Group

Licensed in: All states except AL

Commenced Business: August 1851

Address: 1295 State St, Springfield, MA 01111

Phone: (413) 788-8411 **Domicile State:** MA **NAIC Code:** 65935

Data Date	Rating	RACR #1	RACR #2	Total Assets ($mil)	Capital ($mil)	Net Premium ($mil)	Net Income ($mil)
3-09	A	2.65	1.45	112,015	8,239.8	3,019.9	-155.2
3-08	A	2.82	1.60	119,963	8,442.5	3,243.0	44.0
2008	A	2.84	1.60	114,294	8,462.9	13,234.8	-993.5
2007	A	2.84	1.61	119,086	8,008.1	12,834.0	140.0
2006	A	2.75	1.56	109,221	7,026.8	12,480.8	702.8
2005	A	2.70	1.53	100,694	6,688.5	11,849.8	663.0
2004	A	2.82	1.57	95,586.7	6,290.2	12,495.4	296.6

Adverse Trends in Operations

Decrease in asset base during 2008 (4%)
Decrease in premium volume from 2004 to 2005 (5%)
Increase in policy surrenders from 2004 to 2005 (26%)

MEDICO INS CO   C   Fair

Major Rating Factors: Fair overall results on stability tests (3.2 on a scale of 0 to 10) including fair financial strength of affiliated Ability Resources Inc, negative cash flow from operations for 2008 and fair risk adjusted capital in prior years. Fair profitability (4.5) with operating losses during the first three months of 2009. Return on equity has been fair, averaging 9.3%. Good quality investment portfolio (6.7).

Other Rating Factors: Good liquidity (6.6). Strong capitalization (10.0) based on excellent risk adjusted capital (severe loss scenario).

Principal Business: Individual health insurance (90%) and reinsurance (10%).

Principal Investments: CMOs and structured securities (43%), nonCMO investment grade bonds (39%), common & preferred stock (7%), noninv. grade bonds (5%), and cash (1%).

Investments in Affiliates: 5%

Group Affiliation: Ability Resources Inc

Licensed in: All states except AL, DC, NM, NC, ND

Commenced Business: April 1930

Address: 1515 S 75th St, Omaha, NE 68124

Phone: (402) 391-6900 **Domicile State:** NE **NAIC Code:** 31119

Data Date	Rating	RACR #1	RACR #2	Total Assets ($mil)	Capital ($mil)	Net Premium ($mil)	Net Income ($mil)
3-09	C	4.94	3.82	115.7	44.0	4.2	-0.7
3-08	C	5.63	5.07	130.4	49.3	4.1	-0.4
2008	C	5.10	4.59	117.8	45.5	15.5	-5.1
2007	C	5.56	5.00	127.9	49.3	-131.1	32.7
2006	D+	0.93	0.73	308.1	31.2	58.7	0.4
2005	D	0.89	0.70	283.7	30.3	61.4	8.8
2004	D	0.67	0.52	277.6	21.5	68.4	-2.0

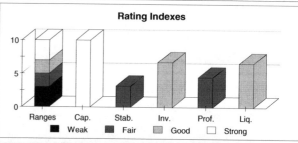

Rating Indexes

MEGA LIFE & HEALTH INSURANCE COMPANY   B-   Good

Major Rating Factors: Good current capitalization (5.8 on a scale of 0 to 10) based on mixed results -- excessive policy leverage mitigated by good risk adjusted capital (severe loss scenario), although results have slipped from the excellent range over the last two years. Fair profitability (3.9). Fair liquidity (4.4).

Other Rating Factors: Fair overall results on stability tests (4.8) including negative cash flow from operations for 2008. High quality investment portfolio (7.3).

Principal Business: Group health insurance (80%), individual health insurance (10%), reinsurance (8%), and individual life insurance (1%).

Principal Investments: NonCMO investment grade bonds (64%), CMOs and structured securities (23%), common & preferred stock (8%), real estate (4%), and misc. investments (2%).

Investments in Affiliates: 8%

Group Affiliation: HealthMarkets

Licensed in: All states except AL, NC

Commenced Business: June 1982

Address: 9151 Grapevine Highway, North Richland Hills, TX 76180

Phone: (817) 255-3100 **Domicile State:** OK **NAIC Code:** 97055

Data Date	Rating	RACR #1	RACR #2	Total Assets ($mil)	Capital ($mil)	Net Premium ($mil)	Net Income ($mil)
3-09	B-	1.21	0.99	702.0	205.0	195.4	16.8
3-08	B	1.01	0.82	967.7	184.7	229.2	-6.8
2008	B-	1.12	0.91	708.3	191.0	849.7	-12.8
2007	B	1.55	1.25	1,061.1	274.9	959.8	31.3
2006	B	1.68	1.35	1,110.1	366.4	1,232.1	288.3
2005	B-	1.59	1.27	1,254.4	366.8	1,346.4	130.8
2004	B-	1.41	1.10	1,269.1	307.5	1,381.3	80.5

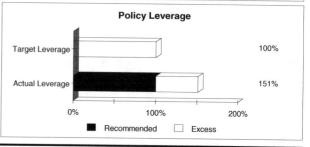

Policy Leverage

MERIT LIFE INSURANCE COMPANY | B | Good

Major Rating Factors: Good quality investment portfolio (5.9 on a scale of 0 to 10) despite significant exposure to mortgages . Mortgage default rate has been low. large holdings of BBB rated bonds in addition to small junk bond holdings. Good overall profitability (6.5). Excellent expense controls. Return on equity has been fair, averaging 8.7%. Fair overall results on stability tests (4.4) including fair financial strength of affiliated American International Group.

Other Rating Factors: Strong capitalization (10.0) based on excellent risk adjusted capital (severe loss scenario). Excellent liquidity (8.6).

Principal Business: Credit health insurance (34%), credit life insurance (29%), individual life insurance (17%), individual health insurance (11%), and other lines (8%).

Principal Investments: NonCMO investment grade bonds (60%), mortgages in good standing (19%), CMOs and structured securities (11%), noninv. grade bonds (7%), and common & preferred stock (2%).

Investments in Affiliates: None

Group Affiliation: American International Group

Licensed in: All states except AL, AZ, NC, VA

Commenced Business: October 1957

Address: 601 NW Second St, Evansville, IN 47708-1013

Phone: (812) 424-8031 **Domicile State:** IN **NAIC Code:** 65951

Data Date	Rating	RACR #1	RACR #2	Total Assets ($mil)	Capital ($mil)	Net Premium ($mil)	Net Income ($mil)
3-09	B	9.65	4.88	647.4	289.1	12.7	9.4
3-08	B+	20.41	10.68	1,106.6	710.4	22.0	4.0
2008	B	13.47	6.97	776.7	408.2	89.3	-16.7
2007	B+	20.32	10.71	1,096.3	707.0	106.6	46.0
2006	B+	20.05	10.56	1,042.4	662.3	101.8	48.4
2005	B+	19.08	9.95	996.9	614.5	95.4	54.8
2004	B+	17.08	8.87	1,024.1	613.5	110.5	56.9

American International Group Composite Group Rating: C+ Largest Group Members	Assets ($mil)	Rating
AMERICAN LIFE INS CO	86338	C-
VARIABLE ANNUITY LIFE INS CO	53699	B
WESTERN NATIONAL LIFE INS CO	45803	B-
AMERICAN GENERAL LIFE INS CO	38638	C+
NATIONAL UNION FIRE INS CO OF PITTSB	33707	B

MERRILL LYNCH LIFE INSURANCE COMPANY | B- | Good

Major Rating Factors: Good quality investment portfolio (6.9 on a scale of 0 to 10) despite mixed results such as: substantial holdings of BBB bonds but moderate junk bond exposure. Fair overall results on stability tests (3.9) including negative cash flow from operations for 2008. Weak profitability (1.9) with operating losses during the first three months of 2009.

Other Rating Factors: Strong capitalization (8.1) based on excellent risk adjusted capital (severe loss scenario). Excellent liquidity (7.1).

Principal Business: Individual annuities (97%) and individual life insurance (3%).

Principal Investments: NonCMO investment grade bonds (43%), policy loans (35%), CMOs and structured securities (14%), noninv. grade bonds (3%), and misc. investments (4%).

Investments in Affiliates: None

Group Affiliation: AEGON USA Group

Licensed in: All states except AL, NC

Commenced Business: December 1986

Address: 425 W Capital Ave Suite 1800, Little Rock, AR 72201

Phone: (800) 535-5549 **Domicile State:** AR **NAIC Code:** 79022

Data Date	Rating	RACR #1	RACR #2	Total Assets ($mil)	Capital ($mil)	Net Premium ($mil)	Net Income ($mil)
3-09	B-	3.43	1.74	9,776.1	294.3	69.3	-59.6
3-08	B	3.63	1.88	12,961.1	359.6	133.9	-8.5
2008	B-	3.90	1.99	10,341.9	356.1	431.3	-259.9
2007	B	3.75	1.96	13,911.0	366.0	744.0	108.8
2006	B	3.91	2.02	14,297.4	418.1	760.8	193.7
2005	B	3.67	1.89	14,062.5	401.0	685.8	117.3
2004	C+	2.82	1.46	14,320.2	284.8	751.9	79.1

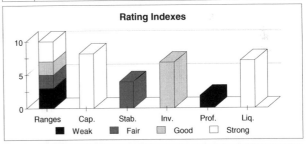

Rating Indexes

Ranges — Cap. — Stab. — Inv. — Prof. — Liq.
■ Weak ■ Fair ▨ Good ☐ Strong

METLIFE INSURANCE COMPANY OF CONNECTICUT | B | Good

Major Rating Factors: Good quality investment portfolio (5.8 on a scale of 0 to 10) despite mixed results such as: substantial holdings of BBB bonds but junk bond exposure equal to 69% of capital. Good overall profitability (6.1) despite operating losses during the first three months of 2009. Return on equity has been good over the last five years, averaging 14.5%. Fair overall results on stability tests (4.7).

Other Rating Factors: Strong capitalization (7.0) based on excellent risk adjusted capital (severe loss scenario). Excellent liquidity (8.8).

Principal Business: Individual annuities (72%), individual life insurance (20%), individual health insurance (7%), and group retirement contracts (1%).

Principal Investments: NonCMO investment grade bonds (46%), CMOs and structured securities (21%), common & preferred stock (8%), mortgages in good standing (8%), and misc. investments (16%).

Investments in Affiliates: 5%

Group Affiliation: MetLife Inc

Licensed in: All states except AL

Commenced Business: April 1864

Address: One Cityplace, Hartford, CT 06103-3415

Phone: (860) 308-7397 **Domicile State:** CT **NAIC Code:** 87726

Data Date	Rating	RACR #1	RACR #2	Total Assets ($mil)	Capital ($mil)	Net Premium ($mil)	Net Income ($mil)
3-09	B	1.50	1.02	65,347.5	4,810.1	1,380.1	-281.3
3-08	B	1.94	1.24	79,833.6	4,433.8	563.8	160.1
2008	B	1.79	1.24	69,829.1	5,471.5	3,062.6	242.3
2007	B	1.74	1.16	83,221.5	4,208.4	2,474.8	1,100.6
2006	B	1.66	1.18	66,375.6	4,089.7	2,691.4	749.3
2005	B	2.27	1.40	68,345.7	4,081.3	4,648.4	1,080.5
2004	B+	1.97	1.45	67,958.0	7,885.8	4,895.7	975.3

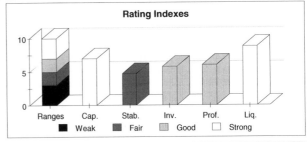

Rating Indexes

Ranges — Cap. — Stab. — Inv. — Prof. — Liq.
■ Weak ■ Fair ▨ Good ☐ Strong

METLIFE INVESTORS INSURANCE COMPANY

B-   **Good**

Major Rating Factors: Good quality investment portfolio (6.1 on a scale of 0 to 10) despite mixed results such as: minimal exposure to mortgages and substantial holdings of BBB bonds but small junk bond holdings. Fair profitability (3.7) with operating losses during the first three months of 2009. Return on equity has been low, averaging -12.9%. Fair overall results on stability tests (4.6) including fair risk adjusted capital in prior years.

Other Rating Factors: Strong capitalization (7.4) based on excellent risk adjusted capital (severe loss scenario). Excellent liquidity (10.0).

Principal Business: Individual annuities (100%).

Principal Investments: NonCMO investment grade bonds (55%), CMOs and structured securities (31%), noninv. grade bonds (3%), mortgages in good standing (3%), and misc. investments (8%).

Investments in Affiliates: None

Group Affiliation: MetLife Inc

Licensed in: All states except AL, MD, NJ, NC, VA

Commenced Business: September 1981

Address: One Tower Lane, Suite 3000, Oakbrook Terrace, IL 60181

Phone: (630) 368-6215 **Domicile State:** MO **NAIC Code:** 93513

Data Date	Rating	RACR #1	RACR #2	Total Assets ($mil)	Capital ($mil)	Net Premium ($mil)	Net Income ($mil)
3-09	B-	2.59	1.25	9,143.0	370.4	563.1	-22.6
3-08	B-	2.72	1.38	11,183.5	340.3	296.1	3.7
2008	B-	3.39	1.72	9,523.4	397.6	1,491.9	-34.9
2007	B-	2.56	1.29	11,882.6	328.6	1,430.3	39.7
2006	B-	2.16	1.09	11,341.8	284.0	1,190.6	115.9
2005	B-	1.08	0.60	9,278.8	175.4	1,179.6	0.5
2004	B-	1.12	0.65	8,480.3	182.4	260.2	-168.4

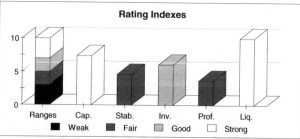

Rating Indexes

Ranges · Cap. · Stab. · Inv. · Prof. · Liq.
■ Weak ■ Fair ▨ Good ☐ Strong

METLIFE INVESTORS USA INSURANCE COMPANY

C+   **Fair**

Major Rating Factors: Fair overall results on stability tests (4.0 on a scale of 0 to 10) including fair risk adjusted capital in prior years. Good quality investment portfolio (5.3) despite mixed results such as: minimal exposure to mortgages and substantial holdings of BBB bonds but small junk bond holdings. Weak profitability (1.2) with operating losses during the first three months of 2009.

Other Rating Factors: Strong capitalization (7.3) based on excellent risk adjusted capital (severe loss scenario). Excellent liquidity (9.2).

Principal Business: Individual annuities (86%), individual life insurance (10%), reinsurance (3%), and group retirement contracts (1%).

Principal Investments: NonCMO investment grade bonds (39%), CMOs and structured securities (23%), mortgages in good standing (5%), noninv. grade bonds (3%), and misc. investments (30%).

Investments in Affiliates: 22%

Group Affiliation: MetLife Inc

Licensed in: All states except AL, NC

Commenced Business: March 1961

Address: 11365 W Olympic Blvd, Los Angeles, CA 90064

Phone: (310) 312-6100 **Domicile State:** DE **NAIC Code:** 61050

Data Date	Rating	RACR #1	RACR #2	Total Assets ($mil)	Capital ($mil)	Net Premium ($mil)	Net Income ($mil)
3-09	C+	2.42	1.21	27,296.1	1,140.2	2,096.6	-253.2
3-08	B-	0.98	0.51	28,970.0	538.2	1,446.6	-71.4
2008	C+	1.53	0.78	26,939.3	760.5	6,811.3	-482.3
2007	B-	1.08	0.55	29,684.1	584.2	7,237.5	-1,106.5
2006	B-	1.31	0.66	24,029.3	575.0	5,385.5	-115.8
2005	B-	1.41	0.71	18,807.8	538.4	4,434.4	-243.7
2004	B	1.83	0.90	14,589.6	381.6	863.0	-200.7

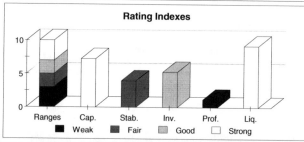

Rating Indexes

Ranges · Cap. · Stab. · Inv. · Prof. · Liq.
■ Weak ■ Fair ▨ Good ☐ Strong

METROPOLITAN LIFE INSURANCE COMPANY

B-   **Good**

Major Rating Factors: Good current capitalization (6.6 on a scale of 0 to 10) based on good risk adjusted capital (severe loss scenario), although results have slipped from the excellent range during the last year. Fair quality investment portfolio (3.7) with substantial holdings of BBB bonds in addition to significant exposure to junk bonds. Exposure to mortgages is significant, but the mortgage default rate has been low. Fair overall results on stability tests (3.7).

Other Rating Factors: Excellent profitability (7.2). Excellent liquidity (7.5).

Principal Business: Group retirement contracts (31%), group life insurance (21%), group health insurance (13%), individual life insurance (12%), and other lines (22%).

Principal Investments: NonCMO investment grade bonds (39%), mortgages in good standing (19%), CMOs and structured securities (18%), noninv. grade bonds (5%), and misc. investments (19%).

Investments in Affiliates: 6%

Group Affiliation: MetLife Inc

Licensed in: All states except AL

Commenced Business: May 1867

Address: 200 Park Avenue, New York, NY 10166-0188

Phone: (212) 578-2211 **Domicile State:** NY **NAIC Code:** 65978

Data Date	Rating	RACR #1	RACR #2	Total Assets ($mil)	Capital ($mil)	Net Premium ($mil)	Net Income ($mil)
3-09	B-	1.81	0.95	278,164	10,601.0	9,196.0	499.7
3-08	B+	2.28	1.22	301,794	13,278.9	6,994.7	-5.4
2008	B	2.15	1.15	289,578	11,592.3	33,867.6	-337.6
2007	B+	2.33	1.25	297,466	13,004.0	26,227.8	2,123.1
2006	B+	2.01	1.08	280,557	9,197.5	25,627.3	1,027.2
2005	B+	2.10	1.15	250,356	8,639.3	26,335.3	2,155.0
2004	A-	2.33	1.24	244,236	8,804.5	26,845.1	2,648.2

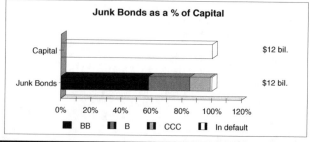

Junk Bonds as a % of Capital

Capital — $12 bil.

Junk Bonds — $12 bil.

0% 20% 40% 60% 80% 100% 120%
■ BB ▨ B ▨ CCC ☐ In default

METROPOLITAN TOWER LIFE INSURANCE COMPANY | B | Good

Major Rating Factors: Good liquidity (6.6 on a scale of 0 to 10) with sufficient resources to handle a spike in claims as well as a significant increase in policy surrenders. Fair quality investment portfolio (3.0). Fair overall results on stability tests (4.3) including negative cash flow from operations for 2008.

Other Rating Factors: Strong capitalization (7.2) based on excellent risk adjusted capital (severe loss scenario). Excellent profitability (7.4) with operating gains in each of the last five years.

Principal Business: Individual life insurance (100%).

Principal Investments: NonCMO investment grade bonds (36%), CMOs and structured securities (24%), real estate (21%), policy loans (7%), and misc. investments (13%).

Investments in Affiliates: 1%

Group Affiliation: MetLife Inc

Licensed in: All states except AL

Commenced Business: February 1983

Address: 200 Park Avenue, New York, NY 10166-0188

Phone: (212) 578-2211 **Domicile State:** DE **NAIC Code:** 97136

Data Date	Rating	RACR #1	RACR #2	Total Assets ($mil)	Capital ($mil)	Net Premium ($mil)	Net Income ($mil)
3-09	B	2.52	1.12	5,171.2	885.3	13.9	-7.6
3-08	B	3.19	1.47	6,183.7	1,158.7	23.0	26.5
2008	B	2.61	1.17	5,511.6	884.8	54.2	212.2
2007	B	3.11	1.42	6,179.1	1,137.8	51.4	103.2
2006	B	4.99	2.44	7,262.0	1,042.8	57.5	2,786.8
2005	B	3.12	1.43	5,806.1	690.3	73.7	352.8
2004	B	3.97	1.82	6,537.9	1,195.2	64.7	144.0

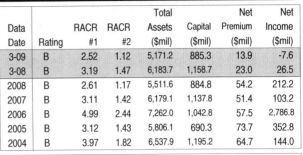

Rating Indexes

MID-WEST NATIONAL LIFE INSURANCE COMPANY OF TN * | B+ | Good

Major Rating Factors: Good overall results on stability tests (5.3 on a scale of 0 to 10) despite negative cash flow from operations for 2008. Other stability subfactors include excellent risk diversification. Good quality investment portfolio (6.8) despite mixed results such as: no exposure to mortgages and substantial holdings of BBB bonds but small junk bond holdings. Good overall profitability (6.1).

Other Rating Factors: Good liquidity (6.6). Strong capitalization (8.6) based on excellent risk adjusted capital (severe loss scenario).

Principal Business: Group health insurance (88%), individual health insurance (9%), and individual life insurance (3%).

Principal Investments: NonCMO investment grade bonds (73%), CMOs and structured securities (20%), noninv. grade bonds (5%), common & preferred stock (1%), and misc. investments (1%).

Investments in Affiliates: 1%

Group Affiliation: HealthMarkets

Licensed in: All states except AL, MD, NJ, NC, VA

Commenced Business: May 1965

Address: 9151 Grapevine Highway, North Richland Hills, TX 76180

Phone: (817) 255-3100 **Domicile State:** TX **NAIC Code:** 66087

Data Date	Rating	RACR #1	RACR #2	Total Assets ($mil)	Capital ($mil)	Net Premium ($mil)	Net Income ($mil)
3-09	B+	2.76	2.08	228.4	101.6	58.5	7.3
3-08	B+	2.60	1.93	391.5	130.7	75.5	11.9
2008	B+	2.57	1.93	218.5	98.3	272.9	38.5
2007	B+	2.88	2.15	374.8	145.3	364.0	72.2
2006	B	2.33	1.75	409.6	142.3	431.7	71.0
2005	B-	2.54	1.91	426.1	154.4	427.7	79.4
2004	C+	2.28	1.69	433.6	140.9	429.5	64.8

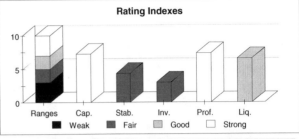

Rating Indexes

MIDLAND NATIONAL LIFE INSURANCE COMPANY * | B+ | Good

Major Rating Factors: Good liquidity (6.1 on a scale of 0 to 10) with sufficient resources to handle a spike in claims as well as a significant increase in policy surrenders. Good overall results on stability tests (6.2). Stability strengths include excellent operational trends, good risk adjusted capital for prior years and excellent risk diversification. Fair quality investment portfolio (4.2).

Other Rating Factors: Strong capitalization (7.1) based on excellent risk adjusted capital (severe loss scenario). Excellent profitability (8.5) with operating gains in each of the last five years.

Principal Business: Individual annuities (58%), individual life insurance (25%), and group retirement contracts (17%).

Principal Investments: NonCMO investment grade bonds (57%), CMOs and structured securities (31%), noninv. grade bonds (5%), common & preferred stock (2%), and misc. investments (5%).

Investments in Affiliates: None

Group Affiliation: Sammons Enterprises Inc

Licensed in: All states except AL, NC

Commenced Business: September 1906

Address: One Midland Plaza, Sioux Falls, SD 57193

Phone: (605) 335-5700 **Domicile State:** IA **NAIC Code:** 66044

Data Date	Rating	RACR #1	RACR #2	Total Assets ($mil)	Capital ($mil)	Net Premium ($mil)	Net Income ($mil)
3-09	B+	2.19	1.05	25,970.2	1,243.6	716.8	24.7
3-08	A-	1.91	0.95	25,670.0	1,106.6	437.9	9.3
2008	B+	2.30	1.12	25,408.8	1,240.3	2,196.1	110.6
2007	A-	1.94	0.96	23,518.2	1,109.4	2,012.0	112.2
2006	A-	1.97	1.00	21,661.6	1,020.0	2,369.5	155.1
2005	A-	2.02	1.03	18,824.1	964.6	2,190.3	186.8
2004	A-	1.96	1.00	16,123.5	811.2	2,181.0	180.8

Adverse Trends in Operations

Decrease in premium volume from 2006 to 2007 (15%)
Increase in policy surrenders from 2005 to 2006 (41%)
Increase in policy surrenders from 2004 to 2005 (27%)

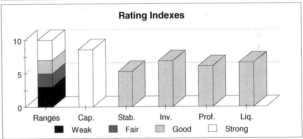

MIDWEST SECURITY LIFE INSURANCE COMPANY

B-   Good

Major Rating Factors: Good current capitalization (5.7 on a scale of 0 to 10) based on mixed results -- excessive policy leverage mitigated by excellent risk adjusted capital (severe loss scenario) reflecting improvement over results in 2008. Good overall profitability (6.0). Excellent expense controls. Return on equity has been excellent over the last five years averaging 19.8%. Good liquidity (5.8).

Other Rating Factors: Fair overall results on stability tests (3.8) including negative cash flow from operations for 2008. High quality investment portfolio (8.4).

Principal Business: Group health insurance (98%) and group life insurance (2%).

Principal Investments: NonCMO investment grade bonds (93%), CMOs and structured securities (11%), and real estate (1%).

Investments in Affiliates: None

Group Affiliation: UnitedHealth Group Inc

Licensed in: AZ, AR, CA, CT, FL, IL, IN, IA, KS, KY, LA, ME, MN, MS, MO, MT, NV, NH, NY, OH, OK, OR, PA, SD, TN, UT, VT, WV, WY

Commenced Business: March 1973

Address: 2700 Midwest Dr, Onalaska, WI 54650-8764

Phone: (608) 783-7130   **Domicile State:** WI   **NAIC Code:** 79480

Data Date	Rating	RACR #1	RACR #2	Total Assets ($mil)	Capital ($mil)	Net Premium ($mil)	Net Income ($mil)
3-09	B-	1.26	1.01	48.9	26.8	25.1	2.5
3-08	B	1.55	1.19	62.6	34.9	31.0	0.1
2008	B-	1.10	0.89	50.3	24.4	118.7	3.0
2007	B	1.54	1.19	64.1	34.8	127.7	4.6
2006	B	1.52	1.18	72.5	40.9	162.5	11.7
2005	B	1.44	1.14	92.1	44.5	221.1	16.7
2004	B+	1.86	1.46	113.5	56.3	239.4	6.4

Policy Leverage

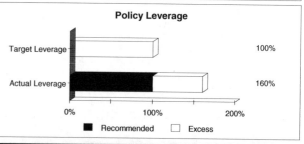

Target Leverage — 100%

Actual Leverage — 160%

0%   100%   200%

■ Recommended   □ Excess

MIDWESTERN UNITED LIFE INSURANCE COMPANY

B   Good

Major Rating Factors: Good overall results on stability tests (5.6 on a scale of 0 to 10) despite fair financial strength of affiliated ING America Ins Holdings Inc and negative cash flow from operations for 2008. Other stability subfactors include excellent operational trends and excellent risk diversification. Good liquidity (6.9) with sufficient resources to handle a spike in claims as well as a significant increase in policy surrenders. Strong capitalization (10.0) based on excellent risk adjusted capital (severe loss scenario).

Other Rating Factors: High quality investment portfolio (7.5). Excellent profitability (7.4) with operating gains in each of the last five years.

Principal Business: Individual life insurance (97%), individual health insurance (1%), and individual annuities (1%).

Principal Investments: NonCMO investment grade bonds (60%), CMOs and structured securities (29%), policy loans (5%), mortgages in good standing (3%), and noninv. grade bonds (2%).

Investments in Affiliates: 1%

Group Affiliation: ING America Ins Holdings Inc

Licensed in: All states except AL, NC

Commenced Business: August 1948

Address: 8605 Kings Mill Pl, Fort Wayne, IN 46804

Phone: (303) 860-1290   **Domicile State:** IN   **NAIC Code:** 66109

Data Date	Rating	RACR #1	RACR #2	Total Assets ($mil)	Capital ($mil)	Net Premium ($mil)	Net Income ($mil)
3-09	B	10.11	7.71	243.4	101.3	1.2	5.8
3-08	A-	9.78	6.61	251.4	97.0	1.2	0.8
2008	B	9.59	7.88	244.7	96.1	4.5	0.7
2007	A-	9.69	6.46	250.4	96.1	4.6	1.5
2006	B	9.50	7.08	252.0	94.7	4.6	5.0
2005	B	8.98	6.51	254.9	89.6	5.0	5.9
2004	B	8.39	5.88	259.1	83.6	5.1	5.7

ING America Ins Holdings Inc
Composite Group Rating: C+
Largest Group Members

	Assets ($mil)	Rating
ING USA ANNUITY LIFE INS CO	64090	C
ING LIFE INS ANNUITY CO	57306	C+
SECURITY LIFE OF DENVER INS CO	24265	B
RELIASTAR LIFE INS CO	20474	B
RELIASTAR LIFE INS CO OF NEW YORK	3207	C+

MINNESOTA LIFE INSURANCE COMPANY

B   Good

Major Rating Factors: Good quality investment portfolio (5.6 on a scale of 0 to 10) despite significant exposure to mortgages . Mortgage default rate has been low. large holdings of BBB rated bonds in addition to small junk bond holdings. Good overall results on stability tests (5.1). Stability strengths include good operational trends and excellent risk diversification. Fair profitability (4.4) with operating losses during the first three months of 2009.

Other Rating Factors: Strong capitalization (7.3) based on excellent risk adjusted capital (severe loss scenario). Excellent liquidity (7.2).

Principal Business: Group retirement contracts (32%), group life insurance (22%), individual annuities (17%), individual life insurance (15%), and other lines (14%).

Principal Investments: NonCMO investment grade bonds (40%), CMOs and structured securities (30%), mortgages in good standing (13%), common & preferred stock (5%), and misc. investments (11%).

Investments in Affiliates: 4%

Group Affiliation: Securian Financial Group

Licensed in: All states except AL, NC

Commenced Business: August 1880

Address: 400 N Robert St, St Paul, MN 55101

Phone: (612) 665-3500   **Domicile State:** MN   **NAIC Code:** 66168

Data Date	Rating	RACR #1	RACR #2	Total Assets ($mil)	Capital ($mil)	Net Premium ($mil)	Net Income ($mil)
3-09	B	1.86	1.19	19,313.5	1,411.3	1,280.7	-16.0
3-08	A-	2.26	1.44	22,925.4	1,719.4	1,211.1	-17.6
2008	B	1.96	1.27	19,697.1	1,432.0	4,634.1	-236.1
2007	A-	2.34	1.50	23,829.0	1,818.1	4,145.5	181.8
2006	A-	2.18	1.40	22,151.1	1,710.9	3,747.5	168.0
2005	A-	2.10	1.34	21,543.6	1,585.3	3,441.8	158.5
2004	A-	2.35	1.43	20,014.4	1,419.4	3,195.4	155.8

Adverse Trends in Operations

Decrease in asset base during 2008 (17%)
Decrease in capital during 2008 (21%)

ML LIFE INSURANCE COMPANY OF NEW YORK   B   Good

Major Rating Factors: Fair overall results on stability tests (3.8 on a scale of 0 to 10). Fair profitability (3.0) with operating losses during the first three months of 2009. Strong overall capitalization (10.0) based on excellent risk adjusted capital (severe loss scenario). Nevertheless, capital levels have fluctuated during prior years.

Other Rating Factors: High quality investment portfolio (7.5). Excellent liquidity (7.4).

Principal Business: Individual annuities (99%) and individual life insurance (1%).

Principal Investments: NonCMO investment grade bonds (46%), policy loans (38%), CMOs and structured securities (15%), common & preferred stock (1%), and noninv. grade bonds (1%).

Investments in Affiliates: None

Group Affiliation: AEGON USA Group

Licensed in: DC, FL, MD, MI, NJ, NM, NC, SC, VA

Commenced Business: March 1974

Address: 4 Manhattanville Rd, Purchase, NY 10577

Phone: (800) 333-6524   **Domicile State:** NY   **NAIC Code:** 82848

Data Date	Rating	RACR #1	RACR #2	Total Assets ($mil)	Capital ($mil)	Net Premium ($mil)	Net Income ($mil)
3-09	B	3.32	2.99	785.2	48.0	0.1	-5.0
3-08	B	4.44	3.89	1,082.7	78.4	2.1	1.8
2008	B	3.59	3.23	835.4	51.9	9.1	-13.1
2007	B	4.35	3.91	1,169.2	76.9	34.8	20.0
2006	B	3.19	2.87	1,219.4	56.7	59.4	17.4
2005	B-	2.52	2.27	1,206.5	43.3	41.2	10.7
2004	C+	1.91	1.72	1,251.4	32.7	74.6	7.1

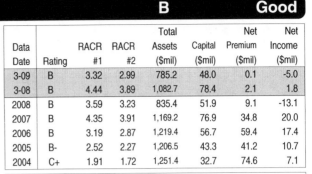

Rating Indexes

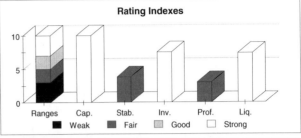

MML BAY STATE LIFE INSURANCE COMPANY *   A   Excellent

Major Rating Factors: Good overall results on stability tests (6.1 on a scale of 0 to 10). Strengths that enhance stability include excellent risk diversification. Good overall profitability (5.8). Return on equity has been good over the last five years, averaging 13.9%. Strong capitalization (10.0) based on excellent risk adjusted capital (severe loss scenario).

Other Rating Factors: High quality investment portfolio (7.4). Excellent liquidity (9.0).

Principal Business: Individual life insurance (100%), group life insurance (1%), and individual annuities (1%).

Principal Investments: NonCMO investment grade bonds (45%), policy loans (34%), CMOs and structured securities (17%), mortgages in good standing (3%), and noninv. grade bonds (2%).

Investments in Affiliates: None

Group Affiliation: Massachusetts Mutual Group

Licensed in: All states except AL, NC

Commenced Business: December 1894

Address: 100 Bright Meadow Blvd, Enfield, CT 06082

Phone: (413) 788-8411   **Domicile State:** CT   **NAIC Code:** 70416

Data Date	Rating	RACR #1	RACR #2	Total Assets ($mil)	Capital ($mil)	Net Premium ($mil)	Net Income ($mil)
3-09	A	4.42	3.12	4,105.4	195.9	10.7	0.1
3-08	A-	3.96	2.94	4,555.2	188.2	9.0	7.1
2008	A	4.20	3.03	4,176.2	191.8	48.1	9.7
2007	A-	3.72	2.76	4,637.0	183.4	51.1	10.8
2006	A-	4.39	3.33	4,549.9	211.6	66.0	37.4
2005	B	4.66	3.50	4,377.4	217.8	75.7	43.5
2004	B	4.81	3.64	4,307.2	222.5	84.1	47.3

Rating Indexes

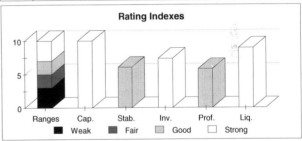

MONUMENTAL LIFE INSURANCE COMPANY   C+   Fair

Major Rating Factors: Fair overall results on stability tests (4.1 on a scale of 0 to 10) including negative cash flow from operations for 2008 and fair risk adjusted capital in prior years. Good capitalization (5.6) based on good risk adjusted capital (moderate loss scenario). Good overall profitability (5.5) despite operating losses during the first three months of 2009.

Other Rating Factors: Low quality investment portfolio (2.8). Excellent liquidity (7.0).

Principal Business: Individual life insurance (26%), group retirement contracts (20%), individual annuities (20%), group health insurance (16%), and other lines (18%).

Principal Investments: NonCMO investment grade bonds (51%), CMOs and structured securities (18%), mortgages in good standing (12%), noninv. grade bonds (7%), and misc. investments (10%).

Investments in Affiliates: 4%

Group Affiliation: AEGON USA Group

Licensed in: All states except AL, NC

Commenced Business: May 1860

Address: 4333 Edgewood Rd NE, Cedar Rapids, IA 52499

Phone: (319) 355-8511   **Domicile State:** IA   **NAIC Code:** 66281

Data Date	Rating	RACR #1	RACR #2	Total Assets ($mil)	Capital ($mil)	Net Premium ($mil)	Net Income ($mil)
3-09	C+	1.39	0.64	32,958.8	1,234.8	486.5	-0.9
3-08	C+	1.18	0.58	37,234.0	819.5	572.4	158.4
2008	C+	1.44	0.68	35,531.2	1,236.2	2,204.0	343.7
2007	C+	1.09	0.54	37,935.2	731.8	2,428.1	361.4
2006	B-	1.07	0.59	19,898.1	876.0	1,215.4	154.8
2005	B-	1.19	0.62	20,222.1	885.0	1,242.6	252.3
2004	B-	1.41	0.70	19,261.2	936.7	1,333.1	328.0

Rating Indexes

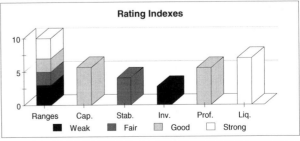

MONY LIFE INSURANCE COMPANY   C   Fair

Major Rating Factors: Fair overall results on stability tests (4.1 on a scale of 0 to 10) including fair financial strength of affiliated AXA Financial Inc, negative cash flow from operations for 2008 and fair risk adjusted capital in prior years. Fair current capitalization (4.1) based on fair risk adjusted capital (moderate loss scenario), although results have slipped from the good range over the last two years. Fair profitability (4.1).

Other Rating Factors: Good quality investment portfolio (5.4). Good liquidity (5.1).

Principal Business: Individual life insurance (85%), individual health insurance (10%), group retirement contracts (2%), individual annuities (1%), and reinsurance (1%).

Principal Investments: NonCMO investment grade bonds (53%), mortgages in good standing (16%), policy loans (11%), common & preferred stock (9%), and misc. investments (12%).

Investments in Affiliates: 5%

Group Affiliation: AXA Financial Inc

Licensed in: All states except AL

Commenced Business: February 1843

Address: 1740 Broadway, New York, NY 10019

Phone: (212) 708-2300   **Domicile State:** NY   **NAIC Code:** 66370

Data Date	Rating	RACR #1	RACR #2	Total Assets ($mil)	Capital ($mil)	Net Premium ($mil)	Net Income ($mil)
3-09	C	0.89	0.64	9,116.7	493.6	104.3	26.7
3-08	B-	1.23	0.96	9,824.4	974.8	114.0	37.9
2008	C+	0.95	0.69	9,161.9	520.7	431.6	2.9
2007	B-	1.23	0.96	9,917.6	961.3	448.9	130.4
2006	C	1.25	0.98	10,270.3	1,069.5	489.2	293.5
2005	C	1.10	0.82	11,022.8	968.6	567.4	142.3
2004	C-	0.85	0.62	11,019.4	830.9	734.1	-307.2

AXA Financial Inc Composite Group Rating: C Largest Group Members	Assets ($mil)	Rating
AXA EQUITABLE LIFE INS CO	111796	C
MONY LIFE INS CO	9162	C+
MONY LIFE INS CO OF AMERICA	4199	C+
AXA CORPORATE SOLUTIONS LIFE REINS	1541	B
COLISEUM REINS CO	619	C

MONY LIFE INSURANCE COMPANY OF AMERICA   C+   Fair

Major Rating Factors: Fair overall results on stability tests (4.6 on a scale of 0 to 10) including fair financial strength of affiliated AXA Financial Inc and negative cash flow from operations for 2008. Fair quality investment portfolio (4.8) with large holdings of BBB rated bonds in addition to moderate junk bond exposure. Good capitalization (5.4) based on good risk adjusted capital (moderate loss scenario).

Other Rating Factors: Good liquidity (6.1). Weak profitability (2.1).

Principal Business: Individual life insurance (83%), individual annuities (12%), group life insurance (3%), and reinsurance (1%).

Principal Investments: NonCMO investment grade bonds (65%), mortgages in good standing (9%), CMOs and structured securities (9%), common & preferred stock (8%), and misc. investments (9%).

Investments in Affiliates: 2%

Group Affiliation: AXA Financial Inc

Licensed in: All states except AL, NC

Commenced Business: June 1969

Address: 1740 Broadway, New York, NY 10019

Phone: (212) 708-2300   **Domicile State:** AZ   **NAIC Code:** 78077

Data Date	Rating	RACR #1	RACR #2	Total Assets ($mil)	Capital ($mil)	Net Premium ($mil)	Net Income ($mil)
3-09	C+	1.25	0.77	3,952.0	177.7	53.3	2.8
3-08	B-	1.73	1.15	5,229.8	282.8	65.1	-3.8
2008	C+	1.36	0.85	4,198.9	191.7	244.7	-68.2
2007	B-	1.81	1.20	5,594.5	291.3	247.6	7.3
2006	C	1.69	1.13	6,004.8	281.3	257.8	27.7
2005	C	1.60	1.01	6,200.4	239.3	396.2	-5.6
2004	C	1.61	0.98	6,362.6	231.5	824.7	-83.4

AXA Financial Inc Composite Group Rating: C Largest Group Members	Assets ($mil)	Rating
AXA EQUITABLE LIFE INS CO	111796	C
MONY LIFE INS CO	9162	C+
MONY LIFE INS CO OF AMERICA	4199	C+
AXA CORPORATE SOLUTIONS LIFE REINS	1541	B
COLISEUM REINS CO	619	C

MOTORISTS LIFE INSURANCE COMPANY   B   Good

Major Rating Factors: Good liquidity (6.5 on a scale of 0 to 10) with sufficient resources to cover a large increase in policy surrenders. Good overall results on stability tests (5.9). Strengths include good financial support from affiliation with The Motorists Group, excellent operational trends and good risk diversification. Fair profitability (3.0) with operating losses during the first three months of 2009.

Other Rating Factors: Strong capitalization (7.9) based on excellent risk adjusted capital (severe loss scenario). High quality investment portfolio (7.0).

Principal Business: Individual life insurance (82%), individual annuities (17%), and group life insurance (1%).

Principal Investments: CMOs and structured securities (49%), nonCMO investment grade bonds (45%), policy loans (3%), common & preferred stock (2%), and noninv. grade bonds (1%).

Investments in Affiliates: None

Group Affiliation: The Motorists Group

Licensed in: GA, HI, IN, IA, LA, MN, OK, RI, SD, TX, WA, WI, WY

Commenced Business: January 1967

Address: 471 E Broad St, Columbus, OH 43215

Phone: (888) 876-6542   **Domicile State:** OH   **NAIC Code:** 66311

Data Date	Rating	RACR #1	RACR #2	Total Assets ($mil)	Capital ($mil)	Net Premium ($mil)	Net Income ($mil)
3-09	B	2.82	1.62	340.5	41.6	15.4	-1.2
3-08	B+	3.43	2.03	336.4	49.3	11.3	-1.0
2008	B	2.95	1.71	334.0	43.1	45.7	-8.3
2007	B+	3.58	2.13	333.6	50.8	42.8	0.7
2006	B+	3.66	2.18	322.5	49.9	40.6	0.7
2005	B+	3.76	2.27	308.6	49.7	38.5	0.0
2004	B+	3.81	2.25	293.2	49.5	38.1	1.4

The Motorists Group Composite Group Rating: B Largest Group Members	Assets ($mil)	Rating
MOTORISTS MUTUAL INS CO	1175	B+
MOTORISTS LIFE INS CO	334	B
AMERICAN HARDWARE MUTUAL INS CO	334	B
IOWA MUTUAL INS CO	80	B
WILSON MUTUAL INS CO	74	B

MTL INSURANCE COMPANY *   B+   Good

Major Rating Factors: Good quality investment portfolio (5.6 on a scale of 0 to 10) despite large holdings of BBB rated bonds in addition to moderate junk bond exposure. Exposure to mortgages is significant, but the mortgage default rate has been low. Good liquidity (5.4) with sufficient resources to cover a large increase in policy surrenders. Good overall results on stability tests (6.2) excellent operational trends and good risk diversification.

Other Rating Factors: Fair profitability (3.2) with operating losses during the first three months of 2009. Strong capitalization (7.3) based on excellent risk adjusted capital (severe loss scenario).

Principal Business: Individual life insurance (93%) and individual annuities (6%).

Principal Investments: NonCMO investment grade bonds (49%), mortgages in good standing (21%), CMOs and structured securities (14%), policy loans (11%), and misc. investments (5%).

Investments in Affiliates: None

Group Affiliation: Mutual Trust Holding Co

Licensed in: All states except AL, AZ, NC

Commenced Business: April 1905

Address: 1200 Jorie Blvd, Oak Brook, IL 60522-9006

Phone: (800) 323-7320 **Domicile State:** IL **NAIC Code:** 66427

Data Date	Rating	RACR #1	RACR #2	Total Assets ($mil)	Capital ($mil)	Net Premium ($mil)	Net Income ($mil)
3-09	B+	2.41	1.23	1,337.3	89.1	36.4	-0.9
3-08	B+	2.39	1.32	1,283.6	105.7	33.9	-0.2
2008	B+	2.47	1.27	1,319.4	89.2	147.8	-11.3
2007	B+	2.44	1.33	1,274.0	105.3	128.3	-0.8
2006	B+	2.94	1.48	1,256.8	106.7	115.5	5.8
2005	B+	3.04	1.52	1,227.2	105.6	106.3	9.9
2004	B+	2.92	1.45	1,177.4	96.6	119.7	7.6

Adverse Trends in Operations

Decrease in capital during 2008 (15%)
Decrease in capital during 2007 (1%)
Increase in policy surrenders from 2005 to 2006 (43%)
Decrease in premium volume from 2004 to 2005 (11%)

MUNICH AMERICAN REASSURANCE COMPANY   C+   Fair

Major Rating Factors: Fair overall results on stability tests (4.4 on a scale of 0 to 10) including fair financial strength of affiliated Munich Re America Corp. Good liquidity (6.8) with sufficient resources to handle a spike in claims as well as a significant increase in policy surrenders. Weak profitability (2.8). Excellent expense controls. Return on equity has been low, averaging -2.7%.

Other Rating Factors: Strong capitalization (7.2) based on excellent risk adjusted capital (severe loss scenario). High quality investment portfolio (8.0).

Principal Business: Reinsurance (100%).

Principal Investments: NonCMO investment grade bonds (77%), CMOs and structured securities (21%), noninv. grade bonds (1%), and common & preferred stock (1%).

Investments in Affiliates: None

Group Affiliation: Munich Re America Corp

Licensed in: All states except AL, CT, MD, MA, MT, NC, OH, SD, VA, PR

Commenced Business: November 1959

Address: 56 Perimeter Ctr E NE Ste 200, Atlanta, GA 30346-2290

Phone: (770) 394-5665 **Domicile State:** GA **NAIC Code:** 66346

Data Date	Rating	RACR #1	RACR #2	Total Assets ($mil)	Capital ($mil)	Net Premium ($mil)	Net Income ($mil)
3-09	C+	1.70	1.14	5,613.3	646.7	322.7	30.5
3-08	C+	1.89	1.26	5,124.5	682.6	279.7	8.6
2008	C+	1.65	1.10	5,506.2	649.2	1,278.0	-58.6
2007	C+	1.80	1.20	5,029.5	673.0	1,164.5	62.6
2006	C	1.54	1.03	4,527.2	544.3	960.2	-60.1
2005	C	1.72	1.16	3,923.1	532.2	822.2	-51.2
2004	C	1.79	1.21	3,344.7	495.8	733.3	1.4

Munich Re America Corp Composite Group Rating: C Largest Group Members	Assets ($mil)	Rating
MUNICH REINSURANCE AMERICA INC	16355	C
MUNICH AMERICAN REASSURANCE CO	5506	C+
HARTFORD SM BOIL INSPECTION INS	1112	B-
AMERICAN MODERN HOME INS CO	909	B+
AMERICAN ALTERNATIVE INS CORP	462	C

MUTUAL OF AMERICA LIFE INSURANCE COMPANY   B   Good

Major Rating Factors: Good quality investment portfolio (6.0 on a scale of 0 to 10) despite mixed results such as: minimal exposure to mortgages and large holdings of BBB rated bonds but small junk bond holdings. Good overall results on stability tests (5.2). Stability strengths include good operational trends and excellent risk diversification. Fair profitability (4.7) with operating losses during the first three months of 2009.

Other Rating Factors: Strong capitalization (7.8) based on excellent risk adjusted capital (severe loss scenario). Excellent liquidity (7.0).

Principal Business: Group retirement contracts (75%), individual annuities (24%), and group life insurance (1%).

Principal Investments: NonCMO investment grade bonds (51%), CMOs and structured securities (40%), real estate (4%), noninv. grade bonds (2%), and misc. investments (4%).

Investments in Affiliates: None

Group Affiliation: None

Licensed in: All states except AL

Commenced Business: October 1945

Address: 320 Park Ave, New York, NY 10022

Phone: (212) 224-1879 **Domicile State:** NY **NAIC Code:** 88668

Data Date	Rating	RACR #1	RACR #2	Total Assets ($mil)	Capital ($mil)	Net Premium ($mil)	Net Income ($mil)
3-09	B	3.18	1.53	10,756.0	779.2	304.3	-3.0
3-08	B+	2.95	1.51	12,424.5	814.3	335.9	-6.0
2008	B	3.35	1.65	10,971.7	783.8	1,371.2	-54.0
2007	B+	3.08	1.58	13,016.9	831.5	1,405.3	7.3
2006	B+	2.82	1.46	12,437.9	811.9	1,282.6	16.8
2005	B+	3.05	1.54	11,838.8	801.8	1,170.1	124.6
2004	B	2.46	1.25	11,486.9	676.7	1,087.2	18.2

Adverse Trends in Operations

Decrease in capital during 2008 (6%)
Decrease in asset base during 2008 (16%)
Decrease in premium volume from 2007 to 2008 (2%)

MUTUAL OF OMAHA INSURANCE COMPANY *   B+   Good

Major Rating Factors: Good overall results on stability tests (6.0 on a scale of 0 to 10). Stability strengths include good operational trends and excellent risk diversification. Good current capitalization (6.4) based on good risk adjusted capital (severe loss scenario), although results have slipped from the excellent range over the last two years. Good quality investment portfolio (5.8).

Other Rating Factors: Excellent profitability (8.6) with operating gains in each of the last five years. Excellent liquidity (7.0).

Principal Business: Individual health insurance (48%), reinsurance (36%), and group health insurance (16%).

Principal Investments: Common & preferred stock (42%), CMOs and structured securities (23%), nonCMO investment grade bonds (22%), mortgages in good standing (5%), and misc. investments (9%).

Investments in Affiliates: 41%

Group Affiliation: Mutual Of Omaha Group

Licensed in: All states except AL

Commenced Business: January 1910

Address: Mutual Of Omaha Plaza, Omaha, NE 68175

Phone: (402) 342-7600 **Domicile State:** NE **NAIC Code:** 71412

Data Date	Rating	RACR #1	RACR #2	Total Assets ($mil)	Capital ($mil)	Net Premium ($mil)	Net Income ($mil)
3-09	B+	0.98	0.92	4,625.4	2,061.9	401.3	10.7
3-08	A-	1.19	1.11	4,538.2	2,217.0	377.7	14.9
2008	B+	1.00	0.94	4,700.1	2,098.6	1,554.3	152.0
2007	A-	1.19	1.11	4,541.7	2,217.4	1,818.7	89.6
2006	A-	1.30	1.20	4,752.9	2,140.9	2,175.1	93.4
2005	A-	1.18	1.08	4,150.2	1,749.4	1,862.6	73.6
2004	A-	1.14	1.05	4,012.0	1,737.8	1,748.8	93.5

Adverse Trends in Operations

Change in premium mix from 2007 to 2008 (4.6%)
Decrease in capital during 2008 (5%)
Decrease in premium volume from 2007 to 2008 (15%)
Decrease in asset base during 2007 (4%)
Decrease in premium volume from 2006 to 2007 (16%)

NATIONAL BENEFIT LIFE INSURANCE COMPANY *   A-   Excellent

Major Rating Factors: Good overall results on stability tests (5.7 on a scale of 0 to 10). Strengths that enhance stability include good operational trends and excellent risk diversification. Good quality investment portfolio (6.6) despite mixed results such as: no exposure to mortgages and large holdings of BBB rated bonds but small junk bond holdings. Strong capitalization (10.0) based on excellent risk adjusted capital (severe loss scenario).

Other Rating Factors: Excellent profitability (7.4) with operating gains in each of the last five years. Excellent liquidity (7.3).

Principal Business: Individual life insurance (73%), group health insurance (24%), group life insurance (2%), and credit life insurance (1%).

Principal Investments: NonCMO investment grade bonds (57%), CMOs and structured securities (34%), noninv. grade bonds (6%), policy loans (3%), and common & preferred stock (1%).

Investments in Affiliates: None

Group Affiliation: Citigroup Inc

Licensed in: All states except AL

Commenced Business: May 1963

Address: 333 West 34th Street, New York, NY 10001-2402

Phone: (212) 615-7500 **Domicile State:** NY **NAIC Code:** 61409

Data Date	Rating	RACR #1	RACR #2	Total Assets ($mil)	Capital ($mil)	Net Premium ($mil)	Net Income ($mil)
3-09	A-	9.78	5.36	738.4	318.1	36.7	3.3
3-08	A-	9.76	5.22	723.0	308.9	35.7	5.3
2008	A-	9.83	5.35	721.5	316.9	131.0	15.1
2007	A-	9.77	5.29	691.2	304.9	215.4	100.7
2006	A	7.67	4.49	834.1	329.5	293.4	36.3
2005	B+	7.41	4.31	809.6	324.1	289.2	36.7
2004	B+	6.70	3.90	781.4	295.4	282.6	34.9

Adverse Trends in Operations

Decrease in premium volume from 2007 to 2008 (39%)
Decrease in premium volume from 2006 to 2007 (27%)
Decrease in asset base during 2007 (17%)
Decrease in capital during 2007 (7%)

NATIONAL FARMERS UNION LIFE INSURANCE COMPANY   B-   Good

Major Rating Factors: Good overall results on stability tests (5.1 on a scale of 0 to 10) despite fair financial strength of affiliated Americo Life Inc and negative cash flow from operations for 2008. Other stability subfactors include good operational trends and good risk diversification. Good quality investment portfolio (6.3) despite mixed results such as: minimal exposure to mortgages and substantial holdings of BBB bonds but minimal holdings in junk bonds. Good liquidity (6.1).

Other Rating Factors: Strong capitalization (8.9) based on excellent risk adjusted capital (severe loss scenario). Excellent profitability (7.5) with operating gains in each of the last five years.

Principal Business: Individual life insurance (70%), reinsurance (29%), and group life insurance (1%).

Principal Investments: NonCMO investment grade bonds (46%), CMOs and structured securities (26%), mortgages in good standing (10%), policy loans (7%), and common & preferred stock (7%).

Investments in Affiliates: None

Group Affiliation: Americo Life Inc

Licensed in: AZ, AR, CA, CO, CT, DE, GA, IL, IN, IA, KS, KY, LA, MN, MS, MO, MT, NE, NV, NH, NY, OH, OK, OR, PA, RI, TN, UT, VT, WA, WV, WY, PR

Commenced Business: April 1938

Address: 500 North Akard, Dallas, TX 75201

Phone: (816) 391-2000 **Domicile State:** TX **NAIC Code:** 66540

Data Date	Rating	RACR #1	RACR #2	Total Assets ($mil)	Capital ($mil)	Net Premium ($mil)	Net Income ($mil)
3-09	B-	4.26	2.29	257.9	42.9	1.8	0.1
3-08	C+	3.67	2.03	284.9	44.1	2.2	1.3
2008	B-	4.02	2.25	262.9	42.3	7.5	6.9
2007	C+	3.64	2.01	272.7	43.0	7.5	7.0
2006	C+	3.42	1.88	281.1	40.6	7.8	5.5
2005	C+	3.28	1.80	291.6	40.6	8.8	7.0
2004	C	3.31	1.81	305.8	39.9	8.7	6.6

Americo Life Inc
Composite Group Rating: C

Largest Group Members	Assets ($mil)	Rating
AMERICO FINANCIAL LIFE ANNUITY INS	3439	C+
INVESTORS LIFE INS CO NORTH AMERICA	755	C-
UNITED FIDELITY LIFE INS CO	572	D+
GREAT SOUTHERN LIFE INS CO	274	C+
NATIONAL FARMERS UNION LIFE INS CO	263	B-

NATIONAL GUARDIAN LIFE INSURANCE COMPANY *   B+   Good

Major Rating Factors: Good current capitalization (5.9 on a scale of 0 to 10) based on good risk adjusted capital (severe loss scenario), although results have slipped from the excellent range over the last two years. Good quality investment portfolio (5.4) despite mixed results such as: large holdings of BBB rated bonds but junk bond exposure equal to 53% of capital. Good liquidity (6.8).

Other Rating Factors: Good overall results on stability tests (5.9) excellent operational trends and excellent risk diversification. Excellent profitability (7.1) with operating gains in each of the last five years.

Principal Business: Group health insurance (33%), group life insurance (32%), individual life insurance (23%), reinsurance (8%), and other lines (4%).

Principal Investments: NonCMO investment grade bonds (62%), CMOs and structured securities (14%), common & preferred stock (8%), mortgages in good standing (7%), and misc. investments (8%).

Investments in Affiliates: 4%

Group Affiliation: NGL Ins Group

Licensed in: All states except AL, NC

Commenced Business: October 1910

Address: 2 E Gilman St, Madison, WI 53703

Phone: (608) 257-5611 **Domicile State:** WI **NAIC Code:** 66583

Data Date	Rating	RACR #1	RACR #2	Total Assets ($mil)	Capital ($mil)	Net Premium ($mil)	Net Income ($mil)
3-09	B+	1.33	0.86	1,663.4	155.3	48.8	2.6
3-08	A-	1.48	0.98	1,515.0	165.5	41.1	1.3
2008	B+	1.36	0.89	1,651.2	160.8	199.1	6.4
2007	A-	1.51	1.01	1,486.0	167.5	165.4	16.5
2006	A-	1.49	1.00	1,393.7	157.4	138.1	17.2
2005	A-	1.33	0.90	1,349.2	139.9	137.7	11.8
2004	A-	1.24	0.85	1,295.3	135.3	158.7	13.9

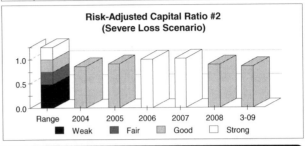

Risk-Adjusted Capital Ratio #2 (Severe Loss Scenario)

Range 2004 2005 2006 2007 2008 3-09
■ Weak ■ Fair ▨ Good □ Strong

NATIONAL INTEGRITY LIFE INSURANCE COMPANY   B-   Good

Major Rating Factors: Good quality investment portfolio (5.5 on a scale of 0 to 10) despite mixed results such as: large holdings of BBB rated bonds but moderate junk bond exposure. Good overall results on stability tests (5.1). Stability strengths include good operational trends and excellent risk diversification. Fair profitability (4.0). Excellent expense controls.

Other Rating Factors: Strong capitalization (7.5) based on excellent risk adjusted capital (severe loss scenario). Excellent liquidity (9.0).

Principal Business: Individual annuities (100%).

Principal Investments: NonCMO investment grade bonds (60%), CMOs and structured securities (27%), noninv. grade bonds (6%), common & preferred stock (3%), and policy loans (3%).

Investments in Affiliates: None

Group Affiliation: Western & Southern Group

Licensed in: DC, DE, GA, MD, NJ, NC, OK, SC, VA

Commenced Business: December 1968

Address: 15 Matthews St Suite 200, Goshen, NY 10924

Phone: (914) 615-1018 **Domicile State:** NY **NAIC Code:** 75264

Data Date	Rating	RACR #1	RACR #2	Total Assets ($mil)	Capital ($mil)	Net Premium ($mil)	Net Income ($mil)
3-09	B-	2.98	1.34	4,163.6	192.0	217.7	0.8
3-08	B+	2.65	1.27	3,761.5	100.6	204.2	10.5
2008	B-	3.21	1.52	4,037.5	184.5	777.6	-56.8
2007	B+	3.83	1.89	3,677.5	142.1	523.2	5.1
2006	B+	3.64	1.84	3,483.2	129.1	528.4	37.9
2005	C+	2.75	1.43	3,049.7	98.3	486.5	7.1
2004	C+	2.67	1.43	2,730.2	98.1	419.1	-4.0

Adverse Trends in Operations

Increase in policy surrenders from 2006 to 2007 (57%)
Increase in policy surrenders from 2005 to 2006 (29%)

NATIONAL LIFE INSURANCE COMPANY   B   Good

Major Rating Factors: Good quality investment portfolio (6.2 on a scale of 0 to 10) despite large holdings of BBB rated bonds in addition to moderate junk bond exposure. Exposure to mortgages is significant, but the mortgage default rate has been low. Good liquidity (5.7) with sufficient resources to cover a large increase in policy surrenders. Good overall results on stability tests (6.3) excellent operational trends, good risk adjusted capital for prior years and excellent risk diversification.

Other Rating Factors: Strong capitalization (7.0) based on excellent risk adjusted capital (severe loss scenario). Excellent profitability (7.3).

Principal Business: Individual life insurance (78%), individual annuities (16%), and individual health insurance (6%).

Principal Investments: NonCMO investment grade bonds (40%), CMOs and structured securities (26%), mortgages in good standing (12%), policy loans (8%), and misc. investments (15%).

Investments in Affiliates: 6%

Group Affiliation: National Life Group

Licensed in: All states except AL

Commenced Business: January 1850

Address: 1 National Life Dr, Montpelier, VT 05604

Phone: (802) 229-3333 **Domicile State:** VT **NAIC Code:** 66680

Data Date	Rating	RACR #1	RACR #2	Total Assets ($mil)	Capital ($mil)	Net Premium ($mil)	Net Income ($mil)
3-09	B	1.40	1.00	7,951.0	789.0	125.5	0.7
3-08	B	1.71	1.21	8,215.5	836.1	114.2	12.7
2008	B	1.41	1.02	7,964.8	792.2	539.2	-4.9
2007	B	1.68	1.18	8,275.6	826.8	507.7	65.0
2006	B	1.66	1.13	8,164.7	708.0	559.2	79.7
2005	B	1.59	1.06	7,901.2	623.5	559.5	91.6
2004	C+	1.46	0.97	7,584.8	542.4	641.1	66.0

Adverse Trends in Operations

Decrease in capital during 2008 (4%)
Decrease in asset base during 2008 (4%)
Decrease in premium volume from 2006 to 2007 (9%)
Increase in policy surrenders from 2005 to 2006 (63%)
Decrease in premium volume from 2004 to 2005 (13%)

NATIONAL TEACHERS ASSOCIATES LIFE INSURANCE COMPAN   B   Good

Major Rating Factors: Good overall results on stability tests (5.3 on a scale of 0 to 10). Stability strengths include excellent operational trends and good risk diversification. Strong capitalization (7.3) based on excellent risk adjusted capital (severe loss scenario). Moreover, capital levels have been consistently high over the last five years. High quality investment portfolio (7.1).

Other Rating Factors: Excellent profitability (9.2). Excellent liquidity (9.3).

Principal Business: Individual health insurance (98%) and individual life insurance (2%).

Principal Investments: CMOs and structured securities (49%), nonCMO investment grade bonds (46%), noninv. grade bonds (2%), and cash (2%).

Investments in Affiliates: None

Group Affiliation: Ellard Enterprises Inc

Licensed in: All states except AL, MI, NJ, NM, NC, SC, VA

Commenced Business: July 1938

Address: 4949 Keller Springs Rd, Addison, TX 75001-5910

Phone: (972) 532-2100 **Domicile State:** TX **NAIC Code:** 87963

Data Date	Rating	RACR #1	RACR #2	Total Assets ($mil)	Capital ($mil)	Net Premium ($mil)	Net Income ($mil)
3-09	B	1.77	1.21	240.7	29.4	20.3	1.8
3-08	B	1.89	1.31	209.3	28.9	18.7	1.8
2008	B	1.70	1.16	229.8	28.0	77.9	-1.1
2007	B	1.80	1.25	198.1	26.9	68.6	1.7
2006	C+	1.88	1.35	166.3	24.4	60.4	3.9
2005	C+	1.72	1.26	134.6	20.3	53.4	3.4
2004	C+	1.66	1.24	106.0	17.0	46.5	3.2

Adverse Trends in Operations

Increase in policy surrenders from 2006 to 2007 (26%)
Increase in policy surrenders from 2004 to 2005 (38%)

NATIONAL WESTERN LIFE INSURANCE COMPANY *   B+   Good

Major Rating Factors: Good quality investment portfolio (6.8 on a scale of 0 to 10) despite mixed results such as: minimal exposure to mortgages and large holdings of BBB rated bonds but small junk bond holdings. Good liquidity (6.2) with sufficient resources to handle a spike in claims as well as a significant increase in policy surrenders. Good overall results on stability tests (5.7) good operational trends and excellent risk diversification.

Other Rating Factors: Strong capitalization (8.5) based on excellent risk adjusted capital (severe loss scenario). Excellent profitability (7.7) with operating gains in each of the last five years.

Principal Business: Individual annuities (50%), individual life insurance (32%), and group retirement contracts (18%).

Principal Investments: NonCMO investment grade bonds (58%), CMOs and structured securities (35%), common & preferred stock (3%), noninv. grade bonds (2%), and misc. investments (3%).

Investments in Affiliates: 3%

Group Affiliation: None

Licensed in: All states except AL, NC

Commenced Business: June 1957

Address: 1675 Broadway #1200, Denver, CO 80202

Phone: (512) 836-1010 **Domicile State:** CO **NAIC Code:** 66850

Data Date	Rating	RACR #1	RACR #2	Total Assets ($mil)	Capital ($mil)	Net Premium ($mil)	Net Income ($mil)
3-09	B+	3.77	2.00	6,175.2	715.0	188.0	5.2
3-08	B-	3.93	2.08	6,094.0	716.0	140.3	8.4
2008	B	3.84	2.06	6,127.0	708.0	575.0	9.6
2007	B-	4.00	2.11	6,078.8	710.9	607.3	32.3
2006	C+	3.93	2.06	5,962.8	673.3	627.5	72.6
2005	C+	3.50	1.84	5,655.2	598.5	673.1	60.1
2004	C+	3.49	1.78	5,293.5	526.1	982.9	54.2

Adverse Trends in Operations

Decrease in premium volume from 2007 to 2008 (5%)
Change in premium mix from 2005 to 2006 (7.5%)
Decrease in premium volume from 2005 to 2006 (7%)
Change in premium mix from 2004 to 2005 (5.5%)
Decrease in premium volume from 2004 to 2005 (32%)

NATIONWIDE LIFE & ANNUITY COMPANY OF AMERICA   B   Good

Major Rating Factors: Good quality investment portfolio (6.8 on a scale of 0 to 10) despite significant exposure to mortgages . Mortgage default rate has been low. substantial holdings of BBB bonds in addition to small junk bond holdings. Good overall profitability (5.6). Return on equity has been good over the last five years, averaging 13.9%. Fair overall results on stability tests (4.5) including negative cash flow from operations for 2008.

Other Rating Factors: Strong capitalization (8.5) based on excellent risk adjusted capital (severe loss scenario). Excellent liquidity (7.1).

Principal Business: Individual life insurance (94%) and individual annuities (6%).

Principal Investments: NonCMO investment grade bonds (45%), CMOs and structured securities (31%), mortgages in good standing (15%), policy loans (7%), and noninv. grade bonds (2%).

Investments in Affiliates: None

Group Affiliation: Nationwide Corp

Licensed in: All states except AL, NC

Commenced Business: October 1959

Address: 300 Continental Dr, Newark, DE 19713

Phone: (610) 407-1056 **Domicile State:** DE **NAIC Code:** 70750

Data Date	Rating	RACR #1	RACR #2	Total Assets ($mil)	Capital ($mil)	Net Premium ($mil)	Net Income ($mil)
3-09	B	3.42	2.01	502.6	43.1	4.3	1.6
3-08	B	5.57	3.12	761.4	84.3	7.2	1.2
2008	B	3.25	1.98	530.3	40.9	25.3	-2.4
2007	B	5.50	3.00	833.1	83.3	30.5	9.4
2006	B-	4.50	2.29	909.9	74.1	29.7	10.2
2005	B-	3.59	1.85	957.7	63.6	29.1	10.0
2004	B-	2.82	1.42	1,052.4	54.5	36.8	12.1

Rating Indexes

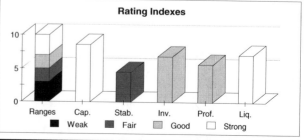

NATIONWIDE LIFE & ANNUITY INSURANCE COMPANY   B   Good

Major Rating Factors: Good capitalization (5.4 on a scale of 0 to 10) based on good risk adjusted capital (moderate loss scenario). Good liquidity (5.1) with sufficient resources to cover a large increase in policy surrenders. Fair quality investment portfolio (3.7) with large holdings of BBB rated bonds in addition to significant exposure to junk bonds. Exposure to mortgages is significant, but the mortgage default rate has been low.

Other Rating Factors: Fair overall results on stability tests (4.8) including negative cash flow from operations for 2008 and fair risk adjusted capital in prior years. Weak profitability (1.4) with operating losses during the first three months of 2009.

Principal Business: Individual annuities (52%), individual life insurance (48%), and group retirement contracts (1%).

Principal Investments: NonCMO investment grade bonds (36%), CMOs and structured securities (29%), mortgages in good standing (22%), and noninv. grade bonds (8%).

Investments in Affiliates: None

Group Affiliation: Nationwide Corp

Licensed in: All states except AL, NC

Commenced Business: May 1981

Address: One Nationwide Plaza, Columbus, OH 43216

Phone: (614) 249-5227 **Domicile State:** OH **NAIC Code:** 92657

Data Date	Rating	RACR #1	RACR #2	Total Assets ($mil)	Capital ($mil)	Net Premium ($mil)	Net Income ($mil)
3-09	B	1.29	0.61	4,342.6	120.8	48.3	-30.3
3-08	B	1.87	0.93	5,012.0	160.4	51.7	-11.3
2008	B	1.24	0.62	4,348.9	81.7	193.0	-87.9
2007	B	1.96	0.97	5,270.4	173.3	150.8	-13.4
2006	B	1.55	0.77	6,481.7	158.6	108.3	-45.6
2005	B	1.95	0.93	7,730.4	209.2	114.7	-17.0
2004	B	1.48	0.75	8,319.2	230.2	166.9	12.5

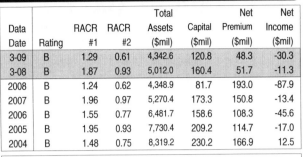

Junk Bonds as a % of Capital

Capital $82 mil.
Junk Bonds $262 mil.

0% 40% 80% 120% 160% 200% 240% 280% 320% 360%

■ BB   ▨ B   ▥ CCC   ▢ In default

NATIONWIDE LIFE INSURANCE COMPANY   B   Good

Major Rating Factors: Fair quality investment portfolio (4.7 on a scale of 0 to 10) with substantial holdings of BBB bonds in addition to junk bond exposure equal to 94% of capital. Exposure to mortgages is significant, but the mortgage default rate has been low. Fair overall results on stability tests (4.6). Weak profitability (2.3) with operating losses during the first three months of 2009.

Other Rating Factors: Strong capitalization (7.0) based on excellent risk adjusted capital (severe loss scenario). Excellent liquidity (9.2).

Principal Business: Individual annuities (49%), group retirement contracts (33%), individual life insurance (8%), group life insurance (5%), and other lines (5%).

Principal Investments: NonCMO investment grade bonds (31%), CMOs and structured securities (24%), mortgages in good standing (21%), noninv. grade bonds (6%), and misc. investments (11%).

Investments in Affiliates: None

Group Affiliation: Nationwide Corp

Licensed in: All states except AL

Commenced Business: January 1931

Address: One Nationwide Plaza, Columbus, OH 43215-2220

Phone: (614) 249-5227 **Domicile State:** OH **NAIC Code:** 66869

Data Date	Rating	RACR #1	RACR #2	Total Assets ($mil)	Capital ($mil)	Net Premium ($mil)	Net Income ($mil)
3-09	B	1.98	1.00	74,462.2	1,927.9	2,211.3	-127.5
3-08	B+	2.06	1.08	93,104.6	2,301.3	2,588.7	32.4
2008	B+	2.54	1.31	77,309.9	2,261.5	9,771.1	-898.3
2007	B+	2.25	1.19	99,016.7	2,501.1	10,732.5	309.0
2006	B+	2.35	1.26	97,060.3	2,682.3	10,923.3	537.5
2005	B+	2.29	1.15	92,685.3	2,601.8	10,213.4	462.5
2004	B+	2.21	1.10	90,735.1	2,391.0	10,237.5	317.7

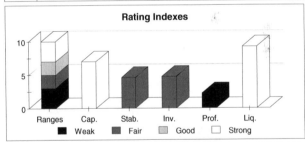

Rating Indexes

10

5

0
Ranges   Cap.   Stab.   Inv.   Prof.   Liq.

■ Weak   ▨ Fair   ▥ Good   ▢ Strong

NATIONWIDE LIFE INSURANCE COMPANY OF AMERICA *   B+   Good

Major Rating Factors: Good overall results on stability tests (5.2 on a scale of 0 to 10). Stability strengths include excellent risk diversification. Good quality investment portfolio (5.9) despite significant exposure to mortgages . Mortgage default rate has been low. substantial holdings of BBB bonds in addition to small junk bond holdings. Good overall profitability (6.4) despite operating losses during the first three months of 2009.

Other Rating Factors: Good liquidity (6.5). Strong capitalization (8.0) based on excellent risk adjusted capital (severe loss scenario).

Principal Business: Individual life insurance (96%), reinsurance (1%), and group life insurance (1%).

Principal Investments: NonCMO investment grade bonds (39%), CMOs and structured securities (26%), mortgages in good standing (17%), policy loans (10%), and misc. investments (9%).

Investments in Affiliates: 2%

Group Affiliation: Nationwide Corp

Licensed in: All states except AL

Commenced Business: June 1865

Address: 1600 Market St, Philadelphia, PA 19103

Phone: (610) 407-1056 **Domicile State:** PA **NAIC Code:** 68225

Data Date	Rating	RACR #1	RACR #2	Total Assets ($mil)	Capital ($mil)	Net Premium ($mil)	Net Income ($mil)
3-09	B+	2.81	1.68	4,826.2	501.7	52.7	-1.7
3-08	B+	2.85	1.81	6,056.6	689.7	58.0	14.8
2008	B+	2.78	1.67	4,993.6	488.4	227.9	27.8
2007	B+	2.82	1.79	6,338.5	674.0	258.0	91.6
2006	B+	2.77	1.73	6,648.5	654.3	275.4	95.3
2005	B	3.05	1.88	6,640.7	660.2	312.0	112.7
2004	B	2.75	1.63	6,657.8	576.5	332.1	126.4

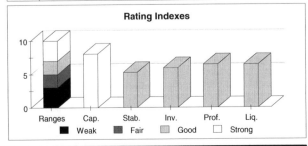

Rating Indexes

10

5

0
Ranges   Cap.   Stab.   Inv.   Prof.   Liq.

■ Weak   ▨ Fair   ▥ Good   ▢ Strong

NEW ENGLAND LIFE INSURANCE COMPANY

B   **Good**

Major Rating Factors: Good quality investment portfolio (6.6 on a scale of 0 to 10) despite mixed results such as: minimal exposure to mortgages and substantial holdings of BBB bonds but small junk bond holdings. Good overall profitability (6.2). Return on equity has been excellent over the last five years averaging 15.9%. Fair overall results on stability tests (4.8).

Other Rating Factors: Strong capitalization (8.1) based on excellent risk adjusted capital (severe loss scenario). Excellent liquidity (8.2).

Principal Business: Individual annuities (60%), individual life insurance (34%), group retirement contracts (4%), group health insurance (1%), and individual health insurance (1%).

Principal Investments: NonCMO investment grade bonds (39%), policy loans (25%), CMOs and structured securities (15%), common & preferred stock (4%), and misc. investments (18%).

Investments in Affiliates: 12%

Group Affiliation: MetLife Inc

Licensed in: All states except AL

Commenced Business: December 1980

Address: 501 Boylston St, Boston, MA 02117

Phone: (617) 578-2000 **Domicile State:** MA **NAIC Code:** 91626

Data Date	Rating	RACR #1	RACR #2	Total Assets ($mil)	Capital ($mil)	Net Premium ($mil)	Net Income ($mil)
3-09	B	3.04	1.73	8,624.0	401.5	366.2	7.4
3-08	B	3.69	2.08	11,559.8	559.0	384.7	3.8
2008	B	3.28	1.86	8,966.1	469.4	1,589.0	27.9
2007	B	3.66	2.06	12,459.0	544.2	1,879.5	121.6
2006	B	2.99	1.69	12,015.5	434.8	1,709.3	109.4
2005	B	2.40	1.36	10,779.1	318.8	1,639.4	50.0
2004	B	2.97	1.70	10,034.1	372.4	1,695.7	72.6

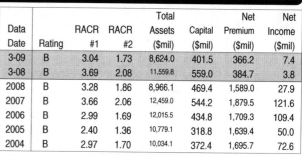

Rating Indexes

NEW ERA LIFE INSURANCE COMPANY

C   **Fair**

Major Rating Factors: Fair capitalization (3.2 on a scale of 0 to 10) based on fair risk adjusted capital (moderate loss scenario). Fair quality investment portfolio (4.6) with significant exposure to mortgages . The mortgage default rate has been low and moderate junk bond exposure. Fair overall results on stability tests (3.2) including negative cash flow from operations for 2008 and fair risk adjusted capital in prior years.

Other Rating Factors: Good overall profitability (5.4) despite operating losses during the first three months of 2009. Good liquidity (5.9).

Principal Business: Individual health insurance (74%), individual annuities (21%), individual life insurance (3%), and reinsurance (2%).

Principal Investments: CMOs and structured securities (33%), nonCMO investment grade bonds (26%), mortgages in good standing (18%), common & preferred stock (15%), and misc. investments (8%).

Investments in Affiliates: 10%

Group Affiliation: New Era Life Group

Licensed in: AK, AR, CO, CT, FL, GA, HI, IA, ME, MO, NY, ND, OR, RI, SD, TN, UT, VT, WI

Commenced Business: February 1971

Address: 200 Westlake Park Blvd, Houston, TX 77079

Phone: (713) 368-7200 **Domicile State:** TX **NAIC Code:** 78743

Data Date	Rating	RACR #1	RACR #2	Total Assets ($mil)	Capital ($mil)	Net Premium ($mil)	Net Income ($mil)
3-09	C	0.75	0.53	300.6	44.7	13.8	0.0
3-08	C-	0.85	0.66	306.7	45.5	19.2	0.5
2008	C	0.76	0.56	301.8	44.6	77.0	-0.9
2007	C-	0.82	0.64	299.8	44.7	117.5	-0.8
2006	C-	0.84	0.66	265.5	39.7	108.8	2.0
2005	D+	0.77	0.62	229.0	35.3	99.5	0.4
2004	D	0.67	0.55	202.2	33.6	110.1	0.4

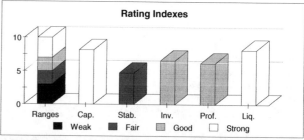

Risk-Adjusted Capital Ratio #1 (Moderate Loss Scenario)

NEW YORK LIFE INSURANCE & ANNUITY CORPORATION *

A-   **Excellent**

Major Rating Factors: Good capitalization (6.3 on a scale of 0 to 10) based on good risk adjusted capital (moderate loss scenario). Capital levels have been relatively consistent over the last five years. Good overall profitability (6.3) despite operating losses during the first three months of 2009. Return on equity has been fair, averaging 6.4%. Good overall results on stability tests (6.3) excellent operational trends and excellent risk diversification.

Other Rating Factors: Fair quality investment portfolio (4.2). Excellent liquidity (7.0).

Principal Business: Individual annuities (82%), individual life insurance (15%), group retirement contracts (1%), and group life insurance (1%).

Principal Investments: NonCMO investment grade bonds (43%), CMOs and structured securities (33%), mortgages in good standing (10%), noninv. grade bonds (7%), and misc. investments (6%).

Investments in Affiliates: 2%

Group Affiliation: New York Life Group

Licensed in: All states except AL

Commenced Business: December 1980

Address: 200 Continental Dr, Newark, DE 19713

Phone: (212) 576-7000 **Domicile State:** DE **NAIC Code:** 91596

Data Date	Rating	RACR #1	RACR #2	Total Assets ($mil)	Capital ($mil)	Net Premium ($mil)	Net Income ($mil)
3-09	A-	1.84	0.89	77,190.7	3,312.1	3,772.5	-206.8
3-08	A	2.13	1.02	73,552.2	2,660.3	2,070.0	25.4
2008	A	2.11	1.04	74,943.6	3,595.8	10,672.8	-386.9
2007	A	2.22	1.06	72,685.5	2,649.9	7,312.2	289.0
2006	A	2.06	0.98	66,967.1	2,323.9	7,279.3	251.6
2005	A	2.02	0.94	60,315.9	2,157.4	6,435.7	231.0
2004	A	1.99	0.93	56,282.5	2,008.8	7,390.8	224.4

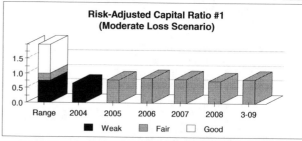

Junk Bonds as a % of Capital

NEW YORK LIFE INSURANCE COMPANY *   A-   Excellent

Major Rating Factors: Good quality investment portfolio (6.0 on a scale of 0 to 10) despite mixed results such as: substantial holdings of BBB bonds but moderate junk bond exposure. Good liquidity (6.6) with sufficient resources to handle a spike in claims as well as a significant increase in policy surrenders. Good overall results on stability tests (6.1) good operational trends and excellent risk diversification.

Other Rating Factors: Strong capitalization (7.1) based on excellent risk adjusted capital (severe loss scenario). Excellent profitability (7.1) despite operating losses during the first three months of 2009.

Principal Business: Individual life insurance (48%), group retirement contracts (29%), group life insurance (10%), reinsurance (5%), and other lines (8%).

Principal Investments: NonCMO investment grade bonds (43%), CMOs and structured securities (20%), mortgages in good standing (10%), policy loans (7%), and misc. investments (20%).

Investments in Affiliates: 9%
Group Affiliation: New York Life Group
Licensed in: All states except AL
Commenced Business: December 1845
Address: 51 Madison Ave, New York, NY 10010
Phone: (212) 576-7000 **Domicile State:** NY **NAIC Code:** 66915

Data Date	Rating	RACR #1	RACR #2	Total Assets ($mil)	Capital ($mil)	Net Premium ($mil)	Net Income ($mil)
3-09	A-	1.42	1.04	114,938	11,091.8	2,920.4	-222.5
3-08	A	1.56	1.15	123,447	11,769.7	2,489.3	-49.0
2008	A-	1.52	1.12	117,306	11,793.5	11,285.9	-564.4
2007	A	1.60	1.19	122,753	11,959.2	9,751.5	856.4
2006	A	1.75	1.25	113,704	11,300.3	9,301.2	794.3
2005	A	1.62	1.17	107,882	10,549.1	9,272.3	1,198.3
2004	A	1.67	1.15	101,304	9,707.8	8,632.9	984.2

Adverse Trends in Operations

Decrease in asset base during 2008 (4%)
Decrease in capital during 2008 (1%)

NIPPON LIFE INSURANCE COMPANY OF AMERICA *   A-   Excellent

Major Rating Factors: Good overall profitability (6.6 on a scale of 0 to 10). Return on equity has been low, averaging 3.4%. Good liquidity (6.5) with sufficient resources to handle a spike in claims. Good overall results on stability tests (6.9) despite negative cash flow from operations for 2008. Strengths that enhance stability include good operational trends and excellent risk diversification.

Other Rating Factors: Strong capitalization (9.9) based on excellent risk adjusted capital (severe loss scenario). High quality investment portfolio (8.0).

Principal Business: Group health insurance (97%) and group life insurance (3%).

Principal Investments: NonCMO investment grade bonds (77%), CMOs and structured securities (22%), common & preferred stock (2%), and mortgages in good standing (2%).

Investments in Affiliates: None
Group Affiliation: Nippon Life Ins Co Japan
Licensed in: All states except AL, MD, NJ, ND, PR
Commenced Business: July 1973
Address: 650 8th St, Des Moines, IA 50309
Phone: (212) 682-3992 **Domicile State:** IA **NAIC Code:** 81264

Data Date	Rating	RACR #1	RACR #2	Total Assets ($mil)	Capital ($mil)	Net Premium ($mil)	Net Income ($mil)
3-09	A-	3.78	2.95	162.8	115.3	54.1	1.7
3-08	B+	3.77	2.97	167.4	116.4	57.1	-0.9
2008	B+	3.73	2.94	159.6	113.9	223.1	-4.0
2007	B+	3.81	3.01	169.5	118.0	229.5	1.3
2006	B+	4.03	3.17	168.7	116.7	213.1	5.3
2005	B-	3.87	3.04	162.9	111.2	211.1	5.0
2004	B-	3.73	2.92	158.6	105.9	208.9	6.7

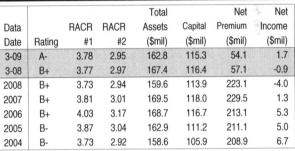

Net Income History
(in thousands of dollars)

NORTH AMERICAN COMPANY FOR LIFE & HEALTH INSURANCE   B   Good

Major Rating Factors: Good liquidity (6.5 on a scale of 0 to 10) with sufficient resources to handle a spike in claims as well as a significant increase in policy surrenders. Good overall results on stability tests (5.6). Stability strengths include excellent operational trends, good risk adjusted capital for prior years and excellent risk diversification. Fair quality investment portfolio (4.6).

Other Rating Factors: Strong capitalization (7.1) based on excellent risk adjusted capital (severe loss scenario). Excellent profitability (7.3) despite modest operating losses during 2008.

Principal Business: Individual annuities (70%), individual life insurance (20%), group retirement contracts (9%), and group life insurance (1%).

Principal Investments: NonCMO investment grade bonds (59%), CMOs and structured securities (31%), noninv. grade bonds (5%), common & preferred stock (1%), and policy loans (1%).

Investments in Affiliates: None
Group Affiliation: Sammons Enterprises Inc
Licensed in: All states except AL, NC
Commenced Business: June 1886
Address: 525 W VanBuren, Chicago, IL 60607
Phone: (312) 648-7600 **Domicile State:** IA **NAIC Code:** 66974

Data Date	Rating	RACR #1	RACR #2	Total Assets ($mil)	Capital ($mil)	Net Premium ($mil)	Net Income ($mil)
3-09	B	2.16	1.06	8,961.9	516.9	505.3	-1.0
3-08	B	1.98	0.97	7,317.3	387.9	292.5	-2.8
2008	B	2.37	1.20	8,446.9	526.6	1,821.5	-18.3
2007	B	2.01	0.98	6,637.3	387.7	1,114.7	2.4
2006	B	2.53	1.27	5,452.0	399.7	769.7	75.4
2005	B	1.90	1.13	5,103.3	432.7	563.3	41.0
2004	B-	1.68	1.09	4,568.7	401.3	580.3	55.3

Adverse Trends in Operations

Increase in policy surrenders from 2007 to 2008 (28%)
Decrease in capital during 2007 (3%)
Increase in policy surrenders from 2006 to 2007 (30%)
Change in premium mix from 2005 to 2006 (4.9%)
Decrease in premium volume from 2004 to 2005 (3%)

NORTHWESTERN LONG TERM CARE INSURANCE COMPANY   B-   Good

Major Rating Factors: Good current capitalization (6.9 on a scale of 0 to 10) based on good risk adjusted capital (severe loss scenario), although results have slipped from the excellent range during the last year. Good quality investment portfolio (5.4) despite mixed results such as: no exposure to mortgages and substantial holdings of BBB bonds but minimal holdings in junk bonds. Good overall results on stability tests (5.1) excellent operational trends, excellent risk adjusted capital for prior years and excellent risk diversification.

Other Rating Factors: Weak profitability (1.9) with operating losses during the first three months of 2009. Excellent liquidity (9.4).

Principal Business: Individual health insurance (100%).

Principal Investments: NonCMO investment grade bonds (58%), CMOs and structured securities (31%), common & preferred stock (10%), and noninv. grade bonds (1%).

Investments in Affiliates: None

Group Affiliation: Northwestern Mutual Group

Licensed in: All states except AL

Commenced Business: October 1953

Address: 720 E Wisconsin Ave, Milwaukee, WI 53202

Phone: (414) 299-3136 **Domicile State:** WI **NAIC Code:** 69000

Data Date	Rating	RACR #1	RACR #2	Total Assets ($mil)	Capital ($mil)	Net Premium ($mil)	Net Income ($mil)
3-09	B-	1.48	0.99	413.1	56.8	43.3	-5.9
3-08	B	1.66	1.11	302.1	54.2	36.5	1.9
2008	B-	1.68	1.13	402.7	63.4	158.9	-17.6
2007	B	1.79	1.21	287.4	53.6	124.6	-3.8
2006	B	2.38	1.61	217.1	58.3	94.1	-8.8
2005	B	3.14	2.13	157.9	62.4	69.1	-2.5
2004	B-	3.71	2.51	114.4	55.3	47.3	-7.0

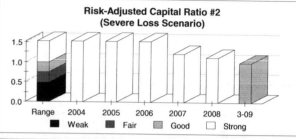

Risk-Adjusted Capital Ratio #2 (Severe Loss Scenario)

Range, 2004, 2005, 2006, 2007, 2008, 3-09
■ Weak ■ Fair ■ Good □ Strong

NORTHWESTERN MUTUAL LIFE INSURANCE COMPANY *   A-   Excellent

Major Rating Factors: Good quality investment portfolio (5.3 on a scale of 0 to 10) despite substantial holdings of BBB bonds in addition to junk bond exposure equal to 74% of capital. Exposure to mortgages is significant, but the mortgage default rate has been low. Good liquidity (6.2) with sufficient resources to handle a spike in claims as well as a significant increase in policy surrenders. Strong capitalization (7.8) based on excellent risk adjusted capital (severe loss scenario).

Other Rating Factors: Excellent profitability (8.5) with operating gains in each of the last five years. Excellent overall results on stability tests (7.3) excellent operational trends and excellent risk diversification.

Principal Business: Individual life insurance (83%), individual annuities (9%), individual health insurance (6%), group retirement contracts (1%), and group health insurance (1%).

Principal Investments: NonCMO investment grade bonds (39%), mortgages in good standing (16%), CMOs and structured securities (16%), policy loans (10%), and misc. investments (19%).

Investments in Affiliates: 4%

Group Affiliation: Northwestern Mutual Group

Licensed in: All states except AL

Commenced Business: November 1858

Address: 720 E Wisconsin Ave, Milwaukee, WI 53202

Phone: (414) 271-1444 **Domicile State:** WI **NAIC Code:** 67091

Data Date	Rating	RACR #1	RACR #2	Total Assets ($mil)	Capital ($mil)	Net Premium ($mil)	Net Income ($mil)
3-09	A-	2.96	1.52	155,607	12,156.8	3,166.3	48.1
3-08	A	3.32	1.64	158,298	12,416.4	3,336.9	436.8
2008	A-	3.05	1.56	154,835	12,401.3	13,336.7	500.8
2007	A	3.49	1.73	156,332	12,106.0	13,065.7	1,003.8
2006	A	3.59	1.81	144,962	11,684.4	11,996.4	838.2
2005	A	3.60	1.80	132,973	10,380.5	11,257.0	926.4
2004	A	3.48	1.70	123,907	8,934.0	10,596.7	823.7

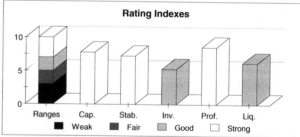

Rating Indexes

Ranges, Cap., Stab., Inv., Prof., Liq.
■ Weak ■ Fair ■ Good □ Strong

NYLIFE INSURANCE COMPANY OF ARIZONA   B   Good

Major Rating Factors: Good liquidity (6.5 on a scale of 0 to 10) with sufficient resources to handle a spike in claims. Good overall results on stability tests (6.0). Strengths include potential support from affiliation with New York Life Group, excellent operational trends and excellent risk diversification. Weak profitability (2.3) with investment income below regulatory standards in relation to interest assumptions of reserves.

Other Rating Factors: Strong capitalization (8.3) based on excellent risk adjusted capital (severe loss scenario). High quality investment portfolio (8.2).

Principal Business: Individual life insurance (99%) and reinsurance (1%).

Principal Investments: NonCMO investment grade bonds (85%), CMOs and structured securities (15%), and noninv. grade bonds (1%).

Investments in Affiliates: None

Group Affiliation: New York Life Group

Licensed in: All states except AL, MD, NC

Commenced Business: December 1987

Address: 4343 N Scottsdale Rd Suite 220, Scottsdale, AZ 85251

Phone: (212) 576-7000 **Domicile State:** AZ **NAIC Code:** 81353

Data Date	Rating	RACR #1	RACR #2	Total Assets ($mil)	Capital ($mil)	Net Premium ($mil)	Net Income ($mil)
3-09	B	2.83	1.88	188.0	39.5	9.3	1.9
3-08	B	2.88	1.91	182.6	37.6	9.5	1.5
2008	B	2.74	1.83	189.6	38.0	39.3	1.6
2007	B	2.82	1.89	178.1	36.1	39.6	-3.7
2006	B-	2.50	1.68	155.5	31.3	42.0	-0.6
2005	C+	2.58	1.73	140.3	29.8	40.2	-7.7
2004	C+	2.96	2.00	125.0	36.2	38.6	-11.6

New York Life Group Composite Group Rating: A Largest Group Members	Assets ($mil)	Rating
NEW YORK LIFE INS CO	117306	A-
NEW YORK LIFE INS ANNUITY CORP	74944	A
NYLIFE INS CO OF ARIZONA	190	B

OCCIDENTAL LIFE INSURANCE COMPANY OF NC   B   Good

Major Rating Factors: Good overall results on stability tests (6.2 on a scale of 0 to 10) despite negative cash flow from operations for 2008. Other stability subfactors include good operational trends and good risk diversification. Good overall profitability (6.3). Return on equity has been excellent over the last five years averaging 16.8%. Good liquidity (6.0).

Other Rating Factors: Strong capitalization (8.3) based on excellent risk adjusted capital (severe loss scenario). High quality investment portfolio (7.5).

Principal Business: Individual life insurance (94%) and individual annuities (5%).

Principal Investments: CMOs and structured securities (70%), nonCMO investment grade bonds (24%), and policy loans (5%).

Investments in Affiliates: None

Group Affiliation: American Amicable Group

Licensed in: All states except AL, NC

Commenced Business: November 1906

Address: 425 Austin Avenue, Waco, TX 76701

Phone: (254) 297-2775 **Domicile State:** TX **NAIC Code:** 67148

Data Date	Rating	RACR #1	RACR #2	Total Assets ($mil)	Capital ($mil)	Net Premium ($mil)	Net Income ($mil)
3-09	B	2.90	1.87	253.9	29.7	7.3	0.6
3-08	B	2.70	2.00	259.2	27.7	7.0	0.0
2008	B	2.79	1.82	259.0	29.0	30.4	3.1
2007	B	2.69	2.00	255.2	27.8	33.0	5.0
2006	B-	2.32	1.78	250.1	23.7	24.3	3.6
2005	C+	2.71	1.81	258.4	27.2	22.5	4.6
2004	C+	2.34	1.31	259.7	23.6	20.6	4.1

Adverse Trends in Operations

Decrease in premium volume from 2007 to 2008 (8%)
Decrease in asset base during 2006 (3%)
Decrease in capital during 2006 (13%)

OHIO NATIONAL LIFE ASSURANCE CORPORATION *   B+   Good

Major Rating Factors: Good overall results on stability tests (6.4 on a scale of 0 to 10). Stability strengths include good operational trends, good risk adjusted capital for prior years and excellent risk diversification. Good overall profitability (6.8). Excellent expense controls. Return on equity has been low, averaging 4.5%. Fair quality investment portfolio (4.8).

Other Rating Factors: Fair liquidity (4.9). Strong capitalization (7.2) based on excellent risk adjusted capital (severe loss scenario).

Principal Business: Individual life insurance (95%) and individual health insurance (5%).

Principal Investments: NonCMO investment grade bonds (54%), mortgages in good standing (20%), CMOs and structured securities (16%), noninv. grade bonds (7%), and misc. investments (4%).

Investments in Affiliates: None

Group Affiliation: Ohio National Life Group

Licensed in: All states except AL, AZ, ID, NC

Commenced Business: August 1979

Address: One Financial Way, Cincinnati, OH 45242

Phone: (513) 794-6100 **Domicile State:** OH **NAIC Code:** 89206

Data Date	Rating	RACR #1	RACR #2	Total Assets ($mil)	Capital ($mil)	Net Premium ($mil)	Net Income ($mil)
3-09	B+	2.16	1.11	2,702.3	259.4	57.8	4.2
3-08	B+	1.63	0.86	2,703.7	188.2	71.0	-1.1
2008	B+	2.29	1.19	2,739.3	267.5	291.0	-43.4
2007	B+	1.67	0.89	2,691.0	188.6	297.1	7.3
2006	B+	1.63	0.87	2,475.1	169.4	356.3	-6.0
2005	B+	1.69	0.88	2,208.6	164.4	280.9	-20.2
2004	B+	1.60	0.83	1,982.8	138.3	236.8	6.7

Adverse Trends in Operations

Decrease in premium volume from 2007 to 2008 (2%)
Decrease in premium volume from 2006 to 2007 (17%)
Increase in policy surrenders from 2005 to 2006 (30%)

OHIO NATIONAL LIFE INSURANCE COMPANY   B   Good

Major Rating Factors: Good current capitalization (6.8 on a scale of 0 to 10) based on good risk adjusted capital (severe loss scenario), although results have slipped from the excellent range during the last year. Good quality investment portfolio (5.7) despite large holdings of BBB rated bonds in addition to junk bond exposure equal to 55% of capital. Exposure to mortgages is significant, but the mortgage default rate has been low. Good overall profitability (5.2) despite operating losses during the first three months of 2009.

Other Rating Factors: Good overall results on stability tests (5.8) good operational trends, excellent risk adjusted capital for prior years and excellent risk diversification. Excellent liquidity (8.1).

Principal Business: Individual annuities (84%), individual life insurance (8%), group retirement contracts (6%), reinsurance (2%), and individual health insurance (1%).

Principal Investments: NonCMO investment grade bonds (55%), CMOs and structured securities (16%), mortgages in good standing (14%), noninv. grade bonds (6%), and misc. investments (9%).

Investments in Affiliates: 5%

Group Affiliation: Ohio National Life Group

Licensed in: All states except AL, AZ, ID, NC

Commenced Business: October 1910

Address: One Financial Way, Cincinnati, OH 45242

Phone: (513) 794-6100 **Domicile State:** OH **NAIC Code:** 67172

Data Date	Rating	RACR #1	RACR #2	Total Assets ($mil)	Capital ($mil)	Net Premium ($mil)	Net Income ($mil)
3-09	B	1.46	0.97	12,098.1	738.3	623.0	-1.0
3-08	B	1.86	1.16	12,828.9	784.7	722.2	3.5
2008	B	1.49	1.00	12,159.8	757.2	2,515.5	-129.6
2007	B	1.90	1.19	13,004.2	794.9	2,732.9	36.9
2006	B	1.97	1.22	11,246.6	791.3	1,877.0	76.1
2005	B	1.78	1.10	10,361.6	749.8	1,306.0	94.4
2004	B	1.77	1.07	9,659.7	686.4	1,164.8	73.5

Risk-Adjusted Capital Ratio #2
(Severe Loss Scenario)

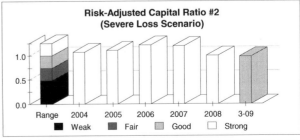

OLD REPUBLIC LIFE INSURANCE COMPANY B Good

Major Rating Factors: Good overall results on stability tests (5.1 on a scale of 0 to 10). Stability strengths include good operational trends and excellent risk diversification. Good overall profitability (5.3). Excellent expense controls. Return on equity has been low, averaging 3.7%. Good liquidity (6.9) with sufficient resources to handle a spike in claims.

Other Rating Factors: Strong capitalization (8.8) based on excellent risk adjusted capital (severe loss scenario). High quality investment portfolio (8.3).

Principal Business: Individual life insurance (45%), group health insurance (38%), and reinsurance (17%).

Principal Investments: NonCMO investment grade bonds (99%), noninv. grade bonds (1%), and policy loans (1%).

Investments in Affiliates: None

Group Affiliation: Old Republic Group

Licensed in: All states except AL, NC

Commenced Business: April 1923

Address: 307 N Michigan Ave, Chicago, IL 60601

Phone: (312) 346-8100 **Domicile State:** IL **NAIC Code:** 67261

Data Date	Rating	RACR #1	RACR #2	Total Assets ($mil)	Capital ($mil)	Net Premium ($mil)	Net Income ($mil)
3-09	B	3.31	2.19	148.8	31.5	6.2	0.2
3-08	B	3.46	2.30	156.8	37.4	7.6	0.1
2008	B	3.69	2.45	154.0	35.1	28.4	0.8
2007	B	3.96	2.64	162.5	43.0	30.4	4.3
2006	B	3.38	2.27	149.3	34.5	32.1	3.4
2005	B	3.06	2.05	142.7	31.8	28.1	1.7
2004	B	1.52	1.16	109.2	23.8	31.0	-2.8

Adverse Trends in Operations

Decrease in asset base during 2008 (5%)
Decrease in premium volume from 2007 to 2008 (7%)
Decrease in capital during 2008 (18%)
Decrease in premium volume from 2004 to 2005 (9%)
Increase in policy surrenders from 2004 to 2005 (161%)

OLD UNITED LIFE INSURANCE COMPANY B- Good

Major Rating Factors: Good overall profitability (6.8 on a scale of 0 to 10). Return on equity has been fair, averaging 6.6%. Fair overall results on stability tests (4.0). Strong overall capitalization (10.0) based on excellent risk adjusted capital (severe loss scenario). However, capital levels have fluctuated somewhat during past years.

Other Rating Factors: High quality investment portfolio (7.2). Excellent liquidity (9.4).

Principal Business: Credit life insurance (54%) and credit health insurance (46%).

Principal Investments: NonCMO investment grade bonds (78%), CMOs and structured securities (14%), common & preferred stock (6%), and noninv. grade bonds (2%).

Investments in Affiliates: None

Group Affiliation: Van Enterprises Group

Licensed in: All states except AL, MD, NJ, NM, NC

Commenced Business: January 1964

Address: 8500 W Shawnee Mission Pky 200, Merriam, KS 66202

Phone: (913) 432-6400 **Domicile State:** AZ **NAIC Code:** 76007

Data Date	Rating	RACR #1	RACR #2	Total Assets ($mil)	Capital ($mil)	Net Premium ($mil)	Net Income ($mil)
3-09	B-	5.05	4.55	70.5	35.7	0.4	1.1
3-08	B-	5.02	4.14	71.9	34.7	1.0	0.4
2008	B-	4.93	4.44	71.4	34.9	5.4	0.1
2007	B-	5.06	4.12	73.5	34.6	9.2	0.6
2006	C+	5.17	4.18	68.8	34.5	9.6	0.5
2005	C+	5.27	4.74	62.3	34.0	3.6	5.3
2004	C+	4.64	4.17	64.7	30.0	5.0	4.2

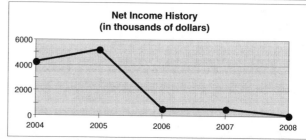

Net Income History
(in thousands of dollars)

OM FINANCIAL LIFE INSURANCE COMPANY C Fair

Major Rating Factors: Fair quality investment portfolio (3.3 on a scale of 0 to 10) with large holdings of BBB rated bonds in addition to junk bond exposure equal to 59% of capital. Fair profitability (3.6). Return on equity has been low, averaging -6.9%. Fair overall results on stability tests (4.2) including fair risk adjusted capital in prior years.

Other Rating Factors: Good capitalization (5.6) based on good risk adjusted capital (moderate loss scenario). Good liquidity (5.9).

Principal Business: Individual annuities (69%), individual life insurance (29%), and reinsurance (2%).

Principal Investments: NonCMO investment grade bonds (65%), CMOs and structured securities (22%), common & preferred stock (8%), noninv. grade bonds (3%), and policy loans (1%).

Investments in Affiliates: 1%

Group Affiliation: Old Mutual plc

Licensed in: All states except AL, NC

Commenced Business: November 1960

Address: 100 E Pratt St, Baltimore, MD 21202

Phone: (410) 895-0100 **Domicile State:** MD **NAIC Code:** 63274

Data Date	Rating	RACR #1	RACR #2	Total Assets ($mil)	Capital ($mil)	Net Premium ($mil)	Net Income ($mil)
3-09	C	1.39	0.71	17,140.4	816.5	216.7	71.8
3-08	C	1.01	0.55	17,972.6	600.4	435.1	-85.5
2008	C	1.38	0.72	17,450.0	802.7	1,793.4	-284.1
2007	C	1.16	0.63	18,202.3	702.7	2,288.3	-41.1
2006	C	1.05	0.58	19,015.4	629.6	2,373.1	-160.3
2005	C	1.14	0.61	17,458.3	654.0	2,327.1	-149.7
2004	C	1.30	0.67	14,974.8	720.6	2,994.5	-39.6

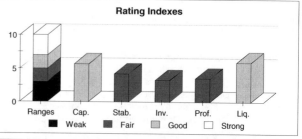

Rating Indexes

■ Weak ▨ Fair ▨ Good ☐ Strong

OM FINANCIAL LIFE INSURANCE COMPANY OF NEW YORK — B- — Good

Major Rating Factors: Good overall profitability (5.5 on a scale of 0 to 10). Excellent expense controls. Return on equity has been fair, averaging 6.7%. Good liquidity (6.1) with sufficient resources to cover a large increase in policy surrenders. Fair overall results on stability tests (4.9) including fair financial strength of affiliated Old Mutual plc.

Other Rating Factors: Fair quality investment portfolio (3.3). Strong capitalization (7.1) based on excellent risk adjusted capital (severe loss scenario).

Principal Business: Individual annuities (94%) and individual life insurance (6%).

Principal Investments: NonCMO investment grade bonds (67%), CMOs and structured securities (20%), common & preferred stock (8%), and noninv. grade bonds (4%).

Investments in Affiliates: None

Group Affiliation: Old Mutual plc

Licensed in: NC

Commenced Business: November 1962

Address: 2500 Westchester Ave, Purchase, NY 10577

Phone: (914) 251-2413 **Domicile State:** NY **NAIC Code:** 69434

Data Date	Rating	RACR #1	RACR #2	Total Assets ($mil)	Capital ($mil)	Net Premium ($mil)	Net Income ($mil)
3-09	B-	2.12	1.04	460.8	35.6	3.5	1.7
3-08	B-	2.19	1.13	495.0	38.6	28.0	0.7
2008	B-	2.05	1.05	472.6	34.8	56.6	-5.9
2007	C+	2.18	1.13	483.9	38.0	49.1	4.9
2006	C	1.87	0.96	487.6	33.1	35.5	-3.2
2005	C	2.05	1.04	493.2	36.8	12.3	3.8
2004	C-	1.74	0.85	509.0	33.1	18.9	2.4

Old Mutual plc
Composite Group Rating: C

Largest Group Members	Assets ($mil)	Rating
OM FINANCIAL LIFE INS CO	17450	C
OM FINANCIAL LIFE INS CO OF NEW YORK	473	B-

OXFORD LIFE INSURANCE COMPANY — B- — Good

Major Rating Factors: Good liquidity (6.7 on a scale of 0 to 10) with sufficient resources to handle a spike in claims as well as a significant increase in policy surrenders. Fair overall results on stability tests (4.9) including negative cash flow from operations for 2008. Strong capitalization (7.9) based on excellent risk adjusted capital (severe loss scenario).

Other Rating Factors: High quality investment portfolio (7.4). Excellent profitability (8.7) with operating gains in each of the last five years.

Principal Business: Reinsurance (38%), individual life insurance (26%), individual health insurance (21%), individual annuities (12%), and group health insurance (2%).

Principal Investments: NonCMO investment grade bonds (53%), CMOs and structured securities (23%), mortgages in good standing (12%), common & preferred stock (10%), and misc. investments (2%).

Investments in Affiliates: 10%

Group Affiliation: Amerco Corp

Licensed in: All states except AL, NC, VA

Commenced Business: June 1968

Address: 2721 N Central Ave, Phoenix, AZ 85004-1120

Phone: (602) 263-6666 **Domicile State:** AZ **NAIC Code:** 76112

Data Date	Rating	RACR #1	RACR #2	Total Assets ($mil)	Capital ($mil)	Net Premium ($mil)	Net Income ($mil)
3-09	B-	2.01	1.62	491.0	130.0	10.4	0.0
3-08	C+	1.91	1.52	528.6	126.2	10.2	0.9
2008	B-	2.01	1.62	502.9	129.7	36.7	9.8
2007	C	1.90	1.52	535.8	124.2	38.8	13.1
2006	C	1.67	1.30	576.3	113.0	33.2	14.9
2005	C-	1.38	1.05	633.2	101.5	41.2	8.0
2004	C-	1.09	0.76	689.4	85.6	47.0	13.0

Rating Indexes

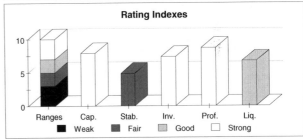

OZARK NATIONAL LIFE INSURANCE COMPANY — B — Good

Major Rating Factors: Good overall profitability (5.9 on a scale of 0 to 10). Return on equity has been excellent over the last five years averaging 24.0%. Good overall results on stability tests (5.9). Stability strengths include excellent operational trends and excellent risk diversification. Strong capitalization (9.4) based on excellent risk adjusted capital (severe loss scenario).

Other Rating Factors: High quality investment portfolio (8.1). Excellent liquidity (7.1).

Principal Business: Individual life insurance (99%).

Principal Investments: CMOs and structured securities (53%), nonCMO investment grade bonds (42%), policy loans (3%), real estate (2%), and cash (1%).

Investments in Affiliates: None

Group Affiliation: CNS Corp

Licensed in: AK, AR, CA, CO, CT, GA, HI, IN, IA, KS, KY, LA, ME, MN, MS, MO, MT, NE, NV, NH, NY, OH, OK, OR, TN, TX, UT, VT, WY, PR

Commenced Business: June 1964

Address: 500 E 9th St, Kansas City, MO 64106

Phone: (816) 842-6300 **Domicile State:** MO **NAIC Code:** 67393

Data Date	Rating	RACR #1	RACR #2	Total Assets ($mil)	Capital ($mil)	Net Premium ($mil)	Net Income ($mil)
3-09	B	4.45	2.63	626.5	99.2	21.7	5.6
3-08	B	4.08	2.42	595.6	89.2	23.1	5.3
2008	B	4.34	2.57	617.6	96.6	89.9	21.1
2007	B	4.00	2.37	586.2	87.1	92.9	21.2
2006	B-	3.78	2.25	554.2	79.1	93.1	20.6
2005	B-	3.40	2.00	522.3	70.4	94.3	17.3
2004	B-	3.10	1.79	493.8	65.7	95.2	16.8

Net Income History
(in millions of dollars)

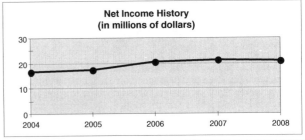

www.thestreetratings.com
171
* Denotes a TheStreet.com Recommended Company

PACIFIC BEACON LIFE REASSURANCE INCORPORATED · C+ · Fair

Major Rating Factors: Fair overall results on stability tests (4.9 on a scale of 0 to 10) including fair risk adjusted capital in prior years. Good quality investment portfolio (6.8) despite mixed results such as: substantial holdings of BBB bonds but moderate junk bond exposure. Good liquidity (6.2) with sufficient resources to handle a spike in claims as well as a significant increase in policy surrenders.

Other Rating Factors: Weak profitability (2.6) with operating losses during the first three months of 2009. Strong capitalization (7.5) based on excellent risk adjusted capital (severe loss scenario).

Principal Business: Reinsurance (100%).

Principal Investments: NonCMO investment grade bonds (65%), CMOs and structured securities (27%), and noninv. grade bonds (5%).

Investments in Affiliates: None

Group Affiliation: California State Auto Group

Licensed in: ID

Commenced Business: June 1999

Address: 745 Fort St Ste 800, Honolulu, HI 96813

Phone: (415) 565-2266 **Domicile State:** HI **NAIC Code:** 84162

Data Date	Rating	RACR #1	RACR #2	Total Assets ($mil)	Capital ($mil)	Net Premium ($mil)	Net Income ($mil)
3-09	C+	2.27	1.32	290.6	38.4	12.6	-0.2
3-08	C	N/A	N/A	N/A	N/A	N/A	N/A
2008	C	2.33	1.36	284.5	40.3	45.1	-7.2
2007	C	1.56	0.90	257.5	23.2	38.0	-3.3
2006	C	1.57	0.89	248.5	21.0	36.5	-8.7
2005	C	1.37	0.80	225.8	14.9	35.4	-4.2
2004	C-	1.17	0.68	203.2	11.2	52.3	-1.4

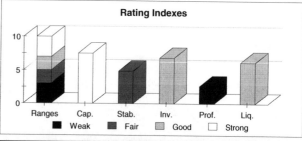

Rating Indexes

PACIFIC CENTURY LIFE INSURANCE CORPORATION · C+ · Fair

Major Rating Factors: Fair overall results on stability tests (4.5 on a scale of 0 to 10). Strong overall capitalization (10.0) based on excellent risk adjusted capital (severe loss scenario). However, capital levels have fluctuated somewhat during past years. High quality investment portfolio (7.4) despite large exposure to mortgages . Mortgage default rate has been low. no exposure to junk bonds.

Other Rating Factors: Excellent profitability (7.0). Excellent liquidity (10.0).

Principal Business: Reinsurance (94%), credit life insurance (5%), and credit health insurance (2%).

Principal Investments: Mortgages in good standing (88%), cash (8%), and nonCMO investment grade bonds (4%).

Investments in Affiliates: None

Group Affiliation: Bank of Hawaii Corp

Licensed in: AR, ID

Commenced Business: February 1982

Address: 2700 N Third St Ste 2000, Phoenix, AZ 85004

Phone: (602) 200-6900 **Domicile State:** AZ **NAIC Code:** 93815

Data Date	Rating	RACR #1	RACR #2	Total Assets ($mil)	Capital ($mil)	Net Premium ($mil)	Net Income ($mil)
3-09	C+	29.95	21.02	335.6	330.7	0.2	2.8
3-08	C+	29.89	19.62	335.1	330.0	0.2	2.9
2008	C+	29.69	21.16	331.4	327.8	0.8	11.3
2007	C	29.63	20.76	331.1	327.0	1.1	10.6
2006	C	N/A	N/A	320.0	316.4	1.1	9.4
2005	C	28.96	20.80	320.7	316.8	1.1	9.8
2004	C	28.93	22.34	320.5	316.6	1.7	9.5

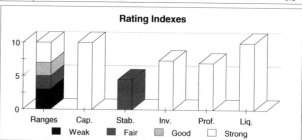

Rating Indexes

PACIFIC GUARDIAN LIFE INSURANCE COMPANY LIMITED * · A- · Excellent

Major Rating Factors: Good quality investment portfolio (6.6 on a scale of 0 to 10) despite large exposure to mortgages . Mortgage default rate has been low. substantial holdings of BBB bonds in addition to no exposure to junk bonds. Good overall profitability (6.9). Return on equity has been fair, averaging 8.3%. Good liquidity (6.2).

Other Rating Factors: Good overall results on stability tests (6.7) excellent operational trends and good risk diversification. Strong capitalization (8.7) based on excellent risk adjusted capital (severe loss scenario).

Principal Business: Individual life insurance (46%), group health insurance (37%), and group life insurance (16%).

Principal Investments: NonCMO investment grade bonds (37%), mortgages in good standing (36%), CMOs and structured securities (18%), policy loans (6%), and misc. investments (4%).

Investments in Affiliates: None

Group Affiliation: Meiji Yasuda Life Ins Co

Licensed in: AZ, AR, CO, CT, ID, IL, KS, ME, MT, NE, NV, NH, NY, OR, PA, TN, UT, VT, WV, PR

Commenced Business: November 1947

Address: 1440 Kapiolani Blvd Ste 1700, Honolulu, HI 96814

Phone: (808) 955-2236 **Domicile State:** HI **NAIC Code:** 64343

Data Date	Rating	RACR #1	RACR #2	Total Assets ($mil)	Capital ($mil)	Net Premium ($mil)	Net Income ($mil)
2008	A-	3.53	2.10	426.8	83.3	74.7	6.1
2007	A-	3.59	2.15	436.7	90.4	69.2	9.2
2006	B+	3.38	2.00	448.7	85.2	65.4	6.9
2005	B+	3.13	1.86	453.0	81.2	61.2	7.3
2004	B+	3.15	1.85	445.0	77.7	57.0	6.0

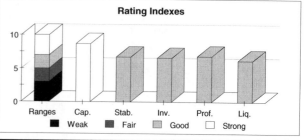

Rating Indexes

PACIFIC LIFE & ANNUITY COMPANY *   A-   Excellent

Major Rating Factors: Good quality investment portfolio (6.7 on a scale of 0 to 10) despite significant exposure to mortgages . Mortgage default rate has been low. large holdings of BBB rated bonds in addition to small junk bond holdings. Good overall results on stability tests (6.2). Strengths include potential support from affiliation with Pacific LifeCorp, good operational trends and excellent risk diversification. Weak profitability (1.9) with operating losses during the first three months of 2009.

Other Rating Factors: Strong capitalization (9.3) based on excellent risk adjusted capital (severe loss scenario). Excellent liquidity (9.7).

Principal Business: Individual annuities (92%), individual life insurance (6%), and reinsurance (1%).

Principal Investments: NonCMO investment grade bonds (63%), CMOs and structured securities (18%), mortgages in good standing (11%), noninv. grade bonds (4%), and common & preferred stock (1%).

Investments in Affiliates: None
Group Affiliation: Pacific LifeCorp
Licensed in: All states except AL
Commenced Business: July 1983
Address: 638 N Fifth Ave, Phoenix, AZ 85003
Phone: (714) 640-3011 **Domicile State:** AZ **NAIC Code:** 97268

Data Date	Rating	RACR #1	RACR #2	Total Assets ($mil)	Capital ($mil)	Net Premium ($mil)	Net Income ($mil)
3-09	A-	5.25	2.56	2,589.4	250.5	141.2	-26.3
3-08	A-	9.59	4.64	2,419.0	371.4	103.7	2.4
2008	A-	6.77	3.35	2,503.7	287.8	521.2	-115.6
2007	A-	10.21	4.94	2,415.3	369.1	593.4	1.9
2006	A-	11.92	5.86	1,851.8	364.5	382.4	5.8
2005	A-	8.94	4.97	1,505.9	359.3	397.6	37.1
2004	A-	4.16	2.67	1,349.0	308.1	934.6	34.7

Pacific LifeCorp Composite Group Rating: A Largest Group Members	Assets ($mil)	Rating
PACIFIC LIFE INS CO	83653	A-
PACIFIC LIFE ANNUITY CO	2504	A-

PACIFIC LIFE INSURANCE COMPANY *   A-   Excellent

Major Rating Factors: Good quality investment portfolio (5.6 on a scale of 0 to 10) despite large holdings of BBB rated bonds in addition to junk bond exposure equal to 55% of capital. Exposure to mortgages is significant, but the mortgage default rate has been low. Good overall results on stability tests (5.6). Strengths that enhance stability include excellent risk diversification. Weak profitability (2.0) with operating losses during the first three months of 2009.

Other Rating Factors: Strong capitalization (7.5) based on excellent risk adjusted capital (severe loss scenario). Excellent liquidity (8.8).

Principal Business: Individual annuities (69%), individual life insurance (21%), and group retirement contracts (10%).

Principal Investments: NonCMO investment grade bonds (39%), CMOs and structured securities (19%), policy loans (17%), mortgages in good standing (13%), and misc. investments (12%).

Investments in Affiliates: 2%
Group Affiliation: Pacific LifeCorp
Licensed in: All states except AL, NC
Commenced Business: May 1868
Address: 1299 Farnam St, Omaha, NE 68102
Phone: (714) 630-3011 **Domicile State:** NE **NAIC Code:** 67466

Data Date	Rating	RACR #1	RACR #2	Total Assets ($mil)	Capital ($mil)	Net Premium ($mil)	Net Income ($mil)
3-09	A-	2.60	1.31	81,524.3	2,869.8	2,144.6	-36.5
3-08	A	3.37	1.83	94,447.4	4,059.5	1,824.9	228.3
2008	A-	2.97	1.57	83,652.6	3,135.8	7,858.6	-1,528.8
2007	A	3.18	1.73	96,551.2	3,708.0	9,354.1	362.2
2006	A	3.07	1.67	86,141.9	3,217.9	10,304.2	362.1
2005	A	2.98	1.61	74,885.5	3,008.8	9,388.1	234.4
2004	A	2.78	1.46	68,467.3	2,814.2	8,758.3	507.7

Rating Indexes

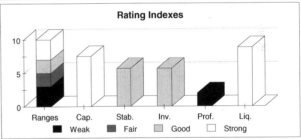

Ranges | Cap. | Stab. | Inv. | Prof. | Liq.
■ Weak ▨ Fair ▨ Good □ Strong

PACIFICARE LIFE & HEALTH INSURANCE COMPANY   B-   Good

Major Rating Factors: Fair overall results on stability tests (3.9 on a scale of 0 to 10) including weak results on operational trends. Strong current capitalization (10.0) based on excellent risk adjusted capital (severe loss scenario) reflecting improvement over results in 2006. High quality investment portfolio (8.5) with no exposure to mortgages and minimal holdings in junk bonds.

Other Rating Factors: Excellent profitability (9.1) with operating gains in each of the last five years. Excellent liquidity (8.4).

Principal Business: Group health insurance (88%) and individual health insurance (12%).

Principal Investments: NonCMO investment grade bonds (78%) and CMOs and structured securities (25%).

Investments in Affiliates: None
Group Affiliation: UnitedHealth Group Inc
Licensed in: All states except AL, NC
Commenced Business: September 1967
Address: 23046 Avenida Dela Carlota 700, Laguna Hills, CA 92653-1519
Phone: (714) 206-5247 **Domicile State:** IN **NAIC Code:** 70785

Data Date	Rating	RACR #1	RACR #2	Total Assets ($mil)	Capital ($mil)	Net Premium ($mil)	Net Income ($mil)
3-09	B-	11.94	8.96	775.6	669.4	85.6	25.8
3-08	B-	4.54	3.56	841.6	603.1	117.7	49.5
2008	B-	11.03	8.35	778.6	642.8	433.7	148.9
2007	B-	3.50	2.76	897.0	552.9	1,333.1	279.6
2006	B-	1.02	0.82	1,077.3	334.3	2,793.2	172.0
2005	B-	1.74	1.42	375.7	147.2	678.7	149.2
2004	C	1.99	1.62	206.2	93.2	385.2	151.5

Adverse Trends in Operations

Decrease in premium volume from 2007 to 2008 (67%)
Decrease in asset base during 2008 (13%)
Change in asset mix during 2007 (11%)
Decrease in premium volume from 2006 to 2007 (52%)
Change in asset mix during 2006 (9.9%)

PAN-AMERICAN LIFE INSURANCE COMPANY   B   Good

Major Rating Factors: Good quality investment portfolio (5.4 on a scale of 0 to 10) despite mixed results such as: large holdings of BBB rated bonds but junk bond exposure equal to 58% of capital. Good overall profitability (5.4). Return on equity has been low, averaging 4.0%. Good liquidity (6.2).

Other Rating Factors: Good overall results on stability tests (6.0) good operational trends and excellent risk diversification. Strong capitalization (7.3) based on excellent risk adjusted capital (severe loss scenario).

Principal Business: Group health insurance (54%), reinsurance (19%), individual life insurance (18%), individual health insurance (6%), and group life insurance (3%).

Principal Investments: NonCMO investment grade bonds (53%), CMOs and structured securities (19%), noninv. grade bonds (11%), policy loans (7%), and misc. investments (11%).

Investments in Affiliates: 4%

Group Affiliation: Pan-American Life

Licensed in: All states except AL, MD, NJ, NC, SC, TN, VA, PR

Commenced Business: March 1912

Address: Pan American Life Center, New Orleans, LA 70130

Phone: (504) 566-1300 **Domicile State:** LA **NAIC Code:** 67539

Data Date	Rating	RACR #1	RACR #2	Total Assets ($mil)	Capital ($mil)	Net Premium ($mil)	Net Income ($mil)
3-09	B	1.99	1.20	1,519.6	264.1	49.6	1.7
3-08	B	2.49	1.54	1,574.5	306.5	49.1	5.2
2008	B	2.07	1.27	1,527.5	267.2	191.7	0.3
2007	B	2.55	1.61	1,582.7	306.5	165.2	25.7
2006	B-	2.51	1.57	1,673.6	289.0	156.4	-7.3
2005	C+	2.40	1.42	1,640.4	269.9	141.7	-5.2
2004	C+	2.17	1.30	1,607.5	222.9	205.7	15.0

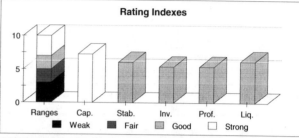

Rating Indexes

PARK AVENUE LIFE INSURANCE COMPANY   B   Good

Major Rating Factors: Good quality investment portfolio (6.2 on a scale of 0 to 10) despite mixed results such as: no exposure to mortgages and large holdings of BBB rated bonds but minimal holdings in junk bonds. Good overall profitability (6.9). Excellent expense controls. Return on equity has been good over the last five years, averaging 10.8%. Good liquidity (6.8).

Other Rating Factors: Good overall results on stability tests (5.6) good operational trends and excellent risk diversification. Strong capitalization (7.5) based on excellent risk adjusted capital (severe loss scenario).

Principal Business: Reinsurance (72%), individual life insurance (27%), and group life insurance (1%).

Principal Investments: NonCMO investment grade bonds (71%), common & preferred stock (22%), noninv. grade bonds (3%), CMOs and structured securities (2%), and misc. investments (2%).

Investments in Affiliates: 22%

Group Affiliation: Guardian Group

Licensed in: All states except AL, ID, NC

Commenced Business: April 1965

Address: 9100 Keystone Crossing Ste 600, Indianapolis, IN 46240

Phone: (212) 598-8179 **Domicile State:** DE **NAIC Code:** 60003

Data Date	Rating	RACR #1	RACR #2	Total Assets ($mil)	Capital ($mil)	Net Premium ($mil)	Net Income ($mil)
3-09	B	1.46	1.32	418.8	146.6	1.2	0.7
3-08	B	1.40	1.28	433.3	150.9	1.7	1.7
2008	B	1.44	1.31	417.8	144.3	6.6	16.9
2007	B	1.40	1.28	434.9	150.5	8.5	15.8
2006	B	1.36	1.24	444.5	152.2	9.5	12.9
2005	B	1.43	1.30	485.3	167.0	11.2	16.1
2004	B	1.49	1.36	494.4	162.3	11.9	29.4

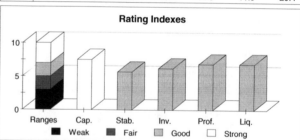

Rating Indexes

PARKER CENTENNIAL ASSURANCE COMPANY   B   Good

Major Rating Factors: Good overall results on stability tests (5.0 on a scale of 0 to 10). Strengths include excellent financial support from affiliation with Sentry Ins Group, good operational trends and excellent risk diversification. Strong overall capitalization (10.0) based on excellent risk adjusted capital (severe loss scenario). However, capital levels have fluctuated somewhat during past years. High quality investment portfolio (8.6).

Other Rating Factors: Excellent profitability (7.1) with operating gains in each of the last five years. Excellent liquidity (10.0).

Principal Business: Group retirement contracts (100%).

Principal Investments: NonCMO investment grade bonds (100%).

Investments in Affiliates: None

Group Affiliation: Sentry Ins Group

Licensed in: All states except AL, CO, DC, MD, MI, MN, NJ, NM, NC, SC, VA

Commenced Business: August 1973

Address: 2345 Waukegan Rd #5210, Bannockburn, IL 60015-1553

Phone: (614) 764-7000 **Domicile State:** WI **NAIC Code:** 71099

Data Date	Rating	RACR #1	RACR #2	Total Assets ($mil)	Capital ($mil)	Net Premium ($mil)	Net Income ($mil)
3-09	B	5.37	4.84	65.7	39.8	0.8	0.3
3-08	B	5.40	4.86	63.5	39.7	1.4	0.2
2008	B	5.33	4.80	64.7	39.5	4.4	0.8
2007	B	5.37	4.83	63.9	39.5	8.6	1.0
2006	B	5.57	5.01	54.4	38.6	6.7	0.9
2005	B	5.68	5.11	49.1	37.7	10.2	0.6
2004	U	6.92	6.23	37.2	37.2	0.0	0.3

Sentry Ins Group Composite Group Rating: A- Largest Group Members	Assets ($mil)	Rating
SENTRY INS A MUTUAL CO	5369	A
SENTRY LIFE INS CO	2882	A
DAIRYLAND INS CO	1213	A+
SENTRY SELECT INS CO	681	B
MIDDLESEX INS CO	657	B

PAUL REVERE LIFE INSURANCE COMPANY   C+   Fair

Major Rating Factors: Fair overall results on stability tests (4.8 on a scale of 0 to 10) including fair financial strength of affiliated Unum Group and negative cash flow from operations for 2008. Fair quality investment portfolio (4.8) with large holdings of BBB rated bonds in addition to junk bond exposure equal to 53% of capital. Good overall profitability (5.3).

Other Rating Factors: Strong capitalization (7.1) based on excellent risk adjusted capital (severe loss scenario). Excellent liquidity (7.8).

Principal Business: Individual health insurance (64%), reinsurance (28%), group health insurance (5%), individual life insurance (2%), and group life insurance (1%).

Principal Investments: NonCMO investment grade bonds (78%), CMOs and structured securities (10%), noninv. grade bonds (5%), common & preferred stock (5%), and mortgages in good standing (1%).

Investments in Affiliates: 3%
Group Affiliation: Unum Group
Licensed in: All states except AL
Commenced Business: July 1930
Address: 18 Chestnut St, Worcester, MA 01608
Phone: (508) 792-6377 **Domicile State:** MA **NAIC Code:** 67598

Data Date	Rating	RACR #1	RACR #2	Total Assets ($mil)	Capital ($mil)	Net Premium ($mil)	Net Income ($mil)
3-09	C+	1.66	1.09	4,714.3	389.8	26.1	21.6
3-08	C+	1.77	1.19	4,824.0	473.2	26.2	32.0
2008	C+	1.52	0.99	4,710.1	340.3	94.9	78.6
2007	C+	1.72	1.15	4,921.0	458.7	99.7	194.2
2006	C+	2.63	1.88	5,286.4	1,034.6	604.6	95.9
2005	C+	2.75	1.98	5,325.9	1,138.1	642.3	130.3
2004	C-	2.60	1.86	5,281.3	1,117.8	576.2	91.1

Unum Group
Composite Group Rating: C+

Largest Group Members	Assets ($mil)	Rating
UNUM LIFE INS CO OF AMERICA	16890	C+
PROVIDENT LIFE ACCIDENT INS CO	7741	C+
PAUL REVERE LIFE INS CO	4710	C+
COLONIAL LIFE ACCIDENT INS CO	1989	C+
FIRST UNUM LIFE INS CO	1933	C+

PAUL REVERE VARIABLE ANNUITY INSURANCE COMPANY   C   Fair

Major Rating Factors: Fair overall results on stability tests (3.8 on a scale of 0 to 10). Good quality investment portfolio (5.7) despite mixed results such as: no exposure to mortgages and large holdings of BBB rated bonds but small junk bond holdings. Weak profitability (2.4) with investment income below regulatory standards in relation to interest assumptions of reserves.

Other Rating Factors: Strong capitalization (8.0) based on excellent risk adjusted capital (severe loss scenario). Excellent liquidity (9.3).

Principal Business: Individual life insurance (100%).

Principal Investments: NonCMO investment grade bonds (89%) and noninv. grade bonds (10%).

Investments in Affiliates: None
Group Affiliation: Unum Group
Licensed in: All states except AL, AZ, NC
Commenced Business: February 1966
Address: 18 Chestnut St, Worcester, MA 01608-0000
Phone: (508) 792-6377 **Domicile State:** MA **NAIC Code:** 67601

Data Date	Rating	RACR #1	RACR #2	Total Assets ($mil)	Capital ($mil)	Net Premium ($mil)	Net Income ($mil)
3-09	C	11.14	8.76	113.5	97.7	0.0	1.9
3-08	C	11.73	8.73	123.0	104.6	0.0	1.4
2008	C	10.80	8.00	110.2	94.7	0.0	1.8
2007	C	12.74	9.67	132.6	114.0	0.0	5.9
2006	C	12.07	9.26	145.7	109.5	0.0	8.4
2005	C	10.70	5.20	140.6	114.9	0.0	8.6
2004	C-	11.01	5.36	147.6	121.2	0.0	8.7

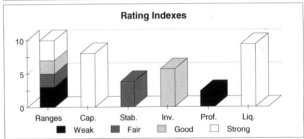

Rating Indexes

PEKIN LIFE INSURANCE COMPANY *   B+   Good

Major Rating Factors: Good overall results on stability tests (6.8 on a scale of 0 to 10). Stability strengths include excellent operational trends and excellent risk diversification. Good overall profitability (6.8) despite operating losses during the first three months of 2009. Return on equity has been fair, averaging 6.4%. Good liquidity (6.5).

Other Rating Factors: Strong capitalization (7.6) based on excellent risk adjusted capital (severe loss scenario). High quality investment portfolio (7.0).

Principal Business: Group health insurance (26%), individual health insurance (24%), individual life insurance (21%), individual annuities (15%), and other lines (14%).

Principal Investments: NonCMO investment grade bonds (60%), CMOs and structured securities (34%), policy loans (2%), noninv. grade bonds (2%), and misc. investments (2%).

Investments in Affiliates: None
Group Affiliation: Pekin Ins Group
Licensed in: IN, IA, KS, LA, MN, MT, OK, WY
Commenced Business: September 1965
Address: 2505 Court St, Pekin, IL 61558
Phone: (309) 346-1161 **Domicile State:** IL **NAIC Code:** 67628

Data Date	Rating	RACR #1	RACR #2	Total Assets ($mil)	Capital ($mil)	Net Premium ($mil)	Net Income ($mil)
3-09	B+	2.26	1.39	863.3	112.9	57.5	-4.2
3-08	B+	2.55	1.58	826.8	121.0	53.5	2.0
2008	B+	2.40	1.48	854.4	117.2	211.4	1.2
2007	B+	2.56	1.59	818.3	120.3	209.6	5.6
2006	B+	2.57	1.62	794.3	119.3	199.7	14.0
2005	B+	2.50	1.58	761.8	108.9	189.9	11.2
2004	B+	2.36	1.51	724.1	101.7	189.2	11.0

Adverse Trends in Operations

Decrease in capital during 2008 (3%)
Increase in policy surrenders from 2006 to 2007 (31%)
Increase in policy surrenders from 2005 to 2006 (66%)

PENN INSURANCE & ANNUITY COMPANY *   B+   Good

Major Rating Factors: Good overall results on stability tests (5.7 on a scale of 0 to 10). Stability strengths include good operational trends and excellent risk diversification. Good overall profitability (5.9) despite operating losses during the first three months of 2009. Return on equity has been good over the last five years, averaging 14.0%. Good liquidity (6.8).

Other Rating Factors: Strong capitalization (7.9) based on excellent risk adjusted capital (severe loss scenario). High quality investment portfolio (7.4).

Principal Business: Individual life insurance (80%), reinsurance (18%), individual annuities (2%), and group life insurance (1%).

Principal Investments: Policy loans (37%), nonCMO investment grade bonds (31%), CMOs and structured securities (30%), and noninv. grade bonds (1%).

Investments in Affiliates: None

Group Affiliation: Penn Mutual Group

Licensed in: All states except AL, NJ, NC

Commenced Business: April 1981

Address: 1209 Orange St, Wilmington, DE 19801

Phone: (215) 956-9177 **Domicile State:** DE **NAIC Code:** 93262

Data Date	Rating	RACR #1	RACR #2	Total Assets ($mil)	Capital ($mil)	Net Premium ($mil)	Net Income ($mil)
3-09	B+	3.08	1.63	1,038.9	104.2	23.0	-1.5
3-08	B+	3.58	1.87	1,103.7	121.4	18.4	4.3
2008	B+	3.21	1.71	1,047.7	107.5	61.7	3.0
2007	B+	3.51	1.83	1,117.5	117.3	37.7	19.5
2006	B+	3.09	1.59	1,143.0	106.5	29.6	18.9
2005	B+	3.20	1.63	1,176.4	110.2	33.0	20.8
2004	B	3.19	1.61	1,222.6	111.8	30.9	23.8

Adverse Trends in Operations

Decrease in asset base during 2008 (6%)
Decrease in asset base during 2007 (2%)
Decrease in premium volume from 2005 to 2006 (10%)
Decrease in capital during 2006 (3%)
Decrease in asset base during 2005 (4%)

PENN MUTUAL LIFE INSURANCE COMPANY *   B+   Good

Major Rating Factors: Good quality investment portfolio (6.7 on a scale of 0 to 10) despite mixed results such as: no exposure to mortgages and substantial holdings of BBB bonds but small junk bond holdings. Good overall profitability (6.2) despite operating losses during the first three months of 2009. Good overall results on stability tests (6.0) good operational trends and excellent risk diversification.

Other Rating Factors: Strong capitalization (8.7) based on excellent risk adjusted capital (severe loss scenario). Excellent liquidity (7.3).

Principal Business: Individual annuities (50%), individual life insurance (45%), group retirement contracts (3%), and individual health insurance (2%).

Principal Investments: NonCMO investment grade bonds (40%), CMOs and structured securities (37%), policy loans (5%), common & preferred stock (3%), and noninv. grade bonds (3%).

Investments in Affiliates: 6%

Group Affiliation: Penn Mutual Group

Licensed in: All states except AL

Commenced Business: May 1847

Address: 600 Dresher Rd, Horsham, PA 19044

Phone: (215) 956-8000 **Domicile State:** PA **NAIC Code:** 67644

Data Date	Rating	RACR #1	RACR #2	Total Assets ($mil)	Capital ($mil)	Net Premium ($mil)	Net Income ($mil)
3-09	B+	3.55	2.11	9,647.6	1,272.0	330.3	-1.4
3-08	B+	3.65	2.22	10,339.6	1,330.6	238.6	-0.5
2008	B+	3.60	2.17	9,688.5	1,285.7	940.5	-49.3
2007	B+	3.58	2.17	10,546.3	1,302.2	1,120.2	-6.0
2006	B+	3.86	2.34	9,972.9	1,295.6	985.1	56.7
2005	B+	3.74	2.26	9,152.6	1,248.2	910.1	184.6
2004	B+	3.64	2.20	8,709.5	1,157.6	903.4	79.8

Adverse Trends in Operations

Decrease in capital during 2008 (1%)
Decrease in premium volume from 2007 to 2008 (16%)
Decrease in asset base during 2008 (8%)

PENNSYLVANIA LIFE INSURANCE COMPANY   D   Weak

Major Rating Factors: Poor current capitalization (0.0 on a scale of 0 to 10) based on excessive policy leverage and weak risk adjusted capital (severe loss scenario), although results have slipped from the good range over the last two years. Weak liquidity (0.1) as a spike in claims or a run on policy withdrawals may stretch capacity. Weak overall results on stability tests (0.2) including weak risk adjusted capital in prior years and negative cash flow from operations for 2008.

Other Rating Factors: Fair quality investment portfolio (4.7). Good overall profitability (5.1) despite operating losses during the first three months of 2009.

Principal Business: Individual health insurance (97%), reinsurance (2%), and individual life insurance (1%).

Principal Investments: CMOs and structured securities (45%), nonCMO investment grade bonds (38%), noninv. grade bonds (12%), cash (3%), and policy loans (2%).

Investments in Affiliates: None

Group Affiliation: Universal American Corp

Licensed in: All states except AL, NC

Commenced Business: January 1948

Address: 525 N Twelfth St, Leymone, PA 17043

Phone: (407) 628-1776 **Domicile State:** PA **NAIC Code:** 67660

Data Date	Rating	RACR #1	RACR #2	Total Assets ($mil)	Capital ($mil)	Net Premium ($mil)	Net Income ($mil)
3-09	D	0.29	0.23	903.0	102.9	597.8	-18.9
3-08	C	0.48	0.38	1,175.1	91.4	542.1	-37.2
2008	D	0.38	0.30	1,102.7	125.5	1,795.2	7.3
2007	C+	1.06	0.81	1,180.3	136.8	676.2	51.1
2006	C	1.58	1.10	964.0	112.4	359.4	22.6
2005	C-	0.79	0.67	579.3	74.4	171.5	9.8
2004	D+	0.77	0.66	544.8	61.2	171.2	12.7

Policy Leverage

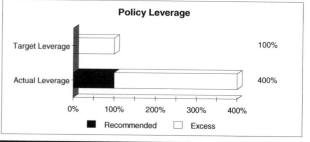

Target Leverage — 100%
Actual Leverage — 400%

0% 100% 200% 300% 400%

■ Recommended □ Excess

PERICO LIFE INSURANCE COMPANY

B **Good**

Major Rating Factors: Good overall results on stability tests (6.0 on a scale of 0 to 10). Stability strengths include excellent operational trends and excellent risk diversification. Strong capitalization (10.0) based on excellent risk adjusted capital (severe loss scenario). Moreover, capital levels have been consistently high over the last five years. High quality investment portfolio (8.9).

Other Rating Factors: Excellent profitability (8.9) with operating gains in each of the last five years. Excellent liquidity (7.5).

Principal Business: Group health insurance (98%), group life insurance (1%), and reinsurance (1%).

Principal Investments: NonCMO investment grade bonds (77%), CMOs and structured securities (13%), and cash (10%).

Investments in Affiliates: None
Group Affiliation: HCC Ins Holdings Inc
Licensed in: All states except AL, NC
Commenced Business: October 1975
Address: 1209 Orange St, Wilmington, DE 19801
Phone: (248) 263-6900 **Domicile State:** DE **NAIC Code:** 85561

Data Date	Rating	RACR #1	RACR #2	Total Assets ($mil)	Capital ($mil)	Net Premium ($mil)	Net Income ($mil)
3-09	B	4.10	3.27	65.5	42.5	18.4	3.1
3-08	B	3.61	2.90	55.5	32.8	12.7	1.3
2008	B	4.23	3.38	61.3	39.5	51.9	7.8
2007	B	3.59	2.91	51.0	31.6	46.8	4.0
2006	B	4.41	3.68	45.4	27.5	31.9	3.0
2005	C+	4.82	4.34	17.3	15.5	0.0	0.3
2004	C	4.56	4.10	17.6	14.8	0.0	2.1

Adverse Trends in Operations

Change in asset mix during 2007 (4%)
Change in asset mix during 2006 (4.2%)
Decrease in asset base during 2005 (2%)

PHL VARIABLE INSURANCE COMPANY

C **Fair**

Major Rating Factors: Fair quality investment portfolio (3.9 on a scale of 0 to 10) with large holdings of BBB rated bonds in addition to junk bond exposure equal to 80% of capital. Fair overall results on stability tests (3.8) including negative cash flow from operations for 2008. Good capitalization (6.4) based on good risk adjusted capital (moderate loss scenario).

Other Rating Factors: Weak profitability (1.6) with operating losses during the first three months of 2009. Excellent liquidity (8.0).

Principal Business: Individual life insurance (51%) and individual annuities (49%).

Principal Investments: NonCMO investment grade bonds (48%), CMOs and structured securities (32%), noninv. grade bonds (9%), common & preferred stock (3%), and policy loans (2%).

Investments in Affiliates: None
Group Affiliation: Phoenix Companies
Licensed in: All states except AL, MD, NC
Commenced Business: July 1981
Address: 200 Park Ave 7th Floor, New York, NY 10166
Phone: (860) 403-1179 **Domicile State:** CT **NAIC Code:** 93548

Data Date	Rating	RACR #1	RACR #2	Total Assets ($mil)	Capital ($mil)	Net Premium ($mil)	Net Income ($mil)
3-09	C	1.90	0.90	4,150.2	214.8	159.8	-70.7
3-08	C	1.51	0.76	5,059.6	154.4	310.4	-53.3
2008	C	2.57	1.27	4,428.5	273.0	1,040.5	-187.0
2007	C	1.66	0.84	5,342.7	167.4	1,051.1	-102.3
2006	C	2.09	1.04	5,133.8	220.3	723.2	-34.0
2005	C	2.23	1.09	5,465.6	264.8	565.7	12.7
2004	C+	2.05	0.99	5,567.3	245.8	629.1	-3.3

Rating Indexes

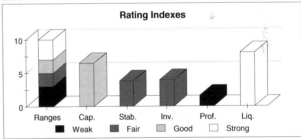

PHOENIX LIFE INSURANCE COMPANY

C+ **Fair**

Major Rating Factors: Fair current capitalization (4.8 on a scale of 0 to 10) based on fair risk adjusted capital (moderate loss scenario), although results have slipped from the good range during the last year. Fair quality investment portfolio (3.7) with large holdings of BBB rated bonds in addition to significant exposure to junk bonds. Fair profitability (4.1) with operating losses during the first three months of 2009.

Other Rating Factors: Fair overall results on stability tests (4.6) including negative cash flow from operations for 2008 and fair risk adjusted capital in prior years. Good liquidity (5.2).

Principal Business: Individual life insurance (92%), individual annuities (4%), and reinsurance (3%).

Principal Investments: NonCMO investment grade bonds (38%), CMOs and structured securities (25%), policy loans (18%), noninv. grade bonds (7%), and common & preferred stock (6%).

Investments in Affiliates: 3%
Group Affiliation: Phoenix Companies
Licensed in: All states except AL
Commenced Business: May 1851
Address: 100 Bright Meadow Blvd, Enfield, CT 06083-1900
Phone: (860) 403-1000 **Domicile State:** NY **NAIC Code:** 67814

Data Date	Rating	RACR #1	RACR #2	Total Assets ($mil)	Capital ($mil)	Net Premium ($mil)	Net Income ($mil)
3-09	C+	0.97	0.57	14,986.3	619.1	174.5	-15.7
3-08	B-	1.36	0.81	16,351.3	797.7	210.8	-22.9
2008	C+	1.14	0.69	15,392.5	758.9	828.2	-82.3
2007	B-	1.48	0.88	16,714.6	848.1	851.5	80.0
2006	B-	1.48	0.91	16,753.0	932.4	891.8	162.0
2005	C	1.39	0.87	16,736.0	885.5	1,058.3	61.0
2004	C	1.19	0.76	16,704.9	809.2	1,115.1	47.1

Junk Bonds as a % of Capital

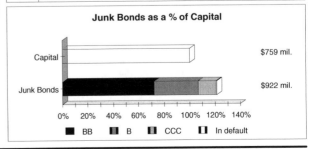

PHYSICIANS LIFE INSURANCE COMPANY *

A-   Excellent

Major Rating Factors: Good overall profitability (6.2 on a scale of 0 to 10) despite operating losses during the first three months of 2009. Return on equity has been low, averaging 3.5%. Good liquidity (5.7) with sufficient resources to handle a spike in claims as well as a significant increase in policy surrenders. Good overall results on stability tests (5.9) despite negative cash flow from operations for 2008 good operational trends and excellent risk diversification.

Other Rating Factors: Fair quality investment portfolio (4.2). Strong capitalization (7.0) based on excellent risk adjusted capital (severe loss scenario).

Principal Business: Individual life insurance (59%), individual health insurance (29%), individual annuities (11%), and reinsurance (2%).

Principal Investments: NonCMO investment grade bonds (65%), CMOs and structured securities (23%), noninv. grade bonds (7%), common & preferred stock (2%), and policy loans (2%).

Investments in Affiliates: None

Group Affiliation: Physicians Mutual Group

Licensed in: All states except AL, NC

Commenced Business: January 1970

Address: 2600 Dodge St, Omaha, NE 68131-2671

Phone: (402) 633-1000 **Domicile State:** NE **NAIC Code:** 72125

Data Date	Rating	RACR #1	RACR #2	Total Assets ($mil)	Capital ($mil)	Net Premium ($mil)	Net Income ($mil)
3-09	A-	2.03	1.02	1,249.3	83.4	51.9	-0.4
3-08	A-	2.13	1.09	1,302.7	79.2	49.4	-1.2
2008	A-	2.22	1.13	1,263.4	87.6	190.2	-1.5
2007	A-	2.28	1.18	1,290.6	84.5	186.0	6.4
2006	A-	2.01	1.04	1,333.8	80.9	239.3	1.2
2005	A-	2.03	1.07	1,334.1	79.1	275.1	2.1
2004	A-	1.99	1.06	1,301.5	78.9	371.3	1.1

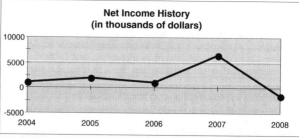

Net Income History (in thousands of dollars)

PHYSICIANS MUTUAL INSURANCE COMPANY *

A+   Excellent

Major Rating Factors: Good quality investment portfolio (6.6 on a scale of 0 to 10) despite mixed results such as: no exposure to mortgages and substantial holdings of BBB bonds but small junk bond holdings. Strong capitalization (10.0) based on excellent risk adjusted capital (severe loss scenario). Furthermore, this high level of risk adjusted capital has been consistently maintained over the last five years. Excellent profitability (8.4) with operating gains in each of the last five years.

Other Rating Factors: Excellent liquidity (7.4). Excellent overall results on stability tests (7.9) excellent operational trends and excellent risk diversification.

Principal Business: Individual health insurance (79%), reinsurance (21%), and group health insurance (1%).

Principal Investments: NonCMO investment grade bonds (60%), CMOs and structured securities (21%), common & preferred stock (11%), noninv. grade bonds (7%), and real estate (1%).

Investments in Affiliates: 7%

Group Affiliation: Physicians Mutual Group

Licensed in: All states except AL

Commenced Business: December 1902

Address: 2600 Dodge St, Omaha, NE 68131-2671

Phone: (402) 633-1000 **Domicile State:** NE **NAIC Code:** 80578

Data Date	Rating	RACR #1	RACR #2	Total Assets ($mil)	Capital ($mil)	Net Premium ($mil)	Net Income ($mil)
3-09	A+	4.75	3.63	1,445.1	769.8	99.5	7.9
3-08	A+	4.72	3.62	1,406.1	754.2	104.9	11.4
2008	A+	4.66	3.61	1,432.8	771.9	403.4	19.0
2007	A+	4.82	3.78	1,389.1	760.0	422.2	32.4
2006	A+	4.82	3.76	1,301.5	752.0	439.0	47.3
2005	A+	4.57	3.61	1,241.3	717.9	461.1	48.0
2004	A+	3.83	2.96	1,202.2	668.5	473.8	49.1

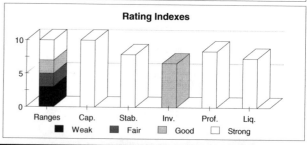

Rating Indexes

Ranges   Cap.   Stab.   Inv.   Prof.   Liq.

■ Weak   ▦ Fair   ▨ Good   □ Strong

PIONEER MUTUAL LIFE INSURANCE COMPANY

B   Good

Major Rating Factors: Good quality investment portfolio (5.1 on a scale of 0 to 10) despite large holdings of BBB rated bonds in addition to moderate junk bond exposure. Exposure to mortgages is significant, but the mortgage default rate has been low. Good liquidity (5.1) with sufficient resources to cover a large increase in policy surrenders. Good overall results on stability tests (5.9) despite negative cash flow from operations for 2008 excellent operational trends and good risk diversification.

Other Rating Factors: Fair profitability (4.3). Strong capitalization (7.2) based on excellent risk adjusted capital (severe loss scenario).

Principal Business: Individual life insurance (94%), individual annuities (5%), and group life insurance (1%).

Principal Investments: NonCMO investment grade bonds (58%), CMOs and structured securities (18%), mortgages in good standing (16%), policy loans (5%), and misc. investments (3%).

Investments in Affiliates: None

Group Affiliation: American United Life Group

Licensed in: All states except AL, AZ, MI, NC, ND

Commenced Business: November 1947

Address: 203 N 10th St, Fargo, ND 58102

Phone: (701) 277-2300 **Domicile State:** ND **NAIC Code:** 67911

Data Date	Rating	RACR #1	RACR #2	Total Assets ($mil)	Capital ($mil)	Net Premium ($mil)	Net Income ($mil)
3-09	B	2.20	1.15	462.6	29.8	9.5	0.5
3-08	B	2.02	1.07	459.5	29.1	7.0	-0.1
2008	B	2.17	1.15	457.2	29.1	34.3	-1.1
2007	B	2.06	1.09	458.6	29.4	32.3	-0.5
2006	B	2.19	1.16	467.3	32.6	33.7	0.6
2005	B	2.13	1.13	465.1	32.0	31.5	2.1
2004	B-	2.06	1.09	464.1	31.7	29.0	2.5

Adverse Trends in Operations

Decrease in capital during 2008 (1%)
Decrease in premium volume from 2006 to 2007 (4%)
Decrease in asset base during 2007 (2%)
Decrease in capital during 2007 (10%)
Increase in policy surrenders from 2005 to 2006 (28%)

PIONEER SECURITY LIFE INSURANCE COMPANY   **B-**   **Good**

Major Rating Factors: Good overall results on stability tests (5.3 on a scale of 0 to 10). Stability strengths include excellent operational trends and good risk diversification. Fair quality investment portfolio (3.8). Strong capitalization (7.3) based on excellent risk adjusted capital (severe loss scenario). Capital levels have been relatively consistent over the last five years.

Other Rating Factors: Excellent profitability (7.2) despite modest operating losses during 2007. Excellent liquidity (7.6).

Principal Business: Individual life insurance (99%) and group life insurance (1%).

Principal Investments: Common & preferred stock (62%), CMOs and structured securities (26%), nonCMO investment grade bonds (11%), and policy loans (1%).

Investments in Affiliates: 62%

Group Affiliation: American Amicable Group

Licensed in: AK, CA, CO, CT, DE, FL, GA, HI, ID, IL, IN, IA, KY, LA, ME, MA, MS, MO, MT, NE, NV, NY, ND, OH, OR, PA, RI, SD, TN, TX, UT, VT, WA, WV, WI, WY

Commenced Business: November 1956

Address: 425 Austin Ave, Waco, TX 76701

Phone: (254) 297-2778 **Domicile State:** TX **NAIC Code:** 67946

Data Date	Rating	RACR #1	RACR #2	Total Assets ($mil)	Capital ($mil)	Net Premium ($mil)	Net Income ($mil)
3-09	B-	1.25	1.22	95.7	74.1	1.2	0.0
3-08	B-	1.22	1.20	94.8	71.7	1.4	2.4
2008	B-	1.24	1.22	95.1	73.6	5.4	2.8
2007	B-	1.20	1.18	91.1	70.5	6.0	-0.8
2006	B-	1.39	1.17	78.9	59.7	6.0	8.3
2005	C	1.09	1.08	84.2	66.8	5.0	1.8
2004	C	1.20	1.18	78.2	62.7	3.7	13.1

Adverse Trends in Operations

Increase in policy surrenders from 2007 to 2008 (57%)
Decrease in premium volume from 2007 to 2008 (11%)
Decrease in capital during 2006 (11%)
Decrease in asset base during 2006 (6%)
Increase in policy surrenders from 2004 to 2005 (38%)

POPULAR LIFE RE   **C**   **Fair**

Major Rating Factors: Fair overall results on stability tests (3.7 on a scale of 0 to 10). Strong capitalization (10.0) based on excellent risk adjusted capital (severe loss scenario). Moreover, capital levels have been consistently high over the last five years. High quality investment portfolio (7.8) with no exposure to mortgages and no exposure to junk bonds.

Other Rating Factors: Excellent profitability (7.8) despite modest operating losses during 2004. Excellent liquidity (9.7).

Principal Business: Reinsurance (100%).

Principal Investments: NonCMO investment grade bonds (87%), common & preferred stock (7%), and cash (6%).

Investments in Affiliates: 4%

Group Affiliation: Popular Inc

Licensed in: (No states)

Commenced Business: December 2003

Address: (No address available)

Phone: (787) 759-0080 **Domicile State:** PR **NAIC Code:** 11876

Data Date	Rating	RACR #1	RACR #2	Total Assets ($mil)	Capital ($mil)	Net Premium ($mil)	Net Income ($mil)
3-09	C	3.91	3.48	55.7	27.1	3.1	1.5
3-08	D+	3.16	2.68	52.1	21.4	4.0	1.3
2008	C	3.70	3.30	54.7	25.6	16.8	5.5
2007	D+	2.97	2.67	51.1	20.2	18.7	5.0
2006	D	2.39	2.15	46.5	15.2	23.8	3.6
2005	D-	2.09	1.65	39.0	11.6	29.2	0.1
2004	D-	2.60	2.14	28.5	11.5	23.3	-6.4

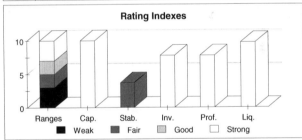

Rating Indexes

Ranges   Cap.   Stab.   Inv.   Prof.   Liq.
■ Weak   ■ Fair   ▨ Good   ☐ Strong

PRESIDENTIAL LIFE INSURANCE COMPANY   **C-**   **Fair**

Major Rating Factors: Fair quality investment portfolio (4.8 on a scale of 0 to 10) with large holdings of BBB rated bonds in addition to junk bond exposure equal to 61% of capital. Fair overall results on stability tests (3.2) including negative cash flow from operations for 2008 and fair risk adjusted capital in prior years. Good capitalization (6.6) based on good risk adjusted capital (severe loss scenario).

Other Rating Factors: Good overall profitability (6.8) despite operating losses during the first three months of 2009. Good liquidity (6.3).

Principal Business: Individual annuities (84%), individual life insurance (10%), group health insurance (5%), and reinsurance (1%).

Principal Investments: NonCMO investment grade bonds (73%), common & preferred stock (8%), CMOs and structured securities (6%), noninv. grade bonds (5%), and policy loans (1%).

Investments in Affiliates: None

Group Affiliation: Presidential Life Corp

Licensed in: All states except AL, NJ

Commenced Business: October 1966

Address: 69 Lydecker St, Nyack, NY 10960

Phone: (914) 358-2300 **Domicile State:** NY **NAIC Code:** 68039

Data Date	Rating	RACR #1	RACR #2	Total Assets ($mil)	Capital ($mil)	Net Premium ($mil)	Net Income ($mil)
3-09	C-	1.90	0.95	3,642.5	281.4	58.7	-6.5
3-08	D+	2.44	1.25	3,891.9	360.5	42.0	12.3
2008	C-	2.18	1.11	3,706.6	329.0	163.7	16.9
2007	D+	2.36	1.22	3,925.7	360.4	146.0	59.1
2006	D+	2.02	1.03	4,277.3	330.1	171.5	75.0
2005	D+	1.64	0.83	4,460.8	291.3	145.6	102.0
2004	D	1.22	0.62	4,329.4	215.4	239.0	-43.6

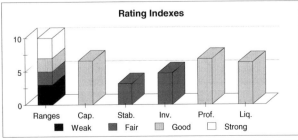

Rating Indexes

Ranges   Cap.   Stab.   Inv.   Prof.   Liq.
■ Weak   ■ Fair   ▨ Good   ☐ Strong

PRIMERICA LIFE INSURANCE COMPANY *

A-   **Excellent**

Major Rating Factors: Good quality investment portfolio (6.1 on a scale of 0 to 10) despite mixed results such as: large holdings of BBB rated bonds but moderate junk bond exposure. Good overall profitability (6.6). Return on equity has been excellent over the last five years averaging 16.4%. Good liquidity (6.9).

Other Rating Factors: Good overall results on stability tests (6.3) good operational trends and excellent risk diversification. Strong capitalization (7.6) based on excellent risk adjusted capital (severe loss scenario).

Principal Business: Individual life insurance (100%).

Principal Investments: NonCMO investment grade bonds (46%), CMOs and structured securities (33%), common & preferred stock (15%), and noninv. grade bonds (5%).

Investments in Affiliates: 18%

Group Affiliation: Citigroup Inc

Licensed in: All states except AL, NC

Commenced Business: January 1903

Address: 3120 Breckinridge Blvd, Duluth, GA 30199-0001

Phone: (770) 381-1000   **Domicile State:** MA   **NAIC Code:** 65919

Data Date	Rating	RACR #1	RACR #2	Total Assets ($mil)	Capital ($mil)	Net Premium ($mil)	Net Income ($mil)
3-09	A-	1.81	1.38	5,765.7	1,155.4	306.7	27.0
3-08	A-	2.65	1.99	6,140.9	1,570.5	296.3	26.1
2008	A-	2.29	1.75	5,959.0	1,472.5	1,190.8	73.6
2007	A-	2.83	2.14	5,896.0	1,654.8	1,154.4	351.0
2006	A-	5.01	3.26	5,549.7	1,665.1	1,183.8	302.9
2005	B+	2.78	2.12	5,437.6	1,702.7	1,130.9	344.3
2004	B+	2.07	1.71	5,553.2	1,817.9	1,102.4	263.0

Rating Indexes

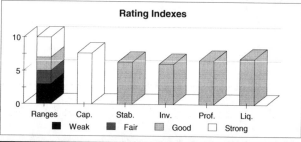

Ranges   Cap.   Stab.   Inv.   Prof.   Liq.

■ Weak   ■ Fair   ▨ Good   ☐ Strong

PRINCIPAL LIFE INSURANCE COMPANY *

A-   **Excellent**

Major Rating Factors: Good overall results on stability tests (5.4 on a scale of 0 to 10). Strengths that enhance stability include good operational trends and excellent risk diversification. Fair quality investment portfolio (4.8) with large holdings of BBB rated bonds in addition to junk bond exposure equal to 69% of capital. Exposure to mortgages is significant, but the mortgage default rate has been low. Strong capitalization (7.2) based on excellent risk adjusted capital (severe loss scenario).

Other Rating Factors: Excellent profitability (7.3) with operating gains in each of the last five years. Excellent liquidity (7.1).

Principal Business: Individual annuities (47%), group health insurance (28%), individual life insurance (16%), group life insurance (4%), and other lines (5%).

Principal Investments: NonCMO investment grade bonds (49%), CMOs and structured securities (17%), mortgages in good standing (16%), noninv. grade bonds (5%), and misc. investments (13%).

Investments in Affiliates: 6%

Group Affiliation: Principal Financial Group

Licensed in: All states except AL

Commenced Business: September 1879

Address: 711 High St, Des Moines, IA 50392-0001

Phone: (800) 986-3343   **Domicile State:** IA   **NAIC Code:** 61271

Data Date	Rating	RACR #1	RACR #2	Total Assets ($mil)	Capital ($mil)	Net Premium ($mil)	Net Income ($mil)
3-09	A-	2.29	1.15	109,924	4,212.2	2,041.4	48.8
3-08	A-	2.45	1.25	132,594	3,821.3	2,100.4	-37.2
2008	A-	2.62	1.34	115,411	4,810.2	8,673.4	83.3
2007	A-	2.45	1.27	135,715	3,697.5	8,323.3	540.2
2006	A-	2.40	1.26	125,532	3,598.6	6,804.7	684.9
2005	A-	2.78	1.42	111,739	3,660.3	6,198.0	666.2
2004	A-	2.47	1.26	101,496	3,046.8	5,950.6	512.7

Adverse Trends in Operations

Decrease in asset base during 2008 (15%)
Increase in policy surrenders from 2005 to 2006 (34%)
Decrease in capital during 2006 (2%)

PROFESSIONAL INSURANCE COMPANY

C   **Fair**

Major Rating Factors: Fair overall results on stability tests (4.2 on a scale of 0 to 10) including negative cash flow from operations for 2008 and fair risk adjusted capital in prior years. Good liquidity (6.8) with sufficient resources to handle a spike in claims. Weak profitability (2.0) with operating losses during the first three months of 2009.

Other Rating Factors: Strong capitalization (7.5) based on excellent risk adjusted capital (severe loss scenario). High quality investment portfolio (7.0).

Principal Business: Individual health insurance (96%) and individual life insurance (4%).

Principal Investments: NonCMO investment grade bonds (72%), CMOs and structured securities (15%), policy loans (6%), common & preferred stock (4%), and misc. investments (3%).

Investments in Affiliates: None

Group Affiliation: Sun Life Assurance Group

Licensed in: All states except AL, AZ, FL, MD, NJ, NM, NC, SC, VA

Commenced Business: September 1937

Address: 4850 Street Road, Trevose, PA 19049

Phone: (800) 730-6484   **Domicile State:** TX   **NAIC Code:** 68047

Data Date	Rating	RACR #1	RACR #2	Total Assets ($mil)	Capital ($mil)	Net Premium ($mil)	Net Income ($mil)
3-09	C	1.85	1.35	103.4	30.7	17.9	-1.5
3-08	C	1.81	1.30	99.9	29.3	17.0	-1.1
2008	C	1.95	1.43	102.2	32.2	69.8	-3.6
2007	C	1.92	1.39	97.3	30.4	65.4	-1.8
2006	C+	1.11	0.79	76.6	19.2	55.2	-2.6
2005	C+	1.02	0.73	70.6	15.6	46.9	-2.3
2004	C+	1.21	0.85	67.3	15.7	38.0	-0.8

Rating Indexes

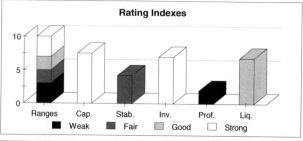

Ranges   Cap.   Stab.   Inv.   Prof.   Liq.

■ Weak   ■ Fair   ▨ Good   ☐ Strong

PROTECTIVE LIFE & ANNUITY INSURANCE COMPANY | B- | Good

Major Rating Factors: Good overall results on stability tests (5.2 on a scale of 0 to 10). Stability strengths include good operational trends and excellent risk diversification. Good overall capitalization (6.8) based on good risk adjusted capital (severe loss scenario). Nevertheless, capital levels have fluctuated during prior years. Good overall profitability (6.3). Excellent expense controls.
Other Rating Factors: Fair quality investment portfolio (3.8). Excellent liquidity (7.2).
Principal Business: Individual annuities (75%), reinsurance (17%), and individual life insurance (8%).
Principal Investments: NonCMO investment grade bonds (71%), policy loans (7%), common & preferred stock (6%), mortgages in good standing (6%), and misc. investments (11%).
Investments in Affiliates: None
Group Affiliation: Protective Life Group
Licensed in: AK, AR, CA, CO, CT, GA, HI, IN, IA, KS, KY, LA, ME, MI, MN, MO, MT, NV, NH, NY, NC, ND, OK, OR, PA, SD, TX, UT, VT, WA, WV
Commenced Business: December 1978
Address: 2801 Highway 280 South, Birmingham, AL 35223
Phone: (205) 268-1000 **Domicile State:** AL **NAIC Code:** 88536

Data Date	Rating	RACR #1	RACR #2	Total Assets ($mil)	Capital ($mil)	Net Premium ($mil)	Net Income ($mil)
3-09	B-	2.02	0.98	790.6	55.9	34.6	2.9
3-08	B-	1.88	0.95	630.9	41.8	13.7	4.0
2008	B-	1.66	0.84	754.5	44.2	163.4	5.7
2007	B-	1.82	0.92	621.0	38.0	78.3	8.8
2006	B-	2.38	1.24	579.8	43.1	25.8	12.8
2005	B	5.49	2.82	660.5	107.4	26.9	16.4
2004	B-	5.26	2.64	672.0	105.4	30.9	14.7

Adverse Trends in Operations

Decrease in capital during 2007 (12%)
Decrease in asset base during 2006 (12%)
Decrease in capital during 2006 (60%)
Decrease in premium volume from 2004 to 2005 (13%)
Decrease in asset base during 2005 (2%)

PROTECTIVE LIFE INSURANCE COMPANY | B- | Good

Major Rating Factors: Fair current capitalization (4.9 on a scale of 0 to 10) based on fair risk adjusted capital (moderate loss scenario), although results have slipped from the good range during the last year. Fair quality investment portfolio (4.8) with large holdings of BBB rated bonds in addition to junk bond exposure equal to 65% of capital. Fair overall results on stability tests (4.5).
Other Rating Factors: Good overall profitability (6.3) despite operating losses during the first three months of 2009. Excellent liquidity (7.4).
Principal Business: Individual annuities (40%), individual life insurance (34%), group retirement contracts (16%), reinsurance (7%), and other lines (2%).
Principal Investments: NonCMO investment grade bonds (40%), CMOs and structured securities (29%), common & preferred stock (13%), mortgages in good standing (8%), and misc. investments (10%).
Investments in Affiliates: 6%
Group Affiliation: Protective Life Group
Licensed in: All states except AL, NC
Commenced Business: September 1907
Address: 1620 Westgate Cir Suite 200, Brentwood, TN 37027-8035
Phone: (205) 879-9230 **Domicile State:** TN **NAIC Code:** 68136

Data Date	Rating	RACR #1	RACR #2	Total Assets ($mil)	Capital ($mil)	Net Premium ($mil)	Net Income ($mil)
3-09	B-	0.99	0.68	24,965.9	1,774.4	594.8	-47.7
3-08	B-	1.26	0.88	26,169.0	1,771.6	727.8	-24.9
2008	B-	1.05	0.76	25,929.5	1,767.7	2,953.1	-300.4
2007	B-	1.29	0.92	25,800.9	1,796.9	1,510.0	350.9
2006	B-	0.89	0.78	19,047.0	1,388.4	1,303.0	451.5
2005	B-	1.22	0.86	18,707.7	1,379.6	1,228.9	41.6
2004	B-	1.51	1.07	17,517.2	1,315.7	1,192.7	235.8

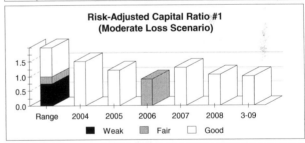

Risk-Adjusted Capital Ratio #1
(Moderate Loss Scenario)

PROTECTIVE LIFE INSURANCE COMPANY OF NEW YORK | C | Fair

Major Rating Factors: Good quality investment portfolio (5.4 on a scale of 0 to 10) despite mixed results such as: large holdings of BBB rated bonds but moderate junk bond exposure. Good overall profitability (5.2) despite operating losses during the first three months of 2009. Return on equity has been low, averaging 3.9%. Good liquidity (6.0).
Other Rating Factors: Weak overall results on stability tests (2.9) including weak results on operational trends and negative cash flow from operations for 2008. Strong capitalization (7.5) based on excellent risk adjusted capital (severe loss scenario).
Principal Business: Individual life insurance (87%) and individual annuities (13%).
Principal Investments: NonCMO investment grade bonds (48%), CMOs and structured securities (47%), noninv. grade bonds (5%), and common & preferred stock (1%).
Investments in Affiliates: None
Group Affiliation: Protective Life Group
Licensed in: NC
Commenced Business: August 2000
Address: 300 Broadhollow Rd Suite 201, Melville, NY 11747
Phone: (847) 930-7505 **Domicile State:** NY **NAIC Code:** 89006

Data Date	Rating	RACR #1	RACR #2	Total Assets ($mil)	Capital ($mil)	Net Premium ($mil)	Net Income ($mil)
3-09	C	2.78	1.35	779.2	96.3	1.0	-0.1
3-08	C	2.94	1.47	1,050.1	128.4	0.8	1.0
2008	C	2.86	1.41	833.3	99.8	2.6	-6.6
2007	C	2.90	1.46	1,119.5	127.5	7.4	2.3
2006	C-	3.56	1.82	989.5	126.5	3.4	14.0
2005	C-	3.02	1.52	1,021.5	111.2	25.4	6.3
2004	C-	2.74	1.35	1,016.3	108.0	145.6	15.2

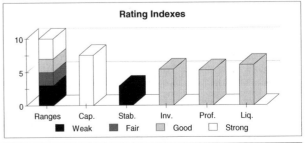

Rating Indexes

PROVIDENT LIFE & ACCIDENT INSURANCE COMPANY   C+   Fair

Major Rating Factors: Fair overall results on stability tests (4.8 on a scale of 0 to 10) including fair financial strength of affiliated Unum Group. Fair quality investment portfolio (3.8) with large holdings of BBB rated bonds in addition to significant exposure to junk bonds. Good capitalization (6.8) based on good risk adjusted capital (severe loss scenario).

Other Rating Factors: Good profitability (5.0). Excellent liquidity (7.2).

Principal Business: Individual health insurance (69%), individual life insurance (25%), group health insurance (3%), group life insurance (2%), and reinsurance (2%).

Principal Investments: NonCMO investment grade bonds (76%), CMOs and structured securities (9%), noninv. grade bonds (7%), mortgages in good standing (4%), and misc. investments (4%).

Investments in Affiliates: None

Group Affiliation: Unum Group

Licensed in: All states except AL, NC

Commenced Business: December 1887

Address: 1 Fountain Square, Chattanooga, TN 37402

Phone: (423) 755-1373 **Domicile State:** TN **NAIC Code:** 68195

Data Date	Rating	RACR #1	RACR #2	Total Assets ($mil)	Capital ($mil)	Net Premium ($mil)	Net Income ($mil)
3-09	C+	1.90	0.98	7,799.2	451.3	250.6	31.6
3-08	C+	2.01	1.04	7,729.4	430.2	237.3	21.5
2008	C+	1.82	0.94	7,741.4	428.4	820.1	118.2
2007	C+	1.97	1.03	7,735.4	435.1	810.3	-17.8
2006	C+	3.92	2.06	7,872.1	1,121.8	1,059.5	70.9
2005	C+	4.01	2.06	7,952.6	1,343.7	1,043.8	122.9
2004	C-	4.05	2.05	7,850.6	1,419.6	1,091.9	329.9

Unum Group
Composite Group Rating: C+
Largest Group Members

	Assets ($mil)	Rating
UNUM LIFE INS CO OF AMERICA	16890	C+
PROVIDENT LIFE ACCIDENT INS CO	7741	C+
PAUL REVERE LIFE INS CO	4710	C+
COLONIAL LIFE ACCIDENT INS CO	1989	C+
FIRST UNUM LIFE INS CO	1933	C+

PROVIDENT LIFE & CASUALTY INSURANCE COMPANY   B-   Good

Major Rating Factors: Good overall results on stability tests (5.2 on a scale of 0 to 10) despite fair financial strength of affiliated Unum Group. Other stability subfactors include excellent operational trends and excellent risk diversification. Good quality investment portfolio (6.6) despite mixed results such as: large holdings of BBB rated bonds but moderate junk bond exposure. Strong capitalization (8.9) based on excellent risk adjusted capital (severe loss scenario).

Other Rating Factors: Excellent profitability (7.4) despite modest operating losses during 2004. Excellent liquidity (7.1).

Principal Business: Individual health insurance (86%), reinsurance (8%), and individual life insurance (6%).

Principal Investments: NonCMO investment grade bonds (74%), CMOs and structured securities (18%), and noninv. grade bonds (7%).

Investments in Affiliates: None

Group Affiliation: Unum Group

Licensed in: AZ, CA, CT, DC, DE, FL, HI, ID, IL, IN, KS, LA, ME, MI, MO, MT, NV, NJ, NM, NY, NC, ND, OH, OK, OR, RI, SC, SD, TN, TX, WA, WV

Commenced Business: December 1952

Address: 1 Fountain Square, Chattanooga, TN 37402

Phone: (423) 755-1373 **Domicile State:** TN **NAIC Code:** 68209

Data Date	Rating	RACR #1	RACR #2	Total Assets ($mil)	Capital ($mil)	Net Premium ($mil)	Net Income ($mil)
3-09	B-	4.01	2.26	709.6	125.1	25.0	3.3
3-08	B-	3.76	2.19	693.9	108.2	22.6	7.7
2008	B-	4.11	2.32	701.1	121.1	83.4	22.6
2007	B-	3.60	2.10	685.5	99.0	79.0	16.4
2006	B-	3.59	2.04	665.2	100.5	75.6	10.3
2005	C+	3.22	1.83	649.3	90.8	76.1	12.7
2004	C	3.07	1.74	640.0	84.6	70.1	-3.2

Unum Group
Composite Group Rating: C+
Largest Group Members

	Assets ($mil)	Rating
UNUM LIFE INS CO OF AMERICA	16890	C+
PROVIDENT LIFE ACCIDENT INS CO	7741	C+
PAUL REVERE LIFE INS CO	4710	C+
COLONIAL LIFE ACCIDENT INS CO	1989	C+
FIRST UNUM LIFE INS CO	1933	C+

PRUCO LIFE INSURANCE COMPANY   C+   Fair

Major Rating Factors: Fair overall results on stability tests (4.5 on a scale of 0 to 10). Good overall capitalization (5.3) based on good risk adjusted capital (moderate loss scenario). Nevertheless, capital levels have fluctuated during prior years. Good quality investment portfolio (5.2) despite substantial holdings of BBB bonds in addition to junk bond exposure equal to 91% of capital. Exposure to mortgages is significant, but the mortgage default rate has been low.

Other Rating Factors: Weak profitability (1.8) with operating losses during the first three months of 2009. Excellent liquidity (8.0).

Principal Business: Individual annuities (58%) and individual life insurance (42%).

Principal Investments: NonCMO investment grade bonds (37%), CMOs and structured securities (25%), policy loans (14%), mortgages in good standing (12%), and misc. investments (12%).

Investments in Affiliates: 4%

Group Affiliation: Prudential Of America

Licensed in: All states except AL, NC

Commenced Business: January 1976

Address: 2999 N 44th St Suite 250, Phoenix, AZ 85018

Phone: (877) 301-1212 **Domicile State:** AZ **NAIC Code:** 79227

Data Date	Rating	RACR #1	RACR #2	Total Assets ($mil)	Capital ($mil)	Net Premium ($mil)	Net Income ($mil)
3-09	C+	1.19	0.69	21,663.3	495.2	717.5	-167.0
3-08	B	1.77	1.03	25,881.1	723.5	733.9	-39.6
2008	C+	1.47	0.86	22,061.4	600.6	3,038.2	-566.2
2007	B	1.86	1.08	27,253.8	772.9	2,959.6	60.6
2006	C+	2.46	1.46	25,360.1	1,020.3	2,503.6	499.2
2005	C	1.36	0.80	23,433.2	540.1	2,235.1	2.0
2004	C	1.47	0.89	22,252.4	571.5	2,087.9	-4.2

Rating Indexes

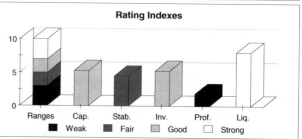

	Weak		Fair		Good		Strong

PRUCO LIFE INSURANCE COMPANY OF NEW JERSEY   C+   Fair

Major Rating Factors: Fair overall results on stability tests (4.3 on a scale of 0 to 10). Good overall capitalization (6.1) based on good risk adjusted capital (moderate loss scenario). Nevertheless, capital levels have fluctuated during prior years. Good quality investment portfolio (5.2) despite large holdings of BBB rated bonds in addition to junk bond exposure equal to 95% of capital. Exposure to mortgages is significant, but the mortgage default rate has been low.

Other Rating Factors: Weak profitability (2.0) with operating losses during the first three months of 2009. Excellent liquidity (7.7).

Principal Business: Individual life insurance (66%) and individual annuities (34%).

Principal Investments: NonCMO investment grade bonds (38%), CMOs and structured securities (26%), policy loans (13%), mortgages in good standing (12%), and noninv. grade bonds (9%).

Investments in Affiliates: 2%

Group Affiliation: Prudential Of America

Licensed in: NM, NC

Commenced Business: December 1982

Address: 213 Washington St, Newark, NJ 07102

Phone: (877) 301-1212 **Domicile State:** NJ **NAIC Code:** 97195

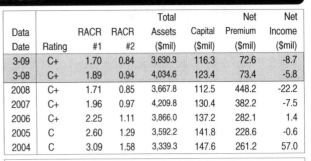

Data Date	Rating	RACR #1	RACR #2	Total Assets ($mil)	Capital ($mil)	Net Premium ($mil)	Net Income ($mil)
3-09	C+	1.70	0.84	3,630.3	116.3	72.6	-8.7
3-08	C+	1.89	0.94	4,034.6	123.4	73.4	-5.8
2008	C+	1.71	0.85	3,667.8	112.5	448.2	-22.2
2007	C+	1.96	0.97	4,209.8	130.4	382.2	-7.5
2006	C+	2.25	1.11	3,866.0	137.2	282.1	1.4
2005	C	2.60	1.29	3,592.2	141.8	228.6	-0.6
2004	C	3.09	1.58	3,339.3	147.6	261.2	57.0

Rating Indexes

PRUDENTIAL ANNUITIES LIFE ASSURANCE CORPORATION   C+   Fair

Major Rating Factors: Fair overall results on stability tests (4.0 on a scale of 0 to 10). Weak profitability (1.9) with operating losses during the first three months of 2009. Strong current capitalization (7.1) based on excellent risk adjusted capital (severe loss scenario) reflecting improvement over results in 2006.

Other Rating Factors: High quality investment portfolio (7.6). Excellent liquidity (10.0).

Principal Business: Group retirement contracts (72%) and individual annuities (28%).

Principal Investments: CMOs and structured securities (68%) and nonCMO investment grade bonds (31%).

Investments in Affiliates: None

Group Affiliation: Prudential Of America

Licensed in: All states except AL

Commenced Business: May 1977

Address: One Corporate Dr, 10th Floor, Shelton, CT 06484

Phone: (800) 628-6039 **Domicile State:** CT **NAIC Code:** 86630

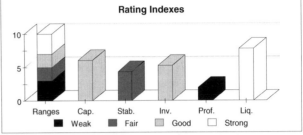

Data Date	Rating	RACR #1	RACR #2	Total Assets ($mil)	Capital ($mil)	Net Premium ($mil)	Net Income ($mil)
3-09	C+	1.44	1.09	34,351.4	454.5	1,503.3	-188.2
3-08	C+	1.08	0.97	41,104.2	414.5	2,051.6	-21.3
2008	C+	2.05	1.55	35,015.0	633.4	7,524.1	-322.6
2007	C+	1.15	1.04	43,236.1	438.3	8,290.8	106.0
2006	C+	1.03	0.92	36,963.1	327.2	6,668.1	110.2
2005	C+	1.32	1.15	31,596.8	367.3	5,265.6	-31.4
2004	C	1.60	1.43	29,302.3	399.0	4,081.2	101.1

Rating Indexes

PRUDENTIAL INSURANCE COMPANY OF AMERICA   C+   Fair

Major Rating Factors: Fair quality investment portfolio (3.6 on a scale of 0 to 10) with large holdings of BBB rated bonds in addition to significant exposure to junk bonds. Exposure to mortgages is significant, but the mortgage default rate has been low. Fair overall results on stability tests (4.1). Good capitalization (5.3) based on good risk adjusted capital (moderate loss scenario).

Other Rating Factors: Good overall profitability (6.4). Excellent liquidity (7.5).

Principal Business: Group retirement contracts (43%), individual life insurance (22%), group life insurance (20%), reinsurance (9%), and other lines (6%).

Principal Investments: NonCMO investment grade bonds (45%), CMOs and structured securities (19%), mortgages in good standing (14%), noninv. grade bonds (9%), and misc. investments (13%).

Investments in Affiliates: 7%

Group Affiliation: Prudential Of America

Licensed in: All states except AL

Commenced Business: December 1875

Address: 751 Broad St, Newark, NJ 07102-3777

Phone: (973) 802-6000 **Domicile State:** NJ **NAIC Code:** 68241

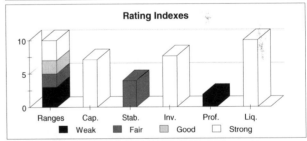

Data Date	Rating	RACR #1	RACR #2	Total Assets ($mil)	Capital ($mil)	Net Premium ($mil)	Net Income ($mil)
3-09	C+	1.19	0.74	227,934	6,392.6	3,499.3	472.1
3-08	B	1.31	0.85	248,830	6,488.0	3,761.5	-238.0
2008	C+	1.23	0.77	237,498	6,432.4	16,129.6	-807.8
2007	B	1.37	0.89	252,761	6,980.8	16,194.3	1,274.3
2006	B	1.17	0.78	245,817	5,972.5	24,068.8	443.9
2005	B	1.45	0.95	221,916	7,065.2	16,510.3	2,170.0
2004	B-	1.60	1.08	207,012	8,420.5	15,453.6	1,877.6

Junk Bonds as a % of Capital

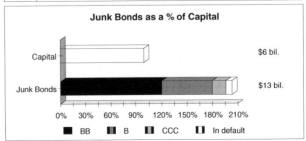

PRUDENTIAL RETIREMENT INSURANCE & ANNUITY   C+   Fair

Major Rating Factors: Fair quality investment portfolio (3.6 on a scale of 0 to 10) with large holdings of BBB rated bonds in addition to significant exposure to junk bonds. Exposure to mortgages is significant, but the mortgage default rate has been low. Fair profitability (4.1) with operating losses during the first three months of 2009. Fair overall results on stability tests (4.5).

Other Rating Factors: Strong capitalization (7.1) based on excellent risk adjusted capital (severe loss scenario). Excellent liquidity (8.2).

Principal Business: Group retirement contracts (88%), individual annuities (10%), and reinsurance (2%).

Principal Investments: NonCMO investment grade bonds (46%), mortgages in good standing (22%), CMOs and structured securities (21%), noninv. grade bonds (9%), and misc. investments (2%).

Investments in Affiliates: None

Group Affiliation: Prudential of America

Licensed in: All states except AL

Commenced Business: October 1981

Address: 280 Trumbull St, Hartford, CT 06103-3509

Phone: (860) 534-2000 **Domicile State:** CT **NAIC Code:** 93629

Data Date	Rating	RACR #1	RACR #2	Total Assets ($mil)	Capital ($mil)	Net Premium ($mil)	Net Income ($mil)
3-09	C+	2.54	1.06	50,465.7	1,196.6	23.0	-9.9
3-08	C+	2.14	0.93	59,010.1	989.5	5.8	-28.1
2008	C+	2.70	1.14	51,851.8	1,208.4	113.9	-12.5
2007	C+	2.11	0.95	61,437.1	945.6	13.4	118.0
2006	C+	2.28	1.13	59,441.3	1,041.5	18.3	224.9
2005	C+	2.28	1.07	52,660.5	989.8	12.2	203.8
2004	C-	2.75	1.37	22,876.7	1,027.4	11.4	122.2

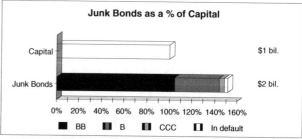

Junk Bonds as a % of Capital

Capital — $1 bil.
Junk Bonds — $2 bil.

0% 20% 40% 60% 80% 100% 120% 140% 160%

■ BB ▨ B ▥ CCC ☐ In default

PYRAMID LIFE INSURANCE COMPANY   C-   Fair

Major Rating Factors: Fair overall capitalization (3.6 on a scale of 0 to 10) based on mixed results -- excessive policy leverage mitigated by fair risk adjusted capital (severe loss scenario). Fair overall results on stability tests (3.0) including negative cash flow from operations for 2008 and fair risk adjusted capital in prior years. Good overall profitability (6.7). Excellent expense controls.

Other Rating Factors: Good liquidity (5.4). High quality investment portfolio (7.8).

Principal Business: Individual health insurance (99%) and individual life insurance (1%).

Principal Investments: NonCMO investment grade bonds (73%), CMOs and structured securities (35%), and noninv. grade bonds (3%).

Investments in Affiliates: None

Group Affiliation: Universal American Corp

Licensed in: AK, AR, CA, CO, CT, FL, GA, HI, IL, IN, IA, KS, KY, LA, ME, MA, MI, MN, MS, MO, MT, NE, NV, NH, NY, ND, OH, OK, OR, PA, RI, SD, TN, TX, UT, VT, WA, WV, WY, PR

Commenced Business: August 1914

Address: 6201 Johnson Dr, Shawnee Mission, KS 66202

Phone: (913) 722-1110 **Domicile State:** KS **NAIC Code:** 68284

Data Date	Rating	RACR #1	RACR #2	Total Assets ($mil)	Capital ($mil)	Net Premium ($mil)	Net Income ($mil)
3-09	C-	0.72	0.58	445.1	167.5	273.8	8.5
3-08	C	0.73	0.59	441.2	152.7	242.5	0.6
2008	C-	0.79	0.63	461.0	178.5	1,016.1	16.5
2007	C	0.73	0.59	462.0	150.5	911.5	10.9
2006	C	1.18	0.87	162.1	29.1	144.5	-1.6
2005	C	1.84	1.33	149.4	41.9	137.4	1.2
2004	C	1.28	0.95	128.0	27.5	136.2	2.1

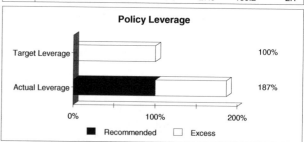

Policy Leverage

Target Leverage — 100%
Actual Leverage — 187%

0% 100% 200%

■ Recommended ☐ Excess

REASSURE AMERICA LIFE INSURANCE COMPANY   C+   Fair

Major Rating Factors: Fair overall results on stability tests (4.7 on a scale of 0 to 10) including fair financial strength of affiliated Swiss Reinsurance Group, negative cash flow from operations for 2008 and fair risk adjusted capital in prior years. Fair current capitalization (4.8) based on fair risk adjusted capital (moderate loss scenario), although results have slipped from the good range during the last year. Fair quality investment portfolio (3.9).

Other Rating Factors: Good overall profitability (6.3) despite operating losses during the first three months of 2009. Good liquidity (5.9).

Principal Business: Individual life insurance (66%), reinsurance (25%), individual health insurance (7%), and group life insurance (2%).

Principal Investments: NonCMO investment grade bonds (47%), CMOs and structured securities (25%), policy loans (20%), common & preferred stock (2%), and misc. investments (7%).

Investments in Affiliates: None

Group Affiliation: Swiss Reinsurance Group

Licensed in: All states except AL, NC

Commenced Business: December 1956

Address: 1700 Magnavox Way, Fort Wayne, IN 46804

Phone: (877) 794-7773 **Domicile State:** IN **NAIC Code:** 70211

Data Date	Rating	RACR #1	RACR #2	Total Assets ($mil)	Capital ($mil)	Net Premium ($mil)	Net Income ($mil)
3-09	C+	0.99	0.48	16,481.2	454.2	95.3	-42.4
3-08	C+	1.32	0.64	17,165.8	507.5	100.0	44.6
2008	C+	1.12	0.55	16,470.3	520.4	439.7	-50.2
2007	C+	1.32	0.64	18,277.0	496.1	495.1	167.9
2006	C+	3.50	1.94	4,464.3	461.2	283.1	161.1
2005	C	3.55	1.89	2,883.4	357.2	194.7	157.4
2004	C	5.16	2.72	3,186.0	553.5	275.4	-166.6

Swiss Reinsurance Group Composite Group Rating: C Largest Group Members	Assets ($mil)	Rating
REASSURE AMERICA LIFE INS CO	16470	C+
SWISS REINSURANCE AMERICA CORP	14402	C
SWISS RE LIFE HEALTH AMER INC	12775	B-
WESTPORT INS CORP	8047	C
NORTH AMERICAN SPECIALTY INS CO	506	C

REGENCE LIFE & HEALTH INSURANCE COMPANY *   B+   Good

Major Rating Factors: Good overall results on stability tests (6.6 on a scale of 0 to 10) despite negative cash flow from operations for 2008. Other stability subfactors include good operational trends and good risk diversification. Good quality investment portfolio (6.8) despite mixed results such as: no exposure to mortgages and substantial holdings of BBB bonds but no exposure to junk bonds. Good liquidity (6.9).

Other Rating Factors: Strong capitalization (7.9) based on excellent risk adjusted capital (severe loss scenario). Excellent profitability (8.2) with operating gains in each of the last five years.

Principal Business: Group health insurance (67%), group life insurance (17%), individual health insurance (14%), and reinsurance (1%).

Principal Investments: NonCMO investment grade bonds (45%), CMOs and structured securities (35%), common & preferred stock (16%), and cash (4%).

Investments in Affiliates: 2%

Group Affiliation: Regence Group

Licensed in: AZ, IL, NE, PA, VT, WV, PR

Commenced Business: July 1966

Address: 100 SW Market St, Portland, OR 97201

Phone: (503) 225-6048 **Domicile State:** OR **NAIC Code:** 97985

Data Date	Rating	RACR #1	RACR #2	Total Assets ($mil)	Capital ($mil)	Net Premium ($mil)	Net Income ($mil)
3-09	B+	2.14	1.60	80.7	37.2	11.2	0.7
3-08	B	2.32	1.66	81.9	39.2	11.0	0.9
2008	B+	2.10	1.54	81.6	37.5	44.7	0.8
2007	B	2.31	1.66	84.9	37.8	42.3	4.4
2006	B	2.15	1.53	84.0	34.1	38.1	2.9
2005	B	1.98	1.43	60.3	30.5	35.0	2.6
2004	B	1.85	1.33	61.5	29.7	35.2	3.3

Adverse Trends in Operations

Decrease in asset base during 2008 (4%)
Decrease in asset base during 2005 (2%)

REINSURANCE CO OF MO INC   C+   Fair

Major Rating Factors: Fair profitability (4.1 on a scale of 0 to 10). Excellent expense controls. Return on equity has been low, averaging -0.2%. Fair overall results on stability tests (4.5). Good current capitalization (6.7) based on good risk adjusted capital (severe loss scenario), although results have slipped from the excellent range during the last year.

Other Rating Factors: Low quality investment portfolio (1.4). Excellent liquidity (7.0).

Principal Business: Reinsurance (100%).

Principal Investments: Common & preferred stock (94%), nonCMO investment grade bonds (3%), and CMOs and structured securities (2%).

Investments in Affiliates: 94%

Group Affiliation: RGA Inc

Licensed in: MT

Commenced Business: December 1998

Address: (No address available)

Phone: (636) 736-7368 **Domicile State:** MO **NAIC Code:** 89004

Data Date	Rating	RACR #1	RACR #2	Total Assets ($mil)	Capital ($mil)	Net Premium ($mil)	Net Income ($mil)
3-09	C+	1.08	0.96	1,128.9	1,061.4	11.4	0.1
3-08	C+	1.07	0.95	1,187.4	1,121.9	10.6	2.3
2008	C+	1.13	1.00	1,174.6	1,107.9	43.2	-2.3
2007	C+	1.13	1.01	1,250.9	1,184.1	35.3	5.2
2006	C+	1.09	0.97	1,137.9	1,045.6	-6.7	68.5
2005	U	0.99	0.94	1,210.8	1,007.4	60.4	-90.1
2004	U	1.17	1.04	897.2	887.7	12.1	6.8

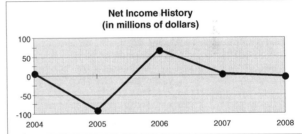

**Net Income History
(in millions of dollars)**

RELIABLE LIFE INSURANCE COMPANY *   B+   Good

Major Rating Factors: Good overall results on stability tests (6.3 on a scale of 0 to 10). Stability strengths include excellent operational trends, excellent risk adjusted capital for prior years and excellent risk diversification. Good current capitalization (6.8) based on good risk adjusted capital (severe loss scenario), although results have slipped from the excellent range during the last year. Good overall profitability (6.9).

Other Rating Factors: Fair quality investment portfolio (4.6). Fair liquidity (4.3).

Principal Business: Individual life insurance (92%), individual health insurance (6%), and reinsurance (2%).

Principal Investments: NonCMO investment grade bonds (59%), CMOs and structured securities (19%), policy loans (8%), common & preferred stock (6%), and misc. investments (7%).

Investments in Affiliates: None

Group Affiliation: Unitrin Inc

Licensed in: All states except AL, ME, NC

Commenced Business: January 1912

Address: 231 W Lockwood Ave, Webster Groves, MO 63119-2327

Phone: (314) 968-4900 **Domicile State:** MO **NAIC Code:** 68357

Data Date	Rating	RACR #1	RACR #2	Total Assets ($mil)	Capital ($mil)	Net Premium ($mil)	Net Income ($mil)
3-09	B+	1.76	0.97	747.4	56.2	28.3	2.7
3-08	A-	1.92	1.11	740.0	61.9	29.3	3.1
2008	B+	1.86	1.03	741.8	56.4	112.2	10.3
2007	A-	1.97	1.15	730.5	58.3	113.2	15.1
2006	A-	2.17	1.27	713.7	55.9	115.1	13.3
2005	A-	2.13	1.29	691.7	54.2	117.3	14.5
2004	B	3.09	1.92	689.0	79.3	116.1	9.7

Adverse Trends in Operations

Decrease in capital during 2008 (3%)
Decrease in premium volume from 2006 to 2007 (2%)
Decrease in premium volume from 2005 to 2006 (2%)
Decrease in capital during 2005 (32%)

RELIANCE STANDARD LIFE INSURANCE COMPANY

B-   **Good**

Major Rating Factors: Good capitalization (5.5 on a scale of 0 to 10) based on good risk adjusted capital (moderate loss scenario). Capital levels have been relatively consistent over the last five years. Fair quality investment portfolio (3.7) with substantial holdings of BBB bonds in addition to junk bond exposure equal to 79% of capital. Fair overall results on stability tests (4.9).

Other Rating Factors: Excellent profitability (8.0) with operating gains in each of the last five years. Excellent liquidity (7.2).

Principal Business: Group health insurance (46%), group life insurance (30%), individual annuities (11%), group retirement contracts (8%), and reinsurance (4%).

Principal Investments: CMOs and structured securities (46%), nonCMO investment grade bonds (33%), noninv. grade bonds (12%), common & preferred stock (3%), and misc. investments (6%).

Investments in Affiliates: 3%

Group Affiliation: Delphi Financial Group Inc

Licensed in: All states except AL, NC

Commenced Business: April 1907

Address: 111 S Wacker Dr Suite 4400, Chicago, IL 60606-4410

Phone: (215) 787-4000   **Domicile State:** IL   **NAIC Code:** 68381

Data Date	Rating	RACR #1	RACR #2	Total Assets ($mil)	Capital ($mil)	Net Premium ($mil)	Net Income ($mil)
3-09	B-	1.31	0.77	3,584.2	489.0	308.9	-11.3
3-08	B-	1.83	1.14	3,183.1	463.1	292.8	11.0
2008	B-	1.49	0.96	3,509.0	511.7	1,233.7	23.3
2007	B-	1.77	1.11	3,240.6	457.5	995.7	54.3
2006	C+	2.11	1.26	2,939.4	416.3	864.2	44.6
2005	C+	1.80	1.11	2,613.5	369.1	762.6	54.2
2004	C+	1.77	1.10	2,420.9	325.4	685.3	27.5

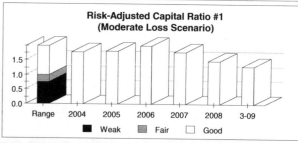

Risk-Adjusted Capital Ratio #1
(Moderate Loss Scenario)

RELIASTAR LIFE INSURANCE COMPANY

B   **Good**

Major Rating Factors: Good quality investment portfolio (5.8 on a scale of 0 to 10) despite substantial holdings of BBB bonds in addition to moderate junk bond exposure. Exposure to mortgages is significant, but the mortgage default rate has been low. Good overall profitability (6.8). Return on equity has been fair, averaging 7.4%. Good liquidity (5.9).

Other Rating Factors: Fair overall results on stability tests (4.3) including fair financial strength of affiliated ING America Ins Holdings Inc. Strong capitalization (7.4) based on excellent risk adjusted capital (severe loss scenario).

Principal Business: Individual life insurance (26%), reinsurance (19%), group life insurance (17%), individual annuities (16%), and other lines (22%).

Principal Investments: NonCMO investment grade bonds (39%), CMOs and structured securities (30%), mortgages in good standing (14%), noninv. grade bonds (5%), and misc. investments (12%).

Investments in Affiliates: 2%

Group Affiliation: ING America Ins Holdings Inc

Licensed in: All states except AL, NC

Commenced Business: September 1885

Address: 20 Washington Ave S, Minneapolis, MN 55401

Phone: (612) 372-5432   **Domicile State:** MN   **NAIC Code:** 67105

Data Date	Rating	RACR #1	RACR #2	Total Assets ($mil)	Capital ($mil)	Net Premium ($mil)	Net Income ($mil)
3-09	B	2.16	1.26	20,409.8	1,995.1	2.4	25.9
3-08	B+	2.05	1.29	21,955.3	2,224.2	717.8	17.6
2008	B	2.24	1.32	20,473.9	2,079.4	2,306.0	-125.2
2007	B+	2.16	1.34	22,384.6	2,325.9	1,970.2	153.1
2006	B	2.17	1.40	22,050.6	2,323.5	3,038.5	129.5
2005	B	1.91	1.22	22,042.6	1,880.1	3,114.4	182.5
2004	B-	1.63	1.02	21,563.4	1,538.5	3,313.8	185.5

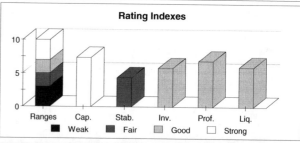

Rating Indexes

RELIASTAR LIFE INSURANCE COMPANY OF NEW YORK

C+   **Fair**

Major Rating Factors: Fair overall results on stability tests (4.5 on a scale of 0 to 10) including negative cash flow from operations for 2008. Good quality investment portfolio (6.1) despite mixed results such as: large holdings of BBB rated bonds but moderate junk bond exposure. Good liquidity (6.6) with sufficient resources to handle a spike in claims as well as a significant increase in policy surrenders.

Other Rating Factors: Weak profitability (1.8) with operating losses during the first three months of 2009. Strong capitalization (7.3) based on excellent risk adjusted capital (severe loss scenario).

Principal Business: Individual annuities (56%), individual life insurance (32%), group retirement contracts (4%), group health insurance (4%), and other lines (4%).

Principal Investments: NonCMO investment grade bonds (52%), CMOs and structured securities (31%), mortgages in good standing (6%), policy loans (5%), and noninv. grade bonds (4%).

Investments in Affiliates: None

Group Affiliation: ING America Ins Holdings Inc

Licensed in: All states except AL

Commenced Business: September 1917

Address: 1000 Woodbury Rd Suite 102, Woodbury, NY 11797

Phone: (516) 682-8700   **Domicile State:** NY   **NAIC Code:** 61360

Data Date	Rating	RACR #1	RACR #2	Total Assets ($mil)	Capital ($mil)	Net Premium ($mil)	Net Income ($mil)
3-09	C+	2.23	1.18	3,182.8	189.6	91.6	-5.4
3-08	B	3.09	1.67	3,239.5	281.3	154.6	-4.3
2008	C+	2.66	1.42	3,207.5	222.0	525.5	-196.9
2007	B	3.13	1.66	3,252.0	287.0	451.1	-12.8
2006	B	3.16	1.76	2,999.3	278.2	423.7	17.9
2005	B	3.23	1.76	2,805.4	279.9	360.2	35.6
2004	B	3.01	1.61	2,679.5	260.9	278.9	18.6

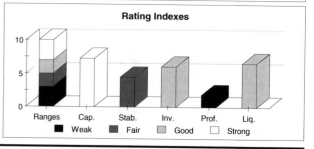

Rating Indexes

RESERVE NATIONAL INSURANCE COMPANY   B   Good

Major Rating Factors: Good overall results on stability tests (5.8 on a scale of 0 to 10). Stability strengths include excellent operational trends and excellent risk diversification. Good liquidity (6.5) with sufficient resources to handle a spike in claims. Fair quality investment portfolio (4.6).

Other Rating Factors: Strong capitalization (7.6) based on excellent risk adjusted capital (severe loss scenario). Excellent profitability (9.3) with operating gains in each of the last five years.

Principal Business: Individual health insurance (93%), group health insurance (7%), and individual life insurance (1%).

Principal Investments: NonCMO investment grade bonds (59%), CMOs and structured securities (13%), common & preferred stock (12%), real estate (11%), and cash (1%).

Investments in Affiliates: None

Group Affiliation: Unitrin Inc

Licensed in: AK, AR, CA, CT, GA, HI, IL, IN, IA, KS, KY, LA, ME, MO, MT, NE, NV, NH, NY, ND, OK, OR, PA, SD, TN, TX, UT, VT, WA, WV, PR

Commenced Business: September 1956

Address: 6100 NW Grand Blvd, Oklahoma City, OK 73118

Phone: (405) 848-7931 **Domicile State:** OK **NAIC Code:** 68462

Data Date	Rating	RACR #1	RACR #2	Total Assets ($mil)	Capital ($mil)	Net Premium ($mil)	Net Income ($mil)
3-09	B	1.98	1.40	106.2	45.3	32.8	0.6
3-08	B	2.01	1.44	108.2	46.1	33.7	0.8
2008	B	1.96	1.40	104.1	45.2	128.6	6.1
2007	B	1.98	1.42	108.3	44.6	129.4	6.4
2006	B	1.88	1.29	104.9	44.3	127.3	18.0
2005	B	1.54	1.18	98.9	34.8	131.9	6.8
2004	B	1.63	1.26	96.8	36.3	127.7	8.8

Adverse Trends in Operations

Increase in policy surrenders from 2007 to 2008 (82%)
Decrease in asset base during 2008 (4%)
Decrease in premium volume from 2005 to 2006 (4%)
Increase in policy surrenders from 2005 to 2006 (128%)
Decrease in capital during 2005 (4%)

RGA REINSURANCE COMPANY   C+   Fair

Major Rating Factors: Fair overall results on stability tests (4.8 on a scale of 0 to 10). Good quality investment portfolio (6.3) despite large holdings of BBB rated bonds in addition to moderate junk bond exposure. Exposure to mortgages is significant, but the mortgage default rate has been low. Good liquidity (5.6) with sufficient resources to handle a spike in claims as well as a significant increase in policy surrenders.

Other Rating Factors: Weak profitability (2.7) with operating losses during the first three months of 2009. Strong capitalization (7.0) based on excellent risk adjusted capital (severe loss scenario).

Principal Business: Reinsurance (100%).

Principal Investments: NonCMO investment grade bonds (41%), CMOs and structured securities (22%), policy loans (15%), mortgages in good standing (11%), and misc. investments (12%).

Investments in Affiliates: None

Group Affiliation: RGA Inc

Licensed in: All states except AL, DC, MD, NJ, NC

Commenced Business: October 1982

Address: 660 Mason Ridge Center Dr, St Louis, MO 63141

Phone: (314) 453-7368 **Domicile State:** MO **NAIC Code:** 93572

Data Date	Rating	RACR #1	RACR #2	Total Assets ($mil)	Capital ($mil)	Net Premium ($mil)	Net Income ($mil)
3-09	C+	1.74	1.00	13,085.6	1,057.1	624.6	-86.5
3-08	B-	1.84	1.09	12,005.4	1,119.6	372.7	-25.6
2008	C+	1.79	1.04	13,009.0	1,103.8	2,854.1	-41.8
2007	B-	1.90	1.13	11,821.5	1,184.1	4,289.0	-41.5
2006	B-	1.86	1.11	11,061.6	1,050.8	3,848.4	-61.5
2005	B-	1.87	1.13	9,778.2	975.1	3,556.7	-62.8
2004	B	1.76	1.07	8,973.2	869.4	1,722.6	117.4

Rating Indexes

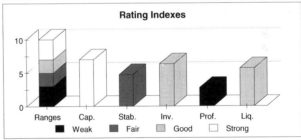

Ranges Cap. Stab. Inv. Prof. Liq.
■ Weak   ▨ Fair   ▨ Good   □ Strong

RIVERSOURCE LIFE INSURANCE COMPANY   B   Good

Major Rating Factors: Good quality investment portfolio (6.0 on a scale of 0 to 10) despite mixed results such as: substantial holdings of BBB bonds but moderate junk bond exposure. Fair overall results on stability tests (4.6). Weak profitability (1.8) with investment income below regulatory standards in relation to interest assumptions of reserves.

Other Rating Factors: Strong capitalization (7.1) based on excellent risk adjusted capital (severe loss scenario). Excellent liquidity (8.1).

Principal Business: Individual annuities (84%), individual life insurance (11%), individual health insurance (4%), and group retirement contracts (1%).

Principal Investments: NonCMO investment grade bonds (48%), CMOs and structured securities (24%), mortgages in good standing (9%), noninv. grade bonds (4%), and misc. investments (15%).

Investments in Affiliates: 2%

Group Affiliation: Ameriprise Financial Inc

Licensed in: All states except AL, NC

Commenced Business: October 1957

Address: 227 AXP Financial Center, Minneapolis, MN 55474

Phone: (612) 671-3131 **Domicile State:** MN **NAIC Code:** 65005

Data Date	Rating	RACR #1	RACR #2	Total Assets ($mil)	Capital ($mil)	Net Premium ($mil)	Net Income ($mil)
3-09	B	1.83	1.08	67,256.2	2,567.3	3,495.2	349.8
3-08	B	2.27	1.28	76,489.9	2,662.0	2,349.0	-93.2
2008	B	1.89	1.13	67,906.2	2,528.6	9,838.1	-1,407.2
2007	B	2.37	1.34	79,870.1	2,820.4	11,711.8	554.7
2006	B	2.51	1.44	74,682.9	3,258.1	11,230.0	513.8
2005	B	1.86	1.25	57,516.5	2,942.2	7,119.1	341.2
2004	B	1.40	0.94	53,108.5	2,276.7	5,803.4	380.0

Rating Indexes

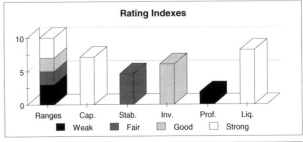

Ranges Cap. Stab. Inv. Prof. Liq.
■ Weak   ▨ Fair   ▨ Good   □ Strong

RIVERSOURCE LIFE INSURANCE COMPANY OF NEW YORK
B-   Good

Major Rating Factors: Good quality investment portfolio (6.0 on a scale of 0 to 10) despite substantial holdings of BBB bonds in addition to junk bond exposure equal to 51% of capital. Exposure to mortgages is significant, but the mortgage default rate has been low. Fair overall results on stability tests (4.9) including negative cash flow from operations for 2008. Weak profitability (2.2) with operating losses during the first three months of 2009.

Other Rating Factors: Strong capitalization (7.4) based on excellent risk adjusted capital (severe loss scenario). Excellent liquidity (7.7).

Principal Business: Individual annuities (81%), individual life insurance (12%), group retirement contracts (4%), and individual health insurance (4%).

Principal Investments: NonCMO investment grade bonds (55%), CMOs and structured securities (24%), mortgages in good standing (11%), noninv. grade bonds (5%), and policy loans (2%).

Investments in Affiliates: None

Group Affiliation: Ameriprise Financial Inc

Licensed in: NC, OH

Commenced Business: October 1972

Address: 20 Madison Avenue Extension, Albany, NY 12203

Phone: (518) 869-8613 **Domicile State:** NY **NAIC Code:** 80594

Data Date	Rating	RACR #1	RACR #2	Total Assets ($mil)	Capital ($mil)	Net Premium ($mil)	Net Income ($mil)
3-09	B-	2.46	1.25	4,196.6	193.5	221.2	-22.3
3-08	B+	3.45	1.76	4,839.2	288.7	146.7	3.2
2008	B-	2.78	1.43	4,197.1	215.6	587.2	-34.0
2007	B+	3.29	1.69	5,025.0	274.3	691.5	34.0
2006	B+	3.73	1.90	4,757.1	331.5	661.1	63.0
2005	B+	3.51	1.83	3,562.1	232.6	441.1	29.5
2004	B+	3.24	1.65	3,284.7	227.0	368.1	34.7

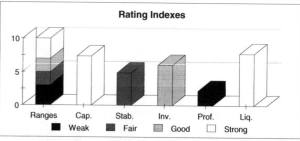

Rating Indexes

ROYAL STATE NATIONAL INSURANCE COMPANY LIMITED
B-   Good

Major Rating Factors: Good overall profitability (5.8 on a scale of 0 to 10). Return on equity has been low, averaging 3.8%. Good overall results on stability tests (5.1). Stability strengths include excellent operational trends and good risk diversification. Strong capitalization (10.0) based on excellent risk adjusted capital (severe loss scenario).

Other Rating Factors: High quality investment portfolio (7.9). Excellent liquidity (9.1).

Principal Business: Group health insurance (50%), group life insurance (35%), individual life insurance (8%), and reinsurance (7%).

Principal Investments: NonCMO investment grade bonds (72%), cash (18%), common & preferred stock (9%), and noninv. grade bonds (1%).

Investments in Affiliates: 4%

Group Affiliation: Royal State Group

Licensed in: ID

Commenced Business: August 1961

Address: 819 S Beretania St, Honolulu, HI 96813

Phone: (808) 539-1600 **Domicile State:** HI **NAIC Code:** 68551

Data Date	Rating	RACR #1	RACR #2	Total Assets ($mil)	Capital ($mil)	Net Premium ($mil)	Net Income ($mil)
3-09	B-	4.33	3.89	47.5	27.2	1.6	0.5
3-08	B-	4.67	4.11	48.9	29.8	1.6	0.5
2008	B-	4.45	4.00	47.1	27.2	6.4	-0.5
2007	B-	4.76	4.13	48.7	29.3	5.9	1.7
2006	B-	4.65	4.19	47.1	28.0	5.1	1.5
2005	B-	4.48	4.04	46.3	26.8	5.3	1.2
2004	C+	4.62	4.16	44.8	27.0	4.9	1.1

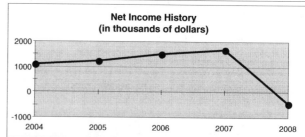

Net Income History
(in thousands of dollars)

SAGICOR LIFE INSURANCE COMPANY
C   Fair

Major Rating Factors: Fair quality investment portfolio (3.8 on a scale of 0 to 10) with large holdings of BBB rated bonds in addition to moderate junk bond exposure. Fair overall results on stability tests (3.3) including negative cash flow from operations for 2008. Good capitalization (5.8) based on good risk adjusted capital (moderate loss scenario).

Other Rating Factors: Good liquidity (6.2). Weak profitability (1.7) with operating losses during the first three months of 2009.

Principal Business: Individual life insurance (61%), individual annuities (20%), reinsurance (18%), and individual health insurance (1%).

Principal Investments: CMOs and structured securities (43%), nonCMO investment grade bonds (39%), policy loans (6%), mortgages in good standing (6%), and misc. investments (6%).

Investments in Affiliates: None

Group Affiliation: Sagicor Financial Corp

Licensed in: All states except AL, AZ, DC, MD, MI, MN, NJ, NC, SC, VA

Commenced Business: April 1954

Address: 2720 E Camelback Rd, Phoenix, AZ 85016

Phone: (800) 531-5067 **Domicile State:** TX **NAIC Code:** 60445

Data Date	Rating	RACR #1	RACR #2	Total Assets ($mil)	Capital ($mil)	Net Premium ($mil)	Net Income ($mil)
3-09	C	1.53	0.77	542.6	29.4	12.7	-3.9
3-08	C	1.89	1.00	527.8	32.1	5.3	-1.3
2008	C	1.55	0.79	538.8	29.2	33.5	-21.2
2007	C	2.09	1.11	527.9	35.1	11.7	-3.5
2006	C	2.26	1.21	479.4	33.9	15.2	-1.2
2005	C-	2.31	1.22	501.4	42.3	24.9	4.8
2004	C-	1.57	0.85	502.4	30.8	28.9	-1.5

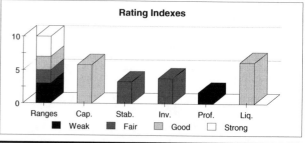

Rating Indexes

SAVINGS BANK LIFE INSURANCE COMPANY OF MA *   B+   Good

Major Rating Factors: Good profitability (5.0 on a scale of 0 to 10). Excellent expense controls. Return on equity has been low, averaging 2.9%. Good liquidity (6.5) with sufficient resources to cover a large increase in policy surrenders. Good overall results on stability tests (6.4). Stability strengths include good operational trends and excellent risk diversification.

Other Rating Factors: Strong capitalization (7.4) based on excellent risk adjusted capital (severe loss scenario). High quality investment portfolio (7.2).

Principal Business: Individual life insurance (90%) and individual annuities (10%).

Principal Investments: NonCMO investment grade bonds (68%), CMOs and structured securities (18%), common & preferred stock (6%), policy loans (4%), and noninv. grade bonds (1%).

Investments in Affiliates: 1%

Group Affiliation: Savings Bank Life Group

Licensed in: AR, CO, CT, DC, DE, FL, HI, IN, IA, MD, MA, MI, MN, NJ, NM, ND, OK, PA, RI, SC, SD, TX, UT, VA, WA, WI

Commenced Business: January 1992

Address: One Linscott Rd, Woburn, MA 01801

Phone: (781) 938-3500 **Domicile State:** MA **NAIC Code:** 70435

Data Date	Rating	RACR #1	RACR #2	Total Assets ($mil)	Capital ($mil)	Net Premium ($mil)	Net Income ($mil)
3-09	B+	1.89	1.26	2,093.4	145.5	45.1	1.3
3-08	A-	2.34	1.58	2,088.9	197.4	48.1	1.2
2008	A-	2.15	1.40	2,130.3	160.9	187.8	-28.6
2007	A-	2.69	1.78	2,056.0	200.0	221.9	8.7
2006	A-	3.44	2.18	1,934.3	195.4	208.0	8.5
2005	A-	3.74	2.38	1,809.1	193.0	203.9	10.1
2004	A-	4.16	2.64	1,697.9	190.0	209.4	9.8

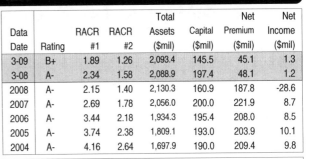

Net Income History
(in millions of dollars)

SBLI USA MUT LIFE INS CO INC   C+   Fair

Major Rating Factors: Fair quality investment portfolio (3.9 on a scale of 0 to 10) with substantial holdings of BBB bonds in addition to junk bond exposure equal to 51% of capital. Fair liquidity (4.8) due, in part, to cash value policies that are subject to withdrawals with minimal or no penalty. Fair overall results on stability tests (4.5).

Other Rating Factors: Good capitalization (5.6) based on good risk adjusted capital (moderate loss scenario). Good overall profitability (5.6) despite operating losses during the first three months of 2009.

Principal Business: Individual life insurance (61%), group life insurance (24%), individual annuities (10%), and reinsurance (4%).

Principal Investments: CMOs and structured securities (43%), nonCMO investment grade bonds (38%), policy loans (8%), common & preferred stock (4%), and misc. investments (7%).

Investments in Affiliates: 1%

Group Affiliation: SBLI USA Group

Licensed in: IN, KS, MN, MO, NJ, NM, NC, ND, OK, RI, TN, VA

Commenced Business: January 2000

Address: 460 W 34th St Suite 800, New York, NY 10001-2320

Phone: (212) 356-0346 **Domicile State:** NY **NAIC Code:** 60176

Data Date	Rating	RACR #1	RACR #2	Total Assets ($mil)	Capital ($mil)	Net Premium ($mil)	Net Income ($mil)
3-09	C+	1.37	0.73	1,467.6	108.5	22.5	-0.6
3-08	C+	1.83	1.04	1,517.4	128.3	22.9	0.6
2008	C+	1.64	0.92	1,486.1	111.6	87.0	-7.2
2007	C+	1.84	1.04	1,526.4	129.5	95.3	4.5
2006	C	1.59	0.92	1,525.1	123.7	99.3	11.5
2005	C	1.62	0.92	1,515.7	119.2	97.2	8.2
2004	C-	1.73	0.98	1,510.1	119.8	135.9	1.8

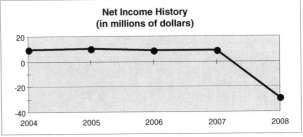

Rating Indexes

Ranges Cap. Stab. Inv. Prof. Liq.
■ Weak ■ Fair ▨ Good □ Strong

SCOR GLOBAL LIFE RE INSURANCE COMPANY OF TEXAS   D+   Weak

Major Rating Factors: Weak overall results on stability tests (1.5 on a scale of 0 to 10) including weak financial strength of affiliated Scor Reinsurance Group, weak results on operational trends and negative cash flow from operations for 2008. Weak profitability (1.9). Excellent expense controls. Return on equity has been low, averaging -20.8%. Good quality investment portfolio (6.7).

Other Rating Factors: Good liquidity (6.6). Strong capitalization (7.1) based on excellent risk adjusted capital (severe loss scenario).

Principal Business: Reinsurance (100%).

Principal Investments: NonCMO investment grade bonds (40%), CMOs and structured securities (31%), and cash (1%).

Investments in Affiliates: None

Group Affiliation: Scor Reinsurance Group

Licensed in: AZ, AR, CA, CO, CT, DE, FL, HI, IL, IN, IA, KS, KY, ME, MA, MN, MS, MO, MT, NE, NV, NH, NY, ND, OH, OK, OR, PA, SD, TN, TX, UT, VT, WV, WI, WY, PR

Commenced Business: May 1977

Address: 26 Century Blvd, Nashville, TN 37214

Phone: (615) 872-4000 **Domicile State:** TX **NAIC Code:** 87017

Data Date	Rating	RACR #1	RACR #2	Total Assets ($mil)	Capital ($mil)	Net Premium ($mil)	Net Income ($mil)
3-09	D+	1.65	1.04	298.6	41.0	8.9	1.1
3-08	D+	1.66	0.98	367.1	43.6	10.8	2.7
2008	D+	1.65	1.04	314.8	41.5	31.2	-5.4
2007	D+	1.62	0.96	376.6	42.6	45.2	-7.1
2006	D+	2.02	1.19	361.7	52.6	28.4	-7.1
2005	D+	2.02	1.20	340.8	61.4	25.3	3.7
2004	D+	0.97	0.64	317.6	37.4	56.4	-28.3

Scor Reinsurance Group Composite Group Rating: D Largest Group Members	Assets ($mil)	Rating
SCOR GLOBAL LIFE US RE INS CO	2011	C-
SCOR REINSURANCE CO	1452	D
GENERAL SECURITY NATIONAL INS CO	317	D
SCOR GLOBAL LIFE RE INS CO OF TX	315	D+
INVESTORS INS CORP	247	D+

SCOR GLOBAL LIFE US RE INSURANCE COMPANY

C- **Fair**

Major Rating Factors: Fair overall results on stability tests (3.1 on a scale of 0 to 10) including potential financial drain due to affiliation with Scor Reinsurance Group and weak risk adjusted capital in prior years. Good current capitalization (5.2) based on good risk adjusted capital (moderate loss scenario) reflecting significant improvement over results in 2004. Good quality investment portfolio (6.4).

Other Rating Factors: Good overall profitability (5.4) although investment income, in comparison to reserve requirements, is below regulatory standards. Excellent liquidity (7.3).

Principal Business: Reinsurance (100%).

Principal Investments: NonCMO investment grade bonds (50%), CMOs and structured securities (39%), common & preferred stock (7%), mortgages in good standing (2%), and noninv. grade bonds (1%).

Investments in Affiliates: 4%

Group Affiliation: Scor Reinsurance Group

Licensed in: All states except AL, NC

Commenced Business: April 1945

Address: 15305 Dallas Parkway Ste 700, Addison, TX 75001

Phone: (972) 560-9500 **Domicile State:** TX **NAIC Code:** 64688

Data Date	Rating	RACR #1	RACR #2	Total Assets ($mil)	Capital ($mil)	Net Premium ($mil)	Net Income ($mil)
3-09	C-	1.13	0.76	2,065.1	174.6	51.1	11.5
3-08	D+	N/A	N/A	N/A	N/A	N/A	N/A
2008	C-	1.06	0.73	2,011.1	163.0	132.5	6.4
2007	D+	1.06	0.68	1,958.2	125.6	78.6	26.0
2006	D	0.95	0.64	1,958.7	126.3	-17.8	-4.6
2005	D-	0.80	0.53	2,129.8	107.1	-60.4	23.0
2004	D-	0.49	0.33	2,219.7	48.7	378.9	-12.7

Scor Reinsurance Group Composite Group Rating: D Largest Group Members	Assets ($mil)	Rating
SCOR GLOBAL LIFE US RE INS CO	2011	C-
SCOR REINSURANCE CO	1452	D
GENERAL SECURITY NATIONAL INS CO	317	D
SCOR GLOBAL LIFE RE INS CO OF TX	315	D+
INVESTORS INS CORP	247	D+

SCOTT LIFE INSURANCE COMPANY

B **Good**

Major Rating Factors: Good overall results on stability tests (5.5 on a scale of 0 to 10) despite fair financial strength of affiliated Wells Fargo Group. Other stability subfactors include good operational trends and excellent risk diversification. Strong capitalization (10.0) based on excellent risk adjusted capital (severe loss scenario). Moreover, capital levels have been consistently high over the last five years. High quality investment portfolio (8.3).

Other Rating Factors: Excellent profitability (8.8) with operating gains in each of the last five years. Excellent liquidity (10.0).

Principal Business: Reinsurance (100%).

Principal Investments: NonCMO investment grade bonds (74%), CMOs and structured securities (19%), cash (4%), and common & preferred stock (4%).

Investments in Affiliates: None

Group Affiliation: Wells Fargo Group

Licensed in: AR

Commenced Business: March 1969

Address: 3300 Valley Bank Center, Phoenix, AZ 85073

Phone: (515) 237-7299 **Domicile State:** AZ **NAIC Code:** 76961

Data Date	Rating	RACR #1	RACR #2	Total Assets ($mil)	Capital ($mil)	Net Premium ($mil)	Net Income ($mil)
3-09	B	10.91	9.82	99.5	97.6	0.1	0.6
3-08	B	10.81	9.73	100.8	95.3	0.1	0.6
2008	B	10.86	9.78	99.1	97.1	0.4	3.5
2007	B	10.54	9.48	97.4	92.5	0.3	3.8
2006	B	10.50	9.45	93.6	90.4	0.3	4.3
2005	B	10.18	9.16	90.7	86.3	0.5	3.4
2004	B	9.82	8.84	92.0	82.4	7.5	6.5

Wells Fargo Group Composite Group Rating: C+ Largest Group Members	Assets ($mil)	Rating
RURAL COMMUNITY INS CO	4387	B-
CENTURION LIFE INS CO	1621	B-
CENTURION CASUALTY CO	383	B
HERITAGE INDEMNITY CO	191	C+
SCOTT LIFE INS CO	99	B

SCOTTISH RE LIFE CORPORATION

D+ **Weak**

Major Rating Factors: Weak profitability (2.5 on a scale of 0 to 10) with operating losses during 2008. Return on equity has been low, averaging -15.0%. Weak overall results on stability tests (2.9) including negative cash flow from operations for 2008. Good quality investment portfolio (6.9) despite mixed results such as: no exposure to mortgages and substantial holdings of BBB bonds but minimal holdings in junk bonds.

Other Rating Factors: Good liquidity (6.3). Strong capitalization (7.1) based on excellent risk adjusted capital (severe loss scenario).

Principal Business: Reinsurance (100%).

Principal Investments: NonCMO investment grade bonds (39%), CMOs and structured securities (30%), common & preferred stock (13%), cash (12%), and misc. investments (6%).

Investments in Affiliates: None

Group Affiliation: Scottish Annuity & Life Holdings Ltd

Licensed in: AR, CA, CO, DE, FL, HI, IL, IN, IA, KS, KY, ME, MI, MN, MO, MT, NV, NH, NM, OK, OR, UT, VT, WV, PR

Commenced Business: October 1979

Address: 1209 Orange St, Wilmington, DE 19801-1120

Phone: (704) 943-2082 **Domicile State:** DE **NAIC Code:** 90670

Data Date	Rating	RACR #1	RACR #2	Total Assets ($mil)	Capital ($mil)	Net Premium ($mil)	Net Income ($mil)
2008	D+	1.63	1.04	521.4	66.4	123.0	-19.4
2007	C-	2.22	1.41	581.3	93.3	128.5	9.8
2006	C-	2.05	1.31	668.0	81.3	109.4	-3.7
2005	U	1.74	1.10	614.7	74.3	114.3	8.8
2004	U	1.39	0.92	628.4	68.6	-44.9	-68.5

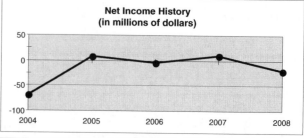

Net Income History
(in millions of dollars)

SEARS LIFE INSURANCE COMPANY   B   Good

Major Rating Factors: Good overall results on stability tests (5.8 on a scale of 0 to 10). Strengths include good financial support from affiliation with Citigroup Inc, good operational trends and excellent risk diversification. Fair profitability (3.0). Return on equity has been low, averaging -0.1%. Strong capitalization (10.0) based on excellent risk adjusted capital (severe loss scenario).

Other Rating Factors: High quality investment portfolio (7.4). Excellent liquidity (8.2).

Principal Business: Group health insurance (60%), group life insurance (29%), individual health insurance (7%), and individual life insurance (4%).

Principal Investments: NonCMO investment grade bonds (62%), CMOs and structured securities (31%), noninv. grade bonds (4%), and cash (3%).

Investments in Affiliates: None

Group Affiliation: Citigroup Inc

Licensed in: All states except AL, DC, NJ, NC

Commenced Business: May 1956

Address: 10255 W Higgins Rd Ste 700, Rosemont, IL 60018

Phone: (817) 348-7565   **Domicile State:** TX   **NAIC Code:** 69914

Data Date	Rating	RACR #1	RACR #2	Total Assets ($mil)	Capital ($mil)	Net Premium ($mil)	Net Income ($mil)
3-09	B	6.82	5.56	75.0	53.1	6.7	2.1
3-08	B	6.63	5.52	72.3	51.8	8.3	0.3
2008	B	6.55	5.27	73.6	51.0	31.9	4.7
2007	B	6.59	5.57	73.7	51.4	31.8	-2.9
2006	B-	6.87	6.18	75.7	54.2	23.3	-6.0
2005	B-	7.64	6.87	77.0	60.7	16.8	1.7
2004	C	7.62	6.86	72.2	59.0	8.4	-1.5

Citigroup Inc
Composite Group Rating: B+

Largest Group Members	Assets ($mil)	Rating
PRIMERICA LIFE INS CO	5959	A-
AMERICAN HEALTH LIFE INS CO	1520	B+
TRITON INS CO	779	B-
NATIONAL BENEFIT LIFE INS CO	721	A-
SEARS LIFE INS CO	74	B

SECURIAN LIFE INSURANCE COMPANY   B   Good

Major Rating Factors: Good overall results on stability tests (5.9 on a scale of 0 to 10). Stability strengths include good operational trends and excellent risk diversification. Strong capitalization (10.0) based on excellent risk adjusted capital (severe loss scenario). Moreover, capital levels have been consistently high over the last five years. High quality investment portfolio (8.3).

Other Rating Factors: Excellent profitability (7.5) despite modest operating losses during 2004. Excellent liquidity (7.5).

Principal Business: Group health insurance (71%), group life insurance (24%), credit life insurance (3%), credit health insurance (2%), and individual life insurance (1%).

Principal Investments: NonCMO investment grade bonds (76%) and CMOs and structured securities (23%).

Investments in Affiliates: None

Group Affiliation: Securian Financial Group

Licensed in: All states except AL, NJ, NC

Commenced Business: December 1981

Address: 400 Robert St N, St Paul, MN 55101

Phone: (651) 665-3500   **Domicile State:** MN   **NAIC Code:** 93742

Data Date	Rating	RACR #1	RACR #2	Total Assets ($mil)	Capital ($mil)	Net Premium ($mil)	Net Income ($mil)
3-09	B	13.21	9.61	144.3	123.0	10.1	1.0
3-08	B	13.01	10.06	142.6	120.4	10.2	1.4
2008	B	13.04	10.03	142.9	122.0	40.5	3.8
2007	B	12.74	10.03	141.5	119.0	38.1	2.3
2006	B	12.69	11.42	122.4	116.4	21.6	3.0
2005	B	12.37	11.14	116.6	113.1	6.9	0.1
2004	B	4.30	3.87	15.9	13.1	0.5	-0.3

Adverse Trends in Operations

Increase in policy surrenders from 2006 to 2007 (264%)
Change in asset mix during 2006 (18.8%)
Change in asset mix during 2005 (17.6%)
Change in premium mix from 2004 to 2005 (11.7%)
Increase in policy surrenders from 2004 to 2005 (82%)

SECURITY BENEFIT LIFE INSURANCE COMPANY   C   Fair

Major Rating Factors: Fair current capitalization (4.1 on a scale of 0 to 10) based on fair risk adjusted capital (moderate loss scenario), although results have slipped from the good range during the last year. Fair quality investment portfolio (3.6) with substantial holdings of BBB bonds in addition to junk bond exposure equal to 60% of capital. Fair overall results on stability tests (3.4) including negative cash flow from operations for 2008 and fair risk adjusted capital in prior years.

Other Rating Factors: Weak profitability (2.2) with operating losses during the first three months of 2009. Excellent liquidity (7.7).

Principal Business: Individual annuities (86%), group retirement contracts (6%), reinsurance (4%), and individual life insurance (4%).

Principal Investments: CMOs and structured securities (34%), nonCMO investment grade bonds (33%), common & preferred stock (5%), cash (4%), and misc. investments (23%).

Investments in Affiliates: 17%

Group Affiliation: Security Benefit Group Inc

Licensed in: All states except AL, NC

Commenced Business: February 1892

Address: One Security Benefit Place, Topeka, KS 66636-0001

Phone: (785) 431-3000   **Domicile State:** KS   **NAIC Code:** 68675

Data Date	Rating	RACR #1	RACR #2	Total Assets ($mil)	Capital ($mil)	Net Premium ($mil)	Net Income ($mil)
3-09	C	0.89	0.45	8,734.3	241.4	79.4	-42.3
3-08	B	2.46	1.26	11,722.8	554.6	258.5	0.7
2008	C	1.12	0.58	9,246.2	300.6	820.1	-317.4
2007	B	3.13	1.60	12,341.3	602.4	1,482.5	19.1
2006	B	2.57	1.35	12,169.9	574.7	1,531.2	38.9
2005	B	2.99	1.51	11,509.6	588.2	1,297.0	36.1
2004	B-	2.81	1.42	10,242.6	591.1	1,328.5	74.0

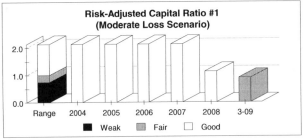

Risk-Adjusted Capital Ratio #1
(Moderate Loss Scenario)

■ Weak   ▨ Fair   □ Good

SECURITY LIFE INSURANCE COMPANY OF AMERICA   C   Fair

Major Rating Factors: Fair overall results on stability tests (3.8 on a scale of 0 to 10) including weak risk adjusted capital in prior years and negative cash flow from operations for 2008. Good current capitalization (5.1) based on mixed results -- excessive policy leverage mitigated by good risk adjusted capital (severe loss scenario) reflecting significant improvement over results in 2004. Good liquidity (5.7).

Other Rating Factors: High quality investment portfolio (8.5). Excellent profitability (8.9) with operating gains in each of the last five years.

Principal Business: Reinsurance (61%), group health insurance (35%), individual life insurance (3%), and group life insurance (1%).

Principal Investments: NonCMO investment grade bonds (81%), mortgages in good standing (9%), cash (8%), policy loans (1%), and CMOs and structured securities (1%).

Investments in Affiliates: None

Group Affiliation: Private Capital Management

Licensed in: All states except AL, DC, MD, MI, NJ, NM, NC, SC, VA

Commenced Business: July 1956

Address: 6681 Country Club Dr, Minneapolis, MN 55427-4698

Phone: (612) 544-2121 **Domicile State:** MN **NAIC Code:** 68721

Data Date	Rating	RACR #1	RACR #2	Total Assets ($mil)	Capital ($mil)	Net Premium ($mil)	Net Income ($mil)
3-09	C	1.09	0.85	82.9	25.6	26.9	1.2
3-08	C	1.17	0.91	83.2	25.3	39.8	1.1
2008	C	0.99	0.78	94.0	25.3	164.6	3.1
2007	C	1.18	0.91	96.5	24.6	138.1	5.1
2006	D+	0.74	0.56	79.1	14.9	111.1	4.2
2005	D	0.64	0.48	83.1	12.4	105.8	2.8
2004	D-	0.63	0.46	74.0	11.8	90.8	3.2

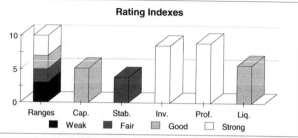

Rating Indexes

SECURITY LIFE OF DENVER INSURANCE COMPANY   B-   Good

Major Rating Factors: Good overall capitalization (5.6 on a scale of 0 to 10) based on good risk adjusted capital (moderate loss scenario). However, capital levels have fluctuated somewhat during past years. Fair overall results on stability tests (3.4) including fair financial strength of affiliated ING America Ins Holdings Inc and weak results on operational trends. Fair quality investment portfolio (3.4).

Other Rating Factors: Excellent profitability (7.4) with operating gains in each of the last five years. Excellent liquidity (7.5).

Principal Business: Reinsurance (52%), individual life insurance (30%), and group retirement contracts (18%).

Principal Investments: CMOs and structured securities (42%), nonCMO investment grade bonds (32%), mortgages in good standing (9%), policy loans (6%), and misc. investments (11%).

Investments in Affiliates: 1%

Group Affiliation: ING America Ins Holdings Inc

Licensed in: All states except AL, NC

Commenced Business: May 1950

Address: 1290 Broadway, Denver, CO 80203-0000

Phone: (303) 860-1290 **Domicile State:** CO **NAIC Code:** 68713

Data Date	Rating	RACR #1	RACR #2	Total Assets ($mil)	Capital ($mil)	Net Premium ($mil)	Net Income ($mil)
3-09	B-	1.37	0.70	22,467.3	1,319.1	258.2	-8.0
3-08	B	1.48	0.79	23,945.8	1,272.8	130.8	8.0
2008	B	1.60	0.84	24,264.7	1,439.0	1,348.0	37.6
2007	B	1.53	0.81	24,222.0	1,305.7	472.5	20.2
2006	B	1.99	1.05	23,761.8	1,595.3	658.1	135.4
2005	B	2.07	1.11	23,814.5	1,529.9	3,549.0	139.4
2004	B	1.60	0.84	21,150.0	1,069.7	1,259.9	41.3

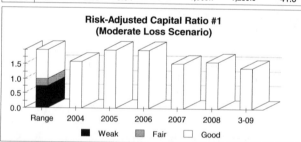

Risk-Adjusted Capital Ratio #1 (Moderate Loss Scenario)

SECURITY MUTUAL LIFE INSURANCE CO OF NEW YORK   B   Good

Major Rating Factors: Good capitalization (5.4 on a scale of 0 to 10) based on good risk adjusted capital (moderate loss scenario). Good quality investment portfolio (5.7) despite mixed results such as: minimal exposure to mortgages and large holdings of BBB rated bonds but minimal holdings in junk bonds. Good overall profitability (5.7) despite operating losses during the first three months of 2009.

Other Rating Factors: Good overall results on stability tests (5.4) despite fair risk adjusted capital in prior years good operational trends and excellent risk diversification. Fair liquidity (4.7).

Principal Business: Individual life insurance (64%), individual annuities (25%), group health insurance (7%), group life insurance (2%), and individual health insurance (1%).

Principal Investments: NonCMO investment grade bonds (59%), CMOs and structured securities (20%), policy loans (10%), mortgages in good standing (9%), and noninv. grade bonds (1%).

Investments in Affiliates: None

Group Affiliation: None

Licensed in: All states except AL

Commenced Business: January 1887

Address: Court House Square, Bimghamton, NY 13901

Phone: (607) 723-3551 **Domicile State:** NY **NAIC Code:** 68772

Data Date	Rating	RACR #1	RACR #2	Total Assets ($mil)	Capital ($mil)	Net Premium ($mil)	Net Income ($mil)
3-09	B	1.29	0.71	2,229.7	108.2	55.3	-1.8
3-08	B	1.57	0.88	2,143.7	115.0	58.0	0.5
2008	B	1.33	0.74	2,221.0	107.9	289.8	-8.8
2007	B	1.58	0.89	2,116.3	114.7	219.9	5.7
2006	B	1.40	0.82	2,041.3	106.8	226.4	7.0
2005	B	1.33	0.77	1,958.4	99.8	251.3	7.3
2004	B	1.28	0.74	1,864.7	94.3	245.7	-3.1

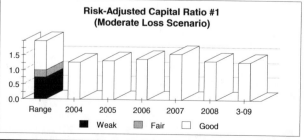

Risk-Adjusted Capital Ratio #1 (Moderate Loss Scenario)

SECURITY PLAN INSURANCE COMPANY   C   Fair

Major Rating Factors: Fair overall results on stability tests (3.5 on a scale of 0 to 10) including potential financial drain due to affiliation with Citizens Inc. Good quality investment portfolio (6.6) despite mixed results such as: minimal exposure to mortgages and substantial holdings of BBB bonds but minimal holdings in junk bonds. Good overall profitability (5.8).

Other Rating Factors: Good liquidity (6.6). Strong capitalization (8.2) based on excellent risk adjusted capital (severe loss scenario).

Principal Business: Individual life insurance (98%) and individual health insurance (2%).

Principal Investments: NonCMO investment grade bonds (72%), CMOs and structured securities (16%), common & preferred stock (8%), policy loans (2%), and misc. investments (3%).

Investments in Affiliates: 1%
Group Affiliation: Citizens Inc
Licensed in: ME, MO
Commenced Business: March 1996
Address: 110 Railroad Ave, Donaldsonville, LA 70346-2520
Phone: (504) 473-8654   **Domicile State:** LA   **NAIC Code:** 60076

Data Date	Rating	RACR #1	RACR #2	Total Assets ($mil)	Capital ($mil)	Net Premium ($mil)	Net Income ($mil)
3-09	C	2.76	1.77	262.9	41.5	7.8	0.4
3-08	C-	3.17	2.10	277.5	56.2	8.0	0.1
2008	C-	2.83	1.82	262.9	42.7	34.5	-8.5
2007	C-	4.00	2.72	273.5	56.7	37.8	7.4
2006	C-	5.24	3.71	269.0	54.6	35.1	4.6
2005	C-	5.15	3.67	264.1	53.3	33.5	7.9
2004	D+	3.92	2.84	260.6	47.2	35.1	8.9

Citizens Inc Composite Group Rating: D+ Largest Group Members	Assets ($mil)	Rating
CICA LIFE INS CO OF AMERICA	404	D+
SECURITY PLAN LIFE INS CO	263	C-
OZARK NATIONAL LIFE INS CO	19	D
CITIZENS NATIONAL LIFE INS CO	12	D+
SECURITY PLAN FIRE INS CO	7	D

SENIOR HEALTH INSURANCE COMPANY OF PENNSYLVANIA   D+   Weak

Major Rating Factors: Low quality investment portfolio (2.5 on a scale of 0 to 10) containing large holdings of BBB rated bonds in addition to significant exposure to junk bonds. Weak profitability (1.4) with operating losses during the first three months of 2009. Return on equity has been low, averaging -47.9%. Weak overall results on stability tests (2.4) including negative cash flow from operations for 2008.

Other Rating Factors: Good capitalization (5.7) based on good risk adjusted capital (moderate loss scenario). Good liquidity (5.6).

Principal Business: Individual health insurance (92%), reinsurance (5%), group health insurance (2%), and individual life insurance (1%).

Principal Investments: NonCMO investment grade bonds (63%), CMOs and structured securities (21%), noninv. grade bonds (9%), mortgages in good standing (5%), and common & preferred stock (1%).

Investments in Affiliates: None
Group Affiliation: Senior Health Care Oversight Trust
Licensed in: All states except AL, DC, NC, SC, VA
Commenced Business: February 1965
Address: 11815 N Pennsylvania St, Carmel, IN 46032
Phone: (317) 817-3700   **Domicile State:** PA   **NAIC Code:** 76325

Data Date	Rating	RACR #1	RACR #2	Total Assets ($mil)	Capital ($mil)	Net Premium ($mil)	Net Income ($mil)
3-09	D+	1.45	0.64	3,288.7	176.4	64.6	-38.0
3-08	D+	1.43	0.76	3,425.9	120.8	79.1	-8.2
2008	D+	2.07	0.99	3,273.0	218.0	297.5	-52.5
2007	D+	1.52	0.82	3,401.1	127.7	322.4	-190.7
2006	D+	1.35	0.74	3,201.5	117.4	343.2	-98.2
2005	D+	1.21	0.68	3,070.3	107.1	364.6	-36.7
2004	D	1.22	0.71	3,002.0	126.3	402.5	-16.4

Junk Bonds as a % of Capital

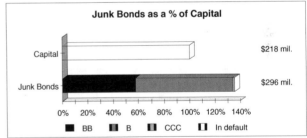

Capital — $218 mil.
Junk Bonds — $296 mil.

0% 20% 40% 60% 80% 100% 120% 140%

■ BB   ▨ B   ▨ CCC   ☐ In default

SENTRY LIFE INSURANCE COMPANY *   A   Excellent

Major Rating Factors: Good overall results on stability tests (6.0 on a scale of 0 to 10). Strengths that enhance stability include excellent risk diversification. Strong capitalization (9.4) based on excellent risk adjusted capital (severe loss scenario). Furthermore, this high level of risk adjusted capital has been consistently maintained over the last five years. High quality investment portfolio (7.6).

Other Rating Factors: Excellent profitability (7.2) with operating gains in each of the last five years. Excellent liquidity (7.0).

Principal Business: Group retirement contracts (89%), individual life insurance (10%), group life insurance (2%), group health insurance (2%), and individual annuities (1%).

Principal Investments: NonCMO investment grade bonds (84%), CMOs and structured securities (13%), policy loans (1%), common & preferred stock (1%), and noninv. grade bonds (1%).

Investments in Affiliates: 1%
Group Affiliation: Sentry Ins Group
Licensed in: All states except AL, NC
Commenced Business: November 1958
Address: 1800 North Point Dr, Stevens Point, WI 54481
Phone: (715) 346-6000   **Domicile State:** WI   **NAIC Code:** 68810

Data Date	Rating	RACR #1	RACR #2	Total Assets ($mil)	Capital ($mil)	Net Premium ($mil)	Net Income ($mil)
3-09	A	4.48	2.60	2,809.8	262.2	77.4	-1.4
3-08	A	4.68	2.59	3,214.3	266.9	76.0	5.2
2008	A	4.40	2.52	2,882.5	262.5	319.5	15.4
2007	A	4.39	2.42	3,338.0	261.7	345.8	17.5
2006	A	4.66	2.68	3,096.6	249.8	317.4	24.3
2005	A	4.45	2.57	2,817.4	233.5	297.4	27.2
2004	A	4.13	2.40	2,623.4	214.5	305.7	23.2

Rating Indexes

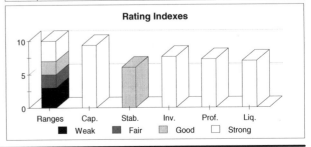

Ranges   Cap.   Stab.   Inv.   Prof.   Liq.

■ Weak   ▨ Fair   ☐ Good   ☐ Strong

SERVICE LIFE & CASUALTY INSURANCE COMPANY   C   Fair

Major Rating Factors: Fair quality investment portfolio (3.3 on a scale of 0 to 10) with significant exposure to mortgages . Mortgage default rate has been low. Good overall profitability (6.6). Return on equity has been good over the last five years, averaging 10.8%. Weak overall results on stability tests (2.9) including weak results on operational trends.

Other Rating Factors: Strong capitalization (7.9) based on excellent risk adjusted capital (severe loss scenario). Excellent liquidity (8.9).

Principal Business: Credit life insurance (66%) and credit health insurance (34%).

Principal Investments: NonCMO investment grade bonds (41%), CMOs and structured securities (18%), real estate (16%), mortgages in good standing (16%), and misc. investments (10%).

Investments in Affiliates: None

Group Affiliation: Service Ins Group

Licensed in: AR, CT, ME, MO, NY, OR, SD, UT

Commenced Business: January 1970

Address: 6907 Capital of Texas Hwy, Austin, TX 78731

Phone: (512) 343-0600   **Domicile State:** TX   **NAIC Code:** 77151

Data Date	Rating	RACR #1	RACR #2	Total Assets ($mil)	Capital ($mil)	Net Premium ($mil)	Net Income ($mil)
3-09	C	3.07	1.60	134.7	34.6	1.7	2.7
3-08	C	N/A	N/A	143.0	33.6	5.7	1.0
2008	C	3.19	1.65	137.8	35.0	13.3	4.6
2007	C	3.27	1.72	149.4	34.2	24.5	2.8
2006	C	3.08	1.63	139.6	35.4	30.6	1.7
2005	C	2.76	1.48	140.1	35.4	32.9	5.1
2004	C	3.08	1.56	142.1	34.7	21.4	7.7

Adverse Trends in Operations

Decrease in premium volume from 2007 to 2008 (46%)
Increase in policy surrenders from 2006 to 2007 (500%)
Decrease in premium volume from 2006 to 2007 (20%)
Decrease in capital during 2007 (3%)
Change in premium mix from 2004 to 2005 (15.8%)

SETTLERS LIFE INSURANCE COMPANY *   B+   Good

Major Rating Factors: Good overall results on stability tests (6.6 on a scale of 0 to 10). Stability strengths include excellent operational trends and good risk diversification. Good quality investment portfolio (6.2) despite mixed results such as: large holdings of BBB rated bonds but moderate junk bond exposure. Strong capitalization (8.1) based on excellent risk adjusted capital (severe loss scenario).

Other Rating Factors: Excellent profitability (7.1) with operating gains in each of the last five years. Excellent liquidity (7.1).

Principal Business: Individual life insurance (77%), group life insurance (21%), and individual health insurance (1%).

Principal Investments: NonCMO investment grade bonds (76%), CMOs and structured securities (11%), noninv. grade bonds (5%), common & preferred stock (4%), and misc. investments (2%).

Investments in Affiliates: None

Group Affiliation: NGL Ins Group

Licensed in: All states except AL, NC

Commenced Business: September 1982

Address: 2 E Gilman St, Madison, WI 53703-1494

Phone: (608) 257-5611   **Domicile State:** WI   **NAIC Code:** 97241

Data Date	Rating	RACR #1	RACR #2	Total Assets ($mil)	Capital ($mil)	Net Premium ($mil)	Net Income ($mil)
3-09	B+	3.38	1.75	417.4	53.8	10.3	1.8
3-08	B+	3.38	1.78	382.7	49.1	9.6	1.1
2008	B+	3.20	1.65	414.2	53.0	39.8	0.8
2007	B+	3.36	1.78	381.8	48.8	37.6	5.9
2006	B	3.48	1.89	373.5	47.0	35.0	5.4
2005	B	2.96	2.66	121.8	24.7	5.6	3.7
2004	B	2.72	2.45	124.8	22.4	11.9	3.3

Adverse Trends in Operations

Change in premium mix from 2005 to 2006 (5.7%)
Increase in policy surrenders from 2005 to 2006 (49%)
Decrease in asset base during 2005 (2%)
Decrease in premium volume from 2004 to 2005 (53%)

SHELTER LIFE INSURANCE COMPANY *   A-   Excellent

Major Rating Factors: Good liquidity (6.5 on a scale of 0 to 10) with sufficient resources to handle a spike in claims as well as a significant increase in policy surrenders. Excellent overall results on stability tests (7.3). Strengths that enhance stability include excellent operational trends and excellent risk diversification. Strong capitalization (9.1) based on excellent risk adjusted capital (severe loss scenario).

Other Rating Factors: High quality investment portfolio (7.4). Excellent profitability (8.3).

Principal Business: Individual life insurance (71%), group health insurance (14%), individual annuities (12%), individual health insurance (1%), and group life insurance (1%).

Principal Investments: CMOs and structured securities (49%), nonCMO investment grade bonds (39%), common & preferred stock (5%), policy loans (3%), and misc. investments (5%).

Investments in Affiliates: 3%

Group Affiliation: Shelter Ins Companies

Licensed in: CA, CT, IN, IA, KS, KY, LA, ME, MO, MT, NV, NH, OR, TX

Commenced Business: March 1959

Address: 1817 W Broadway, Columbia, MO 65218

Phone: (573) 445-8441   **Domicile State:** MO   **NAIC Code:** 65757

Data Date	Rating	RACR #1	RACR #2	Total Assets ($mil)	Capital ($mil)	Net Premium ($mil)	Net Income ($mil)
3-09	A-	3.89	2.43	933.1	170.7	33.7	4.2
3-08	A-	3.80	2.49	924.6	173.4	31.9	1.8
2008	A-	3.71	2.26	920.2	169.5	125.4	-3.3
2007	A-	3.55	2.19	915.4	171.8	115.8	11.9
2006	A-	3.64	2.24	898.3	162.1	110.0	12.1
2005	A-	3.65	2.24	877.8	149.2	102.3	11.4
2004	B+	3.71	2.28	861.9	143.1	99.1	17.6

Adverse Trends in Operations

Decrease in capital during 2008 (1%)

SIERRA HEALTH AND LIFE INSURANCE COMPANY INC   B   Good

Major Rating Factors: Good overall profitability (6.8 on a scale of 0 to 10). Excellent expense controls. Despite its volitility, return on equity has been excellent over the last five years averaging 17.2%. Fair overall results on stability tests (4.0) including weak results on operational trends and fair risk adjusted capital in prior years. Strong capitalization (8.4) based on excellent risk adjusted capital (severe loss scenario).

Other Rating Factors: High quality investment portfolio (8.6). Excellent liquidity (7.9).

Principal Business: Group health insurance (55%), individual health insurance (44%), and group life insurance (1%).

Principal Investments: NonCMO investment grade bonds (100%) and real estate (4%).

Investments in Affiliates: None

Group Affiliation: UnitedHealth Group Inc

Licensed in: All states except AL, GA, MN, MS, NJ, NC, VA, WY

Commenced Business: August 1906

Address: 300 S Grand 22nd Floor, Los Angeles, CA 90071-3132

Phone: (702) 242-7779 **Domicile State:** CA **NAIC Code:** 71420

Data Date	Rating	RACR #1	RACR #2	Total Assets ($mil)	Capital ($mil)	Net Premium ($mil)	Net Income ($mil)
3-09	B	2.42	1.95	127.5	82.0	52.2	4.1
3-08	B	0.70	0.58	113.3	65.5	58.9	1.9
2008	B	2.18	1.75	129.3	76.6	230.5	14.0
2007	B	0.60	0.53	133.5	63.1	424.5	-11.1
2006	B-	0.92	0.75	152.8	63.8	324.9	24.3
2005	B	2.23	1.73	77.2	45.2	109.0	6.5
2004	C	1.92	1.48	74.7	38.4	103.8	12.9

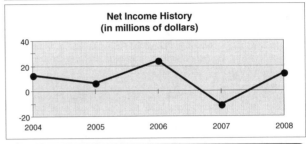

Net Income History
(in millions of dollars)

SOUTHERN FARM BUREAU LIFE INSURANCE COMPANY *   A   Excellent

Major Rating Factors: Good quality investment portfolio (6.3 on a scale of 0 to 10) despite significant exposure to mortgages . Mortgage default rate has been low. large holdings of BBB rated bonds in addition to minimal holdings in junk bonds. Good liquidity (6.2) with sufficient resources to handle a spike in claims as well as a significant increase in policy surrenders. Strong capitalization (8.7) based on excellent risk adjusted capital (severe loss scenario).

Other Rating Factors: Excellent profitability (8.4) with operating gains in each of the last five years. Excellent overall results on stability tests (7.4) excellent operational trends and excellent risk diversification.

Principal Business: Individual life insurance (63%), individual annuities (30%), individual health insurance (4%), group health insurance (2%), and group life insurance (1%).

Principal Investments: NonCMO investment grade bonds (55%), CMOs and structured securities (16%), mortgages in good standing (14%), policy loans (4%), and misc. investments (11%).

Investments in Affiliates: 1%

Group Affiliation: Southern Farm Bureau Group

Licensed in: AK, CA, GA, HI, LA, ME, MO, ND, SD, TX, UT, WA

Commenced Business: December 1946

Address: 1401 Livingston Lane, Jackson, MS 39213

Phone: (601) 981-7422 **Domicile State:** MS **NAIC Code:** 68896

Data Date	Rating	RACR #1	RACR #2	Total Assets ($mil)	Capital ($mil)	Net Premium ($mil)	Net Income ($mil)
3-09	A	3.87	2.11	10,074.1	1,572.6	203.6	-18.0
3-08	A	3.95	2.18	9,974.1	1,599.4	193.4	7.8
2008	A	3.90	2.14	10,019.9	1,570.6	774.1	63.1
2007	A	3.98	2.21	9,949.2	1,587.2	658.6	143.7
2006	A	3.78	2.11	9,680.8	1,483.2	696.2	165.0
2005	A	3.47	1.95	9,270.0	1,292.3	707.9	194.1
2004	A	2.94	1.65	8,776.9	1,116.4	737.0	136.3

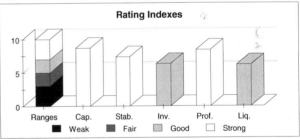

Rating Indexes

Ranges | Cap. | Stab. | Inv. | Prof. | Liq.
■ Weak   ■ Fair   ▨ Good   ☐ Strong

STANDARD INSURANCE COMPANY *   B+   Good

Major Rating Factors: Good quality investment portfolio (6.1 on a scale of 0 to 10) despite large exposure to mortgages . Mortgage default rate has been low. substantial holdings of BBB bonds in addition to small junk bond holdings. Good overall results on stability tests (6.5). Stability strengths include excellent operational trends and excellent risk diversification. Strong capitalization (7.8) based on excellent risk adjusted capital (severe loss scenario).

Other Rating Factors: Excellent profitability (8.2) with operating gains in each of the last five years. Excellent liquidity (7.3).

Principal Business: Group retirement contracts (27%), group health insurance (27%), individual annuities (21%), group life insurance (17%), and other lines (8%).

Principal Investments: NonCMO investment grade bonds (53%), mortgages in good standing (42%), noninv. grade bonds (3%), and CMOs and structured securities (2%).

Investments in Affiliates: None

Group Affiliation: Stancorp Financial Group

Licensed in: All states except AL, NC

Commenced Business: April 1906

Address: 1100 SW Sixth Ave, Portland, OR 97204

Phone: (503) 321-7000 **Domicile State:** OR **NAIC Code:** 69019

Data Date	Rating	RACR #1	RACR #2	Total Assets ($mil)	Capital ($mil)	Net Premium ($mil)	Net Income ($mil)
3-09	B+	2.60	1.55	12,858.1	1,126.6	923.3	54.1
3-08	B	2.50	1.51	13,305.7	1,053.6	1,004.6	53.1
2008	B+	2.57	1.54	12,874.5	1,112.3	4,032.7	134.9
2007	B	2.47	1.52	13,265.3	1,014.4	3,373.8	241.2
2006	B	2.48	1.51	12,148.1	936.7	3,275.1	167.0
2005	B	2.56	1.54	10,810.8	944.5	2,962.2	205.6
2004	B	2.54	1.53	9,688.7	926.2	2,656.6	195.6

Adverse Trends in Operations

Decrease in asset base during 2008 (3%)
Increase in policy surrenders from 2006 to 2007 (29%)
Increase in policy surrenders from 2005 to 2006 (49%)
Increase in policy surrenders from 2004 to 2005 (65%)

STANDARD LIFE & ACCIDENT INSURANCE COMPANY *   A-   Excellent

Major Rating Factors: Good overall results on stability tests (5.5 on a scale of 0 to 10). Strengths that enhance stability include good operational trends and excellent risk diversification. Good quality investment portfolio (5.4) despite mixed results such as: minimal exposure to mortgages and large holdings of BBB rated bonds but minimal holdings in junk bonds. Good liquidity (6.8).

Other Rating Factors: Strong capitalization (9.3) based on excellent risk adjusted capital (severe loss scenario). Excellent profitability (7.6) with operating gains in each of the last five years.

Principal Business: Individual health insurance (67%), reinsurance (12%), individual life insurance (9%), individual annuities (7%), and group health insurance (5%).

Principal Investments: NonCMO investment grade bonds (66%), CMOs and structured securities (12%), common & preferred stock (10%), mortgages in good standing (9%), and noninv. grade bonds (3%).

Investments in Affiliates: None

Group Affiliation: American National Group Inc

Licensed in: All states except AL, MD, NJ, NM, NC, WY

Commenced Business: June 1976

Address: 201 Robert S Kerr Ave Ste 600, Oklahoma City, OK 73102

Phone: (409) 763-4661   **Domicile State:** OK   **NAIC Code:** 86355

Data Date	Rating	RACR #1	RACR #2	Total Assets ($mil)	Capital ($mil)	Net Premium ($mil)	Net Income ($mil)
3-09	A-	4.06	2.51	484.7	187.6	32.6	-8.7
3-08	A-	3.07	2.22	526.2	202.2	33.5	-0.3
2008	A-	4.96	3.11	490.1	201.9	131.8	2.3
2007	A-	3.25	2.36	531.3	210.9	145.1	9.4
2006	B+	3.53	2.48	528.7	211.6	172.7	21.1
2005	B+	3.99	2.58	513.5	198.4	213.9	21.5
2004	B+	3.18	2.24	486.6	187.7	211.9	20.5

Adverse Trends in Operations

Decrease in capital during 2008 (4%)
Decrease in asset base during 2008 (8%)
Decrease in premium volume from 2006 to 2007 (16%)
Decrease in premium volume from 2005 to 2006 (19%)
Increase in policy surrenders from 2005 to 2006 (72%)

STANDARD LIFE INS CO OF NY   B-   Good

Major Rating Factors: Good overall results on stability tests (5.3 on a scale of 0 to 10). Stability strengths include excellent operational trends and excellent risk diversification. Fair profitability (4.8). Return on equity has been low, averaging 0.2%. Strong capitalization (8.6) based on excellent risk adjusted capital (severe loss scenario).

Other Rating Factors: High quality investment portfolio (7.4). Excellent liquidity (7.2).

Principal Business: Group health insurance (62%) and group life insurance (38%).

Principal Investments: NonCMO investment grade bonds (51%) and mortgages in good standing (49%).

Investments in Affiliates: None

Group Affiliation: Stancorp Financial Group

Licensed in: NC

Commenced Business: October 2000

Address: 360 Hamilton Ave Suite 210, White Plains, NY 10601-1871

Phone: (503) 321-7859   **Domicile State:** NY   **NAIC Code:** 89009

Data Date	Rating	RACR #1	RACR #2	Total Assets ($mil)	Capital ($mil)	Net Premium ($mil)	Net Income ($mil)
3-09	B-	3.11	2.08	181.5	42.4	15.1	0.8
3-08	C+	2.87	1.92	149.9	33.7	15.1	0.2
2008	B-	3.06	2.07	176.3	42.3	61.8	1.1
2007	C+	2.85	1.93	141.5	33.4	51.4	-1.7
2006	C+	3.07	2.16	99.0	30.7	44.4	3.8
2005	C	2.48	1.79	71.1	24.2	37.9	2.0
2004	C-	3.17	2.49	35.4	16.3	17.7	-3.5

Adverse Trends in Operations

Change in asset mix during 2005 (5.7%)

STANDARD SECURITY LIFE INSURANCE CO OF NEW YORK *   B+   Good

Major Rating Factors: Good overall results on stability tests (6.2 on a scale of 0 to 10). Stability strengths include excellent operational trends and excellent risk diversification. Good quality investment portfolio (6.8) despite mixed results such as: no exposure to mortgages and substantial holdings of BBB bonds but minimal holdings in junk bonds. Good liquidity (5.7).

Other Rating Factors: Strong capitalization (8.9) based on excellent risk adjusted capital (severe loss scenario). Excellent profitability (7.5).

Principal Business: Group health insurance (77%), reinsurance (22%), and group life insurance (1%).

Principal Investments: NonCMO investment grade bonds (65%), common & preferred stock (19%), CMOs and structured securities (3%), noninv. grade bonds (1%), and cash (1%).

Investments in Affiliates: 13%

Group Affiliation: Geneve Holdings Inc

Licensed in: All states except AL

Commenced Business: December 1958

Address: 485 Madison Ave, New York, NY 10022-5872

Phone: (212) 355-4141   **Domicile State:** NY   **NAIC Code:** 69078

Data Date	Rating	RACR #1	RACR #2	Total Assets ($mil)	Capital ($mil)	Net Premium ($mil)	Net Income ($mil)
3-09	B+	2.91	2.28	365.4	110.3	47.8	1.9
3-08	B+	3.88	3.01	373.6	112.1	52.5	2.1
2008	B+	2.79	2.40	369.7	114.3	197.6	-3.8
2007	B+	3.79	2.88	367.2	109.6	204.7	4.6
2006	B+	4.80	3.57	344.3	107.9	174.7	11.4
2005	B+	3.75	2.89	312.4	110.6	146.1	10.5
2004	B+	4.39	3.50	273.6	105.5	108.2	12.1

Adverse Trends in Operations

Decrease in premium volume from 2007 to 2008 (3%)
Decrease in capital during 2006 (2%)

STATE FARM LIFE & ACCIDENT ASSURANCE COMPANY *

A+   **Excellent**

Major Rating Factors: Good liquidity (6.7 on a scale of 0 to 10) with sufficient resources to handle a spike in claims as well as a significant increase in policy surrenders. Excellent overall results on stability tests (7.9). Strengths that enhance stability include excellent operational trends and excellent risk diversification. Strong capitalization (9.5) based on excellent risk adjusted capital (severe loss scenario).

Other Rating Factors: High quality investment portfolio (8.0). Excellent profitability (7.7).

Principal Business: Individual life insurance (75%) and individual annuities (25%).

Principal Investments: NonCMO investment grade bonds (70%), CMOs and structured securities (18%), policy loans (7%), and noninv. grade bonds (1%).

Investments in Affiliates: None

Group Affiliation: State Farm Group

Licensed in: DC, IN, NC, WY

Commenced Business: July 1961

Address: One State Farm Plaza, Bloomington, IL 61710

Phone: (309) 766-2311 **Domicile State:** IL **NAIC Code:** 69094

Data Date	Rating	RACR #1	RACR #2	Total Assets ($mil)	Capital ($mil)	Net Premium ($mil)	Net Income ($mil)
3-09	A+	4.57	2.66	1,691.4	268.3	50.7	2.0
3-08	A+	5.00	2.92	1,575.8	271.4	41.3	4.8
2008	A+	4.57	2.67	1,660.9	266.5	194.5	-3.4
2007	A+	4.90	2.85	1,549.6	266.5	156.2	10.3
2006	A+	5.03	2.94	1,467.4	255.3	147.3	20.4
2005	A+	5.10	2.97	1,388.8	243.6	143.7	15.6
2004	A+	5.02	2.87	1,296.3	226.0	138.8	9.7

Adverse Trends in Operations

Increase in policy surrenders from 2005 to 2006 (33%)

STATE FARM LIFE INSURANCE COMPANY *

A+   **Excellent**

Major Rating Factors: Good quality investment portfolio (6.7 on a scale of 0 to 10) despite significant exposure to mortgages . Mortgage default rate has been low. substantial holdings of BBB bonds in addition to minimal holdings in junk bonds. Good liquidity (6.4) with sufficient resources to handle a spike in claims as well as a significant increase in policy surrenders. Excellent overall results on stability tests (7.9) excellent operational trends and excellent risk diversification.

Other Rating Factors: Strong capitalization (8.5) based on excellent risk adjusted capital (severe loss scenario). Excellent profitability (7.9) with operating gains in each of the last five years.

Principal Business: Individual life insurance (74%), individual annuities (24%), and group life insurance (1%).

Principal Investments: NonCMO investment grade bonds (54%), CMOs and structured securities (18%), mortgages in good standing (13%), policy loans (8%), and misc. investments (6%).

Investments in Affiliates: 1%

Group Affiliation: State Farm Group

Licensed in: All states except AL, MI, NC, WY

Commenced Business: April 1929

Address: One State Farm Plaza, Bloomington, IL 61710

Phone: (309) 766-2311 **Domicile State:** IL **NAIC Code:** 69108

Data Date	Rating	RACR #1	RACR #2	Total Assets ($mil)	Capital ($mil)	Net Premium ($mil)	Net Income ($mil)
3-09	A+	3.50	1.98	44,978.4	4,924.9	1,190.5	45.3
3-08	A+	3.58	2.05	43,585.2	5,217.3	987.8	67.7
2008	A+	3.52	2.00	44,630.9	5,060.1	4,597.2	185.7
2007	A+	3.57	2.06	43,308.0	5,255.5	3,723.3	382.2
2006	A+	3.63	2.10	42,209.0	5,061.9	3,762.8	388.1
2005	A+	3.56	2.05	39,874.6	4,504.5	3,661.4	317.5
2004	A+	3.47	1.99	37,501.1	4,099.8	3,592.3	237.8

Adverse Trends in Operations

Decrease in capital during 2008 (4%)
Decrease in premium volume from 2006 to 2007 (1%)

STATE LIFE INSURANCE COMPANY

B   **Good**

Major Rating Factors: Good current capitalization (6.2 on a scale of 0 to 10) based on good risk adjusted capital (severe loss scenario) reflecting some improvement over results in 2005. Good overall profitability (6.0). Return on equity has been low, averaging 0.9%. Good overall results on stability tests (5.4) despite fair risk adjusted capital in prior years excellent operational trends and excellent risk diversification.

Other Rating Factors: Fair quality investment portfolio (4.7). Fair liquidity (3.4).

Principal Business: Reinsurance (39%), individual annuities (27%), individual life insurance (22%), and individual health insurance (12%).

Principal Investments: NonCMO investment grade bonds (70%), CMOs and structured securities (19%), mortgages in good standing (7%), noninv. grade bonds (2%), and misc. investments (2%).

Investments in Affiliates: None

Group Affiliation: American United Life Group

Licensed in: All states except AL, AZ, ID, NC, PR

Commenced Business: September 1894

Address: 141 E Washington St, Indianapolis, IN 46204

Phone: (317) 285-1877 **Domicile State:** IN **NAIC Code:** 69116

Data Date	Rating	RACR #1	RACR #2	Total Assets ($mil)	Capital ($mil)	Net Premium ($mil)	Net Income ($mil)
3-09	B	1.74	0.90	2,921.8	183.9	82.8	5.7
3-08	B	1.71	0.90	2,534.0	152.9	53.4	2.9
2008	B	1.71	0.90	2,840.1	177.9	237.4	20.5
2007	B	1.71	0.91	2,504.2	150.8	232.3	19.5
2006	B	1.51	0.81	2,386.1	131.7	207.8	25.6
2005	B	1.26	0.68	2,302.8	108.4	97.5	-57.3
2004	B	3.44	1.84	424.4	46.8	53.2	0.9

Risk-Adjusted Capital Ratio #2 (Severe Loss Scenario)

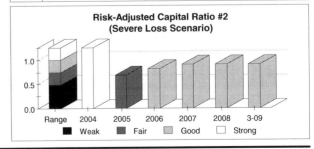

| Range | 2004 | 2005 | 2006 | 2007 | 2008 | 3-09 |

■ Weak ▨ Fair ▧ Good ☐ Strong

STATE MUTUAL INSURANCE COMPANY

C   **Fair**

Major Rating Factors: Fair quality investment portfolio (4.9 on a scale of 0 to 10) with significant exposure to mortgages . Mortgage default rate has been low. Fair overall results on stability tests (4.1). Good current capitalization (5.4) based on good risk adjusted capital (severe loss scenario), although results have slipped from the excellent range over the last two years.

Other Rating Factors: Good overall profitability (5.7). Good liquidity (5.8).

Principal Business: Individual life insurance (46%), individual health insurance (41%), and reinsurance (13%).

Principal Investments: NonCMO investment grade bonds (58%), mortgages in good standing (17%), policy loans (10%), common & preferred stock (6%), and misc. investments (9%).

Investments in Affiliates: 3%

Group Affiliation: State Mutual Ins Group

Licensed in: All states except AL, AZ, CO, DC, MD, MI, MN, NJ, NM, NC

Commenced Business: April 1936

Address: One State Mutual Dr, Rome, GA 30162

Phone: (800) 241-7598 **Domicile State:** GA **NAIC Code:** 69132

Data Date	Rating	RACR #1	RACR #2	Total Assets ($mil)	Capital ($mil)	Net Premium ($mil)	Net Income ($mil)
3-09	C	1.17	0.80	384.0	28.5	8.1	0.6
3-08	C	1.50	1.01	375.9	32.4	7.9	0.8
2008	C	1.22	0.84	386.4	30.1	41.8	3.6
2007	C	1.51	1.03	374.9	30.6	32.3	0.6
2006	C	1.53	1.02	370.5	29.1	26.9	2.2
2005	C	2.06	1.15	358.5	23.2	25.7	2.1
2004	C	1.89	1.05	335.1	22.9	20.4	3.3

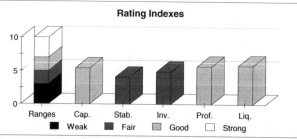

Rating Indexes

Ranges   Cap.   Stab.   Inv.   Prof.   Liq.

■ Weak   ■ Fair   ▨ Good   □ Strong

STONEBRIDGE LIFE INSURANCE COMPANY *

B+   **Good**

Major Rating Factors: Good overall results on stability tests (5.9 on a scale of 0 to 10) despite negative cash flow from operations for 2008 and fair risk adjusted capital in prior years. Other stability subfactors include good operational trends and excellent risk diversification. Good quality investment portfolio (5.4) despite large holdings of BBB rated bonds in addition to junk bond exposure equal to 54% of capital. Exposure to mortgages is significant, but the mortgage default rate has been low. Good overall profitability (6.0).

Other Rating Factors: Good liquidity (6.4). Strong capitalization (7.2) based on excellent risk adjusted capital (severe loss scenario).

Principal Business: Group health insurance (53%), group life insurance (24%), individual life insurance (15%), individual health insurance (6%), and other lines (2%).

Principal Investments: NonCMO investment grade bonds (60%), CMOs and structured securities (16%), mortgages in good standing (11%), noninv. grade bonds (6%), and misc. investments (8%).

Investments in Affiliates: 2%

Group Affiliation: AEGON USA Group

Licensed in: All states except AL

Commenced Business: May 1906

Address: 56 1/2 Merchants Row, Rutland, VT 05702-6564

Phone: (410) 685-5500 **Domicile State:** VT **NAIC Code:** 65021

Data Date	Rating	RACR #1	RACR #2	Total Assets ($mil)	Capital ($mil)	Net Premium ($mil)	Net Income ($mil)
3-09	B+	2.05	1.13	2,089.0	205.8	131.1	30.8
3-08	B	2.94	1.67	2,223.1	304.9	134.2	69.0
2008	B+	1.75	0.98	2,138.2	172.4	518.7	211.0
2007	B	2.35	1.33	2,206.1	241.5	535.0	110.8
2006	B	1.29	0.76	1,885.0	126.0	529.5	126.4
2005	B-	1.41	0.83	1,882.5	142.4	541.8	159.1
2004	B-	1.10	0.65	1,860.4	111.8	590.2	133.5

Adverse Trends in Operations

Decrease in asset base during 2008 (3%)
Decrease in capital during 2008 (29%)
Decrease in premium volume from 2007 to 2008 (3%)
Decrease in capital during 2006 (12%)
Decrease in premium volume from 2004 to 2005 (8%)

SUN LIFE & HEALTH INSURANCE COMPANY

C+   **Fair**

Major Rating Factors: Fair overall results on stability tests (3.2 on a scale of 0 to 10) including fair financial strength of affiliated Sun Life Assurance Group, weak results on operational trends and negative cash flow from operations for 2008. Good quality investment portfolio (6.8) despite mixed results such as: no exposure to mortgages and substantial holdings of BBB bonds but no exposure to junk bonds. Weak profitability (2.2) with investment income below regulatory standards in relation to interest assumptions of reserves.

Other Rating Factors: Strong capitalization (8.0) based on excellent risk adjusted capital (severe loss scenario). Excellent liquidity (9.1).

Principal Business: Group health insurance (74%) and group life insurance (26%).

Principal Investments: NonCMO investment grade bonds (93%) and CMOs and structured securities (22%).

Investments in Affiliates: None

Group Affiliation: Sun Life Assurance Group

Licensed in: All states except AL

Commenced Business: January 1975

Address: 100 Bright Meadow Blvd, Enfield, CT 06083-1900

Phone: (860) 403-1179 **Domicile State:** CT **NAIC Code:** 80926

Data Date	Rating	RACR #1	RACR #2	Total Assets ($mil)	Capital ($mil)	Net Premium ($mil)	Net Income ($mil)
3-09	C+	4.58	2.32	90.5	37.3	0.0	0.4
3-08	B-	3.96	3.13	111.8	36.0	0.0	6.7
2008	C+	2.88	1.51	82.2	23.1	0.0	3.1
2007	B-	3.96	2.59	119.2	35.3	-257.5	338.8
2006	B	2.27	1.57	868.1	254.1	630.5	41.9
2005	B	2.11	1.45	873.3	229.7	611.4	30.3
2004	B	2.12	1.47	843.5	213.0	585.7	20.0

Sun Life Assurance Group
Composite Group Rating: C+
Largest Group Members

	Assets ($mil)	Rating
SUN LIFE ASR CO OF CANADA (US)	39670	C+
SUN LIFE ASR CO OF CANADA	15748	C
SUN LIFE INS ANNUITY CO OF NY	2588	C
INDEPENDENCE LIFE ANNUITY CO	132	B-
PROFESSIONAL INS CO	102	C

SUN LIFE ASR CO OF CANADA   C   Fair

Major Rating Factors: Fair capitalization (3.9 on a scale of 0 to 10) based on fair risk adjusted capital (moderate loss scenario). Fair overall results on stability tests (3.6) including weak risk adjusted capital in prior years. Good liquidity (5.1) with sufficient resources to handle a spike in claims as well as a significant increase in policy surrenders.

Other Rating Factors: Low quality investment portfolio (2.8). Weak profitability (2.0).

Principal Business: Individual life insurance (31%), reinsurance (30%), group health insurance (26%), and group life insurance (14%).

Principal Investments: NonCMO investment grade bonds (42%), mortgages in good standing (23%), CMOs and structured securities (13%), real estate (6%), and misc. investments (16%).

Investments in Affiliates: None

Group Affiliation: Sun Life Assurance Group

Licensed in: All states except AL, NC

Commenced Business: May 1871

Address: One Sun Life Executive Park, Wellesley Hills, MA 02481

Phone: (781) 237-6030 **Domicile State:** MI **NAIC Code:** 80802

Data Date	Rating	RACR #1	RACR #2	Total Assets ($mil)	Capital ($mil)	Net Premium ($mil)	Net Income ($mil)
3-09	C	0.86	0.49	15,401.0	738.3	635.4	20.3
3-08	C	0.67	0.41	15,014.7	561.0	575.3	-14.4
2008	C	0.87	0.50	15,747.9	860.8	2,406.3	-280.9
2007	C	0.59	0.35	14,719.9	550.7	2,440.2	-191.0
2006	C	0.73	0.42	13,566.2	460.9	2,222.6	52.7
2005	C+	1.34	0.73	13,011.4	651.6	1,866.9	179.5
2004	C+	1.17	0.69	12,237.5	670.0	1,674.2	173.9

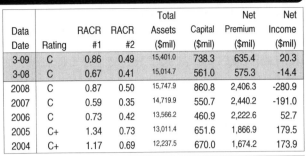

Risk-Adjusted Capital Ratio #1
(Moderate Loss Scenario)

SUN LIFE ASSURANCE COMPANY OF CANADA (US)   C+   Fair

Major Rating Factors: Fair quality investment portfolio (3.8 on a scale of 0 to 10) with large holdings of BBB rated bonds in addition to junk bond exposure equal to 56% of capital. Fair overall results on stability tests (3.3) including negative cash flow from operations for 2008. Good capitalization (5.4) based on good risk adjusted capital (moderate loss scenario).

Other Rating Factors: Weak profitability (1.9) with operating losses during the first three months of 2009. Excellent liquidity (9.3).

Principal Business: Group retirement contracts (49%), individual annuities (26%), group life insurance (15%), and individual life insurance (10%).

Principal Investments: NonCMO investment grade bonds (41%), CMOs and structured securities (33%), mortgages in good standing (10%), policy loans (5%), and misc. investments (11%).

Investments in Affiliates: 2%

Group Affiliation: Sun Life Assurance Group

Licensed in: All states except AL, NC

Commenced Business: December 1973

Address: One Sun Life Executive Park, Wellesley Hills, MA 02181

Phone: (781) 237-6030 **Domicile State:** DE **NAIC Code:** 79065

Data Date	Rating	RACR #1	RACR #2	Total Assets ($mil)	Capital ($mil)	Net Premium ($mil)	Net Income ($mil)
3-09	C+	1.24	0.69	39,760.6	1,178.6	951.4	-143.2
3-08	B-	N/A	N/A	N/A	N/A	N/A	N/A
2008	C+	1.38	0.78	39,669.9	1,267.1	2,831.5	-988.3
2007	B-	1.32	0.75	44,700.8	1,174.1	6,492.1	-55.0
2006	B-	1.42	0.79	42,552.0	1,426.5	3,837.9	171.9
2005	B-	1.47	0.83	40,293.9	1,542.5	3,008.4	146.5
2004	B-	1.33	0.78	39,839.1	1,584.9	3,934.0	230.9

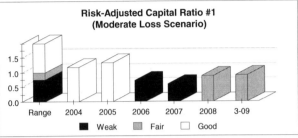

Rating Indexes

SUN LIFE INSURANCE & ANNUITY COMPANY OF NEW YORK   C   Fair

Major Rating Factors: Fair overall results on stability tests (3.8 on a scale of 0 to 10) including negative cash flow from operations for 2008. Good quality investment portfolio (5.9) despite mixed results such as: large holdings of BBB rated bonds but moderate junk bond exposure. Weak profitability (1.8) with operating losses during the first three months of 2009. Return on equity has been low, averaging -19.6%.

Other Rating Factors: Strong capitalization (7.8) based on excellent risk adjusted capital (severe loss scenario). Excellent liquidity (9.1).

Principal Business: Individual annuities (70%), reinsurance (12%), group life insurance (9%), individual life insurance (5%), and group health insurance (5%).

Principal Investments: NonCMO investment grade bonds (78%), mortgages in good standing (8%), CMOs and structured securities (7%), noninv. grade bonds (5%), and cash (1%).

Investments in Affiliates: None

Group Affiliation: Sun Life Assurance Group

Licensed in: NC, SC

Commenced Business: January 1985

Address: 122 E 42nd St Ste 1900, New York, NY 10017

Phone: (212) 983-6352 **Domicile State:** NY **NAIC Code:** 72664

Data Date	Rating	RACR #1	RACR #2	Total Assets ($mil)	Capital ($mil)	Net Premium ($mil)	Net Income ($mil)
3-09	C	2.97	1.56	2,472.8	209.0	149.3	-5.3
3-08	C	2.86	1.60	2,541.0	199.2	94.5	-7.0
2008	C	2.94	1.56	2,587.7	207.3	504.3	-149.5
2007	C	3.04	1.72	2,639.5	207.0	388.1	-25.4
2006	C	1.96	1.03	2,567.3	132.7	275.3	-51.2
2005	B	2.63	1.34	2,585.9	187.0	163.8	-8.6
2004	B	2.54	1.34	2,672.5	192.1	240.3	14.8

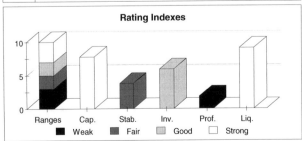

Rating Indexes

SUNAMERICA LIFE INSURANCE COMPANY | C | Fair

Major Rating Factors: Fair current capitalization (4.6 on a scale of 0 to 10) based on fair risk adjusted capital (moderate loss scenario), although results have slipped from the good range over the last two years. Fair quality investment portfolio (4.0) with significant exposure to mortgages . Mortgage default rate has been low. Fair overall results on stability tests (3.0) including fair risk adjusted capital in prior years.

Other Rating Factors: Excellent profitability (7.6). Excellent liquidity (9.9).

Principal Business: Individual life insurance (55%), individual annuities (42%), reinsurance (1%), and group retirement contracts (1%).

Principal Investments: CMOs and structured securities (23%), nonCMO investment grade bonds (23%), common & preferred stock (19%), mortgages in good standing (10%), and noninv. grade bonds (4%).

Investments in Affiliates: 21%

Group Affiliation: American International Group

Licensed in: All states except AL, NC

Commenced Business: June 1890

Address: 1 SunAmerica Center, Los Angeles, CA 90067-6022

Phone: (310) 772-6000 **Domicile State:** AZ **NAIC Code:** 69256

Data Date	Rating	RACR #1	RACR #2	Total Assets ($mil)	Capital ($mil)	Net Premium ($mil)	Net Income ($mil)
3-09	C	0.85	0.70	21,173.1	4,182.5	0.9	391.9
3-08	C+	1.12	0.89	37,926.7	4,299.8	1.6	-330.6
2008	C	0.95	0.80	24,857.5	4,658.8	5.2	-2,231.7
2007	B-	1.24	0.99	39,454.6	4,721.3	3.5	354.0
2006	B-	1.31	0.99	46,889.6	4,462.6	5.0	538.7
2005	B-	0.98	0.68	62,336.6	4,410.0	10.2	259.0
2004	B-	1.28	0.81	68,080.4	5,014.6	14.7	713.5

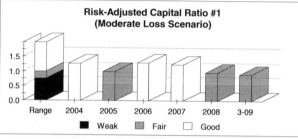

Risk-Adjusted Capital Ratio #1 (Moderate Loss Scenario)

Weak   Fair   Good

SUNSET LIFE INSURANCE COMPANY OF AMERICA | B | Good

Major Rating Factors: Good overall profitability (6.8 on a scale of 0 to 10) despite operating losses during the first three months of 2009. Return on equity has been excellent over the last five years averaging 21.9%. Good liquidity (5.3) with sufficient resources to cover a large increase in policy surrenders. Fair quality investment portfolio (3.7).

Other Rating Factors: Fair overall results on stability tests (4.9) including negative cash flow from operations for 2008. Strong capitalization (7.1) based on excellent risk adjusted capital (severe loss scenario).

Principal Business: Individual life insurance (89%) and individual annuities (11%).

Principal Investments: NonCMO investment grade bonds (56%), CMOs and structured securities (26%), mortgages in good standing (9%), noninv. grade bonds (6%), and misc. investments (4%).

Investments in Affiliates: None

Group Affiliation: Kansas City Life Group

Licensed in: All states except AL, AK, NJ, NM, NC, TX, VA, WY

Commenced Business: May 1937

Address: 3520 Broadway, Kansas City, MO 64121-9532

Phone: (816) 753-7000 **Domicile State:** MO **NAIC Code:** 69272

Data Date	Rating	RACR #1	RACR #2	Total Assets ($mil)	Capital ($mil)	Net Premium ($mil)	Net Income ($mil)
3-09	B	2.21	1.08	403.4	32.9	3.0	-0.9
3-08	B	2.68	1.37	427.6	40.0	3.0	2.4
2008	B	2.37	1.18	408.0	34.9	11.1	5.2
2007	B	2.58	1.31	430.2	38.4	12.7	9.4
2006	B	2.40	1.22	456.7	37.8	17.0	9.2
2005	B	2.34	1.19	479.3	38.0	22.2	11.2
2004	B	2.23	1.14	485.1	35.8	18.9	8.5

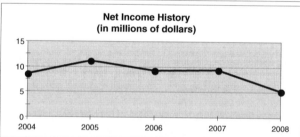

Net Income History (in millions of dollars)

SWISS RE LIFE & HEALTH AMERICA INCORPORATED | B- | Good

Major Rating Factors: Good overall results on stability tests (5.3 on a scale of 0 to 10) despite fair financial strength of affiliated Swiss Reinsurance Group. Other stability subfactors include good operational trends and excellent risk diversification. Good overall capitalization (6.7) based on good risk adjusted capital (severe loss scenario). Nevertheless, capital levels have fluctuated during prior years. Good quality investment portfolio (6.8).

Other Rating Factors: Good overall profitability (6.5) despite operating losses during the first three months of 2009. Good liquidity (6.5).

Principal Business: Reinsurance (100%).

Principal Investments: NonCMO investment grade bonds (56%), CMOs and structured securities (33%), common & preferred stock (7%), noninv. grade bonds (2%), and policy loans (1%).

Investments in Affiliates: 7%

Group Affiliation: Swiss Reinsurance Group

Licensed in: All states except AL, MD, PR

Commenced Business: September 1967

Address: 969 High Ridge Rd, Stamford, CT 06904-2060

Phone: (203) 321-3141 **Domicile State:** CT **NAIC Code:** 82627

Data Date	Rating	RACR #1	RACR #2	Total Assets ($mil)	Capital ($mil)	Net Premium ($mil)	Net Income ($mil)
3-09	B-	1.28	0.96	12,589.8	1,703.5	635.1	-1.6
3-08	B-	1.34	1.01	11,822.3	1,693.3	603.2	48.9
2008	B-	1.30	0.99	12,775.2	1,788.0	2,484.4	375.2
2007	B-	1.20	0.93	11,925.6	1,640.2	2,422.8	277.7
2006	C+	1.26	1.04	11,973.0	2,140.1	2,317.8	233.3
2005	C+	1.15	0.99	12,172.9	2,341.3	2,190.8	441.2
2004	C	0.88	0.77	11,823.4	2,006.6	2,168.6	177.7

Swiss Reinsurance Group Composite Group Rating: C Largest Group Members	Assets ($mil)	Rating
REASSURE AMERICA LIFE INS CO	16470	C+
SWISS REINSURANCE AMERICA CORP	14402	C
SWISS RE LIFE HEALTH AMER INC	12775	B-
WESTPORT INS CORP	8047	C
NORTH AMERICAN SPECIALTY INS CO	506	C

SYMETRA LIFE INSURANCE COMPANY

B   **Good**

Major Rating Factors: Good overall profitability (6.2 on a scale of 0 to 10) despite operating losses during the first three months of 2009. Return on equity has been good over the last five years, averaging 10.4%. Good overall results on stability tests (6.0). Stability strengths include excellent operational trends and excellent risk diversification. Fair quality investment portfolio (4.6).

Other Rating Factors: Strong capitalization (7.2) based on excellent risk adjusted capital (severe loss scenario). Excellent liquidity (7.3).

Principal Business: Individual annuities (69%), group health insurance (19%), individual life insurance (7%), group retirement contracts (4%), and group life insurance (1%).

Principal Investments: NonCMO investment grade bonds (57%), CMOs and structured securities (24%), mortgages in good standing (7%), noninv. grade bonds (6%), and misc. investments (7%).

Investments in Affiliates: None

Group Affiliation: White Mountains Group

Licensed in: All states except AL, NC

Commenced Business: April 1957

Address: 777 108th Ave NE Suite 1200, Bellevue, WA 98004

Phone: (425) 376-8000 **Domicile State:** WA **NAIC Code:** 68608

Data Date	Rating	RACR #1	RACR #2	Total Assets ($mil)	Capital ($mil)	Net Premium ($mil)	Net Income ($mil)
3-09	B	2.16	1.11	19,398.2	1,155.8	1,041.2	-48.9
3-08	B	2.44	1.29	17,975.8	1,202.6	387.5	7.6
2008	B	2.25	1.18	18,646.1	1,179.0	2,275.1	36.7
2007	B	2.51	1.33	18,004.8	1,225.0	1,201.4	134.1
2006	B	2.72	1.39	18,364.6	1,266.2	1,065.6	145.0
2005	B	2.51	1.32	18,824.5	1,260.1	921.4	162.2
2004	B	2.03	1.14	18,887.9	1,138.4	902.9	222.1

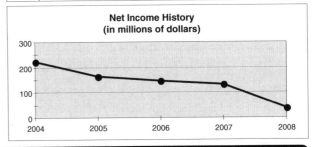

Net Income History
(in millions of dollars)

TEACHERS INSURANCE & ANNUITY ASSOC OF AMERICA *

A+   **Excellent**

Major Rating Factors: Good quality investment portfolio (5.9 on a scale of 0 to 10) despite substantial holdings of BBB bonds in addition to moderate junk bond exposure. Exposure to mortgages is significant, but the mortgage default rate has been low. Good overall results on stability tests (6.9). Strengths that enhance stability include good operational trends and excellent risk diversification. Strong capitalization (9.0) based on excellent risk adjusted capital (severe loss scenario).

Other Rating Factors: Excellent profitability (9.1) despite operating losses during the first three months of 2009. Excellent liquidity (8.3).

Principal Business: Individual annuities (68%), group retirement contracts (29%), and individual life insurance (3%).

Principal Investments: CMOs and structured securities (38%), nonCMO investment grade bonds (37%), mortgages in good standing (11%), noninv. grade bonds (4%), and misc. investments (10%).

Investments in Affiliates: 4%

Group Affiliation: TIAA Family of Companies

Licensed in: All states except AL

Commenced Business: May 1918

Address: 730 Third Ave 7th Floor, New York, NY 10017

Phone: (212) 490-9000 **Domicile State:** NY **NAIC Code:** 69345

Data Date	Rating	RACR #1	RACR #2	Total Assets ($mil)	Capital ($mil)	Net Premium ($mil)	Net Income ($mil)
3-09	A+	4.28	2.31	194,589	16,848.6	2,803.3	-345.6
3-08	A+	4.99	2.79	198,035	18,734.9	2,592.1	91.1
2008	A+	4.48	2.45	195,237	17,754.2	13,377.4	-3,283.4
2007	A+	4.97	2.79	196,409	17,827.1	9,460.1	1,428.7
2006	A+	3.34	2.21	183,698	15,282.2	10,294.2	2,333.8
2005	A+	4.58	2.32	174,921	13,222.6	10,300.3	2,000.8
2004	A+	5.25	2.43	163,564	11,177.4	8,934.6	540.5

Adverse Trends in Operations

Increase in policy surrenders from 2007 to 2008 (62%)
Decrease in premium volume from 2006 to 2007 (8%)
Increase in policy surrenders from 2005 to 2006 (36%)
Increase in policy surrenders from 2004 to 2005 (26%)

TENNESSEE FARMERS LIFE INSURANCE COMPANY *

A   **Excellent**

Major Rating Factors: Good quality investment portfolio (6.0 on a scale of 0 to 10) despite mixed results such as: minimal exposure to mortgages and substantial holdings of BBB bonds but minimal holdings in junk bonds. Good overall profitability (6.8) despite operating losses during the first three months of 2009. Return on equity has been low, averaging 3.1%. Good liquidity (6.4).

Other Rating Factors: Excellent overall results on stability tests (7.4) excellent operational trends and excellent risk diversification. Strong capitalization (7.7) based on excellent risk adjusted capital (severe loss scenario).

Principal Business: Individual life insurance (64%), individual annuities (34%), and reinsurance (2%).

Principal Investments: NonCMO investment grade bonds (70%), common & preferred stock (23%), policy loans (1%), noninv. grade bonds (1%), and misc. investments (4%).

Investments in Affiliates: 21%

Group Affiliation: Tennessee Farmers Ins Companies

Licensed in: TX

Commenced Business: September 1973

Address: 147 Bear Creek Pike, Columbia, TN 38401-2266

Phone: (931) 388-7872 **Domicile State:** TN **NAIC Code:** 82759

Data Date	Rating	RACR #1	RACR #2	Total Assets ($mil)	Capital ($mil)	Net Premium ($mil)	Net Income ($mil)
3-09	A	2.28	1.49	1,318.3	201.6	45.5	-0.2
3-08	A	1.55	1.21	1,269.6	213.8	39.4	2.0
2008	A	2.31	1.52	1,296.0	202.2	138.4	-5.7
2007	A	1.46	1.15	1,072.4	196.0	78.1	9.7
2006	A	1.56	1.25	1,021.5	181.3	53.3	5.4
2005	A	1.59	1.28	970.9	173.3	55.4	4.9
2004	A	1.67	1.33	908.3	163.3	54.1	6.3

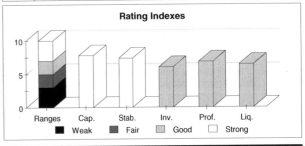

Rating Indexes

Ranges   Cap.   Stab.   Inv.   Prof.   Liq.

■ Weak   ▨ Fair   ▤ Good   □ Strong

TEXAS LIFE INSURANCE COMPANY

B **Good**

Major Rating Factors: Good overall results on stability tests (6.0 on a scale of 0 to 10) despite fair risk adjusted capital in prior years. Other stability subfactors include excellent operational trends and good risk diversification. Good quality investment portfolio (5.8) despite mixed results such as: substantial holdings of BBB bonds but junk bond exposure equal to 58% of capital. Good profitability (5.0) although investment income, in comparison to reserve requirements, is below regulatory standards.

Other Rating Factors: Good liquidity (5.6). Strong capitalization (7.1) based on excellent risk adjusted capital (severe loss scenario).

Principal Business: Individual life insurance (100%).

Principal Investments: NonCMO investment grade bonds (56%), CMOs and structured securities (25%), mortgages in good standing (6%), policy loans (5%), and misc. investments (7%).

Investments in Affiliates: None

Group Affiliation: Wilton Re Holdings Ltd

Licensed in: All states except AL, NC

Commenced Business: April 1901

Address: 900 Washington Ave, Waco, TX 76701

Phone: (254) 752-6521 **Domicile State:** TX **NAIC Code:** 69396

Data Date	Rating	RACR #1	RACR #2	Total Assets ($mil)	Capital ($mil)	Net Premium ($mil)	Net Income ($mil)
3-09	B	1.74	1.06	709.0	38.0	29.5	0.5
3-08	B	1.89	1.10	645.4	47.2	27.8	1.5
2008	B	1.77	1.04	665.0	48.0	129.8	-3.4
2007	B	1.86	1.08	630.9	45.7	112.3	13.2
2006	B	1.53	0.84	1,910.5	39.7	100.1	6.4
2005	B	1.21	0.67	896.4	34.2	90.3	6.4
2004	B	1.07	0.59	874.2	32.2	79.5	4.9

Adverse Trends in Operations

Decrease in asset base during 2007 (67%)

THRIVENT LIFE INSURANCE COMPANY *

B+ **Good**

Major Rating Factors: Good quality investment portfolio (6.0 on a scale of 0 to 10) despite mixed results such as: large holdings of BBB rated bonds but junk bond exposure equal to 60% of capital. Good overall results on stability tests (5.2). Stability strengths include excellent risk diversification. Strong capitalization (7.8) based on excellent risk adjusted capital (severe loss scenario).

Other Rating Factors: Excellent profitability (8.1) with operating gains in each of the last five years. Excellent liquidity (7.9).

Principal Business: Individual annuities (92%) and individual life insurance (8%).

Principal Investments: NonCMO investment grade bonds (51%), CMOs and structured securities (31%), noninv. grade bonds (9%), common & preferred stock (1%), and misc. investments (2%).

Investments in Affiliates: 4%

Group Affiliation: Thrivent Financial for Lutherans Grp

Licensed in: All states except AL, HI, MD, MI, NJ, NC, SC, VA, PR

Commenced Business: December 1982

Address: 625 Fourth Ave S, Minneapolis, MN 55415

Phone: (612) 340-7214 **Domicile State:** MN **NAIC Code:** 97721

Data Date	Rating	RACR #1	RACR #2	Total Assets ($mil)	Capital ($mil)	Net Premium ($mil)	Net Income ($mil)
3-09	B+	3.42	1.55	2,564.9	174.6	33.9	0.2
3-08	B+	4.04	1.90	3,420.3	188.0	32.1	4.2
2008	B+	3.47	1.60	2,689.2	173.6	146.2	20.1
2007	B+	3.67	1.72	3,664.6	178.1	118.2	49.4
2006	B	3.20	1.56	3,731.2	167.5	120.1	34.0
2005	B	2.84	1.43	3,922.5	163.4	146.3	34.5
2004	B	2.44	1.24	3,999.9	134.0	192.7	16.4

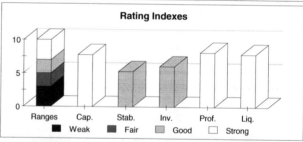

Rating Indexes

TIAA-CREF LIFE INSURANCE COMPANY

B **Good**

Major Rating Factors: Good quality investment portfolio (5.9 on a scale of 0 to 10) despite mixed results such as: minimal exposure to mortgages and large holdings of BBB rated bonds but small junk bond holdings. Good overall profitability (6.2) despite operating losses during the first three months of 2009. Return on equity has been fair, averaging 5.7%. Good liquidity (6.2).

Other Rating Factors: Good overall results on stability tests (6.3) good operational trends and excellent risk diversification. Strong capitalization (8.5) based on excellent risk adjusted capital (severe loss scenario).

Principal Business: Individual annuities (69%), individual life insurance (28%), and individual health insurance (3%).

Principal Investments: NonCMO investment grade bonds (69%), CMOs and structured securities (23%), mortgages in good standing (3%), noninv. grade bonds (2%), and common & preferred stock (2%).

Investments in Affiliates: None

Group Affiliation: TIAA Family of Companies

Licensed in: All states except AL

Commenced Business: December 1996

Address: 730 Third Ave, New York, NY 10017

Phone: (888) 842-5433 **Domicile State:** NY **NAIC Code:** 60142

Data Date	Rating	RACR #1	RACR #2	Total Assets ($mil)	Capital ($mil)	Net Premium ($mil)	Net Income ($mil)
3-09	B	3.75	1.98	3,031.9	342.8	67.7	-10.8
3-08	B	3.80	1.97	3,063.1	323.6	26.1	-11.1
2008	B	3.03	1.59	2,917.6	280.3	168.0	-61.5
2007	B	3.83	1.97	3,115.4	332.1	169.6	10.1
2006	B	3.76	1.93	3,208.4	340.6	136.0	17.3
2005	B	3.07	1.55	3,327.0	324.4	140.6	21.4
2004	B	2.86	1.43	3,376.0	300.1	227.1	25.5

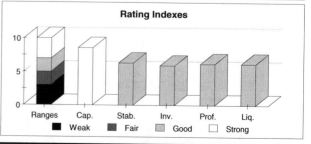

Rating Indexes

TIME INSURANCE COMPANY

B- **Good**

Major Rating Factors: Good current capitalization (5.2 on a scale of 0 to 10) based on mixed results -- excessive policy leverage mitigated by good risk adjusted capital (severe loss scenario), although results have slipped from the excellent range over the last two years. Good quality investment portfolio (5.9) despite large holdings of BBB rated bonds in addition to moderate junk bond exposure. Exposure to mortgages is significant, but the mortgage default rate has been low. Good overall profitability (6.8).

Other Rating Factors: Good liquidity (5.5). Fair overall results on stability tests (4.8) including fair financial strength of affiliated Assurant Inc.

Principal Business: Group health insurance (61%), individual health insurance (35%), and individual life insurance (3%).

Principal Investments: NonCMO investment grade bonds (56%), mortgages in good standing (16%), noninv. grade bonds (10%), common & preferred stock (10%), and misc. investments (9%).

Investments in Affiliates: None
Group Affiliation: Assurant Inc
Licensed in: All states except AL, ID, NC
Commenced Business: March 1910
Address: 501 W Michigan, Milwaukee, WI 53201
Phone: (612) 738-4449 **Domicile State:** WI **NAIC Code:** 69477

Data Date	Rating	RACR #1	RACR #2	Total Assets ($mil)	Capital ($mil)	Net Premium ($mil)	Net Income ($mil)
3-09	B-	1.08	0.82	658.7	207.1	328.8	4.9
3-08	B-	1.39	1.06	808.9	271.5	333.4	21.8
2008	B-	1.10	0.84	678.1	211.8	1,326.0	39.0
2007	B-	1.31	1.00	812.9	254.5	1,350.6	112.5
2006	B-	1.27	0.97	820.8	238.6	1,314.4	99.9
2005	B-	1.37	1.03	879.2	262.3	1,304.5	102.0
2004	B-	1.22	0.93	827.3	246.0	1,407.2	127.8

Policy Leverage

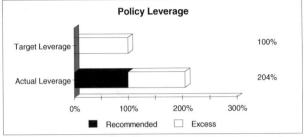

TOWER LIFE INSURANCE COMPANY

C **Fair**

Major Rating Factors: Fair overall results on stability tests (3.8 on a scale of 0 to 10). Good quality investment portfolio (6.9) with minimal exposure to mortgages and minimal holdings in junk bonds. Weak profitability (2.9) with investment income below regulatory standards in relation to interest assumptions of reserves.

Other Rating Factors: Strong capitalization (10.0) based on excellent risk adjusted capital (severe loss scenario). Excellent liquidity (9.0).

Principal Business: Individual life insurance (49%), reinsurance (19%), group health insurance (19%), individual health insurance (8%), and other lines (5%).

Principal Investments: NonCMO investment grade bonds (61%), CMOs and structured securities (13%), real estate (12%), policy loans (10%), and misc. investments (4%).

Investments in Affiliates: None
Group Affiliation: None
Licensed in: NY, OR, UT
Commenced Business: March 1955
Address: 310 St Marys, San Antonio, TX 78205
Phone: (210) 226-7151 **Domicile State:** TX **NAIC Code:** 69493

Data Date	Rating	RACR #1	RACR #2	Total Assets ($mil)	Capital ($mil)	Net Premium ($mil)	Net Income ($mil)
3-09	C	4.77	4.29	75.5	36.8	0.4	0.1
3-08	C	5.12	4.60	78.9	40.2	0.6	0.1
2008	C	4.76	4.29	75.4	36.7	1.9	0.2
2007	C	5.10	4.59	78.6	40.1	2.3	1.2
2006	C	4.96	4.47	79.0	39.1	2.3	1.5
2005	C	4.77	4.30	79.4	37.6	2.7	0.5
2004	C	4.72	4.25	79.0	37.2	2.7	-0.1

Rating Indexes

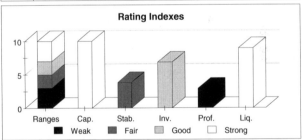

TRANS WORLD ASSURANCE COMPANY

B **Good**

Major Rating Factors: Good quality investment portfolio (6.1 on a scale of 0 to 10) with minimal exposure to mortgages and minimal holdings in junk bonds. Good liquidity (6.4) with sufficient resources to cover a large increase in policy surrenders. Good overall results on stability tests (5.4) excellent operational trends and good risk diversification.

Other Rating Factors: Weak profitability (2.9) with investment income below regulatory standards in relation to interest assumptions of reserves. Strong capitalization (7.7) based on excellent risk adjusted capital (severe loss scenario).

Principal Business: Individual life insurance (87%), reinsurance (11%), and individual annuities (3%).

Principal Investments: NonCMO investment grade bonds (78%), common & preferred stock (11%), real estate (5%), mortgages in good standing (4%), and cash (2%).

Investments in Affiliates: 12%
Group Affiliation: Trans World Asr Group
Licensed in: All states except AL, NJ, NC, VA
Commenced Business: December 1963
Address: 885 South El Camino Real, San Mateo, CA 94402
Phone: (850) 456-7401 **Domicile State:** CA **NAIC Code:** 69566

Data Date	Rating	RACR #1	RACR #2	Total Assets ($mil)	Capital ($mil)	Net Premium ($mil)	Net Income ($mil)
3-09	B	1.73	1.48	336.0	67.9	3.9	1.3
3-08	B	1.60	1.38	333.0	67.1	4.6	0.8
2008	B	1.71	1.46	334.9	67.2	12.7	1.3
2007	B	1.60	1.38	332.0	67.1	15.3	1.0
2006	B	2.56	2.01	323.9	66.6	16.3	0.9
2005	B	4.03	2.88	311.4	64.8	15.1	6.7
2004	B	4.26	3.08	295.9	57.9	15.4	1.8

Adverse Trends in Operations

Decrease in premium volume from 2007 to 2008 (17%)
Decrease in premium volume from 2006 to 2007 (6%)
Decrease in premium volume from 2004 to 2005 (2%)

TRANSAMERICA FINANCIAL LIFE INSURANCE COMPANY   B-   Good

Major Rating Factors: Good current capitalization (6.5 on a scale of 0 to 10) based on good risk adjusted capital (severe loss scenario), although results have slipped from the excellent range during the last year. Good overall results on stability tests (5.0). Strengths include good financial support from affiliation with AEGON USA Group, excellent operational trends, excellent risk adjusted capital for prior years and excellent risk diversification. Fair quality investment portfolio (4.9).

Other Rating Factors: Weak profitability (2.0). Excellent liquidity (9.0).

Principal Business: Group retirement contracts (67%), individual annuities (16%), reinsurance (13%), individual life insurance (2%), and individual health insurance (1%).

Principal Investments: NonCMO investment grade bonds (49%), CMOs and structured securities (24%), mortgages in good standing (13%), noninv. grade bonds (6%), and misc. investments (7%).

Investments in Affiliates: 1%
Group Affiliation: AEGON USA Group
Licensed in: All states except AL
Commenced Business: October 1947
Address: 4 Manhattanville Rd, Purchase, NY 10577
Phone: (914) 697-8000 **Domicile State:** NY **NAIC Code:** 70688

Data Date	Rating	RACR #1	RACR #2	Total Assets ($mil)	Capital ($mil)	Net Premium ($mil)	Net Income ($mil)
3-09	B-	1.91	0.94	19,205.0	780.3	1,332.8	6.2
3-08	B	2.69	1.37	17,598.4	900.4	1,013.2	62.5
2008	B-	2.03	1.02	18,792.4	806.5	4,594.0	-296.9
2007	B	2.54	1.29	17,771.7	813.3	3,539.0	124.8
2006	B	2.65	1.34	16,802.7	888.1	2,586.6	93.3
2005	B	2.49	1.26	16,512.5	802.1	2,519.3	116.7
2004	B	2.28	1.15	15,790.3	690.7	2,137.0	79.3

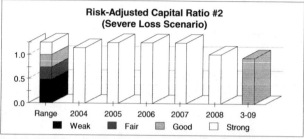

Risk-Adjusted Capital Ratio #2
(Severe Loss Scenario)

Range 2004 2005 2006 2007 2008 3-09
■ Weak ■ Fair ▨ Good □ Strong

TRANSAMERICA LIFE INSURANCE COMPANY   B-   Good

Major Rating Factors: Good current capitalization (6.8 on a scale of 0 to 10) based on good risk adjusted capital (severe loss scenario), although results have slipped from the excellent range during the last year. Fair quality investment portfolio (4.2) with large holdings of BBB rated bonds in addition to significant exposure to junk bonds. Exposure to mortgages is significant, but the mortgage default rate has been low. Fair overall results on stability tests (4.4) including negative cash flow from operations for 2008.

Other Rating Factors: Weak profitability (2.0) with operating losses during the first three months of 2009. Excellent liquidity (7.1).

Principal Business: Individual annuities (46%), group retirement contracts (19%), individual life insurance (16%), reinsurance (12%), and other lines (7%).

Principal Investments: NonCMO investment grade bonds (42%), CMOs and structured securities (23%), mortgages in good standing (15%), noninv. grade bonds (7%), and misc. investments (10%).

Investments in Affiliates: 6%
Group Affiliation: AEGON USA Group
Licensed in: All states except AL, NC
Commenced Business: March 1962
Address: 4333 Edgewood Rd NE, Cedar Rapids, IA 52499
Phone: (319) 398-8511 **Domicile State:** IA **NAIC Code:** 86231

Data Date	Rating	RACR #1	RACR #2	Total Assets ($mil)	Capital ($mil)	Net Premium ($mil)	Net Income ($mil)
3-09	B-	1.94	0.98	99,285.7	4,634.4	2,200.9	-134.6
3-08	B	1.93	0.93	69,758.6	2,093.4	1,447.7	305.5
2008	B-	2.30	1.17	103,872	4,926.9	7,492.2	-528.5
2007	B	1.88	0.91	73,509.1	1,989.7	5,464.0	241.5
2006	B	1.75	0.85	73,929.5	2,042.8	4,898.1	332.4
2005	B	1.80	0.87	68,927.1	2,418.0	5,081.6	298.6
2004	B-	1.87	0.89	44,084.8	1,864.3	3,642.7	128.8

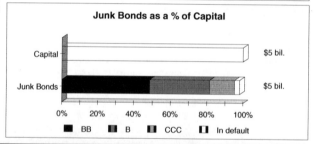

Junk Bonds as a % of Capital

Capital $5 bil.
Junk Bonds $5 bil.

0% 20% 40% 60% 80% 100%
■ BB ▨ B ▥ CCC □ In default

TRIPLE S VIDA INCORPORATED   C+   Fair

Major Rating Factors: Fair liquidity (4.8 on a scale of 0 to 10) as cash from operations and sale of marketable assets may not be adequate to cover a spike in claims or a run on policy withdrawals. Fair overall results on stability tests (4.6) including fair risk adjusted capital in prior years. Good capitalization (5.5) based on good risk adjusted capital (severe loss scenario).

Other Rating Factors: Good quality investment portfolio (6.4). Weak profitability (2.0).

Principal Business: Individual life insurance (57%), individual health insurance (23%), group health insurance (7%), individual annuities (7%), and group life insurance (6%).

Principal Investments: NonCMO investment grade bonds (77%), CMOs and structured securities (13%), common & preferred stock (5%), policy loans (2%), and misc. investments (3%).

Investments in Affiliates: None
Group Affiliation: Triple-S Management Corp
Licensed in: (No states)
Commenced Business: September 1964
Address: 1052 Munoz Rivera Ave, Rio Piedras, PR 00927
Phone: (787) 758-4888 **Domicile State:** PR **NAIC Code:** 73814

Data Date	Rating	RACR #1	RACR #2	Total Assets ($mil)	Capital ($mil)	Net Premium ($mil)	Net Income ($mil)
3-09	C+	1.22	0.81	340.7	47.9	27.2	0.2
3-08	C+	1.32	0.88	317.2	46.9	25.6	1.9
2008	C+	1.26	0.84	329.4	48.7	107.0	2.6
2007	C+	1.07	0.72	309.5	45.1	100.7	8.3
2006	B-	N/A	N/A	293.0	39.3	101.2	7.1
2005	B-	1.40	1.17	207.6	13.2	80.1	15.7
2004	B-	3.19	2.11	228.1	44.8	73.0	10.5

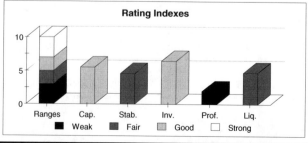

Rating Indexes

Ranges Cap. Stab. Inv. Prof. Liq.
■ Weak ▨ Fair ▥ Good □ Strong

TRUSTMARK INSURANCE COMPANY   B   Good

Major Rating Factors: Good quality investment portfolio (6.0 on a scale of 0 to 10) despite mixed results such as: minimal exposure to mortgages and substantial holdings of BBB bonds but small junk bond holdings. Good overall profitability (6.5). Return on equity has been good over the last five years, averaging 14.5%. Fair overall results on stability tests (4.2).

Other Rating Factors: Strong capitalization (8.0) based on excellent risk adjusted capital (severe loss scenario). Excellent liquidity (7.3).

Principal Business: N/A

Principal Investments: NonCMO investment grade bonds (52%), CMOs and structured securities (31%), common & preferred stock (7%), noninv. grade bonds (3%), and misc. investments (6%).

Investments in Affiliates: 2%

Group Affiliation: Trustmark Group

Licensed in: All states except AL

Commenced Business: January 1913

Address: 400 Field Dr, Lake Forest, IL 60045-2581

Phone: (847) 615-1500 **Domicile State:** IL **NAIC Code:** 61425

Data Date	Rating	RACR #1	RACR #2	Total Assets ($mil)	Capital ($mil)	Net Premium ($mil)	Net Income ($mil)
3-09	B	2.92	1.69	1,147.8	213.0	66.4	7.4
3-08	B	3.19	1.92	1,223.5	241.4	61.4	7.3
2008	B	3.53	2.08	1,168.3	212.2	231.1	46.9
2007	B	3.79	2.26	1,236.9	236.4	164.6	30.1
2006	B-	4.53	2.59	1,282.0	239.8	128.8	42.5
2005	B	4.05	2.38	1,210.2	203.8	146.0	26.2
2004	B	2.80	1.75	1,285.2	174.2	335.5	25.8

Rating Indexes

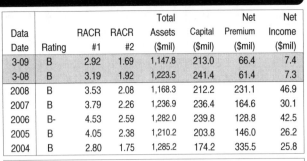

TRUSTMARK LIFE INSURANCE COMPANY   B   Good

Major Rating Factors: Good overall results on stability tests (5.3 on a scale of 0 to 10) despite negative cash flow from operations for 2008. Other stability subfactors include good operational trends, good risk adjusted capital for prior years and excellent risk diversification. Good liquidity (6.2) with sufficient resources to handle a spike in claims. Strong capitalization (10.0) based on excellent risk adjusted capital (severe loss scenario).

Other Rating Factors: High quality investment portfolio (7.6). Excellent profitability (7.1) despite modest operating losses during 2008.

Principal Business: Group health insurance (97%) and group life insurance (3%).

Principal Investments: NonCMO investment grade bonds (75%), common & preferred stock (12%), CMOs and structured securities (12%), and noninv. grade bonds (4%).

Investments in Affiliates: None

Group Affiliation: Trustmark Group

Licensed in: All states except AL, NM, NC

Commenced Business: February 1925

Address: 400 Field Dr, Lake Forest, IL 60045-2581

Phone: (847) 615-1500 **Domicile State:** IL **NAIC Code:** 62863

Data Date	Rating	RACR #1	RACR #2	Total Assets ($mil)	Capital ($mil)	Net Premium ($mil)	Net Income ($mil)
3-09	B	4.47	3.36	362.0	186.4	97.4	3.8
3-08	B	4.68	3.52	352.4	175.1	100.9	3.6
2008	B	4.31	3.25	377.4	183.5	408.0	-14.5
2007	B	4.26	3.20	361.7	171.7	495.5	35.0
2006	B	2.33	1.71	564.6	140.4	619.3	45.5
2005	B-	1.33	0.99	558.4	88.6	721.1	17.7
2004	B-	1.06	0.78	597.1	74.4	632.6	6.9

Adverse Trends in Operations

Decrease in premium volume from 2007 to 2008 (18%)
Decrease in premium volume from 2006 to 2007 (20%)
Decrease in asset base during 2007 (36%)
Decrease in premium volume from 2005 to 2006 (14%)
Decrease in asset base during 2005 (6%)

UBS LIFE INSURANCE COMPANY USA   C+   Fair

Major Rating Factors: Fair overall results on stability tests (4.4 on a scale of 0 to 10). Strong capitalization (10.0) based on excellent risk adjusted capital (severe loss scenario). Capital levels have been relatively consistent over the last five years. High quality investment portfolio (9.6) with no exposure to mortgages and no exposure to junk bonds.

Other Rating Factors: Excellent profitability (8.0) despite operating losses during the first three months of 2009. Excellent liquidity (7.0).

Principal Business: Reinsurance (100%).

Principal Investments: NonCMO investment grade bonds (99%) and cash (1%).

Investments in Affiliates: None

Group Affiliation: UBS AG

Licensed in: All states except AL, DC, NC

Commenced Business: September 1956

Address: 601 6th Ave, Des Moines, IA 50309

Phone: (515) 245-2001 **Domicile State:** CA **NAIC Code:** 67423

Data Date	Rating	RACR #1	RACR #2	Total Assets ($mil)	Capital ($mil)	Net Premium ($mil)	Net Income ($mil)
3-09	C+	6.21	5.59	41.9	36.2	0.1	-0.8
3-08	C+	6.01	5.41	42.4	35.7	0.3	0.1
2008	C+	6.45	5.80	41.4	37.5	1.1	1.7
2007	C	6.11	5.50	42.5	36.3	1.9	3.8
2006	C	5.45	4.91	45.5	33.5	1.2	3.9
2005	C	4.73	4.26	43.5	28.6	3.2	6.6
2004	D	3.98	3.59	38.0	21.7	3.4	2.2

Rating Indexes

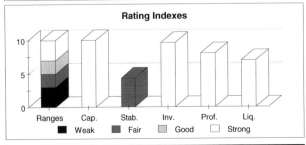

UNICARE LIFE & HEALTH INSURANCE COMPANY | B | Good

Major Rating Factors: Good quality investment portfolio (6.5 on a scale of 0 to 10) despite mixed results such as: substantial holdings of BBB bonds but moderate junk bond exposure. Fair overall capitalization (4.7) based on mixed results -- excessive policy leverage mitigated by good risk adjusted capital (severe loss scenario). Capital levels have been relatively consistent over the last five years. Fair overall results on stability tests (4.5) including negative cash flow from operations for 2008.

Other Rating Factors: Weak liquidity (0.6). Excellent profitability (8.9) with operating gains in each of the last five years.

Principal Business: Individual health insurance (67%), group health insurance (27%), and group life insurance (6%).

Principal Investments: NonCMO investment grade bonds (67%), CMOs and structured securities (24%), noninv. grade bonds (8%), and common & preferred stock (1%).

Investments in Affiliates: None
Group Affiliation: WellPoint Inc
Licensed in: All states except AL
Commenced Business: December 1980
Address: 1209 Orange St, Wilmington, DE 19801
Phone: (877) 864-2273 **Domicile State:** IN **NAIC Code:** 80314

Data Date	Rating	RACR #1	RACR #2	Total Assets ($mil)	Capital ($mil)	Net Premium ($mil)	Net Income ($mil)
3-09	B	1.04	0.79	1,672.9	340.3	644.2	0.6
3-08	B	0.94	0.72	1,836.1	254.3	717.1	-74.9
2008	B	1.06	0.81	1,636.3	361.5	2,832.2	7.1
2007	B	1.11	0.84	1,725.8	344.9	2,554.7	111.6
2006	B	1.01	0.78	1,491.4	278.1	2,328.7	116.2
2005	B	1.48	1.13	1,258.8	288.0	1,574.8	16.2
2004	B	1.68	1.26	1,254.4	300.6	1,491.8	32.5

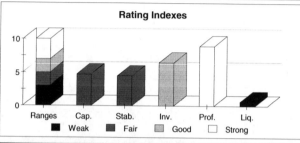

Rating Indexes

UNIMERICA INSURANCE COMPANY | B | Good

Major Rating Factors: Good overall profitability (6.7 on a scale of 0 to 10). Return on equity has been good over the last five years, averaging 12.8%. Fair overall results on stability tests (4.1). Strong capitalization (8.0) based on excellent risk adjusted capital (severe loss scenario). Moreover, capital levels have been consistently high over the last five years.

Other Rating Factors: High quality investment portfolio (8.6). Excellent liquidity (7.1).

Principal Business: Group health insurance (67%), group life insurance (25%), reinsurance (5%), and individual health insurance (4%).

Principal Investments: NonCMO investment grade bonds (78%), CMOs and structured securities (21%), and cash (1%).

Investments in Affiliates: None
Group Affiliation: UnitedHealth Group Inc
Licensed in: All states except AL, NC
Commenced Business: December 1980
Address: 711 High St, Des Moines, IA 50392
Phone: (301) 654-6900 **Domicile State:** WI **NAIC Code:** 91529

Data Date	Rating	RACR #1	RACR #2	Total Assets ($mil)	Capital ($mil)	Net Premium ($mil)	Net Income ($mil)
3-09	B	2.16	1.67	246.9	107.4	62.9	0.1
3-08	B	2.30	1.78	197.5	83.8	59.4	-1.1
2008	B	2.02	1.56	244.4	104.7	255.9	-5.5
2007	B	1.66	1.29	135.2	45.1	146.3	5.3
2006	B-	1.68	1.31	94.3	38.2	83.8	8.9
2005	B-	2.29	1.83	54.8	28.8	54.8	4.3
2004	B-	2.74	2.16	45.6	27.7	43.3	6.2

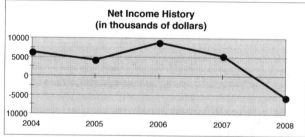

Net Income History
(in thousands of dollars)

UNION CENTRAL LIFE INSURANCE COMPANY | B- | Good

Major Rating Factors: Good overall capitalization (5.3 on a scale of 0 to 10) based on good risk adjusted capital (moderate loss scenario). Nevertheless, capital levels have fluctuated during prior years. Good liquidity (5.2) with sufficient resources to cover a large increase in policy surrenders. Good overall results on stability tests (5.0) good operational trends and excellent risk diversification.

Other Rating Factors: Fair quality investment portfolio (4.4). Weak profitability (2.6) with operating losses during the first three months of 2009.

Principal Business: Group retirement contracts (39%), individual life insurance (33%), individual annuities (18%), individual health insurance (8%), and group health insurance (1%).

Principal Investments: NonCMO investment grade bonds (57%), CMOs and structured securities (20%), mortgages in good standing (12%), common & preferred stock (4%), and misc. investments (7%).

Investments in Affiliates: None
Group Affiliation: UNIFI Mutual Holding Co
Licensed in: All states except AL
Commenced Business: December 1867
Address: 1876 Waycross Rd, Cincinnati, OH 45240
Phone: (513) 595-2200 **Domicile State:** OH **NAIC Code:** 80837

Data Date	Rating	RACR #1	RACR #2	Total Assets ($mil)	Capital ($mil)	Net Premium ($mil)	Net Income ($mil)
3-09	B-	1.21	0.65	6,180.0	202.2	225.5	-70.0
3-08	B	1.82	1.01	6,971.1	309.3	233.7	-6.2
2008	B-	1.50	0.81	6,310.6	267.0	982.3	-156.3
2007	B+	1.93	1.06	7,284.9	321.1	921.5	-0.1
2006	B+	2.19	1.18	7,093.7	327.1	914.3	-9.1
2005	B	2.03	1.05	6,685.1	336.9	889.1	18.3
2004	B-	1.99	1.02	6,499.4	337.7	679.5	10.4

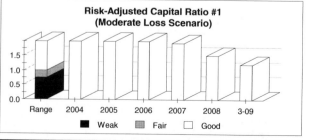

Risk-Adjusted Capital Ratio #1
(Moderate Loss Scenario)

UNION FIDELITY LIFE INSURANCE COMPANY   C-   Fair

Major Rating Factors: Poor current capitalization (2.5 on a scale of 0 to 10) based on weak risk adjusted capital (moderate loss scenario), although results have slipped from the fair range during the last year. Low quality investment portfolio (1.0) containing large holdings of BBB rated bonds in addition to significant exposure to junk bonds. Weak profitability (1.6) with operating losses during the first three months of 2009.

Other Rating Factors: Weak overall results on stability tests (2.5) including weak risk adjusted capital in prior years. Excellent liquidity (9.2).

Principal Business: Reinsurance (80%), group health insurance (9%), group life insurance (7%), individual life insurance (2%), and individual health insurance (2%).

Principal Investments: NonCMO investment grade bonds (78%), mortgages in good standing (6%), CMOs and structured securities (6%), noninv. grade bonds (4%), and misc. investments (7%).

Investments in Affiliates: None
Group Affiliation: General Electric Corp Group
Licensed in: All states except AL
Commenced Business: February 1926
Address: 123 N Wacker Dr, Chicago, IL 60606
Phone: (215) 953-3427   **Domicile State:** IL   **NAIC Code:** 62596

Data Date	Rating	RACR #1	RACR #2	Total Assets ($mil)	Capital ($mil)	Net Premium ($mil)	Net Income ($mil)
3-09	C-	0.69	0.34	18,236.1	387.6	79.1	-48.1
3-08	C	0.92	0.46	17,859.6	409.7	81.0	0.6
2008	C	0.83	0.41	18,264.4	456.3	357.6	-512.1
2007	C	0.93	0.46	18,204.1	414.4	362.4	-41.0
2006	C	1.58	0.80	18,253.6	772.8	394.5	32.7
2005	C	1.68	0.83	19,119.7	891.3	438.7	166.4
2004	C	1.40	0.69	19,298.8	785.0	645.9	-1,765.3

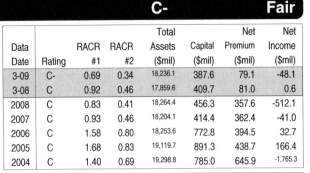

Junk Bonds as a % of Capital

Capital — $456 mil.
Junk Bonds — $709 mil.

0% 20% 40% 60% 80% 100% 120% 140% 160%

■ BB   ▨ B   ▥ CCC   □ In default

UNION LABOR LIFE INSURANCE COMPANY   C+   Fair

Major Rating Factors: Fair profitability (3.3 on a scale of 0 to 10) with investment income below regulatory standards in relation to interest assumptions of reserves. Fair overall results on stability tests (4.8) including negative cash flow from operations for 2008. Strong capitalization (7.4) based on excellent risk adjusted capital (severe loss scenario).

Other Rating Factors: High quality investment portfolio (8.4). Excellent liquidity (7.4).

Principal Business: Reinsurance (32%), group life insurance (30%), group health insurance (25%), individual health insurance (8%), and group retirement contracts (3%).

Principal Investments: CMOs and structured securities (53%), nonCMO investment grade bonds (39%), mortgages in good standing (5%), and common & preferred stock (3%).

Investments in Affiliates: 3%
Group Affiliation: Union Labor Group
Licensed in: All states except AL
Commenced Business: May 1927
Address: 111 Massachusetts Ave NW, Washington, DC 20001-1625
Phone: (202) 682-6690   **Domicile State:** MD   **NAIC Code:** 69744

Data Date	Rating	RACR #1	RACR #2	Total Assets ($mil)	Capital ($mil)	Net Premium ($mil)	Net Income ($mil)
3-09	C+	1.89	1.27	4,145.0	107.1	39.3	3.3
3-08	C+	2.19	1.50	4,152.7	129.8	42.8	4.1
2008	C+	1.86	1.24	4,364.9	107.8	160.3	4.1
2007	C	2.13	1.47	4,058.0	126.2	195.6	-16.5
2006	C	2.46	1.73	3,496.0	139.4	221.7	-0.4
2005	D+	2.39	1.71	3,347.1	139.7	263.7	47.2
2004	D+	1.36	0.97	3,075.7	88.3	292.7	16.6

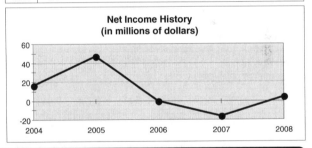

Net Income History
(in millions of dollars)

UNION NATIONAL LIFE INSURANCE COMPANY *   A   Excellent

Major Rating Factors: Good overall profitability (6.8 on a scale of 0 to 10). Excellent expense controls. Return on equity has been good over the last five years, averaging 11.9%. Good liquidity (6.2) with sufficient resources to handle a spike in claims. Excellent overall results on stability tests (7.4) excellent operational trends and excellent risk diversification.

Other Rating Factors: Strong capitalization (8.9) based on excellent risk adjusted capital (severe loss scenario). High quality investment portfolio (7.4).

Principal Business: Individual life insurance (92%) and individual health insurance (8%).

Principal Investments: NonCMO investment grade bonds (62%), CMOs and structured securities (13%), policy loans (9%), cash (7%), and misc. investments (10%).

Investments in Affiliates: None
Group Affiliation: Unitrin Inc
Licensed in: AK, CA, GA, HI, ME, MO, OR, TX, UT
Commenced Business: July 1930
Address: 12115 Lackland Road, St Louis, MO 63146
Phone: (800) 765-0550   **Domicile State:** LA   **NAIC Code:** 69779

Data Date	Rating	RACR #1	RACR #2	Total Assets ($mil)	Capital ($mil)	Net Premium ($mil)	Net Income ($mil)
3-09	A	3.87	2.25	459.3	72.1	21.9	2.8
3-08	A	3.70	2.19	438.2	64.7	21.5	2.2
2008	A	3.80	2.22	448.7	68.7	78.4	10.0
2007	A	3.75	2.23	429.7	62.3	81.9	11.5
2006	A	3.44	2.07	414.1	56.1	87.8	14.9
2005	A	4.73	2.90	444.8	104.8	83.3	10.3
2004	A	4.12	2.52	420.8	85.1	85.3	16.3

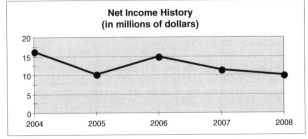

Net Income History
(in millions of dollars)

UNION SECURITY INSURANCE COMPANY

C+   **Fair**

Major Rating Factors: Fair liquidity (3.4 on a scale of 0 to 10) due, in part, to cash value policies that are subject to withdrawals with minimal or no penalty. Fair overall results on stability tests (3.3) including negative cash flow from operations for 2008. Good capitalization (5.6) based on good risk adjusted capital (severe loss scenario).

Other Rating Factors: Good quality investment portfolio (5.4). Good overall profitability (6.1) despite operating losses during the first three months of 2009.

Principal Business: Group health insurance (57%), group life insurance (15%), reinsurance (13%), individual life insurance (8%), and other lines (8%).

Principal Investments: NonCMO investment grade bonds (56%), mortgages in good standing (22%), common & preferred stock (8%), noninv. grade bonds (7%), and misc. investments (6%).

Investments in Affiliates: None

Group Affiliation: Assurant Inc

Licensed in: All states except AL, NC

Commenced Business: September 1910

Address: 500 Bielenberg Dr, Woodbury, MN 55125

Phone: (612) 738-5063 **Domicile State:** IA **NAIC Code:** 70408

Data Date	Rating	RACR #1	RACR #2	Total Assets ($mil)	Capital ($mil)	Net Premium ($mil)	Net Income ($mil)
3-09	C+	1.35	0.83	5,293.4	338.7	277.3	-11.6
3-08	C+	1.71	1.05	6,713.6	454.6	303.0	14.5
2008	C+	1.39	0.85	5,523.8	350.4	1,213.6	1.8
2007	C+	1.67	1.03	7,195.2	438.9	1,255.6	138.5
2006	C+	1.93	1.20	7,494.7	515.1	958.0	212.9
2005	B-	1.73	1.07	8,408.6	535.0	1,802.5	127.1
2004	B-	1.99	1.26	8,129.8	584.2	1,839.2	123.8

Exposure to Withdrawals Without Penalty (as a % of capital)

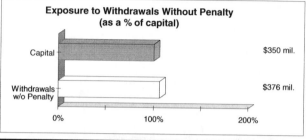

Capital — $350 mil.

Withdrawals w/o Penalty — $376 mil.

0%   100%   200%

UNION SECURITY LIFE INSURANCE COMPANY OF NEW YORK

B   **Good**

Major Rating Factors: Good overall results on stability tests (5.6 on a scale of 0 to 10) despite fair financial strength of affiliated Assurant Inc. Other stability subfactors include good operational trends and excellent risk diversification. Good quality investment portfolio (6.7) despite significant exposure to mortgages . Mortgage default rate has been low. substantial holdings of BBB bonds in addition to small junk bond holdings. Good overall profitability (6.6).

Other Rating Factors: Strong capitalization (9.5) based on excellent risk adjusted capital (severe loss scenario). Excellent liquidity (7.7).

Principal Business: Group health insurance (39%), reinsurance (28%), individual health insurance (11%), group life insurance (9%), and other lines (13%).

Principal Investments: NonCMO investment grade bonds (59%), mortgages in good standing (19%), CMOs and structured securities (9%), common & preferred stock (7%), and misc. investments (6%).

Investments in Affiliates: None

Group Affiliation: Assurant Inc

Licensed in: NC

Commenced Business: April 1974

Address: 220 Salina Meadows Pkwy #255, Syracuse, NY 13212

Phone: (315) 451-0066 **Domicile State:** NY **NAIC Code:** 81477

Data Date	Rating	RACR #1	RACR #2	Total Assets ($mil)	Capital ($mil)	Net Premium ($mil)	Net Income ($mil)
3-09	B	4.00	2.67	168.5	47.0	12.1	1.7
3-08	B	4.20	2.76	177.3	48.7	13.8	2.8
2008	B	3.80	2.57	172.0	46.0	64.8	4.3
2007	B	3.90	2.58	178.6	45.0	59.9	5.7
2006	B	4.51	3.00	179.6	52.1	60.9	14.5
2005	B	4.28	2.87	181.8	49.0	59.0	10.5
2004	C+	3.30	2.26	189.0	43.0	61.4	11.1

Assurant Inc
Composite Group Rating: C+
Largest Group Members

	Assets ($mil)	Rating
UNION SECURITY INS CO	5524	C+
AMERICAN MEMORIAL LIFE INS CO	1996	B-
AMERICAN SECURITY INS CO	1881	B
AMERICAN BANKERS INS CO OF FL	1270	B-
TIME INS CO	678	B-

UNITED AMERICAN INSURANCE COMPANY

B   **Good**

Major Rating Factors: Good quality investment portfolio (5.8 on a scale of 0 to 10) despite mixed results such as: large holdings of BBB rated bonds but moderate junk bond exposure. Good liquidity (6.8) with sufficient resources to cover a large increase in policy surrenders. Fair overall capitalization (3.7) based on mixed results -- excessive policy leverage mitigated by fair risk adjusted capital (moderate loss scenario).

Other Rating Factors: Fair overall results on stability tests (4.1) including fair risk adjusted capital in prior years. Excellent profitability (8.3) with operating gains in each of the last five years.

Principal Business: Individual health insurance (75%), individual annuities (15%), group health insurance (6%), and individual life insurance (4%).

Principal Investments: NonCMO investment grade bonds (81%), common & preferred stock (11%), and noninv. grade bonds (3%).

Investments in Affiliates: 5%

Group Affiliation: Torchmark Corp

Licensed in: All states except AL, NC

Commenced Business: August 1981

Address: 10306 Regency Parkway Dr, Omaha, NE 68114

Phone: (972) 529-5085 **Domicile State:** NE **NAIC Code:** 92916

Data Date	Rating	RACR #1	RACR #2	Total Assets ($mil)	Capital ($mil)	Net Premium ($mil)	Net Income ($mil)
3-09	B	0.81	0.59	1,504.7	130.8	210.8	11.6
3-08	B-	0.88	0.66	1,387.7	151.2	232.8	14.8
2008	B	1.10	0.81	1,384.7	183.1	851.8	78.9
2007	B-	0.96	0.73	1,309.6	168.5	953.0	61.5
2006	B-	1.05	0.79	1,192.6	178.2	950.0	64.6
2005	B	1.41	1.04	1,139.9	189.3	737.1	83.4
2004	B+	1.27	0.93	1,080.0	175.5	758.5	68.6

Rating Indexes

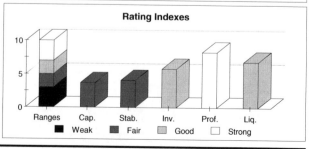

Ranges   Cap.   Stab.   Inv.   Prof.   Liq.

■ Weak   ■ Fair   ▨ Good   ☐ Strong

UNITED FARM FAMILY LIFE INSURANCE COMPANY *   A   Excellent

Major Rating Factors: Good quality investment portfolio (6.5 on a scale of 0 to 10) despite significant exposure to mortgages . Mortgage default rate has been low. substantial holdings of BBB bonds in addition to small junk bond holdings. Good liquidity (6.5) with sufficient resources to handle a spike in claims as well as a significant increase in policy surrenders. Strong capitalization (7.9) based on excellent risk adjusted capital (severe loss scenario).

Other Rating Factors: Excellent profitability (7.0) with operating gains in each of the last five years. Excellent overall results on stability tests (7.4) excellent operational trends and excellent risk diversification.

Principal Business: Individual life insurance (83%), individual annuities (10%), reinsurance (6%), and individual health insurance (1%).

Principal Investments: NonCMO investment grade bonds (49%), CMOs and structured securities (21%), mortgages in good standing (15%), policy loans (6%), and misc. investments (8%).

Investments in Affiliates: 1%
Group Affiliation: Indiana Farm Bureau
Licensed in: IA, OK
Commenced Business: May 1964
Address: 225 S East St, Indianapolis, IN 46202
Phone: (317) 692-7200 **Domicile State:** IN **NAIC Code:** 69892

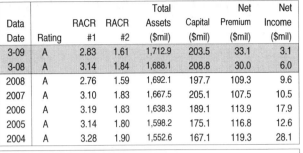

Data Date	Rating	RACR #1	RACR #2	Total Assets ($mil)	Capital ($mil)	Net Premium ($mil)	Net Income ($mil)
3-09	A	2.83	1.61	1,712.9	203.5	33.1	3.1
3-08	A	3.14	1.84	1,688.1	208.8	30.0	6.0
2008	A	2.76	1.59	1,692.1	197.7	109.3	9.6
2007	A	3.10	1.83	1,667.5	205.1	107.5	10.5
2006	A	3.19	1.83	1,638.3	189.1	113.9	17.9
2005	A	3.14	1.80	1,598.2	175.1	116.8	12.6
2004	A	3.28	1.90	1,552.6	167.1	119.3	28.1

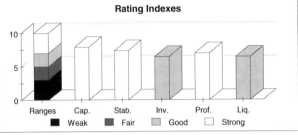

Rating Indexes

Ranges / Cap. / Stab. / Inv. / Prof. / Liq.
■ Weak ■ Fair ▨ Good □ Strong

UNITED FIDELITY LIFE INSURANCE COMPANY   D+   Weak

Major Rating Factors: Poor current capitalization (1.6 on a scale of 0 to 10) based on weak risk adjusted capital (severe loss scenario), although results have slipped from the fair range over the last two years. Weak overall results on stability tests (1.6) including weak risk adjusted capital in prior years and negative cash flow from operations for 2008. Fair quality investment portfolio (3.8).

Other Rating Factors: Fair profitability (3.1) with operating losses during the first three months of 2009. Good liquidity (6.2).

Principal Business: Individual life insurance (48%), reinsurance (47%), individual health insurance (2%), individual annuities (2%), and group life insurance (1%).

Principal Investments: Common & preferred stock (50%), nonCMO investment grade bonds (18%), CMOs and structured securities (12%), mortgages in good standing (8%), and misc. investments (12%).

Investments in Affiliates: 49%
Group Affiliation: Americo Life Inc
Licensed in: All states except AL, DC, ID, MD, MN, MS, NJ, NM, NC, VA
Commenced Business: September 1977
Address: 500 North Akard, Dallas, TX 75201
Phone: (816) 391-2000 **Domicile State:** TX **NAIC Code:** 87645

Data Date	Rating	RACR #1	RACR #2	Total Assets ($mil)	Capital ($mil)	Net Premium ($mil)	Net Income ($mil)
3-09	D+	0.41	0.38	555.0	182.8	2.9	-3.9
3-08	C-	0.47	0.44	599.1	206.9	5.6	-3.0
2008	D+	0.46	0.43	572.1	196.5	25.0	8.9
2007	C-	0.54	0.51	609.7	226.1	28.5	0.2
2006	D	0.51	0.48	612.0	212.5	29.3	4.7
2005	D	0.52	0.48	610.3	201.0	30.1	-38.1
2004	D	0.45	0.42	601.8	173.6	37.9	48.0

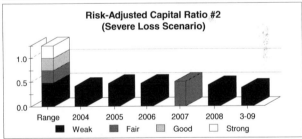

Risk-Adjusted Capital Ratio #2
(Severe Loss Scenario)

Range / 2004 / 2005 / 2006 / 2007 / 2008 / 3-09
■ Weak ■ Fair ▨ Good □ Strong

UNITED HEALTHCARE INSURANCE COMPANY   C+   Fair

Major Rating Factors: Fair overall capitalization (3.2 on a scale of 0 to 10) based on mixed results -- excessive policy leverage mitigated by fair risk adjusted capital (severe loss scenario). Fair overall results on stability tests (3.5) including fair risk adjusted capital in prior years. Weak liquidity (1.5) as a spike in claims may stretch capacity.

Other Rating Factors: High quality investment portfolio (7.4). Excellent profitability (8.7) with operating gains in each of the last five years.

Principal Business: Group health insurance (64%), individual health insurance (23%), and reinsurance (12%).

Principal Investments: NonCMO investment grade bonds (70%), CMOs and structured securities (23%), and common & preferred stock (11%).

Investments in Affiliates: 12%
Group Affiliation: UnitedHealth Group Inc
Licensed in: All states except AL, NC
Commenced Business: April 1972
Address: 450 Columbus Blvd, Hartford, CT 06115
Phone: (860) 702-5000 **Domicile State:** CT **NAIC Code:** 79413

Data Date	Rating	RACR #1	RACR #2	Total Assets ($mil)	Capital ($mil)	Net Premium ($mil)	Net Income ($mil)
3-09	C+	0.71	0.60	10,972.7	2,736.6	9,354.3	461.2
3-08	B	0.75	0.64	10,904.7	2,720.6	8,309.0	434.6
2008	C+	0.61	0.51	10,522.9	2,821.6	32,326.0	1,867.0
2007	B	0.72	0.61	11,425.5	3,104.9	29,378.6	2,290.3
2006	B	0.66	0.57	10,260.2	2,464.3	25,509.3	2,195.1
2005	B	0.68	0.59	7,293.8	1,841.2	17,969.9	1,815.9
2004	B-	0.60	0.52	6,300.5	1,280.4	14,505.9	1,452.4

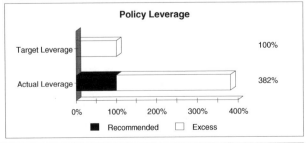

Policy Leverage

Target Leverage — 100%
Actual Leverage — 382%

0% / 100% / 200% / 300% / 400%
■ Recommended □ Excess

UNITED HEALTHCARE INSURANCE COMPANY OF IL | B | Good

Major Rating Factors: Good overall results on stability tests (6.0 on a scale of 0 to 10). Stability strengths include excellent operational trends, excellent risk adjusted capital for prior years and excellent risk diversification. Good overall capitalization (5.9) based on mixed results -- excessive policy leverage mitigated by excellent risk adjusted capital (severe loss scenario). Nevertheless, capital levels have fluctuated during prior years. Good liquidity (6.9).

Other Rating Factors: High quality investment portfolio (8.9). Excellent profitability (7.1) with operating gains in each of the last five years.

Principal Business: Group health insurance (100%).

Principal Investments: NonCMO investment grade bonds (93%) and CMOs and structured securities (7%).

Investments in Affiliates: None

Group Affiliation: UnitedHealth Group Inc

Licensed in: IN

Commenced Business: December 1991

Address: 233 N Michigan Ave, Chicago, IL 60601

Phone: (312) 424-4460 **Domicile State:** IL **NAIC Code:** 60318

Data Date	Rating	RACR #1	RACR #2	Total Assets ($mil)	Capital ($mil)	Net Premium ($mil)	Net Income ($mil)
3-09	B	2.65	2.17	155.4	98.6	79.2	8.4
3-08	B	2.35	1.92	127.2	80.7	72.7	6.4
2008	B	1.94	1.59	122.2	72.4	307.9	22.0
2007	B	2.18	1.79	114.8	74.3	279.0	27.4
2006	B-	2.33	1.90	110.8	73.4	256.6	26.8
2005	B-	2.48	2.03	119.8	82.1	269.0	36.8
2004	B-	2.24	1.83	135.7	88.4	322.5	41.1

Adverse Trends in Operations

Decrease in capital during 2008 (3%)
Decrease in asset base during 2006 (8%)
Decrease in capital during 2006 (11%)
Decrease in premium volume from 2004 to 2005 (17%)
Decrease in asset base during 2005 (12%)

UNITED HEALTHCARE INSURANCE COMPANY OF OH | B- | Good

Major Rating Factors: Fair current capitalization (4.6 on a scale of 0 to 10) based on mixed results -- excessive policy leverage mitigated by excellent risk adjusted capital (severe loss scenario) reflecting significant improvement over results in 2004. Good liquidity (5.4) with sufficient resources to handle a spike in claims. Good overall results on stability tests (5.3) despite fair risk adjusted capital in prior years excellent operational trends and excellent risk diversification.

Other Rating Factors: High quality investment portfolio (8.8). Excellent profitability (8.3) with operating gains in each of the last five years.

Principal Business: Group health insurance (100%).

Principal Investments: NonCMO investment grade bonds (87%) and CMOs and structured securities (13%).

Investments in Affiliates: None

Group Affiliation: UnitedHealth Group Inc

Licensed in: OK

Commenced Business: July 1991

Address: 9200 Worthington Rd, Columbus, OH 43082

Phone: (614) 410-7000 **Domicile State:** OH **NAIC Code:** 73518

Data Date	Rating	RACR #1	RACR #2	Total Assets ($mil)	Capital ($mil)	Net Premium ($mil)	Net Income ($mil)
3-09	B-	1.30	1.07	182.1	81.0	117.9	11.2
3-08	B-	1.19	0.98	170.3	76.3	135.5	7.5
2008	B-	1.08	0.89	154.6	69.7	530.7	27.1
2007	B-	1.09	0.90	159.5	69.9	529.6	34.0
2006	C+	0.89	0.74	112.3	44.4	408.6	18.3
2005	C+	1.22	1.01	108.4	53.1	357.4	29.2
2004	C	0.87	0.72	116.4	45.0	423.5	23.3

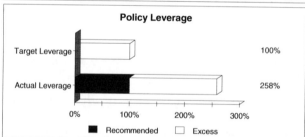

Policy Leverage

Target Leverage — 100%
Actual Leverage — 258%

0%   100%   200%   300%

■ Recommended   ☐ Excess

UNITED HERITAGE LIFE INSURANCE COMPANY | B | Good

Major Rating Factors: Good current capitalization (6.4 on a scale of 0 to 10) based on good risk adjusted capital (severe loss scenario), although results have slipped from the excellent range during the last year. Good overall profitability (6.3) despite operating losses during the first three months of 2009. Return on equity has been fair, averaging 6.7%. Good overall results on stability tests (5.7) excellent operational trends, excellent risk adjusted capital for prior years and good risk diversification.

Other Rating Factors: Fair quality investment portfolio (4.1). Fair liquidity (4.8).

Principal Business: Individual life insurance (56%), individual annuities (34%), group life insurance (5%), group health insurance (3%), and group retirement contracts (2%).

Principal Investments: NonCMO investment grade bonds (46%), CMOs and structured securities (29%), mortgages in good standing (9%), noninv. grade bonds (5%), and misc. investments (11%).

Investments in Affiliates: None

Group Affiliation: United Heritage Mutual Holding co

Licensed in: AZ, AR, CA, CO, CT, ID, IL, IN, IA, KS, KY, ME, MS, MT, NE, NV, NH, NY, OH, OR, PA, TN, UT, VT, WV, WY, PR

Commenced Business: September 1935

Address: 707 East United Heritage Ct, Meridian, ID 83642-3527

Phone: (208) 466-7856 **Domicile State:** ID **NAIC Code:** 63983

Data Date	Rating	RACR #1	RACR #2	Total Assets ($mil)	Capital ($mil)	Net Premium ($mil)	Net Income ($mil)
3-09	B	1.84	0.92	422.8	37.4	14.7	-0.3
3-08	B	2.14	1.12	426.5	40.9	20.9	0.2
2008	B	2.03	1.03	420.5	40.0	56.9	-5.1
2007	B	2.18	1.14	411.7	41.6	62.6	1.7
2006	B	2.47	1.32	409.8	41.2	52.2	2.0
2005	B	2.59	1.39	410.0	41.0	44.7	2.0
2004	B	2.25	1.24	394.1	34.0	46.6	3.7

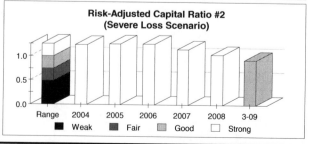

Risk-Adjusted Capital Ratio #2
(Severe Loss Scenario)

1.0

0.5

0.0

Range   2004   2005   2006   2007   2008   3-09

■ Weak   ■ Fair   ▨ Good   ☐ Strong

UNITED INSURANCE COMPANY OF AMERICA

B- **Good**

Major Rating Factors: Good current capitalization (5.7 on a scale of 0 to 10) based on good risk adjusted capital (moderate loss scenario) reflecting some improvement over results in 2008. Good overall profitability (6.6) despite operating losses during the first three months of 2009. Return on equity has been excellent over the last five years averaging 19.6%. Good liquidity (5.6).

Other Rating Factors: Good overall results on stability tests (5.1) despite fair risk adjusted capital in prior years good operational trends and excellent risk diversification. Fair quality investment portfolio (3.1).

Principal Business: Individual life insurance (93%) and individual health insurance (7%).

Principal Investments: NonCMO investment grade bonds (48%), common & preferred stock (11%), CMOs and structured securities (10%), noninv. grade bonds (9%), and misc. investments (21%).

Investments in Affiliates: 2%

Group Affiliation: Unitrin Inc

Licensed in: All states except AL, AZ, NC

Commenced Business: April 1928

Address: One E Wacker Dr, Chicago, IL 60601

Phone: (312) 661-4681 **Domicile State:** IL **NAIC Code:** 69930

Data Date	Rating	RACR #1	RACR #2	Total Assets ($mil)	Capital ($mil)	Net Premium ($mil)	Net Income ($mil)
3-09	B-	1.46	0.80	2,036.1	206.1	50.5	-9.2
3-08	B-	1.61	0.88	2,075.6	206.5	52.0	5.9
2008	B-	1.36	0.74	2,005.0	190.2	201.8	-5.6
2007	B-	1.69	0.95	2,055.2	204.2	213.8	31.9
2006	B	1.73	0.95	2,032.7	208.8	225.8	45.2
2005	B	1.94	1.15	1,959.2	179.8	234.3	-38.6
2004	B+	0.98	0.80	2,025.7	326.1	237.2	63.1

Risk-Adjusted Capital Ratio #1
(Moderate Loss Scenario)

Range 2004 2005 2006 2007 2008 3-09
■ Weak ▨ Fair □ Good

UNITED INVESTORS LIFE INSURANCE COMPANY *

B+ **Good**

Major Rating Factors: Good overall results on stability tests (5.7 on a scale of 0 to 10). Stability strengths include good operational trends and excellent risk diversification. Good quality investment portfolio (6.2) despite mixed results such as: no exposure to mortgages and large holdings of BBB rated bonds but small junk bond holdings. Good liquidity (6.4).

Other Rating Factors: Strong capitalization (10.0) based on excellent risk adjusted capital (severe loss scenario). Excellent profitability (8.9) with operating gains in each of the last five years.

Principal Business: Reinsurance (63%), individual life insurance (33%), and group life insurance (3%).

Principal Investments: NonCMO investment grade bonds (66%), common & preferred stock (21%), noninv. grade bonds (6%), policy loans (3%), and cash (1%).

Investments in Affiliates: 18%

Group Affiliation: Torchmark Corp

Licensed in: All states except AL, NC

Commenced Business: October 1981

Address: 120 S Central Ave, Clayton, MO 63105

Phone: (800) 318-4542 **Domicile State:** MO **NAIC Code:** 94099

Data Date	Rating	RACR #1	RACR #2	Total Assets ($mil)	Capital ($mil)	Net Premium ($mil)	Net Income ($mil)
3-09	B+	6.15	3.29	2,518.4	380.2	94.3	4.4
3-08	B	6.28	3.47	2,987.8	390.4	93.1	10.6
2008	B+	6.64	3.68	2,543.2	421.0	255.1	39.9
2007	B	6.26	3.43	3,058.4	389.6	239.5	62.7
2006	B	6.56	3.63	3,046.8	386.7	203.9	65.8
2005	B	4.38	2.43	3,047.4	298.6	146.8	72.7
2004	B	3.32	1.82	2,966.3	194.5	176.3	54.4

Adverse Trends in Operations

Decrease in asset base during 2008 (17%)
Change in premium mix from 2005 to 2006 (4.8%)
Decrease in premium volume from 2004 to 2005 (17%)

UNITED LIFE INSURANCE COMPANY

B **Good**

Major Rating Factors: Good overall results on stability tests (6.5 on a scale of 0 to 10) despite negative cash flow from operations for 2008. Other stability subfactors include excellent operational trends and excellent risk diversification. Good quality investment portfolio (6.1) despite mixed results such as: large holdings of BBB rated bonds but moderate junk bond exposure. Good liquidity (6.9).

Other Rating Factors: Strong capitalization (7.7) based on excellent risk adjusted capital (severe loss scenario). Excellent profitability (7.9) with operating gains in each of the last five years.

Principal Business: N/A

Principal Investments: NonCMO investment grade bonds (89%), noninv. grade bonds (6%), CMOs and structured securities (3%), common & preferred stock (1%), and misc. investments (2%).

Investments in Affiliates: None

Group Affiliation: United Fire & Casualty Group

Licensed in: AK, AR, CA, CT, GA, IL, IN, IA, KS, KY, ME, MN, MS, MO, MT, NE, NV, NY, OH, OK, OR, TN, TX, UT, VT, WY, PR

Commenced Business: October 1962

Address: 118 Second Ave SE, Cedar Rapids, IA 52401

Phone: (800) 553-7937 **Domicile State:** IA **NAIC Code:** 69973

Data Date	Rating	RACR #1	RACR #2	Total Assets ($mil)	Capital ($mil)	Net Premium ($mil)	Net Income ($mil)
3-09	B	2.90	1.45	1,359.1	153.3	72.0	-0.1
3-08	B	3.07	1.57	1,371.0	164.2	38.1	1.7
2008	B	2.96	1.47	1,322.0	157.0	197.0	0.6
2007	B	3.13	1.61	1,356.7	164.2	194.8	15.1
2006	B	2.87	1.47	1,393.2	151.7	180.1	18.0
2005	B-	2.51	1.25	1,433.1	135.4	99.9	17.6
2004	C+	2.28	1.12	1,396.0	124.5	81.0	16.9

Adverse Trends in Operations

Decrease in capital during 2008 (4%)
Decrease in asset base during 2008 (3%)
Increase in policy surrenders from 2006 to 2007 (2834%)
Decrease in asset base during 2007 (3%)
Decrease in asset base during 2006 (3%)

UNITED OF OMAHA LIFE INSURANCE COMPANY *   B+   Good

Major Rating Factors: Good quality investment portfolio (5.6 on a scale of 0 to 10) despite large holdings of BBB rated bonds in addition to moderate junk bond exposure. Exposure to mortgages is significant, but the mortgage default rate has been low. Good liquidity (6.2) with sufficient resources to cover a large increase in policy surrenders. Good overall results on stability tests (6.4) excellent operational trends and excellent risk diversification.

Other Rating Factors: Fair profitability (4.8) with operating losses during the first three months of 2009. Strong capitalization (7.2) based on excellent risk adjusted capital (severe loss scenario).

Principal Business: Individual life insurance (41%), group health insurance (18%), group life insurance (15%), individual annuities (12%), and other lines (14%).

Principal Investments: CMOs and structured securities (39%), nonCMO investment grade bonds (35%), mortgages in good standing (14%), noninv. grade bonds (5%), and misc. investments (6%).

Investments in Affiliates: 4%

Group Affiliation: Mutual Of Omaha Group

Licensed in: All states except AL, NC

Commenced Business: November 1926

Address: Mutual Of Omaha Plaza, Omaha, NE 68175

Phone: (402) 342-7600 **Domicile State:** NE **NAIC Code:** 69868

Data Date	Rating	RACR #1	RACR #2	Total Assets ($mil)	Capital ($mil)	Net Premium ($mil)	Net Income ($mil)
3-09	B+	1.96	1.12	12,875.0	1,155.9	533.8	-33.8
3-08	B+	2.54	1.45	13,174.6	1,353.7	431.7	-5.3
2008	B+	2.05	1.18	12,879.2	1,196.3	1,854.0	-69.6
2007	B+	2.55	1.46	13,227.9	1,358.1	1,465.0	88.6
2006	B+	2.43	1.36	12,866.3	1,219.9	1,260.3	11.3
2005	B+	2.30	1.25	12,803.8	1,208.2	1,212.2	3.1
2004	B+	2.17	1.12	12,937.2	1,226.3	1,292.3	-50.7

Adverse Trends in Operations

Decrease in asset base during 2008 (3%)
Decrease in capital during 2008 (12%)
Decrease in capital during 2005 (1%)
Increase in policy surrenders from 2004 to 2005 (47%)
Decrease in premium volume from 2004 to 2005 (6%)

UNITED STATES LIFE INSURANCE COMPANY IN NYC   C   Fair

Major Rating Factors: Fair overall results on stability tests (4.1 on a scale of 0 to 10) including fair risk adjusted capital in prior years. Good current capitalization (6.8) based on good risk adjusted capital (severe loss scenario) reflecting some improvement over results in 2008. Good quality investment portfolio (5.2).

Other Rating Factors: Good liquidity (6.1). Weak profitability (1.8).

Principal Business: N/A

Principal Investments: NonCMO investment grade bonds (58%), CMOs and structured securities (22%), mortgages in good standing (8%), noninv. grade bonds (6%), and misc. investments (6%).

Investments in Affiliates: 3%

Group Affiliation: American International Group

Licensed in: All states except AL

Commenced Business: March 1850

Address: 390 Park Ave, New York, NY 10022-4684

Phone: (212) 709-6000 **Domicile State:** NY **NAIC Code:** 70106

Data Date	Rating	RACR #1	RACR #2	Total Assets ($mil)	Capital ($mil)	Net Premium ($mil)	Net Income ($mil)
3-09	C	1.80	0.98	5,259.4	257.9	131.9	13.5
3-08	C	2.46	1.34	5,316.0	417.5	151.0	-59.7
2008	C	1.31	0.71	5,318.3	251.4	631.8	-642.9
2007	C+	2.22	1.20	5,314.7	472.4	812.7	72.3
2006	C+	2.61	1.31	4,252.0	390.1	287.4	47.2
2005	C+	2.48	1.26	4,112.7	337.3	317.6	-140.7
2004	B	3.01	1.52	3,775.2	401.4	313.1	-147.1

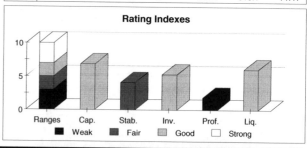

Rating Indexes

Ranges · Cap. · Stab. · Inv. · Prof. · Liq.
■ Weak ■ Fair ▨ Good □ Strong

UNITED TEACHER ASSOCIATES INSURANCE COMPANY   B-   Good

Major Rating Factors: Good overall results on stability tests (5.3 on a scale of 0 to 10) despite fair financial strength of affiliated American Financial Corp. Other stability subfactors include excellent operational trends and excellent risk diversification. Good current capitalization (6.0) based on good risk adjusted capital (severe loss scenario), although results have slipped from the excellent range over the last two years. Good quality investment portfolio (5.6).

Other Rating Factors: Good overall profitability (6.6) despite operating losses during the first three months of 2009. Good liquidity (6.1).

Principal Business: Individual health insurance (72%), group health insurance (12%), reinsurance (8%), group retirement contracts (4%), and individual life insurance (4%).

Principal Investments: NonCMO investment grade bonds (65%), CMOs and structured securities (26%), noninv. grade bonds (5%), policy loans (4%), and real estate (1%).

Investments in Affiliates: None

Group Affiliation: American Financial Corp

Licensed in: All states except AL, NJ, NC, SC, VA

Commenced Business: January 1959

Address: 5508 Parkcrest Dr, Austin, TX 78731

Phone: (512) 451-2224 **Domicile State:** TX **NAIC Code:** 63479

Data Date	Rating	RACR #1	RACR #2	Total Assets ($mil)	Capital ($mil)	Net Premium ($mil)	Net Income ($mil)
3-09	B-	1.41	0.87	512.0	58.5	49.1	-0.4
3-08	B-	1.50	0.97	505.0	60.0	52.0	-3.0
2008	B-	1.45	0.92	506.4	58.6	204.1	-8.0
2007	B-	1.62	1.05	499.3	65.7	217.7	3.0
2006	B-	1.77	1.15	488.1	70.2	231.1	6.4
2005	C+	1.69	1.13	463.8	64.7	232.4	4.2
2004	C+	1.66	1.12	387.0	60.6	227.5	7.2

American Financial Corp
Composite Group Rating: C+

Largest Group Members	Assets ($mil)	Rating
GREAT AMERICAN LIFE INS CO	9628	B-
GREAT AMERICAN INS CO	5642	C
ANNUITY INVESTORS LIFE INS CO	1742	B-
REPUBLIC INDEMNITY CO OF AMERICA	858	B-
NATIONAL INTERSTATE INS CO	730	C+

UNITED WORLD LIFE INSURANCE COMPANY *

B+　**Good**

Major Rating Factors: Good overall results on stability tests (6.7 on a scale of 0 to 10). Stability strengths include excellent operational trends and excellent risk diversification. Strong capitalization (7.6) based on excellent risk adjusted capital (severe loss scenario). Moreover, capital levels have been consistently high over the last five years. High quality investment portfolio (7.4).

Other Rating Factors: Excellent profitability (7.8) with operating gains in each of the last five years. Excellent liquidity (8.2).

Principal Business: Individual health insurance (99%) and individual life insurance (1%).

Principal Investments: NonCMO investment grade bonds (64%), CMOs and structured securities (18%), cash (14%), noninv. grade bonds (3%), and policy loans (1%).

Investments in Affiliates: None

Group Affiliation: Mutual Of Omaha Group

Licensed in: All states except AL, DC, NC

Commenced Business: April 1970

Address: Mutual Of Omaha Plaza, Omaha, NE 68175

Phone: (402) 342-7600　**Domicile State:** NE　**NAIC Code:** 72850

Data Date	Rating	RACR #1	RACR #2	Total Assets ($mil)	Capital ($mil)	Net Premium ($mil)	Net Income ($mil)
3-09	B+	3.33	1.40	114.6	40.3	0.5	0.5
3-08	B+	3.76	1.63	100.4	33.1	0.5	0.7
2008	B+	3.01	1.27	90.6	34.8	2.4	1.9
2007	B	2.72	1.24	91.9	22.6	2.6	2.4
2006	B	2.59	1.76	79.7	20.0	2.8	2.4
2005	B	2.46	2.21	69.1	17.7	3.0	2.2
2004	B	2.49	2.24	64.2	17.5	3.2	2.2

Adverse Trends in Operations

Decrease in premium volume from 2007 to 2008 (8%)
Increase in policy surrenders from 2007 to 2008 (37%)
Decrease in asset base during 2008 (1%)
Decrease in premium volume from 2005 to 2006 (7%)
Decrease in premium volume from 2004 to 2005 (6%)

UNIVERSAL GUARANTY LIFE INSURANCE COMPANY

C-　**Fair**

Major Rating Factors: Fair quality investment portfolio (4.5 on a scale of 0 to 10) with significant exposure to mortgages . Mortgage default rate has been low. Fair overall results on stability tests (3.0) including negative cash flow from operations for 2008 and fair risk adjusted capital in prior years. Good capitalization (5.1) based on good risk adjusted capital (moderate loss scenario).

Other Rating Factors: Good profitability (5.0). Good liquidity (6.0).

Principal Business: Individual life insurance (94%), individual annuities (3%), and group life insurance (2%).

Principal Investments: CMOs and structured securities (28%), common & preferred stock (18%), mortgages in good standing (17%), nonCMO investment grade bonds (16%), and misc. investments (22%).

Investments in Affiliates: 13%

Group Affiliation: UTG Inc

Licensed in: AK, AR, CA, CT, FL, GA, HI, IL, IN, IA, KS, KY, LA, ME, MI, MS, MO, MT, NE, NV, NH, NY, ND, OH, OK, OR, PA, RI, SC, SD, TN, TX, UT, VT, WA, WV, WI, WY

Commenced Business: December 1966

Address: 65 E State St Suite 2100, Columbus, OH 43215-4260

Phone: (217) 241-6300　**Domicile State:** OH　**NAIC Code:** 70130

Data Date	Rating	RACR #1	RACR #2	Total Assets ($mil)	Capital ($mil)	Net Premium ($mil)	Net Income ($mil)
3-09	C-	1.04	0.71	255.8	26.4	2.6	2.2
3-08	C-	1.16	0.81	262.1	32.3	2.6	0.3
2008	C-	1.08	0.74	256.9	27.5	9.4	4.8
2007	C-	1.20	0.84	263.1	30.1	11.2	4.7
2006	C-	1.27	0.93	262.7	31.2	11.8	5.2
2005	C-	1.22	0.83	259.8	25.6	13.1	5.1
2004	D	1.12	0.77	258.9	21.9	14.0	-0.8

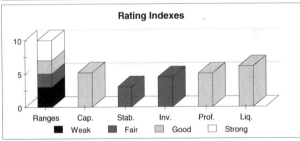

Rating Indexes

Ranges　Cap.　Stab.　Inv.　Prof.　Liq.
■ Weak　　■ Fair　　□ Good　　□ Strong

UNIVERSAL UNDERWRITERS LIFE INSURANCE COMPANY

B-　**Good**

Major Rating Factors: Good liquidity (6.9 on a scale of 0 to 10) with sufficient resources to handle a spike in claims as well as a significant increase in policy surrenders. Fair overall results on stability tests (3.5) including fair financial strength of affiliated Zurich Financial Services Group and negative cash flow from operations for 2008. Strong capitalization (10.0) based on excellent risk adjusted capital (severe loss scenario).

Other Rating Factors: High quality investment portfolio (8.1). Excellent profitability (7.9) with operating gains in each of the last five years.

Principal Business: Individual life insurance (122%), credit health insurance (12%), credit life insurance (10%), and reinsurance (1%).

Principal Investments: NonCMO investment grade bonds (53%), CMOs and structured securities (43%), policy loans (2%), and cash (2%).

Investments in Affiliates: None

Group Affiliation: Zurich Financial Services Group

Licensed in: All states except AL, NC

Commenced Business: October 1965

Address: 1600 McConnor Parkway, Schaumburg, IL 60196-6801

Phone: (847) 874-7400　**Domicile State:** KS　**NAIC Code:** 70173

Data Date	Rating	RACR #1	RACR #2	Total Assets ($mil)	Capital ($mil)	Net Premium ($mil)	Net Income ($mil)
3-09	B-	5.96	4.59	253.7	61.1	2.7	1.5
3-08	B-	4.82	3.85	276.9	52.5	2.6	5.1
2008	B-	5.81	4.79	254.0	59.6	10.7	22.1
2007	B-	4.26	3.18	328.9	46.4	-5.2	8.8
2006	B-	3.72	2.67	387.2	42.4	29.7	0.8
2005	B-	3.66	2.42	287.6	40.2	51.5	8.2
2004	B	8.61	5.57	344.8	101.6	55.4	4.4

Zurich Financial Services Group
Composite Group Rating: C
Largest Group Members

	Assets ($mil)	Rating
ZURICH AMERICAN INS CO	29634	C-
KEMPER INVESTORS LIFE INS CO	13886	C
FARMERS INS EXCHANGE	13368	C
FARMERS NEW WORLD LIFE INS CO	6444	B-
MID-CENTURY INS CO	3273	C-

UNUM LIFE INSURANCE COMPANY OF AMERICA   C+   Fair

Major Rating Factors: Fair overall results on stability tests (4.8 on a scale of 0 to 10) including fair financial strength of affiliated Unum Group. Fair quality investment portfolio (4.5) with large holdings of BBB rated bonds in addition to junk bond exposure equal to 88% of capital. Good overall profitability (5.7). Return on equity has been good over the last five years, averaging 12.2%.

Other Rating Factors: Strong capitalization (7.5) based on excellent risk adjusted capital (severe loss scenario). Excellent liquidity (7.3).

Principal Business: Group health insurance (60%), group life insurance (25%), individual health insurance (11%), reinsurance (3%), and individual life insurance (1%).

Principal Investments: NonCMO investment grade bonds (75%), CMOs and structured securities (10%), noninv. grade bonds (8%), mortgages in good standing (4%), and misc. investments (3%).

Investments in Affiliates: None
Group Affiliation: Unum Group
Licensed in: All states except AL, NC
Commenced Business: September 1966
Address: 2211 Congress St, Portland, ME 04122
Phone: (207) 770-9306 **Domicile State:** ME **NAIC Code:** 62235

Data Date	Rating	RACR #1	RACR #2	Total Assets ($mil)	Capital ($mil)	Net Premium ($mil)	Net Income ($mil)
3-09	C+	2.44	1.34	16,917.0	1,396.9	660.2	65.5
3-08	C+	2.74	1.53	16,524.5	1,474.8	666.8	38.6
2008	C+	2.41	1.33	16,890.1	1,353.3	2,720.1	190.9
2007	C+	2.78	1.56	16,438.5	1,490.5	2,786.6	195.0
2006	C+	2.27	1.44	16,025.9	1,580.1	3,272.1	-14.9
2005	C+	1.94	1.26	15,074.4	1,354.6	2,711.0	249.2
2004	C-	1.68	1.11	12,680.9	1,201.4	2,818.9	63.1

Unum Group
Composite Group Rating: C+
Largest Group Members

	Assets ($mil)	Rating
UNUM LIFE INS CO OF AMERICA	16890	C+
PROVIDENT LIFE ACCIDENT INS CO	7741	C+
PAUL REVERE LIFE INS CO	4710	C+
COLONIAL LIFE ACCIDENT INS CO	1989	C+
FIRST UNUM LIFE INS CO	1933	C+

US FINANCIAL LIFE INSURANCE COMPANY   C   Fair

Major Rating Factors: Fair liquidity (3.5 on a scale of 0 to 10) as cash from operations and sale of marketable assets may not be adequate to cover a spike in claims or a run on policy withdrawals. Fair overall results on stability tests (3.4). Good capitalization (6.2) based on good risk adjusted capital (severe loss scenario).

Other Rating Factors: Good quality investment portfolio (6.8). Weak profitability (2.6).

Principal Business: Individual life insurance (100%).

Principal Investments: NonCMO investment grade bonds (91%), policy loans (3%), noninv. grade bonds (2%), common & preferred stock (1%), and misc. investments (2%).

Investments in Affiliates: None
Group Affiliation: AXA Financial Inc
Licensed in: All states except AL, NC
Commenced Business: September 1974
Address: 6 East Fourth St, Cincinnati, OH 45202
Phone: (513) 287-6805 **Domicile State:** OH **NAIC Code:** 84530

Data Date	Rating	RACR #1	RACR #2	Total Assets ($mil)	Capital ($mil)	Net Premium ($mil)	Net Income ($mil)
3-09	C	1.66	0.90	564.1	51.5	16.3	6.6
3-08	C	1.56	0.86	552.4	45.4	17.7	0.8
2008	C	1.42	0.78	562.7	43.2	65.4	-2.9
2007	C	1.60	0.89	543.7	45.4	73.7	-27.8
2006	C	1.80	1.02	503.9	39.8	84.9	-48.3
2005	C	2.74	1.58	410.1	49.5	34.3	-36.3
2004	C	2.64	1.52	303.5	36.1	52.1	-44.9

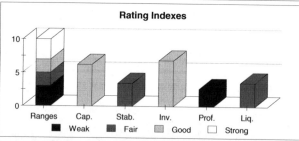

USAA LIFE INS CO OF NEW YORK *   B+   Good

Major Rating Factors: Good quality investment portfolio (5.2 on a scale of 0 to 10) despite mixed results such as: no exposure to mortgages and large holdings of BBB rated bonds but small junk bond holdings. Good overall profitability (6.7) despite operating losses during the first three months of 2009. Return on equity has been fair, averaging 8.2%. Good liquidity (5.7).

Other Rating Factors: Good overall results on stability tests (6.5) good operational trends and excellent risk diversification. Strong capitalization (7.6) based on excellent risk adjusted capital (severe loss scenario).

Principal Business: Individual annuities (70%) and individual life insurance (30%).

Principal Investments: NonCMO investment grade bonds (56%), CMOs and structured securities (30%), common & preferred stock (9%), cash (3%), and misc. investments (2%).

Investments in Affiliates: None
Group Affiliation: USAA Group
Licensed in: NC
Commenced Business: November 1997
Address: 529 Main Street, Highland Falls, NY 10928
Phone: (210) 498-8000 **Domicile State:** NY **NAIC Code:** 60228

Data Date	Rating	RACR #1	RACR #2	Total Assets ($mil)	Capital ($mil)	Net Premium ($mil)	Net Income ($mil)
3-09	B+	2.66	1.38	401.5	39.9	23.3	0.0
3-08	A-	3.18	1.76	334.2	41.1	11.9	0.8
2008	B+	2.66	1.45	377.2	40.1	56.8	1.6
2007	A-	3.15	1.75	321.9	40.3	22.5	2.6
2006	A-	3.80	2.08	306.8	43.4	21.4	3.0
2005	A-	4.20	2.28	296.3	46.4	21.6	5.4
2004	A-	4.01	2.18	281.8	40.9	22.7	4.4

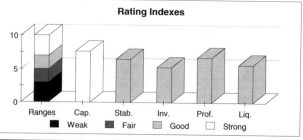

USAA LIFE INSURANCE COMPANY *   A   Excellent

Major Rating Factors: Good quality investment portfolio (6.1 on a scale of 0 to 10) despite mixed results such as: minimal exposure to mortgages and large holdings of BBB rated bonds but small junk bond holdings. Good liquidity (6.2) with sufficient resources to handle a spike in claims as well as a significant increase in policy surrenders. Strong capitalization (8.8) based on excellent risk adjusted capital (severe loss scenario).

Other Rating Factors: Excellent profitability (8.4) with operating gains in each of the last five years. Excellent overall results on stability tests (7.4) excellent operational trends and excellent risk diversification.

Principal Business: Individual annuities (64%), individual life insurance (30%), and individual health insurance (6%).

Principal Investments: NonCMO investment grade bonds (46%), CMOs and structured securities (37%), common & preferred stock (12%), policy loans (1%), and misc. investments (3%).

Investments in Affiliates: 2%

Group Affiliation: USAA Group

Licensed in: All states except AL, NC

Commenced Business: August 1963

Address: 9800 Fredericksburg Rd, San Antonio, TX 78288

Phone: (210) 498-8000 **Domicile State:** TX **NAIC Code:** 69663

Data Date	Rating	RACR #1	RACR #2	Total Assets ($mil)	Capital ($mil)	Net Premium ($mil)	Net Income ($mil)
3-09	A	4.04	2.20	13,463.6	1,144.8	860.7	40.0
3-08	A	4.11	2.41	11,408.6	954.0	472.5	3.0
2008	A	3.88	2.23	12,583.7	1,105.5	1,926.1	23.7
2007	A	4.17	2.47	10,862.3	965.1	1,111.7	103.0
2006	A	4.67	2.72	10,177.3	925.3	962.3	117.8
2005	A	4.46	2.57	10,501.3	875.9	873.3	133.0
2004	A	4.57	2.61	10,117.3	787.2	938.0	129.7

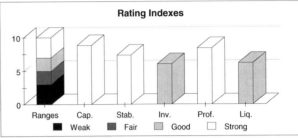

Rating Indexes

Ranges Cap. Stab. Inv. Prof. Liq.
■ Weak ■ Fair ▨ Good □ Strong

USABLE LIFE *   A-   Excellent

Major Rating Factors: Good quality investment portfolio (6.2 on a scale of 0 to 10) with no exposure to mortgages and minimal holdings in junk bonds. Good liquidity (6.5) with sufficient resources to handle a spike in claims. Good overall results on stability tests (6.5). Strengths include excellent financial support from affiliation with Arkansas Bl Cross Bl Shield Group, good operational trends and excellent risk diversification.

Other Rating Factors: Strong capitalization (7.5) based on excellent risk adjusted capital (severe loss scenario). Excellent profitability (8.0) with operating gains in each of the last five years.

Principal Business: Reinsurance (54%), group life insurance (21%), group health insurance (17%), individual health insurance (7%), and individual life insurance (1%).

Principal Investments: NonCMO investment grade bonds (84%), common & preferred stock (14%), policy loans (1%), and noninv. grade bonds (1%).

Investments in Affiliates: None

Group Affiliation: Arkansas Bl Cross Bl Shield Group

Licensed in: All states except AL, AZ, NC

Commenced Business: December 1980

Address: 320 W Capitol Suite 700, Little Rock, AR 72201

Phone: (501) 375-7200 **Domicile State:** AR **NAIC Code:** 94358

Data Date	Rating	RACR #1	RACR #2	Total Assets ($mil)	Capital ($mil)	Net Premium ($mil)	Net Income ($mil)
3-09	A-	1.76	1.32	298.5	113.7	97.8	0.9
3-08	A-	2.34	1.71	265.9	114.9	90.8	-0.7
2008	A-	1.84	1.38	286.7	117.6	366.7	0.4
2007	A-	2.17	1.58	239.5	99.3	205.3	4.3
2006	A-	2.60	1.88	205.0	97.7	155.7	16.9
2005	B+	2.55	1.82	180.1	82.2	116.9	8.5
2004	B+	3.11	2.17	148.9	72.1	82.0	5.4

Arkansas Bl Cross Bl Shield Group
Composite Group Rating: A+

Largest Group Members	Assets ($mil)	Rating
ARKANSAS BLUE CROSS AND BLUE SHIELD	892	A+
USABLE LIFE	287	A-
HMO PARTNERS INC	116	B+
FLORIDA COMBINED LIFE INS CO INC	32	B+

VANTISLIFE INSURANCE COMPANY   C+   Fair

Major Rating Factors: Fair liquidity (4.9 on a scale of 0 to 10) due, in part, to cash value policies that are subject to withdrawals with minimal or no penalty. Fair overall results on stability tests (4.3). Good quality investment portfolio (6.1) despite mixed results such as: minimal exposure to mortgages and large holdings of BBB rated bonds but small junk bond holdings.

Other Rating Factors: Good overall profitability (5.8) despite operating losses during the first three months of 2009. Strong capitalization (7.2) based on excellent risk adjusted capital (severe loss scenario).

Principal Business: Individual annuities (78%), individual life insurance (16%), and group life insurance (6%).

Principal Investments: NonCMO investment grade bonds (71%), CMOs and structured securities (23%), noninv. grade bonds (2%), common & preferred stock (1%), and misc. investments (2%).

Investments in Affiliates: 1%

Group Affiliation: VantisLife Group

Licensed in: All states except AL, NC

Commenced Business: January 1964

Address: 200 Day Hill Rd, Windsor, CT 06095

Phone: (860) 298-5400 **Domicile State:** CT **NAIC Code:** 68632

Data Date	Rating	RACR #1	RACR #2	Total Assets ($mil)	Capital ($mil)	Net Premium ($mil)	Net Income ($mil)
3-09	C+	2.02	1.11	748.5	64.1	92.0	-0.1
3-08	C+	2.95	1.54	675.6	66.9	31.3	0.0
2008	C+	2.16	1.23	669.5	64.6	86.5	-4.7
2007	C+	3.01	1.58	649.5	67.3	28.2	1.1
2006	C+	2.86	1.52	684.4	66.9	27.2	2.2
2005	C+	2.51	1.36	712.8	64.9	46.8	2.2
2004	C	2.57	1.40	691.4	63.5	70.0	1.2

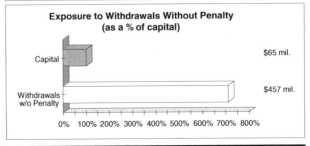

Exposure to Withdrawals Without Penalty
(as a % of capital)

Capital — $65 mil.
Withdrawals w/o Penalty — $457 mil.

0% 100% 200% 300% 400% 500% 600% 700% 800%

VARIABLE ANNUITY LIFE INSURANCE COMPANY   B   Good

Major Rating Factors: Good quality investment portfolio (5.5 on a scale of 0 to 10) despite substantial holdings of BBB bonds in addition to junk bond exposure equal to 71% of capital. Exposure to mortgages is significant, but the mortgage default rate has been low. Good overall profitability (6.6). Return on equity has been excellent over the last five years averaging 17.6%. Good liquidity (6.8).

Other Rating Factors: Fair overall results on stability tests (4.9) including fair financial strength of affiliated American International Group. Strong capitalization (7.6) based on excellent risk adjusted capital (severe loss scenario).

Principal Business: Group retirement contracts (58%), individual annuities (36%), and reinsurance (6%).

Principal Investments: NonCMO investment grade bonds (38%), CMOs and structured securities (30%), mortgages in good standing (13%), noninv. grade bonds (7%), and misc. investments (12%).

Investments in Affiliates: 2%

Group Affiliation: American International Group

Licensed in: All states except AL

Commenced Business: May 1969

Address: 2929 Allen Parkway, Houston, TX 77019

Phone: (713) 522-1111 **Domicile State:** TX **NAIC Code:** 70238

Data Date	Rating	RACR #1	RACR #2	Total Assets ($mil)	Capital ($mil)	Net Premium ($mil)	Net Income ($mil)
3-09	B	2.91	1.38	52,157.7	3,142.5	1,415.5	31.8
3-08	B+	2.85	1.36	61,439.2	2,529.1	1,658.6	-494.5
2008	B	2.68	1.27	53,699.1	2,844.3	6,454.4	-4,497.6
2007	A-	3.19	1.51	63,999.0	2,841.3	6,138.0	302.5
2006	A-	2.98	1.56	61,980.1	3,128.8	5,580.0	616.9
2005	A-	3.00	1.52	58,319.1	2,904.2	5,532.0	726.3
2004	B+	3.00	1.48	55,765.9	2,677.3	5,555.1	644.7

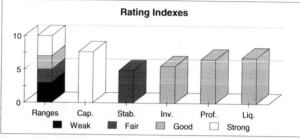

Rating Indexes

Ranges · Cap. · Stab. · Inv. · Prof. · Liq.

■ Weak ■ Fair ▨ Good □ Strong

WASHINGTON NATIONAL INSURANCE COMPANY   D+   Weak

Major Rating Factors: Weak overall results on stability tests (2.7 on a scale of 0 to 10) including potential financial drain due to affiliation with Conseco Group and negative cash flow from operations for 2008. Fair quality investment portfolio (4.6) with large holdings of BBB rated bonds in addition to moderate junk bond exposure. Fair profitability (3.3) with operating losses during the first three months of 2009.

Other Rating Factors: Good capitalization (6.2) based on good risk adjusted capital (severe loss scenario). Good liquidity (6.3).

Principal Business: Individual health insurance (34%), group retirement contracts (20%), individual life insurance (17%), individual annuities (16%), and other lines (13%).

Principal Investments: NonCMO investment grade bonds (47%), common & preferred stock (18%), CMOs and structured securities (15%), noninv. grade bonds (7%), and misc. investments (14%).

Investments in Affiliates: 15%

Group Affiliation: Conseco Group

Licensed in: All states except AL, NC

Commenced Business: September 1923

Address: 300 Tower Parkway, Lincolnshire, IL 60069

Phone: (847) 793-3379 **Domicile State:** IL **NAIC Code:** 70319

Data Date	Rating	RACR #1	RACR #2	Total Assets ($mil)	Capital ($mil)	Net Premium ($mil)	Net Income ($mil)
3-09	D+	1.10	0.90	2,274.6	448.1	51.9	-6.8
3-08	D+	0.92	0.78	2,376.4	408.0	72.1	0.6
2008	D+	1.16	0.96	2,348.2	457.0	254.2	13.5
2007	D+	0.98	0.83	2,473.6	435.6	418.8	-45.2
2006	D+	1.09	0.95	2,609.7	585.8	432.6	4.2
2005	D+	1.12	1.00	2,657.8	762.0	238.1	48.1
2004	D	1.20	1.06	2,768.9	776.0	277.6	101.9

Conseco Group Composite Group Rating: D+ Largest Group Members	Assets ($mil)	Rating
BANKERS LIFE CAS CO	11442	D+
CONSECO LIFE INS CO	4529	D+
CONSECO HEALTH INS CO	2472	D+
WASHINGTON NATIONAL INS CO	2348	D+
CONSECO INS CO	1044	D+

WEA INSURANCE CORPORATION   B   Good

Major Rating Factors: Good overall capitalization (6.7 on a scale of 0 to 10) based on excellent risk adjusted capital (severe loss scenario). However, capital levels have fluctuated somewhat during past years. Good quality investment portfolio (6.4) with no exposure to mortgages and minimal holdings in junk bonds. Good liquidity (6.2).

Other Rating Factors: Good overall results on stability tests (5.7) excellent operational trends, excellent risk adjusted capital for prior years and excellent risk diversification. Excellent profitability (7.5) despite operating losses during the first three months of 2009.

Principal Business: Group health insurance (100%).

Principal Investments: NonCMO investment grade bonds (69%), CMOs and structured securities (18%), and common & preferred stock (13%).

Investments in Affiliates: None

Group Affiliation: WEA Inc

Licensed in: WY

Commenced Business: July 1985

Address: 45 Nob Hill Rd, Madison, WI 53713

Phone: (608) 276-4000 **Domicile State:** WI **NAIC Code:** 72273

Data Date	Rating	RACR #1	RACR #2	Total Assets ($mil)	Capital ($mil)	Net Premium ($mil)	Net Income ($mil)
3-09	B	1.85	1.43	546.2	219.9	214.8	-0.6
3-08	B	1.77	1.34	545.6	231.3	213.1	-2.9
2008	B	1.89	1.46	541.0	223.9	856.3	5.4
2007	B	1.86	1.40	559.1	243.3	897.7	23.4
2006	C+	1.69	1.29	516.8	219.0	909.9	17.5
2005	C	1.63	1.25	478.6	202.0	885.5	0.3
2004	C-	1.74	1.33	461.5	194.0	825.9	22.4

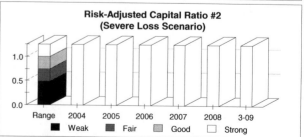

Risk-Adjusted Capital Ratio #2 (Severe Loss Scenario)

Range · 2004 · 2005 · 2006 · 2007 · 2008 · 3-09

■ Weak ■ Fair ▨ Good □ Strong

WEST COAST LIFE INSURANCE COMPANY   C   Fair

Major Rating Factors: Fair overall results on stability tests (4.2 on a scale of 0 to 10). Good overall capitalization (5.3) based on good risk adjusted capital (moderate loss scenario). However, capital levels have fluctuated somewhat during past years. Good quality investment portfolio (5.1) despite large holdings of BBB rated bonds in addition to junk bond exposure equal to 50% of capital. Exposure to mortgages is significant, but the mortgage default rate has been low.

Other Rating Factors: Good liquidity (5.6). Weak profitability (1.9) with operating losses during the first three months of 2009.

Principal Business: Individual life insurance (89%), individual annuities (9%), group retirement contracts (1%), and reinsurance (1%).

Principal Investments: NonCMO investment grade bonds (50%), mortgages in good standing (22%), CMOs and structured securities (14%), common & preferred stock (9%), and misc. investments (6%).

Investments in Affiliates: 4%

Group Affiliation: Protective Life Group

Licensed in: All states except AL, NC

Commenced Business: February 1915

Address: 9140 W Dodge Rd, Omaha, NE 68114

Phone: (415) 591-8200 **Domicile State:** NE **NAIC Code:** 70335

Data Date	Rating	RACR #1	RACR #2	Total Assets ($mil)	Capital ($mil)	Net Premium ($mil)	Net Income ($mil)
3-09	C	1.19	0.75	3,389.4	320.5	52.5	-67.9
3-08	C	1.11	0.76	3,193.7	289.4	47.5	-30.2
2008	C	1.22	0.80	3,400.6	333.3	182.1	-121.1
2007	C	1.17	0.83	3,130.4	299.4	227.9	-49.7
2006	C	1.15	0.87	3,004.3	338.0	200.7	13.0
2005	C	2.37	1.20	2,752.5	260.5	202.5	27.5
2004	C	1.98	1.02	2,497.4	185.9	198.6	-22.3

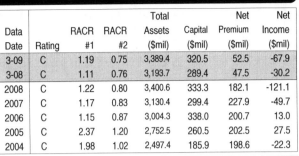

Rating Indexes

WESTERN & SOUTHERN LIFE INSURANCE COMPANY   B   Good

Major Rating Factors: Good overall profitability (6.7 on a scale of 0 to 10). Return on equity has been low, averaging 3.9%. Fair overall results on stability tests (4.7). Fair quality investment portfolio (3.4).

Other Rating Factors: Strong capitalization (7.6) based on excellent risk adjusted capital (severe loss scenario). Excellent liquidity (7.0).

Principal Business: Individual life insurance (67%), reinsurance (22%), individual health insurance (10%), and group life insurance (1%).

Principal Investments: Common & preferred stock (40%), nonCMO investment grade bonds (36%), CMOs and structured securities (10%), policy loans (2%), and misc. investments (12%).

Investments in Affiliates: 31%

Group Affiliation: Western & Southern Group

Licensed in: All states except AL, AZ, DC, MD, MI, NJ, NC, VA

Commenced Business: April 1888

Address: 400 Broadway, Cincinnati, OH 45202

Phone: (513) 357-4000 **Domicile State:** OH **NAIC Code:** 70483

Data Date	Rating	RACR #1	RACR #2	Total Assets ($mil)	Capital ($mil)	Net Premium ($mil)	Net Income ($mil)
3-09	B	1.65	1.39	7,416.9	3,113.1	65.2	9.1
3-08	B+	1.76	1.41	8,533.0	3,661.4	88.2	106.6
2008	B	1.76	1.49	7,727.8	3,302.0	364.0	295.1
2007	B+	1.83	1.47	8,832.3	3,706.0	370.6	264.3
2006	B+	1.88	1.48	9,097.6	3,515.0	382.3	154.0
2005	B+	1.91	1.49	8,308.1	3,070.5	394.4	144.0
2004	B+	1.95	1.48	8,055.2	2,924.5	385.4	182.2

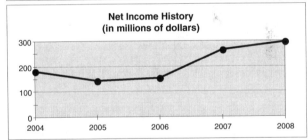

Net Income History
(in millions of dollars)

WESTERN NATIONAL LIFE INSURANCE COMPANY   B-   Good

Major Rating Factors: Good overall capitalization (6.3 on a scale of 0 to 10) based on good risk adjusted capital (moderate loss scenario). Nevertheless, capital levels have fluctuated during prior years. Good overall profitability (6.7) despite operating losses during the first three months of 2009. Return on equity has been fair, averaging 9.3%. Good liquidity (5.3).

Other Rating Factors: Fair overall results on stability tests (4.2) including fair financial strength of affiliated American International Group and negative cash flow from operations for 2008. Fair quality investment portfolio (3.7).

Principal Business: Individual annuities (100%).

Principal Investments: NonCMO investment grade bonds (53%), CMOs and structured securities (25%), noninv. grade bonds (7%), mortgages in good standing (6%), and misc. investments (9%).

Investments in Affiliates: 1%

Group Affiliation: American International Group

Licensed in: All states except AL, NC

Commenced Business: June 1944

Address: 205 E 10th St, Amarillo, TX 79101

Phone: (806) 345-7400 **Domicile State:** TX **NAIC Code:** 70432

Data Date	Rating	RACR #1	RACR #2	Total Assets ($mil)	Capital ($mil)	Net Premium ($mil)	Net Income ($mil)
3-09	B-	1.85	0.87	44,187.0	2,832.5	933.4	-78.1
3-08	B-	2.24	1.07	51,264.6	2,710.8	2,045.2	-944.6
2008	B-	2.00	0.95	45,803.0	3,047.2	5,705.6	-7,901.0
2007	B	2.86	1.37	50,552.6	3,731.3	1,337.3	-104.4
2006	B	2.49	1.30	53,108.0	4,211.9	-240.2	416.5
2005	B	2.32	1.19	54,002.9	3,934.8	206.5	431.4
2004	B	2.22	1.12	50,842.2	3,532.0	796.3	341.3

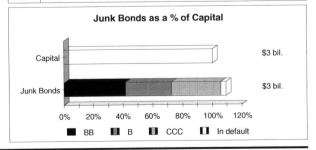

Junk Bonds as a % of Capital

WESTERN RESERVE LIFE ASSURANCE COMPANY OF OHIO   B   Good

Major Rating Factors: Good quality investment portfolio (6.2 on a scale of 0 to 10) with minimal exposure to mortgages and small junk bond holdings. Fair profitability (3.0) with investment income below regulatory standards in relation to interest assumptions of reserves. Fair overall results on stability tests (4.5).

Other Rating Factors: Strong capitalization (7.2) based on excellent risk adjusted capital (severe loss scenario). Excellent liquidity (7.5).

Principal Business: Individual life insurance (65%), individual annuities (31%), and group retirement contracts (3%).

Principal Investments: NonCMO investment grade bonds (38%), policy loans (29%), CMOs and structured securities (21%), noninv. grade bonds (3%), and misc. investments (9%).

Investments in Affiliates: 2%

Group Affiliation: AEGON USA Group

Licensed in: All states except AL, NC

Commenced Business: June 1980

Address: 366 Broad St, Columbus, OH 43215

Phone: (727) 299-1800   **Domicile State:** OH   **NAIC Code:** 91413

Data Date	Rating	RACR #1	RACR #2	Total Assets ($mil)	Capital ($mil)	Net Premium ($mil)	Net Income ($mil)
3-09	B	1.92	1.15	7,262.7	279.2	218.4	15.9
3-08	B	3.15	1.84	10,788.7	499.4	244.4	10.9
2008	B	1.85	1.10	8,127.6	280.1	787.9	-59.1
2007	B	3.01	1.75	11,768.9	488.7	1,013.1	131.7
2006	B-	2.93	1.69	11,528.5	467.1	1,166.2	112.0
2005	B-	2.38	1.44	10,697.7	391.4	1,146.3	104.5
2004	B-	2.00	1.19	10,099.0	277.9	1,148.2	121.4

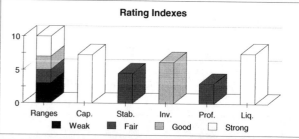

Rating Indexes

Ranges   Cap.   Stab.   Inv.   Prof.   Liq.

■ Weak   ▦ Fair   ▨ Good   □ Strong

WESTERN-SOUTHERN LIFE ASSURANCE COMPANY   B-   Good

Major Rating Factors: Good capitalization (6.4 on a scale of 0 to 10) based on good risk adjusted capital (moderate loss scenario). Capital levels have been relatively consistent over the last five years. Good liquidity (5.5) with sufficient resources to cover a large increase in policy surrenders. Good overall results on stability tests (5.2) excellent operational trends and excellent risk diversification.

Other Rating Factors: Fair quality investment portfolio (4.0). Excellent profitability (8.2).

Principal Business: Individual annuities (90%) and individual life insurance (10%).

Principal Investments: NonCMO investment grade bonds (47%), CMOs and structured securities (32%), noninv. grade bonds (8%), mortgages in good standing (6%), and common & preferred stock (5%).

Investments in Affiliates: 1%

Group Affiliation: Western & Southern Group

Licensed in: All states except AL, AZ, MD, NJ, NC, SC

Commenced Business: April 1981

Address: 400 Broadway, Cincinnati, OH 45202

Phone: (513) 357-4000   **Domicile State:** OH   **NAIC Code:** 92622

Data Date	Rating	RACR #1	RACR #2	Total Assets ($mil)	Capital ($mil)	Net Premium ($mil)	Net Income ($mil)
3-09	B-	1.90	0.91	10,339.3	861.9	406.5	14.0
3-08	B	2.07	1.06	9,568.9	699.4	451.9	3.4
2008	B-	2.06	1.03	10,031.4	868.7	1,306.8	-109.1
2007	B	2.11	1.09	9,294.1	693.7	727.6	40.1
2006	B	2.10	1.07	8,732.4	631.4	830.2	91.2
2005	B	1.95	0.99	9,132.7	578.1	861.9	96.4
2004	B	1.82	0.90	8,898.6	492.9	1,005.7	114.0

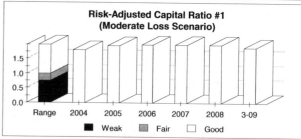

Risk-Adjusted Capital Ratio #1
(Moderate Loss Scenario)

Range   2004   2005   2006   2007   2008   3-09

■ Weak   ▦ Fair   □ Good

WILLIAM PENN LIFE INSURANCE COMPANY OF NEW YORK   C-   Fair

Major Rating Factors: Fair overall results on stability tests (3.1 on a scale of 0 to 10) including potential financial drain due to affiliation with Legal & General America Inc. Weak profitability (2.3). Excellent expense controls. Return on equity has been low, averaging -6.0%. Good liquidity (5.0) with sufficient resources to handle a spike in claims as well as a significant increase in policy surrenders.

Other Rating Factors: Strong capitalization (7.5) based on excellent risk adjusted capital (severe loss scenario). High quality investment portfolio (7.3).

Principal Business: Individual life insurance (99%) and individual annuities (1%).

Principal Investments: NonCMO investment grade bonds (78%), CMOs and structured securities (16%), policy loans (5%), common & preferred stock (1%), and noninv. grade bonds (1%).

Investments in Affiliates: None

Group Affiliation: Legal & General America Inc

Licensed in: DC, DE, GA, IL, MA, NM, NC, OR, PA, RI, SC, SD, TN

Commenced Business: February 1963

Address: 100 Quentin Roosevelt Blvd, Garden City, NY 11530

Phone: (516) 794-3700   **Domicile State:** NY   **NAIC Code:** 66230

Data Date	Rating	RACR #1	RACR #2	Total Assets ($mil)	Capital ($mil)	Net Premium ($mil)	Net Income ($mil)
3-09	C-	2.44	1.36	964.4	97.9	14.1	1.9
3-08	C	2.60	1.45	976.7	101.6	6.6	-13.6
2008	C-	2.39	1.34	965.6	96.0	29.7	-28.4
2007	C	2.87	1.62	977.0	110.5	52.5	-0.5
2006	C	3.32	1.88	989.2	120.7	56.0	17.4
2005	C-	3.24	1.84	999.5	118.9	57.2	21.8
2004	C+	2.92	1.63	1,021.8	107.7	77.3	-57.6

Legal General America Inc Composite Group Rating: D+ Largest Group Members	Assets ($mil)	Rating
BANNER LIFE INS CO	1335	D+
WILLIAM PENN LIFE INS CO OF NEW YORK	966	C-

WILTON REASSURANCE COMPANY　　　　　　　　　D　　Weak

Major Rating Factors: Weak overall results on stability tests (2.0 on a scale of 0 to 10) including weak financial strength of affiliated Wilton Re Holdings Ltd and weak results on operational trends. Weak profitability (1.5) with investment income below regulatory standards in relation to interest assumptions of reserves. Good capitalization (6.8) based on good risk adjusted capital (severe loss scenario).

Other Rating Factors: Good quality investment portfolio (6.3). Excellent liquidity (8.6).

Principal Business: Reinsurance (100%).

Principal Investments: NonCMO investment grade bonds (65%), CMOs and structured securities (15%), common & preferred stock (13%), and cash (6%).

Investments in Affiliates: 16%

Group Affiliation: Wilton Re Holdings Ltd

Licensed in: All states except AL, GA, MD, MN, NJ, NC, ND

Commenced Business: February 1901

Address: 213 Washington St, Newark, NJ 07102-2992

Phone: (201) 802-5807　**Domicile State:** MN　**NAIC Code:** 66133

Data Date	Rating	RACR #1	RACR #2	Total Assets ($mil)	Capital ($mil)	Net Premium ($mil)	Net Income ($mil)
3-09	D	1.13	0.97	670.9	146.1	22.6	30.5
3-08	D	0.86	0.80	314.4	110.8	25.0	13.6
2008	D	1.07	0.96	668.4	126.4	406.1	5.1
2007	D	0.85	0.81	433.5	116.8	105.6	-79.9
2006	D	1.57	1.52	333.7	202.4	69.5	-123.5
2005	U	5.75	5.17	151.5	54.4	49.1	-23.9
2004	U	4.04	3.64	9.4	9.4	0.0	0.4

Wilton Re Holdings Ltd Composite Group Rating: D- Largest Group Members	Assets ($mil)	Rating
WILTON REASSURANCE LIFE CO OF NY	1184	D-
WILTON REASSURANCE CO	668	D

WILTON REASSURANCE LIFE COMPANY OF NEW YORK　　D-　　Weak

Major Rating Factors: Weak profitability (2.8 on a scale of 0 to 10) with operating losses during the first three months of 2009. Return on equity has been low, averaging -8.9%. Weak liquidity (2.5) based on large exposure to policies that are subject to policyholder withdrawals with minimal or no penalty. Weak overall results on stability tests (1.4) including negative cash flow from operations for 2008.

Other Rating Factors: Fair quality investment portfolio (3.9). Good capitalization (5.5) based on good risk adjusted capital (moderate loss scenario).

Principal Business: Individual life insurance (80%), reinsurance (11%), and individual annuities (9%).

Principal Investments: NonCMO investment grade bonds (47%), CMOs and structured securities (40%), common & preferred stock (8%), policy loans (3%), and misc. investments (3%).

Investments in Affiliates: None

Group Affiliation: Wilton Re Holdings Ltd

Licensed in: All states except AL

Commenced Business: November 1956

Address: 320 Park Ave, New York, NY 10022

Phone: (212) 224-1879　**Domicile State:** NY　**NAIC Code:** 60704

Data Date	Rating	RACR #1	RACR #2	Total Assets ($mil)	Capital ($mil)	Net Premium ($mil)	Net Income ($mil)
3-09	D-	1.35	0.72	1,173.2	66.9	13.8	-1.4
3-08	D-	1.90	1.06	1,217.7	89.8	9.8	-0.2
2008	D-	1.42	0.79	1,184.3	70.6	63.3	-26.2
2007	D-	2.02	1.13	1,219.5	93.4	59.7	-15.3
2006	D-	1.90	1.06	1,208.4	84.0	50.6	14.8
2005	D-	1.52	1.37	82.1	9.4	5.6	-10.5
2004	D	2.20	1.98	91.5	15.9	5.2	-8.9

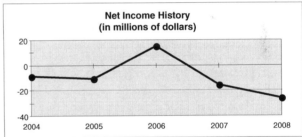

Net Income History (in millions of dollars)

WORLD INSURANCE COMPANY *　　　　　　　　　A-　　Excellent

Major Rating Factors: Good quality investment portfolio (6.0 on a scale of 0 to 10) despite mixed results such as: no exposure to mortgages and substantial holdings of BBB bonds but minimal holdings in junk bonds. Good liquidity (6.6) with sufficient resources to handle a spike in claims. Good overall results on stability tests (6.2) despite negative cash flow from operations for 2008 good operational trends and excellent risk diversification.

Other Rating Factors: Strong capitalization (8.0) based on excellent risk adjusted capital (severe loss scenario). Excellent profitability (7.7).

Principal Business: Individual health insurance (53%), group health insurance (43%), individual life insurance (2%), and reinsurance (1%).

Principal Investments: NonCMO investment grade bonds (51%), CMOs and structured securities (29%), common & preferred stock (16%), policy loans (3%), and noninv. grade bonds (2%).

Investments in Affiliates: 11%

Group Affiliation: American Enterprise Mutual Holding

Licensed in: All states except AL, AZ, MI, NC

Commenced Business: November 1903

Address: 11808 Grant St, Omaha, NE 68164

Phone: (402) 496-8000　**Domicile State:** NE　**NAIC Code:** 70629

Data Date	Rating	RACR #1	RACR #2	Total Assets ($mil)	Capital ($mil)	Net Premium ($mil)	Net Income ($mil)
3-09	A-	2.00	1.64	242.3	104.0	54.9	1.1
3-08	A-	1.80	1.51	218.6	107.7	40.7	0.6
2008	A-	2.11	1.74	210.3	104.1	155.7	-0.9
2007	A-	1.94	1.63	231.5	116.4	171.9	7.9
2006	A-	1.79	1.51	228.9	108.3	173.3	9.6
2005	B	1.67	1.40	222.5	96.6	163.3	18.9
2004	C+	1.41	1.20	211.6	77.4	154.3	3.0

Adverse Trends in Operations

Decrease in asset base during 2008 (9%)
Decrease in capital during 2008 (11%)
Decrease in premium volume from 2007 to 2008 (9%)

XL RE LIFE AMERICA INCORPORATED

D+   **Weak**

Major Rating Factors: Weak profitability (1.8 on a scale of 0 to 10) with operating losses during the first three months of 2009. Return on equity has been low, averaging -11.7%. Weak overall results on stability tests (2.4). Strong overall capitalization (9.7) based on excellent risk adjusted capital (severe loss scenario). Nevertheless, capital levels have fluctuated during prior years.

Other Rating Factors: High quality investment portfolio (8.6). Excellent liquidity (7.0).

Principal Business: Reinsurance (100%).

Principal Investments: NonCMO investment grade bonds (54%), CMOs and structured securities (41%), cash (5%), and noninv. grade bonds (1%).

Investments in Affiliates: None

Group Affiliation: XL Capital Ltd

Licensed in: All states except AL, NC

Commenced Business: September 1963

Address: 200 Hopmeadow St, Simsbury, CT 06089

Phone: (860) 843-5867 **Domicile State:** DE **NAIC Code:** 80586

Data Date	Rating	RACR #1	RACR #2	Total Assets ($mil)	Capital ($mil)	Net Premium ($mil)	Net Income ($mil)
3-09	D+	4.33	2.77	55.9	32.4	2.1	-0.5
3-08	D+	6.64	5.97	57.6	47.0	0.7	-3.1
2008	D+	4.49	2.92	55.5	32.9	5.6	-17.3
2007	D+	6.99	6.29	57.6	49.5	0.9	-4.9
2006	D+	7.72	6.95	59.0	55.2	0.0	-1.0
2005	U	4.28	3.85	11.7	11.2	0.0	0.2
2004	C+	4.23	3.80	11.6	11.0	0.0	0.1

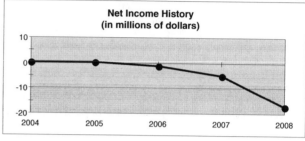

Net Income History
(in millions of dollars)

Section III

TheStreet.com
Recommended Companies

A compilation of those

U.S. Life and Annuity Insurers

receiving a TheStreet.com Financial Strength Rating
of A+, A, A- or B+.

Companies are listed in alphabetical order.

Section III Contents

This section provides a list of recommended carriers along with additional information you should have when shopping for insurance. It contains all insurers receiving a TheStreet.com Financial Strength Rating of A+, A, A-, or B+. If an insurer is not on this list, it should not be automatically assumed that the firm is weak. Indeed, there are many firms that have not achieved a B+ or better rating but are in relatively good condition with adequate resources to cover their risk during an average recession. Not being included in this list should not be construed as a recommendation to surrender policies.

Left Pages

1. **Financial Strength Rating**
Our rating is measured on a scale from A to F and considers a wide range of factors. Highly-rated companies are, in our opinion, less likely to experience financial difficulties than lower rated firms. See *About TheStreet.com Financial Strength Ratings* on page 9 for more information.

2. **Insurance Company Name**
The legally registered name, which can sometimes differ from the name that the company uses for advertising. An insurer's name can be very similar to the name of other companies which may not be on our Recommended List, so make sure you note the exact name before contacting your agent.

3. **Address**
The address of the main office where you can contact the firm for additional financial data or for the location of local branches and/or registered agents.

4. **Telephone Number**
The number to call for additional financial data or for the phone numbers of local branches and/or registered agents.

Right Pages

The right-side pages present the percentage of the company's business that is involved in each type of insurance. Specifically, the numbers shown are the amounts of premium (including certain annuity payments and other deposit funds not technically called premiums) for each line of business as a percent of total premiums. The amounts shown are net premiums and, therefore, include only policies for which the company carries risk.

1. **Domicile State**
The state which has primary regulatory responsibility for the company. It may differ from the location of the company's corporate headquarters. You do not have to be living in the domicile state to purchase insurance from this firm, provided it is licensed to do business in your state.

2. Individual Life   Life insurance policies for individual customers, as opposed to group policies.

3. Individual Health   Health insurance policies for individual customers, as opposed to group policies

4. Individual Annuities Annuity contracts for individual customers which may be fixed and/or variable annuity contracts.

5. Group Life   Life insurance policies for groups such as the employees of a corporation, public institution, or union.

6. Group Health   Health insurance policies for groups such as the employees of a corporation, public institution or union.

7. Group Annuities   Annuity contracts for groups such as the employees of a corporation, public institution or union. These include Guaranteed Interest Contracts (GICs) and other pension products.

8. Credit Life   Life insurance policies designed to protect lenders against the eventual death of the borrower. Typically, if the borrower dies, the policy guarantees repayment of the loan balance.

9. Credit Health   Health insurance policies designed to protect lenders against the sickness of the borrower. Typically, if the borrower becomes ill, the policy guarantees repayment of the loan balance.

10. Supplemental Contracts Policies in which the premium is paid from the benefits of another contract.

TheStreet.com Financial Strength Ratings are not deemed to be a recommendation concerning the purchase or sale of the securities of any insurance company that is publicly owned.

RATING	INSURANCE COMPANY NAME	ADDRESS	CITY	STATE	ZIP	PHONE
A-	ACACIA LIFE INS CO	7315 WISCONSIN AVE	BETHESDA	MD	20814	(800) 444-188
B+	ALFA LIFE INS CORP	2108 EAST SOUTH BLVD	MONTGOMERY	AL	36116	(334) 288-390
B+	ALLSTATE LIFE INS CO	3100 SANDERS RD	NORTHBROOK	IL	60062	(847) 402-500
A-	AMALGAMATED LIFE INS CO	333 WESTCHESTER AVE	WHITE PLAINS	NY	10604	(914) 367-500
B+	AMERICAN FAMILY LIFE ASR CO OF COLUM	1932 WYNNTON RD	COLUMBUS	GA	31999	(706) 323-343
B+	AMERICAN FAMILY LIFE ASR CO OF NY	22 CORPORATE WOODS BLVD #2	ALBANY	NY	12211	(706) 660-720
A+	AMERICAN FAMILY LIFE INS CO	6000 AMERICAN PARKWAY	MADISON	WI	53783	(608) 249-211
A	AMERICAN FIDELITY ASR CO	2000 N CLASSEN BLVD	OKLAHOMA CITY	OK	73106	(800) 654-848
B+	AMERICAN HEALTH & LIFE INS CO	307 WEST 7TH STREET, STE 400	FORT WORTH	TX	76102	(817) 348-750
B+	AMERICAN INCOME LIFE INS CO	8604 ALLISONVILLE RD SUITE 151	INDIANAPOLIS	IN	46250	(254) 761-640
A-	AMERICAN REPUBLIC INS CO	601 SIXTH AVE	DES MOINES	IA	50309	(515) 245-200
B+	AMERICAN UNITED LIFE INS CO	ONE AMERICAN SQUARE	INDIANAPOLIS	IN	46204	(317) 285-187
B+	AMERITAS LIFE INS CORP	5900 O STREET	LINCOLN	NE	68510	(402) 467-1122
A-	AMICA LIFE INS CO	ONE HUNDRED AMICA WAY	LINCOLN	RI	02867	(401) 334-6000
A-	ANTHEM LIFE INS CO	6740 N HIGH ST SUITE 200	WORTHINGTON	OH	43085	(614) 438-3959
B+	ASSURITY LIFE INS CO	1526 K STREET	LINCOLN	NE	68508	(800) 869-0355
B+	ATLANTIC COAST LIFE INS CO	1565 SAM RITTENBERG BLVD	CHARLESTON	SC	29407	(843) 763-868
A	AUTO-OWNERS LIFE INS CO	6101 ANACAPRI BLVD	LANSING	MI	48917	(517) 323-1512
A	BERKSHIRE LIFE INS CO OF AMERICA	700 SOUTH ST	PITTSFIELD	MA	01201	(800) 819-2468
A-	BLUE SHIELD OF CALIFORNIA L&H INS CO	50 BEALE ST	SAN FRANCISCO	CA	94105	(800) 537-0668
B+	BLUEBONNET LIFE INS CO	3475 LAKELAND DRIVE	JACKSON	MS	39208	(601) 932-8269
B+	BOSTON MUTUAL LIFE INS CO	120 ROYALL ST	CANTON	MA	02021	(781) 828-7000
A-	CHARTER NATIONAL LIFE INS CO	3100 SANDERS RD	NORTHBROOK	IL	60062	(847) 402-5000
B+	CHEROKEE NATIONAL LIFE INS CO	2960 RIVERSIDE DR,STE 300	MACON	GA	31204	(912) 477-0400
B+	COLORADO BANKERS LIFE INS CO	5990 GREENWOOD PLAZA BLVD	ENGLEWOOD	CO	80111	(303) 220-8500
B+	COLUMBUS LIFE INS CO	400 E 4TH ST	CINCINNATI	OH	45202	(513) 357-4000
A-	COMPANION LIFE INS CO	2501 FARAWAY DR	COLUMBIA	SC	29219	(800) 753-0404
B+	COMPBENEFITS INS CO	2929 BRIAR PARK SUITE 314	HOUSTON	TX	77042	(800) 342-5209
A-	CONTINENTAL AMERICAN INS CO	2801 DEVINE ST	COLUMBIA	SC	29205	(803) 256-6265
B+	CONTINENTAL LIFE INS CO OF BRENTWOOD	101 CONTINENTAL PLAZA	BRENTWOOD	TN	37027	(615) 377-1300
B+	COTTON STATES LIFE INS CO	244 PERIMETER CTR PKWY NE	ATLANTA	GA	30346	(309) 821-3000
A-	COUNTRY INVESTORS LIFE ASR CO	1701 N TOWANDA AVE	BLOOMINGTON	IL	61701	(309) 821-3000
A+	COUNTRY LIFE INS CO	1701 N TOWANDA AVE	BLOOMINGTON	IL	61701	(309) 821-3000
B+	EASTERN LIFE & HEALTH INS CO	202 NORTH PRINCE ST	LANCASTER	PA	17604	(800) 233-0301
A-	EMPIRE FIDELITY INVESTMENTS L I C	200 LIBERTY ST 1 WORLD FINANCL	NEW YORK	NY	10281	(800) 634-9361
B+	EPIC LIFE INSURANCE CO	PO BOX 14196	MADISON	WI	53708	(608) 221-6882
B+	FAMILY HERITAGE LIFE INS CO OF AMER	6001 E ROYALTON RD SUITE 200	CLEVELAND	OH	44147	(440) 922-5222
B+	FARM BUREAU LIFE INS CO	5400 UNIVERSITY AVE	WEST DES MOINES	IA	50266	(515) 225-5476
A-	FARM BUREAU LIFE INS CO OF MICHIGAN	7373 WEST SAGINAW HWY	LANSING	MI	48909	(517) 323-7000
A-	FARM BUREAU LIFE INS CO OF MISSOURI	701 S COUNTRY CLUB DR	JEFFERSON CITY	MO	65109	(573) 893-1400
A	FEDERATED LIFE INS CO	121 E PARK SQUARE	OWATONNA	MN	55060	(888) 333-4949
A	FIDELITY INVESTMENTS LIFE INS CO	175 E 400 S 8TH FLOOR	SALT LAKE CITY	UT	84111	(800) 634-9361
B+	FIDELITY LIFE ASSN A LEGAL RESERVE	1211 W. 22ND ST., STE 209	OAK BROOK	IL	60523	(630) 522-0392
B+	FIDELITY SECURITY LIFE INS CO	3130 BROADWAY	KANSAS CITY	MO	64111	(816) 756-1060
A-	FIRST AMERITAS LIFE INS CO OF NY	400 RELLA BLVD SUITE 214	SUFFERN	NY	10901	(800) 628-8889
A-	FIRST INVESTORS LIFE INS CO	110 WALL STREET	NEW YORK	NY	10005	(800) 832-7783
A-	FIRST UNITED AMERICAN LIFE INS CO	1020 7TH NORTH ST	LIVERPOOL	NY	13088	(315) 451-2544
B+	FLORIDA COMBINED LIFE INS CO INC	5011 GATE PKWY BLD 200 STE 400	JACKSONVILLE	FL	32256	(800) 370-5856
A-	FORT DEARBORN LIFE INS CO	300 EAST RANDOLPH STREET	CHICAGO	IL	60601	(800) 348-4512
B+	FORT DEARBORN LIFE INS CO OF NY	100 CORPORATE PARKWAY	AMHERST	NY	14226	(716) 832-8678
B+	FRANDISCO LIFE INS CO	213 E TUGALO ST	TOCCOA	GA	30577	(706) 886-7571
B+	GENERAL RE LIFE CORP	30 OAK STREET	STAMFORD	CT	06905	(203) 352-3000
A-	GERBER LIFE INS CO	66 CHURCH ST	WHITE PLAINS	NY	10601	(914) 761-4404
B+	GOVERNMENT PERSONNEL MUTUAL L I C	2211 NE LOOP 410	SAN ANTONIO	TX	78217	(800) 938-4765
A-	GRANGE LIFE INS CO	650 S FRONT ST	COLUMBUS	OH	43216	(614) 445-2820
A-	GREATER GEORGIA LIFE INS CO	THREE RAVINIA DR SUITE 1700	ATLANTA	GA	30346	(877) 864-2273

DOM. STATE	IND. LIFE	IND. HEALTH	IND. ANNU.	GROUP LIFE	GROUP HEALTH	GROUP ANNU	CREDIT LIFE	CREDIT HEALTH	SUP. CONTR.	OTHER	INSURANCE COMPANY NAME
DC	87	0	13	0	0	0	0	0	0	0	ACACIA LIFE INS CO
AL	98	0	2	0	0	0	0	0	0	0	ALFA LIFE INS CORP
IL	30	2	51	1	0	16	0	0	0	0	ALLSTATE LIFE INS CO
NY	3	0	0	81	16	0	0	0	0	0	AMALGAMATED LIFE INS CO
NE	10	87	2	0	0	0	0	0	0	0	AMERICAN FAMILY LIFE ASR CO OF COLUM
NY	1	94	0	0	5	0	0	0	0	0	AMERICAN FAMILY LIFE ASR CO OF NY
WI	88	0	11	1	0	0	0	0	0	0	AMERICAN FAMILY LIFE INS CO
OK	8	24	16	0	52	0	0	0	0	0	AMERICAN FIDELITY ASR CO
TX	1	0	0	16	3	0	40	41	0	0	AMERICAN HEALTH & LIFE INS CO
IN	87	12	0	0	1	0	0	0	0	0	AMERICAN INCOME LIFE INS CO
IA	2	39	0	0	60	0	0	0	0	0	AMERICAN REPUBLIC INS CO
IN	5	0	10	4	6	76	0	0	0	0	AMERICAN UNITED LIFE INS CO
NE	8	0	19	0	41	32	0	0	0	0	AMERITAS LIFE INS CORP
RI	69	0	28	3	0	0	0	0	0	0	AMICA LIFE INS CO
IN	1	0	0	72	27	0	0	0	0	0	ANTHEM LIFE INS CO
NE	48	29	9	2	12	0	0	0	0	0	ASSURITY LIFE INS CO
SC	90	3	5	2	0	0	0	0	0	0	ATLANTIC COAST LIFE INS CO
MI	41	7	43	1	1	7	0	0	0	0	AUTO-OWNERS LIFE INS CO
MA	0	100	0	0	0	0	0	0	0	0	BERKSHIRE LIFE INS CO OF AMERICA
CA	0	41	0	1	58	0	0	0	0	0	BLUE SHIELD OF CALIFORNIA L&H INS CO
MS	1	0	0	97	2	0	0	0	0	0	BLUEBONNET LIFE INS CO
MA	71	2	0	14	13	0	0	0	0	0	BOSTON MUTUAL LIFE INS CO
IL	0	0	0	0	0	0	0	0	0	0	CHARTER NATIONAL LIFE INS CO
GA	0	0	0	0	0	0	69	31	0	0	CHEROKEE NATIONAL LIFE INS CO
CO	67	4	26	0	2	0	0	0	0	0	COLORADO BANKERS LIFE INS CO
OH	62	0	37	0	0	0	0	0	0	0	COLUMBUS LIFE INS CO
SC	0	0	0	17	83	0	0	0	0	0	COMPANION LIFE INS CO
TX	0	0	0	0	100	0	0	0	0	0	COMPBENEFITS INS CO
SC	1	1	0	4	94	0	0	0	0	0	CONTINENTAL AMERICAN INS CO
TN	4	90	0	0	6	0	0	0	0	0	CONTINENTAL LIFE INS CO OF BRENTWOOD
GA	99	0	0	1	0	0	0	0	0	0	COTTON STATES LIFE INS CO
IL	0	0	0	0	0	0	0	0	0	0	COUNTRY INVESTORS LIFE ASR CO
IL	58	15	18	1	7	1	0	0	0	0	COUNTRY LIFE INS CO
PA	0	0	0	16	84	0	0	0	0	0	EASTERN LIFE & HEALTH INS CO
NY	0	0	100	0	0	0	0	0	0	0	EMPIRE FIDELITY INVESTMENTS L I C
WI	0	0	0	41	59	0	0	0	0	0	EPIC LIFE INSURANCE CO
OH	0	100	0	0	0	0	0	0	0	0	FAMILY HERITAGE LIFE INS CO OF AMER
IA	44	0	54	0	0	2	0	0	0	0	FARM BUREAU LIFE INS CO
MI	43	0	56	0	0	1	0	0	0	0	FARM BUREAU LIFE INS CO OF MICHIGAN
MO	75	0	25	0	0	0	0	0	0	0	FARM BUREAU LIFE INS CO OF MISSOURI
MN	69	19	7	5	0	0	0	0	0	0	FEDERATED LIFE INS CO
UT	1	0	99	0	0	0	0	0	0	0	FIDELITY INVESTMENTS LIFE INS CO
IL	93	0	1	6	0	0	0	0	0	0	FIDELITY LIFE ASSN A LEGAL RESERVE
MO	1	0	2	3	88	5	0	0	0	0	FIDELITY SECURITY LIFE INS CO
NY	14	0	4	0	82	0	0	0	0	0	FIRST AMERITAS LIFE INS CO OF NY
NY	79	0	19	2	0	0	0	0	0	0	FIRST INVESTORS LIFE INS CO
NY	32	65	1	0	2	0	0	0	0	0	FIRST UNITED AMERICAN LIFE INS CO
FL	0	98	0	0	2	0	0	0	0	0	FLORIDA COMBINED LIFE INS CO INC
IL	1	0	48	41	10	0	0	0	0	0	FORT DEARBORN LIFE INS CO
NY	0	0	19	31	50	0	0	0	0	0	FORT DEARBORN LIFE INS CO OF NY
GA	0	0	0	0	0	0	31	69	0	0	FRANDISCO LIFE INS CO
CT	45	48	0	1	6	0	0	0	0	0	GENERAL RE LIFE CORP
NY	68	3	0	1	28	0	0	0	0	0	GERBER LIFE INS CO
TX	85	0	3	9	3	0	0	0	0	0	GOVERNMENT PERSONNEL MUTUAL L I C
OH	88	1	8	3	0	0	0	0	0	0	GRANGE LIFE INS CO
GA	2	0	0	75	23	0	0	0	0	0	GREATER GEORGIA LIFE INS CO

RATING	INSURANCE COMPANY NAME	ADDRESS	CITY	STATE	ZIP	PHONE
A	GUARDIAN LIFE INS CO OF AMERICA	7 HANOVER SQUARE	NEW YORK	NY	10004	(212) 598-800
B+	ILLINOIS MUTUAL LIFE INS CO	300 SW ADAMS	PEORIA	IL	61634	(800) 437-735
A-	JOHN HANCOCK LIFE INS CO OF NY	100 SUMMIT LAKE DR 2ND FLOOR	VALHALLA	NY	10595	(914) 921-102
B+	LIFE INS CO OF BOSTON & NEW YORK	277 NORTH AVE SUITE 200	NEW ROCHELLE	NY	10801	(800) 645-231
A	LIFEWISE ASR CO	7007 220TH SW	MOUNTLAKE TERRACE	WA	98043	(206) 670-458
B+	LINCOLN BENEFIT LIFE CO	206 S 13TH ST, SUITE 200	LINCOLN	NE	68508	(800) 525-928
B+	LINCOLN HERITAGE LIFE INS CO	GOVERNMENT CTR 200 PLEASANT ST	MALDEN	MA	02148	(602) 957-165
A	MASSACHUSETTS MUTUAL LIFE INS CO	1295 STATE ST	SPRINGFIELD	MA	01111	(800) 272-221
B+	MID-WEST NATIONAL LIFE INS CO OF TN	9151 GRAPEVINE HIGHWAY	NORTH RICHLAND HILLS	TX	76180	(817) 255-310
B+	MIDLAND NATIONAL LIFE INS CO	ONE MIDLAND PLAZA	SIOUX FALLS	SD	57193	(605) 335-570
A	MML BAY STATE LIFE INS CO	100 BRIGHT MEADOW BLVD	ENFIELD	CT	06082	(800) 272-221
B+	MTL INS CO	1200 JORIE BLVD	OAK BROOK	IL	60522	(800) 323-732
B+	MUTUAL OF OMAHA INS CO	MUTUAL OF OMAHA PLAZA	OMAHA	NE	68175	(402) 342-7600
A-	NATIONAL BENEFIT LIFE INS CO	333 WEST 34TH STREET	NEW YORK	NY	10001	(212) 615-7500
B+	NATIONAL GUARDIAN LIFE INS CO	2 E GILMAN ST	MADISON	WI	53703	(608) 443-5148
B+	NATIONAL WESTERN LIFE INS CO	1675 BROADWAY #1200	DENVER	CO	80202	(512) 836-101
B+	NATIONWIDE LIFE INS CO OF AMERICA	1600 MARKET ST	PHILADELPHIA	PA	19103	(610) 407-105
A-	NEW YORK LIFE INS & ANNUITY CORP	200 CONTINENTAL DR	NEWARK	DE	19713	(212) 576-7000
A-	NEW YORK LIFE INS CO	51 MADISON AVE	NEW YORK	NY	10010	(212) 576-7000
A-	NIPPON LIFE INS CO OF AMERICA	650 8TH ST	DES MOINES	IA	50309	(212) 682-3992
A-	NORTHWESTERN MUTUAL LIFE INS CO	720 E WISCONSIN AVE	MILWAUKEE	WI	53202	(414) 271-1444
B+	OHIO NATIONAL LIFE ASR CORP	ONE FINANCIAL WAY	CINCINNATI	OH	45242	(513) 794-6100
A-	PACIFIC GUARDIAN LIFE INS CO LTD	1440 KAPIOLANI BLVD STE 1700	HONOLULU	HI	96814	(808) 955-2236
A-	PACIFIC LIFE & ANNUITY CO	638 N FIFTH AVE	PHOENIX	AZ	85003	(800) 800-7646
A-	PACIFIC LIFE INS CO	1299 FARNAM ST	OMAHA	NE	68102	(949) 219-3011
B+	PEKIN LIFE INS CO	2505 COURT ST	PEKIN	IL	61558	(309) 346-1161
B+	PENN INS & ANNUITY CO	1209 ORANGE ST	WILMINGTON	DE	19801	(215) 956-8893
B+	PENN MUTUAL LIFE INS CO	600 DRESHER RD	HORSHAM	PA	19044	(215) 956-8893
B+	PHARMACISTS LIFE INS CO	808 HIGHWAY 18 WEST	ALGONA	IA	50511	(800) 247-5930
A-	PHYSICIANS LIFE INS CO	2600 DODGE ST	OMAHA	NE	68131	(800) 228-9100
A+	PHYSICIANS MUTUAL INS CO	2600 DODGE ST	OMAHA	NE	68131	(800) 228-9100
A-	PRIMERICA LIFE INS CO	3120 BRECKINRIDGE BLVD	DULUTH	GA	30199	(770) 381-1000
A-	PRINCIPAL LIFE INS CO	711 HIGH ST	DES MOINES	IA	50392	(800) 986-3343
B+	REGENCE LIFE & HEALTH INS CO	100 SW MARKET ST	PORTLAND	OR	97201	(503) 225-6048
B+	RELIABLE LIFE INS CO	231 W LOCKWOOD AVE	WEBSTER GROVES	MO	63119	(314) 968-4900
B+	SAVINGS BANK LIFE INS CO OF MA	ONE LINSCOTT RD	WOBURN	MA	01801	(781) 938-3500
A	SENTRY LIFE INS CO	1800 NORTH POINT DR	STEVENS POINT	WI	54481	(715) 346-6000
B+	SETTLERS LIFE INS CO	2 E GILMAN ST	MADISON	WI	53703	(276) 645-4300
A-	SHELTER LIFE INS CO	1817 W BROADWAY	COLUMBIA	MO	65218	(800) 743-5837
A	SOUTHERN FARM BUREAU LIFE INS CO	1401 LIVINGSTON LANE	JACKSON	MS	39213	(601) 981-7422
B+	SOUTHERN NATL LIFE INS CO INC	5525 REITZ AVE	BATON ROUGE	LA	70809	(225) 295-2525
B+	STANDARD INS CO	1100 SW SIXTH AVE	PORTLAND	OR	97204	(503) 321-7000
A-	STANDARD LIFE & ACCIDENT INS CO	201 ROBERT S KERR AVE STE 600	OKLAHOMA CITY	OK	73102	(409) 766-6448
B+	STANDARD SECURITY LIFE INS CO OF NY	485 MADISON AVE	NEW YORK	NY	10022	(212) 355-4141
A+	STATE FARM LIFE & ACCIDENT ASR CO	ONE STATE FARM PLAZA	BLOOMINGTON	IL	61710	(309) 766-2311
A+	STATE FARM LIFE INS CO	ONE STATE FARM PLAZA	BLOOMINGTON	IL	61710	(309) 766-2311
B+	STONEBRIDGE LIFE INS CO	56 1/2 MERCHANTS ROW	RUTLAND	VT	05702	(410) 685-5500
B+	SURETY LIFE INS CO	206 S 13TH ST SUITE 300	LINCOLN	NE	68508	(800) 525-9287
A+	TEACHERS INS & ANNUITY ASN OF AM	730 THIRD AVE 7TH FLOOR	NEW YORK	NY	10017	(212) 490-9000
A	TENNESSEE FARMERS LIFE INS CO	147 BEAR CREEK PIKE	COLUMBIA	TN	38401	(931) 388-7872
B+	THRIVENT LIFE INS CO	625 FOURTH AVE S	MINNEAPOLIS	MN	55415	(612) 340-7214
A	UNION NATIONAL LIFE INS CO	12115 LACKLAND ROAD	ST LOUIS	MO	63146	(800) 765-0550
A	UNITED FARM FAMILY LIFE INS CO	225 S EAST ST	INDIANAPOLIS	IN	46202	(317) 692-7200
B+	UNITED INVESTORS LIFE INS CO	120 S CENTRAL AVE	CLAYTON	MO	63105	(800) 340-3787
B+	UNITED OF OMAHA LIFE INS CO	MUTUAL OF OMAHA PLAZA	OMAHA	NE	68175	(402) 342-7600
B+	UNITED WORLD LIFE INS CO	MUTUAL OF OMAHA PLAZA	OMAHA	NE	68175	(402) 342-7600

DOM. STATE	IND. LIFE	IND. HEALTH	IND. ANNU.	GROUP LIFE	GROUP HEALTH	GROUP ANNU	CREDIT LIFE	CREDIT HEALTH	SUP. CONTR.	OTHER	INSURANCE COMPANY NAME
NY	45	0	1	5	49	0	0	0	0	0	GUARDIAN LIFE INS CO OF AMERICA
IL	26	42	31	0	1	0	0	0	0	0	ILLINOIS MUTUAL LIFE INS CO
NY	13	0	49	0	0	39	0	0	0	0	JOHN HANCOCK LIFE INS CO OF NY
NY	90	2	0	1	7	0	0	0	0	0	LIFE INS CO OF BOSTON & NEW YORK
WA	0	0	0	41	59	0	0	0	0	0	LIFEWISE ASR CO
NE	0	0	0	0	0	0	0	0	0	0	LINCOLN BENEFIT LIFE CO
IL	82	7	1	10	0	1	0	0	0	0	LINCOLN HERITAGE LIFE INS CO
MA	29	3	19	2	0	47	0	0	0	0	MASSACHUSETTS MUTUAL LIFE INS CO
TX	0	9	0	0	90	0	0	0	0	0	MID-WEST NATIONAL LIFE INS CO OF TN
IA	25	0	56	0	0	19	0	0	0	0	MIDLAND NATIONAL LIFE INS CO
CT	95	0	1	4	0	0	0	0	0	0	MML BAY STATE LIFE INS CO
IL	93	0	7	0	0	0	0	0	0	0	MTL INS CO
NE	0	84	0	0	16	0	0	0	0	0	MUTUAL OF OMAHA INS CO
NY	66	0	0	1	31	0	1	1	0	0	NATIONAL BENEFIT LIFE INS CO
WI	47	2	2	38	9	1	0	0	0	0	NATIONAL GUARDIAN LIFE INS CO
CO	30	0	52	0	0	18	0	0	0	0	NATIONAL WESTERN LIFE INS CO
PA	97	0	0	2	0	0	0	0	0	0	NATIONWIDE LIFE INS CO OF AMERICA
DE	11	0	87	1	0	1	0	0	0	0	NEW YORK LIFE INS & ANNUITY CORP
NY	50	1	3	12	3	30	0	0	0	0	NEW YORK LIFE INS CO
IA	0	0	0	2	98	0	0	0	0	0	NIPPON LIFE INS CO OF AMERICA
WI	83	6	10	0	0	1	0	0	0	0	NORTHWESTERN MUTUAL LIFE INS CO
OH	98	2	0	0	0	0	0	0	0	0	OHIO NATIONAL LIFE ASR CORP
HI	44	0	0	15	40	0	0	0	0	0	PACIFIC GUARDIAN LIFE INS CO LTD
AZ	7	0	93	0	0	0	0	0	0	0	PACIFIC LIFE & ANNUITY CO
NE	25	0	61	0	0	14	0	0	0	0	PACIFIC LIFE INS CO
IL	20	25	15	9	27	0	2	3	0	0	PEKIN LIFE INS CO
DE	97	0	2	1	0	0	0	0	0	0	PENN INS & ANNUITY CO
PA	42	0	54	0	0	3	0	0	0	0	PENN MUTUAL LIFE INS CO
IA	60	0	40	0	0	0	0	0	0	0	PHARMACISTS LIFE INS CO
NE	85	0	15	0	0	0	0	0	0	0	PHYSICIANS LIFE INS CO
NE	0	99	0	0	1	0	0	0	0	0	PHYSICIANS MUTUAL INS CO
MA	100	0	0	0	0	0	0	0	0	0	PRIMERICA LIFE INS CO
IA	14	2	49	4	28	2	0	0	0	0	PRINCIPAL LIFE INS CO
OR	0	7	0	53	40	0	0	0	0	0	REGENCE LIFE & HEALTH INS CO
MO	94	6	0	0	0	0	0	0	0	0	RELIABLE LIFE INS CO
MA	87	0	13	0	0	0	0	0	0	0	SAVINGS BANK LIFE INS CO OF MA
WI	8	0	1	2	-1	90	0	0	0	0	SENTRY LIFE INS CO
WI	77	1	0	21	0	0	0	0	0	0	SETTLERS LIFE INS CO
MO	69	2	13	1	15	0	0	0	0	0	SHELTER LIFE INS CO
MS	65	1	32	1	1	0	0	0	0	0	SOUTHERN FARM BUREAU LIFE INS CO
LA	1	0	0	50	49	0	0	0	0	0	SOUTHERN NATL LIFE INS CO INC
OR	0	3	22	18	29	28	0	0	0	0	STANDARD INS CO
OK	11	77	8	0	4	0	0	0	0	0	STANDARD LIFE & ACCIDENT INS CO
NY	0	0	0	1	98	0	0	0	0	0	STANDARD SECURITY LIFE INS CO OF NY
IL	75	0	25	0	0	0	0	0	0	0	STATE FARM LIFE & ACCIDENT ASR CO
IL	74	0	24	1	0	0	0	0	0	0	STATE FARM LIFE INS CO
VT	16	5	0	25	53	0	1	1	0	0	STONEBRIDGE LIFE INS CO
NE	0	0	0	0	0	0	0	0	0	0	SURETY LIFE INS CO
NY	3	0	68	0	0	29	0	0	0	0	TEACHERS INS & ANNUITY ASN OF AM
TN	62	0	36	0	2	0	0	0	0	0	TENNESSEE FARMERS LIFE INS CO
MN	8	0	92	0	0	0	0	0	0	0	THRIVENT LIFE INS CO
LA	92	8	0	0	0	0	0	0	0	0	UNION NATIONAL LIFE INS CO
IN	87	1	12	0	0	0	0	0	0	0	UNITED FARM FAMILY LIFE INS CO
MO	33	0	64	3	0	0	0	0	0	0	UNITED INVESTORS LIFE INS CO
NE	40	1	12	16	19	12	0	0	0	0	UNITED OF OMAHA LIFE INS CO
NE	100	0	0	0	0	0	0	0	0	0	UNITED WORLD LIFE INS CO

RATING	INSURANCE COMPANY NAME	ADDRESS	CITY	STATE	ZIP	PHONE
A	USAA LIFE INS CO	9800 FREDERICKSBURG RD	SAN ANTONIO	TX	78288	(210) 498-800
B+	USAA LIFE INS CO OF NEW YORK	529 MAIN STREET	HIGHLAND FALLS	NY	10928	(210) 498-800
A-	USABLE LIFE	320 W CAPITOL SUITE 700	LITTLE ROCK	AR	72201	(800) 370-585
B+	WORLD CORP INS CO	4317 RAMSEY ST	FAYETTEVILLE	NC	28311	(804) 354-732
A-	WORLD INS CO	11808 GRANT ST	OMAHA	NE	68164	(402) 496-800

DOM. STATE	IND. LIFE	IND. HEALTH	IND. ANNU.	GROUP LIFE	GROUP HEALTH	GROUP ANNU	CREDIT LIFE	CREDIT HEALTH	SUP. CONTR.	OTHER	INSURANCE COMPANY NAME
TX	18	7	75	0	0	0	0	0	0	0	USAA LIFE INS CO
NY	19	0	81	0	0	0	0	0	0	0	USAA LIFE INS CO OF NEW YORK
AR	2	8	0	28	62	0	0	0	0	0	USABLE LIFE
NE	0	100	0	0	0	0	0	0	0	0	WORLD CORP INS CO
NE	2	54	0	0	44	0	0	0	0	0	WORLD INS CO

Section IV

TheStreet.com Recommended Companies by State

A compilation of those

U.S. Life and Annuity Insurers

receiving a TheStreet.com Financial Strength Rating
of A+, A, A- or B+.

Companies are ranked by Financial Strength Rating
in each state where they are licensed to do business.

Section IV Contents

This section provides a list of the recommended carriers licensed to do business in each state. It contains all insurers receiving a TheStreet.com Financial Strength Rating of A+, A, A-, or B+. If an insurer is not on this list, it should not be automatically assumed that the firm is weak. Indeed, there are many firms that have not achieved a B+ or better rating but are in relatively good condition with adequate resources to cover their risk during an average recession. Not being included in this list should not be construed as a recommendation to surrender policies.

Companies are ranked within each state by their Financial Strength Rating. However, companies with the same rating should be viewed as having the same relative strength regardless of their ranking in this table. While the specific order in which they appear on the page is based upon differences in our underlying indexes, you can assume that companies with the same rating have differences that are only minor and relatively inconsequential.

1. **Financial Strength Rating**   Our rating is measured on a scale from A to F and considers a wide range of factors. Highly-rated companies are, in our opinion, less likely to experience financial difficulties than lower rated firms. See *About TheStreet.com Financial Strength Ratings* on page 9 for more information.

2. **Insurance Company Name**   The legally registered name, which can sometimes differ from the name that the company uses for advertising. An insurer's name can be very similar to the name of other companies which may not be on our Recommended List, so make sure you note the exact name before contacting your agent.

3. **Domicile State**   The state which has primary regulatory responsibility for the company. It may differ from the location of the company's corporate headquarters. You do not have to be living in the domicile state to purchase insurance from this firm, provided it is licensed to do business in your state.

4. **Total Assets**   All assets admitted by state insurance regulators in millions of dollars. This includes investments, current business assets, and separate accounts.

TheStreet.com Financial Strength Ratings are not deemed to be a recommendation concerning the purchase or sale of the securities of any insurance company that is publicly owned.

Alabama

INSURANCE COMPANY NAME	DOM. STATE	TOTAL ASSETS ($MIL)

Rating: A+

INSURANCE COMPANY NAME	DOM. STATE	TOTAL ASSETS ($MIL)
COUNTRY LIFE INS CO	IL	7,329.3
PHYSICIANS MUTUAL INS CO	NE	1,445.1
STATE FARM LIFE INS CO	IL	44,978.4
TEACHERS INS & ANNUITY ASN OF AM	NY	194,588.7

Rating: A

AMERICAN FIDELITY ASR CO	OK	3,343.9
AUTO-OWNERS LIFE INS CO	MI	2,168.0
BERKSHIRE LIFE INS CO OF AMERICA	MA	2,502.2
FEDERATED LIFE INS CO	MN	978.1
FIDELITY INVESTMENTS LIFE INS CO	UT	11,382.8
GUARDIAN LIFE INS CO OF AMERICA	NY	29,202.2
MASSACHUSETTS MUTUAL LIFE INS CO	MA	112,014.6
MML BAY STATE LIFE INS CO	CT	4,105.4
SENTRY LIFE INS CO	WI	2,809.8
SOUTHERN FARM BUREAU LIFE INS CO	MS	10,074.1
UNION NATIONAL LIFE INS CO	LA	459.3
USAA LIFE INS CO	TX	13,463.6

Rating: A-

ACACIA LIFE INS CO	DC	1,521.4
AMERICAN REPUBLIC INS CO	IA	472.8
AMICA LIFE INS CO	RI	950.4
ANTHEM LIFE INS CO	IN	288.0
CHARTER NATIONAL LIFE INS CO	IL	133.2
COMPANION LIFE INS CO	SC	124.7
CONTINENTAL AMERICAN INS CO	SC	105.0
COUNTRY INVESTORS LIFE ASR CO	IL	192.1
FIRST INVESTORS LIFE INS CO	NY	949.4
FORT DEARBORN LIFE INS CO	IL	2,870.9
GERBER LIFE INS CO	NY	1,568.7
GREATER GEORGIA LIFE INS CO	GA	46.3
NATIONAL BENEFIT LIFE INS CO	NY	738.4
NEW YORK LIFE INS & ANNUITY CORP	DE	77,190.7
NEW YORK LIFE INS CO	NY	114,937.8
NIPPON LIFE INS CO OF AMERICA	IA	162.8
NORTHWESTERN MUTUAL LIFE INS CO	WI	155,607.2
PACIFIC LIFE & ANNUITY CO	AZ	2,589.4
PACIFIC LIFE INS CO	NE	81,524.3
PHYSICIANS LIFE INS CO	NE	1,249.3
PRIMERICA LIFE INS CO	MA	5,765.7
PRINCIPAL LIFE INS CO	IA	109,923.9
STANDARD LIFE & ACCIDENT INS CO	OK	484.7
USABLE LIFE	AR	298.5
WORLD INS CO	NE	242.3

Rating: B+

ALFA LIFE INS CORP	AL	1,087.3
ALLSTATE LIFE INS CO	IL	65,002.0
AMERICAN FAMILY LIFE ASR CO OF COLUM	NE	67,309.5
AMERICAN HEALTH & LIFE INS CO	TX	1,505.6
AMERICAN INCOME LIFE INS CO	IN	1,811.7
AMERICAN UNITED LIFE INS CO	IN	12,264.8
AMERITAS LIFE INS CORP	NE	4,928.5
ASSURITY LIFE INS CO	NE	2,167.6

INSURANCE COMPANY NAME	DOM. STATE	TOTAL ASSETS ($MIL)
ATLANTIC COAST LIFE INS CO	SC	69.9
BLUEBONNET LIFE INS CO	MS	39.2
BOSTON MUTUAL LIFE INS CO	MA	945.5
CHEROKEE NATIONAL LIFE INS CO	GA	30.8
COLORADO BANKERS LIFE INS CO	CO	144.4
COLUMBUS LIFE INS CO	OH	2,512.2
COMPBENEFITS INS CO	TX	62.7
CONTINENTAL LIFE INS CO OF BRENTWOOD	TN	149.3
COTTON STATES LIFE INS CO	GA	281.8
EASTERN LIFE & HEALTH INS CO	PA	44.9
FAMILY HERITAGE LIFE INS CO OF AMER	OH	322.3
FIDELITY LIFE ASSN A LEGAL RESERVE	IL	505.8
FIDELITY SECURITY LIFE INS CO	MO	576.6
FLORIDA COMBINED LIFE INS CO INC	FL	31.8
GENERAL RE LIFE CORP	CT	2,682.0
GOVERNMENT PERSONNEL MUTUAL L I C	TX	783.4
ILLINOIS MUTUAL LIFE INS CO	IL	1,262.3
LINCOLN BENEFIT LIFE CO	NE	2,007.2
LINCOLN HERITAGE LIFE INS CO	IL	629.7
MID-WEST NATIONAL LIFE INS CO OF TN	TX	228.4
MIDLAND NATIONAL LIFE INS CO	IA	25,970.2
MTL INS CO	IL	1,337.3
MUTUAL OF OMAHA INS CO	NE	4,625.4
NATIONAL GUARDIAN LIFE INS CO	WI	1,663.4
NATIONAL WESTERN LIFE INS CO	CO	6,175.2
NATIONWIDE LIFE INS CO OF AMERICA	PA	4,826.2
OHIO NATIONAL LIFE ASR CORP	OH	2,702.3
PENN INS & ANNUITY CO	DE	1,038.9
PENN MUTUAL LIFE INS CO	PA	9,647.6
PHARMACISTS LIFE INS CO	IA	40.4
RELIABLE LIFE INS CO	MO	747.4
SETTLERS LIFE INS CO	WI	417.4
STANDARD INS CO	OR	12,858.1
STANDARD SECURITY LIFE INS CO OF NY	NY	365.4
STONEBRIDGE LIFE INS CO	VT	2,089.0
SURETY LIFE INS CO	NE	13.2
THRIVENT LIFE INS CO	MN	2,564.9
UNITED INVESTORS LIFE INS CO	MO	2,518.4
UNITED OF OMAHA LIFE INS CO	NE	12,875.0
UNITED WORLD LIFE INS CO	NE	114.6
WORLD CORP INS CO	NE	23.2

Alaska

INSURANCE COMPANY NAME	DOM. STATE	TOTAL ASSETS ($MIL)

Rating: A+

INSURANCE COMPANY NAME	DOM. STATE	TOTAL ASSETS ($MIL)
COUNTRY LIFE INS CO	IL	7,329.3
PHYSICIANS MUTUAL INS CO	NE	1,445.1
STATE FARM LIFE INS CO	IL	44,978.4
TEACHERS INS & ANNUITY ASN OF AM	NY	194,588.7

Rating: A

INSURANCE COMPANY NAME	DOM. STATE	TOTAL ASSETS ($MIL)
AMERICAN FIDELITY ASR CO	OK	3,343.9
BERKSHIRE LIFE INS CO OF AMERICA	MA	2,502.2
FIDELITY INVESTMENTS LIFE INS CO	UT	11,382.8
GUARDIAN LIFE INS CO OF AMERICA	NY	29,202.2
LIFEWISE ASR CO	WA	70.2
MASSACHUSETTS MUTUAL LIFE INS CO	MA	112,014.6
MML BAY STATE LIFE INS CO	CT	4,105.4
SENTRY LIFE INS CO	WI	2,809.8
USAA LIFE INS CO	TX	13,463.6

Rating: A-

INSURANCE COMPANY NAME	DOM. STATE	TOTAL ASSETS ($MIL)
AMALGAMATED LIFE INS CO	NY	62.6
AMERICAN REPUBLIC INS CO	IA	472.8
AMICA LIFE INS CO	RI	950.4
ANTHEM LIFE INS CO	IN	288.0
CHARTER NATIONAL LIFE INS CO	IL	133.2
COMPANION LIFE INS CO	SC	124.7
CONTINENTAL AMERICAN INS CO	SC	105.0
COUNTRY INVESTORS LIFE ASR CO	IL	192.1
FIRST INVESTORS LIFE INS CO	NY	949.4
FORT DEARBORN LIFE INS CO	IL	2,870.9
GERBER LIFE INS CO	NY	1,568.7
NATIONAL BENEFIT LIFE INS CO	NY	738.4
NEW YORK LIFE INS & ANNUITY CORP	DE	77,190.7
NEW YORK LIFE INS CO	NY	114,937.8
NIPPON LIFE INS CO OF AMERICA	IA	162.8
NORTHWESTERN MUTUAL LIFE INS CO	WI	155,607.2
PACIFIC GUARDIAN LIFE INS CO LTD	HI	426.8
PACIFIC LIFE & ANNUITY CO	AZ	2,589.4
PACIFIC LIFE INS CO	NE	81,524.3
PHYSICIANS LIFE INS CO	NE	1,249.3
PRIMERICA LIFE INS CO	MA	5,765.7
PRINCIPAL LIFE INS CO	IA	109,923.9
STANDARD LIFE & ACCIDENT INS CO	OK	484.7

Rating: B+

INSURANCE COMPANY NAME	DOM. STATE	TOTAL ASSETS ($MIL)
ALLSTATE LIFE INS CO	IL	65,002.0
AMERICAN FAMILY LIFE ASR CO OF COLUM	NE	67,309.5
AMERICAN HEALTH & LIFE INS CO	TX	1,505.6
AMERICAN INCOME LIFE INS CO	IN	1,811.7
AMERICAN UNITED LIFE INS CO	IN	12,264.8
AMERITAS LIFE INS CORP	NE	4,928.5
ASSURITY LIFE INS CO	NE	2,167.6
BOSTON MUTUAL LIFE INS CO	MA	945.5
COLORADO BANKERS LIFE INS CO	CO	144.4
COLUMBUS LIFE INS CO	OH	2,512.2
FAMILY HERITAGE LIFE INS CO OF AMER	OH	322.3
FIDELITY LIFE ASSN A LEGAL RESERVE	IL	505.8
FIDELITY SECURITY LIFE INS CO	MO	576.6

INSURANCE COMPANY NAME	DOM. STATE	TOTAL ASSETS ($MIL)
GENERAL RE LIFE CORP	CT	2,682.0
GOVERNMENT PERSONNEL MUTUAL L I C	TX	783.4
LINCOLN BENEFIT LIFE CO	NE	2,007.2
LINCOLN HERITAGE LIFE INS CO	IL	629.7
MID-WEST NATIONAL LIFE INS CO OF TN	TX	228.4
MIDLAND NATIONAL LIFE INS CO	IA	25,970.2
MUTUAL OF OMAHA INS CO	NE	4,625.4
NATIONAL GUARDIAN LIFE INS CO	WI	1,663.4
NATIONAL WESTERN LIFE INS CO	CO	6,175.2
NATIONWIDE LIFE INS CO OF AMERICA	PA	4,826.2
PENN INS & ANNUITY CO	DE	1,038.9
PENN MUTUAL LIFE INS CO	PA	9,647.6
REGENCE LIFE & HEALTH INS CO	OR	80.7
RELIABLE LIFE INS CO	MO	747.4
SETTLERS LIFE INS CO	WI	417.4
STANDARD INS CO	OR	12,858.1
STANDARD SECURITY LIFE INS CO OF NY	NY	365.4
STONEBRIDGE LIFE INS CO	VT	2,089.0
SURETY LIFE INS CO	NE	13.2
THRIVENT LIFE INS CO	MN	2,564.9
UNITED INVESTORS LIFE INS CO	MO	2,518.4
UNITED OF OMAHA LIFE INS CO	NE	12,875.0
UNITED WORLD LIFE INS CO	NE	114.6

Arizona

INSURANCE COMPANY NAME	DOM. STATE	TOTAL ASSETS ($MIL)
Rating: A+		
AMERICAN FAMILY LIFE INS CO	WI	3,898.0
COUNTRY LIFE INS CO	IL	7,329.3
PHYSICIANS MUTUAL INS CO	NE	1,445.1
STATE FARM LIFE INS CO	IL	44,978.4
TEACHERS INS & ANNUITY ASN OF AM	NY	194,588.7
Rating: A		
AMERICAN FIDELITY ASR CO	OK	3,343.9
AUTO-OWNERS LIFE INS CO	MI	2,168.0
BERKSHIRE LIFE INS CO OF AMERICA	MA	2,502.2
FEDERATED LIFE INS CO	MN	978.1
FIDELITY INVESTMENTS LIFE INS CO	UT	11,382.8
GUARDIAN LIFE INS CO OF AMERICA	NY	29,202.2
LIFEWISE ASR CO	WA	70.2
MASSACHUSETTS MUTUAL LIFE INS CO	MA	112,014.6
MML BAY STATE LIFE INS CO	CT	4,105.4
SENTRY LIFE INS CO	WI	2,809.8
UNITED FARM FAMILY LIFE INS CO	IN	1,712.9
USAA LIFE INS CO	TX	13,463.6
Rating: A-		
ACACIA LIFE INS CO	DC	1,521.4
AMALGAMATED LIFE INS CO	NY	62.6
AMERICAN REPUBLIC INS CO	IA	472.8
AMICA LIFE INS CO	RI	950.4
ANTHEM LIFE INS CO	IN	288.0
CHARTER NATIONAL LIFE INS CO	IL	133.2
COMPANION LIFE INS CO	SC	124.7
CONTINENTAL AMERICAN INS CO	SC	105.0
COUNTRY INVESTORS LIFE ASR CO	IL	192.1
FIRST INVESTORS LIFE INS CO	NY	949.4
FORT DEARBORN LIFE INS CO	IL	2,870.9
GERBER LIFE INS CO	NY	1,568.7
NATIONAL BENEFIT LIFE INS CO	NY	738.4
NEW YORK LIFE INS & ANNUITY CORP	DE	77,190.7
NEW YORK LIFE INS CO	NY	114,937.8
NIPPON LIFE INS CO OF AMERICA	IA	162.8
NORTHWESTERN MUTUAL LIFE INS CO	WI	155,607.2
PACIFIC GUARDIAN LIFE INS CO LTD	HI	426.8
PACIFIC LIFE & ANNUITY CO	AZ	2,589.4
PACIFIC LIFE INS CO	NE	81,524.3
PHYSICIANS LIFE INS CO	NE	1,249.3
PRIMERICA LIFE INS CO	MA	5,765.7
PRINCIPAL LIFE INS CO	IA	109,923.9
STANDARD LIFE & ACCIDENT INS CO	OK	484.7
USABLE LIFE	AR	298.5
WORLD INS CO	NE	242.3
Rating: B+		
ALLSTATE LIFE INS CO	IL	65,002.0
AMERICAN FAMILY LIFE ASR CO OF COLUM	NE	67,309.5
AMERICAN HEALTH & LIFE INS CO	TX	1,505.6
AMERICAN INCOME LIFE INS CO	IN	1,811.7
AMERICAN UNITED LIFE INS CO	IN	12,264.8
AMERITAS LIFE INS CORP	NE	4,928.5

INSURANCE COMPANY NAME	DOM. STATE	TOTAL ASSETS ($MIL)
ASSURITY LIFE INS CO	NE	2,167.6
BOSTON MUTUAL LIFE INS CO	MA	945.5
COLORADO BANKERS LIFE INS CO	CO	144.4
COLUMBUS LIFE INS CO	OH	2,512.2
COMPBENEFITS INS CO	TX	62.7
CONTINENTAL LIFE INS CO OF BRENTWOOD	TN	149.3
EASTERN LIFE & HEALTH INS CO	PA	44.9
EPIC LIFE INSURANCE CO	WI	42.6
FAMILY HERITAGE LIFE INS CO OF AMER	OH	322.3
FARM BUREAU LIFE INS CO	IA	5,605.0
FIDELITY LIFE ASSN A LEGAL RESERVE	IL	505.8
FIDELITY SECURITY LIFE INS CO	MO	576.6
GENERAL RE LIFE CORP	CT	2,682.0
GOVERNMENT PERSONNEL MUTUAL L I C	TX	783.4
ILLINOIS MUTUAL LIFE INS CO	IL	1,262.3
LINCOLN BENEFIT LIFE CO	NE	2,007.2
LINCOLN HERITAGE LIFE INS CO	IL	629.7
MID-WEST NATIONAL LIFE INS CO OF TN	TX	228.4
MIDLAND NATIONAL LIFE INS CO	IA	25,970.2
MTL INS CO	IL	1,337.3
MUTUAL OF OMAHA INS CO	NE	4,625.4
NATIONAL GUARDIAN LIFE INS CO	WI	1,663.4
NATIONAL WESTERN LIFE INS CO	CO	6,175.2
NATIONWIDE LIFE INS CO OF AMERICA	PA	4,826.2
OHIO NATIONAL LIFE ASR CORP	OH	2,702.3
PENN INS & ANNUITY CO	DE	1,038.9
PENN MUTUAL LIFE INS CO	PA	9,647.6
PHARMACISTS LIFE INS CO	IA	40.4
RELIABLE LIFE INS CO	MO	747.4
SAVINGS BANK LIFE INS CO OF MA	MA	2,093.4
SETTLERS LIFE INS CO	WI	417.4
STANDARD INS CO	OR	12,858.1
STANDARD SECURITY LIFE INS CO OF NY	NY	365.4
STONEBRIDGE LIFE INS CO	VT	2,089.0
SURETY LIFE INS CO	NE	13.2
THRIVENT LIFE INS CO	MN	2,564.9
UNITED INVESTORS LIFE INS CO	MO	2,518.4
UNITED OF OMAHA LIFE INS CO	NE	12,875.0
UNITED WORLD LIFE INS CO	NE	114.6
WORLD CORP INS CO	NE	23.2

Arkansas

INSURANCE COMPANY NAME	DOM. STATE	TOTAL ASSETS ($MIL)

Rating: A+

INSURANCE COMPANY NAME	DOM. STATE	TOTAL ASSETS ($MIL)
COUNTRY LIFE INS CO	IL	7,329.3
PHYSICIANS MUTUAL INS CO	NE	1,445.1
STATE FARM LIFE INS CO	IL	44,978.4
TEACHERS INS & ANNUITY ASN OF AM	NY	194,588.7

Rating: A

INSURANCE COMPANY NAME	DOM. STATE	TOTAL ASSETS ($MIL)
AMERICAN FIDELITY ASR CO	OK	3,343.9
AUTO-OWNERS LIFE INS CO	MI	2,168.0
BERKSHIRE LIFE INS CO OF AMERICA	MA	2,502.2
FEDERATED LIFE INS CO	MN	978.1
FIDELITY INVESTMENTS LIFE INS CO	UT	11,382.8
GUARDIAN LIFE INS CO OF AMERICA	NY	29,202.2
MASSACHUSETTS MUTUAL LIFE INS CO	MA	112,014.6
MML BAY STATE LIFE INS CO	CT	4,105.4
SENTRY LIFE INS CO	WI	2,809.8
SOUTHERN FARM BUREAU LIFE INS CO	MS	10,074.1
UNION NATIONAL LIFE INS CO	LA	459.3
USAA LIFE INS CO	TX	13,463.6

Rating: A-

INSURANCE COMPANY NAME	DOM. STATE	TOTAL ASSETS ($MIL)
ACACIA LIFE INS CO	DC	1,521.4
AMERICAN REPUBLIC INS CO	IA	472.8
AMICA LIFE INS CO	RI	950.4
ANTHEM LIFE INS CO	IN	288.0
CHARTER NATIONAL LIFE INS CO	IL	133.2
COMPANION LIFE INS CO	SC	124.7
CONTINENTAL AMERICAN INS CO	SC	105.0
COUNTRY INVESTORS LIFE ASR CO	IL	192.1
FIRST INVESTORS LIFE INS CO	NY	949.4
FORT DEARBORN LIFE INS CO	IL	2,870.9
GERBER LIFE INS CO	NY	1,568.7
NATIONAL BENEFIT LIFE INS CO	NY	738.4
NEW YORK LIFE INS & ANNUITY CORP	DE	77,190.7
NEW YORK LIFE INS CO	NY	114,937.8
NIPPON LIFE INS CO OF AMERICA	IA	162.8
NORTHWESTERN MUTUAL LIFE INS CO	WI	155,607.2
PACIFIC LIFE & ANNUITY CO	AZ	2,589.4
PACIFIC LIFE INS CO	NE	81,524.3
PHYSICIANS LIFE INS CO	NE	1,249.3
PRIMERICA LIFE INS CO	MA	5,765.7
PRINCIPAL LIFE INS CO	IA	109,923.9
SHELTER LIFE INS CO	MO	933.1
STANDARD LIFE & ACCIDENT INS CO	OK	484.7
USABLE LIFE	AR	298.5
WORLD INS CO	NE	242.3

Rating: B+

INSURANCE COMPANY NAME	DOM. STATE	TOTAL ASSETS ($MIL)
ALFA LIFE INS CORP	AL	1,087.3
ALLSTATE LIFE INS CO	IL	65,002.0
AMERICAN FAMILY LIFE ASR CO OF COLUM	NE	67,309.5
AMERICAN HEALTH & LIFE INS CO	TX	1,505.6
AMERICAN INCOME LIFE INS CO	IN	1,811.7
AMERICAN UNITED LIFE INS CO	IN	12,264.8
AMERITAS LIFE INS CORP	NE	4,928.5
ASSURITY LIFE INS CO	NE	2,167.6

INSURANCE COMPANY NAME	DOM. STATE	TOTAL ASSETS ($MIL)
BLUEBONNET LIFE INS CO	MS	39.2
BOSTON MUTUAL LIFE INS CO	MA	945.5
CHEROKEE NATIONAL LIFE INS CO	GA	30.8
COLORADO BANKERS LIFE INS CO	CO	144.4
COLUMBUS LIFE INS CO	OH	2,512.2
COMPBENEFITS INS CO	TX	62.7
CONTINENTAL LIFE INS CO OF BRENTWOOD	TN	149.3
EASTERN LIFE & HEALTH INS CO	PA	44.9
EPIC LIFE INSURANCE CO	WI	42.6
FAMILY HERITAGE LIFE INS CO OF AMER	OH	322.3
FIDELITY LIFE ASSN A LEGAL RESERVE	IL	505.8
FIDELITY SECURITY LIFE INS CO	MO	576.6
FLORIDA COMBINED LIFE INS CO INC	FL	31.8
GENERAL RE LIFE CORP	CT	2,682.0
GOVERNMENT PERSONNEL MUTUAL L I C	TX	783.4
ILLINOIS MUTUAL LIFE INS CO	IL	1,262.3
LINCOLN BENEFIT LIFE CO	NE	2,007.2
LINCOLN HERITAGE LIFE INS CO	IL	629.7
MID-WEST NATIONAL LIFE INS CO OF TN	TX	228.4
MIDLAND NATIONAL LIFE INS CO	IA	25,970.2
MTL INS CO	IL	1,337.3
MUTUAL OF OMAHA INS CO	NE	4,625.4
NATIONAL GUARDIAN LIFE INS CO	WI	1,663.4
NATIONAL WESTERN LIFE INS CO	CO	6,175.2
NATIONWIDE LIFE INS CO OF AMERICA	PA	4,826.2
OHIO NATIONAL LIFE ASR CORP	OH	2,702.3
PENN INS & ANNUITY CO	DE	1,038.9
PENN MUTUAL LIFE INS CO	PA	9,647.6
PHARMACISTS LIFE INS CO	IA	40.4
RELIABLE LIFE INS CO	MO	747.4
SAVINGS BANK LIFE INS CO OF MA	MA	2,093.4
SETTLERS LIFE INS CO	WI	417.4
STANDARD INS CO	OR	12,858.1
STANDARD SECURITY LIFE INS CO OF NY	NY	365.4
STONEBRIDGE LIFE INS CO	VT	2,089.0
SURETY LIFE INS CO	NE	13.2
THRIVENT LIFE INS CO	MN	2,564.9
UNITED INVESTORS LIFE INS CO	MO	2,518.4
UNITED OF OMAHA LIFE INS CO	NE	12,875.0
UNITED WORLD LIFE INS CO	NE	114.6
WORLD CORP INS CO	NE	23.2

California

INSURANCE COMPANY NAME	DOM. STATE	TOTAL ASSETS ($MIL)
Rating: A+		
AMERICAN FAMILY LIFE INS CO	WI	3,898.0
PHYSICIANS MUTUAL INS CO	NE	1,445.1
STATE FARM LIFE INS CO	IL	44,978.4
TEACHERS INS & ANNUITY ASN OF AM	NY	194,588.7
Rating: A		
AMERICAN FIDELITY ASR CO	OK	3,343.9
BERKSHIRE LIFE INS CO OF AMERICA	MA	2,502.2
FEDERATED LIFE INS CO	MN	978.1
FIDELITY INVESTMENTS LIFE INS CO	UT	11,382.8
GUARDIAN LIFE INS CO OF AMERICA	NY	29,202.2
LIFEWISE ASR CO	WA	70.2
MASSACHUSETTS MUTUAL LIFE INS CO	MA	112,014.6
MML BAY STATE LIFE INS CO	CT	4,105.4
SENTRY LIFE INS CO	WI	2,809.8
UNITED FARM FAMILY LIFE INS CO	IN	1,712.9
USAA LIFE INS CO	TX	13,463.6
Rating: A-		
ACACIA LIFE INS CO	DC	1,521.4
AMALGAMATED LIFE INS CO	NY	62.6
AMERICAN REPUBLIC INS CO	IA	472.8
AMICA LIFE INS CO	RI	950.4
ANTHEM LIFE INS CO	IN	288.0
BLUE SHIELD OF CALIFORNIA L&H INS CO	CA	364.2
CHARTER NATIONAL LIFE INS CO	IL	133.2
CONTINENTAL AMERICAN INS CO	SC	105.0
FIRST INVESTORS LIFE INS CO	NY	949.4
FORT DEARBORN LIFE INS CO	IL	2,870.9
GERBER LIFE INS CO	NY	1,568.7
NATIONAL BENEFIT LIFE INS CO	NY	738.4
NEW YORK LIFE INS & ANNUITY CORP	DE	77,190.7
NEW YORK LIFE INS CO	NY	114,937.8
NIPPON LIFE INS CO OF AMERICA	IA	162.8
NORTHWESTERN MUTUAL LIFE INS CO	WI	155,607.2
PACIFIC GUARDIAN LIFE INS CO LTD	HI	426.8
PACIFIC LIFE & ANNUITY CO	AZ	2,589.4
PACIFIC LIFE INS CO	NE	81,524.3
PHYSICIANS LIFE INS CO	NE	1,249.3
PRIMERICA LIFE INS CO	MA	5,765.7
PRINCIPAL LIFE INS CO	IA	109,923.9
STANDARD LIFE & ACCIDENT INS CO	OK	484.7
USABLE LIFE	AR	298.5
WORLD INS CO	NE	242.3
Rating: B+		
ALLSTATE LIFE INS CO	IL	65,002.0
AMERICAN FAMILY LIFE ASR CO OF COLUM	NE	67,309.5
AMERICAN HEALTH & LIFE INS CO	TX	1,505.6
AMERICAN INCOME LIFE INS CO	IN	1,811.7
AMERICAN UNITED LIFE INS CO	IN	12,264.8
AMERITAS LIFE INS CORP	NE	4,928.5
ASSURITY LIFE INS CO	NE	2,167.6
BOSTON MUTUAL LIFE INS CO	MA	945.5
COLORADO BANKERS LIFE INS CO	CO	144.4

INSURANCE COMPANY NAME	DOM. STATE	TOTAL ASSETS ($MIL)
COLUMBUS LIFE INS CO	OH	2,512.2
FAMILY HERITAGE LIFE INS CO OF AMER	OH	322.3
FIDELITY LIFE ASSN A LEGAL RESERVE	IL	505.8
FIDELITY SECURITY LIFE INS CO	MO	576.6
GENERAL RE LIFE CORP	CT	2,682.0
GOVERNMENT PERSONNEL MUTUAL L I C	TX	783.4
ILLINOIS MUTUAL LIFE INS CO	IL	1,262.3
LINCOLN BENEFIT LIFE CO	NE	2,007.2
LINCOLN HERITAGE LIFE INS CO	IL	629.7
MID-WEST NATIONAL LIFE INS CO OF TN	TX	228.4
MIDLAND NATIONAL LIFE INS CO	IA	25,970.2
MTL INS CO	IL	1,337.3
MUTUAL OF OMAHA INS CO	NE	4,625.4
NATIONAL GUARDIAN LIFE INS CO	WI	1,663.4
NATIONAL WESTERN LIFE INS CO	CO	6,175.2
NATIONWIDE LIFE INS CO OF AMERICA	PA	4,826.2
OHIO NATIONAL LIFE ASR CORP	OH	2,702.3
PENN INS & ANNUITY CO	DE	1,038.9
PENN MUTUAL LIFE INS CO	PA	9,647.6
PHARMACISTS LIFE INS CO	IA	40.4
RELIABLE LIFE INS CO	MO	747.4
SAVINGS BANK LIFE INS CO OF MA	MA	2,093.4
SETTLERS LIFE INS CO	WI	417.4
STANDARD INS CO	OR	12,858.1
STANDARD SECURITY LIFE INS CO OF NY	NY	365.4
STONEBRIDGE LIFE INS CO	VT	2,089.0
SURETY LIFE INS CO	NE	13.2
THRIVENT LIFE INS CO	MN	2,564.9
UNITED INVESTORS LIFE INS CO	MO	2,518.4
UNITED OF OMAHA LIFE INS CO	NE	12,875.0
UNITED WORLD LIFE INS CO	NE	114.6

Colorado

INSURANCE COMPANY NAME	DOM. STATE	TOTAL ASSETS ($MIL)

Rating: A+

INSURANCE COMPANY NAME	DOM. STATE	TOTAL ASSETS ($MIL)
AMERICAN FAMILY LIFE INS CO	WI	3,898.0
COUNTRY LIFE INS CO	IL	7,329.3
PHYSICIANS MUTUAL INS CO	NE	1,445.1
STATE FARM LIFE INS CO	IL	44,978.4
TEACHERS INS & ANNUITY ASN OF AM	NY	194,588.7

Rating: A

INSURANCE COMPANY NAME	DOM. STATE	TOTAL ASSETS ($MIL)
AMERICAN FIDELITY ASR CO	OK	3,343.9
AUTO-OWNERS LIFE INS CO	MI	2,168.0
BERKSHIRE LIFE INS CO OF AMERICA	MA	2,502.2
FEDERATED LIFE INS CO	MN	978.1
FIDELITY INVESTMENTS LIFE INS CO	UT	11,382.8
GUARDIAN LIFE INS CO OF AMERICA	NY	29,202.2
MASSACHUSETTS MUTUAL LIFE INS CO	MA	112,014.6
MML BAY STATE LIFE INS CO	CT	4,105.4
SENTRY LIFE INS CO	WI	2,809.8
USAA LIFE INS CO	TX	13,463.6

Rating: A-

INSURANCE COMPANY NAME	DOM. STATE	TOTAL ASSETS ($MIL)
ACACIA LIFE INS CO	DC	1,521.4
AMALGAMATED LIFE INS CO	NY	62.6
AMERICAN REPUBLIC INS CO	IA	472.8
AMICA LIFE INS CO	RI	950.4
ANTHEM LIFE INS CO	IN	288.0
CHARTER NATIONAL LIFE INS CO	IL	133.2
COMPANION LIFE INS CO	SC	124.7
CONTINENTAL AMERICAN INS CO	SC	105.0
COUNTRY INVESTORS LIFE ASR CO	IL	192.1
FIRST INVESTORS LIFE INS CO	NY	949.4
FORT DEARBORN LIFE INS CO	IL	2,870.9
GERBER LIFE INS CO	NY	1,568.7
NATIONAL BENEFIT LIFE INS CO	NY	738.4
NEW YORK LIFE INS & ANNUITY CORP	DE	77,190.7
NEW YORK LIFE INS CO	NY	114,937.8
NIPPON LIFE INS CO OF AMERICA	IA	162.8
NORTHWESTERN MUTUAL LIFE INS CO	WI	155,607.2
PACIFIC GUARDIAN LIFE INS CO LTD	HI	426.8
PACIFIC LIFE & ANNUITY CO	AZ	2,589.4
PACIFIC LIFE INS CO	NE	81,524.3
PHYSICIANS LIFE INS CO	NE	1,249.3
PRIMERICA LIFE INS CO	MA	5,765.7
PRINCIPAL LIFE INS CO	IA	109,923.9
SHELTER LIFE INS CO	MO	933.1
STANDARD LIFE & ACCIDENT INS CO	OK	484.7
USABLE LIFE	AR	298.5
WORLD INS CO	NE	242.3

Rating: B+

INSURANCE COMPANY NAME	DOM. STATE	TOTAL ASSETS ($MIL)
ALLSTATE LIFE INS CO	IL	65,002.0
AMERICAN FAMILY LIFE ASR CO OF COLUM	NE	67,309.5
AMERICAN HEALTH & LIFE INS CO	TX	1,505.6
AMERICAN INCOME LIFE INS CO	IN	1,811.7
AMERICAN UNITED LIFE INS CO	IN	12,264.8
AMERITAS LIFE INS CORP	NE	4,928.5
ASSURITY LIFE INS CO	NE	2,167.6

INSURANCE COMPANY NAME	DOM. STATE	TOTAL ASSETS ($MIL)
BOSTON MUTUAL LIFE INS CO	MA	945.5
CHEROKEE NATIONAL LIFE INS CO	GA	30.8
COLORADO BANKERS LIFE INS CO	CO	144.4
COLUMBUS LIFE INS CO	OH	2,512.2
COMPBENEFITS INS CO	TX	62.7
CONTINENTAL LIFE INS CO OF BRENTWOOD	TN	149.3
EASTERN LIFE & HEALTH INS CO	PA	44.9
EPIC LIFE INSURANCE CO	WI	42.6
FAMILY HERITAGE LIFE INS CO OF AMER	OH	322.3
FARM BUREAU LIFE INS CO	IA	5,605.0
FIDELITY LIFE ASSN A LEGAL RESERVE	IL	505.8
FIDELITY SECURITY LIFE INS CO	MO	576.6
GENERAL RE LIFE CORP	CT	2,682.0
GOVERNMENT PERSONNEL MUTUAL L I C	TX	783.4
ILLINOIS MUTUAL LIFE INS CO	IL	1,262.3
LINCOLN BENEFIT LIFE CO	NE	2,007.2
LINCOLN HERITAGE LIFE INS CO	IL	629.7
MID-WEST NATIONAL LIFE INS CO OF TN	TX	228.4
MIDLAND NATIONAL LIFE INS CO	IA	25,970.2
MTL INS CO	IL	1,337.3
MUTUAL OF OMAHA INS CO	NE	4,625.4
NATIONAL GUARDIAN LIFE INS CO	WI	1,663.4
NATIONAL WESTERN LIFE INS CO	CO	6,175.2
NATIONWIDE LIFE INS CO OF AMERICA	PA	4,826.2
OHIO NATIONAL LIFE ASR CORP	OH	2,702.3
PENN INS & ANNUITY CO	DE	1,038.9
PENN MUTUAL LIFE INS CO	PA	9,647.6
PHARMACISTS LIFE INS CO	IA	40.4
RELIABLE LIFE INS CO	MO	747.4
SAVINGS BANK LIFE INS CO OF MA	MA	2,093.4
SETTLERS LIFE INS CO	WI	417.4
STANDARD INS CO	OR	12,858.1
STANDARD SECURITY LIFE INS CO OF NY	NY	365.4
STONEBRIDGE LIFE INS CO	VT	2,089.0
SURETY LIFE INS CO	NE	13.2
THRIVENT LIFE INS CO	MN	2,564.9
UNITED INVESTORS LIFE INS CO	MO	2,518.4
UNITED OF OMAHA LIFE INS CO	NE	12,875.0
UNITED WORLD LIFE INS CO	NE	114.6
WORLD CORP INS CO	NE	23.2

Connecticut

INSURANCE COMPANY NAME	DOM. STATE	TOTAL ASSETS ($MIL)

Rating: A+

INSURANCE COMPANY NAME	DOM. STATE	TOTAL ASSETS ($MIL)
COUNTRY LIFE INS CO	IL	7,329.3
PHYSICIANS MUTUAL INS CO	NE	1,445.1
STATE FARM LIFE & ACCIDENT ASR CO	IL	1,691.4
STATE FARM LIFE INS CO	IL	44,978.4
TEACHERS INS & ANNUITY ASN OF AM	NY	194,588.7

Rating: A

INSURANCE COMPANY NAME	DOM. STATE	TOTAL ASSETS ($MIL)
AMERICAN FIDELITY ASR CO	OK	3,343.9
BERKSHIRE LIFE INS CO OF AMERICA	MA	2,502.2
FEDERATED LIFE INS CO	MN	978.1
FIDELITY INVESTMENTS LIFE INS CO	UT	11,382.8
GUARDIAN LIFE INS CO OF AMERICA	NY	29,202.2
MASSACHUSETTS MUTUAL LIFE INS CO	MA	112,014.6
MML BAY STATE LIFE INS CO	CT	4,105.4
SENTRY LIFE INS CO	WI	2,809.8
USAA LIFE INS CO	TX	13,463.6

Rating: A-

INSURANCE COMPANY NAME	DOM. STATE	TOTAL ASSETS ($MIL)
ACACIA LIFE INS CO	DC	1,521.4
AMALGAMATED LIFE INS CO	NY	62.6
AMERICAN REPUBLIC INS CO	IA	472.8
AMICA LIFE INS CO	RI	950.4
ANTHEM LIFE INS CO	IN	288.0
CHARTER NATIONAL LIFE INS CO	IL	133.2
COMPANION LIFE INS CO	SC	124.7
CONTINENTAL AMERICAN INS CO	SC	105.0
COUNTRY INVESTORS LIFE ASR CO	IL	192.1
FIRST INVESTORS LIFE INS CO	NY	949.4
FORT DEARBORN LIFE INS CO	IL	2,870.9
GERBER LIFE INS CO	NY	1,568.7
NATIONAL BENEFIT LIFE INS CO	NY	738.4
NEW YORK LIFE INS & ANNUITY CORP	DE	77,190.7
NEW YORK LIFE INS CO	NY	114,937.8
NIPPON LIFE INS CO OF AMERICA	IA	162.8
NORTHWESTERN MUTUAL LIFE INS CO	WI	155,607.2
PACIFIC LIFE & ANNUITY CO	AZ	2,589.4
PACIFIC LIFE INS CO	NE	81,524.3
PHYSICIANS LIFE INS CO	NE	1,249.3
PRIMERICA LIFE INS CO	MA	5,765.7
PRINCIPAL LIFE INS CO	IA	109,923.9
STANDARD LIFE & ACCIDENT INS CO	OK	484.7
USABLE LIFE	AR	298.5
WORLD INS CO	NE	242.3

Rating: B+

INSURANCE COMPANY NAME	DOM. STATE	TOTAL ASSETS ($MIL)
ALLSTATE LIFE INS CO	IL	65,002.0
AMERICAN FAMILY LIFE ASR CO OF COLUM	NE	67,309.5
AMERICAN FAMILY LIFE ASR CO OF NY	NY	285.0
AMERICAN HEALTH & LIFE INS CO	TX	1,505.6
AMERICAN INCOME LIFE INS CO	IN	1,811.7
AMERICAN UNITED LIFE INS CO	IN	12,264.8
AMERITAS LIFE INS CORP	NE	4,928.5
ASSURITY LIFE INS CO	NE	2,167.6
BOSTON MUTUAL LIFE INS CO	MA	945.5
COLORADO BANKERS LIFE INS CO	CO	144.4

INSURANCE COMPANY NAME	DOM. STATE	TOTAL ASSETS ($MIL)
COLUMBUS LIFE INS CO	OH	2,512.2
EASTERN LIFE & HEALTH INS CO	PA	44.9
FAMILY HERITAGE LIFE INS CO OF AMER	OH	322.3
FIDELITY LIFE ASSN A LEGAL RESERVE	IL	505.8
FIDELITY SECURITY LIFE INS CO	MO	576.6
GENERAL RE LIFE CORP	CT	2,682.0
GOVERNMENT PERSONNEL MUTUAL L I C	TX	783.4
ILLINOIS MUTUAL LIFE INS CO	IL	1,262.3
LINCOLN BENEFIT LIFE CO	NE	2,007.2
LINCOLN HERITAGE LIFE INS CO	IL	629.7
MID-WEST NATIONAL LIFE INS CO OF TN	TX	228.4
MIDLAND NATIONAL LIFE INS CO	IA	25,970.2
MTL INS CO	IL	1,337.3
MUTUAL OF OMAHA INS CO	NE	4,625.4
NATIONAL GUARDIAN LIFE INS CO	WI	1,663.4
NATIONAL WESTERN LIFE INS CO	CO	6,175.2
NATIONWIDE LIFE INS CO OF AMERICA	PA	4,826.2
OHIO NATIONAL LIFE ASR CORP	OH	2,702.3
PENN INS & ANNUITY CO	DE	1,038.9
PENN MUTUAL LIFE INS CO	PA	9,647.6
PHARMACISTS LIFE INS CO	IA	40.4
RELIABLE LIFE INS CO	MO	747.4
SAVINGS BANK LIFE INS CO OF MA	MA	2,093.4
SETTLERS LIFE INS CO	WI	417.4
STANDARD INS CO	OR	12,858.1
STANDARD SECURITY LIFE INS CO OF NY	NY	365.4
STONEBRIDGE LIFE INS CO	VT	2,089.0
SURETY LIFE INS CO	NE	13.2
THRIVENT LIFE INS CO	MN	2,564.9
UNITED INVESTORS LIFE INS CO	MO	2,518.4
UNITED OF OMAHA LIFE INS CO	NE	12,875.0

Delaware

INSURANCE COMPANY NAME	DOM. STATE	TOTAL ASSETS ($MIL)

Rating: A+

COMPANY	DOM. STATE	ASSETS
COUNTRY LIFE INS CO	IL	7,329.3
PHYSICIANS MUTUAL INS CO	NE	1,445.1
STATE FARM LIFE INS CO	IL	44,978.4
TEACHERS INS & ANNUITY ASN OF AM	NY	194,588.7

Rating: A

COMPANY	DOM. STATE	ASSETS
AMERICAN FIDELITY ASR CO	OK	3,343.9
BERKSHIRE LIFE INS CO OF AMERICA	MA	2,502.2
FEDERATED LIFE INS CO	MN	978.1
FIDELITY INVESTMENTS LIFE INS CO	UT	11,382.8
GUARDIAN LIFE INS CO OF AMERICA	NY	29,202.2
MASSACHUSETTS MUTUAL LIFE INS CO	MA	112,014.6
MML BAY STATE LIFE INS CO	CT	4,105.4
SENTRY LIFE INS CO	WI	2,809.8
USAA LIFE INS CO	TX	13,463.6

Rating: A-

COMPANY	DOM. STATE	ASSETS
ACACIA LIFE INS CO	DC	1,521.4
AMERICAN REPUBLIC INS CO	IA	472.8
AMICA LIFE INS CO	RI	950.4
ANTHEM LIFE INS CO	IN	288.0
CHARTER NATIONAL LIFE INS CO	IL	133.2
COMPANION LIFE INS CO	SC	124.7
CONTINENTAL AMERICAN INS CO	SC	105.0
COUNTRY INVESTORS LIFE ASR CO	IL	192.1
FIRST INVESTORS LIFE INS CO	NY	949.4
FORT DEARBORN LIFE INS CO	IL	2,870.9
GERBER LIFE INS CO	NY	1,568.7
NATIONAL BENEFIT LIFE INS CO	NY	738.4
NEW YORK LIFE INS & ANNUITY CORP	DE	77,190.7
NEW YORK LIFE INS CO	NY	114,937.8
NIPPON LIFE INS CO OF AMERICA	IA	162.8
NORTHWESTERN MUTUAL LIFE INS CO	WI	155,607.2
PACIFIC LIFE & ANNUITY CO	AZ	2,589.4
PACIFIC LIFE INS CO	NE	81,524.3
PHYSICIANS LIFE INS CO	NE	1,249.3
PRIMERICA LIFE INS CO	MA	5,765.7
PRINCIPAL LIFE INS CO	IA	109,923.9
STANDARD LIFE & ACCIDENT INS CO	OK	484.7
USABLE LIFE	AR	298.5
WORLD INS CO	NE	242.3

Rating: B+

COMPANY	DOM. STATE	ASSETS
ALLSTATE LIFE INS CO	IL	65,002.0
AMERICAN FAMILY LIFE ASR CO OF COLUM	NE	67,309.5
AMERICAN HEALTH & LIFE INS CO	TX	1,505.6
AMERICAN INCOME LIFE INS CO	IN	1,811.7
AMERICAN UNITED LIFE INS CO	IN	12,264.8
AMERITAS LIFE INS CORP	NE	4,928.5
ASSURITY LIFE INS CO	NE	2,167.6
BOSTON MUTUAL LIFE INS CO	MA	945.5
CHEROKEE NATIONAL LIFE INS CO	GA	30.8
COLORADO BANKERS LIFE INS CO	CO	144.4
COLUMBUS LIFE INS CO	OH	2,512.2
CONTINENTAL LIFE INS CO OF BRENTWOOD	TN	149.3

COMPANY	DOM. STATE	ASSETS
EASTERN LIFE & HEALTH INS CO	PA	44.9
FAMILY HERITAGE LIFE INS CO OF AMER	OH	322.3
FIDELITY LIFE ASSN A LEGAL RESERVE	IL	505.8
FIDELITY SECURITY LIFE INS CO	MO	576.6
GENERAL RE LIFE CORP	CT	2,682.0
GOVERNMENT PERSONNEL MUTUAL L I C	TX	783.4
ILLINOIS MUTUAL LIFE INS CO	IL	1,262.3
LINCOLN BENEFIT LIFE CO	NE	2,007.2
LINCOLN HERITAGE LIFE INS CO	IL	629.7
MID-WEST NATIONAL LIFE INS CO OF TN	TX	228.4
MIDLAND NATIONAL LIFE INS CO	IA	25,970.2
MTL INS CO	IL	1,337.3
MUTUAL OF OMAHA INS CO	NE	4,625.4
NATIONAL GUARDIAN LIFE INS CO	WI	1,663.4
NATIONAL WESTERN LIFE INS CO	CO	6,175.2
NATIONWIDE LIFE INS CO OF AMERICA	PA	4,826.2
OHIO NATIONAL LIFE ASR CORP	OH	2,702.3
PENN INS & ANNUITY CO	DE	1,038.9
PENN MUTUAL LIFE INS CO	PA	9,647.6
PHARMACISTS LIFE INS CO	IA	40.4
RELIABLE LIFE INS CO	MO	747.4
SAVINGS BANK LIFE INS CO OF MA	MA	2,093.4
SETTLERS LIFE INS CO	WI	417.4
STANDARD INS CO	OR	12,858.1
STANDARD SECURITY LIFE INS CO OF NY	NY	365.4
STONEBRIDGE LIFE INS CO	VT	2,089.0
SURETY LIFE INS CO	NE	13.2
THRIVENT LIFE INS CO	MN	2,564.9
UNITED INVESTORS LIFE INS CO	MO	2,518.4
UNITED OF OMAHA LIFE INS CO	NE	12,875.0
UNITED WORLD LIFE INS CO	NE	114.6
WORLD CORP INS CO	NE	23.2

District Of Columbia

INSURANCE COMPANY NAME	DOM. STATE	TOTAL ASSETS ($MIL)

Rating: A+

INSURANCE COMPANY NAME	DOM. STATE	TOTAL ASSETS ($MIL)
PHYSICIANS MUTUAL INS CO	NE	1,445.1
STATE FARM LIFE INS CO	IL	44,978.4
TEACHERS INS & ANNUITY ASN OF AM	NY	194,588.7

Rating: A

INSURANCE COMPANY NAME	DOM. STATE	TOTAL ASSETS ($MIL)
AMERICAN FIDELITY ASR CO	OK	3,343.9
BERKSHIRE LIFE INS CO OF AMERICA	MA	2,502.2
FIDELITY INVESTMENTS LIFE INS CO	UT	11,382.8
GUARDIAN LIFE INS CO OF AMERICA	NY	29,202.2
MASSACHUSETTS MUTUAL LIFE INS CO	MA	112,014.6
MML BAY STATE LIFE INS CO	CT	4,105.4
SENTRY LIFE INS CO	WI	2,809.8
USAA LIFE INS CO	TX	13,463.6

Rating: A-

INSURANCE COMPANY NAME	DOM. STATE	TOTAL ASSETS ($MIL)
ACACIA LIFE INS CO	DC	1,521.4
AMALGAMATED LIFE INS CO	NY	62.6
AMERICAN REPUBLIC INS CO	IA	472.8
AMICA LIFE INS CO	RI	950.4
ANTHEM LIFE INS CO	IN	288.0
CHARTER NATIONAL LIFE INS CO	IL	133.2
COMPANION LIFE INS CO	SC	124.7
CONTINENTAL AMERICAN INS CO	SC	105.0
FIRST INVESTORS LIFE INS CO	NY	949.4
FORT DEARBORN LIFE INS CO	IL	2,870.9
GERBER LIFE INS CO	NY	1,568.7
NATIONAL BENEFIT LIFE INS CO	NY	738.4
NEW YORK LIFE INS & ANNUITY CORP	DE	77,190.7
NEW YORK LIFE INS CO	NY	114,937.8
NIPPON LIFE INS CO OF AMERICA	IA	162.8
NORTHWESTERN MUTUAL LIFE INS CO	WI	155,607.2
PACIFIC LIFE & ANNUITY CO	AZ	2,589.4
PACIFIC LIFE INS CO	NE	81,524.3
PHYSICIANS LIFE INS CO	NE	1,249.3
PRIMERICA LIFE INS CO	MA	5,765.7
PRINCIPAL LIFE INS CO	IA	109,923.9
STANDARD LIFE & ACCIDENT INS CO	OK	484.7
USABLE LIFE	AR	298.5
WORLD INS CO	NE	242.3

Rating: B+

INSURANCE COMPANY NAME	DOM. STATE	TOTAL ASSETS ($MIL)
ALLSTATE LIFE INS CO	IL	65,002.0
AMERICAN FAMILY LIFE ASR CO OF COLUM	NE	67,309.5
AMERICAN HEALTH & LIFE INS CO	TX	1,505.6
AMERICAN INCOME LIFE INS CO	IN	1,811.7
AMERICAN UNITED LIFE INS CO	IN	12,264.8
AMERITAS LIFE INS CORP	NE	4,928.5
ASSURITY LIFE INS CO	NE	2,167.6
BOSTON MUTUAL LIFE INS CO	MA	945.5
COLORADO BANKERS LIFE INS CO	CO	144.4
COLUMBUS LIFE INS CO	OH	2,512.2
COMPBENEFITS INS CO	TX	62.7
EASTERN LIFE & HEALTH INS CO	PA	44.9
FAMILY HERITAGE LIFE INS CO OF AMER	OH	322.3
FIDELITY LIFE ASSN A LEGAL RESERVE	IL	505.8

INSURANCE COMPANY NAME	DOM. STATE	TOTAL ASSETS ($MIL)
FIDELITY SECURITY LIFE INS CO	MO	576.6
GENERAL RE LIFE CORP	CT	2,682.0
GOVERNMENT PERSONNEL MUTUAL L I C	TX	783.4
LINCOLN BENEFIT LIFE CO	NE	2,007.2
LINCOLN HERITAGE LIFE INS CO	IL	629.7
MID-WEST NATIONAL LIFE INS CO OF TN	TX	228.4
MIDLAND NATIONAL LIFE INS CO	IA	25,970.2
MTL INS CO	IL	1,337.3
MUTUAL OF OMAHA INS CO	NE	4,625.4
NATIONAL GUARDIAN LIFE INS CO	WI	1,663.4
NATIONAL WESTERN LIFE INS CO	CO	6,175.2
NATIONWIDE LIFE INS CO OF AMERICA	PA	4,826.2
OHIO NATIONAL LIFE ASR CORP	OH	2,702.3
PENN INS & ANNUITY CO	DE	1,038.9
PENN MUTUAL LIFE INS CO	PA	9,647.6
PHARMACISTS LIFE INS CO	IA	40.4
RELIABLE LIFE INS CO	MO	747.4
SAVINGS BANK LIFE INS CO OF MA	MA	2,093.4
SETTLERS LIFE INS CO	WI	417.4
STANDARD INS CO	OR	12,858.1
STANDARD SECURITY LIFE INS CO OF NY	NY	365.4
STONEBRIDGE LIFE INS CO	VT	2,089.0
SURETY LIFE INS CO	NE	13.2
THRIVENT LIFE INS CO	MN	2,564.9
UNITED INVESTORS LIFE INS CO	MO	2,518.4
UNITED OF OMAHA LIFE INS CO	NE	12,875.0
UNITED WORLD LIFE INS CO	NE	114.6
WORLD CORP INS CO	NE	23.2

Florida

INSURANCE COMPANY NAME	DOM. STATE	TOTAL ASSETS ($MIL)

Rating: A+

INSURANCE COMPANY NAME	DOM. STATE	TOTAL ASSETS ($MIL)
COUNTRY LIFE INS CO	IL	7,329.3
PHYSICIANS MUTUAL INS CO	NE	1,445.1
STATE FARM LIFE INS CO	IL	44,978.4
TEACHERS INS & ANNUITY ASN OF AM	NY	194,588.7

Rating: A

INSURANCE COMPANY NAME	DOM. STATE	TOTAL ASSETS ($MIL)
AMERICAN FIDELITY ASR CO	OK	3,343.9
AUTO-OWNERS LIFE INS CO	MI	2,168.0
BERKSHIRE LIFE INS CO OF AMERICA	MA	2,502.2
FEDERATED LIFE INS CO	MN	978.1
FIDELITY INVESTMENTS LIFE INS CO	UT	11,382.8
GUARDIAN LIFE INS CO OF AMERICA	NY	29,202.2
MASSACHUSETTS MUTUAL LIFE INS CO	MA	112,014.6
MML BAY STATE LIFE INS CO	CT	4,105.4
SENTRY LIFE INS CO	WI	2,809.8
SOUTHERN FARM BUREAU LIFE INS CO	MS	10,074.1
UNION NATIONAL LIFE INS CO	LA	459.3
USAA LIFE INS CO	TX	13,463.6

Rating: A-

INSURANCE COMPANY NAME	DOM. STATE	TOTAL ASSETS ($MIL)
ACACIA LIFE INS CO	DC	1,521.4
AMERICAN REPUBLIC INS CO	IA	472.8
AMICA LIFE INS CO	RI	950.4
ANTHEM LIFE INS CO	IN	288.0
CHARTER NATIONAL LIFE INS CO	IL	133.2
COMPANION LIFE INS CO	SC	124.7
CONTINENTAL AMERICAN INS CO	SC	105.0
COUNTRY INVESTORS LIFE ASR CO	IL	192.1
FIRST INVESTORS LIFE INS CO	NY	949.4
FORT DEARBORN LIFE INS CO	IL	2,870.9
GERBER LIFE INS CO	NY	1,568.7
NATIONAL BENEFIT LIFE INS CO	NY	738.4
NEW YORK LIFE INS & ANNUITY CORP	DE	77,190.7
NEW YORK LIFE INS CO	NY	114,937.8
NIPPON LIFE INS CO OF AMERICA	IA	162.8
NORTHWESTERN MUTUAL LIFE INS CO	WI	155,607.2
PACIFIC LIFE & ANNUITY CO	AZ	2,589.4
PACIFIC LIFE INS CO	NE	81,524.3
PHYSICIANS LIFE INS CO	NE	1,249.3
PRIMERICA LIFE INS CO	MA	5,765.7
PRINCIPAL LIFE INS CO	IA	109,923.9
STANDARD LIFE & ACCIDENT INS CO	OK	484.7
USABLE LIFE	AR	298.5
WORLD INS CO	NE	242.3

Rating: B+

INSURANCE COMPANY NAME	DOM. STATE	TOTAL ASSETS ($MIL)
ALFA LIFE INS CORP	AL	1,087.3
ALLSTATE LIFE INS CO	IL	65,002.0
AMERICAN FAMILY LIFE ASR CO OF COLUM	NE	67,309.5
AMERICAN HEALTH & LIFE INS CO	TX	1,505.6
AMERICAN INCOME LIFE INS CO	IN	1,811.7
AMERICAN UNITED LIFE INS CO	IN	12,264.8
AMERITAS LIFE INS CORP	NE	4,928.5
ASSURITY LIFE INS CO	NE	2,167.6
ATLANTIC COAST LIFE INS CO	SC	69.9

INSURANCE COMPANY NAME	DOM. STATE	TOTAL ASSETS ($MIL)
BOSTON MUTUAL LIFE INS CO	MA	945.5
CHEROKEE NATIONAL LIFE INS CO	GA	30.8
COLORADO BANKERS LIFE INS CO	CO	144.4
COLUMBUS LIFE INS CO	OH	2,512.2
COMPBENEFITS INS CO	TX	62.7
CONTINENTAL LIFE INS CO OF BRENTWOOD	TN	149.3
COTTON STATES LIFE INS CO	GA	281.8
EASTERN LIFE & HEALTH INS CO	PA	44.9
EPIC LIFE INSURANCE CO	WI	42.6
FAMILY HERITAGE LIFE INS CO OF AMER	OH	322.3
FIDELITY LIFE ASSN A LEGAL RESERVE	IL	505.8
FIDELITY SECURITY LIFE INS CO	MO	576.6
FLORIDA COMBINED LIFE INS CO INC	FL	31.8
GOVERNMENT PERSONNEL MUTUAL L I C	TX	783.4
ILLINOIS MUTUAL LIFE INS CO	IL	1,262.3
LINCOLN BENEFIT LIFE CO	NE	2,007.2
LINCOLN HERITAGE LIFE INS CO	IL	629.7
MID-WEST NATIONAL LIFE INS CO OF TN	TX	228.4
MIDLAND NATIONAL LIFE INS CO	IA	25,970.2
MTL INS CO	IL	1,337.3
MUTUAL OF OMAHA INS CO	NE	4,625.4
NATIONAL GUARDIAN LIFE INS CO	WI	1,663.4
NATIONAL WESTERN LIFE INS CO	CO	6,175.2
NATIONWIDE LIFE INS CO OF AMERICA	PA	4,826.2
OHIO NATIONAL LIFE ASR CORP	OH	2,702.3
PENN INS & ANNUITY CO	DE	1,038.9
PENN MUTUAL LIFE INS CO	PA	9,647.6
RELIABLE LIFE INS CO	MO	747.4
SAVINGS BANK LIFE INS CO OF MA	MA	2,093.4
SETTLERS LIFE INS CO	WI	417.4
STANDARD INS CO	OR	12,858.1
STANDARD SECURITY LIFE INS CO OF NY	NY	365.4
STONEBRIDGE LIFE INS CO	VT	2,089.0
SURETY LIFE INS CO	NE	13.2
THRIVENT LIFE INS CO	MN	2,564.9
UNITED INVESTORS LIFE INS CO	MO	2,518.4
UNITED OF OMAHA LIFE INS CO	NE	12,875.0
UNITED WORLD LIFE INS CO	NE	114.6
WORLD CORP INS CO	NE	23.2

Georgia

INSURANCE COMPANY NAME	DOM. STATE	TOTAL ASSETS ($MIL)

Rating: A+

INSURANCE COMPANY NAME	DOM. STATE	TOTAL ASSETS ($MIL)
AMERICAN FAMILY LIFE INS CO	WI	3,898.0
COUNTRY LIFE INS CO	IL	7,329.3
PHYSICIANS MUTUAL INS CO	NE	1,445.1
STATE FARM LIFE INS CO	IL	44,978.4
TEACHERS INS & ANNUITY ASN OF AM	NY	194,588.7

Rating: A

INSURANCE COMPANY NAME	DOM. STATE	TOTAL ASSETS ($MIL)
AMERICAN FIDELITY ASR CO	OK	3,343.9
AUTO-OWNERS LIFE INS CO	MI	2,168.0
BERKSHIRE LIFE INS CO OF AMERICA	MA	2,502.2
FEDERATED LIFE INS CO	MN	978.1
FIDELITY INVESTMENTS LIFE INS CO	UT	11,382.8
GUARDIAN LIFE INS CO OF AMERICA	NY	29,202.2
MASSACHUSETTS MUTUAL LIFE INS CO	MA	112,014.6
MML BAY STATE LIFE INS CO	CT	4,105.4
SENTRY LIFE INS CO	WI	2,809.8
SOUTHERN FARM BUREAU LIFE INS CO	MS	10,074.1
UNION NATIONAL LIFE INS CO	LA	459.3
USAA LIFE INS CO	TX	13,463.6

Rating: A-

INSURANCE COMPANY NAME	DOM. STATE	TOTAL ASSETS ($MIL)
ACACIA LIFE INS CO	DC	1,521.4
AMALGAMATED LIFE INS CO	NY	62.6
AMERICAN REPUBLIC INS CO	IA	472.8
AMICA LIFE INS CO	RI	950.4
ANTHEM LIFE INS CO	IN	288.0
CHARTER NATIONAL LIFE INS CO	IL	133.2
COMPANION LIFE INS CO	SC	124.7
CONTINENTAL AMERICAN INS CO	SC	105.0
COUNTRY INVESTORS LIFE ASR CO	IL	192.1
FIRST INVESTORS LIFE INS CO	NY	949.4
FORT DEARBORN LIFE INS CO	IL	2,870.9
GERBER LIFE INS CO	NY	1,568.7
GRANGE LIFE INS CO	OH	258.2
GREATER GEORGIA LIFE INS CO	GA	46.3
NATIONAL BENEFIT LIFE INS CO	NY	738.4
NEW YORK LIFE INS & ANNUITY CORP	DE	77,190.7
NEW YORK LIFE INS CO	NY	114,937.8
NIPPON LIFE INS CO OF AMERICA	IA	162.8
NORTHWESTERN MUTUAL LIFE INS CO	WI	155,607.2
PACIFIC LIFE & ANNUITY CO	AZ	2,589.4
PACIFIC LIFE INS CO	NE	81,524.3
PHYSICIANS LIFE INS CO	NE	1,249.3
PRIMERICA LIFE INS CO	MA	5,765.7
PRINCIPAL LIFE INS CO	IA	109,923.9
STANDARD LIFE & ACCIDENT INS CO	OK	484.7
USABLE LIFE	AR	298.5
WORLD INS CO	NE	242.3

Rating: B+

INSURANCE COMPANY NAME	DOM. STATE	TOTAL ASSETS ($MIL)
ALFA LIFE INS CORP	AL	1,087.3
ALLSTATE LIFE INS CO	IL	65,002.0
AMERICAN FAMILY LIFE ASR CO OF COLUM	NE	67,309.5
AMERICAN HEALTH & LIFE INS CO	TX	1,505.6
AMERICAN INCOME LIFE INS CO	IN	1,811.7

INSURANCE COMPANY NAME	DOM. STATE	TOTAL ASSETS ($MIL)
AMERICAN UNITED LIFE INS CO	IN	12,264.8
AMERITAS LIFE INS CORP	NE	4,928.5
ASSURITY LIFE INS CO	NE	2,167.6
ATLANTIC COAST LIFE INS CO	SC	69.9
BOSTON MUTUAL LIFE INS CO	MA	945.5
CHEROKEE NATIONAL LIFE INS CO	GA	30.8
COLORADO BANKERS LIFE INS CO	CO	144.4
COLUMBUS LIFE INS CO	OH	2,512.2
COMPBENEFITS INS CO	TX	62.7
CONTINENTAL LIFE INS CO OF BRENTWOOD	TN	149.3
COTTON STATES LIFE INS CO	GA	281.8
EASTERN LIFE & HEALTH INS CO	PA	44.9
FAMILY HERITAGE LIFE INS CO OF AMER	OH	322.3
FIDELITY LIFE ASSN A LEGAL RESERVE	IL	505.8
FIDELITY SECURITY LIFE INS CO	MO	576.6
FLORIDA COMBINED LIFE INS CO INC	FL	31.8
FRANDISCO LIFE INS CO	GA	37.3
GENERAL RE LIFE CORP	CT	2,682.0
GOVERNMENT PERSONNEL MUTUAL L I C	TX	783.4
ILLINOIS MUTUAL LIFE INS CO	IL	1,262.0
LINCOLN BENEFIT LIFE CO	NE	2,007.2
LINCOLN HERITAGE LIFE INS CO	IL	629.7
MID-WEST NATIONAL LIFE INS CO OF TN	TX	228.4
MIDLAND NATIONAL LIFE INS CO	IA	25,970.2
MTL INS CO	IL	1,337.3
MUTUAL OF OMAHA INS CO	NE	4,625.4
NATIONAL GUARDIAN LIFE INS CO	WI	1,663.4
NATIONAL WESTERN LIFE INS CO	CO	6,175.2
NATIONWIDE LIFE INS CO OF AMERICA	PA	4,826.2
OHIO NATIONAL LIFE ASR CORP	OH	2,702.3
PENN INS & ANNUITY CO	DE	1,038.9
PENN MUTUAL LIFE INS CO	PA	9,647.6
PHARMACISTS LIFE INS CO	IA	40.4
RELIABLE LIFE INS CO	MO	747.4
SAVINGS BANK LIFE INS CO OF MA	MA	2,093.4
SETTLERS LIFE INS CO	WI	417.4
STANDARD INS CO	OR	12,858.1
STANDARD SECURITY LIFE INS CO OF NY	NY	365.4
STONEBRIDGE LIFE INS CO	VT	2,089.0
SURETY LIFE INS CO	NE	13.2
UNITED INVESTORS LIFE INS CO	MO	2,518.4
UNITED OF OMAHA LIFE INS CO	NE	12,875.0
UNITED WORLD LIFE INS CO	NE	114.6
WORLD CORP INS CO	NE	23.2

Hawaii

INSURANCE COMPANY NAME	DOM. STATE	TOTAL ASSETS ($MIL)

Rating: A+

INSURANCE COMPANY NAME	DOM. STATE	TOTAL ASSETS ($MIL)
PHYSICIANS MUTUAL INS CO	NE	1,445.1
STATE FARM LIFE INS CO	IL	44,978.4
TEACHERS INS & ANNUITY ASN OF AM	NY	194,588.7

Rating: A

INSURANCE COMPANY NAME	DOM. STATE	TOTAL ASSETS ($MIL)
AMERICAN FIDELITY ASR CO	OK	3,343.9
BERKSHIRE LIFE INS CO OF AMERICA	MA	2,502.2
FIDELITY INVESTMENTS LIFE INS CO	UT	11,382.8
GUARDIAN LIFE INS CO OF AMERICA	NY	29,202.2
MASSACHUSETTS MUTUAL LIFE INS CO	MA	112,014.6
MML BAY STATE LIFE INS CO	CT	4,105.4
SENTRY LIFE INS CO	WI	2,809.8
USAA LIFE INS CO	TX	13,463.6

Rating: A-

INSURANCE COMPANY NAME	DOM. STATE	TOTAL ASSETS ($MIL)
ACACIA LIFE INS CO	DC	1,521.4
AMALGAMATED LIFE INS CO	NY	62.6
AMERICAN REPUBLIC INS CO	IA	472.8
ANTHEM LIFE INS CO	IN	288.0
CHARTER NATIONAL LIFE INS CO	IL	133.2
CONTINENTAL AMERICAN INS CO	SC	105.0
FIRST INVESTORS LIFE INS CO	NY	949.4
FORT DEARBORN LIFE INS CO	IL	2,870.9
GERBER LIFE INS CO	NY	1,568.7
NATIONAL BENEFIT LIFE INS CO	NY	738.4
NEW YORK LIFE INS & ANNUITY CORP	DE	77,190.7
NEW YORK LIFE INS CO	NY	114,937.8
NIPPON LIFE INS CO OF AMERICA	IA	162.8
NORTHWESTERN MUTUAL LIFE INS CO	WI	155,607.2
PACIFIC GUARDIAN LIFE INS CO LTD	HI	426.8
PACIFIC LIFE & ANNUITY CO	AZ	2,589.4
PACIFIC LIFE INS CO	NE	81,524.3
PHYSICIANS LIFE INS CO	NE	1,249.3
PRIMERICA LIFE INS CO	MA	5,765.7
PRINCIPAL LIFE INS CO	IA	109,923.9
STANDARD LIFE & ACCIDENT INS CO	OK	484.7
USABLE LIFE	AR	298.5
WORLD INS CO	NE	242.3

Rating: B+

INSURANCE COMPANY NAME	DOM. STATE	TOTAL ASSETS ($MIL)
ALLSTATE LIFE INS CO	IL	65,002.0
AMERICAN FAMILY LIFE ASR CO OF COLUM	NE	67,309.5
AMERICAN HEALTH & LIFE INS CO	TX	1,505.6
AMERICAN INCOME LIFE INS CO	IN	1,811.7
AMERICAN UNITED LIFE INS CO	IN	12,264.8
AMERITAS LIFE INS CORP	NE	4,928.5
ASSURITY LIFE INS CO	NE	2,167.6
BOSTON MUTUAL LIFE INS CO	MA	945.5
COLORADO BANKERS LIFE INS CO	CO	144.4
COLUMBUS LIFE INS CO	OH	2,512.2
FAMILY HERITAGE LIFE INS CO OF AMER	OH	322.3
FIDELITY LIFE ASSN A LEGAL RESERVE	IL	505.8
FIDELITY SECURITY LIFE INS CO	MO	576.6
GOVERNMENT PERSONNEL MUTUAL L I C	TX	783.4
LINCOLN BENEFIT LIFE CO	NE	2,007.2

INSURANCE COMPANY NAME	DOM. STATE	TOTAL ASSETS ($MIL)
LINCOLN HERITAGE LIFE INS CO	IL	629.7
MID-WEST NATIONAL LIFE INS CO OF TN	TX	228.4
MIDLAND NATIONAL LIFE INS CO	IA	25,970.2
MTL INS CO	IL	1,337.3
MUTUAL OF OMAHA INS CO	NE	4,625.4
NATIONAL GUARDIAN LIFE INS CO	WI	1,663.4
NATIONAL WESTERN LIFE INS CO	CO	6,175.2
NATIONWIDE LIFE INS CO OF AMERICA	PA	4,826.2
PENN INS & ANNUITY CO	DE	1,038.9
PENN MUTUAL LIFE INS CO	PA	9,647.6
RELIABLE LIFE INS CO	MO	747.4
SAVINGS BANK LIFE INS CO OF MA	MA	2,093.4
SETTLERS LIFE INS CO	WI	417.4
STANDARD INS CO	OR	12,858.1
STANDARD SECURITY LIFE INS CO OF NY	NY	365.4
STONEBRIDGE LIFE INS CO	VT	2,089.0
SURETY LIFE INS CO	NE	13.2
THRIVENT LIFE INS CO	MN	2,564.9
UNITED INVESTORS LIFE INS CO	MO	2,518.4
UNITED OF OMAHA LIFE INS CO	NE	12,875.0
UNITED WORLD LIFE INS CO	NE	114.6

Idaho

INSURANCE COMPANY NAME	DOM. STATE	TOTAL ASSETS ($MIL)
Rating: A+		
AMERICAN FAMILY LIFE INS CO	WI	3,898.0
COUNTRY LIFE INS CO	IL	7,329.3
PHYSICIANS MUTUAL INS CO	NE	1,445.1
STATE FARM LIFE INS CO	IL	44,978.4
TEACHERS INS & ANNUITY ASN OF AM	NY	194,588.7
Rating: A		
AMERICAN FIDELITY ASR CO	OK	3,343.9
AUTO-OWNERS LIFE INS CO	MI	2,168.0
BERKSHIRE LIFE INS CO OF AMERICA	MA	2,502.2
FEDERATED LIFE INS CO	MN	978.1
FIDELITY INVESTMENTS LIFE INS CO	UT	11,382.8
GUARDIAN LIFE INS CO OF AMERICA	NY	29,202.2
LIFEWISE ASR CO	WA	70.2
MASSACHUSETTS MUTUAL LIFE INS CO	MA	112,014.6
MML BAY STATE LIFE INS CO	CT	4,105.4
SENTRY LIFE INS CO	WI	2,809.8
USAA LIFE INS CO	TX	13,463.6
Rating: A-		
ACACIA LIFE INS CO	DC	1,521.4
AMALGAMATED LIFE INS CO	NY	62.6
AMERICAN REPUBLIC INS CO	IA	472.8
AMICA LIFE INS CO	RI	950.4
ANTHEM LIFE INS CO	IN	288.0
CHARTER NATIONAL LIFE INS CO	IL	133.2
COMPANION LIFE INS CO	SC	124.7
CONTINENTAL AMERICAN INS CO	SC	105.0
COUNTRY INVESTORS LIFE ASR CO	IL	192.1
FIRST INVESTORS LIFE INS CO	NY	949.4
FORT DEARBORN LIFE INS CO	IL	2,870.9
GERBER LIFE INS CO	NY	1,568.7
NATIONAL BENEFIT LIFE INS CO	NY	738.4
NEW YORK LIFE INS & ANNUITY CORP	DE	77,190.7
NEW YORK LIFE INS CO	NY	114,937.8
NIPPON LIFE INS CO OF AMERICA	IA	162.8
NORTHWESTERN MUTUAL LIFE INS CO	WI	155,607.2
PACIFIC GUARDIAN LIFE INS CO LTD	HI	426.8
PACIFIC LIFE & ANNUITY CO	AZ	2,589.4
PACIFIC LIFE INS CO	NE	81,524.3
PHYSICIANS LIFE INS CO	NE	1,249.3
PRIMERICA LIFE INS CO	MA	5,765.7
PRINCIPAL LIFE INS CO	IA	109,923.9
STANDARD LIFE & ACCIDENT INS CO	OK	484.7
USABLE LIFE	AR	298.5
WORLD INS CO	NE	242.3
Rating: B+		
ALLSTATE LIFE INS CO	IL	65,002.0
AMERICAN FAMILY LIFE ASR CO OF COLUM	NE	67,309.5
AMERICAN HEALTH & LIFE INS CO	TX	1,505.6
AMERICAN INCOME LIFE INS CO	IN	1,811.7
AMERICAN UNITED LIFE INS CO	IN	12,264.8
AMERITAS LIFE INS CORP	NE	4,928.5
ASSURITY LIFE INS CO	NE	2,167.6

INSURANCE COMPANY NAME	DOM. STATE	TOTAL ASSETS ($MIL)
BOSTON MUTUAL LIFE INS CO	MA	945.5
COLORADO BANKERS LIFE INS CO	CO	144.4
COLUMBUS LIFE INS CO	OH	2,512.2
COMPBENEFITS INS CO	TX	62.7
CONTINENTAL LIFE INS CO OF BRENTWOOD	TN	149.3
EASTERN LIFE & HEALTH INS CO	PA	44.9
FAMILY HERITAGE LIFE INS CO OF AMER	OH	322.3
FARM BUREAU LIFE INS CO	IA	5,605.0
FIDELITY LIFE ASSN A LEGAL RESERVE	IL	505.8
FIDELITY SECURITY LIFE INS CO	MO	576.6
GENERAL RE LIFE CORP	CT	2,682.0
GOVERNMENT PERSONNEL MUTUAL L I C	TX	783.4
ILLINOIS MUTUAL LIFE INS CO	IL	1,262.3
LINCOLN BENEFIT LIFE CO	NE	2,007.2
LINCOLN HERITAGE LIFE INS CO	IL	629.7
MID-WEST NATIONAL LIFE INS CO OF TN	TX	228.4
MIDLAND NATIONAL LIFE INS CO	IA	25,970.2
MTL INS CO	IL	1,337.3
MUTUAL OF OMAHA INS CO	NE	4,625.4
NATIONAL GUARDIAN LIFE INS CO	WI	1,663.4
NATIONAL WESTERN LIFE INS CO	CO	6,175.2
NATIONWIDE LIFE INS CO OF AMERICA	PA	4,826.2
OHIO NATIONAL LIFE ASR CORP	OH	2,702.3
PENN INS & ANNUITY CO	DE	1,038.9
PENN MUTUAL LIFE INS CO	PA	9,647.6
PHARMACISTS LIFE INS CO	IA	40.4
REGENCE LIFE & HEALTH INS CO	OR	80.7
RELIABLE LIFE INS CO	MO	747.4
SETTLERS LIFE INS CO	WI	417.4
STANDARD INS CO	OR	12,858.1
STANDARD SECURITY LIFE INS CO OF NY	NY	365.4
STONEBRIDGE LIFE INS CO	VT	2,089.0
SURETY LIFE INS CO	NE	13.2
THRIVENT LIFE INS CO	MN	2,564.9
UNITED INVESTORS LIFE INS CO	MO	2,518.4
UNITED OF OMAHA LIFE INS CO	NE	12,875.0
UNITED WORLD LIFE INS CO	NE	114.6
WORLD CORP INS CO	NE	23.2

Illinois

INSURANCE COMPANY NAME	DOM. STATE	TOTAL ASSETS ($MIL)

Rating: A+

INSURANCE COMPANY NAME	DOM. STATE	TOTAL ASSETS ($MIL)
AMERICAN FAMILY LIFE INS CO	WI	3,898.0
COUNTRY LIFE INS CO	IL	7,329.3
PHYSICIANS MUTUAL INS CO	NE	1,445.1
STATE FARM LIFE & ACCIDENT ASR CO	IL	1,691.4
STATE FARM LIFE INS CO	IL	44,978.4
TEACHERS INS & ANNUITY ASN OF AM	NY	194,588.7

Rating: A

INSURANCE COMPANY NAME	DOM. STATE	TOTAL ASSETS ($MIL)
AMERICAN FIDELITY ASR CO	OK	3,343.9
AUTO-OWNERS LIFE INS CO	MI	2,168.0
BERKSHIRE LIFE INS CO OF AMERICA	MA	2,502.2
FEDERATED LIFE INS CO	MN	978.1
FIDELITY INVESTMENTS LIFE INS CO	UT	11,382.8
GUARDIAN LIFE INS CO OF AMERICA	NY	29,202.2
MASSACHUSETTS MUTUAL LIFE INS CO	MA	112,014.6
MML BAY STATE LIFE INS CO	CT	4,105.4
SENTRY LIFE INS CO	WI	2,809.8
UNITED FARM FAMILY LIFE INS CO	IN	1,712.9
USAA LIFE INS CO	TX	13,463.6

Rating: A-

INSURANCE COMPANY NAME	DOM. STATE	TOTAL ASSETS ($MIL)
ACACIA LIFE INS CO	DC	1,521.4
AMALGAMATED LIFE INS CO	NY	62.6
AMERICAN REPUBLIC INS CO	IA	472.8
AMICA LIFE INS CO	RI	950.4
ANTHEM LIFE INS CO	IN	288.0
CHARTER NATIONAL LIFE INS CO	IL	133.2
COMPANION LIFE INS CO	SC	124.7
CONTINENTAL AMERICAN INS CO	SC	105.0
COUNTRY INVESTORS LIFE ASR CO	IL	192.1
FIRST INVESTORS LIFE INS CO	NY	949.4
FORT DEARBORN LIFE INS CO	IL	2,870.9
GERBER LIFE INS CO	NY	1,568.7
GRANGE LIFE INS CO	OH	258.2
NATIONAL BENEFIT LIFE INS CO	NY	738.4
NEW YORK LIFE INS & ANNUITY CORP	DE	77,190.7
NEW YORK LIFE INS CO	NY	114,937.8
NIPPON LIFE INS CO OF AMERICA	IA	162.8
NORTHWESTERN MUTUAL LIFE INS CO	WI	155,607.2
PACIFIC LIFE & ANNUITY CO	AZ	2,589.4
PACIFIC LIFE INS CO	NE	81,524.3
PHYSICIANS LIFE INS CO	NE	1,249.3
PRIMERICA LIFE INS CO	MA	5,765.7
PRINCIPAL LIFE INS CO	IA	109,923.9
SHELTER LIFE INS CO	MO	933.1
STANDARD LIFE & ACCIDENT INS CO	OK	484.7
USABLE LIFE	AR	298.5
WORLD INS CO	NE	242.3

Rating: B+

INSURANCE COMPANY NAME	DOM. STATE	TOTAL ASSETS ($MIL)
ALLSTATE LIFE INS CO	IL	65,002.0
AMERICAN FAMILY LIFE ASR CO OF COLUM	NE	67,309.5
AMERICAN HEALTH & LIFE INS CO	TX	1,505.6
AMERICAN INCOME LIFE INS CO	IN	1,811.7
AMERICAN UNITED LIFE INS CO	IN	12,264.8

INSURANCE COMPANY NAME	DOM. STATE	TOTAL ASSETS ($MIL)
AMERITAS LIFE INS CORP	NE	4,928.5
ASSURITY LIFE INS CO	NE	2,167.6
BOSTON MUTUAL LIFE INS CO	MA	945.5
COLORADO BANKERS LIFE INS CO	CO	144.4
COLUMBUS LIFE INS CO	OH	2,512.2
COMPBENEFITS INS CO	TX	62.7
CONTINENTAL LIFE INS CO OF BRENTWOOD	TN	149.3
EASTERN LIFE & HEALTH INS CO	PA	44.9
EPIC LIFE INSURANCE CO	WI	42.6
FAMILY HERITAGE LIFE INS CO OF AMER	OH	322.3
FIDELITY LIFE ASSN A LEGAL RESERVE	IL	505.8
FIDELITY SECURITY LIFE INS CO	MO	576.6
GENERAL RE LIFE CORP	CT	2,682.0
GOVERNMENT PERSONNEL MUTUAL L I C	TX	783.4
ILLINOIS MUTUAL LIFE INS CO	IL	1,262.3
LINCOLN BENEFIT LIFE CO	NE	2,007.2
LINCOLN HERITAGE LIFE INS CO	IL	629.7
MID-WEST NATIONAL LIFE INS CO OF TN	TX	228.4
MIDLAND NATIONAL LIFE INS CO	IA	25,970.2
MTL INS CO	IL	1,337.3
MUTUAL OF OMAHA INS CO	NE	4,625.4
NATIONAL GUARDIAN LIFE INS CO	WI	1,663.4
NATIONAL WESTERN LIFE INS CO	CO	6,175.2
NATIONWIDE LIFE INS CO OF AMERICA	PA	4,826.2
OHIO NATIONAL LIFE ASR CORP	OH	2,702.3
PEKIN LIFE INS CO	IL	863.3
PENN INS & ANNUITY CO	DE	1,038.9
PENN MUTUAL LIFE INS CO	PA	9,647.6
PHARMACISTS LIFE INS CO	IA	40.4
RELIABLE LIFE INS CO	MO	747.4
SAVINGS BANK LIFE INS CO OF MA	MA	2,093.4
SETTLERS LIFE INS CO	WI	417.4
STANDARD INS CO	OR	12,858.1
STANDARD SECURITY LIFE INS CO OF NY	NY	365.4
STONEBRIDGE LIFE INS CO	VT	2,089.0
SURETY LIFE INS CO	NE	13.2
THRIVENT LIFE INS CO	MN	2,564.9
UNITED INVESTORS LIFE INS CO	MO	2,518.4
UNITED OF OMAHA LIFE INS CO	NE	12,875.0
UNITED WORLD LIFE INS CO	NE	114.6
WORLD CORP INS CO	NE	23.2

Indiana

INSURANCE COMPANY NAME	DOM. STATE	TOTAL ASSETS ($MIL)

Rating: A+

INSURANCE COMPANY NAME	DOM. STATE	TOTAL ASSETS ($MIL)
AMERICAN FAMILY LIFE INS CO	WI	3,898.0
COUNTRY LIFE INS CO	IL	7,329.3
PHYSICIANS MUTUAL INS CO	NE	1,445.1
STATE FARM LIFE INS CO	IL	44,978.4
TEACHERS INS & ANNUITY ASN OF AM	NY	194,588.7

Rating: A

INSURANCE COMPANY NAME	DOM. STATE	TOTAL ASSETS ($MIL)
AMERICAN FIDELITY ASR CO	OK	3,343.9
AUTO-OWNERS LIFE INS CO	MI	2,168.0
BERKSHIRE LIFE INS CO OF AMERICA	MA	2,502.2
FEDERATED LIFE INS CO	MN	978.1
FIDELITY INVESTMENTS LIFE INS CO	UT	11,382.8
GUARDIAN LIFE INS CO OF AMERICA	NY	29,202.2
MASSACHUSETTS MUTUAL LIFE INS CO	MA	112,014.6
MML BAY STATE LIFE INS CO	CT	4,105.4
SENTRY LIFE INS CO	WI	2,809.8
UNITED FARM FAMILY LIFE INS CO	IN	1,712.9
USAA LIFE INS CO	TX	13,463.6

Rating: A-

INSURANCE COMPANY NAME	DOM. STATE	TOTAL ASSETS ($MIL)
ACACIA LIFE INS CO	DC	1,521.4
AMALGAMATED LIFE INS CO	NY	62.6
AMERICAN REPUBLIC INS CO	IA	472.8
AMICA LIFE INS CO	RI	950.4
ANTHEM LIFE INS CO	IN	288.0
CHARTER NATIONAL LIFE INS CO	IL	133.2
COMPANION LIFE INS CO	SC	124.7
CONTINENTAL AMERICAN INS CO	SC	105.0
COUNTRY INVESTORS LIFE ASR CO	IL	192.1
FIRST INVESTORS LIFE INS CO	NY	949.4
FORT DEARBORN LIFE INS CO	IL	2,870.9
GERBER LIFE INS CO	NY	1,568.7
GRANGE LIFE INS CO	OH	258.2
NATIONAL BENEFIT LIFE INS CO	NY	738.4
NEW YORK LIFE INS & ANNUITY CORP	DE	77,190.7
NEW YORK LIFE INS CO	NY	114,937.8
NIPPON LIFE INS CO OF AMERICA	IA	162.8
NORTHWESTERN MUTUAL LIFE INS CO	WI	155,607.2
PACIFIC LIFE & ANNUITY CO	AZ	2,589.4
PACIFIC LIFE INS CO	NE	81,524.3
PHYSICIANS LIFE INS CO	NE	1,249.3
PRIMERICA LIFE INS CO	MA	5,765.7
PRINCIPAL LIFE INS CO	IA	109,923.9
SHELTER LIFE INS CO	MO	933.1
STANDARD LIFE & ACCIDENT INS CO	OK	484.7
USABLE LIFE	AR	298.5
WORLD INS CO	NE	242.3

Rating: B+

INSURANCE COMPANY NAME	DOM. STATE	TOTAL ASSETS ($MIL)
ALLSTATE LIFE INS CO	IL	65,002.0
AMERICAN FAMILY LIFE ASR CO OF COLUM	NE	67,309.5
AMERICAN HEALTH & LIFE INS CO	TX	1,505.6
AMERICAN INCOME LIFE INS CO	IN	1,811.7
AMERICAN UNITED LIFE INS CO	IN	12,264.8
AMERITAS LIFE INS CORP	NE	4,928.5

INSURANCE COMPANY NAME	DOM. STATE	TOTAL ASSETS ($MIL)
ASSURITY LIFE INS CO	NE	2,167.6
BOSTON MUTUAL LIFE INS CO	MA	945.5
COLORADO BANKERS LIFE INS CO	CO	144.4
COLUMBUS LIFE INS CO	OH	2,512.2
COMPBENEFITS INS CO	TX	62.7
CONTINENTAL LIFE INS CO OF BRENTWOOD	TN	149.3
EASTERN LIFE & HEALTH INS CO	PA	44.9
EPIC LIFE INSURANCE CO	WI	42.6
FAMILY HERITAGE LIFE INS CO OF AMER	OH	322.3
FIDELITY LIFE ASSN A LEGAL RESERVE	IL	505.8
FIDELITY SECURITY LIFE INS CO	MO	576.6
GENERAL RE LIFE CORP	CT	2,682.0
GOVERNMENT PERSONNEL MUTUAL L I C	TX	783.4
ILLINOIS MUTUAL LIFE INS CO	IL	1,262.3
LINCOLN BENEFIT LIFE CO	NE	2,007.1
LINCOLN HERITAGE LIFE INS CO	IL	629.7
MID-WEST NATIONAL LIFE INS CO OF TN	TX	228.4
MIDLAND NATIONAL LIFE INS CO	IA	25,970.2
MTL INS CO	IL	1,337.3
MUTUAL OF OMAHA INS CO	NE	4,625.4
NATIONAL GUARDIAN LIFE INS CO	WI	1,663.4
NATIONAL WESTERN LIFE INS CO	CO	6,175.2
NATIONWIDE LIFE INS CO OF AMERICA	PA	4,826.2
OHIO NATIONAL LIFE ASR CORP	OH	2,702.3
PEKIN LIFE INS CO	IL	863.3
PENN INS & ANNUITY CO	DE	1,038.9
PENN MUTUAL LIFE INS CO	PA	9,647.6
PHARMACISTS LIFE INS CO	IA	40.4
RELIABLE LIFE INS CO	MO	747.4
SAVINGS BANK LIFE INS CO OF MA	MA	2,093.4
SETTLERS LIFE INS CO	WI	417.4
STANDARD INS CO	OR	12,858.1
STANDARD SECURITY LIFE INS CO OF NY	NY	365.4
STONEBRIDGE LIFE INS CO	VT	2,089.0
SURETY LIFE INS CO	NE	13.2
THRIVENT LIFE INS CO	MN	2,564.9
UNITED INVESTORS LIFE INS CO	MO	2,518.4
UNITED OF OMAHA LIFE INS CO	NE	12,875.0
UNITED WORLD LIFE INS CO	NE	114.6
WORLD CORP INS CO	NE	23.2

Iowa

INSURANCE COMPANY NAME	DOM. STATE	TOTAL ASSETS ($MIL)
Rating: A+		
AMERICAN FAMILY LIFE INS CO	WI	3,898.0
COUNTRY LIFE INS CO	IL	7,329.3
PHYSICIANS MUTUAL INS CO	NE	1,445.1
STATE FARM LIFE INS CO	IL	44,978.4
TEACHERS INS & ANNUITY ASN OF AM	NY	194,588.7
Rating: A		
AMERICAN FIDELITY ASR CO	OK	3,343.9
AUTO-OWNERS LIFE INS CO	MI	2,168.0
BERKSHIRE LIFE INS CO OF AMERICA	MA	2,502.2
FEDERATED LIFE INS CO	MN	978.1
FIDELITY INVESTMENTS LIFE INS CO	UT	11,382.8
GUARDIAN LIFE INS CO OF AMERICA	NY	29,202.2
MASSACHUSETTS MUTUAL LIFE INS CO	MA	112,014.6
MML BAY STATE LIFE INS CO	CT	4,105.4
SENTRY LIFE INS CO	WI	2,809.8
USAA LIFE INS CO	TX	13,463.6
Rating: A-		
ACACIA LIFE INS CO	DC	1,521.4
AMERICAN REPUBLIC INS CO	IA	472.8
AMICA LIFE INS CO	RI	950.4
ANTHEM LIFE INS CO	IN	288.0
CHARTER NATIONAL LIFE INS CO	IL	133.2
COMPANION LIFE INS CO	SC	124.7
CONTINENTAL AMERICAN INS CO	SC	105.0
COUNTRY INVESTORS LIFE ASR CO	IL	192.1
FIRST INVESTORS LIFE INS CO	NY	949.4
FORT DEARBORN LIFE INS CO	IL	2,870.9
GERBER LIFE INS CO	NY	1,568.7
GRANGE LIFE INS CO	OH	258.2
NATIONAL BENEFIT LIFE INS CO	NY	738.4
NEW YORK LIFE INS & ANNUITY CORP	DE	77,190.7
NEW YORK LIFE INS CO	NY	114,937.8
NIPPON LIFE INS CO OF AMERICA	IA	162.8
NORTHWESTERN MUTUAL LIFE INS CO	WI	155,607.2
PACIFIC GUARDIAN LIFE INS CO LTD	HI	426.8
PACIFIC LIFE & ANNUITY CO	AZ	2,589.4
PACIFIC LIFE INS CO	NE	81,524.3
PHYSICIANS LIFE INS CO	NE	1,249.3
PRIMERICA LIFE INS CO	MA	5,765.7
PRINCIPAL LIFE INS CO	IA	109,923.9
SHELTER LIFE INS CO	MO	933.1
STANDARD LIFE & ACCIDENT INS CO	OK	484.7
USABLE LIFE	AR	298.5
WORLD INS CO	NE	242.3
Rating: B+		
ALLSTATE LIFE INS CO	IL	65,002.0
AMERICAN FAMILY LIFE ASR CO OF COLUM	NE	67,309.5
AMERICAN HEALTH & LIFE INS CO	TX	1,505.6
AMERICAN INCOME LIFE INS CO	IN	1,811.7
AMERICAN UNITED LIFE INS CO	IN	12,264.8
AMERITAS LIFE INS CORP	NE	4,928.5
ASSURITY LIFE INS CO	NE	2,167.6

INSURANCE COMPANY NAME	DOM. STATE	TOTAL ASSETS ($MIL)
BOSTON MUTUAL LIFE INS CO	MA	945.5
COLORADO BANKERS LIFE INS CO	CO	144.4
COLUMBUS LIFE INS CO	OH	2,512.2
COMPBENEFITS INS CO	TX	62.7
CONTINENTAL LIFE INS CO OF BRENTWOOD	TN	149.3
EPIC LIFE INSURANCE CO	WI	42.6
FAMILY HERITAGE LIFE INS CO OF AMER	OH	322.3
FARM BUREAU LIFE INS CO	IA	5,605.0
FIDELITY LIFE ASSN A LEGAL RESERVE	IL	505.8
FIDELITY SECURITY LIFE INS CO	MO	576.6
GENERAL RE LIFE CORP	CT	2,682.0
GOVERNMENT PERSONNEL MUTUAL L I C	TX	783.4
ILLINOIS MUTUAL LIFE INS CO	IL	1,262.3
LINCOLN BENEFIT LIFE CO	NE	2,007.2
LINCOLN HERITAGE LIFE INS CO	IL	629.7
MID-WEST NATIONAL LIFE INS CO OF TN	TX	228.4
MIDLAND NATIONAL LIFE INS CO	IA	25,970.2
MTL INS CO	IL	1,337.3
MUTUAL OF OMAHA INS CO	NE	4,625.4
NATIONAL GUARDIAN LIFE INS CO	WI	1,663.4
NATIONAL WESTERN LIFE INS CO	CO	6,175.2
NATIONWIDE LIFE INS CO OF AMERICA	PA	4,826.2
OHIO NATIONAL LIFE ASR CORP	OH	2,702.3
PEKIN LIFE INS CO	IL	863.3
PENN INS & ANNUITY CO	DE	1,038.9
PENN MUTUAL LIFE INS CO	PA	9,647.6
PHARMACISTS LIFE INS CO	IA	40.4
RELIABLE LIFE INS CO	MO	747.4
SAVINGS BANK LIFE INS CO OF MA	MA	2,093.4
SETTLERS LIFE INS CO	WI	417.4
STANDARD INS CO	OR	12,858.1
STANDARD SECURITY LIFE INS CO OF NY	NY	365.4
STONEBRIDGE LIFE INS CO	VT	2,089.0
SURETY LIFE INS CO	NE	13.2
THRIVENT LIFE INS CO	MN	2,564.9
UNITED INVESTORS LIFE INS CO	MO	2,518.4
UNITED OF OMAHA LIFE INS CO	NE	12,875.0
UNITED WORLD LIFE INS CO	NE	114.6
WORLD CORP INS CO	NE	23.2

Kansas

INSURANCE COMPANY NAME	DOM. STATE	TOTAL ASSETS ($MIL)
Rating: A+		
AMERICAN FAMILY LIFE INS CO	WI	3,898.0
COUNTRY LIFE INS CO	IL	7,329.3
PHYSICIANS MUTUAL INS CO	NE	1,445.1
STATE FARM LIFE INS CO	IL	44,978.4
TEACHERS INS & ANNUITY ASN OF AM	NY	194,588.7
Rating: A		
AMERICAN FIDELITY ASR CO	OK	3,343.9
AUTO-OWNERS LIFE INS CO	MI	2,168.0
BERKSHIRE LIFE INS CO OF AMERICA	MA	2,502.2
FEDERATED LIFE INS CO	MN	978.1
FIDELITY INVESTMENTS LIFE INS CO	UT	11,382.8
GUARDIAN LIFE INS CO OF AMERICA	NY	29,202.2
MASSACHUSETTS MUTUAL LIFE INS CO	MA	112,014.6
MML BAY STATE LIFE INS CO	CT	4,105.4
SENTRY LIFE INS CO	WI	2,809.8
USAA LIFE INS CO	TX	13,463.6
Rating: A-		
ACACIA LIFE INS CO	DC	1,521.4
AMALGAMATED LIFE INS CO	NY	62.6
AMERICAN REPUBLIC INS CO	IA	472.8
AMICA LIFE INS CO	RI	950.4
ANTHEM LIFE INS CO	IN	288.0
CHARTER NATIONAL LIFE INS CO	IL	133.2
COMPANION LIFE INS CO	SC	124.7
CONTINENTAL AMERICAN INS CO	SC	105.0
COUNTRY INVESTORS LIFE ASR CO	IL	192.1
FIRST INVESTORS LIFE INS CO	NY	949.4
FORT DEARBORN LIFE INS CO	IL	2,870.9
GERBER LIFE INS CO	NY	1,568.7
GRANGE LIFE INS CO	OH	258.2
NATIONAL BENEFIT LIFE INS CO	NY	738.4
NEW YORK LIFE INS & ANNUITY CORP	DE	77,190.7
NEW YORK LIFE INS CO	NY	114,937.8
NIPPON LIFE INS CO OF AMERICA	IA	162.8
NORTHWESTERN MUTUAL LIFE INS CO	WI	155,607.2
PACIFIC LIFE & ANNUITY CO	AZ	2,589.4
PACIFIC LIFE INS CO	NE	81,524.3
PHYSICIANS LIFE INS CO	NE	1,249.3
PRIMERICA LIFE INS CO	MA	5,765.7
PRINCIPAL LIFE INS CO	IA	109,923.9
SHELTER LIFE INS CO	MO	933.1
STANDARD LIFE & ACCIDENT INS CO	OK	484.7
USABLE LIFE	AR	298.5
WORLD INS CO	NE	242.3
Rating: B+		
ALLSTATE LIFE INS CO	IL	65,002.0
AMERICAN FAMILY LIFE ASR CO OF COLUM	NE	67,309.5
AMERICAN HEALTH & LIFE INS CO	TX	1,505.6
AMERICAN INCOME LIFE INS CO	IN	1,811.7
AMERICAN UNITED LIFE INS CO	IN	12,264.8
AMERITAS LIFE INS CORP	NE	4,928.5
ASSURITY LIFE INS CO	NE	2,167.6

INSURANCE COMPANY NAME	DOM. STATE	TOTAL ASSETS ($MIL)
BOSTON MUTUAL LIFE INS CO	MA	945.5
COLORADO BANKERS LIFE INS CO	CO	144.4
COLUMBUS LIFE INS CO	OH	2,512.2
COMPBENEFITS INS CO	TX	62.7
CONTINENTAL LIFE INS CO OF BRENTWOOD	TN	149.3
EASTERN LIFE & HEALTH INS CO	PA	44.9
EPIC LIFE INSURANCE CO	WI	42.6
FAMILY HERITAGE LIFE INS CO OF AMER	OH	322.3
FARM BUREAU LIFE INS CO	IA	5,605.0
FIDELITY LIFE ASSN A LEGAL RESERVE	IL	505.8
FIDELITY SECURITY LIFE INS CO	MO	576.6
GENERAL RE LIFE CORP	CT	2,682.0
GOVERNMENT PERSONNEL MUTUAL L I C	TX	783.4
ILLINOIS MUTUAL LIFE INS CO	IL	1,262.3
LINCOLN BENEFIT LIFE CO	NE	2,007.1
LINCOLN HERITAGE LIFE INS CO	IL	629.7
MID-WEST NATIONAL LIFE INS CO OF TN	TX	228.4
MIDLAND NATIONAL LIFE INS CO	IA	25,970.2
MTL INS CO	IL	1,337.3
MUTUAL OF OMAHA INS CO	NE	4,625.4
NATIONAL GUARDIAN LIFE INS CO	WI	1,663.4
NATIONAL WESTERN LIFE INS CO	CO	6,175.2
NATIONWIDE LIFE INS CO OF AMERICA	PA	4,826.2
OHIO NATIONAL LIFE ASR CORP	OH	2,702.3
PENN INS & ANNUITY CO	DE	1,038.9
PENN MUTUAL LIFE INS CO	PA	9,647.6
PHARMACISTS LIFE INS CO	IA	40.4
RELIABLE LIFE INS CO	MO	747.4
SAVINGS BANK LIFE INS CO OF MA	MA	2,093.4
SETTLERS LIFE INS CO	WI	417.4
STANDARD INS CO	OR	12,858.1
STANDARD SECURITY LIFE INS CO OF NY	NY	365.4
STONEBRIDGE LIFE INS CO	VT	2,089.0
SURETY LIFE INS CO	NE	13.2
THRIVENT LIFE INS CO	MN	2,564.9
UNITED INVESTORS LIFE INS CO	MO	2,518.4
UNITED OF OMAHA LIFE INS CO	NE	12,875.0
UNITED WORLD LIFE INS CO	NE	114.6
WORLD CORP INS CO	NE	23.2

Kentucky

INSURANCE COMPANY NAME	DOM. STATE	TOTAL ASSETS ($MIL)

Rating: A+

INSURANCE COMPANY NAME	DOM. STATE	TOTAL ASSETS ($MIL)
COUNTRY LIFE INS CO	IL	7,329.3
PHYSICIANS MUTUAL INS CO	NE	1,445.1
STATE FARM LIFE INS CO	IL	44,978.4
TEACHERS INS & ANNUITY ASN OF AM	NY	194,588.7

Rating: A

INSURANCE COMPANY NAME	DOM. STATE	TOTAL ASSETS ($MIL)
AMERICAN FIDELITY ASR CO	OK	3,343.9
AUTO-OWNERS LIFE INS CO	MI	2,168.0
BERKSHIRE LIFE INS CO OF AMERICA	MA	2,502.2
FEDERATED LIFE INS CO	MN	978.1
FIDELITY INVESTMENTS LIFE INS CO	UT	11,382.8
GUARDIAN LIFE INS CO OF AMERICA	NY	29,202.2
MASSACHUSETTS MUTUAL LIFE INS CO	MA	112,014.6
MML BAY STATE LIFE INS CO	CT	4,105.4
SENTRY LIFE INS CO	WI	2,809.8
SOUTHERN FARM BUREAU LIFE INS CO	MS	10,074.1
USAA LIFE INS CO	TX	13,463.6

Rating: A-

INSURANCE COMPANY NAME	DOM. STATE	TOTAL ASSETS ($MIL)
ACACIA LIFE INS CO	DC	1,521.4
AMALGAMATED LIFE INS CO	NY	62.6
AMERICAN REPUBLIC INS CO	IA	472.8
AMICA LIFE INS CO	RI	950.4
ANTHEM LIFE INS CO	IN	288.0
CHARTER NATIONAL LIFE INS CO	IL	133.2
COMPANION LIFE INS CO	SC	124.7
CONTINENTAL AMERICAN INS CO	SC	105.0
COUNTRY INVESTORS LIFE ASR CO	IL	192.1
FIRST INVESTORS LIFE INS CO	NY	949.4
FORT DEARBORN LIFE INS CO	IL	2,870.9
GERBER LIFE INS CO	NY	1,568.7
GRANGE LIFE INS CO	OH	258.2
NATIONAL BENEFIT LIFE INS CO	NY	738.4
NEW YORK LIFE INS & ANNUITY CORP	DE	77,190.7
NEW YORK LIFE INS CO	NY	114,937.8
NIPPON LIFE INS CO OF AMERICA	IA	162.8
NORTHWESTERN MUTUAL LIFE INS CO	WI	155,607.2
PACIFIC LIFE & ANNUITY CO	AZ	2,589.4
PACIFIC LIFE INS CO	NE	81,524.3
PHYSICIANS LIFE INS CO	NE	1,249.3
PRIMERICA LIFE INS CO	MA	5,765.7
PRINCIPAL LIFE INS CO	IA	109,923.9
SHELTER LIFE INS CO	MO	933.1
STANDARD LIFE & ACCIDENT INS CO	OK	484.7
USABLE LIFE	AR	298.5
WORLD INS CO	NE	242.3

Rating: B+

INSURANCE COMPANY NAME	DOM. STATE	TOTAL ASSETS ($MIL)
ALLSTATE LIFE INS CO	IL	65,002.0
AMERICAN FAMILY LIFE ASR CO OF COLUM	NE	67,309.5
AMERICAN HEALTH & LIFE INS CO	TX	1,505.6
AMERICAN INCOME LIFE INS CO	IN	1,811.7
AMERICAN UNITED LIFE INS CO	IN	12,264.8
AMERITAS LIFE INS CORP	NE	4,928.5
ASSURITY LIFE INS CO	NE	2,167.6

INSURANCE COMPANY NAME	DOM. STATE	TOTAL ASSETS ($MIL)
ATLANTIC COAST LIFE INS CO	SC	69.9
BOSTON MUTUAL LIFE INS CO	MA	945.5
CHEROKEE NATIONAL LIFE INS CO	GA	30.8
COLORADO BANKERS LIFE INS CO	CO	144.4
COLUMBUS LIFE INS CO	OH	2,512.2
COMPBENEFITS INS CO	TX	62.7
CONTINENTAL LIFE INS CO OF BRENTWOOD	TN	149.3
COTTON STATES LIFE INS CO	GA	281.8
EASTERN LIFE & HEALTH INS CO	PA	44.9
EPIC LIFE INSURANCE CO	WI	42.6
FAMILY HERITAGE LIFE INS CO OF AMER	OH	322.3
FIDELITY LIFE ASSN A LEGAL RESERVE	IL	505.8
FIDELITY SECURITY LIFE INS CO	MO	576.6
GENERAL RE LIFE CORP	CT	2,682.0
GOVERNMENT PERSONNEL MUTUAL L I C	TX	783.4
ILLINOIS MUTUAL LIFE INS CO	IL	1,262.3
LINCOLN BENEFIT LIFE CO	NE	2,007.2
LINCOLN HERITAGE LIFE INS CO	IL	629.7
MID-WEST NATIONAL LIFE INS CO OF TN	TX	228.4
MIDLAND NATIONAL LIFE INS CO	IA	25,970.2
MTL INS CO	IL	1,337.3
MUTUAL OF OMAHA INS CO	NE	4,625.4
NATIONAL GUARDIAN LIFE INS CO	WI	1,663.4
NATIONAL WESTERN LIFE INS CO	CO	6,175.2
NATIONWIDE LIFE INS CO OF AMERICA	PA	4,826.2
OHIO NATIONAL LIFE ASR CORP	OH	2,702.3
PEKIN LIFE INS CO	IL	863.3
PENN INS & ANNUITY CO	DE	1,038.9
PENN MUTUAL LIFE INS CO	PA	9,647.6
PHARMACISTS LIFE INS CO	IA	40.4
RELIABLE LIFE INS CO	MO	747.4
SAVINGS BANK LIFE INS CO OF MA	MA	2,093.4
SETTLERS LIFE INS CO	WI	417.4
STANDARD INS CO	OR	12,858.1
STANDARD SECURITY LIFE INS CO OF NY	NY	365.4
STONEBRIDGE LIFE INS CO	VT	2,089.0
SURETY LIFE INS CO	NE	13.2
THRIVENT LIFE INS CO	MN	2,564.9
UNITED INVESTORS LIFE INS CO	MO	2,518.4
UNITED OF OMAHA LIFE INS CO	NE	12,875.0
UNITED WORLD LIFE INS CO	NE	114.6
WORLD CORP INS CO	NE	23.2

Louisiana

INSURANCE COMPANY NAME	DOM. STATE	TOTAL ASSETS ($MIL)

Rating: A+

INSURANCE COMPANY NAME	DOM. STATE	TOTAL ASSETS ($MIL)
COUNTRY LIFE INS CO	IL	7,329.3
PHYSICIANS MUTUAL INS CO	NE	1,445.1
STATE FARM LIFE INS CO	IL	44,978.4
TEACHERS INS & ANNUITY ASN OF AM	NY	194,588.7

Rating: A

INSURANCE COMPANY NAME	DOM. STATE	TOTAL ASSETS ($MIL)
AMERICAN FIDELITY ASR CO	OK	3,343.9
BERKSHIRE LIFE INS CO OF AMERICA	MA	2,502.2
FEDERATED LIFE INS CO	MN	978.1
FIDELITY INVESTMENTS LIFE INS CO	UT	11,382.8
GUARDIAN LIFE INS CO OF AMERICA	NY	29,202.2
MASSACHUSETTS MUTUAL LIFE INS CO	MA	112,014.6
MML BAY STATE LIFE INS CO	CT	4,105.4
SENTRY LIFE INS CO	WI	2,809.8
SOUTHERN FARM BUREAU LIFE INS CO	MS	10,074.1
UNION NATIONAL LIFE INS CO	LA	459.3
USAA LIFE INS CO	TX	13,463.6

Rating: A-

INSURANCE COMPANY NAME	DOM. STATE	TOTAL ASSETS ($MIL)
ACACIA LIFE INS CO	DC	1,521.4
AMERICAN REPUBLIC INS CO	IA	472.8
AMICA LIFE INS CO	RI	950.4
ANTHEM LIFE INS CO	IN	288.0
CHARTER NATIONAL LIFE INS CO	IL	133.2
COMPANION LIFE INS CO	SC	124.7
CONTINENTAL AMERICAN INS CO	SC	105.0
COUNTRY INVESTORS LIFE ASR CO	IL	192.1
FIRST INVESTORS LIFE INS CO	NY	949.4
FORT DEARBORN LIFE INS CO	IL	2,870.9
GERBER LIFE INS CO	NY	1,568.7
NATIONAL BENEFIT LIFE INS CO	NY	738.4
NEW YORK LIFE INS & ANNUITY CORP	DE	77,190.7
NEW YORK LIFE INS CO	NY	114,937.8
NIPPON LIFE INS CO OF AMERICA	IA	162.8
NORTHWESTERN MUTUAL LIFE INS CO	WI	155,607.2
PACIFIC GUARDIAN LIFE INS CO LTD	HI	426.8
PACIFIC LIFE & ANNUITY CO	AZ	2,589.4
PACIFIC LIFE INS CO	NE	81,524.3
PHYSICIANS LIFE INS CO	NE	1,249.3
PRIMERICA LIFE INS CO	MA	5,765.7
PRINCIPAL LIFE INS CO	IA	109,923.9
SHELTER LIFE INS CO	MO	933.1
STANDARD LIFE & ACCIDENT INS CO	OK	484.7
USABLE LIFE	AR	298.5
WORLD INS CO	NE	242.3

Rating: B+

INSURANCE COMPANY NAME	DOM. STATE	TOTAL ASSETS ($MIL)
ALFA LIFE INS CORP	AL	1,087.3
ALLSTATE LIFE INS CO	IL	65,002.0
AMERICAN FAMILY LIFE ASR CO OF COLUM	NE	67,309.5
AMERICAN HEALTH & LIFE INS CO	TX	1,505.6
AMERICAN INCOME LIFE INS CO	IN	1,811.7
AMERICAN UNITED LIFE INS CO	IN	12,264.8
AMERITAS LIFE INS CORP	NE	4,928.5
ASSURITY LIFE INS CO	NE	2,167.6

INSURANCE COMPANY NAME	DOM. STATE	TOTAL ASSETS ($MIL)
BLUEBONNET LIFE INS CO	MS	39.2
BOSTON MUTUAL LIFE INS CO	MA	945.5
CHEROKEE NATIONAL LIFE INS CO	GA	30.8
COLORADO BANKERS LIFE INS CO	CO	144.4
COLUMBUS LIFE INS CO	OH	2,512.2
COMPBENEFITS INS CO	TX	62.7
CONTINENTAL LIFE INS CO OF BRENTWOOD	TN	149.3
COTTON STATES LIFE INS CO	GA	281.8
EASTERN LIFE & HEALTH INS CO	PA	44.9
FAMILY HERITAGE LIFE INS CO OF AMER	OH	322.3
FIDELITY LIFE ASSN A LEGAL RESERVE	IL	505.8
FIDELITY SECURITY LIFE INS CO	MO	576.6
GENERAL RE LIFE CORP	CT	2,682.0
GOVERNMENT PERSONNEL MUTUAL L I C	TX	783.4
ILLINOIS MUTUAL LIFE INS CO	IL	1,262.3
LINCOLN BENEFIT LIFE CO	NE	2,007.2
LINCOLN HERITAGE LIFE INS CO	IL	629.7
MID-WEST NATIONAL LIFE INS CO OF TN	TX	228.4
MIDLAND NATIONAL LIFE INS CO	IA	25,970.2
MTL INS CO	IL	1,337.3
MUTUAL OF OMAHA INS CO	NE	4,625.4
NATIONAL GUARDIAN LIFE INS CO	WI	1,663.4
NATIONAL WESTERN LIFE INS CO	CO	6,175.2
NATIONWIDE LIFE INS CO OF AMERICA	PA	4,826.2
OHIO NATIONAL LIFE ASR CORP	OH	2,702.3
PENN INS & ANNUITY CO	DE	1,038.9
PENN MUTUAL LIFE INS CO	PA	9,647.6
PHARMACISTS LIFE INS CO	IA	40.4
SETTLERS LIFE INS CO	WI	417.4
SOUTHERN NATL LIFE INS CO INC	LA	16.2
STANDARD INS CO	OR	12,858.1
STANDARD SECURITY LIFE INS CO OF NY	NY	365.4
STONEBRIDGE LIFE INS CO	VT	2,089.0
SURETY LIFE INS CO	NE	13.2
THRIVENT LIFE INS CO	MN	2,564.9
UNITED INVESTORS LIFE INS CO	MO	2,518.4
UNITED OF OMAHA LIFE INS CO	NE	12,875.0
UNITED WORLD LIFE INS CO	NE	114.6
WORLD CORP INS CO	NE	23.2

Maine

INSURANCE COMPANY NAME	DOM. STATE	TOTAL ASSETS ($MIL)

Rating: A+

INSURANCE COMPANY NAME	DOM. STATE	TOTAL ASSETS ($MIL)
COUNTRY LIFE INS CO	IL	7,329.3
PHYSICIANS MUTUAL INS CO	NE	1,445.1
STATE FARM LIFE INS CO	IL	44,978.4
TEACHERS INS & ANNUITY ASN OF AM	NY	194,588.7

Rating: A

INSURANCE COMPANY NAME	DOM. STATE	TOTAL ASSETS ($MIL)
AMERICAN FIDELITY ASR CO	OK	3,343.9
BERKSHIRE LIFE INS CO OF AMERICA	MA	2,502.2
FEDERATED LIFE INS CO	MN	978.1
FIDELITY INVESTMENTS LIFE INS CO	UT	11,382.8
GUARDIAN LIFE INS CO OF AMERICA	NY	29,202.2
MASSACHUSETTS MUTUAL LIFE INS CO	MA	112,014.6
MML BAY STATE LIFE INS CO	CT	4,105.4
SENTRY LIFE INS CO	WI	2,809.8
USAA LIFE INS CO	TX	13,463.6

Rating: A-

INSURANCE COMPANY NAME	DOM. STATE	TOTAL ASSETS ($MIL)
AMALGAMATED LIFE INS CO	NY	62.6
AMERICAN REPUBLIC INS CO	IA	472.8
AMICA LIFE INS CO	RI	950.4
ANTHEM LIFE INS CO	IN	288.0
CHARTER NATIONAL LIFE INS CO	IL	133.2
COMPANION LIFE INS CO	SC	124.7
CONTINENTAL AMERICAN INS CO	SC	105.0
COUNTRY INVESTORS LIFE ASR CO	IL	192.1
FIRST INVESTORS LIFE INS CO	NY	949.4
FORT DEARBORN LIFE INS CO	IL	2,870.9
GERBER LIFE INS CO	NY	1,568.7
NATIONAL BENEFIT LIFE INS CO	NY	738.4
NEW YORK LIFE INS & ANNUITY CORP	DE	77,190.7
NEW YORK LIFE INS CO	NY	114,937.8
NORTHWESTERN MUTUAL LIFE INS CO	WI	155,607.2
PACIFIC LIFE & ANNUITY CO	AZ	2,589.4
PACIFIC LIFE INS CO	NE	81,524.3
PHYSICIANS LIFE INS CO	NE	1,249.3
PRIMERICA LIFE INS CO	MA	5,765.7
PRINCIPAL LIFE INS CO	IA	109,923.9
USABLE LIFE	AR	298.5
WORLD INS CO	NE	242.3

Rating: B+

INSURANCE COMPANY NAME	DOM. STATE	TOTAL ASSETS ($MIL)
ALLSTATE LIFE INS CO	IL	65,002.0
AMERICAN FAMILY LIFE ASR CO OF COLUM	NE	67,309.5
AMERICAN HEALTH & LIFE INS CO	TX	1,505.6
AMERICAN INCOME LIFE INS CO	IN	1,811.7
AMERICAN UNITED LIFE INS CO	IN	12,264.8
AMERITAS LIFE INS CORP	NE	4,928.5
ASSURITY LIFE INS CO	NE	2,167.6
BOSTON MUTUAL LIFE INS CO	MA	945.5
COLORADO BANKERS LIFE INS CO	CO	144.4
COLUMBUS LIFE INS CO	OH	2,512.2
EASTERN LIFE & HEALTH INS CO	PA	44.9
FAMILY HERITAGE LIFE INS CO OF AMER	OH	322.3
FIDELITY LIFE ASSN A LEGAL RESERVE	IL	505.8
FIDELITY SECURITY LIFE INS CO	MO	576.6

INSURANCE COMPANY NAME	DOM. STATE	TOTAL ASSETS ($MIL)
GOVERNMENT PERSONNEL MUTUAL L I C	TX	783.4
ILLINOIS MUTUAL LIFE INS CO	IL	1,262.3
LINCOLN BENEFIT LIFE CO	NE	2,007.2
LINCOLN HERITAGE LIFE INS CO	IL	629.7
MIDLAND NATIONAL LIFE INS CO	IA	25,970.2
MTL INS CO	IL	1,337.3
MUTUAL OF OMAHA INS CO	NE	4,625.4
NATIONAL GUARDIAN LIFE INS CO	WI	1,663.4
NATIONAL WESTERN LIFE INS CO	CO	6,175.2
NATIONWIDE LIFE INS CO OF AMERICA	PA	4,826.2
OHIO NATIONAL LIFE ASR CORP	OH	2,702.3
PENN INS & ANNUITY CO	DE	1,038.9
PENN MUTUAL LIFE INS CO	PA	9,647.6
RELIABLE LIFE INS CO	MO	747.4
SAVINGS BANK LIFE INS CO OF MA	MA	2,093.4
SETTLERS LIFE INS CO	WI	417.4
STANDARD INS CO	OR	12,858.1
STANDARD SECURITY LIFE INS CO OF NY	NY	365.4
STONEBRIDGE LIFE INS CO	VT	2,089.0
SURETY LIFE INS CO	NE	13.2
UNITED INVESTORS LIFE INS CO	MO	2,518.4
UNITED OF OMAHA LIFE INS CO	NE	12,875.0
UNITED WORLD LIFE INS CO	NE	114.6

Maryland

INSURANCE COMPANY NAME	DOM. STATE	TOTAL ASSETS ($MIL)

Rating: A+

INSURANCE COMPANY NAME	DOM. STATE	TOTAL ASSETS ($MIL)
COUNTRY LIFE INS CO	IL	7,329.3
PHYSICIANS MUTUAL INS CO	NE	1,445.1
STATE FARM LIFE INS CO	IL	44,978.4
TEACHERS INS & ANNUITY ASN OF AM	NY	194,588.7

Rating: A

INSURANCE COMPANY NAME	DOM. STATE	TOTAL ASSETS ($MIL)
AMERICAN FIDELITY ASR CO	OK	3,343.9
BERKSHIRE LIFE INS CO OF AMERICA	MA	2,502.2
FEDERATED LIFE INS CO	MN	978.1
FIDELITY INVESTMENTS LIFE INS CO	UT	11,382.8
GUARDIAN LIFE INS CO OF AMERICA	NY	29,202.2
MASSACHUSETTS MUTUAL LIFE INS CO	MA	112,014.6
MML BAY STATE LIFE INS CO	CT	4,105.4
SENTRY LIFE INS CO	WI	2,809.8
UNITED FARM FAMILY LIFE INS CO	IN	1,712.9
USAA LIFE INS CO	TX	13,463.6

Rating: A-

INSURANCE COMPANY NAME	DOM. STATE	TOTAL ASSETS ($MIL)
ACACIA LIFE INS CO	DC	1,521.4
AMALGAMATED LIFE INS CO	NY	62.6
AMERICAN REPUBLIC INS CO	IA	472.8
AMICA LIFE INS CO	RI	950.4
ANTHEM LIFE INS CO	IN	288.0
CHARTER NATIONAL LIFE INS CO	IL	133.2
COMPANION LIFE INS CO	SC	124.7
CONTINENTAL AMERICAN INS CO	SC	105.0
COUNTRY INVESTORS LIFE ASR CO	IL	192.1
FIRST INVESTORS LIFE INS CO	NY	949.4
FORT DEARBORN LIFE INS CO	IL	2,870.9
GERBER LIFE INS CO	NY	1,568.7
NATIONAL BENEFIT LIFE INS CO	NY	738.4
NEW YORK LIFE INS & ANNUITY CORP	DE	77,190.7
NEW YORK LIFE INS CO	NY	114,937.8
NIPPON LIFE INS CO OF AMERICA	IA	162.8
NORTHWESTERN MUTUAL LIFE INS CO	WI	155,607.2
PACIFIC LIFE & ANNUITY CO	AZ	2,589.4
PACIFIC LIFE INS CO	NE	81,524.3
PHYSICIANS LIFE INS CO	NE	1,249.3
PRIMERICA LIFE INS CO	MA	5,765.7
PRINCIPAL LIFE INS CO	IA	109,923.9
STANDARD LIFE & ACCIDENT INS CO	OK	484.7
USABLE LIFE	AR	298.5
WORLD INS CO	NE	242.3

Rating: B+

INSURANCE COMPANY NAME	DOM. STATE	TOTAL ASSETS ($MIL)
ALLSTATE LIFE INS CO	IL	65,002.0
AMERICAN FAMILY LIFE ASR CO OF COLUM	NE	67,309.5
AMERICAN HEALTH & LIFE INS CO	TX	1,505.6
AMERICAN INCOME LIFE INS CO	IN	1,811.7
AMERICAN UNITED LIFE INS CO	IN	12,264.8
AMERITAS LIFE INS CORP	NE	4,928.5
ASSURITY LIFE INS CO	NE	2,167.6
BOSTON MUTUAL LIFE INS CO	MA	945.5
CHEROKEE NATIONAL LIFE INS CO	GA	30.8
COLORADO BANKERS LIFE INS CO	CO	144.4

INSURANCE COMPANY NAME	DOM. STATE	TOTAL ASSETS ($MIL)
COLUMBUS LIFE INS CO	OH	2,512.2
COMPBENEFITS INS CO	TX	62.7
CONTINENTAL LIFE INS CO OF BRENTWOOD	TN	149.3
EASTERN LIFE & HEALTH INS CO	PA	44.9
EPIC LIFE INSURANCE CO	WI	42.6
FAMILY HERITAGE LIFE INS CO OF AMER	OH	322.3
FIDELITY LIFE ASSN A LEGAL RESERVE	IL	505.8
FIDELITY SECURITY LIFE INS CO	MO	576.6
GENERAL RE LIFE CORP	CT	2,682.0
GOVERNMENT PERSONNEL MUTUAL L I C	TX	783.4
ILLINOIS MUTUAL LIFE INS CO	IL	1,262.3
LINCOLN BENEFIT LIFE CO	NE	2,007.2
LINCOLN HERITAGE LIFE INS CO	IL	629.7
MID-WEST NATIONAL LIFE INS CO OF TN	TX	228.4
MIDLAND NATIONAL LIFE INS CO	IA	25,970.2
MTL INS CO	IL	1,337.3
MUTUAL OF OMAHA INS CO	NE	4,625.4
NATIONAL GUARDIAN LIFE INS CO	WI	1,663.4
NATIONAL WESTERN LIFE INS CO	CO	6,175.2
NATIONWIDE LIFE INS CO OF AMERICA	PA	4,826.2
OHIO NATIONAL LIFE ASR CORP	OH	2,702.3
PENN INS & ANNUITY CO	DE	1,038.9
PENN MUTUAL LIFE INS CO	PA	9,647.6
PHARMACISTS LIFE INS CO	IA	40.4
RELIABLE LIFE INS CO	MO	747.4
SAVINGS BANK LIFE INS CO OF MA	MA	2,093.4
SETTLERS LIFE INS CO	WI	417.4
STANDARD INS CO	OR	12,858.1
STANDARD SECURITY LIFE INS CO OF NY	NY	365.4
STONEBRIDGE LIFE INS CO	VT	2,089.0
SURETY LIFE INS CO	NE	13.2
THRIVENT LIFE INS CO	MN	2,564.9
UNITED INVESTORS LIFE INS CO	MO	2,518.4
UNITED OF OMAHA LIFE INS CO	NE	12,875.0
UNITED WORLD LIFE INS CO	NE	114.6
WORLD CORP INS CO	NE	23.2

Massachusetts

INSURANCE COMPANY NAME	DOM. STATE	TOTAL ASSETS ($MIL)

Rating: A+

COUNTRY LIFE INS CO	IL	7,329.3
PHYSICIANS MUTUAL INS CO	NE	1,445.1
TEACHERS INS & ANNUITY ASN OF AM	NY	194,588.7

Rating: A

AMERICAN FIDELITY ASR CO	OK	3,343.9
BERKSHIRE LIFE INS CO OF AMERICA	MA	2,502.2
FEDERATED LIFE INS CO	MN	978.1
FIDELITY INVESTMENTS LIFE INS CO	UT	11,382.8
GUARDIAN LIFE INS CO OF AMERICA	NY	29,202.2
MASSACHUSETTS MUTUAL LIFE INS CO	MA	112,014.6
MML BAY STATE LIFE INS CO	CT	4,105.4
SENTRY LIFE INS CO	WI	2,809.8
UNITED FARM FAMILY LIFE INS CO	IN	1,712.9
USAA LIFE INS CO	TX	13,463.6

Rating: A-

ACACIA LIFE INS CO	DC	1,521.4
AMALGAMATED LIFE INS CO	NY	62.6
AMERICAN REPUBLIC INS CO	IA	472.8
AMICA LIFE INS CO	RI	950.4
ANTHEM LIFE INS CO	IN	288.0
CHARTER NATIONAL LIFE INS CO	IL	133.2
COMPANION LIFE INS CO	SC	124.7
CONTINENTAL AMERICAN INS CO	SC	105.0
COUNTRY INVESTORS LIFE ASR CO	IL	192.1
FIRST INVESTORS LIFE INS CO	NY	949.4
FORT DEARBORN LIFE INS CO	IL	2,870.9
GERBER LIFE INS CO	NY	1,568.7
NATIONAL BENEFIT LIFE INS CO	NY	738.4
NEW YORK LIFE INS & ANNUITY CORP	DE	77,190.7
NEW YORK LIFE INS CO	NY	114,937.8
NIPPON LIFE INS CO OF AMERICA	IA	162.8
NORTHWESTERN MUTUAL LIFE INS CO	WI	155,607.2
PACIFIC LIFE & ANNUITY CO	AZ	2,589.4
PACIFIC LIFE INS CO	NE	81,524.3
PHYSICIANS LIFE INS CO	NE	1,249.3
PRIMERICA LIFE INS CO	MA	5,765.7
PRINCIPAL LIFE INS CO	IA	109,923.9
STANDARD LIFE & ACCIDENT INS CO	OK	484.7
USABLE LIFE	AR	298.5

Rating: B+

ALLSTATE LIFE INS CO	IL	65,002.0
AMERICAN FAMILY LIFE ASR CO OF COLUM	NE	67,309.5
AMERICAN FAMILY LIFE ASR CO OF NY	NY	285.0
AMERICAN HEALTH & LIFE INS CO	TX	1,505.6
AMERICAN INCOME LIFE INS CO	IN	1,811.7
AMERICAN UNITED LIFE INS CO	IN	12,264.8
AMERITAS LIFE INS CORP	NE	4,928.5
ASSURITY LIFE INS CO	NE	2,167.6
BOSTON MUTUAL LIFE INS CO	MA	945.5
COLORADO BANKERS LIFE INS CO	CO	144.4
COLUMBUS LIFE INS CO	OH	2,512.2
FAMILY HERITAGE LIFE INS CO OF AMER	OH	322.3

INSURANCE COMPANY NAME	DOM. STATE	TOTAL ASSETS ($MIL)
FIDELITY LIFE ASSN A LEGAL RESERVE	IL	505.8
FIDELITY SECURITY LIFE INS CO	MO	576.6
GENERAL RE LIFE CORP	CT	2,682.0
GOVERNMENT PERSONNEL MUTUAL L I C	TX	783.4
ILLINOIS MUTUAL LIFE INS CO	IL	1,262.3
LINCOLN BENEFIT LIFE CO	NE	2,007.2
LINCOLN HERITAGE LIFE INS CO	IL	629.7
MID-WEST NATIONAL LIFE INS CO OF TN	TX	228.4
MIDLAND NATIONAL LIFE INS CO	IA	25,970.2
MTL INS CO	IL	1,337.3
MUTUAL OF OMAHA INS CO	NE	4,625.4
NATIONAL GUARDIAN LIFE INS CO	WI	1,663.4
NATIONAL WESTERN LIFE INS CO	CO	6,175.2
NATIONWIDE LIFE INS CO OF AMERICA	PA	4,826.2
OHIO NATIONAL LIFE ASR CORP	OH	2,702.3
PENN INS & ANNUITY CO	DE	1,038.9
PENN MUTUAL LIFE INS CO	PA	9,647.6
RELIABLE LIFE INS CO	MO	747.4
SAVINGS BANK LIFE INS CO OF MA	MA	2,093.4
SETTLERS LIFE INS CO	WI	417.4
STANDARD INS CO	OR	12,858.1
STANDARD SECURITY LIFE INS CO OF NY	NY	365.4
STONEBRIDGE LIFE INS CO	VT	2,089.0
SURETY LIFE INS CO	NE	13.2
UNITED INVESTORS LIFE INS CO	MO	2,518.4
UNITED OF OMAHA LIFE INS CO	NE	12,875.0
UNITED WORLD LIFE INS CO	NE	114.6

Michigan

INSURANCE COMPANY NAME	DOM. STATE	TOTAL ASSETS ($MIL)
Rating: A+		
AMERICAN FAMILY LIFE INS CO	WI	3,898.0
COUNTRY LIFE INS CO	IL	7,329.3
PHYSICIANS MUTUAL INS CO	NE	1,445.1
STATE FARM LIFE INS CO	IL	44,978.4
TEACHERS INS & ANNUITY ASN OF AM	NY	194,588.7
Rating: A		
AMERICAN FIDELITY ASR CO	OK	3,343.9
AUTO-OWNERS LIFE INS CO	MI	2,168.0
BERKSHIRE LIFE INS CO OF AMERICA	MA	2,502.2
FEDERATED LIFE INS CO	MN	978.1
FIDELITY INVESTMENTS LIFE INS CO	UT	11,382.8
GUARDIAN LIFE INS CO OF AMERICA	NY	29,202.2
MASSACHUSETTS MUTUAL LIFE INS CO	MA	112,014.6
MML BAY STATE LIFE INS CO	CT	4,105.4
SENTRY LIFE INS CO	WI	2,809.8
USAA LIFE INS CO	TX	13,463.6
Rating: A-		
ACACIA LIFE INS CO	DC	1,521.4
AMALGAMATED LIFE INS CO	NY	62.6
AMERICAN REPUBLIC INS CO	IA	472.8
AMICA LIFE INS CO	RI	950.4
ANTHEM LIFE INS CO	IN	288.0
CHARTER NATIONAL LIFE INS CO	IL	133.2
COMPANION LIFE INS CO	SC	124.7
CONTINENTAL AMERICAN INS CO	SC	105.0
COUNTRY INVESTORS LIFE ASR CO	IL	192.1
FARM BUREAU LIFE INS CO OF MICHIGAN	MI	1,761.1
FIRST INVESTORS LIFE INS CO	NY	949.4
FORT DEARBORN LIFE INS CO	IL	2,870.9
GERBER LIFE INS CO	NY	1,568.7
GRANGE LIFE INS CO	OH	258.2
NATIONAL BENEFIT LIFE INS CO	NY	738.4
NEW YORK LIFE INS & ANNUITY CORP	DE	77,190.7
NEW YORK LIFE INS CO	NY	114,937.8
NIPPON LIFE INS CO OF AMERICA	IA	162.8
NORTHWESTERN MUTUAL LIFE INS CO	WI	155,607.2
PACIFIC LIFE & ANNUITY CO	AZ	2,589.4
PACIFIC LIFE INS CO	NE	81,524.3
PHYSICIANS LIFE INS CO	NE	1,249.3
PRIMERICA LIFE INS CO	MA	5,765.7
PRINCIPAL LIFE INS CO	IA	109,923.9
STANDARD LIFE & ACCIDENT INS CO	OK	484.7
USABLE LIFE	AR	298.5
WORLD INS CO	NE	242.3
Rating: B+		
ALLSTATE LIFE INS CO	IL	65,002.0
AMERICAN FAMILY LIFE ASR CO OF COLUM	NE	67,309.5
AMERICAN HEALTH & LIFE INS CO	TX	1,505.6
AMERICAN INCOME LIFE INS CO	IN	1,811.7
AMERICAN UNITED LIFE INS CO	IN	12,264.8
AMERITAS LIFE INS CORP	NE	4,928.5
ASSURITY LIFE INS CO	NE	2,167.6

INSURANCE COMPANY NAME	DOM. STATE	TOTAL ASSETS ($MIL)
BOSTON MUTUAL LIFE INS CO	MA	945.5
COLORADO BANKERS LIFE INS CO	CO	144.4
COLUMBUS LIFE INS CO	OH	2,512.2
CONTINENTAL LIFE INS CO OF BRENTWOOD	TN	149.3
EASTERN LIFE & HEALTH INS CO	PA	44.9
EPIC LIFE INSURANCE CO	WI	42.6
FAMILY HERITAGE LIFE INS CO OF AMER	OH	322.3
FIDELITY LIFE ASSN A LEGAL RESERVE	IL	505.8
FIDELITY SECURITY LIFE INS CO	MO	576.6
GENERAL RE LIFE CORP	CT	2,682.0
GOVERNMENT PERSONNEL MUTUAL L I C	TX	783.4
ILLINOIS MUTUAL LIFE INS CO	IL	1,262.3
LINCOLN BENEFIT LIFE CO	NE	2,007.2
LINCOLN HERITAGE LIFE INS CO	IL	629.7
MID-WEST NATIONAL LIFE INS CO OF TN	TX	228.4
MIDLAND NATIONAL LIFE INS CO	IA	25,970.2
MTL INS CO	IL	1,337.3
MUTUAL OF OMAHA INS CO	NE	4,625.4
NATIONAL GUARDIAN LIFE INS CO	WI	1,663.4
NATIONAL WESTERN LIFE INS CO	CO	6,175.2
NATIONWIDE LIFE INS CO OF AMERICA	PA	4,826.2
OHIO NATIONAL LIFE ASR CORP	OH	2,702.3
PEKIN LIFE INS CO	IL	863.3
PENN INS & ANNUITY CO	DE	1,038.9
PENN MUTUAL LIFE INS CO	PA	9,647.6
PHARMACISTS LIFE INS CO	IA	40.4
RELIABLE LIFE INS CO	MO	747.4
SAVINGS BANK LIFE INS CO OF MA	MA	2,093.4
SETTLERS LIFE INS CO	WI	417.4
STANDARD INS CO	OR	12,858.1
STANDARD SECURITY LIFE INS CO OF NY	NY	365.4
STONEBRIDGE LIFE INS CO	VT	2,089.0
SURETY LIFE INS CO	NE	13.2
THRIVENT LIFE INS CO	MN	2,564.9
UNITED INVESTORS LIFE INS CO	MO	2,518.4
UNITED OF OMAHA LIFE INS CO	NE	12,875.0
UNITED WORLD LIFE INS CO	NE	114.6
WORLD CORP INS CO	NE	23.2

Minnesota

INSURANCE COMPANY NAME	DOM. STATE	TOTAL ASSETS ($MIL)

Rating: A+

INSURANCE COMPANY NAME	DOM. STATE	TOTAL ASSETS ($MIL)
AMERICAN FAMILY LIFE INS CO	WI	3,898.0
COUNTRY LIFE INS CO	IL	7,329.3
PHYSICIANS MUTUAL INS CO	NE	1,445.1
STATE FARM LIFE INS CO	IL	44,978.4
TEACHERS INS & ANNUITY ASN OF AM	NY	194,588.7

Rating: A

INSURANCE COMPANY NAME	DOM. STATE	TOTAL ASSETS ($MIL)
AMERICAN FIDELITY ASR CO	OK	3,343.9
AUTO-OWNERS LIFE INS CO	MI	2,168.0
BERKSHIRE LIFE INS CO OF AMERICA	MA	2,502.2
FEDERATED LIFE INS CO	MN	978.1
FIDELITY INVESTMENTS LIFE INS CO	UT	11,382.8
GUARDIAN LIFE INS CO OF AMERICA	NY	29,202.2
MASSACHUSETTS MUTUAL LIFE INS CO	MA	112,014.6
MML BAY STATE LIFE INS CO	CT	4,105.4
SENTRY LIFE INS CO	WI	2,809.8
USAA LIFE INS CO	TX	13,463.6

Rating: A-

INSURANCE COMPANY NAME	DOM. STATE	TOTAL ASSETS ($MIL)
ACACIA LIFE INS CO	DC	1,521.4
AMALGAMATED LIFE INS CO	NY	62.6
AMERICAN REPUBLIC INS CO	IA	472.8
AMICA LIFE INS CO	RI	950.4
ANTHEM LIFE INS CO	IN	288.0
CHARTER NATIONAL LIFE INS CO	IL	133.2
COMPANION LIFE INS CO	SC	124.7
CONTINENTAL AMERICAN INS CO	SC	105.0
COUNTRY INVESTORS LIFE ASR CO	IL	192.1
FIRST INVESTORS LIFE INS CO	NY	949.4
FORT DEARBORN LIFE INS CO	IL	2,870.9
GERBER LIFE INS CO	NY	1,568.7
GRANGE LIFE INS CO	OH	258.2
NATIONAL BENEFIT LIFE INS CO	NY	738.4
NEW YORK LIFE INS & ANNUITY CORP	DE	77,190.7
NEW YORK LIFE INS CO	NY	114,937.8
NIPPON LIFE INS CO OF AMERICA	IA	162.8
NORTHWESTERN MUTUAL LIFE INS CO	WI	155,607.2
PACIFIC LIFE & ANNUITY CO	AZ	2,589.4
PACIFIC LIFE INS CO	NE	81,524.3
PHYSICIANS LIFE INS CO	NE	1,249.3
PRIMERICA LIFE INS CO	MA	5,765.7
PRINCIPAL LIFE INS CO	IA	109,923.9
STANDARD LIFE & ACCIDENT INS CO	OK	484.7
USABLE LIFE	AR	298.5
WORLD INS CO	NE	242.3

Rating: B+

INSURANCE COMPANY NAME	DOM. STATE	TOTAL ASSETS ($MIL)
ALLSTATE LIFE INS CO	IL	65,002.0
AMERICAN FAMILY LIFE ASR CO OF COLUM	NE	67,309.5
AMERICAN HEALTH & LIFE INS CO	TX	1,505.6
AMERICAN INCOME LIFE INS CO	IN	1,811.7
AMERICAN UNITED LIFE INS CO	IN	12,264.8
AMERITAS LIFE INS CORP	NE	4,928.5
ASSURITY LIFE INS CO	NE	2,167.6
BOSTON MUTUAL LIFE INS CO	MA	945.5

INSURANCE COMPANY NAME	DOM. STATE	TOTAL ASSETS ($MIL)
COLORADO BANKERS LIFE INS CO	CO	144.4
COLUMBUS LIFE INS CO	OH	2,512.2
CONTINENTAL LIFE INS CO OF BRENTWOOD	TN	149.3
EASTERN LIFE & HEALTH INS CO	PA	44.9
EPIC LIFE INSURANCE CO	WI	42.6
FAMILY HERITAGE LIFE INS CO OF AMER	OH	322.3
FARM BUREAU LIFE INS CO	IA	5,605.0
FIDELITY LIFE ASSN A LEGAL RESERVE	IL	505.8
FIDELITY SECURITY LIFE INS CO	MO	576.6
GENERAL RE LIFE CORP	CT	2,682.0
GOVERNMENT PERSONNEL MUTUAL L I C	TX	783.4
ILLINOIS MUTUAL LIFE INS CO	IL	1,262.3
LINCOLN BENEFIT LIFE CO	NE	2,007.2
LINCOLN HERITAGE LIFE INS CO	IL	629.7
MID-WEST NATIONAL LIFE INS CO OF TN	TX	228.4
MIDLAND NATIONAL LIFE INS CO	IA	25,970.2
MTL INS CO	IL	1,337.3
MUTUAL OF OMAHA INS CO	NE	4,625.4
NATIONAL GUARDIAN LIFE INS CO	WI	1,663.4
NATIONAL WESTERN LIFE INS CO	CO	6,175.2
NATIONWIDE LIFE INS CO OF AMERICA	PA	4,826.2
OHIO NATIONAL LIFE ASR CORP	OH	2,702.3
PEKIN LIFE INS CO	IL	863.3
PENN INS & ANNUITY CO	DE	1,038.9
PENN MUTUAL LIFE INS CO	PA	9,647.6
PHARMACISTS LIFE INS CO	IA	40.4
RELIABLE LIFE INS CO	MO	747.4
SETTLERS LIFE INS CO	WI	417.4
STANDARD INS CO	OR	12,858.1
STANDARD SECURITY LIFE INS CO OF NY	NY	365.4
STONEBRIDGE LIFE INS CO	VT	2,089.0
SURETY LIFE INS CO	NE	13.2
THRIVENT LIFE INS CO	MN	2,564.9
UNITED INVESTORS LIFE INS CO	MO	2,518.4
UNITED OF OMAHA LIFE INS CO	NE	12,875.0
UNITED WORLD LIFE INS CO	NE	114.6

Mississippi

INSURANCE COMPANY NAME	DOM. STATE	TOTAL ASSETS ($MIL)

Rating: A+

INSURANCE COMPANY NAME	DOM. STATE	TOTAL ASSETS ($MIL)
COUNTRY LIFE INS CO	IL	7,329.3
PHYSICIANS MUTUAL INS CO	NE	1,445.1
STATE FARM LIFE INS CO	IL	44,978.4
TEACHERS INS & ANNUITY ASN OF AM	NY	194,588.7

Rating: A

INSURANCE COMPANY NAME	DOM. STATE	TOTAL ASSETS ($MIL)
AMERICAN FIDELITY ASR CO	OK	3,343.9
AUTO-OWNERS LIFE INS CO	MI	2,168.0
BERKSHIRE LIFE INS CO OF AMERICA	MA	2,502.2
FEDERATED LIFE INS CO	MN	978.1
FIDELITY INVESTMENTS LIFE INS CO	UT	11,382.8
GUARDIAN LIFE INS CO OF AMERICA	NY	29,202.2
MASSACHUSETTS MUTUAL LIFE INS CO	MA	112,014.6
MML BAY STATE LIFE INS CO	CT	4,105.4
SENTRY LIFE INS CO	WI	2,809.8
SOUTHERN FARM BUREAU LIFE INS CO	MS	10,074.1
UNION NATIONAL LIFE INS CO	LA	459.3
USAA LIFE INS CO	TX	13,463.6

Rating: A-

INSURANCE COMPANY NAME	DOM. STATE	TOTAL ASSETS ($MIL)
ACACIA LIFE INS CO	DC	1,521.4
AMERICAN REPUBLIC INS CO	IA	472.8
AMICA LIFE INS CO	RI	950.4
ANTHEM LIFE INS CO	IN	288.0
CHARTER NATIONAL LIFE INS CO	IL	133.2
COMPANION LIFE INS CO	SC	124.7
CONTINENTAL AMERICAN INS CO	SC	105.0
COUNTRY INVESTORS LIFE ASR CO	IL	192.1
FIRST INVESTORS LIFE INS CO	NY	949.4
FORT DEARBORN LIFE INS CO	IL	2,870.9
GERBER LIFE INS CO	NY	1,568.7
GREATER GEORGIA LIFE INS CO	GA	46.3
NATIONAL BENEFIT LIFE INS CO	NY	738.4
NEW YORK LIFE INS & ANNUITY CORP	DE	77,190.7
NEW YORK LIFE INS CO	NY	114,937.8
NIPPON LIFE INS CO OF AMERICA	IA	162.8
NORTHWESTERN MUTUAL LIFE INS CO	WI	155,607.2
PACIFIC LIFE & ANNUITY CO	AZ	2,589.4
PACIFIC LIFE INS CO	NE	81,524.3
PHYSICIANS LIFE INS CO	NE	1,249.3
PRIMERICA LIFE INS CO	MA	5,765.7
PRINCIPAL LIFE INS CO	IA	109,923.9
SHELTER LIFE INS CO	MO	933.1
STANDARD LIFE & ACCIDENT INS CO	OK	484.7
USABLE LIFE	AR	298.5
WORLD INS CO	NE	242.3

Rating: B+

INSURANCE COMPANY NAME	DOM. STATE	TOTAL ASSETS ($MIL)
ALFA LIFE INS CORP	AL	1,087.3
ALLSTATE LIFE INS CO	IL	65,002.0
AMERICAN FAMILY LIFE ASR CO OF COLUM	NE	67,309.5
AMERICAN HEALTH & LIFE INS CO	TX	1,505.6
AMERICAN INCOME LIFE INS CO	IN	1,811.7
AMERICAN UNITED LIFE INS CO	IN	12,264.8
AMERITAS LIFE INS CORP	NE	4,928.5

INSURANCE COMPANY NAME	DOM. STATE	TOTAL ASSETS ($MIL)
ASSURITY LIFE INS CO	NE	2,167.6
ATLANTIC COAST LIFE INS CO	SC	69.9
BLUEBONNET LIFE INS CO	MS	39.2
BOSTON MUTUAL LIFE INS CO	MA	945.5
CHEROKEE NATIONAL LIFE INS CO	GA	30.8
COLORADO BANKERS LIFE INS CO	CO	144.4
COLUMBUS LIFE INS CO	OH	2,512.2
COMPBENEFITS INS CO	TX	62.7
CONTINENTAL LIFE INS CO OF BRENTWOOD	TN	149.3
COTTON STATES LIFE INS CO	GA	281.8
EASTERN LIFE & HEALTH INS CO	PA	44.9
FAMILY HERITAGE LIFE INS CO OF AMER	OH	322.3
FIDELITY LIFE ASSN A LEGAL RESERVE	IL	505.8
FIDELITY SECURITY LIFE INS CO	MO	576.6
GENERAL RE LIFE CORP	CT	2,682.0
GOVERNMENT PERSONNEL MUTUAL L I C	TX	783.4
ILLINOIS MUTUAL LIFE INS CO	IL	1,262.3
LINCOLN BENEFIT LIFE CO	NE	2,007.2
LINCOLN HERITAGE LIFE INS CO	IL	629.7
MID-WEST NATIONAL LIFE INS CO OF TN	TX	228.4
MIDLAND NATIONAL LIFE INS CO	IA	25,970.2
MTL INS CO	IL	1,337.3
MUTUAL OF OMAHA INS CO	NE	4,625.4
NATIONAL GUARDIAN LIFE INS CO	WI	1,663.4
NATIONAL WESTERN LIFE INS CO	CO	6,175.2
NATIONWIDE LIFE INS CO OF AMERICA	PA	4,826.2
OHIO NATIONAL LIFE ASR CORP	OH	2,702.3
PENN INS & ANNUITY CO	DE	1,038.9
PENN MUTUAL LIFE INS CO	PA	9,647.6
PHARMACISTS LIFE INS CO	IA	40.4
RELIABLE LIFE INS CO	MO	747.4
SETTLERS LIFE INS CO	WI	417.4
STANDARD INS CO	OR	12,858.1
STANDARD SECURITY LIFE INS CO OF NY	NY	365.4
STONEBRIDGE LIFE INS CO	VT	2,089.0
SURETY LIFE INS CO	NE	13.2
THRIVENT LIFE INS CO	MN	2,564.9
UNITED INVESTORS LIFE INS CO	MO	2,518.4
UNITED OF OMAHA LIFE INS CO	NE	12,875.0
UNITED WORLD LIFE INS CO	NE	114.6
WORLD CORP INS CO	NE	23.2

Missouri

INSURANCE COMPANY NAME	DOM. STATE	TOTAL ASSETS ($MIL)

Rating: A+

INSURANCE COMPANY NAME	DOM. STATE	TOTAL ASSETS ($MIL)
AMERICAN FAMILY LIFE INS CO	WI	3,898.0
COUNTRY LIFE INS CO	IL	7,329.3
PHYSICIANS MUTUAL INS CO	NE	1,445.1
STATE FARM LIFE INS CO	IL	44,978.4
TEACHERS INS & ANNUITY ASN OF AM	NY	194,588.7

Rating: A

INSURANCE COMPANY NAME	DOM. STATE	TOTAL ASSETS ($MIL)
AMERICAN FIDELITY ASR CO	OK	3,343.9
AUTO-OWNERS LIFE INS CO	MI	2,168.0
BERKSHIRE LIFE INS CO OF AMERICA	MA	2,502.2
FEDERATED LIFE INS CO	MN	978.1
FIDELITY INVESTMENTS LIFE INS CO	UT	11,382.8
GUARDIAN LIFE INS CO OF AMERICA	NY	29,202.2
MASSACHUSETTS MUTUAL LIFE INS CO	MA	112,014.6
MML BAY STATE LIFE INS CO	CT	4,105.4
SENTRY LIFE INS CO	WI	2,809.8
USAA LIFE INS CO	TX	13,463.6

Rating: A-

INSURANCE COMPANY NAME	DOM. STATE	TOTAL ASSETS ($MIL)
ACACIA LIFE INS CO	DC	1,521.4
AMALGAMATED LIFE INS CO	NY	62.6
AMERICAN REPUBLIC INS CO	IA	472.8
AMICA LIFE INS CO	RI	950.4
ANTHEM LIFE INS CO	IN	288.0
CHARTER NATIONAL LIFE INS CO	IL	133.2
COMPANION LIFE INS CO	SC	124.7
CONTINENTAL AMERICAN INS CO	SC	105.0
COUNTRY INVESTORS LIFE ASR CO	IL	192.1
FARM BUREAU LIFE INS CO OF MISSOURI	MO	374.9
FIRST INVESTORS LIFE INS CO	NY	949.4
FORT DEARBORN LIFE INS CO	IL	2,870.9
GERBER LIFE INS CO	NY	1,568.7
GRANGE LIFE INS CO	OH	258.2
NATIONAL BENEFIT LIFE INS CO	NY	738.4
NEW YORK LIFE INS & ANNUITY CORP	DE	77,190.7
NEW YORK LIFE INS CO	NY	114,937.8
NIPPON LIFE INS CO OF AMERICA	IA	162.8
NORTHWESTERN MUTUAL LIFE INS CO	WI	155,607.2
PACIFIC GUARDIAN LIFE INS CO LTD	HI	426.8
PACIFIC LIFE & ANNUITY CO	AZ	2,589.4
PACIFIC LIFE INS CO	NE	81,524.3
PHYSICIANS LIFE INS CO	NE	1,249.3
PRIMERICA LIFE INS CO	MA	5,765.7
PRINCIPAL LIFE INS CO	IA	109,923.9
SHELTER LIFE INS CO	MO	933.1
STANDARD LIFE & ACCIDENT INS CO	OK	484.7
USABLE LIFE	AR	298.5
WORLD INS CO	NE	242.3

Rating: B+

INSURANCE COMPANY NAME	DOM. STATE	TOTAL ASSETS ($MIL)
ALFA LIFE INS CORP	AL	1,087.3
ALLSTATE LIFE INS CO	IL	65,002.0
AMERICAN FAMILY LIFE ASR CO OF COLUM	NE	67,309.5
AMERICAN HEALTH & LIFE INS CO	TX	1,505.6
AMERICAN INCOME LIFE INS CO	IN	1,811.7

INSURANCE COMPANY NAME	DOM. STATE	TOTAL ASSETS ($MIL)
AMERICAN UNITED LIFE INS CO	IN	12,264.8
AMERITAS LIFE INS CORP	NE	4,928.5
ASSURITY LIFE INS CO	NE	2,167.6
BOSTON MUTUAL LIFE INS CO	MA	945.5
CHEROKEE NATIONAL LIFE INS CO	GA	30.8
COLORADO BANKERS LIFE INS CO	CO	144.4
COLUMBUS LIFE INS CO	OH	2,512.2
COMPBENEFITS INS CO	TX	62.7
CONTINENTAL LIFE INS CO OF BRENTWOOD	TN	149.3
EASTERN LIFE & HEALTH INS CO	PA	44.9
EPIC LIFE INSURANCE CO	WI	42.6
FAMILY HERITAGE LIFE INS CO OF AMER	OH	322.3
FIDELITY LIFE ASSN A LEGAL RESERVE	IL	505.8
FIDELITY SECURITY LIFE INS CO	MO	576.6
GOVERNMENT PERSONNEL MUTUAL L I C	TX	783.4
ILLINOIS MUTUAL LIFE INS CO	IL	1,262.3
LINCOLN BENEFIT LIFE CO	NE	2,007.2
LINCOLN HERITAGE LIFE INS CO	IL	629.7
MID-WEST NATIONAL LIFE INS CO OF TN	TX	228.4
MIDLAND NATIONAL LIFE INS CO	IA	25,970.2
MTL INS CO	IL	1,337.3
MUTUAL OF OMAHA INS CO	NE	4,625.4
NATIONAL GUARDIAN LIFE INS CO	WI	1,663.4
NATIONAL WESTERN LIFE INS CO	CO	6,175.2
NATIONWIDE LIFE INS CO OF AMERICA	PA	4,826.2
OHIO NATIONAL LIFE ASR CORP	OH	2,702.3
PEKIN LIFE INS CO	IL	863.3
PENN INS & ANNUITY CO	DE	1,038.9
PENN MUTUAL LIFE INS CO	PA	9,647.6
PHARMACISTS LIFE INS CO	IA	40.4
RELIABLE LIFE INS CO	MO	747.4
SAVINGS BANK LIFE INS CO OF MA	MA	2,093.4
SETTLERS LIFE INS CO	WI	417.4
STANDARD INS CO	OR	12,858.1
STANDARD SECURITY LIFE INS CO OF NY	NY	365.4
STONEBRIDGE LIFE INS CO	VT	2,089.0
SURETY LIFE INS CO	NE	13.2
THRIVENT LIFE INS CO	MN	2,564.9
UNITED INVESTORS LIFE INS CO	MO	2,518.4
UNITED OF OMAHA LIFE INS CO	NE	12,875.0
UNITED WORLD LIFE INS CO	NE	114.6
WORLD CORP INS CO	NE	23.2

Montana

INSURANCE COMPANY NAME	DOM. STATE	TOTAL ASSETS ($MIL)

Rating: A+

INSURANCE COMPANY NAME	DOM. STATE	TOTAL ASSETS ($MIL)
AMERICAN FAMILY LIFE INS CO	WI	3,898.0
COUNTRY LIFE INS CO	IL	7,329.3
PHYSICIANS MUTUAL INS CO	NE	1,445.1
STATE FARM LIFE INS CO	IL	44,978.4
TEACHERS INS & ANNUITY ASN OF AM	NY	194,588.7

Rating: A

INSURANCE COMPANY NAME	DOM. STATE	TOTAL ASSETS ($MIL)
AMERICAN FIDELITY ASR CO	OK	3,343.9
BERKSHIRE LIFE INS CO OF AMERICA	MA	2,502.2
FEDERATED LIFE INS CO	MN	978.1
FIDELITY INVESTMENTS LIFE INS CO	UT	11,382.8
GUARDIAN LIFE INS CO OF AMERICA	NY	29,202.2
LIFEWISE ASR CO	WA	70.2
MASSACHUSETTS MUTUAL LIFE INS CO	MA	112,014.6
MML BAY STATE LIFE INS CO	CT	4,105.4
SENTRY LIFE INS CO	WI	2,809.8
USAA LIFE INS CO	TX	13,463.6

Rating: A-

INSURANCE COMPANY NAME	DOM. STATE	TOTAL ASSETS ($MIL)
ACACIA LIFE INS CO	DC	1,521.4
AMALGAMATED LIFE INS CO	NY	62.6
AMERICAN REPUBLIC INS CO	IA	472.8
AMICA LIFE INS CO	RI	950.4
ANTHEM LIFE INS CO	IN	288.0
CHARTER NATIONAL LIFE INS CO	IL	133.2
COMPANION LIFE INS CO	SC	124.7
CONTINENTAL AMERICAN INS CO	SC	105.0
COUNTRY INVESTORS LIFE ASR CO	IL	192.1
FIRST INVESTORS LIFE INS CO	NY	949.4
FORT DEARBORN LIFE INS CO	IL	2,870.9
GERBER LIFE INS CO	NY	1,568.7
NATIONAL BENEFIT LIFE INS CO	NY	738.4
NEW YORK LIFE INS & ANNUITY CORP	DE	77,190.7
NEW YORK LIFE INS CO	NY	114,937.8
NIPPON LIFE INS CO OF AMERICA	IA	162.8
NORTHWESTERN MUTUAL LIFE INS CO	WI	155,607.2
PACIFIC GUARDIAN LIFE INS CO LTD	HI	426.8
PACIFIC LIFE & ANNUITY CO	AZ	2,589.4
PACIFIC LIFE INS CO	NE	81,524.3
PHYSICIANS LIFE INS CO	NE	1,249.3
PRIMERICA LIFE INS CO	MA	5,765.7
PRINCIPAL LIFE INS CO	IA	109,923.9
STANDARD LIFE & ACCIDENT INS CO	OK	484.7
USABLE LIFE	AR	298.5
WORLD INS CO	NE	242.3

Rating: B+

INSURANCE COMPANY NAME	DOM. STATE	TOTAL ASSETS ($MIL)
ALLSTATE LIFE INS CO	IL	65,002.0
AMERICAN FAMILY LIFE ASR CO OF COLUM	NE	67,309.5
AMERICAN HEALTH & LIFE INS CO	TX	1,505.6
AMERICAN INCOME LIFE INS CO	IN	1,811.7
AMERICAN UNITED LIFE INS CO	IN	12,264.8
AMERITAS LIFE INS CORP	NE	4,928.5
ASSURITY LIFE INS CO	NE	2,167.6
BOSTON MUTUAL LIFE INS CO	MA	945.5

INSURANCE COMPANY NAME	DOM. STATE	TOTAL ASSETS ($MIL)
COLORADO BANKERS LIFE INS CO	CO	144.4
COLUMBUS LIFE INS CO	OH	2,512.2
CONTINENTAL LIFE INS CO OF BRENTWOOD	TN	149.3
EASTERN LIFE & HEALTH INS CO	PA	44.9
FAMILY HERITAGE LIFE INS CO OF AMER	OH	322.3
FARM BUREAU LIFE INS CO	IA	5,605.0
FIDELITY LIFE ASSN A LEGAL RESERVE	IL	505.8
FIDELITY SECURITY LIFE INS CO	MO	576.6
GENERAL RE LIFE CORP	CT	2,682.0
GOVERNMENT PERSONNEL MUTUAL L I C	TX	783.4
ILLINOIS MUTUAL LIFE INS CO	IL	1,262.3
LINCOLN BENEFIT LIFE CO	NE	2,007.2
LINCOLN HERITAGE LIFE INS CO	IL	629.7
MID-WEST NATIONAL LIFE INS CO OF TN	TX	228.4
MIDLAND NATIONAL LIFE INS CO	IA	25,970.2
MTL INS CO	IL	1,337.3
MUTUAL OF OMAHA INS CO	NE	4,625.4
NATIONAL GUARDIAN LIFE INS CO	WI	1,663.4
NATIONAL WESTERN LIFE INS CO	CO	6,175.2
NATIONWIDE LIFE INS CO OF AMERICA	PA	4,826.2
OHIO NATIONAL LIFE ASR CORP	OH	2,702.3
PENN INS & ANNUITY CO	DE	1,038.9
PENN MUTUAL LIFE INS CO	PA	9,647.6
PHARMACISTS LIFE INS CO	IA	40.4
REGENCE LIFE & HEALTH INS CO	OR	80.7
RELIABLE LIFE INS CO	MO	747.4
SETTLERS LIFE INS CO	WI	417.4
STANDARD INS CO	OR	12,858.1
STANDARD SECURITY LIFE INS CO OF NY	NY	365.4
STONEBRIDGE LIFE INS CO	VT	2,089.0
SURETY LIFE INS CO	NE	13.2
THRIVENT LIFE INS CO	MN	2,564.9
UNITED INVESTORS LIFE INS CO	MO	2,518.4
UNITED OF OMAHA LIFE INS CO	NE	12,875.0
UNITED WORLD LIFE INS CO	NE	114.6
WORLD CORP INS CO	NE	23.2

Nebraska

INSURANCE COMPANY NAME	DOM. STATE	TOTAL ASSETS ($MIL)

Rating: A+

INSURANCE COMPANY NAME	DOM. STATE	TOTAL ASSETS ($MIL)
AMERICAN FAMILY LIFE INS CO	WI	3,898.0
COUNTRY LIFE INS CO	IL	7,329.3
PHYSICIANS MUTUAL INS CO	NE	1,445.1
STATE FARM LIFE INS CO	IL	44,978.4
TEACHERS INS & ANNUITY ASN OF AM	NY	194,588.7

Rating: A

INSURANCE COMPANY NAME	DOM. STATE	TOTAL ASSETS ($MIL)
AMERICAN FIDELITY ASR CO	OK	3,343.9
AUTO-OWNERS LIFE INS CO	MI	2,168.0
BERKSHIRE LIFE INS CO OF AMERICA	MA	2,502.2
FEDERATED LIFE INS CO	MN	978.1
FIDELITY INVESTMENTS LIFE INS CO	UT	11,382.8
GUARDIAN LIFE INS CO OF AMERICA	NY	29,202.2
MASSACHUSETTS MUTUAL LIFE INS CO	MA	112,014.6
MML BAY STATE LIFE INS CO	CT	4,105.4
SENTRY LIFE INS CO	WI	2,809.8
USAA LIFE INS CO	TX	13,463.6

Rating: A-

INSURANCE COMPANY NAME	DOM. STATE	TOTAL ASSETS ($MIL)
ACACIA LIFE INS CO	DC	1,521.4
AMALGAMATED LIFE INS CO	NY	62.6
AMERICAN REPUBLIC INS CO	IA	472.8
AMICA LIFE INS CO	RI	950.4
ANTHEM LIFE INS CO	IN	288.0
CHARTER NATIONAL LIFE INS CO	IL	133.2
COMPANION LIFE INS CO	SC	124.7
CONTINENTAL AMERICAN INS CO	SC	105.0
COUNTRY INVESTORS LIFE ASR CO	IL	192.1
FIRST INVESTORS LIFE INS CO	NY	949.4
FORT DEARBORN LIFE INS CO	IL	2,870.9
GERBER LIFE INS CO	NY	1,568.7
NATIONAL BENEFIT LIFE INS CO	NY	738.4
NEW YORK LIFE INS & ANNUITY CORP	DE	77,190.7
NEW YORK LIFE INS CO	NY	114,937.8
NIPPON LIFE INS CO OF AMERICA	IA	162.8
NORTHWESTERN MUTUAL LIFE INS CO	WI	155,607.2
PACIFIC GUARDIAN LIFE INS CO LTD	HI	426.8
PACIFIC LIFE & ANNUITY CO	AZ	2,589.4
PACIFIC LIFE INS CO	NE	81,524.3
PHYSICIANS LIFE INS CO	NE	1,249.3
PRIMERICA LIFE INS CO	MA	5,765.7
PRINCIPAL LIFE INS CO	IA	109,923.9
SHELTER LIFE INS CO	MO	933.1
STANDARD LIFE & ACCIDENT INS CO	OK	484.7
USABLE LIFE	AR	298.5
WORLD INS CO	NE	242.3

Rating: B+

INSURANCE COMPANY NAME	DOM. STATE	TOTAL ASSETS ($MIL)
ALLSTATE LIFE INS CO	IL	65,002.0
AMERICAN FAMILY LIFE ASR CO OF COLUM	NE	67,309.5
AMERICAN HEALTH & LIFE INS CO	TX	1,505.6
AMERICAN INCOME LIFE INS CO	IN	1,811.7
AMERICAN UNITED LIFE INS CO	IN	12,264.8
AMERITAS LIFE INS CORP	NE	4,928.5
ASSURITY LIFE INS CO	NE	2,167.6

INSURANCE COMPANY NAME	DOM. STATE	TOTAL ASSETS ($MIL)
BOSTON MUTUAL LIFE INS CO	MA	945.5
COLORADO BANKERS LIFE INS CO	CO	144.4
COLUMBUS LIFE INS CO	OH	2,512.2
COMPBENEFITS INS CO	TX	62.7
CONTINENTAL LIFE INS CO OF BRENTWOOD	TN	149.3
EASTERN LIFE & HEALTH INS CO	PA	44.9
EPIC LIFE INSURANCE CO	WI	42.6
FAMILY HERITAGE LIFE INS CO OF AMER	OH	322.3
FARM BUREAU LIFE INS CO	IA	5,605.0
FIDELITY LIFE ASSN A LEGAL RESERVE	IL	505.8
FIDELITY SECURITY LIFE INS CO	MO	576.6
GENERAL RE LIFE CORP	CT	2,682.0
GOVERNMENT PERSONNEL MUTUAL L I C	TX	783.4
ILLINOIS MUTUAL LIFE INS CO	IL	1,262.3
LINCOLN BENEFIT LIFE CO	NE	2,007.2
LINCOLN HERITAGE LIFE INS CO	IL	629.7
MID-WEST NATIONAL LIFE INS CO OF TN	TX	228.4
MIDLAND NATIONAL LIFE INS CO	IA	25,970.2
MTL INS CO	IL	1,337.3
MUTUAL OF OMAHA INS CO	NE	4,625.4
NATIONAL GUARDIAN LIFE INS CO	WI	1,663.4
NATIONAL WESTERN LIFE INS CO	CO	6,175.2
NATIONWIDE LIFE INS CO OF AMERICA	PA	4,826.2
OHIO NATIONAL LIFE ASR CORP	OH	2,702.3
PENN INS & ANNUITY CO	DE	1,038.9
PENN MUTUAL LIFE INS CO	PA	9,647.6
PHARMACISTS LIFE INS CO	IA	40.4
RELIABLE LIFE INS CO	MO	747.4
SETTLERS LIFE INS CO	WI	417.4
STANDARD INS CO	OR	12,858.1
STANDARD SECURITY LIFE INS CO OF NY	NY	365.4
STONEBRIDGE LIFE INS CO	VT	2,089.0
SURETY LIFE INS CO	NE	13.2
THRIVENT LIFE INS CO	MN	2,564.9
UNITED INVESTORS LIFE INS CO	MO	2,518.4
UNITED OF OMAHA LIFE INS CO	NE	12,875.0
UNITED WORLD LIFE INS CO	NE	114.6
WORLD CORP INS CO	NE	23.2

Nevada

INSURANCE COMPANY NAME	DOM. STATE	TOTAL ASSETS ($MIL)

Rating: A+

INSURANCE COMPANY NAME	DOM. STATE	TOTAL ASSETS ($MIL)
AMERICAN FAMILY LIFE INS CO	WI	3,898.0
COUNTRY LIFE INS CO	IL	7,329.3
PHYSICIANS MUTUAL INS CO	NE	1,445.1
STATE FARM LIFE INS CO	IL	44,978.4
TEACHERS INS & ANNUITY ASN OF AM	NY	194,588.7

Rating: A

INSURANCE COMPANY NAME	DOM. STATE	TOTAL ASSETS ($MIL)
AMERICAN FIDELITY ASR CO	OK	3,343.9
AUTO-OWNERS LIFE INS CO	MI	2,168.0
BERKSHIRE LIFE INS CO OF AMERICA	MA	2,502.2
FEDERATED LIFE INS CO	MN	978.1
FIDELITY INVESTMENTS LIFE INS CO	UT	11,382.8
GUARDIAN LIFE INS CO OF AMERICA	NY	29,202.2
MASSACHUSETTS MUTUAL LIFE INS CO	MA	112,014.6
MML BAY STATE LIFE INS CO	CT	4,105.4
SENTRY LIFE INS CO	WI	2,809.8
USAA LIFE INS CO	TX	13,463.6

Rating: A-

INSURANCE COMPANY NAME	DOM. STATE	TOTAL ASSETS ($MIL)
ACACIA LIFE INS CO	DC	1,521.4
AMALGAMATED LIFE INS CO	NY	62.6
AMERICAN REPUBLIC INS CO	IA	472.8
AMICA LIFE INS CO	RI	950.4
ANTHEM LIFE INS CO	IN	288.0
CHARTER NATIONAL LIFE INS CO	IL	133.2
COMPANION LIFE INS CO	SC	124.7
CONTINENTAL AMERICAN INS CO	SC	105.0
COUNTRY INVESTORS LIFE ASR CO	IL	192.1
FIRST INVESTORS LIFE INS CO	NY	949.4
FORT DEARBORN LIFE INS CO	IL	2,870.9
GERBER LIFE INS CO	NY	1,568.7
NATIONAL BENEFIT LIFE INS CO	NY	738.4
NEW YORK LIFE INS & ANNUITY CORP	DE	77,190.7
NEW YORK LIFE INS CO	NY	114,937.8
NIPPON LIFE INS CO OF AMERICA	IA	162.8
NORTHWESTERN MUTUAL LIFE INS CO	WI	155,607.2
PACIFIC GUARDIAN LIFE INS CO LTD	HI	426.8
PACIFIC LIFE & ANNUITY CO	AZ	2,589.4
PACIFIC LIFE INS CO	NE	81,524.3
PHYSICIANS LIFE INS CO	NE	1,249.3
PRIMERICA LIFE INS CO	MA	5,765.7
PRINCIPAL LIFE INS CO	IA	109,923.9
SHELTER LIFE INS CO	MO	933.1
STANDARD LIFE & ACCIDENT INS CO	OK	484.7
USABLE LIFE	AR	298.5
WORLD INS CO	NE	242.3

Rating: B+

INSURANCE COMPANY NAME	DOM. STATE	TOTAL ASSETS ($MIL)
ALLSTATE LIFE INS CO	IL	65,002.0
AMERICAN FAMILY LIFE ASR CO OF COLUM	NE	67,309.5
AMERICAN HEALTH & LIFE INS CO	TX	1,505.6
AMERICAN INCOME LIFE INS CO	IN	1,811.7
AMERICAN UNITED LIFE INS CO	IN	12,264.8
AMERITAS LIFE INS CORP	NE	4,928.5
ASSURITY LIFE INS CO	NE	2,167.6

INSURANCE COMPANY NAME	DOM. STATE	TOTAL ASSETS ($MIL)
BOSTON MUTUAL LIFE INS CO	MA	945.5
COLORADO BANKERS LIFE INS CO	CO	144.4
COLUMBUS LIFE INS CO	OH	2,512.2
COMPBENEFITS INS CO	TX	62.7
CONTINENTAL LIFE INS CO OF BRENTWOOD	TN	149.3
EASTERN LIFE & HEALTH INS CO	PA	44.9
EPIC LIFE INSURANCE CO	WI	42.6
FAMILY HERITAGE LIFE INS CO OF AMER	OH	322.3
FARM BUREAU LIFE INS CO	IA	5,605.0
FIDELITY LIFE ASSN A LEGAL RESERVE	IL	505.8
FIDELITY SECURITY LIFE INS CO	MO	576.6
GENERAL RE LIFE CORP	CT	2,682.0
GOVERNMENT PERSONNEL MUTUAL L I C	TX	783.4
ILLINOIS MUTUAL LIFE INS CO	IL	1,262.3
LINCOLN BENEFIT LIFE CO	NE	2,007.2
LINCOLN HERITAGE LIFE INS CO	IL	629.7
MID-WEST NATIONAL LIFE INS CO OF TN	TX	228.4
MIDLAND NATIONAL LIFE INS CO	IA	25,970.2
MTL INS CO	IL	1,337.3
MUTUAL OF OMAHA INS CO	NE	4,625.4
NATIONAL GUARDIAN LIFE INS CO	WI	1,663.4
NATIONAL WESTERN LIFE INS CO	CO	6,175.2
NATIONWIDE LIFE INS CO OF AMERICA	PA	4,826.2
OHIO NATIONAL LIFE ASR CORP	OH	2,702.3
PENN INS & ANNUITY CO	DE	1,038.9
PENN MUTUAL LIFE INS CO	PA	9,647.6
PHARMACISTS LIFE INS CO	IA	40.4
RELIABLE LIFE INS CO	MO	747.4
SAVINGS BANK LIFE INS CO OF MA	MA	2,093.4
SETTLERS LIFE INS CO	WI	417.4
STANDARD INS CO	OR	12,858.1
STANDARD SECURITY LIFE INS CO OF NY	NY	365.4
STONEBRIDGE LIFE INS CO	VT	2,089.0
SURETY LIFE INS CO	NE	13.2
THRIVENT LIFE INS CO	MN	2,564.9
UNITED INVESTORS LIFE INS CO	MO	2,518.4
UNITED OF OMAHA LIFE INS CO	NE	12,875.0
UNITED WORLD LIFE INS CO	NE	114.6
WORLD CORP INS CO	NE	23.2

New Hampshire

INSURANCE COMPANY NAME	DOM. STATE	TOTAL ASSETS ($MIL)

Rating: A+

INSURANCE COMPANY NAME	DOM. STATE	TOTAL ASSETS ($MIL)
PHYSICIANS MUTUAL INS CO	NE	1,445.1
STATE FARM LIFE INS CO	IL	44,978.4
TEACHERS INS & ANNUITY ASN OF AM	NY	194,588.7

Rating: A

INSURANCE COMPANY NAME	DOM. STATE	TOTAL ASSETS ($MIL)
AMERICAN FIDELITY ASR CO	OK	3,343.9
BERKSHIRE LIFE INS CO OF AMERICA	MA	2,502.2
FEDERATED LIFE INS CO	MN	978.1
FIDELITY INVESTMENTS LIFE INS CO	UT	11,382.8
GUARDIAN LIFE INS CO OF AMERICA	NY	29,202.2
MASSACHUSETTS MUTUAL LIFE INS CO	MA	112,014.6
MML BAY STATE LIFE INS CO	CT	4,105.4
SENTRY LIFE INS CO	WI	2,809.8
USAA LIFE INS CO	TX	13,463.6

Rating: A-

INSURANCE COMPANY NAME	DOM. STATE	TOTAL ASSETS ($MIL)
ACACIA LIFE INS CO	DC	1,521.4
AMALGAMATED LIFE INS CO	NY	62.6
AMERICAN REPUBLIC INS CO	IA	472.8
AMICA LIFE INS CO	RI	950.4
ANTHEM LIFE INS CO	IN	288.0
CHARTER NATIONAL LIFE INS CO	IL	133.2
COMPANION LIFE INS CO	SC	124.7
CONTINENTAL AMERICAN INS CO	SC	105.0
FIRST INVESTORS LIFE INS CO	NY	949.4
FORT DEARBORN LIFE INS CO	IL	2,870.9
GERBER LIFE INS CO	NY	1,568.7
NATIONAL BENEFIT LIFE INS CO	NY	738.4
NEW YORK LIFE INS & ANNUITY CORP	DE	77,190.7
NEW YORK LIFE INS CO	NY	114,937.8
NORTHWESTERN MUTUAL LIFE INS CO	WI	155,607.2
PACIFIC LIFE & ANNUITY CO	AZ	2,589.4
PACIFIC LIFE INS CO	NE	81,524.3
PHYSICIANS LIFE INS CO	NE	1,249.3
PRIMERICA LIFE INS CO	MA	5,765.7
PRINCIPAL LIFE INS CO	IA	109,923.9
USABLE LIFE	AR	298.5
WORLD INS CO	NE	242.3

Rating: B+

INSURANCE COMPANY NAME	DOM. STATE	TOTAL ASSETS ($MIL)
ALLSTATE LIFE INS CO	IL	65,002.0
AMERICAN FAMILY LIFE ASR CO OF COLUM	NE	67,309.5
AMERICAN HEALTH & LIFE INS CO	TX	1,505.6
AMERICAN INCOME LIFE INS CO	IN	1,811.7
AMERICAN UNITED LIFE INS CO	IN	12,264.8
AMERITAS LIFE INS CORP	NE	4,928.5
ASSURITY LIFE INS CO	NE	2,167.6
BOSTON MUTUAL LIFE INS CO	MA	945.5
COLORADO BANKERS LIFE INS CO	CO	144.4
COLUMBUS LIFE INS CO	OH	2,512.2
FIDELITY LIFE ASSN A LEGAL RESERVE	IL	505.8
FIDELITY SECURITY LIFE INS CO	MO	576.6
GOVERNMENT PERSONNEL MUTUAL L I C	TX	783.4
ILLINOIS MUTUAL LIFE INS CO	IL	1,262.3
LINCOLN BENEFIT LIFE CO	NE	2,007.2

INSURANCE COMPANY NAME	DOM. STATE	TOTAL ASSETS ($MIL)
LINCOLN HERITAGE LIFE INS CO	IL	629.7
MIDLAND NATIONAL LIFE INS CO	IA	25,970.2
MTL INS CO	IL	1,337.3
MUTUAL OF OMAHA INS CO	NE	4,625.4
NATIONAL GUARDIAN LIFE INS CO	WI	1,663.4
NATIONAL WESTERN LIFE INS CO	CO	6,175.2
NATIONWIDE LIFE INS CO OF AMERICA	PA	4,826.2
OHIO NATIONAL LIFE ASR CORP	OH	2,702.3
PENN MUTUAL LIFE INS CO	PA	9,647.6
RELIABLE LIFE INS CO	MO	747.4
SAVINGS BANK LIFE INS CO OF MA	MA	2,093.4
SETTLERS LIFE INS CO	WI	417.4
STANDARD INS CO	OR	12,858.1
STANDARD SECURITY LIFE INS CO OF NY	NY	365.4
STONEBRIDGE LIFE INS CO	VT	2,089.0
SURETY LIFE INS CO	NE	13.2
UNITED INVESTORS LIFE INS CO	MO	2,518.4
UNITED OF OMAHA LIFE INS CO	NE	12,875.0
UNITED WORLD LIFE INS CO	NE	114.6

New Jersey

INSURANCE COMPANY NAME	DOM. STATE	TOTAL ASSETS ($MIL)

Rating: A+

INSURANCE COMPANY NAME	DOM. STATE	TOTAL ASSETS ($MIL)
PHYSICIANS MUTUAL INS CO	NE	1,445.1
STATE FARM LIFE INS CO	IL	44,978.4
TEACHERS INS & ANNUITY ASN OF AM	NY	194,588.7

Rating: A

INSURANCE COMPANY NAME	DOM. STATE	TOTAL ASSETS ($MIL)
AMERICAN FIDELITY ASR CO	OK	3,343.9
BERKSHIRE LIFE INS CO OF AMERICA	MA	2,502.2
FEDERATED LIFE INS CO	MN	978.1
FIDELITY INVESTMENTS LIFE INS CO	UT	11,382.8
GUARDIAN LIFE INS CO OF AMERICA	NY	29,202.2
MASSACHUSETTS MUTUAL LIFE INS CO	MA	112,014.6
MML BAY STATE LIFE INS CO	CT	4,105.4
SENTRY LIFE INS CO	WI	2,809.8
UNITED FARM FAMILY LIFE INS CO	IN	1,712.9
USAA LIFE INS CO	TX	13,463.6

Rating: A-

INSURANCE COMPANY NAME	DOM. STATE	TOTAL ASSETS ($MIL)
ACACIA LIFE INS CO	DC	1,521.4
AMALGAMATED LIFE INS CO	NY	62.6
AMERICAN REPUBLIC INS CO	IA	472.8
AMICA LIFE INS CO	RI	950.4
ANTHEM LIFE INS CO	IN	288.0
CHARTER NATIONAL LIFE INS CO	IL	133.2
CONTINENTAL AMERICAN INS CO	SC	105.0
FIRST INVESTORS LIFE INS CO	NY	949.4
FORT DEARBORN LIFE INS CO	IL	2,870.9
GERBER LIFE INS CO	NY	1,568.7
NATIONAL BENEFIT LIFE INS CO	NY	738.4
NEW YORK LIFE INS & ANNUITY CORP	DE	77,190.7
NEW YORK LIFE INS CO	NY	114,937.8
NIPPON LIFE INS CO OF AMERICA	IA	162.8
NORTHWESTERN MUTUAL LIFE INS CO	WI	155,607.2
PACIFIC LIFE & ANNUITY CO	AZ	2,589.4
PACIFIC LIFE INS CO	NE	81,524.3
PHYSICIANS LIFE INS CO	NE	1,249.3
PRIMERICA LIFE INS CO	MA	5,765.7
PRINCIPAL LIFE INS CO	IA	109,923.9
USABLE LIFE	AR	298.5
WORLD INS CO	NE	242.3

Rating: B+

INSURANCE COMPANY NAME	DOM. STATE	TOTAL ASSETS ($MIL)
ALLSTATE LIFE INS CO	IL	65,002.0
AMERICAN FAMILY LIFE ASR CO OF COLUM	NE	67,309.5
AMERICAN FAMILY LIFE ASR CO OF NY	NY	285.0
AMERICAN HEALTH & LIFE INS CO	TX	1,505.6
AMERICAN INCOME LIFE INS CO	IN	1,811.7
AMERICAN UNITED LIFE INS CO	IN	12,264.8
AMERITAS LIFE INS CORP	NE	4,928.5
ASSURITY LIFE INS CO	NE	2,167.6
BOSTON MUTUAL LIFE INS CO	MA	945.5
COLORADO BANKERS LIFE INS CO	CO	144.4
COLUMBUS LIFE INS CO	OH	2,512.2
EASTERN LIFE & HEALTH INS CO	PA	44.9
FAMILY HERITAGE LIFE INS CO OF AMER	OH	322.3
FIDELITY LIFE ASSN A LEGAL RESERVE	IL	505.8

INSURANCE COMPANY NAME	DOM. STATE	TOTAL ASSETS ($MIL)
FIDELITY SECURITY LIFE INS CO	MO	576.6
GENERAL RE LIFE CORP	CT	2,682.0
ILLINOIS MUTUAL LIFE INS CO	IL	1,262.3
LINCOLN BENEFIT LIFE CO	NE	2,007.2
LINCOLN HERITAGE LIFE INS CO	IL	629.7
MID-WEST NATIONAL LIFE INS CO OF TN	TX	228.4
MIDLAND NATIONAL LIFE INS CO	IA	25,970.2
MTL INS CO	IL	1,337.3
MUTUAL OF OMAHA INS CO	NE	4,625.4
NATIONAL GUARDIAN LIFE INS CO	WI	1,663.4
NATIONAL WESTERN LIFE INS CO	CO	6,175.2
NATIONWIDE LIFE INS CO OF AMERICA	PA	4,826.2
OHIO NATIONAL LIFE ASR CORP	OH	2,702.3
PENN INS & ANNUITY CO	DE	1,038.9
PENN MUTUAL LIFE INS CO	PA	9,647.6
RELIABLE LIFE INS CO	MO	747.4
SAVINGS BANK LIFE INS CO OF MA	MA	2,093.4
SETTLERS LIFE INS CO	WI	417.4
STANDARD INS CO	OR	12,858.1
STANDARD SECURITY LIFE INS CO OF NY	NY	365.4
STONEBRIDGE LIFE INS CO	VT	2,089.0
SURETY LIFE INS CO	NE	13.2
THRIVENT LIFE INS CO	MN	2,564.9
UNITED INVESTORS LIFE INS CO	MO	2,518.4
UNITED OF OMAHA LIFE INS CO	NE	12,875.0
UNITED WORLD LIFE INS CO	NE	114.6

New Mexico

INSURANCE COMPANY NAME	DOM. STATE	TOTAL ASSETS ($MIL)

Rating: A+

INSURANCE COMPANY NAME	DOM. STATE	TOTAL ASSETS ($MIL)
AMERICAN FAMILY LIFE INS CO	WI	3,898.0
COUNTRY LIFE INS CO	IL	7,329.3
PHYSICIANS MUTUAL INS CO	NE	1,445.1
STATE FARM LIFE INS CO	IL	44,978.4
TEACHERS INS & ANNUITY ASN OF AM	NY	194,588.7

Rating: A

INSURANCE COMPANY NAME	DOM. STATE	TOTAL ASSETS ($MIL)
AMERICAN FIDELITY ASR CO	OK	3,343.9
AUTO-OWNERS LIFE INS CO	MI	2,168.0
BERKSHIRE LIFE INS CO OF AMERICA	MA	2,502.2
FEDERATED LIFE INS CO	MN	978.1
FIDELITY INVESTMENTS LIFE INS CO	UT	11,382.8
GUARDIAN LIFE INS CO OF AMERICA	NY	29,202.2
LIFEWISE ASR CO	WA	70.2
MASSACHUSETTS MUTUAL LIFE INS CO	MA	112,014.6
MML BAY STATE LIFE INS CO	CT	4,105.4
SENTRY LIFE INS CO	WI	2,809.8
USAA LIFE INS CO	TX	13,463.6

Rating: A-

INSURANCE COMPANY NAME	DOM. STATE	TOTAL ASSETS ($MIL)
ACACIA LIFE INS CO	DC	1,521.4
AMERICAN REPUBLIC INS CO	IA	472.8
AMICA LIFE INS CO	RI	950.4
ANTHEM LIFE INS CO	IN	288.0
CHARTER NATIONAL LIFE INS CO	IL	133.2
COMPANION LIFE INS CO	SC	124.7
CONTINENTAL AMERICAN INS CO	SC	105.0
COUNTRY INVESTORS LIFE ASR CO	IL	192.1
FIRST INVESTORS LIFE INS CO	NY	949.4
FORT DEARBORN LIFE INS CO	IL	2,870.9
GERBER LIFE INS CO	NY	1,568.7
NATIONAL BENEFIT LIFE INS CO	NY	738.4
NEW YORK LIFE INS & ANNUITY CORP	DE	77,190.7
NEW YORK LIFE INS CO	NY	114,937.8
NIPPON LIFE INS CO OF AMERICA	IA	162.8
NORTHWESTERN MUTUAL LIFE INS CO	WI	155,607.2
PACIFIC GUARDIAN LIFE INS CO LTD	HI	426.8
PACIFIC LIFE & ANNUITY CO	AZ	2,589.4
PACIFIC LIFE INS CO	NE	81,524.3
PHYSICIANS LIFE INS CO	NE	1,249.3
PRIMERICA LIFE INS CO	MA	5,765.7
PRINCIPAL LIFE INS CO	IA	109,923.9
STANDARD LIFE & ACCIDENT INS CO	OK	484.7
USABLE LIFE	AR	298.5
WORLD INS CO	NE	242.3

Rating: B+

INSURANCE COMPANY NAME	DOM. STATE	TOTAL ASSETS ($MIL)
ALLSTATE LIFE INS CO	IL	65,002.0
AMERICAN FAMILY LIFE ASR CO OF COLUM	NE	67,309.5
AMERICAN HEALTH & LIFE INS CO	TX	1,505.6
AMERICAN INCOME LIFE INS CO	IN	1,811.7
AMERICAN UNITED LIFE INS CO	IN	12,264.8
AMERITAS LIFE INS CORP	NE	4,928.5
ASSURITY LIFE INS CO	NE	2,167.6
BOSTON MUTUAL LIFE INS CO	MA	945.5

INSURANCE COMPANY NAME	DOM. STATE	TOTAL ASSETS ($MIL)
COLORADO BANKERS LIFE INS CO	CO	144.4
COLUMBUS LIFE INS CO	OH	2,512.2
COMPBENEFITS INS CO	TX	62.7
CONTINENTAL LIFE INS CO OF BRENTWOOD	TN	149.3
EASTERN LIFE & HEALTH INS CO	PA	44.9
FAMILY HERITAGE LIFE INS CO OF AMER	OH	322.3
FARM BUREAU LIFE INS CO	IA	5,605.0
FIDELITY LIFE ASSN A LEGAL RESERVE	IL	505.8
FIDELITY SECURITY LIFE INS CO	MO	576.6
GENERAL RE LIFE CORP	CT	2,682.0
GOVERNMENT PERSONNEL MUTUAL L I C	TX	783.4
ILLINOIS MUTUAL LIFE INS CO	IL	1,262.3
LINCOLN BENEFIT LIFE CO	NE	2,007.2
LINCOLN HERITAGE LIFE INS CO	IL	629.7
MID-WEST NATIONAL LIFE INS CO OF TN	TX	228.4
MIDLAND NATIONAL LIFE INS CO	IA	25,970.2
MTL INS CO	IL	1,337.3
MUTUAL OF OMAHA INS CO	NE	4,625.4
NATIONAL GUARDIAN LIFE INS CO	WI	1,663.4
NATIONAL WESTERN LIFE INS CO	CO	6,175.2
NATIONWIDE LIFE INS CO OF AMERICA	PA	4,826.2
OHIO NATIONAL LIFE ASR CORP	OH	2,702.3
PENN INS & ANNUITY CO	DE	1,038.9
PENN MUTUAL LIFE INS CO	PA	9,647.6
PHARMACISTS LIFE INS CO	IA	40.4
RELIABLE LIFE INS CO	MO	747.4
SAVINGS BANK LIFE INS CO OF MA	MA	2,093.4
SETTLERS LIFE INS CO	WI	417.4
STANDARD INS CO	OR	12,858.1
STANDARD SECURITY LIFE INS CO OF NY	NY	365.4
STONEBRIDGE LIFE INS CO	VT	2,089.0
SURETY LIFE INS CO	NE	13.2
THRIVENT LIFE INS CO	MN	2,564.9
UNITED INVESTORS LIFE INS CO	MO	2,518.4
UNITED OF OMAHA LIFE INS CO	NE	12,875.0
UNITED WORLD LIFE INS CO	NE	114.6
WORLD CORP INS CO	NE	23.2

New York

INSURANCE COMPANY NAME	DOM. STATE	TOTAL ASSETS ($MIL)	INSURANCE COMPANY NAME	DOM. STATE	TOTAL ASSETS ($MIL)
### Rating: A+					
PHYSICIANS MUTUAL INS CO	NE	1,445.1			
STATE FARM LIFE & ACCIDENT ASR CO	IL	1,691.4			
TEACHERS INS & ANNUITY ASN OF AM	NY	194,588.7			
### Rating: A					
BERKSHIRE LIFE INS CO OF AMERICA	MA	2,502.2			
FEDERATED LIFE INS CO	MN	978.1			
GUARDIAN LIFE INS CO OF AMERICA	NY	29,202.2			
MASSACHUSETTS MUTUAL LIFE INS CO	MA	112,014.6			
### Rating: A-					
AMALGAMATED LIFE INS CO	NY	62.6			
AMICA LIFE INS CO	RI	950.4			
EMPIRE FIDELITY INVESTMENTS L I C	NY	1,138.6			
FIRST AMERITAS LIFE INS CO OF NY	NY	37.7			
FIRST INVESTORS LIFE INS CO	NY	949.4			
FIRST UNITED AMERICAN LIFE INS CO	NY	126.0			
GERBER LIFE INS CO	NY	1,568.7			
JOHN HANCOCK LIFE INS CO OF NY	NY	6,461.4			
NATIONAL BENEFIT LIFE INS CO	NY	738.4			
NEW YORK LIFE INS & ANNUITY CORP	DE	77,190.7			
NEW YORK LIFE INS CO	NY	114,937.8			
NIPPON LIFE INS CO OF AMERICA	IA	162.8			
NORTHWESTERN MUTUAL LIFE INS CO	WI	155,607.2			
PACIFIC LIFE & ANNUITY CO	AZ	2,589.4			
PRINCIPAL LIFE INS CO	IA	109,923.9			
### Rating: B+					
AMERICAN FAMILY LIFE ASR CO OF NY	NY	285.0			
AMERICAN UNITED LIFE INS CO	IN	12,264.8			
FORT DEARBORN LIFE INS CO OF NY	NY	67.2			
LIFE INS CO OF BOSTON & NEW YORK	NY	72.0			
MUTUAL OF OMAHA INS CO	NE	4,625.4			
NATIONWIDE LIFE INS CO OF AMERICA	PA	4,826.2			
PENN MUTUAL LIFE INS CO	PA	9,647.6			
STANDARD SECURITY LIFE INS CO OF NY	NY	365.4			
STONEBRIDGE LIFE INS CO	VT	2,089.0			
USAA LIFE INS CO OF NEW YORK	NY	401.5			

North Carolina

INSURANCE COMPANY NAME	DOM. STATE	TOTAL ASSETS ($MIL)

Rating: A+

INSURANCE COMPANY NAME	DOM. STATE	TOTAL ASSETS ($MIL)
AMERICAN FAMILY LIFE INS CO	WI	3,898.0
COUNTRY LIFE INS CO	IL	7,329.3
PHYSICIANS MUTUAL INS CO	NE	1,445.1
STATE FARM LIFE INS CO	IL	44,978.4
TEACHERS INS & ANNUITY ASN OF AM	NY	194,588.7

Rating: A

INSURANCE COMPANY NAME	DOM. STATE	TOTAL ASSETS ($MIL)
AMERICAN FIDELITY ASR CO	OK	3,343.9
AUTO-OWNERS LIFE INS CO	MI	2,168.0
BERKSHIRE LIFE INS CO OF AMERICA	MA	2,502.2
FEDERATED LIFE INS CO	MN	978.1
FIDELITY INVESTMENTS LIFE INS CO	UT	11,382.8
GUARDIAN LIFE INS CO OF AMERICA	NY	29,202.2
MASSACHUSETTS MUTUAL LIFE INS CO	MA	112,014.6
MML BAY STATE LIFE INS CO	CT	4,105.4
SENTRY LIFE INS CO	WI	2,809.8
SOUTHERN FARM BUREAU LIFE INS CO	MS	10,074.1
USAA LIFE INS CO	TX	13,463.6

Rating: A-

INSURANCE COMPANY NAME	DOM. STATE	TOTAL ASSETS ($MIL)
ACACIA LIFE INS CO	DC	1,521.4
AMALGAMATED LIFE INS CO	NY	62.6
AMERICAN REPUBLIC INS CO	IA	472.8
AMICA LIFE INS CO	RI	950.4
ANTHEM LIFE INS CO	IN	288.0
CHARTER NATIONAL LIFE INS CO	IL	133.2
COMPANION LIFE INS CO	SC	124.7
CONTINENTAL AMERICAN INS CO	SC	105.0
COUNTRY INVESTORS LIFE ASR CO	IL	192.1
FIRST INVESTORS LIFE INS CO	NY	949.4
FORT DEARBORN LIFE INS CO	IL	2,870.9
GERBER LIFE INS CO	NY	1,568.7
GREATER GEORGIA LIFE INS CO	GA	46.3
NATIONAL BENEFIT LIFE INS CO	NY	738.4
NEW YORK LIFE INS & ANNUITY CORP	DE	77,190.7
NEW YORK LIFE INS CO	NY	114,937.8
NORTHWESTERN MUTUAL LIFE INS CO	WI	155,607.2
PACIFIC LIFE & ANNUITY CO	AZ	2,589.4
PACIFIC LIFE INS CO	NE	81,524.3
PHYSICIANS LIFE INS CO	NE	1,249.3
PRIMERICA LIFE INS CO	MA	5,765.7
PRINCIPAL LIFE INS CO	IA	109,923.9
STANDARD LIFE & ACCIDENT INS CO	OK	484.7
USABLE LIFE	AR	298.5
WORLD INS CO	NE	242.3

Rating: B+

INSURANCE COMPANY NAME	DOM. STATE	TOTAL ASSETS ($MIL)
ALFA LIFE INS CORP	AL	1,087.3
ALLSTATE LIFE INS CO	IL	65,002.0
AMERICAN FAMILY LIFE ASR CO OF COLUM	NE	67,309.5
AMERICAN HEALTH & LIFE INS CO	TX	1,505.6
AMERICAN INCOME LIFE INS CO	IN	1,811.7
AMERICAN UNITED LIFE INS CO	IN	12,264.8
AMERITAS LIFE INS CORP	NE	4,928.5
ASSURITY LIFE INS CO	NE	2,167.6

INSURANCE COMPANY NAME	DOM. STATE	TOTAL ASSETS ($MIL)
ATLANTIC COAST LIFE INS CO	SC	69.9
BOSTON MUTUAL LIFE INS CO	MA	945.5
CHEROKEE NATIONAL LIFE INS CO	GA	30.8
COLORADO BANKERS LIFE INS CO	CO	144.4
COLUMBUS LIFE INS CO	OH	2,512.2
COMPBENEFITS INS CO	TX	62.7
CONTINENTAL LIFE INS CO OF BRENTWOOD	TN	149.3
COTTON STATES LIFE INS CO	GA	281.8
EASTERN LIFE & HEALTH INS CO	PA	44.9
FAMILY HERITAGE LIFE INS CO OF AMER	OH	322.3
FIDELITY LIFE ASSN A LEGAL RESERVE	IL	505.8
FIDELITY SECURITY LIFE INS CO	MO	576.6
FLORIDA COMBINED LIFE INS CO INC	FL	31.8
GENERAL RE LIFE CORP	CT	2,682.0
GOVERNMENT PERSONNEL MUTUAL L I C	TX	783.4
ILLINOIS MUTUAL LIFE INS CO	IL	1,262.3
LINCOLN BENEFIT LIFE CO	NE	2,007.2
LINCOLN HERITAGE LIFE INS CO	IL	629.7
MID-WEST NATIONAL LIFE INS CO OF TN	TX	228.4
MIDLAND NATIONAL LIFE INS CO	IA	25,970.2
MTL INS CO	IL	1,337.3
MUTUAL OF OMAHA INS CO	NE	4,625.4
NATIONAL GUARDIAN LIFE INS CO	WI	1,663.4
NATIONAL WESTERN LIFE INS CO	CO	6,175.2
NATIONWIDE LIFE INS CO OF AMERICA	PA	4,826.2
OHIO NATIONAL LIFE ASR CORP	OH	2,702.3
PENN INS & ANNUITY CO	DE	1,038.9
PENN MUTUAL LIFE INS CO	PA	9,647.6
PHARMACISTS LIFE INS CO	IA	40.4
RELIABLE LIFE INS CO	MO	747.4
SAVINGS BANK LIFE INS CO OF MA	MA	2,093.4
SETTLERS LIFE INS CO	WI	417.4
STANDARD INS CO	OR	12,858.1
STANDARD SECURITY LIFE INS CO OF NY	NY	365.4
STONEBRIDGE LIFE INS CO	VT	2,089.0
SURETY LIFE INS CO	NE	13.2
THRIVENT LIFE INS CO	MN	2,564.9
UNITED INVESTORS LIFE INS CO	MO	2,518.4
UNITED OF OMAHA LIFE INS CO	NE	12,875.0
UNITED WORLD LIFE INS CO	NE	114.6
WORLD CORP INS CO	NE	23.2

North Dakota

INSURANCE COMPANY NAME	DOM. STATE	TOTAL ASSETS ($MIL)
Rating: A+		
AMERICAN FAMILY LIFE INS CO	WI	3,898.0
COUNTRY LIFE INS CO	IL	7,329.3
PHYSICIANS MUTUAL INS CO	NE	1,445.1
STATE FARM LIFE INS CO	IL	44,978.4
TEACHERS INS & ANNUITY ASN OF AM	NY	194,588.7
Rating: A		
AMERICAN FIDELITY ASR CO	OK	3,343.9
AUTO-OWNERS LIFE INS CO	MI	2,168.0
BERKSHIRE LIFE INS CO OF AMERICA	MA	2,502.2
FEDERATED LIFE INS CO	MN	978.1
FIDELITY INVESTMENTS LIFE INS CO	UT	11,382.8
GUARDIAN LIFE INS CO OF AMERICA	NY	29,202.2
LIFEWISE ASR CO	WA	70.2
MASSACHUSETTS MUTUAL LIFE INS CO	MA	112,014.6
MML BAY STATE LIFE INS CO	CT	4,105.4
SENTRY LIFE INS CO	WI	2,809.8
UNITED FARM FAMILY LIFE INS CO	IN	1,712.9
USAA LIFE INS CO	TX	13,463.6
Rating: A-		
ACACIA LIFE INS CO	DC	1,521.4
AMALGAMATED LIFE INS CO	NY	62.6
AMERICAN REPUBLIC INS CO	IA	472.8
AMICA LIFE INS CO	RI	950.4
ANTHEM LIFE INS CO	IN	288.0
CHARTER NATIONAL LIFE INS CO	IL	133.2
COMPANION LIFE INS CO	SC	124.7
CONTINENTAL AMERICAN INS CO	SC	105.0
COUNTRY INVESTORS LIFE ASR CO	IL	192.1
FIRST INVESTORS LIFE INS CO	NY	949.4
FORT DEARBORN LIFE INS CO	IL	2,870.9
GERBER LIFE INS CO	NY	1,568.7
NATIONAL BENEFIT LIFE INS CO	NY	738.4
NEW YORK LIFE INS & ANNUITY CORP	DE	77,190.7
NEW YORK LIFE INS CO	NY	114,937.8
NIPPON LIFE INS CO OF AMERICA	IA	162.8
NORTHWESTERN MUTUAL LIFE INS CO	WI	155,607.2
PACIFIC LIFE & ANNUITY CO	AZ	2,589.4
PACIFIC LIFE INS CO	NE	81,524.3
PHYSICIANS LIFE INS CO	NE	1,249.3
PRIMERICA LIFE INS CO	MA	5,765.7
PRINCIPAL LIFE INS CO	IA	109,923.9
STANDARD LIFE & ACCIDENT INS CO	OK	484.7
USABLE LIFE	AR	298.5
WORLD INS CO	NE	242.3
Rating: B+		
ALLSTATE LIFE INS CO	IL	65,002.0
AMERICAN FAMILY LIFE ASR CO OF COLUM	NE	67,309.5
AMERICAN FAMILY LIFE ASR CO OF NY	NY	285.0
AMERICAN HEALTH & LIFE INS CO	TX	1,505.6
AMERICAN INCOME LIFE INS CO	IN	1,811.7
AMERICAN UNITED LIFE INS CO	IN	12,264.8
AMERITAS LIFE INS CORP	NE	4,928.5

INSURANCE COMPANY NAME	DOM. STATE	TOTAL ASSETS ($MIL)
ASSURITY LIFE INS CO	NE	2,167.6
BOSTON MUTUAL LIFE INS CO	MA	945.5
COLORADO BANKERS LIFE INS CO	CO	144.4
COLUMBUS LIFE INS CO	OH	2,512.2
COMPBENEFITS INS CO	TX	62.7
CONTINENTAL LIFE INS CO OF BRENTWOOD	TN	149.3
EASTERN LIFE & HEALTH INS CO	PA	44.9
EPIC LIFE INSURANCE CO	WI	42.6
FAMILY HERITAGE LIFE INS CO OF AMER	OH	322.3
FARM BUREAU LIFE INS CO	IA	5,605.0
FIDELITY LIFE ASSN A LEGAL RESERVE	IL	505.8
FIDELITY SECURITY LIFE INS CO	MO	576.6
GENERAL RE LIFE CORP	CT	2,682.0
GOVERNMENT PERSONNEL MUTUAL L I C	TX	783.4
ILLINOIS MUTUAL LIFE INS CO	IL	1,262.3
LINCOLN BENEFIT LIFE CO	NE	2,007.2
LINCOLN HERITAGE LIFE INS CO	IL	629.7
MID-WEST NATIONAL LIFE INS CO OF TN	TX	228.4
MIDLAND NATIONAL LIFE INS CO	IA	25,970.4
MTL INS CO	IL	1,337.3
MUTUAL OF OMAHA INS CO	NE	4,625.4
NATIONAL GUARDIAN LIFE INS CO	WI	1,663.4
NATIONAL WESTERN LIFE INS CO	CO	6,175.2
NATIONWIDE LIFE INS CO OF AMERICA	PA	4,826.2
OHIO NATIONAL LIFE ASR CORP	OH	2,702.3
PENN INS & ANNUITY CO	DE	1,038.9
PENN MUTUAL LIFE INS CO	PA	9,647.6
PHARMACISTS LIFE INS CO	IA	40.4
RELIABLE LIFE INS CO	MO	747.4
SETTLERS LIFE INS CO	WI	417.4
STANDARD INS CO	OR	12,858.1
STANDARD SECURITY LIFE INS CO OF NY	NY	365.4
STONEBRIDGE LIFE INS CO	VT	2,089.0
SURETY LIFE INS CO	NE	13.2
THRIVENT LIFE INS CO	MN	2,564.9
UNITED INVESTORS LIFE INS CO	MO	2,518.4
UNITED OF OMAHA LIFE INS CO	NE	12,875.0
UNITED WORLD LIFE INS CO	NE	114.6
WORLD CORP INS CO	NE	23.2

Ohio

INSURANCE COMPANY NAME	DOM. STATE	TOTAL ASSETS ($MIL)

Rating: A+

INSURANCE COMPANY NAME	DOM. STATE	TOTAL ASSETS ($MIL)
AMERICAN FAMILY LIFE INS CO	WI	3,898.0
COUNTRY LIFE INS CO	IL	7,329.3
PHYSICIANS MUTUAL INS CO	NE	1,445.1
STATE FARM LIFE INS CO	IL	44,978.4
TEACHERS INS & ANNUITY ASN OF AM	NY	194,588.7

Rating: A

INSURANCE COMPANY NAME	DOM. STATE	TOTAL ASSETS ($MIL)
AMERICAN FIDELITY ASR CO	OK	3,343.9
AUTO-OWNERS LIFE INS CO	MI	2,168.0
BERKSHIRE LIFE INS CO OF AMERICA	MA	2,502.2
FEDERATED LIFE INS CO	MN	978.1
FIDELITY INVESTMENTS LIFE INS CO	UT	11,382.8
GUARDIAN LIFE INS CO OF AMERICA	NY	29,202.2
MASSACHUSETTS MUTUAL LIFE INS CO	MA	112,014.6
MML BAY STATE LIFE INS CO	CT	4,105.4
SENTRY LIFE INS CO	WI	2,809.8
UNITED FARM FAMILY LIFE INS CO	IN	1,712.9
USAA LIFE INS CO	TX	13,463.6

Rating: A-

INSURANCE COMPANY NAME	DOM. STATE	TOTAL ASSETS ($MIL)
ACACIA LIFE INS CO	DC	1,521.4
AMALGAMATED LIFE INS CO	NY	62.6
AMERICAN REPUBLIC INS CO	IA	472.8
AMICA LIFE INS CO	RI	950.4
ANTHEM LIFE INS CO	IN	288.0
CHARTER NATIONAL LIFE INS CO	IL	133.2
COMPANION LIFE INS CO	SC	124.7
CONTINENTAL AMERICAN INS CO	SC	105.0
COUNTRY INVESTORS LIFE ASR CO	IL	192.1
FIRST INVESTORS LIFE INS CO	NY	949.4
FORT DEARBORN LIFE INS CO	IL	2,870.9
GERBER LIFE INS CO	NY	1,568.7
GRANGE LIFE INS CO	OH	258.2
NATIONAL BENEFIT LIFE INS CO	NY	738.4
NEW YORK LIFE INS & ANNUITY CORP	DE	77,190.7
NEW YORK LIFE INS CO	NY	114,937.8
NIPPON LIFE INS CO OF AMERICA	IA	162.8
NORTHWESTERN MUTUAL LIFE INS CO	WI	155,607.2
PACIFIC LIFE & ANNUITY CO	AZ	2,589.4
PACIFIC LIFE INS CO	NE	81,524.3
PHYSICIANS LIFE INS CO	NE	1,249.3
PRIMERICA LIFE INS CO	MA	5,765.7
PRINCIPAL LIFE INS CO	IA	109,923.9
STANDARD LIFE & ACCIDENT INS CO	OK	484.7
USABLE LIFE	AR	298.5
WORLD INS CO	NE	242.3

Rating: B+

INSURANCE COMPANY NAME	DOM. STATE	TOTAL ASSETS ($MIL)
ALLSTATE LIFE INS CO	IL	65,002.0
AMERICAN FAMILY LIFE ASR CO OF COLUM	NE	67,309.5
AMERICAN HEALTH & LIFE INS CO	TX	1,505.6
AMERICAN INCOME LIFE INS CO	IN	1,811.7
AMERICAN UNITED LIFE INS CO	IN	12,264.8
AMERITAS LIFE INS CORP	NE	4,928.5
ASSURITY LIFE INS CO	NE	2,167.6

INSURANCE COMPANY NAME	DOM. STATE	TOTAL ASSETS ($MIL)
BOSTON MUTUAL LIFE INS CO	MA	945.5
COLORADO BANKERS LIFE INS CO	CO	144.4
COLUMBUS LIFE INS CO	OH	2,512.2
COMPBENEFITS INS CO	TX	62.7
CONTINENTAL LIFE INS CO OF BRENTWOOD	TN	149.3
EASTERN LIFE & HEALTH INS CO	PA	44.9
EPIC LIFE INSURANCE CO	WI	42.6
FAMILY HERITAGE LIFE INS CO OF AMER	OH	322.3
FIDELITY LIFE ASSN A LEGAL RESERVE	IL	505.8
FIDELITY SECURITY LIFE INS CO	MO	576.6
GENERAL RE LIFE CORP	CT	2,682.0
GOVERNMENT PERSONNEL MUTUAL L I C	TX	783.4
ILLINOIS MUTUAL LIFE INS CO	IL	1,262.3
LINCOLN BENEFIT LIFE CO	NE	2,007.2
LINCOLN HERITAGE LIFE INS CO	IL	629.7
MID-WEST NATIONAL LIFE INS CO OF TN	TX	228.4
MIDLAND NATIONAL LIFE INS CO	IA	25,970.2
MTL INS CO	IL	1,337.3
MUTUAL OF OMAHA INS CO	NE	4,625.4
NATIONAL GUARDIAN LIFE INS CO	WI	1,663.4
NATIONAL WESTERN LIFE INS CO	CO	6,175.2
NATIONWIDE LIFE INS CO OF AMERICA	PA	4,826.2
OHIO NATIONAL LIFE ASR CORP	OH	2,702.3
PEKIN LIFE INS CO	IL	863.3
PENN INS & ANNUITY CO	DE	1,038.9
PENN MUTUAL LIFE INS CO	PA	9,647.6
PHARMACISTS LIFE INS CO	IA	40.4
RELIABLE LIFE INS CO	MO	747.4
SAVINGS BANK LIFE INS CO OF MA	MA	2,093.4
SETTLERS LIFE INS CO	WI	417.4
STANDARD INS CO	OR	12,858.1
STANDARD SECURITY LIFE INS CO OF NY	NY	365.4
STONEBRIDGE LIFE INS CO	VT	2,089.0
SURETY LIFE INS CO	NE	13.2
THRIVENT LIFE INS CO	MN	2,564.9
UNITED INVESTORS LIFE INS CO	MO	2,518.4
UNITED OF OMAHA LIFE INS CO	NE	12,875.0
UNITED WORLD LIFE INS CO	NE	114.6
WORLD CORP INS CO	NE	23.2

Oklahoma

INSURANCE COMPANY NAME	DOM. STATE	TOTAL ASSETS ($MIL)

Rating: A+

INSURANCE COMPANY NAME	DOM. STATE	TOTAL ASSETS ($MIL)
COUNTRY LIFE INS CO	IL	7,329.3
PHYSICIANS MUTUAL INS CO	NE	1,445.1
STATE FARM LIFE INS CO	IL	44,978.4
TEACHERS INS & ANNUITY ASN OF AM	NY	194,588.7

Rating: A

INSURANCE COMPANY NAME	DOM. STATE	TOTAL ASSETS ($MIL)
AMERICAN FIDELITY ASR CO	OK	3,343.9
BERKSHIRE LIFE INS CO OF AMERICA	MA	2,502.2
FEDERATED LIFE INS CO	MN	978.1
FIDELITY INVESTMENTS LIFE INS CO	UT	11,382.8
GUARDIAN LIFE INS CO OF AMERICA	NY	29,202.2
MASSACHUSETTS MUTUAL LIFE INS CO	MA	112,014.6
MML BAY STATE LIFE INS CO	CT	4,105.4
SENTRY LIFE INS CO	WI	2,809.8
UNION NATIONAL LIFE INS CO	LA	459.3
USAA LIFE INS CO	TX	13,463.6

Rating: A-

INSURANCE COMPANY NAME	DOM. STATE	TOTAL ASSETS ($MIL)
ACACIA LIFE INS CO	DC	1,521.4
AMALGAMATED LIFE INS CO	NY	62.6
AMERICAN REPUBLIC INS CO	IA	472.8
AMICA LIFE INS CO	RI	950.4
ANTHEM LIFE INS CO	IN	288.0
CHARTER NATIONAL LIFE INS CO	IL	133.2
COMPANION LIFE INS CO	SC	124.7
CONTINENTAL AMERICAN INS CO	SC	105.0
COUNTRY INVESTORS LIFE ASR CO	IL	192.1
FIRST INVESTORS LIFE INS CO	NY	949.4
FORT DEARBORN LIFE INS CO	IL	2,870.9
GERBER LIFE INS CO	NY	1,568.7
NATIONAL BENEFIT LIFE INS CO	NY	738.4
NEW YORK LIFE INS & ANNUITY CORP	DE	77,190.7
NEW YORK LIFE INS CO	NY	114,937.8
NIPPON LIFE INS CO OF AMERICA	IA	162.8
NORTHWESTERN MUTUAL LIFE INS CO	WI	155,607.2
PACIFIC GUARDIAN LIFE INS CO LTD	HI	426.8
PACIFIC LIFE & ANNUITY CO	AZ	2,589.4
PACIFIC LIFE INS CO	NE	81,524.3
PHYSICIANS LIFE INS CO	NE	1,249.3
PRIMERICA LIFE INS CO	MA	5,765.7
PRINCIPAL LIFE INS CO	IA	109,923.9
SHELTER LIFE INS CO	MO	933.1
STANDARD LIFE & ACCIDENT INS CO	OK	484.7
USABLE LIFE	AR	298.5
WORLD INS CO	NE	242.3

Rating: B+

INSURANCE COMPANY NAME	DOM. STATE	TOTAL ASSETS ($MIL)
ALLSTATE LIFE INS CO	IL	65,002.0
AMERICAN FAMILY LIFE ASR CO OF COLUM	NE	67,309.5
AMERICAN HEALTH & LIFE INS CO	TX	1,505.6
AMERICAN INCOME LIFE INS CO	IN	1,811.7
AMERICAN UNITED LIFE INS CO	IN	12,264.8
AMERITAS LIFE INS CORP	NE	4,928.5
ASSURITY LIFE INS CO	NE	2,167.6
BOSTON MUTUAL LIFE INS CO	MA	945.5

INSURANCE COMPANY NAME	DOM. STATE	TOTAL ASSETS ($MIL)
CHEROKEE NATIONAL LIFE INS CO	GA	30.8
COLORADO BANKERS LIFE INS CO	CO	144.4
COLUMBUS LIFE INS CO	OH	2,512.2
COMPBENEFITS INS CO	TX	62.7
CONTINENTAL LIFE INS CO OF BRENTWOOD	TN	149.3
EASTERN LIFE & HEALTH INS CO	PA	44.9
EPIC LIFE INSURANCE CO	WI	42.6
FAMILY HERITAGE LIFE INS CO OF AMER	OH	322.3
FARM BUREAU LIFE INS CO	IA	5,605.0
FIDELITY LIFE ASSN A LEGAL RESERVE	IL	505.8
FIDELITY SECURITY LIFE INS CO	MO	576.6
GENERAL RE LIFE CORP	CT	2,682.0
GOVERNMENT PERSONNEL MUTUAL L I C	TX	783.4
ILLINOIS MUTUAL LIFE INS CO	IL	1,262.3
LINCOLN BENEFIT LIFE CO	NE	2,007.2
LINCOLN HERITAGE LIFE INS CO	IL	629.7
MID-WEST NATIONAL LIFE INS CO OF TN	TX	228.4
MIDLAND NATIONAL LIFE INS CO	IA	25,970.2
MTL INS CO	IL	1,337.3
MUTUAL OF OMAHA INS CO	NE	4,625.4
NATIONAL GUARDIAN LIFE INS CO	WI	1,663.4
NATIONAL WESTERN LIFE INS CO	CO	6,175.2
NATIONWIDE LIFE INS CO OF AMERICA	PA	4,826.2
OHIO NATIONAL LIFE ASR CORP	OH	2,702.3
PENN INS & ANNUITY CO	DE	1,038.9
PENN MUTUAL LIFE INS CO	PA	9,647.6
PHARMACISTS LIFE INS CO	IA	40.4
RELIABLE LIFE INS CO	MO	747.4
SAVINGS BANK LIFE INS CO OF MA	MA	2,093.4
SETTLERS LIFE INS CO	WI	417.4
STANDARD INS CO	OR	12,858.1
STANDARD SECURITY LIFE INS CO OF NY	NY	365.4
STONEBRIDGE LIFE INS CO	VT	2,089.0
SURETY LIFE INS CO	NE	13.2
THRIVENT LIFE INS CO	MN	2,564.9
UNITED INVESTORS LIFE INS CO	MO	2,518.4
UNITED OF OMAHA LIFE INS CO	NE	12,875.0
UNITED WORLD LIFE INS CO	NE	114.6
WORLD CORP INS CO	NE	23.2

Oregon

INSURANCE COMPANY NAME	DOM. STATE	TOTAL ASSETS ($MIL)

Rating: A+

INSURANCE COMPANY NAME	DOM. STATE	TOTAL ASSETS ($MIL)
AMERICAN FAMILY LIFE INS CO	WI	3,898.0
COUNTRY LIFE INS CO	IL	7,329.3
PHYSICIANS MUTUAL INS CO	NE	1,445.1
STATE FARM LIFE INS CO	IL	44,978.4
TEACHERS INS & ANNUITY ASN OF AM	NY	194,588.7

Rating: A

INSURANCE COMPANY NAME	DOM. STATE	TOTAL ASSETS ($MIL)
AMERICAN FIDELITY ASR CO	OK	3,343.9
AUTO-OWNERS LIFE INS CO	MI	2,168.0
BERKSHIRE LIFE INS CO OF AMERICA	MA	2,502.2
FEDERATED LIFE INS CO	MN	978.1
FIDELITY INVESTMENTS LIFE INS CO	UT	11,382.8
GUARDIAN LIFE INS CO OF AMERICA	NY	29,202.2
LIFEWISE ASR CO	WA	70.2
MASSACHUSETTS MUTUAL LIFE INS CO	MA	112,014.6
MML BAY STATE LIFE INS CO	CT	4,105.4
SENTRY LIFE INS CO	WI	2,809.8
USAA LIFE INS CO	TX	13,463.6

Rating: A-

INSURANCE COMPANY NAME	DOM. STATE	TOTAL ASSETS ($MIL)
ACACIA LIFE INS CO	DC	1,521.4
AMALGAMATED LIFE INS CO	NY	62.6
AMERICAN REPUBLIC INS CO	IA	472.8
AMICA LIFE INS CO	RI	950.4
ANTHEM LIFE INS CO	IN	288.0
CHARTER NATIONAL LIFE INS CO	IL	133.2
COMPANION LIFE INS CO	SC	124.7
CONTINENTAL AMERICAN INS CO	SC	105.0
COUNTRY INVESTORS LIFE ASR CO	IL	192.1
FIRST INVESTORS LIFE INS CO	NY	949.4
FORT DEARBORN LIFE INS CO	IL	2,870.9
GERBER LIFE INS CO	NY	1,568.7
NATIONAL BENEFIT LIFE INS CO	NY	738.4
NEW YORK LIFE INS & ANNUITY CORP	DE	77,190.7
NEW YORK LIFE INS CO	NY	114,937.8
NIPPON LIFE INS CO OF AMERICA	IA	162.8
NORTHWESTERN MUTUAL LIFE INS CO	WI	155,607.2
PACIFIC GUARDIAN LIFE INS CO LTD	HI	426.8
PACIFIC LIFE & ANNUITY CO	AZ	2,589.4
PACIFIC LIFE INS CO	NE	81,524.3
PHYSICIANS LIFE INS CO	NE	1,249.3
PRIMERICA LIFE INS CO	MA	5,765.7
PRINCIPAL LIFE INS CO	IA	109,923.9
STANDARD LIFE & ACCIDENT INS CO	OK	484.7
USABLE LIFE	AR	298.5
WORLD INS CO	NE	242.3

Rating: B+

INSURANCE COMPANY NAME	DOM. STATE	TOTAL ASSETS ($MIL)
ALLSTATE LIFE INS CO	IL	65,002.0
AMERICAN FAMILY LIFE ASR CO OF COLUM	NE	67,309.5
AMERICAN HEALTH & LIFE INS CO	TX	1,505.6
AMERICAN INCOME LIFE INS CO	IN	1,811.7
AMERICAN UNITED LIFE INS CO	IN	12,264.8
AMERITAS LIFE INS CORP	NE	4,928.5
ASSURITY LIFE INS CO	NE	2,167.6

INSURANCE COMPANY NAME	DOM. STATE	TOTAL ASSETS ($MIL)
BOSTON MUTUAL LIFE INS CO	MA	945.5
COLORADO BANKERS LIFE INS CO	CO	144.4
COLUMBUS LIFE INS CO	OH	2,512.2
COMPBENEFITS INS CO	TX	62.7
EASTERN LIFE & HEALTH INS CO	PA	44.9
EPIC LIFE INSURANCE CO	WI	42.6
FAMILY HERITAGE LIFE INS CO OF AMER	OH	322.3
FARM BUREAU LIFE INS CO	IA	5,605.0
FIDELITY LIFE ASSN A LEGAL RESERVE	IL	505.8
FIDELITY SECURITY LIFE INS CO	MO	576.6
GENERAL RE LIFE CORP	CT	2,682.0
GOVERNMENT PERSONNEL MUTUAL L I C	TX	783.4
ILLINOIS MUTUAL LIFE INS CO	IL	1,262.3
LINCOLN BENEFIT LIFE CO	NE	2,007.2
LINCOLN HERITAGE LIFE INS CO	IL	629.7
MID-WEST NATIONAL LIFE INS CO OF TN	TX	228.4
MIDLAND NATIONAL LIFE INS CO	IA	25,970.2
MTL INS CO	IL	1,337.3
MUTUAL OF OMAHA INS CO	NE	4,625.4
NATIONAL GUARDIAN LIFE INS CO	WI	1,663.4
NATIONAL WESTERN LIFE INS CO	CO	6,175.2
NATIONWIDE LIFE INS CO OF AMERICA	PA	4,826.2
OHIO NATIONAL LIFE ASR CORP	OH	2,702.3
PENN INS & ANNUITY CO	DE	1,038.9
PENN MUTUAL LIFE INS CO	PA	9,647.6
PHARMACISTS LIFE INS CO	IA	40.4
REGENCE LIFE & HEALTH INS CO	OR	80.7
RELIABLE LIFE INS CO	MO	747.4
SAVINGS BANK LIFE INS CO OF MA	MA	2,093.4
SETTLERS LIFE INS CO	WI	417.4
STANDARD INS CO	OR	12,858.1
STANDARD SECURITY LIFE INS CO OF NY	NY	365.4
STONEBRIDGE LIFE INS CO	VT	2,089.0
SURETY LIFE INS CO	NE	13.2
THRIVENT LIFE INS CO	MN	2,564.9
UNITED INVESTORS LIFE INS CO	MO	2,518.4
UNITED OF OMAHA LIFE INS CO	NE	12,875.0
UNITED WORLD LIFE INS CO	NE	114.6
WORLD CORP INS CO	NE	23.2

Pennsylvania

INSURANCE COMPANY NAME	DOM. STATE	TOTAL ASSETS ($MIL)

Rating: A+

INSURANCE COMPANY NAME	DOM. STATE	TOTAL ASSETS ($MIL)
COUNTRY LIFE INS CO	IL	7,329.3
PHYSICIANS MUTUAL INS CO	NE	1,445.1
STATE FARM LIFE INS CO	IL	44,978.4
TEACHERS INS & ANNUITY ASN OF AM	NY	194,588.7

Rating: A

INSURANCE COMPANY NAME	DOM. STATE	TOTAL ASSETS ($MIL)
AMERICAN FIDELITY ASR CO	OK	3,343.9
AUTO-OWNERS LIFE INS CO	MI	2,168.0
BERKSHIRE LIFE INS CO OF AMERICA	MA	2,502.2
FEDERATED LIFE INS CO	MN	978.1
FIDELITY INVESTMENTS LIFE INS CO	UT	11,382.8
GUARDIAN LIFE INS CO OF AMERICA	NY	29,202.2
MASSACHUSETTS MUTUAL LIFE INS CO	MA	112,014.6
MML BAY STATE LIFE INS CO	CT	4,105.4
SENTRY LIFE INS CO	WI	2,809.8
UNITED FARM FAMILY LIFE INS CO	IN	1,712.9
USAA LIFE INS CO	TX	13,463.6

Rating: A-

INSURANCE COMPANY NAME	DOM. STATE	TOTAL ASSETS ($MIL)
ACACIA LIFE INS CO	DC	1,521.4
AMALGAMATED LIFE INS CO	NY	62.6
AMERICAN REPUBLIC INS CO	IA	472.8
AMICA LIFE INS CO	RI	950.4
ANTHEM LIFE INS CO	IN	288.0
CHARTER NATIONAL LIFE INS CO	IL	133.2
COMPANION LIFE INS CO	SC	124.7
CONTINENTAL AMERICAN INS CO	SC	105.0
COUNTRY INVESTORS LIFE ASR CO	IL	192.1
FIRST INVESTORS LIFE INS CO	NY	949.4
FORT DEARBORN LIFE INS CO	IL	2,870.9
GERBER LIFE INS CO	NY	1,568.7
GRANGE LIFE INS CO	OH	258.2
NATIONAL BENEFIT LIFE INS CO	NY	738.4
NEW YORK LIFE INS & ANNUITY CORP	DE	77,190.7
NEW YORK LIFE INS CO	NY	114,937.8
NIPPON LIFE INS CO OF AMERICA	IA	162.8
NORTHWESTERN MUTUAL LIFE INS CO	WI	155,607.2
PACIFIC LIFE & ANNUITY CO	AZ	2,589.4
PACIFIC LIFE INS CO	NE	81,524.3
PHYSICIANS LIFE INS CO	NE	1,249.3
PRIMERICA LIFE INS CO	MA	5,765.7
PRINCIPAL LIFE INS CO	IA	109,923.9
STANDARD LIFE & ACCIDENT INS CO	OK	484.7
USABLE LIFE	AR	298.5
WORLD INS CO	NE	242.3

Rating: B+

INSURANCE COMPANY NAME	DOM. STATE	TOTAL ASSETS ($MIL)
ALLSTATE LIFE INS CO	IL	65,002.0
AMERICAN FAMILY LIFE ASR CO OF COLUM	NE	67,309.5
AMERICAN HEALTH & LIFE INS CO	TX	1,505.6
AMERICAN INCOME LIFE INS CO	IN	1,811.7
AMERICAN UNITED LIFE INS CO	IN	12,264.8
AMERITAS LIFE INS CORP	NE	4,928.5
ASSURITY LIFE INS CO	NE	2,167.6
BOSTON MUTUAL LIFE INS CO	MA	945.5

INSURANCE COMPANY NAME	DOM. STATE	TOTAL ASSETS ($MIL)
CHEROKEE NATIONAL LIFE INS CO	GA	30.8
COLORADO BANKERS LIFE INS CO	CO	144.4
COLUMBUS LIFE INS CO	OH	2,512.2
CONTINENTAL LIFE INS CO OF BRENTWOOD	TN	149.3
EASTERN LIFE & HEALTH INS CO	PA	44.9
EPIC LIFE INSURANCE CO	WI	42.6
FAMILY HERITAGE LIFE INS CO OF AMER	OH	322.3
FIDELITY LIFE ASSN A LEGAL RESERVE	IL	505.8
FIDELITY SECURITY LIFE INS CO	MO	576.6
GENERAL RE LIFE CORP	CT	2,682.0
GOVERNMENT PERSONNEL MUTUAL L I C	TX	783.4
ILLINOIS MUTUAL LIFE INS CO	IL	1,262.3
LINCOLN BENEFIT LIFE CO	NE	2,007.2
LINCOLN HERITAGE LIFE INS CO	IL	629.7
MID-WEST NATIONAL LIFE INS CO OF TN	TX	228.4
MIDLAND NATIONAL LIFE INS CO	IA	25,970.2
MTL INS CO	IL	1,337.3
MUTUAL OF OMAHA INS CO	NE	4,625.4
NATIONAL GUARDIAN LIFE INS CO	WI	1,663.4
NATIONAL WESTERN LIFE INS CO	CO	6,175.2
NATIONWIDE LIFE INS CO OF AMERICA	PA	4,826.2
OHIO NATIONAL LIFE ASR CORP	OH	2,702.3
PENN INS & ANNUITY CO	DE	1,038.9
PENN MUTUAL LIFE INS CO	PA	9,647.6
PHARMACISTS LIFE INS CO	IA	40.4
RELIABLE LIFE INS CO	MO	747.4
SAVINGS BANK LIFE INS CO OF MA	MA	2,093.4
SETTLERS LIFE INS CO	WI	417.4
STANDARD INS CO	OR	12,858.1
STANDARD SECURITY LIFE INS CO OF NY	NY	365.4
STONEBRIDGE LIFE INS CO	VT	2,089.0
SURETY LIFE INS CO	NE	13.2
THRIVENT LIFE INS CO	MN	2,564.9
UNITED INVESTORS LIFE INS CO	MO	2,518.4
UNITED OF OMAHA LIFE INS CO	NE	12,875.0
UNITED WORLD LIFE INS CO	NE	114.6
WORLD CORP INS CO	NE	23.2

Puerto Rico

INSURANCE COMPANY NAME	DOM. STATE	TOTAL ASSETS ($MIL)
Rating: A+		
TEACHERS INS & ANNUITY ASN OF AM	NY	194,588.7
Rating: A		
MASSACHUSETTS MUTUAL LIFE INS CO	MA	112,014.6
SOUTHERN FARM BUREAU LIFE INS CO	MS	10,074.1
Rating: A-		
CHARTER NATIONAL LIFE INS CO	IL	133.2
GERBER LIFE INS CO	NY	1,568.7
NEW YORK LIFE INS CO	NY	114,937.8
PRIMERICA LIFE INS CO	MA	5,765.7
PRINCIPAL LIFE INS CO	IA	109,923.9
Rating: B+		
ALLSTATE LIFE INS CO	IL	65,002.0
AMERICAN FAMILY LIFE ASR CO OF COLUM	NE	67,309.5
BOSTON MUTUAL LIFE INS CO	MA	945.5
FAMILY HERITAGE LIFE INS CO OF AMER	OH	322.3
LINCOLN HERITAGE LIFE INS CO	IL	629.7
MID-WEST NATIONAL LIFE INS CO OF TN	TX	228.4
MIDLAND NATIONAL LIFE INS CO	IA	25,970.2
MUTUAL OF OMAHA INS CO	NE	4,625.4
NATIONAL WESTERN LIFE INS CO	CO	6,175.2
NATIONWIDE LIFE INS CO OF AMERICA	PA	4,826.2
OHIO NATIONAL LIFE ASR CORP	OH	2,702.3
RELIABLE LIFE INS CO	MO	747.4
STANDARD SECURITY LIFE INS CO OF NY	NY	365.4
UNITED OF OMAHA LIFE INS CO	NE	12,875.0

INSURANCE COMPANY NAME	DOM. STATE	TOTAL ASSETS ($MIL)

Rhode Island

INSURANCE COMPANY NAME	DOM. STATE	TOTAL ASSETS ($MIL)

Rating: A+

INSURANCE COMPANY NAME	DOM. STATE	TOTAL ASSETS ($MIL)
COUNTRY LIFE INS CO	IL	7,329.3
PHYSICIANS MUTUAL INS CO	NE	1,445.1
STATE FARM LIFE INS CO	IL	44,978.4
TEACHERS INS & ANNUITY ASN OF AM	NY	194,588.7

Rating: A

INSURANCE COMPANY NAME	DOM. STATE	TOTAL ASSETS ($MIL)
AMERICAN FIDELITY ASR CO	OK	3,343.9
BERKSHIRE LIFE INS CO OF AMERICA	MA	2,502.2
FEDERATED LIFE INS CO	MN	978.1
FIDELITY INVESTMENTS LIFE INS CO	UT	11,382.8
GUARDIAN LIFE INS CO OF AMERICA	NY	29,202.2
MASSACHUSETTS MUTUAL LIFE INS CO	MA	112,014.6
MML BAY STATE LIFE INS CO	CT	4,105.4
SENTRY LIFE INS CO	WI	2,809.8
USAA LIFE INS CO	TX	13,463.6

Rating: A-

INSURANCE COMPANY NAME	DOM. STATE	TOTAL ASSETS ($MIL)
ACACIA LIFE INS CO	DC	1,521.4
AMALGAMATED LIFE INS CO	NY	62.6
AMERICAN REPUBLIC INS CO	IA	472.8
AMICA LIFE INS CO	RI	950.4
CHARTER NATIONAL LIFE INS CO	IL	133.2
COMPANION LIFE INS CO	SC	124.7
CONTINENTAL AMERICAN INS CO	SC	105.0
COUNTRY INVESTORS LIFE ASR CO	IL	192.1
FIRST INVESTORS LIFE INS CO	NY	949.4
FORT DEARBORN LIFE INS CO	IL	2,870.9
GERBER LIFE INS CO	NY	1,568.7
NATIONAL BENEFIT LIFE INS CO	NY	738.4
NEW YORK LIFE INS & ANNUITY CORP	DE	77,190.7
NEW YORK LIFE INS CO	NY	114,937.8
NIPPON LIFE INS CO OF AMERICA	IA	162.8
NORTHWESTERN MUTUAL LIFE INS CO	WI	155,607.2
PACIFIC LIFE & ANNUITY CO	AZ	2,589.4
PACIFIC LIFE INS CO	NE	81,524.3
PHYSICIANS LIFE INS CO	NE	1,249.3
PRIMERICA LIFE INS CO	MA	5,765.7
PRINCIPAL LIFE INS CO	IA	109,923.9
STANDARD LIFE & ACCIDENT INS CO	OK	484.7
USABLE LIFE	AR	298.5
WORLD INS CO	NE	242.3

Rating: B+

INSURANCE COMPANY NAME	DOM. STATE	TOTAL ASSETS ($MIL)
ALLSTATE LIFE INS CO	IL	65,002.0
AMERICAN FAMILY LIFE ASR CO OF COLUM	NE	67,309.5
AMERICAN HEALTH & LIFE INS CO	TX	1,505.6
AMERICAN INCOME LIFE INS CO	IN	1,811.7
AMERICAN UNITED LIFE INS CO	IN	12,264.8
AMERITAS LIFE INS CORP	NE	4,928.5
ASSURITY LIFE INS CO	NE	2,167.6
BOSTON MUTUAL LIFE INS CO	MA	945.5
COLORADO BANKERS LIFE INS CO	CO	144.4
COLUMBUS LIFE INS CO	OH	2,512.2
CONTINENTAL LIFE INS CO OF BRENTWOOD	TN	149.3
EASTERN LIFE & HEALTH INS CO	PA	44.9

INSURANCE COMPANY NAME	DOM. STATE	TOTAL ASSETS ($MIL)
FAMILY HERITAGE LIFE INS CO OF AMER	OH	322.3
FIDELITY LIFE ASSN A LEGAL RESERVE	IL	505.8
FIDELITY SECURITY LIFE INS CO	MO	576.6
GENERAL RE LIFE CORP	CT	2,682.0
GOVERNMENT PERSONNEL MUTUAL L I C	TX	783.4
ILLINOIS MUTUAL LIFE INS CO	IL	1,262.3
LINCOLN BENEFIT LIFE CO	NE	2,007.2
LINCOLN HERITAGE LIFE INS CO	IL	629.7
MID-WEST NATIONAL LIFE INS CO OF TN	TX	228.4
MIDLAND NATIONAL LIFE INS CO	IA	25,970.2
MTL INS CO	IL	1,337.3
MUTUAL OF OMAHA INS CO	NE	4,625.4
NATIONAL GUARDIAN LIFE INS CO	WI	1,663.4
NATIONAL WESTERN LIFE INS CO	CO	6,175.2
NATIONWIDE LIFE INS CO OF AMERICA	PA	4,826.2
OHIO NATIONAL LIFE ASR CORP	OH	2,702.3
PENN INS & ANNUITY CO	DE	1,038.9
PENN MUTUAL LIFE INS CO	PA	9,647.6
PHARMACISTS LIFE INS CO	IA	40.4
RELIABLE LIFE INS CO	MO	747.4
SAVINGS BANK LIFE INS CO OF MA	MA	2,093.4
SETTLERS LIFE INS CO	WI	417.4
STANDARD INS CO	OR	12,858.1
STANDARD SECURITY LIFE INS CO OF NY	NY	365.4
STONEBRIDGE LIFE INS CO	VT	2,089.0
SURETY LIFE INS CO	NE	13.2
UNITED INVESTORS LIFE INS CO	MO	2,518.4
UNITED OF OMAHA LIFE INS CO	NE	12,875.0
UNITED WORLD LIFE INS CO	NE	114.6

South Carolina

INSURANCE COMPANY NAME	DOM. STATE	TOTAL ASSETS ($MIL)

Rating: A+

INSURANCE COMPANY NAME	DOM. STATE	TOTAL ASSETS ($MIL)
AMERICAN FAMILY LIFE INS CO	WI	3,898.0
COUNTRY LIFE INS CO	IL	7,329.3
PHYSICIANS MUTUAL INS CO	NE	1,445.1
STATE FARM LIFE INS CO	IL	44,978.4
TEACHERS INS & ANNUITY ASN OF AM	NY	194,588.7

Rating: A

INSURANCE COMPANY NAME	DOM. STATE	TOTAL ASSETS ($MIL)
AMERICAN FIDELITY ASR CO	OK	3,343.9
AUTO-OWNERS LIFE INS CO	MI	2,168.0
BERKSHIRE LIFE INS CO OF AMERICA	MA	2,502.2
FEDERATED LIFE INS CO	MN	978.1
FIDELITY INVESTMENTS LIFE INS CO	UT	11,382.8
GUARDIAN LIFE INS CO OF AMERICA	NY	29,202.2
MASSACHUSETTS MUTUAL LIFE INS CO	MA	112,014.6
MML BAY STATE LIFE INS CO	CT	4,105.4
SENTRY LIFE INS CO	WI	2,809.8
SOUTHERN FARM BUREAU LIFE INS CO	MS	10,074.1
USAA LIFE INS CO	TX	13,463.6

Rating: A-

INSURANCE COMPANY NAME	DOM. STATE	TOTAL ASSETS ($MIL)
ACACIA LIFE INS CO	DC	1,521.4
AMALGAMATED LIFE INS CO	NY	62.6
AMERICAN REPUBLIC INS CO	IA	472.8
AMICA LIFE INS CO	RI	950.4
ANTHEM LIFE INS CO	IN	288.0
CHARTER NATIONAL LIFE INS CO	IL	133.2
COMPANION LIFE INS CO	SC	124.7
CONTINENTAL AMERICAN INS CO	SC	105.0
COUNTRY INVESTORS LIFE ASR CO	IL	192.1
FIRST INVESTORS LIFE INS CO	NY	949.4
FORT DEARBORN LIFE INS CO	IL	2,870.9
GERBER LIFE INS CO	NY	1,568.7
GRANGE LIFE INS CO	OH	258.2
GREATER GEORGIA LIFE INS CO	GA	46.3
NATIONAL BENEFIT LIFE INS CO	NY	738.4
NEW YORK LIFE INS & ANNUITY CORP	DE	77,190.7
NEW YORK LIFE INS CO	NY	114,937.8
NIPPON LIFE INS CO OF AMERICA	IA	162.8
NORTHWESTERN MUTUAL LIFE INS CO	WI	155,607.2
PACIFIC LIFE & ANNUITY CO	AZ	2,589.4
PACIFIC LIFE INS CO	NE	81,524.3
PHYSICIANS LIFE INS CO	NE	1,249.3
PRIMERICA LIFE INS CO	MA	5,765.7
PRINCIPAL LIFE INS CO	IA	109,923.9
STANDARD LIFE & ACCIDENT INS CO	OK	484.7
USABLE LIFE	AR	298.5
WORLD INS CO	NE	242.3

Rating: B+

INSURANCE COMPANY NAME	DOM. STATE	TOTAL ASSETS ($MIL)
ALFA LIFE INS CORP	AL	1,087.3
ALLSTATE LIFE INS CO	IL	65,002.0
AMERICAN FAMILY LIFE ASR CO OF COLUM	NE	67,309.5
AMERICAN HEALTH & LIFE INS CO	TX	1,505.6
AMERICAN INCOME LIFE INS CO	IN	1,811.7
AMERICAN UNITED LIFE INS CO	IN	12,264.8

INSURANCE COMPANY NAME	DOM. STATE	TOTAL ASSETS ($MIL)
AMERITAS LIFE INS CORP	NE	4,928.5
ASSURITY LIFE INS CO	NE	2,167.6
ATLANTIC COAST LIFE INS CO	SC	69.9
BOSTON MUTUAL LIFE INS CO	MA	945.5
CHEROKEE NATIONAL LIFE INS CO	GA	30.8
COLORADO BANKERS LIFE INS CO	CO	144.4
COLUMBUS LIFE INS CO	OH	2,512.2
COMPBENEFITS INS CO	TX	62.7
CONTINENTAL LIFE INS CO OF BRENTWOOD	TN	149.3
COTTON STATES LIFE INS CO	GA	281.8
EASTERN LIFE & HEALTH INS CO	PA	44.9
EPIC LIFE INSURANCE CO	WI	42.6
FAMILY HERITAGE LIFE INS CO OF AMER	OH	322.3
FIDELITY LIFE ASSN A LEGAL RESERVE	IL	505.8
FIDELITY SECURITY LIFE INS CO	MO	576.6
FLORIDA COMBINED LIFE INS CO INC	FL	31.8
GENERAL RE LIFE CORP	CT	2,682.0
GOVERNMENT PERSONNEL MUTUAL L I C	TX	783.4
ILLINOIS MUTUAL LIFE INS CO	IL	1,262.3
LINCOLN BENEFIT LIFE CO	NE	2,007.2
LINCOLN HERITAGE LIFE INS CO	IL	629.7
MID-WEST NATIONAL LIFE INS CO OF TN	TX	228.4
MIDLAND NATIONAL LIFE INS CO	IA	25,970.2
MTL INS CO	IL	1,337.3
MUTUAL OF OMAHA INS CO	NE	4,625.4
NATIONAL GUARDIAN LIFE INS CO	WI	1,663.4
NATIONAL WESTERN LIFE INS CO	CO	6,175.2
NATIONWIDE LIFE INS CO OF AMERICA	PA	4,826.2
OHIO NATIONAL LIFE ASR CORP	OH	2,702.3
PENN INS & ANNUITY CO	DE	1,038.9
PENN MUTUAL LIFE INS CO	PA	9,647.6
PHARMACISTS LIFE INS CO	IA	40.4
RELIABLE LIFE INS CO	MO	747.4
SAVINGS BANK LIFE INS CO OF MA	MA	2,093.4
SETTLERS LIFE INS CO	WI	417.4
STANDARD INS CO	OR	12,858.1
STANDARD SECURITY LIFE INS CO OF NY	NY	365.4
STONEBRIDGE LIFE INS CO	VT	2,089.0
SURETY LIFE INS CO	NE	13.2
THRIVENT LIFE INS CO	MN	2,564.9
UNITED INVESTORS LIFE INS CO	MO	2,518.4
UNITED OF OMAHA LIFE INS CO	NE	12,875.0
UNITED WORLD LIFE INS CO	NE	114.6
WORLD CORP INS CO	NE	23.2

South Dakota

INSURANCE COMPANY NAME	DOM. STATE	TOTAL ASSETS ($MIL)
Rating: A+		
AMERICAN FAMILY LIFE INS CO	WI	3,898.0
COUNTRY LIFE INS CO	IL	7,329.3
PHYSICIANS MUTUAL INS CO	NE	1,445.1
STATE FARM LIFE INS CO	IL	44,978.4
TEACHERS INS & ANNUITY ASN OF AM	NY	194,588.7
Rating: A		
AMERICAN FIDELITY ASR CO	OK	3,343.9
AUTO-OWNERS LIFE INS CO	MI	2,168.0
BERKSHIRE LIFE INS CO OF AMERICA	MA	2,502.2
FEDERATED LIFE INS CO	MN	978.1
FIDELITY INVESTMENTS LIFE INS CO	UT	11,382.8
GUARDIAN LIFE INS CO OF AMERICA	NY	29,202.2
MASSACHUSETTS MUTUAL LIFE INS CO	MA	112,014.6
MML BAY STATE LIFE INS CO	CT	4,105.4
SENTRY LIFE INS CO	WI	2,809.8
USAA LIFE INS CO	TX	13,463.6
Rating: A-		
ACACIA LIFE INS CO	DC	1,521.4
AMALGAMATED LIFE INS CO	NY	62.6
AMERICAN REPUBLIC INS CO	IA	472.8
AMICA LIFE INS CO	RI	950.4
ANTHEM LIFE INS CO	IN	288.0
CHARTER NATIONAL LIFE INS CO	IL	133.2
COMPANION LIFE INS CO	SC	124.7
CONTINENTAL AMERICAN INS CO	SC	105.0
COUNTRY INVESTORS LIFE ASR CO	IL	192.1
FORT DEARBORN LIFE INS CO	IL	2,870.9
GERBER LIFE INS CO	NY	1,568.7
NATIONAL BENEFIT LIFE INS CO	NY	738.4
NEW YORK LIFE INS & ANNUITY CORP	DE	77,190.7
NEW YORK LIFE INS CO	NY	114,937.8
NIPPON LIFE INS CO OF AMERICA	IA	162.8
NORTHWESTERN MUTUAL LIFE INS CO	WI	155,607.2
PACIFIC GUARDIAN LIFE INS CO LTD	HI	426.8
PACIFIC LIFE & ANNUITY CO	AZ	2,589.4
PACIFIC LIFE INS CO	NE	81,524.3
PHYSICIANS LIFE INS CO	NE	1,249.3
PRIMERICA LIFE INS CO	MA	5,765.7
PRINCIPAL LIFE INS CO	IA	109,923.9
STANDARD LIFE & ACCIDENT INS CO	OK	484.7
USABLE LIFE	AR	298.5
WORLD INS CO	NE	242.3
Rating: B+		
ALLSTATE LIFE INS CO	IL	65,002.0
AMERICAN FAMILY LIFE ASR CO OF COLUM	NE	67,309.5
AMERICAN HEALTH & LIFE INS CO	TX	1,505.6
AMERICAN INCOME LIFE INS CO	IN	1,811.7
AMERICAN UNITED LIFE INS CO	IN	12,264.8
AMERITAS LIFE INS CORP	NE	4,928.5
ASSURITY LIFE INS CO	NE	2,167.6
BOSTON MUTUAL LIFE INS CO	MA	945.5
COLORADO BANKERS LIFE INS CO	CO	144.4

INSURANCE COMPANY NAME	DOM. STATE	TOTAL ASSETS ($MIL)
COLUMBUS LIFE INS CO	OH	2,512.2
CONTINENTAL LIFE INS CO OF BRENTWOOD	TN	149.3
EASTERN LIFE & HEALTH INS CO	PA	44.9
EPIC LIFE INSURANCE CO	WI	42.6
FAMILY HERITAGE LIFE INS CO OF AMER	OH	322.3
FARM BUREAU LIFE INS CO	IA	5,605.0
FIDELITY LIFE ASSN A LEGAL RESERVE	IL	505.8
FIDELITY SECURITY LIFE INS CO	MO	576.6
GENERAL RE LIFE CORP	CT	2,682.0
GOVERNMENT PERSONNEL MUTUAL L I C	TX	783.4
ILLINOIS MUTUAL LIFE INS CO	IL	1,262.3
LINCOLN BENEFIT LIFE CO	NE	2,007.2
LINCOLN HERITAGE LIFE INS CO	IL	629.7
MID-WEST NATIONAL LIFE INS CO OF TN	TX	228.4
MIDLAND NATIONAL LIFE INS CO	IA	25,970.4
MTL INS CO	IL	1,337.3
MUTUAL OF OMAHA INS CO	NE	4,625.4
NATIONAL GUARDIAN LIFE INS CO	WI	1,663.4
NATIONAL WESTERN LIFE INS CO	CO	6,175.2
NATIONWIDE LIFE INS CO OF AMERICA	PA	4,826.2
OHIO NATIONAL LIFE ASR CORP	OH	2,702.3
PENN INS & ANNUITY CO	DE	1,038.9
PENN MUTUAL LIFE INS CO	PA	9,647.6
PHARMACISTS LIFE INS CO	IA	40.4
RELIABLE LIFE INS CO	MO	747.4
SETTLERS LIFE INS CO	WI	417.4
STANDARD INS CO	OR	12,858.1
STANDARD SECURITY LIFE INS CO OF NY	NY	365.4
STONEBRIDGE LIFE INS CO	VT	2,089.0
SURETY LIFE INS CO	NE	13.2
THRIVENT LIFE INS CO	MN	2,564.9
UNITED INVESTORS LIFE INS CO	MO	2,518.4
UNITED OF OMAHA LIFE INS CO	NE	12,875.0
UNITED WORLD LIFE INS CO	NE	114.6
WORLD CORP INS CO	NE	23.2

Tennessee

INSURANCE COMPANY NAME	DOM. STATE	TOTAL ASSETS ($MIL)

Rating: A+

INSURANCE COMPANY NAME	DOM. STATE	TOTAL ASSETS ($MIL)
COUNTRY LIFE INS CO	IL	7,329.3
PHYSICIANS MUTUAL INS CO	NE	1,445.1
STATE FARM LIFE INS CO	IL	44,978.4
TEACHERS INS & ANNUITY ASN OF AM	NY	194,588.7

Rating: A

INSURANCE COMPANY NAME	DOM. STATE	TOTAL ASSETS ($MIL)
AMERICAN FIDELITY ASR CO	OK	3,343.9
AUTO-OWNERS LIFE INS CO	MI	2,168.0
BERKSHIRE LIFE INS CO OF AMERICA	MA	2,502.2
FEDERATED LIFE INS CO	MN	978.1
FIDELITY INVESTMENTS LIFE INS CO	UT	11,382.8
GUARDIAN LIFE INS CO OF AMERICA	NY	29,202.2
MASSACHUSETTS MUTUAL LIFE INS CO	MA	112,014.6
MML BAY STATE LIFE INS CO	CT	4,105.4
SENTRY LIFE INS CO	WI	2,809.8
SOUTHERN FARM BUREAU LIFE INS CO	MS	10,074.1
TENNESSEE FARMERS LIFE INS CO	TN	1,318.3
UNION NATIONAL LIFE INS CO	LA	459.3
USAA LIFE INS CO	TX	13,463.6

Rating: A-

INSURANCE COMPANY NAME	DOM. STATE	TOTAL ASSETS ($MIL)
ACACIA LIFE INS CO	DC	1,521.4
AMALGAMATED LIFE INS CO	NY	62.6
AMERICAN REPUBLIC INS CO	IA	472.8
AMICA LIFE INS CO	RI	950.4
ANTHEM LIFE INS CO	IN	288.0
CHARTER NATIONAL LIFE INS CO	IL	133.2
COMPANION LIFE INS CO	SC	124.7
CONTINENTAL AMERICAN INS CO	SC	105.0
COUNTRY INVESTORS LIFE ASR CO	IL	192.1
FIRST INVESTORS LIFE INS CO	NY	949.4
FORT DEARBORN LIFE INS CO	IL	2,870.9
GERBER LIFE INS CO	NY	1,568.7
GRANGE LIFE INS CO	OH	258.2
GREATER GEORGIA LIFE INS CO	GA	46.3
NATIONAL BENEFIT LIFE INS CO	NY	738.4
NEW YORK LIFE INS & ANNUITY CORP	DE	77,190.7
NEW YORK LIFE INS CO	NY	114,937.8
NIPPON LIFE INS CO OF AMERICA	IA	162.8
NORTHWESTERN MUTUAL LIFE INS CO	WI	155,607.2
PACIFIC LIFE & ANNUITY CO	AZ	2,589.4
PACIFIC LIFE INS CO	NE	81,524.3
PHYSICIANS LIFE INS CO	NE	1,249.3
PRIMERICA LIFE INS CO	MA	5,765.7
PRINCIPAL LIFE INS CO	IA	109,923.9
SHELTER LIFE INS CO	MO	933.1
STANDARD LIFE & ACCIDENT INS CO	OK	484.7
USABLE LIFE	AR	298.5
WORLD INS CO	NE	242.3

Rating: B+

INSURANCE COMPANY NAME	DOM. STATE	TOTAL ASSETS ($MIL)
ALFA LIFE INS CORP	AL	1,087.3
ALLSTATE LIFE INS CO	IL	65,002.0
AMERICAN FAMILY LIFE ASR CO OF COLUM	NE	67,309.5
AMERICAN HEALTH & LIFE INS CO	TX	1,505.6

INSURANCE COMPANY NAME	DOM. STATE	TOTAL ASSETS ($MIL)
AMERICAN INCOME LIFE INS CO	IN	1,811.7
AMERICAN UNITED LIFE INS CO	IN	12,264.8
AMERITAS LIFE INS CORP	NE	4,928.5
ASSURITY LIFE INS CO	NE	2,167.6
ATLANTIC COAST LIFE INS CO	SC	69.9
BLUEBONNET LIFE INS CO	MS	39.2
BOSTON MUTUAL LIFE INS CO	MA	945.5
CHEROKEE NATIONAL LIFE INS CO	GA	30.8
COLORADO BANKERS LIFE INS CO	CO	144.4
COLUMBUS LIFE INS CO	OH	2,512.2
COMPBENEFITS INS CO	TX	62.7
CONTINENTAL LIFE INS CO OF BRENTWOOD	TN	149.3
COTTON STATES LIFE INS CO	GA	281.8
EASTERN LIFE & HEALTH INS CO	PA	44.9
EPIC LIFE INSURANCE CO	WI	42.6
FAMILY HERITAGE LIFE INS CO OF AMER	OH	322.3
FIDELITY LIFE ASSN A LEGAL RESERVE	IL	505.8
FIDELITY SECURITY LIFE INS CO	MO	576.6
GENERAL RE LIFE CORP	CT	2,682.0
GOVERNMENT PERSONNEL MUTUAL L I C	TX	783.4
ILLINOIS MUTUAL LIFE INS CO	IL	1,262.3
LINCOLN BENEFIT LIFE CO	NE	2,007.2
LINCOLN HERITAGE LIFE INS CO	IL	629.7
MID-WEST NATIONAL LIFE INS CO OF TN	TX	228.4
MIDLAND NATIONAL LIFE INS CO	IA	25,970.2
MTL INS CO	IL	1,337.3
MUTUAL OF OMAHA INS CO	NE	4,625.4
NATIONAL GUARDIAN LIFE INS CO	WI	1,663.4
NATIONAL WESTERN LIFE INS CO	CO	6,175.2
NATIONWIDE LIFE INS CO OF AMERICA	PA	4,826.2
OHIO NATIONAL LIFE ASR CORP	OH	2,702.3
PENN INS & ANNUITY CO	DE	1,038.9
PENN MUTUAL LIFE INS CO	PA	9,647.6
PHARMACISTS LIFE INS CO	IA	40.4
RELIABLE LIFE INS CO	MO	747.4
SAVINGS BANK LIFE INS CO OF MA	MA	2,093.4
SETTLERS LIFE INS CO	WI	417.4
STANDARD INS CO	OR	12,858.1
STANDARD SECURITY LIFE INS CO OF NY	NY	365.4
STONEBRIDGE LIFE INS CO	VT	2,089.0
SURETY LIFE INS CO	NE	13.2
THRIVENT LIFE INS CO	MN	2,564.9
UNITED INVESTORS LIFE INS CO	MO	2,518.4
UNITED OF OMAHA LIFE INS CO	NE	12,875.0
UNITED WORLD LIFE INS CO	NE	114.6
WORLD CORP INS CO	NE	23.2

Texas

INSURANCE COMPANY NAME	DOM. STATE	TOTAL ASSETS ($MIL)

Rating: A+

INSURANCE COMPANY NAME	DOM. STATE	TOTAL ASSETS ($MIL)
AMERICAN FAMILY LIFE INS CO	WI	3,898.0
COUNTRY LIFE INS CO	IL	7,329.3
PHYSICIANS MUTUAL INS CO	NE	1,445.1
STATE FARM LIFE INS CO	IL	44,978.4
TEACHERS INS & ANNUITY ASN OF AM	NY	194,588.7

Rating: A

INSURANCE COMPANY NAME	DOM. STATE	TOTAL ASSETS ($MIL)
AMERICAN FIDELITY ASR CO	OK	3,343.9
AUTO-OWNERS LIFE INS CO	MI	2,168.0
BERKSHIRE LIFE INS CO OF AMERICA	MA	2,502.2
FEDERATED LIFE INS CO	MN	978.1
FIDELITY INVESTMENTS LIFE INS CO	UT	11,382.8
GUARDIAN LIFE INS CO OF AMERICA	NY	29,202.2
MASSACHUSETTS MUTUAL LIFE INS CO	MA	112,014.6
MML BAY STATE LIFE INS CO	CT	4,105.4
SENTRY LIFE INS CO	WI	2,809.8
SOUTHERN FARM BUREAU LIFE INS CO	MS	10,074.1
UNION NATIONAL LIFE INS CO	LA	459.3
USAA LIFE INS CO	TX	13,463.6

Rating: A-

INSURANCE COMPANY NAME	DOM. STATE	TOTAL ASSETS ($MIL)
ACACIA LIFE INS CO	DC	1,521.4
AMALGAMATED LIFE INS CO	NY	62.6
AMERICAN REPUBLIC INS CO	IA	472.8
AMICA LIFE INS CO	RI	950.4
ANTHEM LIFE INS CO	IN	288.0
CHARTER NATIONAL LIFE INS CO	IL	133.2
COMPANION LIFE INS CO	SC	124.7
CONTINENTAL AMERICAN INS CO	SC	105.0
COUNTRY INVESTORS LIFE ASR CO	IL	192.1
FIRST INVESTORS LIFE INS CO	NY	949.4
FORT DEARBORN LIFE INS CO	IL	2,870.9
GERBER LIFE INS CO	NY	1,568.7
NATIONAL BENEFIT LIFE INS CO	NY	738.4
NEW YORK LIFE INS & ANNUITY CORP	DE	77,190.7
NEW YORK LIFE INS CO	NY	114,937.8
NIPPON LIFE INS CO OF AMERICA	IA	162.8
NORTHWESTERN MUTUAL LIFE INS CO	WI	155,607.2
PACIFIC GUARDIAN LIFE INS CO LTD	HI	426.8
PACIFIC LIFE & ANNUITY CO	AZ	2,589.4
PACIFIC LIFE INS CO	NE	81,524.3
PHYSICIANS LIFE INS CO	NE	1,249.3
PRIMERICA LIFE INS CO	MA	5,765.7
PRINCIPAL LIFE INS CO	IA	109,923.9
STANDARD LIFE & ACCIDENT INS CO	OK	484.7
USABLE LIFE	AR	298.5
WORLD INS CO	NE	242.3

Rating: B+

INSURANCE COMPANY NAME	DOM. STATE	TOTAL ASSETS ($MIL)
ALLSTATE LIFE INS CO	IL	65,002.0
AMERICAN FAMILY LIFE ASR CO OF COLUM	NE	67,309.5
AMERICAN HEALTH & LIFE INS CO	TX	1,505.6
AMERICAN INCOME LIFE INS CO	IN	1,811.7
AMERICAN UNITED LIFE INS CO	IN	12,264.8
AMERITAS LIFE INS CORP	NE	4,928.5

INSURANCE COMPANY NAME	DOM. STATE	TOTAL ASSETS ($MIL)
ASSURITY LIFE INS CO	NE	2,167.6
BOSTON MUTUAL LIFE INS CO	MA	945.5
CHEROKEE NATIONAL LIFE INS CO	GA	30.8
COLORADO BANKERS LIFE INS CO	CO	144.4
COLUMBUS LIFE INS CO	OH	2,512.2
COMPBENEFITS INS CO	TX	62.7
CONTINENTAL LIFE INS CO OF BRENTWOOD	TN	149.3
EASTERN LIFE & HEALTH INS CO	PA	44.9
EPIC LIFE INSURANCE CO	WI	42.6
FAMILY HERITAGE LIFE INS CO OF AMER	OH	322.3
FIDELITY LIFE ASSN A LEGAL RESERVE	IL	505.8
FIDELITY SECURITY LIFE INS CO	MO	576.6
GENERAL RE LIFE CORP	CT	2,682.0
GOVERNMENT PERSONNEL MUTUAL L I C	TX	783.4
ILLINOIS MUTUAL LIFE INS CO	IL	1,262.3
LINCOLN BENEFIT LIFE CO	NE	2,007.2
LINCOLN HERITAGE LIFE INS CO	IL	629.7
MID-WEST NATIONAL LIFE INS CO OF TN	TX	228.4
MIDLAND NATIONAL LIFE INS CO	IA	25,970.2
MTL INS CO	IL	1,337.3
MUTUAL OF OMAHA INS CO	NE	4,625.4
NATIONAL GUARDIAN LIFE INS CO	WI	1,663.4
NATIONAL WESTERN LIFE INS CO	CO	6,175.2
NATIONWIDE LIFE INS CO OF AMERICA	PA	4,826.2
OHIO NATIONAL LIFE ASR CORP	OH	2,702.3
PENN INS & ANNUITY CO	DE	1,038.9
PENN MUTUAL LIFE INS CO	PA	9,647.6
PHARMACISTS LIFE INS CO	IA	40.4
RELIABLE LIFE INS CO	MO	747.4
SAVINGS BANK LIFE INS CO OF MA	MA	2,093.4
SETTLERS LIFE INS CO	WI	417.4
STANDARD INS CO	OR	12,858.1
STANDARD SECURITY LIFE INS CO OF NY	NY	365.4
STONEBRIDGE LIFE INS CO	VT	2,089.0
SURETY LIFE INS CO	NE	13.2
THRIVENT LIFE INS CO	MN	2,564.9
UNITED INVESTORS LIFE INS CO	MO	2,518.4
UNITED OF OMAHA LIFE INS CO	NE	12,875.0
UNITED WORLD LIFE INS CO	NE	114.6
WORLD CORP INS CO	NE	23.2

Utah

INSURANCE COMPANY NAME	DOM. STATE	TOTAL ASSETS ($MIL)
Rating: A+		
AMERICAN FAMILY LIFE INS CO	WI	3,898.0
COUNTRY LIFE INS CO	IL	7,329.3
PHYSICIANS MUTUAL INS CO	NE	1,445.1
STATE FARM LIFE INS CO	IL	44,978.4
TEACHERS INS & ANNUITY ASN OF AM	NY	194,588.7
Rating: A		
AMERICAN FIDELITY ASR CO	OK	3,343.9
AUTO-OWNERS LIFE INS CO	MI	2,168.0
BERKSHIRE LIFE INS CO OF AMERICA	MA	2,502.2
FEDERATED LIFE INS CO	MN	978.1
FIDELITY INVESTMENTS LIFE INS CO	UT	11,382.8
GUARDIAN LIFE INS CO OF AMERICA	NY	29,202.2
LIFEWISE ASR CO	WA	70.2
MASSACHUSETTS MUTUAL LIFE INS CO	MA	112,014.6
MML BAY STATE LIFE INS CO	CT	4,105.4
SENTRY LIFE INS CO	WI	2,809.8
USAA LIFE INS CO	TX	13,463.6
Rating: A-		
ACACIA LIFE INS CO	DC	1,521.4
AMALGAMATED LIFE INS CO	NY	62.6
AMERICAN REPUBLIC INS CO	IA	472.8
AMICA LIFE INS CO	RI	950.4
ANTHEM LIFE INS CO	IN	288.0
CHARTER NATIONAL LIFE INS CO	IL	133.2
COMPANION LIFE INS CO	SC	124.7
CONTINENTAL AMERICAN INS CO	SC	105.0
FIRST INVESTORS LIFE INS CO	NY	949.4
FORT DEARBORN LIFE INS CO	IL	2,870.9
GERBER LIFE INS CO	NY	1,568.7
NATIONAL BENEFIT LIFE INS CO	NY	738.4
NEW YORK LIFE INS & ANNUITY CORP	DE	77,190.7
NEW YORK LIFE INS CO	NY	114,937.8
NIPPON LIFE INS CO OF AMERICA	IA	162.8
NORTHWESTERN MUTUAL LIFE INS CO	WI	155,607.2
PACIFIC GUARDIAN LIFE INS CO LTD	HI	426.8
PACIFIC LIFE & ANNUITY CO	AZ	2,589.4
PACIFIC LIFE INS CO	NE	81,524.3
PHYSICIANS LIFE INS CO	NE	1,249.3
PRIMERICA LIFE INS CO	MA	5,765.7
PRINCIPAL LIFE INS CO	IA	109,923.9
STANDARD LIFE & ACCIDENT INS CO	OK	484.7
USABLE LIFE	AR	298.5
WORLD INS CO	NE	242.3
Rating: B+		
ALLSTATE LIFE INS CO	IL	65,002.0
AMERICAN FAMILY LIFE ASR CO OF COLUM	NE	67,309.5
AMERICAN HEALTH & LIFE INS CO	TX	1,505.6
AMERICAN INCOME LIFE INS CO	IN	1,811.7
AMERICAN UNITED LIFE INS CO	IN	12,264.8
AMERITAS LIFE INS CORP	NE	4,928.5
ASSURITY LIFE INS CO	NE	2,167.6
BOSTON MUTUAL LIFE INS CO	MA	945.5

INSURANCE COMPANY NAME	DOM. STATE	TOTAL ASSETS ($MIL)
COLORADO BANKERS LIFE INS CO	CO	144.4
COLUMBUS LIFE INS CO	OH	2,512.2
COMPBENEFITS INS CO	TX	62.7
CONTINENTAL LIFE INS CO OF BRENTWOOD	TN	149.3
FAMILY HERITAGE LIFE INS CO OF AMER	OH	322.3
FARM BUREAU LIFE INS CO	IA	5,605.0
FIDELITY LIFE ASSN A LEGAL RESERVE	IL	505.8
FIDELITY SECURITY LIFE INS CO	MO	576.6
GENERAL RE LIFE CORP	CT	2,682.0
GOVERNMENT PERSONNEL MUTUAL L I C	TX	783.4
ILLINOIS MUTUAL LIFE INS CO	IL	1,262.3
LINCOLN BENEFIT LIFE CO	NE	2,007.2
LINCOLN HERITAGE LIFE INS CO	IL	629.7
MID-WEST NATIONAL LIFE INS CO OF TN	TX	228.4
MIDLAND NATIONAL LIFE INS CO	IA	25,970.2
MTL INS CO	IL	1,337.3
MUTUAL OF OMAHA INS CO	NE	4,625.4
NATIONAL GUARDIAN LIFE INS CO	WI	1,663.4
NATIONAL WESTERN LIFE INS CO	CO	6,175.2
NATIONWIDE LIFE INS CO OF AMERICA	PA	4,826.2
OHIO NATIONAL LIFE ASR CORP	OH	2,702.3
PENN INS & ANNUITY CO	DE	1,038.9
PENN MUTUAL LIFE INS CO	PA	9,647.6
PHARMACISTS LIFE INS CO	IA	40.4
REGENCE LIFE & HEALTH INS CO	OR	80.7
RELIABLE LIFE INS CO	MO	747.4
SAVINGS BANK LIFE INS CO OF MA	MA	2,093.4
SETTLERS LIFE INS CO	WI	417.4
STANDARD INS CO	OR	12,858.1
STANDARD SECURITY LIFE INS CO OF NY	NY	365.4
STONEBRIDGE LIFE INS CO	VT	2,089.0
SURETY LIFE INS CO	NE	13.2
THRIVENT LIFE INS CO	MN	2,564.9
UNITED INVESTORS LIFE INS CO	MO	2,518.4
UNITED OF OMAHA LIFE INS CO	NE	12,875.0
UNITED WORLD LIFE INS CO	NE	114.6
WORLD CORP INS CO	NE	23.2

Vermont

INSURANCE COMPANY NAME	DOM. STATE	TOTAL ASSETS ($MIL)

Rating: A+

INSURANCE COMPANY NAME	DOM. STATE	TOTAL ASSETS ($MIL)
PHYSICIANS MUTUAL INS CO	NE	1,445.1
STATE FARM LIFE INS CO	IL	44,978.4
TEACHERS INS & ANNUITY ASN OF AM	NY	194,588.7

Rating: A

AMERICAN FIDELITY ASR CO	OK	3,343.9
BERKSHIRE LIFE INS CO OF AMERICA	MA	2,502.2
FEDERATED LIFE INS CO	MN	978.1
FIDELITY INVESTMENTS LIFE INS CO	UT	11,382.8
GUARDIAN LIFE INS CO OF AMERICA	NY	29,202.2
MASSACHUSETTS MUTUAL LIFE INS CO	MA	112,014.6
MML BAY STATE LIFE INS CO	CT	4,105.4
SENTRY LIFE INS CO	WI	2,809.8
USAA LIFE INS CO	TX	13,463.6

Rating: A-

ACACIA LIFE INS CO	DC	1,521.4
AMALGAMATED LIFE INS CO	NY	62.6
AMERICAN REPUBLIC INS CO	IA	472.8
AMICA LIFE INS CO	RI	950.4
CHARTER NATIONAL LIFE INS CO	IL	133.2
COMPANION LIFE INS CO	SC	124.7
CONTINENTAL AMERICAN INS CO	SC	105.0
FIRST INVESTORS LIFE INS CO	NY	949.4
FORT DEARBORN LIFE INS CO	IL	2,870.9
GERBER LIFE INS CO	NY	1,568.7
NATIONAL BENEFIT LIFE INS CO	NY	738.4
NEW YORK LIFE INS & ANNUITY CORP	DE	77,190.7
NEW YORK LIFE INS CO	NY	114,937.8
NIPPON LIFE INS CO OF AMERICA	IA	162.8
NORTHWESTERN MUTUAL LIFE INS CO	WI	155,607.2
PACIFIC LIFE & ANNUITY CO	AZ	2,589.4
PACIFIC LIFE INS CO	NE	81,524.3
PHYSICIANS LIFE INS CO	NE	1,249.3
PRIMERICA LIFE INS CO	MA	5,765.7
PRINCIPAL LIFE INS CO	IA	109,923.9
STANDARD LIFE & ACCIDENT INS CO	OK	484.7
USABLE LIFE	AR	298.5
WORLD INS CO	NE	242.3

Rating: B+

ALLSTATE LIFE INS CO	IL	65,002.0
AMERICAN FAMILY LIFE ASR CO OF COLUM	NE	67,309.5
AMERICAN FAMILY LIFE ASR CO OF NY	NY	285.0
AMERICAN HEALTH & LIFE INS CO	TX	1,505.6
AMERICAN INCOME LIFE INS CO	IN	1,811.7
AMERICAN UNITED LIFE INS CO	IN	12,264.8
AMERITAS LIFE INS CORP	NE	4,928.5
ASSURITY LIFE INS CO	NE	2,167.6
BOSTON MUTUAL LIFE INS CO	MA	945.5
COLUMBUS LIFE INS CO	OH	2,512.2
EASTERN LIFE & HEALTH INS CO	PA	44.9
FAMILY HERITAGE LIFE INS CO OF AMER	OH	322.3
FIDELITY LIFE ASSN A LEGAL RESERVE	IL	505.8
FIDELITY SECURITY LIFE INS CO	MO	576.6

INSURANCE COMPANY NAME	DOM. STATE	TOTAL ASSETS ($MIL)
GOVERNMENT PERSONNEL MUTUAL L I C	TX	783.4
ILLINOIS MUTUAL LIFE INS CO	IL	1,262.3
LINCOLN BENEFIT LIFE CO	NE	2,007.2
LINCOLN HERITAGE LIFE INS CO	IL	629.7
MIDLAND NATIONAL LIFE INS CO	IA	25,970.2
MTL INS CO	IL	1,337.3
MUTUAL OF OMAHA INS CO	NE	4,625.4
NATIONAL GUARDIAN LIFE INS CO	WI	1,663.4
NATIONAL WESTERN LIFE INS CO	CO	6,175.2
NATIONWIDE LIFE INS CO OF AMERICA	PA	4,826.2
OHIO NATIONAL LIFE ASR CORP	OH	2,702.3
PENN INS & ANNUITY CO	DE	1,038.9
PENN MUTUAL LIFE INS CO	PA	9,647.6
RELIABLE LIFE INS CO	MO	747.4
SAVINGS BANK LIFE INS CO OF MA	MA	2,093.4
SETTLERS LIFE INS CO	WI	417.4
STANDARD INS CO	OR	12,858.1
STANDARD SECURITY LIFE INS CO OF NY	NY	365.4
STONEBRIDGE LIFE INS CO	VT	2,089.0
SURETY LIFE INS CO	NE	13.2
UNITED INVESTORS LIFE INS CO	MO	2,518.4
UNITED OF OMAHA LIFE INS CO	NE	12,875.0
UNITED WORLD LIFE INS CO	NE	114.6

Virginia

INSURANCE COMPANY NAME	DOM. STATE	TOTAL ASSETS ($MIL)
Rating: A+		
COUNTRY LIFE INS CO	IL	7,329.3
PHYSICIANS MUTUAL INS CO	NE	1,445.1
STATE FARM LIFE INS CO	IL	44,978.4
TEACHERS INS & ANNUITY ASN OF AM	NY	194,588.7
Rating: A		
AMERICAN FIDELITY ASR CO	OK	3,343.9
AUTO-OWNERS LIFE INS CO	MI	2,168.0
BERKSHIRE LIFE INS CO OF AMERICA	MA	2,502.2
FEDERATED LIFE INS CO	MN	978.1
FIDELITY INVESTMENTS LIFE INS CO	UT	11,382.8
GUARDIAN LIFE INS CO OF AMERICA	NY	29,202.2
MASSACHUSETTS MUTUAL LIFE INS CO	MA	112,014.6
MML BAY STATE LIFE INS CO	CT	4,105.4
SENTRY LIFE INS CO	WI	2,809.8
SOUTHERN FARM BUREAU LIFE INS CO	MS	10,074.1
USAA LIFE INS CO	TX	13,463.6
Rating: A-		
ACACIA LIFE INS CO	DC	1,521.4
AMALGAMATED LIFE INS CO	NY	62.6
AMERICAN REPUBLIC INS CO	IA	472.8
AMICA LIFE INS CO	RI	950.4
ANTHEM LIFE INS CO	IN	288.0
CHARTER NATIONAL LIFE INS CO	IL	133.2
COMPANION LIFE INS CO	SC	124.7
CONTINENTAL AMERICAN INS CO	SC	105.0
COUNTRY INVESTORS LIFE ASR CO	IL	192.1
FIRST INVESTORS LIFE INS CO	NY	949.4
FORT DEARBORN LIFE INS CO	IL	2,870.9
GERBER LIFE INS CO	NY	1,568.7
GRANGE LIFE INS CO	OH	258.2
GREATER GEORGIA LIFE INS CO	GA	46.3
NATIONAL BENEFIT LIFE INS CO	NY	738.4
NEW YORK LIFE INS & ANNUITY CORP	DE	77,190.7
NEW YORK LIFE INS CO	NY	114,937.8
NIPPON LIFE INS CO OF AMERICA	IA	162.8
NORTHWESTERN MUTUAL LIFE INS CO	WI	155,607.2
PACIFIC LIFE & ANNUITY CO	AZ	2,589.4
PACIFIC LIFE INS CO	NE	81,524.3
PHYSICIANS LIFE INS CO	NE	1,249.3
PRIMERICA LIFE INS CO	MA	5,765.7
PRINCIPAL LIFE INS CO	IA	109,923.9
STANDARD LIFE & ACCIDENT INS CO	OK	484.7
USABLE LIFE	AR	298.5
WORLD INS CO	NE	242.3
Rating: B+		
ALFA LIFE INS CORP	AL	1,087.3
ALLSTATE LIFE INS CO	IL	65,002.0
AMERICAN FAMILY LIFE ASR CO OF COLUM	NE	67,309.5
AMERICAN HEALTH & LIFE INS CO	TX	1,505.6
AMERICAN INCOME LIFE INS CO	IN	1,811.7
AMERICAN UNITED LIFE INS CO	IN	12,264.8
AMERITAS LIFE INS CORP	NE	4,928.5

INSURANCE COMPANY NAME	DOM. STATE	TOTAL ASSETS ($MIL)
ASSURITY LIFE INS CO	NE	2,167.6
ATLANTIC COAST LIFE INS CO	SC	69.9
BOSTON MUTUAL LIFE INS CO	MA	945.5
CHEROKEE NATIONAL LIFE INS CO	GA	30.8
COLORADO BANKERS LIFE INS CO	CO	144.4
COLUMBUS LIFE INS CO	OH	2,512.2
COMPBENEFITS INS CO	TX	62.7
CONTINENTAL LIFE INS CO OF BRENTWOOD	TN	149.3
COTTON STATES LIFE INS CO	GA	281.8
EASTERN LIFE & HEALTH INS CO	PA	44.9
EPIC LIFE INSURANCE CO	WI	42.6
FAMILY HERITAGE LIFE INS CO OF AMER	OH	322.3
FIDELITY LIFE ASSN A LEGAL RESERVE	IL	505.8
FIDELITY SECURITY LIFE INS CO	MO	576.6
GENERAL RE LIFE CORP	CT	2,682.0
GOVERNMENT PERSONNEL MUTUAL L I C	TX	783.4
ILLINOIS MUTUAL LIFE INS CO	IL	1,262.3
LINCOLN BENEFIT LIFE CO	NE	2,007.2
LINCOLN HERITAGE LIFE INS CO	IL	629.7
MID-WEST NATIONAL LIFE INS CO OF TN	TX	228.4
MIDLAND NATIONAL LIFE INS CO	IA	25,970.2
MTL INS CO	IL	1,337.3
MUTUAL OF OMAHA INS CO	NE	4,625.4
NATIONAL GUARDIAN LIFE INS CO	WI	1,663.4
NATIONAL WESTERN LIFE INS CO	CO	6,175.2
NATIONWIDE LIFE INS CO OF AMERICA	PA	4,826.2
OHIO NATIONAL LIFE ASR CORP	OH	2,702.3
PENN INS & ANNUITY CO	DE	1,038.9
PENN MUTUAL LIFE INS CO	PA	9,647.6
PHARMACISTS LIFE INS CO	IA	40.4
RELIABLE LIFE INS CO	MO	747.4
SAVINGS BANK LIFE INS CO OF MA	MA	2,093.4
SETTLERS LIFE INS CO	WI	417.4
STANDARD INS CO	OR	12,858.1
STANDARD SECURITY LIFE INS CO OF NY	NY	365.4
STONEBRIDGE LIFE INS CO	VT	2,089.0
SURETY LIFE INS CO	NE	13.2
THRIVENT LIFE INS CO	MN	2,564.9
UNITED INVESTORS LIFE INS CO	MO	2,518.4
UNITED OF OMAHA LIFE INS CO	NE	12,875.0
UNITED WORLD LIFE INS CO	NE	114.6
WORLD CORP INS CO	NE	23.2

Washington

INSURANCE COMPANY NAME	DOM. STATE	TOTAL ASSETS ($MIL)
Rating: A+		
AMERICAN FAMILY LIFE INS CO	WI	3,898.0
COUNTRY LIFE INS CO	IL	7,329.3
PHYSICIANS MUTUAL INS CO	NE	1,445.1
STATE FARM LIFE INS CO	IL	44,978.4
TEACHERS INS & ANNUITY ASN OF AM	NY	194,588.7
Rating: A		
AMERICAN FIDELITY ASR CO	OK	3,343.9
AUTO-OWNERS LIFE INS CO	MI	2,168.0
BERKSHIRE LIFE INS CO OF AMERICA	MA	2,502.2
FEDERATED LIFE INS CO	MN	978.1
FIDELITY INVESTMENTS LIFE INS CO	UT	11,382.8
GUARDIAN LIFE INS CO OF AMERICA	NY	29,202.2
LIFEWISE ASR CO	WA	70.2
MASSACHUSETTS MUTUAL LIFE INS CO	MA	112,014.6
MML BAY STATE LIFE INS CO	CT	4,105.4
SENTRY LIFE INS CO	WI	2,809.8
USAA LIFE INS CO	TX	13,463.6
Rating: A-		
ACACIA LIFE INS CO	DC	1,521.4
AMALGAMATED LIFE INS CO	NY	62.6
AMERICAN REPUBLIC INS CO	IA	472.8
AMICA LIFE INS CO	RI	950.4
ANTHEM LIFE INS CO	IN	288.0
CHARTER NATIONAL LIFE INS CO	IL	133.2
COMPANION LIFE INS CO	SC	124.7
CONTINENTAL AMERICAN INS CO	SC	105.0
COUNTRY INVESTORS LIFE ASR CO	IL	192.1
FIRST INVESTORS LIFE INS CO	NY	949.4
FORT DEARBORN LIFE INS CO	IL	2,870.9
GERBER LIFE INS CO	NY	1,568.7
NATIONAL BENEFIT LIFE INS CO	NY	738.4
NEW YORK LIFE INS & ANNUITY CORP	DE	77,190.7
NEW YORK LIFE INS CO	NY	114,937.8
NIPPON LIFE INS CO OF AMERICA	IA	162.8
NORTHWESTERN MUTUAL LIFE INS CO	WI	155,607.2
PACIFIC GUARDIAN LIFE INS CO LTD	HI	426.8
PACIFIC LIFE & ANNUITY CO	AZ	2,589.4
PACIFIC LIFE INS CO	NE	81,524.3
PHYSICIANS LIFE INS CO	NE	1,249.3
PRIMERICA LIFE INS CO	MA	5,765.7
PRINCIPAL LIFE INS CO	IA	109,923.9
STANDARD LIFE & ACCIDENT INS CO	OK	484.7
USABLE LIFE	AR	298.5
WORLD INS CO	NE	242.3
Rating: B+		
ALLSTATE LIFE INS CO	IL	65,002.0
AMERICAN FAMILY LIFE ASR CO OF COLUM	NE	67,309.5
AMERICAN HEALTH & LIFE INS CO	TX	1,505.6
AMERICAN INCOME LIFE INS CO	IN	1,811.7
AMERICAN UNITED LIFE INS CO	IN	12,264.8
AMERITAS LIFE INS CORP	NE	4,928.5
ASSURITY LIFE INS CO	NE	2,167.6

INSURANCE COMPANY NAME	DOM. STATE	TOTAL ASSETS ($MIL)
BOSTON MUTUAL LIFE INS CO	MA	945.5
COLORADO BANKERS LIFE INS CO	CO	144.4
COLUMBUS LIFE INS CO	OH	2,512.2
COMPBENEFITS INS CO	TX	62.7
EASTERN LIFE & HEALTH INS CO	PA	44.9
FAMILY HERITAGE LIFE INS CO OF AMER	OH	322.3
FARM BUREAU LIFE INS CO	IA	5,605.0
FIDELITY LIFE ASSN A LEGAL RESERVE	IL	505.8
FIDELITY SECURITY LIFE INS CO	MO	576.6
GENERAL RE LIFE CORP	CT	2,682.0
GOVERNMENT PERSONNEL MUTUAL L I C	TX	783.4
ILLINOIS MUTUAL LIFE INS CO	IL	1,262.3
LINCOLN BENEFIT LIFE CO	NE	2,007.2
LINCOLN HERITAGE LIFE INS CO	IL	629.7
MID-WEST NATIONAL LIFE INS CO OF TN	TX	228.4
MIDLAND NATIONAL LIFE INS CO	IA	25,970.2
MTL INS CO	IL	1,337.3
MUTUAL OF OMAHA INS CO	NE	4,625.4
NATIONAL GUARDIAN LIFE INS CO	WI	1,663.4
NATIONAL WESTERN LIFE INS CO	CO	6,175.2
NATIONWIDE LIFE INS CO OF AMERICA	PA	4,826.2
OHIO NATIONAL LIFE ASR CORP	OH	2,702.3
PENN INS & ANNUITY CO	DE	1,038.9
PENN MUTUAL LIFE INS CO	PA	9,647.6
PHARMACISTS LIFE INS CO	IA	40.4
REGENCE LIFE & HEALTH INS CO	OR	80.7
RELIABLE LIFE INS CO	MO	747.4
SAVINGS BANK LIFE INS CO OF MA	MA	2,093.4
SETTLERS LIFE INS CO	WI	417.4
STANDARD INS CO	OR	12,858.1
STANDARD SECURITY LIFE INS CO OF NY	NY	365.4
STONEBRIDGE LIFE INS CO	VT	2,089.0
SURETY LIFE INS CO	NE	13.2
THRIVENT LIFE INS CO	MN	2,564.9
UNITED INVESTORS LIFE INS CO	MO	2,518.4
UNITED OF OMAHA LIFE INS CO	NE	12,875.0
UNITED WORLD LIFE INS CO	NE	114.6

West Virginia

INSURANCE COMPANY NAME	DOM. STATE	TOTAL ASSETS ($MIL)

Rating: A+

INSURANCE COMPANY NAME	DOM. STATE	TOTAL ASSETS ($MIL)
COUNTRY LIFE INS CO	IL	7,329.3
PHYSICIANS MUTUAL INS CO	NE	1,445.1
STATE FARM LIFE INS CO	IL	44,978.4
TEACHERS INS & ANNUITY ASN OF AM	NY	194,588.7

Rating: A

INSURANCE COMPANY NAME	DOM. STATE	TOTAL ASSETS ($MIL)
AMERICAN FIDELITY ASR CO	OK	3,343.9
BERKSHIRE LIFE INS CO OF AMERICA	MA	2,502.2
FEDERATED LIFE INS CO	MN	978.1
FIDELITY INVESTMENTS LIFE INS CO	UT	11,382.8
GUARDIAN LIFE INS CO OF AMERICA	NY	29,202.2
MASSACHUSETTS MUTUAL LIFE INS CO	MA	112,014.6
MML BAY STATE LIFE INS CO	CT	4,105.4
SENTRY LIFE INS CO	WI	2,809.8
USAA LIFE INS CO	TX	13,463.6

Rating: A-

INSURANCE COMPANY NAME	DOM. STATE	TOTAL ASSETS ($MIL)
ACACIA LIFE INS CO	DC	1,521.4
AMALGAMATED LIFE INS CO	NY	62.6
AMERICAN REPUBLIC INS CO	IA	472.8
AMICA LIFE INS CO	RI	950.4
ANTHEM LIFE INS CO	IN	288.0
CHARTER NATIONAL LIFE INS CO	IL	133.2
COMPANION LIFE INS CO	SC	124.7
CONTINENTAL AMERICAN INS CO	SC	105.0
COUNTRY INVESTORS LIFE ASR CO	IL	192.1
FIRST INVESTORS LIFE INS CO	NY	949.4
FORT DEARBORN LIFE INS CO	IL	2,870.9
GERBER LIFE INS CO	NY	1,568.7
NATIONAL BENEFIT LIFE INS CO	NY	738.4
NEW YORK LIFE INS & ANNUITY CORP	DE	77,190.7
NEW YORK LIFE INS CO	NY	114,937.8
NIPPON LIFE INS CO OF AMERICA	IA	162.8
NORTHWESTERN MUTUAL LIFE INS CO	WI	155,607.2
PACIFIC LIFE & ANNUITY CO	AZ	2,589.4
PACIFIC LIFE INS CO	NE	81,524.3
PHYSICIANS LIFE INS CO	NE	1,249.3
PRIMERICA LIFE INS CO	MA	5,765.7
PRINCIPAL LIFE INS CO	IA	109,923.9
STANDARD LIFE & ACCIDENT INS CO	OK	484.7
USABLE LIFE	AR	298.5
WORLD INS CO	NE	242.3

Rating: B+

INSURANCE COMPANY NAME	DOM. STATE	TOTAL ASSETS ($MIL)
ALLSTATE LIFE INS CO	IL	65,002.0
AMERICAN FAMILY LIFE ASR CO OF COLUM	NE	67,309.5
AMERICAN HEALTH & LIFE INS CO	TX	1,505.6
AMERICAN INCOME LIFE INS CO	IN	1,811.7
AMERICAN UNITED LIFE INS CO	IN	12,264.8
AMERITAS LIFE INS CORP	NE	4,928.5
ASSURITY LIFE INS CO	NE	2,167.6
BOSTON MUTUAL LIFE INS CO	MA	945.5
CHEROKEE NATIONAL LIFE INS CO	GA	30.8
COLORADO BANKERS LIFE INS CO	CO	144.4
COLUMBUS LIFE INS CO	OH	2,512.2

INSURANCE COMPANY NAME	DOM. STATE	TOTAL ASSETS ($MIL)
COMPBENEFITS INS CO	TX	62.7
CONTINENTAL LIFE INS CO OF BRENTWOOD	TN	149.3
EASTERN LIFE & HEALTH INS CO	PA	44.9
EPIC LIFE INSURANCE CO	WI	42.6
FAMILY HERITAGE LIFE INS CO OF AMER	OH	322.3
FIDELITY LIFE ASSN A LEGAL RESERVE	IL	505.8
FIDELITY SECURITY LIFE INS CO	MO	576.6
GENERAL RE LIFE CORP	CT	2,682.0
GOVERNMENT PERSONNEL MUTUAL L I C	TX	783.4
ILLINOIS MUTUAL LIFE INS CO	IL	1,262.3
LINCOLN BENEFIT LIFE CO	NE	2,007.2
LINCOLN HERITAGE LIFE INS CO	IL	629.7
MID-WEST NATIONAL LIFE INS CO OF TN	TX	228.4
MIDLAND NATIONAL LIFE INS CO	IA	25,970.2
MTL INS CO	IL	1,337.3
MUTUAL OF OMAHA INS CO	NE	4,625.4
NATIONAL GUARDIAN LIFE INS CO	WI	1,663.4
NATIONAL WESTERN LIFE INS CO	CO	6,175.2
NATIONWIDE LIFE INS CO OF AMERICA	PA	4,826.2
OHIO NATIONAL LIFE ASR CORP	OH	2,702.3
PENN INS & ANNUITY CO	DE	1,038.9
PENN MUTUAL LIFE INS CO	PA	9,647.6
PHARMACISTS LIFE INS CO	IA	40.4
RELIABLE LIFE INS CO	MO	747.4
SAVINGS BANK LIFE INS CO OF MA	MA	2,093.4
SETTLERS LIFE INS CO	WI	417.4
STANDARD INS CO	OR	12,858.1
STANDARD SECURITY LIFE INS CO OF NY	NY	365.4
STONEBRIDGE LIFE INS CO	VT	2,089.0
SURETY LIFE INS CO	NE	13.2
THRIVENT LIFE INS CO	MN	2,564.9
UNITED INVESTORS LIFE INS CO	MO	2,518.4
UNITED OF OMAHA LIFE INS CO	NE	12,875.0
UNITED WORLD LIFE INS CO	NE	114.6
WORLD CORP INS CO	NE	23.2

Wisconsin

INSURANCE COMPANY NAME	DOM. STATE	TOTAL ASSETS ($MIL)

Rating: A+

INSURANCE COMPANY NAME	DOM. STATE	TOTAL ASSETS ($MIL)
AMERICAN FAMILY LIFE INS CO	WI	3,898.0
COUNTRY LIFE INS CO	IL	7,329.3
PHYSICIANS MUTUAL INS CO	NE	1,445.1
STATE FARM LIFE & ACCIDENT ASR CO	IL	1,691.4
TEACHERS INS & ANNUITY ASN OF AM	NY	194,588.7

Rating: A

INSURANCE COMPANY NAME	DOM. STATE	TOTAL ASSETS ($MIL)
AMERICAN FIDELITY ASR CO	OK	3,343.9
AUTO-OWNERS LIFE INS CO	MI	2,168.0
BERKSHIRE LIFE INS CO OF AMERICA	MA	2,502.2
FEDERATED LIFE INS CO	MN	978.1
FIDELITY INVESTMENTS LIFE INS CO	UT	11,382.8
GUARDIAN LIFE INS CO OF AMERICA	NY	29,202.2
MASSACHUSETTS MUTUAL LIFE INS CO	MA	112,014.6
MML BAY STATE LIFE INS CO	CT	4,105.4
SENTRY LIFE INS CO	WI	2,809.8
USAA LIFE INS CO	TX	13,463.6

Rating: A-

INSURANCE COMPANY NAME	DOM. STATE	TOTAL ASSETS ($MIL)
ACACIA LIFE INS CO	DC	1,521.4
AMALGAMATED LIFE INS CO	NY	62.6
AMERICAN REPUBLIC INS CO	IA	472.8
AMICA LIFE INS CO	RI	950.4
ANTHEM LIFE INS CO	IN	288.0
CHARTER NATIONAL LIFE INS CO	IL	133.2
COMPANION LIFE INS CO	SC	124.7
CONTINENTAL AMERICAN INS CO	SC	105.0
COUNTRY INVESTORS LIFE ASR CO	IL	192.1
FIRST INVESTORS LIFE INS CO	NY	949.4
FORT DEARBORN LIFE INS CO	IL	2,870.9
GERBER LIFE INS CO	NY	1,568.7
GRANGE LIFE INS CO	OH	258.2
NATIONAL BENEFIT LIFE INS CO	NY	738.4
NEW YORK LIFE INS & ANNUITY CORP	DE	77,190.7
NEW YORK LIFE INS CO	NY	114,937.8
NIPPON LIFE INS CO OF AMERICA	IA	162.8
NORTHWESTERN MUTUAL LIFE INS CO	WI	155,607.2
PACIFIC LIFE & ANNUITY CO	AZ	2,589.4
PACIFIC LIFE INS CO	NE	81,524.3
PHYSICIANS LIFE INS CO	NE	1,249.3
PRIMERICA LIFE INS CO	MA	5,765.7
PRINCIPAL LIFE INS CO	IA	109,923.9
STANDARD LIFE & ACCIDENT INS CO	OK	484.7
USABLE LIFE	AR	298.5
WORLD INS CO	NE	242.3

Rating: B+

INSURANCE COMPANY NAME	DOM. STATE	TOTAL ASSETS ($MIL)
ALLSTATE LIFE INS CO	IL	65,002.0
AMERICAN FAMILY LIFE ASR CO OF COLUM	NE	67,309.5
AMERICAN HEALTH & LIFE INS CO	TX	1,505.6
AMERICAN INCOME LIFE INS CO	IN	1,811.7
AMERICAN UNITED LIFE INS CO	IN	12,264.8
AMERITAS LIFE INS CORP	NE	4,928.5
ASSURITY LIFE INS CO	NE	2,167.6
BOSTON MUTUAL LIFE INS CO	MA	945.5

INSURANCE COMPANY NAME	DOM. STATE	TOTAL ASSETS ($MIL)
COLORADO BANKERS LIFE INS CO	CO	144.4
COLUMBUS LIFE INS CO	OH	2,512.2
CONTINENTAL LIFE INS CO OF BRENTWOOD	TN	149.3
EPIC LIFE INSURANCE CO	WI	42.6
FAMILY HERITAGE LIFE INS CO OF AMER	OH	322.3
FARM BUREAU LIFE INS CO	IA	5,605.0
FIDELITY LIFE ASSN A LEGAL RESERVE	IL	505.8
FIDELITY SECURITY LIFE INS CO	MO	576.6
GENERAL RE LIFE CORP	CT	2,682.0
GOVERNMENT PERSONNEL MUTUAL L I C	TX	783.4
ILLINOIS MUTUAL LIFE INS CO	IL	1,262.3
LINCOLN BENEFIT LIFE CO	NE	2,007.2
LINCOLN HERITAGE LIFE INS CO	IL	629.7
MID-WEST NATIONAL LIFE INS CO OF TN	TX	228.4
MIDLAND NATIONAL LIFE INS CO	IA	25,970.2
MTL INS CO	IL	1,337.3
MUTUAL OF OMAHA INS CO	NE	4,625.4
NATIONAL GUARDIAN LIFE INS CO	WI	1,663.4
NATIONAL WESTERN LIFE INS CO	CO	6,175.2
NATIONWIDE LIFE INS CO OF AMERICA	PA	4,826.2
OHIO NATIONAL LIFE ASR CORP	OH	2,702.3
PEKIN LIFE INS CO	IL	863.3
PENN INS & ANNUITY CO	DE	1,038.9
PENN MUTUAL LIFE INS CO	PA	9,647.6
PHARMACISTS LIFE INS CO	IA	40.4
RELIABLE LIFE INS CO	MO	747.4
SAVINGS BANK LIFE INS CO OF MA	MA	2,093.4
SETTLERS LIFE INS CO	WI	417.4
STANDARD INS CO	OR	12,858.1
STANDARD SECURITY LIFE INS CO OF NY	NY	365.4
STONEBRIDGE LIFE INS CO	VT	2,089.0
SURETY LIFE INS CO	NE	13.2
THRIVENT LIFE INS CO	MN	2,564.9
UNITED INVESTORS LIFE INS CO	MO	2,518.4
UNITED OF OMAHA LIFE INS CO	NE	12,875.0
UNITED WORLD LIFE INS CO	NE	114.6
WORLD CORP INS CO	NE	23.2

Wyoming

INSURANCE COMPANY NAME	DOM. STATE	TOTAL ASSETS ($MIL)

Rating: A+

INSURANCE COMPANY NAME	DOM. STATE	TOTAL ASSETS ($MIL)
AMERICAN FAMILY LIFE INS CO	WI	3,898.0
COUNTRY LIFE INS CO	IL	7,329.3
PHYSICIANS MUTUAL INS CO	NE	1,445.1
STATE FARM LIFE INS CO	IL	44,978.4
TEACHERS INS & ANNUITY ASN OF AM	NY	194,588.7

Rating: A

INSURANCE COMPANY NAME	DOM. STATE	TOTAL ASSETS ($MIL)
AMERICAN FIDELITY ASR CO	OK	3,343.9
BERKSHIRE LIFE INS CO OF AMERICA	MA	2,502.2
FEDERATED LIFE INS CO	MN	978.1
FIDELITY INVESTMENTS LIFE INS CO	UT	11,382.8
GUARDIAN LIFE INS CO OF AMERICA	NY	29,202.2
LIFEWISE ASR CO	WA	70.2
MASSACHUSETTS MUTUAL LIFE INS CO	MA	112,014.6
MML BAY STATE LIFE INS CO	CT	4,105.4
SENTRY LIFE INS CO	WI	2,809.8
USAA LIFE INS CO	TX	13,463.6

Rating: A-

INSURANCE COMPANY NAME	DOM. STATE	TOTAL ASSETS ($MIL)
ACACIA LIFE INS CO	DC	1,521.4
AMERICAN REPUBLIC INS CO	IA	472.8
AMICA LIFE INS CO	RI	950.4
ANTHEM LIFE INS CO	IN	288.0
CHARTER NATIONAL LIFE INS CO	IL	133.2
COMPANION LIFE INS CO	SC	124.7
CONTINENTAL AMERICAN INS CO	SC	105.0
COUNTRY INVESTORS LIFE ASR CO	IL	192.1
FIRST INVESTORS LIFE INS CO	NY	949.4
FORT DEARBORN LIFE INS CO	IL	2,870.9
GERBER LIFE INS CO	NY	1,568.7
NATIONAL BENEFIT LIFE INS CO	NY	738.4
NEW YORK LIFE INS & ANNUITY CORP	DE	77,190.7
NEW YORK LIFE INS CO	NY	114,937.8
NORTHWESTERN MUTUAL LIFE INS CO	WI	155,607.2
PACIFIC GUARDIAN LIFE INS CO LTD	HI	426.8
PACIFIC LIFE & ANNUITY CO	AZ	2,589.4
PACIFIC LIFE INS CO	NE	81,524.3
PHYSICIANS LIFE INS CO	NE	1,249.3
PRIMERICA LIFE INS CO	MA	5,765.7
PRINCIPAL LIFE INS CO	IA	109,923.9
STANDARD LIFE & ACCIDENT INS CO	OK	484.7
USABLE LIFE	AR	298.5
WORLD INS CO	NE	242.3

Rating: B+

INSURANCE COMPANY NAME	DOM. STATE	TOTAL ASSETS ($MIL)
ALLSTATE LIFE INS CO	IL	65,002.0
AMERICAN FAMILY LIFE ASR CO OF COLUM	NE	67,309.5
AMERICAN HEALTH & LIFE INS CO	TX	1,505.6
AMERICAN INCOME LIFE INS CO	IN	1,811.7
AMERICAN UNITED LIFE INS CO	IN	12,264.8
AMERITAS LIFE INS CORP	NE	4,928.5
ASSURITY LIFE INS CO	NE	2,167.6
BOSTON MUTUAL LIFE INS CO	MA	945.5
COLORADO BANKERS LIFE INS CO	CO	144.4
COLUMBUS LIFE INS CO	OH	2,512.2

INSURANCE COMPANY NAME	DOM. STATE	TOTAL ASSETS ($MIL)
CONTINENTAL LIFE INS CO OF BRENTWOOD	TN	149.3
EASTERN LIFE & HEALTH INS CO	PA	44.9
FAMILY HERITAGE LIFE INS CO OF AMER	OH	322.3
FARM BUREAU LIFE INS CO	IA	5,605.0
FIDELITY SECURITY LIFE INS CO	MO	576.6
GENERAL RE LIFE CORP	CT	2,682.0
GOVERNMENT PERSONNEL MUTUAL L I C	TX	783.4
ILLINOIS MUTUAL LIFE INS CO	IL	1,262.3
LINCOLN BENEFIT LIFE CO	NE	2,007.2
LINCOLN HERITAGE LIFE INS CO	IL	629.7
MID-WEST NATIONAL LIFE INS CO OF TN	TX	228.4
MIDLAND NATIONAL LIFE INS CO	IA	25,970.2
MTL INS CO	IL	1,337.3
MUTUAL OF OMAHA INS CO	NE	4,625.4
NATIONAL GUARDIAN LIFE INS CO	WI	1,663.4
NATIONAL WESTERN LIFE INS CO	CO	6,175.2
NATIONWIDE LIFE INS CO OF AMERICA	PA	4,826.2
OHIO NATIONAL LIFE ASR CORP	OH	2,702.3
PENN INS & ANNUITY CO	DE	1,038.9
PENN MUTUAL LIFE INS CO	PA	9,647.6
PHARMACISTS LIFE INS CO	IA	40.4
REGENCE LIFE & HEALTH INS CO	OR	80.7
RELIABLE LIFE INS CO	MO	747.4
SETTLERS LIFE INS CO	WI	417.4
STANDARD INS CO	OR	12,858.1
STANDARD SECURITY LIFE INS CO OF NY	NY	365.4
STONEBRIDGE LIFE INS CO	VT	2,089.0
SURETY LIFE INS CO	NE	13.2
UNITED INVESTORS LIFE INS CO	MO	2,518.4
UNITED OF OMAHA LIFE INS CO	NE	12,875.0
UNITED WORLD LIFE INS CO	NE	114.6
WORLD CORP INS CO	NE	23.2

Section V

All Companies
Listed by Rating

A list of all rated and unrated

U.S. Life and Annuity Insurers

Companies are ranked by TheStreet.com Financial Strength Rating
and then listed alphabetically within each rating category.

Section V Contents

This section sorts all companies by their TheStreet.com Financial Strength Rating and then lists them alphabetically within each rating category. The purpose of this section is to provide in one place all of those companies receiving a given rating. Companies with the same rating should be viewed as having the same relative risk regardless of their order in this table.

1. Financial Strength Rating   Our rating is measured on a scale from A to F and considers a wide range of factors. Highly rated companies are, in our opinion, less likely to experience financial difficulties than lower rated firms. See *About TheStreet.com Financial Strength Ratings* on page 9 for more information.

2. Insurance Company Name   The legally registered name, which can sometimes differ from the name that the company uses for advertising. An insurer's name can be very similar to that of another, so verify the company's exact name and state of domicile to make sure you are looking at the correct company.

3. Domicile State   The state which has primary regulatory responsibility for the company. It may differ from the location of the company's corporate headquarters. You do not have to be living in the domicile state to purchase insurance from this firm, provided it is licensed to do business in your state.

4. Total Assets   All assets admitted by state insurance regulators in millions of dollars. This includes investments, current business assets and separate accounts.

INSURANCE COMPANY NAME	DOM. STATE	TOTAL ASSETS ($MIL)
Rating: A+		
AMERICAN FAMILY LIFE INS CO	WI	3,898.0
COUNTRY LIFE INS CO	IL	7,329.3
PHYSICIANS MUTUAL INS CO	NE	1,445.1
STATE FARM LIFE & ACCIDENT ASR CO	IL	1,691.4
STATE FARM LIFE INS CO	IL	44,978.4
TEACHERS INS & ANNUITY ASN OF AM	NY	194,588.7
Rating: A		
AMERICAN FIDELITY ASR CO	OK	3,343.9
AUTO-OWNERS LIFE INS CO	MI	2,168.0
BERKSHIRE LIFE INS CO OF AMERICA	MA	2,502.2
FEDERATED LIFE INS CO	MN	978.1
FIDELITY INVESTMENTS LIFE INS CO	UT	11,382.8
GUARDIAN LIFE INS CO OF AMERICA	NY	29,202.2
LIFEWISE ASR CO	WA	70.2
MASSACHUSETTS MUTUAL LIFE INS CO	MA	112,014.6
MML BAY STATE LIFE INS CO	CT	4,105.4
SENTRY LIFE INS CO	WI	2,809.8
SOUTHERN FARM BUREAU LIFE INS CO	MS	10,074.1
TENNESSEE FARMERS LIFE INS CO	TN	1,318.3
UNION NATIONAL LIFE INS CO	LA	459.3
UNITED FARM FAMILY LIFE INS CO	IN	1,712.9
USAA LIFE INS CO	TX	13,463.6
Rating: A-		
ACACIA LIFE INS CO	DC	1,521.4
AMALGAMATED LIFE INS CO	NY	62.6
AMERICAN REPUBLIC INS CO	IA	472.8
AMICA LIFE INS CO	RI	950.4
ANTHEM LIFE INS CO	IN	288.0
BLUE SHIELD OF CALIFORNIA L&H INS CO	CA	364.2
CHARTER NATIONAL LIFE INS CO	IL	133.2
COMPANION LIFE INS CO	SC	124.7
CONTINENTAL AMERICAN INS CO	SC	105.0
COUNTRY INVESTORS LIFE ASR CO	IL	192.1
EMPIRE FIDELITY INVESTMENTS L I C	NY	1,138.6
FARM BUREAU LIFE INS CO OF MICHIGAN	MI	1,761.1
FARM BUREAU LIFE INS CO OF MISSOURI	MO	374.9
FIRST AMERITAS LIFE INS CO OF NY	NY	37.7
FIRST INVESTORS LIFE INS CO	NY	949.4
FIRST UNITED AMERICAN LIFE INS CO	NY	126.0
FORT DEARBORN LIFE INS CO	IL	2,870.9
GERBER LIFE INS CO	NY	1,568.7
GRANGE LIFE INS CO	OH	258.2
GREATER GEORGIA LIFE INS CO	GA	46.3
JOHN HANCOCK LIFE INS CO OF NY	NY	6,461.4
NATIONAL BENEFIT LIFE INS CO	NY	738.4
NEW YORK LIFE INS & ANNUITY CORP	DE	77,190.7
NEW YORK LIFE INS CO	NY	114,937.8
NIPPON LIFE INS CO OF AMERICA	IA	162.8
NORTHWESTERN MUTUAL LIFE INS CO	WI	155,607.2
PACIFIC GUARDIAN LIFE INS CO LTD	HI	426.8
PACIFIC LIFE & ANNUITY CO	AZ	2,589.4

INSURANCE COMPANY NAME	DOM. STATE	TOTAL ASSETS ($MIL)
PACIFIC LIFE INS CO	NE	81,524.3
PHYSICIANS LIFE INS CO	NE	1,249.3
PRIMERICA LIFE INS CO	MA	5,765.7
PRINCIPAL LIFE INS CO	IA	109,923.9
SHELTER LIFE INS CO	MO	933.1
STANDARD LIFE & ACCIDENT INS CO	OK	484.7
USABLE LIFE	AR	298.5
WORLD INS CO	NE	242.3
Rating: B+		
ALFA LIFE INS CORP	AL	1,087.3
ALLSTATE LIFE INS CO	IL	65,002.0
AMERICAN FAMILY LIFE ASR CO OF COLUM	NE	67,309.5
AMERICAN FAMILY LIFE ASR CO OF NY	NY	285.0
AMERICAN HEALTH & LIFE INS CO	TX	1,505.6
AMERICAN INCOME LIFE INS CO	IN	1,811.7
AMERICAN UNITED LIFE INS CO	IN	12,264.8
AMERITAS LIFE INS CORP	NE	4,928.5
ASSURITY LIFE INS CO	NE	2,167.6
ATLANTIC COAST LIFE INS CO	SC	69.9
BLUEBONNET LIFE INS CO	MS	39.2
BOSTON MUTUAL LIFE INS CO	MA	945.5
CHEROKEE NATIONAL LIFE INS CO	GA	30.8
COLORADO BANKERS LIFE INS CO	CO	144.4
COLUMBUS LIFE INS CO	OH	2,512.2
COMPBENEFITS INS CO	TX	62.7
CONTINENTAL LIFE INS CO OF BRENTWOOD	TN	149.3
COTTON STATES LIFE INS CO	GA	281.8
EASTERN LIFE & HEALTH INS CO	PA	44.9
EPIC LIFE INSURANCE CO	WI	42.6
FAMILY HERITAGE LIFE INS CO OF AMER	OH	322.3
FARM BUREAU LIFE INS CO	IA	5,605.0
FIDELITY LIFE ASSN A LEGAL RESERVE	IL	505.8
FIDELITY SECURITY LIFE INS CO	MO	576.6
FLORIDA COMBINED LIFE INS CO INC	FL	31.8
FORT DEARBORN LIFE INS CO OF NY	NY	67.2
FRANDISCO LIFE INS CO	GA	37.3
GENERAL RE LIFE CORP	CT	2,682.0
GOVERNMENT PERSONNEL MUTUAL L I C	TX	783.4
ILLINOIS MUTUAL LIFE INS CO	IL	1,262.3
LIFE INS CO OF BOSTON & NEW YORK	NY	72.0
LINCOLN BENEFIT LIFE CO	NE	2,007.2
LINCOLN HERITAGE LIFE INS CO	IL	629.7
MID-WEST NATIONAL LIFE INS CO OF TN	TX	228.4
MIDLAND NATIONAL LIFE INS CO	IA	25,970.2
MTL INS CO	IL	1,337.3
MUTUAL OF OMAHA INS CO	NE	4,625.4
NATIONAL GUARDIAN LIFE INS CO	WI	1,663.4
NATIONAL WESTERN LIFE INS CO	CO	6,175.2
NATIONWIDE LIFE INS CO OF AMERICA	PA	4,826.2
OHIO NATIONAL LIFE ASR CORP	OH	2,702.3
PEKIN LIFE INS CO	IL	863.3
PENN INS & ANNUITY CO	DE	1,038.9
PENN MUTUAL LIFE INS CO	PA	9,647.6

INSURANCE COMPANY NAME	DOM. STATE	TOTAL ASSETS ($MIL)	INSURANCE COMPANY NAME	DOM. STATE	TOTAL ASSETS ($MIL)
Rating: B+ (Continued)			CINCINNATI LIFE INS CO	OH	2,476.6
			CM LIFE INS CO	CT	7,462.3
PHARMACISTS LIFE INS CO	IA	40.4	COLUMBIAN MUTUAL LIFE INS CO	NY	847.6
REGENCE LIFE & HEALTH INS CO	OR	80.7	COMBINED LIFE INS CO OF NEW YORK	NY	391.5
RELIABLE LIFE INS CO	MO	747.4	COMPANION LIFE INS CO	NY	701.5
SAVINGS BANK LIFE INS CO OF MA	MA	2,093.4	CONSUMERS LIFE INS CO	OH	33.2
SETTLERS LIFE INS CO	WI	417.4	CSI LIFE INS CO	NE	19.8
SOUTHERN NATL LIFE INS CO INC	LA	16.2	DELAWARE AMERICAN LIFE INS CO	DE	88.9
STANDARD INS CO	OR	12,858.1	EMPLOYEES LIFE CO MUTUAL	IL	297.5
STANDARD SECURITY LIFE INS CO OF NY	NY	365.4	EMPLOYEES LIFE INS CO	TX	16.0
STONEBRIDGE LIFE INS CO	VT	2,089.0	ERIE FAMILY LIFE INS CO	PA	1,540.7
SURETY LIFE INS CO	NE	13.2	FARM FAMILY LIFE INS CO	NY	1,020.7
THRIVENT LIFE INS CO	MN	2,564.9	FIRST ASR LIFE OF AMERICA	LA	29.2
UNITED INVESTORS LIFE INS CO	MO	2,518.4	FIRST BERKSHIRE HATHAWAY LIFE INS CO	NY	12.4
UNITED OF OMAHA LIFE INS CO	NE	12,875.0	FIRST CENTRAL NATL LIC OF NEW YORK	NY	52.9
UNITED WORLD LIFE INS CO	NE	114.6	FIRST PENN-PACIFIC LIFE INS CO	IN	1,877.8
USAA LIFE INS CO OF NEW YORK	NY	401.5	FIRST RELIANCE STANDARD LIFE INS CO	NY	136.4
WORLD CORP INS CO	NE	23.2	FIRST SECURITY BENEFIT LIFE & ANN	NY	146.6
Rating: B			GARDEN STATE LIFE INS CO	TX	90.4
AAA LIFE INS CO	MI	387.2	GENWORTH LIFE & ANNUITY INS CO	VA	24,891.2
ADVANCE INS CO OF KS	KS	38.6	GLOBE LIFE & ACCIDENT INS CO	NE	2,777.5
AETNA HEALTH & LIFE INS CO	CT	1,654.7	GOLDEN RULE INS CO	IN	665.9
AETNA LIFE INS CO	CT	21,125.8	GREAT WEST LIFE ASR CO	MI	138.0
ALLIANCE HEALTH & LIFE INS CO	MI	37.2	GUARDIAN INS & ANNUITY CO INC	DE	7,143.6
ALLSTATE ASR CO	IL	11.2	HARTFORD INTL LIFE REASR CORP	CT	1,120.7
ALLSTATE LIFE INS CO OF NEW YORK	NY	7,759.9	HCC LIFE INS CO	IN	592.2
ALTA HEALTH & LIFE INS CO	IN	31.6	HEALTH NET LIFE INS CO	CA	653.2
AMERICAN BANKERS LIFE ASR CO OF FL	FL	654.2	HEALTHY ALLIANCE LIFE INS CO	MO	666.9
AMERICAN COMMUNITY MUT INS CO	MI	139.7	HM LIFE INS CO OF NEW YORK	NY	40.4
AMERICAN EQUITY INVESTMENT LIFE NY	NY	117.8	HORACE MANN LIFE INS CO	IL	4,561.7
AMERICAN FARM LIFE INS CO	TX	2.1	HOUSEHOLD LIFE INS CO	MI	813.9
AMERICAN HERITAGE LIFE INS CO	FL	1,317.5	IDEALIFE INS CO	CT	20.5
AMERICAN MATURITY LIFE INS CO	CT	57.0	INS CO OF SCOTT AND WHITE	TX	3.0
AMERICAN MEDICAL SECURITY LIFE INS	WI	122.7	INTRAMERICA LIFE INS CO	NY	27.2
AMERICAN MODERN LIFE INS CO	OH	62.6	JACKSON NATIONAL LIFE INS CO	MI	66,886.5
AMERICAN NATIONAL INS CO	TX	13,984.5	JACKSON NATIONAL LIFE INS CO OF NY	NY	2,554.6
AMERICAN PUBLIC LIFE INS CO	OK	77.0	JOHN HANCOCK LIFE & HEALTH INS CO	MA	2,769.4
AMERICAN REPUBLIC CORP INS CO	NE	10.4	JOHN HANCOCK LIFE INS CO (USA)	MI	102,138.5
AMERICAN-AMICABLE LIFE INS CO OF TX	TX	354.6	JOHN HANCOCK VARIABLE LIFE INS CO	MA	12,033.7
AUTOMOBILE CLUB OF SOUTHERN CA INS	CA	437.5	KANSAS CITY LIFE INS CO	MO	2,950.1
AXA CORPORATE SOLUTIONS LIFE REINS	DE	1,649.4	KENTUCKY HOME LIFE INS CO	KY	5.1
BALBOA LIFE INS CO	CA	44.3	LEADERS LIFE INS CO	OK	5.4
BALBOA LIFE INS CO OF NY	NY	18.1	LIBERTY NATIONAL LIFE INS CO	NE	5,116.8
BALTIMORE LIFE INS CO	MD	836.1	LIFE INS CO OF AL	AL	84.7
BANKERS FIDELITY LIFE INS CO	GA	108.7	LIFE INS CO OF THE SOUTHWEST	TX	6,751.8
BCS LIFE INS CO	IL	178.5	LONDON LIFE INS CO	MI	93.3
BERKLEY LIFE & HEALTH INS CO	IA	27.2	LONDON LIFE REINSURANCE CO	PA	737.6
BEST MERIDIAN INS CO	FL	168.9	MERIT LIFE INS CO	IN	647.4
BLUE CROSS BLUE SHIELD OF KANSAS INC	KS	1,010.3	METLIFE INS CO OF CT (LIFE DEPT)	CT	65,347.5
BROKERS NATIONAL LIFE ASR CO	AR	27.8	METROPOLITAN TOWER LIFE INS CO	DE	5,171.2
CAREAMERICA LIFE INS CO	CA	28.1	MIDWESTERN UNITED LIFE INS CO	IN	243.4
CARIBBEAN AMERICAN LIFE ASR CO	PR	63.1	MINNESOTA LIFE INS CO	MN	19,313.5
CELTIC INS CO	IL	63.8	MISSOURI VALLEY LIFE AND HLTH INS CO	MO	11.5
			ML LIFE INS CO OF NEW YORK	NY	785.2

INSURANCE COMPANY NAME	DOM. STATE	TOTAL ASSETS ($MIL)
Rating: B (Continued)		
MODERN LIFE INS CO OF ARIZONA	AZ	2.6
MOTORISTS LIFE INS CO	OH	340.5
MUTUAL OF AMERICA LIFE INS CO	NY	10,756.0
NATIONAL FARM LIFE INS CO	TX	260.4
NATIONAL INCOME LIFE INS CO	NY	44.9
NATIONAL LIFE INS CO	VT	7,951.0
NATIONAL SECURITY LIFE & ANNUITY CO	NY	86.2
NATIONAL TEACHERS ASSOCIATES L I C	TX	240.7
NATIONWIDE LIFE & ANNUITY CO AMERICA	DE	502.6
NATIONWIDE LIFE & ANNUITY INS CO	OH	4,342.6
NATIONWIDE LIFE INS CO	OH	74,462.2
NEW ENGLAND LIFE INS CO	MA	8,624.0
NORTH AMERICAN CO FOR LIFE & H INS	IA	8,961.9
NYLIFE INS CO OF ARIZONA	AZ	188.0
OCCIDENTAL LIFE INS CO OF NC	TX	253.9
OHIO NATIONAL LIFE INS CO	OH	12,098.1
OLD AMERICAN INS CO	MO	235.9
OLD REPUBLIC LIFE INS CO	IL	148.8
OPTIMUM RE INS CO	TX	72.6
OZARK NATIONAL LIFE INS CO	MO	626.5
PAN AMERICAN ASR CO	LA	23.2
PAN AMERICAN LIFE INS CO OF PR	PR	9.2
PAN-AMERICAN LIFE INS CO	LA	1,519.6
PARK AVENUE LIFE INS CO	DE	418.8
PARKER CENTENNIAL ASR CO	WI	65.7
PERICO LIFE INS CO	DE	65.5
PHPMM INS CO	MI	10.0
PIONEER MUTUAL LIFE INS CO	ND	462.6
PLATEAU INS CO	TN	19.0
PRENEED REINS CO OF AMERICA	AZ	11.4
PRIORITY HEALTH INS CO	MI	25.5
RELIASTAR LIFE INS CO	MN	20,409.8
RESERVE NATIONAL INS CO	OK	106.2
RIVERSOURCE LIFE INS CO	MN	67,256.2
SCOTT LIFE INS CO	AZ	99.5
SEARS LIFE INS CO	TX	75.0
SECURIAN LIFE INS CO	MN	144.3
SECURITY MUTUAL LIFE INS CO OF NY	NY	2,229.7
SENTRY LIFE INS CO OF NEW YORK	NY	50.3
SIERRA HEALTH AND LIFE INS CO INC	CA	127.5
SOUTHERN PIONEER LIFE INS CO	AR	25.2
STARMOUNT LIFE INS CO	LA	35.2
STATE LIFE INS CO	IN	2,921.8
STATE LIFE INS FUND	WI	87.8
SUNSET LIFE INS CO OF AMERICA	MO	403.4
SYMETRA LIFE INS CO	WA	19,398.2
SYMETRA NATIONAL LIFE INS CO	WA	17.4
TEXAS LIFE INS CO	TX	709.0
TIAA-CREF LIFE INS CO	NY	3,031.9
TRANS WORLD ASR CO	CA	336.0
TRUSTMARK INS CO	IL	1,147.8
TRUSTMARK LIFE INS CO	IL	362.0
UNICARE LIFE & HEALTH INS CO	IN	1,672.9
UNIMERICA INS CO	WI	246.9
UNIMERICA LIFE INS CO OF NY	NY	26.2
UNION SECURITY LIFE INS CO OF NY	NY	168.5
UNITED AMERICAN INS CO	NE	1,504.7
UNITED HEALTHCARE INS CO OF IL	IL	155.4
UNITED HERITAGE LIFE INS CO	ID	422.8
UNITED HOME LIFE INS CO	IN	60.6
UNITED LIFE INS CO	IA	1,359.1
UNITED SECURITY ASR CO OF PA	PA	66.8
UNITED TRUST INS CO	AL	5.4
VARIABLE ANNUITY LIFE INS CO	TX	52,157.7
WEA INS CORP	WI	546.6
WESTERN & SOUTHERN LIFE INS CO	OH	7,416.9
WESTERN RESERVE LIFE ASR CO OF OHIO	OH	7,262.7
Rating: B-		
AMERICAN EQUITY INVEST LIFE INS CO	IA	13,999.3
AMERICAN FIDELITY LIFE INS CO	FL	463.5
AMERICAN GENERAL LIFE & ACC INS CO	TN	9,139.2
AMERICAN INVESTORS LIFE INS CO	KS	15,459.9
AMERICAN MEMORIAL LIFE INS CO	SD	1,968.5
AMERICAN NATIONAL LIFE INS CO OF TX	TX	130.9
ANNUITY INVESTORS LIFE INS CO	OH	1,801.4
AUTO CLUB LIFE INS CO	MI	429.0
AXA EQUITABLE LIFE & ANNUITY CO	CO	492.4
BERKSHIRE HATHAWAY LIFE INS CO OF NE	NE	3,595.3
CAMBRIDGE LIFE INS CO	MO	88.7
CANADA LIFE ASSURANCE CO-US BRANCH	MI	4,230.5
CANADA LIFE INS CO OF AMERICA	MI	1,826.7
CENTRAL STATES H & L CO OF OMAHA	NE	318.9
CENTURION LIFE INS CO	IA	1,699.1
CHRISTIAN FIDELITY LIFE INS CO	TX	84.5
CIGNA LIFE INS CO OF NEW YORK	NY	398.2
CITIZENS ACCIDENT & HEALTH INS CO	AZ	3.0
COLONIAL AMERICAN LIFE INS CO	PA	4.9
COMBINED INS CO OF AMERICA	IL	2,421.5
DIRECT GENERAL LIFE INS CO	SC	39.2
EDUCATORS MUTUAL INS ASN	UT	64.3
EQUITABLE LIFE & CASUALTY INS CO	UT	215.2
EQUITRUST LIFE INS CO	IA	7,726.0
FARMERS NEW WORLD LIFE INS CO	WA	6,446.3
FIRST COMMAND LIFE INS CO	TX	19.9
FIRST GREAT-WEST LIFE & ANNUITY INS	NY	698.4
FIVE STAR LIFE INS CO	LA	172.3
GENERAL FIDELITY LIFE INS CO	SC	206.1
GERMANIA LIFE INS CO	TX	44.1
GREAT AMERICAN LIFE INS CO	OH	9,644.4
GREAT WESTERN INS CO	UT	416.0
GREAT-WEST LIFE & ANNUITY INS CO	CO	33,902.1
GUARANTY INCOME LIFE INS CO	LA	423.0
HARTFORD LIFE & ACCIDENT INS CO	CT	13,955.9
HARTFORD LIFE & ANNUITY INS CO	CT	61,552.0
HM LIFE INS CO	PA	358.4

INSURANCE COMPANY NAME	DOM. STATE	TOTAL ASSETS ($MIL)	INSURANCE COMPANY NAME	DOM. STATE	TOTAL ASSETS ($MIL)
			UNION CENTRAL LIFE INS CO	OH	6,180.0
			UNITED HEALTHCARE INS CO OF OH	OH	182.1

Rating: B- (Continued)

INSURANCE COMPANY NAME	DOM. STATE	TOTAL ASSETS ($MIL)
HUMANA INS CO OF KENTUCKY	KY	34.2
HUMANADENTAL INS CO	WI	101.4
INDEPENDENCE LIFE & ANNUITY CO	RI	128.3
JAMESTOWN LIFE INS CO	VA	147.6
JOHN ALDEN LIFE INS CO	WI	481.1
JOHN HANCOCK LIFE INS CO	MA	61,635.9
LAFAYETTE LIFE INS CO	IN	2,043.8
LIBERTY LIFE ASR CO OF BOSTON	MA	11,641.8
LIFE INS CO OF NORTH AMERICA	PA	5,275.1
LIFESECURE INS CO	MI	57.5
LIFESHIELD NATIONAL INS CO	OK	66.3
LINCOLN LIFE & ANNUITY CO OF NY	NY	8,426.1
LINCOLN NATIONAL LIFE INS CO	IN	117,179.0
LOYAL AMERICAN LIFE INS CO	OH	484.3
M LIFE INS CO	CO	169.1
MEDAMERICA INS CO	PA	468.2
MEDICAL BENEFITS MUTUAL LIFE INS CO	OH	20.7
MEGA LIFE & HEALTH INS CO	OK	702.0
MERRILL LYNCH LIFE INS CO	AR	9,776.1
METLIFE INVESTORS INS CO	MO	9,143.0
METROPOLITAN LIFE INS CO	NY	278,164.2
MIDWEST SECURITY LIFE INS CO	WI	48.9
MII LIFE INC	MN	148.7
MOLINA HEALTHCARE INS CO	OH	9.1
NATIONAL FARMERS UNION LIFE INS CO	TX	257.9
NATIONAL INTEGRITY LIFE INS CO	NY	4,163.6
NORTHWESTERN LONG TERM CARE INS CO	WI	413.1
OHIO MOTORISTS LIFE INSURANCE CO	OH	8.6
OLD UNITED LIFE INS CO	AZ	70.5
OM FINANCIAL LIFE INS CO OF NEW YORK	NY	460.8
OXFORD LIFE INS CO	AZ	491.0
PACIFICARE LIFE & HEALTH INS CO	IN	775.6
PEMCO LIFE INS CO	WA	7.2
PERFORMANCE LIFE OF AMERICA	LA	28.8
PHOENIX LIFE & ANNUITY CO	CT	57.5
PIONEER AMERICAN INS CO	TX	48.5
PIONEER SECURITY LIFE INS CO	TX	95.7
PROTECTIVE LIFE & ANNUITY INS CO	AL	790.6
PROTECTIVE LIFE INS CO	TN	24,965.9
PROVIDENT LIFE & CAS INS CO	TN	709.6
RELIANCE STANDARD LIFE INS CO	IL	3,584.2
RIVERSOURCE LIFE INS CO OF NY	NY	4,196.6
ROYAL STATE NATIONAL INS CO LTD	HI	47.5
SAFEHEALTH LIFE INS CO	CA	30.5
SECURITY LIFE OF DENVER INS CO	CO	22,467.3
SENIOR LIFE INS CO	GA	28.3
STANDARD LIFE INS CO OF NY	NY	181.5
SWISS RE LIFE & HEALTH AMER INC	CT	12,589.8
TIME INS CO	WI	658.7
TRANSAMERICA FINANCIAL LIFE INS CO	NY	19,205.0
TRANSAMERICA LIFE INS CO	IA	99,285.7
UNIFIED LIFE INS CO	TX	133.8

INSURANCE COMPANY NAME	DOM. STATE	TOTAL ASSETS ($MIL)
UNION CENTRAL LIFE INS CO	OH	6,180.0
UNITED HEALTHCARE INS CO OF OH	OH	182.1
UNITED INS CO OF AMERICA	IL	2,036.1
UNITED TEACHER ASSOCIATES INS CO	TX	512.0
UNITY FINANCIAL LIFE INS CO	PA	75.4
UNIVERSAL UNDERWRITERS LIFE INS CO	KS	253.7
USA LIFE ONE INS CO OF INDIANA	IN	36.2
WESTERN MUTUAL INS CO	UT	11.6
WESTERN NATIONAL LIFE INS CO	TX	44,187.0
WESTERN-SOUTHERN LIFE ASR CO	OH	10,339.3
WINDSOR LIFE INS CO	TX	2.8
ZALE LIFE INS CO	AZ	10.7

Rating: C+

INSURANCE COMPANY NAME	DOM. STATE	TOTAL ASSETS ($MIL)
AIG LIFE INS CO	DE	9,295.5
AIG SUNAMERICA LIFE ASR CO	AZ	22,319.4
ALLIANZ LIFE INS CO OF NORTH AMERICA	MN	67,509.3
AMERICAN CONTINENTAL INS CO	TN	20.1
AMERICAN GENERAL LIFE INS CO	TX	38,459.0
AMERICAN HOME LIFE INS CO	KS	166.4
AMERICAN INTERNATL LIFE ASR CO OF NY	NY	6,514.9
AMERICO FINANCIAL LIFE & ANNUITY INS	TX	3,389.3
AURORA NATIONAL LIFE ASR CO	CA	3,120.2
AVIVA LIFE & ANNUITY CO	IA	25,060.9
BENEFICIAL LIFE INS CO	UT	3,445.5
CENTRE LIFE INS CO	MA	2,012.1
CHESAPEAKE LIFE INS CO	OK	78.8
CHURCH LIFE INS CORP	NY	203.7
COLONIAL LIFE & ACCIDENT INS CO	SC	2,055.6
CONNECTICUT GENERAL LIFE INS CO	CT	18,317.9
CUNA MUTUAL INS SOCIETY	IA	10,960.4
DESERET MUTUAL INS CO	UT	45.6
EDUCATORS HEALTH PLANS LIFE ACCIDENT	UT	6.2
EMPHESYS INS CO	TX	6.5
FAMILY BENEFIT LIFE INS CO	MO	57.8
FAMILY LIFE INS CO	TX	122.9
FIRST HEALTH LIFE & HEALTH INS CO	TX	726.6
FIRST METLIFE INVESTORS INS CO	NY	2,056.4
FIRST SUNAMERICA LIFE INS CO	NY	7,716.2
FIRST SYMETRA NATL LIFE INS CO OF NY	NY	370.1
FIRST UNUM LIFE INS CO	NY	1,946.2
FORETHOUGHT LIFE INS CO	IN	3,988.5
FUNERAL DIRECTORS LIFE INS CO	TX	574.9
GENERAL AMERICAN LIFE INS CO	MO	11,331.9
GENWORTH LIFE INS CO	DE	33,446.7
GREAT SOUTHERN LIFE INS CO	TX	259.5
GUARANTEE TRUST LIFE INS CO	IL	220.5
HANNOVER LIFE REASSUR CO OF AMERICA	FL	3,405.6
HARLEYSVILLE LIFE INS CO	PA	348.8
HOMESTEADERS LIFE CO	IA	1,626.7
I B A HEALTH & LIFE ASR CO	MI	19.0
ING LIFE INS & ANNUITY CO	CT	54,644.8
INTEGRITY LIFE INS CO	OH	4,942.7
J M I C LIFE INS CO	FL	90.5

INSURANCE COMPANY NAME	DOM. STATE	TOTAL ASSETS ($MIL)	INSURANCE COMPANY NAME	DOM. STATE	TOTAL ASSETS ($MIL)
Rating: C+ (Continued)			ALLIANZ LIFE INS CO OF NY	NY	921.2
KENTUCKY FUNERAL DIRECTORS LIFE INS	KY	12.1	AMERICAN FARMERS & RANCHERS LIFE INS	OK	18.3
LANDCAR LIFE INS CO	UT	33.3	AMERICAN FEDERATED LIFE INS CO	MS	17.4
LIFE INS CO OF LOUISIANA	LA	7.0	AMERICAN GENERAL ASSURANCE CO	IL	189.7
LINCOLN MUTUAL LIFE & CAS INS CO	ND	31.9	AMERICAN LIFE & ACC INS CO OF KY	KY	198.4
MADISON NATIONAL LIFE INS CO INC	WI	800.2	AMERICAN MEDICAL & LIFE INS CO	NY	27.8
MANHATTAN LIFE INS CO	NY	350.6	AMERICAN PHOENIX LIFE & REASSUR CO	CT	25.7
MARQUETTE INDEMNITY & LIFE INS CO	AZ	9.7	AMERICAN PROGRESSIVE L&H I C OF NY	NY	361.6
MEMBERS LIFE INS CO	IA	46.1	AMERICAN SAVINGS LIFE INS CO	AZ	23.1
METLIFE INVESTORS USA INS CO	DE	27,296.1	ASSOCIATED MUTUAL HOSP SVC OF MI	MI	12.9
MONUMENTAL LIFE INS CO	IA	32,958.8	ASSUMPTION MUTUAL LIFE INS CO	MA	10.5
MONY LIFE INS CO OF AMERICA	AZ	3,952.0	AVIVA LIFE & ANNUITY CO OF NY	NY	1,432.1
MOUNTAIN LIFE INS CO	TN	8.9	BANKERS LIFE OF LOUISIANA	LA	13.3
MUNICH AMERICAN REASSURANCE CO	GA	5,613.3	BEST LIFE & HEALTH INS CO	TX	15.7
NATIONAL LIFE INS CO	PR	145.6	BROOKE LIFE INS CO	MI	3,925.2
NATIONAL SAFETY LIFE INS CO	PA	3.1	CENSTAT LIFE ASR CO	AZ	--
OLD SPARTAN LIFE INS CO INC	SC	27.4	CENTRAL AMERICAN LIFE INS CO	LA	17.7
PACIFIC BEACON LIFE REASSUR INC	HI	290.6	CENTRAL RESERVE LIFE INS CO	OH	25.4
PACIFIC CENTURY LIFE INS CORP	AZ	335.6	CENTRAL SECURITY LIFE INS CO	TX	81.2
PAUL REVERE LIFE INS CO	MA	4,714.3	CIGNA WORLDWIDE INS CO	DE	52.6
PHOENIX LIFE INS CO	NY	14,986.3	CITIZENS FIDELITY INS CO	AR	51.5
PHYSICIANS BENEFITS TRUST LIFE INS	IL	19.1	COLUMBIA CAPITAL LIFE REINS CO	DC	139.3
PROVIDENT LIFE & ACCIDENT INS CO	TN	7,799.2	COMMERCIAL TRAVELERS MUTUAL INS CO	NY	33.7
PRUCO LIFE INS CO	AZ	21,663.3	COMMONWEALTH DEALERS LIFE INS CO	VA	13.0
PRUCO LIFE INS CO OF NEW JERSEY	NJ	3,630.3	CONGRESS LIFE INS CO	AZ	58.8
PRUDENTIAL ANNUITIES LIFE ASR CORP	CT	34,351.4	CONSTITUTION LIFE INS CO	TX	87.2
PRUDENTIAL INS CO OF AMERICA	NJ	227,934.5	CONTINENTAL ASSURANCE CO	IL	3,210.9
PRUDENTIAL RETIREMENT INS & ANNUITY	CT	50,465.7	CONTINENTAL GENERAL INS CO	OH	222.8
PURITAN LIFE INS CO	TX	3.0	CROWN LIFE INS CO US BR	MI	336.3
REASSURE AMERICA LIFE INS CO	IN	16,481.2	DALLAS GENERAL LIFE INS CO	TX	9.8
REINSURANCE CO OF MO INC	MO	1,128.9	DIRECT LIFE INS CO	GA	9.6
RELIASTAR LIFE INS CO OF NEW YORK	NY	3,182.8	EMC NATIONAL LIFE CO	IA	692.3
RGA REINSURANCE CO	MO	13,085.6	ENTERPRISE LIFE INS CO	TX	20.7
SBLI USA MUT LIFE INS CO INC	NY	1,467.6	FAMILY LIBERTY LIFE INS CO	TX	27.1
STANDARD LIFE & CAS INS CO	UT	22.4	FEDERAL LIFE INS CO (MUTUAL)	IL	217.5
SUN LIFE & HEALTH INS CO	CT	90.5	FINANCIAL ASSURANCE LIFE INS CO	TX	9.5
SUN LIFE ASR CO OF CANADA (US)	DE	39,760.6	FIRST ALLMERICA FINANCIAL LIFE INS	MA	1,448.0
TEXAS DIRECTORS LIFE INS CO	TX	9.5	FIRST GUARANTY INS CO	AR	47.0
TRIPLE S VIDA INC	PR	340.7	FIRST REHABILITATION LIFE INS AMER	NY	94.9
UBS LIFE INS CO USA	CA	41.9	FRINGE BENEFIT LIFE INS CO	TX	37.3
ULLICO LIFE INS CO	TX	15.2	GENERALI USA LIFE REASSURANCE CO	MO	865.1
UNION BANKERS INS CO	TX	107.4	GENWORTH LIFE INS CO OF NEW YORK	NY	6,936.4
UNION LABOR LIFE INS CO	MD	4,145.0	GREAT CENTRAL LIFE INS CO	LA	17.5
UNION SECURITY INS CO	IA	5,293.4	HEARTLAND NATIONAL LIFE INS CO	IN	5.6
UNITED HEALTHCARE INS CO	CT	10,972.7	HOUSEHOLD LIFE INS CO OF DE	DE	548.7
UNUM LIFE INS CO OF AMERICA	ME	16,917.0	HUMANA INS CO	WI	4,313.0
USIC LIFE INS CO	PR	3.4	HUMANA INS CO OF PUERTO RICO INC	PR	46.1
VANTISLIFE INS CO	CT	748.5	IA AMERICAN LIFE INS CO	GA	30.6
VERSANT LIFE INS CO	MS	6.3	ING USA ANNUITY & LIFE INS CO	IA	60,901.1
Rating: C			INVESTORS CONSOLIDATED INS CO INC	NH	15.8
			INVESTORS HERITAGE LIFE INS CO	KY	337.1
ACE LIFE INS CO	CT	33.3	JEFF DAVIS MORTUARY BENEFIT ASSOC	LA	3.4
ADMIRAL LIFE INS CO OF AMERICA	AZ	14.7	KANAWHA INS CO	SC	823.1
			KEMPER INVESTORS LIFE INS CO	IL	13,503.9

INSURANCE COMPANY NAME	DOM. STATE	TOTAL ASSETS ($MIL)	INSURANCE COMPANY NAME	DOM. STATE	TOTAL ASSETS ($MIL)
			WEST COAST LIFE INS CO	NE	3,389.4
			WESTERN AMERICAN LIFE INS CO	TX	32.7
			WESTPORT LIFE INS CO	AZ	14.5
			WICHITA NATIONAL LIFE INS CO	OK	18.8

Rating: C (Continued)

INSURANCE COMPANY NAME	DOM. STATE	TOTAL ASSETS ($MIL)
EWER LIFE INS CO	MO	27.6
IBERTY LIFE INS CO	SC	3,684.7
IFE ASSURANCE CO INC	OK	7.2
IFE OF THE SOUTH INS CO	GA	63.5
IFECARE ASSURANCE CO	AZ	846.2
MAGNA INS CO	MS	42.2
MANHATTAN NATIONAL LIFE INS CO	IL	212.9
MEDAMERICA INS CO OF NEW YORK	NY	289.2
MEDICO INS CO	NE	115.7
MELLON LIFE INS CO	DE	26.2
MMA INS CO	IN	27.1
MONY LIFE INS CO	NY	9,116.7
MUTUAL SAVINGS LIFE INS CO	AL	429.8
NATIONAL FAMILY CARE LIFE INS CO	TX	14.6
NATIONAL SECURITY INS CO	AL	41.8
NEW ERA LIFE INS CO	TX	300.6
NEW SOUTH LIFE INS CO	MS	6.2
NORTH AMERICAN INS CO	WI	16.2
OHIO STATE LIFE INS CO	TX	9.9
OLD SURETY LIFE INS CO	OK	19.2
OM FINANCIAL LIFE INS CO	MD	17,140.4
PAUL REVERE VARIABLE ANNUITY INS CO	MA	113.5
PHILADELPHIA AMERICAN LIFE INS CO	TX	173.7
PHILADELPHIA-UNITED LIFE INS CO	PA	43.9
PHL VARIABLE INS CO	CT	4,150.2
POPULAR LIFE RE	PR	55.7
PRESIDENTIAL LIFE INS CO	TX	4.4
PROFESSIONAL INS CO	TX	103.4
PROTECTIVE LIFE INS CO OF NY	NY	779.2
RESOURCE LIFE INS CO	IL	64.7
SAGICOR LIFE INS CO	TX	542.6
SECURITY BENEFIT LIFE INS CO	KS	8,734.3
SECURITY LIFE INS CO OF AMERICA	MN	82.9
SECURITY PLAN LIFE INS CO	LA	262.9
SERVCO LIFE INS CO	TX	29.7
SERVICE LIFE & CAS INS CO	TX	134.7
SHERIDAN LIFE INS CO	OK	1.9
SOUTHERN FINANCIAL LIFE INS CO	KY	4.6
SOUTHLAND NATIONAL INS CORP	AL	158.4
STATE MUTUAL INS CO	GA	384.0
SUN LIFE ASR CO OF CANADA	MI	15,401.0
SUN LIFE INS & ANNUITY CO OF NY	NY	2,472.8
SUNAMERICA LIFE INS CO	AZ	21,173.1
T J M LIFE INS CO	TX	12.1
TOWER LIFE INS CO	TX	75.5
TRANS CITY LIFE INS CO	AZ	19.9
TRIANGLE LIFE INS CO	NC	6.0
U S HEALTH & LIFE INS CO INC	MI	30.5
UNITED STATES LIFE INS CO IN NYC	NY	5,259.4
UNITY MUTUAL LIFE INS CO	NY	263.7
UNIVERSAL LIFE INS CO	PR	132.4
US FINANCIAL LIFE INS CO	OH	564.1

Rating: C-

INSURANCE COMPANY NAME	DOM. STATE	TOTAL ASSETS ($MIL)
ABILITY INS CO	NE	515.6
AMALGAMATED LIFE & HEALTH INS CO	IL	7.8
AMBASSADOR LIFE INS CO	TX	11.4
AMERICAN EXCHANGE LIFE INS CO	TX	438.8
AMERICAN LIFE INS CO	DE	82,005.8
AMERICAN PIONEER LIFE INS CO	FL	154.7
ARKANSAS LIFE INS CO	AZ	1.0
ATLANTA LIFE INS CO	GA	81.0
AXA EQUITABLE LIFE INS CO	NY	108,227.8
BIG SKY LIFE INC	MT	1.4
CENTRAL BENEFITS NATL LIFE INS CO	OH	6.8
CHAMPIONS LIFE INS CO	TX	41.3
CINCINNATI EQUITABLE LIFE INS CO	OH	20.3
COLONIAL LIFE INS CO OF TX	TX	16.2
COLUMBIAN LIFE INS CO	IL	240.1
COMMONWEALTH ANNUTIY & LIFE INS CO	MA	5,967.0
CONTINENTAL LIFE INS CO	PA	20.7
COOPERATIVA DE SEGUROS DE VIDA DE PR	PR	358.5
CORNHUSKER LIFE INS CO	NE	2.2
EMPLOYERS REASSURANCE CORP	KS	9,173.0
FAMILY SECURITY LIFE INS CO INC	MS	5.8
FIRST NATIONAL LIFE INS CO OF USA	NE	5.3
FOUNDATION LIFE INS CO OF AR	AR	6.7
FREEDOM LIFE INS CO OF AMERICA	TX	37.2
GULF STATES LIFE INS CO INC	LA	3.0
HALLMARK LIFE INS CO	AZ	1.6
HARTFORD LIFE INS CO	CT	132,572.4
HAWKEYE LIFE INS GROUP INC	IA	15.2
HEALTHPLUS INS CO	MI	21.5
IBC LIFE INS CO	TX	3.3
INDIVIDUAL ASR CO LIFE HEALTH & ACC	MO	45.2
INVESTORS LIFE INS CO NORTH AMERICA	TX	737.8
JEFFERSON LIFE INS CO	TX	4.8
LIBERTY BANKERS LIFE INS CO	OK	877.2
LIBERTY UNION LIFE ASR CO	MI	9.9
LIFE ASR CO OF AMERICA	IL	6.1
LOCOMOTIVE ENGRS&COND MUT PROT ASSN	MI	23.0
MEDAMERICA INS CO OF FL	FL	9.1
MEMORIAL INS CO OF AMERICA	AR	1.2
MEMORIAL LIFE INS CO	LA	2.5
MILILANI LIFE INS CO	HI	2.0
MONITOR LIFE INS CO OF NEW YORK	NY	8.7
NATIONAL FOUNDATION LIFE INS CO	TX	41.0
NEW ERA LIFE INS CO OF THE MIDWEST	TX	42.0
PIONEER MILITARY INS CO	NV	13.2
PORT-O-CALL LIFE INS CO	AR	1.7
PRESIDENTIAL LIFE INS CO	NY	3,642.5
PROVIDENT AMER LIFE & HEALTH INS CO	OH	17.0

INSURANCE COMPANY NAME	DOM. STATE	TOTAL ASSETS ($MIL)
Rating: C- (Continued)		
PYRAMID LIFE INS CO	KS	445.1
REVIOS REINS CANADA LTD	CA	--
S USA LIFE INS CO INC	AZ	14.8
SCOR GLOBAL LIFE US RE INS CO	TX	2,065.1
SELECTED FUNERAL & LIFE INS CO	AR	140.1
SURETY LIFE & CASUALTY INS CO	ND	6.7
TEACHERS PROTV MUTUAL LIFE INS CO	PA	58.7
TEXAS SERVICE LIFE INS CO	TX	10.8
TRANS OCEANIC LIFE INS CO	PR	29.8
UNION FIDELITY LIFE INS CO	IL	18,236.1
UNIVERSAL GUARANTY LIFE INS CO	OH	255.8
USA INS CO	MS	8.0
WESTWARD LIFE INS CO	AZ	13.3
WILLIAM PENN LIFE INS CO OF NEW YORK	NY	964.4
Rating: D+		
ADAMS LIFE INS CO	AL	2.3
ADVANTA LIFE INS CO	AZ	4.4
AGL LIFE ASSURANCE CO	PA	4,084.0
AMERICAN CAPITOL INS CO	TX	66.0
AMERICAN LIFE INS CO	IL	3.2
AMERICAN UNDERWRITERS LIFE INS CO	AZ	74.3
BANKERS LIFE & CAS CO	IL	11,637.0
BANKERS LIFE INS CO	FL	230.5
BANNER LIFE INS CO	MD	1,316.3
BUPA INS CO	FL	106.3
CARDIF LIFE INS CO	KS	60.6
CENTRAL UNITED LIFE INS CO	AR	316.3
CENTURY LIFE ASR CO	OK	9.4
CICA LIFE INS CO OF AMERICA	CO	404.0
CITIZENS NATIONAL LIFE INS CO	TX	11.7
COLONIAL PENN LIFE INS CO	PA	692.4
CONSECO HEALTH INS CO	AZ	2,483.9
CONSECO INS CO	IL	996.8
CONSECO LIFE INS CO	IN	4,511.5
FIRST LIFE AMERICA CORP	KS	33.0
FUTURAL LIFE INS CO	AZ	8.7
GREAT FIDELITY LIFE INS CO	IN	3.1
INVESTORS INS CORP	DE	307.5
LIFE PROTECTION INS CO	TX	13.5
LONGEVITY INS CO	TX	7.6
MAPFRE LIFE INS CO	PR	74.8
MARQUETTE NATIONAL LIFE INS CO	TX	24.6
MID-CONTINENT PREFERRED LIFE INS CO	OK	15.9
PACIFIC UNION ASR CO	CA	28.7
SCOR GLOBAL LIFE RE INS CO OF TX	TX	298.6
SCOTTISH RE LIFE CORP	DE	521.4
SECURITY NATIONAL LIFE INS CO OF LA	LA	2.9
SENIOR HEALTH INS CO OF PENNSYLVANIA	PA	3,288.7
SENTINEL SECURITY LIFE INS CO	UT	49.3
SOUTHERN FINANCIAL LIFE INS CO	LA	64.9
STERLING INVESTORS LIFE INS CO	GA	21.7

INSURANCE COMPANY NAME	DOM. STATE	TOTAL ASSETS ($MIL)
SULLIVAN LIFE INS CO	TX	6.5
TEXAS IMPERIAL LIFE INS CO	TX	25.6
TOWN & COUNTRY LIFE INS CO	UT	5.2
TRINITY LIFE INS CO	OK	3.6
TRUASSURE INS CO	IL	5.4
UNITED FIDELITY LIFE INS CO	TX	555.0
UNIVERSAL FIDELITY LIFE INS CO	OK	9.1
WASHINGTON NATIONAL INS CO	IL	2,274.6
WATEREE LIFE INS	SC	10.4
WILLIAMS PROGRESSIVE LIFE & ACC I C	LA	10.6
WINNFIELD LIFE INS CO	LA	37.9
XL RE LIFE AMERICA INC	DE	55.9
Rating: D		
AMERICAN INDEPENDENT NETWORK INS CO	NY	22.3
AMERICAN LABOR LIFE INS CO	AZ	5.5
ARKANSAS BANKERS LIFE INS CO	AR	4.8
BANKERS CONSECO LIFE INS CO	NY	261.3
CAPITAL RESERVE LIFE INS CO	MO	6.5
COLONIAL SECURITY LIFE INS CO	TX	3.0
CONCERT HEALTH PLAN INS CO	IL	13.2
CONSECO LIFE INS CO OF TX	TX	589.8
COOPERATIVE LIFE INS CO	AR	6.2
DELTA LIFE INS CO	GA	56.6
FIRST VIRGINIA LIFE INS CO	VA	6.9
GOLDEN STATE MUTUAL LIFE INS CO	CA	90.0
GREAT REPUBLIC LIFE INS CO	WA	18.4
GULF GUARANTY LIFE INS CO	MS	17.9
HERITAGE UNION LIFE INS CO	AZ	10.7
INTEGRITY CAPITAL INS CO	IN	7.1
JACKSON GRIFFIN INS CO	AR	10.0
LIFE OF AMERICA INS CO	TX	3.6
MCS LIFE INS CO	PR	49.0
MELANCON LIFE INS CO	LA	6.6
NATIONAL STATES INS CO	MO	75.3
NORTH CAROLINA MUTUAL LIFE INS CO	NC	160.0
NORTH COAST LIFE INS CO	WA	121.2
OZARK NATIONAL LIFE INS CO	AR	19.8
PELLERIN LIFE INS CO	LA	8.0
PENNSYLVANIA LIFE INS CO	PA	903.0
PROFESSIONAL LIFE & CAS CO	IL	72.2
SABINE LIFE INS CO	LA	1.7
SECURITY NATIONAL LIFE INS CO	UT	344.8
SOUTHERN SECURITY LIFE INS CO INC	MS	1.8
SOUTHWEST CREDIT LIFE INC	NM	1.4
TANDY LIFE INS CO	TX	79.6
UNITED FUNERAL BENEFIT LIFE INS CO	OK	33.1
UNITED NATIONAL LIFE INS CO OF AM	IL	7.1
UNITED SECURITY LIFE & HEALTH INS CO	IL	21.6
WILTON REASSURANCE CO	MN	670.9
Rating: D-		
ATLANTIC SOUTHERN INS CO	PR	18.2
BANKERS LIFE INS CO OF AMERICA	TX	5.3

SURANCE COMPANY NAME	DOM. STATE	TOTAL ASSETS ($MIL)
Rating: D- (Continued)		
APITOL SECURITY LIFE INS CO	TX	4.2
ITIZENS SECURITY LIFE INS CO	KY	126.5
RST CONTINENTAL LIFE & ACC INS CO	TX	8.8
AWTHORN LIFE INS CO	TX	9.5
ITERNATIONAL AMERICAN LIFE INS CO	TX	1.9
EFFERSON NATIONAL LIFE INS CO	TX	1,311.3
AFOURCHE LIFE INS CO	LA	22.4
LD RELIANCE INS CO	AZ	3.9
INE BELT LIFE INS CO	MS	2.5
EGAL LIFE OF AMERICA INS CO	TX	14.0
MITH BURIAL & LIFE INS CO	AR	4.7
OUTHWEST SERVICE LIFE INS CO	TX	11.3
NITED ASR LIFE INS CO	TX	1.6
NITED FUNERAL DIR BENEFIT LIC	TX	32.0
VILTON REASSURANCE LIFE CO OF NY	NY	1,173.2
Rating: E+		
COSMOPOLITAN LIFE INS CO	AR	2.6
DESTINY HEALTH INS CO	IL	13.4
VANGELINE LIFE INS CO INC	LA	11.9
IRST AMERICAN LIFE INS CO	TX	9.2
ANDMARK LIFE INS CO	TX	60.2
EWIS LIFE INS CO	TX	1.1
PROVIDENT AMERICAN INS CO	TX	22.3
RABENHORST LIFE INS CO	LA	26.1
RELIABLE LIFE INS CO	LA	6.2
SENIOR AMERICAN LIFE INS CO	PA	20.9
TEXAS INTERNATIONAL LIFE INS CO	TX	7.0
Rating: E		
AF&L INS CO	PA	169.8
ALABAMA LIFE REINS CO INC	AL	45.1
AMERICAN CENTURY LIFE INS CO	OK	32.0
AMERICAN HOME LIFE INS CO	AR	15.0
AMERICAN LIFE & ANNUITY CO	AR	37.2
CASS COUNTY LIFE INS CO	TX	3.6
CONTINENTAL LIFE INS CO OF SC	SC	2.2
DIRECTORS LIFE ASR CO	OK	23.0
MULHEARN PROTECTIVE INS CO	LA	9.0
NETCARE LIFE & HEALTH INS CO	GU	24.1
NORTH AMERICA LIFE INS CO OF TX	TX	102.6
RHODES LIFE INS CO OF LA INC	LA	3.8
Rating: E-		
DIXIE LIFE INS CO INC	LA	14.4
KILPATRICK LIFE INS CO	LA	145.3
LA CRUZ AZUL DE PUERTO RICO INC	PR	39.9
MOTHE LIFE INS CO	LA	40.8
TEXAS MEMORIAL LIFE INS CO	TX	3.5
Rating: F		
AMERICAN FINANCIAL SECURITY L I C	MO	3.1
AMERICAN NETWORK INS CO	PA	123.2

INSURANCE COMPANY NAME	DOM. STATE	TOTAL ASSETS ($MIL)
BENICORP INS CO	IN	--
BENTON LIFE INS CO INC	LA	--
BENTON LIFE INS CO INC	LA	--
BENTON LIFE INS CO INC	LA	--
BENTON LIFE INS CO INC	LA	--
BENTON LIFE INS CO INC	LA	--
BENTON LIFE INS CO INC	LA	--
BENTON LIFE INS CO INC	LA	--
BENTON LIFE INS CO INC	LA	--
BENTON LIFE INS CO INC	LA	--
BENTON LIFE INS CO INC	LA	--
BOOKER T WASHINGTON INS CO INC	AL	--
CAPITOL LIFE INS CO	TX	209.5
ESCUDE LIFE INS CO	LA	2.2
FIDELITY MUTUAL LIFE INS CO	PA	--
FREMONT LIFE INS CO	CA	1.8
JORDAN FUNERAL & INS CO INC	AL	--
LINCOLN MEMORIAL LIFE INS CO	TX	124.0
LONE STAR LIFE INS CO	TX	--
MEMORIAL SERVICE LIFE INS CO	TX	--
MONARCH LIFE INS CO	MA	827.6
MUNICIPAL INS CO OF AMERICA	IL	--
NATIONAL ANNUITY CO	UT	--
NATIONAL HEALTH INS CO	TX	25.8
OLD STANDARD LIFE INS CO	ID	--
PENN TREATY NETWORK AMERICA INS CO	PA	1,001.2
SCOTTISH RE US INC	DE	2,238.8
SECURITY GENERAL LIFE INS CO	OK	--
SHENANDOAH LIFE INS CO	VA	1,614.4
STANDARD LIFE INS CO OF INDIANA	IN	2,088.9
UNIVERSAL LIFE INS CO	AL	13.0
WESTERN UNITED LIFE ASR CO	WA	714.0
Rating: U		
ACME LIFE INS CO	AZ	--
ADAMSON LIFE INS CO	AZ	--
ADVANTAGE LIFE INS CO	TN	--
AGC LIFE INS CO	MO	11,339.4
ALL SAVERS INS CO	IN	4.3
ALL SAVERS LIFE INS CO OF CA	CA	11.6
ALLEGIANCE LIFE INS CO	IL	285.4
ALLIANZ LIFE & ANNUITY CO	MN	16.3
ALLIED FINANCIAL INS CO	TX	0.4
AMERICAN CENTURY LIFE INS CO TX	TX	0.4
AMERICAN CLASSIC REINS CO	AZ	--
AMERICAN CREDITORS LIFE INS CO	DE	17.2
AMERICAN INDUSTRIES LIFE INS CO	TX	3.2
AMERICAN RETIREMENT LIFE INS CO	OH	6.4
AMERICAN SERVICE LIFE INS CO	AR	0.5
AMIL INTERNATIONAL INS CO	TX	--
BANC ONE KENTUCKY INS CO	KY	4.0
BANKERS CAPITAL LIFE INS CO	AZ	--
BASNEY AUTO GROUP LIFE INS CO	AZ	--
BECK LIFE INS CO	AZ	--

INSURANCE COMPANY NAME	DOM. STATE	TOTAL ASSETS ($MIL)	INSURANCE COMPANY NAME	DOM. STATE	TOTAL ASSETS ($MIL)
Rating: U (Continued)			FORETHOUGHT LIFE INS CO OF NY	NY	6.2
BENTON LIFE INS CO	TN	--	FORETHOUGHT NATIONAL LIFE INS CO	TX	200.2
BENTON LIFE INS CO INC	LA	--	FREEDOM FINANCIAL LIFE INS CO	AZ	--
BEVERLY HILLS LIFE INS CO	AZ	--	GENEVA LIFE INS CO	IN	1.5
BIRD INS CO	AZ	0.5	GEORGIA PEOPLES LIFE INS CO	AZ	--
BLUE SPIRIT INS CO	VT	--	GERTRUDE GEDDES WILLIS LIFE INS CO	LA	--
CANYON STATE LIFE INS CO	AZ	--	GMHP HEALTH INS LMTD	GU	1.6
CAPITAL SECURITY LIFE INS CO	OK	--	GOLDEN GATE CAPTIVE INS CO	SC	--
CAPITOL LIFE & ACCIDENT INS CO	AR	0.4	GOLDEN SECURITY LIFE INS CO	TN	3.2
CARLISLE LIFE INS CO	AZ	--	GREAT AMERICAN LIFE ASR CO	OH	20.2
CATERPILLAR LIFE INS CO	MO	155.6	GREAT AMERICAN LIFE INS CO OF NY	NY	46.9
CBI INS CO	AZ	--	GREAT ATLANTIC LIFE INS CO	FL	--
CENTRAL LIFE INS CO	TN	--	GREAT SOUTHEASTERN LIFE INS CO	AZ	--
CENTURY CREDIT LIFE INS CO	MS	32.4	GREAT WESTERN LIFE INS CO	MT	2.0
CHEROB LIFE INS CO	AZ	--	GREATER MISSOURI LIFE INS CO	AZ	--
CITCO LIFE INS CO	AZ	--	GREGG INS CO	AR	--
COMMENCEMENT BAY LIFE INS CO	WA	7.1	GRIFFIN LEGGETT BURIAL INS CO	AR	0.1
COMMERCE NATIONAL INS CO	MS	7.4	GUARANTEE SECURITY LIFE INS CO OF AZ	AZ	0.8
COMMUNITY BANK LIFE & HEALTH INS CO	AR	0.3	HARDIN COUNTY LIFE INS CO	TN	--
CUMBERLAND LIFE INS CO	TN	--	HARRIS LIFE INS CO	AZ	--
DENNIS LIFE INS CO	AZ	--	HEALTHMARKETS INS CO	OK	9.4
DOCTORS LIFE INS CO	CA	35.3	HEALTHSPRING LIFE & HLTH INS CO INC	TX	7.7
DORSEY LIFE INS CO	TX	0.5	HERITAGE LIFE INS CO	AZ	32.7
DUO LIFE INS CO	AZ	--	HIGGINBOTHAM BURIAL INS CO	AR	1.4
DUPAGE LIFE INS CO	AZ	--	HOME SECURITY LIFE INS CO	MS	--
EAGLE AMERICAN LIFE INS CO	LA	--	HOUSEHOLD LIFE INS CO OF AZ	AZ	843.3
EAGLE INS CO	AZ	--	INDEPENDENCE INS INC	DE	1.7
EAGLE LIFE INS CO	IA	6.0	INDEPENDENCE ONE LIFE INS CO	AZ	--
EAST ARKANSAS GEM LIFE INS CO	AZ	--	INDUSTRIAL ALLIANCE PACIFIC LIFE INS	WA	--
EDUCATORS LIFE INS CO OF AMERICA	AZ	0.2	INSOUTH LIFE INS CO	TN	--
ESKAY LIFE INS CO	AZ	--	INTERSTATE BANKERS LIFE INS CO	IL	0.6
FAMILY SERVICE LIFE INS CO	TX	530.6	INVESTORS GROWTH LIFE INS CO	AZ	--
FARMERS LIFE INS CO	TN	--	ISLAND INS CORP	PR	6.1
FIDELITY MUTUAL LIFE INS CO	PA	--	JEFFERSON STANDARD LIFE INS CO	NC	2.7
FIDELITY STANDARD LIFE INS CO	AR	0.7	KELLEY LIFE INS CO	AZ	--
FINANCIAL LIFE INS CO OF GEORGIA	GA	11.6	KEY BANK LIFE INS LTD	AZ	--
FIRST AMTENN LIFE INS CO	AZ	--	LAUREL LIFE INS CO	TX	30.2
FIRST BANK SYSTEM LIFE INS CO	VT	--	LEAFRE REINSURANCE CO	AZ	1.4
FIRST CARTHAGE LIFE INS CO	TN	--	LFG SOUTH CAROLINA REINSURANCE CO	SC	--
FIRST CITIZENS LIFE INS CO	TN	--	M & T LIFE INS CO	AZ	--
FIRST COMMUNITY LIFE INS CO	TN	--	M&I INS CO OF AZ INC	AZ	--
FIRST DIMENSION LIFE INS CO INC	OK	3.8	MAJESTIC LIFE INS CO	LA	--
FIRST DOMINION MUTUAL LIFE INS CO	VA	8.4	MC CARTHY LIFE INS CO	AZ	--
FIRST FINANCIAL ASSURANCE CO	AR	0.1	MCB LIFE INS CO	TN	--
FIRST LANDMARK LIFE INS CO	NE	2.2	MCDONALD LIFE INS CO	TX	0.8
FIRST M & F INS CO	MS	2.3	MIAMI VALLEY INS CO	AZ	--
FIRST MICHIGAN LIFE INS CO	AZ	--	MID AMERICA INS CO	AZ	--
FIRST MIDWEST INS CO	AZ	--	MID STATES LIFE INS CO	AZ	--
FIRST NATIONAL INDEMNITY L I C	TX	1.0	MIDDLE TENNESSEE LIFE INS CO	TN	--
FIRST VOLUNTEER INS CO	AZ	--	MINNETONKA LIFE INS CO	AZ	--
FLEET LIFE INS CO	AZ	25.6	MISSISSIPPI VALLEY LIFE INS CO	AZ	--
FOOTHILLS LIFE INS CO	AZ	--	MOTORSPORT LIFE INS CO	AZ	--
FOR LIFE INS CO	AZ	--	NAP LIFE INS CO	TX	2.2
			NATIONAL HOME LIFE & ACCIDENT INS CO	IN	0.6

Rating: U (Continued)

INSURANCE COMPANY NAME	DOM. STATE	TOTAL ASSETS ($MIL)
NATIONAL MASONIC PROVIDENT ASN	OH	1.3
NEW FOUNDATION LIFE INS CO	AR	2.1
NEW YORK LIFE AGENTS REIN CO	AZ	--
NORLEN LIFE INS CO	AZ	--
NORTH AMERICAN NATIONAL RE INS CO	AZ	--
NORTH AMERICAN NATL LIFE INS CO	AZ	--
NORTHERN NATIONAL LIFE INS CO OF RI	RI	3.9
OAKWOOD LIFE INS CO	AZ	--
OBRIEN NATIONAL LIFE INS CO	AZ	--
OCOEE LIFE INS CO	TN	--
OLD KENT FINANCIAL LIFE INS CO	AZ	--
OLIVIA LIFE INS CO	AZ	--
OMAHA INS CO	NE	10.4
OMAHA LIFE INS CO	NE	10.4
ORANGE SECURITY LIFE INS CO	AZ	--
ORDER UNITED COMM TRAVELERS OF AMER	OH	--
OUACHITA LIFE INS CO	AR	0.1
OVERTON LIFE INS CO	TN	--
PACIFIC CAPTIVE INS CO	SC	--
PAN AMERICAN ASR CO INTL INC	FL	2.6
PARK TWO LIFE INS CO	AZ	--
PATRIOT LIFE INS CO	ME	7.1
PEKIN FINANCIAL LIFE INS CO	AZ	--
PENN OHIO LIFE INS CO	AZ	--
PEOPLES SAVINGS LIFE INS CO	AL	0.4
PHOENIX LIFE & REASSURANCE CO OF NY	NY	13.5
PRAMCO LIFE INS CO	AZ	--
PREFERRED SECURITY LIFE INS CO	TX	4.0
PRESERVATION LIFE INS CO	MO	9.3
PRIDE OF CARROLL LIFE INS CO	LA	--
PRINCIPAL LIFE INS CO IOWA	IA	20.6
PRINCIPAL NATIONAL LIFE INS CO	IA	11.8
REGAL REINSURANCE COMPANY	MA	11.9
REGIONS LIFE INS CO	AZ	--
RELIABLE SERVICE INS CO	LA	0.1
RELIANCE STANDARD LIFE INS CO OF TX	TX	512.4
REMINGTON LIFE INS CO	AZ	--
RESNICK WULBERT & RESNICK LIFE INS	AZ	--
RIDGEWAY LIFE INS CO	TN	--
RIGHTCHOICE INS CO	IL	11.7
RIHT LIFE INS CO	AZ	--
ROCKETT LIFE INS CO	LA	--
ROYAL NEIGHBORS OF AMERICA	IL	--
RUDANDA LIFE INS CO	AZ	--
SCENIC CITY LIFE INS CO	TN	--
SEB TRYGG LIFE USA ASR CO LTD	AZ	0.7
SENTINEL AMERICAN LIFE INS CO	TX	43.5
SEQUATCHIE LIFE INS CO	TN	--
SOUTHEAST FAMILY LIFE INS CO	AZ	--
SOUTHERN CAPITAL LIFE INS CO	MS	6.9
SOUTHERN FIDELITY LIFE INS CO	AR	0.1
SOUTHERN LIFE & HEALTH INS CO	WI	96.6

INSURANCE COMPANY NAME	DOM. STATE	TOTAL ASSETS ($MIL)
SQUIRE REASSURANCE CO LLC	MI	10.1
STARVED ROCK LIFE INS CO	AZ	--
STATE FARM ANNUITY & LIFE INS CO	IL	8.4
SUMMIT CREDIT LIFE INS CO	AZ	--
SUNTRUST INS CO	AZ	16.3
SURENCY LIFE & HEALTH INS CO	KS	2.4
TENNESSEE LIFE INS CO	AZ	--
TEXAS SECURITY MUTUAL LIFE INS CO	TX	1.0
THRIVENT FINANCIAL FOR LUTHERANS	WI	--
TIPPECANOE LIFE INS CO	AZ	--
TRANS-WESTERN LIFE INS CO	TX	0.7
TRANSAM ASR CO	AZ	4.4
TRH HEALTH INS CO	TN	15.3
TWIN LIFE INS CO	AZ	--
UNION LIFE INS CO	AR	0.1
UNITED BENEFIT LIFE INS CO	OH	3.2
UNITED BURIAL INS CO OF WINNSBORO	LA	--
UNITED INTERNATIONAL LIFE INS	OK	2.8
UNIVANTAGE INS CO	UT	1.8
USAA DIRECT LIFE INS CO	NE	9.2
VALUE HEALTH REINS INC	AZ	--
VISTA LIFE INS CO	MI	39.6
WACHOVIA LIFE INS CO	AZ	--
WELLMARK COMMUNITY INS INC	IA	18.3
WESTMARK LIFE INS CO	AZ	--
WILBERT LIFE INS CO	LA	--
WONDER STATE LIFE INS CO	AR	--
WOODMEN OF THE WORLD/ASSURED LIFE	CO	--
WORKMENS LIFE INS CO	AZ	0.5
WORLD SERVICE LIFE INS CO	CO	8.9
XL LIFE INS & ANNUITY CO	IL	82.5
YADKIN VALLEY LIFE INS CO	AZ	--
ZACHARY TAYLOR LIFE INS CO	LA	--

Section VI

Rating Upgrades
and Downgrades

A list of all

U.S. Life and Annuity Insurers

receiving a rating upgrade or downgrade
during the current quarter.

Section VI Contents

This section identifies those companies receiving a rating change since the previous edition of this publication, whether it be a rating upgrade, rating downgrade, newly-rated company or the withdrawal of a rating. A rating may be withdrawn due to a merger, dissolution, or liquidation. A rating upgrade or downgrade may entail a change from one letter grade to another, or it may mean the addition or deletion of a plus or minus sign within the same letter grade previously assigned to the company. Each rating upgrade and downgrade is accompanied by a brief explanation of why the rating was changed. Ratings are normally updated once each quarter of the year. In some instances, however, a company's rating may be downgraded outside of the normal updates due to overriding circumstances. The tables for new and withdrawn ratings will contain some or all of the following information:

1. **Insurance Company Name**

    The legally registered name, which can sometimes differ from the name that the company uses for advertising. An insurer's name can be very similar to that of another, so verify the company's exact name and state of domicile to make sure you are looking at the correct company.

2. **Domicile State**

    The state which has primary regulatory responsibility for the company. It may differ from the location of the company's corporate headquarters. You do not have to be living in the domicile state to purchase insurance from this firm, provided it is licensed to do business in your state.

3. **Total Assets**

    All assets admitted by state insurance regulators in millions of dollars. This includes investments, current business assets, and separate accounts.

4. **New Financial Strength Rating**

    The rating assigned to the company as of the date of this Guide's publication. Our rating is measured on a scale from A to F and considers a wide range of factors. Highly rated companies are, in our opinion, less likely to experience financial difficulties than lower-rated firms. See *About TheStreet.com Fincancial Strength Ratings* on page 9 for more information.

5. **Previous Financial Strength Rating**

    The rating assigned to the company prior to its most recent change.

6. **Date of Change**

    The date that the rating upgrade or downgrade officially occurred. Normally, all rating changes are put into effect on a single day each quarter of the year. In some instances, however, a rating may have been changed outside of this normal update.

New Ratings

INSURANCE COMPANY NAME	DOM. STATE	TOTAL ASSETS ($MIL)	NEW RATING	PREVIOUS RATING	DATE OF CHANGE

No new ratings are being released in this edition.

Withdrawn Ratings

INSURANCE COMPANY NAME	DOM. STATE	TOTAL ASSETS ($MIL)	NEW RATING	PREVIOUS RATING	DATE OF CHANGE
ASHLEY LIFE INS CO	AR	16.4	U	C	08/14/09
CONCORD HERITAGE LIFE INS CO INC	NH	49.2	U	B	08/14/09
MICHIGAN HEALTH INS CO	MI	8.9	U	B	08/14/09
UNITED LIBERTY LIFE INS CO	KY	26.9	U	D	08/14/09

AETNA LIFE INS CO was upgraded to B from B- in August 2009 based on a markedly improved stability index.

CONSTITUTION LIFE INS CO was upgraded to C from C- in August 2009 based on a higher capitalization index, a greatly improved five-year profitability index and a greatly improved stability index., as exemplified by recent upgrade of affiliates: AMERICAN EXCHANGE LIFE INS CO to C- from U. AMERICAN PROGRESSIVE L&H I C OF NY to C from C-. UNION BANKERS INS CO to C+ from C.

CROWN LIFE INS CO US BR was upgraded to C from C- in August 2009 due to continued profitability, improved stability, and strong capitalization

FAMILY LIFE INS CO was upgraded to C+ from C in August 2009 based on a markedly improved capitalization index, a higher investment safety index, a greatly improved five-year profitability index and an improved liquidity index. enhanced financial strength of affiliates in Central United Life Group. Other deciding factors include results on risk-adjusted capital ratio #2 rose to 2.47 from 2.11.

FIDELITY SECURITY LIFE INS CO was upgraded to B+ from B in August 2009 based on a higher capitalization index, an improved investment safety index, a higher liquidity index and a greatly improved stability index.

FIRST COMMAND LIFE INS CO was upgraded to B- from C in August 2009 based on a greatly improved five-year profitability index.

GARDEN STATE LIFE INS CO was upgraded to B from B- in August 2009 based on a greatly improved capitalization index, a markedly improved investment safety index, a higher five-year profitability index, a markedly improved liquidity index and a markedly improved stability index. Other deciding factors include results on risk-adjusted capital ratio #2 rose into the EXCELLENT range.

GREAT REPUBLIC LIFE INS CO was upgraded to D from E+ in August 2009 based on a greatly improved capitalization index, a greatly improved investment safety index, a greatly improved five-year profitability index and a greatly improved stability index. Other deciding factors includ results on risk-adjusted capital ratio #2 rose to 0.77 from 0.32.

GUARANTEE TRUST LIFE INS CO was upgraded to C+ from C in August 2009 based on a markedly improved five-year profitability index.

HEALTHPLUS INS CO was upgraded to C- from D+ in August 2009 based on a greatly improved stability index. composite rating for affiliated HealthPlus of Michigan Group rose to B from E.

LIFE INS CO OF NORTH AMERICA was upgraded to B- from C+ in August 2009 based on a greatly improved stability index. enhanced financial strength of affiliates in CIGNA Group, notably the recent upgrade of affiliated company CONNECTICUT GENERAL LIFE INS CO to C+ from C.

LIFECARE ASSURANCE CO was upgraded to C from C- in August 2009 based on a higher five-year profitability index and a markedly improved stability index.

LOCOMOTIVE ENGRS&COND MUT PROT ASSN was upgraded to C- from D in August 2009 based on a greatly improved capitalization index, a greatly improved investment safety index, a greatly improved five-year profitability index, a greatly improved liquidity index and a markedly improved stability index. Other deciding factors include results on risk-adjusted capital ratio #2 rose to 2.60 from 1.63 and results on risk-adjusted capital ratio #2 rose into the EXCELLENT range during the first 3 months of 2009.

MEMBERS LIFE INS CO was upgraded to C+ from C in August 2009 due to improved risk-adjusted capital. Risk-adjusted capital ratio #1 (moderate economic scenario) increased to 2.05 and risk-adjusted capital ratio #2 (severe economic scenario) increased to 1.84 during the first quarter. Although still suffering a net loss of $284,000 during the quarter, this is an improvement over 2007 and 2008 results.

In August 2009, the rating of MEMBERS LIFE INS CO was confirmed at C+.

Major Rating Factors: Fair overall results on stability tests (4.1 on a scale of 0 to 10) including fair financial strength of affiliated CUNA Mutual Ins Group, negative cash flow from operations for 1997 and fair results on operational trends. Fair profitability (3.8) with operating losses during 1993, 1994, 1995 and 1996. Return on equity has been low, averaging -2.1% over the past five years.

Other Rating Factors: Good quality investment portfolio (6.4). Good liquidity (6.1). Strong current capitalization (7.2).

NATIONAL WESTERN LIFE INS CO was upgraded to B+ from B in August 2009 based onFair overall results on stability tests (4.8 on a scale of 0 to 10). Good liquidity (5.8) with sufficient resources to handle a spike in claims as well as a significant increase in policy surrenders.

NIPPON LIFE INS CO OF AMERICA was upgraded to A- from B+ in August 2009 based on a markedly improved stability index.

OHIO MOTORISTS LIFE INSURANCE CO was upgraded to B- from C- in August 2009 based onWeak overall results on stability tests (2.2 on a scale of 0 to 10) including weak risk diversification exacerbated by a small asset and capital base.

PACIFIC BEACON LIFE REASSUR INC was upgraded to C+ from C in August 2009 based on a greatly improved capitalization index, a greatly improved investment safety index, a markedly improved five-year profitability index, a markedly improved liquidity index and a greatly improved stability index. Other deciding factors include results on risk-adjusted capital ratio #2 rose to 1.36 from 0.90.

SECURITY PLAN LIFE INS CO was upgraded to C from C- in August 2009 based on a markedly improved stability index.

Rating Upgrades (Continued)

SOUTHERN SECURITY LIFE INS CO INC was upgraded to D from E+ in August 2009 based on a greatly improved capitalization index, a greatly improved investment safety index, a greatly improved five-year profitability index and a greatly improved stability index.

STERLING INVESTORS LIFE INS CO was upgraded to D+ from D in August 2009 based on a higher investment safety index, a greatly improved five-year profitability index and a greatly improved stability index.

SYMETRA NATIONAL LIFE INS CO was upgraded to B from B- in August 2009 based on a markedly improved five-year profitability index and a greatly improved liquidity index.

UNION BANKERS INS CO was upgraded to C+ from C in August 2009 based on a greatly improved five-year profitability index and a greatly improved stability index., as exemplified by recent upgrade of affiliates: AMERICAN EXCHANGE LIFE INS CO to C- from U. AMERICAN PROGRESSIVE L&H I C OF NY to C from C-.

WESTERN AMERICAN LIFE INS CO was upgraded to C from C- in August 2009 based on an improved investment safety index. composite rating for affiliated Maximum Corporation Group rose to C from C-.

Rating Downgrades

ALABAMA LIFE REINS CO INC was downgraded to E from D+ in August 2009 due to a substantially lower capitalization index, a declining five-year profitability index, a significant decline in its liquidity index and a substantially lower stability index. Other deciding factors include premium revenues fell off by 91%, return on equity decreased from 8% to 6%, capital & surplus decreased 33%, results on risk-adjusted capital ratio #2 fell into the VERY WEAK range, company size, in terms of admitted assets and shrunk by 6% during the first 3 months of 2009.

ALLIANZ LIFE INS CO OF NORTH AMERICA was downgraded to C+ from B- in August 2009 due to a significant decline in its capitalization index, a substantially lower investment safety index, a declining five-year profitability index, a significant decline in its liquidity index and a declining stability index. Other deciding factors include results on risk-adjusted capital ratio #2 fell into the FAIR range, capital & surplus decreased 18%, operating losses amounted to 32% of capital & surplus and capital & surplus decreased 9% during the first 3 months of 2009.

AMERICAN INCOME LIFE INS CO was downgraded to B+ from A- in August 2009 due to a substantially lower capitalization index, a substantially lower investment safety index and a significant decline in its stability index. Other deciding factors include capital & surplus decreased 32% and results on risk-adjusted capital ratio #2 fell into the GOOD range during the first 3 months of 2009.

AMERICAN NATIONAL INS CO was downgraded to B from B+ in August 2009 due to a substantially lower capitalization index, a substantially lower five-year profitability index, a declining liquidity index and a declining stability index. Other deciding factors include capital & surplus decreased 17%, results on risk-adjusted capital ratio #2 fell into the GOOD range and capital & surplus decreased 7% during the first 3 months of 2009.

AXA EQUITABLE LIFE INS CO was downgraded to C- from C in August 2009 due to a substantially lower capitalization index, a substantially lower investment safety index, a substantially lower five-year profitability index, a declining liquidity index and a substantially lower stability index. Other deciding factors include capital & surplus decreased 52%, holdings in repossessed mortgages increased from zero to $465.2 million, results on risk-adjusted capital ratio #2 fell into the FAIR range, operating losses amounted to 77% of capital & surplus, company size, in terms of admitted assets, shrunk by 22%, capital & surplus decreased 29%, operating losses amounted to 57% of capital & surplus and results on risk-adjusted capital ratio #2 fell into the WEAK range during the first 3 months of 2009.

EQUITRUST LIFE INS CO was downgraded to B- from B in August 2009 due to a significant decline in its capitalization index, a substantially lower investment safety index, a substantially lower five-year profitability index and a declining liquidity index. Other deciding factors include operating losses amounted to 9% of capital & surplus, results on risk-adjusted capital ratio #2 fell into the FAIR range, capital & surplus decreased 7% and operating losses amounted to 9% of capital & surplus during the first 3 months of 2009.

ESCUDE LIFE INS CO was downgraded to F from E- as the company was placed into rehabilitation by the Commissioner of Insurance for the State of Louisiana in April 2009.

FREMONT LIFE INS CO was downgraded to F from E+ as the company was placed into conservatorship by the Insurance Commissioner of the State of California in June 2009.

ILLINOIS MUTUAL LIFE INS CO was downgraded to B+ from A- in August 2009 due to a substantially lower capitalization index, a substantially lower investment safety index, a substantially lower five-year profitability index and a significant decline in its stability index. Other deciding factors include capital & surplus decreased 9%, return on equity decreased from 7% to 5%, results on risk-adjusted capital ratio #2 fell into the GOOD range and capital & surplus decreased 6% during the first 3 months of 2009.

LIBERTY BANKERS LIFE INS CO was downgraded to C- from C in August 2009 due to a substantially lower capitalization index, a substantially lower investment safety index and a significant decline in its stability index. Other deciding factors include results on risk-adjusted capital ratio #2 fell into the FAIR range, results on risk-adjusted capital ratio #2 fell into the WEAK range and capital & surplus decreased 7% during the first 3 months of 2009.

LINCOLN MEMORIAL LIFE INS CO was downgraded to F from C as the preneed cemetery and funeral services company was placed into liquidation by the Iowa Insurance Division in September 2008.

MANHATTAN NATIONAL LIFE INS CO was downgraded to C from C+ in August 2009 due to a substantially lower capitalization index, a substantially lower investment safety index, a substantially lower five-year profitability index, a declining liquidity index and a substantially lower stability index. Other deciding factors include capital & surplus decreased 84%, company size, in terms of admitted assets and shrunk by 19%.

MARQUETTE NATIONAL LIFE INS CO was downgraded to D+ from D in August 2009 due to a substantially lower capitalization index, a lower investment safety index, a declining five-year profitability index, a substantially lower liquidity index and a substantially lower stability index. Other deciding factors include capital & surplus decreased 35%, results on risk-adjusted capital ratio #2 fell into the VERY WEAK range, operating losses amounted to 166% of capital & surplus, company size, in terms of admitted assets and shrunk by 26% during the first 3 months of 2009.

Rating Downgrades (Continued)

METROPOLITAN LIFE INS CO was downgraded to B- from B in August 2009 due to a significant decline in its capitalization index, a substantially lower investment safety index, a significant decline in its five-year profitability index and a substantially lower stability index. Other deciding factors include mix of premium types by product line changed drastically, capital & surplus decreased 11%, return on equity decreased from 13% to 4%, results on risk-adjusted capital ratio #2 fell into the GOOD range and capital & surplus decreased 9% during the first 3 months of 2009.

MONY LIFE INS CO was downgraded to C from C+ in August 2009 due to a substantially lower capitalization index, a declining investment safety index, a substantially lower five-year profitability index, a significant decline in its liquidity index and a substantially lower stability index. In addition, the composite rating for affiliated AXA Financial Inc Group fell to C from B. Other deciding factors include capital & surplus decreased 46%, results on risk-adjusted capital ratio #2 fell into the FAIR range, company size, in terms of admitted assets, shrunk by 8% and capital & surplus decreased 5% during the first 3 months of 2009.

NATIONWIDE LIFE INS CO was downgraded to B from B+ in August 2009 due to a declining capitalization index, a substantially lower investment safety index, a substantially lower five-year profitability index, a declining liquidity index and a substantially lower stability index. Other deciding factors include operating losses amounted to 27% of capital & surplus, company size, in terms of admitted assets, shrunk by 22%, capital & surplus decreased 10%, operating losses amounted to 56% of capital & surplus and capital & surplus decreased 15% during the first 3 months of 2009.

NEW YORK LIFE INS & ANNUITY CORP was downgraded to A- from A in August 2009 due to a significant decline in its capitalization index, a lower investment safety index, a substantially lower five-year profitability index and a significant decline in its stability index. Other deciding factors include return on equity deteriorated from a gain of 11% to a loss of 3%, results on risk-adjusted capital ratio #2 fell into the GOOD range, capital & surplus decreased 8% and operating losses amounted to 7% of capital & surplus during the first 3 months of 2009.

RABENHORST LIFE INS CO was downgraded to E+ from D in August 2009 due to a substantially lower capitalization index, a declining investment safety index, a declining five-year profitability index, a significant decline in its liquidity index and a substantially lower stability index. Other deciding factors include capital & surplus decreased 41%, results on risk-adjusted capital ratio #2 fell into the WEAK range, operating losses amounted to 11% of capital & surplus, capital & surplus decreased 29%, operating losses amounted to 49% of capital & surplus and results on risk-adjusted capital ratio #2 fell into the VERY WEAK range during the first 3 months of 2009.

SAVINGS BANK LIFE INS CO OF MA was downgraded to B+ from A- in August 2009 due to a significant decline in its capitalization index, a significant decline in its investment safety index, a substantially lower five-year profitability index and a significant decline in its stability index. Other deciding factors include capital & surplus decreased 20%, return on equity deteriorated from a gain of 3% to a loss of 2% and capital & surplus decreased 10% during the first 3 months of 2009.

SECURITY LIFE OF DENVER INS CO was downgraded to B- from B in August 2009 due to a declining capitalization index, a substantially lower investment safety index and a significant decline in its stability index. In addition, the composite rating for affiliated ING America Ins Holdings Inc Group fell to C+ from B. Other deciding factors include mix of premium types by product line changed drastically, capital & surplus decreased 8%, results on risk-adjusted capital ratio #2 fell into the FAIR range, company size, in terms of admitted assets, shrunk by 7% and capital & surplus decreased 8% during the first 3 months of 2009.

UNION FIDELITY LIFE INS CO was downgraded to C- from C in August 2009 due to a substantially lower capitalization index, a substantially lower investment safety index, a lower liquidity index and a substantially lower stability index. Other deciding factors include capital & surplus decreased 29%, operating losses amounted to 42% of capital & surplus, operating losses amounted to 21% of capital & surplus and capital & surplus decreased 15% during the first 3 months of 2009.

UNIVERSAL LIFE INS CO was downgraded to F from E as the company was placed into rehabilitation by the State of Alabama Commissioner of Insurance in April 2009.

Appendix

State Guaranty Associations

The states have established insurance guaranty associations to help pay claims to policyholders of failed insurance companies. However, there are several cautions which you must be aware of with respect to this coverage:

1. Most of the guaranty associations do not set aside funds in advance. Rather, states assess contributions from other insurance companies after an insolvency occurs.

2. There can be an unacceptably long delay before claims are paid.

3. Each state is governed by its own legislation, providing a wide range of coverage and conditions that may apply. According to the National Organization of Life and Health Guaranty Associations (NOLHGA), the issues are extremely complex with unique variables for each individual state.

4. The table on the following page is designed to help you sort out these issues. However, it is not intended to handle all of them. If your carrier has failed and you need a complete answer, we recommend you contact your State Insurance Official (see page 320 for phone numbers) or NOLHGA at 703-481-5206.

Following is a brief explanation of each of the columns in the table.

1. **Non-Resident Coverage**

   Resident coverage means that the individual state's guaranty fund will cover those policyholders residing in that state. This essentially means that each individual state is responsible for policyholders residing in that state, no matter where the insolvent insurer is domiciled.

   Non-resident coverage (marked Y) is provided only under certain circumstances listed in the state's statutes. The general conditions are as follows:

   a) The insurer of the policyholder must be domiciled and licensed in the state in which the non-resident is seeking coverage;

   b) When the contracts were sold, the insurers that issued the policies were not licensed in the state in which the policyholder resides;

   c) The non-resident policyholder is not eligible for coverage from his or her state of residence;

   d) The state where the policyholder resides must have a guaranty association similar to that of the state in which he or she is seeking non-resident coverage.

   Warning: Be sure to contact your state guaranty fund association for any furthur information. Conditions and limitations subject to individual state statutes.

2. Death Benefits   The maximum amount payable by the State Guaranty Fund to cover death benefits for life insurance policies, including individual life policyholders as well as certificate holders on group life policies.

3. Life Insurance Cash Value   The maximum amount payable by the State Guaranty Fund to cover cash values accumulated under life insurance policies for individual life policyholders as well as certificate holders on group life policies.

4. Annuity Contracts   The maximum amount payable by the State Guaranty Fund to cover annuity contracts, including variable annuities. However, for variable contracts, most states will cover only the money you have paid in and, in some cases, a portion of interest accrued. Most states also only cover present value of annuities and may annuitize the payments over ten years.

5. Health and Disability   The maximum amount payable by the State Guaranty Fund to cover health and disability benefits, including most accident and disability, as well as individual and group health.

6. Blue Cross Blue Shield (BCBS) Plans   Indicates whether or not the states' Blue Cross Blue Shield plans are currently covered by the State Guaranty Association.

If Blue Cross Blue Shield plans are covered (marked Y), then they are licensed within the state and a member of the Guaranty Fund Association. Coverage is only provided for certain policies. Check with the state Guaranty Fund Association for exact coverage.

If Blue Cross Blue Shield plans are not covered (marked N), then they are not a member of the state's Guaranty Fund Association.

7. Aggregate Benefits   The maximum total amount payable by the State Guaranty Fund per policyholder.

8. Unallocated Annuity Contracts   The maximum amount payable by the State Guaranty Fund to cover any annuity contract or group annuity certificate which is not owned by an individual. This includes most GICs and other similar pension products.

States marked "excluded" either do not have provisions currently in their statutes or the statutes specifically deny any coverage for unallocated annuities.

9. Notes   See the notes on page 318 regarding peculiarities in state coverages.

Coverage of State Guaranty Funds

State	Non-Resident Coverage	Death Benefits ($000)	Life Ins Cash Value ($000)	Annuity Contracts ($000)	Health And Disability ($000)	Blue Cross Blue Shield Plans	Aggregate Benefits ($000)	Unallocated Annuities ($000)	Notes
Alabama	Y	300	100	300	300	N	300	excluded	
Alaska	Y	300	100	100	Tier Model	N	300	5,000	(1, 2)
Arizona	Y	300	100	100	300	N	300	excluded	
Arkansas	Y	300	300	300	300	Y	300	1,000	
California	Y	250	100	100	200	N	250	excluded	(3, 4)
Colorado	Y	300	100	100	Tier Model	N	300	excluded	(1, 2)
Connecticut	Y	500	500	500	500	Y	500	5,000	
Delaware	Y	300	100	100	Tier Model	N	300	1,000	(1, 2)
D.C.	Y	300	100	300	100	Y	300		
Florida	Y	300	100	100	300	Y	300	excluded	
Georgia	Y	300	100	100	300	N	300	5,000	
Hawaii	Y	300	100	100	100	N	300	excluded	
Idaho	Y	300	100	300	300	Y	300	excluded	(5)
Illinois	Y	300	100	100	300	Y	300	5,000	
Indiana	Y	300	100	300	300	Y	300	5,000	
Iowa	Y	300	100	300	300	Y	300	1,000	
Kansas	Y	300	100	100	100	Y	300	excluded	
Kentucky	Y	300	100	100	100	Y	300	1,000	
Louisiana	Y	300	100	100	100	Y	300		(6, 7)
Maine	Y	300	100	100	Tier Model	Y	300	5,000	(1)
Maryland	Y	300	100	100	300	Y	300	excluded	(8)
Massachusetts	Y	300	100	100	100	N	300	excluded	(9)
Michigan	Y	300	100	100	100	N	300	5,000	(10)
Minnesota	Y	300	100	100	300	Y	300	7,500	
Mississippi	Y	300	100	100	Tier Model	Y	300	5,000	(1, 2)
Missouri	Y	300	100	100	100	Y	300	excluded	
Montana	Y	300	100	100	Tier Model	N	300	5,000	(10)
Nebraska	Y	300	100	100	500	Y	300	5,000	(10)
Nevada	Y	300	100	100	Tier Model	N	300	5,000	(1, 2, 10)
New Hampshire	Y	300	100	100	100	N	300	5,000	
New Jersey	Y	500	100	500	No Maximum	Y	500	2,000	(9)
New Mexico	Y	300	100	100	100	N	300	excluded	
New York	Y	500	500	500	500	N	500	1,000	(11, 12, 13)
North Carolina	Y	300	300	300	300	Y	300	5,000	
North Dakota	Y	300	100	100	100	Y	300	5,000	
Ohio	Y	300	100	100	100	Y	300	1,000	
Oklahoma	Y	300	100	300	300	Y	300	excluded	
Oregon	Y	300	100	100	100	N	300	5,000	(14)
Pennsylvania	Y	300	100	100	100	N	300	5,000	
Puerto Rico	Y	300	100	100	100	Y	300	excluded	(15)
Rhode Island	Y	300	100	100	Tier Model	N	300	5,000	
South Carolina	Y	300	300	300	300	Y	300	excluded	
South Dakota	Y	300	100	100	Tier Model	Y	300	5,000	(10, 16)
Tennessee	Y	300	100	100	100	N	300		(9)
Texas	Y	300	100	100	Tier Model	Y	300	5,000	(10)
Utah	Y	500	200	200		Y	500	5,000	(17)
Vermont	Y	300	100	100	300	N	300	1,000	
Virginia	Y	300	100	100	300	Y	300	excluded	
Washington	Y	500	500	500	500	N	500	5,000	(18)
West Virginia	Y	300	100	100	100	Y	300	1,000	
Wisconsin	Y					N	300		(19)
Wyoming	Y	300	100	100	100	N	300	Excluded	

NOTES

1.   For tiered health and disability coverage, the coverage is separated and listed as the following:

   Health –excludes major medical, surgical or basic hospital services; coverage is provided up to a maximum of $100,000 with exception for Maine, maximum of $300,000 and Texas, maximum of $200,000.

   Disability - coverage is provided up to a maximum of $300,000.

   Basic Hospital/Medical/Surgical and/or Major Medical - coverage is provided up to a maximum of $500,000.

2.   For states that have tiered health, disability and major medical models, the aggregate coverage is subject to change with the exceptions of major medical expenses covered. However, the increased aggregate amount only applies to the allotted maximum of the health benefits.

3.   An aggregate limit of $5 million per policyholder exists, regardless of the number of policies. A 20% deductible in the limits for life insurance and annuity policies exists. The limits for health insurance can increase or decrease depending upon inflation.

4.   Coverage for Health and Disability is subject to Moody's Index of interest rates, rollbacks and adjustments. The California Life and Health Guaranty Fund Association can only determine a maximum in health and disability coverage.

5.   Annuities are covered up to a maximum of $300,000 if they are in pay out on or before the date of the impairment or insolvency; otherwise, a maximum coverage of $100,000 is provided.

6.   Does not provide coverage for unallocated annuities, except any unallocated annuity or defined contribution government plans qualified under Section 403(b) of the U.S Internal Revenue Code

7.   PPO Indemnity plans of Blue Cross Blue Shield are covered.

8.   Covers contractual obligations of impaired insurers for all lines of business. If health care is received after the date of impairment or insolvency, the corporation is not liable.

9.   For unallocated annuities, coverage is provided for net present value only.

10.   The aggregate limit of $300,000 excludes the aggregate amount of $500,000 for health benefits.

11.   New York state statutes defines a "resident" as someone who resided in New York at the time the insurer became insolvent or when the policy was issued by a member insurer.

12.   The aggregate limit does not apply to group or blanket health policies; however, in the event an insurer becomes insolvent there are only 180 days for coverage, allowing for an employer to have stop-gap coverage until they find another insurer.

13.   Health and disability policies are only covered if they have been purchased through a life insurance company, not a property and casualty insurance company.

14. There is an aggregate limit of $5 million, subject to the limits of any one specific policy or contract. This aggregate limit does not apply to governmental retirement plans established under Section 401, 403(b) or 457 of the U.S. Internal Revenue Code.

15. There is currently only one company identified as Blue Cross and Blue Shield; this plan has recently converted into a stock ownership company. The date of coverage by the Puerto Rico Guaranty Association became effective the date of Blue Cross and Blue Shield's conversion.

16. Group policies are covered under the non-resident coverage, within the state's other limitations mentioned in the statutes.

17. The maximum coverage for health benefits under the Utah Guaranty Fund Association is $200,000. The maximum coverage for disability and basic hospital/medical/surgical and/or major medical is a combined total of $500,000.

18. The $500,000 death benefit limit includes cash values. The $500,000 present value of annuities limit also applies to annuities established under Section 403(b) of the U.S. Internal Revenue Code. The $5 million unallocated annuities limit applies to unallocated annuities and governmental retirement plans established under Section 401 or 457 of the U.S. Internal Revenue Code.

19. Has a $200 deductible. Wisconsin statute §646.31(4) only lists liability for the aggregate amount of a single life, loss, or risk. Contact the Wisconsin Guaranty Fund Association for further information.

Information provided in the Coverage of State Guaranty Funds chart was compiled from data obtained by the National Organization of Life and Health Guaranty Associations (NOLHGA), the National Association of Insurance Commissioners (NAIC), and state statutes.

State Insurance Commissioners'
Departmental Phone Numbers

State	Official's Title	Website Address	Phone Number
Alabama	Commissioner	www.aldoi.org	(334) 269-3550
Alaska	Director	www.dced.state.ak.us/insurance/	(907) 465-2515
Arizona	Director	www.id.state.az.us	(800) 325-2548
Arkansas	Commissioner	www.insurance.arkansas.gov	(800) 282-9134
California	Commissioner	www.insurance.ca.gov	(800) 927-4357
Colorado	Commissioner	www.dora.state.co.us/insurance/	(800) 930-3745
Connecticut	Commissioner	www.ct.gov/cid/	(860) 297-3800
Delaware	Commissioner	www.state.de.us/inscom/	(302) 674-7300
Dist. of Columbia	Commissioner	disr.dc.gov/disr/	(202) 727-8000
Florida	Commissioner	www.fldfs.com	(800) 342-2762
Georgia	Commissioner	www.gainsurance.org	(800) 656-2298
Hawaii	Commissioner	www.hawaii.gov/dcca/areas/ins/	(808) 586-2790
Idaho	Director	www.doi.idaho.gov	(800) 721-3272
Illinois	Director	www.idfpr.com/doi/	(217) 782-4515
Indiana	Commissioner	www.ia.org/idoi/	(317) 232-2385
Iowa	Commissioner	www.iid.state.ia.us	(877) 955-1212
Kansas	Commissioner	www.ksinsurance.org	(800) 432-2484
Kentucky	Executive Director	www.doi.ppr.ky.gov/kentucky/	(800) 595-6053
Louisiana	Commissioner	www.ldi.state.la.us	(800) 259-5300
Maine	Superintendent	www.maine.gov/pfr/insurance/	(800) 300-5000
Maryland	Commissioner	www.mdinsurance.state.md.us	(800) 492-6116
Massachusetts	Commissioner	www.mass.gov/doi/	(617) 521-7794
Michigan	Commissioner	www.michigan.gov/cis/	(877) 999-6442
Minnesota	Commissioner	www.commerce.state.mn.us	(651) 296-4026
Mississippi	Commissioner	www.doi.state.ms.us	(800) 562-2957
Missouri	Director	www.insurance.mo.gov	(800) 726-7390
Montana	Commissioner	www.sao.state.mt.us	(800) 332-6148
Nebraska	Director	www.nebraska.gov	(402) 471-2306
Nevada	Commissioner	doi.state.nv.us	(775) 687-4270
New Hampshire	Commissioner	www.nh.gov/insurance/	(800) 852-3416
New Jersey	Commissioner	www.state.nj.us/dobi/	(800) 446-7467
New Mexico	Superintendent	www.nmprc.state.nm.us/id.htm	(888) 427-5772
New York	Superintendent	www.ins.state.ny.us	(800) 342-3736
North Carolina	Commissioner	www.ncdoi.com	(800) 546-5664
North Dakota	Commissioner	www.nd.gov/ndins/	(800) 247-0560
Ohio	Director	www.ohioinsurance.gov	(800) 686-1526
Oklahoma	Commissioner	www.oid.state.ok.us	(800) 522-0071
Oregon	Insurance Administrator	www.cbs.state.or.us/ins/	(503) 947-7980
Pennsylvania	Commissioner	www.ins.state.pa.us/ins/	(877) 881-6388
Puerto Rico	Commissioner	www.ocs.gobierno.pr	(787) 722-8686
Rhode Island	Superintendent	www.dbr.state.ri.us	(401) 222-2223
South Carolina	Director	www.doi.sc.gov	(800) 768-3467
South Dakota	Director	www.state.sd.us/drr2/reg/insurance/	(605) 773-3563
Tennessee	Commissioner	www.state.tn.us/commerce/insurance/	(800) 342-4029
Texas	Commissioner	www.tdi.state.tx.us	(800) 252-3439
Utah	Commissioner	www.insurance.utah.gov	(800) 439-3805
Vermont	Commissioner	www.bishca.state.vt.us	(802) 828-3301
Virgin Islands	Lieutenant Governor	www.ltg.gov.vi	(340) 774-7166
Virginia	Commissioner	www.scc.virginia.gov/division/boi/	(877) 310-6560
Washington	Commissioner	www.insurance.wa.gov	(800) 562-6900
West Virginia	Commissioner	www.wvinsurance.gov	(304) 558-3386
Wisconsin	Commissioner	oci.wi.gov	(800) 236-8517
Wyoming	Commissioner	insurance.state.wy.us	(800) 438-5768

Risk-Adjusted Capital for Life and Annuity Insurers in TheStreet.com Rating Model

Among the most important indicators used in the analysis of an individual company are our two risk-adjusted capital ratios, which are useful tools in determining exposure to investment, liquidity and insurance risk in relation to the capital the company has to cover those risks.

The first risk-adjusted capital ratio evaluates the company's ability to withstand a moderate loss scenario. The second ratio evaluates the company's ability to withstand a severe loss scenario.

In order to calculate these risk-adjusted capital ratios, we follow these steps:

1. Capital Resources

First, we add up all of the company's resources which could be used to cover losses. These include capital, surplus, the Asset Valuation Reserve (AVR), and a portion of the provision for future policyholders' dividends, where appropriate. Additional credit may also be given for the use of conservative reserving assumptions and other "hidden capital" when applicable.

2. Target Capital

Next, we determine the company's target capital. This answers the question: Based upon the company's level of risk in both its insurance business and its investment portfolio, how much capital would it need to cover potential losses during a moderate loss scenario? In other words, we determine how much capital we believe this company *should* have.

3. Risk-Adjusted Capital Ratio #1

We compare the results of step 1 with those of step 2. Specifically, we divide the "capital resources" by the "target capital" and express it in terms of a ratio. This ratio is called RACR #1. (See next page for more detail on methodology.)

If a company has a Risk-Adjusted Capital Ratio of 1.0 or more, it means the company has all of the capital we believe it requires to withstand potential losses which could be inflicted by a moderate loss scenario. If the company has less than 1.0, it does not currently have all of the basic capital resources we think it needs. During times of financial distress, companies often have access to additional capital through contributions from a parent company, current profits or reductions in policyholder dividends. Therefore, an allowance is made in our rating system for firms with somewhat less than 1.0 Risk-Adjusted Capital Ratios.

4. Risk-Adjusted Capital Ratio #2

We repeat steps 2 and 3, but now assuming a severe loss scenario. This ratio is called RACR #2.

5. Capitalization Index

We convert RACR #1 and #2 into an index. It is measured on a scale of zero to ten, with ten being the best and seven or better considered strong. A company whose capital, surplus and AVR equal its target capital will have a Risk-Adjusted Capital Ratio of 1.0 and a Risk-Adjusted Capital Index of 7.0.

How We Determine Target Capital

The basic procedure for determining target capital is to ask these questions:

1.   What is the breakdown of the company's investment portfolio and types of business?

2.   For each category, what are the potential losses which could be incurred in the loss scenario?

3.   In order to cover those potential losses, how much in capital resources does the company need? It stands to reason that more capital is needed as a cushion for losses on high-risk investments, such as junk bonds, than would be necessary for low-risk investments, such as AAA-rated utility bonds.

      Unfortunately, the same questions we have raised about Wall Street rating systems with respect to how they rate insurance companies can be asked about the way they rate bonds. However, we do not rate bonds ourselves. Therefore, we must rely upon the bond ratings of other rating agencies. This is another reason why we have stricter capital requirements for the insurance companies. It accounts for the fact that they may need some extra protection in case an AAA-rated bond may not be quite as good as it appears to be.

      Finally, target capital is adjusted for the company's spread of risk in the diversification of its investment portfolio, the size and number of the policies it writes and the diversification of its business.

Table 1 on the next page shows target capital percentages used by the National Association of Insurance Commissioners (NAIC) in relation to TheStreet.com Risk-Adjusted Capital Ratios #1 and #2 (RACR #1 and RACR #2).

The percentages shown in the table answer the question: How much should the firm hold in capital resources for every $100 it has committed to each category? Several of the items in Table 1 are expressed as ranges. The actual percentages used in the calculation of target capital for an individual company may vary due to the levels of risks in the operations, investments or policy obligations of that specific company.

Table 1. Target Capital Percentages

Asset Risk	TheStreet.com Ratings RACR#1 (%)	RACR#2 (%)	NAIC
Bonds			
Government guaranteed bonds	0	0	0
Class 1	.5-.75	1-1.5	0.4
Class 2	2	5	1.3
Class 3	5	15	4.6
Class 4	10	30	10
Class 5	20	60	23
Class 6	20	60	30
Mortgages			
In good standing	0.5	1	0
90 days overdue	1.7-20	3.8-25	0.1-18
In process of foreclosure	25-33	33-50	1.4-23
Real Estate			
Class 1	20	50	15
Class 2	10	33	23
Preferred Stock			
Class 1	3	5	1.1
Class 2	4	6	3.0
Class 3	7	9	7.2
Class 4	12	15	15
Class 5	22	29	20
Class 6	30	39	15
Class 7	3-30	5-39	22.5-45
Common Stock			
Unaffiliated	25	33	22.5-45
Affiliated	25-100	33-100	22.5-45
Short-term investment	0.5	1	0.4
Premium notes	2	5	6.8
Collateral loans	2	5	6.8
Separate account equity	25	33	11 **
Other invested assets	5	10	6.8
Insurance Risk			
Individual life reserves*	.06-.15	.08-.21	.09-.23
Group life reserves*	.05-.12	.06-.16	.08-.18
Individual Health Premiums			
Class 1	12-20	15-25	10-16.5
Class 2	9.6	12	6.7-12
Class 3	6.4	8	3.5/$50,000
Class 4	12-28	15-35	23.1-53.9
Class 5	12-20	15-25	10.8-38.5
Group Health Premiums			
Class 1	5.6-12	7-15	9-15
Class 2	20	25	25
Class 3	9.6	12	6.7-12
Class 4	6.4	8	3.5/$50,000
Class 5	12-20	15-25	4.6-23.1
Managed care credit	5-40	6-50	NAIC calculation
Premiums subject to rate guarantees	100-209	120-250	2.4-6.4
Individual claim reserves	4	5	5-7.7
Group claim reserves	4	5	5-7.7
Reinsurance	0-2	0-5	0.8
Interest Rate Risk			
Policy loans	0-2	0-5	1.1
Life reserves	1-2	1-3	0.7-1.1
Individual annuity reserves	1-3	1-5	0.7-1.1
Group annuity reserves	1-2	1-3	0.7-1.1
Guaranteed interest contract reserves	1-2	1-3	0.7-1.1

All numbers are shown for illustrative purposes. Figures actually used in the formula vary annually based on industry experience.

*Based on net amount at risk.

**Risk-based capital for separate account assets that are not tied to an index = 100% of the risk-based capital of assets in the accounts.

Investment Class

Descriptions

Investment Class		Descriptions
Government guaranteed bonds		Guaranteed bonds issued by U.S. and other governments which receive the top rating of state insurance commissioners.
Bonds	Class 1	Investment grade bonds rated AAA, AA or A by Moody's or Standard & Poor's or deemed AAA - A equivalent by state insurance commissioners.
	Class 2	Investment grade bonds with some speculative elements, rated BBB or equivalent.
	Class 3	Noninvestment grade bonds, rated BB or equivalent.
	Class 4	Noninvestment grade bonds, rated B or equivalent.
	Class 5	Noninvestment grade bonds, rated CCC, CC or C or equivalent.
	Class 6	Noninvestment grade bonds, in or near default.
Mortgages		Mortgages in good standing
		Mortgages 90 days past due
		Mortgages in process of foreclosure
Real Estate	Class 1	Properties acquired in satisfaction of debt.
	Class 2	Company occupied and other investment properties.
Preferred stock	Class 1	Highest quality unaffiliated preferred stock.
	Class 2	High quality unaffiliated preferred stock.
	Class 3	Medium quality unaffiliated preferred stock.
	Class 4	Low quality unaffiliated preferred stock.
	Class 5	Lowest quality unaffiliated preferred stock.
	Class 6	Unaffiliated preferred stock, in or near default.
	Class 7	Affiliated preferred stock.
Common stock		Unaffiliated common stock.
		Affiliated common stock.
Short-term investments		All investments whose maturities at the time of acquisition were one year or less.
Premium Notes		Loans for payment of premiums.
Collateral loans		Loans made to a company or individual where the underlying security is in the form of bonds, stocks, or other marketable securities.
Separate account assets		Investments held in an account segregated from the general assets of the company, generally used to provide variable annuity benefits.
Other invested assets		Any invested assets that do not fit under the main categories above.
Individual life reserves		Funds set aside for payment of life insurance benefits under an individual contract rather than a company or group, underwriting based on individual profile.
Group life reserves		Funds set aside for payment of life insurance benefits under a contract with at least 10 people whereby all members have a common interest and are joined for a reason other than to obtain insurance.
Individual health premiums	Class 1	Usual and customary hospital and medical premiums which include traditional medical reimbursement plans that are subject to annual rate increases based on the company's claims experience.
	Class 2	Medicare supplement, dental, and other limited benefits anticipating rate increases.
	Class 3	Hospital indemnity plans, accidental death and dismemberment policies, and other limited benefits not anticipating rate increases.
	Class 4	Noncancellable disability income.
	Class 5	Guaranteed renewable disability income.

Group health premiums	Class 1	Usual and customary hospital and medical premiums which include traditional medical reimbursement plans that are subject to annual rate increases based on the company's claims experience.
	Class 2	Stop loss and minimum premium where a known claims liability is minimal or nonexistent.
	Class 3	Medicare supplement, dental, and other limited benefits anticipating rate increases.
	Class 4	Hospital indemnity plans, accidental death and dismemberment policies, and other limited benefits not anticipating rate increases.
	Class 5	Disability Income.
Managed care credit		Premiums for HMO and PPO business which carry less risk than traditional indemnity business. Included in this credit are provider compensation arrangements such as salary, capitation and fixed payment per service.
Premiums subject to rate guarantees		Health insurance premiums from policies where the rate paid by the policyholder is guaranteed for a period of time, such as one year, 15 months, 27 months or 37 months.
Individual claim reserves		Accident and health reserves for claims on individual policies.
Group claim reserves		Accident and health reserves for claims on group policies.
Reinsurance		Amounts recoverable on paid and unpaid losses for all reinsurance ceded; unearned premiums on accident and health reinsurance ceded; and funds held with unauthorized reinsurers.
Policy loans		Loans against the cash value of a life insurance policy.
Life reserves		Reserves for life insurance claims net of reinsurance and policy loans.
Individual annuity reserves		Reserves held in order to pay off maturing individual annuities or those surrendered before maturity.
Group annuity reserves		Reserves held in order to pay off maturing group annuities or those surrendered before maturity.
GIC reserves		Reserves held to pay off maturing guaranteed interest contracts.

Table 2. Bond Default Rates - potential losses as a percent of bond portfolio

Bond Rating	(1) Moody's 15 Yr Rate (%)	(2) Moody's 12 Yr Rate (%)	(3) Worst Year (%)	(4) 3 Cum. Recession Years (%)	(5) TheStreet.com Ratings 15 Year Rate (%)	(6) Assumed Loss Rate (%)	(7) Losses as % of Holdings (%)	(8) RACR #2 Rate (%)
Aaa	2.80	1.60	0.10	0.30	1.89	50	0.95	1.00
Aa	2.00	1.60	0.20	0.60	2.19	50	1.09	1.00
A	3.30	2.50	0.40	1.20	3.67	55	2.02	1.00
Baa	7.20	5.50	1.10	3.26	8.58	60	5.15	5.00
Ba	20.10	17.90	8.40	23.08	36.47	65	23.71	15.00
B	33.70	32.50	21.60	50.80	62.24	70	43.57	30.00

Comments On Target Capital Percentages

The factors that are chiefly responsible for the conservative results of our Risk-Adjusted Capital Ratios are the investment risks of bond Classes 2 - 6, mortgages, real estate and affiliate common stock as well as the interest rate risk for annuities and GICs. Comments on the basis of these figures are found below. Additional comments address factors that vary, based on particular performance or risk characteristics of the individual company.

Bonds

Target capital percentages for bonds are derived from a model that factors in historical cumulative bond default rates from the last 20 years and the additional loss potential during a prolonged economic decline. The continuance of post-World War II prosperity is by no means certain. Realistic analysis of potential losses must factor in the possibility of severe economic reversal. **Table 2** shows how this was done for each bond rating classification. A 15-year cumulative default rate is used (column 1), due to the 15-year average maturity at issue of bonds held by life insurance companies. These are historical default rates for 1970-1990 for each bond class, taken from *Moody's Studies Loss Potential of Life Insurance Assets*.

To factor in the additional loss potential of a severe three-year-long economic decline, we reduced the base to Moody's 12-year rate (column 2), determined the worst single year experience (column 3), spread that experience over three years (column 4), and added the historical 12-year rate to the 3-year projection to derive TheStreet.com Ratings 15-year default rate (column 5). Note: Due to the shrinking base of nondefaulted bonds in each year, column 4 may be somewhat less than three times column 3, and column 5 may be somewhat less than the sum of column 2 and column 4.

The next step was to determine the losses that could be expected from these defaults. This would be equivalent to the capital a company should have to cover those losses. Loss rates were assigned for each bond class (column 6), based on the fact that higher-rated issues generally carry less debt and the fact that the debt is also better secured, leading to higher recovery rates upon default. Column 7 shows losses as a percent of holdings for each bond class.

Column 8 shows the target capital percentages that are used in RACR #2 (Table 1, RACR #2 column, Bonds - classes 1 to 6).

Regulations limiting junk bond holdings of insurers to a set percent of assets are a tacit acknowledgement that the 10% and 20% maximum reserve requirements used by State Insurance Commissioners (Table 1, NAIC column, Bonds-classes 4, 5 and 6) are inadequate. If the figure adequately represented full loss potential, there would be no need to limit holdings through legislation since an adequate loss reserve would provide sufficient capital to absorb potential losses.

Mortgages
Mortgage default rates for the Risk-Adjusted Capital Ratios are derived from historical studies of mortgage and real estate losses in selected depressed markets. The rate for RACR #2 (Table 1, RACR #2 column, Mortgages – 90 days overdue) will vary between 3.8 and 25%, based on the performance of the company's mortgage portfolio in terms of mortgage loans 90 days or more past due, in process of foreclosure and foreclosed during the previous year.

Real Estate
The 33% rate (Table 1, RACR #2 column, Real Estate – Class 2) used for potential real estate losses in TheStreet.com ratios is based on historical losses in depressed markets. It avoids the commonly made assumption that the continuous appreciation of property values experienced since World War II must inevitably continue.

Affiliate Common Stock
The target capital rate on affiliate common stock for RACR #2 can vary between 33% and 100% (Table 1, RACR #2 column, Common stock - Affiliate) depending on the financial strength of the affiliate and the prospects for obtaining capital from the affiliate should the need arise.

Insurance Risk
Calculations of target capital for insurance risk vary according to categories. For individual and group life insurance, target capital is a percentage of net amount at risk (total amount of insurance in force less reserves). Individual and group health insurance risk is calculated as a percentage of premium. Categories vary from "usual and customary hospital and medical premiums" where risk is relatively low, because losses from one year are recouped by annual rate increases to "noncancellable disability income" where the risk of loss is greater because disability benefits are paid in future years without the possibility of recovery.

Reinsurance
This factor varies with the quality of the reinsuring companies and the type of reinsurance being used (e.g. co-insurance, modified co-insurance, yearly renewable term, etc.).

Interest Rate Risk On Annuities
The 1 - 5% rate on individual annuities as a percentage of reserves (Table 1, RACR #2 column 3, Individual annuity reserves) and the 1 - 3% rate for group annuities as a percentage of reserves (Table 1, RACR #2 column 3, Group annuity reserves and GICs) are derived from studies of potential losses that can occur when assets and liabilities are not properly matched.

Companies are especially prone to losses in this area for one of two reasons: (1) They promise high interest rates on their annuities and have not locked in corresponding yields on their investments. If interest rates fall, the company will have difficulties earning the promised rate. (2) They lock in high returns on their investments but allow policy surrenders without market value adjustments. If market values decline and surrenders increase, liquidity problems can result in substantial losses.

The target capital figure used for each company is based on the surrender characteristics of its policies, the interest rate used in calculating reserves and the actuarial analysis found in New York Regulation 126 filing or similar studies where applicable.

RECENT INDUSTRY FAILURES

2009

Institution	Headquarters	Industry	Date of Failure	Total Assets ($Mil)	Financial Strength Rating
				At Date of Failure	
American Network Ins Co	Pennsylvania	L&H	01/06/09	125.8	D+ (Weak)
Consumer First Ins Co	New Jersey	P&C	04/22/09	10.7	D- (Weak)
Coral Ins Co	Florida	P&C	04/09/09	15.4	E+ (Very Weak)
Escude Life Ins Co	Louisiana	L&H	04/27/09	3.0	E- (Very Weak)
First Commercial Insurance Co	Florida	P&C	07/10/09	87.1	E+ (Very Weak)
First Comm. Transp & Prop Ins Co	Florida	P&C	07/10/09	19.6	E+ (Very Weak)
Insurance Corp of New York	New York	P&C	06/29/09	87.3	
NSA Rrg Inc	Vermont	P&C	03/09/09	23.4	N/A
Penn Treaty Network America Ins Co	Pennsylvania	L&H	01/06/09	1037.6	C- (Fair)
Physicians Assurance Corp	Ohio	HMO	08/18/09	3.4	D+ (Weak)
Preferred Health	Puerto Rico	HMO	07/30/09	16.2	D- (Weak)
Scottish RE US Inc	Delaware	L&H	01/05/09	2950.6	D (Weak)
Shenandoah Life Ins Co	Virginia	L&H	02/12/09	1735.0	B (Good)
Texas Memorial Life Ins Co	Texas	L&H	06/10/09	3.80	E- (Very Weak)
Universal Life Insurance Co	Alabama	L&H	04/24/09		E (Very Weak)

2008

Institution	Headquarters	Industry	Date of Failure	Total Assets ($Mil)	Financial Strength Rating
				At Date of Failure	
Americas Hlth Choice Med. Plans Inc.	Florida	HMO	08/06/08	N/A	U
Austin Indemnity Lloyds Ins Co	Texas	P&C	12/29/08	5.5	E+ (Very Weak)
Fremont Life Ins Co.	California	L&H	06/05/08	6.1	E+ (Very Weak)
Jordan Funeral and Ins Co, Inc	Alabama	L&H	09/12/08		U
Lincoln Memorial Life Ins Co.	Texas	L&H	05/14/08	124.0	C (Fair)

MD Medicare Choice, Inc.	Florida	HMO	09/29/08	N/A	U
MDNY HealthCare, Inc.	New York	HMO	07/31/08	10.3	E (Very Weak)
Medical Savings Ins Co	Indiana	HMO	12/01/08	43.5	
Memorial Service Life Ins Co.	Texas	L&H	05/14/08	23.4	D+ (Weak)
Standard Life Ins Co	Indiana	L&H	12/18/08	2021.1	

2007

| | | | | At Date of Failure | |
Institution	Headquarters	Industry	Date of Failure	Total Assets ($Mil)	Financial Strength Rating
Beacon Insurance Co.	North Carolina	P&C	12/03/07		N/A
Benicorp Insurance Co	Indiana	L&H	06/05/07	53.4	D (Weak)
Colonial Indemnity Ins. Co	New York	P&C	9/6/2007	N/A	U
Community Health Plan Inc	New York	HMO	08/30/07	N/A	U
Lincoln Memorial Life Ins Co	Texas	L&H	10/24/07	N/A	C+ (Fair)
Lion Ins. Co	New York	P&C	09/06/07	N/A	U
Memorial Service Life Ins Co	Texas	L&H	10/24/07	N/A	D+ (Weak)
Municipal Ins. Co of America	Illinois	L&H	10/24/07	12.6	D (Weak)
National Annuity Co	Utah	L&H	03/23/07	N/A	E (Very Weak)
NW Nat.Ins Co of Milwaukee, WI	Wisconsin	P&C	03/08/07	N/A	U
Patriot Health Ins Co Inc	New Hampshire	HMO	12/12/07	N/A	U
Suncoast Physicians Hlth Plan, Inc	Florida	HMO	08/10/07	2.1	U
Vanguard Fire & Casualty	Florida	P&C	1/19/2007	47.8	E (Very Weak)
Universal Health Care Ins Co Inc	Florida	HMO	02/21/07	N/A	U

2006

Institution	Headquarters	Industry	Date of Failure	At Date of Failure	
				Total Assets ($Mil)	Financial Strength Rating
Atlantic Preferred	Florida	P&C	05/01/06	63.4	D (Weak)
Booker T Washington Ins	Alabama	L&H	03/02/06	54.3	E (Very Weak)
DoctorCare Inc	Florida	Health	11/20/06	11.4	U
Family Life Ins Co of Am	Texas	L&H	08/24/06	N/A	U
Florida Preferred Prop	Florida	P&C	05/25/06	63.4	E+ (Very Weak)
Florida Select Ins Co	Florida	P&C	06/30/06	38.6	D (Weak)
Hawaiian Ins & Guaranty	Hawaii	P&C	06/30/06	26.4	D (Weak)
Municipal Mutual Ins Co	California	P&C	10/24/06	N/A	E (Very Weak)
NJ Exchange	New Jersey	P&C	07/10/06	3.6	E+ (Very Weak)
Phoenix Fund Inc	No Carolina	P&C	10/17/06	29	E (Very Weak)
Security General Life Ins	Oklahoma	L&H	09/29/06	6.2	B- (Good)
Shelby Casualty Ins Co	Illinois	P&C	06/30/06	29.3	D (Weak)
Southern Family Ins Co	Florida	P&C	04/25/06	56.1	D (Weak)
Texas Select Lloyds Ins	Texas	P&C	06/30/06	47.5	D (Weak)
The Shelby Ins Co	Illinois	P&C	06/30/06	29.0	D (Weak)
Ultimed HMO Michigan	Michigan	Health	01/25/06	2.7	D- (Weak)
Universal Ins Exchange	Texas	P&C	01/26/06	10.0	D (Weak)
Valor Ins Co	Montana	P&C	08/03/06	3.8	U
Vesta Fire Ins Co	Illinois	P&C	06/30/06	344.1	D (Weak)
Vesta Insurance Corp	Illinois	P&C	06/30/06	19.4	D (Weak)

2005

Institution	Headquarters	Industry	Date of Failure	Total Assets ($Mil)	Financial Strength Rating
				At Date of Failure	
Amil Int'l, Inc.	Texas	Health	03/07/05	9.9	E (Very Weak)
Benton Life Ins Co Inc	Louisiana	L&H	06/23/05	N/A	U
Commercial Mutual Ins	Georgia	P&C	06/15/05	18.7	E (Very Weak)
Consolidated Am Ins Co	So Carolina	P&C	03/08/05	4.0	D (Weak)
Cornerstone Mutual Ins	Georgia	P&C	06/15/05	28.5	D- (Weak)
Employers Life Ins Co	S Carolina	L&H	07/24/05	12.1	E- (Very Weak)
Financial Life & Acc Ins	Florida	L&H	04/18/05	10.6	U
Hospitality Mutual Captive	Georgia	P&C	08/24/05	4.1	E+ (Very Weak)
Lone Star Life Ins Co	Texas	L&H	08/18/05	N/A	U
MagnaHealth of NY Inc	New York	Health	08/24/05	2.4	D (Weak)
North America Life Ins	Texas	L&H	06/30/05	N/A	E (Very Weak)
Old Am.Cnty Mutual Fire Ins Co	Texas	P&C	11/07/05	N/A	E+ (Very Weak)
Omnicare Health Plan	Tennessee	Health	04/21/05	12.3	C+ (Fair)
PrimeGuard Ins Co RRG	Hawaii	P&C	12/19/05	3.3	D- (Weak)
Realm National Ins Co	New York	P&C	06/15/05	31.2	U
Reliant American Ins Co	Texas	P&C	05/06/05	21.5	E- (Very Weak)
Senior Citizens Mutual	Florida	P&C	05/09/05	21.9	C- (Fair)
South Carolina Ins Co	So Carolina	P&C	03/08/05	19.3	E+ (Very Weak)
States General Life Ins Co	Texas	L&H	03/09/05	7.5	D- (Weak)
Texas Int'l Life Ins Co	Texas	L&H	06/29/05	N/A	E (Very Weak)
Top Flight	Oklahoma	P&C	05/10/05	5.9	E+ (Very Weak)
Union American Ins Co	Florida	P&C	02/09/05	11.0	D (Weak)

2004

| Institution | Headquarters | Industry | Date of Failure | At Date of Failure | |
				Total Assets ($Mil)	Financial Strength Rating
Acadian Life Ins Co	Louisiana	L&H	08/31/04	16.0	E- (Very Weak)
American Superior Ins Co	Florida	P&C	09/29/04	13.5	D (Weak)
American Skyline Ins Co	Maryland	P&C	11/30/04	6.0	E+ (Very Weak)
Assoc of Trial Lawyers	Illinois	P&C	10/14/04	1.5	U
Capitol Life Ins Co	Texas	L&H	03/03/04	304.8	D (Weak)
Carrol Cnty Mutual Fire Ins Co	Maryland	P&C	04/12/04	N/A	D (Weak)
Cascade National Ins Co	Washington	P&C	11/30/04	27.3	D (Weak)
Colorado Western Ins Co	Colorado	P&C	05/27/04	17.2	D- (Weak)
Cumberland Cas & Surety	Florida	P&C	02/26/04	12.1	D (Weak)
Family Health Care Plus	Mississippi	Health	07/15/04	25.3	U
Financial Ins Co of Am	Texas	P&C	05/03/04	10.6	D (Weak)
Foundation Insurance Co	So Carolina	P&C	05/17/04	25.5	E (Very Weak)
Hospital Casualty Co	Oklahoma	P&C	03/31/04	6.5	E (Very Weak)
Interboro Mutual Indem	New York	P&C	04/06/04	58.4	E- (Very Weak)
L&H Ins Co of America	Pennsylvania	L&H	07/02/04	47.9	E- (Very Weak)
Mack H Hannah Life Ins	Texas	L&H	07/23/04	N/A	U
Metrowest Health Plan	Texas	Health	06/10/04	7.2	B (Good)
MIIX Insurance Co	New Jersey	P&C	08/27/04	813.0	U
National Health Ins Co	Texas	L&H	03/03/04	873.8	E (Very Weak)
New America Ins Co	Florida	P&C	07/01/04	10.9	C- (Fair)
Physicians Liability Ins	Oklahoma	P&C	03/31/04	1.5	E+ (Very Weak)
Pinnacle Cas Assur Corp	Alabama	P&C	02/02/04	3.4	E (Very Weak)
PrimeHealth of Alabama	Alabama	Health	02/13/04	3.7	E (Very Weak)
State Capital Ins Co	No Carolina	P&C	06/21/04	8.7	D- (Weak)
Statewide Insurance Co	Illinois	P&C	01/06/04	33.1	D- (Weak)
Twin Falls Mutual Ins Co	Idaho	P&C	10/29/04	2.1	D- (Weak)

Glossary

This glossary contains the most important terms used in this publication.

Admitted Assets　　The total of all investments and business interests that are acceptable under statutory accounting rules.

Asset/Liability Matching　　The designation of particular investments (assets) to particular policy obligations (liabilities) so that investments mature at the appropriate times and with appropriate yields to meet policy obligations as they come due.

Asset Valuation Reserve (AVR)　　A liability established under statutory accounting rules whose purpose is to protect the company's surplus from the effects of defaults and market value fluctuation on stocks, bonds, qmortgages and real estate. This replaces the Mandatory Securities Valuation Reserve (MSVR) and is more comprehensive in that it includes a mortgage loss reserve, whereas the MSVR did not.

Average Recession　　A recession involving a decline in real GDP which is approximately equivalent to the average of the postwar recessions of 1957-58, 1960, 1970, 1974-75, 1980 and 1981-82. It is assumed, however, that in today's market, the financial losses suffered from a recession of that magnitude would be greater than those experienced in previous decades. (See also "Severe Recession.")

Capital　　Strictly speaking, capital refers to funds raised through the sale of common and preferred stock. Mutual companies have capital in the form of retained earnings. In a more general sense, the term capital is commonly used to refer to a company's equity or net worth, that is, the difference between assets and liabilities (i.e., capital and surplus as shown on the balance sheet).

Capital Resources　　The sum of various resources which serve as a capital cushion to losses, including capital, surplus and Asset Valuation Reserve (AVR).

Capitalization Index　　An index, expressed on a scale of zero to ten, with seven or higher considered excellent, that measures the adequacy of the company's capital resources to deal with a variety of business and economic scenarios. It combines Risk-Adjusted Capital Ratios #1 and #2 as well as a leverage test that examines pricing risk.

Cash and Demand Deposits　　Includes cash on hand and on deposit. A negative figure indicates that the company has more checks outstanding than current funds to cover those checks. This is not an unusual situation for an insurance company.

Collateralized Mortgage Obligation (CMO)	Mortgage-backed bond that splits the payments from mortgage pools into different classes, called tranches. The investor may purchase a bond or tranche that passes through to him or her the principal and interest payments made by the mortgage holders in that specific maturity class (usually two, five, 10 or 20 years). The risk associated with a CMO is in the variation of the payment speed on the mortgage pool which, if different than originally assumed, can cause the total return to vary greatly.
Common and Preferred Stocks	See "Stocks".
Deposit Funds	Accumulated contributions of a group out of which immediate annuities are purchased as the individual members of the group retire.
Direct Premiums Written	Total gross premiums derived from policies issued directly by the company. This figure excludes the impact of reinsurance.
Financial Strength Rating	TheStreet.com Financial Strength Ratings grade insurers on a scale from A (Excellent) to F (Failed). Ratings are based on five major factors: investment safety, policy leverage, capitalization, profitability and stability of operations.
Five-Year Profitability Index	See "Profitability Index."
Government Securities	Securities issued and/or guaranteed by U.S. and foreign governments which are rated as highest quality (Class 1) by state insurance commissioners. Included in this category are bonds issued by governmental agencies and guaranteed with the full faith and credit of the government. Regardless of the issuing entity, they are viewed as being relatively safer than the other investment categories. See "Investment Grade Bonds" to determine which items are excluded from this category.
Health Claims Reserve	Funds set aside from premiums for the eventual payment of health benefits after the end of the statement year.
Insurance Risk	The risk that the level of claims and related expenses will exceed current premiums plus reserves allocated for their payment.
Interest Rate Risk	The risk that, due to changes in interest rates, investment income will not meet the needs of policy commitments. This risk can be reduced by effective asset/liability matching.
Invested Assets	The total size of the firm's investment portfolio.
Investment Grade Bonds	This covers all investment grade bonds other than those listed in "Government Securities" (above). Specifically, this includes: (1) nonguaranteed obligations of governments; (2) obligations of governments rated as Class 2 by state insurance commissioners; (3)

state and municipal bonds; plus (4) investment grade corporate bonds.

Investment Safety Index   Measured on a scale of zero to ten, with ten being the best and seven or better considered strong. Each investment area is rated as to quality and vulnerability during an unfavorable economic environment (updated using quarterly data when available).

Investments in Affiliates   Includes bonds, preferred stocks and common stocks, as well as other vehicles which many insurance companies use to invest in—and establish a corporate link with—affiliated companies

Life and Annuity Claims Reserve   Funds set aside from premiums for the eventual payment of life and annuity claims.

Liquidity Index   An index, expressed on a scale from zero to ten, with seven or higher considered excellent, which measures the company's ability to raise the necessary cash to meet policyholder obligations. This index includes a stress test which considers the consequences of a spike in claims or a run on policy surrenders. Sometimes a company may appear to have the necessary resources, but may be unable to sell its investments at the prices at which they are valued in the company's financial statements.

Mandatory Security Valuation Reserve (MSVR)   Reserve for investment losses and asset value fluctuation mandated by the state insurance commissioners for companies registered as life and health insurers. As of December 31, 1992, this was replaced by the Asset Valuation Reserve.

Moderate Loss Scenario   An economic decline from current levels approximately equivalent to that of the average postwar recession.

Mortgages in Good Standing   Mortgages which are current in their payments (excludes mortgage-backed securities).

Net Premiums Written   The total dollar volume of premiums retained by the company. This figure is equal to direct premiums written, plus reinsurance assumed less reinsurance ceded.

Noninvestment Grade Bonds   Low-rated issues, commonly known as "junk bonds," which carry a high risk as defined by the state insurance commissioners. These include bond Classes 3 - 6.

Nonperforming Mortgages   Mortgages which are (a) 90 days or more past due or (b) in process of foreclosure.

Other Investments   Items not included in any of the other categories such as premium notes, collateral loans, short-term investments and other miscellaneous items.

Other Structured Securities   Nonresidential mortgage related and other securitized loan-backed or asset-backed securities. This category also includes CMOs with noninvestment grade ratings.

Policy Leverage	A measure of insurance risk based on the relationship of net premiums to capital resources.
Policy Loans	Loans to policyholders under insurance contracts.
Profitability Index	Measured on a scale of zero to ten, with ten being the best and seven or better considered strong. A composite of five factors: (1) gain or loss on operations; (2) consistency of operating results; (3) impact of operating results on surplus; (4) adequacy of investment income as compared to the needs of policy reserves; and (5) expenses in relation to industry averages. Thus, the overall index is an indicator of the health of a company's current and past operations.
Purchase Money Mortgages	Mortgages written by an insurance company to facilitate the sale of property owned by the company.
Real Estate	Direct real estate investments including property (a) occupied by the company; (b) acquired through foreclosure and (c) purchased as an investment.
Reinsurance Assumed	Insurance risk acquired by taking on partial or full responsibility for claims on policies written by other companies. (See "Reinsurance Ceded.")
Reinsurance Ceded	Insurance risk sold to another company.
Risk-Adjusted Capital	The capital resources that would be needed in a worsening economic environment (same as "Target Capital").
Risk-Adjusted Capital Ratio #1	The capital resources which a company currently has, in relation to the resources that would be needed to deal with a moderate loss scenario. This scenario is based on historical experience during an average recession and adjusted to reflect current conditions and vulnerabilities (updated using quarterly data when available).
Risk-Adjusted Capital Ratio #2	The capital resources which a company currently has, in relation to the resources that would be needed to deal with a severe loss scenario. This scenario is based on historical experience of the postwar period and adjusted to reflect current conditions and the potential impact of a severe recession (updated using quarterly data when available).
Separate Accounts	Funds segregated from the general account and valued at market. Used to fund indexed products, such as variable life and variable annuity products.
Severe Loss Scenario	An economic decline from current levels in which the loss experience of the single worst year of the postwar period is extended for a period of three years. (See also "Moderate Loss Scenario".)
Severe Recession	A prolonged economic slowdown in which the single worst year of the

postwar period is extended for a period of three years. (See also "Average Recession".)

Stability Index   Measured on a scale of zero to ten. This integrates a wide variety of factors that reflects the company's financial stability and diversification of risk.

State of Domicile   Although most insurance companies are licensed to do business in many states, they have only one state of domicile. This is the state which has primary regulatory responsibility for the company. Use the state of domicile to make absolutely sure that you have the correct company. Bear in mind, however, that this need not be the state where the company's main offices are located.

State Guaranty Funds   Funds that are designed to raise cash from existing insurance carriers to cover policy claims of bankrupt insurance companies.

Stocks   Common and preferred equities, including ownership in affiliates.

Surplus   The difference between assets and liabilities, including paid-in contributed surplus, plus the statutory equivalent of "retained earnings" in non-insurance business corporations.

Target Capital   See "Risk-Adjusted Capital."

Total Assets   Total admitted assets, including investments and other business assets. See "Admitted Assets."

TheStreet.com Ratings'

THESTREET.COM RATINGS' REPORTS AND SERVICES

See pricing below for each report and service.

Ratings Online — An on-line summary covering an individual company's TheStreet.com Financial Strength Rating or an investment's unique TheStreet.com Investment Rating with the factors contributing to that rating; available 24 hours a day by visiting www.thestreet.com/tscratings/.

Unlimited Ratings Research — The ultimate research tool providing fast, easy online access to the very latest TheStreet.com Financial Strength Ratings and Investment Ratings. Price: $559 per industry.

THESTREET.COM RATINGS' CUSTOM REPORTS

TheStreet.com Ratings is pleased to offer two customized options for receiving our data. Each taps into our vast data repositories and is designed to provide exactly the data you need. Choose from a variety of industries, companies, data variables, and delivery formats including print, Excel, SQL, Text or Access.

Customized Reports - get right to the heart of your company's research and data needs with a report customized with just the data you need.

Complete Database Download - we design and deliver the database; you're then free to sort it, recalculate it, and format your results to suit your specific needs.

To Place your Reports Order

❶ Call TheStreet.com at (800) 289-9222

❷ Order Online at www.thestreet.com/ratings

Business Information ◆ **Ratings Guides** ◆ General Reference ◆ Education ◆
Statistics ◆ Demographics ◆ Health Information ◆ Canadian Information

Grey House Publishing

TheStreet.com Ratings Guide to Health Insurers

TheStreet.com Ratings Guide to Health Insurers is the first and only source to cover the financial stability of the nation's health care system, rating the financial safety of more than 6,000 health insurance providers, health maintenance organizations (HMOs) and all of the Blue Cross Blue Shield plans – updated quarterly to ensure the most accurate information. The Guide also provides a complete listing of all the major health insurers, including all Long-Term Care and Medigap insurers. Our *Guide to Health Insurers* includes comprehensive, timely coverage on the financial stability of HMOs and health insurers; the most accurate insurance company ratings available–the same quality ratings heralded by the U.S. General Accounting Office; separate listings for those companies offering Medigap and long-term care policies; the number of serious consumer complaints filed against most HMOs so you can see who is actually providing the best (or worst) service and more. The easy-to-use layout gives you a one-line summary analysis for each company that we track, followed by an in-depth, detailed analysis of all HMOs and the largest health insurers. The guide also includes a list of TheStreet.com Ratings Recommended Companies with information on how to contact them, and the reasoning behind any rating upgrades or downgrades.

> *"With 20 years behind its insurance-advocacy research [the rating guide] continues to offer a wealth of information that helps consumers weigh their healthcare options now and in the future." -Today's Librarian*

Issues published quarterly, Softcover, 550 pages, $499.00 for four quarterly issues, $249.00 for a single issue

TheStreet.com Ratings Guide to Life & Annuity Insurers

TheStreet.com Safety Ratings are the most reliable source for evaluating an insurer's financial solvency risk. Consequently, policy-holders have come to rely on TheStreet.com's flagship publication, *TheStreet.com Ratings Guide to Life & Annuity Insurers*, to help them identify the safest companies to do business with. Each easy-to-use edition delivers TheStreet.com's independent ratings and analyses on more than 1,100 insurers, updated every quarter. Plus, your patrons will find a complete list of TheStreet.com Recommended Companies, including contact information, and the reasoning behind any rating upgrades or downgrades. This guide is perfect for those who are considering the purchase of a life insurance policy, placing money in an annuity, or advising clients about insurance and annuities. A life or health insurance policy or annuity is only as secure as the insurance company issuing it. Therefore, make sure your patrons have what they need to periodically monitor the financial condition of the companies with whom they have an investment. The TheStreet.com Ratings product line is designed to help them in their evaluations.

> *"Weiss has an excellent reputation and this title is held by hundreds of libraries. This guide is recommended for public and academic libraries." -ARBA*

Issues published quarterly, Softcover, 360 pages, $499.00 for four quarterly issues, $249.00 for a single issue

TheStreet.com Ratings Guide to Property & Casualty Insurers

TheStreet.com Ratings Guide to Property and Casualty Insurers provides the most extensive coverage of insurers writing policies, helping consumers and businesses avoid financial headaches. Updated quarterly, this easy-to-use publication delivers the independent, unbiased TheStreet.com Safety Ratings and supporting analyses on more than 2,800 U.S. insurance companies, offering auto & homeowners insurance, business insurance, worker's compensation insurance, product liability insurance, medical malpractice and other professional liability insurance. Each edition includes a list of TheStreet.com Recommended Companies by type of insurance, including a contact number, plus helpful information about the coverage provided by the State Guarantee Associations.

> *"In contrast to the other major insurance rating agencies...Weiss does not have a financial relationship worth the companies it rates. A GAO study found that Weiss identified financial vulnerability earlier than the other rating agencies." -ARBA*

Issues published quarterly, Softcover, 455 pages, $499.00 for four quarterly issues, $249.00 for a single issue

TheStreet.com Ratings Consumer Box Set

Deliver the critical information your patrons need to safeguard their personal finances with *TheStreet.com Ratings' Consumer Guide Box Set*. Each of the eight guides is packed with accurate, unbiased information and recommendations to help your patrons make sound financial decisions. TheStreet.com Ratings Consumer Guide Box Set provides your patrons with easy to understand guidance on important personal finance topics, including: *Consumer Guide to Variable Annuities, Consumer Guide to Medicare Supplement Insurance, Consumer Guide to Elder Care Choices, Consumer Guide to Automobile Insurance, Consumer Guide to Long-Term Care Insurance, Consumer Guide to Homeowners Insurance, Consumer Guide to Term Life Insurance,* and *Consumer Guide to Medicare Prescription Drug Coverage.* Each guide provides an easy-to-read overview of the topic, what to look out for when selecting a company or insurance plan to do business with, who are the recommended companies to work with and how to navigate through these often-times difficult decisions. Custom worksheets and step-by-step directions make these resources accessible to all types of users. Packaged in a handy custom display box, these helpful guides will prove to be a much-used addition to any reference collection.

Issues published twice per year, Softcover, 600 pages, $499.00 for two biennial issues

Business Information ◆ <u>**Ratings Guides**</u> ◆ **General Reference** ◆ **Education** ◆
Statistics ◆ **Demographics** ◆ **Health Information** ◆ **Canadian Information**

Grey Hou⌐
Publishir

TheStreet.com Ratings Guide to Stock Mutual Funds

TheStreet.com Ratings Guide to Stock Mutual Funds offers ratings and analyses on more than 8,800 equity mutual funds – more than any other publication. The exclusive TheStreet.com Investment Ratings combine an objective evaluation of each fund's performance and risk to provide a single, user-friendly, composite rating, giving your patrons a better handle on a mutual fund's risk-adjusted performance. Each edition identifies the top-performing mutual funds based on risk category, type of fund, and overall risk-adjusted performance. TheStreet.com's unique investment rating system makes it easy to see exactly which stocks are on the rise and which ones should be avoided. For those investors looking to tailor their mutual fund selections based on age, income, and tolerance for risk, we've also assigned two component ratings to each fund: a performance rating and a risk rating. With these, you can identify those funds that are best suited to meet your - or your client's – individual needs and goals. Plus, we include a handy Risk Profile Quiz to help you assess your personal tolerance for risk. So whether you're an investing novice or professional, the *Guide to Stock Mutual Funds* gives you everything you need to find a mutual fund that is right for you.

> *"There is tremendous need for information such as that provided by this Weiss publication. This reasonably priced guide is recommended for public and academic libraries serving investors." -ARBA*

Issues published quarterly, Softcover, 655 pages, $499 for four quarterly issues, $249 for a single issue

TheStreet.com Ratings Guide to Exchange-Traded Funds

TheStreet.com Ratings editors analyze hundreds of mutual funds each quarter, condensing all of the available data into a single composite opinion of each fund's risk-adjusted performance. The intuitive, consumer-friendly ratings allow investors to instantly identify those funds that have historically done well and those that have under-performed the market. Each quarterly edition identifies the top-performing exchange-traded funds based on risk category, type of fund, and overall risk-adjusted performance. The rating scale, A through F, gives you a better handle on an exchange-traded fund's risk-adjusted performance. Other features include Top & Bottom 200 Exchange-Traded Funds; Performance and Risk: 100 Best and Worst Exchange- Traded Funds; Investor Profile Quiz; Performance Benchmarks and Fund Type Descriptions. With the growing popularity of mutual fund investing, consumers need a reliable source to help them track and evaluate the performance of their mutual fund holdings. Plus, they need a way of identifying and monitoring other funds as potential new investments. Unfortunately, the hundreds of performance and risk measures available, multiplied by the vast number of mutual fund investments on the market today, can make this a daunting task for even the most sophisticated investor. This Guide will serve as a useful tool for both the first-time and seasoned investor.

Editions published quarterly, Softcover, 440 pages, $499.00 for four quarterly issues, $249.00 for a single issue

TheStreet.com Ratings Guide to Bond & Money Market Mutual Funds

TheStreet.com Ratings Guide to Bond & Money Market Mutual Funds has everything your patrons need to easily identify the top-performing fixed income funds on the market today. Each quarterly edition contains TheStreet.com's independent ratings and analyses on more than 4,600 fixed income funds – more than any other publication, including corporate bond funds, high-yield bond funds, municipal bond funds, mortgage security funds, money market funds, global bond funds and government bond funds. In addition, the fund's risk rating is combined with its three-year performance rating to get an overall picture of the fund's risk-adjusted performance. The resulting TheStreet.com Investment Rating gives a single, user-friendly, objective evaluation that makes it easy to compare one fund to another and select the right fund based on the level of risk tolerance. Most investors think of fixed income mutual funds as "safe" investments. That's not always the case, however, depending on the credit risk, interest rate risk, and prepayment risk of the securities owned by the fund. TheStreet.com Ratings assesses each of these risks and assigns each fund a risk rating to help investors quickly evaluate the fund's risk component. Plus, we include a handy Risk Profile Quiz to help you assess your personal tolerance for risk. So whether you're an investing novice or professional, the *Guide to Bond and Money Market Mutual Funds* gives you everything you need to find a mutual fund that is right for you.

> *"Comprehensive... It is easy to use and consumer-oriented, and can be recommended for larger public and academic libraries." -ARBA*

Issues published quarterly, Softcover, 470 pages, $499.00 for four quarterly issues, $249.00 for a single issue

TheStreet.com Ratings Guide to Banks & Thrifts

Updated quarterly, for the most up-to-date information, *TheStreet.com Ratings Guide to Banks and Thrifts* offers accurate, intuitive safety ratings your patrons can trust; supporting ratios and analyses that show an institution's strong & weak points; identification of the TheStreet.com Recommended Companies with branches in your area; a complete list of institutions receiving upgrades/downgrades; and comprehensive coverage of every bank and thrift in the nation – more than 9,000. TheStreet.com Safety Ratings are then based on the analysts' review of publicly available information collected by the federal banking regulators. The easy-to-use layout gives you: the institution's TheStreet.com Safety Rating for the last 3 years; the five key indexes used to evaluate each institution; along with the primary ratios and statistics used in determining the company's rating. *TheStreet.com Ratings Guide to Banks & Thrifts* will be a must for individuals who are concerned about the safety of their CD or savings account; need to be sure that an existing line of credit will be there when they need it; or simply want to avoid the hassles of dealing with a failing or troubled institution.

> *"Large public and academic libraries most definitely need to acquire the work. Likewise, special libraries in large corporations will find this title indispensable." -ARBA*

Issues published quarterly, Softcover, 370 pages, $499.00 for four quarterly issues, $249.00 for a single issue

Business Information ♦ **Ratings Guides** ♦ General Reference ♦ Education ♦
Statistics ♦ Demographics ♦ Health Information ♦ Canadian Information

TheStreet.com Ratings Guide to Common Stocks

TheStreet.com Ratings Guide to Common Stocks gives your patrons reliable insight into the risk-adjusted performance of common stocks listed on the NYSE, AMEX, and Nasdaq – over 5,800 stocks in all – more than any other publication. TheStreet.com's unique investment rating system makes it easy to see exactly which stocks are on the rise and which ones should be avoided. In addition, your patrons also get supporting analysis showing growth trends, profitability, debt levels, valuation levels, the top-rated stocks within each industry, and more. Plus, each stock is ranked with the easy-to-use buy-hold-sell equivalents commonly used by Wall Street. Whether they're selecting their own investments or checking up on a broker's recommendation, TheStreet.com Ratings can help them in their evaluations.

"Users... will find the information succinct and the explanations readable, easy to understand, and helpful to a novice." -Library Journal

Issues published quarterly, Softcover, 440 pages, $499.00 for four quarterly issues, $249.00 for a single issue

TheStreet.com Ratings Ultimate Guided Tour of Stock Investing

This important reference guide from TheStreet.com Ratings is just what librarians around the country have asked for: a step-by-step introduction to stock investing for the beginning to intermediate investor. This easy-to-navigate guide explores the basics of stock investing and includes the intuitive TheStreet.com Investment Rating on more than 5,800 stocks, complete with real-world investing information that can be put to use immediately with stocks that fit the concepts discussed in the guide; informative charts, graphs and worksheets; easy-to-understand explanations on topics like P/E, compound interest, marked indices, diversifications, brokers, and much more; along with financial safety ratings for every stock on the NYSE, American Stock Exchange and the Nasdaq. This consumer-friendly guide offers complete how-to information on stock investing that can be put to use right away; a friendly format complete with our "Wise Guide" who leads the reader on a safari to learn about the investing jungle; helpful charts, graphs and simple worksheets; the intuitive TheStreet.com Investment rating on over 6,000 stocks — every stock found on the NYSE, American Stock Exchange and the NASDAQ; and much more.

"Provides investors with an alternative to stock broker recommendations, which recently have been tarnished by conflicts of interest. In summary, the guide serves as a welcome addition for all public library collections." -ARBA

Issues published quarterly, Softcover, 370 pages, $499.00 for four quarterly issues, $249.00 for a single issue

TheStreet.com Ratings' Reports & Services

- Ratings Online — An on-line summary covering an individual company's TheStreet.com Financial Strength Rating or an investment's unique TheStreet.com Investment Rating with the factors contributing to that rating; available 24 hours a day by visiting www.thestreet.com/tscratings or calling (800) 289-9222.
- Unlimited Ratings Research — The ultimate research tool providing fast, easy online access to the very latest TheStreet.com Financial Strength Ratings and Investment Ratings. Price: $559 per industry.

Contact TheStreet.com for more information about Reports & Services at www.thestreet.com/tscratings or call (800) 289-9222

TheStreet.com Ratings' Custom Reports

TheStreet.com Ratings is pleased to offer two customized options for receiving ratings data. Each taps into TheStreet.com's vast data repositories and is designed to provide exactly the data you need. Choose from a variety of industries, companies, data variables, and delivery formats including print, Excel, SQL, Text or Access.

- Customized Reports - get right to the heart of your company's research and data needs with a report customized to your specifications.
- Complete Database Download – TheStreet.com will design and deliver the database; from there you can sort it, recalculate it, and format your results to suit your specific needs.

Contact TheStreet.com for more information about Reports & Services at www.thestreet.com/tscratings or call (800) 289-9222

Business Information ♦ Ratings Guides ♦ General Reference ♦ Education ♦
Statistics ♦ Demographics ♦ Health Information ♦ Canadian Information

Grey House
Publishing

The Directory of Business Information Resources, 2009

With 100% verification, over 1,000 new listings and more than 12,000 updates, *The Directory of Business Information Resources* is the most up-to-date source for contacts in over 98 business areas – from advertising and agriculture to utilities and wholesalers. This carefully researched volume details: the Associations representing each industry; the Newsletters that keep members current; the Magazines and Journals - with their "Special Issues" - that are important to the trade, the Conventions that are "must attends," Databases, Directories and Industry Web Sites that provide access to must-have marketing resources. Includes contact names, phone & fax numbers, web sites and e-mail addresses. This one-volume resource is a gold mine of information and would be a welcome addition to any reference collection.

"This is a most useful and easy-to-use addition to any researcher's library." –The Information Professionals Institute

Softcover ISBN 978-1-59237-399-4, 2,500 pages, $195.00 | Online Database: http://gold.greyhouse.com Call (800) 562-2139 for quote

Hudson's Washington News Media Contacts Directory, 2009

With 100% verification of data, *Hudson's Washington News Media Contacts Directory* is the most accurate, most up-to-date source for media contacts in our nation's capital. With the largest concentration of news media in the world, having access to Washington's news media will get your message heard by these key media outlets. Published for over 40 years, Hudson's Washington News Media Contacts Directory brings you immediate access to: News Services & Newspapers, News Service Syndicates, DC Newspapers, Foreign Newspapers, Radio & TV, Magazines & Newsletters, and Freelance Writers & Photographers. The easy-to-read entries include contact names, phone & fax numbers, web sites and e-mail and more. For easy navigation, Hudson's Washington News Media Contacts Directory contains two indexes: Entry Index and Executive Index. This kind of comprehensive and up-to-date information would cost thousands of dollars to replicate or countless hours of searching to find. Don't miss this opportunity to have this important resource in your collection, and start saving time and money today. Hudson's Washington News Media Contacts Directory is the perfect research tool for Public Relations, Marketing, Networking and so much more. This resource is a gold mine of information and would be a welcome addition to any reference collection.

Softcover ISBN 978-1-59237-407-6, 800 pages, $289.00 | Online Database: http://gold.greyhouse.com Call (800) 562-2139 for quote

Nations of the World, 2009 A Political, Economic and Business Handbook

This completely revised edition covers all the nations of the world in an easy-to-use, single volume. Each nation is profiled in a single chapter that includes Key Facts, Political & Economic Issues, a Country Profile and Business Information. In this fast-changing world, it is extremely important to make sure that the most up-to-date information is included in your reference collection. This edition is just the answer. Each of the 200+ country chapters have been carefully reviewed by a political expert to make sure that the text reflects the most current information on Politics, Travel Advisories, Economics and more. You'll find such vital information as a Country Map, Population Characteristics, Inflation, Agricultural Production, Foreign Debt, Political History, Foreign Policy, Regional Insecurity, Economics, Trade & Tourism, Historical Profile, Political Systems, Ethnicity, Languages, Media, Climate, Hotels, Chambers of Commerce, Banking, Travel Information and more. Five Regional Chapters follow the main text and include a Regional Map, an Introductory Article, Key Indicators and Currencies for the Region. As an added bonus, an all-inclusive CD-ROM is available as a companion to the printed text. Noted for its sophisticated, up-to-date and reliable compilation of political, economic and business information, this brand new edition will be an important acquisition to any public, academic or special library reference collection.

"A useful addition to both general reference collections and business collections." –RUSQ

Softcover ISBN 978-1-59237-273-7, 1,700 pages, $180.00

The Directory of Venture Capital & Private Equity Firms, 2009

This edition has been extensively updated and broadly expanded to offer direct access to over 2,800 Domestic and International Venture Capital Firms, including address, phone & fax numbers, e-mail addresses and web sites for both primary and branch locations. Entries include details on the firm's Mission Statement, Industry Group Preferences, Geographic Preferences, Average and Minimum Investments and Investment Criteria. You'll also find details that are available nowhere else, including the Firm's Portfolio Companies and extensive information on each of the firm's Managing Partners, such as Education, Professional Background and Directorships held, along with the Partner's E-mail Address. *The Directory of Venture Capital & Private Equity Firms* offers five important indexes: Geographic Index, Executive Name Index, Portfolio Company Index, Industry Preference Index and College & University Index. With its comprehensive coverage and detailed, extensive information on each company, The Directory of Venture Capital & Private Equity Firms is an important addition to any finance collection.

"The sheer number of listings, the descriptive information and the outstanding indexing make this directory a better value than ...Pratt's Guide to Venture Capital Sources. Recommended for business collections in large public, academic and business libraries." –Choice

Softcover ISBN 978-1-59237-398-7, 1,300 pages, $565/$450 Lib | Online DB: http://gold.greyhouse.com Call (800) 562-2139 for quote

Business Information ✦ **Ratings Guides** ✦ **General Reference** ✦ **Education** ✦
Statistics ✦ **Demographics** ✦ **Health Information** ✦ **Canadian Information**

Grey House
Publishing

The Encyclopedia of Emerging Industries

*Published under an exclusive license from the Gale Group, Inc.

The fifth edition of the *Encyclopedia of Emerging Industries* details the inception, emergence, and current status of nearly 120 flourishing U.S. industries and industry segments. These focused essays unearth for users a wealth of relevant, current, factual data previously accessible only through a diverse variety of sources. This volume provides broad-based, highly-readable, industry information under such headings as Industry Snapshot, Organization & Structure, Background & Development, Industry Leaders, Current Conditions, America and the World, Pioneers, and Research & Technology. Essays in this new edition, arranged alphabetically for easy use, have been completely revised, with updated statistics and the most current information on industry trends and developments. In addition, there are new essays on some of the most interesting and influential new business fields, including Application Service Providers, Concierge Services, Entrepreneurial Training, Fuel Cells, Logistics Outsourcing Services, Pharmacogenomics, and Tissue Engineering. Two indexes, General and Industry, provide immediate access to this wealth of information. Plus, two conversion tables for SIC and NAICS codes, along with Suggested Further Readings, are provided to aid the user. *The Encyclopedia of Emerging Industries* pinpoints emerging industries while they are still in the spotlight. This important resource will be an important acquisition to any business reference collection.

"This well-designed source…should become another standard business source, nicely complementing Standard & Poor's Industry Surveys. It contains more information on each industry than Hoover's Handbook of Emerging Companies, is broader in scope than The Almanac of American Employers 1998-1999, but is less expansive than the Encyclopedia of Careers & Vocational Guidance. Highly recommended for all academic libraries and specialized business collections." –Library Journal

Hardcover ISBN 978-1-59237-242-3, 1,400 pages, $495.00

Encyclopedia of American Industries

*Published under an exclusive license from the Gale Group, Inc.

The Encyclopedia of American Industries is a major business reference tool that provides detailed, comprehensive information on a wide range of industries in every realm of American business. A two volume set, Volume I provides separate coverage of nearly 500 manufacturing industries, while Volume II presents nearly 600 essays covering the vast array of services and other non-manufacturing industries in the United States. Combined, these two volumes provide individual essays on every industry recognized by the U.S. Standard Industrial Classification (SIC) system. Both volumes are arranged numerically by SIC code, for easy use. Additionally, each entry includes the corresponding NAICS code(s). The *Encyclopedia's* business coverage includes information on historical events of consequence, as well as current trends and statistics. Essays include an Industry Snapshot, Organization & Structure, Background & Development, Current Conditions, Industry Leaders, Workforce, America and the World, Research & Technology along with Suggested Further Readings. Both SIC and NAICS code conversion tables and an all-encompassing Subject Index, with cross-references, complete the text. With its detailed, comprehensive information on a wide range of industries, this resource will be an important tool for both the industry newcomer and the seasoned professional.

"Encyclopedia of American Industries contains detailed, signed essays on virtually every industry in contemporary society. ... Highly recommended for all but the smallest libraries." -American Reference Books Annual

Two Volumes, Hardcover ISBN 978-1-59237-244-7, 3,000 pages, $650.00

Encyclopedia of Global Industries

*Published under an exclusive license from the Gale Group, Inc.

This fourth edition of the acclaimed *Encyclopedia of Global Industries* presents a thoroughly revised and expanded look at more than 125 business sectors of global significance. Detailed, insightful articles discuss the origins, development, trends, key statistics and current international character of the world's most lucrative, dynamic and widely researched industries – including hundreds of profiles of leading international corporations. Beginning researchers will gain from this book a solid understanding of how each industry operates and which countries and companies are significant participants, while experienced researchers will glean current and historical figures for comparison and analysis. The industries profiled in previous editions have been updated, and in some cases, expanded to reflect recent industry trends. Additionally, this edition provides both SIC and NAICS codes for all industries profiled. As in the original volumes, *The Encyclopedia of Global Industries* offers thorough studies of some of the biggest and most frequently researched industry sectors, including Aircraft, Biotechnology, Computers, Internet Services, Motor Vehicles, Pharmaceuticals, Semiconductors, Software and Telecommunications. An SIC and NAICS conversion table and an all-encompassing Subject Index, with cross-references, are provided to ensure easy access to this wealth of information. These and many others make the *Encyclopedia of Global Industries* the authoritative reference for studies of international industries.

"Provides detailed coverage of the history, development, and current status of 115 of "the world's most lucrative and high-profile industries." It far surpasses the Department of Commerce's U.S. Global Trade Outlook 1995-2000 (GPO, 1995) in scope and coverage. Recommended for comprehensive public and academic library business collections." -Booklist

Hardcover ISBN 978-1-59237-243-0, 1,400 pages, $495.00

To preview any of our Directories Risk-Free for 30 days, call (800) 562-2139 or fax (518) 789-0556
www.greyhouse.com books@greyhouse.com

Business Information ◆ Ratings Guides ◆ General Reference ◆ Education ◆ Statistics ◆ Demographics ◆ Health Information ◆ Canadian Information

Grey House Publishing

The Directory of Mail Order Catalogs, 2009

Published since 1981, *The Directory of Mail Order Catalogs* is the premier source of information on the mail order catalog industry. It is the source that business professionals and librarians have come to rely on for the thousands of catalog companies in the US. Since the 2007 edition, *The Directory of Mail Order Catalogs* has been combined with its companion volume, *The Directory of Business to Business Catalogs*, to offer all 13,000 catalog companies in one easy-to-use volume. Section I: Consumer Catalogs, covers over 9,000 consumer catalog companies in 44 different product chapters from Animals to Toys & Games. Section II: Business to Business Catalogs, details 5,000 business catalogs, everything from computers to laboratory supplies, building construction and much more. Listings contain detailed contact information including mailing address, phone & fax numbers, web sites, e-mail addresses and key contacts along with important business details such as product descriptions, employee size, years in business, sales volume, catalog size, number of catalogs mailed and more. *The Directory of Mail Order Catalogs*, now with its expanded business to business catalogs, is the largest and most comprehensive resource covering this billion-dollar industry. It is the standard in its field. This important resource is a useful tool for entrepreneurs searching for catalogs to pick up their product, vendors looking to expand their customer base in the catalog industry, market researchers, small businesses investigating new supply vendors, along with the library patron who is exploring the available catalogs in their areas of interest.

"This is a godsend for those looking for information." –Reference Book Review

Softcover ISBN 978-1-59237-396-3, 1,700 pages, $350/$250 Lib | Online DB: http://gold.greyhouse.com Call (800) 562-2139 for quote

Sports Market Place Directory, 2009

For over 20 years, this comprehensive, up-to-date directory has offered direct access to the Who, What, When & Where of the Sports Industry. With over 20,000 updates and enhancements, the *Sports Market Place Directory* is the most detailed, comprehensive and current sports business reference source available. In 1,800 information-packed pages, *Sports Market Place Directory* profiles contact information and key executives for: Single Sport Organizations, Professional Leagues, Multi-Sport Organizations, Disabled Sports, High School & Youth Sports, Military Sports, Olympic Organizations, Media, Sponsors, Sponsorship & Marketing Event Agencies, Event & Meeting Calendars, Professional Services, College Sports, Manufacturers & Retailers, Facilities and much more. The Sports Market Place Directory provides organization's contact information with detailed descriptions including: Key Contacts, physical, mailing, email and web addresses plus phone and fax numbers. *Sports Market Place Directory* provides a one-stop resources for this billion-dollar industry. This will be an important resource for large public libraries, university libraries, university athletic programs, career services or job placement organizations, and is a must for anyone doing research on or marketing to the US and Canadian sports industry.

"Grey House is the new publisher and has produced an excellent edition...highly recommended for public libraries and academic libraries with sports management programs or strong interest in athletics." -Booklist

Softcover ISBN 978-1-59237-418-2, 1,800 pages, $225.00 | Online Database: http://gold.greyhouse.com Call (800) 562-2139 for quote

Food and Beverage Market Place, 2009

Food and Beverage Market Place is bigger and better than ever with thousands of new companies, thousands of updates to existing companies and two revised and enhanced product category indexes. This comprehensive directory profiles over 18,000 Food & Beverage Manufacturers, 12,000 Equipment & Supply Companies, 2,200 Transportation & Warehouse Companies, 2,000 Brokers & Wholesalers, 8,000 Importers & Exporters, 900 Industry Resources and hundreds of Mail Order Catalogs. Listings include detailed Contact Information, Sales Volumes, Key Contacts, Brand & Product Information, Packaging Details and much more. *Food and Beverage Market Place* is available as a three-volume printed set, a subscription-based Online Database via the Internet, on CD-ROM, as well as mailing lists and a licensable database.

"An essential purchase for those in the food industry but will also be useful in public libraries where needed. Much of the information will be difficult and time consuming to locate without this handy three-volume ready-reference source." –ARBA

3 Vol Set, Softcover ISBN 978-1-59237-361-1, 8,500 pages, $595 | Online DB: http://gold.greyhouse.com Call (800) 562-2139 for quote

The Grey House Performing Arts Directory, 2009

The Grey House Performing Arts Directory is the most comprehensive resource covering the Performing Arts. This important directory provides current information on over 8,500 Dance Companies, Instrumental Music Programs, Opera Companies, Choral Groups, Theater Companies, Performing Arts Series and Performing Arts Facilities. Plus, this edition now contains a brand new section on Artist Management Groups. In addition to mailing address, phone & fax numbers, e-mail addresses and web sites, dozens of other fields of available information include mission statement, key contacts, facilities, seating capacity, season, attendance and more. This directory also provides an important Information Resources section that covers hundreds of Performing Arts Associations, Magazines, Newsletters, Trade Shows, Directories, Databases and Industry Web Sites. Five indexes provide immediate access to this wealth of information: Entry Name, Executive Name, Performance Facilities, Geographic and Information Resources. *The Grey House Performing Arts Directory* pulls together thousands of Performing Arts Organizations, Facilities and Information Resources into an easy-to-use source – this kind of comprehensiveness and extensive detail is not available in any resource on the market place today.

"Immensely useful and user-friendly ... recommended for public, academic and certain special library reference collections." –Booklist

Softcover ISBN 978-1-59237-376-5, 1,500 pages, $185.00 | Online Database: http://gold.greyhouse.com Call (800) 562-2139 for quote

To preview any of our Directories Risk-Free for 30 days, call (800) 562-2139 or fax (518) 789-0556
www.greyhouse.com books@greyhouse.com

Business Information ✦ **Ratings Guides** ✦ **General Reference** ✦ **Education** ✦
Statistics ✦ **Demographics** ✦ **Health Information** ✦ **Canadian Information**

Grey House
Publishing

The Environmental Resource Handbook, 2009/10

The Environmental Resource Handbook is the most up-to-date and comprehensive source for Environmental Resources and Statistics.
Section I: Resources provides detailed contact information for thousands of information sources, including Associations &
Organizations, Awards & Honors, Conferences, Foundations & Grants, Environmental Health, Government Agencies, National Parks &
Wildlife Refuges, Publications, Research Centers, Educational Programs, Green Product Catalogs, Consultants and much more.
Section II: Statistics, provides statistics and rankings on hundreds of important topics, including Children's Environmental Index,
Municipal Finances, Toxic Chemicals, Recycling, Climate, Air & Water Quality and more. This kind of up-to-date environmental data, all
in one place, is not available anywhere else on the market place today. This vast compilation of resources and statistics is a must-have
for all public and academic libraries as well as any organization with a primary focus on the environment.

> *"...the intrinsic value of the information make it worth consideration by libraries with
> environmental collections and environmentally concerned users." –Booklist*

Softcover ISBN 978-1-59237-433-5, 1,000 pages, $155.00 | Online Database: http://gold.greyhouse.com Call (800) 562-2139 for quote

New York State Directory, 2009/10

The New York State Directory, published annually since 1983, is a comprehensive and easy-to-use guide to accessing public officials
and private sector organizations and individuals who influence public policy in the state of New York. *The New York State Directory*
includes important information on all New York state legislators and congressional representatives, including biographies and key
committee assignments. It also includes staff rosters for all branches of New York state government and for federal agencies and
departments that impact the state policy process. Following the state government section are 25 chapters covering policy areas from
agriculture through veterans' affairs. Each chapter identifies the state, local and federal agencies and officials that formulate or
implement policy. In addition, each chapter contains a roster of private sector experts and advocates who influence the policy process.
The directory also offers appendices that include statewide party officials; chambers of commerce; lobbying organizations; public and
private universities and colleges; television, radio and print media; and local government agencies and officials.

> *"This comprehensive directory covers not only New York State government offices and key personnel but pertinent U.S. government
> agencies and non-governmental entities. This directory is all encompassing... recommended." -Choice*

New York State Directory - Softcover ISBN 978-1-59237-420-5, 800 pages, $145.00
Online Database: http://gold.greyhouse.com Call (800) 562-2139 for quote
New York State Directory with *Profiles of New York* – 2 Volumes, Softcover ISBN 978-1-59237-421-2, 1,600 pages, $225.00

The Grey House Homeland Security Directory, 2010

This updated edition features the latest contact information for government and private organizations involved with Homeland Security
along with the latest product information and provides detailed profiles of nearly 1,000 Federal & State Organizations & Agencies and
over 3,000 Officials and Key Executives involved with Homeland Security. These listings are incredibly detailed and include Mailing
Address, Phone & Fax Numbers, Email Addresses & Web Sites, a complete Description of the Agency and a complete list of the
Officials and Key Executives associated with the Agency. Next, *The Grey House Homeland Security Directory* provides the go-to
source for Homeland Security Products & Services. This section features over 2,000 Companies that provide Consulting, Products or
Services. With this Buyer's Guide at their fingertips, users can locate suppliers of everything from Training Materials to Access
Controls, from Perimeter Security to BioTerrorism Countermeasures and everything in between – complete with contact information and
product descriptions. A handy Product Locator Index is provided to quickly and easily locate suppliers of a particular product. This
comprehensive, information-packed resource will be a welcome tool for any company or agency that is in need of Homeland Security
information and will be a necessary acquisition for the reference collection of all public libraries and large school districts.

> *"Compiles this information in one place and is discerning in content. A useful purchase for public and academic libraries." –Booklist*

Softcover ISBN 978-1-59237-365-9, 800 pages, $195.00 | Online Database: http://gold.greyhouse.com Call (800) 562-2139 for quote

Business Information ◆ Ratings Guides ◆ General Reference ◆ Education ◆
Statistics ◆ Demographics ◆ Health Information ◆ Canadian Information

Grey Hous
Publishir

The Grey House Safety & Security Directory, 2009

The Grey House Safety & Security Directory is the most comprehensive reference tool and buyer's guide for the safety and security industry. Arranged by safety topic, each chapter begins with OSHA regulations for the topic, followed by Training Articles written by top professionals in the field and Self-Inspection Checklists. Next, each topic contains Buyer's Guide sections that feature related products and services. Topics include Administration, Insurance, Loss Control & Consulting, Protective Equipment & Apparel, Noise & Vibration, Facilities Monitoring & Maintenance, Employee Health Maintenance & Ergonomics, Retail Food Services, Machine Guards, Process Guidelines & Tool Handling, Ordinary Materials Handling, Hazardous Materials Handling, Workplace Preparation & Maintenance, Electrical Lighting & Safety, Fire & Rescue and Security. Six important indexes make finding information and product manufacturers quick and easy: Geographical Index of Manufacturers and Distributors, Company Profile Index, Brand Name Index, Product Index, Index of Web Sites and Index of Advertisers. This comprehensive, up-to-date reference will provide every tool necessary to make sure a business is in compliance with OSHA regulations and locate the products and services needed to meet those regulations.

> *"Presents industrial safety information for engineers, plant managers, risk managers, and construction site supervisors..."* –Choice

Softcover ISBN 978-1-59237-375-8, 1,500 pages, $165.00

The Grey House Transportation Security Directory & Handbook

This is the only reference of its kind that brings together current data on Transportation Security. With information on everything from Regulatory Authorities to Security Equipment, this top-flight database brings together the relevant information necessary for creating and maintaining a security plan for a wide range of transportation facilities. With this current, comprehensive directory at the ready you'll have immediate access to: Regulatory Authorities & Legislation; Information Resources; Sample Security Plans & Checklists; Contact Data for Major Airports, Seaports, Railroads, Trucking Companies and Oil Pipelines; Security Service Providers; Recommended Equipment & Product Information and more. Using the *Grey House Transportation Security Directory & Handbook*, managers will be able to quickly and easily assess their current security plans; develop contacts to create and maintain new security procedures; and source the products and services necessary to adequately maintain a secure environment. This valuable resource is a must for all Security Managers at Airports, Seaports, Railroads, Trucking Companies and Oil Pipelines.

> *"Highly recommended. Library collections that support all levels of readers, including professionals/practitioners; and schools/organizations offering education and training in transportation security."* -Choice

Softcover ISBN 978-1-59237-075-7, 800 pages, $195.00

The Grey House Biometric Information Directory

This edition offers a complete, current overview of biometric companies and products – one of the fastest growing industries in today's economy. Detailed profiles of manufacturers of the latest biometric technology, including Finger, Voice, Face, Hand, Signature, Iris, Vein and Palm Identification systems. Data on the companies include key executives, company size and a detailed, indexed description of their product line. Information in the directory includes: Editorial on Advancements in Biometrics; Profiles of 700+ companies listed with contact information; Organizations, Trade & Educational Associations, Publications, Conferences, Trade Shows and Expositions Worldwide; Web Site Index; Biometric & Vendors Services Index by Types of Biometrics; and a Glossary of Biometric Terms. This resource will be an important source for anyone who is considering the use of a biometric product, investing in the development of biometric technology, support existing marketing and sales efforts and will be an important acquisition for the business reference collection for large public and business libraries.

> *"This book should prove useful to agencies or businesses seeking companies that deal with biometric technology. Summing Up: Recommended. Specialized collections serving researchers/faculty and professionals/practitioners."* -Choice

Softcover ISBN 978-1-59237-121-1, 800 pages, $225.00

Business Information ◆ Ratings Guides ◆ General Reference ◆ Education ◆
Statistics ◆ Demographics ◆ Health Information ◆ Canadian Information

Grey House Publishing

The Rauch Guide to the US Adhesives & Sealants, Cosmetics & Toiletries, Ink, Paint, Plastics, Pulp & Paper and Rubber Industries

The Rauch Guides save time and money by organizing widely scattered information and providing estimates for important business decisions, some of which are available nowhere else. Within each Guide, after a brief introduction, the ECONOMICS section provides data on industry shipments; long-term growth and forecasts; prices; company performance; employment, expenditures, and productivity; transportation and geographical patterns; packaging; foreign trade; and government regulations. Next, TECHNOLOGY & RAW MATERIALS provide market, technical, and raw material information for chemicals, equipment and related materials, including market size and leading suppliers, prices, end uses, and trends. PRODUCTS & MARKETS provide information for each major industry product, including market size and historical trends, leading suppliers, five-year forecasts, industry structure, and major end uses. Next, the COMPANY DIRECTORY profiles major industry companies, both public and private. Information includes complete contact information, web address, estimated total and domestic sales, product description, and recent mergers and acquisitions. *The Rauch Guides* will prove to be an invaluable source of market information, company data, trends and forecasts that anyone in these fast-paced industries.

"An invaluable and affordable publication. The comprehensive nature of the data and text offers considerable insights into the industry, market sizes, company activities, and applications of the products of the industry. The additions that have been made have certainly enhanced the value of the Guide." –Adhesives & Sealants Newsletter of the Rauch Guide to the US Adhesives & Sealants Industry

Paint Industry: Softcover ISBN 978-1-59237-428-1 $595 | Plastics Industry: Softcover ISBN 978-1-59237-445-8 $595 | Adhesives and Sealants Industry: Softcover ISBN 978-1-59237-440-3 $595 | Ink Industry: Softcover ISBN 978-1-59237-126-6 $595 | Rubber Industry: Softcover ISBN 978-1-59237-130-3 $595 | Pulp and Paper Industry: Softcover ISBN 978-1-59237-131-0 $595 | Cosmetic & Toiletries Industry: Softcover ISBN 978-1-59237-132-7 $895

Research Services Directory: Commercial & Corporate Research Centers

This ninth edition provides access to well over 8,000 independent Commercial Research Firms, Corporate Research Centers and Laboratories offering contract services for hands-on, basic or applied research. Research Services Directory covers the thousands of types of research companies, including Biotechnology & Pharmaceutical Developers, Consumer Product Research, Defense Contractors, Electronics & Software Engineers, Think Tanks, Forensic Investigators, Independent Commercial Laboratories, Information Brokers, Market & Survey Research Companies, Medical Diagnostic Facilities, Product Research & Development Firms and more. Each entry provides the company's name, mailing address, phone & fax numbers, key contacts, web site, e-mail address, as well as a company description and research and technical fields served. Four indexes provide immediate access to this wealth of information: Research Firms Index, Geographic Index, Personnel Name Index and Subject Index.

"An important source for organizations in need of information about laboratories, individuals and other facilities." –ARBA

Softcover ISBN 978-1-59237-003-0, 1,400 pages, $465.00

International Business and Trade Directories

Completely updated, the Third Edition of *International Business and Trade Directories* now contains more than 10,000 entries, over 2,000 more than the last edition, making this directory the most comprehensive resource of the worlds business and trade directories. Entries include content descriptions, price, publisher's name and address, web site and e-mail addresses, phone and fax numbers and editorial staff. Organized by industry group, and then by region, this resource puts over 10,000 industry-specific business and trade directories at the reader's fingertips. Three indexes are included for quick access to information: Geographic Index, Publisher Index and Title Index. Public, college and corporate libraries, as well as individuals and corporations seeking critical market information will want to add this directory to their marketing collection.

"Reasonably priced for a work of this type, this directory should appeal to larger academic, public and corporate libraries with an international focus." –Library Journal

Softcover ISBN 978-1-930956-63-6, 1,800 pages, $225.00

Business Information ◆ Ratings Guides ◆ <u>General Reference</u> ◆ Education ◆
Statistics ◆ Demographics ◆ Health Information ◆ Canadian Information

Grey Hous
Publishir

The Value of a Dollar 1860-2009, Fourth Edition

A guide to practical economy, *The Value of a Dollar* records the actual prices of thousands of items that consumers purchased from the Civil War to the present, along with facts about investment options and income opportunities. This brand new Third Edition boasts a brand new addition to each five-year chapter, a section on Trends. This informative section charts the change in price over time and provides added detail on the reasons prices changed within the time period, including industry developments, changes in consumer attitudes and important historical facts. Plus, a brand new chapter for 2005-2009 has been added. Each 5-year chapter includes a Historical Snapshot, Consumer Expenditures, Investments, Selected Income, Income/Standard Jobs, Food Basket, Standard Prices and Miscellany. This interesting and useful publication will be widely used in any reference collection.

*"Business historians, reporters, writers and students will find this source...
very helpful for historical research. Libraries will want to purchase it." –ARBA*

Hardcover ISBN 978-1-59237-403-8, 600 pages, $145.00 | Ebook ISBN 978-1-59237-173-0 www.greyhouse.com/ebooks.htm

The Value of a Dollar 1600-1859, The Colonial Era to The Civil War

Following the format of the widely acclaimed, *The Value of a Dollar, 1860-2004*, *The Value of a Dollar 1600-1859, The Colonial Era to The Civil War* records the actual prices of thousands of items that consumers purchased from the Colonial Era to the Civil War. Our editorial department had been flooded with requests from users of our *Value of a Dollar* for the same type of information, just from an earlier time period. This new volume is just the answer – with pricing data from 1600 to 1859. Arranged into five-year chapters, each 5-year chapter includes a Historical Snapshot, Consumer Expenditures, Investments, Selected Income, Income/Standard Jobs, Food Basket, Standard Prices and Miscellany. There is also a section on Trends. This informative section charts the change in price over time and provides added detail on the reasons prices changed within the time period, including industry developments, changes in consumer attitudes and important historical facts. This fascinating survey will serve a wide range of research needs and will be useful in all high school, public and academic library reference collections.

"The Value of a Dollar: Colonial Era to the Civil War, 1600-1865 will find a happy audience among students, researchers, and general browsers. It offers a fascinating and detailed look at early American history from the viewpoint of everyday people trying to make ends meet. This title and the earlier publication, The Value of a Dollar, 1860-2004, complement each other very well, and readers will appreciate finding them side-by-side on the shelf." -Booklist

Hardcover ISBN 978-1-59237-094-8, 600 pages, $145.00 | Ebook ISBN 978-1-59237-169-3 www.greyhouse.com/ebooks.htm

Working Americans 1880-1999
Volume I: The Working Class, Volume II: The Middle Class, Volume III: The Upper Class

Each of the volumes in the *Working Americans* series focuses on a particular class of Americans, The Working Class, The Middle Class and The Upper Class over the last 120 years. Chapters in each volume focus on one decade and profile three to five families. Family Profiles include real data on Income & Job Descriptions, Selected Prices of the Times, Annual Income, Annual Budgets, Family Finances, Life at Work, Life at Home, Life in the Community, Working Conditions, Cost of Living, Amusements and much more. Each chapter also contains an Economic Profile with Average Wages of other Professions, a selection of Typical Pricing, Key Events & Inventions, News Profiles, Articles from Local Media and Illustrations. The *Working Americans* series captures the lifestyles of each of the classes from the last twelve decades, covers a vast array of occupations and ethnic backgrounds and travels the entire nation. These interesting and useful compilations of portraits of the American Working, Middle and Upper Classes during the last 120 years will be an important addition to any high school, public or academic library reference collection.

*"These interesting, unique compilations of economic and social facts, figures and graphs will support multiple research needs.
They will engage and enlighten patrons in high school, public and academic library collections." –Booklist*

Volume I: The Working Class Hardcover ISBN 978-1-891482-81-6, 558 pages, $150.00 | Volume II: The Middle Class Hardcover ISBN 978-1-891482-72-4, 591 pages, $150.00 | Volume III: The Upper Class Hardcover ISBN 978-1-930956-38-4, 567 pages, $150.00 | www.greyhouse.com/ebooks.htm

Working Americans 1880-1999 Volume IV: Their Children

This Fourth Volume in the highly successful *Working Americans* series focuses on American children, decade by decade from 1880 to 1999. This interesting and useful volume introduces the reader to three children in each decade, one from each of the Working, Middle and Upper classes. Like the first three volumes in the series, the individual profiles are created from interviews, diaries, statistical studies, biographies and news reports. Profiles cover a broad range of ethnic backgrounds, geographic area and lifestyles – everything from an orphan in Memphis in 1882, following the Yellow Fever epidemic of 1878 to an eleven-year-old nephew of a beer baron and owner of the New York Yankees in New York City in 1921. Chapters also contain important supplementary materials including News Features as well as information on everything from Schools to Parks, Infectious Diseases to Childhood Fears along with Entertainment, Family Life and much more to provide an informative overview of the lifestyles of children from each decade. This interesting account of what life was like for Children in the Working, Middle and Upper Classes will be a welcome addition to the reference collection of any high school, public or academic library.

Hardcover ISBN 978-1-930956-35-3, 600 pages, $150.00 | Ebook ISBN 978-1-59237-166-2 www.greyhouse.com/ebooks.htm

**To preview any of our Directories Risk-Free for 30 days, call (800) 562-2139 or fax (518) 789-0556
www.greyhouse.com books@greyhouse.com**

Business Information ♦ Ratings Guides ♦ **General Reference** ♦ Education ♦
Statistics ♦ Demographics ♦ Health Information ♦ Canadian Information

Grey House Publishing

Working Americans 1880-2003 Volume V: Americans At War

Working Americans 1880-2003 Volume V: Americans At War is divided into 11 chapters, each covering a decade from 1880-2003 and examines the lives of Americans during the time of war, including declared conflicts, one-time military actions, protests, and preparations for war. Each decade includes several personal profiles, whether on the battlefield or on the homefront, that tell the stories of civilians, soldiers, and officers during the decade. The profiles examine: Life at Home; Life at Work; and Life in the Community. Each decade also includes an Economic Profile with statistical comparisons, a Historical Snapshot, News Profiles, local News Articles, and Illustrations that provide a solid historical background to the decade being examined. Profiles range widely not only geographically, but also emotionally, from that of a girl whose leg was torn off in a blast during WWI, to the boredom of being stationed in the Dakotas as the Indian Wars were drawing to a close. As in previous volumes of the *Working Americans* series, information is presented in narrative form, but hard facts and real-life situations back up each story. The basis of the profiles come from diaries, private print books, personal interviews, family histories, estate documents and magazine articles. For easy reference, *Working Americans 1880-2003 Volume V: Americans At War* includes an in-depth Subject Index. The Working Americans series has become an important reference for public libraries, academic libraries and high school libraries. This fifth volume will be a welcome addition to all of these types of reference collections.

Hardcover ISBN 978-1-59237-024-5, 600 pages, $150.00 | Ebook ISBN 978-1-59237-167-9 www.greyhouse.com/ebooks.htm

Working Americans 1880-2005 Volume VI: Women at Work

Unlike any other volume in the *Working Americans* series, this Sixth Volume, is the first to focus on a particular gender of Americans. *Volume VI: Women at Work*, traces what life was like for working women from the 1860's to the present time. Beginning with the life of a maid in 1890 and a store clerk in 1900 and ending with the life and times of the modern working women, this text captures the struggle, strengths and changing perception of the American woman at work. Each chapter focuses on one decade and profiles three to five women with real data on Income & Job Descriptions, Selected Prices of the Times, Annual Income, Annual Budgets, Family Finances, Life at Work, Life at Home, Life in the Community, Working Conditions, Cost of Living, Amusements and much more. For even broader access to the events, economics and attitude towards women throughout the past 130 years, each chapter is supplemented with News Profiles, Articles from Local Media, Illustrations, Economic Profiles, Typical Pricing, Key Events, Inventions and more. This important volume illustrates what life was like for working women over time and allows the reader to develop an understanding of the changing role of women at work. These interesting and useful compilations of portraits of women at work will be an important addition to any high school, public or academic library reference collection.

Hardcover ISBN 978-1-59237-063-4, 600 pages, $145.00 | Ebook ISBN 978-1-59237-168-6 www.greyhouse.com/ebooks.htm

Working Americans 1880-2005 Volume VII: Social Movements

Working Americans series, Volume VII: Social Movements explores how Americans sought and fought for change from the 1880s to the present time. Following the format of previous volumes in the Working Americans series, the text examines the lives of 34 individuals who have worked -- often behind the scenes --- to bring about change. Issues include topics as diverse as the Anti-smoking movement of 1901 to efforts by Native Americans to reassert their long lost rights. Along the way, the book will profile individuals brave enough to demand suffrage for Kansas women in 1912 or demand an end to lynching during a March on Washington in 1923. Each profile is enriched with real data on Income & Job Descriptions, Selected Prices of the Times, Annual Incomes & Budgets, Life at Work, Life at Home, Life in the Community, along with News Features, Key Events, and Illustrations. The depth of information contained in each profile allow the user to explore the private, financial and public lives of these subjects, deepening our understanding of how calls for change took place in our society. A must-purchase for the reference collections of high school libraries, public libraries and academic libraries.

Hardcover ISBN 978-1-59237-101-3, 600 pages, $145.00 | Ebook ISBN 978-1-59237-174-7 www.greyhouse.com/ebooks.htm

Business Information ✦ Ratings Guides ✦ <u>General Reference</u> ✦ Education ✦
Statistics ✦ Demographics ✦ Health Information ✦ Canadian Information

Grey Hous
Publishin

Working Americans 1880-2005 Volume VIII: Immigrants

Working Americans 1880-2007 Volume VIII: Immigrants illustrates what life was like for families leaving their homeland and creating a new life in the United States. Each chapter covers one decade and introduces the reader to three immigrant families. Family profiles cover what life was like in their homeland, in their community in the United States, their home life, working conditions and so much more. As the reader moves through these pages, the families and individuals come to life, painting a picture of why they left their homeland, their experiences in setting roots in a new country, their struggles and triumphs, stretching from the 1800s to the present time. Profiles include a seven-year-old Swedish girl who meets her father for the first time at Ellis Island; a Chinese photographer's assistant; an Armenian who flees the genocide of his country to build Ford automobiles in Detroit; a 38-year-old German bachelor cigar maker who settles in Newark NJ, but contemplates tobacco farming in Virginia; a 19-year-old Irish domestic servant who is amazed at the easy life of American dogs; a 19-year-old Filipino who came to Hawaii against his parent's wishes to farm sugar cane; a French-Canadian who finds success as a boxer in Maine and many more. As in previous volumes, information is presented in narrative form, but hard facts and real-life situations back up each story. With the topic of immigration being so hotly debated in this country, this timely resource will prove to be a useful source for students, researchers, historians and library patrons to discover the issues facing immigrants in the United States. This title will be a useful addition to reference collections of public libraries, university libraries and high schools.

Hardcover ISBN 978-1-59237-197-6, 600 pages, $145.00 | Ebook ISBN 978-1-59237-232-4 www.greyhouse.com/ebooks.htm

Working Americans 1770-1896 Volume IX: From the Revolutionary War to the Civil War

Working Americans 1770-1869: From the Revolutionary War to the Civil War examines what life was like for the earliest of Americans. Like previous volumes in the successful Working Americans series, each chapter introduces the reader to three individuals or families. These profiles illustrate what life was like for that individual, at home, in the community and at work. The profiles are supplemented with information on current events, community issues, pricing of the times and news articles to give the reader a broader understanding of what was happening in that individual's world and how it shaped their life. Profiles extend through all walks of life, from farmers to merchants, the rich and poor, men, women and children. In these information-packed, fun-to-explore pages, the reader will be introduced to Ezra Stiles, a preacher and college president from 1776; Colonel Israel Angell, a continental officer from 1778; Thomas Vernon, a loyalist in 1776, Anna Green Winslow, a school girl in 1771; Sarah Pierce, a school teacher in 1792; Edward Hooker, an attorney in 1805; Jeremiah Greenman, a common soldier in 1775 and many others. Using these information-filled profiles, the reader can develop an understanding of what life was like for all types of Americans in these interesting and changing times. This new edition will be an important acquisition for high school, public and academic libraries as well as history reference collections.

Hardcover ISBN 978-1-59237-371-0, 660 pages, $145.00

Working Americans 1880-2009 Volume X: Sports & Recreation

Working Americans 1880-2009 Volume X: Sports & Recreation focuses on the lighter side of life in America. Examining professional sports to amateur sports to leisure time and recreation, this interesting volume illustrates how Americans had fun from the Civil War to the present time. Intriguing profiles in each decade-long chapter are supplemented with information on current events, community issues, pricing of the times and news articles to give the reader a broader understanding of what was happening in that individual's world and how it shaped their life. To further explore the life and times of these individuals, each chapter includes several other helpful elements: Historical Snapshots, Timelines, News Features, Selected Prices, and Illustrations. Readers will be able to examine the growth of professional sports and how ticket prices changed over the years, look at what games were popular, find out how early Americans spent their leisure time and get and understanding of the importance of recreation in any time period.

Hardcover ISBN 978-1-59237-441-0, 600 pages, $145.00

The Encyclopedia of Warrior Peoples & Fighting Groups

Many military groups throughout the world have excelled in their craft either by fortuitous circumstances, outstanding leadership, or intense training. This new second edition of *The Encyclopedia of Warrior Peoples and Fighting Groups* explores the origins and leadership of these outstanding combat forces, chronicles their conquests and accomplishments, examines the circumstances surrounding their decline or disbanding, and assesses their influence on the groups and methods of warfare that followed. Readers will encounter ferocious tribes, charismatic leaders, and daring militias, from ancient times to the present, including Amazons, Buffalo Soldiers, Green Berets, Iron Brigade, Kamikazes, Peoples of the Sea, Polish Winged Hussars, Teutonic Knights, and Texas Rangers. With over 100 alphabetical entries, numerous cross-references and illustrations, a comprehensive bibliography, and index, the *Encyclopedia of Warrior Peoples and Fighting Groups* is a valuable resource for readers seeking insight into the bold history of distinguished fighting forces.

"Especially useful for high school students, undergraduates, and general readers with an interest in military history." –Library Journal

Hardcover ISBN 978-1-59237-116-7, 660 pages, $165.00 | Ebook ISBN 978-1-59237-172-3 www.greyhouse.com/ebooks.htm

Business Information ◆ Ratings Guides ◆ <u>General Reference</u> ◆ Education ◆
Statistics ◆ Demographics ◆ Health Information ◆ Canadian Information

Grey House Publishing

Speakers of the House of Representatives, 1789-2009

Beginning with Frederick Muhlenberg in 1789 and stretching to Nancy Pelosi, the first female Speaker of the House, this new reference work provides unique coverage of this important political position. Presiding over the House of Representatives and second the United States presidential line of succession, this position has particular influence over US politics. Features include: thoughtfully-written Biographies of each of the 52 Speakers of the House, all with photos; several full-length Essays, each covering an interesting and thought-provoking topic pertinent to the formation, history and current events surrounding the Speaker; Primary Documents, for added sources of research, include important articles, resignation letters, speeches and letters; several helpful Appendices: Years Served in Congress before Becoming Speaker, Speakers & Party Control of the Presidency, Dates of Election & States Represented, Speaker Firsts; a Chronology of Elections and Important Events, a comprehensive Bibliography and a cumulative Index. This new resource brings together a wealth of information on individual Speakers, the history of the position and its changing role in US politics. This resource will be a valuable addition to public libraries, high schools, university libraries along with history and political science collections.

Hardcover ISBN 978-1-59237-404-5, 500 pages, $135.00 | Ebook ISBN 978-1-59237-483-0 www.greyhouse.com/ebooks.htm

The Encyclopedia of Rural America: the Land & People

History, sociology, anthropology, and public policy are combined to deliver the encyclopedia destined to become the standard reference work in American rural studies. From irrigation and marriage to games and mental health, this encyclopedia is the first to explore the contemporary landscape of rural America, placed in historical perspective. With over 300 articles prepared by leading experts from across the nation, this timely encyclopedia documents and explains the major themes, concepts, industries, concerns, and everyday life of the people and land who make up rural America. Entries range from the industrial sector and government policy to arts and humanities and social and family concerns. Articles explore every aspect of life in rural America. *Encyclopedia of Rural America*, with its broad range of coverage, will appeal to high school and college students as well as graduate students, faculty, scholars, and people whose work pertains to rural areas.

"This exemplary encyclopedia is guaranteed to educate our highly urban society about the uniqueness of rural America. Recommended for public and academic libraries." -Library Journal

Two Volumes, Hardcover, ISBN 978-1-59237-115-0, 800 pages, $250.00

The Encyclopedia of Invasions & Conquests, From the Ancient Times to the Present

This second edition of the popular *Encyclopedia of Invasions & Conquests*, a comprehensive guide to over 150 invasions, conquests, battles and occupations from ancient times to the present, takes readers on a journey that includes the Roman conquest of Britain, the Portuguese colonization of Brazil, and the Iraqi invasion of Kuwait, to name a few. New articles will explore the late 20th and 21st centuries, with a specific focus on recent conflicts in Afghanistan, Kuwait, Iraq, Yugoslavia, Grenada and Chechnya. In addition to covering the military aspects of invasions and conquests, entries cover some of the political, economic, and cultural aspects, for example, the effects of a conquest on the invade country's political and monetary system and in its language and religion. The entries on leaders – among them Sargon, Alexander the Great, William the Conqueror, and Adolf Hitler – deal with the people who sought to gain control, expand power, or exert religious or political influence over others through military means. Revised and updated for this second edition, entries are arranged alphabetically within historical periods. Each chapter provides a map to help readers locate key areas and geographical features, and bibliographical references appear at the end of each entry. Other useful features include cross-references, a cumulative bibliography and a comprehensive subject index. This authoritative, well-organized, lucidly written volume will prove invaluable for a variety of readers, including high school students, military historians, members of the armed forces, history buffs and hobbyists.

"Engaging writing, sensible organization, nice illustrations, interesting and obscure facts, and useful maps make this book a pleasure to read." –ARBA

Hardcover ISBN 978-1-59237-114-3, 598 pages, $165.00 | Ebook ISBN 978-1-59237-171-6 www.greyhouse.com/ebooks.htm

Encyclopedia of Prisoners of War & Internment

This authoritative second edition provides a valuable overview of the history of prisoners of war and interned civilians, from earliest times to the present. Written by an international team of experts in the field of POW studies, this fascinating and thought-provoking volume includes entries on a wide range of subjects including the Crusades, Plains Indian Warfare, concentration camps, the two world wars, and famous POWs throughout history, as well as atrocities, escapes, and much more. Written in a clear and easily understandable style, this informative reference details over 350 entries, 30% larger than the first edition, that survey the history of prisoners of war and interned civilians from the earliest times to the present, with emphasis on the 19th and 20th centuries. Medical conditions, international law, exchanges of prisoners, organizations working on behalf of POWs, and trials associated with the treatment of captives are just some of the themes explored. Entries are arranged alphabetically, plus illustrations and maps are provided for easy reference. The text also includes an introduction, bibliography, appendix of selected documents, and end-of-entry reading suggestions. This one-of-a-kind reference will be a helpful addition to the reference collections of all public libraries, high schools, and university libraries and will prove invaluable to historians and military enthusiasts.

"Thorough and detailed yet accessible to the lay reader. Of special interest to subject specialists and historians; recommended for public and academic libraries." - Library Journal

Hardcover ISBN 978-1-59237-120-4, 676 pages, $165.00 | Ebook ISBN 978-1-59237-170-9 www.greyhouse.com/ebooks.htm

---

To preview any of our Directories Risk-Free for 30 days, call (800) 562-2139 or fax (518) 789-0556
www.greyhouse.com books@greyhouse.com

Business Information ✦ Ratings Guides ✦ <u>General Reference</u> ✦ Education ✦
Statistics ✦ Demographics ✦ Health Information ✦ Canadian Information

Grey Hous
Publishin

From Suffrage to the Senate, America's Political Women

From Suffrage to the Senate is a comprehensive and valuable compendium of biographies of leading women in U.S. politics, past and present, and an examination of the wide range of women's movements. This reference work explores American women's path to political power and social equality from the struggle for the right to vote and the abolition of slavery to the first African American woman in the U.S. Senate and beyond. The in-depth coverage also traces the political heritage of the abolition, labor, suffrage, temperance, and reproductive rights movements. The alphabetically arranged entries include biographies of every woman from across the political spectrum who has served in the U.S. House and Senate, along with women in the Judiciary and the U.S. Cabinet and, new to this edition, biographies of activists and political consultants. Bibliographical references follow each entry. For easy reference, a handy chronology is provided detailing 150 years of women's history. This up-to-date reference will be a must-purchase for women's studies departments, high schools and public libraries and will be a handy resource for those researching the key players in women's politics, past and present.

"An engaging tool that would be useful in high school, public, and academic libraries looking for an overview of the political history of women in the US." –Booklist

Two Volumes, Hardcover ISBN 978-1-59237-117-4, 1,160 pages, $199.00 | Ebook ISBN 978-1-59237-227-0
www.greyhouse.com/ebooks.htm

An African Biographical Dictionary

This landmark second edition is the only biographical dictionary to bring together, in one volume, cultural, social and political leaders – both historical and contemporary – of the sub-Saharan region. Over 800 biographical sketches of prominent Africans, as well as foreigners who have affected the continent's history, are featured, 150 more than the previous edition. The wide spectrum of leaders includes religious figures, writers, politicians, scientists, entertainers, sports personalities and more. Access to these fascinating individuals is provided in a user-friendly format. The biographies are arranged alphabetically, cross-referenced and indexed. Entries include the country or countries in which the person was significant and the commonly accepted dates of birth and death. Each biographical sketch is chronologically written; entries for cultural personalities add an evaluation of their work. This information is followed by a selection of references often found in university and public libraries, including autobiographies and principal biographical works. Appendixes list each individual by country and by field of accomplishment – rulers, musicians, explorers, missionaries, businessmen, physicists – nearly thirty categories in all. Another convenient appendix lists heads of state since independence by country. Up-to-date and representative of African societies as a whole, An African Biographical Dictionary provides a wealth of vital information for students of African culture and is an indispensable reference guide for anyone interested in African affairs.

"An unquestionable convenience to have these concise, informative biographies gathered into one source, indexed, and analyzed by appendixes listing entrants by nation and occupational field." –Wilson Library Bulletin

Hardcover ISBN 978-1-59237-112-9, 667 pages, $165.00 | Ebook ISBN 978-1-59237-229-4 www.greyhouse.com/ebooks.htm

African American Writers

A timely survey of an important sector of American letters, *African American Writers* covers the role and influence of African American cultural leaders, from all walks of life, from the 18th century to the present. Readers will explore what inspired various African-American writers to create poems, plays, short stories, novels, essays, opinion pieces and numerous other works, and how those writings contributed to culture in America today. With 200 new entries, over 35% larger than the previous edition, this edition features over 100 new Author biographies, for a total of 500, with illustrations, cover the important events in a writer's life, education, major works, honors and awards, and family and important associates; more Genre Tables, covering newspapers, journals, book publishers, online resources, illustrators and more, each with an introduction and listings of top authors in each genre, their pen names, key publications and awards; new Topical entries, including writing collaboratives, book clubs, celebrity authors and self-publishing; new Author Tables, covering additional authors in multiple genres, with author name, pen name, birth year, genre and more; an Appendix of Writers by Genre; a Chronology of Writers; a Chronology of Firsts, with interesting facts, from the first narrative written by an African-American slave, to the first African-American to receive the Nobel prize for literature; a list of Abbreviations and a Cumulative Index. More than a collection of biographies, this important work traces the evolution of African-American writers, their struggles, triumphs, and legacy, this volume is not to be missed. A comprehensive, easy to use source that will complement the reference collection of any public, high school or university library, and will prove useful to all university humanities and African American studies reference collections.

"No other single work seeks to include all past and present African American writers of significance in such an affordable format ... an appealing choice for all public and academic libraries." –Library Journal

Hardcover ISBN 978-1-59237-291-1, 667 pages, $165.00 | Ebook ISBN 978-1-59237-302-4 www.greyhouse.com/ebooks.htm

American Environmental Leaders, From Colonial Times to the Present

A comprehensive and diverse award winning collection of biographies of the most important figures in American environmentalism. Few subjects arouse the passions the way the environment does. How will we feed an ever-increasing population and how can that food be made safe for consumption? Who decides how land is developed? How can environmental policies be made fair for everyone, including multiethnic groups, women, children, and the poor? *American Environmental Leaders* presents more than 350 biographies of men and women who have devoted their lives to studying, debating, and organizing these and other controversial issues over the last 200 years. In addition to the scientists who have analyzed how human actions affect nature, we are introduced to poets, landscape architects, presidents, painters, activists, even sanitation engineers, and others who have forever altered how we think about the environment. The easy to use A–Z format provides instant access to these fascinating individuals, and frequent cross references indicate others with whom individuals worked (and sometimes clashed). End of entry references provide users with a starting point for further research.

"Highly recommended for high school, academic, and public libraries needing environmental biographical information." –Library Journal/Starred Review

Two Volumes, Hardcover ISBN 978-1-59237-119-8, 900 pages $195.00 | Ebook ISBN 978-1-59237-230-0
www.greyhouse.com/ebooks.htm

World Cultural Leaders of the Twentieth & Twenty-First Centuries

World Cultural Leaders of the Twentieth & Twenty-First Centuries is a window into the arts, performances, movements, and music that shaped the world's cultural development since 1900. A remarkable around-the-world look at one-hundred-plus years of cultural development through the eyes of those that set the stage and stayed to play. This second edition offers over 120 new biographies along with a complete update of existing biographies. To further aid the reader, a handy fold-out timeline traces important events in all six cultural categories from 1900 through the present time. Plus, a new section of detailed material and resources for 100 selected individuals is also new to this edition, with further data on museums, homesteads, websites, artwork and more. This remarkable compilation will answer a wide range of questions. Who was the originator of the term "documentary"? Which poet married the daughter of the famed novelist Thomas Mann in order to help her escape Nazi Germany? Which British writer served as an agent in Russia against the Bolsheviks before the 1917 revolution? A handy two-volume set that makes it easy to look up 450 worldwide cultural icons: novelists, poets, playwrights, painters, sculptors, architects, dancers, choreographers, actors, directors, filmmakers, singers, composers, and musicians. *World Cultural Leaders of the Twentieth & Twenty-First Centuries* provides entries (many of them illustrated) covering the person's works, achievements, and professional career in a thorough essay and offers interesting facts and statistics. Entries are fully cross-referenced so that readers can learn how various individuals influenced others. An index of leaders by occupation, a useful glossary and a thorough general index complete the coverage. This remarkable resource will be an important acquisition for the reference collections of public libraries, university libraries and high schools.

"Fills a need for handy, concise information on a wide array of international cultural figures."-ARBA

Two Volumes, Hardcover ISBN 978-1-59237-118-1, 900 pages, $199.00 | Ebook ISBN 978-1-59237-231-7
www.greyhouse.com/ebooks.htm

Political Corruption in America: An Encyclopedia of Scandals, Power, and Greed

The complete scandal-filled history of American political corruption, focusing on the infamous people and cases, as well as society's electoral and judicial reactions. Since colonial times, there has been no shortage of politicians willing to take a bribe, skirt campaign finance laws, or act in their own interests. Corruption like the Whiskey Ring, Watergate, and Whitewater cases dominate American life, making political scandal a leading U.S. industry. From judges to senators, presidents to mayors, *Political Corruption in America* discusses the infamous people throughout history who have been accused of and implicated in crooked behavior. In this new second edition, more than 250 A–Z entries explore the people, crimes, investigations, and court cases behind 200 years of American political scandals. This unbiased volume also delves into the issues surrounding Koreagate, the Chinese campaign scandal, and other ethical lapses. Relevant statutes and terms, including the Independent Counsel Statute and impeachment as a tool of political punishment, are examined as well. Students, scholars, and other readers interested in American history, political science, and ethics will appreciate this survey of a wide range of corrupting influences. This title focuses on how politicians from all parties have fallen because of their greed and hubris, and how society has used electoral and judicial means against those who tested the accepted standards of political conduct. A full range of illustrations including political cartoons, photos of key figures such as Abe Fortas and Archibald Cox, graphs of presidential pardons, and tables showing the number of expulsions and censures in both the House and Senate round out the text. In addition, a comprehensive chronology of major political scandals in U.S. history from colonial times until the present. For further reading, an extensive bibliography lists sources including archival letters, newspapers, and private manuscript collections from the United States and Great Britain. With its comprehensive coverage of this interesting topic, *Political Corruption in America: An Encyclopedia of Scandals, Power, and Greed* will prove to be a useful addition to the reference collections of all public libraries, university libraries, history collections, political science collections and high schools.

"...this encyclopedia is a useful contribution to the field. Highly recommended." - CHOICE
"Political Corruption should be useful in most academic, high school, and public libraries." Booklist

Two Volumes, Hardcover ISBN 978-1-59237-297-3, 500 pages, $195.00 | Ebook ISBN 978-1-59237-308-6
www.greyhouse.com/ebooks.htm

**Business Information ♦ Ratings Guides ♦ <u>General Reference</u> ♦ Education ♦
Statistics ♦ Demographics ♦ Health Information ♦ Canadian Information**

Grey House
Publishing

Encyclopedia of Religion & the Law in America

This informative, easy-to-use reference work covers a wide range of legal issues that affect the roles of religion and law in American society. Extensive A–Z entries provide coverage of key court decisions, case studies, concepts, individuals, religious groups, organizations, and agencies shaping religion and law in today's society. This *Encyclopedia* focuses on topics involved with the constitutional theory and interpretation of religion and the law; terms providing a historical explanation of the ways in which America's ever increasing ethnic and religious diversity contributed to our current understanding of the mandates of the First and Fourteenth Amendments; terms and concepts describing the development of religion clause jurisprudence; an analytical examination of the distinct vocabulary used in this area of the law; the means by which American courts have attempted to balance religious liberty against other important individual and social interests in a wide variety of physical and regulatory environments, including the classroom, the workplace, the courtroom, religious group organization and structure, taxation, the clash of "secular" and "religious" values, and the relationship of the generalized idea of individual autonomy of the specific concept of religious liberty. Important legislation and legal cases affecting religion and society are thoroughly covered in this timely volume, including a detailed Table of Cases and Table of Statutes for more detailed research. A guide to further reading and an index are also included. This useful resource will be an important acquisition for the reference collections of all public libraries, university libraries, religion reference collections and high schools.

Hardcover ISBN 978-1-59237-298-0, 500 pages, $135.00 | Ebook ISBN 978-1-59237-309-3 www.greyhouse.com/ebooks.htm

The Religious Right, A Reference Handbook

Timely and unbiased, this third edition updates and expands its examination of the religious right and its influence on our government, citizens, society, and politics. This text explores the influence of religion on legislation and society, while examining the alignment of the religious right with the political right. The coverage offers a critical historical survey of the religious right movement, focusing on its increased involvement in the political arena, attempts to forge coalitions, and notable successes and failures. The text offers complete coverage of biographies of the men and women who have advanced the cause and an up to date chronology illuminate the movement's goals, including their accomplishments and failures. Two new sections complement this third edition, a chapter on legal issues and court decisions and a chapter on demographic statistics and electoral patterns. To aid in further research, *The Religious Right*, offers an entire section of annotated listings of print and non-print resources, as well as of organizations affiliated with the religious right, and those opposing it. Comprehensive in its scope, this work offers easy-to-read, pertinent information for those seeking to understand the religious right and its evolving role in American society. A must for libraries of all sizes, university religion departments, activists, high schools and for those interested in the evolving role of the religious right.

" Recommended for all public and academic libraries." - Library Journal

Hardcover ISBN 978-1-59237-113-6, 600 pages, $165.00 | Ebook ISBN 978-1-59237-226-3 www.greyhouse.com/ebooks.htm

Human Rights in the United States: A Dictionary and Documents

This two volume set offers easy to grasp explanations of the basic concepts, laws, and case law in the field, with emphasis on human rights in the historical, political, and legal experience of the United States. Human rights is a term not fully understood by many Americans. Addressing this gap, the new second edition of *Human Rights in the United States: A Dictionary and Documents* offers a comprehensive introduction that places the history of human rights in the United States in an international context. It surveys the legal protection of human dignity in the United States, examines the sources of human rights norms, cites key legal cases, explains the role of international governmental and non-governmental organizations, and charts global, regional, and U.N. human rights measures. Over 240 dictionary entries of human rights terms are detailed—ranging from asylum and cultural relativism to hate crimes and torture. Each entry discusses the significance of the term, gives examples, and cites appropriate documents and court decisions. In addition, a Documents section is provided that contains 59 conventions, treaties, and protocols related to the most up to date international action on ethnic cleansing; freedom of expression and religion; violence against women; and much more. A bibliography, extensive glossary, and comprehensive index round out this indispensable volume. This comprehensive, timely volume is a must for large public libraries, university libraries and social science departments, along with high school libraries.

"...invaluable for anyone interested in human rights issues ... highly recommended for all reference collections."
- American Reference Books Annual

Two Volumes, Hardcover ISBN 978-1-59237-290-4, 750 pages, $225.00 | Ebook ISBN 978-1-59237-301-7
www.greyhouse.com/ebooks.htm

The Comparative Guide to American Elementary & Secondary Schools, 2009/10

The only guide of its kind, this award winning compilation offers a snapshot profile of every public school district in the United States serving 1,500 or more students – more than 5,900 districts are covered. Organized alphabetically by district within state, each chapter begins with a Statistical Overview of the state. Each district listing includes contact information (name, address, phone number and web site) plus Grades Served, the Numbers of Students and Teachers and the Number of Regular, Special Education, Alternative and Vocational Schools in the district along with statistics on Student/Classroom Teacher Ratios, Drop Out Rates, Ethnicity, the Numbers of Librarians and Guidance Counselors and District Expenditures per student. As an added bonus, *The Comparative Guide to American Elementary and Secondary Schools* provides important ranking tables, both by state and nationally, for each data element. For easy navigation through this wealth of information, this handbook contains a useful City Index that lists all districts that operate schools within a city. These important comparative statistics are necessary for anyone considering relocation or doing comparative research on their own district and would be a perfect acquisition for any public library or school district library.

*"This straightforward guide is an easy way to find general information.
Valuable for academic and large public library collections." –ARBA*

Softcover ISBN 978-1-59237-436-6, 2,400 pages, $125.00 | Ebook ISBN 978-1-59237-238-6 www.greyhouse.com/ebooks.htm

The Complete Learning Disabilities Directory, 2009

The Complete Learning Disabilities Directory is the most comprehensive database of Programs, Services, Curriculum Materials, Professional Meetings & Resources, Camps, Newsletters and Support Groups for teachers, students and families concerned with learning disabilities. This information-packed directory includes information about Associations & Organizations, Schools, Colleges & Testing Materials, Government Agencies, Legal Resources and much more. For quick, easy access to information, this directory contains four indexes: Entry Name Index, Subject Index and Geographic Index. With every passing year, the field of learning disabilities attracts more attention and the network of caring, committed and knowledgeable professionals grows every day. This directory is an invaluable research tool for these parents, students and professionals.

"Due to its wealth and depth of coverage, parents, teachers and others… should find this an invaluable resource." -Booklist

Softcover ISBN 978-1-59237-368-0, 900 pages, $150.00 | Online Database: http://gold.greyhouse.com Call (800) 562-2139 for quote

Educators Resource Directory, 2009/10

Educators Resource Directory is a comprehensive resource that provides the educational professional with thousands of resources and statistical data for professional development. This directory saves hours of research time by providing immediate access to Associations & Organizations, Conferences & Trade Shows, Educational Research Centers, Employment Opportunities & Teaching Abroad, School Library Services, Scholarships, Financial Resources, Professional Consultants, Computer Software & Testing Resources and much more. Plus, this comprehensive directory also includes a section on Statistics and Rankings with over 100 tables, including statistics on Average Teacher Salaries, SAT/ACT scores, Revenues & Expenditures and more. These important statistics will allow the user to see how their school rates among others, make relocation decisions and so much more. For quick access to information, this directory contains four indexes: Entry & Publisher Index, Geographic Index, a Subject & Grade Index and Web Sites Index. *Educators Resource Directory* will be a well-used addition to the reference collection of any school district, education department or public library.

"Recommended for all collections that serve elementary and secondary school professionals." –Choice

Softcover ISBN 978-1-59237-397-0, 800 pages, $145.00 | Online Database: http://gold.greyhouse.com Call (800) 562-2139 for quote

Profiles of New York | Profiles of Florida | Profiles of Texas | Profiles of Illinois | Profiles of Michigan | Profiles of Ohio | Profiles of New Jersey | Profiles of Massachusetts | Profiles of Pennsylvania | Profiles of Wisconsin | Profiles of Connecticut & Rhode Island | Profiles of Indiana | Profiles of North Carolina & South Carolina | Profiles of Virginia | Profiles of California

The careful layout gives the user an easy-to-read snapshot of every single place and county in the state, from the biggest metropolis to the smallest unincorporated hamlet. The richness of each place or county profile is astounding in its depth, from history to weather, all packed in an easy-to-navigate, compact format. Each profile contains data on History, Geography, Climate, Population, Vital Statistics, Economy, Income, Taxes, Education, Housing, Health & Environment, Public Safety, Newspapers, Transportation, Presidential Election Results, Information Contacts and Chambers of Commerce. As an added bonus, there is a section on Selected Statistics, where data from the 100 largest towns and cities is arranged into easy-to-use charts. Each of 22 different data points has its own two-page spread with the cities listed in alpha order so researchers can easily compare and rank cities. A remarkable compilation that offers overviews and insights into each corner of the state, each volume goes beyond Census statistics, beyond metro area coverage, beyond the 100 best places to live. Drawn from official census information, other government statistics and original research, you will have at your fingertips data that's available nowhere else in one single source.

"The publisher claims that this is the 'most comprehensive portrait of the state of Florida ever published,' and this reviewer is inclined to believe it...Recommended. All levels." –Choice on Profiles of Florida

Each Profiles of... title ranges from 400-800 pages, priced at $149.00 each

America's Top-Rated Cities, 2009

America's Top-Rated Cities provides current, comprehensive statistical information and other essential data in one easy-to-use source on the 100 "top" cities that have been cited as the best for business and living in the U.S. This handbook allows readers to see, at a glance, a concise social, business, economic, demographic and environmental profile of each city, including brief evaluative comments. In addition to detailed data on Cost of Living, Finances, Real Estate, Education, Major Employers, Media, Crime and Climate, city reports now include Housing Vacancies, Tax Audits, Bankruptcy, Presidential Election Results and more. This outstanding source of information will be widely used in any reference collection.

"The only source of its kind that brings together all of this information into one easy-to-use source. It will be beneficial to many business and public libraries." –ARBA

Four Volumes, Softcover ISBN 978-1-59237-410-6, 2,500 pages, $195.00 | Ebook ISBN 978-1-59237-233-1
www.greyhouse.com/ebooks.htm

America's Top-Rated Smaller Cities, 2008/09

A perfect companion to *America's Top-Rated Cities*, *America's Top-Rated Smaller Cities* provides current, comprehensive business and living profiles of smaller cities (population 25,000-99,999) that have been cited as the best for business and living in the United States. Sixty cities make up this 2004 edition of America's Top-Rated Smaller Cities, all are top-ranked by Population Growth, Median Income, Unemployment Rate and Crime Rate. City reports reflect the most current data available on a wide-range of statistics, including Employment & Earnings, Household Income, Unemployment Rate, Population Characteristics, Taxes, Cost of Living, Education, Health Care, Public Safety, Recreation, Media, Air & Water Quality and much more. Plus, each city report contains a Background of the City, and an Overview of the State Finances. *America's Top-Rated Smaller Cities* offers a reliable, one-stop source for statistical data that, before now, could only be found scattered in hundreds of sources. This volume is designed for a wide range of readers: individuals considering relocating a residence or business; professionals considering expanding their business or changing careers; general and market researchers; real estate consultants; human resource personnel; urban planners and investors.

"Provides current, comprehensive statistical information in one easy-to-use source... Recommended for public and academic libraries and specialized collections." –Library Journal

Two Volumes, Softcover ISBN 978-1-59237-284-3, 1,100 pages, $195.00 | Ebook ISBN 978-1-59237-234-8
www.greyhouse.com/ebooks.htm

Profiles of America: Facts, Figures & Statistics for Every Populated Place in the United States

Profiles of America is the only source that pulls together, in one place, statistical, historical and descriptive information about every place in the United States in an easy-to-use format. This award winning reference set, now in its second edition, compiles statistics and data from over 20 different sources – the latest census information has been included along with more than nine brand new statistical topics. This Four-Volume Set details over 40,000 places, from the biggest metropolis to the smallest unincorporated hamlet, and provides statistical details and information on over 50 different topics including Geography, Climate, Population, Vital Statistics, Economy, Income, Taxes, Education, Housing, Health & Environment, Public Safety, Newspapers, Transportation, Presidential Election Results and Information Contacts or Chambers of Commerce. Profiles are arranged, for ease-of-use, by state and then by county. Each county begins with a County-Wide Overview and is followed by information for each Community in that particular county. The Community Profiles within the county are arranged alphabetically. *Profiles of America* is a virtual snapshot of America at your fingertips and a unique compilation of information that will be widely used in any reference collection.

A Library Journal Best Reference Book "An outstanding compilation." –Library Journal

Four Volumes, Softcover ISBN 978-1-891482-80-9, 10,000 pages, $595.00

To preview any of our Directories Risk-Free for 30 days, call (800) 562-2139 or fax (518) 789-0556
www.greyhouse.com books@greyhouse.com

Business Information ✦ Ratings Guides ✦ General Reference ✦ Education ✦
Statistics ✦ **Demographics** ✦ Health Information ✦ Canadian Information

Grey House
Publishing

The Comparative Guide to American Suburbs, 2009/10

The Comparative Guide to American Suburbs is a one-stop source for Statistics on the 2,000+ suburban communities surrounding the 50 largest metropolitan areas – their population characteristics, income levels, economy, school system and important data on how they compare to one another. Organized into 50 Metropolitan Area chapters, each chapter contains an overview of the Metropolitan Area, a detailed Map followed by a comprehensive Statistical Profile of each Suburban Community, including Contact Information, Physical Characteristics, Population Characteristics, Income, Economy, Unemployment Rate, Cost of Living, Education, Chambers of Commerce and more. Next, statistical data is sorted into Ranking Tables that rank the suburbs by twenty different criteria, including Population, Per Capita Income, Unemployment Rate, Crime Rate, Cost of Living and more. *The Comparative Guide to American Suburbs* is the best source for locating data on suburbs. Those looking to relocate, as well as those doing preliminary market research, will find this an invaluable timesaving resource.

"Public and academic libraries will find this compilation useful…The work draws together figures from many sources and will be especially helpful for job relocation decisions." – Booklist

Softcover ISBN 978-1-59237-432-8 1,700 pages, $130.00 | Ebook ISBN 978-1-59237-235-5 www.greyhouse.com/ebooks.htm

The American Tally: Statistics & Comparative Rankings for U.S. Cities with Populations over 10,000

This important statistical handbook compiles, all in one place, comparative statistics on all U.S. cities and towns with a 10,000+ population. *The American Tally* provides statistical details on over 4,000 cities and towns and profiles how they compare with one another in Population Characteristics, Education, Language & Immigration, Income & Employment and Housing. Each section begins with an alphabetical listing of cities by state, allowing for quick access to both the statistics and relative rankings of any city. Next, the highest and lowest cities are listed in each statistic. These important, informative lists provide quick reference to which cities are at both extremes of the spectrum for each statistic. Unlike any other reference, *The American Tally* provides quick, easy access to comparative statistics – a must-have for any reference collection.

"A solid library reference." -Bookwatch

Softcover ISBN 978-1-930956-29-2, 500 pages, $125.00 | Ebook ISBN 978-1-59237-241-6 www.greyhouse.com/ebooks.htm

The Asian Databook: Statistics for all US Counties & Cities with Over 10,000 Population

This is the first-ever resource that compiles statistics and rankings on the US Asian population. *The Asian Databook* presents over 20 statistical data points for each city and county, arranged alphabetically by state, then alphabetically by place name. Data reported for each place includes Population, Languages Spoken at Home, Foreign-Born, Educational Attainment, Income Figures, Poverty Status, Homeownership, Home Values & Rent, and more. Next, in the Rankings Section, the top 75 places are listed for each data element. These easy-to-access ranking tables allow the user to quickly determine trends and population characteristics. This kind of comparative data can not be found elsewhere, in print or on the web, in a format that's as easy-to-use or more concise. A useful resource for those searching for demographics data, career search and relocation information and also for market research. With data ranging from Ancestry to Education, *The Asian Databook* presents a useful compilation of information that will be a much-needed resource in the reference collection of any public or academic library along with the marketing collection of any company whose primary focus in on the Asian population.

"This useful resource will help those searching for demographics data, and market research or relocation information… Accurate and clearly laid out, the publication is recommended for large public library and research collections." -Booklist

Softcover ISBN 978-1-59237-044-3, 1,000 pages, $150.00

The Hispanic Databook: Statistics for all US Counties & Cities with Over 10,000 Population

Previously published by Toucan Valley Publications, this second edition has been completely updated with figures from the latest census and has been broadly expanded to include dozens of new data elements and a brand new Rankings section. The Hispanic population in the United States has increased over 42% in the last 10 years and accounts for 12.5% of the total US population. For ease-of-use, *The Hispanic Databook* presents over 20 statistical data points for each city and county, arranged alphabetically by state, then alphabetically by place name. Data reported for each place includes Population, Languages Spoken at Home, Foreign-Born, Educational Attainment, Income Figures, Poverty Status, Homeownership, Home Values & Rent, and more. Next, in the Rankings Section, the top 75 places are listed for each data element. These easy-to-access ranking tables allow the user to quickly determine trends and population characteristics. This kind of comparative data can not be found elsewhere, in print or on the web, in a format that's as easy-to-use or more concise. A useful resource for those searching for demographics data, career search and relocation information and also for market research. With data ranging from Ancestry to Education, *The Hispanic Databook* presents a useful compilation of information that will be a much-needed resource in the reference collection of any public or academic library along with the marketing collection of any company whose primary focus in on the Hispanic population.

"This accurate, clearly presented volume of selected Hispanic demographics is recommended for large public libraries and research collections."-Library Journal

Softcover ISBN 978-1-59237-008-5, 1,000 pages, $150.00

Business Information ◆ Ratings Guides ◆ General Reference ◆ Education ◆
Statistics ◆ Demographics ◆ Health Information ◆ Canadian Information

Grey Hous
Publishir

Ancestry in America: A Comparative Guide to Over 200 Ethnic Backgrounds

This brand new reference work pulls together thousands of comparative statistics on the Ethnic Backgrounds of all populated places in the United States with populations over 10,000. Never before has this kind of information been reported in a single volume. Section One, Statistics by Place, is made up of a list of over 200 ancestry and race categories arranged alphabetically by each of the 5,000 different places with populations over 10,000. The population number of the ancestry group in that city or town is provided along with the percent that group represents of the total population. This informative city-by-city section allows the user to quickly and easily explore the ethnic makeup of all major population bases in the United States. Section Two, Comparative Rankings, contains three tables for each ethnicity and race. In the first table, the top 150 populated places are ranked by population number for that particular ancestry group, regardless of population. In the second table, the top 150 populated places are ranked by the percent of the total population for that ancestry group. In the third table, those top 150 populated places with 10,000 population are ranked by population number for each ancestry group. These easy-to-navigate tables allow users to see ancestry population patterns and make city-by-city comparisons as well. This brand new, information-packed resource will serve a wide-range or research requests for demographics, population characteristics, relocation information and much more. *Ancestry in America: A Comparative Guide to Over 200 Ethnic Backgrounds* will be an important acquisition to all reference collections.

"This compilation will serve a wide range of research requests for population characteristics ... it offers much more detail than other sources." –Booklist

Softcover ISBN 978-1-59237-029-0, 1,500 pages, $225.00

Weather America, A Thirty-Year Summary of Statistical Weather Data and Rankings

This valuable resource provides extensive climatological data for over 4,000 National and Cooperative Weather Stations throughout the United States. Weather America begins with a new Major Storms section that details major storm events of the nation and a National Rankings section that details rankings for several data elements, such as Maximum Temperature and Precipitation. The main body of Weather America is organized into 50 state sections. Each section provides a Data Table on each Weather Station, organized alphabetically, that provides statistics on Maximum and Minimum Temperatures, Precipitation, Snowfall, Extreme Temperatures, Foggy Days, Humidity and more. State sections contain two brand new features in this edition – a City Index and a narrative Description of the climatic conditions of the state. Each section also includes a revised Map of the State that includes not only weather stations, but cities and towns.

"Best Reference Book of the Year." –Library Journal

Softcover ISBN 978-1-891482-29-8, 2,013 pages, $175.00 | Ebook ISBN 978-1-59237-237-9 www.greyhouse.com/ebooks.htm

Crime in America's Top-Rated Cities

This volume includes over 20 years of crime statistics in all major crime categories: violent crimes, property crimes and total crime. *Crime in America's Top-Rated Cities* is conveniently arranged by city and covers 76 top-rated cities. Crime in America's Top-Rated Cities offers details that compare the number of crimes and crime rates for the city, suburbs and metro area along with national crime trends for violent, property and total crimes. Also, this handbook contains important information and statistics on Anti-Crime Programs, Crime Risk, Hate Crimes, Illegal Drugs, Law Enforcement, Correctional Facilities, Death Penalty Laws and much more. A much-needed resource for people who are relocating, business professionals, general researchers, the press, law enforcement officials and students of criminal justice.

"Data is easy to access and will save hours of searching." –Global Enforcement Review

Softcover ISBN 978-1-891482-84-7, 832 pages, $155.00

The Complete Directory for People with Disabilities, 2009

A wealth of information, now in one comprehensive sourcebook. Completely updated, this edition contains more information than ever before, including thousands of new entries and enhancements to existing entries and thousands of additional web sites and e-mail addresses. This up-to-date directory is the most comprehensive resource available for people with disabilities, detailing Independent Living Centers, Rehabilitation Facilities, State & Federal Agencies, Associations, Support Groups, Periodicals & Books, Assistive Devices, Employment & Education Programs, Camps and Travel Groups. Each year, more libraries, schools, colleges, hospitals, rehabilitation centers and individuals add *The Complete Directory for People with Disabilities* to their collections, making sure that this information is readily available to the families, individuals and professionals who can benefit most from the amazing wealth of resources cataloged here.

"No other reference tool exists to meet the special needs of the disabled in one convenient resource for information." –Library Journal

Softcover ISBN 978-1-59237-367-3, 1,200 pages, $165.00 | Online Database: http://gold.greyhouse.com Call (800) 562-2139 for quote

The Complete Learning Disabilities Directory, 2009

The Complete Learning Disabilities Directory is the most comprehensive database of Programs, Services, Curriculum Materials, Professional Meetings & Resources, Camps, Newsletters and Support Groups for teachers, students and families concerned with learning disabilities. This information-packed directory includes information about Associations & Organizations, Schools, Colleges & Testing Materials, Government Agencies, Legal Resources and much more. For quick, easy access to information, this directory contains four indexes: Entry Name Index, Subject Index and Geographic Index. With every passing year, the field of learning disabilities attracts more attention and the network of caring, committed and knowledgeable professionals grows every day. This directory is an invaluable research tool for these parents, students and professionals.

"Due to its wealth and depth of coverage, parents, teachers and others… should find this an invaluable resource." -Booklist

Softcover ISBN 978-1-59237-368-0, 900 pages, $150.00 | Online Database: http://gold.greyhouse.com Call (800) 562-2139 for quote

The Complete Directory for People with Chronic Illness, 2009/10

Thousands of hours of research have gone into this completely updated edition – several new chapters have been added along with thousands of new entries and enhancements to existing entries. Plus, each chronic illness chapter has been reviewed by a medical expert in the field. This widely-hailed directory is structured around the 90 most prevalent chronic illnesses – from Asthma to Cancer to Wilson's Disease – and provides a comprehensive overview of the support services and information resources available for people diagnosed with a chronic illness. Each chronic illness has its own chapter and contains a brief description in layman's language, followed by important resources for National & Local Organizations, State Agencies, Newsletters, Books & Periodicals, Libraries & Research Centers, Support Groups & Hotlines, Web Sites and much more. This directory is an important resource for health care professionals, the collections of hospital and health care libraries, as well as an invaluable tool for people with a chronic illness and their support network.

"A must purchase for all hospital and health care libraries and is strongly recommended for all public library reference departments." –ARBA

Softcover ISBN 978-1-59237-415-1, 1,200 pages, $165.00 | Online Database: http://gold.greyhouse.com Call (800) 562-2139 for quote

The Complete Mental Health Directory, 2008/09

This is the most comprehensive resource covering the field of behavioral health, with critical information for both the layman and the mental health professional. For the layman, this directory offers understandable descriptions of 25 Mental Health Disorders as well as detailed information on Associations, Media, Support Groups and Mental Health Facilities. For the professional, The Complete Mental Health Directory offers critical and comprehensive information on Managed Care Organizations, Information Systems, Government Agencies and Provider Organizations. This comprehensive volume of needed information will be widely used in any reference collection.

"… the strength of this directory is that it consolidates widely dispersed information into a single volume." –Booklist

Softcover ISBN 978-1-59237-285-0, 800 pages, $165.00 | Online Database: http://gold.greyhouse.com Call (800) 562-2139 for quote

Business Information ◆ Ratings Guides ◆ General Reference ◆ Education ◆
Statistics ◆ Demographics ◆ **Health Information** ◆ Canadian Information

Grey House
Publishin

The Comparative Guide to American Hospitals, Second Edition

This new second edition compares all of the nation's hospitals by 24 measures of quality in the treatment of heart attack, heart failure, pneumonia, and, new to this edition, surgical procedures and pregnancy care. Plus, this second edition is now available in regional volumes, to make locating information about hospitals in your area quicker and easier than ever before. The Comparative Guide to American Hospitals provides a snapshot profile of each of the nations 4,200+ hospitals. These informative profiles illustrate how the hospital rates when providing 24 different treatments within four broad categories: Heart Attack Care, Heart Failure Care, Surgical Infection Prevention (NEW), and Pregnancy Care measures (NEW). Each profile includes the raw percentage for that hospital, the state average, the US average and data on the top hospital. For easy access to contact information, each profile includes the hospital's address, phone and fax numbers, email and web addresses, type and accreditation along with 5 top key administrations. These profiles will allow the user to quickly identify the quality of the hospital and have the necessary information at their fingertips to make contact with that hospital. Most importantly, *The Comparative Guide to American Hospitals* provides easy-to-use Regional State by State Statistical Summary Tables for each of the data elements to allow the user to quickly locate hospitals with the best level of service. Plus, a new 30-Day Mortality Chart, Glossary of Terms and Regional Hospital Profile Index make this a must-have source. This new, expanded edition will be a must for the reference collection at all public, medical and academic libraries.

> *"These data will help those with heart conditions and pneumonia make informed decisions about their healthcare and encourage hospitals to improve the quality of care they provide. Large medical, hospital, and public libraries are most likely to benefit from this weighty resource."-Library Journal*

Four Volumes Softcover ISBN 978-1-59237-182-2, 3,500 pages, $325.00 | Regional Volumes $135.00 |
Ebook ISBN 978-1-59237-239-3 www.greyhouse.com/ebooks.htm

Older Americans Information Directory, 2008

Completely updated for 2008, this sixth edition has been completely revised and now contains 1,000 new listings, over 8,000 updates to existing listings and over 3,000 brand new e-mail addresses and web sites. You'll find important resources for Older Americans including National, Regional, State & Local Organizations, Government Agencies, Research Centers, Libraries & Information Centers, Legal Resources, Discount Travel Information, Continuing Education Programs, Disability Aids & Assistive Devices, Health, Print Media and Electronic Media. Three indexes: Entry Index, Subject Index and Geographic Index make it easy to find just the right source of information. This comprehensive guide to resources for Older Americans will be a welcome addition to any reference collection.

> *"Highly recommended for academic, public, health science and consumer libraries..." –Choice*

1,200 pages; Softcover ISBN 978-1-59237-357-4, $165.00 | Online Database: http://gold.greyhouse.com Call (800) 562-2139 for quote

The Complete Directory for Pediatric Disorders, 2009/10

This important directory provides parents and caregivers with information about Pediatric Conditions, Disorders, Diseases and Disabilities, including Blood Disorders, Bone & Spinal Disorders, Brain Defects & Abnormalities, Chromosomal Disorders, Congenital Heart Defects, Movement Disorders, Neuromuscular Disorders and Pediatric Tumors & Cancers. This carefully written directory offers: understandable Descriptions of 15 major bodily systems; Descriptions of more than 200 Disorders and a Resources Section, detailing National Agencies & Associations, State Associations, Online Services, Libraries & Resource Centers, Research Centers, Support Groups & Hotlines, Camps, Books and Periodicals. This resource will provide immediate access to information crucial to families and caregivers when coping with children's illnesses.

> *"Recommended for public and consumer health libraries." –Library Journal*

Softcover ISBN 978-1-59237-430-4, 1,200 pages, $165.00 | Online Database: http://gold.greyhouse.com Call (800) 562-2139 for quote

The Directory of Drug & Alcohol Residential Rehabilitation Facilities

This brand new directory is the first-ever resource to bring together, all in one place, data on the thousands of drug and alcohol residential rehabilitation facilities in the United States. The Directory of Drug & Alcohol Residential Rehabilitation Facilities covers over 1,000 facilities, with detailed contact information for each one, including mailing address, phone and fax numbers, email addresses and web sites, mission statement, type of treatment programs, cost, average length of stay, numbers of residents and counselors, accreditation, insurance plans accepted, type of environment, religious affiliation, education components and much more. It also contains a helpful chapter on General Resources that provides contact information for Associations, Print & Electronic Media, Support Groups and Conferences. Multiple indexes allow the user to pinpoint the facilities that meet very specific criteria. This time-saving tool is what so many counselors, parents and medical professionals have been asking for. *The Directory of Drug & Alcohol Residential Rehabilitation Facilities* will be a helpful tool in locating the right source for treatment for a wide range of individuals. This comprehensive directory will be an important acquisition for all reference collections: public and academic libraries, case managers, social workers, state agencies and many more.

> *"This is an excellent, much needed directory that fills an important gap..." –Booklist*

Softcover ISBN 978-1-59237-031-3, 300 pages, $135.00

Grey House
Publishing

The Directory of Hospital Personnel, 2009

The Directory of Hospital Personnel is the best resource you can have at your fingertips when researching or marketing a product or service to the hospital market. A "Who's Who" of the hospital universe, this directory puts you in touch with over 150,000 key decision-makers. With 100% verification of data you can rest assured that you will reach the right person with just one call. Every hospital in the U.S. is profiled, listed alphabetically by city within state. Plus, three easy-to-use, cross-referenced indexes put the facts at your fingertips faster and more easily than any other directory: Hospital Name Index, Bed Size Index and Personnel Index. *The Directory of Hospital Personnel* is the only complete source for key hospital decision-makers by name. Whether you want to define or restructure sales territories… locate hospitals with the purchasing power to accept your proposals… keep track of important contacts or colleagues… or find information on which insurance plans are accepted, *The Directory of Hospital Personnel* gives you the information you need – easily, efficiently, effectively and accurately.

"Recommended for college, university and medical libraries." -ARBA

Softcover ISBN 978-1-59237-402-1, 2,500 pages, $325.00 | Online Database: http://gold.greyhouse.com Call (800) 562-2139 for quote

The HMO/PPO Directory, 2009

The HMO/PPO Directory is a comprehensive source that provides detailed information about Health Maintenance Organizations and Preferred Provider Organizations nationwide. This comprehensive directory details more information about more managed health care organizations than ever before. Over 1,100 HMOs, PPOs, Medicare Advantage Plans and affiliated companies are listed, arranged alphabetically by state. Detailed listings include Key Contact Information, Prescription Drug Benefits, Enrollment, Geographical Areas served, Affiliated Physicians & Hospitals, Federal Qualifications, Status, Year Founded, Managed Care Partners, Employer References, Fees & Payment Information and more. Plus, five years of historical information is included related to Revenues, Net Income, Medical Loss Ratios, Membership Enrollment and Number of Patient Complaints. Five easy-to-use, cross-referenced indexes will put this vast array of information at your fingertips immediately: HMO Index, PPO Index, Other Providers Index, Personnel Index and Enrollment Index. *The HMO/PPO Directory* provides the most comprehensive data on the most companies available on the market place today.

"Helpful to individuals requesting certain HMO/PPO issues such as co-payment costs, subscription costs and patient complaints. Individuals concerned (or those with questions) about their insurance may find this text to be of use to them." -ARBA

Softcover ISBN 978-1-59237-369-7, 600 pages, $325.00 | Online Database: http://gold.greyhouse.com Call (800) 562-2139 for quote

Medical Device Register, 2009

The only one-stop resource of every medical supplier licensed to sell products in the US. This award-winning directory offers immediate access to over 13,000 companies - and more than 65,000 products – in two information-packed volumes. This comprehensive resource saves hours of time and trouble when searching for medical equipment and supplies and the manufacturers who provide them. Volume I: The Product Directory, provides essential information for purchasing or specifying medical supplies for every medical device, supply, and diagnostic available in the US. Listings provide FDA codes & Federal Procurement Eligibility, Contact information for every manufacturer of the product along with Prices and Product Specifications. Volume 2 - Supplier Profiles, offers the most complete and important data about Suppliers, Manufacturers and Distributors. Company Profiles detail the number of employees, ownership, method of distribution, sales volume, net income, key executives detailed contact information medical products the company supplies, plus the medical specialties they cover. Four indexes provide immediate access to this wealth of information: Keyword Index, Trade Name Index, Supplier Geographical Index and OEM (Original Equipment Manufacturer) Index. *Medical Device Register* is the only one-stop source for locating suppliers and products; looking for new manufacturers or hard-to-find medical devices; comparing products and companies; know who's selling what and who to buy from cost effectively. This directory has become the standard in its field and will be a welcome addition to the reference collection of any medical library, large public library, university library along with the collections that serve the medical community.

"A wealth of information on medical devices, medical device companies… and key personnel in the industry is provide in this comprehensive reference work... A valuable reference work, one of the best hardcopy compilations available." -Doody Publishing

Two Volumes, Hardcover ISBN 978-1-59237-373-4, 3,000 pages, $325.00

The Directory of Health Care Group Purchasing Organizations, 2008

This comprehensive directory provides the important data you need to get in touch with over 800 Group Purchasing Organizations. By providing in-depth information on this growing market and its members, *The Directory of Health Care Group Purchasing Organizations* fills a major need for the most accurate and comprehensive information on over 800 GPOs – Mailing Address, Phone & Fax Numbers, E-mail Addresses, Key Contacts, Purchasing Agents, Group Descriptions, Membership Categorization, Standard Vendor Proposal Requirements, Membership Fees & Terms, Expanded Services, Total Member Beds & Outpatient Visits represented and more. Five Indexes provide a number of ways to locate the right GPO: Alphabetical Index, Expanded Services Index, Organization Type Index, Geographic Index and Member Institution Index. With its comprehensive and detailed information on each purchasing organization, *The Directory of Health Care Group Purchasing Organizations* is the go-to source for anyone looking to target this market.

"The information is clearly arranged and easy to access…recommended for those needing this very specialized information." –ARBA

1,000 pages; Softcover ISBN 978-1-59237-287-4, $325.00 | Online Database: http://gold.greyhouse.com Call (800) 562-2139 for quote

**To preview any of our Directories Risk-Free for 30 days, call (800) 562-2139 or fax (518) 789-0556
www.greyhouse.com books@greyhouse.com**

Business Information ◆ Ratings Guides ◆ General Reference ◆ Education ◆
Statistics ◆ Demographics ◆ Health Information ◆ **Canadian Information**

Grey House
Publishing

Canadian Almanac & Directory, 2009

The Canadian Almanac & Directory contains sixteen directories in one – giving you all the facts and figures you will ever need about Canada. No other single source provides users with the quality and depth of up-to-date information for all types of research. This national directory and guide gives you access to statistics, images and over 100,000 names and addresses for everything from Airlines to Zoos - updated every year. It's Ten Directories in One! Each section is a directory in itself, providing robust information on business and finance, communications, government, associations, arts and culture (museums, zoos, libraries, etc.), health, transportation, law, education, and more. Government information includes federal, provincial and territorial - and includes an easy-to-use quick index to find key information. A separate municipal government section includes every municipality in Canada, with full profiles of Canada's largest urban centers. A complete legal directory lists judges and judicial officials, court locations and law firms across the country. A wealth of general information, the *Canadian Almanac & Directory* also includes national statistics on population, employment, imports and exports, and more. National awards and honors are presented, along with forms of address, Commonwealth information and full color photos of Canadian symbols. Postal information, weights, measures, distances and other useful charts are also incorporated. Complete almanac information includes perpetual calendars, five-year holiday planners and astronomical information. Published continuously for 160 years, *The Canadian Almanac & Directory* is the best single reference source for business executives, managers and assistants; government and public affairs executives; lawyers; marketing, sales and advertising executives; researchers, editors and journalists.

Hardcover ISBN 978-1-59237-370-3, 1,600 pages, $325.00

Associations Canada, 2009

The Most Powerful Fact-Finder to Business, Trade, Professional and Consumer Organizations
Associations Canada covers Canadian organizations and international groups including industry, commercial and professional associations, registered charities, special interest and common interest organizations. This annually revised compendium provides detailed listings and abstracts for nearly 20,000 regional, national and international organizations. This popular volume provides the most comprehensive picture of Canada's non-profit sector. Detailed listings enable users to identify an organization's budget, founding date, scope of activity, licensing body, sources of funding, executive information, full address and complete contact information, just to name a few. Powerful indexes help researchers find information quickly and easily. The following indexes are included: subject, acronym, geographic, budget, executive name, conferences & conventions, mailing list, defunct and unreachable associations and registered charitable organizations. In addition to annual spending of over $1 billion on transportation and conventions alone, Canadian associations account for many millions more in pursuit of membership interests. *Associations Canada* provides complete access to this highly lucrative market. *Associations Canada* is a strong source of prospects for sales and marketing executives, tourism and convention officials, researchers, government officials - anyone who wants to locate non-profit interest groups and trade associations.

Hardcover ISBN 978-1-59237-401-4, 1,600 pages, $325.00

Financial Services Canada, 2009/10

Financial Services Canada is the only master file of current contacts and information that serves the needs of the entire financial services industry in Canada. With over 18,000 organizations and hard-to-find business information, Financial Services Canada is the most up-to-date source for names and contact numbers of industry professionals, senior executives, portfolio managers, financial advisors, agency bureaucrats and elected representatives. Financial Services Canada incorporates the latest changes in the industry to provide you with the most current details on each company, including: name, title, organization, telephone and fax numbers, e-mail and web addresses. *Financial Services Canada* also includes private company listings never before compiled, government agencies, association and consultant services - to ensure that you'll never miss a client or a contact. Current listings include: banks and branches, non-depository institutions, stock exchanges and brokers, investment management firms, insurance companies, major accounting and law firms, government agencies and financial associations. Powerful indexes assist researchers with locating the vital financial information they need. The following indexes are included: alphabetic, geographic, executive name, corporate web site/e-mail, government quick reference and subject. *Financial Services Canada* is a valuable resource for financial executives, bankers, financial planners, sales and marketing professionals, lawyers and chartered accountants, government officials, investment dealers, journalists, librarians and reference specialists.

Hardcover ISBN 978-1-59237-416-8, 900 pages, $325.00

Directory of Libraries in Canada, 2009/10

The Directory of Libraries in Canada brings together almost 7,000 listings including libraries and their branches, information resource centers, archives and library associations and learning centers. The directory offers complete and comprehensive information on Canadian libraries, resource centers, business information centers, professional associations, regional library systems, archives, library schools and library technical programs. *The Directory of Libraries in Canada* includes important features of each library and service, including library information; personnel details, including contact names and e-mail addresses; collection information; services available to users; acquisitions budgets; and computers and automated systems. Useful information on each library's electronic access is also included, such as Internet browser, connectivity and public Internet/CD-ROM/subscription database access. The directory also provides powerful indexes for subject, location, personal name and Web site/e-mail to assist researchers with locating the crucial information they need. *The Directory of Libraries in Canada* is a vital reference tool for publishers, advocacy groups, students, research institutions, computer hardware suppliers, and other diverse groups that provide products and services to this unique market.

Hardcover ISBN 978-1-59237-427-4, 850 pages, $325.00

To preview any of our Directories Risk-Free for 30 days, call (800) 562-2139 or fax (518) 789-0556
www.greyhouse.com books@greyhouse.com

Business Information ✦ Ratings Guides ✦ General Reference ✦ Education ✦
Statistics ✦ Demographics ✦ Health Information ✦ **Canadian Information**

Grey House
Publishing

Canadian Environmental Directory, 2009

The Canadian Environmental Directory is Canada's most complete and only national listing of environmental associations and organizations, government regulators and purchasing groups, product and service companies, special libraries, and more! The extensive Products and Services section provides detailed listings enabling users to identify the company name, address, phone, fax, e-mail, Web address, firm type, contact names (and titles), product and service information, affiliations, trade information, branch and affiliate data. The Government section gives you all the contact information you need at every government level – federal, provincial and municipal. We also include descriptions of current environmental initiatives, programs and agreements, names of environment-related acts administered by each ministry or department PLUS information and tips on who to contact and how to sell to governments in Canada. The Associations section provides complete contact information and a brief description of activities. Included are Canadian environmental organizations and international groups including industry, commercial and professional associations, registered charities, special interest and common interest organizations. All the Information you need about the Canadian environmental industry: directory of products and services, special libraries and resource, conferences, seminars and tradeshows, chronology of environmental events, law firms and major Canadian companies, *The Canadian Environmental Directory* is ideal for business, government, engineers and anyone conducting research on the environment.

Softcover ISBN 978-1-59237-374-1, 900 pages, $325.00

Canadian Parliamentary Guide, 2009

An indispensable guide to government in Canada, the annual *Canadian Parliamentary Guide* provides information on both federal and provincial governments, courts, and their elected and appointed members. The Guide is completely bilingual, with each record appearing both in English and then in French. The Guide contains biographical sketches of members of the Governor General's Household, the Privy Council, members of Canadian legislatures (federal, including both the House of Commons and the Senate, provincial and territorial), members of the federal superior courts (Supreme, Federal, Federal Appeal, Court Martial Appeal and Tax Courts) and the senior staff for these institutions. Biographies cover personal data, political career, private career and contact information. In addition, the Guide provides descriptions of each of the institutions, including brief historical information in text and chart format and significant facts (i.e. number of members and their salaries). The Guide covers the results of all federal general elections and by-elections from Confederations to the present and the results of the most recent provincial elections. A complete name index rounds out the text, making information easy to find. No other resources presents a more up-to-date, more complete picture of Canadian government and her political leaders. A must-have resource for all Canadian reference collections.

Hardcover ISBN 978-1-59237-417-5, 800 pages, $184.00